Arguing the Modern Jewish Canon
Essays on Literature and Culture in Honor of Ruth R. Wisse

Ruth R. Wisse

ARGUING THE MODERN JEWISH CANON
Essays on Literature and Culture in Honor of Ruth R. Wisse

edited by
Justin Cammy
Dara Horn
Alyssa Quint
Rachel Rubinstein

Center for Jewish Studies, Harvard University
distributed by
Harvard University Press
Cambridge, Massachusetts and London, England
2008

Published by the Center for Jewish Studies at Harvard University
with the generous support of
the Yanoff-Taylor Lecture and Publication Fund

Library of Congress Cataloging-in-Publication Data

Arguing the modern Jewish canon : essays on literature and culture in honor of Ruth R.
Wisse / edited by Justin Cammy... [et al.].
    p. cm.
ISBN 978-0-674-02585-1
1. Jewish literature--History and criticism. 2. Literature, Modern--Jewish authors--History and criticism. 3. Hebrew literature--History and criticism. 4. Hebrew language. 5.
Yiddish language. 6. Judaism and literature. 7. Canon (Literature) 8. Jews in literature.
I. Cammy, Justin Daniel. II. Wisse, Ruth R. III. Title.

PN842.A74 2008
809'.88924–dc22   2007047941

Book production and design by CDL Press, POB 34454, Bethesda, MD 20827
Cover design by Catherine Lo
Artwork utilized on cover and chapter pages by Yosl Bergner
Publisher: Harvard University Center for Jewish Studies

ISBN 978-0-674-02585-1

TABLE OF CONTENTS

Introduction
THE EDITORS

1

I. MAKING A CANON

Writing Jewish
HILLEL HALKIN

11

*Knocking on Heaven's Gate:
Hebrew Literature and Wisse's Canon*
ALAN MINTZ

23

*Holocaust Literature:
Foreshadowings and Shadowings*
DAVID ABERBACH

35

Of Jews and Canons: Further Thoughts
ILAN STAVANS

55

A Jewish Artistic Canon
EZRA MENDELSOHN

61

Judging The Judgment of Shomer:
Jewish Literature versus Jewish Reading
JUSTIN CAMMY

85

The Judgment of Shomer
or
The Jury Trial of All of Shomer's Novels
SHOLEM ALEICHEM
(TRANSLATED AND ANNOTATED BY JUSTIN CAMMY)

129

II. ELABORATIONS: READING WISSE'S CANONICAL AUTHORS

Daniel Deronda:
"The Zionist Fate in English Hands" and
The Liberal Betrayal of the Jews
EDWARD ALEXANDER
189

The Pleasure of Disregarding Red Lights:
A Reading of Sholem Aleichem's Monologue "A Nisref"
DAN MIRON
201

The Hershele Maze:
Isaac Babel and His Ghost Reader
SASHA SENDEROVICH
233

The Open Suitcases:
Yankev Glatshteyn's Ven Yash Iz Gekumen
AVRAHAM NOVERSHTERN
255

Seductions and Disputations:
Pseudo-Dialogues in the Fiction of Isaac Bashevis Singer
MIRIAM UDEL-LAMBERT
299

Gimpel the Simple and on Reading from Right to Left
DAVID G. ROSKIES
319

Isaac Bashevis Singer's Short Story "Androgynous"
SUSANNE KLINGENSTEIN
341

Building Bridges Destined to Fall:
Biological and Literary Paternity in Appelfeld's The Ice Mine
PHILIP HOLLANDER
357

Life/Writing:
Aharon Appelfeld's Autobiographical Work
and the Modern Jewish Canon
NAOMI B. SOKOLOFF
371

Henry Roth, Hebrew, and the Unspeakable
HANA WIRTH-NESHER
387

The Modern Hero as Schlemiel:
The Swede in Philip Roth's American Pastoral
MICHAEL KIMMAGE
401

III. CONVERSATIONS: ACROSS CANONS AND BETWEEN TEXTS
Innovation by Translation:
Yiddish and Hasidic Hebrew in Literary History
KEN FRIEDEN
417

Creating Yiddish Dialogue for
"The First Modern Yiddish Comedy"
MARION APTROOT
427

The Smoke of Civilization:
The Dialectic of Enlightenment
in Sh. Y. Abramovitsh's Di Klyatshe
MARC CAPLAN
445

Yiddish Canon Consciousness and
the Dionysiac Spirit of Music
JED WYRICK
467

Joyce's Yiddish:
Modernism, Translation, and the Jews
RACHEL RUBINSTEIN
487

The Transmission of Poetic Anger:
An Unexploded Shell in the Jewish Canon
JANET HADDA
505

Guilt, Mourning, Idol Worship, and Golem Writing:
The Symptoms of a Jewish Literary Canon
EMILY MILLER BUDICK
517

IV. INTERVENTIONS: EXPANDING WISSE'S CANON

What's So Funny about Yiddish Theater?
Comedy and the Origins of Yiddish Drama
JEREMY DAUBER
535

Naked Truths:
Avrom Goldfaden's The Fanatic or the Two Kuni-Lemls
ALYSSA QUINT
551

Memory as Metaphor:
Meir Wiener's Novel Kolev Ashkenazi *as*
Critique of the Jewish Historical Imagination
MIKHAIL KRUTIKOV
579

Shmuel Nadler's Besht-Simfonye:
At the Limits of Orthodox Literature
BEATRICE LANG CAPLAN
599

Chava Rosenfarb and The Tree of Life
GOLDIE MORGENTALER
613

Fiddles on Willow Trees:
The Missing Polish Link in the Jewish Canon
MONIKA ADAMCZYK-GARBOWSKA
627

The Kvetcher in the Rye:
J. D. Salinger and Challenges to the Modern Jewish Canon
LEAH GARRETT
645

Israeli Identity in a Post-Zionist Age
YARON PELEG
661

V. WRITERS, CRITICS, AND CANONS

Bellow's Canon
JONATHAN ROSEN
677

The Eicha Problem
DARA HORN
687

The Grand Explainer
CYNTHIA OZICK
701

RUTH WISSE BIBLIOGRAPHY
707

CONTRIBUTORS
717

Introduction

> *My model was the five rabbis [mentioned in the Haggadah]
> who, according to the legend, tell about the departure from
> Egypt all night long, until their disciples come to them and
> say, 'Masters, the time has come to read the morning she-
> ma.' For years I pictured myself as a participant in that all-
> night session where the talk would be so stimulating that
> dawn would catch us unawares...Throughout my teens and
> far beyond, I took the discussion of life to be its essential
> part.*[1]

It is not surprising that Ruth Wisse, in recounting her early intellectual models, cites a rabbinic tradition of disputation and discussion. Nor is it surprising that the subject under discussion in this model of argument is the founding moment of Jewish peoplehood, the exodus from Egypt, for Wisse has devoted her career to a passionate conversation with minds past and present on the art and destiny of *'am yisrael*. And yet Wisse demonstrates her ease and passion in *both* a Jewish and American tradition of argument as, in the next breath, she adds, "Edmund Wilson [was] then my ideal intellectual."[2] It would be inaccurate to say that these two statements are a reflection of an intellectual with a foot in "both worlds." The truth is far more dynamic: Wisse is a thinker whose work and world is all of a piece, a lifelong demonstration of the indispensability of Jewish life to the existence of creative civilization, and of the necessity of creative civilization to the existence of Jewish life.

Wisse's first critical work, *The Schlemiel as Modern Hero* (1971), which traced the evolution of a Jewish folk type across Yiddish and American culture, was her first sustained attempt in writing to argue for the centrality of Jewish creative expression to Western civilization. At the same time, early in her university career, she transformed McGill University's English department by introducing Yiddish language and literature courses into the regular curriculum. "In proposing to teach Jewish literature," she would later recall, "I argued that an expanded humanities curriculum would broaden

---

1. Ruth Wisse, "Between Passovers," *Commentary* (December 1989), 42.
2. Ibid.

the university's coverage of Western culture, legitimating the university's claim to be teaching Western, rather than Christian, civilization."[3]

In a moment when the ascendant ethos of many humanities departments is a severe critique of Western culture, and even its outright rejection, it might be difficult to see just how radical Wisse's project was. It has inspired students and colleagues and has provided the animating energy for the wide array of intellectual and scholarly endeavors she has undertaken for the last several decades. Breadth of knowledge—of literature, intellectual history and Jewish history—enrich her tightly focused book on Yiddish author and intellectual I. L. Peretz (*I.L. Peretz and the Making of Modern Jewish Culture*, 1991), while *A Little Love in Big Manhattan* (1988) has become required reading for anyone hoping to appreciate not just the works of American Yiddish poets Mani Leyb and Moyshe Leyb Halpern, but the astonishingly vibrant creative and intellectual life of Yiddish-speaking immigrants in the first decades of the twentieth century.

These works, as well as the curricular transformations she encouraged and implemented at McGill and later Harvard University, would in turn necessitate her work as a translator and anthologizer. That is to say, her scholarship inspired increasing numbers of students to explore Yiddish literature, but few texts were available in translation. Thus Wisse has served as editor or co-editor of *The Best of Sholem Aleichem, The Penguin Book of Modern Yiddish Verse, A Shtetl and Other Yiddish Novellas, The I.L. Peretz Reader*, and a soon-to-be-published edition of Yankev Glatshteyn's novels. Examples of meticulous translation on levels both linguistic and cultural, these anthologies provide lay readers reliable access to works that resist the sentimentalization of Jewish Eastern Europe. *A Shtetl and other Yiddish Novellas* is a case in point. Compiled as a result of a course she taught at McGill on Yiddish literature in translation, which attracted students "whose curiosity exhausted the available materials and left us wishing for more,"[4] *A Shtetl* offers translations of masterworks by writers as different in artistic temperament as S.Y. Abramovitsh is from Dovid Bergelson and Sh. Anski. In her anthology, the shtetl is revealed as an evolving and constantly shifting imagined homeland, where political engagement and cultural conflict play themselves out against the backdrop of dissolving tradition.

The Modern Jewish Canon is a culmination of Wisse's anthologizing drive, which we can understand as a continuation of the Jewish cultural project that H. N. Bialik called *kinus*, or "ingathering": the bringing together

---

3. Ruth Wisse, *The Modern Jewish Canon: A Journey Through Language and Culture* (New York: The Free Press, 2000), ix. See her preface to *The Modern Jewish Canon* for the best account of her entry as a scholar and teacher into the field of Yiddish literature.

4. Wisse, preface to *A Shtetl and Other Yiddish Novellas* (New York: Behrman House, 1973), 1.

of literary treasures in such a way that a new generation can find further meaning in them. This is not even to mention Wisse's voluminous output of literary and critical essays (still to be collected in one volume), which have probed the work of many of the most significant Yiddish, American-Jewish, and Hebrew writers of the last century. Of increasing sociological and historical significance, Wisse's autobiographical essays record her coming of age in Montreal, in a milieu infused, in particular, by her mother's Yiddishist life in Vilna, which had been cut short by the war, and where prominent Yiddish intellectuals were part of the landscape—Melech Ravitch attended Passover seders, for instance, and none other than the great Yiddish poet Abraham Sutzkever would urge her toward her career as a Yiddish scholar.

As everyone familiar with her work knows well, Wisse does not devote herself solely to academic writing. Indeed, she considers her polemical essays to be an integral part of her cultural program. Her fierce, politically engaged articles defending Israel against multiplying enemies both within and without the Jewish fold, and her daring, argumentative works, *If I am Not For Myself: The Liberal Betrayal of the Jews* and its newly published companion, *Jews and Power*, are the product of someone willing to risk notoriety to say what she feels must be said. A great many of these articles first appeared in *Commentary*, an organ of Jewish intellectual discourse with which she has enjoyed a long and fruitful relationship. A recent contribution serves to remind us of her political commitments even as it attests to the thoughtfulness and natural range she lends to everything she writes. At the core of her memorial essay "An Unheralded Zionist," about her colleague and Hebrew critic Gershon Shaked, is the argument that though his Zionism was idiosyncratic, it ultimately was unshakable. But "An Unheralded Zionist" also brims with fascinating asides and observations (such as on Shaked's fellow European-born contemporaries, Aharon Appelfeld and Saul Friedlander), offers an intriguing peek into Shaked's otherwise forgotten novel, and features a personal reflection on Shaked that Wisse had jotted down at the 1982 conference in Bellagio, Italy, where they first met, describing him as "the most honest and wholesome among us and the most carefully nuanced in his judgments."[5] In the few minutes spent reading an essay by Wisse, the reader has gained so much.

Wisse's style is instantly recognizable; well-versed in critical theory, she nevertheless purposely eschews trendy theoretical language and scholarly jargon in favor of historical literacy, analytic clarity, and the more than occasional polemical thrust. A self-described "skeptical rationalist of Lithuanian

---

5. Wisse, "An Unheralded Zionist," *Commentary* (June 2007). Gershon Shaked was in the process of writing an essay for this festschrift, "The Weakness of Strength and the Strength of Weakness," at the time of his passing, attesting to the fact that the respect between these two friends was as a mutual as their scholarly interests. We regret that we were not able to include the essay in this volume.

stock" rather than a "Hasidic enthusiast,"[6] Wisse has carefully taught her students and readers that the study of modern Jewish literatures must be informed by literacy of a broader scope, including proficiency in Hebrew language and texts, ancient and modern, and an acquaintance with the other national literary traditions with which Jewish writers so frequently interact. It is no wonder that present-day "Hasidic enthusiasts" of Yiddish, for whom sentimentality, nostalgia, anti-Zionism, or radical leftism have colored their approaches to it, find—in Wisse's work—no purchase.[7]

Wisse has touched a chord in generations of students in a way few university professors do. The number of former, and even current, students whose contributions fill this volume is testament to the steady stream of new scholarship that Wisse has inspired. "Education is a bit like love, don't you think?" Wisse once wrote in a note to a student. One measure of Wisse's talent as a teacher is that so many of her students have fallen in love with a literature that they often encounter, for the first time, through a chance meeting with Wisse's scholarship—in an elective course taken because it happened to fit into a difficult schedule, or in a book or article read while browsing in the library. Wisse's offhand comments intrigue even the most casual listener. Consider her observation, for instance, while presenting a Chelm story: "Yiddish literature is the history of Jewish mistakes." Or her human insight layered into literary analysis, such as the warning on romantic relationships that she issued while dissecting a scene in a novel by Yisroel Rabon: "Never get involved in a rescue operation." Or an entire world of political commentary enveloped into a single literary phrase, such as her announcement in a class on *Tevye the Dairyman* that the final line of the Hodel episode, when Tevye weeps at the exile of his daughter and communist son-in-law and asks permission to discuss something more cheerful ("How is the cholera epidemic in Odessa?") is actually "the saddest line in the history of Jewish literature"—not as an expression of a father's grief for his daughter, but as a premonition of the disaster that communism would bring the Jews after so many had committed themselves to it. Or her comment, in a discussion of Yiddish theater, on the painfully bad melodrama that became the very last Yiddish play she saw with her family in Montreal, and how much she had loathed it—but: "What would one give to be back in that theater again, sitting in that audience, living in that world? A year of one's life, at least."

---

6. See *I.L. Peretz and the Making of Modern Jewish Culture* (Seattle: University of Washington Press, 1991), xvii.

7. For more on this, see Wisse, "Yiddish: Past, Present, Imperfect," *Commentary* (November 1997), 32–39.

The editors of this volume (and a good number of its contributors), who have had the privilege of being Wisse's students at McGill and Harvard, each remember the moment when they found themselves falling intractably in love with the literature she taught and, more powerfully, with the larger world of ideas it revealed, only to follow her out of the seminar room to continue the conversation. Wisse's inspired students have gone on to write, teach, translate, and devote themselves to other forms of ingathering, as Aaron Lansky did in establishing the National Yiddish Book Center, which collects, catalogues, and makes available the Yiddish texts that Wisse's first graduate students so sorely lacked.

Students often come to know Wisse first by reputation, as a teacher and scholar who does not march in step with the dominant ethos of the liberal academy. Though the passion and force of her ideas invariably generate heated reactions, students appreciate the competing perspectives she brings to campus. Those colleagues who casually dismiss her ideas invariably do a disservice to themselves by diminishing the culture of argument itself. Though Wisse's interests in the "moral pitch" of a work of literature or in such concepts as dignity, loyalty, and heroism may strike some as old-fashioned, students are refreshed and challenged by her boldness, as when she writes in the preface to *If I Am Not for Myself*: "I wanted to explore the contrast in attitudes to love and loyalty between the traditional religiously inspired determination to contain evil and the modern idea that men and women should be liberated from their civilizing constraints....I found my subject [in] the connecting dramatic link between moral courage in personal life and in politics."[8] Ironically, though Wisse critiques "intellectuals [for] boast[ing] of their iconoclasm," it is she who, more often than not, can be counted on for her independence of mind: "The opposite of loyalty is disloyalty, a rotten quality, whatever attractive notions it holds of itself. Psychologically, it breeds selfishness; intellectually, it rewards lying; socially, it cultivates irresponsibility; politically, it invites tyranny."[9]

Wisse's students also quickly discover that she is a famously generous and kind teacher and mentor. Her intellectual rigor isn't a sign of stubbornness, but rather of a mind that takes ideas so seriously that it will not ignore or take lightly new challenges, particularly from students. For Wisse, students and the intellectual energy of the classroom are to be taken as seriously as her most erudite academic colleagues and the most prestigious public forum. More than once, she invited the students in her undergraduate seminar in American Jewish literature to dinner at her home in Cambridge in lieu of the last class meeting; there, students were told in advance, they

---

8. Ruth Wisse, *If I am Not for Myself: The Liberal Betrayal of the Jews* (New York: The Free Press, 1992), xiii.

9. Ibid., 219.

would hold the course's final discussion on Saul Bellow's novella *The Bella-rosa Connection*. Each student was shocked to arrive in Wisse's dining room and discover Saul Bellow himself seated at the head of the table, ready to lead the discussion. For her graduate students, Wisse has been the staunchest advocate. They remember her 8:30 A.M. phone calls to discuss their papers (always knowing that she had been waiting since her usual pre-dawn walk-up time for an hour when it might be remotely acceptable to try to reach a student), or the invitations to her office, where she might usher in visitors wearing fuzzy bedroom slippers on a cold winter afternoon. Her passionate rhetoric dazzles, but not by design; there is no showmanship in her personality. Her political, literary, and personal candor, her students learn, are all of a piece: when one takes ideas seriously, one becomes com-fortable with them, showing them an intimacy that comes only from pro-found respect.

> *A book on the canon is by definition open-ended. Let read-ers take it as an invitation to set out on their own journeys through Jewish language and culture.*[10]

Our decision to fasten, as the organizing principle for her *festschrift*, upon Wisse's *The Modern Jewish Canon: A Journey Through Language and Culture* (2000), was largely the result of her invitation in that work to continue, so to speak, the conversation. Indeed, Wisse energetically lob-bied us to adopt "argument" as the theme for the *festschrift* (as if we did not already know how much she valued argument). Wisse's sensibility, as we have seen, is fundamentally dialogic: built on conversation, disagreement, and thus transcendence. The "primary scene" of modern Jewish literature, Wisse has said, is "two Jews talking." In this volume, we have thirty-six writ-ers "talking"—with Wisse, with previous scholarship, and often, without being aware of it, with each other. Some use specific moments, texts, or perceived lacunae in *The Modern Jewish Canon* as jumping-off points for their arguments; others refer to Wisse obliquely in providing new readings in and of literary fields that she has pioneered. We asked scholars both established and just launching their careers to contribute; we asked stu-dents, colleagues, and friends. In a sense, this book collects the musings of an extended family.

We have structured the volume around the narrative, so to speak, of *The Modern Jewish Canon*; thus, we begin with a number of meditations on canon-formation. This section addresses both terms in "Jewish canon": some pieces encourage opening up the Jewish canon even further, geo-graphically, linguistically, and aesthetically, while others address the specif-ic issue of Jewishness in creating a canon. We include the first full transla-

---

10. Wisse, *The Modern Jewish Canon*, 348.

tion into English of *Shomers mishpet*, Sholem Aleichem's mock-trial of a fellow Yiddish writer and one of the first efforts to argue for Yiddish literature's competitiveness, as Wisse would say, as a world literature.

The essays in "Elaborations" offer re-readings of Wisse's canonical authors, from George Eliot to Philip Roth. We are fortunate to have three distinct examinations of Isaac Bashevis Singer (including a thorough reconsideration of that most canonical Bashevis story, "Gimpel the Fool," by Wisse's brother and fellow scholar, David Roskies) and two of Aharon Appelfeld, thus making very explicit the degree to which argument and conversation provide for the fullest account of literary history. In "Conversations," essays begin to open up to other national and linguistic canons, examining the ways in which Jewish texts construct themselves in relation to other texts and aesthetic media both within and without their own traditions. These essays compare "canons" across time, across languages, and across genres.

In closing *The Modern Jewish Canon*, Wisse writes: "In taking leave of my subject let me reiterate that this book is only a signpost on an unfinished road. I myself am already in the position of the incredulous reader who will say, 'How could you have failed to write about *that*?!'"[11] The essays in "Interventions" address precisely *that*: those texts that, these authors argue, were excluded from Wisse's "unfinished" discussion. Finally, we close with a number of meditations on the role of the critic, moral and otherwise, vis-à-vis the literary civilization about which she writes. It is important not to confuse, Wisse writes, "universalism, which seeks to eliminate tribal categories, with universality, which is the global resonance of a tribal work."[12] Wisse defends the distinctiveness of Jewish literature as an expression of the choice of Jews to remain distinct, and also acknowledges the challenges of assuming this position:

> *The concept of modern Jewish literature would have no value whatsoever if one were not prepared to respect the autonomy of Jewishness, and respect for that autonomy would have to be implicit in any work of Jewish literature. But how does one establish criteria for Jewishness in the arts when the Jews have changed so much in the twentieth century and the arts continually reinvent themselves?*[13]

The essays in this volume take up this very question, arguing with Wisse even as they are founded upon the very same premise: a defense of a distinctively Jewish literary tradition, one that ranges across languages and national contexts.

---

11. Ibid., 347.

12. Ibid., 19.

13. Ibid., 10–11.

It is our hope that this book will express some small fraction of our gratitude to the person who has given us the key to a *genizah* full of arguments and ideas, and who still gives us new reasons to read, rediscover, and reinvent its contents. May she continue to provoke many more discussions that will continue until the dawn catches us unawares, refreshed and renewed by her insight.

We acknowledge with gratitude the support of the Yanoff-Taylor Lecture and Publication Fund of the Center for Jewish Studies at Harvard University. In particular, we thank Professor Jay Harris, former director of the CJS, for approving the publication of this celebratory volume, and Rachel Rockenmacher, CJS administrator, for her patience and assistance.

Yosl Bergner, one of Israel's leading artists and a longtime friend of Ruth Wisse, generously volunteered the original sketches that grace the cover and interior of this volume. We thank him for his enthusiasm and for coming up with images that reflect the theme of this book.

And of course, we thank Ruth Wisse for her friendship, encouragement, and wisdom.

The Editors
Jerusalem and New York City
July 2007

I.
MAKING A CANON

Writing Jewish

HILLEL HALKIN

In his 1913 essay "The Hebrew Book," the prominent Hebrew poet and literary figure Chaim Nachman Bialik elaborated on an idea that had been preoccupying him for several years. Termed by him *kinus*, literally a "gathering" or "bringing together," this was to select, edit, and publish in attractively affordable editions a large number of classical, nonsacred Jewish texts hitherto inaccessible to the general reader. The project was ambitious because, unlike the sacred component of Jewish literature, which had always circulated widely, much of the material Bialik was thinking of (ancient religious poetry, medieval prose romances, medieval and postmedieval Hebrew verse, works of Jewish philosophy, and so forth) was out of print or had never been printed.

Bialik conceived of this undertaking, which today we would call establishing and promulgating a secular Jewish canon, as part of the cultural program of Zionism, a national effort to recover a Jewish literary tradition that, far from having been restricted to the religious sphere alone, had embraced the full range of human experience. In setting forth a practical proposal for *kinus*, he divided the texts in question into seven categories: the apocryphal books of the Bible, the medieval corpus of Judeo-Arabic literature, writing in modern Jewish vernaculars like Yiddish, and so on. Concerning the sixth of these categories, which he described as "[modern] works of a universal nature written by Jewish writers in non-Jewish languages," Bialik observed:

> For the moment, I propose that [this] category be omitted, since its inclusion in the project of *kinus* is premature. This is not because it lacks national importance—on the contrary!—but because of the special problems it involves.

Bialik did not dwell on these "problems," even though they may not have been obvious to his readers, who in 1913 could have named but a few of the prominent "Jewish writers of a universal nature in non-Jewish languages" familiar to us today. There was, of course, the seminal case of Spinoza. And Heine, if one overlooked or forgave his conversion to Christianity. Likewise, Disraeli. And a small number of contemporary Jewish authors writ-

---

ing for predominantly non-Jewish audiences, including Lev Shestov in Russian, Max Nordau and Arthur Schnitzler in German, and Ferenc Molnar in Hungarian. Perhaps a handful of Bialik's readers had even heard of such new talents as the Russian poet Osip Mandelstam or the half-Jewish Marcel Proust, the first volume of whose *Remembrance of Things Past* appeared in the same year as Bialik's essay. But it would have taken a degree of prescience even then to foresee that this still thin trickle of Jewish literary talent into the languages of Europe was about to become a major deluge.

Franz Kafka, Italo Svevo, Isaac Babel, Elias Canetti, Albert Cohen, Joseph Roth, Julian Tuwim, Antoni Slonimski, Ilya Ehrenburg, Elsa Lasker-Schüler, Hermann Broch, Bruno Schulz, Walter Benjamin, Nelli Sachs, Paul Celan, Primo Levi, Vasily Grossman, Saul Bellow, Nadine Gordimer, Joseph Brodsky, Philip Roth: even a partial list of major Jewish writers of our times amply illustrates the problems Bialik had in mind. Some of these authors were born to two Jewish parents, some to one, some to parents baptized before their birth. Some converted to Christianity themselves. Some were raised as Jews and others were not. Some dealt explicitly with Jewish themes in their writing, some inferentially, some to all appearances not at all. Some felt comfortable with their Jewishness. Some did not. Some were ambivalent or indifferent.

Moreover, although these distinctions sometimes form consistent patterns—a strong Jewish identity, for instance, often goes together with clear Jewish concerns in the work—this is not always the case. Kafka, intensely involved with being a Jew, never used the word in his fiction, whereas Proust made Jews into key characters in his seven-volume masterpiece while never coming forth as one himself. Slonimsky, born a Polish Catholic to converted parents, came to value a Jewish heritage that Joseph Roth, raised in a Galician shtetl, repudiated. Primo Levi, sent to Auschwitz as a Jew, appears to have considered his Jewishness as a fact of life that was to be neither regretted nor overly valued.

Who of these writers belongs in a Jewish canon? Bialik's reluctance to enter such a conceptual thicket is understandable.

And not only Bialik's. The subject continued to be shied away from long after him. In the United States, as Ruth Wisse points out in *The Modern Jewish Canon* the notion of a multilingual corpus of twentieth-century writing usefully considered Jewish was still regarded as outlandish even when she was a graduate student at Columbia in the 1960s. Books, articles, and academic courses on a modern Hebrew or Yiddish literature that transcended national boundaries, yes—such disciplines were no different from English, Spanish, or German literature, which were likewise not confined to a single country. But a modern *Jewish* literature, defined neither by the religious beliefs, nationality, nor language of its authors but by a nebulous assumption of secular Jewish character or peoplehood (which many of these authors would have rejected), hardly seemed a serious proposition.

Even at the height of acclaim in the 1960s and early 1970s for the "American Jewish fictional renaissance," when writers such as Bellow, Roth, and Bernard Malamud were being freshly hailed for their contribution to American culture, it was that culture to which they were seen, and saw themselves, as belonging—a judgment acceded to by an American Jewry that often tended to view them less as an asset than as a threat to its carefully nurtured image. In Europe, countries struggling to disown a legacy of totalitarianism and anti-Semitism were even more anxious to claim leading Jewish writers as their own. A Kafka, Babel, or Schulz (Babel murdered by the Communists, Schulz by the Nazis) was a monument to a "different" Germany, Russia, or Poland only if his achievements could be attributed to a native culture.

In Israel, where Bialik's project of *kinus*, though never systematically implemented, was carried out ad hoc on a book-by-book basis, the situation was similar for different reasons. Though secular Jewish peoplehood was a Zionist axiom, its literary expression was taken to be Hebrew, the "national language" of the Jews. It was thus only, or at least predominantly, in Hebrew that Jewish literature was to be sought. Works written in other languages were either a tragic miscalculation—as was the case with Yiddish literature, many of whose authors had known Hebrew well and even started their careers in it before switching to the doomed East-European Jewish vernacular—or a consequence of Jewish cultural unraveling in modern times, as was the case with writers who, deprived of a traditional Jewish education, never had Hebrew as an option. And although the Sholom Aleichems and I.L. Peretzes could be regained for high Jewish culture by translation from the "low" medium of Yiddish into Hebrew (just as Maimonides' *Guide for the Perplexed* or Yehuda Halevi's *Kuzari*, originally written in Judeo-Arabic, had been rescued by their Hebraization in medieval Spain), modern writers operating entirely beyond Jewish linguistic bounds were viewed as marginal. At best, they could await their turn.

This turn, it would seem, has now come at last. Wisse's book is one formidable indication of an upsurge of interest over the last decade in the Jewishness of twentieth-century writers. Though it far surpasses them in ambition and achievement, it joins books like Leslie Fiedler's *Essays on Literature and Jewish Identity* (1991), Alice Stone Nakhimovsky's *Russian-Jewish Literature and Identity* (1992), Eugenia Prokop-Janiec's *Interwar Polish-Jewish Literature as a Cultural and Artistic Phenomenon* (1992), Hana Wirth-Nesher's *What Is Jewish Literature?* (1994), and Giuliano Baioni's *Kafka, Literature, and Judaism* (1994). Recent years have also seen a host of articles in literary journals and anthologies on such diverse subjects as "Identity and Diaspora: A Cross-Cultural Subversion and Redefinition of Nationhood" and "The Marrano Epic in the Literary Sephardism of Argentina"; university courses such as "Diaspora and Jewish Fiction" and "Literature and Politics: The Case of Zionism"; and even the introduction into the curricula of Jewish secondary schools of authors such as Philip Roth and Primo Levi. Suddenly, "Jewish writers on universal themes in non-Jewish languages" are "in."

Some of the reasons for this may be obvious. One is the gradual discovery and dissemination by literary critics of once-esoteric Jewish authors such as Kafka, Babel, Schulz, Celan, and Walter Benjamin, who today have become de rigueur. Another is the influence of multiculturalism, with its interest in hybrid identities cutting across clear ethnic and national lines. The spread in Israel of post-Zionism, for which the primacy of Hebrew is no longer an issue, is also a contributing factor, as is the growth of a "neo-Diasporism" in America that is on the lookout for reformulations of Jewish identity within the framework of minority status. Concomitantly, a decreased fear of anti-Semitism has made Jews less defensive toward Jewish writing critical of Jewish life. And finally, the postmodernist assault on the "Western canon," which it has demanded be "opened" to allegedly excluded groups like women and minorities, has made canon-formation itself a hotly debated issue.

As if to put an official stamp of cultural entrepreneurship on all this activity, the well-funded and well-publicized National Yiddish Book Center of Amherst, Massachusetts, significantly expanding its activities beyond its original mandate, has now announced a "Great Jewish Books Program," culminating in an international panel of seven judges that will pick "the 100 great Jewish books of modern times in all languages."[1] Once the selection process is completed, declares a recent press release, the program will turn to "reissuing out-of-print Jewish books, commissioning new English translations, and developing educational initiatives based on the list"—in other words, systematically introducing this vast body of material into the consciousness of American Jews. Ironically, it is in English rather than Hebrew that the sixth category of Bialik's *kinus* has at last found a willing sponsor.

As one of the judges selected to serve on the panel of the Great Jewish Books Program, I have in my possession a shortlist from which the 100 winners are to be chosen. Drawn up in consultation with Jewish critics and teachers of literature from all over the world, it is in fact a dauntingly long list. Alphabetically arranged in it are 445 authors from Pearl Abraham, Hermann Adler, Shmuel Yosef Agnon, and Woody Allen to Herman Wouk, Louis Zukofsky, Arnold Zweig, and Stefan Zweig, and close to 2,500 individual titles. Of these, I have perhaps read 150, and while the batting average of other panelists may be better, one book in five would be an impressive achievement for anyone.

---

1. The finished list has since been released and is available via the National Yiddish Book Center. [eds.]

Looking at the columns of titles, in which appear such entries as two books in Spanish by Alcina Lubitch Domecq, six books in Russian by Osip Dymov, eight books in French by Armand Lunel, and twenty-eight books in English by Marge Piercy, all authors that in my ignorance I have never heard of, I wonder what is to be gained from even attempting the task of picking the lucky few. Agreeing as I do with Harold Bloom, who argues in his *The Western Canon* that great books are made by authors, not by committees or hegemonic power structures, I can think of no other qualified judge of literary greatness than Time. Since Time will not be a significant participant in the National Yiddish Book Center's panel, whose final decisions are due next year, what will those decisions be worth?

Just why we often have to wait a generation or two (though rarely more) after an author's death to arrive at a reliable judgment of his work is a puzzling question. Perhaps this has to do with the background noise of contemporary culture, which must fade before the solo authorial voice can be heard with sufficient clarity. In any event, while cultivated readers and even professional critics may overlook great works of their age while being taken in by more mediocre competitors—not to mention those most tragic of ultimately forgotten books, the very good but not uniquely outstanding ones—this rarely happens when going back in time. There, we have more perfect pitch. Though literary taste has its fashions, and Byron will sometimes be preferred to Wordsworth and Wordsworth sometimes to Byron for as long as Romantic poetry is read, the remarkable thing about the literature of the past, as opposed to that of the present, is how little disagreement there is regarding it. The Latin poet Persius complained that "thick-headed Rome" preferred one Attius Labeo to his contemporary Juvenal, but who would take up cudgels for Attius today? And for all the voguish talk about unfairly neglected women, blacks, and "minor-literature" authors of the past, can one point to a single deserving representative of such groups who was not seated with the immortals long ago?

No doubt the skittishness of still new reputations troubled Bialik, too. The contemporary books whose ratings we fight over will one day fall into rank by themselves; why not then rely on the literary marketplace, that is, on the slowly stabilizing preferences of readers, critics, publishers, and educators, to tell the distance runners from the sprinters? Give Homer enough time and, mysteriously enough, he will outsell even Harry Potter.

Indeed, long-term popularity has always made canons, which, conspiracy theory notwithstanding, tend to be little more than after-the-fact recognitions of a literary tradition's favorite works. Even the Hebrew Bible, the first and arguably the most important body of canonically defined literature in history, appears to have been consolidated on such a basis. Although we are ignorant of the exact process of its formation, we do know that its books were widely read, copied, and taught long before the final rabbinic seal of approval was put on them in the early years of the Common Era—far more

widely than texts not included in holy writ, such as the Apocrypha or the
Dead Sea Scrolls. While there is every indication, for example, that the Dead
Sea sectaries knew and revered the same biblical books that the rabbis did,
there is no sign that their own literature was read or appreciated by anyone
but themselves.

Thus, while much of what failed to enter the Bible was unacceptably het-
erodox in any case, Robert Alter is surely correct to observe in his *Canon
and Creativity* that "it seems plausible that there were Hebrew texts
excluded from the canon not for doctrinal reasons but because they were
inferior as literature." If one takes even the most verbally accomplished of
the Dead Sea writings, the poems of the "Scroll of Thanksgiving," and compares them to the biblical Psalms they were modeled on, this inferiority is
evident at a glance. The same is true of the Apocrypha. The Book of Tobit
has its charms, but these do not compare to Esther's or Ruth's; Jubilees is a
dull and windy retelling of Genesis; next to the compiler of Proverbs, Ben-
Sira is priggish and trite; Isaiah glows from its collision with a transcendent
reality whereas Enoch is flaccid with self-spun fantasy. In every case, it is
the stronger book that ended up in the canon.

Alter is also just to remark on the converse, namely, that some books of
the Bible, such as Job and the Song of Songs, presented doctrinal problems
themselves and were canonized not because of their contents but in spite of
them and by virtue of their literary power. The Song of Songs is a particularly good example because of the extravagant lengths to which the rabbis'
reading of it went in order to justify its inclusion in the Bible, turning a highly sensual love poem into a religious allegory; and while it was their allegorization of the poem that made its canonization possible, it was their determination to canonize it, one feels, that (unconsciously, it may be) led to its
allegorization. For a man like Rabbi Akiva, who held that "if all the Bible is
holy, the Song of Songs is the holy of holies," the prospect of losing its rare
beauty must have been, if not sufficient reason for admitting it to the protective sanctuary of Scripture, sufficient reason for finding a reason.

But is the situation different with modern authors such as Kafka and
Proust? Although, three-quarters of a century after their deaths, their greatness is beyond question, might we not be reading them extravagantly, too,
when we interpret this greatness as singularly Jewish? Are we seeking to
appropriate them for a tradition to which they do not intrinsically belong?
And how is one to establish their relationship to this tradition? Using what
criteria? We are back to the entanglements of Bialik's sixth category.

Yes to Kafka, no to Proust: such is Ruth Wisse's verdict in *The Modern
Jewish Canon*.

Wisse, who teaches Yiddish literature at Harvard and is well known to
Commentary readers for her superb essays on Jewish culture and politics,
begins her brief dismissal of Proust with an even briefer one of the American Jewish literary critic Lionel Trilling, whom she quotes as having

remarked when a young man: "Being a Jew is like walking in the wind or swimming: you are touched at all points and conscious everywhere." Wisse then declares, "Had this insight informed [Trilling's] fiction, he would have secured a place of honor in the modern Jewish canon." But, she points out, Trilling's only novel, *The Middle of the Journey*, despite being set in a world of left-wing New York intellectuals that was in reality heavily Jewish, has not a Jew in it. Whether because Trilling "neutered" his main characters "to make [them] more purely American or because he could not find an aesthetic means of integrating Jewishness into his story, its consideration as a Jewish book," Wisse writes with genuine regret, "is precluded." And she goes on:

> If it hurts to omit Trilling, it aches to leave out Proust. Some critics consider Proust a Jewish writer despite the fact that he was baptized a Catholic and received communion when he was twelve. They may do so because Proust's mother, Jeanne Weil, came from a Jewish family in Metz in northeastern France, whose members he stayed in touch with all his life. Proust was deeply influenced by his mother and, through her, by his Jewishness. The social matrix of his work owes much to his firsthand knowledge of French Jewry....[But] though Proust derives from the Jews and shows sympathy with their condition, he is at pains in his writing to show that he does not share in their fate....[His] first-person narrator emphasizes his own exclusion from [the Jewish people]....Though the narrator is also detached from the French majority...he is much more sorrowfully and explicitly estranged from the Jews. Proust's familiarity and sympathy do not translate into a novel of Jewish experience, however deep and persuasive its knowledge of the subject.

For Wisse, then, Trilling and Proust have stepped out of bounds by crossing opposite sidelines. The first does not belong in a Jewish canon because, while possessing a Jewish identity, he did not write about Jews; the second because, while writing about Jews, he did not possess a Jewish identity. Each represents a class in which other Jewish writers can be placed.

But what, then, of Kafka, who felt Jewish like Trilling but like Trilling kept Jews out of his fiction? Where is the logic in including him?

The logic, Wisse might reply, begins with Kafka's having kept many things out of his fiction, the "abstractness" of which has been frequently commented on. Since there are practically no Christians in it, either, or Czechs, Germans, names of countries, cities, or streets, or references to contemporary events, the lack of Jews merely follows a general rule. Jews must be looked for in Kafka symbolically—but when they are, one finds them everywhere.

Thus, Wisse contends in a chapter on Kafka's novel *The Trial*, the book's protagonist Joseph K., finding himself unreasonably and powerlessly under arrest one day, is in the typical situation of the "liberal Jew, who, having come to trust that reason *was* power, had forfeited the protection of God without shoring up any political alternative." In fact, Joseph K.'s basic guilt

is being Jewish, or, more precisely, a Jew amid a German culture and language in which (like Kafka) he feels himself an intruder, so that his being
put to death at the novel's end with the self-loathing knowledge that "the
shame of it must outlive him" is, Wisse writes, "the price [he] pays for living
in German, and the shame will outlive him because he has acquiesced in its
terms."

There are other possible "Jewish" interpretations of *The Trial*, starting
with the fact that "the Law" (*Das Gesetz*), the mysterious presence before
which Joseph K. stands accused, is a term commonly used in German no
less than in English for the Mosaic commandments—commandments that,
according to Christian theology, are so beyond the human capacity for obedience that they render all men guilty by their very existence. Yet in a climactic section of the novel often reprinted separately as "the Parable of the
Law," it is suggested to Joseph K. that the rigors of "the Law" are in reality
accessible to everyone and even uniquely tailored to our individual needs,
the difficulty being not their pitiless remoteness but a false illusion of this
that deters us from approaching their "inextinguishable radiance." Read this
way, *The Trial* is indeed a deeply Jewish book.

This raises a problem, however. "The Law" in *The Trial* can also be read,
and has been read by most critics, as standing for other things, such as the
bureaucratic apparatus of the modern state, the ruthless pseudo-justice of
twentieth-century totalitarianism, the guilt-inducing operations of the
superego, and so forth. This overdetermination is part of the brilliance of
the novel, the various interpretations of which, far from canceling each
other out, are mutually enriching. Certainly, therefore, there is no bar to
construing *The Trial* in terms of Jewish themes as well, especially as we
know from Kafka's letters and journals that these absorbed him greatly. Yet
since doing so means choosing one set of possibilities out of many, and
sometimes (as with other interpretations) reading against the grain (the
"Parable of the Law" is related to Joseph K. by a Catholic priest, one of the
few characters in Kafka's fiction whose religion is made explicit), can we
not do this with other authors too?

Why not with Proust, for example? Taken at face value, the many passages about Jews in *Remembrance of Things Past* do confirm Wisse's judgment that the novel's narrator is "at pains to show that he does not share
their fate." But the same can be said of the many passages dealing with sexual inversion, a condition gradually revealed in the novel's course to affect
more and more of its characters but never—though Proust's homosexuality
was common knowledge in his lifetime—the narrator himself. Since no
sophisticated reader would point to this as proof that Proust did not identify
himself as a homosexual, why should the narrator's distancing himself from
Jews demonstrate Proust's nonidentification as a Jew? There is even a
lengthy passage in *Remembrance of Things Past* in which Jews are compared to homosexuals as social outcasts forced to choose between desper-

ately concealing their true selves in order to "pass" or clannishly flaunting them in defensive self-segregation. What is to prevent one from pushing this analogy a step further, as some literary critics have done, by assuming the writer of this passage to have been not only Proust the homosexual, but also Proust the Jew?

Wisse herself is clearly aware of the fragility of resting the case for Jewish canonicity on the twin supports of Jewish subject matter and Jewish identity, each of which can be coaxed from the other, for much of her book is an argument for a standard that is stricter if also vaguer—namely, the insistence that both these aspects of a writer's Jewishness be, in some sense, enhancing of Jewish life. Not only, one suspects, would the failure to meet this standard be her fallback position on Proust, it is her express reason for excluding other writers—the seemingly arch-Jewish Bernard Malamud, for example, to whom she ascribes a caricaturized version of the Jew, ever doomed to be either the hapless shlemiel or the Christ-like sufferer.

This too is problematic, however. It is not that Wisse is unsubtle in her discriminations. Far from it; her discussions of the writers on her far-ranging list are both delicate and wonderfully penetrating, and taken together they make a strong case for the multilingual Jewish literature whose existence she sets out to prove. (Among these writers are Sholom Aleichem; Mendele; Kafka; Babel; Grossman; Primo Levi; the Polish novelist Henryk Grynberg; the Hebrew authors Yosef Haim Brenner, S.Y. Agnon, and Aharon Appelfeld; the Yiddish novelist Isaac Bashevis Singer, the Yiddish poets Yakov Glatstein and Moshe Kulbak; the Canadian poet A.M. Klein; and the Americans Abraham Cahan, Henry and Philip Roth, Bellow, and Cynthia Ozick.) She can take a novelist such as Brenner, accused by some Hebrew critics of "Jewish self-hatred" despite his practical commitment to Zionism, and explain why, by having "clear[ed] away the detritus of sickly guilt" clogging the Jewish soul, he qualifies for inclusion. And, writing against her own conservative political views, she can admiringly explicate the short stories in Babel's *Red Cavalry*, written by a committed Bolshevik, and demonstrate how well they probe this same soul.

In the final analysis, though, one doubts whether her criteria, while they work well for her, are generally applicable. Although it may seem reasonable to expect a Jewish canon to serve Jewish needs, it is less reasonable to make it contingent on them; for even were it possible to agree on what those needs are, it makes little sense to demand recognition for "modern Jewish literature" on a basis of parity with other literatures while judging it by standards uniquely its own. What English critic would bar D.H. Lawrence from the English canon because he despised England and wanted nothing to do with it, or argue that, because Joyce refused to step on Irish soil for the entirety of his adult life, only a close examination of the attitudes toward Ireland in his fiction can determine whether he belongs to Irish literature?

Shall we then abandon this line of approach and look for another—perhaps a more formal one, like that taken by Alter in his *Canon and Creativity*? This slim volume is a study of how, even in modern times, the ancient Jewish canon of the Bible has gone on exerting its influence on major writers. For his purposes, Alter has chosen three very different texts: one, Bialik's long narrative Hebrew poem "The Dead of the Desert," written by a man raised and educated in the world of East-European Jewish Orthodoxy; a second, Kafka's *Amerika*, whose author was the product of a partially assimilated Jewish home in Central Europe; and a third, Joyce's *Ulysses*, the work of a renegade Irish Catholic with a polymath's knowledge of European culture. While the question of a modern Jewish canon is not explicitly raised by him, Alter's project is relevant to Wisse's because, by tracing the ways in which the Bible has remained productive in modern authors, it seems to suggest a solution to our dilemma.

Predictably, Alter's analysis of "The Dead of the Desert" is the least surprising, for not only is Bialik's immersion in the Bible evident in all he wrote, the poem itself takes off from a rabbinic legend based on the Bible. More illuminating is the chapter on Kafka's *Amerika*, the plot of which, Alter shows, contains numerous parallels with the books of Genesis and Exodus. But most intriguing is the section on *Ulysses*, a novel famous for being patterned on Homer's *Odyssey* even though its main character, Leopold Bloom, is a Jew. By dissecting key images, Alter demonstrates that the Bible is "a necessary complement to Homer in Joyce's literary scheme," the two working together to enable Joyce "to take stock of the literary origins of the Western tradition," so that "in the extraordinarily supple and varied uses to which the Bible is put in *Ulysses*, it is converted into a secular literary text, but perhaps not entirely secular, after all, because it is reasserted as a source of value and vision."

As Alter observes, canonicity sets in motion a self-reinforcing dynamic. Originally conferred on certain books because they are more resonant than others, it compels us to pay them a different kind of attention, one that teases out their riches in the form of new books that become the objects of further creative exegesis, and so on and so forth. Why not base our modern Jewish canon, then, on books that form a link in this chain, of which the Bible is forever the prime mover?

A promising idea, but no more than that; for the fact that we find a voice like Joyce's taking part in this collective conversation (there are even allusions to rabbinic literature in *Ulysses*) shows how unsatisfactory a diagnostic tool it is. Surely Joyce does not belong in a modern Jewish canon because of this, any more than he does because Leopold Bloom is a Jew.

This suggests an interesting thought experiment. Suppose a biographer were to unearth the fact that, unbeknownst to him, Joyce had had a Jewish grandparent who died before he was born: would this win him a place in a Jewish canon? If yes, why should a trivial biographical fact make a difference? If no, how many Jewish grandparents would it take? And suppose the reverse were true, and Joyce had written *Ulysses* under the mistaken impression that a grandparent of his was Jewish—what then? Or suppose *Ulysses* had been published anonymously and we did not know who its author was?

Such questions are absurd. They are a sign that something is wrong with our thinking.

Let us try another experiment, this time by going back to the biblical book of Job. A curious thing about this book is that there is nothing in it to prove that its author was an Israelite or even particularly familiar with biblical religion, some of the premises of which he sharply calls into question. Indeed, one theory about him (now rather discredited) has been that he was not a Jew and did not write his book in Hebrew, a language into which it was later translated. Suppose that a new archeological or textual find were to prove that this theory was correct. Would Jews have to excise Job from the Hebrew canon?

Obviously not. The book of Job, even if it turns out to have originally been "a work of universal nature written in a non-Jewish language," is an integral part of Jewish literary tradition. The issue of its provenance is irrelevant to its place in this tradition, just as irrelevant as is the fact that, Christian and Western culture having appropriated Job for themselves, most non-Jews would not consider it a Jewish book.

This should be our answer. We have in a sense been barking up the wrong tree. The question of provenance—who wrote a given text, with what personal background, motives, and opinions—cannot ultimately determine a modern Jewish canon, any more than it can determine a text's worth. What matters is less where a book is coming from than where it is going: to, or not to, a lasting engagement with other Jewish books.

Of course, provenance matters. Kafka stands a better chance of entering such an engagement than Proust because he wrestled with Jewish issues more strenuously. And if, despite its literary greatness and Jewish subject matter, Jews do not feel that *Ulysses* is a book they must address as Jews, this may indeed be because Joyce was raised as an Irish Catholic, or because, as Wisse remarks in unfavorably comparing the novel with George Eliot's *Daniel Deronda*, there is nothing Jewishly enhancing about it. But although *Ulysses* will probably never become a Jewish book, that is not something that can be determined *a priori*: one can, after all, conceive of a future in which *Ulysses* would be so widely read and responded to by Jews that it would be considered a necessary part of a Jewish education. Time, the one arbiter of literary greatness, will decide whether to capture such greatness for a Jewish orbit—which is all the more reason to give Time a prod on behalf of the books we most care about.

There are Jews who might wonder who needs a modern Jewish canon at all. I can imagine one such Jew regarding me right now, his hand resting on an open Talmud. "So!" he says with an ironic gleam. "The Bible you already know! The Mishnah and Gemara you've learned by heart! Would that all Jews had studied as much and had time for your Kafka and your Proust!"

I do not make light of this man. He pricks a sore conscience. But that is neither here nor there. Bialik heard similar words from his teachers at the yeshiva of Volozhin in Lithuania over a hundred years ago, and his conscience, to judge from his poetry, was in a worse state than ours. It is too late in the day to reopen that old argument. All that needs to be observed is that, since all Jewish arguments that are, as the rabbis put it, "for the sake of heaven" are in some sense over books, it is better for them to be over the same books.

If one looks at the great schisms in Jewish history, the breaking point has always been textual: writings accepted as canonical by one side but not by the other. To some, this may be a reason for not seeking to expand the Jewish canon beyond its traditional bounds. But if modern Jews are going to converse with each other and not only with tradition, they will need common great books of their own. Otherwise, they will be talking to the wall.

Knocking on Heaven's Gate:
Hebrew Literature
and Wisse's Canon

ALAN MINTZ

It is perhaps inevitable that at the turn of the millennium Ruth Wisse should have mounted a counter-attack against the assault on the canon that had been building during the last two decades of the old century. Although *The Modern Jewish Canon* is, of course, principally concerned with Jewish literature, the position it takes about canon making was mobilized in reaction to the turmoil in American Studies that came to a head in the 1980s. This was a heady time when oral narratives by slaves and American Indians were being discovered and great numbers of unknown or forgotten works by women, African American, Asian American, and Chicano writers widely published. The curricular cartel of Poe, Hawthorne, Melville, Twain, James, Faulkner, and company had to be cracked open, it was claimed, to embrace, or at least to represent, the diversity of American literatures, which no longer deserved to be relegated to separate categories labeled minority or ethnic. In the face of this claim, figures such as E. D. Hirsch and Harold Bloom reasserted the need for a common core of literary works whose universal interest and unimpeachable aesthetic achievement would provide a coherent basis for a shared national culture.[1]

When Wisse set out her vision of the modern Jewish canon, she was turning in two directions at the same time: toward the conservative camp in the culture wars in the American academy and toward her colleagues in Jewish studies. In the case of the former, Wisse generally applauded the will to set standards and to assign to great books an authoritative role in culture and schooling. Yet, as a Jew engaged in the study of Jewish literature, Wisse had to demur when it came to the universal and deracinated portrayal of the human condition in most versions of the western canon. National context is not merely background and setting for strong works of art but the deep soil in which they grow and make sense and in which human struggle becomes most human. In presenting a modern *Jewish* canon, then, Wisse did not see herself filing a report from a provincial outpost of Western literature. Rather, the Jewish works she presented in her volume are great precisely because they are entangled in the parochial predicaments of a group whose transactions with modernity should be of interest to all.

---

1. Harold Bloom, *The Western Canon; The Books and School of the Ages* (New York: Harcourt Brace, 1994); E. D. Hirsch, *Cultural Literacy; What Every American Needs to Know* (Boston: Houghton Mifflin, 1987).

A related kind of entanglement gave Wisse reason to contest positions held by some members of her own party in the national debates about the canon. She had no problem joining the chorus of voices deploring the manipulation of the curriculum to further (radical) social ends, and she did not disagree with advocating allegiance to enduring aesthetic standards. But she would not join Harold Bloom in declaring that true essence of the canon rests only upon the sovereign autonomy of the aesthetic and the private pleasures of reading. The best works of Jewish literature are wholly embroiled in the ferment of Jewish historical forces and ideologies, and their extra-literary dimensions cannot be extracted without doing violence to their integrity.

Yet, after the fashion of a family feud, Wisse's fiercest polemical energies are brought back home. Although modern Jewish literature may enjoy recognition in both the public mind and Jewish studies, it is nevertheless set apart in a gauzy aesthetic zone of its own and denied the authority accorded to works of Jewish history and thought. Wisse sought to upend this hierarchy by demonstrating through strong readings of strong texts that it is the modern Jewish novel, as a complex and multivocal act of historical understanding that, in fact, provides the fullest and most profound account available of modern Jewish experience. "It is the most complete way of knowing the inner life of Jews," Wisse avers.[2] Although Wisse does not gainsay the pleasures of the novel—its humor and aesthetic effects—she does insist on its ultimate seriousness.

As such, in Wisse's view, the modern Jewish novel legitimately deserves to be called canonical in something more than a figurative sense. When modern literary scholars talk about the canon, whether to debunk or defend it, they are usually borrowing a figure from the codification of the Hebrew and Greek scriptures to suggest the sway implicitly exercised by works of art. To be sure, some books may be enshrined in school curricula, but the use of the term canon is at most an image or a *façon de parler* used to convey the way a consensus of taste privileges some works over others. For Wisse, by contrast, the way in which the twenty-four books of the Hebrew Bible were drawn together and sealed into an authoritative package is more than a metaphor. It is, after all, *our* bible, and Wisse sees in the flowering of Jewish literature in many languages in the nineteenth and twentieth centuries a reemergence of the same kind of imaginative creativity displayed in the Hebrew Bible. It is as if some deep-running wellspring of national imagination had been unstoppered. The fact that the products of this upsurge are modern works of art rather than inspired religious scriptures does not mean, to her lights, that we are free to treat the former with less rigor and seriousness of purpose than the latter.

---

2. *The Modern Jewish Canon*, 4; henceforth referred to simply by page numbers in parenthesis in the body of the text.

With this new gift of spirit come responsibilities. Like the members of the Sanhedrin in antiquity, we cannot shirk our duty to decide which works of modern art–analogues, perhaps, to the vexing border cases of Job and the Song of Songs–deserve, or do not deserve, to be essential components of the cultural patrimony we transmit to future generations. "This modern list," Wisse opines, "will probably never be as firmly redacted as the twenty-four books of the Hebrew Bible, because no contemporary community is as confident as its ancestors, and because moderns are generally warier of any process that smacks of authority" (4). Yet despite these obstacles, the critic-scholar is not free to desist from the kind of critical argument that would draw lines and enforce distinctions rather than erase them.

The Modern Jewish Canon is a powerful instance of a scholar discharging this responsibility. In her vigorously argued analyses of Sholem Aleichem, Brenner, Kafka, Babel, Agnon and many others, Wisse lays out the justification for including each work according to her dual criteria: each is an accomplished work of art that succeeds in representing the historical experience of the Jewish people in its age. Wisse is no theorist, and although the introductory chapter of her book adroitly explains her approach to her project and makes various qualifications and clarifications that affect her choices, she means for the proof to be in the pudding. Rather than appealing to a set of abstract principles, Wisse is content to let the interpretive argument wrapped around each canonical work bear the burden of persuasion.

Canon making, at least of the sort practiced by Wisse, is a combination of drawing the list and then mounting arguments to defend the choices. As a scholar who does not speak on behalf of an institution–however much she may feel accountable to the Jewish people–she is free to make her own nominations to the modern Jewish canon. "My criteria are largely aesthetic and personal," Wisse admits. "In this book I set out some of my favorite Jewish works as a way of inviting others to continue discussion over them" (5). Yet beneath the breezy rhetoric of personal preference lies a bold assertion of power. Give heed and obeisance, it proclaims, to these–my decisions about those works that most urgently deserve to be transmitted to the future and those that do not. Without the willingness to make these assertions–and to accept the exposure to resistance and criticism that unavoidably goes along with it–there is ultimately, Wisse would argue, no culture. Yet the hard work of canon making lies not in listing the choices but in defending them. The greatness of *The Modern Jewish Canon*, to my lights, lies less in the probity of the list than in the critical discussions that justify the choices and connect them together into a grand argument. The fine intelligence and committed passion of these arguments are the truest sources of authority for the claims made on behalf of the works.

In the spirit of these spirited arguments, it strikes me that one can discover something of the rough-and-tumble democracy found in the Talmud.

Even though they are treating matters of grave import, the sages see no need to wear kid gloves as they search for the truth by knocking one proof against another to see which rings true. Being in the game means being willing to have your position scrutinized for consistency, utility, and elegance. The goal is not the triumph of individual authority but the clarification of God's will through the instruments of human ingenuity. In *The Modern Jewish Canon* Wisse plays by similar rules. Although she is not shy about projecting her opinions, her goal is not to seal the impress of her authority and secure humbled assent. Rather, she writes to provoke other serious minds into serious argument about serious matters of Jewish culture. She would, I think, prefer to be shown wrong in her championing of a particular work of literature if the counter-argument shed expanded light on the enterprise of the Jewish imagination. She seems ready to take her chances with all comers—if only they would come.

In the spirit of this dialectical openness, I propose to think about Wisse's canon from the vantage point of a student of modern Hebrew literature. It will be generally conceded, I think, that modern Hebrew literature from the Haskalah through the founding of the State of Israel on into the present is a crucial, even privileged, corpus within the catholic embrace of modern Jewish literature. Yet the student of modern Hebrew literature has to take some deep breaths upon discovering just how catholic Wisse's conception truly is. Hebraists and Zionists of the old school would claim that the revival of the ancient national tongue and its blossoming into rich modern literature deserve to be regarded as the one great drama of Jewish literature. Yiddishists of the old school, pointing to Yiddish as the great indigenous flower of the diaspora, would make a similarly exclusivist claim. Although she is a native daughter of the latter and profoundly sympathetic to the former, Wisse would tell the proponents of each camp to simmer down and get used to the fact that Jewish literature has moved on to circulate in a wider orbit that includes Russian, German, Polish, French, Italian, and, most of all, English. Wisse's canon is a meritocracy in which there are no protected slots reserved for works in Jewish languages; each place is awarded solely on the strength of a work's aesthetic assets and its imaginative power in representing Jewish historical experience.

Even playing by these rules, Wisse's treatment of modern Hebrew literature is deeply problematic. Part of the problem stems from the criteria Wisse has established for the shape and nature of her canon, and part of the problem stems from her deep ambivalence to Israeli literature. I will take these up under three heads.

The first is Wisse's seigniorial decision to limit her canon to novels and to exclude poetry, short fiction, and drama. True, it is Wisse's canon and she can lay down her own principles, and surely the novel is a legitimate and formidable genre. Yet if the goal is to represent what is greatest in modern Jewish literature—here and throughout I will use the test case of modern

Hebrew literature—it must be admitted that a great deal of greatness is left out if the novel is the only entry ticket. When it comes to a critical argument justifying her decision, there is none to be found aside from a fleeting assertion that the novel "more than poetry pronounces its social context and cultural affinity" (5). Now, from the rich readings of individual works in the body of her book, a serious reader, equipped with a little learning from the abundance of critical work on the history of the novel, would not have much trouble inferring nuanced claims Wisse might make on behalf of the novel's special place in modern Jewish culture. Yet, regrettably, these are arguments that are never undertaken.

As estimable a cultural achievement as is the novel, it is the not the genre through which the greatest works of Hebrew literature were realized. Hebrew literature does boast some fascinating novels, but, like Brenner's astonishing *Bahoref* ["In Winter," 1900], their artistic force is purchased by a self-conscious parodic play with conventions of the novel that are recognized at the outset as irrelevant to Jewish society. The novel as a phenomenon in European culture was perfected in the nineteenth century in such national cultures as France, England, and Russia, where a settled social order was being destabilized by forces that allowed individuals to move across class lines. Against the background of the "hum and buzz of implication" in the manners of social institutions, novelists explored themes of individual will, romantic love, marriage, property, and family. However, because East European Jewish life at the end of the nineteenth century was characterized by pauperization, crumbling religious authority, anti-Semitism, and mass immigration, the conditions that nurtured novels were simply not present. The exact nature of those enabling conditions remains a tantalizing object of scholarly discussion. My notions on the subject were formed by the work of Ian Watt, Georg Lukacs, and Lionel Trilling, but more recent scholarship has productively barked up many different trails. Investigations of the role of female readers as consumers of novels have been particularly illuminating. Yet even as our knowledge of the origins of the novel grows, the stubborn fact of the genre's stunted appearance in Hebrew literature remains.

That the novel is not Hebrew literature's long suit does not mean that it lacks brilliant examples of prose fiction. These are ample, but they are forms of *short* fiction, including the sketch, the short story, the long short story, and the novella, and, as such, do not qualify for the canon. Take, for example, the case of Micha Yosef Berdichevsky, the prolific polymath who engaged in provocative Semitic scholarship in addition to writing some of the most important fiction of the Hebrew Revival. Although Berdichevsky's work is not analyzed in the body of *The Modern Jewish Canon*, his novel *Miriam*, his only novel and a problem work, is included in the list of recommended books in the volume's appendix. (The novel has been translated into English, another necessary condition in Wisse's scheme, about which more shortly.) The fact is that any one of a dozen stories of Berdichevsky's is far superior to *Miriam*. But wanting to do the right thing by this writer, as she should, Wisse is stuck with a lesser example of his fiction because it is a novel. At least Berdichevsky has a novel to be chosen. Pity the case of Uri Nissan Gnessin and Devora Baron, the finest Hebrew prose writers of the early part of the twentieth century, who have only their superb short fiction to offer. There are profound historical and aesthetic reasons for the superiority of short fiction over the novel in classic modern Hebrew literature and a strong case to be made that the short forms are the truest and most characteristically Jewish prose expressions of the age. Yes, the novel has prestige, but it can also be seen as a form alien to the Jewish imagination at this time. Superimposing a novel-based schema upon the vitality of Hebrew literature means, by definition, that its finest achievements cannot shine forth. From what I know of Yiddish literature, moreover, the case is similar. When it comes to picking a work of Sholem Aleichem's for analysis, for example, Wisse declines to go to works like *Stempenyu*, which are truly novels and rely on the conventions of sentimental fiction; instead, she writes one of the most brilliant chapters of her book on the cycle of the Tevye stories. Although this may indeed be Sholem Aleichem's masterpiece, calling this series of monologues a novel requires a prodigiously elastic conception of the genre.

The largest problem by far is the case of poetry. Aside from Brenner and Agnon, many would agree that the greatest Hebrew writers of the twentieth century are Chaim Nachman Bialik, Shaul Tchernichovsky, Uri Zvi Greenberg, Natan Alterman, and Yehuda Amichai. They happen to be poets. Again, it is not happenstance but serious historical and aesthetic conditions that account for the unequal distribution of greatness among the genres of modern Hebrew literature. These poets are great for some of the same reasons that Wisse is drawn to the novel: their poetry embodies the historical experience of the Jewish people and provides deep insights into the inner lives of Jews. Yet the poetry does something that the prose rarely does. It stages the most acute confrontations in modern Jewish experience (tradition v. modernity, particular v. universal, individual v. collective) *within* the drama of language. The language, of course, is Hebrew, and, as anyone who has read a Bialik poem knows, the ability of the modern Hebrew poet to play the variegated historical layers of the language in concert and in conflict with one another produces extraordinary possibilities of meaning. Similarly, no one who is familiar with Wisse's scholarly career could seriously think that she is unsympathetic to poetry or undervalues the great Hebrew poets. Her exclusion of poetry from her canon project, one assumes, has to do with the fact that it does not travel well in translation and cannot be presented in a way that will be persuasive to a general reader. Be that as it may—the issue of translation will addressed directly—we are left with a modern Jewish canon that does not mention Bialik, Tchernichovsky, Greenberg,

Alterman, and Amichai.[3] The problem is not so much that Hebrew literature is not given its "due credit," but that the meaningfulness of the entire endeavor is diminished by the absence.

The second major issue is the decision to include only works translated into English. Writing in America and addressing an English-speaking audience in an era in which English has become a global medium, Wisse need make no apology for the priority of English. But the translation-only policy requires more clarification, and one wishes that Wisse had been more self-reflective on this critical decision. From the outset, one infers, Wisse conceived of her project as an act of public education and public responsibility. The implied reader of *The Modern Jewish Canon* is a general reader who, however intellectually curious and broadly cultured, comes to the book without specialist knowledge of Jewish literature and without Jewish languages. Students of Yiddish and Hebrew literature may have a lot to learn from this book, but they are not its intended audience. Hence the rationale for hewing to works translated into English; even if the translations are not currently in print, of which quite a number are not, they exist in libraries and can be accessed. Now, this is a perfectly understandable and principled stance that speaks to the vocation and responsibilities of the scholar and public intellectual. Yet the overall success of the enterprise must be judged by the integrity of the final product. By integrity I mean the question of whether the public account of the modern Jewish canon bears a true relationship, as to proportionality and emphasis, to the account given by scholars in the field after all the adjustments have been made. Speaking, again, from the perspective of Hebrew literature, it seems to me that, once one eliminates poems and short stories and all works that have not yet been translated into English, the result runs the danger of conveying a distorted map of modern Jewish literature. Although the intelligible and stimulating public presentation of Jewish culture is a goal of paramount importance, the question is whether this approach does or does not end in becoming a classic case of *yatsa sekharo behefsedo*, the gain being erased by the loss (Mishnah Avot 5:11).

What would happen, it's very much worth wondering, if the English-only stricture were breached? Let us say, for argument's sake, that Wisse shared my view that Brenner's as-yet-untranslated first novel *In Winter* is superior to his last novel *Breakdown and Bereavement*, which has been translated, and she then went on to make a stirring case for the importance

---

3. Amichai's novel *Lo me'akhshav, lo mikan* ["Not of This Time, Not of This Place"] (1963) is included among the supplementary works in the appendix, "Suggested Reading from the Modern Jewish Canon." (384) But, again, the novel template forces Wisse to ignore the enormous achievements of a writer's verse in favor of an anomalous and far from successful prose work.

of his early novel while mentioning along the way the writings of Brenner's—stories in addition to the late novel—that could be found in English. In addition to producing a more accurate account of Brenner's achievement, an intellectually stimulating discussion of the untranslated novel would likely create a buzz of interest that would eventually result in the novel's being translated and published in English. Ruth Wisse on the ten greatest untranslated Jewish novels—now that would be a formidable list indeed! One should never underestimate the efficacious curiosity of intelligent readers who have been told that something valuable has been withheld from them. Sticking only to works available in English means accepting the extant map of Jewish literature as conveyed under this severe and potentially distorting limitation rather than preparing the ground for a fuller and more accurate account. Admittedly, the loss of immediate access is a disadvantage, but considered on balance, there is a strong argument for seeing here the possibility of reversing the lamentable scenario mentioned above and turning it into a happy case of *yatsa hefsedo bisekharo,* the loss being redeemed by the gain.

Even within the general audience to which *The Modern Jewish Canon* is aimed Hebrew plays a privileged role that it would be a shame not to exploit. Although the "demographic" of the audience can never be precisely known, it is safe to say that among the younger lay and professional leadership cadres of the American Jewish community a certain amount of Hebrew literacy can be assumed. While I would not exaggerate what average day school graduate or Jewish Studies major can accomplish in Hebrew, I would say that there are many who, with the help of annotation and translation, could grasp the meaning of a contemporary Hebrew poem or a short prose text. Hebrew is the only language of the many tongues represented in Wisse's volume about which this can be said, and it is, of course, no coincidence. As a community, we have not invested in German or French or even, for that matter, in Yiddish; but we have invested considerable resources in Hebrew literacy because we see in Hebrew an irreplaceable link both to the classical past and to Israeli culture and society.[4] We are unique in this regard; I know of no other community in America in which numbers of young people can read their ancient texts in the original. Yet there remains a disconnect between this inchoate knowledge of Hebrew and Wisse's great books. For if there is one thing that our Hebrew-literate American Jewish leader is unlikely to be able to do is polish off a Hebrew novel whole. If this version of the modern Jewish canon had room for poems and short stories, there would be putative points of entry, and many aids—and why not

---

4. Of Wisse's commitment to Hebrew there is no mistake. See her "The Hebrew Imperative" in Alan Mintz, ed., *Hebrew in America: Perspective and Prospects* (Detroit: Wayne State University Press, 1993), 265–276. The essay first appeared in *Commentary* 89, no. 6 (June 1990), 34–39.

computer-assisted aids?—could be deviscd to makc this first-hand encounter with great Jewish culture accessible. But if the only real currency of Jewish culture remains the novel, then the encounter is destined always to be mediated through translation.

My third and final animadversion concerns the perplexingly scant attention given to Israeli literature. Now, admittedly Wisse has set out to assemble a canon of individual great books and not to write a history of Jewish literature. Her intention absolves her of the need to draw maps of literary movements, trace connections among key figures, and mark off periods of development. Nevertheless, she must take responsibility for the fact that, like it or not, a narrative account of modern Jewish literature emerges from her project. Rather than analyzing the substance of this narrative, I will suggest its contours by contrasting it to a very different account. Israeli historiography points to the gathering body of creative Hebrew writing from the period of the Yishuv through the founding of the state to the present and argues that, taken together, it represents, not to put too fine a point on it, the greatest flowering of Jewish culture since the time of the Bible and the Mishnah. There are many assumptions, of course, that are packed into this assertion and many ways that one could disagree with it. Yet any refutation would have to come to terms with the brute fact of the scores upon scores of Hebrew writers who have populated Israel's active literary life. Wisse accords places to six in her supplemental list (Yehuda Amichai, Aharon Appelfeld, Shulamith Hareven, Amos Oz, Yaakov Shabtai, and A. B. Yehoshua) and discusses only Shabtai in the body of the book. Yet letting my eyes graze over my office bookshelves and overcoming the strong urge to include scores and scores of poets and playwrights, I see the names of not a fcw Israeli prose writers who have won deserved places in the national literary culture: Eli Amir, Gavriella Avigur-Rotem, Shimon Balas, Hannah Bat-Shahar, Haim Be'er, Hanoch Bartov, Yehoshua Bar-Yosef, Yitzhak Ben-Ner, Yosel Berstein, Orli Caster-Bloom, Amir Gotfreund, David Grossman, Yehudit Hendel, Yoel Hoffman, Amalia Kahana-Carmon, Yehudit Katzir, Yehosua Kenaz, Etgar Keret, Yeshayahu Koren, Abba Kovner, Saviyon Librecht, Ronit Matalon, Aharon Megged, Sami Michael, Haim Sabato, Dan Benaya Seri, Natan Shaham, David Shahar, Meir Shalev, Moshe Shamir, Yuval Shimoni, David Shutz, Dan Tsalka, and S. Yizhar. The point of this very partial list—on which, it should be added, there are many translations into English—is not to impress with numbers but to indicate that, even with sundry reservations and qualifications, there is something undeniably huge going on here.

The title Wisse gives to the final chapter of *The Modern Jewish Canon*, which is devoted to Israeli literature, is "A Chapter in the Making." After tracing the miraculous invention of modern Hebrew and the establishment of a full and proliferating literary culture in Israel, Wisse concludes that it is too soon to establish a canon of Israeli literature; she gives her chapter the title she does "because it would require another book to contain the subject of Israeli literature" (29). Although the chapter contains a brilliant comparison between Abramovitsh's *Di klyatshe* ["The Mare," 1873–1909] and Shabtai's *Zikhron devarim* ["Past Continuous," 1970], Shabtai's novel remains the only work of Israeli literature discussed in the volume. This is, to my mind, as if an entire galaxy had somehow slipped off the map of the heavens. Moreover, the acknowledgment that another book would be required fails to convey a profound or promissory sense of conviction. My perplexity stems from the difficulty in squaring this vague absence with Wisse's universally recognized advocacy of Israel. She is, simply, the most articulate American intellectual on behalf of Israel. What, then, are we to make of this gap? Does she believe that Israeli literature, like Israeli politics, should not be criticized or assessed by Jews living outside the country? Does she contend that the critical politics implied in much Israeli fiction undermines its literary force? Does she feel that the broad failure of Israeli literature to engage Jewish tradition similarly disqualifies it? One is forced to look for answers between the lines, and on this subject there are, alas, few lines to read between. But one imagines that this discreet recoil from Israeli literature derives in the end from the not-so-discreet recoil of Israeli authors from the use of Jewish power. It is no secret that from its origins in the Haskalah Hebrew literature has been an "enlisted" literature that takes as its vocation the critique of national and social institutions, and in this quality it resembles nothing so much as American and British literature and many another national literature. One's stance toward Hebrew literature will depend largely on whether one views it, as the maskilim did, as a continuation of the prophetic tradition of being a "watchman to the house of Israel" or whether, like Wisse, one views it as a betrayal of the intellectuals. Wisse's position is clear, principled, and consistent, yet, to my mind, it is reductive in a way that demands renouncing extraordinary aesthetic achievements that shake us up and make us continually rethink our positions. I am repulsed, for example, by many of the political positions dramatized in the poetry of Uri Zvi Greenberg even as I am enthralled by the imaginative power of his verse. Figuring out such a contradiction is the work we literary scholars have to do.

Taken together, all the issues I have raised are by way of wishing that Wisse had written an even larger and even more ambitious book than the already imposing volume she has produced. I am aware of the niggardliness entailed in ignoring the splendid and shining chapters on Sholem Aleichem, Babel, the Singers, Bellow, and many others in favor of an argument on behalf of other, perhaps alternative, goals the project might have accomplished. Although as a specialist rather than a general reader I am not the main audience for *The Modern Jewish Canon*, I feel inspired, challenged, and goaded into seeing my role as a scholar in a new way. Wisse's volume joins together with the essays gathered by David Stern in *The Anthology in*

Jewish Literature[5] to create an awareness of how thoroughly our work as scholars is permeated by acts of selecting and excerpting and the critical arguments that justify our decisions. Every time we teach a class or prepare a syllabus we are participating in the central endeavor of picking and presenting that has characterized the making of Jewish culture since the books of Proverbs and Psalms. There is virtually no aspect of our work as scholars that is untouched by the anthological impulse and, inevitably and ineluctably, we make our canons as we go.

What Wisse has done is to take this everyday act and write it large and write it with force. On the one hand, she has simply—oh that is were so simple!—taken a wonderful university course that has been developed and refined over time and invested with enormous intellectual passion and turned it into a book. On the other hand, she has done what few others of us Jewish literature professors have done: she has projected her views into the public realm and called it a canon. This is an exercise of power that should be neither underestimated nor unappreciated. Wisse is not, to be sure, of the party of Michel Foucault and his disciples, who see the iron fist of hegemony at work in every institutionally sanctioned cultural norm. When it comes to motives, she would prefer to see herself as sailing under the motto from Deuteronomy, "Thou shall teach them diligently unto thy children," which actually appears on the opening page of her Introduction. Nonetheless, make no mistake. *The Modern Jewish Canon* is a work of great entrepreneurial force. When all is said and done, Wisse gets to tell the canon *her* way.

It is just this willingness to be willful that is the shining example to all of us. I will conclude with an example from my own work. For some years know I have studying the American Hebraist movement; these are the writers, critics, educators and especially poets who, beginning in earnest around World War I, attempted to create a serious Hebrew culture in America. The American Hebrew writers hoped to play an active role in a global Hebrew literature centered in the Yishuv even as they worked to raise a younger generation of Hebraists in America. Instead, they incurred a double rebuff. They were ignored in the literary journals and cafes of Tel Aviv, and at home their efforts were thrust aside by the galloping steed of Americanization. By the time the founding of Israel engendered in American Jewry a new excitement about spoken Hebrew, the decades of Hebrew creativity in America had either been forgotten or come to be viewed as a quaint Haskalah survival. I came to this literature because I was fascinated by encounter it stages between the Hebrew language (and it all it brings with it) and American history and the American landscape. Dusting off these

---

5. Oxford University Press, 1974. The book began as several special numbers of *Prooftexts; A Journal of Jewish Literary History.*

tomes and reading them afresh, I found much to admire on aesthetic terms and much to take hold of as the work of my precursors here in America.

Here's the rub. As much as I believe that the double marginality endured by these writers is unfair, as much as I believe that fruits of American Hebrew literature should be widely available to American Jews and appreciated by them, and as much as I believe that anyone teaching Hebrew literature in the United States, be they Israeli or American, has the duty to place these cultural artifacts before their students, believing all this does not make it so. Railing against injustice and undeserved obscurity persuades no one that the American Hebrew writers warrant inclusion in some division of the modern Jewish canon, be it is modern Hebrew literature or American Jewish literature. The only way to achieve this goal is to gather, republish, anthologize and translate their works, to create occasions and venues where scholars can become familiar with them, and, most of all, to write critical studies that demonstrate their aesthetic and historical interest. To whine about the justice of inclusion and exclusion is to behave as if someone other than ourselves is in charge of the canon. As Ruth Wisse has shown us, the canon belongs to all of us who take the trouble.

Holocaust Literature:
Foreshadowings and Shadowings
DAVID ABERBACH

Before the Holocaust, European culture rumbled with hints and warnings of impending catastrophe, and after the Holocaust the aftershocks have continued. Joseph Conrad's late-nineteenth-century novella *Heart of Darkness* (1899) was a devastating warning. Its condemnation of the Enlightenment and its barbarism leading to mass murder—and European guilt—was prophetic. Literature above all, from both before and after the Holocaust, challenges the belief that the plague of racial hatred and intolerance can ever be vanquished. As Camus states at the end of his allegorical novel *The Plague* (1947), written in the shadow of the Holocaust: *"Le bacille de la peste ne meurt ni ne disparait jamais"* ("the plague bacillus never dies or disappears for good").[1]

Holocaust literature can be defined as limited to the Holocaust itself, to poetry, fiction, drama, and autobiographical works of survivors such as Elie Wiesel, Primo Levi, Abraham Sutzkever, and Aharon Appelfeld, and works specifically about the Holocaust. These have become part of the canon of Jewish writings. Yet Holocaust literature can be interpreted also as including works not relating to the war or to anything specifically Jewish. There are pre-Holocaust works that in some ways foreshadow the Holocaust—for example, Armenian poetry of the Turkish genocide in World War I. Also, some post-Holocaust works, such as Arthur Miller's *The Crucible*, shadow the Holocaust in the sense that although they are on totally different topics, they might not have been written in the same way, if at all, if not for the Holocaust.

The case against this broader interpretation of Holocaust literature is implicit in the view of historians such as Jacob Katz, Yehuda Bauer, and Bernard Wasserstein that the Holocaust had no precedent and, in its savage detail, was totally unpredictable. Wasserstein writes: "the agony of European Jewry was enacted in a separate moral arena, a grim twilight world where their conventional moral code did not apply."[2] The idea of the "concentration camp universe" cut off from morality and ordinary history might imply the necessary segregation of literature deriving from this catastrophe or, in Adorno's words apropos Celan's *Todesfuge*, the rejection of poetry after Auschwitz as barbaric.

---

1. Trans. S. Gilbert (Harmondsworth, Middlesex: Penguin Books, 1968), 252.

2. *Britain and the Jews of Europe* (Oxford University Press, 1988 [1977]), 357.

Yet most Holocaust writers would probably not agree. The fact that they are writing at all means that they are part of a literary tradition in which the value of civilization is paramount. There are, in any case, few atrocities and hardly any aspect of grief among Holocaust victims without precedent.[3] The Holocaust was one of several major genocides in modern times and, contrary to what is sometimes claimed, it was predicted, though not in the exact form in which it took place. It is appropriate, therefore, that certain literary works, mostly in the fifty years or so preceding the Holocaust, should be considered alongside literature of the Holocaust itself. Kafka's *The Trial* (1925), after all, has nothing to do with the Holocaust, yet it might be seen as part of the social transformation that made the Holocaust possible: it shows the Goddess of Justice becoming the Goddess of the Hunt, with human beings her target.[4]

It is, in any case, undeniable that many literary works, particularly in the half-century before World War II but even before that, give glimpses of what was to become, in combination, the Holocaust: the hatred of Jews in European folk tales; the murderous potential of so-called representatives of European Enlightenment in Conrad's *Heart of Darkness* (1899); increasing Jewish isolation from Europe in Schnitzler's *The Way to the Open* (1908); the steep devaluation of human life observed by World War I writers such as Stefan George, Wilfred Owen, and Erich Maria Remarque (on the first day of the battle of the Somme, far more died than on the worst days at Auschwitz); the critique of the belief in progress and humanity in the novels of Hermann Broch; the suicidal despair in Werfel's *The Mirror Man* (1920) and Toller's *Such is Life!* (1927); the rise of pathological racial hatred in Joseph Roth's *The Spider Web* (1923); Shoffman's unique Hebrew stories of the Austrian peasantry, with its deep-rooted Jew-hatred; the depiction of mass expulsions of Jews in novels such as Hugo Bettauer's *The City without Jews* (1922); and Artur Landsberger's *Berlin without Jews* (1925); the workings of a murderous bureaucracy in Kafka's *The Trial* (1925) and *The Castle* (1925); the failure of Jewish assimilation in Leon Feuchtwanger's *Jud Süss* (1925); the abuse of power in Arnold Zweig's *The Dispute over Sergeant Grischa* (1927); predictions of mass slaughter in Döblin's *Berlin Alexanderplatz* (1930) and *Babylonische Wanderung* (1934); the Turkish genocide against the Armenians during World War I in Franz Werfel's historical novel *The Forty Days of Musa Dagh* (1933); and the genocidal rage of Russian and Polish peasants as depicted in the stories of Babel. This is apart from the

---

3. See David Aberbach, *Surviving Trauma: Loss, Literature, and Psychoanalysis* (New Haven and London: Yale University Press, 1989), ch. 1. On Jewish responses to catastrophe, see David G. Roskies, *Against the Apocalypse: Responses to Catastrophe in Modern Jewish Culture* (Cambridge, Mass., and London: Harvard University Press, 1984).

4. Trans. W. and E. Muir (New York: Schocken Books, 1977), 163.

East European Hebrew and Yiddish writers who, drawing on a long history and literature of catastrophe, often had the sharpest antennae for the perilous Jewish future, uniquely concerned as they were with Jewish national interests and uninhibited in predicting the worst, especially after the Russian pogroms of 1881–82.

Genocide in Pre-Holocaust literature

The horror of the Holocaust, Yehuda Bauer reminds us, is that it did not deviate from human norms.[5] In the three generations prior to World War II, there were genocides in Bulgaria, the Belgian Congo, Armenia, Soviet Russia, and the Far East, with millions of victims. World War I exposed the brutal extremes to which nominally civilized Christian European countries were prone. Joseph Conrad, in *Heart of Darkness*, describes the genocide of millions of African slaves in the Belgian Congo. He condemns European Enlightenment as an illusion and fraud; it claimed to represent justice and progress to the natives but instead brought wickedness and mass murder. Kurtz, the superlatively gifted and cultured colonial trader, is transformed from being an apostle of Enlightenment, an "emissary of pity and science and progress," into a homicidal maniac: "'Exterminate all the brutes!" In his twisted idealism and destructiveness, Kurtz represents Europe: "All Europe contributed to the making of Kurtz."[6]

In retrospect, *Heart of Darkness* bears out the post-Holocaust recognition that the Nazi exterminations can be traced, in distorted form, to the Enlightenment and the Romantic movement. The Holocaust was carried out in the name of nationalist ideals, "not out of individual self-interest, but in fulfilment of a duty, for the general good, in pursuit of purification and beauty"; nor was the Holocaust entirely alien to the mainstream of European thought; rather, in some ways "it is a continuation of the Enlightenment, and...part of the Romantic reaction to it."[7] Even Hitler's *Mein Kampf*, for all its anti-Jewish lies and hatred, was, according to one interpretation, not deviant but "firmly rooted in European intellectual orthodoxy"[8]—the ortho-

---

5. *Rethinking the Holocaust* (New Haven and London: Yale University Press, 2001), 43.

6. R. Hampson, ed. (Harmondsworth, Middlesex: Penguin Books, 1995), 47, 83, 84. Zola's *Germinal* (1885) is an earlier fictional warning of a cataclysm set off by extreme social and economic injustice. Shortly after the novel appeared, Zola wrote: "There may still be time to avoid total catastrophe. But hasten to be just, or else disaster looms: the earth will open at our feet and all nations will be swallowed up in one of the most terrible upheavals ever to take place in the course of human history." Trans. and ed. R. Pearson (London: Penguin Books, 2004), xxxlx; the Holocaust would not have surprised Zola (ibid. xxx).

7. Ernest Gellner, "The Coming of Nationalism and Its Interpretation: The Myths of Nation and Class," in G. Balakrishnan, ed., *Mapping the Nation* (London: Verso, 1992), 122.

8. John Carey, *The Intellectuals and the Masses* (London: Faber, 1992), 208.

doxy of prejudice and violence. Hitler's precursors as prophets of the doom of European Jewry were well-known and respected anti-Semites (whose writings often sold well), including Friedrich Fries, Heinrich von Treitschke, Eugen Karl Dühring, and Paul de Lagarde. And, of course, Hitler's racial demonization of Jews as the evil source of morality, justice, and equality, the decadent antithesis of the pagan, primordial natural order, who had to be fought and eradicated together with their values, had a long germination in the history of the Church. The genocidal language of Hitler's *Mein Kampf* was little different from that of other writers and speakers on the *völkisch* Right going back well before World War I.[9]

Throughout Europe, racial prejudice and genocidal language were widespread. Anti-Semitic language was not much different from other racist language. The stereotype of pushy, morally contaminated, usurious, cunning, dishonest, lascivious, vermin-like, disease-ridden Jews, contemptuous of authority, conspiring against non-Jews, had many parallels. Other peoples were seen by Germans in stereotypical terms. There were the "envious" English; the "decadent" "archenemy" France; the "materialist" U.S.A.; "barbaric" Russia; "backward" Poles and Czechs; and "primitive" Africans.[10] Americans, including eminent figures such as Thomas Jefferson and Theodore Roosevelt, had "justified extermination" of native American Indians.[11] The British, too, were susceptible to stereotypes of hatred. During World War I, for example, Rudyard Kipling condemned the Germans in language later used by Hitler against the Jews, as "germs of any disease...typhoid or plague—Pestis Germanicus."[12] Practically everyone was tarred with the nationalist-racist brush. As patriots, Jews used identical language. During World War I, *Im Deutschen Reich*, the official paper of the *Centralverein deutscher Staatsbürger jüdischen Glaubens* (C.V.), which represented the majority of German Jews, condemned "Russian malice," "French thirst for revenge" "English deviousness," and "Serbian lust for murder"; Eugen Fuchs, chairman of the C.V., used even stronger language, as befitted a

---

9. Ian Kershaw, *Hitler*, vol. 1 (New York: W.W. Norton, 1998), 244.

10. David Blackbourne, *The Fontana History of Germany 1780–1918: The Long Nineteenth Century* (London: Fontana, 1997), 308, 437, 440; also see 426, 435, 454.

11. Michael Mann, *The Dark Side of Democracy: Explaining Ethnic Cleansing* (Cambridge University Press, 2005), ix.

12. Andrew Lycett, *Rudyard Kipling* (London: Weidenfeld and Nicolson, 1999), 474. Those who think Nazi atrocities such as the manufacture of lamp shades of human skin or soap from human fat were "unimaginable" prior to the Holocaust should consider that Allied propaganda in World War I falsely accused Germany precisely of such horrors. On 16 June 1915, Cynthia Asquith, daughter-in-law of the prime minister, related a conversation over dinner: "We discussed the rumour that the Germans utilise even their corpses by converting them into glycerine with the by-product of soap" *Diaries 1915–18* (London: Hutchinson, 1968), 44.

"German down to my bones": "murderous Russia," "insidious England," "bloodthirsty France," Japan's "yellow highway robbers."[13] Continent-wide language of contempt for and murderous hatred of foreign countries and ethnic groups contributed to both world wars.

Misanthropy and Genocide in Western Civilization

Racism and anti-Semitism are linked to a deep-rooted misanthropic tradition in Western culture. It is not just the Jews who are wicked and demonic but the human race generally. In the Hebrew Bible "The imagination of man's heart is evil from his youth" (Gen 8:21), and though he be "little lower than the angels" (Ps 8:6), "the heart is crooked above all things" (Jer 17:9). Swift's attack on the Brobdingnagians in *Gulliver's Travels* (1726, Part 2, end of ch. 6) reflects his generally low view of the human species, as "the most pernicious Race of little odious Vermin that Nature ever suffered to crawl upon the Surface of the Earth."[14] Human nature in William Blake's "A Divine Image" is scarcely any better:[15]

> Cruelty has a human heart,
> And Jealousy a human face;
> Terror the human form divine,
> And secrecy the human dress.

All humans, according to Christian theology, are guilty of Original Sin and, as Nietzsche notes in *The Gay Science* (1882) (III 130), "The Christian decision to find the world ugly and bad has made the world ugly and bad," though, like other nineteenth-century liberal thinkers, he found the origins of the alleged flaws of Christianity in Judaism (137): "A Jesus Christ was possible only in a Jewish landscape."[16] Joseph Conrad in *Under Western Eyes* (1911) portrays an elderly female Russian revolutionary radicalized by the "grotesque horror" of social injustice by which (in an echo of a scene in the Congo in *Heart of Darkness*) half of Russia is preoccupied with its petty affairs while the other half starves: "a belief in a supernatural source of evil is not necessary; men alone are quite capable of every wickedness" (II 4). In his *Autobiography* (1924), Mark Twain, an arch-misanthrope, summed up

---

13. Amos Elon, *The Pity of It All: A History of Jews in Germany 1743 – 1933* (New York: Henry Holt and Company, 2002), 306–307.

14. P. Turner, ed. (Oxford University Press, 1971), 126.

15. Trans. J. Nauckhoff (Cambridge University Press, 2001), 123, 126. Mendele Mocher Sefarim, the leading Jewish novelist of the 1881–1917 period, used blatant stereotyping to depict Jews, their alleged corruption and immorality, uncleanliness and unhygienic manners, ridiculous appearance (including their "Jewish" noses), and love of money. David Aberbach, *Realism, Caricature and Bias: The Fiction of Mendele Mocher Sefarim* (Oxford: The Littman Library, 1993).

16. P. Kirschner, ed. (Harmondsworth, Middlesex: Penguin Books, 1999), 108.

his view of man as the most malicious and detestable of animals, "below the rats, the grubs, the trichinae...the only creature that inflicts pain for sport, knowing it to be pain."[17]

In the expression of contempt for human life, one scene in *Heart of Darkness* seems especially "prophetic" of the Holocaust and the cold bureaucracy exemplified by Eichmann. It describes the European chief accountant at work in his jungle hut. Impeccably dressed, he is surrounded by dying African slaves, "black shadows of disease and starvation." The accountant is upset, not by this atrocity but because the sounds of the dying men interfere with his work: "The groans of this sick person distract my attention. And without that it is extremely difficult to guard against clerical errors in this climate."[18] New here is the extent to which life is devalued by Christian Europeans, though their continent had been free of major wars since the time of Napoleon.

This moral callousness was shown in other genocides prior to the Holocaust. During World War I, about 60,000 Russian Jews, driven from their homes, died from exposure and hunger. During the Russian civil war (1918–20), a "raw genocide" of 30,000—rising eventually to a total of as many as 150,000 Jewish civilians who died of their wounds or as a result of disease contracted during the pogroms—was carried out in the Ukraine by Petliura's and Denikin's White armies and, to a lesser extent in East Galicia, by the Polish army led by Pilsudski.[19] The Hebrew poet Uri Zvi Greenberg, a survivor both of the war and the pogroms, warned repeatedly of the danger faced by the European Jews.

In the stories of *Red Cavalry*, based on his experiences riding with the Cossacks in the Soviet army during the civil war, Babel has the revelation of the genocidal Jew-hatred on all sides, among the Poles as well as the Russians. "Gedali" tells of an old Jew in Zhitomir, owner of a curiosity shop and believer in the Revolution as an ideal of goodness and joy, now shocked and disillusioned by what he has seen:

---

17. New York and London: Harper and Brothers Publishers, II 7.

18. Op. cit., 35, 37. Bureaucracy and brutal mass slaughter are juxtaposed, too, in Hašek's description of the office of Judge Advocate Bernis in *The Good Soldier Svejk* (1923), its walls covered with photographs of Austrian army atrocities, charred cottages, and trees sagging with the weight of the hanged: "Particularly fine was a photograph from Serbia of a whole family strung up—a small boy with his father and mother. Two soldiers with bayonets were guarding the tree, and an officer stood victoriously in the foreground smoking a cigarette. On the other side in the background a field kitchen could be seen in full operation." Trans. C. Parrott (Harmondsworth, Middlesex: Penguin Books, 1978), 93.

19. Howard Morley Sachar, *Dreamland: Europeans and Jews in the Aftermath of the Great War* (New York: Alfred A. Knopf, 2002), 12, 18, 25.

"A Pole closed my eyes," whispered the old man, in a voice that was scarcely audible. "The Poles are bad-tempered dogs. They take the Jew and pluck out his beard, the curs! That is splendid, that is the Revolution! And then those who have beaten the Poles say to me: "Hand your gramophone over to the State, Gedali..." "I am fond of music, Pani," I say to the Revolution. "You don't know what you are fond of, Gedali. I'll shoot you and then you'll know. I cannot do without shooting, because I am the Revolution."[20]

Similar atrocities sear the writings of Armenian poets such as Daniel Varoujan (1884–1915) and Siamanto (1878–1915), both later killed by the Turks. Siamanto's poem, "The Dance" (1909), recalls massacres of Armenians by the Turks, anticipating Nazi degradations:[21]

> Someone brought a bucket
> Then, of kerosene. O human justice
> I spit at your forehead. Then they
> Doused those twenty brides, shouting
> "You must dance..."

Werfel's best-selling novel on the Armenian genocide in World War I, *The Forty Days of Musa Dagh* (1933), had clear implications in the 1930s. The language used by the Turks to describe the Armenians—"There can be no peace between human beings and plague germs"—is identical to that of the Nazis on the Jews; and the Armenian genocide is described in Werfel's novel as "the worst crime in recorded history so far."[22] This genocide is alluded to also in Döblin's novel *Babylonische Wandrung* (1934), a picaresque fantasy of an exiled Babylonian ex-god named Konrad, who has visions in Paris of a government-planned genocide against the "Romans":

> Down on the marketplace, in the streets, there was an indescribable hubbub. A vast, gruesome cry arose, a screaming, as when animals are being slaughtered. People came pouring out of the houses...They did not escape. All were without weapons. Massacre, massacre. The bodies screamed, turned, sank to the ground. "There is no point in turning away, Konrad. Just this is what you must watch quietly. Quietly. You think that people are being slaughtered here. That is incidental. What is happening here is very clear, premeditated and according to plan. Actions are being taken, order is being created. These are Romans, the women, children, all of them Romans, rich merchants, bankers, whatever you like, officials, businessmen...They are being exterminated. The Romans are being annihilated. You believe that defenseless people, especially women and children, are being ruthlessly slaughtered. Nothing of the

---

20. *Collected Stories* (Harmondsworth, Middlesex: Penguin Books, 1974), 62.

21. Diana Der Hovanessian and Marzbed Margossian, trans. and eds., *Anthology of Armenian Poetry* (New York: Columbia University Press, 1978), 144.

22. (New York: Carroll and Graf, 1990), 190, 531.

sort! We're not talking about people. These are Romans, political enemies...being destroyed in the course of official operations."[23]

Döblin, an army doctor in World War I, condemns through satire the dehumanization that turns people into "political enemies," the slaughter of whom is legitimized. His novel, though ostensibly concerned with an imaginary past, predicts a future of equal, if not greater, horror.

Anti-Semitism in European Literature

Anti-Semitism in European literature gave ideological justification to the Holocaust. From Fichte to T.S. Eliot, anti-Semitism in European literature warned that the Jews would be betrayed and sacrificed. Even Goethe, for all his humanism, his sympathy for individual Jews (at one time he even learned some Yiddish) and admiration for the Hebrew Bible, disparaged the Jews as a people. Goethe opposed Jewish emancipation as a threat to Christian civilization. In *Wilhelm Meisters Wanderjahre* ("Wilhelm Meister's Years of Travel," 1795–96), Goethe expressed intolerance toward the Jews as they lived in a Christian society, yet rejected the Savior: "We tolerate no Jew in our midst; for how should we permit him a share in the highest cultural phenomenon since he rejects its origin and tradition."[24]

As violent German chauvinism increased, Heine virtually predicted a form of mass slaughter. If the demonic anti-Semitic elements prevailed, he wrote, "there will break over the heads of the poor Jews a storm of persecution, which will far surpass even their previous sufferings."[25] The prevalence of Jew-hatred prevented many Germans from admitting that Heine was the greatest German poet after Goethe's death. Heine took refuge in France, but French writers turned out to be even worse than the German ones: Bourget, Rimbaud, Edmond de Goncourt, Gide, Valles, Daudet, even Maupassant and Zola, presented the Jew in a negative light as unassimilable, materialistic, shifty, manipulative, cold, intellectually abstract, socially corrosive. A sign of the extent to which anti-Jewish prejudice permeated French society by the late nineteenth century was the fact that Émile Zola, later Dreyfus's main defender, was influential in giving credence to the libel of a Jewish conspiracy. The collapse of the Union Générale bank in 1882 triggered an unprecedented explosion of Jew-hatred in France, where blame was put on an international conspiracy of Jewish financiers of German origin, headed by the Rothschilds. Zola's novel *L'Argent* (1891), based on the Union

---

23. Frederik V. Grunfeld, *Prophets without Honour: A Background to Freud, Kafka, Einstein and Their World* (New York: Holt, Rinehart and Winston; Philadelphia: Jewish Publication Society of America, 1979), 279–280.

24. Trans. H.M. Waidson (London: John Calder; New York: Riverrun Press, 1982), 75.

25. Israel Tabak, *Judaic Lore in Heine: The Heritage of a Poet* (Baltimore: The Johns Hopkins Press, 1948), 197.

Générale scandal, portrays a Jewish banker, transparently based on James de Rothschild, as a legitimate target of hatred as he belongs to

> that accused race that no longer has its own country, no longer has its own prince, which lives parasitically in the home of nations, feigning to obey the law, but in reality only obeying its own God of theft, of blood, of anger... fulfilling everywhere its mission of ferocious conquest, to lie in wait for its prey, suck the blood out of everyone, [and] grow fat on the life of others.[26]

Zola gave "literary credibility to the idea that the Union Générale really had been destroyed by the Rothschilds, as well as to the canard that the French Rothschilds had pro-German sympathies."[27]

Resentment of Jewish assimilation was felt by French writers, many of whom were infected by prevailing anti-Jewish prejudice. In 1914, André Gide confessed in his diary dismay at the Jewish contribution to French literature, for the Jews were not French:

> There is today in France a Jewish literature that is not French literature...For what does it matter to me that the literature of my country should be enriched if it is so at the expense of its significance? It would be far better, whenever the Frenchman comes to lack sufficient strength, for him to disappear rather than to let an uncouth person play his part in his stead and in his name.[28]

However, few approached the hysterical calls of Céline in the 1930s for the destruction of the Jews. Céline's *Bagatelles pour un massacre* (1937) is "possibly the most vicious anti-Jewish tirade in modern Western literature."[29]

Similarly, most nineteenth-century Russian writers were tainted by the pervasive Jew-hatred in their society, though they were otherwise an enclave of liberal enlightenment in a backward, totalitarian empire. Lermontov's play *The Spaniards*, Turgenev's story "The Jew," Gogol's novels *Taras Bulba* and *Dead Souls*, Tolstoy's *Anna Karenina*, and, most strikingly, Dostoevsky's writings betray the deep anti-Jewish prejudice and hatred nourished by the Church and kept alive in the popular imagination. Russian writers rarely contemplated a Jew without medieval associations of money-lending, miserliness, trickery, and extortion. The anti-Semitism in Dostoevsky's major writings, though muted in comparison to the hatred in his

---

26. Niall Ferguson, *The House of Rothschild, The World's Banker, 1849–1998* (Harmondsworth, Middlesex: Penguin Books, 2000), 263.

27. Ibid., 264.

28. *Journals 1889–1949* (Harmondsworth, Middlesex: Penguin, 1978), 194ff.

29. Saul Friedlander, *Nazi Germany and the Jews: The Years of Persecution 1933–39* (London: Weidenfeld and Nicolson, 1997), 213.

publicistic works,[30] did incalculable harm in view of the novelist's vast
moral authority. Most striking is the moment in *The Brothers Karamazov*
(1880) when the invalid child, Lisa Khokhlakov, asks Alyosha, "Is it true that
at Easter the Jews steal a child and kill it?" Here was an opportunity to refute
a hateful libel that caused the deaths of thousands of innocent people,
including many in Russia. Yet, pandering to the prejudices of his Russian
readers, Dostoevsky refuses to let even the saintly Alyosha admit the truth.
Instead he says, "I don't know."[31]

Even English writers of the late nineteenth and early twentieth centuries,
such as Joseph Conrad, D.H. Lawrence, Hilaire Belloc, G.K. Chesterton,
Rudyard Kipling, and, notoriously, T.S. Eliot, expressed anti-Semitic views
typical of the period. Some were influenced by the new racial anti-Semitism.[32]

Joseph Roth's German novel *The Spider's Web* (1923) is an unusually
clear warning of the alarming rise of Jew-hatred after World War I. The novel, set in Germany in the early years of Nazism, is an exposé of the psychology of Jew-hatred, a warning of the failure of emancipation. It opens with a
portrait of a society in chaos, with rampant anti-Semitism and growing popularity of Hitler, whose danger is recognized in the novel. Theodor Lohse, a
humble tutor in a wealthy Jewish home, is a prime candidate for the Nazi
Party, an ex-serviceman with few prospects and, typically, much envy
toward Jews for their alleged wealth and power, and their corrupting influence and lust for world domination as revealed in the tsarist anti-Semitic
forgery *The Protocols of the Elders of Zion*, recently translated into German
and a best-seller:

> Everything was sharp practice. Glaser's learning was as dishonestly
> come by as the [Jewish] jeweller's fortune. There was something wrong
> with things when Private Grunbaum was granted leave or when Efrussi made
> a deal. The revolution was a swindle, the Kaiser had been betrayed, the
> [Weimar] Republic was a Jewish conspiracy. Theodor could see all this for
> himself, and other people's opinions confirmed his impressions. Clever men
> like Wilhelm Tieckmann, Professor Koethe, Bastelmann the lecturer, the
> physicist Lorranz and the ethnologist Mannheim all made a point of exposing
> the harmful nature of the Jewish race during lecture evenings at the Union
> of German Law Students, as well as in their own books, which were on
> display in the reading room of the "Germania."

30. See David I. Goldstein, *Dostoyevsky and the Jews* (Austin, Texas, and London: Univer-
    sity of Texas Press, 1981 [1976]).

31. Fyodor Dostoevsky, *The Brothers Karamazov*. Trans. Constance Garnett, revised and
    edited by Ralph F. Matelow (New York: W.W. Norton and Co., 1976), 552.

32. See Bryan Cheyette, *Constructions of "The Jew" in English Literature and Society:
    Racial representations, 1875–1945* (Cambridge University Press, 1993).

Father Lohse had often enough warned his daughters against any contact with young Jews during their dancing classes. He could give examples, yes, examples! At least twice a month, Jews from Posen, the worst of the lot, would try to cheat him. During the war they had been classified as unfit for active service, and were to be found as writers in field hospitals and area headquarters. In the seminars on jurisprudence they would always push themselves forward and think up new conundrums, in which Theodor would find himself all at sea and which would drive him to new, disagreeable and difficult labours.

They had destroyed the army now, they had taken over the State, discovered socialism and that one should love one's enemy. It was written in The Elders of Zion—a book which was issued to the officer reservists on Fridays, along with the vegetables—that they aimed at world dominion. They had the police in their pockets and were persecuting the nationalist organizations. And one was reduced to educating their sons, to living off them, badly. And how did they themselves live?

Oh! They lived in style. The Efrussi mansion was separated from the common street by a shining, silvery railing, and surrounded by a broad, green lawn. The gravel gleamed white and the steps up to the door were even whiter. Pictures in gold frames hung in the hall and a footman in green and gold livery bowed as he escorted you in...[33]

The novel ends with a warning to escape, though Roth rightly saw East European Jews as more likely than the more assimilated German Jews to seek refuge elsewhere: "One could say a single word to any Jew from Lodz, and he would understand. Jews from the east needed no explanations."[34]

Kafka's works, though seemingly set in a fantasy world divorced from history, are firmly grounded in the social and psychological realities of the European Jews prior to the Holocaust. The premise of *The Trial*—that a man, Joseph K., can be charged as guilty without ever finding out why—has particular relevance to European Jews, whose existence, as Kafka well knew, was counted by their enemies as a crime. Kafka mocks widespread beliefs such as those in which Jews were associated with particular physical characteristics and condemned as an inferior race. In one of many scenes in which K. tries to find out the charges against him, he is told that the courts are full of superstition: "one of the superstitions is that you're supposed to tell from a man's face, especially the line of his lips, how his case is going to turn out."[35] On this basis, K. has evidently been found guilty. In *The Castle*, Kafka shows with similarly sharp prophetic satire how bureaucracy can destroy human rights. Joseph K. has been sent an invitation from Klamm, a high official, to be surveyor at the castle. Though tolerated in the town, he is

---

33. Trans. J. Hoare (London: Chatto and Windus, 1988), 6–7.

34. Ibid., 111.

35. Trans. W. and E. Muir (New York: Schocken Books, 1977), 193.

not admitted to the castle and refused permission to practice his profession. K. is reduced to "an unofficial, totally unrecognized, troubled, and alien existence"[36] and the mayor's response to his insistence that he wants his rights resonates with the unfolding tragedy of European Jewry:

> "I don't want any act of favour from the castle but my rights."
> "Mitzi," the mayor said to his wife, who still sat pressed against him and, lost in a daydream, was playing with Klamm's letter, which she had folded into the shape of a little boat. K. snatched it from her in alarm.
> "Mitzi, my foot is beginning to throb again. We must renew the compress."[37]

Zionist Warnings of Catastrophe

Zionists, more consistently and emphatically than any other group (except rabid anti-Semites), criticized or denounced Jewish patriotism and predicted an impending Jewish catastrophe. Moses Hess, for example, wrote in *Rome and Jerusalem* (1862) that Judaeophobia, particularly among Germans, would lead to a catastrophic "blow from without" against the Jews.[38] In the 1870s, the Russian pioneer of Zionism, Peretz Smolenskin, identified a recurrent cycle in Jewish history of attempted assimilation followed by violence against Jews. Smolenskin feared that the 1881 pogroms were just a prelude to the slaughters to come.[39] Leon Pinsker, in his pamphlet *Auto-Emancipation* (1882), warned that the lack of a Jewish homeland inevitably attracted violence against the Jews: "Though you prove yourselves patriots a thousand times, you will still be reminded at every opportunity of your Semitic descent."[40] Herzl became fully aware of the threat of racial anti-Semitism as a student at the University of Vienna in the early 1880s when he read Dühring's attack on the Jews as a parasitical race that the superior Nordic race must destroy by "killing and extermination" (*durch Ertötung und Ausrottung*).[41] In Herzl's view, Dühring's call for the extermination of the Jews was a declaration of war. In his diary on February 9, 1882, Herzl condemned Duhring and other racial anti-Semites in

---

36. Trans. W. and E. Muir (New York: Schocken Books, 1994), 75.

37. Ibid., 96.

38. Moses Hess, *The Revival of Israel: Rome and Jerusalem, the Last Nationalist Question*, trans. M. Waxman (Lincoln and London: University of Nebraska Press, 1995), 177–178.

39. *Essays* [Hebrew] (Jerusalem: Cooperatif Dfus Hapoalim, 1925), I 60; and G. Elkoshi, "Smolenskin and the Hibbat Zion Movement" in S. Briman, ed., *The Smolenskin Book* [Hebrew] (Jerusalem: Ahiasaf, 1952), 189, 193.

40. Robert Chazan and M. L. Raphael, eds., *Modern Jewish History: A Source Book* (New York: Schocken Books, 1974), 169.

41. Paul Johnson, *A History of the Jews* (London: Phoenix, 2002 [1987]), 394.

imagery reminiscent of medieval times and prophetic of the Holocaust. Old Christian Jew-hatred was weakening; racial anti-Semitism was a more efficient "modern fuel" for making a cheerful fire to incinerate the Jews, and sending up the "sweet smell of crackling Jew-fat." As head of the World Zionist Organization twenty years later, Herzl had no doubt that the threats of anti-Semites had to be acted upon. The Jews, he wrote on July 5, 1902, must "die or get out" (sterben oder weg müssen).[42]

Others, too, were drawn to Zionism as they realized that Herzl was right to warn of the failure of Jewish assimilation and of a potential catastrophe. Chaim Weizmann at the age of eleven contrasted Continental Europe with England: "Why should we look to the Kings of Europe for compassion? ...In vain! All have decided the Jews must die."[43] Herzl's colleague, Max Nordau, wrote in June 1897 in Die Welt that in some places anti-Semitism threatened the Jews with extermination (Vernichtung); bad as it was, it "would get worse, much worse."[44] The Russian Hebrew writer J.H. Brenner was similarly aware of imminent catastrophe. In 1900 he wrote to his friend and fellow Hebrew writer, U.N. Gnessin, "Don't you know that our people is going to die?"[45] In 1934, the Hebrew poet H.N. Bialik, using the Hebrew word shoah, wrote that European Jewry "is on the verge of destruction,"[46] a view powerfully articulated at the time by the Revisionist Zionist leader, Vladimir Jabotinsky.

In his commentary on the Chumash (The Five Books of Moses), first published in one volume in 1936, the British Chief Rabbi, Joseph Hertz, a staunch Zionist (though at the same time a religiously patriotic British imperialist) warned similarly of a coming catastrophe.[47]

Warnings in Hebrew and Yiddish Literature

East European Hebrew and Yiddish writers, who wrote exclusively for Jews, were less vulnerable to the illusory beliefs of West European Jewish writers such as the young Jakob Wassermann or Simone Weil that they were no longer defined by their Jewish identity. Yiddish and Hebrew literature

---

42. Theodor Herzl, Briefe und Tagebücher, 6 vols., eds. J. Wachten et al. (Vienna: Propylaen Verlag, 1983), I 614, III 407.

43. Chaim Weizmann, Letters and Papers, vol. 1. L. Stein, ed. (London: Oxford University Press, 1968), I 37.

44. Elon, op. cit., 325.

45. Gershon Shoffman, Collected Works (Hebrew) 4 vols. (Tel Aviv: Am Oved, 1952), IV 141.

46. H.N. Bialik, Letters (Hebrew) 5 vols. (1937–1939), ed. F. Lachower (Tel Aviv: Dvir, 1939), V 307.

47. Pentateuch and Haftorahs. 2nd edition (London: Soncino Press, 1972 [1936]), 747.

expressed the solidarity of fear with particular intensity after the pogroms
of 1871, 1881–82, 1903–6 and 1918–21. *The Mare*, the Yiddish satiric allegory by Mendele Mocher Sefarim, first published in 1873 (Hebrew version,
1909), is unusual in nineteenth-century Jewish writing, as it recognizes "the
protean force and unbridled joy of anti-Semitism."[48] Written after the Odessa pogrom of 1871, it warns that Jew-haters would "wipe you out and tear
the soul from your body!"[49] In reaction to the pogroms of 1881–82, the
Hebrew poet Naphtali Herz Imber (best known as the author of the Jewish
national anthem, *Hatikva*) wrote a poem, *Himmalet ha-Harah* ("Escape to
the Mountain," 1886), in which he predicted catastrophe, warning the Jews
to escape to the "mountain," i.e., the Land of Israel:[50]

> Let me be like the Gentiles, you say,
> live with them, choose their way.
> They want your money, not you.
> Get to the mountain in the cry and hue.
>
> Europe is a flaming coal that burns you dry;
> fire and brimstone of hate
> rain from its sky:
> Quick, to the mountain, escape.
>
> For the day may come...where will you go?
> Round you the storm will grow.
> My helpless people, from catastrophe run,
> escape to the mountain!

Far more influential than Imber's poem was Bialik's *Al Ha-Shechitah*
("On the Slaughter"), written at the time of the Kishinev pogrom in 1903,
one of a wave of hundreds of anti-Semitic outbursts in Russia from 1903 to
1906:[51]

> Heaven, beg mercy for me!
> If you have a God, and he can be reached
> - but I've not found him -
> pray for me!
> My heart is numb, my prayer gone,
> I've lost my strength and hope -
> how long, till when, how long?

---

48. Ruth Wisse, *The Modern Jewish Canon: A Journey through Language and Culture*
    (New York: The Free Press, 2000), 335.

49. In Joachim Neugroschel, ed., *Great Works of Jewish Fantasy* (London: Picador,
    1978), 255.

50. *Collected Poems* (Hebrew) (Tel Aviv: Newman, 1950), 50–51.

51. In *Bialik: a bilingual anthology*, ed. and trans. D. Aberbach (New York: Overlook,
    2004), 76.

On the eve of World War I, the Hebrew poet Zalman Shneour (1887–1959) warned in a poem prophetically entitled *Yeme ha-Beinayim Mitkarvim* ("The Middle Ages Are Coming," 1913) that Europe was moving backward to barbarism. If the Jews were to be destroyed, he wrote, they should join forces and die fighting:[52]

> If everything is coming to an end,
> if the day does not dawn,
> if the cruel wheel sweeps you up,
> grinds you in its teeth forever,
> greases its axle with your blood,
> if the nations make a covenant of murder,
> to drag you into their savage world,
> prevent you from going on alone,
> to fulfil your vision on this earth –
> what then do you want with peace?
>
> ...Stop being martyrs. Learn to be heroes –
> The Middle Ages are coming!

Uri Zvi Greenberg, perhaps the leading Hebrew poet of the interwar period, was driven to Zionism by anti-Semitism. During the 1918 pogrom in Lemberg, anti-Semites lined him and his family against a wall in a mock-execution. As he put it, he felt the soil on which he had grown up burning under his feet, for the anti-Jewish hatred of the *goyim*—the murderous Polish and Ukrainian Gentiles—would not stop until it destroyed its victims. In *Yerushalayim shel Matah* ("Earthly Jerusalem"), written shortly after his arrival in Palestine in 1923, Greenberg describes Europe as a paradise turned into Hell by Jew-hatred:[53]

> Forced to leave all we valued, we dressed for exile,
> slung satchel on shoulder...
> We were forced to go.
> The earth screamed under our feet, rattling our beds.
>
> We were forced to hate what we loved:
>
> ...Wrenched from the shtetls, we saw our houses
> in fire-filled tears, knowing
> they would burn in the end...

David Vogel's Hebrew novel *Married Life* (1929–30) warns, similarly, that despite, perhaps because of, a considerable increase in assimilation and intermarriage, anti-Semitism threatened the future of European Jews. Written in Paris, the novel tells of Gurdweill, a Jewish writer from Poland, who marries an impecunious Austrian baroness in Vienna after the war. Gurd-

---

52. Zalman Schneour, *Poems* (Hebrew), 4 vols. (1958–1959), (Tel Aviv: Dvir, 1958), I 161.

53. David Aberbach, "Fanatic Heart: The Poetry of Uri Zvi Greenberg," *Journal of the Central Conference of American Rabbis* (Spring 2003), 20–21.

weill's marriage is a mirror of the failure of Jewish-Christian relations. The sado-masochism of wife and husband recalls the entire history of Christian cruelty to Jews who are "married" to the countries where they live. Gurdweill become increasingly frustrated by anti-Semitism. In a small but telling scene repeated countless times throughout Europe, he is riding on a tram with his Jewish friends, Lotte and Dr. Mark Astel, when he encounters a typical anti-Semite:

> A big, heavy man with a broad, red face, a long brown Virginia cigar stuck in his mouth and a bowler hat on his head, got in, dragging a skinny little woman behind him. They sat down directly opposite Gurdweill and his friends. The big man blew out puffs of delicate, almost invisible smoke and stared fixedly at Lotte. Suddenly, he addressed his wife in a voice loud enough for the whole coach to hear:
> "These Poles, you can't get away from them!"
> The three friends pretended not to hear. Lotte sat there petrified. She felt that something was going to happen and wanted to tell her companions to get off the tram. But she said nothing. The man, seeing that his words had missed their aim, now addressed them directly:
> "Yes, yes, I mean you!" he said in a Viennese accent and a voice as coarse as a butcher's. "Why are you staring at me? I mean Jews! You're Jews, aren't you?"
> Dr. Astel and Gurdweill jumped up together. The blood rushed to Gurdweill's head and his face went red and then white.
> "You, you," spluttered Dr. Astel, furiously waving his fist in the fat man's face, "you shut your mouth! Or else I'll throw you off the tram!"
> "Who? You'll throw me off the tram?" growled the man, jumping to his feet.
> "Me? A Viennese? You go back to Galicia where you came from!"[54]

Vogel, unlike most other Hebrew writers, did not heed the warning in his own writings. He stayed in France and was trapped there during the war. In 1944 he was caught and presumably died in an extermination camp.

Shadowings and "The Crucible"

European culture in the half-century prior to the Holocaust—especially its expression of post–1918 despair, fragmentation, grief, anxiety, alienation and fears—foreshadowed the coming war and the Holocaust. The new dark mood in Western culture continued to affect post-Holocaust literature, which, even if not concerned directly with the Holocaust, often alludes to it in ways that bring to mind the ominous adumbrations of interwar literature. Samuel Beckett's *Waiting for Godot* (1951), for example, contains passages that seem to echo T.S. Eliot's *The Hollow Men* (1926). Beckett's play on one level communicates the author's grief for Jewish friends killed by the Nazis;

---

54. Trans. D. Bilu (London: Peter Halban, 1988), 301–302.

the character Estragon was originally called Levy.[55] Similarly, William Golding's novel *Lord of the Flies* (1954), though influenced by Richard Hughes's interwar novel of castaway children who succumb to evil, *A High Wind in Jamaica* (1929), was written under the impact of the author's wartime experiences while serving in the British navy and his awareness that a few miles away atrocities were being committed.

Harold Pinter's *The Caretaker* (1960), likewise, has no open reference to the Holocaust (nor mention of Jews or anti-Semitism), yet the basic premise of the play, the frustration of a desperate wish to be accepted, recalls interwar works such as Kafka's *The Castle* and Schnitzler's *Dream Story* (1926). In this literary context, Pinter's play can be seen as an enactment in miniature of the pattern of Jewish experience in Europe. A tramp, Davies, is taken into a derelict house; he seems to be on the way to acceptance (though he is terrified of being gassed), but his efforts to adapt are resisted and, after a power struggle, he is evicted. The play is filled with language of racial hatred, the aggressive intolerance of "foreigners," with which Pinter was familiar from the London East End in the 1930s and 1940s. Pinter recalled how anti-Semitism affected his view of language as a form of defence after the war, in the East End, when the fascists were coming back to life in England:

> I got into quite a few fights down there. If you looked remotely like a Jew, you might be in trouble. Also, I went to a Jewish club, by an old railway arch, and there were quite a lot of people often waiting with broken milk bottles in a particular arch we used to walk through. There were one or two ways of getting out of it—one was a purely physical way, of course, but you couldn't do anything about the milk bottles —*we* didn't have any milk bottles. The best way was to talk to them, you know, sort of "Are you all right?" "Yes, I'm all right." "Well, that's all right then, isn't it?" And all the time keep walking toward the lights of the main road.[56]

The cruel interrogatory style to which Davies and other characters in Pinter's plays are subjected recalls, Pinter admits, the "terrorising through words of power" of the Gestapo: "I was a boy in the last war...and the sense of the Gestapo was very strong in England. They weren't here but we as children knew about them."[57]

---

55. Richard Ellmann, *Four Dubliners: Wilde, Yeats, Joyce, and Beckett* (London: Cardinal, 1988), 82. Ionesco's Absurd play *Rhinocéros* (1959), too, has no overt reference to the Holocaust but can be read as a satiric condemnation of Romanian acquiescence to Nazism and Nazi anti-Semitism during the war. In a diary entry of 1940, written in French, Ionesco, whose mother was Jewish, declared, "Vous êtes le seul homme parmi les rhinocéros. [...] est-ce vrai que le monde était conduit par des hommes?" *Present passé, Passé present* (Mercure de France, 1968), 114.

56. In Ian Smith, *Pinter in the Theatre* (London: Nick Hern Books, 2005), 61.

57. Ibid., 83.

Among other post-war works shadowing the Holocaust, Arthur Miller's *The Crucible* stands out. This was Miller's best-selling, most widely translated and internationally performed play. Its immediate historical context was the Cold War following World War II and the anti-Communist hysteria in the United States. The "crucible" refers to the testing of American democracy, and the purging of prejudice and intolerance, both among the seventeenth-century Puritans in Salem, Massachusetts, where the play is set, and in reaction to the McCarthyist "witch-hunt" of suspected Communists—including Miller himself—many of them Jews.

Yet Miller was first attracted to the subject of the Salem witch trials long before the McCarthy era, in the 1930s, when Jews were being persecuted in Europe.[58] An early play of his, "The Golden Years" (1939), set in sixteenth-century Mexico, is an anguished, if immature, response to the futile attempts to appease Hitler. At this time, American anti-Semitism reached its height, and Miller felt it personally. "Since the early thirties," he recalled,

> ...we had lived under the threat not just of Nazism, but American racism. It was terrifying, and anti-Semitism was very strong in the United States. The more it surfaced in Germany, the worse it got here. It became OK to be anti-Semitic, and we had some terrible incidents, and I thought it was getting worse all the time. I thought personally that we would be destroyed by it one day, if a reaction against it didn't materialize.[59]

Anti-Semitism is the subject of Miller's only novel, *Focus* (1945), leading to *The Crucible*. Both present the hysterical degeneration of a terrified society, the complex social and psychological roots of the need for a scapegoat, and the creeping nature of persecution until it becomes a social norm.

The Crucible in some ways goes much further than *Focus* and has greater emotional force: exposing suppressed desires unleashed in a deeply repressed society; the use of the witch-hunt to "solve" problems by killing a scapegoat; awareness of complex social and political causes in the late seventeenth century; the role of personal grievance, jealousy and spite; the charge of ritual murder; the virtual impossibility of proving innocence; and the defenselessness of the victims.

The parallels between Salem and the Holocaust are explicit in one of Miller's main historical sources, Marion Starkie's *The Devil in Massachusetts* (1949). According to Starkie, the Salem witch hunt of 1692 was not confined to the distant past: "It has been revived on a colossal scale by replacing the medieval idea of malefic witchcraft by a pseudo-scientific concept like 'race' [and] 'nationality'."[60] Starkie's view of the witch-hunt as "an

58. In Matthew C. Roudane, ed., *Conversations with Arthur Miller* (Jackson and London: University Press of Mississippi, 1987), 109.

59. In Christopher Bigsby, *Arthur Miller and Company* (London: Methuen, 1990), 29–30.

60. Marion Starkie, *The Devil in Massachusetts: A Modern Enquiry into the Salem Witch Trials* (London: Robert Hale Limited, 1952 [1949]), 11.

allegory of our times" was adopted by Miller. It was appropriate that on the 300th anniversary of the trials, in 1992, the Auschwitz survivor, Elie Wiesel, was invited to dedicate the monument to the victims at Salem.

Speaking of the world of *The Crucible*, with its Puritan intolerance of difference, Miller admitted that he made the connection with concentration camps as "the statement of people who were against the idea of a mixed society, where people have the opportunity to do anything they choose to do....I think the purging of the Jews was a logical consequence of the desire to make all people part of a single larger organism."[61]

The purging of "witches" in *The Crucible* is on one level symbolic of the purging of Jews (traditionally associated in Christian Europe with witchcraft, the devil, and demonic possession) and of any group different from the majority by a prejudiced, intolerant society. Though anti-Semitism may be the biographical base of *The Crucible*, it represents a universal evil. The extraordinary international fascination with *The Crucible* suggests that in being hated and discriminated against, the Jews are like everyone else, only more so.

The Crucible, then, can be read as a milestone in the growth of cultural pluralism. It marks the point at which American Jewish writers began to achieve something no group of Jewish writers had hitherto achieved, certainly not in genocidal Europe: acceptance as an ethnic group contributing to the cultural mainstream. The Holocaust defined in extreme form not just what America stood for and fought against but also what it would not tolerate in future. Amid unprecedented prosperity and growth, America after the Holocaust largely rejected European-style Jew-hatred as, by the early eighteenth century, it had rejected the hysteria of the witch trials that in Europe over the centuries had led to the deaths of far more women than Jews. Unlike most European Jewish writers, Miller sees intolerance as something to be fought and defeated—in the name of American democracy (in *Focus*, the anti-Semites are driven away with baseball bats). Miller gained recognition as an American writer in a way that Heine or Kafka, for example, never did as German writers. [62]

---

61. Roudane, op. cit., 379–380.

62. *The Crucible* spawned a group of plays by Miller—none quite as good—that openly deal with, or allude to, anti-Semitism and the Holocaust: *After the Fall*, *Incident at Vichy*, *Playing for Time* (set in Auschwitz), and *Broken Glass*. *Broken Glass*, set at the time of *Kristallnacht* in 1938, explores the painful entanglements of anti-Semitism and paralyzing Jewish self-hate—a theme familiar among pre-Holocaust writers such as Kafka and Schnitzler—leading the author at the age of 80 to an admission of Jewish pride hard to imagine at the time of *Death of a Salesman*: "something in me suspects that there must continue to be Jews in the world or it will somehow end." Martin Gottfried, *Arthur Miller: His Life and Work* (Cambridge Mass.: De Capo Press, 2003), 441.

Of Jews and Canons:
Further Thoughts

ILAN STAVANS

In 1998 I edited *The Oxford Book of Jewish Stories*, which afforded me the opportunity to think comprehensively about Jewish literature in transnational, multilingual terms. A native of Mexico, I had emigrated to the United States in 1985. My perspective, thus, was that of an outsider to the English-speaking world, and I allowed that viewpoint to be filtered into my selection criteria. Yiddish, Hebrew, English, German, Polish, and Russian were showcased in the volume's content. But I also made space for Brazilian, South African, Yugoslavian, Canadian, and Argentine authors.

In subsequent years, the topic of canonicity remained ingrained in my mind. In lectures and in print, I asked questions: What is a Jewish book? Is it defined by content or context? Then, on January 28, 2000, I published in *The Forward* a brief essay—more like a modest proposal *à la* Jonathan Swift—summarizing my opinions and inviting people to establish a library of world Jewish classics. The piece was entitled "Of Jews and Canons." Collected in my book *The Inveterate Dreamer* (2001), it read:

> Samuel Johnson said that we are less in need of discovering new truths than of remembering old ones. He, of course, was the quintessential canonizer, a major force in the drive to systematize what is memorable in English literature. He spent his days not only codifying the language of his day but also scrutinizing the authors who mattered, from Shakespeare to Milton and onward to his own contemporaries, Dryden and Pope. But Dr. Johnson lived in a less skeptical age than ours, one in which Truth, undeniable and absolute, was written with a capital T. That is no longer the case, and today, canons (from the Greek *kanön*, meaning rule) are seen as tricky strategies. They are under heavy-artillery attack, particularly in liberal circles, relentlessly portrayed by the press and by academics as capricious and authoritarian. Canon-makers are perceived as fools with flair, self-promoters who are no better than the anthologist for whom literature is a limitless river in desperate need of a cut-and-paste job. Who on earth gives them the right to endorse and obliterate?
>
> I must confess to being one of those fools myself, guilty of constantly telling people what is or is not good in literature, and also guilty of generating "portable mini-libraries," as I often find myself describing anthologies. In the past few years, though, I have come to believe that this fanciful urge of mine—to judge books to be the most precious objects in the universe and to be certain that among them only a handful are worthy of sacrifice—is genetic, a hand-me-down, easily traceable to remote times. It makes me smile that nowadays, in academic debates about the canon, there are always

more than enough Jews to make a minyan. But why are they not debating
the formation of a Jewish literary canon?

Many of these thoughts sprang into my mind not long ago as a result of
a happy coincidence. In a secondhand bookstore, I stumbled upon a copy
of *Sefer Ha-Aggadah*, an anthology co-edited by Hayyim Nahman Bialik, the
poet of the Hebrew renaissance. I acquired it along with another volume that
is more easily accessible: Harold Bloom's *The Western Canon*. As I delved
into them, more or less simultaneously, I realized how interconnected they
are in their overall message. Bialik was a fervent Zionist, but his dream was
not only the physical relocation of the Jews to the Promised Land. He also
sought their spiritual and cultural rebirth, and his anthology of rabbinic
legend and lore, originally published in Odessa from 1908 to 1911, was part
of that project. He was helped by Yehoshua Hana Ravnitzky, another early
Zionist and a founder of modern Hebrew journalism. The volume was but
a part, albeit a magisterial one, of a larger project that Bialik had in mind. He
called it *kinus*, the "ingathering" of a Jewish literature that was dispersed
over centuries of Diaspora life. That library, much like its readers, needed
to be centralized in a single, particular place, Israel, and in a single tongue,
Hebrew: a centripetal canon.

Bloom, on the other hand, sees literature as centrifugal. He does not
reach out to other cultures; instead, he waits for those other cultures to
reach him. His book, more than five hundred pages in length, is made up of
erudite disquisitions on twenty-six classic authors and on the schools that
shaped them, from John Milton to Samuel Beckett, with Shakespeare at the
heart of it. A successor to Matthew Arnold (and one of his stronger promot-
ers these days), Bloom does not see the canon as a nationalistic heritage, but
rather as a universal one. This is a trick, of course. Days after I finished the
book, I found, on the web site amazon.com, a reaction from a reader in
Madrid: "This isn't the Western canon," it said, "but an English-language
one." And it is true; in the table of contents, the British, Irish, and Americans
listed total thirteen, half of Bloom's library for the ages.

Bialik's concept of *kinus* suggests that at some point in its development,
Israel would produce a real library of Jewish classics in inexpensive editions,
just like the paperbacks of *Hamlet*, *Middlemarch*, and *Ulysses*, easily available in bookstores across America. But such a publishing enterprise has not
yet been implemented. Sholem Aleichem, Isaac Babel, and Saul Bellow, who
have all been translated into Hebrew at some point, remain inaccessible in
popular formats for Israeli readers. They are either out of print or in editions
that are not quite suitable for the educational market. The truce between
Zionism and the Diaspora is still being forged. Israelis are only now recognizing, half a century into their history, that Jews elsewhere on the globe
live fruitful lives and that most are not about to make aliyah. As a result, much
of the literature produced in gentile milieus, especially from the Enlightenment on, has yet to be digested.

What is puzzling, though, is that no such library exists in English either,
and English is the lingua franca of the Jews at the dawn of the third millennium of the Common Era, exactly as Aramaic was in Palestine and Babylonia
in late antiquity. Just as they were in antiquity, Jews in America today are
undergoing a tremendous intellectual revival. The reading list, however, is

frighteningly insular, intra-Ashkenazic and monolinguistic. It starts with the
Bible and then jumps haphazardly to the Yiddish masters, Abramovich,
Sholem Aleichem, and Peretz, only to focus its attention on New York immigrants such as Abraham Cahan and Anzia Yezierska, Holocaust writers such
as Paul Celan and Primo Levi, and contemporary voices like that of Philip
Roth. Medieval Spain does not exist at all and neither does France, let alone
a place as peripheral—in other words, as barbaric—as Brazil.

The experience of reading Bloom and Bialik together was nothing short
of enlightening. It led me to ponder the identity of Jews as canon-makers of
Western civilization and their utter avoidance of the task of shaping a Jewish
canon for themselves, one that is truly international. Why shape other
people's libraries and not our own? Have we not reached a time in which
the universalist and particularist trends can be reconciled? What unites secular Jews the world over, especially at a time when a considerable portion of
them is nonaffiliated? The answer, I often hear, is moral values or a common
heritage. Freud spoke of the "psychological Jew" as an entity with a clear
moral code and a reservoir of intellect. But how common is that heritage in
the global village? What links us together when in one corner of the world
the work of someone such as the German-writing Sephardic master Elias
Canetti or the French philosopher Edmond Jabes is cardinal, yet in another
one it is utterly unknown?

Kanön plus *kinus:* Bialik envisioned the canon as an instrument for
harvesting the universal elements in his own people, to help them along on
the road to normalizing their national status. Almost a century later, the same
instrument ought to be recast for the intellectual consciousness of a Diaspora
that no longer has any boundaries. The duty of our generation is to shape a
balanced canon that transcends time and place, first and foremost in English
but also in other diaspora languages and in Hebrew—the finest, most influential of our books available to everyone in affordable editions. Its main criterion ought to be the power to make the particular universal and vice versa.
And its purpose should be the ingathering of the Jews, at home in the world.

Almost a decade later, I still believe a homogenized library of Jewish classics in English, one modeled after the French imprint La Pléïade, is worth
pursuing. It isn't an easy task, given the dynamics of the publishing industry.
Scores of books are already available in disparate, at times substandard editions. Copyright ownership is sometimes difficult to identify and availability
of translations makes it difficult to bring out a competing version. Still, the
kinus Bialik talked about has yet to take place.

In any case, a short time after I published my brief piece, Ruth R. Wisse
came out with *The Modern Jewish Canon* (2000), pushing the discussion
on Jews and books to another level. Her argument wasn't in favor of consol-
idating an effort to republish the classics. Her interests were more academic; she wanted to delineate the boundaries of the ingathering: who is in,
who is out. Until a few years prior, my interaction with Wisse had been
largely tangential. I studied with her brother Dovid Roskies at the Jewish
Theological Seminary. I had read her work on the schlemiel as modern hero
as well as on Isaac Leib Peretz. And on occasion I came across her articles in

The New Republic. Then, in 1998, the two of us were part of an international panel of judges (others included Robert Alter and Gershom Shaked) organized by the National Yiddish Book Center, in Amherst, Mass., to select a list
of the one hundred most important Jewish books. The debate at the judging
table had been invigorating. The panel trimmed from a large pull of titles by
means of intense, informed, argumentative debate. The consensus was easy
to reach on a dozen entries, but then it was open field. Time was given for
people to get themselves acquainted with unfamiliar novels, memoirs, collections of essays, and poetry. I quickly learned from the occasion—no surprise!—that Ashkenazic (principally Yiddish) letters were, as I stated it in
"On Jews and Canons," on everyone's radar, and that American (the two
Roths, Bellow, Malamud, Paley), European (Kafka, Babel, Schulz, Canetti,
Levi) and Israeli (Bialik, Agnon, Oz, Yehoshua) letters also carried fundamental weight. The judges were less acquainted with the oeuvre of authors
from other diasporas (the Ottoman Empire, India, Australia, South Africa,
Canada, Brazil, Argentina) and languages (Ladino, Turkish, Arabic, Spanish,
Portuguese). Given the geographical and cultural background of the judges,
the inclusion of entries from these regions became more contested.

Reading Wisse's book, I was immediately taken by her breadth of knowledge and her attempt to look at the Jewish bookshelf broadly and comprehensively. (I articulated my thoughts in a review for *The Nation*.) I found
particularly inspiring her discussion on the Holocaust, the Singer siblings
(Israel Joshua, Isaac Bashevis, and Esther Kreitman), and the American
immigrant novel (Cahan, Yezierska). And her suggestions for further reading (pages 382–84) encouraged her audience to expand its horizon even
further. My qualm, expectedly, was, yet again, with Wisse's narrow view of
Ashkenazic literature. The ingathering from other diasporas was left out.
Needless to say, this type of complaint is often targeted toward anthologists
(and I've done my share of them). What's included in is closely scrutinized
against what's left out. Why isn't there a more serious consideration of Anne
Frank's diary? And why were Piotr Rawicz, Chaim Grade, and Arthur Koest-
ler left out? There's no satisfying everybody, nor should there be.

We owe Wisse the building of a global Jewish canon. Her contribution has been essential in enabling us to read the past as a mosaic. But,
again, our responsibility is to read more widely if not also, and excuse
the pun, more wisely. Lionel Trilling, in *The Liberal Imagination,* says
that "literature is the human activity that takes the fullest and most precise
account of *variousness, possibility,* complexity, and difficulty." But his
famous 1950 collection, though not devoted to Jews, hardly goes beyond
Kipling and Henry James, F. Scott Fitzgerald and Mark Twain, an orbit of
interests ad hoc to Trilling's countrified times. I emphasize two of his
nouns because, in the same piece, he added that criticism is the task of
bringing awareness to that complexity and difficulty, though he forgets
to insert the words variousness and possibility. In the twentieth centu-

ry, Jewish life was turned on its head: a massive movement of people took place from east to west; the tragic destruction of European communities in the hands of the Nazis erased an entire culture; the state of Israel was established; and reaction against secularism and toward religion manifested itself. Ironically, as we move away from those events, it becomes clear that almost every diaspora was somehow affected. Why do we know so little about the Jewish experience in those regions? When will the triangle United States–Eastern Europe–Israel be broken? Are we able to take full advantage of Trilling's terms: variousness and possibility?

I'm concerned with the work of Sephardic authors, which go largely unread. In 2005 I edited *The Schocken Book of Modern Sephardic Literature*, which starts in eighteenth-century London and concludes in present-day Israel. And, more specifically, I'm worried about the lack of representation in the Jewish canon of writers from the Hispanic world. Since 1994, when I published the anthology *Tropical Synagogues*, three years before the first title appeared in the "Jewish Latin America" series I edited for the University of New Mexico Press, which included twenty-five titles and lasted from 1997 to 2006, I began devoting an important part of my time and energy to making those literatures better known. Alberto Gerchunoff from Argentina, Moacyr Scliar from Brazil, and Isaac Goldemberg from Peru were included in the list of "100 most important Jewish books." They are the tip of the iceberg, though. The Jewish-Argentine shelf includes hundreds of books, among which is fiction by Marcos Aguinis, Mario Goloboff, Mario Szichman, and Perla Suez. Venezuela, Colombia, Costa Rica, Guatemala, Cuba, and Mexico each contain a rich well of narrative gems. In these countries, Jewish literature dates back to the colonial period, when marranos and crypto-Jews arrived, escaping the might of the Holy Inquisition. Contemporary scholars have not even begun to explore these texts in a systematic manner.

However, in the last few years my anxiety has moved in another direction. Literature as a whole is obviously losing its gravitas. It doesn't matter anymore, at least not in the way it did in the heart of the twentieth century. And the writer is less of a public figure. Indeed, as of late, Jews, while they are vigorous readers, seem to have become more adept at producing movie and television artifacts, even graphic novels, than at remaining loyal to the written word. Might the people of the book be transforming themselves into the people of the image (in spite of the ancient prohibition against idols)? As I look into the future, I wish the Jewish canon to become more elastic, less parochial. But I'm also concerned with the viability of experience through words themselves. I'm afraid a literate Jew today is less in need of being acquainted with Bellow's *Humboldt's Gift* than with the tenor of Jerry Seinfeld's long-running television show. Equally, the legacy of Bernard Malamud appears to be far less relevant than that of Mel Brooks. I wonder whether when discussing the Jewish canon our debate hasn't been futile, even preposterous. Does it still matter who reads what? Should we not be thinking about Jewish literacy in larger, more comprehensive ways, reaching beyond books into other media: film, music, radio, television, theater, dance, video games, and the internet? If so, our discriminating taste should once more be applied not only to canonize American pop culture but to appreciate the material from other corners of the globe: masterful movies in Dutch, soap operas from France, Yiddish tangos and mariachi from Argentina and Mexico, stage dramas from South Africa, graphic novels from Germany and Japan, and so on. For the way Jews, and the public in general, appreciate the past now is through a sophisticated configuration of outlets and channels. Thinking reflectively is still the goal, but digesting information is nowadays achieved through various forms.

One Jewish tradition, many decentralized artistic expressions...to find their common thread is to create a narrative.

A Jewish Artistic Canon

EZRA MENDELSOHN

Efforts to establish a modern Jewish literary canon have been going on for some time now. This is a highly contentious enterprise. Should such a canon consist only of writings in Jewish languages, meaning above all Hebrew and Yiddish, or should it include Jewish authors who wrote in the languages of the countries in which they lived but who were interested, to one degree or another, in Jewish subjects? For that matter, might it even include works by non-Jews on Jewish themes, such as George Eliot, author of the great proto-Zionist novel *Daniel Deronda*, and Henry Wadsworth Longfellow, who wrote a beautiful and moving poem about the Jewish cemetery at Newport? Israeli literary scholars in recent years have been discussing the question of which works deserve to be found on "the Jewish bookshelf" (*madaf hasefarim hayehudi*) and, of course, the honorée of this collection of essays has made this question the subject of an important and much acclaimed recent book.[1] The debate among literary scholars and critics goes on, paralleling similar debates on what constitutes the canon of American, British, French, and other literatures.

What of a modern Jewish artistic canon? By this I mean a catalogue of images made by Jewish painters, photographers, and sculptors who have attained or deserve to attain a special status in the world of Jewish culture by depicting, in a particularly successful way, the modern Jewish experience. So far as I know, Jewish historians or Jewish art historians have not yet proposed such a list.[2] In what follows I take up this task, and suggest a number of Jewish images that, I believe, qualify for inclusion in a pantheon of "Jewish art," however we may define it.

My thanks to my son, Amitai Mendelsohn, for his comments on this essay.

1. See especially her discussion in *The Modern Jewish Canon* of how to select such a canon (4ff.). One prominent Israeli scholar who has written on this is Hannan Hever. See his *Producing the Modern Hebrew Canon. Nation Building and Minority Discourse* (New York: 2002). See also Yedidia Z. Stern, *Making the Jewish Canon Accessible to Our Generation* (Ramat Gan: 2003). Longfellow's poem, "The Jewish Cemetery at Newport," was written in 1852 and published two years later.

2. I have already discussed the case for proposing such a canon in my brief note in *Images* 1/1 (2007), 22–23. One possible exception is the important work by Avram Kampf, *Jewish Experience in the Art of the Twentieth Century* (New York: 1976).

So far as western art in general is concerned, it is obvious that certain works have, by general consensus, attained canonical or, to use the term preferred by art historians, iconic status. In American art, for example, perhaps the most famous example is Grant Wood's "American Gothic" of 1930 [fig. 1]. This painting, depicting a mid-Western (Iowan) farm couple, has been designated, in the sub-title of a recent study devoted entirely to it, "America's most famous painting."[3] It has been endlessly reproduced and often lampooned—a certain sign of iconic status, since in order for the joke

FIG. 1
Grant Wood, *American Gothic*, 1930
oil on beaver board, 30 11/16 × 25 11/16 in.
Friends of American Art Collection, 1930.934. The Art Institute of Chicago
Photography c/o The Art Institute of Chicago

---

3. Steven Biel, *American Gothic: A Life of America's Most Famous Painting* (New York: 2005). See also Jane C. Milosch, ed., *Grant Wood's Studio: Birthplace of* American Gothic, (Munich., et al.: 2005). On American icons in general, see John Carlin and Jonathan Fineberg, *Imagining America: Icons of 20ʰ-Century American Art* (New Haven and London: 2005).

to work the image must be instantly recognizable. It owes its unique place in the history of American art to its success in conveying something quintessential about America and in particular about the American heartland: its spareness and loneliness, and the self-reliance and individualism of its white, Protestant inhabitants. Its creator was a leading member of the American regional school of the 1930s, which specialized in painting, in various styles, accessible scenes of American life far removed from the big city.

Another artist whose work obviously qualifies for inclusion in the American canon is Norman Rockwell, whose images of Americana graced the covers of the *Saturday Evening Post* in the 1950s and 1960s. A well-known example is his "Breaking Home Ties" of 1954, which displays a young man prepared to leave his home somewhere in the American heartland and go off to college. He is flanked by his hard-working father, a weather-beaten

FIG. 2
Norman Rockwell, *Breaking Home Ties*, 1954
oil on canvas
cover of *Saturday Evening Post*, September 1954
printed by permission of the Norman Rockwell Family Agency,
copyright c/o 1954, the Norman Rockwell Family Entities,
licensed by The Curtis Publishing Company, Indianapolis, Indiana

laborer or farmer who obviously never enjoyed a university education, and by his faithful collie [fig. 2].[4]

For iconic images of urban America and its marvels one might turn to Alfred Stieglitz's celebrated 1903 photograph of the Flatiron building, an early New York skyscraper, or to Italian-born Joseph Stella's modernist paintings depicting the Brooklyn Bridge.[5] As for paintings celebrating America's glorious history, probably the most famous is the work of an obscure German-American artist, Emanuel Leutze's "Washington Crossing the Delaware" (1851). To this should be added, no doubt, Gilbert Stuart's series of portraits of George Washington, one of which decorates the one-dollar bill.

Drawing somewhat closer to our particular interest, it is also possible to identify iconic images of certain American minority groups. In the case of African Americans, for example, we have "The Awakening of Ethiopia" (ca. 1910), the work of the sculptor Meta Warrick Fuller [fig. 3]. This sculpture,

FIG. 3
Meta Warrick Fuller,
The Awakening of Ethiopia (sculpture),
ca. 1910,
Schomburg Center for Research in Black Culture,
The New York Public Library

4. It is reproduced in Christopher Finch, *Norman Rockwell's America* (New York: 1975), 69, and discussed in Laura Claridge, *Norman Rockwell. A Life* (New York: 2001), 399–400.

5. See Katherine Hoffman, *Stieglitz: A Beginning Light* (New Haven and London: 2004), 208–212; Stella's first representation of the Brooklyn Bridge was completed in 1919 or 1920; see Irma B. Jaffe, *Joseph Stella* (Cambridge, Mass.: 1970), 55.

now on display at the Schomburg Center for Research in Black Culture in New York, has been interpreted as a representation of "the new Negro," a figure as vital to the Harlem Renaissance movement of the 1920s and 1930s as was the "new Jew" to Zionism.[6]

Turning to Europe, a number of strong candidates for membership in the artistic canon are easy to identify. Edvard Munch's "The Scream" of 1893, for example, qualifies because it "has come to be seen as a painting of the dilemma of modern man, a visualization of Nietzsche's cry, 'God is dead, and we have nothing to replace him.'"[7] Picasso's "Guernica" is doubtless the most familiar image of the cruelty of modern warfare, while the greatest Polish artist of the nineteenth century, Jan Matejko, produced in his "Battle at Grunwald" (1878) what is certainly the most famous image in the history of his country's art, an image of early fifteenth-century Polish heroism and defiance, painted at a time when Polish independence had long been lost and when Russia, Germany, and Austria ruled the Polish lands [fig. 4].[8] Another well-known East European image is Ilya Repin's "Volga Boatmen"

FIG. 4
Jan Matejko, *The Battle at Grunwald*, 1878
oil on canvas, 426 × 987 cm
National Museum, Warsaw, photograph T. Zoltowska

6. See David Driskell, "The Flowering of the Harlem Renaissance: The Art of Aaron Douglas, Meta Warrick Fuller, Palmer Haydon and William H. Johnson," *Harlem Renaissance: Art of Black America* (New York: 1987), 108. On relations between blacks and Jews in the sphere of art, see Milly Heyd, *Mutual Reflections: Jews and Blacks in American Art* (New Brunswick, N.J.: 1999).

7. Sue Prideaux, *Edvard Munch: Beyond the Scream* (New Haven and London: 2005), 151.

8. There is an extensive literature on this image. See, for example, Krystyna Sroczyńska, ed., *Matejko. Obrazy olejne* (Warsaw: 1993), 151–157.

of 1872, which depicts a group of desperately poor, bedraggled Russian men dragging a boat to shore. Eugène Delacroix's "Liberty Leading the People" (1830) is surely the most celebrated image of the French revolutionary tradition, and perhaps of the modern European revolutionary tradition in general.

These modern images have attained canonical status because they succeed in representing some essential aspect of humankind's condition, or of a nation's history or psyche, or of the mood of a particular era. "The Scream" captures the anxiety of the *fin de siècle*, "Volga Boatmen" represents age-old Russian suffering, and, to cite another example not mentioned above, Andy Warhol's renditions of Marilyn Monroe symbolize America's obsession with female beauty and the manufacturing of celebrity. The process by which these particular images have come to be recognized as canonical is rather mysterious. Is the "decision" made from above, by critics, museum curators, and other shapers of opinion, or is it determined from below, by a popular groundswell of opinion? These are complicated questions having to do with the shaping of taste and the role of cultural elites and mass media, and we cannot deal with them here. What we can say with certainty is that such images are invested by the artist himself, and by those who observe them, with great symbolic significance, with meaning that links the onlooker to something much larger than himself, be it his nation, his religion, his social class, an ideology, or an important human emotion. It is also certain that canonical images do not necessarily have to be works of "great art," as defined by the critics and the leading museums. Norman Rockwell is not usually beloved by art critics, who accuse him of pandering to vulgar taste and of creating nothing more than kitsch. Yet who can deny the iconic status of his works? In this case "the people" have made their decision. Not many critics would rank Joseph Stella among the major American artists, but his renditions of the bridge connecting Manhattan to Brooklyn are nonetheless iconic. We might say the same thing about literature. Emma Lazarus was probably not a great poet, but who would gainsay the canonical status of her sonnet inscribed on the base of the Statue of Liberty, a poem learned by heart by generations of New York schoolchildren?

Now let me proceed to the central theme of this essay: Which works of art, sculpture, and photography qualify as belonging to a modern Jewish canon of images? Inevitably, the choices that follow are personal, and perhaps even eccentric, but they do take into account the views both of the shapers of opinion within the world of Jewish culture and the "Jewish masses." They are limited to images created by Jews and to the realm of what is often called "high culture."

One way of going about this controversial but interesting task is to define certain major aspects of the Jewish experience and to search for images that best represent them. Thus, no one could deny the centrality of "wandering," in general, and of immigration to the New World, in particular, in modern Jewish history. Richard Cohen gathered for a Paris exhibition several years ago a number of modern images of the legend of the "wandering Jew," including works made by Jews that might be considered for inclusion in our canon.[9] Another strong candidate is Raphael Soyer's well-known "Dancing Lesson" of 1926, which depicts three generations of a Russian-Jewish family: the grandparents, whose photographs are to be seen the wall, the parents sitting on a couch, one of them with a Yiddish newspaper (*Der Tog*) in her hand, and the children dancing in the new American fashion [fig. 5]. This is a penetrating portrayal of the immigration experience and of the inevitable process of Americanization of the youngsters, who are clearly dancing away from the Judaism of their elders.[10]

FIG. 5
Raphael Soyer, *Dancing Lesson*, 1926, oil on canvas, 24 × 20 in.
c/o Estate of Raphael Soyer, courtesy of Forum Gallery, New York.

---

9. It has been published as *Le Juif érrant: Un témoin du temps* (Paris: 2001).

10. See my book *On Modern Jewish Politics* (New York: 1993), 9. This painting was featured in the invitations to the conference on American Jewish history honoring Professor Arthur Goren, held at Columbia University in 1990. It is often shown in American Jewish art calendars.

Another possibility, the one that I choose for inclusion in my pantheon, is the famous 1907 photograph by Alfred Stieglitz entitled "The Steerage" [fig. 6]. This image appears to depict immigrants coming to America, inhabiting the lowest (and cheapest) accommodations on the boat, the "steerage," a place that became a byword for the often traumatic passage of the "new immigrants," including East European Jews, to pre-World War I America. The destination of the boat, presumably, was Ellis Island, where the immigrants would be inspected and then, finally, allowed to enter the promised land.

There are a number of ironies here. Stieglitz, American-born of German Jewish origin, was not only a great photographer but also the apostle of modern American art, and among his protégés were several Jewish artists interested in Jewish subject matter, most notably Max Weber. However, so far as I know, he himself took no interest in Jewish matters whatsoever,

FIG. 6
Alfred Stieglitz, *The Steerage*, 1907, Gelatin silver print
gift of Augusta and Arnold Newman, New York,
to American Friends of the Israel Museum. 693.78.
Collection, The Israel Museum, Jerusalem. Photo, The Israel Museum, Jerusalem
photogravure, in or before 1913, 33.2 × 26.4 cm
Alfred Stieglitz Collection, 1949.3.292, National Gallery of Art.

including Jewish culture. Moreover, we know that in the case of this photograph what interested him was its formal attributes, its adherence to a Cubist aesthetic, and not its ostensible subject. As he himself put it, "You may call this a crowd of immigrants...To me it is a study in mathematical lines and in balance, in a pattern of light and shade."[11] Although Stieglitz did admit a social subtext here—himself a passenger on the ship, he wished to distance himself from his well-to-do shipmates to observe the lower-class families traveling in steerage—he had no interest in capturing on film a significant historical movement. Moreover, although "many have interpreted the photograph as an image that memorialized the New York immigrant experience," the immigrants depicted here are not immigrants at all, since the ship was sailing from New York to Europe. They are, presumably, former immigrants returning to Europe after spending some time in the New World.[12] Furthermore, the "immigrants" depicted here cannot be safely identified as Jews. The central figure, back turned to us, is wearing a shawl, not a *talit*, and it is a woman, not a man.

Nonetheless, this image has been widely received as a portrayal, indeed *the* portrayal, of Jewish immigration to America. A recent album on American Jewish art makes this claim. Its author, Ori Soltes, writes that "the teeming masses of Eastern European immigrants (including Orthodox Jews wrapped in their prayer shawls, praying) are seen from the close but not *internal* perspective of the long-since arrived (and not from Eastern Europe) photographer."[13] To this we can only add: *se non è vero, è ben trovato* (even if not true, it is well conceived). Alfred Kazin, the American Jewish literary critic and memoirist, went so far as to decide that the woman in the picture was none other than his mother:[14]

> I dimly knew that Stieglitz had taken the photograph going to Europe. The figures in the photograph were returning, but no matter. The woman is wearing a long wide skirt, and she has draped herself head and back with a long white towel with a double-striped border that puts her at the center of the picture...She is my mother—in that picture and for that year...She is the ugly duckling in a family of just too many girls. She arrives with a beloved handsome older brother who will unwillingly return on the pleas of a wife too pious to flee the Nazis and who will be shot by them right on her doorstep.

11. Alfred Stieglitz, "How *The Steerage* Happened," as reprinted in Richard Whelan, *Stieglitz on Photography* (New York: c. 2000), 197.

12. Hoffman, *Stieglitz*, 237. See also the comments on these "immigrants" in Whelan, *Stieglitz*, 197.

13. See Ori Z. Soltes, *Fixing the World: Jewish American Painters in the Twentieth Century* (Hanover and London: 2003), 25–26.

14. Alfred Kazin, *New York Jew* (New York: 1978), 16.

Kazin kept a reproduction of this photograph on his desk, and insisted upon viewing Stieglitz, the champion of photography as high art and of American artistic modernism, as a "Jewish prophet, who had created in this photograph an unforgettable image of the sufferings, and the indomitable strength, of the Jewish people."[15] It is interesting and entirely in keeping with its reception in the Jewish world that this image is reproduced in a recent volume devoted to the masterpieces of the Jewish Museum in New York.[16]

What of icons of Jewish heroism, Jewish versions of the images by Matejko and Leutze mentioned above? It is striking how few such images exist. Of course, most of Jewish history, unlike that of Poland and America, and indeed of most modern nations, is not marked by decisive military battles. For that one has to go back to the Bible, to the Maccabees, or to Bar Kochba, or to leap forward to 1948 and the wars of the State of Israel. But even these cases do not seem to have engaged the interest of many Jewish artists. There is Boris Schatz's lost work "Matityahu," and Alfred Nossig's "Judah Maccabee," a forgotten sculpture by a forgotten sculptor.[17] And what important Jewish artist has painted the wars of King David, the wars against Rome, or the victories of 1948 and 1967? It may well be that biblical epics and the wars of the Maccabees were appropriated by Christian artists (and composers). Moreover, by the twentieth century most artists had ceased to paint great battle scenes in the manner of previous centuries, as practiced by Matejko and his contemporaries in nineteenth-century Eastern Europe. Has any great American artist painted the Battle of the Bulge or some other great campaign of World War II? These bloody events have been immortalized by the camera, not by the artist's brush. The most famous image of World War II, after all, is the photograph of American soldiers raising the flag at Iwo Jima in 1945.

To find an iconic representation of Jewish heroism we must turn to the Warsaw Ghetto Monument of the sculptor Nathan Rapoport [fig. 7]. It was revealed to the public at a ceremony held in the Polish capital in 1948, and is situated on the place where the ghetto once stood. It has also been copied and installed at Yad Vashem in Jerusalem (in 1976). This monument to Jewish heroism is also a monument to Jewish martyrdom, since it depicts not only the heroic fighters but also, in bas relief, images of unfortunate Jews

---

15. Ibid., 91.

16. Kazin's attitude toward this image is expressed also in an exchange of letters in *The New York Review of Books*, vol. 25, no. 12, July 20, 1978, 50. A. David Wunsch takes to task Robert Towers, author of a review of Kazin's memoir, *New York Jew*, for apparently accepting the idea that these are immigrants coming to America. Towers rejects this accusation in his reply. Interestingly, both appear to agree that the figures in the photograph are Jews.

17. See Richard Cohen, *Jewish Icons* (Berkeley: 1998), 243–244.

FIG. 7
Nathan Rapoport, *Warsaw Uprising Monument*
Photo courtesy of Yad Vashem, Jerusalem

being driven by their unseen tormentors to a terrible fate. There is, of course, an association in the Jewish tradition between heroism and martyrdom, well expressed in the Israeli decision to link officially the commemoration of the Shoah with *gvurah*.

In the words of the foremost scholar of Holocaust monuments, Rapoport's work is, for better or for worse, "the most widely known, celebrated, and controversial" of all Holocaust memorials, reproduced everywhere, derided as "proletarian pap," and as "archaic," but still and all a true "memorial icon."[18] It is, obviously, the product of an aesthetic that is not only com-

18. James Young, *The Texture of Memory: Holocaust Memorials and Meaning* (New Haven and London: 1993), 156. Chapter six of this book is devoted to Rapoport's memorial.

pletely outdated but is also completely discredited, namely Soviet socialist realism. Rapoport, a Polish-born sculptor, fled to the Soviet Union after the Nazi invasion of his country, and worked there during the war years as a state-sponsored artist, making busts of Soviet war heroes. After the war he left the Soviet Union, but remained true to its aesthetic values.

In the sculptor's own words, "My purpose was to give back, at least spiritually, what had been taken away by deadly destruction. My task was to recreate shadows of mothers and fathers, young and old; the epic and tragic end of their lives should be remembered for generations to come."[19] It is noteworthy that the main figure among the fighters, representing Mordechai Anielewicz, member of the Zionist youth movement Hashomer Hatsair and leader of the Jewish fighting force in the Ghetto, has nothing ostensibly Jewish about him. He could just as easily be the "new Soviet man" as the "new Jewish man," and, in fact, his depiction is reminiscent of certain popular renditions of "the new Jew" in Palestine in the interwar period, also heavily influenced by the Soviet aesthetic.[20] It may well be that since military valor was so foreign to the Jewish experience in exile, it was necessary to make the figures into "Non-Jewish Jews." Moreover, as has been noted by others, despite the fact that Anielewicz and most of his comrades in the uprising were Zionists, there does not seem to be anything "Zionist" about the figures: no allusions to Eretz Yisrael and no intimation of the fighters' Jewish political allegiance. Anielewicz is a proletarian hero, not a Jewish nationalist.[21] The female, partly undressed figure reminds Young of Delacroix's "Liberté," and if this is a correct attribution she alludes to the French revolutionary tradition, not to any specifically Jewish phenomenon (her breast, by the way, was covered up in the Jerusalem version of the monument).[22] All this obliges us to recall that the monument was made to be displayed in a country ruled by communism and controlled by the Soviet Union.

As for the figures in the bas-relief on the other side of the monument, Young believes that there is an allusion here to the Triumphal Arch of Titus in Rome, which celebrates the defeat of the Jewish revolt in 70 A.D. Whatever the case, these figures, unlike the fighters, are readily identifiable as

19. Nathan Rapoport, "Memoir of the Warsaw Ghetto Monument," in Young, ed., *The Art of Memory: Holocaust Memorials in History* (Munich and New York: 1994), 106.

20. See the catalogue of an exhibition at the Israel Museum in Jerusalem on this theme: Batia Donner, ed., *Taamulah vehazon: Omanut sovietit veyisraelit 1930–1955* (Jerusalem: 1997).

21. Young, *Texture of Memory*, 174.

22. This change was insisted upon by Yitzhak Arad, the head of Yad Vashem, who also wanted to make the heroic figures look more Jewish. See Judith Tydor Baumol, "'Rachel Laments her Children'—Representation of Women in Israeli Holocaust Memorials," *Israel Studies*, 1 (1996), 112.

Jews, and include a man carrying a Torah scroll, presumably a rabbi. Perhaps they are not only marching to their death, but also exiting from Jewish history altogether, to make room for the non-Jewish Jewish heroes. If this was the artist's intent, then perhaps we can, in fact, find here a Zionist message, somewhat reminiscent of Ephraim Lilien's famous 1901 image contrasting the old Jew of exile to the new Jews of Palestine.[23] But the truth is that we are not sure of the cause for which Rapoport's heroes are fighting. Is it for Palestine, for international socialism, or for communism, or, as I think most likely, for the noble cause of Jewish dignity? It is fascinating that despite these ambiguities, and despite their lack of any identifiably Jewish markers, the fighters depicted on this monument have become the accepted collective face of modern Jewish courage in the face of insurmountable odds.

Since Zionism has played so huge a role in modern Jewish history no canon of Jewish images can be complete without an explicitly Zionist one. A non-controversial choice, I think, would be the famous photograph by Ephraim Moses Lilien of Theodor Herzl on the balcony in Basel, made at the time of the fifth Zionist Congress in 1901 [fig. 8]. Lilien was by far the best-

FIG. 8
Ephraim Moses Lilien, *Herzl*, photograph, 1901
from front cover of *Jüdische Rundschau*, September, 1904
courtesy of George Washington University Special Collections, Gelman Library.

---

23. It is discussed in Michael Berkowitz, *Zionist Culture and West European Jews before the First World War* (Cambridge and New York: 1993), 127–129. See also the discussion on Lilien and Zionism in Michael Stanislawski, *Zionism and the Fin de Siècle: Cosmopolitanism and Nationalism from Nordau to Jabotinsky* (Berkeley: 2001), 98–115.

known artist to be associated with Zionism in its early years, and the creator of a number of famous images associated with the aspirations of this new political force in the Jewish world. His photograph of Herzl is surely the most familiar image of the father of the movement, and has been called "the most recognizable Zionist icon of all times."[24]

Why is this the case? It seems that the image manages to convey, in its profile of Herzl, a potent combination of nobility and Jewishness. It may suggest, too, the parallel between the Rhine, Germany's sacred river, with the Jews' own sacred river, the Jordan, over which they must pass on their way to the "old new land." The central message here, however, is undoubtedly one of vision, or prophecy. Herzl is portrayed as a visionary; he sees the future, a future of terrible anti-Semitism in his own Europe, leading to the Holocaust, but also of Jewish renewal in the ancestral fatherland. In this image Herzl is obviously linked to the ancient prophets; he is a modern prophet, ridiculed and despised by many of his Jewish contemporaries as "king of the Jews," and yet in possession of some secret knowledge. He is, in the well-known Hebrew phrase taught to every Israeli schoolchild, "*hozeh hamedinah*," the seer of the Jewish state, the idea of which in his own time seemed to be a foolish, even harmful fantasy. At the same time, he is, as his dress signifies, the "assimilated" West European Jew who in contrast to other *Westjuden* clearly perceived the tragic state not only of the Jewish masses of Eastern Europe (the *Ostjuden*), but of all Jews.

It is time now to choose an image that represents the Zionist enterprise in Palestine/Eretz Israel. I am tempted to suggest the famous 1939 statue by Itzhak Danziger entitled "Nimrod" [fig. 9]. This is the most famous artistic representation of the so-called "Canaanite" movement in the *yishuv*, which rejected any connection between the new "Hebrews" of Palestine and the Jews of the Exile—thus the importance of the choice of Nimrod, a "mighty hunter" of biblical times, a "Semite," but not a Jew.[25]

This is clearly an iconic sculpture, but I would propose as a more mainstream candidate for inclusion in our visual canon a work by the most popular and influential Jewish artist active in Palestine in the time of the British mandate, Reuven Rubin.[26] This Romanian-born artist, who settled in Pales-

---

24. David Katz, review of Michael Berkowitz's *The Jewish Self-Image in the West* in *The American Historical Review,* 107, no. 1 (Feb. 2002): 163.

25. On this work see Mordecai Omer, *Itzhak Danziger* (Tel Aviv: 1996), 96–101. On the Canaanite movement in general, see Yehoshua Porath, *Shelah veet biyado. Sipur hayav shel Uriel Shelah (Yonatan Ratosh)* (Tel Aviv, 1989).

26. There is an interesting link between Stieglitz and Rubin; it was the former who arranged Rubin's exhibition in New York in 1921. See Dalia Manor, *Art in Zion: The Genesis of Modern National Art in Jewish Palestine* (London and New York: 2006), 216 n. 62. On Stieglitz's relationship with Rubin and in general on this painter, see also Amitai Mendelsohn, *Prophets and Visionaries: Reuven Rubin's Early Years, 1914–*

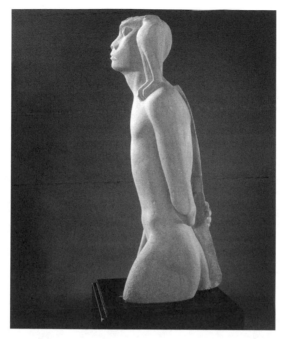

FIG. 9
Itzhak Danziger, *Nimrod*, 1939, Nubian sandstone, 95 × 33 × 33 cm
gift of Dr. David H. Orgler, The Israel Museum, Jerusalem

tine in the early 1920s, contrived to present a picture of a land in which
tranquility reigned, where the "locals" (Arabs) and the Jews were effortless-
ly integrated into the peaceable landscape. A splendid example of his work
from the 1920s is his triptych "The First Fruits" ("Perot rishonim") of 1923
[fig. 10].[27] The painting's name recalls the festival of Shavuot, which for this
Zionist was above all an agricultural festival, not a religious one commemorating the giving of the Torah. Jewish agriculture was, of course, of tremendous symbolic importance to Zionism, signifying the return of the Jews to

23 (Jerusalem: 2006), the catalogue of an exhibition of Rubin's early work at the Israel
Museum, 2006; and Carmela Rubin, ed., *Makom halom. Reuven Rubin vehamifgash
im erets yisrael betsiyurav mishnot ha-20 veha-30* (Tel Aviv: 2007).

27. My thanks to Amitai Mendelsohn of the Israel Museum for suggesting this image to me.
See on this painting the important essay by Gideon Ofrat, "Haperot harishonim 1923,"
in *Beit Reuven. Sefer habayit* (Tel Aviv: 1993), 33–38, in which he calls it "undoubt-
edly one of the most important paintings ever created in Israel" (p. 33). There is an
English version of this article in the same book. See also the analysis in Manor, *Art in
Zion*, 94–98.

FIG. 10
Reuven Rubin, *First Fruits*, Triptych:
The Fruit of the Land, oil on canvas, 188 × 202 cm;
The Shepherd, oil on canvas, 188 × 102 cm;
Rest (The Bedouin), oil on canvas, 188 × 102 cm
Rubin Museum, Tel Aviv

the soil and to a natural, healthy life of productive labor. Jewish farming in
the Land of Israel also justified the right of the Jews to repossess the land,
since they were "making the desert bloom" after centuries of what they considered to be neglect at the hands of the Ottoman rulers and the Arab inhabitants.

The image, in fact three separate paintings, displays two *halutsim* (pioneers), "new men" of the Zionist (not the Canaanite or Soviet) variety, Zionist "saints" in the words of Gideon Ofrat, reaping the fruits of their labor in
the fields, alongside a Yemenite family, the man bearded and with side-
locks, the woman all covered up, in contrast to the bare-breasted new Jewish woman and her bare-chested, heroically proportioned companion. The
issue of dress is obviously important here. The Yemenite Jewish adults are
covered from head to toe, in the traditional style of the exile, whereas the
Ashkenazi Zionists bare their healthy bodies to the life-giving sun of their
new home. How the Yemenite baby will dress when he or she grows up is
an open question. This central image in the triptych is flanked by portrayals
of "native" Arabs, one asleep with his camel in the desert, conveying, no
doubt, the passivity and unchanging character of the backward but mysterious East, the other, a shepherd, playing his flute as his sheep gather round.
These are, no doubt, "orientalist" depictions, in contrast to the dynamic
new Jewish couple in the center, who are building the new Jewish homeland. Yet all three sides of the triptych fit together into a seamless whole, for
these are the different "types" who will come to constitute the new society
being built in the Land of Israel, which embraces both its native inhabitants
and Jews of East and West.

Rubin, not widely known outside Israel, remained an active painter into
the 1970s, but it was his paintings of the 1920s and 1930s that established
him as the artist who gave visual expression to a basically romantic view of
Palestine and to the possibility of harmonious life in the welcoming "old-
new land" among its various inhabitants. This was, of course, a vision that
became more and more difficult to portray as relations between Jews and
Arabs deteriorated, particularly after 1929.[28]

Leaving Palestine/Eretz Israel behind, let us now suggest a canonical
depiction of diaspora Jewish spirituality or, in broader terms, of Judaism
itself. Not surprisingly, numerous modern Jewish artists have portrayed
Jews at prayer, either together, usually in the synagogue, or as individuals.
Indeed, Jewish genre painting is largely composed of such depictions since,
after all, the single most obvious thing that marks the Jews as different is
their way of serving God. This is one "Jewish subject" that has long fascinated non-Jewish artists. A fine early example is the Dutch painter Emanuel De
Witte's portrayal of the Portuguese synagogue in Amsterdam, dating to the

---

28. As pointed out by Ofrat, *One Hundred Years of Art in Israel*, trans. Peretz Kidron
    (Boulder, Co.: 1998), 59.

mid-seventeenth century.[29] In the nineteenth century numerous Polish (non-Jewish) artists painted Jews at their devotions, and some of these portrayals, in particular Aleksander Gierymski's "Festival of the Trumpets" of 1890, are both beautiful and moving.[30]

Faced with many plausible choices, I will propose Maurycy Gottlieb's "Jews Praying in the Synagogue on Yom Kippur" of 1878 [fig. 11]. This image, too, has been reproduced countless times, and has even been made into a jigsaw puzzle, an ultimate accolade for any work of art. Among the characters depicted in the painting is the artist himself, seen both as a boy and as a young man. Famously, the inscription on the Torah mantle proclaims that the painter himself is deceased. Indeed, the artist died a year later, rather mysteriously, at the tender age of 23.[31]

FIG. 11
Maurycy Gottlieb, *Jews Praying in the Synagogue on Yom Kippur*, 1878
oil on canvas, 245 × 192 cm
Tel Aviv Museum of Art, gift of Sidney Lamon.

29. See Steven Nadler, *Rembrandt's Jews* (Chicago: 2004), 179.

30. For a survey of these images, see Halina Nelken, *Images of a Lost World: Jewish Motifs in Polish Painting 1770–1945* (London and New York: 1991).

31. For a study of this artist, see my *Painting a People. Maurycy Gottlieb and Jewish Art* (Hanover and London: 2002), also available in Hebrew: *Maurycy Gottlieb: Omanut, historia, vezikaron* (Jerusalem: 2006). See also Nehama Guralnik, ed., *In the Flower of Youth: Maurycy Gottlieb 1856–1879* (Tel Aviv: 1991).

Maurycy Gottlieb was certainly a father of "Jewish art." He was a Galician Jew by birth, pupil and disciple of the above-mentioned Jan Matejko in Kraków, and ambitious to be both a Polish artist and an artist of European Jewry. In a way, this canvas is a Jewish answer to Matejko's "Battle at Grunwald," for if the Polish painter's monumental work depicts the Polish nation at war, Gottlieb's is a depiction of the Jewish nation at prayer. The moving expressions of extreme piety on the faces of the large cast of characters in this painting have no doubt made it popular, as has its mysterious aura, in part related to the prophetic inscription. It has been interpreted in various and conflicting ways. For some, the painting is a nostalgic representation of the Jewish past, noble, admirable, but in inexorable decline.[32] For others it is a celebration of that intense Jewish spirituality that has preserved this ancient people over the centuries of their exile, despite all efforts to destroy it. In the post-Holocaust era it has come to be seen as an authentic portrayal of a once vibrant East European Jewish life that was forever destroyed by the Nazis, making it all the more worthy of reverent remembrance. Gottlieb's Jewish heroes are not the "new Jews" of Rapoport or of Rubin's "First Fruits," but men and women faithful to their traditions, to their Jewishness, who in the not too distant future would be martyred for their faith. This may not be the greatest painting of Jews at prayer, just as Gottlieb was not the greatest of all artists of Jewish origin, but certainly in the popular mind it reigns supreme over all its rivals.[33]

Jewish life in "the old home," meaning pre-World War II, pre-Shoah Eastern Europe, has been associated in the modern Jewish consciousness, most particularly in America, with the *shtetl*, the small, mostly Jewish town. This is partly the result of the remarkable popularity of the musical "Fiddler on the Roof," loosely based on the work of Sholem Aleichem, a charter member of the Jewish literary canon. The artist who best represented this aspect of Jewish life was, of course, Marc Chagall, one of the few artists of the modern era who combined a strong interest in and knowledge of Jewish culture with great success in the general world of European art. My candidate for a particular work is his "Green Violinist." The image shown here is an early version of this work, made in 1918; the best-known version dates from 1923–24, and was painted in Paris, his "second Vitebsk" [fig. 12].[34]

---

32. Mendelsohn, *Painting a People*, 145–148.

33. A version of it was shown at the Diaspora Museum in Tel Aviv as part of an exhibition of visual images of Jewish holidays—but with the women omitted! This too, I suppose, is a form of tribute, a back-handed compliment. See Pnina Lahav, "A Chandelier for Women. A Tale about the Diaspora Museum and Maurycy Gottlieb's 'Day of Atonement'–Jews Praying on Yom Kippur," *Israel Studies*, 11, no. 1 (Spring 2006): 108–142.

34. Benjamin Harshav, *Marc Chagall and His Times. A Documentary Narrative* (Stanford: 2003), 317. "Paris–'My Second Vitebsk'" is the title of chapter nine of this important book.

FIG. 12
Marc Chagall, *Green Violinist*, Study for the mural of the Jewish Theatre, 1918.
Watercolor, pencil, gouache, 24.7 × 13.3 cm
Musée National d'Art Moderne, Centre Georges Pompidou, Paris. CNAC/MNAN/Dist.
Réunion des Musées Nationaux/Art Resource, N.Y.
Photo Bertrand Prévost. c/o Artists Rights Society (ARS), New York/ADAGP, Paris.

Vitebsk was really a small city, not at all a "shtetl," but Chagall's renditions of his home town have come to be seen as quintessential representations of the East European small town, with its quaint, shabby buildings,
orthodox but eccentric inhabitants, and supernatural goings-on. This violinist on the roof, or roofs, may be both a representation of traditional East
European Jewish life (as represented by the folksy klezmer musician) and a
reflection of the fact that so many sons of East European Jewry actually
became famous classical violinists. In this sense he may be looking both
backward, to the hey-day of traditional Jewish culture in the nineteenth century, and forward, to the rise to prominence of Jews (such as Chagall himself) in high European culture. Whatever the case, its picturesqueness, its
magical qualities, and, I think, the atmosphere of nostalgia and sadness that
it presents to the onlooker (well aware, today, of the tragic fate that overcame the Jews of the *shtetlakh*) make this work, like Gottlieb's portrayal of
Jews at prayer, an iconic image of a lost Jewish world, which at the very

time that this painting was made was being swept away by the brutal and ruthless Soviet regime.

I would like to conclude this essay by suggesting an image that expresses another ideological stream within modern Jewry that emerged during the nineteenth century, along with and in competition to most varieties of Jewish nationalism. I have in mind the ideology of universalism, the idea that the true message of Judaism, and of the Jewish people, is the brotherhood of man, the equality of all nations and religions, an end to intolerance and persecution. This was an idea promoted by such disparate groups as classic Reform Judaism and by some specifically Jewish left-wing organizations, such as the Russian and Polish Bund. It represented a world outlook that professed optimism regarding relations between Jews and Gentiles; eventually, so its adherents believed, anti-Semitism would give way to toleration and respect, while Jewish hostility toward the Gentiles would likewise disappear into the ashcan of history. In the Israeli context this meant (and still means) a belief in the inevitability of reconciliation between Jewish Israelis and Arabs and a sharing, in some way or another, of the land that both inhabit.

I have suggested in a recent essay that there exists a Jewish artistic tradition of representing universalism.[35] Among the artists who have been involved in this project are Gottlieb, Chagall, the Americans R. B. Kitaj and Raphael Soyer, the Israeli Jacob Steinhardt, and many others, including those openly identified with the general and Jewish left in Europe, America, and Israel. An early example, one I propose for inclusion in our canon, is Moritz David Oppenheim's "Felix Mendelssohn-Bartholdy Plays before Goethe" of 1864 [fig. 13].

Oppenheim, as Ismar Schorsch has shown in a brilliant essay, was the artist of nineteenth-century German-Jewish integration.[36] Very much on the periphery of German artistic life, and most definitely absent from the canon of German art, he attained considerable fame in the Jewish world of Central Europe. In his canvases, most particularly in his popular series "Scenes from Traditional Jewish Family Life," he managed to convey both pride in his Jewishness and in Jewish traditional ceremonies, such as marriage, the celebration of the holidays, and circumcision, and a belief in the progressive integration of Jews into German life and the transformation of Jews into patriotic Germans.

---

35. Ezra Mendelsohn, "Jewish Universalism. Some Visual Texts and Subtexts," in Jack Kugelmass, ed., *Key Texts in American Jewish History* (New Brunswick and London: 2003), 163–184. See also Mendelsohn, *Painting a People*, 208–222.

36. Ismar Schorsch, "Art as Social History: Oppenheim and the German Jewish Vision of Emancipation," in his collection of essays *From Text to Context: The Turn to History in Modern Judaism* (Hanover and London: 1994), 93–117.

FIG. 13
Moritz Oppenheim, *Felix Mendelssohn-Bartholdy Plays Before Goethe*, 1864
oil on canvas, 85 × 62 cm, Jüdisches Museum Frankfurt
on permanent loan from Alexander Tesler, Photograph by Ursula Seitz-Gray.

In the painting under discussion we are shown two famous, historical figures—a celebrated member of the Mendelssohn family, the brilliant composer Felix, grandson of Moses Mendelssohn, father of the Jewish Enlightenment movement and patron saint of German Jewish integrationism, and Johann Wolfgang von Goethe, the greatest of all German writers and hero of the German *Aufklärung*. As the young Mendelssohn plays for Goethe, the German sage seems lost in thought, perhaps amazed at the miracle of a scion of a prominent Jewish family so splendidly making his way in the art form most closely identified with German genius: music. Such an encounter between the *Wunderkind* and the sage of Weimar actually took place, but we do not know what piece Mendelssohn played for him, perhaps something by Bach, whose immortal "St. Matthew Passion," a masterpiece of Christian music, he so famously revived at a performance in Berlin in 1829.[37]

I read this painting as emblematic of the universalistic and integrationist hopes of nineteenth-century German Jewry. Having finally been given a chance to enter European high culture, Jews—as represented by the preco-

---

37. This event is portrayed in a remarkable drawing by the Russian-Jewish artist Leonid Pasternak of 1930; see Mendelsohn, *Painting a People*, 213.

cious Mendelssohn—are fulfilling their destiny and proving that they can be true Europeans. Music, in this case, is the essential bridge that can link Jews and Gentiles together. No longer segregated in their ghettos, whether physical or spiritual, the Jews have come out into the light of day, and have proved themselves worthy of the Gentiles' respect. In the end, universal values, those of the *Aufklärung* and the *Haskalah*, the vision of the prophets as maintained by German-born modern Judaism, will prevail.

There is, of course, a problem with this interpretation. Felix Mendelssohn was, at an early age, converted by his parents to Christianity. He, like the "immigrants" in Stieglitz's iconic photograph, was, in fact, not Jewish. But in truth Felix Mendelssohn, despite his adherence to Christianity (which was profound), despite even his composing Christian liturgical music, was an honored figure among German (and other) Jews, and often seen as "one of them." The whole world, after all, knew of his distinguished Jewish origins, and his unparalleled achievements made him a godsend for German Jewry. Perhaps being singled out for particular disdain by Richard Wagner in his infamous anti-Semitic screed of 1850 contributed to this attitude (later on, his music was banned by the Nazis). Mendelssohn's music was played at Jewish occasions, especially at Jewish marriages.[38] He is often considered a "Jewish composer," whatever that might mean.[39] Only two generations removed from the ghetto, he is emblematic of the triumph of universalist values, although, unlike Moritz Oppenheim, he did not remain loyal to Judaism.

The painters, photographers, and sculptors discussed in this essay are a variegated lot, that includes Stieglitz, the non-Jewish Jew, and such East European Jewish insiders as Gottlieb and Chagall, the Zionists Lilien and Rubin, and the integrationist Oppenheim. They are men of very different reputations, ranging from Rapoport, a sculptor whose stylistic language seems almost grotesque today, to such renowned modernists as Stieglitz and Chagall. Taken together, they present us with visual images of Jewish heroism and martyrdom, Jewish spirituality, and various aspects of Zionism and Jewish universalism. Their works reflect the hopes and dreams of modern Ashkenazi Jews, and represent ways of portraying Jewish identity and Jewish history

It might be interesting, as a coda, to suggest a musical Jewish canon to accompany these visual images. Thus, one of Aaron Copland's rare ventures

---

38. In the Tlomacka synagogue in Warsaw during the interwar years Jews were married to the tune of Mendelssohn's famous wedding march. See Aleksander Gutterman, *Mehitbolelut leleumiyut. Perakim betoldot beyt hakeneset hagadol hasinagoga bevarsha, 1806–1943* (Jerusalem: 1993), 126.

39. For an example, see Alex Ross, "American Sublime," *The New Yorker* (June 19, 2006), 87.

into "Jewish music," his "Vitebsk (Study on a Jewish Theme)" of 1928, would make a perfect companion to Chagall's "Violinist."[40] For commemorating the Holocaust, Arnold Schoenberg's "A Survivor from Warsaw" comes immediately to mind, while the new world of Jewish Palestine in the Mandate period received musical expression in such works as Stefan Wolpe's beautiful song settings from the "Palestinian Notebook" of 1939 and the compositions of the Romanian-born Israeli composer Alexander Boskovitch, such as his "Semitic Suite" (an example of the so-called "Mediterranean" style, first performed in 1946).[41] As for the ideology of Jewish universalism, why not admit into the canon the musical "West Side Story" of 1957. True, this retelling of the story of Romeo and Juliet does not deal with Jews, but its creators—Bernstein, Sondheim, and Robbins—were all Jewish, and it does appear that, originally, this was supposed to be the tale of tribal tensions between Jews and Polish Catholics in New York.[42] As for canonical musical renditions of Jewish spirituality, it is hard to best Max Bruch's "Kol Nidrei" (composed in 1880) for cello and orchestra, a piece that attained tremendous popularity in the Jewish world. Unfortunately, Bruch was not Jewish, but since the melodies he arranged are most definitely those of the synagogue, we may be permitted to make an exception in this case. At any rate, what more appropriate music could be played while observing Gottlieb's "Jews Praying in the Synagogue on Yom Kippur," painted only a few years earlier?[43] I cannot think of a suitable musical companion to "The Steerage," but perhaps one day a Jewish composer will write a symphony based on the Jewish immigration saga or, even better, an opera. The Jewish cultural canon is most definitely still a work in progress.

---

40. See the remarks in Gail Levin and Judith Tick, eds., *Aaron Copland's America: A Cultural Perspective* (2000), and Tick and Carol J. Oja, *Aaron Copland and His World* (Princeton and Oxford: 2005), especially the article by Beth E. Levy, "From Orient to Occident: Aaron Copland and the Sagas of the Prairie," 307–349.

41. See Jehoash Hirshberg, "Alexander U. Boskovitch and the Quest for an Israeli National Musical Style," in Mendelsohn, ed., *Modern Jews and Their Musical Agendas*, *Studies in Contemporary Jewry*, vol. 9 (New York: 1990), 102–104.

42. Stephen Whitfield, "Fiddling with Sholem Aleichem," in Kugelmass, *Key Texts*, 108.

43. On this piece, see Christopher Fifield, *Max Bruch. His Life and Work* (N.Y.: 1988), 169–172. Bruch has been claimed, in various publications, for the Jewish people, but he was, in fact, a German Protestant.

Judging *The Judgment of Shomer*
Jewish Literature
versus Jewish Reading

JUSTIN CAMMY

When Nahum-Meir Shaykevitsh, better known as Shomer,[1] was at the height of his popularity in 1887, a critical controversy erupted in the Yiddish press over the virtues and perils of the sentimental popular fiction that had made him a household name across Yiddish-speaking Eastern Europe. Sholem Aleichem[2] used the dispute as fodder for *The Judgment of Shomer* (1888), an important document of early Yiddish literary criticism. This essay is intended to provide both the context of *The Judgment of Shomer* and a history of its uses and abuses in the decades following its publication. It is meant to be read in conjunction with my annotated translation of the document that is included in this volume. I begin by asking where *The Judgment* fits into Sholem Aleichem's own development as a writer, and why he felt

My appreciation to my co-editors and Olga Litvak for their comments on earlier drafts of this essay. Some readers may benefit from first reading my translation of *The Judgment of Shomer* that follows, and then return to my discussion of it here.

1. Shomer (1846–1905) was an acronym based on letters of Shaykevitsh's name. He began publishing his Yiddish novelettes in 1876, and by the mid-1880s he was the most productive and successful producer of mass Yiddish fiction. By the time Sholem Aleichem's *The Judgment of Shomer* appeared in 1888, Shomer was the author of more than 50 Yiddish romances (some critics estimate the number is much higher), and by the time of his death, he had published in excess of 200 Yiddish novels, 50 Yiddish plays, and several early works in Hebrew. Shomer's novels included both historical narratives and stories set in far-off lands, in addition to works set in Eastern Europe. However, it was his sentimental fiction that secured his reputation. It featured passionate love affairs, sensational plot lines (often including murder, theft, betrayal, and other scandals), and moralistic conclusions in which good was rewarded and evil met its come-uppance. Though Shomer was read by all segments of the public, he was particularly popular among "new women readers," whose reading habits in Yiddish shifted away from traditional, didactic literature to sentimental fiction as the bonds of tradition weakened. Among such readers, Yiddish came to be associated with the pleasures of escapist fiction, whereas for maskilic (Enlightenment) writers it continued to serve a didactic purpose. See Iris Parush, *Reading Jewish Women: Marginality and Modernization in Nineteenth-Century Eastern European Jewish Society* (Brandeis, 2004), 243.

2. Sholem Aleichem (1859–1916), the pen name of Sholem Rabinovitsh, first published Yiddish fiction in 1883 in the newspaper *Yudishes folksblat.* By the time of his death, and especially in the interwar period, literary historians canonized him as one of the "classic" figures of modern Yiddish literature.

the need to attack a peddler of popular sentimental fiction so forcefully. How did it establish the author's credentials among fellow Jewish intellectuals? My reading suggests that *The Judgment of Shomer* was employed strategically by Sholem Aleichem so that he could redefine the terrain of Yiddish literature on his own terms. The document reveals a young, ruthless ingénue determined to rout the competition in order to clear space for himself. As Dan Miron has argued, Sholem Aleichem's invention of a villain for this emergent vernacular literature in *The Judgment of Shomer* was intimately balanced against his careful creation of a respectable genealogy in which he cast himself as the legitimate heir, or "grandson," to S.Y. Abramovitsh, whom he recognized as the "grandfather" of modern Yiddish literature.[3] This juxtaposition of Shomer and Abramovitsh was designed to introduce an intermediate category of Yiddish fiction for the masses that was neither derivative of European fiction nor elite in its aesthetic standards. In 1888, there were not yet measures in place to determine where lowbrow fiction ended and highbrow literature began. The purpose of *The Judgment of Shomer* was to establish legitimate categories and measures for Yiddish popular fiction (*folks-literatur*), and to bring needed prestige to the efforts of its writers (*folks-shraybers*).

In the second half of this essay my attention broadens from the initial discussion of what *The Judgment of Shomer* tells us about Yiddish polemics in Sholem Aleichem's day to subsequent efforts to revisit the justice of the initial verdict among three differing groups of interwar writers and critics. My overview of their exchanges will suggest that as the fate of Yiddish shifted through the first half of the twentieth century, so too did the responses to *The Judgment of Shomer,* as subsequent literary figures reengaged with it to express their competing ideological, aesthetic, or cultural agendas and anxieties.

The Initial Firestorm

From 1887 to 1888, prior to the publication of *The Judgment of Shomer,* a pitched debate about the merits of Yiddish sentimental fiction played out over seventeen issues of St. Petersburg's *Yudishes folksblat.* A Yiddish weekly founded in 1881, the *Folksblat* aspired to be a highbrow forum for new Yiddish writing and discussion of literary and cultural matters. The controversy enabled the paper to secure its credentials among intellectuals, one of its core constituencies, by attacking a symbol of lowbrow culture, all while feeding the sale of papers with juicy accusations of literary impropriety and transgression. While the paper's contributors honed in on Shomer as a scapegoat for all that was aesthetically and morally corrupt in popular Yiddish fiction, they were not the first to question his artistic legitimacy. As

---

3. Dan Miron, *A Traveler Disguised: The Rise of Modern Yiddish Fiction in the Nineteenth Century* (Syracuse University Press, 1996), 27–30.

early as 1880, Shomer poked good-natured fun at his critics in his chap-books, suggesting that he already had his detractors several years before the controversy exploded later that decade. For instance, he prefaced his Yid-dish novel *Der baal tshuve, oder der falsher khosen* (1880) with a Hebrew poem in which he attacked his critics as "foolish" and "stupid." In 1886 he introduced the second half of his novel *Der raykher betler* with a fable in which he portrayed his critics as failed novelists who howl like dogs trying to get attention.[4] Such responses were typical of the way in which Shomer dealt with his critics. He regularly called them names or accused them of jealousy or greed in an attempt to discredit them. He never engaged the sub-stance of their critique.

Shomer began to take negative appraisals of his writing more seriously when David Frishman, in the Hebrew paper *Hayom*,[5] and Shimon Dubnov, writing under the pseudonym Criticus in the Russian-Jewish periodical *Voskhod*, published harsh critiques of his work. Dubnov's article, a review of Shomer's Yiddish chapbook *Der rayhker betler* (1886) and his Hebrew novel *Ha-nidahat* (1886) anticipated several charges that Sholem Aleichem would later build upon in *The Judgment,* including the accusations that Shomer's novels lacked authenticity, corrupted the Yiddish language through an over-reliance on Germanisms, and trivialized the contemporary drama of Jewish life by offering up cheap escapist fairy-tales. He prodded Shomer: "Is Jewish life so impoverished that there is not enough material in it for true creativity?"[6]

Several months after the publication of Dubnov's *Voskhod* review, the controversy spilled over to the *Yudishes folksblat.* The fact that it took a Russian-language Jewish periodical to prompt a Yiddish newspaper to inves-tigate the state of Yiddish popular fiction says a great deal about the self-respect of Yiddish writing in this period. From the outset, the *Yudishes folksblat* staged and managed the controversy (anticipating the court scene in *The Judgment*) by providing space to voices that were both for and against Shomer, including anonymous editorials by his detractors and rebut-

---

4. Shmuel Niger, "Shomers mishpet–af Sholem Aleykhemen," *Di tsukunft* (February 1947), 111–112. It is possible that Shomer invented (or anticipated) some of his own critics in order to secure his reputation with the masses as someone who provided them with the type of literature that elites, presumably, would not want them to have access to. That is, Shomer's reputation benefited from criticism–real or imagined–that enabled him to play the embattled defender of the ordinary Yiddish reader.

5. See Letter III of "Mihtavim al davar ha-sifrut," *Hayom*, 257–258 (1887), 2–3; 2–4.

6. Criticus, "Literaturnaia Letopis" (Literary Chronicles: The Poverty of Contemporary Jewish Belles-Lettres), *Voskhod* (May 1887). Portions of Dubnov's argument were translated from Russian into Yiddish and published in *Yudishes folksblat* 27–28 (1887).

tals by Shomer himself. For instance, issues 1 and 3 of the paper in 1887 featured a sympathetic feuilleton by Sh. Berdichevski in which Shomer was called a "rare" writer whose oeuvre includes many realistic descriptions of Jewish life and whose critics attack him out of jealousy for his success.[7] The paper's editor, Alexander Tsederboym, wedged Y.M. Volfson's sharp critique of Shomer's novel *Der shlimazldiker hoz* (1886)[8] between installments of Berdichevski's piece, giving the appearance of a burgeoning controversy. Tsederboym also felt free to take sides: "What is the purpose of [your] manufactured love stories and fantasies, copied from the French novels of the 1840s....We are living in different times; people today do not need fantasies. Real life provides enough material on its own..."[9] Yiddish intellectuals were rallying around realism as what was most needed to establish artistic legitimacy for Yiddish fiction.

The *Folksblat* gave the appearance of fairness by providing multiple perspectives, but in reality the tone of the discussion was overwhelmingly critical of Shomer, who initially defended himself in the form of a letter to the editor. He personalized his response to Volfson's comments by calling him "childish," and attempted to embarrass the editor of the paper for daring to publish critiques without having read Shomer's works himself.[10] He reminded Tsederboym that when he had translated one of his early stories into Hebrew and sent it to Y.L. Gordon, then the editor of one of Tsederboym's other newspapers, *Ha-melits,* Gordon published it and invited Shomer to send him additional materials. Given Gordon's standing as the most accomplished Hebrew poet and Jewish Enlightenment figure of his generation, Shomer suggested that Gordon's opinion must stand for something: "If my stories are so bad, why did you publish [them] in your own newspaper *Ha-melits*?" Tsederboym retreated somewhat, conceding that he had not read Shomer's writing closely enough to be able to offer a personal assessment of them, and acknowledged that "I know for sure that writers such as you, Mr. Shomer, are in good standing with the people and are useful [to them]."[11]

---

7. Sh. Berdichevski, ""Erinerungen un gedanken vegn ertsiung un literatur," *Yudishes folksblat* 1 (1887), 3-9; 3 (1887), 35-38.

8. Y.M. Volfson, "Der shlimazldiker hoz," *Yudishes folksblat* 2 (1887), 24-26.

9. Quoted in Z. Reyzin, "Shomer," *Leksikon fun der yidisher literatur, prese un filologie,* vol. 4 (Vilna: Kletskin, 1929), 778.

10. Shomer, "Korespondentsies: A briv tsu der redaktsie," *Yudishes folksblat* 10 (1887), 150-151.

11. Shomer, *Yehi or: a literarishe kampf* (New York, 1898), 2. Though Shomer took Tsederboym's comments as an admission that he had been wrongly smeared, he failed to recognize the slight inherent in Tsederboym's apology, in which the latter readily admitted that he had not bothered to read Shomer's novels.

It was Shomer's misfortune that the *Yudishes folksblat* was sold during the controversy to another publisher, Yisroel Levi, whose own attitudes toward Yiddish were highly vexed (he often used the paper to attack Yiddish, to the frustration of other intellectuals who were hoping to use its pages to bring the language greater esteem amid accusations that it was little more than jargon). As a journalist, Levi recognized that controversy was the bread and butter of selling newspapers. He quickly fueled the controversy's fire by penning his own attack on Shomer under the pseudonym Der yudisher gazlen (The Jewish Thief), in which he accused Shomer's novels of corrupting young readers with their implausible plots. He translated segments from Dubnov's earlier Russian critique of Shomer that had appeared in *Voskhod* and republished them in Yiddish.[12] Since Shomer was under the impression that he had put such criticism to rest only months earlier, the renewed attacks enraged him. In his feuilleton "A Blow for a Blow," he responded to Dubnov by suggesting that "he must have written these words out of jealousy, hatred, or perhaps simply because he is a little out of his mind (it shouldn't happen to us)." He neither concealed his condescension toward his critics ("I am not interested in the criticism of fresh-baked little writers. They cannot destroy me in any way") nor did he hold back his patronizing attitude toward his readership ("One must provide a child with something sweet, even when one wants to give him bitter medicine. I know that if I had just provided my readers with moralistic writings they would not have picked up a single book. As the saying goes, '*Od na'ar yisrael*'—the Jewish people is still naïve"). Shomer also penned a letter to Levi demanding to know why his paper seemed to have it in for him, and threatened that if the latter did not respond, "I promise you that I too have a pen that can pour out my wrath."[13] Levi responded to him within days with the admission that personally he had never read Shomer's works because they were difficult to obtain in St. Petersburg. This was not only untrue, but also a backhanded apology because it suggested that Shomer's novels were well beneath the standards of writers and other intellectual readers in that city.[14] Shomer assumed that Levi's response put an end to the matter, and was shocked when, a short time later, critical reviews of his latest novels by Volfson, Yehoshua Ravnitski, and Sholem Aleichem surfaced anew in the *Folksblat*. He was incensed that the new editor provided space to an upstart writer with the "sweet name"[15] Sholem Aleichem, who was trying to make a repu-

---

12. Der yudisher gazlen, "Kritik," *Yudishes folksblat* 27 (1887), 419–422; 28 (1887), 435–440.

13. "A patsh far a patsh," *Yudishes folkslat* 30 (1887), 483–488.

14. *Yehi or*, 2–3. See also Der yudisher gazlen, "Der yudisher gazlen iz esh-halev," *Yudishes folksblat* 34 (1887), 563–568.

15. *Yehi or*, 4.

tation for himself at Shomer's expense, and especially by the paper's unfair-
ness in publishing anonymous reviews.[16] In the foreword to his historical
novel *Der letster yudisher kenig* (which appeared in 1888, prior to *The
Judgment*) he crafted a pun on Sholem Aleichem's pen name, suggesting
that although the name was convivial, his stories left much to be desired:
*"Vet nit zayn keyn Sholem Aleichem, vet zayn Aleichem Sholem ober men
zol khotsh kenen lezen a halbe shtunde un nit genetsin."* ("If there is no
Mr. How-Do-You-Do then there will be Mr. Fine-Thank-You-and-You, but
may we at least be able to read for a half hour without yawning!") In the
same novel, he chastised the entire editorial board of the *Folksblat* for providing space for Sholem Aleichem's "clownish pranks" and "prattling," and
provided a fable called "The Mites and the Lion," in which he cast himself in
the role of the heroic king of the jungle while the contributors to the *Folksblat* were his annoying pests.[17]

   The debate about the merits of Shomer's writing that occupied pages of
Folksblat in 1887–88 provides us with the necessary context for understanding both the tone and central contentions of *The Judgment of Shomer*.
Sholem Aleichem's literary trial of Shomer did not appear *ex nihilo*, but was
the result of several years of attacks, counter-attacks, and mutual invective.
Nonetheless, Sholem Aleichem's achievement in *The Judgment of Shomer*
was one of both synthesis and style. It brought together criticisms about
Shomer that had been first introduced by others, and packaged them in
such an entertaining way that readers forgot they were reading literary criticism. *The Judgment*'s fiction of a mock-trial provided a patina of neutrality,
which only added to the bite of its partiality. In the late 1880s, literary criticism could not afford to be objective, especially when it saw itself at the
center of a campaign to create a Yiddish literary high art.

   By casting himself in *The Judgment* as court stenographer, Sholem Aleichem borrowed from a long tradition of "found texts" in European literature.[18] It was a gesture that enabled him to masquerade as someone who

---

16. For a sense of the exchange, see Pri ets ha-hayim (Y.M. Volfson), "Kritik af kritik,"
    Yudishes folksblat 32 (1887), 541–542; Sholem Aleichem, "Fun vayte medines,"
    Yudishes folksblat 33 (1887), 547–552; Rav-katsin (Y.Kh. Ravnitski), "An eysek mit
    shmates," *Yudishes folksblat*, supplement to issue 4 (1888), 13–15; 5 (1888), 32–33;
    Anonymous, "Retsenzie," *Yudishes folksblat*, supplement to issues 11–12 (1888),
    355–361; Eyner fun di mitarbeter, "Retsenzie: Di goldene kelber," *Yudishes folksblat*
    16 (1888), 455–467. It is likely that Levi himself was one of the anonymous reviewers.
    By writing under several different covers, he was able to orchestrate the debate to
    ensure maximum controversy.

17. Shomer, *Der letster yudisher kenig: a historisher roman* (Vilna, 1888).

18. Sholem Aleichem was also responding to a fascination with public trials, which
    became a novelty after the Russian judicial reforms of 1874. Several contemporary
    Russian writers, including Dostoyevski and Tolstoy, included trials in their work.

was simply providing his readers with a service by transcribing the proceedings. In reality, the document was part of a deliberate agenda to establish new aesthetic hierarchies that corresponded to his own preference for the intimacy of vernacular experience. Though *The Judgment* was intended for a rarefied audience of fellow writers and was never widely disseminated, it later would prove to be an important turning point in the way Yiddish literary history understood its own maturation.

Sholem Aleichem's Anxiety of Influence

The Judgment of Shomer was one of several important texts in Sholem Aleichem's ideological coming of age as a writer. Indeed, it would be difficult to understand what he was attempting to accomplish without reading it alongside several other essays and literary works of the same period; as a group, these texts enable us to understand not only what kind of fiction he was attempting to uproot by attacking Shomer, but also the kind of fiction he proposed to replace it. These efforts constituted the first steps in what would be recognized later by literary historians as a project of Yiddish canonical self-definition.

The Judgment of Shomer was a public exorcism of Sholem Aleichem's own demons as a writer. It liberated him from his own sentimental desires by deliberately choosing a foil in Shomer against which to redefine his own writing.[19] Sholem Aleichem clearly had Shomer's brand of fiction in mind in the following meta-fictional moment that appeared in one of his earliest novels, *Natasha* (published as an insert in the *Yudishes folksblat* in 1884):

> Our Yiddish readers have come to expect that the hero of a novel must either be an angel or a devil; he must be so good, so honest, so pure, like an angel in heaven...who only does good. And since the world is sinful this poor angel finds himself pursued to the ends of the earth. For his love he is repaid with hatred; for his honesty—with murder. And this is how this poor innocent character is blackened. Until the novel concludes. Then he suddenly is repaid a hundred times over for his good deeds, and the murderer, the evil protagonist, gets his comeuppance from the author....The reader praises the bright author for his pretty fairytale, for throwing together such fantastic stories that enrage and terrify us....But let us not talk badly about our manufacturer [of fiction], our Paul de Kock.[20]

This passage anticipates the kind of arguments Sholem Aleichem refined a few years later in *The Judgment of Shomer*, establishing that, from his ten-

---

19. Ironically, it was an exorcism that kept the ghost alive. The continued strength of the market for lowbrow fiction, especially in the interwar period in the Yiddish press, suggests that although Sholem Aleichem forged a reputation off the struggle against Shomer, he lost the larger battle to reform mass reading habits and tastes. See Chone Shmeruk, "Letoldot sifrut ha-'shund' be-Yiddish," *Tarbitz* 52 (1983), 325–354.

20. Quoted in Shmeruk, 343. Charles Paul de Kock (1793–1871) was a disseminator of lowbrow French sentimental novels.

tative first steps as a Yiddish writer in the early 1880s, he was already working out ways to discipline himself.

In the period between the publication of *Natasha* and *The Judgment of
Shomer*, the demands of the market outpaced even Shomer's productivity,
giving rise to a school of hack imitators. What started in Sholem Aleichem's
early imaginative universe of *Natasha* as a sarcastic jab at a much more successful and established competitor gradually morphed into an obsessive
campaign over legitimate and illegitimate forms of Yiddish popular fiction.[21] As he wrote to his friend and fellow writer Y.H. Ravnitski during the
composition of *The Judgment of Shomer*: "With God's help, Sholem Aleichem will soon do away with Shomer, that beloved transformer of paper
into rags, cut him up, atomize him, destroy all traces of his bones, innards,
and arteries, so that the public knows once and for all who and what he really is."[22] Sholem Aleichem's rhetoric here speaks of evisceration, pointing to
an emotional over-entanglement with the fate of a fellow writer. The battle
was for nothing less than the future character of Yiddish fiction.

The Judgment of Shomer appeared at the same moment that Sholem Aleichem worked through a new definition for himself of the so-called "Jewish
novel" and launched a new literary anthology, *Di yudishe folks-bibliotek*
(The Jewish People's Library, 1888–1889). Together, these works provide a
full portrait of Sholem Aleichem's artistic thinking at this transitional
moment, when he emerged from his first tentative steps as a Yiddish writer
into a decisive aesthetic force and guiding critical voice.

The Judgment of Shomer is organized around concerns over the appro-
priateness of Shomer's plots, characterizations, and language. Sholem Aleichem's overriding apprehension was that Shomer's writing represented the
derivativeness of Yiddish popular fiction. He accused its plots of being hackneyed adaptations of European dime novels. He determined that the anti-
realist base of Yiddish popular fiction had a corrosive effect on the masses
because it prevented them from seeing their own lives reflected in literature
and distracted them from the social changes that were going on all around

---

21. For instance, in a list he compiled under the pseudonym Solomon Esbikher, he showed
     that of the seventy-eight Yiddish books published between 1887 and 1888, almost 40%
     were penned by Shomer and his imitators, whereas only one was penned by S.Y. Abra-
     movitsh, whom he considered his mentor. A similar list published a year later included
     a total of thirty-five books by Shomer, compared to two by S.Y. Abramovitsh. Sholem
     Aleichem's list-making was not only an attempt to take stock of what was being
     published, but was intended to force his fellow intellectuals to acknowledge that they
     were being out-read, in part, because they were being severely out-published. See
     Solomon Esbikher, "A reyster iber ale zhargonishe bikher vos zenen opgedrukt gevorn
     inem yor TRM"Kh [1887/1888]," *Di yudishe folksbibliotek* 1 (1888), 469–473; see
     also the list published for 1888/1889 in *Di yudishe folksbibliotek* 2 (1889), 135–139.

22. Letter from Sholem Aleichem to Y.H. Ravnitski, 20 February 1888 in *Briv fun Sholem-
     Aleykhem,* ed. Abraham Lis (Perets farlag, 1995), 178.

them.[23] As he saw it, Jewish fiction ought to reflect the rhythms—religious, economic, political, linguistic—of lived Jewish experience. Sholem Aleichem was neither a cultural nationalist nor even a populist at this stage; rather, he believed that language was constitutive and that because Yiddish was the language spoken by Eastern European Jewry, its literature ought to reflect that distinct experience. At the same time, where Sholem Aleichem differed from many of his fellow intellectuals was in his desire to break free in his own writings from the small, elite audiences who were the consumers of maskilic Yiddish fiction up until that point. Sholem Aleichem's search for a new definition of *folks-literatur,* or literature of the people, sought to bridge the divide between elite and lowbrow audiences by establishing a category of popular literature that was both aesthetically refined, representative of lived reality, and accessible.

Though Sholem Aleichem never invoked the word *shund* (trash)[24] in *The Judgment of Shomer* (he refers to Shomer's writing in the document as *mist*, or garbage) no writer in the history of Yiddish literature was more responsible for establishing *shund* as a literary category that put the appetites of the mass market in competition with the talents of emerging artists. Prior to the emergence of Sholem Aleichem, the audience for secular Yiddish literature was divided. On the one hand, there was a mass audience (which included many women) that was spread out over the market towns

---

23. A close reading of Shomer's fiction reveals that Sholem Aleichem's evidence in *The Judgment* is highly selective. He bases his discussion on two dozen works by Shomer, most written in the years and months immediately preceding the composition of *The Judgment.* Recent scholarship argues that Shomer's novels, even those cited by Sholem Aleichem, contain the valuable portraits of contemporary Jewish life that Sholem Aleichem insists are missing. In these studies Shomer emerges as a populist maskil who takes on religious extremism and the Jewish aristocracy, attacks anachronistic customs, and delves into Jewish history for inspiration. For a balanced discussion of the fairness and shortcomings of Sholem Aleichem's criticisms in *The Judgment of Shomer,* see Sophie Grace Pollack, "Shomer le-or *Shomers mishpet* le-Sholem Aleichem," *Hulyot* 5 (1999), 109–159.

24. Chone Shmeruk concludes that because Sholem Aleichem did not use the term *shund* in *The Judgment of Shomer*, the term must not have become the accepted way of defining lowbrow fiction in Yiddish until a short time after 1888. Shmeruk underscores the difficulty of coming to a precise definition of *shund*, in part because trash fiction meant different things in different national literatures. For instance, while Lessing used the term broadly to refer to writing that was worthless in his opinion, others associated it more narrowly with the presence of titillating or erotic elements. For Sholem Aleichem, *shund* included literature that lacked both aesthetic and moral depth. Sholem Aleichem consistently refers to Shomer as a *romanmakher* (a producer or maker of novels), a label that focuses solely on the economic function of his trade and denies it any aesthetic value. He believed that the speed with which Shomer published his books was an indication that Shomer did not consider writing a form of art but rather an industry. See Shmeruk, 325–354.

and cities of Eastern Europe. This was the market for lowbrow works of escapist fantasy. These readers turned to Yiddish literature for its entertainment value. On the other hand, a more educated (mainly male) audience of aspiring intellectuals, based mainly in the Russian Empire's urban centers, consumed novels and dramas that were innovative in their narrative style, disseminated Enlightenment values, and held a mirror up to Jewish society. Sholem Aleichem's desire was to co-opt the first audience, and especially the female readers, for himself. He recognized that most Jewish intellectuals would always first turn to Hebrew or to European literature due to their cultural prestige, and saw Yiddish instead as means through which to create a broad-based *folks-literatur* that could bridge the gap between the intellectuals and a potential mass readership by attracting both groups to the same vernacular texts.[25] Indeed, this is played out by the opening scene of *The Judgment of Shomer*, which features a courtroom filled with Shomer's fans, "simple Jews...married women, girls, half-educated young ladies, schoolboys." Sholem Aleichem peoples the courtroom audience with representatives of what he hopes to claim as his eventual audience, even though the

---

25. Alyssa Quint recently pointed to the memoirs of Ephraim Deinard (1831–1930) and Menashe Halpern (1871–1960) to argue that there were two distinct beginnings to modern Yiddish literature. The first, which we might call the standard or "maskilic" version, took place during the first three-quarters of the nineteenth century. It reached for the "highbrow" and "elite," and included figures such as Aksenfeld, Linetski, and Abramovitsh. However, Quint argues that there is also a sub-canonical origin that began only in the late 1870s. It was "audience-driven," "lowbrow," "popular," and much more connected to the Yiddish book trade than elite Yiddish fiction, which found its outlet first in manuscripts circulated among intellectuals and then in intellectual journals. In Deinard's *Memories of My People* (1920), the Odessa-based Hebrew bookstore owner recalls with some bitterness that there was no local market for Yiddish literature until the emergence of Shomer and the playwright Goldfaden. "[Shomer]...discovered a bookshop in Odessa owned by a couple of shoemakers who bought everything his pen vomited because they did not read Yiddish and could not understand the garbage that Shomer wrote. It was enough for them that the filth would be sold, paid in full... There was not one maiden, one wagon driver from Odessa to Berdichev, from Warsaw to Vilna, who did not have Shomer's name on his or her lips." (Quint, 62) In recalling the reading habits of his town in his memoir *Parmetn* (1952), Halpern adds: "Putting aside the charges fairly or unfairly leveled against Shomer, he has retained the distinction of having taught the masses how to read and for having made from them a large reading circle....The common man was attracted to Shomer's novels like a magnet." (Quint, 74–75) If Quint is correct in asserting that both Deinard's and Halpern's comments prove that the masses did not consume (or even know about) most of the maskilic Yiddish texts or writers who have been prominent in our understanding of the origins of modern Yiddish fiction, then what she is calling for is the creation of a parallel narrative of origins (or the delineation of a popular canon) in which Shomer would occupy a privileged position. See Alyssa Quint, "'Yiddish Literature for the Masses?' A Reconsideration of Who Read What in Jewish Eastern Europe," *AJS Review* 29:1 (2005), 61–89.

actual readership of *The Judgment of Shomer* was limited to his fellow intellectuals.

Sholem Aleichem's paternalistic contempt for the existing tastes of the literary marketplace prompted his need to distinguish between what we would today call canonical and non-canonical writing. This necessitated the demonization of the Yiddish *shundroman*. In so doing, he argued that there were aesthetic and moral differences between writers who were market-driven and catered to the uncultivated desires of the masses and those who regarded themselves as artists. This might explain why *The Judgment of Shomer* expresses a particular disdain for escapist plots that had no anchor in Jewish life, or for registers of language—especially the use of *daytshmerish* (an inflated use of Germanisms in literary Yiddish)[26]—that seemed overly contrived or pretentious. They signaled a slavishness and aesthetic laziness that, in Sholem Aleichem's view, reflected a depressing acceptance of Yiddish's status as a secondary culture.

The Judgment of Shomer was also an opportunity for Sholem Aleichem to describe the creative process of storytelling in a way that enabled him to crystallize his own thinking as a stylist. In pausing to take account of the way Shomer constructs dialogue and characters, or by comparing the similarity of his plot lines to those of French sentimental romances, he taught himself the craft of writing. Though he easily could have made his point about Shomer in a much shorter essay, he seems to have enjoyed quoting from Shomer's works as a way to hone his critical skills, develop his own ideas about the way a work of literature communicates, and express his anxiety about Yiddish as a language of plagiarists that has not yet realized its own self-worth. These satiric riffs enable him to work out his frustration over his failure to achieve popular success at the same time that they psychologically expose Sholem Aleichem in unexpected ways. For instance, he plays up a bourgeois sense of propriety in his comments on vulgarity and sexuality in Shomer's works as a way to distinguish himself as more refined than his competitor. Sholem Aleichem's frequent use of ellipses and allusive language when speaking about the consummation of love in Shomer's romances feign prudishness as a means of undermining the false propriety in Shomer's happy endings.[27]

---

26. *Daytshmerish,* a conscious imitation of German within Yiddish, is an indeterminate category that came to take on negative connotations only with the rise of Yiddishism in the late nineteenth century. Yiddishism was hyper-conscious about effacing the language's links to its German determinant. See Max Weinreich, *History of the Yiddish Language,* trans. Shlomo Noble (University of Chicago, 1980), 418 and Mordkhe Schaechter, "The 'Hidden Standard': A Study of Competing Influences in Standardization," *The Field of Yiddish* 3 (Mouton & Co., 1969), 284.

27. At times, Sholem Aleichem's own readings in *The Judgment* strain credulity. For instance, in *The Judgment of Shomer* he contrasts an unflattering episode in Shomer's

Sholem Aleichem worked through an emerging definition of the Jewish novel at the same time that he was composing *The Judgment of Shomer*, offering his own contemporaneous novels as counter-texts to Shomer's fiction. For instance, *Sender Blank,* serialized in 1888 in the *Yudishes folksblat,* is suddenly interrupted by a meta-fictional commentary:

> I am overjoyed that I have the opportunity to begin this chapter like a genuine novelist, and to present my dear reader with heart-rending scenes and moving portraits, just like my literary friends who have long been famous and with whom I can in no way compare myself because their small finger is larger than my loins. Even if I lived a hundred years I would not be able to compose as many pretty romances about which our literature has nothing to be ashamed....And I hope that with God's help there will come a time in which these nice romances are gathered in wagons and are hauled far, far away, because those who trade them in will earn a pretty penny from turning them into pulp....I think about the sad situation of these writers (if they even survive), with their suffering faces as they watch their most interesting works packed up in sacks...and tossed into the wagon! Away, all you blond heroes, frightening criminals, Jewish counts and barons, wild millionaires, clumsy usurers...who were created by those who call themselves writers...
>
> But since much time may pass between now and then, until the moment our public looks up and notices that they have been reared on rags and given straw to chew just like animals, in the interim these enablers will return to their old habits and take up their scribbling. But until that fortunate time arrives let us also attempt, if only for a minute, to borrow this style and provide the reader with the bonus of a surprise romantic scene in this novel.
>
> And so: It was a rare summer night...[28]

Sholem Aleichem here performs a self-referential intervention that draws attention to the reader's expectations and desires, all the while undermin-

---

novel *Paltiel Ox*, in which the father of a Jewish girl who has gotten pregnant out of wedlock greedily accepts hush money to keep quiet about her condition, against Turgenev's story *The Jew* (1846), in which a Jewish spy uses his beautiful daughter as bait to gain favor with an army official, all the while standing outside his tent to make sure her modesty is not violated. Sholem Aleichem argues that Turgenev's story is a more sympathetic representation of Jewish values because it emphasizes the primacy of family and the willingness of even the most corrupt Jewish father to protect his daughter. Sholem Aleichem's interpretation willfully ignores the fact that Turgenev's story portrays the Jew in Russian literature as a greedy betrayer of the mother country, describes Yiddish (the language in which his sketches of the army camp are annotated) as a secret, subversive language, and that in the end the Jew does offer up his daughter to the Russian colonel if it will save him from execution.

28. *Sender blank un zayn gezindl: A roman on a roman* (composed in 1887, published in 1888 under the title *Reb Sender Blank un zayn fulgeshetste familie*: *a roman on a libe* in *Ale verk fun Sholem Aleykhem* 21 (Sholem Aleykhem folksfond, 1925), 94–95.

ing the conventions of the Yiddish popular novel. The passage opens ironically, with self-deprecation bordering on self-emasculation as he compares the paucity of his own artistic productivity to that of his senior colleagues (the reference to the "most interesting" works of such writers is a direct attack on Shomer, who often included those very words on his own works as a form of self-advertising). The passage imagines a moment when the marketplace will correct itself by having no more interest in such sentimental novels, but recognizes that this remains a distant dream. In order to speed the process of reform, he crafts an extended parody of Shomer in the saccharine scene that follows the excerpt above. It allows Sholem Aleichem to demonstrate that he could write like Shomer if he really wanted to, but that he has elected to set higher standards for himself. The parody also shows readers the degree to which their own desires and expectations of Yiddish fiction have been constructed and managed by the sentimental novel. The entire scene is a masterful example of early Yiddish meta-fiction, in which prevailing ways of writing are satirized within a competing narrative to demonstrate their artlessness.

Sholem Aleichem includes a similar moment in *Stempenyu* (1888), performing his own anxieties about the frustration and disappointment his readers must be experiencing as they work through the failed love story between the refined and pious Rokhele and a musician that is at the heart of his newest "Jewish romance." *Stempenyu* is the best example of his attempt to upset the conventions of the Yiddish sentimental novel by crafting a story featuring characters who were recognizable Jewish types:

> "A tame story!," the reader may possibly explain, feeling highly dissatisfied with the fare I have set before him, because of the fact that he has been brought up on the "highly interesting romances" in which there is hanging, drowning, poisoning, and shooting on every page. Or in which perhaps a poor teacher becomes a duke, and a servant-girl a princess, and an assistant farmer a troubadour. But, what can I do? Am I to blame if amongst our people there are neither dukes nor princesses? If amongst us there are only ordinary women and musicians, plain young women with no dreams of marvelous transformations, and working men who live from hand to mouth?[29]

---

29. Sholem Aleichem, *Stempenyu,* trans. Hannah Berman (Methuen and Co., 1913), 275. In both this and the previous citation from *Sender Blank,* Yiddish literature enters into the discussion initiated by Flaubert in *Madame Bovary* (1856), a novel that pitches its realism against the sentimental novels read by its heroine, Emma. Her views of life and love are shaped by the types of novels she reads (or misreads) in her convent school. Emma's melancholy and her unhappy marriage are blamed on the fact that she inhabits an imaginative world of fantasy that has no connection to what is possible in her everyday life. Flaubert's description of what Emma reads is not so different from Sholem Aleichem's descriptions of Shomer's romances: "They were all love, lovers, sweethearts, persecuted ladies fainting in lonely pavilions, postilions killed at every stage, horse-ridden to death on every page, somber forests, heartaches, vows, sobs, tears and

In attempting to find a literary voice that could stand up to the popularity of the Yiddish sentimental novel, Sholem Aleichem looked to his relationship with S.Y. Abramovitsh. A short time earlier, Sholem Aleichem had recognized Abramovitsh as the "grandfather" of modern Yiddish fiction. He saw Abramovitsh as a consummate stylist, one whose stories were rooted in the economic and social realities of everyday Eastern European Jewish life. The celebration of Abramovitsh's silver anniversary a few years earlier in the Russian-language Jewish press was the first time that a Yiddish writer had been held up as a model for a "national writer."[30] These Russian-Jewish intel-

---

kisses, little skiffs by moonlight, nightingales in shady groves, 'gentlemen' brave as lions, gentle as lambs, virtuous as no one ever was, always well dressed, and weeping like fountains." (42) The more Emma reads, the more the nuns worry that Emma is "slipping" (43) from them, "with nothing more to learn, and nothing more to feel." (45) In order to free Emma from her melancholy, "it was decided to stop Emma from reading novels....Would they not have a right to apply to the police if the librarian persisted all the same in his poisonous trade?" (146) Elsewhere in the novel, after her husband complains that "Although my wife has been advised to take exercise she prefers always sitting in her room reading," (96) Flaubert inserts an interlocutor for Emma (and for the reader) to underscore that although her escapist fiction may contain "noble characters, pure affectations, and pictures of happiness...they miss, it seems to me, the true end of art." (97) Gustave Flaubert, *Madame Bovary,* trans. Eleanore Marx Aveling (Modern Library, 1918). Both Flaubert and Sholem Aleichem are particularly concerned about the situation of female readers, who are assumed to be the consumers of such fiction, though the difference between the bourgeois consumers of sentimental fiction imagined by Flaubert and the housemaids held up by Sholem Aleichem as Shomer's audience suggests that the sentimental novel served a different class of readers in European society than it did in Jewish society.

Sholem Aleichem's insistence in the passage above that Yiddish literature could not draw on the same romantic past that fed the European literary imagination finds a parallel in Henry James's biographical study *Hawthorne* (1879), in which he discusses the emergence of American literature. James elaborated upon a comment Nathaniel Hawthorne included in the preface to *The Marble Faun* (1860) in which he stated that as an American he comes from a country that is bereft of a romantic past. James understood this to mean that as American literature struggled to achieve its independence from English literature, it needed to take into account that it could not draw on the same sources that European literature took for granted—royal families, high society, world-class universities, the Church, architecturally distinguished cities, and so forth.

30. According to Olga Litvak, the celebratory essays in 1884 emphasized Abramovitsh's literary talents and the roots of his fiction in popular experience. In him, they found a Yiddish writer who could both withstand "criticism" and command "popular interest." Her discussion of a biographical essay by his friend Lev Binshtok shows how Abramovitsh had a hand in managing his own myth as a national writer who functions as "a new kind of folk hero...a maskil who transcended the material inducements of emancipation in order to suffer alongside his own impoverished people." See Olga Litvak, *Conscription and the Search for Modern Russian Jewry* (Indiana University Press, 2006), 129–132.

lectuals provided Sholem Aleichem with a reason to ally himself with Abramovitsh, and to embrace the people's vernacular as a language worthy of creative expression.

On 28 June, 1888, Abramovitsh wrote a letter to his "grandson" in which he famously advised Sholem Aleichem, via a play on the word *roman* (which in Yiddish means either a novel or a romance), "not to write romances. You have an entirely different style. After all (as you yourself say), you are my grandson. Do you comprehend what this means? Understand it and obey your grandfather and, with God's help, you will become something special. In general, all Yiddish romances are worthless. They make me want to vomit. If there are romances among our people, they are entirely different from those that exist among other peoples. One must understand this and write entirely differently."[31] Sholem Aleichem took this advice to heart, in part because it corresponded to what he had already undertaken with the publication of *The Judgment of Shomer* several months earlier. As the self-styled inheritor of Abramovitsh's commitment to writing as an artistic calling (rather than as a way to make money), Sholem Aleichem took it as his duty to domesticate the meaning of the Yiddish *roman,* even if it necessitated the writing of "*a roman on a roman*" (a novel without a romance[32]). His response to Abramovitsh's letter appeared as the preface to *Stempenyu*:

> Your words sank deep into my heart; and I began to realize by how much and in what way a Jewish novel must differ from all other novels. The truth is that the circumstances under which a Jew falls in love and declares his passions are altogether different from the circumstances which control the lives of other men. Besides, the Jewish nation has its own peculiarities—its own habits, and manners, and customs....And these too must have their place in the Jewish novel if it is to bear a true resemblance to Jewish life.[33]

He continued a short while later: "Over any work, you wrote to me in another letter, over any piece of work, dear grandchild, one must sweat and toil. One must ...chisel every separate episode to perfection..." He then added: "I should like that in a book there should not only be beauty of form, but also truth, and depth, and sympathy, as we find in life itself. There should be something to think about, as well as to amuse."[34] Sholem Aleichem here advances a Flaubertian case for the artfulness of a realism native to Jewish experience, arguing that Jewish experience is not only worthy of realistic representation in literature, but that such a representation, rather than demoting literature to the supposed humbleness of its characters, would, in fact, elevate the status of such literature to that of respectable art.

---

31. Quoted as Letter #110 in *Dos mendele bukh*, ed. Nahman Mayzel (Ikuf, 1959), 156.

32. This became the paradoxical subtitle of *Stempenyu.*

33 Sholem Aleichem, *Stempenyu: a idisher roman* (Sholem-Aleykhem folksfond oysgabe, 1925), 123.

34. *Stempenyu,* trans. Hannah Berman (Methuen and Co., 1913), 5, 7.

Collectively, these statements provide a succinct definition of Sholem Aleichem's aesthetic views about his own writing. They established his belief in the distinctiveness of Jewish life that necessitated the distinctiveness of Yiddish fiction. The recognition that Jews were different from the co-territorial populations among whom they lived made it all the more important that Yiddish literature—as the people's vernacular—reflect this consciousness in its settings, characterizations, plots, and ethical vision. This was a direct attack on pulp fiction writers like Shomer, who produced works at an astonishing pace and contended that the sole goal of their fiction was to entertain and distract readers from the challenges of their daily lives. Inherent in the creation of a new standard for Yiddish fiction, was the venue in which *Stempenyu* appeared: a supplement to Sholem Aleichem's own new anthology of Yiddish literature *Di yudishe folks-bibliotek: a bukh far literatur, kritik un visnshaft* (The Jewish Popular Library: An Anthology of Literature, Criticism, and Scholarship). In undertaking this editorial endeavor (and putting his own money behind it), Sholem Aleichem signaled that the only way to transform the landscape of Yiddish publishing was to find ways to disseminate higher-quality Yiddish fiction. The *Folks-bibliotek* was conceived as an elegant product that would accord Yiddish literature with prestige. Sholem Aleichem managed to publish only two volumes of the anthology prior to the loss of his fortune in October 1890. Nonetheless, for the first time Yiddish literature had a figure who persuaded both established writers and figures who were reticent to publish in Yiddish to send him their best work so that they could be published together in one volume. The first issue of the *Folks-bibliotek* included both a revised edition of the first half of Abramovitsh's *Dos vintshfingerl* (The Wishing Ring), I.L. Peretz's debut in Yiddish literature with the narrative poem "Monish," and pieces by David Frishman and Simon Frug, who had previously published mainly in Hebrew or Russian. Aside from Sholem Aleichem's own *Stempenyu* (itself something of an artistic manifesto), the first volume of the *Folks-bibliotek* also included a short essay in which he explored the need to standardize Yiddish orthography and grammar so as to facilitate reading and comprehension. This revealed Sholem Aleichem's eagerness to manage the process of bringing Yiddish out of its chaotic infancy to a more mature understanding of itself as a literature that needed to take itself seriously.[35] He understood that the process of shifting reading habits among the public would be incremental, as evidenced by the fact that the initial runs of his

---

35. The second volume of the *Folks-bibliotek* further expanded the coterie of writers who were prepared to sign on to Sholem Aleichem's program, most of whom came to occupy a dignified place in Yiddish literary history as the process of its canonization later unfolded. The second volume included Sholem Aleichem's newest novel *Yosele Solovey,* which, like *Stempenyu* before it, was crafted as a self-consciously "Jewish" romance in which the values of self-restraint, modesty, and collective responsibility were pitched against individual self-fulfillment.

Folks-bibliotek still paled in comparison to the lowbrow Yiddish romances that continued to flood the market.[36]

Much of Sholem Aleichem's thinking about this new aesthetic standard crystallized in his essay "A Letter to a Close Friend,"[37] which appeared in the second volume of the *Folks-bibliotek*. The piece is worth quoting at length, not only because it reveals Sholem Aleichem's fear that a commitment to a Jewish realism might be a turn-off to readers, but also because of the way it elaborates upon the conversation initiated by *The Judgment of Shomer* a year earlier:

> My critics do not want to forgive me in any way for two things. First, they ask me, as is the custom among Jews: *ma nishtano?* How is a Jewish novel different than any other novel in the world? One of them, who appears to be quite educated, wrote to me: "Until physiology proves that the Jew was created with a different heart, blood-type, or nerves, I will not understand how there can be such a thing as a Jewish or a non-Jewish novel."
>
> Everyone admits that Jewish life implies a different type of existence. So why can't they understand that the novel, in which life is portrayed, should not have a different complexion? Why should they not want to understand that every novel must have its own expression and physiognomy so that it reveals an accurate reflection of the life of the people that is described in it...[38]

Having established his understanding that every national literature must be as distinct as the nation from which it emerges, Sholem Aleichem anticipates that his portrayal of Jewish love may at first bore those who are used to the flights of fantasy and dramatic confrontation between "good" and "evil" typical of Yiddish popular fiction:

> It is worth mentioning that a Jewish young woman is not the same as any other young woman. Raised and reared among Jews...a Jewish girl knows that she must first love God, then her parents, then her husband and children....A Jewish heroine...contains her desires, forgets her caprices, abandons her passions for someone else....This is the nature of Jewish heroism.[39]

Where Shomer was determined to play up romantic suffering, jealousy, intrigue, and betrayal among casts of characters who found themselves in

---

36. Alyssa Quint observes that in 1888, 3,200 issues of *Di yudishe folks-bibliotek* were published, compared to 96,000 copies of Shomer's works. These figures suggest that the market in this period for serious Yiddish fiction was still immature and limited to elite readers. See Quint, 81.

37. "A briv tsu a gutn fraynt," *Di yudishe folks-bibliotek* 2 (Kiev, 1889), 304–310. This work should be read in conjunction with his short pamphlet *Der yidisher dales in di beste verk fun undzere folks-shriftshteler* (Jewish Poverty in the Best Works of Our National Writers) (St. Petersburg, 1888) in which he holds up Abramovitsh's *Fishke the Lame* as a model of the type of Yiddish realism that addresses the socio-economic conditions of Jewish life and resists the escapism and fantasies offered up by sentimental fiction.

38. "A briv," 304.

situations completely foreign to Eastern European Jewish life, Sholem Aleichem contended that Shomer's idealization of love at all costs was artistically false and socially offensive to the values by which Jews love and live. This
enables him to explain and defend his artistic decision in *Stempenyu* to
short-circuit the romance between the modest Rokhele and the unrefined
eponymous musician. Her decision to resist his amorous advances after
reading his garbled attempt at a love letter privileges Jewish literacy over
sentimentality. This embedded mockery of Shomer's style dashes the expectations of readers, and seems to offer a new heroism of self-restraint in its
place. Sophisticated readers would have caught on to the irony of Sholem
Aleichem's prescriptions, given the author's own biography as someone
who initiated a secret affair with a young woman whose father had hired
him to serve as her tutor. His "advice" to Jewish girls in the novel that it is
more heroic to control their desires and behaviors out of respect for traditional standards of modesty was actually intended to portray the deleterious
effects of the suppression of desire as it actually existed in Jewish society. At
first reading, he comes across as a cultural conservative, protective of young
female readers who might otherwise be inclined to run off with inappropriate lovers because of the influence of Shomer's novels. Upon reflection,
however, the radical undertow of his writing emerges.

Sholem Aleichem's choice of two musicians as his male protagonists in
Stempenyu and *Yosele Solevey* also performed a kind of cultural service:

> A klezmer musician? A cantor? I wanted to show how artists and poets
> discover themselves in this world...and how low these great talents among
> us have fallen, how they go unrecognized. Such a talent as Stempenyu would
> have been acclaimed as a great talent, as a virtuoso among any other people,
> but among us how is he treated? As nothing more than a folk musician.
> Talents such as Stempenyu and Yosele Solevey are numerous among us but
> they are shunned....And if one of them manages to pop up to demonstrate
> his fire, nobody understands him....So their lives are very lonely...[40]

Sholem Aleichem underscores the degree to which the achievements of the
Jews' native artists come into conflict with dominant social conventions
that minimize or denigrate their importance.[41] Both *klezmer* musicians and
traditional cantors, models of native creativity, occupied a relatively low
position in a society that privileged the refinement of intellectual achievement and wealth as signs of social status. However, Sholem Aleichem self-
identifies with them as marginal figures whose artistic independence necessarily comes into conflict with societal mores. He was attempting to

---

39. Ibid., 305.

40. Ibid., 306–307.

41. For more on this, see Anita Norich, "Portraits of the Artist in Three Novels by Sholem
   Aleichem," *Prooftexts* 4:3 (1984), 237–251.

enhance the status of the Jewish artist among a readership for whom such talents had never before had any importance. "The people must know what powers it has, what rarities wander among it,"[42] he explained elsewhere, furthering his contention that a central function of the Jewish writer was to provide audiences with an awareness of their own talents and self-worth. As the people's vernacular, Yiddish—much more so than Hebrew or Russian—was ideally suited to represent the cadences of Jewish life among the masses, and in the process to enable readers to better understand themselves. Sholem Aleichem recognized that elevating the tastes of readers so that they would come to desire quality Jewish fiction would be a long process that needed to be carefully nurtured. If he was going to be successful in convincing readers that their lives were the legitimate stuff of a literature worth reading, he first needed to justify for himself, via *The Judgment of Shomer,* why the Yiddish popular romance was no longer legitimate, despite its seductions.

"Let There Be Light": Shomer Responds

The publication of *The Judgment of Shomer* was only the beginning of a polemical battle that would rage, on and off, for decades. Shomer was so infuriated by the belief that he was being scapegoated by Russian Jewish intellectuals (and so attracted to the new possibilities of a mass market of Yiddish immigrants in New York) that he moved across the Atlantic the year following its publication, in 1889. Despite the new distance between them, Shomer rallied to his own defense almost as soon as he could digest Sholem Aleichem's verdict. In the preface to his novel *Der mord oys libe* (1890) Shomer raised the populist flag in an attempt to portray Sholem Aleichem and his supporters as being out of touch with the reading masses: "You empty critics can say what you want, scream in the streets that my novels are foolish, pass verdicts against me as much as your hearts desire. I will do what I do, I will continue to write fairy tales for my readers which, thank God, are helpful to thousands of people and will continue to be more useful than the prattling of your foolish critics."[43] Shomer himself fanned the flames of controversy by continually referring to *The Judgment* in an obsessive effort to discredit it. For instance, in the story "Yudke shmerkes dertseylung" we find the first suggestion (repeated later in his 1898 pamphlet *Yehi or*) that Sholem Aleichem was a charlatan who used his new found wealth to purchase the talent of others and publish their work under his own name. In 1890, Shomer published an extensive overview of the development of Yiddish literature in the nineteenth century in the pages of *Der mentshnfraynd* (issues 28–48), the paper he founded soon after his arrival

---

42. "A briv," 308.

43. Z. Reyzin, "Shomer," *Leksikon fun der yidisher literatur, prese, un filologye*, vol. 4 (Vilna: Kletskin, 1929), 783.

in New York, in which he had generous words for almost every major Yiddish writer of the nineteenth century—with the significant exception of Sholem Aleichem, in whom he did not find a trace of literary talent. The review essay seems to have been designed, through supposedly disinterested analysis, to write Sholem Aleichem out of the emerging literary canon in much the same way that he felt Sholem Aleichem had attempted to exclude him.[44] His criteria for being a good writer included "talent to tell a story...so that the reader will want to read it." This was intended as a not-so-subtle attack on Sholem Aleichem's early novels.[45] Similarly, Shomer's foreword to *Ester* (1891) lashes out sarcastically: "I am sure that this small tale will greatly interest our reading public. They certainly will enjoy it more than the hefty *Kindershpiln* and *Sender Blankn,* and perhaps even more than the fat *Folks-bibliotek,* which are so overweight with wisdom that no mortal could possibly have the privilege of appreciating them..."[46] His bitterness was also evident in his preface to *Di amerikanishe glikn: a roman fun yidishn lebn in amerike* (1895):

> So how are you, our Yiddish writers in Russia? I thought that by leaving Russia I would have left you the field wide open to show off your talents. I assumed that as soon as they were rid of me they would show off what they were all about, but until now they have been mute, and from across the ocean I now hear the complaints of the Russian booksellers: "Woe! Send us new novels, [Shomer]. Our customers are tearing us apart, complaining that they have nothing to read, but we have nothing to give them. So what are you up to, you Yiddish critics, you Sholem Aleichems...who with one hand compose verdicts and with the other something else...?"[47]

---

44. Shmuel Niger, "Shomers mishpet—af Sholem Aleykhemen," *Di tsukunft* (April 1947), 233.

45. In summarizing the articles from *Der mentshnfraynd,* Kalmen Marmor shows that Shomer had no patience for Sholem Aleichem's efforts to reinvent the "Jewish romance." Were Sholem Aleichem truly a talent, for instance, Shomer explained that *Stempenyu* would have ended with more drama. Rokhele's strong attraction to Stempenyu should have triumphed over her modesty, prompting her to run away with him and break down class distinctions. Or she ought to have suffered so much in realizing that Stempenyu was not an appropriate match for her that she would have died of heartbreak. Shomer was so comfortable in the genre of the sentimental potboiler that he dismissed the possibility that ordinary readers would find anything else interesting. Marmor shows how Shomer had no understanding of Sholem Aleichem's desire to create a fiction that reflected the values, experiences, and limitations (as opposed to the fantasies) of Jewish life. See Kalmen Marmor, "Shomer pruv aruntertsuraysn Sholem-Aleykhems romanen," *Morgn frayheyt* (February 12, 1939), 3, 6.

46. Shomer here is referring to two of Sholem Aleichem's early novels, and to his anthology of Yiddish literature, The Jewish People's Library. Quoted by A. Veviorke, "Shomer un Shomerizm," *Di royte velt* (August 1929), 126.

47. Veviorke, "Shomer un Shomerizm," 126.

The accusation that his critics were not potent enough to satisfy the desire of Yiddish readers and the innuendo about masturbation may be a transference of his own public emasculation in light of the controversy. However, it is also an insightful reading of Sholem Aleichem, which suggests that much of what he was producing was for his own onanistic pleasures. Sholem Aleichem, despite casting himself as a "writer of the people," remained his own ideal audience.

Shomer's 1894 essay, "Le-mi ani amel" (its title references the Hebrew maskilic poem of 1871 by Y.L. Gordon in which he despaired for the future of Hebrew literature) opens with an echo of the male protagonist of the biblical book of Lamentations:

> *Ani ha-gever*, I am a living witness to how badly our public deals with the writer who toils on its behalf. Everyone knows that I am special for having written over 200 novels and stories in Hebrew and Yiddish for the people of Israel. Everyone, except for my worst enemies, admits that my novels have had a tremendous impact on readers....And what is the outcome of my efforts? The public looks on with pleasure as coarse young snots toss stones at me. And nobody intervened [on my behalf]. Just the opposite—many applauded "Bravo."[48]

Despite the overblown rhetorical flourish of comparing his fate to that of a witness to the destruction of the Temple, Shomer's fears were not borne out by reality. He still outsold Sholem Aleichem by tremendous amounts, even though the newer generation of writers such as Sholem Aleichem and Warsaw's Peretz garnered the respect of intellectuals, pockets of middle-class urban readers and, in the case of Peretz, young radicals. Nonetheless, Shomer continued to stoke the controversy as a way to maintain his relevance in a rapidly expanding literary landscape.

He marked the tenth anniversary of Sholem Aleichem's verdict with the pamphlet *Yehi or: A literarishe kampf* (Let There Be Light: A Literary Controversy), a twenty-eight-page diatribe that swung between desperation and rage. The essay appeared about the same time as a public debate at New York's Free Jewish People's Theater (*folksbine*) in which Shomer's son, Avrom, defended his father against playwrights Leon Kobrin and Jacob Gordin, who were attempting to stake out New York's theatrical audiences for themselves by arguing that Yiddish theater could ill afford a *shund* writer of Shomer's ilk in its midst.[49] The pamphlet's title appeals both to a divine

---

48. The article appeared in *Land khokhem* 10 (July 1894). See Reyzin, *Leksikon*, 783–784.

49. Shomer's contribution to the American Yiddish theater is beyond the scope of this essay, though he wrote more than three dozen plays. See Andrey Bredstein, "Nokhem-Meyer Shaykevitsch: Another Classic of Yiddish Theater," *Studies in Jewish Civilization* 16 (2005), 203–216; Roze Shomer-Batshelis, *Undzer foter Shomer* (Ikuf, 1950), 85–94, 159–161, 167–168. Z. Reyzin's bibliography at the end of Shomer Batshelis' book includes a list of Shomer's dramas.

source of creative inspiration and to the maskilic call for enlightenment. However, its address to "my critics"—"those swindlers and liars"[50] and the "dishonest means they employ to tarnish me"[51]—underscores Shomer's real desire to defend himself from stigmatization by discrediting his antagonists and offering his own counter-narrative of the controversy. He attributes Sholem Aleichem's attack against him to jealousy rather than to a commitment to aesthetic principles, and asserts that *The Judgment of Shomer* was an immature, disproportionate reaction ("an explosive, hellish fire, like a bomb") to a few words that Shomer had included in an earlier novel that suggested that the *Folksblat* "ought not fill its pages with garbage and with Sholem Aleichem's crazy articles."[52] In revisiting in great detail the history of the literary controversy about him, Shomer occasionally borders on the conspiratorial, climaxing with the accusation that David Frishman ghost-wrote *The Judgment of Shomer* for payment:

> This is a true fact that I can prove through letters from prominent Yiddish writers who with their own eyes saw how Frishman wrote *The Judgment of Shomer*. Sholem Aleichem himself cannot write. Anything that is good in his work is not his, but rather the result [of editorial revisions by] Abramovitsh and Ravnitski, whom Sholem Aleichem paid handsomely to correct his works. This is what the typesetters of [Sholem Aleichem's novels] *Stempenyu* and *Yosele Solevey* admit.[53]

Though Shomer does not produce copies of such testimonies by "prominent Yiddish writers" and the "typesetters," he imagines a premeditated effort among intellectuals, editors, and writers—financed by Sholem Aleichem's wealth and machinations—to rearrange the literary landscape from above for unsuspecting readers.[54]

At no point in the pamphlet does Shomer recognize that the struggle between him and his critics was part of an effort to define new borders between an emerging Yiddish literature that aspired for artistry and his variety of lowbrow popular fiction, nor does he entertain the possibility that any of the criticisms launched against him have any merit.[55] In his mind, he

---

50. *Yehi or*, 1.

51. Ibid., 28.

52. Ibid., 4.

53. Ibid., 4. Shomer repeats the claim again on page 23.

54. He cites letters by editors of *Yudishes folksblat,* Alexander Tsederboym and then Yisroel Levi, in which both admit that they did not personally read any of his novels prior to publishing critical essays about him. This leads Shomer to assume that there was an elitist cabal determined to do him in: "An editor of a newspaper screams that my novels make our youngsters unhappy and in the end he admits that he personally has never read them!" *Yehi or,* 2.

55. Sholem Aleichem was attempting to refine the image of Yiddish literature by taming the type of shameless self-promotion that had long been a staple of its popular market-

had masses of Yiddish readers on his side as the most potent element in his defense.

Unfortunately, *Let There Be Light* was more therapy for Shomer than an attempt to really engage his critics. It enabled him to release more than a decade of pent-up frustrations, and to lament how competitive, political, and petty the Yiddish literary world had become ("Among us Jews, when one falls upon a writer and makes a pile of rubble of him, all his other colleagues applaud"[56]), and take leave of the controversy with a self-righteous "pure conscience."[57] Despite protestations to the contrary, Shomer's continued engagement in a debate that Sholem Aleichem had long since moved beyond proved that he never really psychologically recovered from the verdict of *The Judgment of Shomer*.

Rehabilitation and Revision

With the passing of the generation of "classic Yiddish writers" during World War I, Yiddish literature was poised to reassess the function of popular (or sub-canonical) fiction in the creation of a modern Yiddish reader and a self-supporting Yiddish republic of letters. The question was how such a history would be written, by whom, and how it would evaluate Shomer's contributions. What is remarkable about the verdict in *The Judgment of Shomer* is the extent to which it continued being a source of contention decades after it was published. Though Sholem Aleichem never sanctioned its republication in any of the authorized collections of his works (he reputedly found it shrill), Yiddish critics continued to accept it as a founding document, essential to any serious discussion of distinctions between *shund* and legitimate fiction, and thus a central work of Yiddish canonical self-definition. We might divide up such debates as occurring both within and among three critical camps: the Yiddishist,[58] the Soviet, and the modernist.

---

ing, and Shomer resented the intervention: "The critics make fun of the fact that in one of my novels I wrote that the novel contains everything that the reader loves and that many other writers praise the name Shomer and even borrow it [to sell their own works]....Frishman (aka Sholem Aleichem) considers this a sin and compares it to peddlers hawking their wares. But all writers, even the holy rabbis, write introductions with the goal of enticing readers to read their works. Authors from other peoples do even better; when they publish a book they take out advertisements in the newspapers....But when Shomer praises himself with a few words in one of his forwards it is considered a heavenly transgression." (Ibid., 14) In truth, Sholem Aleichem was only slightly more subtle in his own self-referentiality.

56. Ibid., 17.

57. Ibid., 28.

58. "Yiddishist" is a rather slippery term, referring both to advocates and producers, as well as to experts in varieties of secular Yiddish culture. Yiddishists also shared, to varying degrees, a commitment to humanism and to the autonomy of Yiddish as a secular Jewish cultural system.

Yiddishist Circles

One of the earliest revisionist interventions on behalf of Shomer's reputation was offered up in the form of an ode to Shomer by Eliokim Tsunzer
(1836–1913), himself among the last of the Yiddish folk bards. For Tsunzer,
Shomer represented a more innocent moment when ordinary readers could
still turn to Yiddish literature as a source of entertainment and leisure without having to fear the censure of the critics:

Vu iz zayn getlekher gayst nit ge{floygn?	Where did your sacred spirit not soar?
In Bovl, Mitsrayim geven,	Your heavenly eyes roamed
in Shpanye gekukt mit di gaystike oygn,	From Babylon and Egypt to Spain,
geshildert undz alts mit zayn pen.	Your pen described everything for us.
Levi, Ben-Ezre, un Hurduses palats	Levi, Ben Ezra, and Herod's palace,
Zahare un kaltn Sibir,	Sahara and frigid Siberia,
harems fun sultans, hayzer fun dales	Sultans' harems, impoverished homes
fotografirt af papir.[59]	All photographed on paper.

Tsunzer here sharply resists the standard of contemporary realism imposed
by Sholem Aleichem in *The Judgment of Shomer*. Though Shomer's plots
may seem derivative to elite readers, he suggests that they did do important
cultural work by bringing the Eastern European popular Jewish imagination
to exotic worlds of the Jewish past, thereby asserting their value as historical fiction.

Shomer's death also precipitated what we might call a reassessment of
the history of Yiddish reading. Zalmen Reyzin, in his *Lexicon of Yiddish Literature, Press, and Philology* (1929) writes that "after [I.M.] Dik, Shomer
was the first to provide the public with material to read, and also the first to
write not only story books, but also to create thick works—novels—and
through these he had a great influence on the Yiddish masses."[60] Reyzin's
bold proclamations and positive words ("It is possible to find in Shomer's
novels realistic characters, talented depictions, psychological insights, in
short all the elements that we associate with the content of a true literary
work") marked a significant step forward in the rehabilitation of Shomer
within Yiddishist circles. The very fact that his lexicon entry on Shomer
amounted to almost fifty pages[61] signaled a move on the part of some inter-

59. Eliokim Tsunzer, "Shomer," reprinted in Shomer-Batshelis, *Undzer foter Shomer*, 193.

60. Z. Reyzin, *Leksikon,* 768–769.

61. Postwar general histories of Yiddish literature published in English have not been as generous in acknowledging Shomer's accomplishments, contributing to the replica-

war intellectuals to challenge Sholem Aleichem's unilateral efforts to exclude Shomer from Yiddish fiction's canonical borders. Reyzin believed that by downplaying the history of Yiddish reading, the canonical narrative of Yiddish literary history would represent only elite tastes. Others concurred in arguing that Yiddish literature could not have developed without him: "His [Shomer's] name is the history of the Yiddish reading public and its taste..."[62] Kalmen Marmor added: "He taught the Jewish masses to read Yiddish and thus prepared the base for the new Yiddish literature. He was above all a teacher to the masses."[63] Y.Y. Sigal went even further, suggesting "that Shomer was the one who gathered the audience which later became Sholem Aleichem's."[64]

Such comments are supported time and again in the Yiddish memoiristic literature. In her memoir of her childhood, Rokhl Feynberg asserts: "Above all else I wanted to read Shomer....But it was very hard to get a hold of [his novel] because it was always being read by someone else." She emphasizes the degree to which she read and reread Shomer, because although she was a voracious reader "apart from Shomer the other [Yiddish writers] interested me very little."[65]

As Avrom Reyzin's memoirs confirm, it is an elite misconception that Shomer's popularity was limited to women or to a less-educated class of men:

> In the tall library at home, stuffed between several German books...were a
> few small volumes in Yiddish that my mother bought from an itinerant

tion of Sholem Aleichem's early canonizing efforts and the effacement of tensions between mass and elite tastes in understanding the development of Yiddish fiction. For instance, A.A. Roback's *The Story of Yiddish Literature* (1940) dedicates a few paragraphs (in a book of over 400 pages) to Shomer's contribution to the emergence of Yiddish fiction; Charles Madison's *Yiddish Literature: Its Scope and Major Writers* (New York 1968) mentions Shomer in passing on three separate occasions in a work of more than 500 pages. Though Sol Liptzin's *A History of Yiddish Literature* (Jonathan David, 1972) includes a little more than a page out of more than 500 about Shomer, his history at least provides the reader with an understanding of why his "entertaining" fiction "aroused the wrath of intellectuals," suggesting to readers that a history of Yiddish reading would look very different from his study of canonical Yiddish writers (53–54).

62. Shmuel Niger, "Shomer," *Leksikon fun der nayer yidisher literatur*, vol. 8 (New York: Alveltlekhn kultur-kongres, 1981), 744.

63. Kalmen Marmor, *Morgn frayheyt* (New York, December 20, 1923). Quoted by Shmuel Niger, "Shomers mishpet–af Sholem Aleykhemen: a kapitl yidishe kultur geshikhte," *Di tsukunft* (January 1947), 46.

64. *Kanade odler* (Montreal, November 9, 1930). Quoted by Niger, *Di tsukunft* (January 1947), 44.

65. Quoted in Sophie Grace Pollack, "Hashpaato shel Shomer al korei Yiddish," *Hulyot* 10 (2006), 71, 73.

peddler who went house to house, like a beggar, to sell Yiddish chapbooks....These books...were the most beloved in our home. The first book
I had the energy to read was by Shomer, *Der raykher betler,*....I cannot
describe for you how great Shomer's name was in our household, so much
so that my mother handed over an entire gulden to purchase this book....As
a boy I would hear [Shomer's] novel[s] read out loud by father on Friday
evenings to the entire family. My mother would openly weep during the
scenes when the evil protagonist and his wife beat the poor orphan. We read
Der raykher betler over and over. For a time, it was the most beloved book
in our home. Even the neighbors borrowed it endlessly. If this book was not
the first novel I read by Shomer or even the first I read in Yiddish, it was the
first to have an impact on me. I knew entire chapters by heart. Its power
rested on a simple fable: good would be rewarded and evil punished, not in
the next world but in our own lifetime ...Of course the book was naïve. Even
illogical in some ways. But did anyone complain? Life then was so gray and
monotonous... Shomer was an event, a holiday...

So to me the name Shomer is still dear. One of the most beloved parts
of my youth, its greatest joy, was to read a book. Since reading books is still
a pleasure, it is worth reminding ourselves of our first sweet memories of
reading, reading the legendary Shomer.[66]

Reyzin's perspective is valuable because it emerges out of a personal
experience of reading that contextualizes Shomer as a transitional, yet critical literary figure in opening up the pleasures of Yiddish reading to an entire
generation, including future Yiddish writers like himself.[67]

Shomer's influence on his readers was also conjured in Y.L. Peretz's
short sketch "Di lezerin" (The Female Reader). The setting for the story is
the house of an impoverished water-carrier. The only respite for his oldest
daughter from her misery occurs on the Sabbath eve, when the rest of the
family is asleep. Then she escapes with a popular Yiddish romance: "Her
eyes burn. Her sad bosom heaves. Her thin hands tremble....She is reading a
romance by Shomer by the candlelight. Her lips tremble with impa-
tience."[68] These memoirists and fiction writers challenge the fixed borders
of margin and center by crediting the marginality of so-called sentimental
popular literature for creating the audience necessary for a canonical center
to later emerge. All of them take note of Shomer's popular appeal among
women, which allows us to conclude that Yiddish reading habits in this
period were significantly influenced by gender. Avrom Reyzin credits his

---

66. Avrom Reyzin, "Tsum 25stn yortsayt fun Shomer," *Forverts* (New York, December 6,
1930); reprinted in Shomer-Batshelis, *Undzer foter shomer,* 199–205.

67. According to Pollack, the noted Israeli literary scholar Dov Sadan admitted in a private
letter from the 1950s that he read all of Shomer in his youth. "Hashpaato," 74. See also
Sadan's brief introduction to *Shirei Shomer ve'zikhronotav,* ed. Roze Shomer-Batshelis (Jerusalem: Ahiasef, 1952), 7–8.

68. Y.L. Peretz, "Di lezerin," *Ale verk* II (New York, CYCO, 1947), 108.

mother as having been the conduit that brought Yiddish sentimental fiction into the household, and in turn introduced him to the pleasures of Yiddish reading that would eventually influence his decision to become a Yiddish writer.

Zalmen Reyzin's entry on Shomer in the *Lexicon* in 1929, along with his comments a year later on the twenty-fifth anniversary of Shomer's death that "perhaps we are on the verge of a major Shomer rehabilitation in Yiddish literary history,"[69] reflected the willingness of Yiddish literary scholars to reopen the verdict against Shomer and anticipated the re-evaluation that would continue unabated in the ensuing years. Reyzin's recognition of Shomer's role in helping to create a Yiddish reader, and his concession that "if it difficult from the standpoint of refined literature to find something positive in his novels, one must admit that his earlier stories are at a high level, and some of them contain vivid portraits of Jewish life in the past,"[70] were proof to some critics that Sholem Aleichem had tarnished the reputation of a Yiddish literary "pioneer" who—unlike other writers, especially those who emerged out of the Haskalah and earned their reputations by mocking the deficiencies of Jewish life—was at least sympathetic to Jews in his writing.[71]

Critical discussion of Shomer in the interwar period ranged widely, from attempts to discover positive aspects of Shomer's writing to investigations of Sholem Aleichem's own motivations and critical shortcomings. Thus, Kalman Marmor is among the earliest critics who rejects Sholem Aleichem's accusation that Shomer severely harmed the Yiddish language with his Germanisms and instead suggests that "his short stories of Jewish life are filled with folklore. His novels, without overlooking their shortcomings, enriched the Yiddish language with many new words and expressions."[72] In a different vein, Shaul Ginsburg attacks the prosecution in *The Judgment* for its ignorance about the way literatures develop and for its lack of attention to differences between benign and corrosive varieties of popular culture.

> *The Judgment* was misguided...[because] it never made a distinction between *shund* and entertainment. What is *shund*? It is that which appeals to one's lowest instincts, that which calls up immoral feelings. *Shund* is pornographic. But entertainment is not immoral. It has a noble purpose—to provide spiritual respite, to allow those who are exhausted to re-energize....All healthy world literatures have within them authors who specialize in popular entertainment.[73]

69. *Morgn zhurnal* (May 24, 1930). Quoted by Niger, *Di tsukunft* (January 1947), 43.

70. Z. Reyzin, *Leksikon*, 770.

71. See Gershom Bader, "A nayer vikuekh vegn Shomer," *Yidishe togblat* (New York, February 29, 1929); republished in Shomer-Batshelis, 228–231.

72. *Morgn frayhayt* (December 20, 1923); quoted by Niger, *Di tsukunft* (January 1947), 46.

73. Shaul Ginzberg, "Shomer un zayne kritikers," *Di tsukunft* (November 1940); reprinted in Shomer-Batshelis, 219.

Not all interwar Yiddishists were prepared to jump onto the rehabilitation bandwagon. As early as 1927, Yisroel Shtern published a feuilleton in Poland's leading Yiddish literary weekly, *Literarishe bleter,* in which he seemed to mock Shomer and his defenders in a staged conversation between himself and the writer:

-"How did it happen that you lost the trial?"

-Shomer responded: "In the end people will investigate who was right. Truth will swim up like oil on water."

-I told him: "Mr. Shomer, that time has already arrived....Not a single family can get on without you. They mention you at every table....You have many followers. You have your own school in Yiddish literature called: Shomerism....It is the strongest school of all."

Shomer cannot believe his ears. He thinks he is being lied to or mocked.

-"Yes, maestro, you are rehabilitated."[74]

Shtern here was responding, sarcastically, to the prevalence of pulp fiction in the interwar Yiddish daily press in Poland. This explosion of lowbrow fiction—which was the diet of most contemporary readers—was of serious concern to critics and intellectuals, who traced such works to Shomer's transgressions.[75]

In an altogether different approach to Sholem Aleichem's judgment of Shomer's work, Shmuel Niger's psychological reading of Sholem Aleichem anticipates Harold Bloom by suggesting that *The Judgment* was a way for him to work through an anxiety of influences that had S.Y. Abramovitsh's *yetser tov* (good impulse) of literary realism and Shomer's *yetser hara* (evil impulse) of escapist fiction dueling for his artistic soul. According to Niger, Sholem Aleichem set for himself the task of freeing the Yiddish reader from the *klipa* (husk) of *shund*. It is interesting that Niger employs a mystical term to explain Sholem Aleichem's motivations; just as the Lurianic kabbalist sets for himself the task of rescuing the sparks of divinity from the husk of materiality, so too does Niger attribute an almost otherworldly impulse—an aesthetic calling—to Sholem Aleichem's own artistic birth. In Niger's view, the unforgiving tone and sarcasm of *The Judgment* was a form of overcompensation and penance for literary sins committed at the outset of his own career in such early works such as "Tsvey shteyner," "Natashe," and "Kinder shpil," in which one could find the stain of sentimentality.[76]

Avrom Reyzin, however, was far less generous in finding psychological excuses for what he read as a vicious personal attack that damaged the

---

74. Yirsoel Shtern, "Unzer lezerin oder Shomer hot gevunen," *Literarishe bleter* 4 (April 8, 1927), 265–268.

75. For more on this, see Shmeruk, 325–354.

76. Shmuel Niger, *Geklibene verk* 3 (New York: Yidisher kultur farlag, 1928), 20–29.

career of a fellow writer.[77] With the advantages of hindsight, Reyzin argued that *The Judgment of Shomer* had been "unnecessary" because "a new era in Yiddish literature was already well underway with the publication of Spektor's *Hoyzfraynd*, Sholem Aleichem's *Folks-bibliotek*, and later Peretz's *Yudishe bibliotek*," all of which introduced a more sophisticated editorial standard that transformed Yiddish into a competitive, world-class literature.[78] Reyzin's point is that had Sholem Aleichem just ignored Shomer, his influence would have undergone a more natural decline as the quality of the Yiddish writing that Sholem Aleichem hoped to produce and disseminate garnered attention, especially from an expanding middle-class audience that was prepared to be challenged in its reading. More recently, scholar Chone Shmeruk added that even without Sholem Aleichem's intervention, the *shund* chapbook dried up in Eastern Europe by the end of the 1890s due to the emergence of a mass-circulation Yiddish press. As editors recognized that trash fiction was a lucrative way to provoke readers to buy papers, *shund* found a new home in serialization. This left the Yiddish book publishing industry much less vulnerable to market pressures from below and provided room for it to turn its attention to the dissemination of a higher-quality product.[79]

By the time Niger returned to the question of Shomer in a series of three articles in *Di tsukunft* (1947),[80] he exhibited a certain frustration over having to restate his position about the function of sentimental Yiddish fiction in the emergence of the Yiddish reader. His comments were prompted by what he considered the apologetics of articles that had appeared in the American Yiddish press in 1940, on the thirty-fifth anniversary of Shomer's death. Niger went to great lengths to separate the social function of popular literature (which he recognized as a transitional necessity) and his opinion of Shomer as a writer. On the one hand, as Iris Parush explains, "even Niger expressed a certain recognition of the significance of popular Yiddish literature...the popular novels helped form habits of reading."[81] On the other hand, Niger went on the offensive by claiming that "the opinion that Shomer was one of the victims and not the victimizer is entirely false: that which Dubnov, Sholem Aleichem, Frishman, Ravnitski, and others wrote about Shomer was temperate compared to the cheap and false accusations that

---

77. Shomer managed to reestablish himself in New York as a fiction writer and playwright, though never with the same dominance over the market that he had enjoyed in Russia.

78. Reyzin, "Shomer un zayne romanen" *Forverts* (N.Y., November 17, 1940), republished in Shomer-Batshelis, 210.

79. Shmeruk, 335.

80. Niger, "Shomers mishpet – af Sholem Aleykhemen," *Di tsukunft* 1 (January 1947), 41–47; 2 (Feb. 1947), 111–116; 4 (April 1947), 232–236.

81. Parush, *Reading Jewish Women*, 154.

Shomer launched against them."[82] Niger provided his readers, many of whom had not grown up reading Shomer, with a detailed history of the attacks and counterattacks launched between Shomer and his critics from the early 1880s until his death in 1905, hoping that his would be the last word about this episode in Yiddish literary history. Niger recontextualized Sholem Aleichem's motivation for questioning the standards of Yiddish popular fiction: "Sholem Aleichem...could not be as objective as we are. He felt and had to feel that the cheap novels were a danger to young Yiddish literature, that the "most interesting novels" would weaken the influence of better Yiddish writers to gradually raise [the tastes of] the Yiddish reading public..."[83] Niger also resisted the notion, suggested by Shaul Ginzburg as late as 1940, that there had not yet been an honest effort to annul the "unfair verdict." [84] He reminded his readers of the many efforts to rehabilitate Shomer in the interwar period, rehearsing sympathetic comments made by such ideologically diverse writers as the modernist poet Yankev Glatshteyn, the Soviet critic Veviorke (both of whom we shall discuss below), and the Yiddishists Zalmen Reyzin and Kalmen Marmor. He sarcastically concluded that "those who are knocking for a revision are banging on an open door."[85]

A few years later, in response to the publication of *Undzer foter Shomer* (Our father Shomer, 1950)—a biography and collection of sympathetic essays edited by Shomer's daughter Roze Shomer-Batshelis—Niger conceded yet again that "of course, if [Shomer] had not been so popular, his critics would not have so fiercely opposed him."[86] In his articles in *Di tsukunft*, Niger had already conceded that "I am not trying to minimize the role Shomer played in the life of the ordinary Jew, who first had to learn how to read chapbooks... Shomer, to a larger extent than Dik, pulled the greatest numbers of simple Jews to Yiddish reading..."[87] Nonetheless, Niger was eager to introduce a distinction between the history of Yiddish literature (which he implicitly understood as the history of canonical texts) and the history of Yiddish reading: "Shomer can rightfully inscribe his name in the history of the Yiddish reading public and its taste, *but not in the history of the literature itself* [my emphasis]."[88] Niger was reacting to what he considered to be overblown revisionist claims by Shomer's daughter, such as "before he [my

---

82. *Di tsukunft* 1 (January 1947), 41–42.

83. *Di tsukunft* 2 (February 1947), 115.

84. *Di tsukunft* 1 (January 1947), 43. Niger here is referring to Ginzberg's article that appeared in *Di tsukunft* (November 1940).

85. *Di tsukunft* 2 (January 1947), 47.

86. Niger, "A naye revizye fun Shomers mishpet," *Idisher Kempfer* (March 23, 1956), 34.

87. *Di tsukunft* 1 (January 1947), 47.

88. Niger, "A naye revizye," 33, 35.

father] started writing, there was no such thing as the Yiddish 'reading masses.'"[89] Niger responded in frustration: "It is not true that there were no readers before him. [Yankev] Dinezon's second novel *Der shvartser yungermantshik* was published in Vilna in 1877 when Shomer had not yet written his first novel. Dinezon's novel was distributed in ten thousand copies. The Yiddish masses did not need to wait for Shomer to create a reading public....Dik sold no less than one hundred thousand books in 1861 alone."[90]

To what extent was Niger's resistance to lowbrow popular fiction a reflection of a long-standing gendered and classist readings of Yiddish literary history, which privileged works by maskilic writers whose audience was composed of fellow (male) intellectuals and middle-class readers over popular writers who were read more widely by women and the impoverished masses? Parush has argued that the reading habits of Jewish women in the nineteenth century were often disregarded because of a lack of interest in their intellectual development. Women thus had the "benefit of marginality"[91] in being free to consume escapist, popular fiction published both in Yiddish and in other European languages. Such reading habits enabled secular influences to filter down to women and gain widespread currency throughout society, thus serving as an important way-station on Jewish society's road to modernity. Since many of Shomer's novels featured women who were rebelling against traditional society or young couples who were victims of its traditional values, Shomer's heroes elicited a natural response among women and the working class, who were left behind by society's religious, intellectual, and economic hierarchies. These "social groups deemed 'marginal' in terms of class and gender"[92] were the core audience of Yiddish popular fiction that Sholem Aleichem intended to co-opt as his own. By establishing the female reader as instrumental to the development of this mass Yiddish audience, Parush destabilizes and reorganizes Yiddish literary history in such a way that Shomer, rather than the maskilic Yiddish writers who constitute its early canonical figures, inevitably emerges as one of its founding fathers.

---

89. Shomer-Batshelis, *Undzer foter shomer*, 62.

90. Niger, "A naye revizye," 35. Iris Parush distinguishes between the "old reading women"—consumers of traditional Yiddish texts to whom Dik's *mayse bikhlekh* (chapbooks) appealed—and the "new reading women," who gravitated toward Shomer's escapist fiction. She thus differentiates between Shomer's "modern" (or transitional) audience and Dik's traditional one.

91. Iris Parush, "'The Whole Trouble is the Fault of the Little Story Books: Women Who Read Yiddish," *Reading Jewish Women*, 242.

92. Parush, 241.

The Soviet Debate

By far the most explosive rehearsal of the controversy emerging out *The Judgment of Shomer* occurred between the Soviet critics Avrom Veviorke and Meir Viner. Veviorke's attempts to rehabilitate Shomer were first introduced in two articles in *Di royte velt*, which he then expanded in a long essay in his volume *Revizye* (Revision).[93] Veviorke attributes Sholem Aleichem's contempt for Shomer to the class struggle between the bourgeois tastes of an emerging Yiddishist intelligentsia and the working masses. He argues that the point of departure for any analysis of Shomer ought to take into account his audience: "If Shomer himself has no worth or interest for literary research, at least...hundreds of thousands of his readers must. He was the first Yiddish writer who had (and created) a mass of readers in the fullest sense of the word....Thus, even if Shomer himself, the writer, is not of interest to us, then at least Shomer's social base must be!"[94] On the basis of demographics alone, then, Veviorke accords Shomer a central place in the canon. He adds elsewhere: "The time has come to shed new light on *The Judgment of Shomer* and to conduct a historical retrospective and rehabilitation about that which was positive in him....This can only be accomplished if we separate *The Judgment of Shomer* from his socio-historical function, if we are prepared to recognize his social optimism...despite his primitive form."[95] According to Veviorke, Shomer's writing was part of a social mission to provide a welcome distraction for the working masses from their poverty and suffering. His happy, improbable endings—the cause of so much controversy and criticism—provided joy to his readers by fulfilling the moral fantasy of allowing them to believe that goodness ultimately prevails and evil is punished. In so doing, Shomer provided "the abused servant girl" with encouragement and hope by "driving her from the kitchen to enchanted palaces."[96] In Shomer's happy endings, Veviorke sees the writer's "deep faith in the lowest classes," his commitment to the creation of a "class consciousness that must in the end set things right so that the swindler...sooner or later gets his due," and his rejection of "the epidemic of sad endings found in the newly fashionable novels that is a type of fatalism which he checked with optimism."[97] Veviorke suggests that Sholem Aleichem's defense of aesthetic standards in *The Judgment of Shomer* was largely a distraction from the larger ideological campaign between bour-

---

93. A. Veviorke, "Shomer un Shomerizm," *Di royte velt* (August 1929), 108–120; "Shomer un Sholem Aleykhem," *Di royte velt* (October 1929), 123–128; *Revizye* (Kharkov-Kiev: Literatur un kunst, 1931).

94. *Revizye,* 7–8.

95. "Shomer un Sholem Aleykhem," 138.

96. "Shomer un Shomerizm," 115.

97. Ibid., 115.

gcois (hence reactionary) and progressive forces in contemporary Eastern European Jewish society that remained engaged in a pitched battle for the Jewish street:

> Shomer appealed to the lowest classes of the *shtetl* who sought an outlet from their social position. Sholem Aleichem came in the name of a Jewish middle class which was already entrenched in the Yehupetses [the cities], already socially and culturally on a higher level, but which was at the same time in the hold of Jewish medieval modesty....Shomer represented youth and servant-girls whereas Sholem Aleichem represented students of Torah and pious virgins, the learned householders to whom his theory of...the Jewish novel appealed.[98]

Veviorke here probes the link between the development of Yiddish proletarian literature and *shund*. He sees Shomer as a critical "transfer station" for nineteenth-century Yiddish literature whose "rails lead to proletarian literature in one direction and to petit-bourgeois literature in the other."[99] Whereas Shomer and later proletarian writers shared the same social base and offered a vision of revolutionary societal change, Sholem Aleichem "demanded that a Jewish literary work contain a Jewish idea, *yidishkeyt* (Jewishness) as his class interpreted it."[100] Veviorke explains: "[since] Shomer was the liberator of the masses from the Jewish plutocracy and the rabbis,"[101] "the householders, who saw it as their duty to protect the Jewish vineyard, wanted to annihilate his influence and trumped up a trial against him."[102] Veviorke's central claim, then, was that the fight waged by Sholem Aleichem against Shomer was not based on principles of literary quality at all. Rather, it reflected an ideological dispute between the muted class struggle inherent in Shomer's brand of escapist pulp fiction and Sholem Aleichem's own establishment values.[103]

---

98. "Shomer un Sholem Aleykhem," 129.

99. *Revizye*, 8.

100. Ibid., 60.

101. Ibid., 54.

102. Ibid., 56.

103. For more on Veviorke's understanding of the way petit-bourgeois tastes determined the borders of the emerging Yiddish canon, see his essay "Arop mitn kleynbirglekhn kheyrem" (Away with the Petit-Bourgeois Ban), April 10, 1927. My summary above ignores other aspects of Veviorke's close literary analysis, in which he attempts to deconstruct many of Sholem Aleichem's critiques. For instance, he accords great significance to Shomer's early stories, especially those in the series featuring the beggar Yudke Shmerkes, which "have no connection to *shund*....Among them are several that have great literary, historical, and cultural worth, with portraits of characters from Jewish life back then...and sharp folk-humor and biting satire directed against those with status and power....It was not an accident that they were loved by the so-called lower classes and hated in respectable society. Yudke told stories that he

Veviorke's defense of Shomer prompted a swift and harsh response by the noted Soviet critic Meir Viner. In two articles published in Moscow's *Emes* in February 1932, then at a symposium of the Institute for Jewish Proletarian Culture (April 25–30, 1932), and finally in a long essay in the volume *Problems of Criticism*,[104] Viner asks: "Is Shomer really a writer whose rehabilitation ought to be connected to the demands of great Bolshevik art?"[105] Offended by Veviorke's suggestion that Shomer and his school could be seen as precursors of proletarian literature, Viner argues that Shomer's happy endings and unbelievable plots were themselves reactionary because they addicted the working class to an escapist brand of pulp fiction that promoted the lowest aesthetic standard of "*shmireray*" (scribbling)[106] and diverted attention away from class struggle: "The struggle on behalf of Shomer is a struggle on behalf of trash (*shund*) in our contemporary proletarian literature. And the fight against the rehabilitation of *shund* is a fight against such trashy contraband in our proletarian cultural revolution."[107] He adds: "The happy endings are an example of the reactionary tendencies of the petit-bourgeoisie of that time. They had the function of dampening the thought of the masses, and halting the development of social consciousness among workers....Trashy literature has a similar function today in capitalist countries."[108] Though Viner admits that Sholem Aleichem's program for the development of the "Jewish novel" contained within it a "reactionary nationalistic streak wedded to national 'originality'...one must also recognize in it the struggle for the realistic novel of self-criticism that stood against both thievery from other sources and "trashy [*shundish*]

---

heard from the people, funny and tragic stories [about the abuses of the rich]." ("Shomer un shomerizm," 109, 110) Elsewhere, he claims that the attack on Shomer's use of Germanisms was overblown, given that many of Shomer's works were composed in a folk-language that was "juicy and popular" and that ultimately enriched the language ("Shomer un shomerizm," 112). Although many Yiddish writers employed Germanisms in their writing, Veviorke asserts that Sholem Aleichem chooses only to criticize Shomer. He then implies that Sholem Aleichem is guilty of hypocrisy, given that his own works are filled with Slavicisms.

104. Meir Viner, "Far marksistisher revizye—kegn kleynbirglekhe legendes (Pre-Marxist Revisions—Against Petit-Bourgeois Legends)," *Emes* (February 2, 1932), 2; (February 5, 1932), 4; "Materialn tsu A. Veviorke's Shomer-legende (Materials on A. Veviorke's Shomer Legend," in *Problemes fun kritik*, ed. M. Viner and A. Gurshteyn (Moscow: Emes, 1933).

105. *Emes* (February 2, 1932), 2.

106. "Vegn Kh. Veviorke's *Revizye* (About Comrade Veviorke's *Revision*)," *Farn leninishn etap in der literatur-kritik* (Kiev: Notes from a Plenary of the Literary Section, 1932), 47.

107. "Materialn," 240.

108. "Vegn Kh. Veviorke's *Revizye*," 49.

attempts to polish palaces of fantasy."[109] Viner rejects Veviorke's distinction between a "good" Shomer, represented by a handful of early short stories, and the bulk of his literary production, which was represented by his sentimental romances. He cites Shomer's own words from the introduction to his novel *Der kheyrem* (1892) ("I do not write for you [the reader], but rather for your money"[110]) as evidence that he was a crass opportunist whose works "have no ideological or artistic worth" and who deserves to remain in the "garbage pail of history."[111] The dispute between Veviorke and Viner demonstrates that Soviet critics were just as divided among themselves as were their Yiddishist colleagues. Both groups used the contest between Sholem Aleichem and Shomer to work through ongoing ambivalences about the place and function of popular fiction and the way they related to contested narratives about the borders of the Yiddish canon.

A Modernist Intervention

The most sophisticated artistic effort to rehabilitate Shomer in the interwar period was undertaken by the American Yiddish modernist poet and literary critic Yankev Glatshteyn in his poem "Shomer"[112] (1930) and in his essay "Unzer elter feter Shomer" (Our Great Uncle Shomer).[113] That these works appeared on the anniversaries of Shomer's death suggests that Glatshteyn imagined them as revisionist interventions designed to shift the terms of critical discourse about Shomer.

"Shomer" was composed in the same period as another Glatshteyn poem of literary homage, "Moyshe leybs kol,"[114] dedicated to the memory of the modernist troubadour Moyshe Leyb Halpern. Though Glatshteyn is interested in exploring creative debts in both, the focus of "Moyshe leybs kol" was on the creative personality of Halpern, whereas "Shomer" was more concerned with exploring the bond between its subject and his readers. What did a leading modernist poet of interwar New York have in common with

---

109. "Materialn," 261.

110. Ibid., 236.

111. Ibid., 262.

112. Yankev Glatshteyn, "Shomer," *Undzer bukh* 4:4 (October 1930), 97–99; republished in *Inzikh* (1934), *Yidishtaytshn* (Warsaw: Brzoza, 1937), 70–72, and *Fun mayn gantser mi* (New York, 1956), 278–279. References to the poem are from the version published in *Yidishtaytshn*. For more on the poem, see readings by Janet Hadda, *Yankev Glatsteyn* (Boston: Twayne Publishers, 1980), 54–56 and Avrom Novershtern, "In di videranandn fun yidishn modernizm," *Yivo bleter* 1 (1991), 199–248.

113. "Unzer elter feter Shomer," *Morgn zhurnal* (24 November 1940); republished in Glatshteyn's *Prost un poshet* (New York, 1978), 130–134 and in Shomer-Batshelis, *Undzer foter Shomer*, 223–227. All citations here are from the reprint of the article in *Prost un poshet*.

114. See *Fun mayn gantser mi*, 276–277.

the literature's most legendary transgressor against literary propriety? It was one thing for modernists to seek out and creatively betray folk sources, quite another to seek kinships with accused peddlers of trash fiction. Nevertheless, in the same way that Sholem Aleichem's *The Judgment of Shomer* was more about Sholem Aleichem's efforts to eke out a place for his own brand of writing as it was about the accused, so too was Glatshteyn's poem as much a reflexive vehicle through which he sought to comment on the condition of Yiddish in America and the fate of his own modernist enterprise as it was about its subject.

The poem opens by drawing our attention to Shomer's style, both through its inflated, Germanized diction ("Der mond bashtralt mit varer libe dos shtikl mer...") and the overly sentimentalized atmosphere it creates.[115] At first, the diction seems designed to mock Shomer, especially when the speaker shifts in the second line to a more colloquial contemporary Yiddish. This linguistic destabilization poses an immediate interpretive challenge. Is it meant to ridicule Shomer by playing up his style, or to call attention to different registers of language, breaking down distinctions between appropriate and "inappropriate" Yiddish, a favorite modernist technique? Glatshteyn confuses matters further by blurring the boundary between fantasy and reality, as when the speaker compares himself in the opening stanza to an "absurd hero of yours," a self-description that seems to make him as unbelievable as one of Shomer's sentimental and unbelievable fictional creations. At one and the same time, the poem seems to mock Shomer's style and identify with it. Though Glatshteyn was only thirty-four when "Shomer" first appeared, the speaker's references to his age ("these temples of mine are turning gray") and to the performative burden of the contemporary Yiddish writer ("I am breaking from the exertion / of playing the prince among your maids and teamsters..."; "I walked on stilts through the Jewish street, wore a dress coat and top hat and said G'day, all in order to perfume the stench...") point to an artist who feels himself prematurely anachronistic.[116] The poet-

---

115. Novershtern disputes Janet Hadda's suggestion that Glatshteyn's poem was an intervention into the aforementioned dispute between Veviorke and Viner. Though Veviorke's articles about Shomer in *Di royte velt* (1929) may have influenced Glatshteyn, "Shomer" was composed before the debate between the Soviet critics was published. Rather, Novershtern posits that Glatshteyn may have been provoked more by Veviorke's harsh criticism of his own *Inzikh* (Introspectivist) modernist poetic group. By calling attention in the poem to Shomer's inflated diction and his fantastic plots, Glatshteyn argues that *Inzikh* is the inheritor of this interest in language play and resistance to realism. See Novershtern, 247–248 (n35).

116. As early as Glatshteyn's maiden collection of poems in 1921, we find hints (as in the poem "Arteriosclerosis" or in the section "Passing") of the young poet's fear of being devoured by forces beyond his control. See also Jeffrey Shandler's discussion of postvernacular Yiddish in his *Adventures in Yiddishland: Postvernacular Language and Culture* (University of California, 2005) in which he suggests that well before the

ic persona that emerges through the speaker allows Glatshteyn to external-
ize his own creative pressures and anxieties, as when he constructs a neologism around the very subject of the poem, *shund*: "Ikh hob shoyn bald
durkhgeshundevet mayn lebn" (I've already trashed my way through my
life). This gesture exposes the fear that his own modernist experimentation
might meet the same fate as Shomer's popular fantasies. At the same time
that the poet-speaker casts himself as an outlandish figure ("Don Quixotic,
like a hero of yours"), he identifies with "one of the heroes of your romances in two parts" because the modernist enterprise strives for a similar escapist experience. What, Glatshteyn teases us, could be more quixotic, more
beyond belief, more outrageous, than a Yiddish high-modernist in America?

The imagined bond between Shomer's sentimental fantasies and Glatshteyn's modernist escapism allows the poet-speaker to acclaim Shomer as
"liber, gotzeltiger elter-feter mayner" (dear, blessed, great uncle of mine).
By inviting Shomer back into the founding family of Yiddish literature, Glatshteyn evokes and then expands the borders of the family constellation set
up by Sholem Aleichem when he proclaimed Abramovitsh the grandfather
of modern Yiddish literature and himself its legitimate heir as grandson
(Peretz was referred to by a later critic as "the father of another literary family"). Since there is a distinction between a grandfather as an idealized figure
and the progenitor of a direct line of descendants, and a fun-loving uncle
who may provide occasional relief from propriety, the speaker's public celebration of his filial relations with Shomer marks a revision of the Yiddish
meta-narrative away from the canonical grandfather-grandson myth to an
extended family of cousins. By adding this link to the founding genealogy of
Yiddish, Glatshteyn portrays Shomer as an influence (conscious or not) on
all later Yiddish writers. In this, Glatshteyn himself may have been influenced by the Russian formalist critic Victor Shklovsky, who, in 1923, moved
away from a linear approach to defining the dynamics of literary influence
by suggesting that "in the history of art the legacy is transmitted not from
father to son, but from uncle to nephew."[117] Ultimately what this suggests
is that it is necessary to break free from the established reading of canons by
offering counter-canons. Glatshteyn's poetic homage to Shomer as uncle
underlines just how knotty and convoluted literary dynamics are, and seeks
nothing less than to trace the origins of his brand of Yiddish modernism
back to *shund*, since both ultimately reject the requirement (embraced by
Abramovitsh and Sholem Aleichem) that Yiddish literature represent Jewish
reality:

Holocaust, Yiddish writers were self-consciously obsessed with the fate of the
language.

117. Cited by V. Erlich, *Russian Formalism: History-Doctrine* (The Hague, 1965), 260.

Like you, I wanted to flee from *Fishke the Lame*.
You, conjuror, beat the stone of Jewish life
And out flowed the hot tears of warm,
unhappy servant-girls far away from home,
of the orphans, poor things, who moistened your golden pages.
Those who were repressed, humiliated
by the boss in the silken caftan,
kissed and fondled in the dark.
Along with the holy Sabbath, you provided a little peace
for their tired, worn-out feet.
They sat in the corner, and read with their lips, like mutes,
and sobbed and dreamed of true love.
O comfort giver, transformer of wretched days and nights,
you blew incense into the stew-filled air and ennobled those cursed days
with the angel-pure heart of your hero...

Glatshteyn here embraces Shomer's anti-mimetic thematic while also sketching a portrait of Shomer's readership and the social function of his writing. He imagines Shomer sacrificing his potential as a serious writer for the sake of his audience, evidence of a true people's artist. The poem forces recognition that Shomer's work was a refuge for his readers, especially women who were overworked and without means of social advancement. Thus, Shomer's *shund* was not the corrosive, destructive force imagined by Sholem Aleichem, but rather provided a form of cultural resistance from the vagaries of daily life. The speaker's rejection of realist texts depicting Jewish poverty such as Abramovitsh's *Fishke the Lame* (1869/1888) is an aversion to allowing Jewish social reality to define the boundaries of Yiddish literature and the imagination of its readers. He identifies with Shomer's ability to dampen the stench of reality with the perfumed "incense" of his chapbooks. Far from being an enemy of the people, as Sholem Aleichem would have it, Shomer, through his decision to provide an escape to those who were economically and physically abused by the Jewish establishment, was "a comfort-giver" and leader to his generation. The therapeutic function of escapist fiction here is celebrated as serving the emotional needs of the people, while at the same time laying the groundwork for a non-mimetic Yiddish literary aesthetics of which Glatshteyn's modernism is a direct descendant.

As the poem eventually reveals, the speaker's concern about the relevance of the Yiddish writer in America is symbiotically related to the disappearance of the Yiddish reader, "our dead inheritance." If Shomer was responsible, as some critics have suggested, for the creation of a mass readership, then his excision from the canon marked the beginning of the end of this same popular audience. When Shomer followed his own readers across the Atlantic, he unwittingly participated in a process that would, within a generation, witness the disappearance of a mass audience for Yiddish culture as the children of these immigrants adjusted to their condition as

English-speaking Americans. For Glatshteyn, the evaporation of new, young sources of Yiddish readers was not only a sign of sociological transformation but of moral redefinition as well. While Shomer's female reader could only fantasize about true love when stealing away with one of his potboilers on the Sabbath, her granddaughters in America no longer need Shomer because in America they were free to act upon their amorous desires: "Ober dayne dinstmeydn zenen shoyn mer nisht umgliklekh / · zey hobn gehey ratetet - / un zeyere tekhter varelibn zikh oyf griltsndikn english in di oyto-mobiln." (But your servant-girls are no longer unhappy -/ they married up - / and their daughters practice true love in grating English in automobiles.) Glatshteyn passes moral judgment through his diction. He invents the ironic verb "varelibn zikh" (to indicate a fleeting sexual encounter), which contrasts sharply with the purity of the poem's opening line (in which Shomer's readers dream, if sentimentally, of old-fashioned true love under the moonlight). Glatshteyn suggests that the social and material improvement resulting in the move across the ocean was accompanied by a betrayal of the values of Jewish modesty. Where Shomer's chapbooks provided innocent escapist fantasy, he is no longer relevant because the subsequent, not-so-innocent generations of young Jewish readers can act out their desires without him. Furthermore, the choice here to replace the more intimate Yiddish term for marriage "khasene gehat" with the Germanism "geheyratetet" underscores the desire of young Jews in America to "marry up," not only out of poverty but perhaps, more snobbishly, out of Jewishness as well. More to the point, to the speaker's ear it is not Yiddish that jars one's sensibilities but English, now a symbol of cheap arriviste mores. From the poem's perspective, immigrant English has displaced Yiddish as the new jargon of an American Jewish life, which privileges self-gratification over self-refinement, individualism over community. Glatshteyn implies that Yiddish only functions as a meaningful language for modern Jews so long as they behave and think of themselves as Jews. Once this self-consciousness is gone, Germanisms are poetically invoked to symbolize the new idiom of the culturally and morally deracinated. Shomer often invoked Germanisms in his fiction to mock the assimilationist pretensions of an aspiring Jewish "high society" (he rarely used them to characterize the way simple Jews or women spoke). Glatshteyn builds upon this legacy to show the ways in which language signals a move from Jewish to "Gentile" behavior and self-definition. What such comments provoke is the understanding that Yiddish readers bear part of the responsibility for Shomer having been given an ignominious "donkey's burial," because a people that does not honor its writers ultimately lacks self-respect. This speaks directly to Glatshteyn's anxieties about the fate of the Yiddish writer in America. Indeed, the speaker predicts that he will suffer the same fate as his great-uncle. If Shomer's popular readership evaporated as the tastes of Yiddish readers grew more sophisticated in the 1890s, then the danger to Glatshteyn is from the opposite end of the spectrum. He sees

threats both within and without, as Yiddish literary high culture (and especially his brand of Yiddish modernism) finds itself challenged not only from
a lack of serious Yiddish readers, but also from the communist Yiddish left
via *Proletpen* ("they are building gallows for us all/...and mocking us with
their red tongues"). By labeling those who besiege him because his modernist verse is not enough engaged in the class struggle for the Jewish street as
modern-day Haidamaks,[118] he transforms them from the radicals they imagine themselves to be into the cultural reactionaries they are.

The poet-speaker's imagined relations with Shomer are a natural out-
growth of their shared experience of being labeled irrelevant in their
respective ages. If early Yiddish critics scolded Shomer's work for being
nothing more than fantasy, this charge is internalized by Glatshteyn to such
a degree that the modernist Yiddish poet in America feels himself to be no
less an absurdity than Shomer's outrageous protagonists. Both are, so to
speak, beyond the pale. This allows for the poem's remarkable concluding
tribute to Shomer as "Du, unzer eynuneyntsiker / yidisher naiver un far ale
tsaytn eybiker modernist" (You, our one and only / Yiddish naïf and for all
time eternal modernist). While the yoking together of naïveté with modernism may seem odd, it underlines the extent to which Glatshteyn used Shomer to prompt a reconsideration of distinctions between high and low. Was
it Glatshteyn's modernism that was naïve in remaining true to itself despite
the absence of an audience and a surplus of sentimentality? Or was it American Jewry that was naïve in believing that, in translating itself out of its Jewishness, it might just realize the happy endings that Shomer had once dan-
gled before Yiddish readers?

By posthumously inviting Shomer into the modernist fold, Glatshteyn
legitimates Shomer's precedent of inventing fantastic scenarios without any
concern for social mimesis in his writing. Shomer's resistance to transforming his art into a vehicle for discussing the politics of his age was a model
that the modernists of Glatshteyn's generation appropriated for themselves.
Having avoided the constraints of ideology and the realities of contemporary society in his writing, Glatshteyn shows himself to be a kindred spirit
with Shomer in so far as both resisted politics and literary realism from
opposite ends of the high-low continuum. Glatshteyn's counter-narrative of
Yiddish literary history opens with the sentimentalist Shomer and concludes with his great-nephew, the Yiddish modernist poet in New York.

Shklovsky's uncle-nephew theory, first adopted in the ode "Shomer,"
was so provocative to Glatshteyn that he expanded on it in the essay "Our
Great Uncle Shomer" (1940). His argument begins with a meditation on the
ways in which time is an even greater judge than human beings in its ability
to heal old wounds, imagining that Sholem Aleichem and Shomer probably

---

118. Haidamaks were roving bands of armed peasants in Polish Ukraine responsible for
      pogroms against Jews in the seventeenth century.

buried the hatchet long ago in the next world while critics continue their partisan bickering here on earth. He then attempts to provide a comparative perspective on the controversy by referencing another contemporaneous literary controversy of the late nineteenth century, that launched by Mark Twain against James Fenimore Cooper. In 1895 (seven years after the appearance of *The Judgment of Shomer*) Twain—the American Sholem Aleichem—published "Fenimore Cooper's Literary Sins," in which he attempted to tarnish his colleague's reputation by accusing him of corrupting literary taste by providing unrealistic characterization, plots, and dialogue, and demonstrating a lack of original style. Glatshteyn's audience might have recognized these charges as remarkably similar to those that Sholem Aleichem had used to indict Shomer. Despite the similarities between *The Judgment* and "Fenimore Cooper's Literary Sins," Glatshteyn observes that more than forty years later, the American literary canon proved itself self-confident and elastic enough to make room for both Twain and Fenimore Cooper within its ranks of leading nineteenth-century writers. Surely the Yiddish canon, Glatshteyn intimates, could eke out an honorary footstool for Shomer: "Without a doubt, this phenomenal creator who authored the best-sellers of his day cannot be chased entirely from our literary palace. Just the opposite: in a greater literature, such an interesting figure would already have rows of monographs and biographies [about him] that would provide a helpful portrait of Shomer in the context of the generation that devoured his novels."[119] Like other critics before him, Glatshteyn pressed his case for Shomer's rehabilitation through an acknowledgment of his importance in having created a broad, popular base of readers that extended beyond the ranks of intellectuals whose maskilic fiction rarely reached beyond that rarefied group: "Yiddish literature in his time was masculine. Shomer also spoke to the Yiddish woman."[120] By calling attention to the relationship between gender and readership, Glatshteyn casts Shomer as an early populist who liberated Yiddish fiction from a male elite and helped to transform it into a truly popular forum of national culture.

---

119. "Unzer elter feter Shomer," *Prost un poshet*, 131.

120. Ibid. Niger, who was at the forefront of those resisting rehabilitation of Shomer, sharply contested Glatshteyn's conclusions about Shomer and the creation of the female reader: "From a historical standpoint, this is simply incorrect. [I.M.] Dik spoke to Yiddish women much earlier. It was Dik—not Shomer—who was the first to create both a [Yiddish reader] and a [Yiddish] woman reader." Niger went on to suggest that Glatshteyn's belief that Yiddish literature owes Shomer a debt is misguided. "The same thing was said by Leyeles. But both are at such a distance from the Yiddish popular reader—from Shomer's reader—that they really cannot judge...[this is a type of] reverse snobbism. It contains within it a kind of literary slumming." Niger, "Shomers mishpet—af Sholem Aleykhemen," *Di tsukunft* (January 1947), 43.

Glatshteyn contended that Sholem Aleichem cooked up an attack on Shomer not so much because he was offended by what he was producing, but because he wanted ownership over the readers that Shomer had created. By discrediting Shomer as a writer, the young upstart hoped to gain a ready-made mass market for his own career and to reinvent himself as a "folks-shrayber" (a writer for the people). Glatshteyn's essay suggests that Sholem Aleichem (and his defenders) did not fully appreciate that the tension between high and popular fiction is a necessity for a healthy literary system, and that by attempting to eradicate figures such as Shomer, Yiddish literature now belatedly was paying the price: "Where is he now, this mature, intelligent, ideal reader, who hungers and thirsts after our words with passion? How did we allow that reader to slip away?"[121] The result of the campaign by the self-styled guardians of the canon against Shomer and popular fiction demonstrated an ongoing disconnect between the elite and the street over the function of literature. For the latter, literature is a form of entertainment and escapism, whereas for the former it is an aesthetic calling. Ultimately, Glatshteyn—whose modernist lyrics were certainly not intended for unsophisticated readers—recognized that the sustenance of a literary high culture appreciative of the type of writing he practiced depended on the concomitant development of a mass base from which to cultivate readers. According to Glatshteyn, the delegitimization of this mass, consumerist Yiddish-speaking base through attacks on lowbrow popular fiction did not improve the fate of Yiddish literature but placed it in precarious danger: "Shomer never pretended to enter the salon where intellectuals sat playing chess, debating the state of the world. But if you watched closely you might notice some of those very same chess players sneaking into the kitchen for a break with the maids to play out Shomer's fantastic yarns until dawn."[122] He deflates the pretensions of the guardians of high canon by accusing them of hypocrisy; though they criticize Shomer's works as beneath their dignity in public, they still enjoy its forbidden pleasures in private. Ironically, then, it was the modernist Glatshteyn who hoped to provoke renewed attention to the imperative of popular fiction, both in Shomer's day and our own, as a necessary component of a healthy republic of letters.[123]

---

121. "Unzer elter feter Shomer," 134.

122. Ibid., 134.

123. Of course, Glatshteyn was well aware that the thinning of a market for sophisticated Yiddish literature could not be blamed on elite attitudes toward mass tastes, but was more the result of linguistic assimilation in both America and Eastern Europe, the Russification of Soviet Jewry, and the politicization of the Jewish street. In the same way that Shomer's readers were comforted by his fantastic tales that resisted reality, so too does Glatshteyn's explanation of his own fall into irrelevance draw on a kind of sentimental comfort that ignores the more uncomfortable social realities of the moment.

Though Ruth Wisse's *The Modern Jewish Canon*—the study that inspired this festschrift—has very little to say about sub-canonical (or popular) Jewish literature,[124] I suggest that it too is part of the process that began in earnest with *The Judgment of Shomer,* when Sholem Aleichem initiated conversation about the legitimate borders of Yiddish fiction. *The Judgment* provided her—and the rest of us—with a rudimentary (if imperfect) vocabulary for the Jewish canonizing project that anticipated her attention to the link between language and identity, and the universal resonances of Jewish particularism. When the editors of this volume approached her about publishing a collection of essays in her honor, Wisse's natural instinct was to propose that we organize it around the theme of argument.[125] That the argument initiated by Sholem Aleichem 120 years ago remains relevant to the way we understand the modern Jewish canon suggests that the jury of *The Judgment of Shomer* is still deliberating.

---

124. The exception to this is her discussion of Leon Uris' *Exodus,* the best-selling American novel about the birth of Israel. Wisse shows that even *Exodus*—despite its sentimental romance and clichéd characters—was serious about popularizing the story of a transformative moment in contemporary Jewish experience, something that Sholem Aleichem accuses Shomer's novels of failing to do. Jewish literary history would benefit from increased attention to the modern Jewish best-seller in order to complement Wisse's study with the contours of a popular canon.

125. Wisse has suggested elsewhere that argument is a central organizing feature of modern Jewish texts. See "Two Jews Talking: A View of Modern Yiddish Literature," *Prooftexts* (January 1984): 35–48.

The Judgment of Shomer
or
The Jury Trial of All of Shomer's Novels

Transcribed word for word
by Sholem Aleichem

Translated from the Yiddish and annotated by Justin Cammy

Berdichev
Jacob Sheftil, Publisher
1888

Strike the capitals so that the thresholds quake.[1]
(Amos 9:1)

Fleece the flock and the lambs tremble.
(Yiddish proverb)

My thanks to Alan Astro and Avraham Novershtern for their assistance on questions of translation. Olga Litvak, Alyssa Quint, Dara Horn, and Ernest Benz were kind enough to read a draft of the translation and to offer their advice. Titles of works mentioned by Sholem Aleichem first appear both in Yiddish transliteration and in my English translation; subsequent mention of the same work appears only in translation. I preserved Sholem Aleichem's editorial decision to have Shomer's name appear in bold throughout the text. [JC]

1. The full verse reads: "I saw my Lord standing by the altar and He said: Strike the capitals so that the thresholds quake, and make an end of the first of them all. And I will slay the last of them with the sword; not one of them shall escape, and not one of them shall survive." (Jewish Publication Society translation)

In a large hall, at the head of a green table, sits the presiding judge, an old man. Two other magistrates are seated on either side. The prosecutor, an irascible young man with fiery eyes, is seated on one side, to the left, at a small table. The defense counsel, a good-natured, spirited young man, is opposite him, to the right, also at a small table. The secretary is a little bit farther away at a large table, upon which are scattered dozens of the *"most interesting novels by Shomer,"* and also various works by Abramovitsh,[2] Linetski,[3] Dik,[4] Spektor,[5] Bukhbinder,[6] Bekerman,[7] Ulrikh Kalmus,[8] Tsim-

---

2. Sholem Yankev Abramovitsh (183[6]-1917), widely acknowledged as one of the three classic writers of modern Yiddish fiction and also one of the founders of modern Hebrew fiction. Sholem Aleichem affectionately called him the "grandfather" of modern Yiddish literature. He is often referred to by the name of his most famous literary creation, Mendele Moykher Sforim (Mendele the Bookpeddler).

3. Yitskhok Yoel Linetski (1839–1915), Yiddish novelist, essayist and translator. His picaresque novel *Dos poylishe yingl* (The Polish Boy), which first appeared serially in *Kol-mevaser* (1867), was a popular and biting satire of Hasidism. Along with Avrom Goldfaden (see note 14), he published the weekly *Yisrolik* (1875–76), which included his unfinished novel *Der litvisher bokher* (The Lithuanian Boy). *Der vorem in khreyn* (The Worm in Horseradish), a sequel to *Dos poylishe yingl,* appeared in volumes 1 and 2 of Sholem Aleichem's *Di yudishe folksbibliotek* (1888–89). Linetski also published several collections of feuilletons.

4. Isaac Meir Dik (1807–93), the first popular writer of Yiddish fiction, and one of its most productive. At the height of his fame, his chapbooks (*mayse-bikhlekh*) sold tens of thousands of copies and were eagerly consumed by ordinary Jewish men and women.

5. Mordecai Spektor (1858–1925), Yiddish novelist, journalist, and editor. His first novel, *A roman on a nomen* (A Novel Without a Title), was published serially in *Yudishes folksblat* in 1883. His second novel, *Der yidisher muzhik* (The Jewish Peasant, 1884) was influenced by the Zionist ideology of Hibat Zion and advocated that the Jews return to productive labor. Later, Spektor become the editor of *Der hoyz-fraynd* (The Family Friend, 1888–89), and edited (along with I.L. Peretz and David Pinski) the first issue of the anthology *Yontev bletlekh* (Holiday Pages, 1894).

6. Avrom Yitskhok Bukhbinder (186?-97), journalist; author of numerous novels in the style of Shomer, and several works on the condition of Jewish pioneers in the Land of Israel, including *Vi geyt es unzer brider in Palestine* (The Condition of Our Brethren in Palestine, 1888).

7. Shimon Bekerman (dates unknown), author of such popular novels such as *Meshiekhs tsaytn oder der freylekher Tishebov* (Messianic Times, or the Happy Day of Mourning, 1887); *Di shreklikhe nakht* (The Terrifying Night, 1887); *Di kortn-varferke oder di opgeshosene hant* (The Tarot Card Reader, or the Chopped-Off Hand, 1888); beginning in 1883, editor of the satirical journal *Der ployder zak* (The Charlatan).

8. Ulrikh Kalmus (dates unknown), Yiddish journalist, author of literary sketches,

bler,[9] Oyzer Bloshteyn,[10] Marakhovski,[11] and others. Next to the lawyer, under arrest, on the bench reserved for the accused, sits the defendant **Shomer**, a man who is not very old or very young, not very dark or very fair, not totally ugly but also not very handsome. Opposite him, on twelve stools, are the twelve jurors, each representing a different segment of society, rich and poor, young and old.

The hall is packed. The audience consists of simple Jews, common peo ple who do not understand any language except Yiddish.[12] It also is full of married women, girls, half-educated young ladies, and schoolboys.

It is so quiet in the room that one can hear the flies buzzing! All eyes are fixed on **Shomer**, the accused, who comports himself smugly, like a man

and dramatist, most productive during the 1870s and 1880s. His writings appeared in such publications as *Kol-mevaser* and *Yisrolik* (edited by Linetski). His play *A zeltener bris un a genarte khasene* (A Rare Circumcision and a Fraudulent Wedding, Odessa, 1871; Warsaw, 1882) was an anti-Hasidic farce composed in the earthy dialect of Polish Jewry.

9. Khayim Bunim Tsimbler (dates unknown), well-known wedding musician and performer, and author of several collections of chapbooks, including *Di gener-alshe, oder der puster benyokhed* (The General's Wife, or The Only Son, 1887).

10. Oyzer Bloshteyn (1840–98), in his day one of the most popular writers of trashy Yiddish novels. From 1878, he published more than fifty novels and stories. He vigorously defended Yiddish against accusations that it was nothing more than a Jewish jargon. He also published a Russian-Yiddish dictionary, and Russian trans-lations of the weekday and High Holiday prayer books, as well as of the Passover Haggadah.

11. Moyshe Marakhovski (dates unknown), author of several collections of satiric poetry, including *Der elnter yosem* (The Lonely Orphan, 1872); *Hagode in hayn-tiker tsayt* (The Contemporary Haggadah, 1885), and *Yontevdike lider: a kritik in ferzn fun dem lebn* (Holiday Poems: A Verse-Critique of Life, 1886).

12. Sholem Aleichem uses the term *zhargon*, or "jargon," throughout *The Judgment of Shomer* to refer to Yiddish. This was an accepted term for Yiddish in his day. However, in certain places where Sholem Aleichem did not intend the pejorative connotations that the term carries with it today, I elected to translate *zhargon* as Yiddish. Dan Miron explains: "...it was only at the end of the nineteenth century and in the twentieth century that the language...had become universally known as Yiddish—the language of the Jews (*Yidn*). In the previous century it had first been called *Yidish-daytsh* (Judeo-German) and, later (until the time of Sholem Aleichem and Peretz), *Zhargon* ("jargon"), the former name designating the language as a corrupt German spoken by Jews and the latter degrading it further to the class of sublanguages, incoherent mechanisms of linguistic communica-tion, gibberation," *A Traveler Disguised: The Rise of Modern Yiddish Fiction in the Nineteenth Century* (1996), 47. Max Weinreich notes that though zhargon was used by proponents of enlightenment (*maskilim*) pejoratively, Yiddish writ-ers such as Sholem Aleichem employed it neutrally until the language wars between Hebrew and Yiddish rendered the term entirely pejorative. See *History of the Yiddish Language* (Chicago 1980), 315–27.

who is aware of his own importance. The secretary rises and begins to read out the indictment:

"It has been nearly twenty years since Yiddish began to show signs of becoming a language, to stretch its limbs and demonstrate some forward movement. Three giants in Poland[13]–Abramovitsh, Linetski, Goldfaden[14]–and Isaac Meir Dik in Lithuania boldly stood Yiddish on its own two feet, and carried it over from the language of Bible translations in the *Tsenerene*[15] to a living literature, from the *Bove-mayse*[16] to the novel, from the hasidic hagiography of *Shivhei ha-Besht*[17] to poetry, from the supplicatory prayers of *tkhines*[18] to satire. These four giants, these great individuals, forged a new language and breathed the European spirit into our old jargon. And masses of new readers sprung up! The public took up Yiddish with enthusiasm, with all the passion of the Jewish people. There was barely a Jewish home in which people were not clutching their sides with laughter, reading Linetski's *Dos poylishe yingl* (The Polish Boy),[19] published in the

13. Sholem Aleichem's reference to Poland and Lithuania in this line does not refer to the current borders of these countries but to a basic north-south dichotomy in the geography of Jewish Eastern Europe under the Russian tsars. Poland included much of Jewish Ukraine (and was seen to be far more under the influence of Hasidism), while Lithuania included significant parts of Belarus (and was understood to be the territory of Misnagdism, or rationalist tradition).

14. Abraham (Avrom) Goldfaden (1840–1905), Yiddish dramatist, widely acknowledged as the founder of modern Yiddish theater and a celebrated folk poet. In describing the modernization of Yiddish literature Sholem Aleichem deliberately leaves the Yiddish theater unmentioned, a telling sign of his bourgeois literary tastes.

15. *Tsenerene* (lit. "Come and See," 1622), popular Yiddish adaptation of narrative sections of the Bible. It was the most significant book for generations of Ashkenazic Jewish women.

16. *Bove-mayse*, Yiddish expression for a fantastic or unbelievable tale. Sholem Aleichem is referring here to the Yiddish chivalric romance by Elijah Levita (Elye Bokher), *Bove-bukh* (1507). Several chapbook editions of *Bove-bukh* appeared later under the title *Bove-mayse*. Over time, the proximity of "Bove" to "bobe" (the Yiddish word for grandmother) transformed *Bove-mayse* from the title of a specific work in the pre-modern Yiddish literary canon into a common expression for the types of stories grandmothers tell, or old wives' tales.

17. *Shivhei ha-Besht* (In Praise of the Baal Shem Tov), hagiographic tales first published in 1814–15 about the life and spiritual achievements of Israel ben Eliezer Ba'al Shem Tov (c.1700–60), the founder of Hasidism.

18. *Tkhines*, Yiddish supplicatory prayers recited mainly by Ashkenazic women. Eastern European varieties of *tkhines* were published in small pamphlets and provide invaluable insight into women's religious lives. *Tkhines* were among the most widespread publications of Yiddish devotional literature.

19. See note 3. Alyssa Quint has argued that Sholem Aleichem shows his distance from the reading habits of the masses by overstating their interest in such manifesta-

first Yiddish newspaper *Kol-mevaser,* edited by Tsederboym;[20] did not sing the immortal sweet songs of Goldfaden; did not ingest, declaim, and perform by heart the wonderful scenes from Abramovitsh's *Di takse.*[21] In short, it was a bright moment in the history of the language, a fortunate slice of time in Jewish life in general[22] that Jews still recall with fondness.

"But bright sun brings its own dark shadows. Mushrooms sprout in the same spot as fruit trees, and one can always find thorns next to roses. In every literature, the cripple who has not succeeded in anything follows in the steps of great talent. After the most beautiful hero, after the lion, a small worm creeps in. If a great talent in the form of a genius were to exist forever and protect literature under its wings, a worm would cease to have any reason to live. Although it happens infrequently, a large worm sometimes develops out of a small worm, and its damage is so great that the public starts looking for ways to smoke it out, along with any memory of it. But this doesn't always happen so smoothly. In our case, the famous writers mentioned earlier put down their weapons, and the people gradually began to forget them.[23] At that point, small worms began to emerge from their holes.

---

tions of "highbrow" Yiddish literature. See "'Yiddish Literature for the Masses'? A Reconsideration of Who Read What in Jewish Eastern Europe," *AJS Review* 29: 1 (2005) 61–89.

20. *Kol-mevaser* (The Herald), Yiddish supplement to the first Hebrew weekly *Ha-Melits* (The Advocate). *Kol-mevaser* first appeared in 1862; from 1869–72 it was published on its own. As the first modern Yiddish paper in Russia, *Kol-mevaser* played a significant role in raising the prestige of Yiddish by demonstrating that it was more than a popular folk "jargon," and could function as a medium for modern intellectual and literary discussion. Alexander Tsederboym (1816–93), pioneering figure of the Jewish press in Russia, published *Ha-Melits,* beginning in 1860; in 1881 he began to edit the Yiddish newspaper *Yudishes folksblat.*

21. *Di takse, oder der bande shtot baley toyves* (The Meat Tax, or the Band of Community Benefactors, 1869), S.Y. Abramovitsh's satiric drama that took aim at the corruption of community leaders in Berdichev.

22. A reference to the liberalization of attitudes toward the Jews during the early reign of Tsar Alexander II (1855–81). Alexander II's ascension to the throne was a moment of great hope for Jewish enlighteners, who felt that their internal efforts at modernization of Jewish society would be reciprocated by their integration into Russian society. A wave of pogroms against Russian Jewry beginning in the 1870s and peaking in 1881–82 following the tsar's assassination destroyed the idealism of the Haskalah and marked the beginning of a chaotic period that witnessed mass Jewish emigration from the Russian empire, the disintegration of the shtetl, rapid urbanization, and the rise of modern Jewish politics.

23. A possible reference to the gap between the publication of S.Y. Abramovitsh's *Kitser masoes binyomin hashlishi* (The Abridged Travels of Benjamin the Third, 1878) and a revised version of *Dos kleyne mentshele* (The Little Man, 1879) and his drama *Der priziv* (The Draft, 1884). In that five-year period, Abramovitsh did not publish any new works in Yiddish.

They laid eggs and multiplied. All types of cockroaches, one insect after another, crept out of the corners and infected Yiddish with such ugliness that it would need to purify and cleanse itself for quite some time until it managed to return to respectability.

"Yiddish writers, writers of the people,[24] fabricators of sentimental romances came pouring forth like sand and garbage, and Yiddish was suddenly overflowing with novels. What kind of novels?! The world was flooded with them, and they dulled the literary taste of the reading public to such an extent that no one dreamt of touching anything else! But that is not the end of it. Every reader became a writer; many young good-for-nothings proclaimed themselves novelists! It was enough for anybody to read a book, a foreign novel, and soon enough he proclaimed himself a novelist. He just changes the names of the heroes, slips in a few Jewish names, and sells this "most interesting novel in four parts with an epilogue" for the price of a bagel to the latest itinerant peddler who happens by. The itinerant peddler publishes it, the young snot becomes a popular writer, a novelist, the masses accept this shoddy merchandise, and there is no stopping things.

"The greatest, the most productive, the richest of all of these cockroaches, centipedes, and worms is the so-called novelist **Shomer**, our accused.

"This fellow took it upon himself, and not as a joke, to inundate Yiddish with his unbelievable, insubstantial novels, with their wild, strange concoctions that are beneath any possible criticism, and that are as dangerous as poison to the reader. He has corrupted the sensibilities of his readers by providing them with dreadful fantasies, wild ideas, and heart-rending scenes that our people would have had no idea about had they not been exposed to them in his works.

"This became problematic for our community representatives, and they named a commission to investigate more than fifty such novels by **Shomer**. The commission came to the following conclusions:

---

24. Sholem Aleichem's repeated use of the term "folks-shrayber" (from the Russian *narodnyi*) is particularly challenging to translate. I am uncomfortable rendering it as "popular writer," if only because Sholem Aleichem did not interpret "popular" in the way we do today, as necessarily low-brow. Rather, I prefer Miron's suggestion of "writer of the people," despite its clumsiness in English: "A folks-shrayber writes for the people, about the people, and in order to educate the people while entertaining them." See *A Traveler Disguised,* 276 (n77). The translator encounters the same problem with Sholem Aleichem's frequent invocation of the concept "undzer folks-literatur" ("our literature for the people"), which he understood as literature intended for the entire population, not just for a highly educated elite. The Yiddish "folk" cannot be translated into English either as "folk" (which sounds too primitive) or as "national" (because at that time only Hebrew was understood to have the status of a "national" language). Moreover, Russian does not use the term "*narodnaia literatura*" but rather "*narodnoe tvorchestvo*" (literally, "folk creativity"), which is used as a synonym for the internationalism "folklore."

1. Almost all of his novels are, pardon the expression, stolen from foreign literatures.

2. All his novels are of the same cut.

3. This so-called novelist does not provide a realistic, authentic picture of Jewish life.

4. As a result, his novels have no connection to the Jews whatsoever.

5. These romances ignite the imagination, but provide no ethical direction, no moral.

7. They contain obscenity and cynicism.

8. They are very poorly constructed.

9. The author appears to be an ignoramus.

10. Under no circumstances should such novels be given to our schoolboys or teenage girls.

11. It would be a great act of charity if he and all of his fantastic and uncouth novels were expunged from our literature by means of serious, clear-headed criticism.

"Fifty-some novels by this so-called novelist are strewn before you on this table. They are the best manifestation of this writer's ignorance, of the ignorance of his readers, and of the silence of our critics who allow such a novelist to exist among the people."

When the secretary finished reading the indictment, the crowd began to cast glances back and forth. The presiding judge then turned to the accused and asked him if he considered himself guilty according to the terms of the indictment. To this **Shomer** responded:

"Your Honor, the entire indictment is a lie from A to Z, a total fabrication. It is the product of one of my enemies who is undoubtedly jealous of my talent, my achievements in Yiddish, and my books, which the public laps up like hot noodles. I am telling you the plain truth. Your Honor, this is all about envy. I tell you in all sincerity, it is entirely about jealousy!"

The presiding judge winked at the prosecutor, who rose and turned to the court with the following indictment:

"Honored judges and jurors! Before us sits an accused who is neither a thief, nor a bandit, nor a scoundrel. He did not commit any crimes. He did not insult anyone, cheat anyone, or reduce anyone to poverty. Yet now he is on the stand as a true offender, as a defendant. So what is this all about? What is the matter with him? In my opinion, your honors, he is guiltier than a thief, a bandit, or a killer. True, this rascal did not set off to kill with a sword, a spear, or a club. He trampled on our innocent Yiddish literature with nothing more than a pen in his hand. Slowly but surely he murdered it.

He corrupted the taste of the public. He harmed our simple readers, poor things, who are not expert enough to know the difference between good and bad literature, who lose themselves in the dark without a critic to guide them, and who cannot yet differentiate between the value of works by Abramovitsh and the garbage peddled by our accused **Shomer**. Fooling someone, stealing his money, and killing him are, in my opinion, lesser crimes than tricking an entire people, murdering an entire literature, and ruining the literary taste of thousands of readers. Because in the first case, only a single individual is harmed. But this is about the suffering of the public, of the masses, of a whole society.

"Consider what this fabricator of novels brought to our community. **Shomer** corrupted the feelings and taste of our ordinary readers to such a degree that our working men, housewives, and young women are so taken with his empty, wild, nutty novels that their minds are pulsating with his crazy fantasies. They will no longer even pick up a decent book, an ethical tract, a work with some moral direction. All they want are the kind of entanglements and intrigues, the moving and heart-stirring scenes found in **Shomer**'s "most interesting novels," in which people steal, loot in broad daylight, dig up bodies from the grave, fight, battle to the death over a beautiful brunette or over a fine blond fellow, and other such wild fantasies imported from various vapid Russian, German, or French novels by Xavier de Montépin,[25] Paul de Kock..."[26]

"Your Honor!," the accused interjected, jumping up from the bench, "Your Honor! It is a lie! All lies! My enemies have trumped up the charges because of their great jealousy, their envy of me..."

"Mr. Accused!," the chief judge interrupted, "you must not forget that in a court-room one must sit with respect. If you are not being questioned, you must remain silent and seated!"

The prosecutor continued without even casting a glance at **Shomer**.

"Paul de Kock, Dumas,[27] Ponson du Terrail,[28] and others like them... our accused steals material from these worthless writers for his clumsy novels.

---

25. Xavier de Montépin (1823–1902) authored more than twenty popular French serial novels and feuilletons; collaborated with Alexandre Dumas on *Tour de Saint-Jacques;* his novel *Simon y Maria* appeared in translation in Ladino in 1889.

26. Charles Paul de Kock (1793–1871), writer of French popular novels, many dealing with middle- to lower-class Parisian life.

27. Alexandre Dumas (1802–70), one of the most important nineteenth-century French novelists. Among his famous works are *The Count of Monte Cristo*, *The Three Musketeers*, and *The Man in the Iron Mask.*

28. Pierre Alexis, vicomte Ponson du Terrail (1829–71), a popular author of serialized fiction who began publishing in the French press in the 1850s. His nine books in the Rocambole series marked the transition between the Gothic novel and the rise of the French mystery and adventure novel.

He serves up these wretched works to the reading public who swallows them without any discretion. The people ingest this rotten food and do harm to their innards for years to come.

"I trust, honored jurors, that you are aware of the sacred purpose of literature. As every reader knows, fine literature—for instance, a decent novel drawn from real life—employs various shades to portray the positive and negative qualities of a character with the purpose of providing the reader some intimacy with man's spiritual nature. Since this kind of writing can sometimes be boring, like an ethical tract that tires the reader, writers created sublime poetry, they invented the novel, they made things up, a kind of theater in which the writer introduces his artificial heroes who speak, travel about, walk, sit, laugh, sing, cry, and so on. In order to keep the attention and interest of the reader, the writer's imagination fabricates different tales, coincidences, stories (and sometimes even very complicated ones), miracles and wonders, moving scenes that are either happy or sad and over which we pour out our tears.

"But when do the writer and his work realize their purpose? When he provides us with scenes that are recognizable to us, to which we have a connection, and that can more or less occur in real life. But when, for example, a writer tells us a story about a poker that fell in love with a shovel that then upset the jealous feather-duster, so that the latter roused all the geese and turkeys... I ask you, what benefit, what moral value, what lesson does such a tale provide? Whose heart will it touch? Who will understand it? Who will draw pleasure from it, and to whom will it cause pain? Our novelist **Shomer** indulges in fantasy to such a degree that in his universe an ordinary teacher, a *melamed*, becomes a lord; a chimney-sweep becomes a count; death becomes life and life becomes death. In his works, millions in diamonds lie around like garbage. Servant-boys and girls play out love affairs (or, as **Shomer** prefers, their "flirtations") over which they drown themselves, shoot themselves, hang themselves, and so on. In the same way that we have become accustomed to the cheerfulness of French novels, so too if you were to read one of **Shomer**'s novels would you think that Berdichev had been carried over to Paris, and that Chaim, Yosl, and Avreml are strangers to worldly affairs. They have never heard of business, a ruble, a broker, a nobleman, or rates of interest; they just wander about in search of "love." Never in their lives have Hannah, Mira, and Brayndl been made aware that in this world there are such things as a store, a shop, a tavern, Yiddish translations of the Bible—no! Hannah, Mira and Brayndl recline on soft velvet divans, with little white dogs in their arms, singing sweet, sentimental songs about "love"... But people are always fond of hearing a tall tale, and when there is no fish people will eat potatoes, and when there is nothing better they will chew on straw...That explains why the common people chew straw. That explains why ordinary Jews and simple Jewesses pick up a novel by **Shomer**. On the Sabbath day after the tsholent,[29] when one can cast aside momentarily the burden of worrying about a living, when it is possible to forget that there are such things as a shop or a store to run, a broker to whom one owes money, or a nobleman and his little lady to whom one owes homage...at that moment women, teenage boys and young girls gather round to hear one of **Shomer**'s wild, bizarre, awkward stories about the miracles and wonders of the *melamed* who is now a lord, the chimney-sweep who has become a count, the love between Yankl the blond student and Rokhl the brunette with cheeks as red as roses, and the pretty songs they sing and the passionate tears they pour out under the pale light of the moon. They experience the sighs and the moans of the unhappy lovers whose hearts are united but who suffer at the hands of their murderous parents who want to separate them, make their lives miserable, and drive them from this world."

The accused cried out again: "This is hearsay, your Honor! Pure jealousy and hatred!"

The presiding judge requested that he sit down and conduct himself with respect, and the prosecutor continued with his indictment.

"Love, honored jurors, love is an old story in literature, an ancient song! Every writer and reader understands that the best material for a novel is love, especially love among youth. It is a sacred feeling, a tender feeling, a gift from God, and without Him, without this sacred, tender feeling, we human beings would not be any better than animals. But there are many different modes and varieties of love. For instance, the love of parents for a child, and vice versa, of a child for his parents; love between brothers, sisters, and friends; love between best friends; love for all of humanity, for nature, for enlightenment, for things that are known to be good or bad. However, the love between a young man and a young woman is known to be the type of love that novelists from around the world take up. Thousands upon thousands of books have already been written about this type of love. A boy and a girl, a young man and a young woman—these are the fundamental elements in almost every novel. The young man is in love with the young woman. She is in love with him. They are in love with each other. Their hearts are united. Their souls are close. But they are torn apart, they are physically separated. Still, they seek the means through which they can quickly and easily realize their only goal in life, their only wish—to be reunited, to come together in the strongest of eternal bonds. The disputes, the struggles, the fights, the sufferings and the pleasures of this battle in pursuit of their ideal become the canvas upon which the writer designs the scenes of his novel. Just as no two places are alike, the same is true of love. Love comes into contact with all kinds of obstacles, occurs for different reasons,

---

29. Traditional hearty stew, prepared prior to the Sabbath and slowly simmered, eaten by Ashkenazic Jews on the Sabbath day after synagogue.

unfolds in miserable or happy circumstances. Here the parents are for it and there they are against it; here the groom is liked and the bride is not liked; here they encounter a plague of an uncle, a relative, a gossipy neighbor, and the whole story is turned around. Usually they cannot achieve their ultimate goal. They become full of anger and fury, tears begin to flow, disasters unfold, God help us. The groom hangs himself, the bride drowns herself, howling and grief, confusion ensues...Or, just the opposite. Everything is overcome, thank God. The bride and groom marry—Mazl tov! Congratulations!—This is how many writers conclude their novels.

"One has to be naive, like a young child, to believe that the plot of a novel is its most essential element, that the only thing that matters is whether the guy gets the girl. I told you earlier, honored jurors, that the entire purpose of literature is to illustrate the positive and negative aspects of human nature. Aside from providing us with pleasure through the plausibility of their descriptions, works by real writers and by educated novelists also provide a lesson—to each reader according to his comprehension and his abilities. In this way they ennoble our emotions, answer some of our fundamental questions regarding life, show us how it can be lived well or badly, and develop for us the finest feelings of mercy, sympathy, and humanity, and so on.

"This is relevant when speaking about the educated writer, the upstanding novelist. But we do not experience this in the works of our own accused, Mr. **Shomer**. There, on the table before you, in the novel *Der blutiger adieu*[30] (The Bloody Adieu) this so-called novelist takes the liberty to state the following: "*In writing my novel, I did not aim for you to derive a pretty lesson from my words, as other novelists do. No, I swear on my beard and sidelocks*[31] (What do you make of such a witticism!) *that I did not intend anything of the sort...I wrote the novel with the sole purpose of entertaining you...*"

"We shall soon examine the type of entertainment provided to us by **Shomer**'s pretty, wonderful stories. But at this point I am still focused on the ethical aspect of our so-called novelist who has the audacity to express himself openly with the decorative phrase "*on my beard and sidelocks*," admitting that he has no moral objective; his sole goal is to entertain.

---

30. *Der blutiger adieu!, oder gift in gliksbekher: eyn vunderlikher rirender roman, velkher verdet dem lezer fil fargenigen farshafen* (The Bloody Adieu, or Poison in the Goblet of Happiness), Vilna 1879, 1883.

31. A reference to the beard and sidelocks (*peyes* or *pey'ot*) worn by traditional Jewish men in observance of the biblical commandment (Lev 19:27): "Do not round off the hair on the corners of your head..." In English, the translation should more appropriately read: "I swear on all that is holy." I decided on a literal translation because Sholem Aleichem takes offense at Shomer's expression.

"Elsewhere, such as in the novel *Dos antikl, oder di koshere metsie* (The Precious Find, or A Heck of a Bargain)[32] **Shomer** expresses himself in the pretty language of a court servant: *"Dear readers, purchase this exquisite merchandise. You will derive great pleasure from it, and it will teach you a great deal regarding how much you owe your family..."*

"This preface made me quite happy, and in order to discover how it teaches "a great deal regarding how much we owe our family," I read the book from cover to cover. And what did I discover? Listen up!

"A young man, Izak Windman,[33] witnesses the beautiful actress, Zinaida, on the theater stage. A wild desire overcomes him. He makes her acquaintance and falls in love immediately, just like the rest of **Shomer**'s heroes whenever they see a woman. He gets rid of his wife and spends night and day with this singer Zinaida. He buys her presents, brings her bouquets, sings her songs, and kisses her red lips until his wealth is reduced by some two thousand rubles. Who is this Zinaida, what is this Zinaida? A Jew or a Christian? Who is Izak? What was he before, and what is he now? We never know: the author does not want to disclose matters. All he tells us is that she made Izak buy her a bracelet for her birthday—something exquisite, engraved with two letters: S W—for which the jeweler Marcus at first wanted five thousand rubles, but which our hero Izak, who was a good bargainer, managed to haggle down to two thousand rubles. The bargaining itself occupies such a good chunk of the novel that it makes you sick to the stomach....In the end, when Izak obtains *the most sparkling of the best diamonds*[34] (to quote the author verbatim), and wants to run to his beloved Zinaida to buy her passionate love, suddenly (this is the manner in which every idea occurs in **Shomer**), suddenly another thought occurs to him: he has a wife who is *twenty times more beautiful than Zinaida, and if she put on rouge and powder*—says **Shomer**—*just like Zinaida put on rouge and powder, she would be a hundred times more beautiful. As for my money? Let her suffer as much as she wants. I am not going to give her a dime!* All of a sudden our fine Izak becomes a penitent. Since God helps penitents, the following miracle occurs to him: the two letters on the bracelet with the sparkling diamonds, Z and W, correspond precisely to his wife's initials, "Zelda Windman"!

"There is no end to God's wonders! As he approached his wife Zelda, she was in the middle of singing a pretty song by "that" Jewish poet:

---

32. *Dos antikl oder di koshere metsie: a moderner roman*, Vilna 1888.

33. Windman: windbag.

34. The original ("di burlianten fun di tayere dimanten") is purposely satiric due to its circular locution and its mistaken spelling. I render it below, for the sake of clarity, as "sparkling diamonds."

Als shpigl kent ir mikh meydlekh hobn,
Kukt zikh nor gut in mir ayn,
Beser zolt ir zikh bagrobn,
Eyder hayratn mit a sharlatn!

Use me for a mirror, girls
Gaze into me deeply,
Better to dig yourself a grave
Than to marry a charlatan!

"I don't know the identity of the poet who composed this special song.
Perhaps "that" poet is **Shomer** himself, because almost all of his novels
begin with a poem in our holy language, Hebrew. But our hero Izak is so
moved that he throws himself around his wife's neck and with tears in his
eyes he gives Zelda the precious find, the bracelet with the sparkling diamonds.

"But the greatest miracle of all consists of the fact that the precious find,
the bracelet with the sparkling diamonds for which Izak paid two thousand
rubles, was in truth worth five thousand rubles! So our hero earned three
thousand rubles off the entire deal! You can conclude from this that God
should only be so kind as to bless all Jews and all young people in love with
such bargains...

"This is the moral provided by this fabricator of novels. Such a novel is
read by the common people, by ordinary folks, by simple readers who have
no ability to read between the lines. **Shomer** calls this vile product a novel,
and a novel with a moral to boot! I ask you, honored jurors, is this not a desecration? Is it not heartbreaking that for the sake of the two gulden **Shomer**
will earn from this work, an entire literature, a young literature, will be corrupted? In my opinion, our accused deserves the strongest punishment, the
harshest penalty for this "precious find."

"But let us continue. Here is another of **Shomer**'s novels, entitled *Gvald,
vu iz mayn bord*[35] (Help! Where's My Beard). On the front cover there is an
illustration of a drunken Gentile lass wearing a top hat and a Russian holding
a big pair of scissors. It turns out that the Gentile lass with the top-hat is not
a lass at all but rather a Hasid, whose beard and side-curls have been shorn.
In the novel, **Shomer** goes on to explain *"that the pious Reb Todres who
has a liking for pretty young women always took great pride in his beard,
just as a fashionable modern woman prides herself on her wide behind*
(that's how **Shomer** puts it), *and his side-curls were like two mouse tails..."*

"Our talented novelist considers this satire. Our people are raised on this
nice satire to laugh at a Jew with a beard. If one can laugh at a Jewish beard,
it is a sign that one is already educated, sophisticated, Westernized, as the
saying goes.

---

35. *Gvald vu iz mayn bord!: eyn roman,* Vilna 1886, 1888.

"In retelling you the entire story of "the beard," which actually is an adaptation of a Russian vaudeville sketch by Solovyov[36] entitled "Gospoda Sobachkiny"[37] (The Sobachkins), no one can imagine that even when **Shomer** is serious and thinks that he is being earnest he is tolerable; but when he falls into satire and begins to crack jokes, when he tries to be funny like a young rascal who is a bit tipsy, then he is really insufferable. No matter how many times I tossed the book aside, no matter how much it repelled me, no matter how much it nauseated me, despite all my pain and suffering I still had to read it and all these other novels through to the end. It would take a weak person more than half a year to return to himself after the exquisite marvels of **Shomer**'s novels. Nor would I wish on any friend of mine the punishment of reading fifty-some books by **Shomer**.

"One can better understand how **Shomer** interprets the meaning and purpose of satire from what he says in his small satirical work *A sheyne reyne kapore*[38] (It Serves Him Right). *"These days, satire is in vogue: for instance, mocking a good friend to his face, laughing at a beggar—in one word, laughter, people should let it all out."* But at the same time that **Shomer** is being satiric, he requests that he should not be made fun of...Now that's satire!

"In order for you to have some concept of **Shomer**'s satiric talents and jokes I will relate several of his witticisms from his novel about "The Beard." For example: *"He is full, excuse the expression, with learning"*... *"Ha, ha, ha, right in the kisser..."* *"Hanele's bris, Amen congratulations"*... *"Even old men like a young woman"*... *"Jews today, because of our many sins, only love young girls"*... *"He whose hand I did not wash* (What is our **Shomer** thinking here?) *should with His righteous hand preserve all Jewish beards from such a misfortune as befell poor Todres' beard. Amen to that!...*"[39]

"I do not believe that shopkeepers in the marketplace jabber among themselves in this way, let alone cobblers' apprentices. Such chatter can only be the product of a talented humorist, a cheerful satirist like **Shomer**, who offers up these obscenities to the world so that it can laugh and be merry!

"I will have the honor more than once of returning to the unique satirical talents of our accused **Shomer**. But I cannot hold myself back and stay silent, having experienced with my very own eyes such a masterwork as *Der tayvl khapt dem melamed: a vare sheyne ertseylung*[40] (Devil Kidnaps the Teacher: A Pleasant True Story) by **Shomer**.

---

36. Vsevolod Solovyov (1849–1903), a Russian historical novelist.

37. All Russian quotations appear in the Cyrillic alphabet in Sholem Aleichem's original.

38. *A sheyne reyne kapore*, Vilna 1886.

39. Sholem Aleichem here quotes these lines out of context to provide examples of what he considers Shomer's failed attempts at humor.

40. *Tayvl khapt dem melamed: a vare sheyne ertseylung*, Vilna 1886.

"**Shomer** declares piously: *"We must thank and praise God who gives our hand the strength to write, our eyes the power to observe, and our what's-it-called...to sit on..."*

"Do you understand, honored jurors? This is how an author, a novelist who writes books for the people chooses to express himself! Understand me well: **Shomer** thanks and praises the One whose name he is not worthy of pronouncing for bestowing upon him a "what's-it-called" to sit on!!! Such a desecration of God's name, such blasphemy is not even permitted in a tavern among drunks and hooligans. The use of such ugly words deserves to be punished with great severity. In our Yiddish literature people read such jokes and obscenities and they are delighted. This great **Shomer** is not only a novelist, he is a jokester, a prankster, a humorist, a type of Heine,[41] Börne,[42] and Shchedrin,[43] pardon the comparison.

"*Devil Kidnaps the Teacher*, that pleasant little work, is full of such satiric pearls. For example, in this novel the cantor prays like a cat, the women jabber through the heart of the Rosh Hashanah service, and the teacher Tsadok Zerakh butchers his German...As to the depth of **Shomer**'s own knowledge of German we will return a bit later...But do you understand the salt of the satire? The teacher Tsadok Zerakh wrote "chamapagnerie" instead of champagne, and instead of "you should send me some port wine" the teacher wrote "you should do to send me port-whine," which is as realistic as the rest of **Shomer**'s scenes.

"Near the beginning of this satiric work, **Shomer** provides us with the following scene of pure comedy:

The door opened and Hannah-Beyle entered.

-"Good morning, Leybele! Have you already become a tailor?"

-"Yes, auntie! Perhaps you would like me to sew you a shroud?"

-"Go to hell! You have a special way of making fun of everyone."

-"Who's making fun? He who laughs first is punished first. How old are you? Sixty? What about our matriarch Sarah who celebrated the circumcision of her son at the age of ninety?"

-"Go to hell!"

-"Auntie, you are angry...Treat me to a slice of bread and a sour pickle."

---

41. Heinrich Heine (1797–1856), one of the most important German Romantic poets, known for his acid satire. Heine converted to Lutheranism in 1825. His Jewish background prompted him to take up Jewish themes in several important works, including *Almansor* (about Catholic persecution of Jews and Muslims in medieval Grenada), *Der Rabbi von Bacherach*; *Hebraeische Melodien*; and *Jehuda ben Halevy*.

42. Ludwig Börne (Juda Löb Baruch, 1786–1837), German-Jewish humorist and political commentator who converted to Christianity and lived in exile in Paris.

43. M.E. Saltykov-Shchedrin (1826–89), a leading Russian nineteenth-century satirist.

-"Enough of your jokes..."

-"Just like that? Perhaps your goat died or the cow gave birth? Congratulations!"

-"Chatterbox, just shut up! Anyhow, all jokes aside..."

"This is what passes for witty dialogue in **Shomer**!

"Later, we overhear the following conversation between Leybke the jokester, what a devil, and David, a rabbinic judge:

-"Welcome! A visit from Reb Leyb!"

-"Yes, rabbi. I came to ask you a question... I was sewing, you should pardon my expression, my pants. I was holding the needle in my mouth and I swallowed it suddenly. Now it is stuck in my stomach. I want to know, am I kosher or unkosher?"

-"Such an animal as you is always unkosher."

-"Very well put, rabbi, indeed. You understand why I like you so much...An ox like you is an expert in cows..."

"The rabbi tells Leybele that he is a cow, and Leybele replies that the rabbi is an ox... Where does a rabbi, a judge, a pious Jew speak in such a manner? In **Shomer**'s novels, which our people read! **Shomer** calls this a joke. **Shomer** is a happy-go-lucky fellow. You can see the white of his teeth while he laughs, and he wants the reader to laugh along with him. But it is not funny, honored jurors. It is no laughing matter. It would be more appropriate to cry and to weep than to laugh! Cry because among Jews a rabbi is treated with more disrespect that any servant; any tailor can insult him. Weep because in a literature for the people like our Yiddish literature, one can find such simple lowlifes who call themselves "novelists," who corrupt any decent feeling within the general public, damage its taste, and destroy the language itself.

"So, shall I continue with the interesting contents of this so-called novel by **Shomer**? Shall I provide you with its juicy details, like how the teacher Tsadok Zerakh flirted with the servant girl Tsipe-Krayne (all of **Shomer**'s heroes flirt); how he pulled her to his chest, kissed her, and embraced her; how they spoke about going into the fields in the morning where there is a barn, this teacher and this servant girl....Do you follow?

"No! It is no longer possible for me to speak calmly about **Shomer**'s satire, humor and moral lessons! I am putting an end to the discussion and turning our attention now to the matter of his fantasy, to his serious, earnest, great, important writings, to his *most interesting novels*, because those that we have mentioned thus far are only "pretty and happy stories, moralistic and satirical works, nice simple stories for the people..." And now we will consider his *"most interesting novels in two parts"* where the talent of our great novelist generously unfurls itself in all its greatness. It occurs to me that I do not see before me **Shomer** but rather the famous French pseudo-novelists Xavier de Montépin, Ponson di Terrail, Paul de

Kock, and others. The difference between them is that these fantasists used their own imaginations to invent their unbelievable heroes and wild stories, whereas **Shomer**, our fabricator of novels, picked it all up from them and transported their heroes from Paris to Nyesvizh,[44] from Marseilles to Berdichev,[45] and from Bordeaux to Eyshishok![46] Indeed, **Shomer**'s heroes have as much connection to Jewish life as Marseilles has to Berdichev. Consequently, **Shomer**'s most interesting novels stick to us in the same way that a pea sticks to the wall. Let us select one of **Shomer**'s best novels from the table: *Der oremer milyoner*[47] (The Poor Millionaire), a most interesting novel in two parts.

"Honored jurors, this most interesting novel is a reworking, a reformulation, an imitation, a mimicry of the famous novel *Mystères de Paris* by the well-known French novelist Eugène Sue.[48] * Whether or not Eugène Sue's

---

44. Nyesvizh: Shomer's hometown, a Belorussian shtetl in the region between Vilna and Minsk.

45. Berdichev: The quintessential Jewish city of the Ukraine; Jews constituted the majority of its inhabitants in the late nineteenth century.

46. Eyshishok: Lithuanian shtetl famous for its level of observance of Jewish tradition.

47. *Der oremer milyoner: eyn hekhst interesanter roman in tsvey teyln*, Warsaw 1883 or 1884.

48. Eugène Sue (1804–57), sensationalist French novelist, best remembered for his serialized novels *Les Mystères de Paris* (Mysteries of Paris, 1842–43) and *Le Juif Errant* (The Wandering Jew, 1844–45). *Les Mystères de Paris* was a bestselling French melodramatic novel that focused on intrigues among the lowest strata of Parisian society.

* It seems as if the prosecutor was unfamiliar with Alexandre Dumas' work *The Count of Monte Cristo*. Had he read it, he would have seen that *The Poor Millionaire* was a precise reworking of Dumas' work, with only the French names of the characters put into Yiddish. It is incredible that the stenographer, Mr. Sholem Aleichem, did not notice this! Or perhaps he was so grateful to the prosecutor for his defense of Yiddish that he did not want to interrupt his presentation. What does it matter to the reader what it is an imitation of, as long as it is not original...

The Typesetter

AUTHOR'S NOTES:

Khatati, aviti, pashati, I transgressed, I offended, I sinned! I am guilty, guilty, guilty! I believe the typesetter—who has expertise in these matters—when he says that in *The Poor Millionaire* Shomer patched over the wrong side of *The Count of Monte Cristo*. Ahhh. I would trade a sack of beets and all fifty of Shomer's most interesting novels to get a hold of *The Count of Monte Cristo* at this moment! But who is guilty, if not Shomer alone? Who is responsible for tracing and controlling his works? The author himself should be responsible for pointing out the source of his fine pelts. For example, here before our eyes are three "historical" novels by Shomer:

novel is good or bad is not my concern at this time. A well-known Hebraist, Kalmen Shulman,[49] loved the novel. He took it upon himself to translate it into our holy tongue, and it was a solid translation. Had **Shomer** done the same—translate *Mystères de Paris* into Yiddish—that would have been enough! But no, our accused does not just want to be a simple translator. That does not suit him. So what did he do? He "made" his own novel with Eugène Sue's heroes and gave it the title *The Poor Millionaire*. Whereas in Eugène Sue's work the lead character is Prince Rudolf, the same role here is played by the Jew Glazvald, a millionaire. Glazvald who? Glazvald what? It is none of our business. Just as Prince Rudolf travels around Paris incognito in search of his lost family, so does Glazvald wander about the city of Nyesvizh in search of his lost family. As you well know, in the end Prince Rudolf finds his lost daughter Maria, and Mr. Glazvald finds his lost son Naftali the watchmaker. Just as there is a terrifying bandit, Jacques Ferrand,[50] in Eugène Sue, so too in **Shomer** do we find the usurer Hertsnshteyn,[51] the murderous thief Shpin,[52] a viper by the name of Gilon from Paris, an Elizabeth, and many other heroes. Since there is a poor miserable family Morel in Eugène Sue's Paris, why shouldn't **Shomer** include the same poor miserable family of

---

(1) *Der gemakhter yoyresh* (The Would-Be Heir), *a historical novel;*

(2) *Khosen damim* (Bridegroom of Blood), *a historical novel* [ed. The phrase Khosen damim appears in Exodus 4:25–26; Zipporah, wife of Moses, uses these enigmatic words to refer to the circumcision of her son at a moment when Moses seems to be in grave danger.];

(3) *Der falsher hertsog* (The Fake Duke), *a historical story.*

On all three books we find the printed statement: "written by Shomer" (not translated?). I was astonished: Where does Shomer get off writing a historical novel? In order to create a historical novel one must first know something about history, and in order to know history one must know a thing or two...So I was doubtful about their connection to history, since they were not, God forbid, revamped like the rest of Shomer's novels...In the end, I put aside these three "historical" novels, several other pearls by Shomer, and those fifty other devils who dance after Shomer and imitate his style—works that my good friends sent me—long may they live... Until the next time, God willing, soon and with happy hearts. Amen.

Sholem Aleichem

49. Kalmen Shulman (1819–99), Hebrew maskilic writer and translator. His abridged Hebrew translation of *Mystères de Paris* (1857–60) proved extremely popular and went through several editions. The translation introduced contemporary French fiction to Hebrew readers and helped to demonstrate that Hebrew could function as a modern literary language.

50. Jacques Ferrand, the evil notary of *Mystères de Paris* who betrays the novel's heroine, Fleur-de-Marie.

51. Hertsnshteyn: "heart of stone."

52. Shpin: "spider."

Tsipe and Leah in Nyesvizh? Whereas Rudolf comes and rescues the family from its poverty, here Glazvald comes and sits over Leah's bed. What's the difference?

"I repeat: had **Shomer** wanted to translate that confusing story in its entirety into Yiddish, he would have been able to preserve his good name. We would not have had any right to comment on it. We would have only spoken about Eugène Sue, not about our accused. But as soon as **Shomer** slapped a new name on the work and published it as if it were his own creation, then we are obliged to abandon Eugène Sue and discuss the merits of *The Poor Millionaire* as a Jewish work, as a novel by **Shomer.**

"Unfortunately, there is not a single Jewish type, not a single Jewish scene, not a grain of Jewishness in the entire novel. The author conducts himself like a performer: he parades before us an entire series of mannequins, artificial characters who wander about, run, sit, speak. This one loves that one; that one is in love with this one. This one is an angel, something extraordinary, a benevolent man; that one is a rogue, a bandit, a killer. This one is wise; that one is an idiot. This one is a beautiful caring woman with long blond hair; that one is ugly, disgusting, like death incarnate. **Shomer** orders this or that hero to fall on his knees and declare: "I love you, my angel!" So he falls on his knees and declares: "I love you, my angel!"

"No, this is not quite a novel. It is more like an organ belonging to a street performer. **Shomer** cranks the handle and out comes: "Love!" Everyone is in love in his world, and they all love in the same way. Elizabeth falls unconscious, the seamstress swoons...everyone is constantly fainting and they are all equally deceived by their love, they are all equally despondent, they are all equally trusting. The heroes are so alike that if it were not for their different names we would not be able to perceive any differences between the wealthy Elizabeth and the poor Leah; between the millionaire Glazvald and the watch-maker Naftali; between Hertsnshteyn the usurer and Shpin-Hekht-Fayerfan the bandits. According to **Shomer**, a bandit is someone who kills people, robs people in broad daylight, disinters bodies from their graves, or disguises himself with various aliases. That's how it is with Shpin the bandit, Hekht the shady businessman, and Fayerfan the seamstress's husband. Wherever he goes, he finds a rich bride with a substantial dowry and piles of money. According to **Shomer**, money is as common as garbage—millions pile up in every corner!

"In **Shomer**'s universe, an evil character must be a bandit. He does not understand that a bad character can be a good Jew, a respected householder, not someone hiding behind three different names. He does not understand that someone can be evil even if he does not poison, kill, rob in the dark of night, drag bodies from the grave—things that do not even occur among Jews! I cannot imagine that there are still readers among us who are such fools that they would accept this as it is and continue to have faith in this writer.

"As soon as a novel does not relate to real life, it is no longer a novel but rather a *Bove-mayse*, a tall-tale, a story about a prince and a princess, a rabbi and his wife, about twelve brothers and twelve castles, about an Old English sheep-hound and a werewolf, and so on.

"**Shomer**'s novels would not be such a great disaster were they just empty and useless to our readers, like his tale about the sheep-dog and the werewolf. But as I demonstrated earlier and I will point out to you, God willing, in a few moments, apart from these shortcomings they also are harmful from a moral perspective.

"As long as we are on the subject of fantasy, let us continue and open another of **Shomer**'s "most interesting" novels, *Di agune*[53] (The Abandoned Wife). I was delighted by its introduction, in which **Shomer** writes: "*I can tell you with complete confidence that all of my characters are taken from real life...*" It gave me tremendous pleasure to learn that **Shomer** at least recognizes that characters in a novel must have a connection to real life. But a man is his own worst enemy, and **Shomer**'s tongue does him in. In the same prologue he later says with self-praise: "*I know that if you read this novel you will applaud just as thunderously as you did in response to my earlier novels (?). And whoever does not enjoy my novel is not going to ruin things for me by reporting me to the religious authorities in an attempt to prevent me from being showered with synagogue honors...*"

"After reading this comment about "thunderous applause" and "showered with synagogue honors," I immediately lost my trust and any regard for this "most interesting" novel in two parts.

"Let us consider what kinds of real-life characters **Shomer** crafts for us here. He wants to persuade us that such rogues exist in Lithuania among the Jews (He swears this in *The Abandoned Wife*). But promises do not matter, and no one is obliged to believe **Shomer**. So I began to search the entire novel for a single living person who is not just some mannequin, but a familiar type, for one true scene of Jewish life. But what did I find? Another angel; another ideal-type; a saint, poor thing, who pays for other people's sins; another thief, bandit, and rogue (you only find rogues in **Shomer**!); a barbarian who steals, plunders, rakes in money, lives it up, and who is unexpectedly defeated in the end to the pleasure of the author and the reader, who know that all evil characters in **Shomer** come to a bad end and that the righteous will recover, with God's help, in good time— Amen... That is how it is in **Shomer**'s The Abandoned Wife, *Di khalitse*[54] (The Levirate Marriage), *Di*

---

53. *Di agune: a hekhst interesanter roman*, Vilna 1881, 1887.

54. *Di khalitse: eyn interesanter roman*, Vilna 1883, 1884. *Halizah* (Hebrew) refers to the ceremony associated with biblical laws of levirate marriage in which a brother who normally would be obliged to marry his sister-in-law after his brother's death is released from his duties, allowing the woman to remarry according to her desires.

yerushe[55] (The Inheritance), *Der tiranisher bruder*[56] (The Tyrannical Brother), *Der baal tshuve*[57] (The Penitent), *Der oremer milyoner,* (The Poor Millionaire), *Der raykher betler*[58] (The Rich Beggar), *Der oytser*[59] (The Treasure), *Di hayntmodishe kale*[60] (The Stylish Bride), and *Di farkoyfte kale*[61] (The Sold-Off Bride). That is how it is with all the characters in **Shomer**'s "most interesting" novels, which are all, in truth, one grand unending novel in which only the names and locales are switched around; here the villain is called Hertsnshteyn whereas there he is Feldboym; here he is Perets while there he is Velvl Vokhernik[62] or Daniel Pintl—but they are all rogues, they are all thieves, brigands, greedy bloodsuckers, vampires, hypocrites. They are all involved in intrigues. They defraud everyone they come across. They have all been married several times and have buried several beautiful innocent demoiselles. They are pals with the underworld and consort with the Jewish gravediggers, who rob the graves of the dead (Have you ever heard of such a thing among Jews?). In a word, **Shomer**'s heroes—those rogues—are not heroes, not real people, not even wild beasts; rather they are vipers, half fish and half men, werewolves, royal couriers, eight-legged horses, and other such strange, wild, terrifying creatures intended to frighten young children, adapted from fairy tales and *A Thousand and One Nights.*

"That is how it is with all of his villains, and that is how it is with every one of his heroes—the angels, the righteous ones—each a variant of the same prototype, the same character with different names. They are all good, honest, decent, pure, handsome, refined, unblemished, brave, courageous young men, educated children, faithful and devoted to the end. They all write passionate letters with the same words. They all speak about holy love in the same style, in the same tone, as if coached by a book to recite by heart: "Oh! I love you, my angel!" "Oh, I love you, my darling!" **Shomer** stands at the back and prompts his hero: "Say, 'Oh, I love you my angel,'" and the hero says, "Oh, I love you my angel!" But they are words without any soul, without any feeling. They seem automatic, as if sputtered from a machine.

---

55. *Di raykhe yerushe, oder a mayse on a sof*, Vilna 1886.

56. *Der tiranisher bruder oder der opekun*, Warsaw 1883.

57. *Der baal tshuve: roman*, Vilna 1880.

58. *Der raykher betler: a roman in tsvey teyln*, Vilna 1884(?), 1886 .

59. *Der oytser oder der kalter gazlen: roman in tsvey teyln*, Vilna 1884.

60. *Di hayntmodishe kale oder ver iz shuldik:* roman, Warsaw 1881 or 1882, 1887.

61. *Di farkoyfte kale: roman*, Warsaw 1886.

62. Vokhernik: a usurer.

"Though **Shomer**'s heroines conduct themselves differently, they all act in the same way too, according to the same program, according to the same instructions. They all cast their eyes upward, searching for their ideal floating in the distant heavens, and in every novel they sing sweet, sentimental songs, a variety of which I now present to you from different novels by **Shomer**:[63]

"In the novel *The Poor Millionaire* Elizabeth sits at the piano and sings

> *Ikh vil shoyn mer do nit lebn*
> *Keyn zakh iz mir zis*
> *Ikh vil tsu mayn libn shvebn*
> *Ahin in paradiz!*

> I no longer want to live here
> Nothing is sweet to me
> I want to soar to my love
> There in paradise!

"In the same novel, Leah the seamstress sits and sings in the same vein:

> *Dort in himl tsvishn di shtern*
> *Shpatsirt mayn engel lustik fray*
> *Er zet shoyn nit mayne trern*
> *Er iz mir shoyn umgetray!...*

> There in the heavens, among the stars
> My angel strolls happily and free
> He no longer sees my tears
> He is no longer faithful to me!

"In *The Penitent* Dina goes so far as to sing in "pure" German:[64]

> *Ich steh am einsamen Hugel*
> *Und schaue noch dir zurück*
> *Es schenkt die senkende Sonne*
> *Dir eben den letzten Glück.*

"In *The Treasure* Itke sings the following:

> *In der stiller Abendstunde*
> *Wenn der blasser Mond strallt herab, usw.*

"In *The Tyrannical Brother* the hero Perets begins to write poetry to his bride (do you understand the meaning of "writing poetry"?):

---

63. One of the reasons Sholem Aleichem cites these songs is to showcase their lack of artistry and sophistication. For this reason I provide the original Yiddish along with my literal (non-rhyming) translations.

64. German readers will discover several mistakes in the German cited below. Sholem Aleichem sought out such examples as part of his struggle against daytshmerish (Germanisms) in literary Yiddish. See note 105.

Di schone Sonne mit ire shtraln
Darfn tsu dayne fis faln
Zey darfn ziftsn shrayen (Ver?) *oy vey!*
Den du bist fil schöner fun zey!...(Fun vemen?)

The beautiful sun and its rays
Ought to fall at your feet
They (*whom does he mean?*) should sigh and cry: Woe is me!
Because you are more beautiful than they (*than who?*)...

"In *The Rich Beggar* Helena Flantsberg sings:

Er iz eyn engel fun got geshikt
Dos werde ikh zogn biz mayn toyt
Mayn fershmakhtes herts hot er derkvikt
Geretet hot er mikh fun mayn noyt.

He is my angel sent by God
I will say this to the day I die
He revived my faint heart
He rescued me from my dire condition.

"In *Der kosherer yid*[65] (The Pious Jew) Lize's servant-girl sings:

Mayn liber iz vayt fun danen
Ikh bin geblibn aleyn,
Ale meydlekh hobn manen
Nor ikh, nebekh, zits un veyn.

My love is far away
I remain behind alone,
Other girls have fiancés
But I, poor thing, sit and cry...

"In *Der kheyrem*[66] (The Excommunication) Rivke sits under a tree and sings:

Mayn brust iz mit leydn voll
Du must libender verlassen mikh
Vielleicht iz haynt dos letste mol
Vos ikh ze mayn lebn dikh...

My heart is full of suffering
You, my love, must leave me
Perhaps today is the last time
That I ever see you, my darling.

---

65. *Der kosherer yid, oder tsvey kets in eyn zak,* date of first publication unknown. There was a reprint published in Vilna in 1891.

66. A later edition of this novel was published in Warsaw in 1897. I have not been able to locate the edition to which Sholem Aleichem is referring.

"In *Tsvishn tsvey flamen* (Between Two Flames)[67] Perele sings the following:

> *Af mayne lipn fil ikh zayn kus*
> *Ikh her zayn zisn kol*
> *Dos iz geven vi tsuker-zis*
> *Akh! Vu nem ikh im nokh a mol!...*

> I feel his kiss on my lips
> I hear his sweet voice
> It was as sweet as sugar
> Oh! Where can I find him again! ...

"In *Di blinde yesoyme*[68] (The Blind Orphan Girl) Lisette sings to Itsik melancholically:

> *Oder in libe shtekt dayn shmerts*
> *Zi hot dikh tiranish antzogt*
> *Iz dos di urzakhe fun dayn shmerts*
> *Bist darum farveynt, ferklogt...*

> Or perhaps your sorrow comes from love
> She rejected you tyrannically
> And that is the source of your suffering
> That is why you cry and mourn...

"Honored jurors, from these cultured pearls you understand that our accused **Shomer** is not only a great novelist, moralist, and satirist but also a wonderful poet for old maids, for grown-up brides, for foolish boys—perhaps even a prominent poet. One cannot say that he is a poet like Goldfaden. He is more like Moyshe Marakhovski from Boslov[69] who modeled himself on Goldfaden's style and reworked Goldfaden's songs from "Yudele"[70] so artfully that it enlivens the soul:

> *Mayn vayb vigt mikh in vigl*
> *Far dem shtikl kigl...*
> *Zi shrayt gvald*
> *Ikh zol ir geben bald...*

> My wife is rocking me in the cradle
> For a piece of kugel...
> She cries out, "Help!"
> So that I will give her some soon..."

(Contemporary Poems by Moyshe Marakhovski from Boslov)

---

67. *Tsvishn tsvey flamen, oder der hefker-yung: roman in tsvey teyln*, Vilna, 1887–88.

68. *Di blinde yesoyme oder tsvishn tigren: eyn roman*, Vilna 1880.

69. Boslov (or Boguslav), town south of Kiev in the Ukraine. See note 11 for more on Marakhovski.

70. *Dos yudele* (The Little Jew, 1866), anthology of Yiddish poetry and songs edited by Goldfaden.

"Mr. Prosecutor!," the Chief Justice cried out, "I ask you to stay on point. You began by discussing **Shomer**'s novel *The Abandoned Wife* and you have digressed to Moyshe Marakhovski's poetry..."

"Yes, jurors, in all honesty the poetic talents of our accused so mesmerized me, so enchanted me that I forget entirely about **Shomer**'s *The Abandoned Wife*...

"Our talented novelist, who had already written many novels in his lifetime, achieved something new in *The Abandoned Wife* in order to interest the public. **Shomer**'s innovation was: Scandal. This is nothing new in other literatures. For example, the Parisian penny novels that are published almost daily in impressive quantities are lapped up like hot noodles because the French audience loves a good scandal. But among Jews, in Yiddish literature, this an important innovation, and this innovation is due to **Shomer** alone.

"Consider the following pretty story:

"*Ish hoyo be-kitnevits,* there was a Jew in Kitnevits, and his name was Benjamin. He was nothing more than a dealer in wagons, a pauper, God save us. But suddenly—that's how it always is with **Shomer**, all of a sudden, miracles and wonders around every corner!—suddenly this Benjamin the pauper becomes enormously wealthy off real estate and precious metals. This Benjamin had a son, Aaron Feldboym. Aaron Feldboym, as is usually the case, was a knave, a thief, a scoundrel—in a word, a complete rogue! He made many women miserable...His first victim was a married woman, Hannah-Rachel, who was left an *agune,* an abandoned wife, because of him. Aaron Feldboym also burned her father's house to the ground. This same Aaron Feldboym also robbed a church (can you believe these terrible deeds?). A little later, this rich bandit married, but he quickly did away with his unfortunate wife, and then he...What do you think? Poisoned her? Slaughtered her? Burned her? God forbid! He just threw a loaf of bread at her head and she went out of her mind...you get it? Such tragedies can occur only in **Shomer**. Aaron Feldboym went on to have three more wives.

"Do you think that was the end of it? Absolutely not! Aaron Feldboym cast his eye upon the beautiful Malke. But this Malke loved Hannah-Rachel's son, Avrom. The progress of this wonderful relationship is worth considering. Avrom taught Malke all about "love." He engaged her in long conversations, in philosophical discussions, and concluded with the statement from the holy Torah "Thou shalt not covet another man's wife." But just to have a good time with her, without "meaning any harm"...**Shomer** persuades us that this is permissible. If it is a question of a woman who does not even have a husband, it is 100% kosher! The long and the short of it is that Malke ended up turning her eyes to the heavens:

...tsvishn di shtern
Shpatsirt ir engel lustik fray,
Er zet shoyn mer nit ire trern
Er iz ir shoyn ungetray

...among the stars
Her angel strolls happily and free,
He no longer sees her tears
He is no longer faithful to her!

"Now let us leave these two lovebirds behind, leave Malke and her "angel," and return to the villain Aaron Feldboym. This little devil, you may recall, had already cast his eye on his next victim, Reb Hershl's beautiful daughter Yente, whom the bastard quickly trapped in his net. **Shomer** relates how Yente began to visit Aaron secretly at night...one thing led to another, until she began to feel that she soon ought to ...in a word, the accursed lout got her into trouble and even accused her of fooling around with David the musician... But you haven't heard anything yet! In Kitnevits there was a barber-surgeon, Leybke, who was an expert at abortions. Aaron ordered a "potion" from him for Yente, from which she ultimately died...

"But since the powers that be have decided that **Shomer**'s rogues must suffer their hell in *this* world, Aaron began to have terrifying nightmares with hallucinations. It did not occur to him to repent. Just the opposite: his roguish instincts burned even stronger, and he went off to war in Romania, where he managed to finagle millions by the shovelful, and made even more people miserable. **Shomer** brings the remaining characters in the novel to Bucharest, where the author shows us "the source whence all had gotten their money," and "the veritable paradise that was the cafe in the magnificent Grand Hotel...""

"Such details led me to believe that **Shomer** himself was probably in Bucharest at that time, together with his novels, and I might have hoped that the author would have provided us with true scenes and interesting stories of our brothers in Bucharest.[71] At the time, there was a lot of material about Jewish life that might have been depicted from many different angles and illuminated from all possible sides. We could have anticipated this from a real writer, from a writer of the people like Spektor, for example, who loves to observe Jewish life and faithfully depict its scenes and types, to the extent that his talent permits. But we could not demand such things from one who churns out novels like **Shomer**. **Shomer** is preoccupied with bandits and intrigues, with vipers and werewolves, so how could Mr. Khaykl or Spektor's Mr. Traytl[72] be of any value to him? Where Spektor would have

---

71. Sholem Aleichem is being coy here in that he knows that Shomer was in Bucharest as a contractor for the Russian army during the Russo-Turkish war (1876–77) and that these contractors (most of whom were Jews) were living large at a hotel similar to the one he describes. Sholem Aleichem may also be hinting at the early Yiddish theater, whose early productions took place in Bucharest.

72. M. Spektor, *Reb Traytl: ertseylung in tsvey teyln* (Warsaw 1889); another revised version of the novel was published in *Der hoyz-fraynd* 4 (1895), 1–148. It is likely that Sholem Aleichem is referring to an excerpt from the novel that appeared prior to its publication in book form in 1889, though I have not been able to find the

taken the time to describe the coachman with his two horses, **Shomer** creates ten bandits, seven angels, five innocent souls, three disinterred bodies, a Jewish teacher engaged in an affair with a Gentile lass under the moonlight, a duel between Yakelzon and Khatsklzon, a vial of poison, a noose, impassioned letters, sugary songs, eyes beseeching the heavens, terrifying dreams, buckets of tears, and a lot of blood!...Where Spektor would have said a few sincere, heartfelt words to take pity on the people—the suffering and poverty of the Jewish masses that includes millions of *"paupers and beggars"*[73] and a few wealthy ones...in place of Spektor's touching words that come from the heart and affect the reader deeply, **Shomer** would have churned out countless puffed-up, empty ringing phrases sweetened by his own philosophical insights.

"In the second part of *The Abandoned Wife*, **Shomer** states: *"Were we to consider the world and all creation with an open critical mind, we would see that life is always bound to death, and that luck is always connected to misfortune...Of that, we do not need to adduce any particular proof; it is already a well-known fact. That is why the old sages* said: It is a wheel of fortune, where one wins, and then another... We see the same in the Crimean war..."*

What a parable!

> *"Once upon a time there were two brothers, one was wise, studious, learned in Torah, and the other was called Benjamin and had a yellow beard—and that's the way it is..."*

"I am so accustomed to **Shomer**'s "philosophy" that I almost know it by heart. Almost every one of his chapters begins with an elevated philosophical statement in which the author gets so excited that he speaks with the echoing authority of a barrel-maker. It is not for nothing that **Shomer** writes the following in *The Levirate Marriage*:

> *"I have already entangled myself enough in these tangential subjects. Readers would surely hold it against me if I were to drive them crazy with my somber philosophizing. Poor things, they pay good money for the story itself. So I have to make them happy and return to the story..."*

"But **Shomer** does not do what the reader wants. On almost every page he offers up—as he calls it—his "somber" philosophizing, and he often says

---

source. The wordplay with the names Khaykl and Traytl also may be a nod to two works by Isaac Meir Dik: "Reb Traytl der kleynshtetisher noged," *Varshoyer yudishe tsaytung* (1867–68); *Khaytsikl aleyn: a sheyne un vare geshikhte, vi azoy eltern zoln zeyere kinder ertsien* (Vilna, 1887).

73. M. Spektor, *Aniyim ve'evyoynim, oder gliklikhe un umgliklikhe* (Petersburg, 1885).

* Which old sages? Where is this written?—It is a total fabrication.

The Typesetter

these things with such conviction, with such open insolence, that one wants to burst with frustration. *"Practice teaches us that...poor parents love their children with greater warmth and tenderness than the rich..."* (*The Abandoned Wife*)

"I will not explicate every one of **Shomer**'s philosophical thoughts, but rather provide you with a full page of his words of wisdom that are based on history, astronomy, psychology, anthropology, phrenology, and so on. That which **Shomer** refers to as his "somber philosophizing" was called "*krantse-folye*" or folderol by a big ignoramus who is an acquaintance of mine...[74]

"Listen to some of his pearls of wisdom:

> *"Just as the honest man has no concept of how a robber comes to steal...so too does the thief not understand how the honest man can live peacefully and survive through business alone..."* (The Blind Orphan Girl)

> *"When a person has a lot of worries and he does not know which one he should deal with first, at that moment he finds himself face to face with the greatest worry of all...And as the second worry passes, the third and fourth worries come along, and so on, until he has been confronted with all his worries. At that instant it is possible for us to say that he stands before the final worry in the same state of despair as he stood before his very first worry..."* (The Rich Beggar)

"Just as the sea has no bottom, so is **Shomer**'s philosophy groundless. Even if I had the opportunity to speak to you for three days and three nights, I still could only provide you with a tenth of what our accused has written in his hundred-some novels. Nothing to sneeze at—a full hundred novels!!! There are thirty to forty characters in every one of **Shomer**'s novels (there is never a shortage of characters with **Shomer**). That is to say, there is a total of some four thousand heroes, four thousand different characters with different souls, personalities, perceptions, thoughts, talents, inclinations, habits, qualities and deficiencies, all derived from nature and from their education. In short, it is not an easy task. One must have a special talent in order for each and every book to be carefully chiseled. It requires a lot of blood, sweat and tears, not to mention the fact that you also need that God-given gift called talent. Before the author publishes each book, he must first go through it carefully, think about it ten times over, improve it, correct it, freshen it up and rework it so that it reaches the level of a work of literature,

---

74. I elected to translate "*krantsefolye*" (crowning folly) as "folderol." In Sholem Aleichem's early novella *Taybele* (1884), the wealthy ignoramus Gershon Shpringer employed this word to refer dismissively to the Haskalah (the Jewish Enlightenment). Sholem Aleichem playfully explained to his readers in that novella: "We searched for the meaning of *krantsefolye* in all of the new and old dictionaries but we could not find such a word. Therefore we ask our readers to memorize the word *krantsefolye* so that it will remain for generations to come" (*Ale verk fun Sholem Aleykhem*, vol. 20 [Vilna and Warsaw: Kletskin, 1926], 35).

so that it is gleams and sparkles, so that it seems alive, so that its words speak both to the mind and to the heart.

"Our accused **Shomer** does not understand his responsibilities in this way. He began to treat Yiddish—our literature for the people—as a game, as if churning out a new novel* every day was some kind of business transaction through which he could become an entrepreneur, a supplier of novels to Yiddish publishers. The public looked upon this with indifference, and the critics took notice and remained silent: "Whatever... it is only for the people, for the masses, for common folk who are perfectly willing to chew on straw... What does it matter?!" This is how the masses are exploited. They hand over their money and are given grass in return, and nobody dares to say a word. "But you are talking about **Shomer**...**Shomer**! He has already written a hundred novels, and the public reads them, so there must be something to them!" When the well-known critic in *Voskhod*,[75] Mr. Criticus,[76] attempted to comment on and appraise the value of one little book by **Shomer**,[77] the great novelist responded with an article of his own in the *Yudishes folksblat*[78] in which **Shomer** proved that he is **Shomer**...[79]

Honored jurors, I cannot be satisfied with the novels we have enumerated up to now, because they are all older works, sins of youth.[80] Who knows,

---

* Shomer takes pride in the fact that he can finish a large novel in two nights.

The Typesetter

75. *Voskhod,* Jewish periodical for the intelligentsia, published in Russian in St. Petersburg (1881–1906).

76. *Criticus,* pseudonym used by the historian Shimon Dubnov (1860–1941) in his critical writings about Yiddish literature.

77. Criticus's article, "Literaturnaia Letopis" (Literary Chronicles: The Poverty of Contemporary Jewish Belles-Lettre), *Voskhod,* May 1887, was a critique of both Shomer's *Der raykher betler* and his Hebrew work *Ha-nidahat*. Excerpts (in Yiddish translation) from Criticus's article later appeared in *Yudishes folksblat* 27–28 (1887). Criticus anticipated many of the criticisms that Sholem Aleichem would incorporate into *The Judgment of Shomer*. For instance, he asserted that since Shomer's work lacked authenticity, both in terms of its description of Jewish life and in its portrayal of Jewish characters, "there is nothing one can really say about it artistically." He challenged Shomer: "Is Jewish life so impoverished that there is not enough material in it for true creativity?" He also called attention to the grammatical flaws in Shomer's Germanized Yiddish.

78. *Yudishes folksblat,* Yiddish weekly, published in Petersburg beginning in 1881 and edited by Alexander Tsederboym.

79. A reference to Shomer's article "A patsh far a patsh" (A blow for a blow), *Yudishes folksblat* 30 (1887), 483–88, in which Shomer responded to Criticus and other critics by commenting: "He must have written these words out of jealousy, hatred, or perhaps simply because he is a little out of his mind—it shouldn't happen to us."

80. The term Sholem Aleichem employs for sins of youth, *Hate'ot Ne'urim*, was also

perhaps we will find a different **Shomer** in the later works? Frequently, talented writers retreat, whereas those who begin as invalids improve and make such great strides forward that it is difficult to recognize them. So now let us open one of his latest works, a novel with the fine title *Paltiel Ox*, published in Vilna in 1887—it is fresh and right out of the hopper, something that enlivens the soul.

"In the preface to this fine novel, **Shomer** writes: *"The many plaudits I receive every day from readers..."* In simple Yiddish, he might as well just say: "Come on, buyers! Over here, buddy! It's good here! Get a deal here! It's fresh here! Neighbor, come on over!"

"...my novel contains everything that the Jewish audience demands: moving scenes, great intrigues, secret romances, surprise encounters..."

"Buttons, sticks, raisins, whips,
Shirts, ties, cookies, material,
Bagels, pins, thread, and soap!...[81]

"In a word, **Shomer** knows what the public demands. **Shomer** knows that the masses love razzle-dazzle and hocus-pocus, so he gives it to them. The audience loves scandals, so he gives them scandals, each more spectacular than the next. But we will return to this matter shortly. I want to get back to his "introduction":

"I once again ask my readers that when they pick up one of my works they check on the first page to ensure that my real name appears on the cover, because people have begun to exploit my name and slap it on various rags in order to confuse readers..."

"As they say in Russian: *Osteregaites' poddelki!*, or watch out for thieves!...A poor lot has fallen upon our young Yiddish literature if indeed there are writers and publishers who aspire to imitate **Shomer**! We can console him with the words of a Russian poet:[82]

---

the title of the autobiography (1873–76) of the Hebrew writer, critic, and journalist Moses Leib Lilienblum (1843–1910), in which he described the struggles of his youth, his sexual awakening, and the development of his beliefs. The reference would have been obvious to sophisticated readers.

81. Sholem Aleichem is mocking Shomer's self-promotion as something more appropriate for a street hawker shouting out his wares than for a writer.

82. A reference to I.M. Dmitriev. The first line cited by Sholem Aleichem is somewhat different in Dmitriev's version, and words are reordered for the sake of rhyme:

ЭПИГРАММА

–«Я разорился от воров!»
–«Жалею о твоем я горе».
–«Украли пук моих стихов!»
–«Жалею я об воре»

-Uvy! Menia obobrali.
-Zhaleiu o tvoem ia gore.
-Puk moikh stikhov ukrali!
-Zhaleiu ia o vore...

"which translates into Yiddish as:

-"Alas! Robbers have fleeced me."
-"I'm sorry, that's terrible."
-"They've stolen a bunch of my poems!"
-"Pity the thief..."

"Too bad for the thief, too bad for Yiddish, too bad for our people!

"How about this for a scandal: Benjamin Fridfish was the only son of Levi Fridfish, a wealthy man from the city of Bobruisk.[83] When Benjamin turned nineteen, **Shomer** told him that it was time for him to fall in love. So he went off and fell in love with the beautiful Maria, the only daughter of the police inspector Samuel Bergtal (almost every hero in **Shomer** is an only son and almost every heroine is an only daughter). Benjamin began to pay frequent visits to the beautiful Maria. Her parents, who knew that Benjamin's family was well-off, took notice and helped matters along a little so that their "love would ignite." Indeed, their love was sparked, until shortly thereafter the beautiful Maria joyfully informed our fine Benjamin that, with God's help, he soon would be a father...

"Of course, this good news was not at all pleasant to our Benjamin. To fall in love, to fool around with a girl... that's one thing, why not? But to be a father at the age of nineteen, yuck! That is the way it is, explains **Shomer** in his somber philosophy, or folderol: *...Love is the most sacred thing until one partakes of her fruits... But when the lovers allow themselves to enjoy her fruits...*"

"You get it?

"*Beys ho-hi,* by the time Benjamin was enjoying the fruits of love, a teacher had already got there before him, and he was followed by a small-time accountant, a lout, a yeshiva student who ran away from his wife, a scholar, a recluse, a beggar, a good-for-nothing, a robber, a rogue, a butcher, a werewolf, a viper, a rascal from **Shomer**'s cast of rascals—and his blessed name was Paltiel Ox.

"Our fine Benjamin revealed his secret to Paltiel Ox: he had already tasted the fruits of love and he had gotten himself into a nasty bit of business, God save us, such that soon he was going to be a father...

-"Ha, ha, ha! You're such a child!" - Paltiel Ox answered him - "What a joke on Samuel, his wife, and his daughter..."

-"What type of advice have you got for me, Reb Paltiel?"

---

83. Bobruisk, large Belorussian shtetl.

-"My advice is simple. Spit into his clean-shaven face! ...What do you have to worry about? For five rubles I can find you a guy who will swear that Maria is pregnant with his child..."

-"You can do that?"—Benjamin asked, delighted.

-"It's nothing!"—Paltiel responded.

-"Oh! You are my savior, my best friend in the entire world!" -Benjamin cried, embracing Paltiel and kissing him through his tears.

"The next day Paltiel Ox came to Samuel the Inspector General and talked with him about his daughter Maria, who had for all intents and purposes got herself married without a ceremony...And he let it be known that Benjamin could not be of any assistance, except to help *"wipe away the stain on the family honor"*...

-"Let your daughter go to Warsaw, and let her remain there quietly until she gives birth...That is the beginning of all wisdom. [84] In addition, you will not be destroying a living creature because the child, poor thing, isn't guilty of anything..."

-"Aren't you forgetting how much money one must have for all of this?"...- Samuel answered dispassionately.

-"You are entirely correct," Paltiel answered him, "I reckon that 500 rubles would cover things?"

-"Not nearly enough," Samuel shot back. "My daughter is only in her fourth month...with today's expenses..."

-"A thousand rubles will surely be enough?"

-"Yes, a thousand rubles should cover things..."

-"So, in the meantime, good night!..."

"Honored justices and jurors, what can one say about such a scene? What can one say about this denunciation of an entire people? A Jew wrote this, a Jewish author, a Jewish belletrist, one of our writers of the people, and he portrays for us how a Jewish parent first sells his only daughter into prostitution, and then assuages his wounds with a thousand rubles. There no longer remains any feeling among them except for money. What happened to the family life that had been the pride of Jews among all nations? There is no love, no loyalty, no compassion—nothing at all except for money, nothing except for a thousand rubles!...Only a Jew-baiter, a Judeophobe, only the Jews' worst enemy could offer up such a scene! Such an incident has never even been heard of among Jews. Listen to how the immortal Turgenev writes about this in his story *"Zhid."* [85] It is worthwhile

---

84. An ironic reference to the biblical verse "The fear of God is the beginning of wisdom." (Ps 111:10) Also, *Reishit hohmah* (The Beginning of Wisdom) was a classical tract of Jewish mysticism, ethics, and morality written by the sixteenth-century scholar Rabbi Elijah de Vidas.

85. Ivan Sergeyevich Turgenev (1818–83), one of the most important nineteenth-

to consider how a Christian portrays almost the same scene that **Shomer** offered up in his *Paltiel Ox*.

"Who among us does not remember Red Hirshl, the middleman?[86] Turgenev tells us that this Hirshl was nothing more than a spy who permitted the officer to look at his pretty daughter Sara, but just to look at her, nothing more, for a fistful of golden coins!

"When the officer ordered him to leave and his daughter to remain behind in the tent, Hirshl responded: "Oh, no, no. It is strictly forbidden, not permitted. I'll stay outside, around the corner, it is forbidden!..."

"And this is how Hirshl the agent managed the officer for a while. He squeezed a small fortune out of him, promised him mounds of gold–and the officer could only look at the beautiful Sara, gaze into her big black eyes, admire her pretty shining face–and nothing more...

"The great artist Turgenev showed us through the use of his talented pen how the worst and most corrupt father possesses a love for his child that is

---

century Russian realists; author of the classic novel *Fathers and Sons* (1862). Turgenev's early story "Zhid" (Kike) first appeared in 1846.

86. Turgenev introduces the protagonist of his story as follows: "This Jew, whose name was Hirshl, was continually hanging about our camp, offering his services as an agent, getting us wine, provisions, and other such trifles. He was a thinish, red-haired little man, marked with smallpox; he blinked incessantly with his diminutive little eyes, which were reddish too; he had a long crooked nose, and was always coughing." In Turgenev's narrative, the Jew tempts the Russian officer with the promise of providing him with services, including tempting him with an attractive young woman. He carefully manages their interactions, ensuring that the officer's desire for her intensifies (thereby increasing his reliance on the Jew) while not allowing for the sexual consummation of that desire. Only at the end of the story, when Hirshl is about to be hanged as a spy, is it revealed that the woman is his daughter Sara. Sholem Aleichem's reading of Turgenev's story is problematic in that he emphasizes Turgenev's sensitivity to the primacy of the Jewish family and to the value of female modesty, while leaving out the fact that, in the end, Hirshl does offer to trade sex for clemency:

"Your honor," he began muttering, "look, your honor, look . . . she, this girl, see–you know–she's my daughter."

"I know," I answered, and turned away again.

"Your honor," he shrieked, "I never went away from the tent! I wouldn't for anything . . ."

He stopped, and closed his eyes for an instant. . . . "I wanted your money, your honor, I must own . . . but not for anything . . ."

"But now, if you save me," the Jew articulated in a whisper, "I'll command her . . . I . . . do you understand? . . . everything . . . I'll go to every length . . ."

See "The Jew" in Ivan Turgenev, *The Jew and Other Stories,* translated from the Russian by Constance Black Garonett (London: William Heinemann, 1899).

greater than any other emotion, even for such a greedy lowlife as Hirshl the spy who lost his life over a few coins (he was caught with a sketch of the Russian camp and he was hanged). Turgenev's great genius allowed him to recognize that Jewish respect for family life was so great, and that the innocence of a Jewish daughter was so strongly protected, so sacred, that...

"Now let us compare: Turgenev's story was written by a Russian author for the Russian people, whereas **Shomer**'s was written by a Jewish writer for the Jewish people! How can that be? Because Turgenev is a real writer, a genius, an artist, a poet, and on top of it a humanist with an aesthetic sensibility, with a sensitive spirit, with good taste. In short, he has all those important attributes with which God blesses only the chosen few from among His servants.

"This is true in Turgenev's case, as well as in the case of other writers among other peoples, including the Jews, but not in the case of **Shomer**. By contrast, the decency and honor of a Jewish woman is masterfully portrayed by the Jewish poet Gordon.[87] Consider Gordon's "The Tip of the Yud."[88] Admire the way the poem describes the piety, honesty, and innocence of the beautiful Bat-Shu'a who has never been fortunate enough to experience a single lucky day in her entire life. Her husband Hillel abandons her in his search to earn a living. Suddenly, in an instant, the bright sun shines down upon the unfortunate Bat-Shu'a and a passion ignites in her heart, a fire of love for the widower Fayvish, who notices her in the store and attracts her with tenderness, without any of the scandals or "tasting the fruits of love" that are a staple in **Shomer**'s works. Even when their entire blissful plan is destroyed over the tip of the letter yud—over a missing point on a letter in one of the names on the writ of divorce, thereby rendering it invalid—even then when the unfortunate Bat-Shu'a realizes that she will remain a grass widow, and a shopkeeper in Ayalon[89] exposed to suffering, poverty, and disaster...even then this Bat-Shu'a remains a daughter of Israel, a decent, innocent Jewish woman until the day of her death, until the grave! Gordon understands this, but not **Shomer**.

"To be a writer of the people one must be both talented and patriotic. One must be a humanist and a lover of one's people, and whether in reproof

---

87. Judah Leib Gordon (1831–92), Hebrew poet, critic, journalist, social advocate, and outstanding exponent of the Jewish enlightenment. His poem "Hakitsah 'ami" (Awake, My People) was the motto of a generation of maskilim, while his "Le-mi ani 'amel" (For Whom Do I Toil, 1871) despaired of the future of Hebrew culture: "Perhaps I am the last of Zion's poets / and you the last readers."

88. "Kotso shel yod" (The Tip of the Yud, 1876), famous poem by Gordon in which he champions the rights of women. The poem criticizes extremist exponents of tradition who would deny a woman happiness by leaving her "chained" to her husband based on a minute technicality in the writ of divorce.

89. Ayalon: an anagram, based on its Hebrew letters, for the city of Vilna.

or in laughter, one must have faith in the people, one must be devoted to them and love them, just like Abramovitsh whose heart, whether he is laughing or mocking, bleeds for them.

"When I write about my unfortunate people," confesses Abramovitsh in a private letter to an acquaintance, "my heart bleeds for them. I laugh for the sake of appearances, but it is a bitter laughter mixed with bile, and a feverish form of writing in which I am consumed until I extinguish like a candle..."

"This may be how Abramovitsh writes, but not **Shomer**. **Shomer** looks only for filthy scandals that he hopes will prompt his audience to break out in thunderous "Bravos"! If they don't, it does not bother him one way or the other whether he is showered with honors in the synagogue.

"The other great Yiddish writer Linetski, who toils, outdoes himself, and expends his rare satiric talent on entertaining little fragments that the public loves in order to earn himself some bread—this Linetski who laughs and contorts himself like a clown before his audience, at great pain to himself, bleeds for our poor Jewish people whenever he speaks, writes, or thinks of them. There is nothing sadder in the world than one who must bring himself to laugh when he really wants to cry, and who must climb walls while a fire rages in his heart, while his head is who knows where, and all along, behind his back, the angel of death lies constantly in wait...

"But this has to do with Linetski, not **Shomer**, who confesses in his novel *The Penitent* that "because I am so soft-headed, I do not remember how I got from here to there."

"I will take him at his word. One can also become soft-headed after experiencing some fifty so-called novels by **Shomer,** which I read with such trembling that to this day I still dream of werewolves, vipers, rogues, angels, old maids with their eyes turned to the heavens, their sentimental, cloying songs, **Shomer**'s "somber philosophy," or "folderol"...

"Let us move from that most interesting novel *Paltiel Ox* to an even finer one: *A sheyne mayse nor a kurtse*[90] (A Story, Short but Sweet) written by **Shomer** in 1887.

"*A few weeks ago,*" writes **Shomer** in the introduction, "*I was in Warsaw, and I was staying in Hotel Danzig located at Nalewki 18. Since I come to Warsaw quite often, I am as familiar to the hotel employees as a plugged nickel, and I know them...*"

"Thanks to the fact that **Shomer** knows all of the clerks at Warsaw's Nalewki 18, we now have the privilege of reading *A Story, Short but Sweet*. If **Shomer** were not notorious, God forbid, among the servants and clerks at Warsaw's Nalewki 18, then Yakub, the chief valet of Hotel Danzig, would not have been able to tell him the following fine tale, **Shomer** would not

---

90. *A sheyne mayse nor a kurtse*, Vilna 1887.

have printed it, and we would not be privileged to read it...The story is truly short but sweet, though it should have been a bit shorter! Here it is:

"First, Yakub the valet recounts a merry tale about a couple from Lodz, who were staying in room 52, and a couple from Kovne, who were staying in room 62. The guest from Kovne had an old wife and the guest from Lodz had a young wife. The guest from Kovne, who left his room on some other matter... was led astray and visited the younger woman in 52. So, you understand...in short, punches, cries for help, tears...

"This is simply a merry little story, a satiric scene. The real stew follows.

"Yakub, our fine young hotel valet, arrived in the town of Mezeritsh after nightfall, and could not find a single soul. As if he did not already have enough problems, he fell down, could not get up, and cried out: "Help me!" Suddenly...suddenly a Jew appeared out of nowhere... You are probably thinking it was just some ordinary Jew? No, it was a Jew with a lantern! This Jew with the lantern rescued him. He saved his life! But Yakub the valet was destined to suffer, because the old man, whose name was Isaac Dreykop,[91] and his wife mistakenly identified Yakub as their son-in-law Yankl, who had long ago cast away their daughter Sheyne-Feygl...

"One way or another, they did not let Yakub the valet return to his wife and children! They watched his every step. He was given a separate room with Sheyne-Feygl, the wife foisted upon him, and his new mother-in-law lavished him with gold[92] (that's what **Shomer** writes, literally). Her long-lost son-in-law now had to live "on proper footing" with her daughter. And he, Yakub the valet, was forced to remain there, without any residence permit to boot, until the real Yankl turned up. Only then was Yakub the valet able to return home to his little lady, to his wonderful guests at Hotel Danzig 18, where **Shomer** stays whenever he visits Warsaw.

"Of course, you probably think that this is the core of the novel? You are mistaken. It would have been better had the whole story ended with that. But this entire narrative about Yakub's mistaken identity is only a canvas for **Shomer**, a prelude, an introduction. The real affair is just getting started!

"Since Yakub the valet remained with Sheyne-Feygl alone in a room and began to philosophize with her about the bitter circumstances in which he now found himself (poor thing!), Sheyne-Feygl also had an opportunity to pour out her bitter heart and to tell Yakub the valet about her most interesting biography.

"Sheyne-Feygl—are you following?—was in love with the bookkeeper David Fridvald, a rare personage who dressed in the latest Western fashion.

---

91. Dreykop: someone who wheels and deals in business, thought usually not with great success.

92. A more idiomatic version of this ironic expression would be "showered him with kindness."

The romance between them had been going on for some time. She wrote passionate letters, sang sweet songs, and carried on until the lovers settled on a rendezvous, a place where they could meet face-to-face. That place was Trokhim's garden. And so the lovers met every day in Trokhim's garden... until her parents were warned... Her parents had intended to marry her off to the Rebbe's grandson, whose face radiated a divine countenance and who dressed according to the latest styles published in the rabbinical journals (word for word). But Sheyne-Feygl put her foot down and said that she would rather die than marry this other man. She only would agree to marry David the bookkeeper!

"Or so Sheyne-Feygl believed. David the bookkeeper apparently thought differently. This character was involved simultaneously with two beauties—with Sheyne-Feygl and with Khavele (and perhaps with Trokhim's daughter too, though I am only guessing...). He wrote the same poems for both of them, he led them on and he tasted the fruits of love with both of them...

"So what did they do? The betrayal led them to establish a bond with one another, and they agreed to play a prank on him. Sheyne-Feygl promised him that if he dressed up like a woman, she would go with him to the village of Flaruntshik where they could enjoy the fruits of their love...

"The plan went off without a hitch. David dressed up like a noblewoman, excuse the comparison, and waited by the church for his beloved Sheyne-Feygl. The young demoiselles he had deceived then appeared. They informed the town gentiles that there was a horse-thief dressed as a woman hanging around behind the church. The gentiles caught him and threw him in jail.

"But David was soon released. He left the town safely and over the course of six years married three times (he remarried every two years). Yes, David the bookkeeper is one of **Shomer**'s rogues, the type of person who leads people astray, like all of **Shomer**'s heroes.

"In the end, Sheyne-Feygl married the Rebbe's grandson, the precious Yankele, who cast her off, as we already know...

"What a procedure it is to trudge one's way through **Shomer**'s novel! Couldn't he have just told the story of this rascal, this knave David and his affairs with Sheyne-Feygl, Khavele, Trokhim's daughter (that gentile lass), and the many other unfortunate women whom he asphyxiated like a polecat strangles chickens? No, instead he led us in and out of the forest, over hills and through valleys. First he had to tell us some story about a guest from Kovne in room 62 who happened to stray with the young wife of the guest from Lodz in room 52... And after that, we were told about Yakub the poor valet who fainted, who was "lavished with gold," and who had a strange woman foisted upon him (not that ugly, mind you, even if she was another man's wife)... And why is the story about Yakub necessary? Because Sheyne-Feygl needs a character to appear suddenly to whom she can reveal her most interesting life story, from which one can derive a moral exemplum.

"In my opinion, this nice story, like the rest of **Shomer**'s most interesting novels, could have been a bit shorter, in this way:

> Once upon a time there was a hen and a rooster–
> The story begins;
> Once there was a cow and a calf –
> The story is half done!
> Once there was a cat and a mouse –
> The story concludes...[93]

"One story ends, and another begins, a brand new one...but it is actually an old one—rearranged inside-out, haphazardly stitched, hurriedly patched, and mixed together from scraps and bits—so long as the end product is a big book, a novel in two parts with an epilogue.

"This is precisely what the famous Hebrew critic David Frishman[94] remarked in the Jewish newspaper *Hayom*[95] when he said that the narratives in **Shomer**'s novels are not well-connected and that they do not relate to one another. Rather, he added, they are threaded together like beads on a string or apples on a piece of twine; they have no real relationship to one another. But does our fabricator of novels care what a Frishman or a Criticus or anyone else says about him? **Shomer** responds that any criticism is the result of jealousy and hatred, and that he will not allow himself to be discouraged.[96]

---

93. Sholem Aleichem bases this on a popular Russian folk rhyme:

> *Zhili-byli dve mochely*
> *Vot i skazochke nachalo*
> *Zhili-byli dva pingvina*
> *Vot i skazke seredina*
> *Zhili-byli dva gusia*
> *Vot i skazochka ivsia.*

94. David Frishman (1859–1922), one of the major writers and critics of the renaissance of modern Hebrew literature, and a champion of art for art's sake.

95. *Hayom* (The Day), first Hebrew daily newspaper published in Russia (1886–88). Frishman's review of Shomer's novel *Hanidahat* appeared as Letter III of "Mihtavim al davar ha-sifrut," *Hayom*, 257–258 (1887), 2–3; 2–4. See also David Frishman, *Mihtavim al sifrut: Kol kitvei David Frishman* (Jerusalem: M. Neuman, 1968), 21–37.

96. Shomer was not shy in defending himself against his critics during this period. A vigorous debate among his critics and defenders occurred in 1887–88 in the pages of *Yudishes folksblat* (for a list of the relevant articles and essays, see note 126). In a letter to the editor of the *Yudishes folksblat* 10 (1887) he asserted: "One must provide a child with something sweet, even when one wants to give him bitter medicine. I know that if I had just provided my readers with moralistic writings they would not have picked up a single book." In his feuilleton "A patsh af a patsh," *Yudishes folksblat* 30 (1887), he attacked the new generation of critics: "I am not

"I nearly forgot to tell you that the novel *A Story, Short but Sweet* also includes a saccharine-sweet song that the two heroines sing with their eyes rolled to the heavens (sweet David wrote the song):

Nobody knows how miserable I am,
How my heart desires you,
Fly quickly, my beautiful angel,
Come quickly. Oh, revive me...and so on.

"This is just the place for such a song by Goldfaden:[97]

I am Jacob the valet
To live without a drink is useless,
I know the Pentateuch and the Bible too:
The Righteous Haman had a good head,
And Korah was a first-class drunk,
Whereas Lot, for whom alcohol had no value,
was swallowed by the earth
Pharaoh put on a banquet for Haman
And Abraham our Patriarch was there too,
And Jethro stood on the other side of the door
And Esther was hanged,
Woe is me!

"These are the types of songs, in fact, that would have been written by such heroes as David and the rest of the servants who figure so prominently in **Shomer**'s works, rather than the inflated, sentimental and philosophical poems we encounter in almost every one of his novels.

"Yes, **Shomer** "knows the Pentateuch and the Bible too"... This is quite evident from the citations he borrows from Ecclesiastes and from Hebrew poetry to begin his novels...

"Honored jurors! A writer of the people—a true artist and poet—is a mirror in which the rays of his epoch and generation are reflected. He portrays and reflects life in the same way that a pool of pure water reflects the rays of the sun. That is why vision is first born in the soul of a talented writer who is a leader of the human community. That is why whenever some disaster occurs, some punishment from God, some misfortune, the refined sensibility of the poet, the veritable conscience of the people, is the first to feel it.

---

interested in the criticism of freshly-baked little writers. They cannot destroy me in any way." In the foreword to his historical novel *Der letster yudisher kenig* (which appeared in 1888 prior to *The Judgment of Shomer*) he singled out Sholem Aleichem by taking to task the editorial staff of the *Folksblat* for providing space for his "clownish pranks....Is there nothing better than Sholem Aleichem's prattling?"

97. Sholem Aleichem is being ironic here. To the best of my knowledge, this is not a song from Goldfaden's repertoire.

Similarly, at a redemptive moment or when a piece of good news or celebration comes to pass, the first to announce it is the inspired writer who is blessed by God with a rich spirit, with elevated comprehension, with refined understanding, with a soft, warm heart. This is why there is a strong, eternal bond between a writer and his people. This is why the writer is a servant of God, a priest, a prophet, and an advocate, and every people loves such a servant who comforts it through its misfortunes, celebrates its joys, and guides it through its various ideas, thoughts, strivings, hopes, and so on. This is why, I submit, not a single event can come to pass within the life of a people, neither a celebration nor a disaster, that the writer does not address fully down to its very essence.

"Lately, Jews have been through bitter times. There have been many occurrences, changes, difficulties, and much suffering. This bitter period has affected every writer, and prompted them to be among the first to respond. And respond they did. Open any Jewish book or newspaper—either in Hebrew, Yiddish or Russian—and in it you will find a trace of the times, you will discover that the Jewish world did not doze off: we debated, conversed, took action, planned gatherings, raised money, built colonies in the Land of Israel, emigrated to America, whispered about Spain... in general we went for it! Whether it did any good or not, that's a different question. What matters is that everyone got worked up. Most active of all was that small group who grabbed for the pen, picked up on all the nuances, worried about the masses, and remained interested in the fate of their poor brothers who had been left behind.

"Though **Shomer** is a cripple and a bad writer, he is a writer nevertheless. He, too, holds a pen in hand, consumes impressive quantities of ink, and ruins a lot of paper. Is it possible that the last few years have not had any impact on him? Is it possible that no Jewish matter affected him apart from werewolves, vipers, uninhibited Cecilias with their "sparkling diamonds," "Lisettes," usurers, and rogues? No! In his last novel (or should I say, in the most recent of his latest novels, in case he writes some more!) I read the following words with great delight: "Palestine," "patriotism," "Jewish Question," "pioneer." I devoured the novel right down to the bones. But it came back up on me, it poisoned my head, damaged my stomach, caused me heartache, and destroyed my appetite.

"This nice novel full of national sentiment has the lovely title *Di goldene kelber*[98] (The Golden Calves). It passes itself off as a novel of Kiev, as a reflection of the holy city of Kiev. But it is related to Kiev to the same degree that the rest of **Shomer**'s novels are related to Jewish life. If it were not for the fact that in the novel there was mention of the Podol and Hotel Belle-

---

98. *Di goldene kelber oder der katsav in salon: roman in tsvey teyln*, Vilna 1887.

vue, it could have taken place in Krisielevke,[99] Shepetivke,[100] Lahishin,[101] Jerusalem, Philadelphia, or even on the other side of the Sambatyon, behind the mountains of darkness, among the so-called red Jews.[102] That is how natural its scenes are. That is how believably the characters come across... But why don't we turn to the novel itself?

"In this latest novel, **Shomer** made great strides forward, a major achievement. In short, there are no rogues. Instead of a rogue, there is a tyrant. The worst of all tyrants in *The Golden Calves* is the speculator Yoyne Faygshteyn. Like the rest of **Shomer**'s heroes, Yoyne Faygshteyn was a yeshiva student, a nobody, a little snot before he became filthy rich. Of course, he made the life of his first wife so miserable that she died of consumption, and after her death he flirted with some fifty girls (how's that for a scoundrel?). He courted all the available young misses in Kiev, but he set his sights on the most beautiful Helena, daughter of Abraham Risfeld. Perhaps you are wondering why he desired her more than any of the other girls in Kiev? This is how **Shomer** explains it to us in his folderol:

> *We accept that one is willing to spend a lot of money on a diamond. If you were to ask someone: why do you love that diamond so much? Is it because of its luster? And why is it worth a thousand rubles? — Why? Because everyone likes a diamond!...In the same way, one does not get engaged because the bride-to-be pleases him, but rather because she is desired by everyone else. The opposite is also true. One takes an aversion to a woman if she does not appeal to others. In a word, in the practical world we have thousands of examples that tell us that... and so forth.*

"What a foolish lesson. Why does one want a diamond? Because it is desired by everyone else too. Why did Yoyne set his eyes on Helena?

---

99. Close in sound to Krasilovka, a town near Kiev where Sholem Aleichem resided during the composition of *The Judgment of Shomer*. The name later became the inspiration for his fictional shtetl of Kasrilevke.

100. Shepetivke (also Shepetovka): shtetl in the Western Ukraine, burial place of the hasidic rebbe Pinhas of Koretz.

101. Lahishin (also Lohiszyn): small shtetl located in several kilometers northwest of Pinsk, in Belarus.

102. The Sambatyon is part of Jewish mythical geography. It is believed to be the river beyond which the ten Lost Tribes of Israel were exiled by the Assyrians. The Talmud describes how the river rages during the week and is calm only on the Sabbath; this has prevented the lost tribes from crossing it to return from their exile. Over the centuries, the Sambatyon has captured the imagination of Jewish mystics, messianists, and travellers. The "red Jews" (natives) refer to those peoples, both in Asia and in the New World, whom various Jewish travellers have believed to be descendents of the Lost Tribes. S.Y. Abramovitsh's *The Abridged Travels of Benjamin the Third* (1878), one of the most important satiric novels of classic Yiddish fiction, is a mock epic about a *luftmentsh* who sets out from his shtetl in search of the red Jews across the Sambatyon.

Because she was the desire of Zisblum, the attorney. If Zisblum had not been attracted to Helena, then Yoyne would not been attracted to her either. In that case, Helena would have married, Yoyne would have done whatever he wanted, Zisblum would still be an attorney, and **Shomer** would have been left, God forbid, without a novel!

"Who is this Helena? Helena is a girl, pretty as a picture, like a rose in the month of May... She is exactly like Lisette, Elizabeth, Zinaida and all of the other pretty girls in **Shomer**'s novels. **Shomer** writes: "She was well-educated and smart but she did not like Jews. She always read anti-Semitic newspapers such as *Kievlianin* [103] and *Novoe vremia* [104] But suddenly (always suddenly?!) something changed in Helena. She was transformed from being a self-hating Jew who wanted to be baptized into a passionate Jewish nationalist, all thanks to the attorney Zisblum who opened her eyes to the fact that the *Kievlianin* was a big lie (may its name be blotted out!). Together with her native pride, there sparked within her a sacred love for the upstanding lawyer. It burned so passionately that soon enough she found herself at the piano singing sweet songs... This hero Zisblum was so good and so honest that he did not allow himself, like some of **Shomer**'s other heroes, to partake of the fruits of love. As he states: "I have never been an idealist. I have always been a realist..." However, in order for you to understand the nature of Zisblum's realism, I am obliged to read you an entire scene from *The Golden Calves:*

---

103. *Kievlianin* (1864–1918), a semi-official Russian anti-Semitic periodical, edited by V. Ia. Shulgin (until 1878) and then his student D.I. Pikhno. Initially founded to promote Russification, the journal quickly concerned itself with the so-called "Jewish Question." It regularly published critical articles on aspects of Jewish education, culture, economics, and political power. In 1873, its pages published "The Jewish Cemetery in Prague" (a translation from the German novel *Biarritz*), which later inspired the famous anti-Semitic forgery *The Protocols of the Elders of Zion.*

104. *Novoe Vremia* (New Times, 1868–1917) one of the most influential conservative newspapers in the Russian empire. It increasingly adopted an anti-Semitic course after it was purchased by A.S. Suvorin in 1876, who transformed it into a mass-market nationalist publication. It was a leading proponent of the Blood Libel and blamed Jewish economic practices for the pogroms launched against them in 1881. The year before Sholem Aleichem published *The Judgment of Shomer*, the newspaper characterized the "Jew" as follows: "He directs all his inner strength toward disturbing that foundation of religious, political, and civil life upon which are based the contemporary states that give him equal rights... The Jew remains the same enemy of the rest of the world that he has been from the time of the exodus from Egypt. With political and civil rights, he possesses additional means and resources to harm his enemy, to trample on him and to seek his destruction" (August 26, 1887, quoted in J. Klier *Imperial Russia's Jewish Question* (Cambridge University Press, 1995), 447–48).

Yoyne Faygshteyn knocked at room 6, Hotel Bellevue, Kiev.

-"Ah! Mr. Faygshteyn," Zisblum called out warmly. "I came to see your accommodations and to inquire about your well-being."

-"I have a wonderful room and, thank God, I am healthy."

-"Have you had a chance to see our Kiev?"

-"Yes, Kiev is a fine city, but it does not compare to Warsaw."

-"Have you visited anyone?"

-"Yes, I have already been to Mr. Risfeld's..."

-"Really? So you have already caught a glimpse of your future bride?"

-"I had the pleasure of speaking with her."

-"So what is your opinion of her?"

-"She is a rare beauty, and intelligent to boot; one can make a lady of her."

-"It seems to me that it would be appropriate then to wish you congratulations?"

-"From my perspective, yes. But I don't know whether the other side is going to agree."

-"Oh! Don't worry about it!" - Yoyne said - "She will consider herself fortunate if she marries you because she has already been around the block..."

-"What do you mean by that?"

-"You ought to know that...today she likes this man and tomorrow she prefers that one. She promises one that she is going to be his wife, and then becomes his wife... You get it? And the next day she goes for someone different, falls in love with him, and also becomes his wife, and so forth..."

-"What are you talking about?"

-"Exactly what you hear!"

-"This is totally disgusting," Zisblum shouted and spit. "You are a true friend. I am indebted to you! You saved me..."

Zisblum remained seated, absorbed in his thoughts. Suddenly... another knock on the door! Risfeld's servant entered and brought with him a notecard.

-"Forgive me, Sir. I have something to ask you."

-"Ask."

-"Was Mr. Faygshteyn here?"

-"Yes, he was."

-"And he must have told you who-knows-what about Fräulein Helena, because moments before her arrival here she drove him from her home."

-"Why did she throw him out?," Zisblum asked surprised.

-"Because he is a dishonest, vile man... No doubt he spoke ill of Helena... she had just thrown him out... I can promise you that this golden lass has no equal. I swear, she is a girl with all the best virtues."

-"This is the first time I have ever heard a servant speaking well about his employer."

-"Not all servants are the same. Just as there are fine and abject people, so are there many servants, *"feine Charaktere und niederträchtige"* (the servant speaks philosophically in in-your-face German)."[105]

-"If that is the case, I will pay a visit to Fräulein Helena later today..."

"This is the type of character that **Shomer** calls a "realist." This is one of the best heroes in his repertoire. For him such a character is an angel, a wise man, an ideal, and this incarnation of the ideal is embodied by Zisblum the realist with whom **Shomer** sympathizes so strongly. This idiot takes it upon himself to educate and improve Fräulein Helena, who has grown up on a diet of the *Kievlianin* and the *Novoe Vremia*, and he begins to converse with her about Palestine and colonization, and expresses himself not as a lawyer but like a talmudic bench-warmer, jumping from Bismarck to the Turks and back to the Ishmaelites.

-"As I see it," Helena said to him, "you have already become an idealist."

-"No, I am speaking very realistically!" Zisblum responded, "I tell you, I have firmly decided to become a settler in Palestine."

-"But how will you work the land, when you have to sit hovering over books?"

-"I will get accustomed to working the land the same way I have gotten used to hovering over books."

-"And how can you be sure that you will not be driven from Palestine?"

-"First, the Turks do not drive people from their territories. Second, if there was an attempt to get rid of us, the European governments would stand up for us..."

At that moment a servant arrived...

"Whenever **Shomer** finds himself in strange territory, confused, stuck, and he cannot find his way out of it, he falls back on the strategy (crafty lad!) of sending in a servant, or a servant girl, or a policeman to get him out of the

---

105. The term employed in the original is *mekhteyse daytsh*. For the sake of readability in English, I opt to translate it throughout the text as "in-your-face German." Other possible translations might have included "there's German for you," "pompous German," or "German with pleasure." Throughout *The Judgment of Shomer*, Sholem Aleichem criticizes Shomer's decision to employ *daytshmerish* (a conscious imitation of German) in his writing. Sholem Aleichem had both artistic and national reasons for opposing the *daytshmerish* influence in modern Yiddish letters. Shomer's Germanisms seemed overly inflated and constructed, obscuring Sholem Aleichem's own interest in creating a natural-sounding Yiddish that reflected the everyday vernacular of ordinary Jews. However, as linguist Max Weinreich explains, Sholem Aleichem's antipathy toward *daytshmerish* was a relatively recent phenomenon: "The concept of daytshmerish...came into being gradually only in the nineteenth century. Up to that time the attitude toward the German determinant was neutral. Utilizing more German-component elements was a question of style *within the boundary* of Yiddish" (*History of the Yiddish Language,* 418).

thicket... Thanks to this servant who interrupts the action, we never really know how familiar **Shomer** is with the question of Palestine, about which many other writers have already poured out substantial quantities of ink, broken many pencils, and consumed heaps of paper... **Shomer** saw or heard that the world was speaking of Palestine and colonization, so he also tossed in a word about Palestine and colonization, and he doesn't come back to it again. At the end of the novel he informs us that Zisblum is in a settlement in Palestine and that he and all the colonists are living there happily, as in the days of King Solomon (literally), each one sitting in his vineyard and under his fig tree (that's what he writes, word for word). And that is all. With those few words, he has acquitted himself of the matter. And now we know that **Shomer** is also a nationalist and an admirer of Palestine. So what do people have against him?

"It would have been fine had **Shomer** actually provided us with flesh-and-blood characters, with real-life Jews, whether in Palestine or America, as long as they are flesh-and-blood and not just broomsticks, fireplace pokers, and shovels, not a cast of puppets performing for little children who dance, jump, fight among themselves, spin, and fall apart to the audience's delight.

"In this novel there is only one contemporary figure—Mr. Zisblum. Another character, Miss Zina, is also an interesting type. It is worth getting acquainted with her...

"**Shomer** heard that one should laugh at the assimilated—that is, at those who say that Jews ought to mix in with all other peoples. So he went and inserted into *The Golden Calves* a strange kind of creature, the Jewish girl Zina who was half man and half woman (that's how **Shomer** refers to her). Her idée-fixe, her obsession, was female emancipation. That is to say, she wanted to educate women and give them all the same rights as their husbands. In one word, she was a kind of androgyne—half male and half female, with short hair, always talking about books, emancipation, and so forth.

"But since this androgyne Zina still had the delicate heart of a woman, she fell in love with one of **Shomer**'s tyrants, Judah Krum, an aristocrat from Kiev. This Krum asked her to rob her father, the rich usurer Pleyter. He persuaded her that they should then flee Kiev together and live it up elsewhere. Of course, this rogue Judah Krum tricked Zina out of her few rubles and never really loved her. They tasted the fruits of love and Zina got...you get it?

"But do you think that this is the end of Zina's epic? No, **Shomer** wants to take revenge on this educated woman Zina and on all women who dare to speak about education, emancipation, freedom, and so on. So he sent her another miserable pest: a gambler, a drunk, a pickpocket by the name of Brandvelt,[106] who began to court our beautiful Zina. Here is an episode from their strange courtship:

---

106. Brandvelt: a variation on *brent a velt* ("burn the world").

-"Good morning! You know, my darling Zina," Brandvelt said to her once Judah had left, "I am ready for our journey. I want to run away with you tonight, my love..."

Zina was silent.

-"Why aren't you answering me, my angel? As long as we are not together, my life is not a life. You know how passionate my love is for you. You are my very soul. So what do you say, shall we take off tonight...?"

""Good morning! Here's a groschen, give me a candle! Are you going to give it to me or not?" It is with such enthusiasm that these lovers, the viper Brandvelt and the androgyne Zina, converse. Their passionate love ends with their robbing the tyrant Judah Krum and escaping. This is when Zina's sad tale really begins, full of troubles, disasters, and blows of misfortune. For the gambler Brandvelt is an even greater rogue (still more rogues?) than Judah Krum. He is prepared to kill both the miserable Zina and the child fathered by her first lover Judah Krum... Suddenly... suddenly a police officer appears and brings with him the usurer Pleyter, who is now going by the new name Kopelberg and who recognizes his miserable daughter. Tears flow by the river-full... In short, a big deal, a tumult, a din, money flying around, a policeman, someone going to jail, a rogue, werewolves, vipers, dragons!!!...

"But this novel is not exactly my main point.[107] It is like the rest of **Shomer**'s novels: the villain meets his downfall and the good guy is saved... I only wanted to show you the degree to which **Shomer** pursued the latest fashion and took it upon himself to produce a "contemporary" novel about how Jews live today. **Shomer** attempted to portray figures from both categories: a patriot and an assimilated woman, a lover of Palestine and a... what? Even he does not know! **Shomer** hears the tune but he can't sing on key...

"In the story "*Aheym*" (Homeward), published in *Der veker*[108] in 1887, the new Yiddish writer Marie Lerner[109] also tried to portray one of these Jewish women whose education took her so far afield that she almost forgot that she was a daughter of Israel, and, boy, did she get burned because of it.

---

107. Sholem Aleichem here is playfully acknowledging the influence of S.Y. Abramovitsh, whose character Mendele the Book Peddler frequently employed the expression "nishto bin ikh oysn" ("but that's not what I'm getting at") as an ironic rhetorical strategy.

108. *Der yudisher veker*, Yiddish miscellany published in Odessa, politically allied with the Zionist Hovevei Zion.

109. Marie Lerner (nee Miriam Rabinovitsh, 1860–1927), Yiddish short story writer and playwright. During the 1880s her stories appeared in such publications as *Der veker* and *Yudishes folksblat*. Her play *Di agune* appeared in the second volume of Spektor's *Hoyz-fraynd*. Before World War II, several of her plays (in manuscript) from the early 1880s were found in the YIVO archives in Vilna.

"Now is not the proper time to discuss whether this woman was a realistic character or how "Homeward" stands up to criticism. But at the very least Marie Lerner offered us a portrait of a Jewish girl, a flesh-and-blood person, and we now understand with whom we are dealing. We have some concept of such a person. We can say whether such a character is good or bad. But what can one say about **Shomer**'s androgyne? What kind of creature did he dream up? What kind of comedy is it?! *The Golden Calves* is not comedy, it is a vaudeville sketch, a type of Purim play, even worse than vaudeville! But **Shomer** loves vaudeville. Here on the table is another of **Shomer**'s vaudevillian numbers, a true story taken from his consumptive portfolio: *A khasene on a kale* [110] (A Wedding Without a Bride). It tells the important story of how a rabbi attempted to marry his "precious" son to an attractive girl, and only after the ceremony did it become clear that the bride was not a girl but rather Moshke the servant! A satire? Why aren't you laughing?

"It is amazing that when **Shomer** wants us to laugh, we do not laugh; and when he is trying to be earnest, sober, or tragic, then we want to explode with laughter. For example, in the novel *It Serves Him Right,* **Shomer** says that the names of the characters are a good clue for the reader that they will have something to laugh about. I was not lazy and I read the entire book about Hantsi Dreyze the tavern keeper, Shmaye Fayfer and Berke Tsimbler the musicians, Mr. Eplkvas, [111] and many others. I was not moved to crack a smile.

"So now you are familiar with **Shomer**'s satiric talent, here in *The Golden Calves* and in his other serious novels that he fiercely prevents from being reprinted (God forbid) without his permission. However, I insist that there *is* actually something to laugh about, seeing how **Shomer** imitates the French novelists Dumas, Paul de Kock, and others. He is raving mad, he gets lost in strange happenings, he jams the locks full of wax, he brings dead characters back to life, people are poisoned along the way, children are abandoned in broad daylight, millions are withdrawn from banks under false pretenses, letters are stolen from the post office, little children are kidnapped, there are duels, arson, spilt blood... This all takes place where? In Kiev, in Odessa, in Bobruisk, in Nyesvizh, all before our very eyes. We remain silent! I ask you: isn't this something to laugh about? Could we demand any greater satire than this from **Shomer**?

"Honored jurors, now that we have familiarized ourselves with our accused from various angles, now that we know, thank God, that **Shomer** is a moralist, a satirist, a poet, a philosopher, a belletrist and a psychologist, let

---

110. *A khasene on a kale: a vare geshikhte, aroysgenumen fun tshakhatker pinkes*, Vilna 1884 or 1885.

111. Fayfer: one who blows (on a musical instrument); Tsimbler: one who bangs on cymbals or other percussion instruments; Eplkvas: apple cider.

us now consider him from an aesthetic perspective too. I mean by this his style, his language. If the bride is neither smart nor educated, neither pious nor rich, at least let her be pretty! In every literature one finds uselessness, nonsense, empty chatter. If the rhetoric itself is beautiful, then perhaps it might be beneficial to the reader in that sense. But this quality is also absent from **Shomer**, who has his own language, his own variety of Yiddish that one must refer to by the name: in-your-face German. His jargon is neither Yiddish nor Russian nor German, but rather "half German and half *goyish*." I doubt if ten percent of his readers understand his in-your-face German, with its "*Bräutigame, Kamaraden, Frauenemanzipation...*," "*Immer erworben Respekt*"... "*duftenhayt*," "*Richard hat sich bewaffent mit sein künftigen Ehrennamen...*" "*Sogar schön diktiert die Reden vos er wird tragen...*" "*Jemanden beschuldigen ohne zu wenden...*" "*Sie hot feind gehat seine Physionomie mit die Manieren...*" "*Sympathieren*" (sympathize?). To extract all such in-your-face German words from all of **Shomer**'s novels is an impossible task. He also often uses Russian, and translates skillfully. For example: "*Benjamin and Aaron robbed a church and both smelled of hard labor.*" (Oni oba pakhli katorzhnymi rabotami?) "The ordinary Ulman was lying on the edge of the abyss... (Ulman nakhodilsya vozlye dynki propasti?)... "Daniel softened him with his tears..." "The clock struck midnight..." "... the root cause of the terrible situation..." "The convict..." "The understudy...," and so on.

"All of **Shomer**'s male heroes are cut from the same cloth as regards beauty: a picture-perfect blond, tall, blue eyes, and so on. This is how all his heroines are portrayed: "*She was eighteen years old, a beauty in the full sense of the word; her alabaster white face, her long black hair like black sparkling velvet cascaded down over her shoulders, and her black fiery eyes reminded one of Venus.*" (from *The Pious Jew*)

"Nature in **Shomer** is also described implausibly and with in-your-face German. For example: "*Das war in Monat Mai. Die ganze Natur war geschmuckt wie a schöne Kalleh in Rojsen, es war a prächtige Landshaft...die Sonne strahlt so prächtig, so meistetisch, so lieblich, punkt wie dos engelisches Gesicht ihr geliebten Tanzenwald...*" [112]

"I have in my hands a different Yiddish novel by Spektor, *Der yudisher muzhik* (The Jewish Peasant). [113] Let us compare how this writer describes nature in simple Yiddish, without resorting to **Shomer**'s in-your-face German:

---

112. "It was the month of May. All of nature was bejeweled like a beautiful bride in roses, it was a splendid landscape... the sun shone magnificently, so majestically, so lovely, just as her angelic face shone toward her beloved Tanzenwald." In the citation above, Sholem Aleichem is drawing attention not only to Shomer's overblown rhetoric and mangled German diction, but also to specific mistakes. For instance, there is no such word in German as *meistetish* (*meisterisch* and *majestätisch* do exist).

113. See note 5.

It was a very hot day in the month of Tamuz, one of those burning hot days about which schoolkids say: "God revealed the celestial orb." Humans and other creatures find such days hard to bear. They look forward to the cool night. Small children splash in the river like ducks, but the annoying flies and nasty bugs thank and praise God for such a warm day—they crawl over man and beast and every living thing, sucking out their warm blood. It is impossible to escape the annoyance. In the marketplace in the middle of the city of N–v, people were moving about slowly and quickly, here and there...Merchants, shop-wives, peddlers, and hawkers were all sitting on the earth frying in the sun, looking for customers... Everyone was consumed by his own affairs: the salesperson was running to purchase a bushel of wheat or a measure of millet from the peasant, with the hope that he could earn a groschen for bread. The porter carefully transported his cargo in order to receive ten groschens for food. The pauper wandered around begging for a tiny morsel... Small children ran home from school to eat lunch. The teacher's assistant carried a basketful of greasy meat and milk pots to the house mistress for which he would probably receive his monthly payment... It was steaming, sweat flowed, but people wiped the sweat with their sleeves and carried on...

"In a word, you have before you a familiar scene from actual Jewish life. The shopkeepers in search of buyers, the hungry school kids, the teacher's assistant with the dishes... It is familiar, we recognize it, we remember it—it is as true as truth itself. It is clear as day. And everything is the way it should be. This is what aesthetics, poetry, art demand. This is how one should compose descriptive scenes. All authors should be required to provide these types of descriptions—only what is possible, only that which can be found in real life. Not like **Shomer**'s marvelous paradise: Jewish counts, girls named Elizabeth, angels or rogues of whom we can't even imagine because they have nothing to do with our lives, they have no relationship to us whatsoever. Since everything is borrowed from Paris, it comes across as strange in Kiev, Odessa, Bobruisk, Eyshishok, like a monkey in a tuxedo with a top-hat, as natural as a clown with Queen Esther among Purim players who yell and shriek and confuse to such an extent that one is glad to be rid of them at last. **Shomer**'s rogues, angels, old maids, werewolves, vipers, and remaining cast of characters also yell and shriek and confuse us, and we are also delighted when we can finally be rid of them.

"I still have something to say about a few remaining points, about several special nuggets contained in these fifty novels by **Shomer** that are spread on the table before us. Only God knows whether I will be able to mention all of the wonders that prove that **Shomer** is an expert in the Trivium and the Quadrivium, in all seventy tongues[114] —all knowledge is on the tip of his tongue—Talmud, history, mythology, law, medicine, philosophy, and so on.

---

114. A reference to a talmudic tradition according to which there are seventy primary nations and languages in the world, derived from the list of Noah's grandsons. A midrash teaches that Moses taught the Torah in seventy languages.

"In the novel *Di ayzerne froy*[115] (The Iron Lady), he translates the Hebrew *"ayelet ohavim"* as the goddess of beauty—Aurora. But it seems to me that every schoolchild who has glanced at a book of ancient mythology knows that the goddess of beauty is Venus, and that Aurora is the morning star, or *"ayelet ha-shahar,"* and that the God of love is Amour, not Aurora...

"In the novel *Di umgliklikhe libe*[116] (Unhappy Love) he translates the Hebrew word "vanity" as fanaticism. So how would he translate the verse from Ecclesiastes: "Vanity of vanities, all is vanity"?—Fanaticism of fanaticism, everyone is a fanatic?

"In the novel *The Rich Beggar* **Shomer** says: *"Even a génie like the poet Luzatto..."* The reader asks himself, what kind of species is that, a génie? But **Shomer** is a Frenchman. We read in his *"Di tsidkonyes"*[117] (Pious Woman): *"bonjour and bonsoir,"* good morning and good evening.

"Le-mi ani 'amel? For whom do I toil?[118] *This is a talmudic question,"* says **Shomer** in his novel *The Treasure*. But where does such a citation appear among our sages? Who said it? History is silent in this regard...

"**Shomer** is a great Talmudist, but he is an even better Hebrew poet. His Hebrew poems, which he provides at the beginning of every novel, are a beautiful gift, a type of bonus to the novel itself, and today people are really wild for bonuses! But the majority of such Hebrew bonuses from **Shomer** are... since it's not connected to Yiddish, I'll hold my tongue.

"In the novel *Der shlimazldiger hoz*[119] (The Unlucky Hare), **Shomer** writes offhandedly: *"It was prophesied about Reb Bereniu from Koretz that he must be the messiah because you would have to look far and wide to find such an idiot, such a golem.* "Quite a notion of the messiah! We should show it to our most talented, nationalist Jewish writers—what would they have to say about it?

"In the novel *Between Two Flames*, **Shomer** says that Nathan was brought up in *"milk and in honey"*—have you every heard a metaphor like this?

"In one of his most interesting novels (I've already forgotten which one) **Shomer** writes that *"the heroine was ruined because she could not get married before the age of twenty. It was forbidden, according to Russian*

---

115. *Di ayzerne froy oder dos farkoyfte kind: eyn vunder-sheyner roman*, 1882.

116. *Di umgliklekhe libe oder der kosherer mamzer: roman in tsvey teyln*, Warsaw 1882.

117. *Di tsidkonyes oder gut shabes Yakhne: a vare hekhst interesante ertseylung*, Vilna 1884 or 1885.

118. Title of a famous poem (1871) by the Hebrew enlightenment poet Judah Leib Gordon in which he laments the lack of a Hebrew readership and critiques Russification among segments of the Jewish intellectual elite.

119. *Der shlimazldiker hoz: a varer hekhst interesanter roman*, Vilna 1886.

law..." Who does not know that according to Russian law a man cannot marry before the age of eighteen, and a woman before the age of sixteen?

"In *Der spekulant*[120] (The Speculator) **Shomer** writes: "*Today's ordinary Jews who have reached the summit of happiness have taken an aversion to their religion. Who gave them their horns?—The speculator did!*" This is already related to psychology and to the political economy with which **Shomer** is entirely at home... Is it possible to catch all such precious finds which are scattered throughout **Shomer**'s novels? You can demand such insights from a true writer, but in the case of a scribbler like **Shomer**...

"Honored jurors, now that I have proven the degree to which our accused is a manufacturer of novels, now that I have shown you what kind of "writer of the people" **Shomer** really is, I hope that your good judgment, your taste and your pure conscience will point you to the conclusion that you need to deal with him sternly, that you should not spare him, because that is what is rightfully earned by such a harmful writer, such a murderer of the people. Therefore you can do two good deeds: you can condemn a literary huckster, and you can protect our poor young Yiddish from other such parasites. I am not saying this for my own sake, honored jurors. I am telling you this in the name of literature, in the name of readers, in the name of our entire people!"

* * *

The prosecutor took his seat and **Shomer**'s attorney rose, cleared his throat, and began his defense in the following words:

"Honored judges and jurors! My talented opponent, the prosecutor, certainly painted you a pretty picture. He presented my client, Mr. **Shomer**, as a terrible parasite, as a murderer of the people, as a butcher, as a thief. But that is simply not true. His interpretation is completely tendentious. He is the type of prosecutor who snoops around and seeks out only the worst. In my opinion, it is no great achievement to besmirch even the purest man. If we look hard enough we can find plenty of faults and imperfections in anyone. Everything must have its boundary, its limits. It is no great art to toss an entire mountain of shortcomings at someone, to search, rummage, and dig around, all in order to ruin the reputation of an author who has written so much for his people. To be honest, I will not tell you that my client is a great, highly praised belletrist. But neither will I pronounce that he is not a writer at all, or that he does not have a speck of talent. A hundred novels, honored jurors, a hundred novels are no small thing. It is not so easy to create plots for several thousand heroes! The prosecutor says that they are all hackneyed versions of French novels. Even if this were the case, it is more difficult to adapt a hundred novels than to be a prosecutor! Especially since

---

120. *Der spekulant oder tsvey meysim geyen tantsn: a vare geshikhte*, Vilna 1886.

not all of them are adapted. The majority are the product of **Shomer**'s own imagination. The prosecutor cannot deny this. Even if they have little connection to Jewish life, this does not mean that **Shomer** is guilty. The public, the uneducated class of readers, demands his type of merchandise, and the booksellers, the itinerant salesmen, seek out his variety of novels, nothing better—the only criterion is that they be cheap and plentiful! Sirs, I ask you, how is **Shomer** guilty if people come to him and pay him by the sheet to write such-and-such a work by such-and-such a title? It is purchased by the warehouse-full, the public reads it—people probably need it! If it were not needed, people would not buy it. But since people are willing to hand over their hard-earned money for it, why should they not be able to have it? There is a saying among the gentiles: "A fool gives, and the clever one takes"...

"The prosecutor makes a comparison between my client and Abramovitsh, Linetski, Goldfaden, and so forth. Woe is me! Who said that **Shomer** should be compared to them? Even **Shomer** himself would never say such a thing! He is not such an idiot as to persuade himself of such a pile of rubbish. The prosecutor calls him a murderer, a butcher, a robber. Honored jurors, take a look at my client. Does he have the face of a murderer, a butcher, a robber? What kind of evil, God forbid, could **Shomer** have intended with his novels? He does not mean any harm, God forbid, to anyone. He does not want to provoke anyone or to ruin anyone's livelihood. If a businessman wants to earn a ruble, why shouldn't he? Have you imagined what is possible for a Jewish writer to earn from his writing? I would not wish it on any of my enemies. I am certain that were my client to have something of a decent income—a store, a commission, a position—he would gladly forfeit his name, his reputation, his literary career, along with everything else.* But what is he supposed to do, honored jurors? He has to live, he has to eat! A Jewish writer also has a stomach. The prosecutor demonstrates that **Shomer** is not a moralist, not a satirist, not a poet, not a belletrist, not a psychologist, not a philosopher, and not an aesthete. Very well, I agree. I concede that to him. But I would be interested to know who that writer is who contains within him all of these aforementioned virtues? One must be a serious pedant to demand all of this from a single person. So what is this really all about? Is there not among the fifty or so novels that the prosecutor has mentioned a single work that has some value, a chapter, or even a single page? It cannot be! It cannot be! On the contrary, I know from my own experience that

---

* In the novel *The Treasure*, **Shomer** explicitly says that he would do business with the fools who would have erected an iron monument in his honor after his death; in his lifetime he would take from them a third of what the monument should cost... Shomer has desires! Napoleon once said: "A man is not a soldier if he never has the ambition of becoming a general."

Sholem Aleichem

many young ladies who read **Shomer's** most interesting novels have cried countless tears. No doubt, if they weep over his work, it must be worth something! We have further proof that his works have something of value to them: there are many imitators who make use of **Shomer**'s name on their creations. I have here in my portfolio a nice rag, a novel with the title *Di aristokratke*[121] (The Aristocrat) by Abraham Isaac Bukhbinder from Odessa. The name of the real author appears in small letters, and above it, printed in big letters, we read: composed in the style of **Shomer** (in really big letters!).

"The second treasure is *Di hadase,*[122] a drama in four acts by Shimon Bekerman, also from Odessa, and also written in the style of **Shomer** (printed in big letters). In order for it to seem precisely like one of **Shomer**'s works, on which there always appears the statement "reprint strictly forbidden," Shimon Bekerman added the following statement at the bottom, though it came out a little differently: "Re print strict for bidden!"

"Not long ago, a new type of writer, some fellow with the name Ulrikh Kalmus (perhaps from Odessa also?) reworked **Shomer**'s novel *A patsh fun zayn libn nomen*[123] (A Slap from the Lord) about the householder who married the cook after winning the lottery. But this Ulrikh Kalmus published it as a drama (a real treat!) under the title *Der groyser trefer*[124] (The Great Fortune Teller), and with such beautiful language that he is welcome to warm himself by **Shomer**'s hearth. The content itself is also very interesting in that all of Ulrikh Kalmus's heroes drink only coffee. It seems that Ulrikh Kalmus enjoys coffee, and coffee is the kind of drink that does not spoil..."

"Mr. Defense Counsel!," the presiding judge suddenly broke in, "I must ask you to speak to the issue at hand and not wander so far off course!"

"Pardon me! Honored jurors, it should be as clear as day to you that **Shomer**'s novels do contain something of worth, even though the prosecutor absolutely denies it. I can provide you with further proof in the fact that the public reads more of **Shomer**'s novels than Abramovitsh's or other similar works. For what reason? Why, I ask you? It is probably not an accident.

---

121. I was unable to find the date of this novel. See note 6 for additional information on Bukhbinder.

122. A reference to *Hadase di khalutse: a drame in 4 aktn, ferfast af dem ort fun Shomer*, Odessa 1884.

123. A possible reference to *A gebentshter patsh: a vare ertseylung*, Berdichev, 1887. A novel by the same title as the one cited by Sholem Aleichem above was republished in Warsaw in 1897.

124. Sholem Aleichem is referring here to Kalmus's *Der groyser trefer oder der gevins fun di 200,000 rubl* (The Great Fortune-Teller, or the 200,000 Ruble Windfall, a Yiddish drama in four acts), *Yudishes folksblat* 6–12 (1888). Sholem Aleichem found the vulgarity of Kalmus' Yiddish unacceptable.

Perhaps there is something to them. I assert that there is a kind of bond between **Shomer** and his readership, something that makes their feelings coincide with his works. It would appear that **Shomer** understands what the public likes. How can **Shomer** be guilty if the public does not understand? What should **Shomer** do if the masses prefer such fairy tales—as the prosecutor refers to them—full of rogues, vipers, and werewolves? The masses, the ordinary folk, are like small children who cannot fall asleep without such a fairy tale. They adore such stories. They get frightened at the sound of "Boo," and they demand precisely to get frightened!

"**Shomer** understands this very well, and you can see how he acquired great fame as a result. Wherever you happen to be in a Jewish town, drop in on the shop attendant, the servant girl, the artisan, the female cook, the woman who sells fruit...You will hear the delight with which they respond to your inquiries about **Shomer**. Ask the same cooks or fruit-sellers or servants about Abramovitsh or Linetski and their mouths will open and their ears will prick up. They will not understand what an Abramovitsh or a Linetski even is... So what is the story with them? The story is the following: Abramovitsh, Linetski and others like them are writers for the intelligentsia, for the chosen few, for the educated or partly educated classes, whereas **Shomer** is a writer for everyone, a novelist for shopkeepers, servant girls, cooks, coachmen, and women who peddle goods at the market. Yes, honored jurors, for such an audience **Shomer** is a nice writer, a fine belletrist, just as Moshe Marakhovski from Boslov is a decent poet, and Ulrikh Kalmus is a decent playwright who crafts dramas and comedies, and Ozer Bloshteyn and Bekerman, and Khayim Bunim Tsimbler and Fishzon the jester, and all the other hacks are considered major writers by the ordinary folk... I see that the prosecutor is looking at me askance, as if I am offending the masses and casting aspersions on the people. What am I to do? I am also eager for the masses to take up the kinds of Yiddish works that the intellectuals are reading. I also want to see what the scullery maid has to say about Abramovitsh, Linetski, and other such authors. I also want to hear what the servant girl has to say about one of Spektor's novels. I also would like to live so long as to experience a time when this audience chases after a real book, seeks out a Jewish newspaper, a journal, understands what a critic is all about and why critics are necessary... Only God knows whether I and the prosecutor and you will live to see such a day. Only God knows whether something will be learned from today's proceedings that are being taken down by our stenographer Sholem Aleichem and will probably be reprinted in a separate pamphlet—God knows whether anyone will know of it!...No, honored jurors, you must not be so severe with my client, because it is not **Shomer** who is guilty for being a **Shomer**. The public is guilty that there is such a thing as a **Shomer**. A certain man of science once said that everything is a product of its time, of its circumstances. Whatever we see, whatever we find in the world must be the way it is; it cannot be otherwise because then it would not be....Therefore, we must conclude, we must be reconciled to the fact that writers such as **Shomer**, Bekerman, Ulrikh Kalmus, Moshe Marakhovski from Boslov, Oyzer Bloshteyn, Khayim Bunim Tsimbler and others must be part of our literature, and the more we persecute them, the more we want to hound them, the more they will breed, be fruitful and multiply, sprout like green grass and grow like toadstools. Let them be, and they will probably cease to exist on their own. Leave the public alone to choose what material it wants to read. The audience, I repeat, is like a little child. It will grow up, it will get smarter. You will not be holding back anyone in the least, and true talents, important writers will not be harmed. God's world is vast. Beautiful nature and human intelligence co-exist with scoundrels and insects, worms and cockroaches, frogs and lice, darkness and plague... and they do not destroy God's world.

"Therefore, honored jurors, I hope that your intelligence and your conscience will not permit you to deal too harshly with my client, Mr. **Shomer**, who is now in your hands and who begs you to judge him fairly and with compassion, as a man equal to others. I rest my case."

* * *

"What is your response?," the presiding justice turned to the prosecutor.

"After such a statement, after such a "defense" presented by my opponent, the counsel for the plaintiff, I have nothing further to add."

This is what the prosecutor said and he sat down.

"The Accused! You may now put in a last word."

Thus the presiding justice turned to **Shomer**, who rose and began to speak in a trembling voice:

"Honored judges and jurors. I am supposed to react both to the prosecutor as well as to my own lawyer, but my health does not allow it. I will not assert that I am a major belletrist. But I can tell you that in my place and time I play an important enough role... A new generation has arisen. New Yiddish writers have appeared: educated men who possess a good knowledge of Hebrew and have advanced degrees... All of them have taken to writing in our homey language. It has become the rage to criticize Yiddish works. It was never like this before. Nobody ever said a single bad word about my writing. Just the opposite: I was praised, I was thanked, I was paid—so long as I continued to write novels. Now that a Yiddish newspaper has been established, now that there is criticism, everyone is suddenly concerned with me, everyone is piling on... "Mr. Criticus" is on my case; the "Yudisher gazlen"[125] in the *Yudishes folksblat* is against me, Frishman and Sholem

---

125. *Der yudisher gazlen* (The Jewish Thief) pseudonym of Yisroel Levi (1842–1905). Levi's St. Petersburg press put out *Yudishes folksblat* from 1881–90. Though the

Aleichem are no better inclined towards me.[126] Everyone is getting in on the action. Why me and not others? Because they are jealous of me, they begrudge my success. Honored jurors, in my life I have written close to a hundred novels. It was not easy. The prosecutor says that I adapted them from French. I swear to you, I do not know French! What kind of reward will I live to see from the common people? Long ago I wrote in one of my novels that I will spare them the trouble of erecting me a cast-iron monument after my death. I have toiled so much and in the end they will ruin me. Honored jurors, have pity!"

At this point **Shomer**'s voice broke and a sobbing cry could be heard in the hall. Two scullery maids and a servant girl were crying. The rest of the audience also sat sadly and several among them had red, damp eyes.

"So, honored jurors," the presiding justice said, "now you must go to your deliberation room. You must determine your judgment of our accused, which consists of three possibilities:

1. If you find according to the prosecutor's accusation that **Shomer** is entirely guilty, you will indicate: "Yes, he is guilty."

2. If you find according to the defense that **Shomer** is entirely innocent, you will indicate: "Not guilty."

3. And if you determine that **Shomer** is guilty but with extenuating circumstances, and you want to treat him with mercy, compassion, and pity, you will indicate: "He is guilty, but he deserves leniency."

* * *

---

paper published some of the best contemporary writers (for instance, Sholem Aleichem, Spektor, and Yankev Dinezon), in Levi's own articles he often defamed Yiddish, to the chagrin of those writers and intellectuals who were struggling to establish respect for it as a competitive literature.

126. A reference to the heated exchanges that took place in the pages of *Yudishes folksblat* (hereafter *YF*) among Shomer, his critics, and his defenders. See Sh. Berdichevski, "Erinerungen un gedanken vegn ertsiung un literatur," *YF* 1 (1887), 3–9; 3 (1887), 35–38; Y.M. Volfson, "Der shlimazldiker hoz," *YF* 2 (1887), 24–26; Shomer, "Korespondentsyes: A briv tsu der redaktsye," *YF* 10 (1887), 150–51; Der yudisher gazlen, "Kritik," *YF* 27 (1887), 419–22; 28 (1887), 435–40; Shomer, "A patsh far a patsh," *YF* 30 (1887), 483–88; Pri ets ha-hayim (Y.M. Volfson), "Kritik af kritik," *YF* 32 (1887), 541–42; Sholem Aleichem, "Fun vayte medines," *YF* 33 (1887), 547–52; Der yudisher gazlen, "Der yudisher gazlen iz eysh-lehove," *YF* 34 (1887), 563–68; Rav-kotsn (Y.Kh. Ravnitski), "An eysek mit shmates," *YF*, supplement to issue 4 (1888), 13–15; 5 (1888), 32–33; Anonymous, "Retsenzye," *YF*, supplement to issues 11–12 (1888), 355–61; Eyner fun di mitarbeter, "Retsenzye: Di goldene kelber," *YF* 16 (1888), 455–67; Shomer, "Di shlimazldike knishiklekh," *YF* 16 (1888), 449–55; 17 (1888), 481–88; 18 (1887), 525–37.

A half-hour later the twelve jurors came back with their verdict: "Yes, he is guilty, but he deserves leniency."

The prosecutor and the defense counsel exchanged a few more words, during which time the prosecutor demanded that **Shomer** be driven from the literary world and that he be forbidden from writing any more novels for the common people. The defense argued that this was somewhat excessive, that to forbid someone from writing was too harsh, and that the verdict itself was already punishment enough for **Shomer**.

The presiding judge and the two magistrates rose and left to consider the verdict, and there was a significant commotion and tumult in the hall. People conversed, complained, grumbled. This one said that they were going to send him to hard labor, and that one determined that it smelled more like Siberia. The women spoke more than anyone, all at once, like geese. Several were on **Shomer**'s side, and some on the opposite. Several old maids gazed at **Shomer** with pity, compassion, and love.

Finally, the presiding judge and the justices came out and read the following decision, consisting of five points:

1. The court determines that **Shomer** is not truly a Yiddish writer.
2. Following the careful deliberation of twelve individuals whose responsibility it was to judge him, we proclaim that **Shomer** is not a belletrist, a poet, an artist, a moralist, a philosopher, a satirist, or an aesthete.
3. Every new work that is published by **Shomer** immediately must be submitted to the critics who will go over it in great detail.
4. A request that **Shomer** should have compassion on our poor Yiddish language and should, at the very least, refrain from reprinting any of his old rags, so that his "most interesting" novels should go off to the same place where our beloved holy Sabbath goes at sunset.
5. This verdict, which is being copied word for word by our stenographer Sholem Aleichem, should be printed quickly and without delay in several thousand copies and distributed among Yiddish readers at the cheapest possible price.

II.
ELABORATIONS:
READING WISSE'S CANONICAL AUTHORS

Daniel Deronda:
"The Zionist Fate in English Hands" and
The Liberal Betrayal of the Jews

EDWARD ALEXANDER

In Chapter Seven of *The Modern Jewish Canon*, "The Zionist Fate in English Hands," Ruth Wisse veers slightly from her attempt to define the canon to a consideration of how well English literature has been able to admit the autonomy of the modern Jewish people. Wisse limits her canon, the reader may remember, to Jewish writers who, whether they write in Yiddish, Hebrew, or some Gentile tongue, evince respect for the autonomy of Jewishness and the centrality of Jewish national experience. Their work must "attest to the indissolubility of the Jews," although not necessarily in a positive way. Another requirement for admission to Wisse's canon is that "in Jewish literature the authors or characters know and let the reader know that they are Jews." But here she announces that before considering how Jewish literature has dealt with the Zionist enterprise she will discuss two works by non-Jewish authors, George Eliot's *Daniel Deronda* (1876), "the classic of Zionism," and James Joyce's *Ulysses* (1922), "the classic of modernism," to discover "how Jews can, and cannot, survive the dilemma of English generosity."[1]

   In the event, Wisse gives a low grade to Joyce and a very high one to George Eliot, whose novel (begun in 1874) she deems "the imaginative equivalent of the Balfour Declaration" (238), which in 1917 gave the British government's formal recognition of a historical Jewish claim to Palestine and so provided the basis for the Palestine Mandate given to Britain in 1920. One might also add that the novel anticipated the rationale for a Jewish state given in the same year by the most important Englishman of modern times, Winston Churchill: "If, as may well happen, there should be created in our own lifetime by the banks of the Jordan a Jewish State under the protection of the British Crown which might comprise three or four millions of Jews, an event will have occurred in the history of the world which would from every point of view be beneficial, and would be especially in harmony with the truest interests of the British Empire."[2]

---

1. *The Modern Jewish Canon: A Journey through Language and Culture* (New York: The Free Press, 2000), 239. Subsequent references to this work appear in parentheses in the text. Perhaps Wisse should have qualified her allusions to the apparently welcoming arms of "English generosity" with mention of the fact that the most vividly realized Jewish character in nineteenth-century English fiction, Fagin, an ancestor of Nazi anti-Semitic caricature, was the creation of the ardently liberal Charles Dickens.

2. *Illustrated Sunday Herald*, 8 February 1920. Quoted in Martin Gilbert, *Exile and*

Wisse did not raise the question of whether *Deronda* itself, by virtue of the fact that some of its characters do know and let the reader know they are Jews, belongs in the Jewish canon, even though written by a non-Jew who—with one notable exception—knew little from experience about Jews except for the deracinated ones who, then as now, frequented intellectual coteries. "Is it not," George Henry Lewes observed, "psychologically a fact of singular interest that she was never in her life in a Jewish family, at least never in one where Judaism was still a living faith and Jewish customs kept up? Yet the Jews all fancy she must have been brought up among them."[3]

George Eliot as the celebrator of Jewish autonomy and indissolubility, and nearly an honorary Jew! Who that looked over her shoulder as she wrote her letters or diary entries in 1848 could have predicted this? At age twenty-nine, Mary Ann Evans (Eliot's real name), infuriated by the idea of "race fellowship" among Jews, which she thought she detected in Benjamin Disraeli's novel *Coningsby* (1844), told a friend that she was "almost ready to echo Voltaire's vituperation. I bow to the supremacy of Hebrew poetry, but much of their early mythology and almost all their history, is utterly revolting. Their stock has produced a Moses and a Jesus but Moses was impregnated with Egyptian philosophy, and Jesus is venerated and adored by us only for that wherein he transcended or resisted Judaism...Everything specifically Jewish is of a low grade." This being so, she could even ruminate about how "Extermination...seems to be the law for inferior races," including "even the Hebrew caucasian."[4]

Nevertheless, a mere twenty-eight years later the young Lithuanian Jew Eliezer ben-Yehuda was telling his friends that what they had derided as his "new heresy" of the rebirth of the people Israel, speaking its own language (Hebrew) in its own land was, in his view, being massively endorsed by the English novelist George Eliot, who had written of "a man who had a vision similar to my own." "After I had read the story a few times [!]," Ben-Yehuda wrote in his autobiography, "I went to Paris...to learn and equip myself there with the information needed for my work in the Land of Israel."[5]

Return (Philadelphia: J. P. Lippincott, 1978), 128–129. Many years later, Churchill said that the creation of the State of Israel would in time be considered the major historical event of the twentieth century. Churchill no doubt respected the fact that virtually no nation-state anywhere in the world was more solemnly founded in international consent than Israel. Yet his words strongly suggest that the significance of the State is rooted in deeper and more ancient foundations than those modern covenants or the modern Zionist movement: "The coming into being of a Jewish state...is an event in world history to be viewed in the perspective not of a generation or a century, but in the perspective of a thousand, two thousand or even three thousand years."

3. Richard Owen, *The Life of Richard Owen*, 2 vols. (London, 1894), I, 231–232.

4. J. W. Cross, *Life of George Eliot* (New York: Thomas Y. Crowell & Co., 1884), 84, 87, 88.

5. Eliezer Ben-Yehuda, *The Dream Come True*, trans. T. Muraoka, ed. George Mandel (Boulder, Co.: Westview Press, 1993), 27.

And exactly one hundred years after Mary Ann Evans's Voltairean fulminations of 1848, the three main cities of the newly founded state of Israel—Jerusalem, Tel Aviv, and Haifa—all boasted a George Eliot Street. (None of which should be taken as confirmation of the absurdities of Edward Said, who in *The Question of Palestine* (1979) based his entire discussion of the origins of Zionism on Eliot's novel, to which he devoted six pages while ignoring Pinsker, Herzl, Smolenskin, Ahad Ha'am, Gordon, Syrkin, Jabotinsky, and Ben-Gurion.) The development of Eliot's Jewish sympathies was made possible by her turn, not taken until 1857, when she was almost thirty-eight, from discursive writing to fiction, at whose heart, she believed, was the capacity for imaginative sympathy. "If Art does not enlarge men's sympathies, it does nothing morally. I have had heart-cutting experience that opinions are a poor cement between human souls, and the only effect I ardently long to produce by my writings, is that those who read them should be better able to *imagine* and to *feel* the pains and the joys of those who differ from themselves in everything but the broad fact of being struggling erring human creatures."[6]

In 1858 she and Lewes, with whom she was by now living happily in sin, traveled to Prague, where she found that "the most interesting things" in the city were the Jewish burial ground (Alter Friedhof) and the old (Altneu) synagogue. The multitude of quaint tombs in the cemetery struck her as the existential realization of Jewish history, "the fragments of a great building...shaken by an earthquake." But could these fragments still live? Perhaps. "We saw a lovely dark-eyed Jewish child here, which we were glad to kiss in all its dirt. Then came the somber old synagogue, with its smoked groins, and lamp forever burning. An intelligent Jew was our cicerone and read us some Hebrew out of the precious old book of the law."[7]

But, as everyone now knows, the real turning point in George Eliot's attitude toward "everything specifically Jewish" came in 1866, when she met Emanuel Deutsch, a talmudic scholar born in Prussian Silesia and educated both by the University of Berlin in theology and by his rabbinic uncle in Talmud. He gave her weekly Hebrew lessons and also conveyed to her the excitement he felt upon visiting the Holy Land in 1869. When he saw Jews leaning against the western wall in prayer he thought less of the past than of the future, and expressed his conviction that the destiny of "the once proscribed and detested Jews...is not yet fulfilled."[8] ("*Od lo avdah tikvateinu.*")

---

6. *Letters of George Eliot*, ed. G. S. Haight (New Haven: Yale University Press, 1954–1955), III, 111.

7. Cross, 274–275.

8. *Literary Remains of the Late Emanuel Deutsch*, ed. Emily Strangford (London: John Murray, 1874), 169.

So intimate did the relationship between Deutsch and the novelist become that Eliot, during the years when her friend began to suffer terribly from the cancer that would eventually, in 1873, kill him, felt personally obligated to keep him from suicide. This she did, in part, by casting herself as "a fellow Houyhnhnm who is bearing the yoke with you" and who had herself (perhaps) once considered self-destruction. "I have been ailing and in the Slough of Despond too...[but] remember, it has happened to many to be glad they did not commit suicide, though they once ran for the final leap."[9]

Although it is generally supposed that Deutsch's vision of national revival first made itself felt in the character of Mordecai in *Daniel Deronda* (1876), there is evidence that, for whatever reasons, Eliot was being drawn toward the affirmation of a national idea some years earlier. One hint of the forces stirring within her appears in the famous Prelude to *Middlemarch* (1871–1872), the novel Eliot began to work on in 1867, the year after she met Deutsch. The Prelude's opening sentences allude to the way in which Spain's national identity was forged in an ostensibly religious struggle against Muslim Arabs; but they do so by briefly telling the story of Saint Theresa as a little girl, "walking forth one morning hand-in-hand with her still smaller brother, to go and seek martyrdom in the country of the Moors." Their children's hearts were "already beating to a national idea."[10]

Given the prominence of the "national idea" on the first page of the novel, one looks, but in vain, for its development in the nearly 900 pages of *Middlemarch*. The novel's heroine Dorothea Brooke yearns intensely for "something...by which her life might be filled with action at once rational and ardent; and since the time was gone by for guiding visions and spiritual directors, since prayer heightened yearning but not instruction, what lamp was there but knowledge?" (Chapter 10, 112–13). But since, unlike Theresa, she lives in the nineteenth rather than the sixteenth century, her yearning can be satisfied (and, as it happens, not very well at all) only in marriage. Fulfillment of a protagonist's larger spiritual ambitions was not to come until *Deronda*.

When she began *Middlemarch*, Eliot would also have been aware of a recently published novel dealing with Jewish-Christian relations called *Nina Balatka* (1867), by Anthony Trollope. Trollope concealed his authorship of the book, but gave a curious hint of it by naming its Jewish protagonist Anton Trendellsohn. Set in both the Christian and Jewish sections of Prague, including the very Altneu synagogue ("the oldest place of worship

---

9. *Letters of George Eliot*, V, 160–161.

10. *Middlemarch*, ed. W. J. Harvey (New York: Penguin Books, 1965), 25. Subsequent references to this work appear in parentheses in the text. Was Eliot aware, one wonders, of Theresa's Jewish ancestry?

belonging to the Jews in Europe"[11] and the location for its most powerful scene) that had engaged Eliot's interest and sympathy, *Nina Balatka* can be linked, though by contrast as much as by likeness, to *Daniel Deronda.*[12]

Although Trollope displays at least as much knowledge of and sympathetic attention to the existing Jewish community (of Prague, at any rate) as will be found in *Deronda*, he follows the convention of marrying his Jewish protagonist to the Christian heroine: Catholic Nina wins out (in part because she does not have black hair and dark eyes) over her Jewish rival Rebecca. The novel acknowledges that "the Jews of Prague were still subject to the isolated ignominy of Judaism" and that "in Prague a Jew was still a Pariah" (69) but also assumes that raw, violent Jew-hatred is a thing of the past: "In her time but little power was left to Madame Zamenoy to persecute the Trendellsohns other than that which nature had given to her in the bitterness of her tongue" (3-4). *Nina Balatka*'s awareness of Jewish national aspirations in Palestine does not go beyond such comments as "most of us [Jews] are dark here in Prague. Anton says that away in Palestine our girls are as fair as the girls in Saxony" (10). So much for this Jewish hero's Zionism. A good deal of what has come to be called the "Zionist part" of *Daniel Deronda* is actually no more than what the writer Avi Erlich calls "ancient Zionism," that is, traditional orthodox beliefs about the importance of the Holy Land in Jewish ethics and self-definition that may underlie political Zionism but could have been held (then) by many Orthodox Jews who opposed political Zionism as itself a thinly veiled form of assimilation.[13]

The book of Ezekiel, for example, promises that "I will take you from among the nations, and gather you out of all the countries, and will bring you into your own land" (Ezekiel 36: 24). Nevertheless, there is a specifically political Zionist element in the novel, both in the few scenes in which Mordecai holds forth and in Deronda's own aspirations and ideals. Here, for example, is Mordecai's proposal for a Jewish national revival, an expression of the idea that the Jews are, as the late Emil Fackenheim used to say, a dispersed but not a dismembered people:

> Revive the organic centre: let the unity of Israel which has made the growth
> and form of its religion be an outward reality. Looking toward a land and a
> polity, our dispersed people in all the ends of the earth may share the dignity

---

11. *Nina Balatka*, ed. Robert Tracy (New York: Oxford University Press, 1991), 9. Subsequent references to this work will be given in parentheses in the text.

12. See Murray Baumgarten's excellent discussion of the two novels in "Seeing Double: Jews in the Fiction of F. Scott Fitzgerald, Charles Dickens, Anthony Trollope, and George Eliot," in *Between Race and Culture*, ed. B. Cheyette (Palo Alto, Calif.: Stanford University Press, 1996), 44–61.

13. Avi Erlich, *Ancient Zionism: The Biblical Origins of the National Idea* (New York: Free Press, 1995). David Mesher's unpublished work on this topic has also been of great use to me.

of a national life that has a voice among the peoples of the East and the West—
which will plant the wisdom and skill of our race so that it may be, as of old,
a medium of transmission and understanding.[14]

This is quite different from both the Christian "Zionism" of Victorian English
Evangelicals who proposed the Jews' return to the Holy Land—the better to
convert them to Christianity—and from that of Moses Montefiore, who wanted "the return of thousands of our brethren to the land of Israel" to better
observe their own religion.[15]

Mordecai, who also resembles Emanuel Deutsch in being fatally ill, sets
forth his ideas in the discussions at the "Hand and Banner" workingmen's
club, discussions that are remarkable in their prescient foreshadowing of
the modern war of ideas over the Jewish state. Two of Mordecai's antagonists, for example, sound very like Arnold Toynbee condemning Jews as a
culturally degenerate historical "fossil" or like Tony Judt disparaging the
state of Israel as an "anachronism" and the only impediment to a post-
nationalist world, or like modern "progressive" Jews who believe that liberalism and Judaism are the same thing:

> "Whatever the Jews contributed at one time, they are a standstill people,"
> said Lilly. "They are the type of obstinate adherence to the superannuated.
> They may show good abilities when they take up liberal ideas, but as a race
> they have no development in them." (Chapter 42, 590)

When Mordecai envisions a time when the Jews, no longer a dispersed people, "shall have a defence in the court of nations, as the outraged Englishman or American" (595), one thinks immediately of the rationale for the
trial in Jerusalem of Adolf Eichmann for "crimes against the Jewish people."
Already the Zionist idea that the Jews should be not a chosen people but
k'chol ha-goyim, like the Gentiles, in the sense of belonging to the family of
nations, was being derided by those who believed that the era of nationality
was (almost) at an end, a belief as chimerical in 1876 as it is in 2008. A good
deal less prescient or sophisticated is the process whereby Daniel discovers
his Jewish identity. Although reared as an English aristocrat and believing
himself to be of Spanish "blood," he finds himself drawn, by apparent acci-
dents that prove to be inevitabilities, to other Jews. This movement of the
novel, as Lionel Trilling acerbically complained in 1939,[16] shows Eliot's sus-
ceptibility to Victorian race-thinking (of the sort exhibited, for example, in
Matthew Arnold's Oxford lectures *On the Study of Celtic Literature*).
Indeed, Daniel is often asked by London Jews, within five minutes of meet-

---

14. *Daniel Deronda*, ed. Barbara Hardy (Baltimore: Penguin Books, 1967), Chapter 42,
    592. Subsequent references to this work appear in parentheses in the text.

15. See Naomi Shepherd, *The Zealous Intruders* (San Francisco: Harper & Row, 1987),
    229, 239.

16. Lionel Trilling, *Matthew Arnold* (New York: Columbia University Press, 1939).

ing him, whether he belongs to their "race." He eventually discovers his Jewish identity, and not by looking down.[17]

Rather, in the novel's great ironic moment, Daniel hears his mother (whose melding of [Jewish] Jew-hatred with feminism is yet another prescient touch of George Eliot's) boast of how she (now turned Christian) saved him from his Jewish fate, or, as Daniel sees the matter, deprived him of his birthright. "And the bondage I hated for myself I wanted to keep you from. What better could the most loving mother have done? I relieved you from the bondage of having been born a Jew" (Chapter 51, 689). Wisse correctly observes that "though the book's thematic sympathies are not with the princess [Daniel's mother], Eliot invests her with the dramatic and intellectual powers to express this position better than it has ever been done in fiction."[18]

Daniel, once sure of his Jewish identity, offers a more specifically English rationale than Mordecai's for a Jewish national home: "restoring a political existence to my people, making them a nation again, giving them a national centre, such as the English have, though they too are scattered over the face of the globe" (Chapter 69, 875). Here Daniel raises the question of the relation between the potentiality of Jewish nationhood and the actuality (which is shown to be in a very dismal state in the novel) of English nationhood.

Eliot seems to have looked to the Jewish tradition, more specifically to the Zionist version of national renaissance, an idea brought to ruin—at least according to *Daniel Deronda*—in Victorian England by its system of dehumanized relations, epitomized in the treatment of Gwendolen by Grandcourt. In the famous fifteenth chapter of *Middlemarch* Eliot had expressed her dissatisfaction with the English novel's endless obsession with "romance" and her intention to direct it toward a nobler subject, that of "vocation." She was, of course, not entirely successful in doing so; four romances are still at the heart of that novel, despite its massive exploration of one protagonist's calling to medicine, the "noblest of professions." But one senses Eliot's earnestness about changing the genre's direction in the way she baffled Victorian readers by keeping the novel's true heroine, Dorothea, and the novel's true hero, Dr. Lydgate, on quite separate romantic-marital tracks. Similarly, in *Deronda*, the romantic attraction between Daniel and Gwendolyn is overcome (on his part) by "vocation," except that Daniel is called not to medicine or to law but to the Jewish national idea.

Daniel's linkage of a yet unrealized Jewish national idea to a tarnished and desiccated English one also implicitly raises the by now endlessly discussed question of the relation between the "English" and the "Jewish"

---

17. On the intriguing subject of whether Daniel was circumcised as an infant, see John Sutherland, "Is Daniel Deronda Circumcised?" in *Can Jane Eyre Be Happy?* (New York: Oxford University Press, 1997), 169–176.

18. *The Modern Jewish Canon*, 242.

halves of the novel in which he appears. Eliot herself complained, right from the beginning, so to speak, that readers "cut the book into scraps and talk of nothing in it but Gwendolen."[19]

Some of the hostility to what Henry James derided as the "Jewish" part of the novel, and later critics, especially English ones writing after 1948 (when the yishuv drove the British from Palestine), as the "Zionist" part derive from genuinely aesthetic motives or principles. After all, H. M. Daleski, the Israeli critic (and also hero of the War of Independence), while arguing for the essential thematic unity of the novel, also observed that "the Gwendolen Harleth part must surely rank as among the best things George Eliot ever did, while the Jewish part has no mean claim to being among the worst."[20] Barbara Hardy also wrote in good faith when she criticized Eliot for suspending her characteristic critical irony and humor (exercised even at the expense of such heroines as Dorothea Brooke) in presenting the relentlessly solemn Daniel.[21]

Irving Howe, to whom Ruth Wisse attributed perfect pitch as a literary critic, and who, though a non-(but not anti-) Zionist, could hardly be accused of hostility to Jewishness, objected that Daniel is "abundantly virtuous but only intermittently alive....No wonder he comes to seem a mere figment of will or idea, a speechmaker without blood, a mere accessory to the prophetic Mordecai, the dying spokesman of Jewish rebirth."[22]

But there has always been another, less "aesthetic," far nastier, *a priori* hostility to the "Jewish/Zionist" element of the novel, and one that appears to foreshadow today's fierce hostility of England's liberal and learned classes to the state of Israel. In a now famous letter, Eliot wrote to her American friend Harriet Beecher Stowe in 1876:

> As to the Jewish element in *Deronda*, I expected from first to last in writing it that it would create much stronger resistance and even repulsion than it has actually met with. But precisely because I felt that the usual attitude of Christians toward Jews is—I hardly know whether to say more impious or more stupid when viewed in the light of their professed principles, I therefore felt urged to treat Jews with such sympathy and understanding as my nature and knowledge could attain to....Can anything be more disgusting than to hear people called "educated" making small jokes about eating ham, and showing themselves empty of any real knowledge as to the relation of their own social and religious life to the history of the people they think

19. Letters of George Eliot, VI, 290.

20. "Owning and Disowning: The Unity of *Daniel Deronda*," *Daniel Deronda: A Centenary Symposium*, ed. Alice Shalvi (Jerusalem: Jerusalem Academic Press, 1976), 67.

21. Introduction to *Daniel Deronda*, 20.

22. *Irving Howe: Selected Writings, 1950–1990* (New York: Harcourt Brace Javanovich, 1990), 361.

themselves witty in insulting?...I find men educated at Rugby supposing that Christ spoke Greek.[23]

To George Eliot's inner circle, that "Rugby" allusion might have called to mind her young admirer (and later to be husband) J. W. Cross, who had been educated at Rugby (and whose lack of Hebrew—he "knew little of *hiphil* and *huphal*"—she sometimes lamented). But to the general reader that letter, when it appeared, is more likely to have suggested the most famous of all Rugby figures, Dr. Thomas Arnold. Arnold, earlier in the century, had been the spiritual (and political) leader of the Liberal or Broad Church movement within the Church of England and a major figure in liberalism more generally. He displayed a notable shortage of sympathy in the Jewish direction. The Jews, in his view, had no right to British citizenship or to its privileges. England, he argued, was the land of Englishmen, not of "lodgers" who had claims to nothing more than an honorary citizenship. "'Religion,' in the king's mouth," Arnold insisted, "can mean only Christianity." He was outraged by the notion of a Jew serving as one of the governors of the Christ's Hospital School, and in 1838 resigned his position on the University of London's board of examiners rather than countenance the admission of Jews to a university whose "nonsectarianism" (i.e., admission of Dissenters) had, ironically, been a scandal to Arnold's High Church enemies.

Of course Dr. Arnold, had he lingered in the world long enough to read *Daniel Deronda*, might have said of Daniel and his bride Mirah as they sail off to the Holy Land, "good riddance to them." No need to guess what Henry James said of the novel's Jewish protagonist through one of his invented characters (one Pulcheria) in "Daniel Deronda: A Conversation": "I am sure Daniel had a nose, and I hold that the author has shown great pusillanimity in her treatment of it." But James's unpleasantness has no political dimension, as does that of the formidable liberal Leslie Stephen, father of Virginia Woolf, whose discussion of Daniel's Jewish quest, according to Eliot's biographer Frederick Karl, "borders on a barely controlled anti-Semitism."[24]

Eliot's own critique of what Ruth Wisse would later call "the liberal betrayal of the Jews," (the subtitle of Wisse's book *If I Am Not for Myself...*) comes in her essay of 1878: "The Modern Hep! Hep! Hep!" In it Eliot observes that English liberals often seem keen to promote every nationalism except the Jewish one. The new crop of what she calls "anti-Judaic advocates" are "liberal gentlemen," who "belong to a party which has felt itself glorified in winning for Jews, as well as Dissenters and Catholics, the full privileges of citizenship, laying open to them every path to distinction." In this sense, they are far different from Dr. Arnold. But now, she says, they have been brought up short by the prospect of Jewish autonomy and the

---

23. *Letters of George Eliot*, VI, 301–302.

24. Frederick R. Karl, *George Eliot: Voice of a Century* (New York: W. W. Norton, 1995), 556n.

desire of (some) Jews to retain a culture and an inner world of their own. "Too late enlightened by disagreeable events," these liberal gentlemen now regret that they were mistaken and the foes of emancipation correct. They are eager to celebrate the dignity of populations of which they have never seen a single specimen—she cites as an instance the liberal glorification of "grim marriage customs of the native Australians"—but "sneer at the notion of a renovated national dignity for the Jews," and impatiently demand (as the youthful Mary Anne Evans had) the "complete fusion" of the Jews with the various peoples among whom they are dispersed.[25]

Lest there be any doubt that she is alluding not just to typically English social prejudices and snobbishness but to sanctified liberal doctrine, Eliot proposes to "nationalize" the sacred text of English individuality, John Stuart Mill's *On Liberty* (1859). "A modern book on Liberty has maintained that from the freedom of individual men to persist in idiosyncrasies the world may be enriched. Why should we not apply this argument to the idiosyncrasy of a nation, and pause in our haste to hoot it down?" (423). Showing no patience with the utopian liberal fantasy—the antithetical twin of the aforementioned liberal respect for newly formed nationalities—that the nation-state is about to disappear, Eliot argues that the "organized memory" and distinctive national consciousness of the Jews require, if they are to be preserved and expressed in the modern world, a sovereign state:

> Are there, in the political relations of the world, the conditions present or approaching for the restoration of a Jewish State planted on the old ground as a centre of national feeling, a source of dignifying protection, a special channel for special energies, which may contribute some added form of national genius, and an added voice in the councils of the world (422)?

However painful to Eliot the "resistance" and "repulsion" with which the Zionist element of *Deronda* was met in 1878, they were a mere pinprick compared to the fusillades that the Zionist idea and the State of Israel provoke in England today. Indeed, the very title of Wisse's chapter, "The Zionist Fate in English Hands," which seemed innocent enough when *The Modern Jewish Canon* appeared in 2000, today (2008) seems ghoulishly ironic, especially when viewed in the light of Wisse's allusion to "the world's most hospitable culture." If we take "English hands" to refer to England itself, then the Zionist fate is in mortal danger. Contemporary England, most especially its literary culture, and within that culture most particularly its liberals and battlers against "racism," has declared war upon Zionism and the Jewish state and its inhabitants (unless they happen to be Israeli Arabs). London today has a mayor who considers vituperative abuse

---

25. "The Modern Hep! Hep! Hep!" *Impressions of Theophrastus Such* [1879] (New York: Doubleday Page & Co., 1901), 413, 421. Subsequent references to this work appear in parentheses in the text.

of Israel (and of British Jews) one of his primary municipal duties. England as a whole has become the most anti-Zionist and perhaps most anti-Semitic country in Europe, although it falls behind France (and only France, among European nations), with its much larger Muslim population, in acts of physical violence.[26]

Such animosity is not entirely new in England. As far back as 1982 the *Observer* reporter who attended the London performance of George Steiner's *The Portage to San Cristobal of A.H.* said that it was received with raucous applause; and he wondered how much of that applause was intended for Hitler's monologue justifying himself and declaring that he, not Herzl, founded the Jewish state. Years later, when Norman Finkelstein's squalid tract *The Holocaust Industry* (2001), which depicted the Holocaust as in essence a Jewish-Zionist invention, appeared in England, every major British paper devoted at least a full page to this updated version of *The Protocols of the Learned Elders of Zion*, and the book was actually serialized in the *Guardian*. By 2003 a columnist in that paper's sister publication *The Observer* was demanding that Jewish journalists declare their "racial" origins when writing about the Middle East: "I have developed a habit," announced Richard Ingrams, "when confronted by letters to the editor to look at the signature to see if the writer has a Jewish name. If so, I tend not to read it."[27] In 2002 it was English intellectuals who organized the boycott of Israeli academics and researchers. The English (also Jewish) playwright Harold Pinter spoke for a great number of English writers when he called Israel "the central factor in world unrest" and accused it of using nuclear weapons against the Palestinians.

Back in the summer of 1947, at the height of Jewish resistance to British rule in Palestine, the anti-Jewish riots in London, Glasgow, and Manchester were largely the work of working class thugs. Today the battle against Israel and British Jewry more generally is conducted by the devotees of George Eliot's own Religion of Humanity, humanists adept in the reversal of memory, passionate defenders of Islamic suicide bombers, who are called "the victims of victims." The equation of Zionism with Nazism, a commonplace slander among British colonial officials as early as 1941, is now a central dogma of British liberals and leftists. Indeed, England's chief rabbi Jonathan Sacks labeled it "one of the most blasphemous inversions in the history of the world's oldest hate."[28]

Amidst this ocean of English hostility to the Zionist idea and its realization in Israel, the pointed omission of "The Modern 'Hep! Hep! Hep!'" from

---

26. See Robert Wistrich, "Cruel Britannia: Anti-Semitism among the Ruling Elites," *Azure* (Summer 2005), 100–124.

27. See Julie Burchill, "Good, Bad and Ugly," *Guardian*, November 29, 2003.

28. Jonathan Sacks, "A New Anti-Semitism?" in Paul Iganski and Barry Kosmin, eds., *A New Anti-Semitism?* (London: Profile, 2003), 46. The most thorough and sophisticated

A. S. Byatt's 1990 edition of Eliot's *Selected Essays, Poems and Other Writings* constitutes no more than a ripple, but one worth noticing in this context. Eliot's essay first appeared in what was to be her last book, *Impressions of Theophrastus Such*, a collection of eighteen pieces, ostensibly edited by Eliot. Although most Eliot scholars consider the "Jewish" essay by far the strongest in the collection, Byatt, a member in good standing of England's literary establishment (and not one of its ardent Israel-haters[29]) finds space for selections of nine of those essays but none at all for so much as a word from "The Modern 'Hep! Hep! Hep!'" On this particular subject, the voice of George Eliot is not welcome in the contemporary British world of letters.

And yet the voice continues to resonate. If, for example, we wonder what the author of *Daniel Deronda* would have made of this resurgence of Jew-hatred precisely in the midst of "the world's most hospitable culture," we need not do so for long. In May of 2004 the literary section of a New York newspaper carried a lengthy essay entitled "The Modern 'Hep! Hep! Hep!'" which linked past and present:

> As an antisemitic yelp, *Hep*! is long out of fashion. In the eleventh century it was already a substitution and a metaphor: Jerusalem meant Jews, and "Jerusalem is destroyed" was, when knighthood was in flower, an incitement to pogrom. Today, the modern *Hep*! appears in the form of Zionism, Israel, Sharon. And the connection between vilification and the will to undermine and endanger Jewish lives is as vigorous as when the howl of *Hep*! was new. The French ambassador to Britain, his tongue unbuttoned in a London salon, hardly thinks to cry *Hep*!; instead, he speaks of "that shitty little country." European and British scholars and academicians, their Latin gone dry, will never cry *Hep*!; instead they call for the boycott of Israeli scholars and academicians....Lies shoot up from the rioters in Gaza and Ramallah. Insinuations ripple out of the high tables of Oxbridge. And steadily, whether from the street or the salon, one hears the enduring old cry: *Hep! Hep! Hep!*[30]

The words are those of Cynthia Ozick, the vision still that of the noble, long-nosed, omnipresent sibyl: George Eliot.

---

study of contemporary liberal anti-Semitism in England is Bernard Harrison, *The Resurgence of Anti-Semitism: Jews, Israel, and Liberal Opinion* (Lanham, Md.: Rowman & Littlefield, 2006).

29. By English standards, she is something of a trimmer. She has said (in the *Guardian*, 27 April 2002) that she "[understands] the anxieties of American Jews who, while not supporting all of Israel's actions, are disappointed by the way disapproval in Europe seems to shade very easily into anti-semitism."

30. Cynthia Ozick, *The New York Observer*, May 10, 2004.

The Pleasure of Disregarding Red Lights:
A Reading of
Sholem Aleichem's Monologue "A Nisref"

DAN MIRON

> *The road now stretched across open country, and it oc-*
> *curred to me—not by a way of protest, not as a symbol, or*
> *anything like that, but merely as a novel experience, that*
> *since I had disregarded all laws of humanity, I might as*
> *well disregard the rules of traffic. So I crossed to the left side*
> *of the highway and checked the feeling, and the feeling was*
> *good.—Passing through a red light was like a sip of forbid-*
> *den Burgundy when I was a child.*

Vladimir Nabokov, *Lolita*, chapter 36

We are used to reading Sholem Aleichem's stories in the order and within the contexts the author himself imposed upon them by dividing them
among the various volumes of his collected works and by placing each one
of them in its specific niche within the respective volume to which it was
allocated. Thus our reading of the stories is greatly influenced by the two
canonical editions of the writer's *oeuvre*, the so-called "Progress" edition,
which appeared in his lifetime (Warsaw, 1910–14), and the posthumous
"Folksfond" edition (New York, 1917–23), which, though edited by Sholem
Aleichem's son-in-law, the Hebrew-Yiddish writer I.D. Berkovitsh, nevertheless was based on the author's own revised texts, as well as on his general
plan for a comprehensive, if not exhaustive, edition of his works in forty
volumes (only twenty-eight of which appeared). Both editions placed "A
nisref" ("Burned Out," 1903), one of the many short stories Sholem Aleichem had cast in the mold of a monologue, as the fifteenth of the twenty
monologues of which the volume *Ayzenban geshikhtes* (Railway Stories;
originally titled *Ksovim fun a komi-voyazher*, Writings of a Commercial
Traveler, with "ayzenban geshikhetes" serving as a subtitle) was comprised.
Thus we tend to read this story as one of the *Railway Stories*, which inevitably imbues our understanding of it with the general color or tonality of
this late masterpiece.

The general tonality of *Railway Stories* is a peculiarly wistful, bittersweet one. The majority of the stories (to be exact, fourteen of the twenty),
and certainly those that strike us as the "quintessential" among them, were
written from 1909–11, as the author was slowly convalescing from the dire
health crisis he had experienced in summer 1908, when his hectic tour of
the Jewish pale in the Ukraine and Byelorussia as a solo performer-reader of
his own works to packed halls was cut short by a violent spell of open pul-

monary tuberculosis. After months of inactivity the writer, who for many years had been producing new works at a dizzying pace and whose writing also constituted his sole source of income, took again to the pen, writing in bed on pads supported by his raised knees and, at least for a time, investing his energies mainly in the *Railway* project, which thus was suffused with the mood of a person who, as Sholem Aleichem himself put it, had been granted an audience with his majesty Death himself.

It was not by any measure an overtly tragic mood. On the contrary, there was something distinctly bright and restful about it. Inherently deeply pessimistic in their assessment of the human condition, the stories nevertheless exhibited an uncannily smooth, relaxed, albeit ironic, surface, as if the writer had reconciled himself to the chaos and absurdities of existence. Thus two otherwise completely different, indeed polarized and antagonistic, masterpieces, the heartbreaking "Happiest Man in All Kodny" and the poisonously sweet "Man from Buenos Aires," were quite similar in their unhurried pace and relatively simple plot line. Both, at surface level, were strangely calm (though both recorded events and described situations that were inherently either tragic or chaotic and morally repugnant) and smoothly flowing. In this, the two, as well as many of the other stories written more or less together with them, distinctly differed from the author's well-known earlier masterpieces cast in the monologue matrix, such as "The Pot" (1901), "Seventy-five Thousand" (1902), and "Advice" (1904), agitated, meandering, nervous tales of sound and fury told by monologists who were writhing with pain and angst, could not keep to the topic or goal they tried to focus on, got themselves entangled in zigzag-like plot lines, repeatedly fell into narrative traps, were unable to reach real denouements and closures, and generally gave the impression of being carried away by uncontrollable currents of frenzied speech.

A close reading of "A nisref," as well as of some of the other monologues that found their place in the *Railway Stories,* demands, however, that we free ourselves of the mindset prescribed by the series as a whole, cast off the peculiar bittersweet mood with which it is informed, and realize that some of the texts of which the series consists do not organically belong in it. The author's decision to include them in this segment of his collected works was based on the premise that they could be easily fitted into the general rhetorical framework of a series of tales heard or overheard in train compartments and then recorded by a bored itinerant *komi-voyazher* (commercial traveler) who spent too many "dead" hours in uncomfortable, often crowded, trains, traveling from one Jewish provincial center to another with his samples of whatever merchandise he promoted. The presence of this commercial agent who dabbled in writing, through which all the tales of the *Railway Stories* were purportedly refracted, formed the rhetorical axis of the series as a whole, hence the prominence of the "komi-voyazher" in its original title. It supplied the author with a situational and narrative framework that vouchsafed the continuity and unity not only of the stories he wrote mainly in 1909–10 but also of some earlier monologues that could be presented as verbatim recordings of stories told by train passengers. Thus, as Sholem Aleichem prepared the *Writings of a Commercial Traveler* for their first publication in book form as the eighth volume (1911) of the "Progress" edition of his collected works, he searched and found among his older works written in monologue form six that had either been originally presented as told during a train voyage (including "Funem priziv" [Back from the Draft Check-up], "Driter klas" [Third Class], and particularly "A nisref," in which the fact that the story was told to a captive audience in a crowded train compartment was particularly significant) or, although devoid of specifically indicated locations of the narration, could be easily presented as such with the help of a few additional introductory sentences (such were "Gimnazye" [High School]; "Afikoymen," an intentional twisting of the word *apikun*, which means "trustee" or "fiduciary guardian"; and a title that was replaced in 1911 by "Bashert an umglik" [Fated to Misfortune]). These stories were now "planted" in the *Railway* series, forming its rear part, so as to enable the chapters written in 1909–10 to leave an indelible imprint on the mind of the readers before these earlier and quite different chapters were reached in the process of an orderly reading of the book. Although the latter shared with the other episodes important common motifs and mental characteristics, such as the motif of travel by train and the peculiar ambiguity of confessional tales told by anonymous narrators to total strangers who were not in a position to either believe or doubt their veracity, they were, in many ways, also utterly at variance with the more recently written episodes.

For one thing, the additional stories, written at an earlier phase in the author's career (1902–03), were based on a substantially different approach to the monologue as a narrative-dramatic subgenre. Having explored the potential of this subgenre during the 1890s in the first three stories in the *Tevye der milkhiker* (Tevye the Dairyman) series, Sholem Aleichem discovered the full range of its artistic possibilities in "Dos tepl" ("The Pot," 1901), which triggered the writing of a host of other monologue-stories throughout the first half of the first decade of the new century. In the best of these the subgenre yielded an almost inexhaustible array of psychological insights and nuances that were generated by the juxtaposition of the overt narrated text and the covert (silenced, or only partially articulated) sub-text. The monologue was actually told by two or three voices: one official and assertive and the others repressed and subversive; one advocating the monologist's case and the others "inadvertently" weakening it through self-contradictions, Freudian slips, and unintentional *double entendres*, as well as through what looked like uncontrollable redundancy and penchant for digression. The narrative and psychological potential thus discovered was of a magnitude that justified the temporary deflection of the better part of the writer's creative energy from other subgenres toward the monologue, his *forme maîtresse* during those years. It particularly made him "forget" (or almost forget), for a while, his ambition to write the great "Jewish" novel of the age, preferring the dramatized, unreliable, "disorderly," hurried, and mostly unintellectualized talk of common men and women crying from the midst of the maelstrom of their hectic mundane lives to the epic, integrative, "true," and explanatory telling of the omniscient narrators of his novels, who, immune to life's fitful fevers, were in a position to make perceptive comments on, and often to also poke fun at, the vicissitudes of fate and fortune experienced by the novels' protagonists.

The potential of the convoluted monologue with its complexities of plot and structure was so alluring that in 1902 the writer came up with a plan that would allow for revving it up to the highest possible intensity. The plan had the general title "Peklekh," which literally means "bundles" or "bags," but metaphorically signifies big troubles consisting of many smaller ones, conglomerates of misfortunes and entanglements heaped on each other and together forming a big heavy "bundle" a person had to carry on his sagging shoulders. A Jew with a *"pekl"* was a man beset by this kind of mega-trouble. Sholem Aleichem's idea was to create a series of characters burdened with *"peklekh,"* who would, so to speak, unburden themselves by confiding their tales of cumulative woes to occasional listeners, starting with a minor inconvenience or a surmountable difficulty, and then quickly and uncontrollably spiraling through all sorts of minor and major disasters, assuming the dimensions of a true *"pekl."* This, of course, would have made for monologue-stories that progressively became more chaotic and complex, since the monologists, quite overwhelmed by their respective *peklekh,* were not only unfocused but also often unwilling to straightforwardly point to their own share in or responsibility for the troubles that plagued them. Sometimes, in their self-righteousness and self-pity, they were not even altogether conscious of their considerable contributions to the mess. Thus the *Peklekh* series was to sound the discordant tonalities produced by the juxtaposition of contradictory overt and covert messages, of text versus sub-text, at an unprecedented high pitch.

The first story conceived as part of the *Peklekh* series was the magisterial "Finf un zibetsik toyzend" (Seventy-five Thousand), the author's longest and, in many ways, most complex story, cast in the monologue form, in which the theme of craving for unearned, "miraculous" riches (to which Sholem Aleichem repeatedly came back throughout his writing career) yielded its farthest-reaching "metaphysical" implications. It was published in 1902 and was immediately followed by four much shorter *Peklekh* stories: "Afikoymen," "A nisref," "Der daytsh" (The German [meaning a westernized Jew]), and "Tsu der shkhite" (Taken to Slaughter [the original title of the story better known as "Gimnazye"]). In 1903 another story was added to the series, "Me tor nit zayn keyn guter" (It Doesn't Pay to Be Good). For reasons unknown to us, Sholem Aleichem did not continue the writing of the *Peklekh* series and decided not to keep the stories he had already written as a distinct unit in his collected works. Perhaps he felt that when huddled together these stories, with their endless complications, brought the reader to the verge of emotional asphyxiation. In any case, he found places for the six stories in different volumes of his collected works. Four of them ("Bashert an umglik," "A nisref," "Gimnazye," and "Me tor nit zayn keyn guter") were eventually relegated to the *Railway Stories*, where, while technically conforming to the rhetorical framework of the volume, they actually formed a distinct and separate unit within it, in many ways out of sync with what preceded or followed them. It is important to remember this textual history and its ramifications as we embark upon the reading of any of the four stories, and of "A nisref," perhaps, more than the others. Clearly, the *Peklekh* context is by far more conducive to the understanding of this extraordinary masterpiece of a monologue-story than that of the *Railway Stories* or, indeed, that of any other group of the many generic and thematic groups into which the author divided the vast corpus of his short stories.

II.

Like all the other *Peklekh* stories, "A nisref" is a tale of stark juxtapositions and discordant tonalities. Indeed, it stands out even within the *Peklekh* context as particularly rife with dissonance and contradictions. Above all else, the reader does not have to read far into it in order to realize that here is a story rooted in self-contradiction, since its narration—its pace, rhythms, the stylistic peculiarities of the telling—is at variance with the narrative's contents. In other words, what the story tells does not dovetail with the way it is being told.

In terms of content, "A nisref" is truly a story of a "*pekl*," a mega-trouble consisting of many smaller ones. It is told by a merchant and member of the Jewish community of Bohuslav, a *shtetl* stuck in the heart of the Ukraine, not far from the eastern bank of the river Dnieper. He is a storekeeper whose store (and probably his adjacent living quarters as well) has recently been burned out, totally consumed by fire. The conflagration occurred on a night when he was away from home celebrating in a nearby town the engagement of his niece, "the middle daughter," he takes the trouble to tell, of his "one and only sister."[1] A telegram cut short his stay with his sister's

---

1. All references to and quotations from the story are based on the version included in volume XXVIII of the "Folksfond" edition (New York 1923), 231–42. Page numbers will consistently refer to that version. "A nisref," together with the other *Ayzenban geshikhtes*, was translated into English by Hillel Halkin (Sholem Aleichem, *Tevye the Dairyman and the Railroad Stories*, Schocken Books, New York 1987, 247–55). While the translation is very readable, it is sometimes inaccurate, and, therefore,

family, and hurriedly coming home, he discovered that he had just lost everything he possessed. His only consolation, he says, was that at least none of his family members had been harmed; but actually he also had another consolation: the store had been insured for the large sum of ten thousand rubles, which many said had exceeded by far the real value of the damaged inventory. So he could be optimistic, and perhaps even more than merely optimistic. As a matter of fact, he unabashedly tells his listeners, a random group of train passengers, that when the insurance money arrives he will not only refurbish his store and be once again the businessman he used to be, but also extricate himself from other tight spots. For instance, he had recently betrothed his dearly beloved daughter to a worthy young man of good family. The wedding, however, had been indefinitely postponed because he did not have the money necessary not only for depositing (with a third party) the dowry to which he had committed himself, but even for paying the matchmaker's fee. As soon as he receives "his few rubles" (236), he says, he will throw a grand wedding party "*asher loy khosoynu avoysey-nu*" ("as none of our ancestors had 'weddinged'," 242).

The trouble, however, is that he is not going to get this money anytime soon. Why? Because the fire that consumed his store was very suspicious. In other words, nobody believes it was not self-inflicted, not necessarily by the monologist (who betook himself out of town) personally, but by a hired mercenary. Our merchant's store had already been burned down on an earlier occasion under suspicious circumstances. Then, too, he just happened to be out of town. But the insurance company, unable to prove any culpability on his part, had to respect his claim. This time, however, it refused to do so. It sent one of its best and most thorough investigators, who was also, alas, incorruptible (could not be bribed) and "a mean bastard" ("My luck!" the protagonist complains), who warns: "Don't think that getting us to pay up will be easy." (234) The local police then conducts an investigation of its own, threatening the suspect with criminal proceedings. Everything about the fire looks non-kosher. The store had been insured only two weeks before the fire for an exaggerated sum and by an inexperienced and naïve insurance agent. Uncharacteristically, everything in the store was destroyed by the fire, not leaving any material evidence that would have enabled the investigators to reconstruct the fire's origin. Moreover, the telegram that brought the monologist helter-skelter back home ("wife sick, kids sick, mother-in-law sick, very dangerous," 233) did not make sense (why was he not told about the fire?) unless it contained a previously agreed upon coded message. If the suspicions of the insurance company and the police were not enough, the narrator must also face accusations made by his fellow Bohuslaver Jews, who say that he himself made the "*boyre me'oyrey*

cannot always be used in a literary analysis. I allowed myself to use it wherever I found it convenient, but have often replaced it by glosses of my own.

ho'esh" benediction ("Blessed be He who creates the lights of fire," the benediction pronounced when the Sabbath departs and one kindles the *havdole*, the plaited wax candle that is lit as darkness descends, and blesses Him who separated the holy from the mundane). Everyone in town is aware of the narrator's financial difficulties and assumes that he committed arson in order to collect the insurance money. Some maintain that a person holding a burning torch was seen near the store on the night of the fire, others that the merchandise in the store was not worth half the sum it had been insured for and that the books supporting his insurance claim were "cooked." The accusers write letters to the company and visit its headquarters in order to bear witness to their fellow Bohuslaver's guilt, which, they say, they can prove. In short, our narrator is under tremendous pressure. Also, he is unable to go on with his life. Time flies by. Money for business, or even for basic daily needs, gets scarcer from day to day. The various investigations are not brought to a determination, one way or the other. And the monologist has even been made to sign a document forbidding him to leave town. Of course, as he well knows, all these restrictions have a flip-side, as indications that the charge of arson, as much as it offers the only sensible explanation of the circumstances of the fire, has yet to be proved and probably never will rest on evidence solid enough for criminal proceedings to be brought. However, he says, "*dervayle iz shlekht, shlekht, bizn ek arayn shlekhet!*" ("In the meantime it's bad, bad, bad from top to bottom!" 240). Undoubtedly, he is a Jew with a *pekl*, and what a *pekl*!

Yet he neither talks nor behaves like a man with a *pekl*. Strangely, he is neither frightened nor depressed. He does not share with some of the other *Peklekh* narrators ("High School," "Seventy-five Thousand," and "It Doesn't Pay to Be Good," for instance) their characteristic low spirits and disorientation (which in "Seventy-five Thousand" mushrooms into an enveloping sense of unreality) or their whining and self-pity. Rather, the delivery of his story is informed by vigor, energy, and a positive (even grandiose) self-image. Instead of evincing fear and moodiness, his "ruling passions" are anger, optimism, and self-confidence. Clearly, he is a manic character, not a depressive one. He is never lachrymose, never confused, always on top of what he is telling or doing. By no means is he going to play the game by the rules set by his adversaries, be they the authorities, the insurance company, or his Bohuslaver detractors. That is proved by the very location of the narration in "A nisref," a train compartment. As mentioned earlier, the monologist had been forced to sign an order prohibiting him from leaving the narrow confines of his town. So how can his presence in a moving train, and probably at a good distance from Bohuslav, be explained? Only by his conscious decision to defy that order, a decision to which he triumphantly calls his listeners' attention, taking the risk of incriminating himself, as he says:

> They cannot scare me—I travel around day and night, just to spite those Bohuslav Jews! "*Koyl dikhfin yesey veyitsrokh*"—what's the translation?—

whoever wants can travel in my wake and let them invite me to "*unesane toykef*!" [i.e., a nonexistent tribunal or authority]. (239)

This declaration reveals much more than defiance and courage. It reveals not only the protagonist's overflow of energy and self-confidence, but also the unique quality of his tale as a "railroad" story. As he relates it, we suddenly understand how this tale differs from all other *Ayzenban geshikhtes*. For here we have, for the first and only time in the author's stories supposedly told in a moving train, a passenger who is not a passenger at all. He did not board the train as all passengers do, that is, with the intention of traveling from whatever points of departure to specific destinations. He travels for the sake of traveling, boarding trains not with the intention of arriving somewhere, but as means of making a point and, in the process, asserting his determination. Traveling becomes his source of unlimited number of new pairs of ears to absorb his story. In his hometown he cannot find the audiences he seeks, for there not only is the story "old hat," but those who do show interest in it, such as the son of the local *gevir* (rich man), cannot be trusted. Thus the protagonist, who must repeatedly tell his story, has to travel far away from his hated hometown for the purpose of finding "objective" and fair-minded, that is, impersonal and unconcerned, audiences. Clearly, only trains can supply such ever-changing audiences, and that, he admits, is why he is to be found on them day and night. We, or rather the commercial traveler, chance to meet him during one of his random voyages and, like it or not, we become part of that audience he seeks to convince (not necessarily of his innocence, as we shall see). Everything in his story—the provocations, the witticisms, the well-structured funny vignettes—bears witness to the fact that he has already told it many times under similar circumstances, suddenly standing up in a crowded train compartment, and, uninvited, provoking a random group of indifferent people, tired and busy with their own affairs, into listening, quite attentively, to whatever he wants to tell them. Contrary to Hillel Halkin's translation, he does not talk to any specific individual. While Sholem Aleichem launched the story with the sentence: "—Our Jews—I hear a Jew preaching behind my back and passengers cock their ears—our Jews" etc. (231), Halkin's translation begins the story with "May God not punish me for saying this, I heard a Jew behind me tell some passengers, 'but our Jews, our Jews....'" The original sentence did not present the narrator as "telling" his story to "some passengers." Rather it presented him as suddenly "sermonizing" or "preaching" (*darshenen*) like a speaker on a podium, a *magid* of sorts. His sudden declaration regarding "Our Jews," which surprises everybody, including the commercial traveler, manages to silence for a while all passengers who were engaged in conversations of their own, and turns the general attention toward the speaker ("*pasazhirn heren im tsu*"). This is the gist of the dramatic opening of the story: the sudden unsolicited and loud proclamation on the part of the speaker and the ensuing silence and listening, and not the interjection "May God not punish me," which in the original opening sentence comes far behind the "*Undzere yidn*" opening salvo, after an additional clause that had been completely deleted from the English version:

> Our Jews, do you hear me, it is quite inappropriate to say so, may God not punish for the words, they are "*amo pezizo*"—what's the translation? A Jew is good only for sharing a noodle pudding, for praying with him from one *siddur*, lying near him in one graveyard, and let the devil take their father, and that's it!

By changing the meaning and the order of the opening sentence, the English translation obscures the dramatic point the author makes, which is that the narrator made a "splash," bombarding the passengers with a provocative declaration so as to get their attention, which he would try to hold onto by telling his story his way.

For our "burned out" protagonist is not just a person who unburdens himself of a woeful story of toil and trouble. If he is anything, he is a performer, with an inborn sense of dramatic surprise and suspense, an actor of sorts who chooses the train compartment as his stage and its always changing flow of passengers—a generalized, impersonal group representing fair and objective humanity at large—as a representative audience he wants to manipulate and influence. Of course, he is a Jewish actor, whose main tool is his wonderfully fluent Yiddish, and who would make clever use of his Jewish "erudition," appealing to "Jewish" values, such as a father's need to marry off a ripe-and-ready daughter and to educate his sons. Of course, he would travel only in areas that are densely strewn with Jewish *shtetlekh*, so he could count on finding in any train compartment he might board enough Yiddish speakers who would also follow a reference to the daily prayer or to tractate *Avot* in the Mishna. That does not mean that his delivery of his "text" (and it should be read as a text, rehearsed and performed) lacks spontaneity and genuine emotion. Like all good actors, the narrator is both spontaneous and well prepared, emotionally direct and consciously histrionic. If we don't understand that, we miss the point of the story as a whole, its structure, style, performative élan, brilliance, and relative brevity; for "A nisref" is a monologue of a person who knows that whatever he says, whatever he reveals or conceals, he must first and foremost entertain, titillate, create tension and surprises, keep his listeners interested, curious, and never overstay his welcome as somebody who can make people forget, for a while, the tedium and inconvenience of a long train voyage and as well as their own personal troubles and difficulties. Although he is a Jew with a heavy *pekl*, he has learned to carry it lightly. His shoulders do not sag and his back is not bent. He must and he wants to come through as bright, strong, almost wildly strong. "*Ikh bin, darft ir visn, a yid a gazlen!*" ("I am, you have to know, a robber of a Jew," 240), he says; and later on, toward the end of the story, and as part of the imaginary description of his daughter's sensational wedding: "That's the kind of Jew I am! You don't know me at all. Do you hear what I am telling you? You don't even begin to know me! I, when I get wild, then money is nothing in my eyes!" (242)—all that, of course, not only out of sheer exuberance, but, as said before, for the purpose of making a point, of expressing an idea that he regards as a universal truth, and for which he cunningly seeks the approval and conviction of his listeners.

III.

The story, then, starts with an intentional provocation. What the protagonist actually says is that Jews are untrustworthy, treacherous. One should cooperate with them only in matters pertaining to the religious ritual, where they can be counted on to follow the *din* (halakhic law or regulation). That is why one is allowed to eat together with another Jew from the same dish of noodle pudding—because it has undoubtedly been prepared according to the strict regulations of *kashres* (ritual cleanliness)—or share with him the same graveyard, because the other Jew, no matter how devious and malicious, can be counted on to have been buried in a properly consecrated ground, an official Jewish cemetery run by the *khevro kadisho* (the holy company; a group of volunteers that took care of burying the Jewish dead) according to all the pertinent regulations. In all other matters the proximity of a Jew is bad news and should be shunned. This is proclaimed by a Jew facing a Jewish audience and in the homiletic manner of a traditional Jewish *darshen* (preacher). It is, of course, an outburst, an expression of a tremendous rage. At the same time, however, it is also a rhetorical ploy, a means for attracting attention through shocking; and the narrator does not let go of it until he has milked its shock effect to the last drop. Adding hyperbole to hyperbole, he continues his attack on the "Jews," promising his listeners that would they had undergone at the hands of their fellow Jews what he underwent at the hands of his fellow Bohuslaver Jews,[2] they would regard the fact that he limited himself to verbal abuse to be an indication of his mildness and readiness for compromise.

This elaborate developing of the opening remark goes on (among other vilifications) with the narrator contending that "sending" somebody to Bohuslav and making him stay there is a punishment worse than sentencing

---

2. It is appropriate to mention here the fact that the choice of Bohuslav as the town of the story was not accidental. The author had a personal account to settle with this Ukrainian *shtetl* that was the hometown of his late mother Khaye Ester. After her death in the cholera epidemic of 1872—Sholem was then a mere *bar mitsve* boy— he was sent, together with his siblings, to Bohuslav, to stay there with their maternal grandparents while his father was looking for a new spouse. The description of their few months there in Sholem Aleichem's autobiographical novel *Funem yarid* (Back From the Fair), although it records mixed impressions, is essentially one of disappointment and alienation. After a short time the children felt unwanted and "superfluous." In spite of their grandfather (a strange mixture of a cabbalist and a pawnbroker) being supposedly "rich," they were looked upon, particularly by their

him to incarceration in a Siberian prison camp (232). However, it cannot go on without becoming tedious, and the narrator knows he needs to bring it to an end. He does that, pretending that he is about to properly present himself to his listeners, who still don't know who he is, as well as finally start telling the story he keeps promising his listeners ("*hert a mayse*," 231), but he does neither. He still does not reveal his name; actually he will never do that, although, later on, he would seem to drop it as if unintentionally, by a slip of the tongue, referring to himself in the third person, as tells his listeners about the telegram and his hasty home-bound trip: "*gekhapt di fis oyf di pléytses, un holakh Moyshe Mordkhe aheym*" ("Placing his feet on his shoulders, off went Moshe Mordechai back home," 233). Here the protagonist supposedly, and as if by accident, reveals his name, which is never mentioned anywhere else in his monologue. Actually, this accidental self-identification is deceptive, since "*holakh Moyshe Mordkhe*" is a prevalent expression that indicates nothing more than total and quick leave taking. Tevye the Dairyman applies it to himself when he wants to convey the idea that he made himself scarce, "took his feet on his shoulders" and disappeared. Thus the narrator does not really identify himself nor does he really turn to the actual events that he supposedly would unfold later, starting with the fatal night of the engagement party and the fire. Instead he regales his listeners with a *tour de force*: a series of riddles, jokes and quotations. First he presents them with a riddle. He is, he says, an unfortunate man who was hit by "a triple misfortune"; what can he mean? Is he about to tell of the three separate misfortunes of which his *pekl* consists? Not at all! The "triple misfortune" is a clever construct presenting the condition of the protagonist in terms of a funny hierarchy of negativity: (a) he is a Jew, and that is negative in itself; (b) he is a Jew from Bohuslav, which is much worse; and (c) he is a Bohuslaver Jew who is also a *nisref*, i.e., one who has just been burned out and lost everything he owned.

With this witty definition of the misfortune succinctly delivered and, undoubtedly, relished by the listeners, the protagonist is now looking for a trope that would enable him to convey the extent of the damage inflicted upon him by the fire. He has to tell about all this in a manner that would elicit empathy from his listeners and, at the same time, heighten the entertainment bar of his discourse. He does that with so much untranslatable brilliance that the following lines must be quoted in the original Yiddish. He is, he says, a *nisref*

un nokh vos far a nisref—fun di emese "porim hanisrofim" vos in sider! Ikh bin, heyst es, hayntikes yor opgebrent gevorn. Vi azoy, meynt ir? vi a

---

uncle and aunt, as eating the family out of house and home, and heard sarcastic remarks about their unusually developed *apetitlekh*. They were greatly relieved when called back home, although they were to face there a stepmother (See the Bohuslav chapters [38–44] in volume XXVI of the "Folksfond" edition [New York, 1923], 227–265).

shtroyener dakh! Ikh bin aroys mamesh bekharbi uvekashti—vos iz di
taytsh?—vi di mame hot mikh gehat. (232)

The narrator begins by referencing a source with which his listeners are
familiar: the daily morning prayer book. He was, he says, burnt to a cinder
just like the bulls sacrificed as whole offerings on the first day of each
month in the Jerusalem Temple. These bulls, mentioned in the Bible (Num
28:9), are referred to in Tractate *Zevakhim* of the Mishna, where all the
technical details of the ritual (the location of slaughtering, the place for dis-
posing of the remaining ashes, the manner of collecting the bulls' blood in a
special vessel, and then sprinkling it on the golden altar in the temple, etc.)
are meticulously discussed. However, it is not the relatively lesser-known
mishnaic source to which the narrator refers, but rather to the excerpts
embedded within the daily morning prayer in the siddur, which every traditional Jew knows by heart. Since with the destruction of the Temple and the
cessation of its rituals, the sacrificed animals had been replaced by prayer
(based on Hos 14:2-3: "Return, O Israel, to the Lord your God—Take words
with you and return to the Lord. Say to Him: Forgive all guilt and accept
what is good; instead of bulls we will pay [the offering of our] lips"), the
offering of the bulls, as well as other animals, is mentioned in the prayer,
where the mishnaic source is directly quoted. By comparing himself to the
"emese porim hanisrofim" ("the genuine bulls that are burned," i.e.,
burned completely, no part of their meat being left to the priests) our narrator does five different things at one and the same time: (1) he bonds with his
listeners as a Jew, a member of a religious community to which they all
belong; (2) he conveys the extent of the damage he suffered by mentioning
the bulls that were totally consumed on the altar; (3) he presents himself as
a pure and passive victim, a sacrifice of the highest degree of sanctity, since
the bulls, as whole offerings, unlike other offerings that as tokens of personal or collective atonement for specific sins, were of a more "practical" use,
expressed total and unconditional faith and loyalty; (4) he makes a witty and
original linguistic connection between the mundane *nisref* he is and the elevated *nisrofim* of the Mishna and the prayer, that is, he legitimizes himself
as an entity mentioned in the holy scriptures; and (5) he comically compares himself to a bull, which somewhat diffuses the harsh hyperbole of his
dire accusations aimed at Jews, in general, and at the Jews of Bohuslav, in
particular. Thus he manages by one lucky metaphorical strike to get close to
his listeners (when everything is said and done, aren't we all good, loyal
Jews?), to pleasantly poke fun at himself (look, I am like a bull!), to seriously
convey the idea that the fire had totally devastated him, and to indirectly
refer not only to his innocence and "sanctity," but also to his victimization,
to his being "sacrificed," possibly by a sinister force.

But that is not enough of a witty performance for our narrator. He goes
on to convey the extent of his loss by a Yiddish proverb. He has burned, he
says, like a "straw thatched roof." Thus he brings his listeners from the

heights of scripture and prayer to the mundane reality of loss by fire, and he does that not only by linguistic means (replacing the Hebrew quotations with a juicy Yiddish idiom: *brenen vi a shtroyener dakh*), but also by a direct reference to daily life in small eastern European towns, hamlets, and villages, where most homeowners did not possess the means to construct shingled roofs, and, therefore, most houses were thatched with straw, which, in the dry hot summer season, could easily catch fire, and once on fire could not be saved. This idiomatic comparison confirms the innocence of the narrator as a passive victim (can a straw roof protect itself?), which has already been asserted through the use of the verb *opbrenen* (to burn out, completely) together with the auxiliary verb *vern*, which here signifies the passive case: "*opgebrent gevorn*" can mean only burned out by somebody else, be it a force of nature or a human agent.

However, our narrator does not stop even at this point. Immediately he soars from the reality of the Yiddish idiom and the straw roofs of the Ukrainian village to a seemingly inappropriate biblical quotation. He came out of the holocaust, he says, veritably "*bekharbi uvekashti*" ("with (or by) my sword and bow"). This is a tidbit, a delicacy, the monologist offers the more knowledgeable and quick-witted among his listeners. Of course, hearing the ancient Hebrew words, which they encountered in the *parshah* (the weekly portion of the Torah read in the synagogue on Sabbath) or the *haftorah* (the selection from the books of prophecy, which in the Hebrew Bible include many of the historical books, added to the *parshah*), these erudite listeners cannot but wonder about the connection between the narrator's misfortune and those ancient victories in battle in the biblical verses he quotes (such as Jacob's promise to bequeath to Ephraim and Menasseh, Joseph's sons, lands "that I took out of the hands of the Amorites with my sword and with my bow," [Gen 48: 22], or the miraculous victory reported in the book of Joshua: "And I sent the hornet [or the plague] ahead of you, and it drove them out before you—just like the two Amorite kings—not by your sword and your bow" [24:12] etc.). The narrator certainly intends to raise questions and make his listeners wonder whether he really understands the verses he quotes; but he also counts on some of them being able to follow his brilliant association connecting the word *kashti* ("my bow," first-person singular conjugation of the substantive *keshet*) to the Hebrew word *kash,* "straw," the same straw that was featured metaphorically in the Yiddish idiom. Perhaps he also expects some of them to follow the connection between *harbi* ("my sword") and *harev* ("destroy") and *hurban* ("destruction," "demolition"), for all these words derive from the same root *h-r-v*, which, when used as a transitive verb, indicates destruction inflicted upon somebody else, but when used intransitively, indicates one's own destruction by somebody else. The cleverness of the quotation, which at face value seems completely out of context, reveals itself not only in the narrator's original associative manipulation of the Hebrew language, but also in the intentional or, perhaps, semi-intentional ambivalent light he sheds on his situation as a *nisref*: on the one hand he is destroyed (*h-r-v*), burned like dry straw (*kash*); on the other hand he is a warrior, a heroic fighter, who, wielding his sword (*harbi*) and bow (*kashti*), i.e., his brains and dexterity, will have the upper hand and squeeze out of the insurance company the ten thousand rubles he is confident it will have to pay him eventually. The same ambivalence characterizes the "translation" of the biblical quotation by "*vi di mame hot mikh gehat.*" Again we have a Yiddish idiom, meaning totally stripped of everything, naked as at birth (the idiom is based on a biblical source, Job's resounding dictum "Naked came I out of my mother's womb, and naked shall I return there" [Job 1: 21]). As much as the somber idiom indicates the protagonist's destitution (he is totally naked, bereft of all possessions), it also covertly suggests the idea of rebirth. Our narrator thinks of the burning of his store not only in terms of disaster, but also, perhaps mainly, as his great second (or third) chance, a rebirth of sorts.

This multiple-page analysis of four lines in the Yiddish text sounds a warning. Were we to dwell as closely on the narrator's many other flights of wit through association and quotation, our discourse may assume book-length dimensions. Just one more example of the narrator's extraordinary cleverness, as well as his ability to talk from both sides of his mouth, will have to suffice before we turn to other issues presented by "A nisref." It is taken from the section in the story in which the monologist tells about his very unpleasant encounter with Zaynvl, the insurance agent he used to work with. When he came to him and stated his intention to re-insure his store (just a few weeks, as it turns out, before it is burned out a second time), the agent welcomed him with "a strange smile." Asked for the meaning of his grin, Zaynvl cryptically answered: "I am feeling so good and so bad..." and went on to explain himself by saying "bad because I insured you before, and good because I'm not doing it again" (236–37). This, of course, infuriated the narrator, who saw his good name as a merchant and a householder besmirched by his agent. To the extent that he planned to set the store on fire and collect the insurance money once again, the agent's unconcealed derision should alert him as to how the affair will be looked upon and judged by everybody. Nevertheless, being the courageous and crafty man he is, he is neither deterred nor crestfallen. Since the town is full of insurance agents ("*vi di hint,*" "like dogs," the narrator says), among them inexperienced and naïve youngsters until now supported by their in-laws, he is confident that he will finally catch the fish he is looking for. In an outburst of proud self-confidence he rhetorically asks: "*hamibli eyn pegorim bemitsrayim?*" ("Are there no cadavers in Egypt?" 237). This sounds like a biblical quotation. The truth is that it is and it is not, or rather that it is a twisted quotation. In the Bible the question is superficially similar: "*hamibli eyn kevorim bemitsayim?*" (Exod 14:11: "Are there no graves in the land of Egypt?"). The question is asked by the rebellious Hebrews, maligning Moses for having taken them out of the house of bondage only to let them die in the empty desert, where they lacked food and water. Why had he "liberated" them and marched them into the wasteland where they would die? Hillel Halkin assumed that Sholem Aleichem himself did not remember the quotation correctly and he silently "corrected" the text, replacing "*pegorim*" by "*kevorim.*" But, of course, Sholem Aleichem as well as his protagonist knew what they were doing. When the latter encountered Zaynvl's offensive grin he retorted by a question every bit as offensive: "*Vos shmeykhelst du—vi a peger umgevashen?!*" (236): "Why do you smile—like a cadaver before cleansing?!" The question is based on a very earthy and unceremonious expression that refers to the strange expression on the face of dead people (which can be understood as a weird grin), and that those who take care of the body and prepare it for burial try as best they can to erase, working the dead face into a somnolent expression of unworldly repose. The custom of beautifying the face of the dead is not Jewish, and the expression "*a peger umgevashen*" would never be used in reference to the lifeless body of a Jew. Using it among Jews in the framework of a metaphorical comparison, as the narrator does here, would indicate extreme disrespect and be considered uncommonly rude, which was, of course, exactly how the narrator wanted his question to sound. However, as the short conversation evolves, the expression assumes a somewhat different significance. This agent, the narrator quickly realizes, was, as far as his plan of re-insuring the store was concerned, "dead" and done with. Moreover, he was to him a "*peger*," a mere cadaver, also in the sense that he, the one who seeks insurance, had "buried" him (as the agent himself complained), that is, undermined him, by making him responsible for the first unwise insurance that had eventually cost the company a considerable sum of money, and certainly had not elevated Zaynvl's status as an experienced and careful agent. What was needed now was another "*peger*," a new agent who would unwittingly repeat Zaynvl's mistake. Hence the twisting of the biblical verse followed almost automatically. What would the word *kevorim* (graves) mean in this context? Little, if anything. In contrast, the word *pegorim* reveals the narrator's intention and motives perhaps more than he cares to reveal them. In any case, by replacing one Hebrew word with another, he endows the basic idea that there are enough insurance agents in town with a rich plethora of nuances and additional significance.

IV.

One can proceed through the story and see how the narrator continually finds new ways of entertaining his listeners, holding them in suspense, and, at the same time, projecting the event of the fire and its consequent complications in ambiguous terms. For instance, the narrator replicates in some detail his encounters with the investigators, particularly with the police detective, quoting in full their questions and his answers, replete with a

Schweik-like pretense of dumbness, by which he cleverly dodges questions.
He is fully aware of the comic effect of the altercations (234):

> "What makes you burn again and again?"
>
> "Fire does, your Excellency."
>
> "Why did not one item of the damaged merchandise survive the fire?"
>
> "Oh, that's exactly my own complaint."
>
> "Why did he insure the store only two weeks before the fire?"
>
> "Would you have liked me to do that two weeks later?" ...
>
> "Why was he away from home on the night of the fire?"
>
> "Would it have made you feel better, sir, if I were at home?"
>
> "Why did the telegram mention dead relatives [the police detective inciden-
> tally 'kills' the mother-in-law, who in the original telegram was described
> only as dangerously sick] rather than the fire itself?"
>
> "So as not to frighten me!"

At the same time he is certainly out to show his listeners how astute and
cunning he was, and how easily he had led those bloodhounds by the nose.
In the section dealing with the abrasive conversation with the insurance
agent, the fun and ambivalence inhere in the already mentioned cadaver-
joke, by which the narrator, once again, both entertains and asserts his dominance and control as a live person of supreme mobility among immobile
"cadavers." This leads to another joke by which the narrator expresses his
feelings of disgust and contempt for his fellow Bohuslavers in general and
particularly for the sanctimonious son of the local *gevir*, a saintly hypocrite
who pretends to be truly interested in the narrator's difficulties, whereas
really he just wants to pry out his secrets, make him reveal his true emotions
(this is, at least, the narrator's understanding of the young man's intentions).
In any case, determined to fend off the false (or genuine) empathy of the
man and keep the pretense of high spirits and self-confidence, the narrator
buttresses himself with a famous quote from *Avot*: "*Peshot neveylo—ve'al
titsoreykh...*" (239) Seemingly unrelated to the case in point, this admonition urging one not to count on charity and perform even the basest of
menial jobs (flay the skin of an animal's carcass found in the marketplace)
and retain one's financial independence rather than live on the bounty of
others, does not really say what its "translation" purports to say ("tweak
your own cheeks to make them look ruddy and healthy," that is, keep up
pretenses and do not reveal your troubles to others). Rather it interjects into
the scene the self-image of the narrator as a person who, having stepped on
a carcass of an animal—the hated young man who stopped him in the market
place—he must undergo the disgusting and debasing experience of flaying
its hide, that is, controlling himself and keeping up a normal conversation,
rather than doing what he really wants, which is to slap the man's face as
one would shove aside a stinking carcass by kicking it out of the way. The

listeners, presumably, enjoy this innovative, if quite inelegant interpretation of the sage's saying. To the same extent they enjoy the narrator's equating of the insurance company to the biblical Haman of the book of Esther. He does that indirectly by presenting his decision not to compromise with the company and wait till they have no choice but to pay him the full sum of his insurance policy, as based on the "philosophy" or attitude encapsulated in the premonition of Zeresh, Haman's wife, who knows intuitively that in his confrontation with his rival, Mordechai (at this point we cannot dismiss the idea that the protagonist's name perhaps *was* Moyshe Mordkhe, and his name referred not only to the concept of absconding, making oneself scarce, as the proverbial "*holakh Moyshe Mordkhe*" suggested, but also to that of a biblical namesake, the Mordechai of the book of Esther), her husband is going to emerge the loser: "*Heykhiloso linpoyl—nofoyl tipoyl*" (240; Esth 6:13): "You have begun to fall, then you will fall before him to your ruin." Thus the protagonist imbues the struggle he is embroiled in with the colors of the archetypal Haman-Mordechai conflict, and projects his eventual victory as a repetition of the miracle of Purim, the quintessential Jewish model for the narrative of a dire situation and a mortal danger resulting in success, dominance, and great festivity, with much eating and drinking.

Accordingly the story will end with a description of exactly such a festivity, a sensational wedding celebration. As much as the story line started with the festivity of engagement, it must end with one of matrimony. Since that earlier celebration was cut short and undermined by the fire, the eventual victory over the insurance company, the police, and all the Bohuslaver enemies must culminate in a re-instated one by which the interim and therefore shaky position of a betrothal would be canceled and replaced with the permanent nuptial union. Thus the narrator concludes his story by projecting into the future a typical scene of comic closure in which the tensions, fears, and misunderstandings that had informed the comic plot, supplying it with the necessary complications and tensions, are drowned in great quantities of food and liquor (as well as the tacitly suggested sexuality of the newlyweds) and trampled by the feet of exhilarated dancers. However, even this final imagined scene of victorious denouement is not devoid of a residue of the ambivalence that is the staple characteristic of the story as a whole. The narrator parades here his future generosity and open-handedness, his communal charity, contributions to the synagogue (when called up to the Torah on the Sabbath), the grandiose wedding party he would throw, never mind the expenses, the presents he would give on that occasion to the beggars of the entire neighborhood, etc. His tone is excited and self-congratulatory; his posture is that of a wild celebrant hardly in control of his own munificence. However, when we pay attention to the details, we soon discover that he is not as careless and above petty calculations as he pretends to be. How much would he contribute to the synagogue? He carefully refrains from putting a number on his pledge. He would give, he says,

not less than others (241), which may not be that much. What will he
donate to the local hospital? The fee of a proper physician, medicines, comfortable beds? "Half a dozen shirts" for the sick and destitute patients (for
only the destitute members of the community passed away in a traditional
Jewish hospital, or *hekdesh*; all the others died at home, in their beds).
What about a present to the *talmud toyre* (the community-supported
school for the sons of those who cannot pay for their children's education)?
A set of new *talis kotns* (the fringed undergarment) for the kids. As for the
feast for the beggars at the wedding, we hear only about a small *challah*
bread for each, some brandy, and an alms of five pennies "for every two of
them" (242). All in all, the narrator would not carelessly spend his money.
And the wedding party itself would be, more than anything else, an act of
revenge, in which all the narrator's detractors would be made to drink and
dance at their enemy's victorious celebration until they split their sides and
burst open. In the Yiddish original this concept of a joyous and sweet
revenge is encapsulated in a linguistic twist, a play on words. Those who
wanted "*im dertrinken*" ("to drown him") would have to "*tsezetst vern
trinkendik*" ("burst from overdrinking"). The narrator ends his story with a
quote, none other than Samson's final wild call of anguish and revenge thun-
dering over the heads of the Philistines gathered in the temple of their god,
Dagon, as the blinded giant toppled the temple's roof and walls and crushed
the thousands of celebrants: "*tamus nafshi im plishtim*!" "Let me die with
the Philistines" (Judg 16:29). The mood with which the story ends is, therefore, not that different from the mood with which it started with the impre-
cation against "*undzere yidn*," one of manic rage and self-assertion.

V.

With all these and many other fascinating details inviting us to further
explore each of the sections of "A nisref," we nevertheless must turn away
from them and examine the major issues that form the core of the story's
ambiguous message. Superficially, the issue that seems to be more important than all the others presents itself through the simple question: Is our
protagonist guilty or not guilty of the charge of self-inflicted arson? Is he a
genuine *nisref* or a disingenuous one, a mere pretender? Since the narrator
never directly answers this question himself, it seems to be left hanging in
the balance, thus supplying the story as a whole with much of its inherent
tension. Certainly the listening passengers would have liked to know the
truth, one way or another. But here, as in all other aspects of the story, ambiguity seems to be the order of the day. As we observed earlier, it is not clear
whether the narrator revealed his true name or hid behind the proverbial
name of the person who absconded, as he did by leaving his town in spite of
his commitment to stay in it.

The narrator himself never admits to any culpability on his part. At the
same time, he never convinces—nor, it would seem, tries too hard to con-

vince—his listeners (and through them us, the readers) of his innocence. At the beginning, as we noticed, he assumes the role of the innocent victim of a disaster augmented and protracted by a complex legal entanglement. He is one of the *"porim hanisrofim,"* an *"opgebrent gevorn"* unfortunate man left in the world "as naked as he was born." He is also the victim of the malice, ill-will, and false accusations of the people of his hometown, upon whose heads he pours his boiling verbal rage. He proclaims his innocence and quotes as proof the fact that he was away from home on the night of the fire, celebrating in a nearby town the engagement of the "middle daughter" of his one and only sister. In the next section of the story, which focuses on the investigations to which he has been subjected, he cleverly dodges the investigators' questions and responds to the threats of the police detective with a highly pathetic and forceful *cri du coeur* of an absolutely innocent victim:

> What do you want from me? You take a perfectly innocent man and devastate him! It is not a big deal to cut someone's throat! You want to slaughter me—go ahead, slaughter!. You forget that there is law on earth and a God in heaven. (234)

This call "from the depths" is immediately followed by what soon becomes one of the two "refrains" of the story (in almost all of Sholem Aleichem's monologues, as well as in many of his stories written in different techniques, the "refrain," or the oft-repeated formulaic sentence, plays a very important structural and musical role). While the first, shorter, and more pervasive one, couched in down-to-earth marketplace terms, expresses the narrator's rage and defiance *("un a rukh in zey in taten, un gornit!"* "Let the devil take their father, and that's it!"), the second, somewhat longer and stylistically florid one affirms the narrator's innocence: *"Nor vos her ikh im, az ikh bin reyn, reyn vi gingold"* ("But why should I pay attention to him when I am clean, pure as the purest gold?" 254–55).

This is the highest point reached by the tide of affirmations of innocence on the part of the narrator. However, as soon as this point has been reached, the movement in the opposite direction, that of the low ebb, starts. Perhaps it can be said to have started before the ceremonial formula was fully uttered, for there is something hyperbolic, exaggerated, and unconvincing about the narrator's use of the literary, old Yiddish word *gingold,* which will from now on appear whenever the second refrain is sounded. Somehow the "pure as the purest gold" is weaker, more formulaic, and less credible than the much simpler "I am clean." Moreover, the narrator adds to his first *gingold* declaration one of his queer misquotations, which, when carefully examined, seem to undermine whatever preceded them. The monologist once again quotes *Avot* (with which Jews of limited erudition were better acquainted than with any another section in the Mishna): *"Al tehi boz lekhol bosor"* ("Do not treat with disdain any flesh," in the sense of flesh and blood, a living person). The actual saying in *Avot,* ascribed to the sage Rabbi

Shimon bar Azai, is: "*Al tehi baz lekhol adam*" ("Do not treat with disdain [or underestimate] any person"). Why does our narrator twist the quotation, replacing the word *adam*, which in the given context makes perfect sense, with the word *basar*, which demands an unnecessary effort of interpretation? The answer to this is given in his funny "translation" or Yiddish interpretation of the Hebrew saying "*az me est nit keyn knobl, hert zikh nit nokh*" ("When one doesn't eat garlic, one's mouth doesn't smell." 235). The narrator, it seems, understands the word *basar* (*bosor* in the Ashkenazi pronunciation) quite literally as meat. If you don't spike the taste of your meat dish with garlic, he says, no telltale bad breath will reveal the fact that you ate it, and you will save yourself an inconvenience and a social embarrassment. Somehow the narrator fancifully equates the very strong and pungent Hebrew verb *b-u-z* (to disrespect, to disdain) to the act of eating garlic, and arrives at the conclusion that as much as garlic renders the cooked dish tastier, its negative consequences are deplorable, and, therefore, one should give it up. If we translate this kitchen wisdom in terms of the narrator's situation (of being accused of arson) and argument (that he is "pure as the purest gold") we must understand this quaint Yiddish interpretation of the mishnaic dictum in the following manner: If you want to keep your "purity" and avoid bad breath, i.e., avoid leaving evidence that would incriminate you, you have to be careful and think three steps ahead. You are allowed to eat your "meat," i.e., to make your kill, but keep away from the garlic, and then your "purity" (innocence) would withstand close scrutiny and not be disproved. In short, the narrator as much as says, albeit in a very roundabout and unclear manner, that he can insist on his innocence, because he took good care not to leave any telltale evidence, and his guilt cannot be proved.

The narrator's official position ("I'm clean") is further eroded as he attempts, in the following section, to point out the absurdity of the accusation that he himself had started the fire (or idiomatically, that he had made the "Blessed be He who creates the lights of fire" benediction). Taking this accusation in its most literal sense (he himself lit the match that started the fire), he reverts to and elaborates upon his alibi, his being away from home. As an ultimate proof he puts a series of rhetorical questions to his listeners:

> I have an only sister—she's marrying off her middle daughter, should I have not gone to the betrothal party? Would that have been an appropriate behavior? I ask you yourselves: let's say you had a one and only sister who would celebrate her middle daughter's engagement, would you have stayed at home and refrain from participating in the party?! (235–36)

Playing this rather simplistic game of making his listeners "themselves" pronounce his alibi ironclad, the narrator adds another "proof" that totally undermines his argument. The inanity of ascribing to him the direct responsibility for the fire is also proved, he says, by the well-known fact that nobody who intends to do "such a thing" (that is, start a fire for the purpose of collecting insurance money) does it with one's own hands when one can hire for three rubles a "good angel" who would do it for him. "The dumbest child understands this." (235) But is the narrator himself dumb? Does he not realize that by this additional "proof" of his innocence he has actually as much as pointed out the way the arson was perpetrated and to the hollowness of his alibi? Of course, he did not start the fire with his own hands. Instead, knowing beforehand that within a short time he would have a perfectly legitimate reason to spend a night away from his hometown, he carefully prepared the arson, starting with the re-insuring of his store and then proceeding to the hiring of the "good angel" who did the dirty work for him in his absence.

But our monologist, admittedly a braggart, is, nevertheless, not a fool. He could not have spilled the beans, undermining his professed position, by sheer mistake. He must have intended his listeners to understand the meaning of his all but self-incriminating remark; for having made it, he goes on to ask these listeners: "Isn't that how it's done where you come from?" by which question he seems not only to share with them his criminal "secret," but also to tacitly ask for their complicity. As people who live in the real world they should not pretend not to have known the truth all along. After all, what he has done is being done everywhere. Each of his listeners knows of cases of self-inflicted arson that took place in his or her town. Perhaps some of them committed the same "crime" themselves. If not, they certainly have given it a thought. As practical people they cannot but see that people who find themselves *in extremis*, as did the narrator, often have no recourse but to commit "such a thing"' or break the law in other ways. This, he says, is common knowledge, as much as it is a common practice. "Such things" are done on a daily basis by normal, God-fearing people when they have no other choice.

If so, then, our narrator, while persisting in his protestations and insisting on his technical innocence, does not really want to lie to his listeners. Rather he wants them to silently understand what he did and tacitly approve of it or "accept" it. He wants to turn them into accomplices with sealed lips. This is proved later in the story as he tells them, quite incidentally it seems, as a mere item in his long list of troubles, that he is being blackmailed by one Dovid Hersh, who must have seen something that renders his silence worth paying for. "All of us together should earn in one week what I had to pay him to keep his mouth shut," he says (241). Clearly, the narrator has answered in the affirmative the question of whether he was responsible for the arson. Indeed, his "innocence" is a mere façade. Everybody knows he is guilty. The police and the insurance company, being unable to prove his guilt, play a game of cat and mouse with him, which will probably end with his victory over them. With them, however, he must hold onto his technical innocence for dear life, and being the crafty man he is, he knows how to play the game better than they do by pretending to be dumb and, as he says, "*got di neshume shuldik*" ("com-

pletely innocent," 234). But with his captive audience, the silent train passengers, he does not play dumb, nor does he flaunt the façade of his innocence in their faces for the purpose of misleading them. As a matter of fact,
he progressively renders this façade as transparent as he possibly can. The
innocence/guilt ambiguity is superficially kept alive throughout the story
for purposes of titillation and entertainment, but it is only the garlic, the
condiment for the meat of his narrative. The much more serious issue he
wants to bring up has to do with the boiling rage that seethes under the
comic surface of his narrative from its very inception (*"undzere yidn"*) to its
conclusion with *"tomus nafshi im plishtim!"* It is by focusing on this other
issue that we shall fully grasp the significance of "A nisref," the essence of
its moral ambivalence, and its role in the author's overall narrative and ideational world.

VI.

The protagonist is a folksy "philosopher," a moralist of sorts. He is described
at the beginning of his story not as "telling" or "speaking" but as "preaching" (*"darshenen"*), that is, holding a *droshe,* a lecture, a sermon, a moral
disquisition. Indeed "A nisref," on top of being a hilarious story, is also a lecture or sermon. Of course, the protagonist's arguments are neither couched
in abstract terms nor presented as generalizations, and they are also not
"objective" and universally applicable. No one knows better than he that he
has a personal ax to grind, and a big one at that. But all this does not dimin-
ish the seriousness of the ideational core of his arguments, nor does the fact
that he pleads for himself, trying to justify his own questionable behavior,
nullify in advance the more general significance of his "sermon."

What prodded him to take the risk of boarding trains (when he was legal-
ly committed to staying in his hometown) and talk about his "deed" almost
candidly with groups of strangers, who, for all he knew, might have called
the first gendarme they bumped into in a nearby train station and point him
out as a fugitive criminal, was, among other things, a sense of mission, a
search for justice. The protagonist has no quarrel with the police or the
insurance company. He expects them to do what they do, as much as he
expects himself to dodge and defeat their investigative maneuvers. It is a
game (a very dangerous one, to be sure) both parties play, each expecting
the other to act predictably. The only unexpected move, from the perspective of the narrator, was the investigator's rejection of bribery, his "inexplicable" honesty. That, as far as he was concerned, went against the "rules" of
the game, and had to be ascribed to sheer "bad luck" (*"oyf mayn glik"*).
Otherwise the cat-and-mouse chase the story describes is conducted in a
manner informed by all but mathematical objectivity, almost like a cat-and-
mouse scene in a Warner Brothers cartoon. Strong emotions or moral indignation have no place in it. The narrator's already mentioned *cri du coeur*
(*"vilst koylen–koyle!"* "You want to slaughter–slaughter!") is not a genuine

one; it is a mere histrionic gesture, an expected replica in the confrontational drama acted by himself and the police detective, whereas the latter's more genuine *cri de colere*, his outburst of rage, is more than anything else an indication of his awareness of being overpowered and outmaneuvered by his antagonist.

But the protagonist is genuinely appalled and infuriated by the behavior of the members of his own community, the Jews of Bohuslav. Under no circumstances will he admit, or even entertain the thought, that their motives for accusing him and informing the "company" about him have anything to do with morality or even with sheer legality, for the Jews of Bohuslav, as far as he is concerned, have no role to play in the legal game in which he participates. Of course, he knows he has committed what is called a crime; he broke the law and continues to break it on a daily basis (*"tog vi nakht"*). However, his view of the matter (which he fully trusts most "normal" people share) is that crime, in and of itself, is, at least under certain circumstances, not only unavoidable but also acceptable and justifiable; and criminal behavior, as long as it undermines only the abstraction called "the law" and not "real" people in "real" life situations, is legitimate and even normative. For "the law" as an intellectual, moral, and institutional entity is so remote, so distant from that horrific melee, the jungle of daily strife for survival in which most people live and act, as to be morally inapplicable to their deeds and actions—so much so that its role in that jungle-like reality can only be that of one of the beasts of prey that live and prosper there by devastating weaker creatures, slashing their throats, as the protagonist tells the police detective to his face, and eating them alive. A big and fearful beast of prey it certainly is, but still, as part of the jungle and not as an entity that inheres beyond and above it, it can be beaten at its own bloody game, provided one possesses, as the superbly intelligent mice of the Warner Brothers cartoons do, the necessary cunning and dexterity, which the protagonist evidently possesses. That is why one is, as long as one can beat the beast, really and truly "clean, pure like the purest gold," not only technically (because the clumsy law cannot catch one who is cleverer and nimbler), but also in the full moral sense of the metaphor, for how can the mouse who managed to make the cat slip, fall on its face, or burn its own fur be blamed or regarded as tarnished and unclean? On the contrary, the success of the mouse's stratagems should be celebrated with a feast of victory similar to the one described by the narrator as the story reaches a happy (albeit, in our case, still imaginary) closure.

True, the protagonist mentions the law in terms that are as sublime as they are disingenuous. Remember, he warns the police inspector: *"s'iz faran a zakon un s'iz a got oyf der velt"* ("there is a civil law and there is God in the world," 234). But this is only part of his pretense of being innocent, a mealy-mouthed equating of the state's law and God's justice offered to a representative of the former in an exclamation that mixes protest with flattery. The narrator sees no connection between God's justice and the Russian civil law represented by the detective, and his clear differentiation between the two is linguistically highlighted by the irreconcilability of the very Russian (*"zakon"*) and the quintessentially Yiddish (*"Got oyf der velt"*) words he uses. For by using the word *zakon* he is not only trying to appeal to the Russian detective whose duty is to enforce the law but at the same time also to abide by it; he also throws it at his Jewish listeners, who should remember whose law has been broken. Is it not the law of a despotic and anti-Semitic state that meted to its Jewish "subjects" (for they have not yet been elevated to the status of citizens) a travesty of a justice? If so, what was so blameworthy about breaking the *zakon* of this state, if one could only get away with it?

The narrator truly and unhesitatingly believes his disrespect for the *zakon* to contain a universal as well as a Jewish truth that cannot be refuted, and that is the source of his rage. He believes every objective and fair-minded person who knows life for what it is, a veritable *"emek habakha"* ("vale of tears"), would support this view and acknowledge this truth. Hence the audacious exercise he undertakes, boarding trains for the purpose of unfolding his story in the presence of listeners who, unlike the malicious members of his own community, are expected to be at one and the same time objective and fair-minded, Jewish, and existentially experienced people, i.e., people living in the real world. He, therefore, approaches this audience with a thought-through and intellectually principled rationale that he hides underneath his entertaining and histrionically delivered story. The entertainment is necessary because people's attention and interest must be courted and then kept alive; but the hidden rationale is what informs and shapes the infrastructure of the tale. Why, the protagonist asks, shouldn't his act of arson be greeted with consent and approval as long as it has been "perpetrated" with consideration for the following three conditions?

Condition number one: the arson did not cause any "real," i.e., personal, suffering or loss. It did not harm or negatively impact on anyone who was really alive and was susceptible to harm in the way living and real people were susceptible to it. It would seem that while preparing for the conflagration the protagonist took every precaution necessary to limit the damage to his own property. We do not hear complaints from his neighbors about the fire spreading and engulfing their homes or stores, or having incidentally harmed any one and anything with the exception of its intended target. Therefore, the fire did not "really" undermine any relevant system of justice, let alone the law, which, on top of its abstraction and indifference to the plight of real people, was devised and enforced by an inimical entity, as every Jew living in the Czarist Empire knew. As for the insurance company, it was about to sustain a loss of ten thousand rubles, but even this loss was hardly a "real" one. For starters, the "company" was almost as remote and abstract as the law. It was probably a corporation, not belonging to any one person and, in any case, it was fabulously rich, and the money it would eventually cough up would be of no financial consequence to it. It would not become poorer, he says, because of his "few rubles" ("*iber mayne etle-khe kerblekh vet zi oremer nit vern,*" 236). Besides, the company entered the speculative game of insurance against fire fully aware of the probability that people would try to cheat it, and it certainly had taken that probability into its calculations, stretching its margin of profits wide enough to discount in advance the eventual loss to a successful arsonist. In all these the narrator speaks in the name of the "natural justice," which he regards as self-evident. A "real" crime, according to his home-spun existentialist ethics, consists of inflicting harm upon a real person within the context of a real-life situation.

Condition number two: the "crime" was perpetrated *in extremis*, i.e., under circumstances that rendered it unavoidable. Even the abstract and alien law had to be respected (or at least feared) as long as one was not coerced to break it. But when one was caught by the cogwheels of cruel circumstances, self-salvation was to be preferred to adherence to laws and regulations. The narrator makes sure his listeners are aware of the reality of his predicament. He invites them "*arayngeyen in zayne polozhenye*" (that is, "step into his shoes," 238). Once they imagine themselves in his position, they would certainly absolve him. Let them see themselves as the fathers of daughters ripe for marriage and motherhood but barred from performing their physiologically natural and socially approved functions because of pressing financial difficulties. Let them taste the bitterness of not being able to deposit the dowry money and pay the matchmaker's fee—two transactions that had to take place before their daughter's marriage was consummated. Let them project themselves into the quandary of a father of a bright and highly motivated son whose education was stalled because of lack of capital. Let them experience in their imagination the sleepless nights, the feeling of being physically consumed by worries (the protagonist presents himself as one subjected to an incessant torture that sucks the marrow out of his bones; one who "*mutshet zikh—tsit fun zikh di kley,*" 238). In all this the narrator speaks in the name of a Jewish justice or, to be exact, of traditionalist Jewish middle-class justice, for not everyone would regard the socially and financially proper marrying off of daughters and the responsibility for the education of one's sons as existential *sine qua nons;* but members of the traditional Jewish middle class, proper *balebosim* (householders), would certainly agree with the narrator that there was no nunnery in Judaism and, therefore, Jewish girls had to marry and procreate—there was no other role for them in the traditional Jewish life scheme—and that talented Jewish boys who wished to study had to be allowed to learn. They would, therefore, also have to agree that the narrator's violation of the law, looked at from this Jewish middle-class perspective, could fit the elevated category of a *mitsve* (understood as a good deed, or a prescribed good deed), since it was not done for the purpose of egotistic self-enrichment but rather for that of achieving familial goals that are regarded as "sacred." The money he would get, the protagonist contends, is not his; it is his children's money, and the insurance company has no right to dispossess the children of what is theirs. He purposefully uses the word *mitsve* ("*tomer iz gor a mitsve?*" 238) in a somewhat ambiguous context that allows for two different (but complementary) interpretations, as referring both to other people's empathy and moral support (*arayngeyen in yenems polozhenye*) and to his own illegal action. In any case, he makes it clear that decent and God-fearing Jews, unlike his fellow Bohuslaver ones, should approve of this action. If not approving of the action itself, at least evince an empathic understanding of the circumstances that caused it and approve of its very kosher goals. Granted that all these amount to a *mitsve*, then the malice and ill-will shown by the members of his own community amount to an *aveyre*, which is the opposite of the Jewish *mitsve*.

Condition number three: Being *in extremis*, and careful not to harm any third party, the narrator was following the all-important principle of activity in the face of adversity. Whether this activity is technically legal or illegal was of secondary (if any) significance. The rule was: when threatened by a situation of devastating potential, a person should become active and help himself rather than wait for help to arrive from some external source. Indeed, one should even condescend to flaying a carcass of an animal (i.e., dirty one's hands by an illegal action) rather than count on people's charity. As stinking as the carcass must be, there is no real loss of one's honor in flaying it as long as one is actively fending off disaster. The narrator asserts this "rule" of "*im eyn ani li mi li?*" ("If I don't help myself, who will?") through the very tempo and rhythm of his narrative, which, as mentioned earlier, continuously conveys vigor, strength, and volition. In this, in spite of the quotes from the ancient sources, the protagonist speaks primarily as a "modern" Jew or, rather, he caricatures Jewish modernity; modernity—not in the sense of atheism or secularism but rather in the humanistic sense of individual activism, the opposite of what the modernists (starting with the exponents of the Enlightenment) regarded as the endemic passivity of the traditional Jew, expecting dire exigencies to be somehow removed by an external force, be it the traditional messiah suddenly descending from the clouds complete with a white donkey and a shofar, or the folksy "magic ring," the yearning for which drew the fire of Sh.Y. Abramovitsh's satire. That modern Jewish humanism affirmed, as a matter of course, the unconditional obligation to abide by the law when it is based on the "moral principle" (Kant's "*moralisches Gesetz*") does not concern the narrator, for he is, as already indicated, an "existentialist" rather than an "essentialist" thinker.

In any case, abiding by these three conditions, he regards himself as absolutely in the right and his detractors as absolutely in the wrong. Indeed, their being in the wrong seems to him so clear and self-evident, that he is unable to understand their motivation. Not for a single minute would he believe them to have acted as law-abiding members of the community who know how detrimental to society criminal activity must in the final analysis be, even when it does not seem to inflict harm on any individual as such. He would not give the slightest thought to the possibility, no matter how remote and theoretical, that this, indeed, triggered their actions against him. Rather, they must have been prompted to action by envy. But why would established, secure, well-off members of the community be envious of a failed merchant? This is a riddle for which the protagonist has no solution. He is quite ready to understand and forgive the malicious envy of people poorer than himself, owners of degraded, penny-worth grocery stands: "*Oremelayt zenen mekane, lemay ikh nem gelt un zey nit*" ("Poor people are envious: how come I get money and they don't?" 239). Such envy is at least a natural human affect, an understandable if ungenerous reaction on the part of the unsuccessful to someone else's success. The protagonist, an "existentialist," to whom nothing human is alien, understands and accepts such envy. However, that cannot explain the ill-will of the *negidim* (the rich people). Why should his prospective ten thousand rubles concern them? "Was it any skin off their noses if some cash came my way?—I ask you: What of it? What? Why should anyone's head ache because of it? The man burns? Let him burn! You can also burn, may fire reduce you to a cinder!" (238) Thus the malice shown by these people cannot be understood as motivated by anything other than "sheer" evil, a transcendental rather than a psychological entity. Indeed, these enemies, the "great saints," are portrayed by the protagonist as satanic emissaries. Since as human beings their behavior is inexplicable, they must be devils.

VII.

At this point in our discussion some readers may raise the question: Was Sholem Aleichem himself, or even the non-personal "implied author" of his story, in agreement with the protagonist? Was he, in other words, justifying criminal behavior? The question is actually an illegitimate one and should not be asked at all. However, once the question has been asked, it can be helpful in pointing to a significant, perhaps central, feature of the author's best works. Sholem Aleichem, of course, was neither justifying nor criticizing his protagonist's behavior. By choosing both the form and the contents of his best works (the monologues, including those of Tevye, definitely forming the very upper crust of his *oeuvres*), he committed himself, both artistically and philosophically, to a non-judgmental position. We may even say that he committed himself to an anti-judgmental position. In these best works of his (some of them, like our story, veritable masterpieces), he took upon himself to fully and unconditionally articulate his protagonists' subjective experiences, their sense of existence. He, therefore, let them speak for themselves and present themselves by talking to other people. Of course, the presence of these (in most cases silent) interlocutors entangled the speaking protagonists in all the possible coils of groping for some advantage, superimposing upon their narration different self-serving agendas, trying to hide blatant biases through strict selection of the facts they narrate and the tone and order of their narration, lying, trying to curry favor, indulging in imaginary polemics, evading realities that are too difficult to face, and other brands of *mauvaise faites*. At the same time it endowed their talk with a situational authenticity in the existentialist sense of the term. These protagonists were not doing their talking only within the framework of fictional or rhetorical agreements between authors and readers called omniscient narration, or first-person confessional, or stream-of-consciousness fiction. They were performing in the real world of human interactions and, therefore, even their lies and self-serving arguments formed part of their reality.

Sholem Aleichem committed himself as an artist to this reality. His intensive and highly accomplished practicing of the monological narrative mode was not only the result of a carefully thought-out artistic choice, but, as all important artistic choices are, also that of a philosophical or, to put it in humbler terms, an ideational choice. According to this choice, a writer's "right" attitude toward the binary opposition or equation of life versus art was to strictly abide by the rules of art to the extent that they enhanced or made possible the articulation of the existential reality of authentic life-situations. Such an attitude precluded, both for purposes of the artistic tenability of the narration and for those of narrowing as much as possible the gap between narration and the situational reality it represented, the application to the narrated situation of any extrinsic norms of moral or factual truth, that is, all norms that have not been internalized by the protagonists themselves in the processes of their socialization, education, etc. Thus it was only to the speaking protagonists themselves that the right to judge, praise, condemn, or justify was given.

Obviously, the protagonists' mental worlds were replete with judgmental prejudices, biased cognition, and normative or pseudo-normative ideation. They were, after all, normal people who were born into a certain community, had been suffused with the presuppositions of a certain culture or religion, and were taught to respond in certain ways to the vicissitudes of individual and collective existence. And yet, more often than not, the author became intensely interested in fictional people who, as domesticated by their native culture as they were, also harbored consciously or semiconsciously a strong resentment aimed at the norms that controlled their social and emotional lives, a rebellious awareness, intellectually dim as it may be, of the fact that these were norms extrinsic to their own interior being, imposed by others and of service to those others and not at all to themselves. Thus, a whole crowd of women in Sholem Aleichem's works (best represented perhaps by Yente, the garrulous protagonist of "The Pot"), as religiously devout and totally controlled by the values of traditionalist Jewish way of life as they were, felt in the depth of their hearts that these values cruelly restricted their existential maneuvering space and often facilitated their exploitation and debasement. Half-knowingly these women rebelled against the *halakhah* and its exponents—rabbis, "saintly" people and erudite husbands who used the universally acknowledged value of "learning" as a pretext for secluding themselves, making themselves emotionally inaccessible, and shirking responsibility, letting their wives shoulder the heavy burden of daily existence.

Similarly, in stories focusing on post-traditional or semi-modern Jewish society Sholem Aleichem often looked for protagonists who thumbed their noses at the entire array of contemporary normative ideologies, such as humanism as propagated by modern Hebrew and Yiddish literatures, nationalism, Socialism, or even Zionism (although Sholem Aleichem himself was officially a Zionist and wrote Zionist novels and even Zionist propaganda brochures). The author let these protagonists, whom all these ideologies purported to educate and guide, question their applicability to the realities that they, the protagonists, had to contend with. As sociologically and psychologically different from each other as these protagonists were, their common denominator was their closeness to "things as they actually were" or as they existentially experienced them. As such they always spoke in the name of the mundane or "average" man and woman, who had to navigate his or her life through the stormy seas of often unspeakably difficult exigencies. And these people, often very much aware of the fact that, judged by the criteria of this or that normative ideology, they did not look good at all, explicitly or implicitly registered their protests against the norms. They usually criticized them for being fine and dandy in theory, but impracticable in or inapplicable to mundane reality. Their protests and critique of the norms sometimes reached a boiling point when they channeled themselves into sharp attacks—verbal but on some occasions also physical—on those regarded as the exponents of the norms.

The author, as we have seen, neither justified nor criticized these protests. Judging them was not his role, and he strictly forbade himself the indulgence in either apologetics or homiletics. His role was to let his protagonists speak for themselves, and he played this role even when dealing with characters who were totally reprehensible from both the moral and the aesthetic perspectives, such as, for instance, the "Man from Buenos Aires," an underworld coordinator of the "white flesh" industry, i.e., the orderly supply of duped or kidnapped European young women (among them many eastern European Jewish women) to brothels in various parts of the world, and particularly in South America. Even such a person was allowed to project reality as he experienced it, to justify himself as having been totally neglected by family and society in his childhood, to present his "profession" in the most attractive hues possible, and generally spin his crude social-Darwinist "philosophy." Here too, the role of the writer was subsumed by the meticulous articulation of the protagonist's subjective view of himself and of others.

Playing this role, Sholem Aleichem had to constantly practice a severe reduction or even truncation of the representation of his own subjectivity. This entailed a self-limitation that was not devoid of dangerous pitfalls, for such self-limitation could result in aridity and loss of credibility; and it was an indication of Sholem Aleichem's unique artistic greatness that in most of his works this did not happen. At the same time this creative self-curtailment, which ran in a direction opposite to that in which Yiddish literature in general moved as it entered modernity, gradually rendered him, in spite of his huge popularity with the readers, a lonely and excluded writer among his contemporary peers; for subjectivity became the order of the day in a literature in which Romanticism, Symbolism, and Impressionism all but coincided during the fifteen or so years in which Sholem Aleichem wrote his best works (1899–1912 or 1913).

To see the clear difference between his manner of narration and that of others we have only to compare our story to those sections (16 and 17) in I. L. Peretz's "Impressions of a Journey through the Tomazsow Region" that focus on the theme of insurance against fire, self-inflicted arsons, fires, and so forth. Peretz's famous series of vignettes and character sketches was written in the early 1890s as a result of the author's participation in a "statistic expedition," a project financed by an assimilated Polish Jewish magnate whose goal was to dispel through the objective means of statistics the anti-Semitic accusations of the Jewish inhabitants of small Polish towns amassing riches at the expense of the local Polish peasantry. It was a groundbreaking work of tremendous vitality exactly because it replaced the epic vein of much of nineteenth century Yiddish fiction with the unmistakable personal voice of a narrator who was a modern, urban, nervous, self-aware, and auto-ironic person. Eventually this person, in the role of an amateur statistician and a public "benefactor," could not but see the absurdity of his mission as the dire poverty he witnessed engulfed his consciousness. At an accelerating pace he vacillated among lyrical, satirical, matter-of-fact, and sheer disoriented manners of narration. When he approached the topic of criminal behavior on the part of some of the Jews (particularly in matters of arson and illegal brewing of alcoholic beverages) he waxed apologetic:

> While medical science has perfected an instrument for recording the heartbeat, statistical science toys with inane numbers. Does it know the frequency, strength, and intensity of the heartache suffered by a descendant of an exiled Jewish hidalgo or by the author of a work on the laws governing kosher slaughter, or, for that matter, by an ordinary householder, before any of them did what the law says should not be done? Does it know how long their hearts continued to bleed afterward? Can it count the sleepless nights that preceded and followed the first illegal act, or the times when the chil-

dren writhed with hunger cramps and limbs tossed with fever before the first glass of unlicensed liquor was poured?[3]

Sholem Aleichem would have none of these questions unless they were asked directly by the people concerned and, in general, he was averse to allowing the vein of complaint and apology overpower the mood of the narrative, nor would he allow the presuppositions this vein conveyed (confirming the "sanctity" of the law and the inevitable anguish caused by its violation) to cloud the narrative's ideational horizon. His attitude, essentially anarchistic, was by far more revolutionary than that of Peretz, although it was the latter who was favored by the Jewish revolutionary movements of the day (such as the Bund). Sholem Aleichem would invest himself in the wild élan of a fugitive "Moshe Mordechai," in his equivocations and hilarious twisting of the sacrosanct texts rather than talk about the miseries of a descendant of an exiled Jewish hidalgo. His protagonist was not only a man who broke the law without being either ashamed of or pained by his deed, but also a man who dared to intellectually challenge the legitimacy of the law under current existential circumstances. As this man's author, Sholem Aleichem did not for a second let embarrassment or the fear of being accused of enhancing the "case" of anti-Semitic propaganda make him flinch from fully articulating his protagonist's sense of victory against all odds. Whether he personally condoned this protagonist's behavior is absolutely beside the point he was out to make, which was that of putting his formidable talent at the disposal of the "Moshe Mordechais," and unabashedly conveying the mental vigor released in them by overcoming the law, a vigor that resembled the almost erotic pleasure Nabokov's Humbert Humbert experienced as he drove on the wrong side of the road and disregarded all traffic regulations, including red lights.

---

3. Ruth R. Wisse (ed.), *The I.L. Peretz Reader*, Schocken Books (New York 1990), 60. The translation is by Milton Himmelfarb.

The Hershele Maze:
Isaac Babel and His Ghost Reader

SASHA SENDEROVICH

> *My reader lives in my soul,*
> *but since he's been there for quite a long time,*
> *I have fashioned him in my own image.*
>
> Isaac Babel[1]

Writing about *Red Cavalry* in *The Modern Jewish Canon*, Ruth Wisse comes close to hinting at one of the hidden clues in Isaac Babel's war stories. Like other critics, she sees Babel's narrator as a figure that belongs to, and is thus able to interpret, two seemingly antithetical historical milieus: Jewish and Cossack.[2] He can claim to be at home in both contexts, writes Wisse, "because the Revolution is in the process of crushing the differences between them, and yet he can interpret Lenin to the Cossacks and Hershele

---

I would like to thank the participants of the following conferences where various stages of this project have been presented: the colloquium "Imagining Jewish Modernities" organized by the Jewish Studies Graduate Student Association at the University of Illinois at Urbana-Champaign in 2005 and the graduate student workshop organized by the American Academy for Jewish Research at Stanford University in 2006. I am indebted to my fellow participants of the panel "Heteroglossia, Soviet Style" at the American Association for the Advancement of Slavic Studies in Washington, D.C. in 2006: Bella Grigoryan, Anna Wexler Katsnelson, Jane Taubman, and Boris Wolfson; members of the audience at that panel also asked helpful and insightful questions: Cathy Popkin, Robert Rothstein, and Val Vinokurov. I am thankful to Svetlana Boym, Galit Hasan-Rokem, Harriet Murav, Gabriella Safran, William Mills Todd III, Janneke van de Stadt, and Steven Zipperstein for reading different versions of this essay, and to Liora Halperin for her editorial help.

1. From Babel's meeting with his readers at the Union of Soviet Writers on September 28, 1937. The transcript of the conversation was published in *Nash sovremennik* 4 (1964), 96–100. For the English translation see Isaac Babel, *You Must Know Everything: Stories 1915–1937*, trans. Max Hayward and ed. Nathalie Babel (New York: Farrar, Straus and Giroux, 1969), 205–221. The quotation is on page 100 in the Russian, and on page 220 in the English. Later in this essay the English text is referred to as Babel 1969.

2. Lionel Trilling was one of the first American scholars to speak of Babel's "forbidden dialectic" in his introduction to the 1955 translation of Babel's work: "For him the Cossack was indeed the noble savage, all too savage, not often noble, yet having in his savagery some quality that might raise strange questions in a Jewish mind." See the reprint of the essay: Lionel Trilling, "The Forbidden Dialectic: Introduction to *The Collected Stories*" in Harold Bloom (ed.), *Isaac Babel* (New York, New Haven, and

Ostropolier to the Jews."[3] I read in Wisse's turn of phrase an implied comparison between the narratives of two stories in the *Red Cavalry* cycle. One is "My First Goose," in which the narrator, Liutov, while traveling with the Cossack division as a propagandist for a Red Army newspaper (as Babel himself did), conveys Lenin's message from *Pravda* to the illiterate Cossacks. The second story is "Rebbe," in which Liutov offers a puzzling response to a question posed by Motale Bratslavskii, the Hasidic rebbe in Zhitomir, when he describes his occupation as "putting into verse the adventures of Hershele Ostropolier."[4]

Liutov's occupation, as he describes it, is an act of both creativity and interpretation. The focus on interpretation as both an action and a product of that action is crucial to these stories, yet Wisse stops short of exploring this theme beyond the conclusion that "in his [Liutov's] search for merriment he is putting Hershele Ostropolier into verse."[5] Efraim Sicher sees Liutov's answer to the rebbe as "a cultural referent which identifies Liutov as a fellow Jew rather than a marauding soldier from the invading revolutionary forces."[6] However, the exchange offers more than a reference to a specific piece of cultural knowledge that identifies the ambivalent Liutov as a Jew to his Hasidic hosts; a great deal more than merriment is at stake here. Enough is strange and estranging in the story "Rebbe" to cast doubt on any straightforward interpretation of Liutov's seemingly straightforward answers to the *tsadik*.

In this essay I would like to explore the relationship between Isaac Babel and an ideal reader constructed in his stories. I intend to follow the puzzling clues set in the story "Rebbe," by tracing what I will call the "Hershele maze" of the Babelian text. Hershele Ostropolier, a trickster figure from Yiddish folklore, is central to Babel. The subtext suggested by references to

---

    Philadelphia: Chelsea House Publishers, 1987), 29.

3. Ruth R. Wisse, *The Modern Jewish Canon: A Journey through Language and Culture* (Chicago: The University of Chicago Press, 2003), 113.

4. Isaak Babel', *Sochineniia* (Moscow: Khudozhestvennaia literatura, 1990), vol. 2, 36. Throughout the essay, I quote from three separate editions of Babel's work: the above-mentioned two-volume Russian edition, against which the translations from two editions that are currently in print are verified and the best is given. This exchange is also translated in Isaac Babel, *Collected Stories*, ed. Efraim Sicher and trans. David McDuff (London: Penguin books, 1994), 124; and in Isaac Babel, *Red Cavalry*, ed. Nathalie Babel and trans. Peter Constantine (New York and London: W. W. Norton & Company, 2002), 71. Below I refer to these three editions as, respectively, Babel' 1990, Babel 1994 and Babel 2002. All translations from Babel' 1990, and from other Russian and Yiddish sources, are my own.

5. Wisse, 113.

6. Efraim Sicher, "Babel's 'Shy Star': Reference, Inter-reference and Interference," *New Zealand Slavonic Journal* 36 (2002): 259.

Yiddish folklore adds a flavor of Hershele's trickery to Babel's persona in the Russian-language text of *Red Cavalry*. Babel constructs a figure of the reader inside the text who can understand the crux of his project: not so much the interpretation of Lenin to the Cossacks and Hershele to the Jews, but rather the interpretation of Lenin by way of Jewish discourse, and of becoming a Cossack as Hershele's act of trickery. This figure of the reader inside the text is neither equivalent to any actual readers outside the text, nor does it explain the entirety of the enigmatic and vast phenomenon that is Isaac Babel. In this article I hope to delineate a particular kind of reader constructed in Babel's text to understand one aspect of the author/narrator's own experience: being a disguised Jew during the Soviet-Polish War of 1920.

I.

The story "Rebbe" is inspired by the same entry from Babel's 1920 diary as the story "Gedali." Both resulting narratives are set on a Friday evening in Zhitomir, at the beginning of the Sabbath, but are separated in *Red Cavalry* by the story "My First Goose." All *Red Cavalry* stories were written separately and in retrospect, as a number of critics point out,[7] yet the sequential arrangement of the stories in book form sets up a puzzle about the way these stories fit together in the larger cycle of *Red Cavalry*.[8]

---

7. Efraim Sicher writes, for example, that the *Red Cavalry* stories were composed in retrospect and "at some distance from the material collected in his 1920 Diary. Lyutov [sic] is a composite figure who actually never fully develops, but remains a fictional persona used with irony by the implied author as an intermediary eye." See: Efraim Sicher, *Style and Structure in the Prose of Isaac Babel* (Columbus: Slavica Publishers, 1985), 12.

8. Of the critical works that deal with the sequence of stories "Gedali," "My First Goose," and "Rebbe" as a cycle, three are of note. Charles Rougle sees "My First Goose" as a rupture between the narrative thread that goes from "Gedali" to "Rebbe", noting that the latter picks up where the former left off, with "the abruptness of the break with the intervening narrative ['My First Goose'] serving to emphasize the duality of the narrator's consciousness." See Charles Rougle, "Isaac Babel and His Odyssey of War and Revolution," in Charles Rougle (ed.), *Red Cavalry: A Critical Companion* (Evanston, Ill.: Northwestern University Press, 1996), 41. Edyta M. Bojanowska's approach to *Red Cavalry* as a cycle defines "three structural-thematic blocks": the first block of the initial ten stories establishes the whole cycle's themes and motifs by concentrating on life behind the front line; the second block of twenty-three stories deals with the front-line experience; and the final block of one to three stories, depending on the edition, "reconnects with the opening stories, thus foregrounding the work's cyclical structure"; see: Edyta M. Bojanowska, "*E Pluribus Unum*: Isaac Babel's *Red Cavalry* As a Story Cycle," *The Russian Review* 59 (July 2000) 373. Evgenii Dobrenko creates a very thorough reading of *Red Cavalry* as a cycle in his article "The Logic of the Cycle." Dobrenko sees the events of "My First Goose" as a trial of a person who must relinquish his individuality and merge with the "herd consciousness" [*roevoe soznanie*]; the

The Zhitomir rebbe asks Liutov a number of questions when Liutov joins the Hasidim at their meal, but Liutov answers more in this story than he is asked. We must assume that the conversation between Liutov (the character) and his hosts takes place in Yiddish and is "translated" into Russian by Liutov (the implied author) for the sake of the Russian-language readers of Isaac Babel, the author of *Red Cavalry*. When Liutov-the-character answers the rebbe's questions, his answers reveal something about the implied author—who is strikingly similar to Babel—as well.

One of the rebbe's questions, *"Otkuda priekhal evrei?"* ("Where did the Jew come from?"),[9] might be seen as a direct translation into Russian of the Yiddish idiom *"fun vanen kumt a yid?"* At first glance, the wording of the rebbe's question seems no more than a faithful rendering of the implied Yiddish original into the writer's native tongue. However, the Yiddish *a yid* of the idiom does not mean *"evrei"* or "Jew": in a language that, in its traditional environment, assumes all its speakers to be Jews, *a yid* means no more than "a person" and is used in several idioms instead of the second-person singular pronoun. If the Yiddish idiom were to be idiomatically translated into another language, the translation would have been: "Where did you come from?" The difference is significant, because the rebbe's question, rendered in Russian, is the only instance in *Red Cavalry* when someone else explicitly refers to Liutov as a Jew. It is also the only instance in the cycle where by the mere fact of replying to such a question and engaging this literally translated idiom, Liutov unambiguously identifies himself as a Jew—not to the rebbe in Zhitomir, who must understand that his interlocutor is Jewish because he is linguistically and culturally conversant in Yiddish, but to the readers of *Red Cavalry*.

Upon hearing that Liutov comes from Odessa, the rebbe produces an unexpected reply: "A devout town [...] The star of our exile, the reluctant well of our afflictions!'"[10] That a Hasidic rebbe would make such a reverent statement about Odessa, known in the Jewish world at the time as a city of sin,[11] is puzzling. Does the rebbe mean what he says? Should the reader

---

identity defines itself only after it has emerged from this trial. This trial is the reason, claims Dobrenko, why the unified narrative texture of "Gedali" and "Rebbe" is interrupted by "My First Goose." "Rebbe" becomes "My First Goose" in reverse: it speaks of the difficulty in entering not the new world, but the old one, not of succumbing to the "herd consciousness" but rather to the consciousness that is elegiac. See E.A. Dobrenko, "Logika tsykla" in G.A. Belaia, E.A. Dobrenko, and I.A. Esaulov, *"Konarmiia" Isaaka Babelia* (Moscow: Rossiiskii universitet, 2004), 55.

9. Babel' 1990, v. 2, 35.

10. Babel 2002, 71.

11. Steven J. Zipperstein, *The Jews of Odessa: A Cultural History, 1794–1881* (Stanford: Stanford University Press, 1986), 1.

assume that the rebbe's characterization of Odessa as a "devout town" [*blagochestivyi gorod*] is a sign of the decadence in this Hasidic court[12] or simply a game of pretense and a "fabric of lies" in which the rebbe does not really mean what he says?[13] I suggest that the proper interpretation of the rebbe's words lies in the Yiddish subtext of his reply. The phrase "star of our exile" [*zvezda nashego izgnaniia*] could be approximately translated back into its implied Yiddish original: *likht fun goles*–"the light of exile" (in Hebrew, *ma'or ha-golah*). The phrase then becomes more than it literally means: the expression is an honorific applicable not to places, but to sages who distinguished themselves in the art of religious learning and textual commentary.[14]

Such a reading is confirmed in the cryptic phrase that follows in the rebbe's response to Liutov's assertion that he is "putting into verse the adventures of Hershele Ostropolier": "A great task [...] The jackal moans when it is hungry, every fool has foolishness enough for despondency, and only *the sage* shreds the veil of existence with laughter..."[15] Commentators of Babel's style have spoken about the poetics of the writer's prose and of the need to read his references on a level that cuts somewhere underneath the text and holds the text together.[16] One of Babel's earliest critics defined this feature of Babel's style as "*vnutrennaia fabula*" or "*zakulisnaia fabula*" ("internal *fabula*" or "backstage *fabula*")–a kind of internal development of the story that occurs beneath the surface of the text through the interlinking associations that separate words and phrases evoke.[17] If there is such an internal *fabula* in the story "Rebbe," then the word "sage" (*mudrets*) can be read as a synonym of the implied Yiddish idiom *likht fun goles*.

Of course, an entirely different and, to the speakers of Yiddish, more obvious reading of the word "sage" is possible here. When translated into the implied Yiddish original that the rebbe must have used in Babel's story,

---

12. Wisse, 102.

13. Alice Stone Nakhimovsky, *Russian-Jewish Literature and Identity: Jabotinsky, Babel, Grossman, Galich, Roziner, Markish* (Baltimore and London: The Johns Hopkins University Press, 1992), 95.

14. Yitshok Niborsky, *Verterbukh fun loshn-koydesh-shtamike verter in yidish* (Paris: Medem-Bibliotheque, 1999), 145.

15. Babel 2002, 71 [my emphasis].

16. On the "ornamental" aspects of Babel's prose see, for example, James E. Falen, *Isaac Babel: Russian Master of the Short Story* (Knoxville: The University of Tennessee Press, 1974), 42–45; and an illuminating analysis of Babel's "poetic prose" in Efraim Sicher, *Style and Structure in the Prose of Isaac Babel* (Columbus: Slavica Publishers, 1985), 26–38.

17. Nik. Stepanov, "Novella Babelia," in *I.E. Babel': Statii i materialy* (Leningrad: Academia, 1928), 37.

the word in question becomes *khokhem*. As such the word can be interpreted as a mocking epithet; after all, the Yiddish idiom *"er iz a khokhem"*
("he is [such] a sage," or even "what a sage he is!") means precisely the
opposite: the sage of the phrase is dismissed as a fool. Here, however, I have
ventured to suggest a new reading that does not treat the puzzling exchange
between the Zhitomir rebbe and Liutov as a mere joke. I would like to imagine that the rebbe means what he says, that Liutov understands the elder's
cryptic message, and that the word "sage" is synonymous with the expression "a star/light of exile." I claim that the *khokhem* in question is linked
with Odessa, and that the point of contact between this epithet and this top-
onym provides us with two crucial hidden meanings. The first of these
meanings hints at an alternative etymology of the word *khokhem* that is not
as dismissive and mocking as that of the folk idiom. I am thinking here of
khakhmey Odes, "the sages of Odessa," as the prominent Russian-Jewish
thinkers, artists, and men of letters residing in Odessa in the latter part of
the nineteenth century came to be known.[18]

The second concealed meaning involves Babel's programmatic understanding of his native city as a place whence Russia's literary messiah would
emerge. As Gabriella Safran noted, Babel's description of Odessans in his
1916 manifesto[19]—men of sunshine and youthful vigor—coincided with
Maksim Gorkii's imperative to create positive new Jewish characters in Russian literature.[20] Though Liutov may wish to be more vigorous than he can
actually be in his circumstances, he appears before the Zhitomir rebbe as a
writer from Odessa, similar to those other Odessans who bring with them
some vital "blood-freshening" spirit.[21] With the Polish-Soviet war in the
background and with Hasidism driven to the brink of extinction, the figure
of a Jew from Odessa carries a glimmer of hope even for the Zhitomir rebbe.
On June 3, 1920 Babel notes the following exchange between him and the
Zhitomir rebbe, the clear prototype of the *tsadik* in *Red Cavalry*:

> "Where are you from, young man?"
> "From Odessa."
> "How do people live there?"
> "People are alive there." [*"Tam liudi zhivy"*]
> "And here it's terrible." [*"A zdes' uzhas"*][22]

---

18. See, for example, Dan Miron's introduction in S.Y. Abramovitsh, *Tales of Mendele the
Book Peddler*, Dan Miron and Ken Frieden, eds., trans. Ted Gorelick and Hillel Halkin
(New York: Schocken Books, 1996), xxiii.

19. See "Odessa" in Babel' 1990, vol. 1, 62–65.

20. Gabriella Safran, "Isaak Babel's El'ia Isaakovich as a New Jewish Type," *Slavic Review*
61, no. 2 (Summer 2002): 257.

21. Babel' 1990, vol. 1, 65.

22. Babel' 1990, vol. 1, 363. Peter Constantine translates the exchange in Babel 2002 (p.

Zhitomir and Odessa are at the opposite ends of historical experience, one "here" and another "there," with a contrastive conjunction emphasizing the world of difference that lies between them. Yet, it is not Odessa's staunch secularism that is cast here against the rebbe's piety: Liutov is a *khokhem* from Isaac Babel's *Odes,* a sage from an idiosyncratically optimistic city who lightens the mood in the midst of destruction.

"Reb Motale says that while animals and simpletons may be able to express the misery of the human condition, only laughter can get beyond the limits of reality to ultimate freedom," writes Ruth Wisse in her interpretation of the puzzling passage from "Rebbe." She continues to state that "[t]he rebbe ascribes to Hershele Ostropolier a spiritual function as high as his own, and when Lyutov [sic] finds himself seated among the other Hasidim [...] he includes himself in their inspired brotherhood."[23] However, it is not Hershele, or, at least, not *only* Hershele, whom the rebbe credits with sagely wisdom for the ability to illuminate existence with his saving laughter. The sage of Odessa in this passage is Liutov himself, Liutov who claims to be the interpreter of Hershele's adventures, Liutov who doesn't so much adapt these adventures into verse, but rather adopts them into his own life.

Like Hershele Ostropolier, who entertained the melancholy rebbe of Medzhibozh with witty stories about his own trickery, Liutov must have earned the respect of the Zhitomir rebbe and his court by telling them similar stories. A "sage" from Odessa, Liutov would likely have told the Hasidim a story about Hershele—or a Hershele-like story—to earn his place at their table. Despite the fact that no such storytelling happens in the plot of "Rebbe," the internal *fabula* of the work suggests a possibility of Liutov's storytelling that may have been implied between the lines.

We might begin to understand Babel's conception of Hershele by looking at the one story in Babel's oeuvre that is explicitly marked as a Hershele narrative, "Shabos-Nakhamu."[24] That story, written in 1918 at the beginning of Babel's career, bears a subtitle: "From the Hershele cycle." Though no other stories explicitly belong to this "cycle," there is at least one other story that resembles a Hershele narrative: "My First Goose," which, as has been mentioned, precedes "Rebbe" in the *Red Cavalry* cycle. Babel does

---

202) but the last two lines of the dialogue translated as "People are alive" and "Here it's terrible" leave out the words "there" in reference to Odessa, and the conjunction "and," which, in the Russian original ("a") expresses contrast rather than equivalence. Babel's diary entry is clear about the contrast between Zhitomir and Odessa that the rebbe is trying to capture and emphasize through his choice of words (or, rather, through the words that Babel the diarist puts in his mouth).

23. Wisse, 102.

24. The original publication according to Efraim Sicher's very useful bibliography is: "Shabos-nakhamu (Iz tsikla *Gershele*)," *Vecherniaia zvezda* [Petrograd] March 16, 1918.

have a "Hershele cycle" that implicitly runs through much of his total text. This cycle itself becomes a kind of internal *fabula* that illuminates the writer's many works.

II.

In order to define more precisely what a "Hershele story" is, we must take a brief look at the place of Hershele Ostropolier in the context of Yiddish folklore. In Nathan Ausubel's description, Hershele is one of the "wags and wits" of Yiddish folklore.[25] Hershele is a poor man whose wit originates not so much in his smarts as in the pressing economic and social conditions in which he must exist. As Ausubel puts it: "He was an impish likeable *schlimazl* [sic] whose misfortunes did not, by any means, arise from his own personal character weaknesses but rather from the illogic of the topsy-turvy world he lived in."[26] That is to say, Hershele is mischievous not only for the sake of mischief. His impoverishment and his hunger lead him to engage in a play of wits in order to deceive those who are capable of being duped and to obtain something that is forbidden to him.

In one representative Hershele story, Hershele finds himself in a pub, penniless and badly in need of food. The owner refuses to feed him without receiving payment, saying that she has no food left to put on the table. After a moment of thought, Hershele says, "In that case, I'm afraid I'll have to do what my father did." The owner, frightened, asks for clarification, but gets none. "Never mind," Hershele says, "my father did what he did!" In fear, the owner finds food and feeds Hershele a full dinner. After he has finished eating and the potential trouble has been avoided, the owner insists on clarification. "Oh, my father?" replie[s] Hershele innocently. "Whenever my father didn't have any supper he went to bed without it."[27]

---

25. Nathan Ausubel, ed., *A Treasury of Jewish Folklore* (New York: Crown Publishers, 1949), 286. For a structural study of Hershele stories see: Toby Blum-Dobkin, "Yiddish Folktales about Jesters: A Problem in Structural Analysis and Genre Definition," *Working Papers in Yiddish and East European Jewish Studies,* no. 22 (New York: Max Weinreich Center for Advanced Jewish Studies, YIVO, 1977). For a useful introduction to Hershele stories, see commentaries in Dan Ben-Amos, ed., *Folktales of the Jews,* vol. 2 (Philadelphia: The Jewish Publication Society, 2007), 329–333.

26. Ausubel, 287.

27. Ibid., 313. This particular story, as well as many other Hershele stories, shares its motifs with other narratives in the international repertoire of trickster tales. Some other Hershele stories could be placed into the specific cultural context of subversive narratives within the tradition of Hasidic storytelling. In one such story, Hershele tricks a devotee of Rebbe Borukh (who was Hershele's employer in the town of Medzhibozh) into believing that his worn-out shoes are, in fact, "holy" because they had once belonged to the rebbe himself. The ensuing exchange leaves Hershele with the wealthy Hasid's new boots; this feat is accomplished because Hershele exploits his interlocutor's blind devotion to and unquestioning reverence of Rebbe Borukh. The

On close examination, this model of storytelling is instructive for Babel. Hershele's inventiveness enables him to bypass the required means (money) to achieve the desired goal (food). Babel establishes a similar model of inventiveness in "My First Goose," a story that is placed between "Gedali" and "Rebbe." "My First Goose" is the story of Liutov's acceptance by the Cossacks, who are suspicious of and unfriendly to a bespectacled intellectual Jew with a typewriter who has entered their environment of masculinity, courageousness, and physical crudeness. However, the story is more than simply an initiation narrative. I propose to read it as a story, addressed to someone inside the text of *Red Cavalry*, in which Liutov hopes to justify his lesser act of violence through a narrative of trickery.

Liutov is given a hint on how to be accepted: he must "mess up a lady"—"and a good lady at that" in order to earn respect from the soldiers.[28] Rape here is the means that must be utilized in order to achieve the end-goal of acceptance. As it were, Liutov is presented with a kind of a riddle that he needs to solve or else be beaten. (His acceptance by the Cossacks rests on the expected act of cruelty and violence, which he is unwilling to commit.) Johan Huizinga, the author of the classic study of the elements of play in culture, comments on such riddles in the archetypal settings of play:

> The answer to an enigmatic question is not found by reflection or logical reasoning. It comes quite literally as a sudden solution—a loosening of the tie by which the questioner holds you bound. The corollary of this is that by giving the correct answer you strike him powerless. In principle, there is only one answer to every question. It can be found if you know the rules of the game. These are grammatical, poetical, or ritualistic as the case may be. You have to know the secret language of the adepts and be acquainted with the significance of each symbol....Should it prove that a second answer is possible, in accord with the rules but not suspected by the questioner, then it will go badly with him: he is caught in his own trap.[29]

Only one answer is possible here: an act of violence must be committed. But, even though Liutov is trying to pass for a Cossack, he is an intellectual and a Jew who experiences pangs of conscience. He is morally incapable of committing the brutal act of rape and thus earning respect from the soldiers.

---

holey/holy shoes represent that kind of reverential narrative about Hasidic *tsadikim* that Hershele's witticism works against. For the complete narrative summarized above, see: Valerii Dymshitz, ed., *Evreiskie narodnye skazki: Predaniia, bylichki, rasskazy, anekdoty sobrannye E.S. Raize* (St. Petersburg: Symposium, 2000), 236–237. For other Hershele narratives, see, among others, the following collection: M. Stern, ed., *Hershele Ostropoler un Motke Habad: zayere anekdoten, vitsen, stsenes un shtukes* (New York: Star Hebrew Book Co., [n.d.]).

28. Babel' 1990, vol. 2, 33.

29. Johan Huizinga, *Homo Ludens: A Study of the Play Element in Culture* (Boston: The Beacon Press, 1955), 110.

Instead, in an instant, he comes to understand that there is also a second answer "in accord with the rules but not suspected by the questioner." Liutov here engages in a kind of subversion as inventive as Hershele's: instead of raping a woman, he kills a goose and asks the landlady to cook it for him. He subverts the soldiers' expectation because he is unwilling to commit an act of violence but is capable of playful invention. The killing of the goose earns him the respect of the soldiers and his goal is achieved.

Efraim Sicher observes that "[t]he colorful imagery and unusual metaphors conceal a deep concern for morality built into the structure of Babel''s short stories."[30] If Liutov were to tell the story of his acceptance by the Cossacks to the Hasidim in Reb Motale's court, he would have proven to them that he was a Jew who was able to retain his sense of what is right even in the conditions of extreme violence. Only a certain type of reader would have understood the particularly Jewish plays of identity communicated through this Hershele-like story about acceptance by the Cossacks. I would like to propose that this reader, Babel's reader constructed in the text, was present at this imagined storytelling that Friday night in the court of Reb Motale Bratslavskii.

III.

A comparison between Isaac Babel and Nikolai Gogol may aid our understanding of certain elements in Babel's work. Babel himself perceived a literary kinship with Gogol, who preceded him by almost a century. He invokes Gogol when contemplating his own origins in the south of the Russian Empire. "Do you remember the life-giving [*plodorodiashchee*] bright sun of Gogol, a man who came from Ukraine?" Babel writes, "If there are such descriptions—then they are merely episodes. But 'The Nose,' 'The Overcoat,' 'The Portrait' and 'Notes of a Madman' are not episodes. Petersburg defeated Poltava [*Poltavshchina*] [...]"[31] Thinking of himself as Rus-

---

30. Sicher 1985, 10.

31. Babel' 1990, vol. 1, 64. Besides Babel's own professed affinity with Gogol's southern origins and his creative project, there is an ample amount of additional evidence for comparing the two writers. There is a degree of similarity in their relation to folkloric motifs, as I suggest in this essay. Much also remains to be said about the way that each came to represent urban spaces of Petersburg and Odessa (see note 32 below). An additional obvious commonality has to do with the way that each represented the Cossacks. Maksim Gorkii was among the first who has noted the common thread. Publicly defending Babel from the attacks of the Red Army general Semion Budennyi (who criticized Babel for the misrepresentation of Cossack soldiers in Budennyi's First Cavalry division), Gorkii positively compared *Red Cavalry* to Gogol's *Taras Bulba*; see Maksim Gorkii, "Rabselkoram i voenkoram o tom, kak uchilsia pisat," *Pravda* Sept 30, 1928, 3–4. For the critical treatment of the Cossack myth in Russian culture in Gogol, Babel, and other writers, see Judith Deutsch Kornblatt, *The Cossack Hero in Russian Literature: A Study in Cultural Mythology* (Madison: The University of Wisconsin Press, 1992).

sia's literary "messiah" who arrived from Odessa, Babel sees in Gogol his literary forerunner whose "Poltavan" style succumbed to the linguistic demands of Russia's imperial capital.[32]

Two elements of Donald Fanger's classic study of Gogol are applicable to my analysis of Babel: the notion of a cluster of themata that is woven through and thereby illuminates an oeuvre; and, second, the notion that a folkloric motif in literature can reflect a psychological state of the writer that is central to his works and text. The intersection of these two elements helps illuminate the Babelian text further.

Fanger proposes that all Gogol's works, as well as his biography, can be understood as one single text: "the text is Gogol and Gogol is the text, simultaneously compelling recognition and resisting definition."[33] Fanger elaborates further that the reader can recognize not merely particular Gogolian locutions and style:

> What we rather recognize is the unique thematic resonance his phrases take on from their participation in the characteristic workings of the larger Gogolian text. By theme here I mean something more fundamental than those recurrent objects of concern—rank, stupidity, greed, moral vacuousness [...]—all of which may be found in "reality" and in his writings alike. Behind them, organizing the rival reality that is Gogol's poetic universe and expressing only *its* laws, are certain pervasive entities that cannot be reduced to propositional statements. In fact, they manifest themselves textually as dynamic tendencies, modalities of concern, patterns of relationship. Because they comprise key elements in Gogol's artistic code and because they are not to be confused with themes as usually construed, I propose to use the terms "thema" and "themata."[34]

Fanger further speaks of "clusters of themata" organized around such large notions as "metamorphosis," "evasion," "identity," and "recognition" that are central to the Gogolian text and that can serve as loose cluster headings for a number of works in which "[n]one of its [the cluster's] members is clearly privileged" and in which "[e]ach of its shifting relations to the others contributes to an implication."[35] Each thema offers an entry point into the entirety of an oeuvre, and each cluster of themata allows for a number of individual works to be grouped in a particular way that reveals something

---

32. However, we should keep in mind that Babel hardly practices what he preaches. If his own stories that belong to the so-called "Childhood Stories" cycle are an indication, then we do not exactly find that southern sun that the writer claims to have associated with his native city. This idiosyncratic Odessa is nearly as grim, grotesque, and alienating as is Gogol's Petersburg.

33. Donald Fanger, *The Creation of Nikolai Gogol* (Cambridge, Mass. and London: The Belknap Press of Harvard University Press, 1979), 239.

34. Ibid.

35. Ibid., 240.

about the properties of each cluster, as well as its implication for the entire-ty of the author's text.[36]

Hershele, I argue, is one theme in a cluster of themata constituted by meta-literary situations. In their book-length study of three of Babel's sto-ries, "A Note," "My First Fee," and "Guy de Maupassant," Mikhail Iampolskii and Alexander Zholkovskii argue that all three stories have in common a meta-literary setting, a situation that draws attention to the writing process and the relationship between a writer and a reader. In the case of these three stories, a writer or a writer figure takes advantage of a "reader figure" and receives both monetary and sexual favors from her by possessing or guarding knowledge that would help her understand the writer. By identify-ing this cluster of meta-literary themata, Iampolskii and Zholkovskii position these stories, generally viewed as marginal, at the center of Babel's oeuvre.[37]

I would like to add the story "Shabos-Nakhamu" to this cluster of meta-lit-erary situations in Babel by showing that the Hershele story contemplates the encounters between writers and readers. In the story, which is usually seen only as an adaptation of a Yiddish folkloric tale accidental in Babel's oeuvre,[38] Hershele Ostropolier encounters the pregnant wife of an absent tavern owner, who tells him that she is waiting for Shabos Nakhamu. Her-shele realizes that the woman does not understand what Shabos Nakhamu is (the term "Shabos-Nakhamu," "the Sabbath of consolation," in fact refers to

---

36. Other critics also choose to approach Gogol's oeuvre by identifying a number of themes that are chosen as prisms through which one sees much of the writer's total text. Instructive for my particular interest in Babel's "folkloric imagination" is the treat-ment of Gogol's story "A Terrible Vengeance" included in his *Dikanka* cycle. Through his reading of the story, Robert Maguire identified the problem of "bounded space," the organic vitality of which is destroyed by the intrusion of outside forces; see Robert Maguire, *Exploring Gogol* (Stanford: Stanford University Press, 1994), 9. Yuri Mann, in his *Poetika Gogolia* (Moscow: Khudozhestvennaia literatura, 1988 [1978]) also commented on the problem of an individual's separation from the organic community (41), as well as on the presence of uncontrolled evil forces that create a kind of prede-termination against which an individual's will is powerless (47). Both critics place the reading of this "folkloric" story (which Gogol wrote at the start of his career) at the beginning of their studies, identifying in it those themes (bounded space, intrusion of mythic forces) that would come to dominate much of the writer's oeuvre.

37. See A.K. Zholkovskii and M.B. Iampolskii, *Babel'/Babel* (Moscow: Carte Blanche, 1994).

38. See, for example, Falen 1974, 31–33. I disagree with Falen's claim that Babel never continued the "Hershele cycle" because the circumstances of his life—his experiences during the war and working for the Cheka—made it inevitable that "the saga of Hershele may have ceased to occupy the forefront of his mind" (33). I claim in this essay that Hershele continued to be very much on Babel's mind during and after the experiences that Falen thinks to have displaced the writer's interest in the folkloric trickster. For a different treatment of folkloric themes in Babel, see Safran 2002, 253–272 (268–272 in particular).

the Saturday following the fast day of Tisha b'Av), and replies that he is in fact "Shabos Nakhamu." The woman understands her guest to be a visitor from the other world, serves him a lavish meal, and sends him away with a bag of clothes that he claims he will take to her dead relatives in the world-to-come. In this situation, Hershele exploits the woman's ignorance of Jewish ritual to gain the hospitality he desires.

The situation in "Shabos-Nakhamu" is typologically similar to the situation in two stories, "My First Fee" (and "The Note," which is a version of "My First Fee") and "Guy de Maupassant." In the former, the narrator invents a story about himself and withholds from his "reader," the prostitute Vera, the information that would enable her to understand that he is fabricating this story.[39] In "Guy de Maupassant," the narrator, who is hired as a helper in a translation project, is able to achieve material gain and sexual favors by understanding the nuances of French and Russian better than does Raisa Benderskaia, the hired translator of Maupassant's stories into Russian.[40] In all three of these stories we can see the same meta-literary thema: the stories construct a reader who knows less than a writer and thus is forever incapable of understanding the irony of his or her situation. In "My

---

39. Babel' 1990, vol. 2, 245–253. The story fabricated by the narrator of "My First Fee" presents him as a male prostitute—that is, Vera's "little sister"—who is utterly inexperienced with women. The prostitute believes his story and takes pity on the narrator, teaching him the tricks of her trade and charging him nothing for her services. The narrator, thus, earns his first literary fee, a payment for fabricating a story and making it believable.

40. Babel' 1990, vol. 2, 217–223. Benderskaia's husband is a publisher, and it is clear from the story that she gets the translation job through her connections rather than through any special talent. It must be remarked that the gender relations in these stories are of crucial importance: in "Guy de Maupassant," "My First Fee," and "Shabos-Nakhamu" the duped readers and reader-figures are all women. In the same interview from which I quoted in the epigraph, Babel noted that he often imagined his reader as a woman: "Generally speaking, I feel that a short story can be read properly only by a very intelligent woman—the better specimens of this half of the human race sometimes have absolute taste, just as some people have absolute pitch" (in Babel 1969, 220). It is interesting to read this line in conjunction with Antonina Pirozhkova's reminiscences in her memoirs about Isaac Babel: in one of the entries Pirozhkova notes the way in which Babel, through his gifts of books to her and through his reading suggestions shaped her, as it were, into a kind of an ideal reader. See: A. N. Pirozhkova, *At His Side: The Last Years of Isaac Babel*, trans. by Anne Frydman and Robert L. Busch (South Royalton, Vt.: Steepforth Press, 1996), 45–46. For an illuminating discussion of gender in Babel's oeuvre see Eliot Borenstein, *Men Without Women: Masculinity and Revolution in Russian Fiction, 1917–1929* (Durham and London: Duke University Press, 2000), 73–124. Though gender is not my focus in this article, the noticeable coincidence between gender and Babel's ideal reader makes this a highly relevant matter that I would like to discuss on another occasion.

First Fee" and "Guy de Maupassant" the meta-literary thema is exercised straightforwardly; in "Shabos-Nakhamu" this thema is only implied.

Fanger writes, secondly, that the use of folkloric references in creative work can reveal a certain psychological state of the writer. Though the scholarship on Babel tends to ascribe his use of the Hershele trope merely to his familiarity with Jewish folklore, Fanger suggests through his reading of Gogol the possibility of a more nuanced reading of the folkloric elements in Babel's work. Quoting from Abram Tertz's/Andrei Siniavskii's *In Gogol's Shadow* [*V teni Gogolia*], he writes that "Gogol draws patterns of experience from his own psyche that are identical to those of folklore." By claiming folkloric origins for the stories that comprise, among others, the *Dikan'ka Stories* cycle, Gogol thus "signal[s] a kind of authenticity but seeks transparently to disown its intimate provenance by passing off as an impersonal product what is actually the objectification of a personal psychological state."[41]

For Gogol, the "personal psychological state" manifest in the usage of Ukrainian folklore in his Russian-language stories may concern the evasion, absence, and displacement that Fanger so eloquently contemplates in his monograph. In Babel, the Hershele trope is an indication of a "psychological state" of an entirely different variety. I have so far cited two of the three instances when Hershele is mentioned in the Babelian text. The third is a reference that comes from Babel's 1920 diary. One paragraph in Babel's entry for July 23, 1920 deserves to be quoted in full:

> The Dubno synagogues. Everything destroyed. Two small anterooms remain, centuries, two minute little rooms, everything filled with memories, four synagogues in a row, and then the pasture, the fields, and the setting sun. The synagogues are pitiful, squat, ancient, green and blue little buildings, the Hasidic one, inside, no architecture whatsoever. I go into the

---

41. Fanger 1979, 100. Gogol himself was not particularly familiar with Ukrainian folklore. Having come to Petersburg at the time when stories about Ukraine were incredibly popular, Gogol implored his mother to send him detailed descriptions of folk customs and rituals in her letters from home. However, Tertz/Siniavskii claims that Gogol far surpassed his seeming lack of knowledge about folklore on a deeply personal level, achieving a kind of understanding that placed a certain folkloric imagination inside him as a kind of a "terrible pain that cuts through the heart of the writer." In a particularly illuminating passage, Tertz writes: "In Gogol, folklore is torn apart (and is justified) by the facts of the subconscious, and imagination is subjugated to truth that the author carries in his own soul while not making anything up but rather searching for the object of his visions. The assimilation of an existing tradition gives way to the unrelenting process of remembrance about it as a living event. The encounter with folklore takes place on the level of inner experience, whence the knowledge—identified as a fairy tale—is drawn. This knowledge is more reliable and deeper than the fairy tale itself; it supports it from below, from the inside as its authentic original or an underlining meaning." See: Abram Tertz/Andrei Siniavskii, *V teni Gogolia* in *Sobranie sochinenii v dvukh tomakh* (Moscow: Start, 1992) vol. 2, 331–332 [my translation].

Hasidic synagogue. It's Friday. What stunted little figures, what emaciated faces, for me everything that existed in the past 300 years has come alive, the old men bustle about the synagogue, there is no wailing, for some reason they all run back and forth, the praying is extremely informal. It seems that Dubno's most repulsive-looking Jews have gathered. *I pray, rather, I almost pray, and think about Hershele, this is how I should describe him* [sic!]. A quiet evening in the synagogue, this always has an irresistible effect on me, four synagogues in a row. Religion? No decoration at all in the building, everything is white and plain to the point of asceticism, everything is incorporeal and bloodless to a monstrous degree, to grasp it fully you have to have the soul of a Jew. But what does this soul consist of? Is it not bound to be our century in which they will perish?[42]

A modification to this translation by Peter Constantine is necessary. When Babel mentions Hershele, the original Russian omits the direct object of the sentence's second part: "*Ia molius', vernee, pochti molius' i dumaiu o Gershele, vot kak by opisat'.*"[43] The correct, even if awkward, translation then should be: "I pray, rather, I almost pray and think about Hershele, *how would I [ever] describe.*" Babel's language throughout the text of the diary is schematic; some sentences are mere sketches rather than complete statements. The clause that comes after his mention of Hershele's name signals not an assertive full stop but an obviated question mark. Babel is not thinking about how he *should* describe Hershele, as Constantine's translation has it; rather, he is invoking Hershele as he thinks about how to describe the collapsing state of the Dubno synagogues and of much of traditional Jewish life that he is witnessing around him.[44]

Babel does not completely regret the passing of traditional Jewish life. After all, it is clear from the example quoted above that his diary is not so flattering in the way it describes the Jews of Dubno (and other towns). However, what is both regrettable and mournful to Babel is the disappearance of some elusive element of Jewishness nurtured by and rooted in the Jewish tradition. The quoted passage is one of Babel's frankest admissions not only of the fact that traditional Jewish life is in an utter state of disrepair, but that he laments the passing of *dusha evreia*, the "soul of a Jew" that is capable of understanding and, in fact, mourning, this destruction.

The entry is made two days before Tisha b'Av, the 9th of the Hebrew month of Av, on which the destruction of both ancient temples occurred (in

---

42. Babel 2002, 230 [my emphasis].

43. Babel' 1990, vol. 1, 386.

44. Another extant translation of Babel's 1920 diary is equally misleading when it comes to the July 23 entry. H. T. Willets' version, which is very similar to Constantine's, goes like this: "I pray, or rather almost pray, thinking of Hershele and how to describe him." See Isaac Babel, *1920 Diary*, Carol J. Avins, ed., H. T. Willets, trans. (New Haven and London: Yale University Press, 2002 [1995]), 33.

586 BCE and in 70 CE respectively) and is traditionally observed. This resonance of this date does not elude Babel. He is conscious of it when, a day later, on July 24, he recalls remaining silent when his Cossack companion forces the Jews to fry potatoes despite the arrival of the fast the following day,[45]
and again two days later, on July 25, when he writes of the "two torturous
hours" (*muchitel'nye dva chasa*) when the Jewish women of Demidovka
were awakened at four o'clock in the morning and forced to boil "Russian
meat, and this on Tisha b'Av."[46]

When Babel thinks of Hershele in Dubno, he is aware of the Jewish liturgical calendar and the period of traditional mourning over the events that
had signaled that beginning of Jewish exile. The story "Shabos-Nakhamu"—
the work explicitly about Hershele—is set either right before or right after
Tisha b'Av. The story "Rebbe," in which the most enigmatic Hershele reference occurs, originates from the diary entry that precedes Tisha b'Av by a
month. However, its setting in a Hasidic court comprising a space "empty as
a morgue" amid the men who reassert vitality of the Jewish tradition despite
the fact that "in the ardent house of Hasidism the windows and doors have
been torn out"[47] makes a clear link to the kind of Jewish destruction
mourned on Tisha b'Av. The "psychological state" that is signaled in Babel
by references to Hershele Ostropolier is rooted in a specifically Jewish
understanding of destruction that draws on traditional imagery and thus
cannot be shared with the wider reading public.

I first linked the Hershele motif to the thema of meta-literary situations in
Babel's oeuvre. Second, I established the permanent link between Hershele
and the state of mourning for Jewish destruction that the folkloric trickster
signals in Babel. Now the intersection of these two clusters of themata
becomes apparent. Hershele-like trickery, implied by Liutov's exchange
with Reb Motale, signals a veiled reference to Liutov's understanding of himself as a Jew who can mourn Jewish destruction despite his acceptance by
the Cossacks. But this insight can be understood only in the eyes of the
implied reader who, as in the story "Shabos-Nakhamu," is smarter than the
deceived protagonist, the tavern owner's wife who is duped because she
does not understand a crucial piece of cultural knowledge. The only person
who understands the linguistic punning that eludes that female protagonist
in "Shabos-Nakhamu" is outside the text: he or she is the reader who possesses enough knowledge about Jewish culture to laugh at the one who
expects "Shabos-Nakhamu" to be a person rather than a day on the liturgical
calendar. In "Rebbe" this implied reader is constructed as a character in the
text itself: this character is Ilia, the rebbe's rebellious son, who profanes the

45. Babel' 1990, vol. 1, 386.

46. Ibid., 388.

47. Babel' 1990, vol. 2, 35.

Sabbath by "smoking and twitching like an escaped convict."[48] Ilia is caught up in the same circumstances as Liutov (and Babel). As someone who understands both the Jewish and Cossack milieus, he is the kind of reader whom Babel counts on to understand the difficulty of being positioned between the Communist project that excites him and the Jewish world that still claims him.

IV.

In an oft-cited passage from the *Red Cavalry* story "Rebbe's Son," Liutov enumerates the possessions of the dying Ilia Bratslavskii, who was introduced briefly in the story "Rebbe":

> Here everything was dumped together[49]–the mandates of the agitator and the mementos of the Jewish poet. Portraits of Lenin and Maimonides lay side by side–the gnarled steel of Lenin's skull[50] and the tarnished silk of the portraits of Maimonides. A strand of female hair had been placed in a book of the resolutions of the Sixth Party Congress, and in the margins of communist leaflets swarmed crooked lines of ancient Hebrew verse. In a sad and meager rain they fell on me–pages of the Song of Songs and revolver cartridges.[51]

This passage has been interpreted as evidence of a Jew's ambivalent dual identity: he is inspired by the Revolution's cause but is still unable to break free from the Jewish tradition in which he was raised.[52] These interpretations accuse Ilia twice: once for insufficient participation in the Soviet project, and again for half-abandoning his Jewish practice. I propose here, rather, to look more closely at Ilia's scattered possessions for the evidence of a positively construed double identity.

Besides the lock of a woman's hair and revolver cartridges–a pair of metonymic reminders of *eros* and *thanatos*–all Ilia's possessions are texts. Their owner, a rebbe's son who attempts to join the revolution, must have had the ability to read Lenin and Maimonides, the Party manifestos and the Song of Songs. Ilia shares the ability to read both kinds of texts with Liutov (and with Babel, who was exposed to traditional Jewish learning in his

---

48. Babel 2002, 71.

49. Babel 1994, 226. The two translations of Babel's work currently in print, the McDuff and the Constantine editions, differ considerably. Here I work with the Russian text to find the translation closest to the original. For the Russian text see Babel' 1990, vol. 2, 129.

50. Babel 2002, 168.

51. Babel 1994, 226-227.

52. For the discussion of this passage, see, for example, Nakhimovsky, 96-97; Wisse, 116-117.

childhood).[53] References to similar pairs of texts—Lenin's writings and Jewish commentaries—are scattered throughout the stories discussed in this article. In "Gedali," for example, Liutov is overtaken by "the dense sorrows of memory" on the eve of the Sabbath in Zhitomir, where he remembers how his "grandfather's yellow beard caressed the volumes of Ibn Ezra,"[54] a reference to the commentaries of the twelfth-century Spanish Jewish philosopher and exegete. In "My First Goose," Liutov reads "Lenin's speech at the Second Congress of the Comintern,"[55] first by himself and, once he is accepted in the Cossacks' midst, to the fighters of the First Cavalry. The kinship between Ilia and Liutov is first and foremost the kinship experienced among readers who had the ability to read both traditional Jewish and new Revolutionary texts. Such a group of Russian readers would have been limited to the generation of Jews transitioning from traditional life toward Communism.

On closer examination, the encounter between Liutov and Ilia in "Rebbe's Son" is facilitated by a text, and Liutov's appropriation of Ilia's possessions speaks to the porous nature of the boundary—and the kinship—between a writer and a reader who share a particular set of experiences and abilities. In "Rebbe's Son," Liutov speaks of the potatoes that he has been throwing from the train to defeated soldiers of the Soviet army: "And after twelve versts when I had no potatoes left, I threw a heap of Trotskii leaflets at them. But only one of them stretched out a dirty, dead hand for the leaflet. And I recognized Ilia, the son of the Zhitomir rebbe."[56] Implied here is a fact made clear in other stories of *Red Cavalry*: while many of the Cossacks in the Red Army were illiterate, at times asking Liutov to write letters for them and to read the newspaper to them, the dying son of the Zhitomir rebbe is both interested in and capable of reading a political text. The most explicit affirmation of Liutov's Jewish kinship in *Red Cavalry* is the moment when he extends a leaflet written by Trotskii to a fellow Jew who has forfeited his right to be the inheritor of his father's Hasidic court.

This kinship is affirmed not only through Liutov's receiving of his "brother's last breath" and his burial of the rebbe's son, but also by his appropriation of Ilia's possessions. Twice in *Red Cavalry* Babel mentions Liutov's trunk.[57] In "My First Goose," his trunk is thrown onto the street by one of

53. See, for example, Gregory Freidin, "Isaac Babel," *European Writers*, vol. 11, *The Twentieth Century: Walter Benjamin to Yuri Olesha*, ed. George Stade (New York: Charles Scribner's Sons, 1990), 1890–1891.

54. Babel 2002, 63.

55. Babel 2002, 68.

56. Babel' 1990, vol. 2, 128–129.

57. Several readers of the passage that enumerates Ilia Bratslavskii's possessions have misread a crucial detail: the trunk into which the possessions are, in the end, collected

the Cossacks: "I went down on my hands and knees and gathered up *the manuscripts* and the old, tattered clothes that had fallen out of my suitcase."[58] In "Rebbe's Son," Liutov says: "I, who had seen him during one of my vagabond nights, began packing into the trunk the scattered belongings of the Red Army soldier, Ilia Bratslavskii."[59] This is a meta-literary moment; here, the political and the Jewish texts that belonged to Ilia join Liutov's manuscripts, which are also both political (his articles for *The Red Trooper*) and personal. We might assume that Babel's wartime diary, full of many reflections on the fate of the Jews, is also an item in Liutov's trunk.

But the "crooked lines of ancient Hebrew verse" that Ilia scribbles in the margins of a Communist pamphlet also comprise a part of these texts. The Jewish reader, caught between two worlds, is akin to the Jewish writer: Ilia interprets the Communist pamphlets through his Jewish mind and the lines of Hebrew verse through his affiliation with the Russians. Liutov and Ilia's shared cultural code is rooted in their ability to explain each of these two opposing cultural contexts in terms of the other: the Communist manifesto with the help of Hebrew verse, and the acceptance by the Cossacks through a particularly Jewish form of subversion, which I have identified as a Hershele narrative. Liutov acknowledges this kinship when Ilia's texts—his own writings and others'—join Liutov's conflicted manuscripts in one and the same piece of luggage. By the same token, Ilia is constructed in the text as the kind of a reader whom Babel, in his 1937 interview, describes as living in "[his] soul." "But since he's been there for quite a long time," adds Babel, "I have fashioned him in my own image."[60]

It is fitting to remember what Babel writes in his 1920 diary about the destruction of Jewish life around him: "to grasp it fully you have to have the soul of a Jew. But what does this soul consist of? Is it not bound to be our century in which they will perish?"[61] The Jewish soul that can alone comprehend this destruction in Jewish terms is Ilia's soul and, by extension, the soul of the ideal reader whom Babel anticipates and hopes for in *Red Cavalry*. Ilia alone can understand Liutov's trickery and his balancing act between his Jewishness and the Revolution. But the readers who are in possession of such a soul would, as Babel intimates, perish in "our century": the ideal reader that Babel constructs in his text exists in *Red Cavalry* as a mere trace

---

is Liutov's, not Ilia's. Liutov does not simply pick up Ilia's very carefully arranged trunk; rather, the various objects in Ilia's possessions are gathered by Liutov and paired next to each other in a seemingly dichotomous way by Liutov's language. This detail, I believe, is crucial; I explain it in the current paragraph.

58. Babel 2002, 68 [my emphasis].

59. Babel' 1990, vol. 2, 129.

60. Babel 1969, 220.

61. Babel 2002, 230.

of someone who is already disappearing and of whose disappearance the writer is painfully aware.[62]

A powerful hidden reference to impending Jewish destruction is also present in "Rebbe" and "Rebbe's Son." Maurice Friedberg writes about the paradox in these two stories: the stories mention the rebbe—a head of a Hasidic dynasty—and his son, who is referred to as "the last prince" of this dynasty, both of whom share the last name Bratslavskii. The last name implies that the rebbe and his son belong to Hasidism's Bratslav dynasty, which had not had a new rebbe since the death of the dynasty's famed founder, Rebbe Nakhman, in 1810. For this reason the Bratslaver Hasidim are often referred to as *di toyte khsidim,* or "dead Hasidim."[63] By placing the issue of inheritance of a Hasidic dynasty at the forefront of the two stories, Babel might be hinting at a hidden subtext. In Marc Chagall's 1908

---

62. Ilia Bratslavskii may be Liutov's ideal reader, but he is different from Liutov in at least one very important way. Liutov is an intellectual, an urban Jew from Odessa traveling through much more traditional areas in Poland; he is displaced from traditional Jewish context and estranged from traditional Jewish practice. His estrangement makes him the character that he is: he may have deeply personal reflections at times, but he is often a removed observer whose private feats of imagination do not translate into passionate action. Ilia, on the other hand, is a young man of the extremes, he is either the misbehaving "last prince" of a Hasidic dynasty or an engaged soldier of the Revolution. He is an active participant in events whereas Liutov is careful to always remain on the sidelines, not to compromise the much more stable middle ground that he may have already struck, and which Ilia might have yet figured out (were it not for his early death).

Leo Strauss's view on the matter in his *Persecution and the Art of Writing* (Chicago and London: The University of Chicago Press, 1988 [1952]) is illuminating here. In his seminal essay Strauss advances an idea that writers working under the threat or the experience of persecution create a kind of literature that is addressed "not to all readers, but to trustworthy and intelligent readers only" (25). It is a literature produced with the help of "a peculiar technique of writing" that relies on "writing between the lines" (24). But those to whom such writing is truly addressed are "neither the unphilosophic majority nor the perfect philosopher as such, but the young men who might become philosophers: the potential philosophers are to be led step by step from the popular views that are indispensable for all practical and political purposes to the truth that is merely and purely theoretical, guided by certain obtrusively enigmatic features in the presentation of popular teaching—obscurity of the plan, contradictions, pseudonyms, inexact repetitions of earlier statements, strange expressions, etc. Such features do not disturb the slumber of those who cannot see the wood for the trees, but act as awakening stumbling blocks for those who can" (36). This is a crucial point that I would like to investigate further on a later occasion: Ilia, the passionate young man of extremes, is the *potential* of an ideal reader in Babel's text; he is a reader who is to be guided away from these extremes to a more dispassionate middle ground that Liutov himself might already occupy. That Ilia is the potential of a reader whose development is halted by his death is the real tragedy of Isaac Babel and his creative oeuvre.

63. Maurice Friedberg, "Yiddish Folklore Motifs in Isaac Babel's *Konarmija,*" in Bloom 1987, 192.

painting "The Dead Man," the dead person in the middle of the street can be seen as a metonymic realization of the idiom *di toyte shtot*, "a dead town," representing the collapse of a communal entity larger than any single man.[64] Similarly, Babel's Hasidim, celebrating the Sabbath in a room cold and empty as a morgue, realize the cultural idiom as the "dead" Hasidim. Ilia, Babel's ideal reader and the last prince of the dynasty that is already "dead," himself dies in the end. Still "alive" among the "dead" in the story "Rebbe," where Liutov needs him to understand the ambiguities communicated by his mentioning of Hershele Ostropolier, Ilia appears as a ghostly figure, a figure who makes the text possible and haunts it at the same time.

We may remember that the narrative of "Rebbe's Son" is framed as a monologue delivered by Liutov and addressed to one Vasilii, whom we have not met before and who is nowhere to be seen in the story itself. Liutov, telling Vasilii about the death of the rebbe's son, implores his enigmatic interlocutor to remember the night in Zhitomir when both had presumably first met Ilia at Reb Motale's court. But there is no character named Vasilii in the story "Rebbe" in which Ilia is first mentioned. Carol J. Avins argues persuasively that Vasilii (whose name is the same as Liutov's patronymic: Vasilievich) is another Jew of a background similar to Liutov's "who, like Lyutov, uses a conspicuously Russian pseudonym."[65] Avins reads Vasilii as Liutov's alter ego, as someone closer to Liutov than Ilia. I would like to propose that the existence of Vasilii may be somewhat further removed from reality than the distance of a literary character from his alter ego.

In the *fabula* of "Rebbe's Son" the death of Ilia Bratslavskii precedes Liutov's telling about this death to Vasilii. Addressing the enigmatic interlocutor about a death that happens in real time but also, as I suggested above, acts out a cultural idiom, is akin to addressing a ghost. Vasilii is, indeed, a ghostly presence, someone who is not a corporeal being, someone whose existence cannot be traced to anything but Liutov's imagination and his desire to continue addressing someone who could understand him after Ilia, the ideal reader, has died. Avins suggests that Vasilii may even be closer to Liutov than to the dead Bratslavskii because, unlike Bratslavskii, both Liutov and Vasilii are Jews hiding under gentile names and masks.[66] I suggest that Vasilii may be that ideal reader whom Liutov now seeks after Ilia has died.

---

64. Critics have observed that in some of his works Chagall often depicted a number of Yiddish idioms. See: Ziva Amishai-Maisels, "Chagall's Jewish In-Jokes," *Journal of Jewish Art* 5 (1982), 76–93; Seth L. Wolitz, "Vitebsk versus Bezalel: A Jewish *Kulturkampf* in the Plastic Arts," in Zvi Gitelman, ed., *The Emergence of Modern Jewish Politics: Bundism and Zionism in Eastern Europe* (Pittsburgh: University of Pittsburgh Press, 2003), 151–177.

65. Carol J. Avins, "Kinship and Concealment in *Red Cavalry* and Babel's 1920 Diary," *Slavic Review* 53, no. 3 (Fall 1994): 708.

66. Ibid.

Vasilii is identical to Liutov in what he can understand between the lines. He is, however, a reader who is merely imagined. The address to Vasilii reveals a confused Liutov—and, through him, a confused figure of a Jewish writer who feels compelled to narrate the death of his ideal reader to an imagined listener who is himself no more than a ghost. Liutov's words are addressed to someone who does not exist and are greeted by silence. In that moment at least there is no one who is even remotely close to talking back.

The Open Suitcases:
Yankev Glatshteyn's
Ven Yash Iz Gekumen

AVRAHAM NOVERSHTERN

A Polyphony in a Polish Jewish Resort Hotel

> *Afile fun der blote vel ikh zingen tsu dir, mayn got, afile fun der blote.*
>
> Even from the mud will I sing to you, my God, even from the mud.[1]

Yankev Glatshteyn's *Ven Yash iz gekumen* opens with the human voice: a short, pithy sentence noteworthy for its tone of defiance and its close links to Jewish tradition. While derived from the well-known verse, "From the depths I have called You, O Lord," the phrase "from the depths" is replaced by "from the mud," a ubiquitous feature of Eastern European Jewish towns. This last lends the statement an emphatically prosaic, earthy quality.

The verb "sing," instead of "call," by contrast, belongs more appropriately to the discourse of art than to that of prayer, and it is doubtful whether the average speaker of Yiddish would have deployed the two interchangeably. The book's opening cry thus invokes a synthesis of cultures: whereas its first element might have been uttered by a character like Tevye the Dairyman, the second is more fitting for the modern Jew aligned with secular culture, even if he is not supposed to identify with it fully. While the linguistic flexibility displayed here draws on Sholem Aleichem's presentation of Yiddish as reflecting a particular cultural synthesis, the sentence takes a significant step toward the complexity of the modern world. And although the opening statement bears a clearly spiritual, almost mystical quality and is repeated as a sort of chorus, the narrator immediately provides a broad situational context that mitigates the force of its passion:

> *Men hot shoyn gehaltn baym sof fun der vetshere. A tsol gest hobn shoyn farlozt dos estsimer. Andere zaynen nokh gezesn bay zeyere tishn un zikh kalupet di tseyn, dertrunken dos glezl tey un zikh gefoylt uftsuheybn.*
>
> *Eyn tish iz nokh geven in gantsn bazetst. Keyner hot zikh nisht gerirt fun ort. A man, mit a kapl afn shpits kop, iz gezesn oybn on un gefirt tish un a zibn-akht mener hobn him gekukt in moyl arayn. Etlekhe hobn*

---

1. All Yiddish quotations are from *Ven Yash iz gekumen* (New York, 1940). The page numbers refer to this edition. I thank my friend and colleague David Roskies for translating the Yiddish citations and for his careful reading of a draft of this article. The book was translated into English by Norbert Guterman as *Homecoming at Twilight* (New York, 1962).

gelasn gegesn dem kompot, ober zey hobn afile nit gezen di kleyne teler-
lekh. Zey hobn genogt un genogt dos letste bisl zaft fun di harte floymen-
kern un zey arumgevorfn in moyl fun der linker bak tsu der rekhter. Ober
beemes hanoe hobn zey gehat fun dem man mit dem kapl. Zey hobn fun
im di oygn nit aruntergenumen.

> Supper was nearly over. A number of guests had already left the dining
> room. Those who were lingering on at their tables picked their teeth, nursed
> their glasses of tea and were too lazy to get up.
> At one of the tables every seat was still occupied. No one moved from
> his spot. A man in a skullcap sat at the head of it and held forth. The seven
> or eight other men at that table were hanging on his every word, occasionally
> dipping a spoon into their stewed fruit without looking at it, slowly sucking
> and rolling the prune pits on their tongues. But what they really delighted
> in was the man in the skullcap. Never for a moment did they take their eyes
> off him. (7)

Thus the concise opening statement is followed by a detailed down-to-earth
description that tracks the physiological act of eating and the accompanying
social ceremony of a meal. The entire scene has a quality of hedonism:
before the reader is fully aware of the setting—a resort hotel in Poland—its
(all male) participants are presented as casually noncommittal, sitting idly
around in a relaxed end-of-day mood. Those who hear this resoundingly
spiritual call no doubt "enjoy" it, but surely fail to delve into its meaning, if
they are even expected to do so. In any case, they are passive listeners who
neither respond to the speaker's words nor enter into a dialogue with him.
His call remains hanging in the air without evoking a response, which only
serves to amplify its power.

Is this scene constructed as a modern stylization of the Hasidic "tish" or
as a parody thereof? The answer must be an equivocal one. Regarding the
speaker, it does not state "er pravet tish," but rather "er firt tish," a less common expression when referring to the Hasidic way of life. The speaker's
own description throws this question into sharp relief: true Hasidim would
never have seen their rabbi as "a man mit a kapl" ("a man with a skullcap"),
since for them the wearing of a head-covering was taken for granted. Only a
modern narrator would need to refer to this detail so as to mark his protagonist with a clear cultural identity. This clue recurs time and again, and only
later is the reader made aware of the family name, Steinman, by which the
protagonist will be identified throughout the novel.

A few pages into the book, a chance meeting occurs in the hotel between Steinman and a man "*mit a sametn, rabonish kapelyushl*" ("wearing
a rabbi's velvet hat," 20), immediately followed by his encountering another
character, "*oykh mit a rabonishn kapelyushl*" ("also in a rabbi's hat," 21),
accentuating the cultural meaning of the head-covering and the differences
between them. In retrospect it becomes plain that the yarmulke on Steinman's head at that dinner indicates his allegiance to the class of the traditionally observant. However, whether he is a strict observer of *mitzvot*

remains unknown—certainly he does not belong to the rabbinic class. Nor is the use of the protagonist's surname a culturally neutral choice. It does not merely imply distance and a certain foreignness, as an inexperienced reader might think. In the Jewish cultural milieu of Eastern Europe, calling someone by their surname rather than by their first name was a sign of upward mobility, a use of urbane manners inimical with traditional Jewish communal and small-town practice.

Only much later, after the character of Steinman has been sharply delineated, is the reader made aware of the novel's other central protagonist—the first-person narrator. The difference between their manner of representation is striking. The narrator makes his oblique appearances from the shadows; neither his name nor his business is made known to the reader anywhere in the text: "*Kumt, yunger-man! Mayn nomen iz Shteynman. Vi heyst ir?*" ("Let's go, young man. My name is Steinman. What's yours?" 17). Steinman's question is left unanswered, with the narrator offering no response whatsoever to his words. Even the reasons for his arrival are only later made apparent, and then only grudgingly:

> *Do-o vel ikh zikh es darfn opruen fun etlekhe vokhn Poyln, afn veg tsurik. Tsvantsik yor az ikh hob gebenkt nokh di etlekhe vokhn .*

> This is the place where I would rest up from my several weeks in Poland, on my way back. For twenty years I have been yearning for these weeks. (33)

Admittedly, *Ven Yash iz gekumen*, published in 1940, is supposed to be read as a sequel to *Ven Yash iz geforn*, published two years earlier. The "informed reader" is supposed to recall from the first volume the circumstances that brought the narrator to Poland—he came to visit his mother on her deathbed. Yet the opening of *Ven Yash iz gekumen* provides a highly significant "blank slate"; its beginning *in medias res* forgoes the presentation of that important event, the son returning to his mother for the final moments of her life. The setting is not that of the narrator's house or birthplace but another place altogether, a resort hotel located somewhere in Poland, never precisely pinpointed on a map. Like the previous novel, *Ven Yash iz gekumen* is a first-person narrative, yet its opening hides the narrator's presence while focusing on a different character.

The same tone of defiance found in that saying of Steinman's with which the novel began also features at its end, in momentous and poignant scenes that portray his gradual demise and the moment of his death. With one exception, Steinman is present in each of the book's six chapters, and his character serves to tie its various parts together. Here lies the essential difference between the two "Yash" volumes. In the first, *Ven Yash iz geforn*, the narrator encounters and strikes up conversations with the many people on the boat taking him to his homeland of Poland. Yet none of these characters he chances upon can be seen as potential protagonists. *Ven Yash iz gekumen* presents an alternative artistic design. The hotel takes up the function of the boat of the first volume as the provisional meeting-place where the paths of numerous central figures cross. But now the narrator has provided a protagonist of sorts, focusing on the character, story, and fortune of Steinman.

The novel's concluding chapter, in which the narrator and Steinman re-encounter each other, is particularly relevant in this context. Transformed into a rousing final chorus, the last moments of Steinman's life, one of the climaxes of the book, form a subtle contrast to the opening scene. At the outset of the novel, the narrator appears in the hotel after the (undescribed) death of his mother. Thus, an understated tension is fashioned between presence and absence, between the narrator's descriptions and his silences. His complete silence regarding the death of his mother, the person supposedly closest to him, as opposed to the great attention he pays to the depiction of Steinman's last moments, is one of the clearest proofs of Glatshteyn's artistic decision to deploy a narrative technique that diverts both text and reader from the narrator's private world, from his personal experiences at the crucial moments of his life and from the direct expression of his emotional state. In the novel's concluding paragraph the narrator faces his loneliness in his temporary quarters in the hotel:

> *Ikh hob farloshn di likht, der ufgevakhter bloy fun fentster hot fun gantsn fintsern tsimer oysgeteylt di tsvey ibergepakte, tseefnte valizes. Zey zaynen geven di sharfste un kontikste zakhn in gantsn tsimer.*

> When I turned off the light, the awakened blue that filtered through the window dilated upon the two bulging, open valises. They were the most sharply drawn and familiar objects in the whole room. (304)

The book's final sentence focuses on those inanimate objects that perfectly represent the transitory: the suitcases, pointedly described as wide open. The touch of a skilled writer is evident in this concluding tableau, which is both vague and delicate. It presents a liminal atmosphere: the early morning hours, in his hotel room just before his departure. We heard the deafening cries of Steinman's only daughter just a few lines earlier, as she is left alone in the wake of the death of her father. In contrast to this emotional outburst, the narrator does not allow himself the direct, meaningful expression of his inner feelings; he focuses on the inanimate objects that symbolizes his leaving, without providing an outlet for human emotion.

The novel's concluding paragraph supplies an unmistakably different atmosphere to that of the previous pages, in which the gradual death of Steinman is portrayed as a public event, with all those surrounding him serving as participants. They weep for him and eulogize him as though he were a Hasidic rabbi: *"er is nifter gevorn vi a groyser tsadik"* ("he passed away like a great zaddik," 302). This is no mere bombastic expression. Steinman's final moments are, indeed, described as something of an epiphany. His last request is directed to the narrator, who comes to visit him on his deathbed: *"men zol epes zingen, a khsidishe zakh, a freylekhs"* ("one should sing something, a Hasidic song, some lively set-piece," 293). At first his words

are taken as an inexplicable and surprising request, which the narrator passes on to the group crowded around his deathbed: *"vi ikh volt far zey geley-
ent an umgleyblekhn tekst, oder ibergezetst fun a toyter shprakh"* ("as if I
were reading them an unbelievable text, translated from a dead language").
Yet eventually, after some hesitation, they fulfill the last request of the dying
man. Thus the end of the novel is clearly linked to its beginning, with both
of these key literary sections praising the "power of the melody": *"dos
brumt men dem zelbn nign, vos men hot gezungen, ven ikh hob tsum
ershtn mol derzen Shteynmanen, vi er hot gefirt tish"* ("they were hum-
ming the same melody that they were singing when I first caught sight of
Steinman as he was holding forth," 294). Steinman's last request embodies
the widespread assumption in contemporary Jewish culture that melody
and music hold a unique place in the Hasidic experience. And what could
be more suitable for Steinman, who functions as a kind of Hasidic rabbi,
than to end his life with a melody? *Nign* refers to a wordless melody, presented as the loftiest expression of an ecstatic experience. At several important junctures the novel makes use of motifs from the world of music,[2] and
the "melody" that breaks out during Steinman's last moments adds an
important aspect to this theme. It embodies the primal emotions at the final
moments of human existence.

There is no question that Steinman's last request and the artistic shaping
of his final moments provide one of the most poignant scenes of the novel,
perhaps the most touching of all. Yet immediately afterward, the narrator
attempts to play down its great emotional charge, aware as he always is of
the other side of human experience. There follows a banal chronicle of
events that occur in the hotel in the wake of Steinman's death, before he is
laid to rest: vacationing couples go out for their love strolls as is their wont;
and even the Jew whose job it is to spend the night reciting psalms before
the burial is very much aware of his own primary physiological needs: *"Vel
darfn zitsn baym mes a gantse nakht, iz khalesht mir shoyn dos harts, a
pshite shoyn shpeter. Farvalgert zikh efsher a shtikl hering? A kelishikl tsu
derkhapn s'harts?"* ("I am supposed to stay with the corpse the whole night
and I'm already starved. It will be worse later on. Could I have a piece of her-
ring? And a glass of vodka to pick me up?" 303). The opening of the book
suggests a fine balance between the ecstatic cry and the minute descriptions of those sitting round the dinner table. The book's conclusion offers
another example of this balance: melody and food, the night before the
burial that is also a night of love. Spiritual inspiration goes hand in hand with
basic physiological urges. The text of *Yash* links the spiritual and the earth-

---

2. The comparison of the structure of *Ven Yash iz gekumen* and musical forms features
   in many critical writings on the book. Regarding the network of allusions to the world
   of music, see Jan Schwarz, *Imagining Lives: Autobiographical Fiction of Yiddish
   Writers* (Madison, 2005), 111.

ly, the lofty and the lowly. The description of the climax of spiritual inspiration goes hand in hand with the account of the urge to satisfy basic needs, and thus the book offers a polyphonic approach toward the conflicting poles of human experience.

A comparison of two texts in Yiddish literature that connect death to music will illustrate Glatshteyn's unique approach in this regard. The description of Steinman's death might, indeed, recall the portrayal of death in Peretz's well-known story "A klezmertoyt" ("A Musician's Death"), as Jan Schwarz claims. The essential difference between the texts, however, is of no less significance than their superficial resemblance. Peretz's story recounts the deathbed confession of a musician to his wife concerning his erotic adventures and sins, while he asks his sons to accompany this confession with music. The story, in fact, ends with an unequivocal statement: "*Di fir-eylndike shtub iz gevorn ful mit muzik*" ("The tiny house filled with music").[3] The neoromantic Peretz extols the power of music in the face of death in a clear-cut fashion. Glatshteyn the modernist, by contrast, strikes a different note in his treatment of this widespread cultural motif of the meeting of art and death. In Glatshteyn's version, after some brief moments of inspiration, life goes on as before.

The final pages of *Ven Yash iz gekumen* suggest an underlying tension between the "strong ending," unambiguous in its treatment of the key events—the complex scenes depicting Steinman's death—and the open, "weak ending"—the narrator departing without allowing the slightest insight into his emotional state. This is the ultimate textual proof of the novel's overall reluctance to focus on anything that touches on the narrator's emotional world, a pronounced textual feature that can even be viewed as a sign of self-denial. The novel's *in medias res* opening and its conclusion together underline the narrator's refusal to show his face or his feelings, and the extent to which he pushes himself aside to the margins of the story.

Who is the narrator, how did he get there, and what of his inner world, his spiritual identity and his cultural horizons? These questions are not easy to answer, and the text's silence in this regard is vital to an understanding of the artistic intent of the novel as a whole. In this context it is appropriate to introduce a wider perspective, to place *Ven Yash iz gekumen* beside its predecessor, *Ven Yash iz geforn*, and examine the biographical and cultural circumstances of their writing.

Is There a Home for the Jewish Writer?

When read in sequence, the two "Yash" novels reveal an unusual and intriguing feature of the presentation of the narrator. In the first part, which takes place mostly on the boat transporting him to his native Poland, the narrator begins by putting himself forward as a writer and intellectual

---

3. Y.L. Perets, *Ale verk, II: Dertseylungen, mayselekh, bilder* (New York, 1947), 98.

engaged in the world of Yiddish letters. However, this aspect of the narrator's self-representation becomes less marked as the text progresses. In the second book, *Ven Yash iz gekumen,* the narrator's cultural identity is presented as a "blank slate." While staying in Poland, the narrator, as we shall see, is surrounded by artists and writers of various kinds; however, it is at this stage that he paradoxically chooses to conceal most of the details that might have allowed us a glimpse into his cultural and spiritual world.

It is no coincidence that the identity of the first-person narrator as a Jewish writer and intellectual is emphasized in the first parts of *Ven Yash iz geforn.* The reasons for this can be found in the book's publication history. Its chapters were published in installments in the monthly *Inzikh* journal between the years 1934–1937 and subsequently brought out in book form without any major changes. *Ven Yash iz gekumen* was published in installments in the weekly *Yidisher kemfer* of 1939. However, one section published in the journal *Inzikh* (in October 1934) is missing from the books: its preface, an illuminating literary document whose highly revelatory nature likely led to its removal. The preface begins by mentioning the homecoming trip of the American author, Louis Adamic, originally from Slovenia (the preface calls him "a Yugoslav"). Adamic's novel, *The Native Son,* was published in 1934, the very same year in which Glatshteyn traveled to Poland, and it achieved instant success. The fact that Glatshteyn chose to open his preface with a comparison of his trip to that of Louis Adamic indicates the extent to which Glatshteyn saw himself first and foremost as a writer who measured himself against other writers. But it also indicates that the travel report was designed to serve as a contemporary account, so much so that it refers to a recently published work. By the time *Ven Yash iz geforn* was published in book form, four years later (1938), the comparison would no longer have carried the same weight and Glatshteyn probably sensed it was better left out. Yet there is no question that the *Yash* novels were originally written with the first-person narrator's awareness of his own status as a professional writer, whether as a journalist or as an author of *belles-lettres.*

The excised preface is of interest for another reason: the book bears a dedication to the memory of the narrator's mother. Although the particular circumstances that led to the trip are not at first detailed in the text, after a short few pages we are told that the narrator had received urgent messages from New York calling him to his mother's deathbed. The preface, by contrast, offers a completely different perspective on the circumstances surrounding his trip to Poland. It is not presented as involving any personal crisis or distress, and there is certainly no mention of mourning or loss. The first-person narrator of the preface represents himself primarily as a writer. He compares himself to a well-known American author and imagines that he will receive a royal welcome. When his illusions are shattered, he reacts with disappointment:

> *Kh'gedenk shoyn nisht vegn velkhn yidishn shrayber men hot dos der-*
> *tseylt, az ven er iz gekumen tsurik aheym tsu zikh in shtetl, hobn di*
> *shtetldike oysgeshpant di ferd un zikh aleyn ayngeshpant in vogn (...)*
> *Efsher hob ikh in zinen gehat aza tryumfaln aheymfor, ven ikh hob in*
> *mayn briv geshribn vegn dem moment, ven ikh vel "dershaynen" vi a*
> *prints.*

> I no longer remember of which Yiddish writer it was told that when he
> returned to his native shtetl, his townspeople unharnessed their horses and
> harnessed themselves to the wagon (....) Perhaps I had such a triumphant
> return in mind when I wrote in my letter about the moment when I would
> "appear" like a prince.[4]

Greater obstacles still, we learn from the excised preface, lie in the way of
the Yiddish writer's chronicle of homecoming. While Adamic's record of
his visit to his home country is full of descriptive passages, and at times
offers an exotic folkloristic appeal, the Yiddish writer cannot choose this
path:

> *Vi azoy kon ikh ober kumen tsu a yidishn oylem un im servirn ekzotik*
> *fun shtetl, vos er ken aleyn tsu nudne gut. Men hot shoyn dos shtetl bazun-*
> *gen, bagramt un bafefert. Ikh ken zikh nisht farlozn in foroys oyf der*
> *nayger fun yidishn lezer, ven men vet im dertseyln vegn "yidishe natsyo-*
> *nale kostyumen."*

> How can I possible appear before a Yiddish reader and serve him up the exot-
> icism of the shtetl, which he himself knows only too well? The shtetl has
> already been serenaded, rhymed and seasoned. I cannot rely on the Yiddish
> reader's curiosity to learn about "Jewish national costumes."[5]

Glatshteyn thus rejects out of hand the possibility that a novel that focuses
on a visit to Poland might provide a descriptive account of its Jewish cultural life. The *shtetl* can no longer serve as the central background for such a
story. This distinction provides one of the keys to the evident difference in
literary style between the two *Yash* volumes. The journalistic, "factual"
approach is more pronounced in the first book, in which the majority of the
characters portrayed are far removed from the world of the Yiddish reader.
The literary technique of *Ven Yash iz gekumen* is slightly different; the very
fact that the cultural landscape portrayed in the book is so familiar to the
Yiddish reader leads the narrator to deploy various strategies of estrangement.

As Ruth Wisse and other critics have noted, there is no doubt that in the
overall history of twentieth-century Jewish literature, a unique place must
be given to a pair of well-known novels published almost simultaneously,
both describing journeys to Poland: *'Oreakh nata' lalun* ("A Guest for the
Night") by S.Y. Agnon, and Yankev Glatshteyn's *Ven Yash iz gekumen*. In

---

4. *Inzikh*, no. 6 (October 1934), 178–179.

5. Ibid.

recent years much critical attention has indeed been focused on the relationship between the two.[6] Yet it must be kept in mind that the very possibility of their being evaluated against one another is the result of a later perspective. Glatshteyn's work should be viewed first and foremost within its contemporary cultural framework.

From the early 1920s onward, there were many cases of writers, journalists, and intellectuals from the Yiddish cultural scene in the United States who returned to Eastern Europe and provided detailed accounts of their experiences, whether in the form of newspaper articles, travel narratives, or both. This is one of the most prominent forms of expression in a wider phenomenon that can be termed travel reports in modern Yiddish culture (as opposed to migration accounts), a literary corpus that invites comprehensive critical attention. These trips were at times motivated by personal concerns, such as an effort to reunite with parents and other family members whom the writer had not seen for many years. At other times, they served as journalistic missions, designed to produce a series of articles reflecting the intellectual adventures of involved modern Jews who wished to keep an eye on events in the Old Country. Similarly, they might have included a series of lectures in which Yiddish writers whose careers had developed in the United States received a warm welcome "back home." The list of Yiddish writers and journalists from New York who set out on these trips is long and varied, starting with senior, recognized, and popular figures such as Morris Vinchevsky, David Pinski, Abraham Cahan, and Abraham Reisen, and continuing through second and third-generation writers, such as Joseph Opatoshu, Baruch Glazman, H. Leivick, A. Leyeles, and Moyshe Nadir.

The majority of these trips were planned as visits to the sites of a kind of Jewish utopia, where traditional Jewish life had undergone drastic changes. By this I refer first and foremost to trips to the Soviet Union that have been pithily referred to as journeys "back to the future."[7] Such travels were also

6. In this regard it is revealing that the first to draw a comparison of the two works was the Hebrew-Yiddish poet Abraham Regelson, in a newspaper article on *A Guest For The Night*: "A hebreysh bukh vegn yidn in Poyln tsvishn di velt-milkhomes," *Morgn-frayhayt*, Jan. 2 1944. In recent years this comparison has been discussed by Dan Miron, Ruth Wisse, and Riki Ophir. See Dan Miron, *The Dark Side of Sholem Aleichem's Laughter* (Hebrew) (Tel Aviv, 2004), 231–249 (originally published in 1994 as an afterword to his translation of *Ven Yash iz geforn*); Ruth R. Wisse, *The Modern Jewish Canon: A Journey Through Language and Culture* (New York, 2000), 163–189; Riki Ophir, "The Jewish Odyssey, Or Where Is Ithaca?: Place, Journey and Home in S. Y. Agnon's *A Guest For the Night* and Yankev Glatshteyn's *Ven Yash iz geforn* and *Ven Yash iz gekumen*" (thesis paper, Tel Aviv University 2005); Dan Miron, "The Nightingale's Song in the Depths of the Forest," afterword to his translation of *Ven Yash iz gekumen* (Tel Aviv, 2006), 251–286.

7. See Daniel Soyer, "Back to the Future: American Jews visit the Soviet Union in the 1920s and 1930s," *Jewish Social Studies*, vol. 6, no. 3 (Spring-Summer 2000), 124–

undertaken in the 1920s by Yiddish writers from nearby Poland, including I. J. Singer and H. D. Nomberg. A few writers also reached Palestine, visits that significantly affected their attitude toward the Zionist movement (such as Abraham Cahan's documented visit of 1925). Most of the authors passed through Poland on their way to the Soviet Union, yet it is important to note that most of the Yiddish travel accounts are dedicated to visits to the Soviet Union, with only a few focused on Jewish Poland. The writers probably assumed—correctly at the time—that Yiddish readers would prefer to encounter a new world, such as the construction of the new society of the Soviet Union and the fate of its Jews, rather than read another description of the Jewish world in Poland, with which they had first-hand familiarity. It is true that the Polish Jewry of the 1920s and 1930s was very different from the one that most Yiddish readers in America would have recalled from when they left their native provinces before World War I. Yet, on the whole, these changes were for the worse—impoverishment, crises, outspoken anti-Semitism, and a sense of hopelessness. For Yiddish readers, the "news" regarding Jewish life in Poland was hardly interesting, heartwarming, or joyous. The life with which they were painfully well acquainted had deteriorated, but this did not offer any essential novelty. The Soviet Union, on the other hand, was for them the most palpable example of the construction of a new society, a historical experiment of the highest ideological and human dimensions. A fundamental and at times highly charged dispute centered on this experiment; with the stormy discussions and endless arguments it bred, any additional information on the subject was always welcome. Coverage of events in Jewish Poland was typically of an entirely different nature: it aroused in the reader emotional identification with the oppressed and persecuted Jewish minority, but not intellectual curiosity as such.

For some American Yiddish writers the trips turned into victory parades, bringing them into close contact with a readership familiar with their writings, and finally providing their readers in Europe with the opportunity to meet their favorite authors in person. These meetings strengthened the faith of the American Yiddish writers in the ultimate meaning of their literary endeavors, a belief that might have been shaken by the palpable process of linguistic and cultural assimilation in their American milieu. The trips invariably followed a regular format: festive welcoming committees; lectures in front of packed halls; highly laudatory articles in the daily and weekly papers; newspaper interviews in which the guests presented their thoughts on the state of Yiddish literature in America, as well as on a variety of current literary and public issues; visits to Yiddish schools, and, of

---

159. See also his article "Revisiting the Old World: American Jewish Tourists in Interwar Eastern Europe," in Michael Berkowitz et al., *Forging Modern Jewish Identities: Public Faces and Private Struggles* (London, 2003), 16–38.

course, face-to-face meetings with Eastern European Yiddish writers. For most of the writers, these trips endured as powerful and enriching biographical experiences.

Glatshteyn's 1934 visit to Poland did not fit this pattern. After living in New York for twenty years, Glatshteyn left for Poland for painful personal reasons. From the outset, the nature of his trip lay somewhere between the private visit and the journey of a writer who had earned a modest measure of recognition in the Yiddish world. Yet if Glatshteyn retained the secret hope that despite the particular circumstances of his visit he would still be granted a grand reception in the Yiddish cultural circles, he was disappointed:

> *Ikh, Yash, vel dervayl in mayn araynfir makhn a shvayg iber dem groysn ufnem, vos ikh hob gekrogn. Kh'vel bloyz tsugebn, az a hon hot nisht gekreyt un keyn hunt hot nisht gebilt.*

> In my preface, I, Yash, will keep mum for the time being about the grand reception that awaited me. I will merely note that no rooster crowed and no dog let out a bark.[8]

Literarishe bleter, the foremost literary journal of Yiddish in Poland, did, indeed, mention Glatshteyn's visit in a brief notice in its list of literary events, and published three of his poems, Glatshteyn's first publications in the weekly. The wording of the short announcement, however, shows how much of an unknown quantity Glatshteyn was, even for the most loyal followers of Yiddish literature in Poland:

> *S'iz gekumen keyn Poyln un bazukht Varshe der dikhter Yankev Glatshteyn, mitredaktor fun nyu-yorker zhurnal 'Inzikh'. Y. Glatshteyn shtamt fun Lublin, fun vanet er iz opgeforn mit tsvantsik yor tsurik. Donershtik dem 29stn hayntikn khoydesh vet forkumen a khaverisher tsuzamentref funem varshever Pen-Club mitn gast. Y. Glatshteyn vet haltn a fortrag iber aktuele literarish gezelshaftlekhe fragn un oykh leyenen zayne lider.[9]*

> The poet Yankev Glatshteyn has come to Poland and visited Warsaw. A co-editor of the New York-based journal *Inzikh*, Y. Glatshteyn hails from Lublin, which he left twenty years ago. On Thursday the 29th of this month, a cordial get-together with our guest will take place at the Warsaw PEN Club. Y. Glatstheyn will deliver a lecture about current literary and social issues as well as read from his poetry.

Glatshteyn is presented to the magazine's readers as a writer with whom they were not expected to be familiar, which is why the biographical-personal aspect is emphasized. Note that there is no mention of an evening in honor of the poet in the popular writers' club located at Tlomackie 13, an occasion that would likely have attracted a large gathering. Rather, a more

---

8. *Inzikh*, 179.

9. *Literarishe bleter*, Jul. 20 1934, 466.

intimate meeting was meant to take place with an elite group, members of
the Yiddish PEN club. Apparently, however, even this modest event in the
end did not take place, due to Glatshteyn's refusal to participate. This can
be inferred from a letter he wrote to Melech Ravitch, then active secretary
of the "Union of Yiddish Writers and Journalists in Warsaw," and the chief
promoter of literary and cultural events at the writers' club:

> *Kh'hob keyn mol nisht dervart az der varshever Pen vet in mir aroysrufn*
> *mer varemkeyt. Ikh bin bikhlal geforn keyn Poyln nisht vi der dikhter mit*
> *di ongeklepte shlifes ayntsupakn pudn koved. Ikh bin geforn vi a zun tsu*
> *tate-mame, vi a bruder tsu brider, shvester, shvegerins, kuzines, plimeni-*
> *kes un plimenitses, libe voyle mentshn un kinder vos gleybn mir afn vort*
> *az fun Yanklen iz gevort a layt.*[10]

> I never expected myself to warm to the Warsaw PEN. The whole purpose
> of my trip to Poland was not to appear like a poet wearing pasted epaulets
> in order to have heaps of honors piled upon him. I traveled as a son to his
> parents, as a brother to his siblings, to his sisters-in-law, cousins, nephews
> and nieces, great and lovable people all of them, who take me at my word
> that Yankl amounted to something.

This letter does not reveal the reason for Glatshteyn's refusal to attend the
event arranged in his honor, but a note of complaint can be detected
between the lines. His three poems published in *Literarishe bleter* and an
interview in the Bundist literary weekly *Vokhnshrift far literatur kunst un*
kultur are apparently the only literary evidence of Glatshteyn's visit to
Poland.[11] Even Lublin's Yiddish daily newspaper *Lubliner togblat* did not
consider its talented son's return to his birthplace worthy of a serious mention, although its silence might have been a result of the painful circumstances of his visit.[12]

Glatstheyn did not need to invoke Louis Adamic in order to underscore
his own non-reception in Jewish Poland. Indeed, a mere two months prior
to his trip, Jewish Warsaw had rolled out the red carpet in honor of well-
known prose writer Joseph Opatoshu, who went there as part of a wide-
ranging trip that also included the Soviet Union and Palestine. "Joseph Opatoshu is with Us Once Again!" ran the lead article in *Literarishe bleter* by

10. Undated letter to Melech Ravitch (Glatshteyn did not typically date his letters), Ravitch
    collection, Jewish National and University Library, Jerusalem.

11. "Vegn politik, lebn un poetn: A shmues mitn poet Y. Glatshteyn, dem redaktor fun
    amerikaner *Inzikh*," *Vokhnshrift far literatur kunst un kultur*, no. 31 (180), 19 July
    1934, 1-2.

12. Only a short announcement appeared: "Dikhter Yankev Glatshteyn in Lublin": "Keyn
    Lublin iz er gekumen in private inyonim un veylt bay zayn nonte familye" ("He came
    to Lublin on private matters and spends his time with his close relatives") (*Lubliner*
    togblat, Jul. 30, 1934). The announcement appeared a few days before his mother's
    passing. The paper makes no later reference to the writer's stay in his hometown.

the editor N. Mayzil.[13] The Yiddish cultural world in Poland treated a recognized writer of prose with a very different measure of hospitality to that meted out to the modernist poet. The "media silence" that greeted Y. Glatshteyn in Poland casts a harsh light on the marginal status granted to modernist poetry within the contemporaneous Yiddish literary scene.

Glatshteyn's visit to Poland, in short, did not merit the status of a public literary event. The author in him surrendered to the idea that this visit was primarily personal, and one of the artistic choices he had to make when drawing on this visit for fictional purposes concerned the character of the novel's narrator. Should he appear as a journalist reporting to his readers on events in those provinces he visits (Glatshteyn had worked for a number of years as a professional journalist), or rather as a Polish Jew returning to his birthplace after a lengthy and significant absence of twenty years? Should he present himself as a man of letters? A writer? An intellectual? An average Jew? Perhaps a "citizen of the world"? What *is* Yash's spiritual identity? To what extent does the text focus on the character of the narrator in his various guises?

A partial if problematic hint of an answer is already suggested by the epigraph to *Ven Yash iz gekumen* for which Glatshteyn selected an excerpt from a Polish poem by popular writer Maria Konopnicka (1842–1910) without providing a Yiddish translation.[14] It contrasts the very different fates of a king and a regular soldier going out to war: while the soldier falls in battle, the king returns to his realm with his spirits raised. The very fact that a writer in Yiddish chose to quote a Polish poem as an epigraph to his novel can be considered as a statement promoting the author's broad cultural horizons. It seems that the reader of Yiddish literature of the time would have raised an eyebrow at the choice, even though the Polish poem is selected as an epigraph for a book describing a visit to Poland. That Konopnicka was known for her philo-Semitic views would partly have mitigated the surprise that this decision would have aroused, but it would not have dispelled it entirely. Moreover, it is not clear which part of the text itself is the analogy to the epigraph. Is Yash, the first-person narrator who sets out on the trip, ultimately to be considered as the soldier who died in battle? Or perhaps he should be viewed ironically as the king returning victorious at the expense of his fallen men? What is the counterpart to the poem's "battle"? Perhaps it is a mistake to search for an analogy in the first place. Although the expunged preface does not quote the poem, it can be claimed that it indirectly refers to it. Its description of the rift between the writers Louis Adam-

---

13. "Yoysef Opatoshu vider mit undz!" *Literarishe bleter*, 11 (1934), 188; See also ibid., 407–408, 421–422, 509.

14. Abraham Reisen translated the poem into Yiddish: "Iz avek tsu krig der meylekh..." Abraham Reisen, *Shriften*, I: *Gezamelte lieder* (Warsaw, 1913), 284.

ic and Yankev Glatshteyn includes the following: "*Azoy iz der 'kenig' geforn aheym tsu zayne landslayt. Un az Yash iz geforn—ober dos iz gornisht antkegn dem vos es hot zikh opgeton, ven der 'kenig' iz tsurikgekumen!*" ("Thus did 'his royal highness' return home to his fellow citizens. And when Yash set forth—but this is nothing when compared to what happened when 'his royal highness' returned!")[15] Thus the wording of the preface suggests a vague allusion to a poem it does not quote,[16] whereas in the text itself, in which, as stated, there is no mention of the preface, the epigraph serves as an enigmatic opening. It equates the fates of "hero" and "antihero," while leaving it unclear whether, and how, this comparison can be made relevant to the character and fate of the narrator Yash. The epigraph to this novel does not offer the reader any reliable clues, and the questions it raises regarding its meaning remain unanswered.

The Narrator as Writer: Words and Silence

The fact that the expunged preface to *Ven Yash iz geforn* dealt with literary questions and presented the narrator first and foremost as a writer had a direct influence on the narrator's presentation in the opening chapters of the book. As a result, a somewhat paradoxical pattern can be discerned in the two novels. *Ven Yash iz geforn*, as stated, unfolds on a boat on its way to Europe. In the cosmopolitan atmosphere of such a trip, the narrator encounters a large number of characters, Jews and non-Jews alike, only a few of whom speak Yiddish. Even if they are "regular people" and even if they earn their livelihood from some sort of intellectual capacity (such as teaching), not a single one of them has literary pretensions. By contrast, in the very first chapter the narrator identifies himself as an intellectual and a Yiddish poet. *Ven Yash iz gekumen* is different in this regard—the diametrical opposite, in fact. As we will see below, in the resort hotel in which the narrator is staying, he is surrounded by men with literary and artistic ambitions, and even a few genuine writers. Yet it is in these surroundings that he decides to hide his spiritual identity behind a veil of silence.

Although we are provided with few details by which to identify the narrator of *Ven Yash iz geforn*, they are in line with what we know of Glatshteyn's biography. For example, in the novel's very first paragraph he mentions that he was a law student (9) and provides a detailed description of his miserable and grotesque status as a teacher of Yiddish in a community of boorish and coarse New York Jews (34-35).[17] Immediately following this

---

15. *Inzikh*, 178.

16. I thank Ophir Dines for this insight.

17. In an undated letter to Kalmen Marmor, in which he asks him to publish his contributions in the embryonic New York Yiddish Communist newspaper *Frayhayt*, he describes his work as a teacher in a Jewish school: "*Kh'hob tsu ton mit zeyer fargrebte mentshn fun dem min vos darfn nokh yern tsu dergreykhn di madreyge fun a*

description he offers another scene, which, in light of the fact that the characters involved were identifiable and familiar, is surprisingly direct. He recalls his deep sense of humiliation upon turning to the editor of the Yiddish paper where he had worked for "eight years" and meekly requesting a vacation to travel to Europe, an occasion so demeaning that he forgot *"[m]ayn oysgeglaykhtkeyt, mayn talent, mayne dray oreme liderbikher, mayn ayngeredkeyt"* ("my stature, my talent, my pitiful three volumes of verse, my conceit," 36). Indeed, B. Alkvit, a colleague of Glatshteyn's at *Inzikh*, was on the mark when he noted in his review of *Ven Yash iz geforn* that *"Glatshteyn git undz do dem ershtn kinstlerishn dokument fun di ekonomishe gilgulim fun a yidishn inteligent in Amerike"* ("Glatshteyn provides us with the first artistic document of the financial experiences of a Jewish intellectual in America").[18]

The speaker's literary work is not only mentioned as background detail; he remains a writer throughout his sea journey as well. The first chapter of *Ven Yash iz geforn* concludes with the speaker's attempt to compose a poem about what he has seen so far. The attempt fails because the atmosphere is too far removed from his native cultural milieu, and hence the poem *"iz aroysgekumen spetsifish nisht-yidish un tsu Mansfild-mesik"* ("came out being especially un-Yiddish and much too Mansfield-like," 25). The second chapter ends also with a reference to the Yiddish cultural world, but from a different perspective: *"A yid fun Bogota"* ("A Jew from Bogota"), the first character on the boat to approach the narrator, retells in his colorful Yiddish his life in distant Colombia, a life of material comfort without the semblance of anything Jewish. To his question of what he should invest in were he to move to New York, the narrator responds, in a semi-comical vein, that he can become a publisher at a *"[a] yidishe tsaytung, a gut yidish vokhnblat"* ("a Yiddish newspaper, a good Yiddish weekly"), since *"[b]ildung un aroysgeberay fun a yidisher tsaytung darfn davke nisht zayn keyn geshvesterkinder. Men ken zikh on bildung gants sheyn bageyn, men darf nisht geyn in di klasn. Es iz a biznes vi ale biznes"* ("Education and putting out a Yiddish newspaper aren't necessarily close cousins. You can manage quite well without education, and you don't need to attend class. It's a business like every other business," 61–62). The narrator's ties to the Yiddish cultural world are thus a recognized and established fact in *Ven Yash iz geforn*, although this aspect is neither emphasized nor developed due to the textual framework of interactions between the narrator and other passengers on board, who are rarely concerned with literature.

---

bavustzinikn Shomer-lezer" ("I have dealings with the coarsest people imaginable, of the kind who must still aspire to reach the level of a self-conscious reader of pulp fiction"). (K. Marmor Collection, YIVO Library).

18. B. Alkvit, "Yankev Glatshteyns nay bukh," *Inzikh*, no. 46 (May 1938), 103.

On the other hand, in *Ven Yash iz gekumen*, the novel in which the narrator is situated on the fertile terrain of Jewish Poland surrounded by various types of artists, he does not ascribe himself to their party at all. How are we to understand the great chasm separating this novel's narrator from its author? Is it a symptom of literature's inability to offer an intellectual and meaningful stance toward the complexity of the human landscape on display? Does the visit to Poland provide the narrator with the opportunity for some soul-searching, an opportunity to "rediscover himself," or does it repress his introspective leanings? In order to answer these questions we must examine the narrator's place amongst the gallery of colorful figures he encounters at the resort hotel somewhere in the middle of Poland, especially his relationship with the one character who figures so prominently throughout the novel.

Steinman: The Elusive Man of Letters

The scenes portraying Steinman's death, as in the opening episode in *Ven Yash iz gekumen*, suggest a kind of Hasidic master, or at least his surrogate. Throughout the text he is, in fact, presented as a full-fledged Jewish intellectual whose spiritual horizons blur the gap between both worlds, the traditional and the modern. Yet his is not mere abstract intellectualization, since he both introduces and defines himself as a professional writer: *"Ikh shrayb,—hot er mir masbir geven —khsidishe mayses in di gazetn"* ("'I write,' he explained to me, 'Hasidic stories in the newspapers,'" 24). While journalistic pieces are his main source of livelihood, he retrospectively disparages that practice as a waste of his intellectual powers, an activity that leaves his creative potential largely untapped. His central monologue, devoted to reflections on the nature of Jewish literature, begins as follows:

> *Gehat hob ikh gor groyse ambitsyes, ober gevorn bin ikh nisht keyn shrayber, nor a mayse-dertseyler fun khsidishe heyfn un rabeyshe dinastyes. Meynt nisht, az ikh farklener kholile mayne fardinstn. Mir zaynen geborn gevorn bay an orem folk un mir hobn gemuzt ton undzer flikht.* (218)

> I once had great ambitions, but instead of becoming a writer I became a teller of tales about Hasidic courts and rabbinic dynasties. You shouldn't think that I'm minimizing my accomplishments. We were born into a poor people and we had to do our duty.

Steinman's skeptical view of the value of his own work is no display of false modesty. In the eyes of the ultra-traditional Jew, *belles-lettres* possess no lasting value, which is why one of the novel's most prominent representatives of the traditional world, a unique and even eccentric Hasidic youth whom the narrator meets on one of his strolls, admits that Steinman's writings are, to him, *"puste mayses"* ("frivolous stories," 157). As we will see, that young man harbors literary ambitions of his own, but this merely reinforces his denouncement. Steinman actually unknowingly agrees with this judgment, and his attitude toward his own writing highlights the problematic status of *belles-lettres* in the Jewish society. Steinman sees himself first and foremost as a writer who owes a debt to his readers. This view does not, of course, stem from traditional Jewish sources, but is rather in keeping with the approach toward the function of literature shared by nineteenth-century Russian realism and Polish positivism, according to which the artistic work must be addressed to the people, not necessarily in the crude manner of serving as a mirror to reality, but as an expression of the profound moral ties that supposedly link the writer to his countrymen.

Steinman's character shares certain features with I. L. Peretz, a comparison that has, indeed, been developed in several studies of the novel.[19] Less obvious are the significant differences between the fictional character and his possible real-life prototype. It is absolutely clear, for example, that I. L. Peretz would not have presented himself as a writer of "khsidishe mayses in di gazetn," even though this is a basically accurate "factual" description of his writings. While his series of stories entitled *Hasidut/Khsidish* ("Hasidism/Hasidic-style"), written in Yiddish and Hebrew, is at the core of his oeuvre, Peretz himself would hardly have singled it out as the finest of his diverse output. Most important, Steinman's comments regarding the publication of his stories in newspapers places him among those writers dependent on the daily press. Admittedly, Peretz, like many others, first published his stories in periodicals, but he viewed this as the first step toward their publication in book form. Steinman, by contrast, is never able to polish his writings and arrange them into a book. Moreover, he does not feel the need to do so, or at least he never gives that impression to his attentive audience. Steinman spends the last days of his life busily sorting his papers (216), but even then he never considers publishing a book of his own, since his basic approach regarding the ultimate aim of literature for Jewish society is fundamentally at variance with that of the full-fledged modern author.

An air of mystery envelops this elusive character. Above all, he is a dedicated Jewish intellectual who traverses the twilight area between the traditional Jewish and modern worlds. Any informal mention of a Jewish issue is close to his heart or conversation, and he will associatively link diverse subjects, moving from character to character, from one cultural field to another. A spiritual man with inexhaustible cultural riches at his disposal, he nonetheless finds it very difficult to produce a work of value. His strength lies in casual chat and does not lend itself to systematic intellectual and spiritual endeavors. His status as professional writer living by his pen is secondary to the main feature of his character, which is his enthusiasm for anything Jewish. As a result, the modern version of Jewish literature is seen through his prism as marginal and even problematic in the face of the broad-

---

19. For example, Dan Miron (see note 6 above, 245) writes that Steinman is "a sort of caricature of I. L. Peretz," an identification echoed by Leah Garrett in "The Self as Marrano in Jacob Glatstein's Autobiographical Novel," *Prooftexts*, 18 (1998), 211.

er historical scope of the Jewish cultural experience. Steinman comes across as an idiosyncratic figure, yet his perspective is central to the entire structure of the book. His many creative projects and their failure to get off the ground form pieces of a mosaic whose parts are never meant to merge into an artistic whole.

On the one hand, one should not look for many common traits between Steinman and the narrator, since the latter, as discussed earlier, reveals next to nothing of his personality. On the other hand, an implicit yet momentous comparison is set up between Steinman's personality and the composition of *Ven Yash iz gekumen*, a heterogeneous, fragmented text that challenges classical notions regarding the wholeness of the work of art.

Steinman comes across as a Jewish intellectual who would never entirely cut himself off from his traditional Jewish sources, but would prefer to forever remain suspended between different worlds. Shmuel Niger insightfully noted that three literary and cultural generations merge in this unique character: the man of the *Haskalah*, the *hasid*, and the neo-Hasidic writer.[20] Steinman is also gifted with a sophisticated sense of historical awareness (he mentions that some of his works were historical popularizations, 219), and is thus conscious of his status as a singular cultural model who will not have a successor. Not only does his yearning for male heirs fail to materialize (the daughter who nurses him in his frail health is of no importance in his eyes), but he also has doubts regarding the lasting value of his intellectual efforts: "*Ikh aleyn zukh oykh a yoyresh. Zet ir, az ir vet mikh fregn, vos azoyns hot men bay mir tsu yarshenen, af dem vet shoyn zayn shver tsu entfern*" ("I too am looking for an heir, though if you ask me what I have to bequeath, I would find it hard to reply," 57). His aptitude for storytelling lies in the verbal spell he casts over his listeners rather than his readers, and he basically fulfills the role of the folk narrator in traditional societies. The reader encounters him for the first time dining with a yarmulke on his head, yet a few pages later the narrator goes out of his way to offer a significant variation of this theme:

> Der man, vos hot ersht gefirt tish, hot geshpant hin un tsurik, ober itst hot er gefirt a gantse tshate vayber. Er hot shpatsirt in bloyzn kop.

> The man who had just held forth was now pacing back and forth, only now he was leading a whole flock of womenfolk and was walking with his head uncovered. (15)

Steinman's spiritual experience is thus notable for the freedom with which he moves between worlds. The scene also includes a slightly ironic acknowledgment of the hero's powerful charismatic appeal, a strength he retains when he exchanges male society for its female counterpart. Apparently, the border dividing the traditional Jewish and modern worlds is ill-

---

20. S. Niger, "Fraye proze," *Der tog*, Jan. 12 1941.

defined for Steinman himself, and hence his passage from one to the other is smooth and imperceptible. The spiritual quandary that preoccupied Peretz—the nature and destiny of secular Judaism—does not concern Steinman in the least. The underlying differences between the two cannot be traced back to their spiritual stature or measure of public influence, but are rather a result of fundamental disparities between the cultural worlds to which they each belong.

The fact that Steinman is the novel's chief exemplar of the professional writer underlines the unique perspective from which Glatshteyn chose to illuminate the status of Jewish literature. For this purpose he does not employ a modern author of Yiddish poetry or prose, among other reasons because such a character would immediately have the reader searching for its biographical prototype. Yet the result of this decision is of the utmost significance: *Ven Yash iz gekumen* is loaded with observations regarding the nature, status, and future of Jewish literature in general and Yiddish literature in particular (the term *yidishe literatur* refers equally to both fields), but these do not include any direct mention of the modern face of contemporary Yiddish writing, and certainly not of its modernist tendencies. Accordingly, a clear movement can be detected in this regard, involving a significant thematic shift away from the novel's author, who is supposed to be fully positioned within the modernist camp, toward the portrayal of a writer who represents an amalgamation of earlier literary epochs.

The topics of Steinman's diverse ruminations range over a variety of subjects, including juicy episodes from his biography, the current status of Polish Jewry, and musings over the future of Jewish literature. His discussions are never "focused." His speech is intended to serve as an example of the associative nature of the Jewish intellectual's talk, freed from any cultural labels or ideological commitment, and it stands as a paradigmatic case of a kind of seemingly random "stream of consciousness" monologue. Notwithstanding, certain subtle threads link Steinman the writer to his listener, the first-person narrator. These pertain to two very different areas: his meditations on literature on the one hand, and the biographical episodes he recounts on the other.

Steinman's aforementioned sober observations on his own literary career and, specifically, the gap between his ambitions and achievements function as a segue to a discussion on the state of Yiddish literature and Jewish literature, generally. These insights are worth special attention even if they appear to present a non-committed torrent of words:

> *Say vi, darft ir visn, iz bay undz dervayl nishto keyn ort far literatur fun groysn farnem. Vayl—veyst ir far vos? Vayl literatur fun groysn farnem iz a literatur fun kleynikaytn: fun kleyne fargenigns, kleyne zorgn, kleyne tog-teglekhe gesheenishn, kleyne mentshelekh, zeyere zorgelekh, zeyere haselekh, zeyere libelekh, zeyere vaybelekh, zeyere kinderlekh, zeyer arbet un zeyer ru.* (218)

> Anyway, you should know that there is no room in our world for literature
> with major scope. That's because—do you know why? Because a literature
> of major scope is one made up of small things: little pleasures, little worries,
> little everyday happenings, little people, their little worries, their little
> hatreds, their little loves, their little wives, their little children, their work
> and their leisure.

The reference to the *"kleyne mentshelekh"* ("the little people") sheds light
on Steinman's approach to one of the central issues in the development of
Yiddish literature. The inaugural work of modern Yiddish literature is S. Y.
Abramovitsh's *Dos kleyne mentshele* (*The Little Man*, first published in
1864), a title echoed in the heading of Sholem Aleichem's well-known
series *Di shtot fun di kleyne mentshelekh* (*The Town of the Little People*,
1901–1902). Modern Yiddish literature, indeed, began by placing the "little
man" at the center of its world. It is true that Steinman neither advocates a
considered literary approach nor mentions his predecessors. Despite all its
idiosyncratic mannerisms and obvious ties to traditional Judaism, however,
his is a frame of mind that takes into consideration secular literature. Moreover, his language is modern. For instance, it is hard to picture Mendele or
Sholem Aleichem coining phrases such as *"zeyere zorgelekh, zeyere hase-
lekh, zeyere libelekh,"* notwithstanding the familiarity of these everyday
words and their broad reliance on the common Yiddish diminutive. This is
another instance of Steinman's idiosyncratic language. It should be noted
that in his view the principle task of literature is, in fact, *"kleyne fargenigns"* ("little pleasures"), an approach that removes Yiddish creativity
from those great national and social functions certain circles had burdened
it with. Yet Steinman is surprisingly supportive of those opinions, widespread in his day, that the very nature and status of Yiddish literature
requires of it a "realist" approach, and is convinced that it must sprout from
the fertile soil of daily life. It should neither depict larger-than-life heroes
nor an intellectually or emotionally rich and intricate world. Steinman's
approach is definitively anti-heroic and anti-romantic. For him, the purpose
of Yiddish literature is not to provide expression for the world of the individual, but to allow for a profound, mystical link to its source—the multifaceted Jewish world from which it draws its power.

This approach would seem to be diametrically opposed to the literary
views of Glatshteyn, the modernist poet whose poems develop the delicate
and complex expression of the individual life. Yet are these ideas really a
foreign implant grafted onto the prose work *Ven Yash iz gekumen*? Perhaps Steinman's comments can be seen as an overt expression of the artistic
intention regarding both content and structure of the book as a whole. It
appears that in this case Glatshteyn prefers a highly intricate and tricky
approach. From the moment he centered his work on Polish Jewry of the
1930s he would have been well aware that he had chosen a subject loaded
with weighty historical and ideological implications, and he tried to treat

these substantial aspects with a somewhat lighter touch. We spoke earlier of his method of merging references to meaningful acts and inspirational speeches, on the one hand, with observations of the minor details of daily reality, on the other. Such a synthesis, indeed, testifies to his ambitions of creating "*a literatur fun kleynikeytn,*" a literature of small, even miniscule, and, at times, enigmatic parts of a complex and fragmented reality that can never be fully encompassed, about which there are no grounds to assume the existence of any sort of unifying principle that links together its various facets.

Thus the two *Yash* volumes should not be viewed as the dividing line between Glatshteyn's early modernism and his later works, with their more direct language, their tendency toward weighty statements, and their emphasis of Jewish themes. This approach was, indeed, once the accepted view of Glatshteyn's artistic development,[21] but while it is partly true, it does not nearly exhaust the significance of *Ven Yash iz gekumen*. The novel makes use of familiar material from Yiddish literature to create an unmistakably modernist work of art—one associative, fragmented, aimless and apparently lacking in structure—while at the same time dissolving the boundaries between genres. The book is designed as Yiddish *modernist prose*, with all that this label entails.[22] Every aspect of the novel is influenced by a modernist sensibility, especially in regards to the autobiographical self-reflections offered by its two protagonists, Steinman and the first-person narrator.

Steinman is not presented as someone who wishes to put the story of his life on display and offer it as a smooth progression that contains any sort of meaning. Certainly he has no intention of "confessing" to the narrator or of establishing an intimate relationship with him. This becomes evident when we realize that the "gaps" in the description of Steinman's life easily outnumber the biographical details provided. More interesting and surprising is the fact that the information we are given is comprised of a thorough mixture of important and representative episodes with less significant, marginal and even incidental ones. Steinman's autobiographical memories concentrate on four characters who have absolutely nothing in common, not their historical value, nor their importance to Polish Jewry, nor even their influence on the subject himself.

The decision to open Steinman's memories with the mention of the German Orthodox leader Azriel Hildesheimer might appear justified from a purely biographical perspective, as Steinman is relating how the latter's trip

---

21. See for example Dov Sadan's comments in the introduction to the Hebrew translation of Glatshteyn's collected poems, *Of All My Toil* (Jerusalem, 1964): "The 'Yash' stories are important not only in their own right, but as the watershed between his earlier and later books of poetry," xix.

22. This aspect of the novel has already been noted by Shmuel Niger (see note 20), whose review of the book carries the title "*Fraye proze*" ("Free Prose").

to Poland led him to Germany, where he became acquainted with broader secular culture. Yet from a novelistic point of view the choice is unexpected. Is there really some special importance to this character that leads Steinman to commence his sequence of recollections with him? Not only do the choices of characters themselves raise unanswered questions, but so do the transitions between them. For example, the associative logic connecting Azriel Hildesheimer to the historian Heinrich Graetz is very clear. Both are presented in the book as faithful to Judaism as a historical or halakhic entity while nonetheless failing to keep a warm place in their hearts for the flesh-and-blood Jew, especially those of that cast most pitiable in their eyes, namely, the traditional Polish Jew. The function of the episodes in which Steinman encounters these individuals thus seems to represent the well-known and established mental distance separating the *Ostjude* from the *Westjude*, and to defend the besmirched honor of Polish Jewry. But if this is the case, how can one explain why the next subject of these reminiscences is the Yiddish dramatist Yankev Gordin? Steinman recollects the most bizarre episode of Gordin's biography in Eastern Europe before he became a Yiddish dramatist: his leadership of a disreputable religious sect that tried to synthesize Judaism with Christianity. The incident in question is in fact a negligible and peculiar episode in the life of Yankev Gordin, one that left no discernible traces on Eastern European Jewry. Why then mention this particular fact and place it beside the portrayal of Herzl (90–91) and Steinman's impressions as a minor participant in the First Zionist Congress, one of the founding events of modern Jewish history?

The chain of associations surprises in its variety and in the diverse modes of characterization and represents the rich cultural world of its bearer. Herzl is the only character whose genuine historical achievements have left an indelible impression on Steinman, and he is portrayed as a founding figure in the latter's spiritual world. But the other figures have had only a minor effect on Steinman, and his sharp criticism of them highlights the less flattering sides of their personalities. The mention of Yankev Gordin is all the more unusual in this context, as Steinman's acquaintance with him was merely superficial, which is why he does not appear in any personal recollections. These are the only historical characters to whom Steinman devotes significant space, and it is odd that this authentic Polish Jew fails to mention in all his recollections a single person related to the world of Polish Jewry. Steinman's associative sequence thus negates any possible distinction between "central" and "marginal," between "significant" and "incidental," providing us with a prime example of a Jewish intellectual's "stream of consciousness," in which any aspect of Jewish existence in his time might occupy him and attract his attention. He considers his own Zionist activity in the wake of Herzl first and foremost a cultural endeavor, specifying the "literary" quality of the Zionist activity to which he was devoted: "*Mir zaynen gevorn poetn, statistiker, finantsistn, magidim, matifim, darshonim,*"

("We became poets, statisticians, masters of finance, preachers of every conceivable ilk," 96). In Steinman's eyes, the story of his life is first and foremost a "story" that works its magic on his listeners: "*Ir vart avade af dem sof fun der mayse, ober ven ikh zits azoy un dertseyl aykh toyznt mit eyn tog, volt di mayse alts keyn sof nisht gehat*" ("I'm sure you're waiting for the end of the story. But even if I were to sit here and tell you tales for 1001 days, the story would still never be finished," 97). Yet this associative and random sequence performs a clear function in the composition of the novel: in this manner, Glatshteyn the modernist undermines one of the accepted truths of his generation: the belief that time and history have a direction and meaning.

Away from the Self

Steinman is the most important example of a writer or artist in *Ven Yash iz gekumen*, yet he is by no means the only one to harbor creative ambitions, including literary ones. By way of generalization we can state that all the characters have one attribute in common: the enigmatic nature of their personalities and writings. These include a fresh-faced youngster, one of a group of youths staying at the hotel, who places himself right in that twilight region between the halakhic, normative Jewish world and an undefined, unnameable spiritual realm. While this youngster has literary aspirations, he certainly does not see *belles-lettres* as a clear and well-defined corpus: "*Mir zaynen di filosofn tsvishn di rabeym un di sheynreder*" ("We are the philosophers among the Hasidic rabbis and the polished orators," 158). At the same time he offers a fierce criticism of the spiritual horizons of modern Yiddish literature. He presents himself both as a burgeoning writer and a visionary, while the divide between the two (like the one delineating Steinman's Zionist activity) remains hazy and indistinct. In his eyes he is not a poet in the full meaning of the term, but someone with "*a gezang*" ("a song") rolling off his tongue. When he quotes a number of his poems, the reader is left in no doubt that they are juvenile and naïve works, especially when they touch on the erotic (162).

The inclusion of such a character in the fabric of *Ven Yash iz gekumen* can be explained as a reference to certain trends in Yiddish literature of the 1930s, specifically as a biting and sarcastic dismissal of the growth of Yiddish religious literature in *belles-lettres* among Orthodox circles of Poland, much of it of highly debatable aesthetic value.[23] But this does not exhaust the significance of this character, because the cultural world of the Hasidic youth is not cut of one cloth. While his poems can only raise a chuckle from the reader, this would not appear to be the appropriate response to his

---

23. On this subject, see the chapter entitled "The Place of Belle-lettres in the Orthodox Community" in Nathan Cohen's *Books, Writers and Newspapers: The Jewish Cultural Center in Warsaw, 1918–1942* (Hebrew) (Jerusalem, 2003), 178–186.

efforts to compose prayers in stylized Yiddish (170). Furthermore, notwithstanding the dubious worth of his writings, his daydreams display an intrigu-
ingly enigmatic quality. He recounts to the narrator one of his experiences,
a hallucinatory and weird encounter with the false messiahs Shabbetai Zvi
and Jacob Frank, illustrating how their characters and fates remain an open
wound for this dreamy ultra-Orthodox youth.[24] In other words, whereas his
writings receive an unequivocally negative judgment, the passing glance at
this youth's complex mental world leaves the reader with a sense of mysterious depth. In this case, "life" is far more absorbing and interesting than
"literature."

The diverse gallery of artists from various fields presented in the novel
also includes the plastic arts, such as the highly diverse set of painters
whom the narrator meets during his visit to the town of Kazimierz, a central
segment of the book to which we shall return. Even his English teacher
from night school in the Lower East Side, who introduced the narrator to
English literature, is described as a frustrated poet unable to fulfill either his
creative or his erotic potential: "*Er hot gehat a myes vayb un er hot far
tsaytfartrayb geshribn heyse geshlekhtlekhe lider, vos er hot gedrukt in
Grinitsh Viledzsh vinkl-zhurnaln*" ("He had an ugly wife and to kill time he
wrote passionate erotic verse, which he published in obscure Greenwich
Village magazines," 48).

This impressive list of writers and artists makes the issue of the narrator's
self-presentation all the more imperative. Can we draw a parallel between
him and the author Yankev Glatshteyn, the modernist Yiddish poet who
was a professional journalist in the 1920s and 1930s as well as an occasional
literary critic? The reader will search in vain for a clear indication of a link
between the two; the novel's first-person narrator does not present himself
anywhere as a professional writer. "Yash," the name that features only in
the title of the book and is not repeated in the text itself, is not Yankev Glatshteyn, a fact that has far-reaching repercussions for an understanding of
Ven Yash iz gekumen.

This distinction goes beyond the obvious difference between author and
narrator. The relevant question here is how to deal with the fact that the
narrator's own experiences are detached from the spheres of both literature
and intellectual activity in general, a subject that occupies such a central
place in the structure of *Ven Yash iz gekumen*. A possible clue to an answer
lies in one of the most puzzling sections of the book, in which the narrator
reverts to his Lublin childhood. Here alone the narrator actually presents
himself as a writer, yet it occurs when he returns to his childhood days, in
the context of the theatrical world. In his hallucination he sees himself in a

---

24. Avraham Novershtern, *The Lure of Twilight: Apocalypse and Messianism in Yiddish
    Literature* (Hebrew) (Jerusalem, 2003), 264–267.

theater, but is unable to identify the play being performed. The first rejected possibility, in fact, concerns his own "play": "*Es iz geven klor, az dos shpilt men nisht mayn Purim-pyese, vos ikh hob ongeshribn tsu akht yor un vos ikh hob forgeshpilt far mayne khaveyrim, in der mames shenste kleyder, nokh dem vi zey hobn gekoyft tsu groshn a bilet*" ("Clearly, they were not performing the Purim play that I had written when I was eight years old and that I had put on before my friends, wearing Mother's prettiest clothes, after they had each purchased a ticket for a groschen," 119). The text continues to eliminate one-by-one various possibilities regarding the authorship and the very nature of this play being performed on a provincial Lublin stage:

> *Neyn, oykh nisht "Di shvue" iz itst geshpilt gevorn in der ofener, likhtiker tir, af der zaytik avekgeshtelter bine. In der pyese, vos men hot geshpilt, hob ikh a bisl derkent mayn loshn, nor di aktyorn zaynen mir geven in gantsn umbakant.* (121)

> No. "The Oath" was also not being played in the bright open door, on the hastily constructed stage. In the play they were performing I did recognize my lines, but the actors were total strangers to me.

In a clearly modernist fashion, all divisions separating "real" memory from hallucinations are collapsed, which makes any identification problematic. It is clear to the author of these memories (or hallucinations, or dreams) that it is not a performance of *Di shvue*, Jacob Gordin's play, popular largely among amateur troupes both in Eastern Europe and Yiddish communities around the world. In a grotesque episode, amusing and shocking at the same time, the first-person narrator originally sees himself on stage as a prompter (one of the lowliest positions in the theatrical hierarchy), but fails at the task, since in his great excitement he forgets the text of the play. Subsequently he appears on stage as one of the play's characters, yet it is entirely unclear as to who is the "real" author of this play. Is it he himself? The question of the "ownership" of the literary work remains unresolved, and the first-person narrator can see himself only as the possible author of an immature, juvenile work. The fact that his parents are watching the play adds a further grotesque element to the entire scene, as the "child" senses that they will not be proud of a work that does not meet their demands. The mother will view any play lacking her beloved Goldfaden songs as deficient, while the father will judge his son's play by completely different criteria:

> *Lomir zen, vos far a plonter er vet do onplontern, Peretz mit di pintelekh – ongepintlt, ongetintlt. Far vos zol er nisht shraybn azoy, az a tate zol oykh farshteyn?* (121)

> Let's see what kind of mess he'll cook up here, like Peretz with his ellipses: dots and ink spots signifying nothing. Why can't he write in a way that a father might also be able to grasp the meaning?

The child's place in this grotesque nightmare appears to fall somewhere in between the two demands. His father's familiarity with Peretz notwithstanding, he is likely to complain of the text's unintelligibility. However, the reader is immediately made aware that this is not a before-its-time modernist text of some Eastern European child prodigy. The novel quotes some pages of this "play," and they reveal nothing that would justify their inclusion in *Ven Yash iz gekumen*. It is a very minor and uncertain work, whose only merit lies in its heroes' folksy turns of phrase. Certainly this is not a text that a sophisticated modernist poet such as Yankev Glatshteyn would have been proud of, even as a childhood effort. Yet this juvenile composition is the only one that the first-person narrator of *Ven Yash iz gekumen* claims as his own.[25] Right through the book he refrains from identifying himself as a writer or artist, either to himself or to others, and his reflections when closely observing his surroundings do not bring to his mind any significant literary associations.[26] What portrait of the first-person narrator emerges from the novel?

Spurred by the intense debate on issues of self-presentation in the literary text, especially in the genres of autobiographical writing, a significant number of recent studies of the *Yash* books have approached it from this angle. Jan Schwarz, for instance, deals with *Ven Yash iz gekumen* in a book that focuses on autobiographical writings of Yiddish authors. Furthermore, the blurb on the novel's new Hebrew translation (by Dan Miron, Tel Aviv, 2006), presents it as "a unique autobiographical novel by the most talented and sharpest poet of Yiddish modernism in America." Yet it is highly doubtful whether a close perusal of the complex network that is *Ven Yash iz gekumen* would confirm this categorization of the book's genre. A medley of lively autobiographical fragments sprinkled throughout the novel does not transform it into an "autobiographical novel," much less justify a focus on this aspect of the book alone, without reference to the function and context of such material in the text as a whole.

These autobiographical sections, few in number, are geared primarily to underscore the modernist nature of the work. They vary widely in type.

---

25. Several of the characters that feature in this dramatic sequence reappear in the only chapter published from the third volume, which would have been called *Ven Yash iz tsurikgeforn*: "Fragment fun '*Ven Yash iz tsurikgeforn*'," *Di tsukunft*, Nov. 1941, 82–84. Yankev Glatshteyn republished this chapter some years later: "Nakhmen zeyger-makher," *Di goldene keyt*, no. 30 (1958), 256–261. The publication included the following note: "Fragment fun *Ven Yash iz tsurikgeforn*, driter teyl fun trilogye vos vert tsugegreyt." It indicates that Glatshteyn never abandoned his plans to write a third volume, even though he was unable to bring them to fruition. A. Sutzkever, editor of *Di goldene keyt*, would probably not have published the chapter had he known that it had been printed before.

26. A rare literary association offered by the narrator of *Ven Yash iz gekumen* brings together two very different cultural worlds in a description of Steinman's face in his last days: "Er iz itst geven shtark enlekh tsu di bilder fun Anatole France" ("He bore a strong resemblance to Anatole France's pictures," 239).

Some depict "formative moments" in the speaker's life, such as the journey to America and the shock of his first impression of the modern and alien city of New York. Others, by contrast, cast their light on the shadows, focusing on more marginal episodes from the speaker's experiences, such as the narrator's recollections of his night school studies in New York as a new immigrant, reminiscences centered not on himself but on his grotesque teacher, the frustrated poet who died suddenly at a young age (45–49). The status of the first-person narrator differs greatly in these two passages. He is the main protagonist of the first, as from a later period in time he recounts his hopes, fears, and the young immigrant's sense of insult, shared by so many others. In the second piece the narrator is reduced to the status of an observer, witness to an unusual character and an unexpected event. Thus the autobiographical memories of *Ven Yash iz gekumen* elude all categorization; the incidental and bizarre are included alongside formative, representative experiences.

Even upon first inspection it is evident that the autobiographical episodes function in the text as prime examples of the "stream of consciousness" technique. The textual links between narrative present and autobiographical memory are typically absent, coincidental or of secondary importance. Sometimes these connections present a challenge to the reader's accepted cultural values. The best example of this is the series of associations leading to the first set of recollections in the text, describing the event closest to the narrative present: the preparations for his mother's funeral. The narrator, idly waiting near the resort hotel, observes the picture of a Christian saint hanging on a tree, which transports him from his present state to the world of the New Testament, and from there to the Pentateuch: "*Ikh hob zikh dermont, az ersht nisht lang tsurik iz mir bashert geven ibertsushpiln a shtikl Khumesh, vos gehert tsu a sakh a fartsaytikerer epokhe, vi dos ponem fun dem heylikn*" ("I was reminded that not too long ago it was my fate to reenact a bit of the Bible, which partakes of a far more ancient epoch than the visage of this saint," 34). The haggling in the community offices over the burial price reminds the narrator of Abraham's attempts to buy the Cave of Machpelah as a burial plot. We thus have a narrator who is not afraid to follow a chain of associations leading from the image of the Christian saint before him to the arrangements preceding his mother's burial. The very fact that the description of the haggling with the community members is related with ironic wit turns it into the finest example in the novel of that emotional reticence that is the hallmark of most of the autobiographical fragments incorporated into the text. The same narrator who is completely silent when it comes to describing the final moments of his mother's life and his encounter with his closest family members on that highly charged occasion, all of which is passed over in silence by the text, delves into every detail of the bargaining over the funeral price in the premises of the Jewish community, an event that is far less taxing emotionally. The result is a sharpening of the reader's awareness of the largest and most significant gap in the novel's sequences of memories.

The narrator's past is presented in a very different light from that of Steinman's. He does not encounter a single historical figure of import and although his memories are, of course, rooted in the Eastern European Jewish world and his move to the United States, the immediate historical context is absent. The main bulk of memories appearing in *Ven Yash iz geforn* center on a major historical event: the repercussions of the 1905 revolution as seen through the eyes of a child (76–96). *Ven Yash iz gekumen* does mention certain historical events that occurred during the narrator's lifetime, but these are incidental references. Historical and personal memories are not intermingled in this book.

Several of the autobiographical pieces of *Ven Yash iz gekumen* are particularly charged emotionally. For example, the episode immediately following the aforementioned scene of the burial preparations focuses on the speaker's childhood memories of a lengthy walk across a field in order to bring a pot of food to his father, who was serving in the czar's army (36–39). The piece offers a wonderful blend of elegant lyricism and primordial fear. Yet the narrator's life, as depicted in the novel, does not feature many remarkable events and lacks dramatic or emotional content. It is hard to point to any biographical episodes that are exceptionally uplifting or, at the other extreme, to traumatic memories. These are memories of *"kleyne fargenigns, kleyne zorgn, kleyne tog-teglekhe gesheenishn"* ("little pleasures, little worries, little everyday happenings"), the stuff of literature itself, according to Steinman. Glatshteyn thus faces a unique challenge: to maneuver the narrator away from the ordinary and to find the unique, even idiosyncratic, angle to his biographical episodes; to avoid the drift into sentimentality while preserving emotional restraint. Were the reader to undertake the intellectual exercise of combining these few autobiographical pieces, he would undoubtedly discover that they fail to present the narrator's autobiography as a meaningful sequence or as a psychological whole. The rifts are as pronounced as its points of continuity.

When the narrator encounters a character from his past who performed a significant role in the shaping of his character, the meeting also illuminates the inherent limitations of memory. For instance, he receives a visit in the hotel resort from his private Hebrew teacher, who sought to merge traditional and modern Jewish culture with its secular counterpart. This visit triggers one of the most detailed recollections in the novel, characteristically devoted to that autobiographical chapter that was of great importance in the life of every Eastern European Jewish youth: the narrator's *cheder* and *melamed* (183–208). The average reader of Yiddish literature is likely to approach this section with extremely low expectations: What more can be said of such a well-worn topic? Hence the encounter with the former teacher (who was not necessarily a traditional *melamed*) begins by stressing the power of forgetfulness—and the destructive march of time—rather than the strength of memory, for the narrator fails at first to identify his teacher (183–84). Moreover, the teacher does not open the conversation with his former student by reminding him of his studies, but rather by mentioning a most idiosyncratic personal detail, that after many years he had finally managed to divorce the wife that had embittered his life! With the aid of this device the author sidesteps the literary stumbling-block placed in his path; the danger that we will be given a stereotypical portrayal of an Eastern European teacher or *melamed* is avoided, and a mysterious and idiosyncratic character takes its place.

These fragments of memory might serve to reinforce a modernist, perhaps even post-modernist, conception of the self. They seem to frustrate any possibility of granting the narrator psychological or spiritual unity. The individual past does not affect, explain, or illuminate the present, mainly because the personal portrait of the narrator in his current state is so sparse and vague, leaving very little to "explain." Two contradictory impulses grapple in each autobiographical memory, with self-revelation opposed to concealment. There is no doubting which of them has the upper hand in *Ven Yash iz gekumen.*

Herein lie both the similarities and the differences between Glatshteyn the poet and Glatshteyn the author of the *Yash* books, although the distinction is more complicated than it would seem at first glance. Glatshteyn, the quintessential Yiddish modernist of the 1920s and 1930s, indeed centers his poetry on his internal world, yet it should be noted that he does not focus on the singular individual event, and he certainly does not center it on any details of a quasi-autobiographical stance. Regarding this poetic option Glatshteyn had his say in the witty poem, "*Oytobyografye*" ("Autobiography"),[27] which mocks the penchant common among his contemporary Yiddish poets for cultivating a rhetorical stance of honesty and self-revelation:

> *Ikh hob nekhtn opgeshtekt mayn zun di dozike geshikhte:*
> *Az mayn tate iz geven a tsiklop un, farshteyt zikh, mit eyn oyg,*
> *Az mayne fuftsn brider hobn mikh gevolt uffresn,*
> *Hob ikh zikh koym aroysgeratevet fun zeyere hent*
> *Un zikh genumen kayklen iber der velt.*

> ·Yesterday I dumped on my son the following story:
> That my father was a cyclops and, of course, had one eye,
> That my fifteen brothers wanted to devour me,
> So, I barely got myself out of their clutches
> And started rolling all over the world.

27. "Oytobyografye," *Kredos* (New York, 1929), 70. The poem was first published in 1928. English translation by Benjamin Harshav, *American Yiddish Poetry* (Berkeley, 1986), 247.

The poem is built around an imaginary "story" related by a father to his son, and it is no accident that the poet uses the word *geshikhte*, which bears the double meaning of "history" and "story." The speaker in the poem fiercely opposes the urge to immortalize the individual and collective pasts, which had already left its mark on the contemporary Yiddish cultural scene. He tells his son an entirely fictional "story," woven as it is from the most formulaic material: a family portrait, an immigration saga. On top of that, it seems that an entirely different cultural phenomenon is being mocked here: the modernist tendency to mythologize the self. However, the poem does not just make use of patently imaginary material. At its conclusion it incorporates an authentic biographical detail, referring to the speaker's status after all that has occurred to him:

> *Nokh der khasene hot mayn gut opgebrent*
> *Bin ikh gevorn an oremer tsaytung-shrayber.*

> After the marriage, my estate burned down.
> So, I became a poor newspaper writer.

This "autobiography" is thus not entirely imaginary. Its conclusion provides an accurate detail from the speaker's current life, for Glatshteyn indeed worked in journalism during this period. Yet there is no real connection between past and present, between the imaginary biographical history and the speaker's current reality. In similar fashion, the undue emotional self-restraint of the narrator of *Ven Yash iz gekumen* and the manner in which he integrates a few biographical sketches into the larger text can be seen as an extreme instance of a quality also found in Glatshteyn's poetry of the same period. They function so as to prevent the various autobiographical episodes from combining in a way that would inject a sense of continuity and meaning into the speaker's life.

Yash *as Travel Literature*

It would be unfair to say that the *Yash* books depart from the accepted conventions of the contemporary Yiddish autobiography, particularly the tradition that developed in wake of the memoirs of the *klasikers*—Mendele, Sholem Aleichem, and Peretz. After all, these books make absolutely no pretense of using the text to foreground the autobiographical material. However, a different genre category is certainly applicable to them: the travel narrative. The very inclusion in the title of words connected to "journey" and "arrival" clearly set up such an expectation.

Yet rather than continuity between these two stages of the trip, we find that the books create a chasm between them. As stated, *Ven Yash iz gekumen* nowhere depicts the son's return to his home and family. The only scene that unfolds in the narrator's hometown is the aforementioned haggling prior to his mother's funeral, while his meeting with her is not described at all. Ruth Wisse correctly notes that "Glatstein's emphasis falls on the caesura, on the empty space between the anticipation and the aftermath of homecoming."[28] The decentering tendency of the novel (that, for instance, moves us away from the narrator) is reflected in the actual space and situation of its characters. The resort hotel situated somewhere in Central Poland, in which the narrator stays through most of the novel, does not embody his actual return to the familiar surroundings of his formative years; at best it serves as a watered-down version of such a homecoming. Since it is a new place for him, the narrator is unable to single out any particular aspect of it as relating to his past.

As other readers have noted,[29] the narrator's stay at the hotel should certainly not arouse mistaken expectations of a novel like Vicki Baum's *Grand Hotel* (1929), an extremely popular work of its time. Admittedly, on a number of occasions the text offers flashes of the easy and non-committal atmosphere that pervades among the guests, including a tangible sexual tension. Yet the very choice of such a place as the main site of the narrator's visit to Poland has an obvious effect: as in every hotel, the protagonists of the novel are removed from their natural surroundings and their regular existence— their place of residence, their work environment and their families. This has far-reaching implications in the context of the Yiddish prose of the time, which was decisively tilted toward realism (occasionally of the stricter variety) and preferred to place its characters in their usual and natural environments. The protagonists of *Ven Yash iz gekumen*, by contrast, are released from the shackles of the everyday. As Steinman puts it, "*dreyt men zikh arum tsvishn zin un umzin. S'iz a moshl kegn gantsn lebn*" ("You twirl about between sense and senselessness. It's a parable of one's whole life," 24). Life at the hotel in an ideal end-of-summer ambience necessarily lessens the great sense of crisis enveloping Polish Jewry at the time, palpably evident in the comments of various characters who turn to the narrator for help in receiving assistance from their relatives in the United States. As opposed to the mood of the monologues, it is noticeable that the stay in the resort hotel provides the narrator himself a measure of economic comfort, of bourgeois lethargy and hedonism. The question bothering many of those who lay out their complaints before the narrator—literally how they can sustain themselves and their family members—is not shared by the narrator or the other hotel guests, who do not suffer the scarcity that surrounds them. Likewise, throughout his long stay in the hotel the narrator fails to display any sign of his private grief for the loss he so recently experienced. The place is explicitly geared toward senile patients, yet it successfully maintains an air of idyllic calm, real or imaginary, alongside the presence of disease and death.

---

28. See Wisse, 173.

29. Abraham Regelson, "A farkalekhter dor," *Di tsukunft*, Dec. 1941, 181; Dan Miron (note 4, above), 239.

Ven Yash iz gekumen should be considered both a continuation and elaboration of the physical and human space at the heart of *Ven Yash iz geforn*, which, as Leah Garrett states, "has no private space—everything is in public, and everything is in motion."[30] In the hotel, whose occupants had no prior acquaintance with one another, an essentially similar set of human relationships to that of the ship is constructed, only with a more nuanced diversity. During the weeks of the narrator's stay he serves as Steinman's constant auditor until the key event of the latter's sickness and death, an episode that is harder to imagine occurring during the journey at sea. Likewise, although he does receive visits from notable individuals who embody his biographical past, such as the aforementioned Hebrew teacher, most of the characters the narrator encounters at the hotel are new to him. These meetings provide for the type of re-encounters that could not have been arranged in the first volume of the *Yash* books. The speaker's complete anonymity among the ship's passengers in *Ven Yash iz geforn* is replaced by a more complex set of circumstances in *Ven Yash iz gekumen*, a blend of the strange and the intimate. Yet both cases involve temporary relationships, which are not intended to last beyond his departure from that place.

In one aspect we find an essential difference between the two *Yash* volumes: by its very nature the transatlantic trip bears an international flavor. Its passengers include a group of Soviet youths returning to their country after a period of studies in the United States, a teacher from Wisconsin taking her yearly trip to Paris, and a Dutchman trying to hide his Jewish identity. Only one character can be said to be fully conversant with the narrator: the "Jew from Bogota," who recounts his life story in colorful Yiddish. In this sense *Ven Yash iz gekumen* offers entirely new artistic possibilities: all (or almost all) of its protagonists speak Yiddish. In many ways the hotel is an emotionally neutral location for the narrator, but the Yiddish spoken within its walls transforms this neutral space into "home." Physically, this is not his "birthplace," yet the language to a certain extent turns it into one.

The text makes much use of stylistic differentiation as a means of characterizing its various protagonists, and their monologues create a spectacular polyphony of diverse linguistic registers. The simple Jew who heaps curses on his brother who became wealthy in the States but fails to assist him as he should (136–38), the modern provincial intellectual who laces his speech with superficial slogans (146–47), the Hasidic youth with pretentious literary ambitions—all these turn the text not only into a virtuoso stylistic display, but also into a demonstration of the versatility of contemporary Yiddish. The same language is used in the novel to express the thoughts of characters from different cultural worlds. A simple Jew, a Hasidic scholar, a

---

30. Leah Garret, *Journeys Beyond the Pale: Yiddish Travel Writing in the Modern World* (Wisconsin, 2003), 149.

modern intellectual, a woman well-versed in both Yiddish and general literature, all speak Yiddish. This is a scenario with which the Yiddish prose of
the previous generation was not equipped to deal, as its focus was mainly
on the language of the folksy Jew. Although one can occasionally observe
the narrator assimilating the other characters' speech into his own, and at
times they speak "Glatshteynish,"[31] he is generally careful to avoid this artistic hazard. Along this linguistic spectrum, it is clear that Steinman's speech
sets the desired standard. It is at once anchored in both Jewish tradition and
the modern world, and incorporates both the animated tone of everyday
conversation and the abstract written word of essayist and journalist. The
"Jew from Bogota" in *Ven Yash iz geforn* praises the narrator time after time
in that "*ir hot a por goldene oyern*" ("you have a pair of golden ears," 172).
Yet this quality of the narrator's is fully displayed only in *Ven Yash iz gekumen*, a book that justly deserves a key place in the development of Yiddish
prose. It integrates the linguistic achievements of several literary generations, from Sholem Aleichem[32] to contemporary prose.

The narrator of *Ven Yash iz gekumen* is no tourist; his talent for *listening* to people and for grasping the meaning of their small-scale actions is
immeasurably greater than his ability to *see* places. Yet in a significant passage in the novel, toward its end, this pattern is disrupted. On only one
occasion does the narrator leave the hotel grounds—in order to visit the picturesque town of Kazimierz, famous for its connection to the legend of the
relationship between King Casimir the Great and his Jewish lover,
Esterke.[33] This visit provides for a highly significant reference to the historical dimensions of Polish Jewry. Here, for the first time, the present confronts the mythic past. Consider, for example, the conversation on the way
to Kazimierz. The narrator's companion on this trip is Nayfeld, a lawyer
excited at the prospect of seeing the place once again. Over the course of
the journey he offers a pertinent and sober survey of the state of Polish Jewry, mainly focusing on the problems of widespread conversion to Christianity and intermarriage among the youth—topics that directly touch on the
relationship between Casimir and Esterke.[34] Meanwhile, the trip to Kazimierz prompts the narrator to delve into one of the founding legends of the

---

31. S. Niger makes this observation in his review of the book (see note 20 above).

32. A number of critics have noted this connection to Sholem Aleichem, including S. Niger
in his review of Glatshteyn's novel for adolescents, *Emil and Karl*: "Nokh do mentshn
af der velt," *Der tog*, June 16, 1940. See also Glatshteyn's comments below.

33. See the anthology *Kazimierz vel Kuzmir*, ed. Monika Adamcyk-Garbowska (Lublin,
2006).

34. Dan Miron noted this connection in his essay of 2006 (note 4, above), 283.

Jewish community in Poland.[35] But Kazimierz, that charming town with its historical sites and local legends, with its unique Jewish characters who draw their livelihood from this tradition, that same place that aroused so much enthusiasm in Nayfeld, leaves the narrator skeptical and unconvinced. The place fails to inspire him, and he soberly reflects on both the nature of the legend and the "politics of memory" that it incorporates. The special function of this trip to Kazimierz in the overall fabric of *Ven Yash iz gekumen* emphasizes the novel's uniqueness as a "travel narrative"; hikes across landscapes and plains are not its concern. The physical space in which most of the novel unfolds is restricted and localized, whereas its depictions of various life experiences spread far and wide.

The Metapoetical Strand

The gradual yet steady changes in the narrator's character as the text progresses embody a complex cultural meaning. Throughout the entire first book, the speaker identified himself as a Yiddish writer and poet as he traveled in the modern ambience of the ship. When, however, he is faced with the range of personalities and cultures of Polish Jewry, at once rich and decaying, he conceals his identity. The complexities of this world and the narrator's inability to grasp it in its entirety or to divine its fate cause him to curtail his intellectual profile. There is a hidden lesson here in intellectual and emotional humility, which includes more than a little hesitation and confusion. Because the *Yash* novels are such an important landmark in Glatshteyn's oeuvre, we must strive to understand them in all their diverse aspects. A useful guide is the middlebrow writer Z. Vaynper, who in a cross between a critical and biographical essay provides us with a keen sense of the figure that Glatstheyn cut at the time:

> *Epes vi a ger iz Yankev Glatshteyn in undzer yidisher poezye. Er farmogt aza vunderlekhn yidish un dokh ringlt epes a min fremdkayt arum yedes vort, vos er zogt tsu undz. (...) Geboyrn un gelebt di frye yunge yorn in der poylish-yidisher shtot Lublin, getsertlt gevorn mistome fun a mamen, geven avade unter der hashgokhe fun a tatn, ober keyn simen fun yenem lebn vet ir nisht gefinen in zayn lid.[36]*

> Yankev Glatshteyn is something of a proselyte in our Yiddish poetry. Even though he possesses such a marvelous Yiddish, a kind of foreignness surrounds each and every word that he utters....Born and bred in the Polish-Jewish city of Lublin, most probably pampered by a [Jewish] mother, most certainly raised under the stern eye of a father, yet not a sign of that life can be discerned in his poetry.

---

35. Chone Shmeruk devotes a monograph to this fascinating topic. See Chone Shmeruk, *The Esterke Story in Yiddish and Polish Literature* (Jerusalem, 1985). Glatshteyn's novel is mentioned only in an aside (77, note 11).

36. Z. Vaynper, *Yidishe shriftshteler*, I (New York, 1933), 60–61.

Ven Yash iz gekumen does not offer a response to the challenges raised by Vaynper, as it nowhere provides a straightforward biographical account of events. The reader who anticipates a comprehensive picture of Glatshteyn's life in Lublin, his childhood and youth, education and family, will finish the book only half-satisfied—if even that. It is true that the first-person narrator fits Vaynper's characterization: he is, indeed, occasionally seen as "alien" to his surroundings, a short-term guest, even if he himself does not convey such a feeling. On more than one occasion in his modernist poetry Glatshteyn gives expression to the gulf separating him from his surroundings. Yet when the narrator of this prose work displays excessive restraint regarding his self-characterization, this distance is greatly narrowed, as the attenuation of his own presence provides more room for numerous and varied other human voices. The narrator stands alone in a fragmented and disintegrated world. This seems to be the central literary-cultural significance of *Ven Yash iz gekumen* in the context of Yiddish literature of the time.[37]

Sh. Niger was the major contemporary critic who pointed out the highly original character of the book, although he himself was known for his conservative literary tastes and his very lukewarm appraisal of Yiddish modernism in general and the work of the *Inzikh* writers in particular. He entitled his critical review of the novel "Fraye proze" ("Free Prose"), which is, of course, a play both on the term "free verse" as well as on the title of Glatshteyn's second book of poems, *Fraye ferzn* (1926). Yankev Glatshteyn responded to him privately:

> **Ken zayn az mayn bukh iz es take un ir zent gerekht.** Nor, oyb ir zent gerekht, bin ikh durkhgefaln, vayl ikh hob durkh mayn bukh gevolt esn vetshere tsuzamen mit Sholem-Aleykhemen, Peretsn un Mendelen un nisht vartn afn moment ven di yidishe literatur vet mikh, dem kunstfrant, araynrufn af farbaysekhts un a tshashke tey.
>
> Es iz mir keyn mol nisht gegangen in oysteyln zikh fun klal un vern a literarisher prishtshik rakhmone litslan (vi groys der onvaks zol nisht zayn), nor mir hot zikh gekholemt, az mayne oysteylungen un andershkeytn farmogn genug koyekh tsu vern a teyl fun gantsn, vi shkotsevate zey zoln nisht oyszen afn ershtn ontap oder baym ershtn barir.[38]
>
> **Perhaps my book is what you say it is and you are right.** But if you right, then I have failed, because through my book I wanted to share a festive meal with Sholem Aleichem, Peretz, and Mendele, and not wait for the moment when Yiddish literature will see fit to invite the art-dandy, me, in for some dessert and a glass of tea.

---

37. This would suggest an essential difference in the narrator's status in the novels of Glatshteyn and Agnon, but a full comparison of these two seminal works is beyond the scope of this paper.

38. Glatshteyn's undated letter to S. Niger, S. Niger collection, YIVO Archives. The emphasis is in the original.

> It was never my intention to separate myself from the collective and become, if you'll pardon the expression, a literary facial mole (however large a size its size), but rather I dreamed that my separateness and differences have sufficient power to become a part of the whole, however prankish they may appear to be at first glance or upon first touch.

It should be kept in mind that Glatshteyn wrote these comments alert to the cultural background of his addressee, the authoritative Yiddish literary critic with a conservative taste, at a time when the former sought a reconciliation of sorts after years of tense, even hostile relations.[39] Hence he overemphasizes the "Yash" books' ties to the Yiddish literary tradition. Nonetheless, we can assume that Glatshteyn's comments on his own work contain a revealing and profound statement regarding the dialectical nature of the *Yash* volumes, and an indication of the extent to which they were devised as a new and innovative phase of Yiddish prose. Indeed, they are indissolubly linked to one of the central models of modern Yiddish literature since the work of S. Y. Abramovitsh—the loaded, tense, and enriching encounter between the modern Jewish intellectual on the one hand and a broad array of characters from various strands of society on the other. Yet how great is the difference between the imposing presence of a Mendele the Book Peddler in the novels of S. Y. Abramovitsh and that of the narrator in *Ven Yash iz gekumen*! The bulk of the novel touches upon the complex relations between the narrator and his environment. Their unraveling comprises the very core of the book, and this is the main reason why the second volume in the series exceeds the first in cultural importance and literary achievement.

Ven Yash iz gekumen represents a crowning of the most significant trends in modern Yiddish prose; numerous sections of variegated monologues in which the richness of spoken Yiddish is gloriously expressed are embedded in an open-ended, plotless modernist text, one that refuses to give credence to any possibility of "progress" or "change." One of the most illuminating fragments of the text makes a suggestive reference to this artistic structure, creating a powerful symbol. On the way to Kazimierz, in the heart of nature, along that sole trip during which the narrator leaves the hotel, the passengers hear the song of the nightingale. The impression this song leaves on its listeners offers an indirect account of the novel's literary underpinnings, the most significant of its kind in the book:[40]

> *Er hot gezungen trukn, etlekhe kurtse treln, vos hobn zikh ibergekhazert, vi er volt ayngeshtelt di teme, ober glaykh nokh dem iz er zikh fargangen in lengere monologn (...) Dos zingen iz arumgeringlt gevorn mit azoy fil*

---

39. On this see Yankev Glatshteyn's article, "Krig un fridn mit Sh. Nigern," *Yidisher kemfer*, Passover issue 1957, 25–31. The article includes lengthy quotations from S. Niger's correspondence with him, dating back to 1940.

40. Dan Miron concludes his essay on *Ven Yash iz gekumen* (note 6, above) with an analysis of the significance of this scene.

shvaygn, vos hot gemakht a vare far dem eyntsikn bisl gezang. (...) Es iz nisht geven keyn simen fun degradirndiker ziskeyt in dem nakhtigals gezang, fun arunterlozn zikh tsu ongenumene geshmakn, farkert – es iz geven perfektsye fun oysdruk. Es hot poshet gerisn baym hartsn, vos men hot dem foygl azoy baleydikt, farsakharint un farlakritst far der velt, beeys er hot aza umpopulere un kluge muzikalishe ivre. (249)

Crisply it gave a few short trills, repeated as though the singer wanted to stress the theme, but soon it went on to elaborate in lengthier monologues (...) The singing was encircled by such a degree of silence that the way was opened for a single piece of song (...) There was no trace of degrading sweetness in the nightingale's song, no concession to debased popular taste. To the contrary, this was the perfection of musical expression. It was outrageous to think that this bird was so despised and had the reputation of a "sweet" singer when its musical language was so intellectual, so sophisticated.

It is here, more than in any other portion of the book, that the narrator reveals his closeness to the world of art and literature. The narrator is able to express his artistic views through his attention to the nightingale's song, that wordless music. His ambition is to create a work that integrates isolated patches of "song" surrounded by "silence." Likewise, the composition of *Ven Yash iz gekumen* is based on the dialectical tension between the sounding of a variety of human voices and the narrator's meaningful silence.[41] It is because these voices in the novel often attest to a reality of deprivation, poverty, and stifled material and spiritual existence in the shadow of persecutions that it is important to the narrator to avoid all forms of sentimentality. As a modernist author he seeks to write "cleverly," and is also aware that the work is not supposed to be "popular." Although the temptation is to associate the nightingale with the poet, the more instructional comparison is the one between the nightingale and the text itself.

The narrator is well aware that the song of the nightingale is a hackneyed motif that appears in countless literary works, including poems of a largely sentimental nature. Yet he is not deterred, trusting as he does in his ability to provide an original approach to this literary motif and transform it into a fresh and renewed symbol. The nightingale's fragmented song has no clearly defined "subject," but its listener can detect its virtuosic ability to vary its voice. The nightingale and its song are also comparable to the fate of the modernist artist in their respective environments. The implied question of the nightingale's song is left unanswered:

---

41. Years later, in an interview with the poet and critic A. Tabachnik, Glatshteyn would define poetry as "*an organizirt shvaygn*" ("an organized silence"): Y. Glatshteyn, "Poezye un poetn," *Di goldene keyt*, No. 57 (1966), 79 (abridged English translation: *Yiddish*, vol. 1, no. 1 [Summer 1973], 41)

Er hot ibergekhazert tsvey frazn, ober di tsveyte fraze hot zikh dershpitst tsu a frage, vos iz geblibn opgehakt, vartndik af a tshuve. Di tshuve iz nisht gekumen. Er iz antshvign gevorn.

The nightingale repeated two phrases, but on repetition the second had pointedly become a question waiting for an answer. No answer came, and the singer fell silent.

Each one of the nightingale's listeners interprets its song by his own terms, yet none of them is awarded any kind of response. *"Es iz geven a sheyn shtikl shire tsum riboyne-shel-oylem, hot der balegole es gemakht kurts"* ("'It was a fine hymn of praise to the Almighty,' said the driver curtly"). The words belong to the coachman, a simple Jew whose language and behavior are reminiscent of Tevye the dairyman. Later he, in fact, begins to hum passages of liturgy. Yet his words offer more than a characterization of his cultural milieu; they are directly linked to Steinman's declaration at the very outset of the novel (*"afile fun der blote vel ikh zingen tsu dir, mayn Got, afile fun der blote"*). His observation thus indirectly confirms the sense that the religious theme is a very minor presence in *Ven Yash iz gekumen*. The interpretation of the second listener could not be more different: *"Es iz efsher geven a [...]*[42] *lekoved aykh, hot Nayfeld gezogt mit a shmeykhl"* ("'Maybe it was a [...] in your honor,' said Nayfeld with a smile). Nayfeld, one of the representatives of the "Modern Jew" in the novel, views man as the sole addressee of the work of art. Nonetheless he is capable of a certain reservation from his own comments, showing awareness of the extent to which they voice the hubris of modern man. By contrast the narrator himself does not believe that the nightingale's song is addressed to anyone or has a meaning, yet he exercises all his senses in an effort to grasp and explain its nature. The song of the nightingale in the woods, that familiar symbol of absolute freedom, sounds like a disjointed sequence, yet the narrator still does not abandon his resolve to find within it a hidden order and artistic pattern.

The Modernistic Jewish Encyclopedia

Ven Yash iz gekumen enjoys a unique place in the framework of contemporary Yiddish literature. Familiar and even trite literary material is granted a new artistic configuration in a modernist framework. This depiction of a visit to Jewish Poland is mainly located in an atypical site for the landscape of Yiddish literature. The *shtetl*, that quintessential Jewish space, is almost completely absent from this travelogue to Jewish Poland (apart from the short visit to Kazimierz).The text does not offer an account of life in the city either, and even the familiar theme of the train journey that plays such a significant role in *Ven Yash iz geforn* is absent here. Narrating in the

---

42. A word is missing here in both published versions of the work.

first person, the narrator conceals both his presence and spiritual identity, only occasionally allowing his voice to be heard. The book has been dubbed "a novel of return without the return itself."[43] Admittedly, in one particular aspect, the novel approaches the conventional form of the contemporary Yiddish travel narrative: *Ven Yash iz gekumen* does, indeed, offer a panoramic overview of Polish Jewry with its hopes and fears. Yet even here the narrator forges a distinctive path, for the characters depicted in the book do not conform to any easy cultural or ideological classifications. Rather than introducing clearly defined representatives of parties or ideological currents, he presents us with figures that traverse cultural worlds. The writer Steinman is one such example, and to a great extent the Hasidic youth with his literary aspirations also fits into this category. Thus the familiar human landscape of Yiddish literature undergoes in *Ven Yash iz gekumen* a delicate process of sophisticated estrangement.

The *Yash* books, the first sustained prose works of the modernist poet Yankev Glatshteyn, thus present a difficult challenge for the critic who attempts to place them in their relevant framework, involving as it does two or even three divergent contexts: Glatshteyn's oeuvre, the relationship between prose and poetry within Yiddish modernism on the one hand and within American Yiddish literature on the other. Yankev Glatshteyn was never entirely unfamiliar with prose writing, but it presented him with particular problems. "I began my literary career with short stories," he told Yankev Pat in a late interview:

> *Es iz geven in yener tsayt a Reyzenisher derekh—derfirn a dertseylung oder a lid tsu a final, tsu a shpits. Zogn baym sof a shtik pikkhes. Hot ober gefelt der shpits fun der mayse, hot di mayse nit getoygt. Unter a fremdn nomen, Y. Yungman, hob ikh gedrukt in 'Morgen zhurnal' arum hundert dertseylungen. Ikh hob zikh bakent mit der amerikaner moderner proze un poezye, un bin gevor gevorn az me kon shraybn on shpitsn un on vitsn.*[44]

> In those days it was the Reisen thing to do: to build a story or poem up to a grand finale, a punchline. Articulate something really clever at the end. If the story lacked that kind of punchline, then it was no good. Under a penname, Y. Yungman, I published around a hundred stories in the *Morgen zhurnal*. But when I became acquainted with American prose and poetry I discovered that one can write without punchlines and one-liners.

This disparaging comment notwithstanding, there exists a complex relationship between the different genres in Glatshteyn's work from the outset of his literary career. His first story was published immediately upon his arrival in the United States in 1914 as a youngster of eighteen. Yet five years

---

43. Riki Ophir (note 6, above), 46.

44. Yankev Pat, *Shmuesn mit yidishe shrayber* (New York, 1954), 86. Glatshteyn went back to this topic in his interview with A. Tabachnik (see above, note 41), 86.

of creative sterility (at least as far as publication is concerned) passed before Glatshteyn's significant breakthrough into the Yiddish literary scene with his first modernist poems, published in 1919. In the 1920s Glatshteyn devoted most of his creative efforts to poetry, yet he did not entirely renounce other genres—as early as 1920, then a burgeoning poet, he published an article proclaiming the need to revitalize the literary feuilleton.[45] Beginning in 1925 he worked steadily as a journalist. The daily newspaper also served as a major outlet for his prose, not all of which has survived. There is no question that Glatshteyn valued this facet of his writing and saw it as a respectable form of his creativity, beyond the economic necessity of providing the paper with written copy. Thus for example, in 1936 (after the completion of the first *Yash* volume) he planned to write "*a lengere dertseylung*" ("a longer story") for the first volume of *Zamlbikher,* to be published under the editorship of H. Leivick and Y. Opatoshu, although he eventually penned an apology over his inability to make good on his promise.[46] In *Ven Yash iz gekumen* there is mention of "*a bukh kurtse noveln un dertseylungen*" ("a book of short novellas and stories"; the genre distinction is not altogether clear) as a book ready for publication, while in a letter from 1944 to S. Niger he notes: "*Ikh farmog gornisht mer in mir, vi mayn dritn bukh* Yash, *nokh etlekhe lider, a novele un a drame*" ("I have nothing left inside of me, other than the third volume of *Yash*, another few poems, a short story and a play").[47] Glatshteyn, then, continued writing prose for at least two decades and intended to collect it in book form, quite apart from the *Yash* volumes and his novel for adolescents, *Emil un Karl*, also published in 1940.

Glatstheyn's turn to prose, then, was not a whim, an accidental feature in his career, but rather a significant aspect from the very outset. His early prose efforts reveal a struggle between two contradictory impulses as far as their artistic qualities and target audiences are concerned. His widely accessible realistic stories were printed mainly in the New York Yiddish daily newspapers. At the same time, Glatshteyn's attempts at modernist and experimental prose in Yiddish were published in elitist literary journals; the best known of these pieces bear the defiant title "*Ven Joys volt geshribn yidish*" ("If Joyce Wrote in Yiddish").[48]

It would seem that this disparity is not confined to a particular case. On the one hand it illustrates the inherent difficulty in writing modernistic Yiddish prose in general, especially in the United States. On the other hand, it testifies to Glatshteyn's persistent efforts to try his hand at this form.

---

45. "Shotns," *Baym fayer*, no. 3–4 (Nov.-Dec. 1920), 1–3.

46. Undated letter to H. Leivick [1936] (H. Leivick Collection, YIVO Archives).

47. Letter to S. Niger, Jan. 25 1944 (S. Niger Collection, YIVO Archives).

48. "Ven Joys volt geshribn yidish: A parode," *In zikh*, July 1928, 68–70; "Ven Joys volt geshribn yidish," *Undzer bukh*, July-Aug. 1929, 218–220.

Already in the first volume of *In zikh* (January 1920), A. Leyeles wrote that the group is open to, and even interested in developing, "*introspektive proze*," "*vos zol bafridikn undzer introspektivn kredo*" ("introspective prose," "that will fulfill the principles of our introspectivism"), but as of yet they have not found the like.[49] With hindsight it can, indeed, be said that this search continued for many years and achieved its most important artistic expression in Glatshteyn's *Yash* books. These books were acclaimed as such in the circles of Yiddish modernist poets and their ilk, in reviews by B. Alquit, J. L. Teller, Eliezer Greenberg, Gabriel Preil, and others.

It was in Glatshteyn's prose works that the most significant breakthrough in Yiddish modernism occurred, as Glatshteyn the prose writer merged with Glatshteyn the journalist. This fusion is not, however, intended to lead the reader into any sort of safe harbor. In an essay of 1937 (after the completion of the first *Yash* book), "*Zhurnalizm un poezye*" ("Journalism and Poetry"), Glatshteyn speaks of a new synthesis between these two modes of expression. He refers to the unique status and characteristics of Yiddish journalism (although the historical accuracy of his account is highly suspect), concluding with an explicit statement of his own credo:

> *Nisht faran keyn ris tsvishn der moderner zhurnalistik un der moderner poezye. Farkert, in der moderner zhurnalistik zenen faran di shenste meglekhkaytn far moderner poezye. Moderne zhurnalistik bafridikt dem elementarn hunger nokh publitsistishn oysdruk un lozt iber dem emesn poet mit der shverer ufgabe tsu shafn fun klorn un blitsikn materyal a naye, haynttsaytike misterye.*[50]

> There exists no split between modern journalism and modern poetry. To the contrary. In modern journalism one can find the finest possibilities for modern poetry. Modern journalism satisfies the elementary hunger for current events and leaves the real poet with the difficult task of fashioning out of clear and flashing items a new, contemporary mystery.

Indeed, the essayistic segments of the *Yash* books do not dispel the sense of perplexity that takes hold of the reader as the complexities of reality are revealed to the narrator, but rather serves to heighten this very confusion. In his review of *Ven Yash iz gekumen*, S. Niger comments on its intricate play of genres: "*Iz es a rayze-bashraybung? Iz es a kapitl zikhroynes? Zaynen es fragmentn fun an oytobyografye? Oder efsher iz es gor a dertseylung?*" ("Is it a travelogue? A chapter from a memoir? Can they be fragments from an autobiography? Or maybe it's a story?")[51] Shloyme Bickel expressed himself in similar terms, claiming that one of the novel's major achievements is its merging of four "forms": "*rayze-bashraybung, roman,*

---

49. A. Leyeles, "Introspektive proze," *In zikh*, Jan. 1920, 45.

50. Yankev Glatshteyn, "Zhurnalizm un poezye," *Inzikh*, Oct. 1937, 71.

51. S. Niger, "Fraye proze," *Der tog,* Jan. 12 1941.

memuaristik un publitsistik" ("travelogue, novel, memoir, and journalism").[52]

S. Niger even tried to back up his case from the book itself. It should be
noted, however, that the proof remains somewhat ambiguous: as the first-
person narrator conceals the fact of his being a writer, the meta-poetic
reflections of the work are formulated by others, who can in no way be
viewed, of course, as spokesmen for the narrator or the author himself. As
will be recalled, among the characters with literary aspirations encountered
by the narrator in the resort hotel, pride of place goes to that over-ambitious
Hasidic youth with his juvenile writings and resolute, unyielding opinions
in literary matters. His spiritual horizons stretch much farther than the
closed walls of the ultra-Orthodox world, and his words display the original,
innocent, impulsive enthusiasm of the fresh-faced youngster who has lifted
himself up to get a cultural glimpse "beyond the fence." Nonetheless, his is
not a typical case of one who "left the fold." Quite the opposite. Here is the
atypical situation of a youth from the traditional world who claims to be
thoroughly familiar with modern Yiddish literature and "nonetheless" stays
loyal to Jewish beliefs. A generation earlier, the natural expectation of a
youth of his kind was that he would first acquaint himself with Hebrew literature and then abandon the traditional path. But the cultural dynamic of
Polish Jewry in the 1930s allowed the narrator to include an Orthodox
youth who refers to Yiddish literature. When one considers this cultural
background, it comes as no surprise that the youth's reservations about the
nature and value of this literature should first and foremost be directed
against Peretz's Hasidic stories:

> *Ikh hob durkhgeleyent di gantse yidishe literatur. Ikh ken alemen un alts.*
> *Ober vos farmogn zey akhuts loshn? Peretses khsidishe mayses zaynen*
> *anekdotn mit a moral. Es iz fun droysn arayngekukt durkhn shlisllokh*
> *un getantst kodesh. Ikh vil kumen fun ineveynik. Ikh vil banayen dem*
> *gantsn yidishn gedank. Koydem, darft ir farshteyn, muzn mir opshafn di*
> *goyishe formen. Undzers a shafung muz koylel zayn alts: Poezye, proze,*
> *filosofye, drame, psikhologye, astronomye, epigram— alts. Vos darfn mir*
> *di kleyne shakhtelekh? Mir darfn vern a sheferishe entsiklopedye.* (159)

I have read through all of Yiddish literature. I know the writers from start
to finish. But what have they got except for language? Peretz's Hasidic Tales
are mere anecdotes with a moral tacked on. It's like peeping through a
keyhole and then performing hosanahs. I want to come from the inside. I
want to renew all of Jewish thought. First off, you understand, we must abol-

---

52. Shlomo Bickel, *Detaln un sakh-haklen* (New York, 1943), 198. It is of interest that
    Bickel wrote this as a complaint over S. Niger's omission of *Ven Yash iz gekumen* in
    his encyclopedic survey of twentieth-century Yiddish literature, published in 1942,
    unaware that the latter had expressed elsewhere a similar opinion regarding Glat-
    shteyn's book.

ish the gentile forms. A work of ours must contain everything: poetry, prose, philosophy, drama, psychology, astronomy, epigram—everything. What do we need those tiny boxes for? We must become a creative anthology.

The fact that Peretz is the only Jewish writer to merit serious attention in the novel is highly revealing. The criticism voiced by the youth is based on the supposed "lack of authenticity" in Peretz's stories. Yet the latter's very dedication to *belles-lettres* serves as an impetus for the youth to suggest, in his naïve and dismissive tone, a far more ambitious project, one that would break down all categorical divides between the various genres of literature and other fields of intellectual inquiry. To his mind, Jewish spiritual creativity must go beyond the literary and fulfill a completely different role to the one it serves for the other nations. It is no coincidence that the youth later mentions the figure of Rabbi Nahman of Bratslav, implicitly contrasting him with Peretz. The opposition rests on the gap between the counterfeit and the real—Peretz's stylized writing in contrast to an authentic, unmediated creativity. Moreover, it is clear that this provincial lad views Peretz as "merely" a writer, while Rabbi Nahman is presented as a true spiritual leader. Unlike the disparaging attitude Peretz receives, Rabbi Nahman occupies an important place in the spiritual world of this Hasidic youth.

The fact that literary opinions, like other topical matters for Polish Jewry, are voiced by varied and strange characters without explicit endorsement from the narrator, adds to the atmosphere of uncertainty that is one of the fundamental qualities of the entire text. On the one hand, the Hasidic youth and his opinions are presented as an idiosyncratic and somewhat bizarre element in the human tapestry of *Ven Yash iz gekumen*. On the other hand, the innovative idea that Yiddish literature should not be identical to that of "the Gentiles," and should, indeed, serve as a "creative encyclopedia," provides a call of defiance from within the text. It suggests that if Yiddish literature is supposed to bear unique qualities, then the artistic structure of the *Yash* books should perhaps be considered in a different light. Perhaps it should be seen as the end result of that aspiration to create a kind of "encyclopedic work" that blurs the accepted boundaries of the various literary genres in an attempt to integrate them afresh. It seems then that the *Yash* volumes in their own way embody Glatshteyn's deep-seated conviction that if Yiddish literature is to fulfill its destiny in the tragic circumstances of the late 1930s, then it must indeed be "different."

Shloyme Bickel also pointed to an additional dimension of the *Yash* books, a literary achievement with spiritual and cultural dimensions: the synthesis "*tsvishn idyom un neologizm*" ("between idiom and neologism"). A linguistic polyphony is, indeed, the watermark of the book. On the one hand, we find the colorful diction of folk characters, from the likes of the "Jew from Bogota" from the first volume down to simple Jews who come to describe their dire economic state to the narrator and ask him to try to locate their relatives in the United States. On the other hand, the book also presents the language of Steinman, a man of letters from the previous generation deeply rooted in the various layers of Jewish culture, as well as the speech of the young Hasid with his fledgling literary ambitions. To these we should add the narrator himself—a modern Jewish intellectual, whether he reveals himself or not.

The complex, even elusive nature of the *Yash* books positions them as the most challenging works in Glatshteyn's oeuvre. These prose works aim to break down the boundaries between different genres, fulfilling a unique function in the context of the Yiddish culture of the time. They put into question the very ability of the Yiddish writer to fashion a coherent and meaningful picture of the surrounding Jewish world; they do not completely rule out such a possibility, but they nonetheless leave the question in place. It seems that these prose works, in which Glatshteyn significantly broadened the limits of his literary world by turning to subjects of general topical interest as well as contemporary Jewish issues, are, in fact, the most modernist of all his multifaceted writings. They represent Glatshteyn's boldest artistic experiment, and perhaps as such it should be admitted that ultimately they raise certain doubts about the quality of the literary achievement they embody. The books upset most of the reader's expectations: a travel description that does not constitute a "travelogue," a highly personal work that is not an "autobiographical novel." The unique literary character of the *Yash* books carries a demand of its own: the ambition that Yiddish literature must venture beyond the purely belletristic so as to remain loyal to its nature and destiny. Yet at the very same time they depict the Yiddish writer as refusing to fashion structures of any sort of continuity and meaning, even concerning himself or his environment. Yankev Glatshteyn's *Yash* books are at once the most ambitious and most unassuming Yiddish literary works of their time.

Translated from the Hebrew by Avi Steinhart

Seductions and Disputations:
Pseudo-Dialogues in the Fiction of
Isaac Bashevis Singer

MIRIAM UDEL-LAMBERT

A theme that Ruth Wisse has often taken up in her scholarship[1] is the necessity of Eastern European Jewish writers' crafting their fictions and poetry with materials near at hand—and the marvelous inventions born of that necessity. In a seminar called in "In the Folk Manner" taught at Harvard University, she argued that otherwise dissimilar Yiddish writers shared the technique of plundering and embroidering Yiddish folk forms, whether ballads, wonder tales, or fables. Yiddish modernism was bound to differ from other European modernisms if only because of the historical compression under which it developed as a modern literature.[2] While many other national literatures ambled gradually into the twentieth century, Yiddish caromed from folksy traditionalism to full-blown modernism (and anti-modernism) in just over three-quarters of a century, ensuring greater logical and chronological proximity than is usual between modern authors and the raw folk materials of their cultural inheritance.[3] A phenomenon affecting choices of

1. This theme may be detected in *The Schlemiel as Modern Hero* (Chicago: University of Chicago Press, 1971), 6–14, 32–33; *A Little Love in Big Manhattan* (Cambridge: Harvard University Press, 1988), 27–29, 66–68, 135; and *The Modern Jewish Canon* (New York: The Free Press, 2000), 158–159. Here is a representative passage from "Di Yunge and the Problem of Jewish Aestheticism": "In their search for simplicity, purity of expression, melodious flow of language, they had to uncover the natural folk voice upon which they could play their own variations" (270), *Jewish Social Studies* Volume 38 (1976), no. 3–4, 265–276.

2. See David G. Roskies, "The Achievement of American Yiddish Modernism" in *Go and Study: Essays and Studies in Honor of Alfred Jospe*, ed. Raphael Jospe and Samuel Z. Fishman (Washington, D.C.: B'nai Brith Hillel Foundations, 1980), 353–368. "It was, for lack of a better term, the European Connection, when a hundred years of cultural development were compressed into ten." (354)

3. Many Yiddish writers, including Bashevis Singer, were just a generation removed from traditional religious piety with its accompanying wellsprings of liturgy and legend. Moreover, long-ago events—especially of an apocalyptic nature—were kept fresh in the Jewish collective consciousness by continuing episodes of violence. Avraham Novershtern writes that the chronicle *Yeven Metsulah* (treating the Chmielnitzky massacres) "never lost any of its immediacy: Its readers could always compare its descriptions of the terrible events of the past to the atrocities continually perpetrated during their own time." See "History, Messianism, and Apocalypse in Bashevis's Work" in *The Hidden Isaac Bashevis Singer*, ed. Seth L. Wolitz (Austin: University of Texas Press, 2001), 29.

theme as well as genre, this literary adaptation of folk materials and styles has secured for the fantastic a special place within the Jewish canon. In particular, the denizens of the underworld—Satan and his demonic host—have found their most full-throated voice in Yiddish literature.[4]

Nowhere do demons speak more eloquently and more disturbingly than in the fiction of Isaac Bashevis Singer. With one foot in the study house even as the other strode into the Warsaw PEN Club,[5] this author explored the sophisticated, modern use of the fantastic. In his stories, perspicacious *dybbuks* and demons, as well as instances of prophecy and possession, all form part of a moral vocabulary with ultimate metaphysical stakes. Although Bashevis Singer's devils are unfailingly witty and often quite funny, this demonic menagerie is put to serious literary use. By reposing the voice of evil in a set of discrete supernatural characters, the storyteller externalizes and dramatizes[6] the moral struggle. Resisting the tendency of his times to locate the conflict between good and evil within a singular consciousness— as seen in the discourses of both literary modernism[7] and psychology[8]— Bashevis Singer sculpts a battle in the round between distinct speakers. In his fantastic fiction, he refuses the modernist burden of depicting interiori-

---

4. This is the thesis of David G. Roskies's article in a forthcoming festschrift for Chava Turniansky, *"Di shprakh fun derekh-hasam: vi der sotn redt af yidish": "...nit gekukt deraf vos der sotn un zayne meshortim farnemen aza khoshev ort in gang fun der yiddisher geshikhte, iz ersht af yidish un bloyz af yidish hobn zey bakumen loshn..."* (1).

5. Thus does he emerge from Wisse's concise, vivid portraits of him, as well as in longer biographical treatments by others. See Wisse's introduction to *Satan in Goray*, trans. Jacob Sloan (New York: Farrar, Straus and Giroux, 1995), material later adapted in *The Modern Jewish Canon*. See also her article "Isaac Bashevis Singer's Paradoxical Progress" in *Isaac Bashevis Singer: A Reconsideration*. For a full-length biography, see Janet Hadda's *Isaac Bashevis Singer: A Life* (New York: Oxford University Press, 1997). It is also well worth consulting Ilan Stavans's *Isaac Bashevis Singer: An Album* (New York: Library of America, 2004).

6. This calculus is explicit in the novel *Shosha* (1978), in which the author's alter ego, the playwright Aaron Greidinger, solves a dramaturgical challenge by having his play's protagonist fall in love with the *dybbuk* who possesses her.

7. For an especially skillful account of the modernist exploration of consciousness, see Dorrit Cohn's *Transparent Minds: Narrative Modes for Presenting Consciousness in Fiction* (Princeton, N.J.: Princeton University Press, 1978). Bashevis Singer's relation to literary modernism is a complicated one. He might best be referred to as an antimodernist; his distinctive aesthetic-ideological response to modernity has been characterized as "(neo)conservative" by Novershtern, p 36.

8. Bashevis Singer's accounts of possession (see below) contain some eerie similarities to clinical descriptions of neurological maladies, such as Tourette's Syndrome. See Donald J. Cohen, *Life is With Others*, ed. Robert King and Andrés Martin (New Haven: Yale University Press, 2006), xvii–xviii.

ty, constructing instead a figured world[9] where evil is no less real for being portrayed in supernatural terms external to the human psyche. The fact that he does depict characters' internal emotional lives much more fully in his later, realistic fiction may be adduced as evidence of a deliberate aesthetic choice.[10]

A writer who was "never more playful, youthful, or hopeful than when writing as a demon," as David Roskies perceptively points out, Bashevis Singer created demonic characters of unaccustomed "venality, vulgarity, and malevolence."[11] Yet there is a critical tendency to be confounded by the simultaneous meanness and the moral seriousness of these demons, so that many interpreters find it impossible to treat his *sheydim* with a straight face even when these supernatural characters are painted in a serious rather than a comical light.[12] Others exorcise Bashevis Singer's demons too precipitately by rushing to flattening psychological interpretations of them.[13]

---

9. To borrow a key phrase from Dorothy Holland, William Lachicotte, Jr., Debra Skinner, Carole Cain, *Identity and Agency in Cultural Worlds* (Cambridge, Mass.: Harvard University Press, 1998). See especially ch. 3, "Figured Worlds." They define a "figured world" as "a socially and culturally constructed realm of interpretation in which particular characters and actors are recognized, significance is assigned to certain acts, and particular outcomes are valued over others. Each is a simplified world populated by a set of agents...who engage in a limited range of meaningful acts or changes of state...as moved by a specific set of forces..." (53) One of the examples furnished is of a cultural system where ghosts have "a psychological reality that denotes nothing about a person's sanity or insanity—as it might in a culture where such beings are considered figures of fantasy, imagination, and superstition." (54) With reference to the work of Bashevis Singer, I would quibble only with the phrase "psychological reality," arguing that his ghosts and demons variously inhabit both psychological and material realms.

10. Novershtern ascribes the lack of interiority to a concern for historical verisimilitude, 41.

11. See *A Bridge of Longing: The Lost Art of Yiddish Storytelling* (Cambridge: Harvard University Press, 1995), 268-269. Roskies isolates Der Nister and Bashevis Singer as lone swimmers against the tide of an overwhelming tendency toward celebratory demonological tales that served the interests of secular humanism.

12. Chone Shmeruk identifies in the demonic narrators of the *Yeytser-hore mayses* "that element of humour and buffoonery which belongs to the nature of demons who do not act from malice towards man. In this way we feel that behind the demonic, there is a touch of clowning and cleverness, corresponding to the use of the word *shed* in Yiddish as applied to human beings." I argue elsewhere that the association is more fruitfully reversed: behind clowning and cleverness Bashevis Singer perceives a touch of the demonic. See "The Use of Monologue as a Narrative Technique in the Stories of Isaac Bashevis Singer," which serves as an introduction to *Der shpigl un andere dertseylungen*, ed. Chone Shmeruk (Tel Aviv: Shamgar Press, 1975), xix-xx.

13. Even a perceptive analysis like that of Seth L. Wolitz refers to Rechele's "becoming 'possessed' in mind and body," placing the term in absorptive quotation marks. See his

According to these readings, the wickedness that Bashevis Singer sculpts in the round comes merely to stand in for the only evil that really counts—that buried within the human psyche.

Bashevis Singer has always provoked readerly discomfiture,[14] whether we speak of the audience of secular Eastern European Jews who originally bestowed on him equal measures of fame and notoriety, or of the vast worldwide readership he has achieved in translation. As modern readers who have staked much of our moral identity on our engagement with literature, we tend to identify with our canons, and we expect them to resemble us and our values. Our canon, one instinctively feels, ought to be rational, forward-looking, universalistic—like us. When literary exegetes are confronted with unsettling classics, there is a propensity toward strategic reinterpretation, as Barbara Herrnstein Smith explains:

> ...features that conflict intolerably with the interests and ideologies of subsequent subjects (and, in the West, with those generally benign 'humanistic' values for which canonical works are commonly celebrated)—for example, incidents or sentiments of brutality, bigotry, and racial, sexual, or national chauvinism—will be repressed or rationalized, and there will be a tendency among humanistic scholars and academic critics to 'save the text' by transferring the locus of its interest to more formal or structural features and/or allegorizing its potentially alienating ideology to some more general ('universal') level where it becomes more tolerable and also more readily interpretable in terms of contemporary ideologies. Thus we make texts timeless by suppressing their temporality.[15]

"Satan in Goray as Parable," *Prooftexts* (January 1989), 20. For a Freudian account of *Satan in Goray*, see Karl Malkoff's "Demonology and Dualism: The Supernatural in Isaac Singer and Muriel Spark" in *Critical Views of Isaac Bashevis Singer*, ed. Irving Malin (New York: NYU Press, 1969), 157. For psychological readings of his work in general, see Hadda's biography.

14. The discomfiture that surfaces with regard to Bashevis Singer's use of the supernatural and occult is akin to the scathing criticism he received from both traditional and revolutionary sectors of the community on account of his treatment of sexuality. Wisse has been especially eloquent on this point, arguing that his pornography was a legitimate artistic device to create an otherwise non-existent vocabulary for manifold forms of evil. See her introduction to *Satan in Goray*, xxiii–xxv.

15. Barbara Herrnstein Smith, "Contingencies of Value" in *Canons*, ed. Robert von Hallberg (Chicago: University of Chicago Press, 1984), 32. In his close reading of the short story "Zaydlus der ershter," Joseph Sherman demonstrates how this suppression could also be effected through sanitizing translation practices. See "Bashevis/Singer and the Jewish Pope" in *The Hidden Isaac Bashevis Singer*: 13–27 (cited above). Sherman's close analysis ends with a critique of the author for cynical and greedy complicity in the marketing of his altered work to non-Yiddish reading audiences. For a further development of this critique, see Irving Saposnik's essay "A Canticle for Isaac: A *Kaddish* for Bashevis" in the same volume (3–12).

Smith refers to classics that were "acceptable" when written but have since come to be regarded as problematic. How much more intractable is the case of a mischievous contrarian such as Bashevis Singer, who, in rejecting the Enlightenment promise of rational progress,[16] purposely wrote against the "interests and ideologies" of his primary audience, the increasingly secular and progressive Jews of Eastern Europe![17] The existence of "difficult" authors, whether the difficulty is ideological or aesthetic, argues for the occasional necessity of a different approach to canonicity: a hermeneutic not of automatic identification but of assumed distance. Often, in fact, we stand to learn the most by reading canonical texts as a challenge to our moral assumptions and predilections, and by honestly gauging the divergences.[18] Singer's deliberately irrational narrative elements must be held up as a mirror to contemporary humanistic values.

Allowing ourselves to enter Bashevis Singer's figured world of *dybbuks* and Satanic possession, we soon recognize that these grotesqueries animate one of this author's most abiding preoccupations: a theory of language whereby speech is less an ordered expression of consciousness than an unruly power unto itself. In short, language can be demonic. Thus Bashevis Singer employed a demonic vocabulary[19]—hearkening back to rabbinic demonology by way of kabbalah and European folklore[20]—to tap directly into a universe where utterance can come uncoupled from rational thought or human control and where speech constitutes the most potent possible kind of action. Though it will recur throughout his career in both fantastic and naturalistic guises, the theme of the power of language to harm is developed most fully in Bashevis Singer's first novel, *Satan in Goray.* Concentrat-

---

16. Dan Miron. "Passivity and Narration: The Spell of Bashevis Singer," trans. Uriel Miron, *Judaism* 41:1 (Winter 1992), 7–9. See also Novershtern, p. 52.

17. The fact that Bashevis Singer's (originally) oppositional and off-putting supernaturalism came to be viewed as tokens of a "quaint" folksiness as he moved into the literary mainstream through translation has to be one of the great cosmic jokes of twentieth-century literary history. Roskies details the simplification and bowdlerization of Bashevis Singer's later, American-period work to suit his newly expanded but deracinated audience. See *Bridge,* 304–306.

18. For more on the value of a vital canon that challenges the dominant culture, see Charles Altieri's *Canons and Consequences: Reflections on the Ethical Force of Imaginative Ideals* (Evanston, Ill.: Northwestern University Press, 1990),10.

19. "Demonic vocabulary" denotes more than the use of actual demonic characters. Indeed, Bashevis Singer's realistic fiction is rife with references to *dybbuks* and demonic possession, particularly in connection to speech that is candid, harmful, or inexplicable to the speaker. Even beyond these references, the author explores the evil element he sees as inherent to social conversation.

20. To my knowledge, no one has yet undertaken the work of pinpointing his folkloric sources systematically. This would doubtless be a fascinating study.

ing on this tale set in 1666—with its elements of possession and seduction, and its sharp rhetorical switchbacks—the present essay will trace the contours of Bashevis Singer's demonic view of speech. In so doing, our aim is less to catalogue various aspects of the author's uniqueness than to appreciate his usefulness in constructing an account of an anti-Enlightenment theory of language.

Possession, Seduction, and the Power of Speech

Bashevis Singer's ideas about language represented one of the most retrograde aspects of his art. Enlightenment, both secular and Jewish, was bound up in the notion that people are rational actors with full agency whose words directly voice their thoughts; words and deeds are separate and separately controllable. While earlier Yiddish authors surely were aware of liabilities inherent in the human use of language, such as dishonesty and futility, those concerns were nonetheless premised on the idea of a consciousness attempting (and succeeding ominously or else utterly failing at) expression—not on linguistic expression as independent of consciousness. However, Bashevis Singer continually recurred to the ways in which language can *deprive* people of agency and possibilities. The starkest portrayal of this deprivation is the phenomenon of possession, which subjects the mind to occupation by a foreign presence. Consider this climactic scene from *Satan in Goray*:

> For a long time now someone inside her had been thinking twistedly, someone had been asking questions, and replying—as though a dialogue went on in her mind, complicated, tedious, with neither start nor conclusion. For days and nights on end the argument extended. Lofty words were spoken, the Torah was explained meticulously, as well as secular works; the disputants were obdurate. Often Rechele tried to comprehend the grounds of the dispute and later to recall them; but they were elusive, like words in a dream.[21]

Rechele's possession by warring forces of good and evil allows for the estrangement of what transpires even within the boundaries of her own consciousness. She cannot comprehend, much less control, the conversation taking place within and eventually, through her. As the novel continues, the voice of evil gains the uppermost, and a *dybbuk*'s speech issues from Rechele's mouth. The speaker inhabiting the young woman is demonstrably alien, "For her voice was a woman's voice and the *dybbuk* cried with the voice of a man with such weeping and wailing that terror seized all that were there and their hearts dissolved with fear and their knees trembled" (222). Rechele's speech is involuntary, an action apart from and at

---

21. *Satan in Goray*, edition cited in fn. 4, 206. All citations of the novel are from this edition.

odds with her intentions. The sense of extreme linguistic determinism represented so starkly by the device of possession was both cause and symptom of the passivity and pessimism that have been so skillfully documented in Bashevis Singer's prose.[22]

The devil that possesses Rechele is one of the most coercive in Bashevis Singer's corpus. Indeed in *Satan in Goray* the demonic voice, characterized variously in different parts of the novel as belonging to Satan or to a *dybbuk*, completely overrides and muffles Rechele's capacity for self-expression. But this total hegemony is only the most extreme end of a spectrum of influencing or controlling others through speech that runs throughout the novel and Bashevis Singer's fiction more broadly. Usually, his underworldly persuaders proceed, silver-tongued, to win the consent of a victim in his or her own destruction.[23] Bashevis Singer's later, realistic fiction offers further evidence for the register in which we ought to read his early demons. In the realistic stories, the author translates the imagery of demons into more abstract manifestations; nevertheless, he continues to portray speech and conversational banter as exhibiting a demonic potency quite without respect to intentions or moral character. Nor is it correct to say that demons are entirely absent from those more conventional, inward-looking novels, for human beings are portrayed in demonic terms with surprising frequency. Lurking somewhere between metaphor and reality, Bashevis Singer's demons are the spokesmen for a complex brand of irony, and irony, according to one critic, "provides a ludic space in which reason and imagination cavort, neither succumbing to the other."[24] For Bashevis Singer, truth hovers in that imagined space between play and fright.

In the dark world of Goray, seduction is the speech-act par excellence,[25] and it is practiced by demons and humans alike: Rechele seduces Itche

---

22. Chiefly by Dan Miron in "Passivity and Narration" (7–9) and by Ruth Wisse in her introduction to *Satan in Goray* (xxxvii–xxxviii).

23. Bashevis Singer's demonic speakers reach the peak of their eloquence (that is to say, their power) in the series of *Yeytser-hore mayses* (*Memoirs of the Evil One*) narrated by *sheydim* or Satan himself. As Chone Shmeruk explains, Bashevis Singer intended to publish as a unified series his several tales with supernatural narrators, as indicated by the subtitle "From a Series of Stories: The Memoirs of the yeytser-hore," but ended up dividing these stories between books ("Use of Monologue," xvi).

24. Michael Saler, "Modernity, Disenchantment, and the Ironic Imagination," *Philosophy and Literature*. Dearborn: April 2004 (28:1), 137–149.

25. It is important to note that seduction would not have to be construed as a speech-act at all. One of the most famous seductions in Yiddish literature, that of Y.L. Peretz's eponymous *Monish* (1888), occurs through the visual medium and through the aural quality of the sweet and song-like voice of the *daytsh*'s daughter. However, until the final, climactic scene, there is no authorial attention to any specific words uttered by that mellifluous voice.

Mates, Gedaliya seduces both Rechele and the town of Goray, the devil seduces Rechele, and the dybbuk attempts to seduce everyone into letting him remain. Seduction is a dual form of speech that constitutes both an act *of* saying something and an act *in* saying something–to borrow the terms of J.L. Austin's classic discussion in *How to Do Things with Words.*[26] That is, the conversational exchange attending a seduction is simultaneously *representational*, or "about" something–philosophy, the beauty of the seduced, the palace of Lilith and Asmodeus, or the sin of adultery–and *executive*, or "doing" something–namely persuading the seduced to the will of the seducer. Unlike possession, in which a body and a mind are simply overtaken by an alien presence, seduction involves two parties in conversation, creating the appearance of a dialogue. But as we shall see, this hardly implies parity between the speakers; in the case of demons who can harness the omniscience and near omnipotence of Satan, especially, the exchange is hardly equal. With respect to the fiction of Bashevis Singer, in which seduction tends toward the hegemonic control of another person, these conversations might more accurately be termed a form of pseudo-dialogue. To seduce literally means to "lead aside," an etymology underscoring the fact that seduction is really about the creation of a differential power dynamic rather than the adultery, blasphemy, or other sins that are its proximate and putative aims. Seduction works not only because the delights that it promises are compelling, but also because its representative qualities mask its executive power. The apparent neutrality of conversation, the assumed dichotomy between talk and action, offers persuaders a kind of immunity as they pose provocative questions and utter sweet blandishments. Seduction, then, is the quintessential showcase for the power of language.

Filling the Vacuum of Silence

Rechele Babad, embodying her town, spends her brief life as an inarticulate victim. Eighteen years after Bogdan Chmielnitzky's catastrophic pogroms of 1648, she returns to Goray with her father, a mere shell of the man who was once the town's wealthiest citizen and lay leader. Rechele, his only remaining child, prefers confinement in her father's half-ruined house to venturing among the townspeople who seek to arrange a marriage for her. At seventeen, she is a woman apart from the town, marked as different by her silence, her intellectual pursuits, and her current of unchanneled sexual energy: "To the young wives and girls who came to call on her she said nothing, driving them away with her indifference. From early morning till night she sat alone, knitting stockings or merely reading in the Hebrew volumes she had brought from abroad. Sometimes she would stand at the

---

26. J. L. Austin, *How to Do Things With Words* (Cambridge, Mass.: Harvard University Press, 1975).

window braiding her hair."[27] By age seventeen, she has endured a lifetime's worth of suffering. Not only does the pogrom reach Goray just weeks after her birth, but her mother dies when she is five, and her father consigns her to the care of relatives in Lublin. Those relatives include her widowed uncle, a ritual slaughterer, and his mother-in-law, a crone who regularly beats Rechele and contains the girl's budding "wantonness" by keeping her in a perpetual state of terror with frightful tales of the beasts, goblins, robbers, and monsters that lie beyond the locked door of the ancient stone house where they live.

Rechele's childhood is a saga of inexpressible feelings and experiences exacerbated by a keen sense of lurking supernatural harms. After the minutely rendered illness and spooky death of her "Granny," Rechele is left alone with her uncle, who in his own pain or haste stifles any mutual solace he and his niece might have found. After the funeral, he blesses her according to a traditional formulation invoking the matriarchs. Then, "Rechele opened her lips to answer, but Uncle violently thrust the door open, and rushed out, almost extinguishing the candles."[28] Denied the opportunity for verbal exchange, Rechele soon loses the ability for verbal expression. That night, the eve of Yom Kippur, she is terrified at home alone while her uncle attends synagogue. But she remains isolated in her unchosen silence: "Rechele wanted to go out into the street and call people to her, but she was afraid to open the door in the dark passageway. She pursed her lips to shout, but the cry would not leave her throat."[29] It is on this night that Rechele experiences her first supernatural visitation. The departed Granny comes calling to her in a dream, haggard and bloody. The eeriness does not subside upon waking: "She awoke, drenched with sweat. There was a ringing in her ear, and she felt a sharp stab in her breast. She tried to cry but could not...There was a scarlet glow on the walls. Everything seethed, burst, crackled, as though the whole house were aflame."[30] A key aspect of her experience is that she is forcibly silenced, unable to cry out. Her uncle arrives home and discovers her lying in a fetal position with glazed eyes and clenched teeth.[31] Her recovery from this episode is slow and incomplete. One leg is paralyzed, laming her for life. There is other damage too. Thus far her desire to speak has been thwarted in various ways, but now she loses the physical capacity to speak altogether: "In the beginning Rechele could not speak at all. Later she regained her speech, but she suffered from all

---

27. *Satan in Goray*, 9.

28. Ibid., 63.

29. Ibid., 66.

30. Ibid., 67.

31. Ibid.

sorts of illnesses."[32] Lacking a logos of her own, Rechele's mind is a vessel waiting to be filled by the speech of others. Later in the novel, when she is possessed by a sequence of other voices—of prophecy, of disputation, of a demonic *dybbuk*, and of Satan himself—it is as if this unbidden speech comes to fill Rechele's long-standing vacuum of silence.[33]

But Rechele is not alone in her silence. "Less a heroine than a foil of events," as Professor Wisse puts it in her introduction to the novel,[34] Rechele's experience mirrors that of the town. Her appalling childhood is inseparable from the lasting damage done by Chmielnitzky's *haidamak* hordes, and as she comes under Satan's grip, the town comes under the grip of an Idea,[35] namely the idea that the Turkish Jew Sabbatai Zevi is the messiah who will imminently redeem the suffering of Israel and usher in an idyllic era. Sweeping across the map of European Jewry, Sabbatianism catches up both major metropolitan centers and sleepy little hamlets like the remote Goray, "the town at the end of the world."[36] Rechele's representative quality is fulfilled especially vividly in the arena of speech. If Satan fills a vacuum of silence in her pathetic existence, so too does he exploit an uneasy silence in the collective life of Goray. Just as her silence "invites" other voices to possess and speak through her,[37] so too the town's defensive posture of silence invites "possession" by the Sabbatian heresy.

"Silence is seemly for the wise"

The Goray to which the Babads return is a town bereft of any healthy or robust discourse, a town cowed by fear and awed by superstitious wonder into maintaining a pathological quietude. Before the pogroms, Rabbi Benish Ashkenazy had represented the town's vigorous, normative discourse of legal decision-making in a humane, rationalist tradition. A listing pillar, he manages to restore ritual order to the lives of his congregants but is unable to impose domestic order on his own warring family. By nature both studi-

---

32. Ibid.

33. Roskies also points out that "in her whole unhappy life, Rekhele has barely uttered an independent word" before she is seized by the spirit of prophecy (Turniansky festschrift, 13).

34. *Satan in Goray*, xxi.

35. The phrase is Sanford Pinsker's. See "Satan in Goray and the Grip of Ideas" in *Studies in American Jewish Literature*, ed. Daniel Walden (Albany: SUNY Press, 1981) 14–23.

36. *Satan in Goray*, 3.

37. In the novel's final section, the *dybbuk* offers this simple causal account of how he came to inhabit Rechele: "For one morning the woman desired to start a fire with two flint stones and the sparks would not light the wick; And she cried out the name of Satan: And the moment I heard this I entered her body." (227)

ous and personable, he withdraws by degrees from the fray and begins keeping to his room. He grows so impatient with the evil speech in his household that he demands silence:

> On the rare occasions when a member of his family came into his room to begin tattling and informing, Rabbi Benish would rise to his full height; his beard leaping like a living thing, one hand beating on the oaken table, the other pointing to the door.
>
> "Get—out!" he would shout. "I've heard enough. Pests!"[38]

As troubling to Rabbi Benish as the bickering at home are the "extraordinary rumors"[39] circulating abroad that the end of days is near. The rabbi "knew of these rumors and tales, but he heeded the verse in Amos: 'Therefore the prudent doth keep silence in such a time'—and he kept silent."[40] Instead of exerting himself as he had previously done to contain the influence of messianic zealots, the rabbi succumbs to diffidence and passivity, taking refuge in the classical Jewish regard for virtuous silence.[41]

His foes, most of whom are well-intentioned, also embrace silence both as part of their quest for sanctity and out of a fear of the evil to which speech may lead. When the devoutly ascetic Sabbatian packman Reb Itche Mates arrives in town, he is shown hospitality by a sympathizer, Reb Godel Chasid. All night long, Reb Godel hears the drone of his scholarly guest's lucubration, and himself sleepless, looks over to see the peddler bathed in supernal light. Confronted at daybreak with this evidence of his saintliness, Itche Mates cites the rabbinic adage "Silence is seemly for the wise."[42] At once a demurral and an adjuration to Reb Godel to keep secret that which he has witnessed, this dictum could serve as the motto for the town's Sabbatians with their shrouded, mystical expectations. The sect craves signs of the immanence of holiness, seeking it even, or especially, in circumstances or activities deemed suspect according to classical constructions of the Law. Thus, at the party celebrating Rechele's betrothal to Itche Mates, the bridegroom begins to dance with a woman known as Chinkele the Pious. Although dancing with members of the opposite sex is strictly proscribed, the skeptics present soon admit that extenuating, mystical circumstances obtain: "But soon they were silenced, sensing that his dance was not a simple one: great things were transpiring. So profound did the silence become that candle flames could be heard sputtering."[43] The holy must be protec-

---

38. *Satan in Goray*, 18.

39. Ibid., 19.

40. Ibid., 23.

41. See, for example, *Avot* 1:15, 1:17, and 3:17.

42. *Satan in Goray*, 74.

43. Ibid., 101.

tively enshrouded in silence. As the New Year approaches with its promise of redemption, the messianic fervor grows into frenzy and Sabbatai Zevi's adherents see portents everywhere, including in a protean cloud hovering in the sky to the east of Goray. Members of the sect make much of this cloud among themselves, but they squelch their excitement, for "all seemed to feel that at such a moment silence was best."[44] Here silence preserves the feelings of mystery and sectarian intimacy that would dispel all too easily at the slightest skeptical murmurings.

Not only is silence regarded as virtuous within the culture that Bashevis Singer portrays, but speech is attended by an aura of danger. Indeed, Rabbi Benish receives an impossibly convoluted letter from a rabbinical colleague warning him about the messianists generally and about the impious and harmful activities of Itche Mates specifically. In her introduction to the novel, Ruth Wisse characterizes the letter's rhetoric as "the stylistic antithesis to the narrator's uninflected prose." She continues, "Studded with formalities, slowed by circumlocutions, inflated by hyperbole, the Hebrew epistle from the great rabbi in Lublin takes far too long to get to the point of delivering its warning about the messengers of the false messiah, and finally offers its recipient too little ammunition to stop them."[45] The author of the letter chooses delay and obfuscation where clear, forceful speech is needed. Dismissing the apocalyptic intimations found by the Sabbatians in kabbalistic works, the diffident correspondent borrows rabbinic language to write, "I shall keep a curb on my mouth, that I may not be burned by their speech, for their bite is as the bite of the fox and their sting is as the sting of the scorpion...."[46] He goes on to say of Itche Mates, "...his lips drip with deceit. With a tongue of blandishment he doth speak, and the poison is under his gums."[47] Not only does this passage demonstrate the assumption that speech is harmful (almost physically so, like poison or a scorpion's sting), but it also reveals a problem with which the novel is continually concerned the imprecise application of ready-made language to complicated situations. Until this point in the story, Itche Mates has been portrayed as a sincere if misguided individual. There is, indeed, a deceitful utterer of blandishments in the tale, but this is not the melancholy packman. Rather it is the glib ritual slaughterer Reb Gedaliya who takes Rabbi Benish's vacated place as the town's ritual authority and who displaces Itche Mates as Rechele's husband. Excessive caution about the dangerous *aura* of speech hinders necessary communication, while truly demonic speech proliferates unsuspected and

---

44. Ibid., 178.

45. Ibid., xxxiv–xxxv.

46. Ibid., 87.

47. Ibid., 91.

unchecked. Through their righteous silence, the townsmen have paved the way for the demonic speech to come.

Pseudo-dialogues: Seduction and Disputation

Reb Gedaliya, a treacherously adept speaker, fills Goray's vacuum of silence just as the devil will fill Rechele's. He arrives in town with a winsome manner and fabulous stories of Sabbatai Zevi's exploits, all recounted with rich folk imagery. His prosperous girth and merry ways are the opposite of Itche Mates's bony asceticism, and the people find him charismatic: "His robust figure and sympathetic words won them over immediately."[48] He addresses each segment of Goray society in language it can appreciate: "For the scholars he had learned explications; ordinary people were delighted with his witticisms."[49] With his credentials as a ritual slaughterer, he once again makes meat available in Goray, which has had to subsist on a vegetarian diet since the pogroms. He seems to be a force for good. After all, "Never since Goray first became a town had the rich given so much to the poor. Reb Gedaliya completely overwhelmed the wealthy with his smooth tongue, and enchanted them with his grand manner."[50] Yet he is a seducer, and his smooth tongue is not reserved for noble goals. Gedaliya's verbal flow corresponds to images of overflow and inappropriate mixing, both evincing a lack of proper restraint. Animal blood runs freely from the tip of his smooth knife, and wine runs freely at his table; he is heedless of the Hasidic interdiction against mixing matzah with liquid at Passover time or the social taboo of seating women with men at a feast.[51] The special aim of Reb Gedaliya's smooth talk is to bring about the sexual liberation of Goray, a purpose for which he uses the pulpit:

> On the Great Sabbath before Passover, after Levi's explication, Reb Gedaliya preached a sermon that was full of admonitions and consolations.... He scolded them that so many young men and girls were still unmarried. Such neglect of the principle of fruitfulness would delay their redemption. He demonstrated by means of cabala that all the laws in the Torah and the Shul-

---

48. Ibid., 141.

49. Ibid., 143.

50. 146. In the original: *"Reb Gedaliye hot zey greylekh ibergeredt mit zayn geshlifener tzung un farblift mit zayn hadras-ponim."* (119) The verb *ibergeredt* is significant. He overwhelms people with speech.

51. The *seder* that Gedaliya hosts is described as follows: "The women sat with the menfolk, as Reb Gedaliya had bidden. They mingled the unleavened bread with the meats, the dumplings with the pancakes, and all ate and drank together, like one family." (150) This imagery resonates with the midrashic correlation between a man's bread and his wife. The improper overstepping of boundaries in this regard is palpable in Reb Gedaliya's seating Rechele (still married to Itche Mates) at his right hand at this very meal and complimenting her beauty.

chan Aruch referred to the commandment to be fruitful and multiply; and that, when the end of days was come not only would Rabbi Gershom's ban on polygamy become null and void, but all the strict "Thou shalt nots," as well.... Reb Gedaliya explained all these things in a pleasant way and with many parables. He recited from memory whole sections from the Zohar and other works of cabala and adorned his speech with mystical combinations and permutations.[52]

This chain of logic is pure sophistry. Under the guise of moral exhortation, he incites the people to sin, and he does so with the kind of rhetorical skill that characterizes the demonic narrators in the "Memoirs of the Evil One," which Bashevis Singer would begin to publish a decade later. In Bashevis Singer's world, verbal license is closely allied with sexual license, and oral depravity leads inexorably to sexual depravity. Gedaliya's sermon serves as the prologue to his own appropriation of Itche Mates's wife.

This is not to say that Rechele is an innocent victim. In fact, she makes such an attractive target for satanic possession because a licentious streak animates her otherwise disaffected existence. Her first encounter with Itche Mates is a small-scale study in Bashevian seduction. The peddler, who is also something of a scribe, goes from door to door checking the ritual fitness of the *mezuzah* scroll on the doorpost. Arriving at the Babad residence, he finds an almost feral girl with a wild laugh, disheveled hair full of feathers and straw, bare feet, a torn dress, and mad eyes. Clutching the household's unusually blemished *mezuzah*, he asks,

> "Are you a married woman, or a maiden?"
> "A maiden," answered Rechele brazenly. "Like Jeptha's daughter, a sacrifice to God!"
> The *mezuzah* fell out of Reb Itche Mates's hand. Never in his whole life, not since he had first stood on his feet, had he heard such talk.[53]

This brief seduction, which results in Itche Mates's proposal of marriage, proceeds through a conversational topic that appears to be sanctioned, a Bible story. But the effect is nearly obscene, as indicated by the fact that Itche Mates drops a holy object upon hearing Rechele's unholy riposte. The conversation hinges on the dual sense of the Hebrew/Yiddish word *besule*, rendered here as "maiden." Itche Mates employs the word to inquire after her social status; she replies by invoking the same word to refer to her sexual status. It is as if he asked casually, "Are you single or married?" and she responded gleefully, "I'm a virgin!" Rechele's speech here has great power, but Rechele does not have the power of speech.

With precipitous speed, however, the seducer becomes the seduced. The middle section of the novel details the twin seductions that Rechele and

---

52. *Satan in Goray*, 147–148.

53. Ibid., 75 (English); 67–68 (Yiddish).

the town undergo at the hands of the ritual slaughterer. When the news finally reaches Goray that Sabbatai Zevi is a false messiah and has converted to Islam, the town greets the intelligence with its typical silence: "The people of Goray were completely taken aback. They were too shocked to open their mouths; they seemed to have lost the power of speech."[54] This ashamed quietism is all the invitation Satan needs to "dance in the streets."[55] The dejected town falls into chaos, with war raging between the Sabbatians and their opponents, and theologically motivated sin rampant among the Sabbatians.[56]

Corresponding to the town's schism, Rechele's psyche plays reluctant host to a disputation (*shtreyt*) between the sacred, which "had a face, but no body"[57] and the profane, which "grew stronger from day to day, entangling her."[58] The disputation is a literary trope based on a historical reality. During the Middle Ages, Jews were called on by Christian and Muslim rulers under whose sovereignty they lived to respond to polemical attacks on their faith. At their height, the disputations were formal, public performances, the content of which was subsequently recorded by the participants or witnesses, writing for each side. The disputation was formally dialogic, but this was just a pretense, and sometimes even the pretense was weak. The Christian account of the Barcelona disputation of 1263, the most publicly open event of its kind, emphasizes that the outcome of the debate was a foregone conclusion, since the certainty of Christianity "cannot be subjected to debate" (*que propter sui certitudinem non est in disputatione ponenda*).[59]

---

54. Ibid., 191.

55. Ibid., 200.

56. As the novel itself explains this perverse twist on Lurianic kabbala, "According to those who supported this interpretation, the generation before redemption had to become completely guilty; consequently, they went to great lengths to commit every possible offense. They were secretly adulterous, ate the flesh of the pig and other unclean foods, and performed those labors expressly forbidden on the Sabbath as most to be avoided." (197)

57. *Satan in Goray*, 206.

58. Ibid., 208.

59. Bashevis Singer, in employing the trope of the disputation, did not have to reach all the way back to the medieval period. Haim Hillel Ben-Sasson writes that "As late as 1933, a representative of Protestant Christianity, Karl Ludwig Schmidt, declared to his Jewish partner, as representative of German Jewry, the Zionist and philosopher Martin Buber, in a Christian-Jewish dialogue before a gathering of Jews: 'The evangelical theologian who has to talk to you, must talk to you as a member of the Church of Jesus Christ, must endeavor to talk in a manner that will convey the message of the Church to Jewry. He must do this even if you would not have invited him to do so. The assertion of a mission to you may have a somewhat bitter taste as if intending an attack; but such an attack precisely involves caring about you as Jews—so that you may live with us as

The best result for which the representatives of the Jewish community could hope in these antagonistic conversations was a draw. The numerous works chronicling disputations tend to present polished, hermetic argumentation that served more to affirm the faith of the believers than to convince the other side.[60]

Bashevis Singer refashions this trope so that the disputants are not members of different religions but the universally warring forces of holiness and impurity, or as Jacob Sloan's translation styles them, "the Sacred" and "the Profane." Just as the medieval Jew was bound to lose the ritualized argument before bishop or king, so too it is only a matter of time before the Sacred gives way to the Profane. The Sacred, with his "grandfatherly grace" and his litany of blessings and pious tales, cannot stand up against the irresistible pornographic allure of the Profane, who "jested and mocked profusely" enough to bring "Rechele to the verge of laughter, though she knew that to be sinful."[61] Skillfully weaving together visual depiction with oral titillation,

> The Profane called the nether parts of men and women by their crudest names: he showed Rechele vile sights, and discovered obscene meanings in Biblical verses. Nor did he spare the patriarchs and King David, Bathsheba and Queen Esther. He depicted the copulation of beasts and animals, an ox with a woman, and a man with a sow. He told tales of women who lay at night with monstrous men, and of girls who had assignations with goblins and evil spirits.[62]

The Profane does not create wild, new obscenities *ex nihilo*. Rather, he traffics in words and scenes that are latent in her consciousness, such as crude names for body parts or images of fornication. He simply unleashes existing language that is normally suppressed. By rendering his obscenities explicit, the Profane uses the representative function of language as cover for the executive function of gaining control over Rechele. Just as sexuality is a latent force in human culture, Bashevis Singer suggests, messianism is a latent force in Jewish culture—all the more potent and vital for its long periods of disuse. The Profane works through indirection, through irresistible but gross humor, as when he playfully rhymes on Rechele's name: "*Rekhele, du host a l....*"[63] Rendered literally as "Rechele, you have a *l...*," the rhyme makes clear that the missing word is *lekhele*, translating as "opening" or,

---

our brethren in our German fatherland as throughout the world'" *(Theologische Blaetter,* 12 [1933], 258 as cited in *Encyclopedia Judaica s.v.* "Disputation").

60. Ibid.

61. *Satan in Goray*, 207.

62. Ibid., 208.

63. Yiddish, 167. All Yiddish citations are from *Der sotn in goray un andere dertseylungen* (Tel Aviv: Y.L. Perets, 1955).

crudely speaking, "vagina." So completely does the Profane appropriate Rechele that he incorporates his obscenity into her very name. Bashevis Singer's disputation is seduction by other means. Both verbal processes have the appearance of a dialogue, but both are ultimately hegemonic and inexorable. This is the perfect image for the author, who wishes to conjure an irresistible messianism that knows no half-measures. Once its latent power is set loose, it will not be contained until its force is spent and Goray is reduced to abject misery.

The Critique of Available Language

The devil's own seductive speech—his verbal slideshow of pornographic images—is the book's starkest portrait of the latent power of a ready, resonant discourse. More subtly, this question is addressed throughout the tale and even embedded in its very narration. Most discussions of the novel's narration have dwelt on the disjunction between "the naïve and unreliable observer" who recounts all but the final two chapters, and the finale penned by a "pious fanatic"[64] writing in the manner of a Yiddish morality tract.[65] Yet one distinctive rhetorical feature that cuts across the book's sections, sub-genres[66] and narrative modes has received little attention. That is the use of epic catalogues, extensive lists of heaped-up details, usually of either a wondrous or a grotesque nature. The subjects of these catalogues include the *haidamak* atrocities of 1648, the miraculous deeds attributed to Sabbatai Zevi, the abominations of the Sabbatians after receiving word of Sabbatai Zevi's apostasy, the torments Rechele undergoes at the hands of Satan and her possessing *dybbuk*, the antics of that *dybbuk* among the townsfolk, and the torments that he fears at the hands of "the outer ones." These catalogues display the secretarial sensibility of a narrator who does not feel responsible for sifting through the information he provides. Although sometimes he uses distancing language such as "was reported" and "as the legend went," he just as often reports the most fantastic details with deadpan immediacy, betraying no sense of questioning irony. With a studied neutrality that masks his lack of responsibility, the narrator calls them as he sees them.

Unleashing these paratactic floods—writing in what Miron calls "a free-flowing and evenly rhythmed narrative sequence"[67]—Bashevis Singer channels deep wells of Jewish rhetoric. Consider the opposition between the pro-Sabbatian rhetoric that Gedaliya brings with him to Goray, versus the

---

64. Both phrases are cited from Wolitz, 17.

65. See Wolitz ibid.; Wisse xxxiii–xxxvi; and Miron, 15–16.

66. Wolitz offers the most probing discussion of the novel's use of traditional Yiddish genres. See especially 15–16.

67. Miron, 16.

subsequent account of the sectarians' devolution into total sin after their messiah has proved false. The narrator attributes speech to Gedaliya, and then steps out of the way, relating the details through free indirect discourse:

> Sabbatai Zevi—he related—having already, with God's help, been revealed as the Messiah, had departed for Stamboul to claim the crown of the Sultan who ruled the Land of Israel. Not through the might of hosts had Sabbatai Zevi conquered, but through the power of lords and prophets from the other side of the River Samation [sic] who accompanied him riding on the backs of elephants, leopards, and water oxen. Sabbatai Zevi himself (may his name be praised!) rode before them on a wild lion, wearing garments of purple and spun gold and numerous precious stones that shone in the darkness. A sash of pearls girded his loins. His right hand clasped a scepter, and he was fragrant as the Garden of Eden. The sea parted before him, as it had in days of old for our Master Moses (peace be with him!), and he walked upon dry land in the midst of the waters, he and those that were with him. A pillar of fire went before him to show the way, and angels flew after him, singing hymns in his praise. At first the kings and princes of the earth had dispatched hosts of giants with drawn swords against Sabbatai Zevi, that they might take him prisoner. But a torrent of great stones rained from heaven as had been promised for the day of Gog and Magog, and all the giants perished. The world was astounded.... The Holy Temple would be restored, the Tables of the Law returned to the Holy Ark, and a High Priest would enter the Holy of Holies. Sabbatai Zevi, the redeemer, would reign throughout the world....[68]

These references weave together motifs from the long history of Jewish literature. Some formulations evoke biblical style ("Not through the might...") or events (the crossing of the Red Sea); others conjure folktales (the River Sambation); still others, talmudic and kabbalistic legends about the end of days. Rhetoric used to the opposite effect, to express fascination at the sect's abominations, similarly smacks of differing historical periods and genres. Legal prohibitions meld with folk traditions in painting a portrait of the ultimate in Jewish corruption:

> And the deeds of the [Sabbatian] Faithful were truly an abomination. It was reported that the sect assembled at a secret meeting place every night; extinguishing the candles, they would lie with each other's wives. Reb Gedaliya was said to have secreted a whore sent him by the sect in Zamosc somewhere in his house without the knowledge of his wife, Rechele. A copper cross hung on his breast, under the fringed vest, and an image lay in his breast pocket. At night Lilith and her attendants Namah and Machlot visited him, and they consorted together. Sabbath eve, dressing in scarlet garments and a fez, like a Muslim, he accompanied his disciples to the ruins of the old castle near Goray. There Samael presented himself to them, and they all prostrated

---

68. *Satan in Goray*, 138.

themselves together before a clay image. Then they danced in a ring with torches in their hands. Rabbi Joseph de la Reina, the traitor, descended from Mount Seir to join them in the shape of a black dog. Afterward, as the legend went, they would enter the castle vaults and feast on flesh from the living—rending live fowl with their hands, and devouring the meat with the blood. When they had finished feasting, fathers would know their daughters, brothers their sisters, sons their mothers....[69]

This rhetoric reverberates in the Jewish consciousness because it too is a latent verbal force within Jewish culture. Should one wish to portray the messiah's advent, one may call on a host of vivid images associated with the eschaton; should one wish to discredit an opponent, powerful language stands at the ready. With these catalogues of wonders and grotesqueries, Bashevis Singer explores the problematics of readily available language, so resonant and so susceptible to abuse. Like a garment of whole cloth ready to be donned, this language awaits the man or the demon who will utter the words that must lead inexorably to frenzy. The narrator's nonchalance actually masks a perilous diffidence; his willingness to apply ready-made language to a situation is of a piece with his failure to analyze and question. He slaps on pre-existing rhetoric to describe and dispatch a situation rather than trying to understand its particular nuances. This tactic evades moral responsibility for speech and for verbal discrimination even as it pronounces moral judgments. Readily available language is a seduction waiting to happen, and through his neutrality, the narrator abets—even perpetrates—this seduction.

There are liabilities, Bashevis Singer suggests, in harboring a deep-seated collective discourse, a strain of rhetoric sure to set every heart thumping and turn every hand toward action. The most consequential seductions are not those between individuals but those on a national scale: the Sabbatianism that grips Goray and the communism that the author views as its twentieth-century analogue. Modernist authors have typically retreated from the political sphere into the exploration of individual subjectivity and consciousness. In choosing a highly figural means of representation, one that externalizes moral conflict, Bashevis Singer insists on political engagement. He does so not in earnest, direct fashion like the social realists or sweatshop poets, but through folkloric means, deployed with a measure of ludic irony.

"Why demons," asks the narrator of Bashevis Singer's story "The Last Demon," "when man himself is a demon? Why persuade to evil someone who is already convinced?"[70] Why demons, indeed, asks the author himself, as he shifts from the Old World to the new, and from the fantastic to the realistic modes. Throughout his career, Bashevis Singer would present

---

69. Ibid., 201.

70. *The Collected Stories* (New York: Farrar, Straus, and Giroux, 1982), 179.

speech as a potently destructive force independent of thought or human will. His starkest portrayals of this force involve demonic possession; however, even in his realistic novels, Singer probes the structure of seduction, which remains for him the defining human speech-act. The underworld of demons and *dybbuks* is surprisingly close to the underworld of criminality and even to the fashionable moral bankruptcy to which the enlightened salon culture of conversation inevitably leads in his novels. Over the course of a lifetime, Bashevis naturalized the fantastic in both senses of the word: he integrated it seamlessly into the realistic world,[71] and he conferred on his *dybbuks* a secure citizenship in not only the modern Jewish canon but the modern canon, period.

---

71. This is a point that I take up elsewhere, but that can be conveniently encapsulated by tracing the *dybbuk* imagery in the novel *Shadows on the Hudson*.

Gimpel the Simple and
on Reading from Right to Left

DAVID G. ROSKIES

Jewish texts had always been read from right to left. Even when there was recourse to translation—into Judeo-Arabic, Yiddish or Judezmo—the same Hebrew alphabet was used. Came the era of Emancipation (or the hope thereof) and the direction changed from left to right. Mendelssohn's *Biur*, his collaborative translation of the Hebrew Bible into Hochdeutsch, still appeared in Hebrew characters and in the medieval Yiddish typeface. But before long, what was not written *a priori* in *galkhes*, a non-Jewish alphabet, was rendered accessible, both to non-Jews and to rapidly acculturating Jews, through translation into a coterritorial language. A reading strategy in which Jewish texts both classical and modern were read first in one direction then in the other became the next best thing, a cultural holding pattern.

Where bilingual editions of a Jewish classic exist—the prayer book or the Pentateuch, for example—the common practice is for the Hebrew-character text to be laid out on the right-hand side of the page and the Roman-character translation to appear on the left. Opening as they do from right-to-left, these editions signal their "Jewishness," even as their bilingual format trumpets the integration of the Hebraic canon into the print culture of the West. Yet the actual, I would argue, dyslexic layout makes the comparison of text and translation exceedingly difficult. What purports to be a bilingual edition is functionally monolingual, "two solitudes," as they were wont to say in Canada. The reader needs a wide-angle lens—or a finger on opposite sides of the book—to move from text to translation. Imagine, if you will, a reverse procedure. Placing the right-to-left version where it visually belongs, on the left-hand side of the page, is a way of granting it equality, encouraging the modern reader, for once, to read *competitively* along a justified margin that does not privilege one direction over another. Which way the book opens is no longer culturally relevant. I call this a postintegrationist reading of a Jewish classic.

* * *

By any measure, the short list of modern Yiddish classics includes Isaac Bashevis Singer's "Gimpel the Fool." Yet its canonical status was achieved at a price. When, in 1950, Singer made his first bid to compete on the world literary stage with the publication by Knopf of *The Family Moskat*, he failed, both because his ambitious family saga was upstaged by Knopf's

319

other "Jewish" offering of the season, John Hersey's *The Wall*, and because
the few "slots" reserved for a Yiddish novelist in English were still occupied
by his late brother, I. J. Singer, and his bête noire, Sholem Asch.[1] Three
years passed and Singer was reborn as a teller of droll and demonic tales
from the Old Country. This happened, as everyone knows, when Saul Bellow's translation of "Gimpel the Fool" appeared in the May 1953 issue of
The Partisan Review in advance of being anthologized in the enormously
influential Howe and Greenberg *Treasury of Yiddish Stories* (Viking, 1954).
As a result, I. B. Singer all but occluded Yitskhok Bashevis; Bellow's translation was universally believed to have inaugurated Singer's American career,
and the left-to-right reading of "Gimpel the Fool" assumed cultural primacy,
supremacy, and exclusivity.[2] Whereas the Yiddish audience contented itself
with reading Bashevis's novels in installments, rarely, if ever, in book form,
and could purchase only two commercially published collections of his stories, I. B. Singer's long and short fiction was available in bookstores and
supermarkets everywhere. The right-to-left reading of Bashevis's "*Gimpl
tam*," as a consequence, was relegated to antiquarian study.

1. Compensatory Readings

Readers of "Gimpel the Fool" in Bellow's translation can be divided into
two categories: those who have benefited from Ruth Wisse's chapter on
"Gimpel the Fool" in *The Schlemiel as Modern Hero* and those who have
not.[3] Those who have not find it impossible to resist patronizing a character
who speaks with a Yiddish accent. They cannot view him other than as a
parodic figure.

The most common practice is to lay Gimpel on the couch. Here is a character who avoids confrontation because he cannot effect change. His is a
delusionary way of coping by denying reality. His repression of anger and
his practice of "rationalizing" his behavior and that of others represent the
male Jewish coping mechanism. Gimpel in this scheme is either a species of
Jewish pathology or of "ghetto Jew."[4] Janet Hadda, thus far the lone psycho-
therapist to have treated Gimpel in his mother tongue, labels him a masoch-
ist, but does not lay the blame on the sins of his tribe. Rather, it is Gimpel's
orphanhood that Hadda sees at the root of his behavior, as she tracks the
progress of his life from repressed mourning, anger, and ambivalence to

---

1. See Janet Hadda, *Isaac Bashevis Singer: A Life* (New York and Oxford: Oxford Univer-
    sity Press, 1997), chap. 7.

2. Ibid., 124; Sidra DeKoven Ezrahi, *Booking Passage: Exile and Homecoming in the
    Modern Jewish Imagination* (Berkeley: University of California Press, 2000), 202.

3. Ruth R. Wisse, "Holocaust Survivor," in *The Schlemiel as Modern Hero* (Chicago: The
    University of Chicago Press, 1971), chap. 4.

4. On 67–68 of *The Schlemiel as Modern Hero*, Wisse summarizes some of these argu-
    ments.

mental health.[5] All attempts to lay Gimpel on the couch begin with the premise that there is something very wrong with him.

Those, in contrast, whose point of departure is Wisse's definition of Gimpel as a hero-in-defeat, the schlemiel who "becomes a hero when real action is impossible and reaction remains the only way a man can define himself," have generated a number of extremely provocative "compensatory readings." For Sidra DeKoven Ezrahi, Gimpel, precariously situated between faith and memory, remembering and forgetting, is the ideal culture bearer for the postwar American Jew. Gimpel also occupies a place of honor in her project of charting "exile and homecoming in the modern Jewish imagination." As the narrator of his own hapless fate, Gimpel becomes nothing less than the cultural ambassador of East European Jewry, and as a self-professed wandering teller of tales he embodies the homelessness endemic to the Jewish condition.[6]

Subjecting Bellow's translation to a careful and theoretically sophisticated analysis, Hana Wirth-Nesher reveals the compensatory strategies of a master negotiator between Jewish and Christian cultures. She demonstrates, for example, how the seven Yiddish words that Bellow retained in his translation serve as authenticating markers of the lost culture of Jewish Eastern Europe, point to the growing visibility of Jewish symbols in American culture, and bespeak postwar nostalgia for the world of the "shtetl."[7]

Both Ezrahi and Wirth-Nesher draw special attention to the gaps between the Yiddish and English versions of the story. As first noted by Chone Shmeruk, Bashevis carefully distinguished between the semantic fields of *nar, narishkeyt,* and *makhn tsu nar* on the one hand, and Gimpel's self-understanding as a *tam,* a simpleton, or person of simple faith, on the other.[8] By creating this semantic distinction, Gimpel can distance and protect himself from a world that judges his behavior as mere foolishness. This marker of his innocence, the key word, *tam,* which carries deep theological and literary-historical echoes (of which more below), was sacrificed in Bellow's translation. "Gimpel the Simple" would have rendered the title utterly laughable. Contrariwise, Wirth-Nesher makes much of an avoidable gap, the mildly anti-Christian phrase about "Baby Jesus" that disappeared between the Yiddish and English versions. Whether the editorial excision was the

---

5. Janet Hadda, "Gimpel the Full," *Prooftexts* 10 (1990): 283–295.

6. DeKoven Ezrahi, 202, 206–207; "compensatory readings" is her felicitous phrase.

7. Hana Wirth-Nesher, *Call It English: The Languages of Jewish American Literature* (Princeton and Oxford: Princeton University Press, 2006), 103–104.

8. Chone Shmeruk, "The Use of Monologue as a Narrative Technique in the Stories of Isaac Bashevis Singer," in Yitskhok Bashevis-Zinger, *Der shpigl un andere dertsey-lungen* (Jerusalem: The Hebrew University of Jerusalem Yiddish Department, 1975), n. 35. Full of disdain for left-to-right readings of Bashevis, Shmeruk relegated this critical observation to a footnote!

work of Saul Bellow or Eliezer Greenberg (I vote for Greenberg), Wirth-Nesher sees it as a sign of the "timid reemergence of Jewish American liter-ature in the shadow of the Holocaust," which did not as yet "take the risk of being unecumenical."[9] Both of these extended readings, for all that they have recourse to the Yiddish original, go from left-to-right. Both strive to recontextualize the story within a Jewish American discourse of the early 1950s. Such readings are indispensable if we are to understand how Singer was later to become an American classic, the first non-English author to be included in the prestigious Library of America. But because both readings focus on the traditional locutions that were sacrificed in translation, on words or phrases that somehow resisted transmission, they privilege certain interpretive possibilities over others. "Gimpel the Fool," they argue, was meant to be read as an emblem of loss, a transcript of equivocal faith, an act of cultural mediation—if not by Singer himself, then most assuredly by Bel-low, Greenberg, and Howe.

So successful were Bellow and Howe that Gimpel's ironic sensibility has been absorbed into the American mainstream. Jimmy Carter can quote from it verbatim. Thanks to Ezrahi, Wirth-Nesher and other students of Jewish American literature, moreover, the challenge laid down by Wisse's *The Schlemiel as Modern Hero* has been taken up and validated. In the tran-script of Jewish American fiction, Singer's schlemiel-hero occupies center stage. When properly decoded, this fiction yields a rich Yiddish palimpsest. Yet the autonomous, right-to-left version of the story that lies on the oppo-site page, perhaps because it was never meant to be there, or was meant to be superseded, remains illegible.

2. Competitive Readings

Gimpel is clearly a throwback, an anachronism. The question is, A throwback to what? Wisse was the first to demonstrate that the return to storytelling, monologue, comic exegesis, allegory, and other pre-maskilic forms of self-expression in modern Yiddish culture was accompanied by a concomitant retrieval of anti-heroic models of behavior. Sobered by the cri-sis of emancipation, Yiddish writers, beginning with Abramovitsh in the 1870s, discovered alternative coping strategies in their own backyard. Among the several lines of literary lineage that can be said to converge in the figure of Gimpel *tam* is I. L. Peretz's "Bontshe Shvayg."[10] Written in

---

9. Ibid., 106: Blaming Eliezer Greenberg for the omission, Naomi Seidman sees it as a sign of "Jewish Americanization." Contrariwise, she sees the reference to Baby Jesus as key to a subversive retelling of the Gospels meant for Jews alone. See "Who's the Fool? Gimpel in English," in *Faithful Renderings: Jewish-Christian Differences and the Politics of Translation* (Chicago and London: The University of Chicago Press, 2006), 255–263.

10. For a recent translation, see "Bontshe Shvayg," trans. Hillel Halkin, in *The I. L. Peretz Reader*, ed. Ruth R. Wisse, 2nd ed. (New Haven: Yale University Press, 2002), 146–152.

1894, it appears to be the cradle-to-grave story of a hidden saint, a *lamed-vovnik,* who suffers in this world in order to receive his reward in the world-to-come. Like Gimpel, Bontshe is the whipping boy of society. Among the many indignities he is made to suffer, Bontshe is rendered impotent by a botched circumcision, such that his benefactor sires his only son, who in turn kicks Bontshe out of the house. Bontshe ends his mortal existence in a charity ward, surrounded by strangers. Gimpel suffers a remarkably similar fate. Read contextually, however, as a product of Peretz's so-called Radical Period, "Bontshe Shvayg" is a screed on the hallowed ideal of passivity. It ends with a call for the Bontshes of this world to throw off their shackles. Key to its subversive message is the absolute dichotomy between the pitiless world below and the sentimental world above.[11] Key to Gimpel's triumph, as we shall see, is the blurring of all such distinctions. Gimpel, Dan Miron has argued, is Bontshe's positive reincarnation.[12]

It is a measure of Bashevis's literary self-confidence that he chose Peretz as the precursor worthy of taking on.[13] It is a measure of his confidence in reaching a competent Yiddish reader that he placed his bet on a seemingly innocent monologue in the folk vein. "*Gimpel tam,*" we learn from Shmeruk's text-critical edition of Bashevis's monologues, first appeared in the Passover 1945 issue of the New York-based *Yidisher kemfer.* A Labor Zionist weekly, the *Kemfer,* as it was fondly known, catered to a more discriminating reader, especially through its rich holiday supplements. Thus "*Gimpl tam*" was intended for Judaically literate readers who were committed to some form of Jewish national identity.[14]

11. My coming of age as a Jewish reader began the day my sister, Ruth Wisse, fresh from Columbia University with a Masters in Yiddish and Comparative Literature, let me sit in on one of her classes, conducted at the local Y, where they just happened to be studying this Peretz story—a staple of the Folkshule, the Yiddish-Hebrew Day School, curriculum we had both completed. Here, among grown-ups, she revealed that the point of Bontshe's request for a *bulke mit puter,* a hot buttered roll each morning, was not to extol pacifism but precisely the opposite, to burlesque Jewish passivity. For more on Peretz's radical period, see David G. Roskies, *A Bridge of Longing: The Lost Art of Yiddish Storytelling* (Cambridge, Mass.: Harvard University Press, 1985), 99–114.

12. See Dan Miron, "Passivity and Narration: The Spell of Bashevis Singer," in *The Image of the Shtetl and Other Studies of the Modern Jewish Literary Imagination* (Syracuse: Syracuse University Press, 2000), 340.

13. In August 1943, Bashevis divided Polish-Yiddish literature into two rival camps, one that had followed the narrowly conceived "ridicule" of Mendele, or the "path breaking," "profoundly Jewish" and "eternal" path inaugurated by Peretz. See "Concerning Yiddish Literature in Poland," trans. Robert Wolf, *Prooftexts* 15 (1995): 119.

14. The *Kemfer* was a folio-sized journal, printed in double columns, averaging 20 to 22 pages an issue. The Passover edition for 1945 (No. 593), by contrast, was 96 pages long. "*Gimpl tam*" appeared in fourth place, following Yiddish translations of Moses'

However they read Bashevis's intent, whether merely to conjure up and memorialize a simpler time or to beat the master Yiddish folk stylist I. L. Peretz at his own game, or whether they greeted Gimpel as a welcome guest at their seder table or as the first in an uncomfortable flow of Holocaust survivors, one thing was clear to the readers of Yiddish: Gimpel did not speak with an accent.

Read from right-to-left, a Jewish classic must allow for multiple interpretations. Here then are three possible readings of "*Gimpl tam*": one grounded in the mock heroic genre, and therefore profoundly indebted to Wisse; one grounded in the story's orality, and therefore profoundly indebted to Bakhtin; and one grounded in its intertextuality, and therefore profoundly indebted to Rabbi Nahman of Braslav. These Yiddish-in-Yiddish readings, it will be seen, add up to one cumulative, anthological, Mikra'ot Gedolot, which in turn contribute to an extremely competitive reading across a justified margin.

3. Gimpel as a Love Story

As the boldest in a series of pranks and orchestrated hoaxes, Gimpel the baker's apprentice is bullied into marrying Elka, the town whore. That Gimpel is the obvious fall-guy is signaled by his name, which in German means "dunce, ninny, simpleton," and who in Frampol is called by seven other nicknames. The timing of his marriage is also significant. The whole town gets involved in marrying him off when Gimpel has just about had enough. "*Kh'hob shoyn gevolt avek in an ander shtot, ober dervayl hot der oylem mir genumen redn a shidekh. S'heyst geredt? M'hot mir di poles opgerisn*" ("I wanted to go off to another town, but then everyone got busy matchmaking, and they were after me so they nearly tore my coat tails off").[15] Normally, the role of *redn a shidekh*, "negotiating [lit. talking] a match" is relegated to the parents of the bride and groom. But Gimpel is an orphan, an additional comic flaw. Moreover, he realizes, the bride herself "was no chaste maiden, but they told me she was a virgin pure." Resorting to verbal bullying, the townspeople "talked at me and talked until I got water on the ear." Gimpel sizes up the situation perfectly well. Realizing that his destined bride is a whore with a bastard child, he reconsiders in light of three pragmatic considerations: (1) acting against the collective will of the people of Frampol is impossible; (2) Elka presumably agrees to be bound by the social conventions of matrimony; and (3) who is he to argue

---

Song at the Sea, and an excerpt from the talmudic tractate Pesahim. Also appearing for the first time in this rich holiday supplement was Aaron Zeitlin's remarkable "Monologue in Plain Yiddish."

15. All Yiddish quotations are from "*Gimpl tam*," in Bashevis-Zinger, *Der shpigl un andere dertseylungen*, 33–47. For the English version, the reader may consult any edition of Singer's stories.

with life? "No one," he says, citing a Yiddish idiom, "dies with his fringed undergarment on."

> *Kh'hob gezen, az kh'el shoyn keyn gantser fun zeyere hent nisht aroys, trakht ikh: mayn kapore iz es. Ikh bin der mantsbil, nisht zi. Oyb s'iz ir lib, iz mir nikhe. Tsveytns, m'kon dokh nisht shtarbn in laybserdakl.*
>
> I saw then that I wouldn't escape them so easily and I thought: They're set on making me their butt. But when you're married the husband's the master, and if that's all right with her it's agreeable to me too. Besides, you can't pass through life unscathed, nor expect to.

Irony is predicated on the ability to balance two competing truth systems. Here, one truth invokes the norms of a patriarchal society wherein he will be lord and master. The other truth, equally gendered (for only men are required by Jewish law to wear *tzitzith*), invokes the School of Hard Knocks. You die as you live, without your sacred trappings. No one is privileged, male or otherwise. This is the first of several proverbial phrases that Gimpel will invoke when recapping the vicissitudes of his life. How fitting that it appears in the context of matrimony.

The next step is for the bride and groom to meet. A more perfunctory, comical, courtship can hardly be imagined: he finds her doing the wash and the stench is overwhelming. Rhetorically too Elka assumes an offensive posture, vigorously denying all the rumors, claiming to be a virgin, and insisting that the little boy is her brother. Then, turning social convention on its head, she demands that Gimpel be the one to provide a dowry. "Don't bargain with me," she says, cutting off all discussion, "Either a flat 'yes' or a flat 'no'—go back where you came from."

Elka's plainspokenness (of which more, anon) adds to her sex appeal. Not only is she barefoot and rustically clad, she also has her hair in braids pinned up on both sides of her head, "*vi, lehavdil, a shikse*" ("like a shiksa, pardon the proximity"). By excising this homey observation, Bellow erased the link between Gimpel and a long line of Bashevis's male lovers, who take up with honest-to-goodness Polish shiksas—long live the proximity—wearing identical hairdos.

The last obstacle is overcome when Frampol pools its resources on the couple's behalf, further motivated by the fear of death. The wedding ceremony is held at the cemetery gates, the extreme measure of marrying off two orphans to ward off the plague. Bashevis's readers no doubt recalled an identical scene in Book Two of I. J. Singer's *Yoshe Kalb*. Singer Senior had died suddenly in 1944. Alternatively, they recalled the grotesque shotgun wedding of Fishke the Lame to a blind beggarwoman in Abramovitsh's famous novel. Thus Frampol rejoices doubly, in a carnivalesque mix of fasting and feasting, Eros fused and confused with Thanatos. Gimpel alone is privy to a moment of sobriety. As the *ketubah* is read out under the canopy, he learns that Elka is both a widow and divorced. When amidst the tradition-

al showering of wedding gifts Gimpel is presented with a crib, he understands that his bride is already with child.

The next chapter of Gimpel's marital life, which may be subtitled "The
Crisis of Infidelity," is recounted in a compressed and comical manner, for
as Wisse reminds us, the cuckolded husband is the oldest plot in folklore
and literature. When Gimpel's first child is born four months after the wedding, he is openly mocked in the House of Prayer. In a replay of the wedding, the circumcision feast is cause for universal revelry. "I ate and drank as
much as anyone and they all congratulated me."

In private, however, Gimpel confronts his wife with the evidence, asking pointedly, "*Vi makht men dos a mantsbil tsum nar?*" ("'How can you
make such a fool,' I said, 'of one who should be lord and master?'"). Here,
for the first time, Gimpel drops the semantic shield and refers to himself as a
nar, defining his foolishness as *makh[n] a mantsbil tsum nar,* i.e., being
taken in by one's wife. To underscore Gimpel's sense of humiliation, Bellow, hearing the echo of Gimpel's earlier, prenuptial, bravado, translates
mantsbil as "one who should be lord and master."

Gimpel eventually comes around. What changes his mind is not Elka's
claim that the birth of their child seventeen weeks after the wedding was a
genetic quirk; not the schoolmaster's mock-biblical proof text about Adam
and Eve ("Two they went up to bed, and four they descended. 'There isn't a
woman in the world who isn't the granddaughter of Eve,' he said."); and not
the example of Jesus' conception ("Who knows? I've heard it said that Baby
Jesus didn't have any father at all.")—the famous excised passage. All these
leave Gimpel unconvinced. Gimpel is swayed by his love for the newborn
child and, above all, his love for Elka.

What Gimpel loves most about her is her invective.

> *Haynt ire reydelekh! Zi shit mit pekh un shvebl un s'iz mole-kheyn, oys-*
> *tsukushn yedes vort. Zi krikht dir arayn in der zibeter rip un du ligst afn*
> *pyekelik in gehakte vundn un vilst nokh, elehey a gebrotns.*

> And her orations! Pitch and sulphur, that's what they were full of, and yet
> somehow also full of charm. I adored her every word. She gave me bloody
> wounds though.

Listening to her invective, says Gimpel in Yiddish but alas not in English, is
akin to lying on a tile stove begging to be served yet another serving of suc-
culent meat. Gimpel, in other words, "eats it up." Though her verbal aggression also is akin to taking a beating, Elka cannot be accused of spousal
abuse: "*Zi krikht dir arayn in der zibeter rip*" is the Yiddish equivalent of
"she gets under your skin." And this makes a difference, because in effect
and in affect Elka is acting out Gimpel's aggression. Her constant barrage of
words is a way of articulating the gratuitous cruelty that Gimpel suffers day-
in, day-out. Her rage helps Gimpel compensate for being the butt of everyone's joke. If this is pathology, it is the pathology of your typical Jewish mar-

riage of a passive man with a "passionate," super-aggressive woman.[16] If this is masochism, self-punishing behavior, then it answers a deep-felt need for catharsis.[17] What remains unclear is whether any of that pent-up aggression gets played out in the marital bed. Put simply: Has their marriage yet been consummated?

"I had to sleep away from home all during the week, at the bakery," he recalls. "On Friday nights when I got home she always made an excuse of some sort." Adding injury to insult, "this little brother of hers, the bastard," gives him regular beatings, with Elka's blessings. *An anderer af mayn ort volt antlofn vu der shvartser fefer vakst; ober ikh bin beteve a farsh-vayger. Nu, haklal, vos zol men ton? Az got git pleytses muz men shlepn dem pak.* ("Another man in my place would have taken French leave and disappeared. But I'm the type that bears it and says nothing. What's one to do? Shoulders are from God, and burdens too.") So for the second time Gimpel accepts his less-than-perfect marital situation by invoking a piece of Yiddish folk wisdom. ("French leave" is, of course, a Bellowism. The Yiddish reads: "would have fled to where the black pepper grows," a folk idiom.) Quoted by Jimmy Carter, "Shoulders are from God, and burdens too" bespeaks the fatalism common to many folk cultures; none more so than that of East European Jews.

Only when he finds her in bed with another man is Gimpel forced to acknowledge, "There's a limit even to the foolishness of a fool like Gimpel; *tsu Gimpls narishkeyt iz oykh do a grenets.*" The line, the *grenets* that has been crossed is also halachic. Once he turns to the rabbi for advice, Gimpel is forced to sue for divorce. And only when cut off from her entirely does he fully appreciate the extent of his loss. "A longing took me, for her and for the child." "I wanted to be angry," he continues the self-analysis, "but that's my misfortune exactly, I don't have it in me to be really angry." So what if he made a fool of himself? "*Mayle a mentsh banarisht zikh.*" The prolonged separation is cause for intense introspection, punctuated by his weeping helplessly into the flour where he lies at night. Gimpel finally recants before the rabbi, which ushers in a nine-month-long halakhic process.

Two things happen during this moratorium: another child is born, occasioning more revelry at his expense, and Gimpel makes the leap of faith. "*Ober ikh hob bay mir opgepast fun haynt on alts tsu gleybn. Vos kumt aroys az du gleybst nisht? Haynt gleybstu nish' dem vayb, morgn vestu nisht gleybn in got.*" ("However I resolved that I would always believe what I was told. What's the good of not believing? Today it's your wife you don't

---

16. See Janet Hadda, *Passionate Women, Passive Men: Suicide in Yiddish Literature* (Albany: SUNY Press, 1988).

17. "Although he is unable to avoid pain," Hadda concludes, "he has discovered that he needs Elka for her vitality and fearlessness, that being around her gives him a sense of worth, liveliness and courage." Hadda, "Gimpel the Full," 291.

believe; tomorrow it's God himself you won't take stock in.") Gimpel pred-
icates his faith in God on faith in his promiscuous wife. His relationship to
her becomes the sole measure of his relationship to God. The love that is
the source of his weakness becomes the source of his strength. His back-
and-forthing about marital relations, about trust, about life, yields a profession of faith, however fraught, however questionable in the light of what
has already transpired. For this faith to become unequivocal it must be tested anew.

So when the rabbis rule in Gimpel's favor and our hero returns home
unexpectedly, only to be met with a repeat performance of marital infidelity, this time with the apprentice from Gimpel's bakery, the very one who
has been delivering his gifts these many months, Elka easily tricks her husband into checking on the goat, then throws up a smoke screen of invective. Her "brother" gives him a *zets* for good measure, and the next day the
apprentice denies everything. Repetition makes it easier, rather than harder, for Gimpel to believe. As for his standing in society, "Gimpel chooses a
life with love but without dignity over a life with dignity but without
love."[18] The choice, in fact, has already been made through a prior leap of
faith and a painful introspective journey.

At this critical juncture, moving as we do from a plot-driven to a thought-
driven discourse in the final chapter, Gimpel's faith is put to the ultimate
test. On her deathbed, Elka confesses that none of the children were his. "I
imagined that, dead as she was, she was saying 'I deceived Gimpel. That was
the meaning of my brief life. *S'dukht zikh mir, az zi zogt toyterhayt:
kh'hob opgenart Gimplen. Dos iz geven der takhlis fun mayne farshnitene
yorn....*"[19] Gimpel's subsequent crisis of faith is bracketed by two dreams,
one in which he is seduced by the Devil and is persuaded to wreak revenge
by urinating in the dough, and a counter-dream in which he sees Elka suffering for her deceptions. "The whole world deceives you," says the Devil to
provoke him, "and you ought to deceive the world in your turn. (*Az di gantse velt nart dikht, nar du di velt.*)" "*Du tam,*" says Elka in dramatic counterpoint, distinguishing by her choice of words between his innocence and
her falsehood. "'You fool!' she said. 'You fool! Because I was false is everything false too? I never deceived anyone but myself.'" ("*Un az Elke iz falsh
iz shoyn alts lign? Ikh aleyn hob oykh keynem nisht opgenart akhuts
mikh aleyn.*") "There is no world-to-come," proclaims the Devil. "They've
sold you a bill of goods and talked you into believing you carried a cat in
your belly. What nonsense! (*S'iz nishto keyn yene velt. M'hot dir ayngeredt*

18. Wisse, 62.

19. Hadda sees this as an expression of his anger at Elka for having abandoned him; ibid.,
    292.

a kats in boykh.)" Is faith contingent upon human proofs? comes Elka's counter-argument from the other world.[20]

The two sides of Gimpel's psyche battle it out in his dreams: the id disguised as a Devil "with a goatish beard and horns, long-toothed, and with a tail," and the superego in the guise of his penitent dead wife, her face blackened by hellish torture. By this point in his life Gimpel is fully equipped to withstand the cheap psychological victory offered by the Devil. Thanks to "Elka's" intervention he can go beyond the earlier syllogism (love of God is as love for one's wife) to articulate the first stirrings of a transcendental faith ("Because I was false is everything false too?"). Acting upon that faith, Gimpel not only buries the polluted dough in the frozen ground, but he also renounces the material world and goes into exile. So doing, Gimpel also renounces his children, the very children for whose sake he presumably stayed in an abusive marriage. How can he now pick up and abandon them?[21]

Elka's death is the moment of truth both on the interpersonal and theological plane. At one and the same juncture Gimpel articulates his faith in God and actualizes his love of Elka. As he wanders through the world he dreams constantly of Elka, and she answers all his queries. Her presence becomes his surrogate home and emotional anchor.[22] Only now does he achieve true communion with her soul, with her memory, for this is a love that *cannot be falsified*. A love beyond death is the touchstone of truth.

Revisiting Gimpel in his dreams, Elka appears as she first did, standing by the washtub, "but her face is shining and her eyes are as radiant as the eyes of a saint." Whereas in life, she uttered nothing but curses and calumny, now, after death, "she speaks outlandish words to me, strange things." Whereas in the midst of his loneliness, he wet the flour sacks with tears of longing, in his dreams, "Sometimes she strokes and kisses me and weeps upon my face. When I awaken I feel her lips and taste the salt of her tears."

How, Bashevis asked himself, can one achieve love in a world hell-bent on evil and deception? Beginning with "The Spinoza of Market Street" in 1944, followed by *The Slave* (1961), "Taibele and her Demon" (1962) and *Shosha* (1974), his answer was to conjure up the love relationship of a usually misanthropic intellectual and a simple woman—a theme that hearkened back to such writers as Dostoevsky and W. Somerset Maugham. In "*Gimpl tam*" (1945), uniquely, the roles were reversed. Elka runs circles around her

---

20. Hadda interprets Elka's rejoinder as also expressing Gimpel's anger and ambivalence (ibid., 292–293).

21. Hadda, who tracks Gimpel's ever-growing self-confidence and understanding of the world against the backdrop of his orphanhood, glosses over the abandonment of his children, which functionally renders them orphans.

22. Hadda, "Gimpel the Full," 293.

marital partner every step of the way. Yet Gimpel does achieve a true love relationship: because of his simplicity, because he is salt of the earth, a mere baker of bread; because he is empathic, deeply caring, and incapable of anger; because of his unheroic, unmanly behavior. Whether or not that love was ever consummated, it becomes for him a metaphysical reality.

To whom should Elka be compared if she were viewed "competitively" across a justified margin? Surely not to Dante's Beatrice or Petrarch's Laura, the chaste love from afar, who leads her male suitor to God by being beautiful and genteel. Elka leads Gimpel to God by being anything but. Though Gimpel briefly toys with the notion of the Virgin Birth, a virgin is surely not what our shtetl lover has in mind. Nor, like the mock-epic knight errant, is the baker's apprentice from Frampol engaged in a quest for his Dulcinea. If anything, poor Gimpel is bullied into *marrying* the peasant wench Aldonza Lorenzo (*lehavdil*), this very real and earthly union initiating him into travails of a different kind.[23] Elka prefers to sleep with any man in Frampol—provided he's not her husband. Like the People Israel, Elka persists in acting the harlot, but Gimpel, emulating God, faithfully loves Israel, his promiscuous wife. Psychologically and spiritually, it is as a cuckolded husband that Gimpel achieves true self-knowledge. Through celibate marriage that produces no biological children and no true heir, Gimpel is led to a transcendent love that cannot be falsified. From the genealogy of the schlemiel as modern hero we arrive at the schlemiel as immaculate lover.

4. Gimpel as Double-Voiced Monologue

Most obviously, the genre to which "*Gimpl tam*" belongs is that of the monologue; obvious, that is, after Shmeruk published his text-critical edition of *Der shpigl un andere dertseylungen* in 1975, which showcased Bashevis as a master of that most venerable and protean genre. Shmeruk's arrangement of the twenty monologues, by subgenre and in loose chronological order, was also highly instructive, because it stimulated the reader to become culturally competent: to distinguish the "written monologue" of a Devil, erudite and highly subversive, from the confessional monologue of someone like Gimpel; a female speaker with her repertoire and stylistic register from a male; a learned Hasid from a shtetl lowlife; a live monologue from a memoir.

Why Bashevis invested his best efforts in mimicking the oral qualities of Yiddish only after immigrating to the United States is something that Shmeruk left unexplored. But the answer is not hard to find, for in 1943, the year that saw the republication of *Der sotn in Goray* and the appearance of a series of demonic narratives he tentatively titled "*Dos gedenkbukh fun yeyster-hore*" (The Devil's Diary), was the year that Bashevis emerged from

---

23. My thanks to Hana Wirth-Nesher for this comparison to traditions of courtly love.

a seven-year-long writer's block with both fists flying. In an essay disarming-
ly titled "Problems of Yiddish Prose in America," he exposed the debasement and diminution of American Yiddish culture, the failed project of Yiddish secularism, and the artistic impasse of the American Yiddish writer.
"Hebrew," he concluded ruefully, "is now more a living language, with all
the attributes, than is our mother tongue, Yiddish." So fiercely controversial
was this essay, published in the second issue of a little magazine called
Svive, that the editors reserved the right to publish a rebuttal.[24]

Before signing off, however, Bashevis called upon the surviving Yiddish
writers in America to rededicate themselves to their true cultural calling.
"We believe that the Jewish attachment to the past can accommodate an
extremely progressive outlook," he wrote, "for the history of the Jewish
people is the history of an ongoing revolution against the powers of darkness. *Mir gloybn, az...di yidishe tsugebundnkeyt tsum over geyt tsuzamen
mit groyser progresivitet, vayl di geshikhte fun dem yidishn folk iz di
geshikhte fun a permanenter revolutsye akegn di koykhes fun fintster-
nish.*" How different Bashevis sounded when breaking his silence in the
midst of the Second World War for the sake of his fellow Jews from the
speech he would deliver in Stockholm in 1978 extolling his mother tongue
as the language of the landless, the meek, and the lovers of peace!

Whatever Gimpel's message, it must have something to do with the
author's restorative-revolutionary program, his desire to revive the dead
through the power of their living language. What liberated Bashevis, both
from the constraints of an obsolescent language limited to an ever-shrinking
sector of American Jewry, and from the manifest failures to emancipate Yiddish from its religious and regional moorings, was the return to a fully re-
imagined Yiddish-speaking past. "*Gimpl tam*" exemplifies this reactionary
modernism.[25]

Formally, we learn from Shmeruk, "*Gimpl tam*" is a "closed" monologue, a deathbed confession to a group of beggars in a poorhouse.[26] It is
"closed" insofar as we do not know who they are or how they respond. In
other monologues, Shmeruk reminds us, the first-person speaker is the
Devil, which is to say, an omniscient narrator, or there is some response on
the part of the addressee. Here, by contrast, Gimpel recapitulates his whole
life, from boyhood to old age, and for all we know, this confession falls on

24. Yitskhok Bashevis, "Problemen fun der yidisher proze in Amerike," *Svive* 2 (March-
     April, 1943): 2–13; trans. Robert H. Wolf in *Prooftexts* 9 (1989): 5–12.

25. "Reactionary modernism" is the phrase Elliot Y. Neamann uses to describe Ernst
     Junger. See "The Problem of 'Inner Immigration,'" in *A New History of German Liter-
     ature*, ed. David E. Wellbery et al. (Cambridge, Mass.: Harvard University Press, 2004),
     805–809. Reactionary modernism, it seems, makes strange bedfellows.

26. Shmeruk, "The Use of Monologue as a Narrative Technique in the Stories of Isaac
     Bashevis Singer," xxi.

deaf ears. Unlike the fantastical stories that Gimpel, the storyteller-sage, recounts to eager children, this true-life monologue is a solipsistic exercise.

But is it really "closed"? Is it a species of *skaz*, of uncultivated, obsessive speech that feeds only on itself? Once before in the annals of Yiddish literature, the most abject of men ended his earthly existence surrounded by a motley crew of down-and-outs. But unlike Bontshe Shvayg, Gimpel seeks out their company. What's more, while Bontshe is apprised of his life through the giving of testimony, through cross-examination in the heavenly tribunal, through back-referencing and variant stories recounted in full public forum, Gimpel arrives at an understanding of his life that answers to no interrogation and emphatically requires no corroboration. Bontshe proves by his final utterance that he has learned nothing; he was and always will be bereft of a religious imagination. Gimpel proves by his final utterance that the life he has just narrated is the life he has authored, thanks to his dialogical imagination.

"*Ikh bin Gimpl tam*" ("I am Gimpel the Simple") he says by way of introduction. "*Ikh halt mikh nisht far keyn nar*. I don't think myself a fool." I-for-myself, as Bakhtin would have parsed it, is distinct from myself-for-others, i.e., how my self looks and feels to my own consciousness is separable from how my self appears to those outside it.[27] If in our first reading of "*Gimpl tam*" as a love story we have seen (with Shmeruk's blessing) how the mature Gimpel erects a consistent semantic barrier between his self-perception as a *tam* and the world that makes a fool of him, that considers his behavior *narishkayt*, now, in our second reading, and with Bakhtin's blessing, we shall see how Gimpel enters into dialogue with different kinds of utterance, four to be exact. Recasting these utterances in his own words, he produces an "innerly persuasive" discourse. The selfhood that he, a seasoned storyteller, projects from this last of his stories is not a particular voice within, but a particular way of combining various voices within.[28]

COMMUNAL UTTERANCE

Frampol speaks with many voices but with a single purpose. Comical nicknames were common in every shtetl; indeed, Gimpel has seven. Children are famously gullible. Gimpel's classmates make fooling him into their favorite cocurricular activity. "They said, 'Gimpel, you know, the rabbi's wife has been brought to childbed?' *M'hot gezogt: Gimpl, du veyst, di rebetsin iz gelegn gevorn*." Worse yet, Gimpel never outgrows his reputation and pretty soon, everyone gets into the act—young and old, male and female, learned and ignorant.

---

27. Gary Saul Morson and Caryl Emerson, *Mikhail Bakhtin: Creation of a Prosaics* (Stanford: Stanford University Press, 1990), 180.

28. Ibid., 221.

*Az di akhbroshim hobn dershmekt, az kh'loz mikh **narn**, hot yeder eyner gepruvt s'mazl. Gimpl, der keyser kumt keyn Frampol; Gimpl, di levone iz aropgefaln in Turbin; Gimpl, Hodele Shmoysh hot gefunen an oytser hintern bod.*

When the pranksters and leg-pullers found that I was easy to fool, every one of them tried his luck with me. "Gimpel, the Czar is coming to Frampol; Gimpel, the moon fell down in Turbeen; Gimpel, little Hodel Furpiece found a treasure behind the bathhouse."

Frampol invests its collective creativity in orchestrating fantastical rumors that only a fool would believe, each one accompanied by an appropriate taunt: "Gimpel, there's a fair in heaven; Gimpl, the rabbi gave birth to a calf in the seventh month; Gimpel, a cow flew over the roof and laid brass eggs." Many of these taunts are in fact common folk expressions, but when thrown in the face of a certified idiot, clichés suddenly take on a literal significance. Because they are met by Gimpel's incomprehension, they are defamiliarized: *"Gimpl, oyfn himl iz a yarid. Gimpl, der rov hot zikh opgekelbt un gehat a zibele. A ku iz gefloygn ibern dakh un geleygt meshene eyer."* As recorded and assembled by Gimpel, communal speech is dialogical, revealing sparks of poetic imagination that lie buried in the folk.[29] Yet how this poetic imagination has run amok! Speech acts that began discretely become, in due course, monomaniacal. Frampol speaks with one voice, and that voice is parodic, satiric, abusive, and cruel.

LEARNED UTTERANCE

When the world is too much with him, Gimpel consults with a rabbinic authority. Punctuating his monologue and in stark opposition to the communal voice are three instances of learned speech. "I went to the rabbi to get some advice," says Gimpel, recalling his first impasse with the entire community.

He said, "It is written, better to be a fool all your days than for one hour to be evil. You are not a fool. They are the fools. For he who causes his neighbor to feel shame loses Paradise himself."

Zogt er: S'shteyt: beser zay a shoyte ale yorn eyder eyn sho a roshe. Du bist, zogt er, nish' keyn nar. Di naronim zenen zey, vayl az m'farshemt dem andern, farlirt men yene velt.

In Yiddish, the chief marker of learned speech is the presence of *Loshn-koydesh*, Hebrew-Aramaic terms drawn from the world of the study house. The rabbi's brief responsum is a pastiche of quotes that are precisely on point. The first draws an absolute distinction between *shoyte* and *roshe*, a "fool" and an "evil-doer," both terms drawn from the same semantic field of

---

29. Cf. Bakhtin's discussion of "incomprehension": ibid., 360–361.

Loshn-koydesh. Foolishness, quoth the rabbi, is not a characterological flaw but a moral bulwark; it protects one from perpetrating evil. As for those who ridicule such behavior, they are mere *naronim*. The second is a partial quote and paraphrase of B. Sanhedrin 99a: Whoever shames a fellow human being in public [*hamalbin pnei ḥaveiro berabim*], may he even be armed with Torah and good deeds, will have no place in the world-to-come. Alas, this exalted teaching is immediately undercut by the behavior of the rabbi's daughter. She cannot resist making a fool of him, and even Gimpel must admit that it was a clever trick.

The next time Gimpel seeks rabbinic advice is after Elka gives birth "prematurely." In his world a mere *melamed*, translated "the schoolmaster" by Bellow, can also impart wisdom. Said "schoolmaster," we recall, cites the mock-biblical precedent of Adam and Eve and ends with a folksy, slightly off-color flourish, "*Nu, yeder ishe iz der muter Khaves an ureynikl*; There isn't a woman in the world who is not the granddaughter of Eve;" scratch a woman and you'll find the archetypal temptress and progenitor of sin. Whether or not Gimpel catches the double entendre, he is inspired by the schoolmaster's example to come up with a precedent of his own: the Virgin Birth of baby Jesus; "*Un tsurikgeshmuest, ver veyst? Ot zogt men dokh, az s'Yoyizl hot in gantsn keyn tatn nisht gehat.*"[30]

Years pass. Marital infidelities are exposed and forgiven. Gimpel resolves in his own mind, "I believed and that's all," underscored by what the rabbi has recently said to him, "Belief in itself is beneficial. It is written that a good man lives by his faith. *Az du gleybst, iz voyl dir. S'shteyt, az a tsadik lebt mit zayn emune.*" Gimpel's credulity and gullibility are here recast as the foundations of faith, which in turn is the surest protection against perpetrating evil. The rabbi, citing Habakkuk 2:4, compares his behavior to that of a *tsadik*, a supremely righteous person. Whereas communal speech is drawn from oral lore, learned speech is drawn from the textual tradition. Whereas communal speech is reductionist and monolithic, learned speech recasts the particular phenomenon into universal—and eternal—categories of meaning.

SHREWSPEECH

The turning point in Gimpel's life, as we have seen, is his arranged marriage to Elka. At their first encounter, however, he is scandalized by her vulgarity. "No bread," he concludes, "will be baked from this dough!" He falls in love with her invective, becoming, in his own words, a glutton for punishment. The generic- and gendered-Yiddish name for Elka's speech is *mayne-loshn*, which I would translate as "shrewspeech."

---

30. The metadiscursive *tsurikgeshmuest* betokens the rhetoric of talmudic debate, which Gimpel unconsciously adopts from his learned male interlocutor.

So long as Elka is alive and kicking, her voice represents one of two instances in Gimpel's monologue of "talking bad." This verbal aggression, as I hear it, contributes mightily to his psychological well-being. Elka continues to speak to him from beyond the grave, her *mayne-loshn* transformed into "outlandish words," "strange things." When he awakens, unfortunately, he has forgotten them, but while the dream lasts, he is comforted.

DEVILSPEECH

The other instance of talking bad is devilspeech. Unlike "The Devil's Diary," the ambitious series in which the center of consciousness is the Devil himself, here he makes but a cameo—and comical—appearance. From first to last, Gimpel cuts the Devil down to size; first, by answering his challenge with a joke, and last, by trying to catch him by the tail. "*Gimpl, vos shlofstu?*" he asks, "Gimpel, why do you sleep?" "*Zog ikh: Vos zol ikh ton? Esn kreplekh?* I said, 'What should I be doing? Eating *kreplach*?" Still, the Devil is up to his old tricks, urging Gimpel to beat Frampol at its own game. "'The whole world deceives you,' he said, 'and you ought to deceive the world in your turn.' *Az di gantse velt **nart** dikh, **nar** du di velt.*"

Devilspeech is vulgar and subversive. "Let the sages of Frampol eat filth," he says, *à propos* his devilish plan to urinate into the communal dough. "*Zoln zey, zogt er, fresn umreynkeyt, di frampoler khakhomim.*" "There is no world-to-come," he proclaims, in answer to Gimpel's fear of divine punishment. "They've sold you a bill of goods and talked you into believing you carried a cat in your belly." "There is no God either," he states, pulling out all the stops. What is there? "A thick mire. *A tife blote.*"

During Elka's lifetime, Gimpel's unconditional love for her was transmuted into an absolute faith in God. Her death and deathbed confession are what trigger a momentary denial of God. How better to articulate that fearful, heretical thought than through an aggressive and parodic voice that speaks to him in the dead of night? At the risk of over-schematization, it is possible to group the four utterances we have heard thus far into two pairs: the communal vs. the learned, shrewspeech vs. devilspeech. Within each pair, the first operates in the realm of the mundane. The second speaks from within the realm of the metaphysical.

GIMPEL'S SPEECH

This leaves Gimpel himself, who is more than the sum of his disparate, neatly-paired voices. As Yiddish folk narrators go, he is no Tevye. The few learned, second-hand citations that he has woven into his life story are no match for Tevye's ad-libbed performances of comic exegesis. Yet Gimpel is a species of proverbial Jew. His two most memorable sayings—"You can't pass through life unscathed, nor expect to" and "Shoulders are from God, and burdens, too"—bespeak a qualified fatalism that we have come to identify with Yiddish irony.

Gimpel's monologue, as Wisse was the first to recognize, follows a developmental pattern, from boyhood to cuckoldhood to wise old age. By the fourth and last chapter he has turned into a voluntary exile, whose own speech waxes contemplative and who endows his dead wife's speech with extraordinary tenderness. At the end of the road, our naïve folk narrator claims ownership of the metaphysical realm. In Bakhtinian terms, the balance he achieves between the I-for-myself and the I-for-others gives way to I-for-the-Other. "When the time comes," proclaims Gimpel on his deathbed, "I will go joyfully. Whatever may be there, it will be real, without complication, without ridicule, without deception. God be praised: there even Gimpel cannot be deceived. *Mertshishem, az di tsayt vet kumen, vel ikh geyn ahin mit freyd. Vos s'zol dort nisht zayn, alts iz vor, on fardrey-enishn, on letsones un shvindl. Got tsu danken: dort kon men afile Gim-plen oykh nisht opnarn.*"

Mertshishem, which Bashevis spells phonetically, signals that Gimpel remains in the same folk register as before. (Spelled etymologically, "*im yirtse hashem,* God willing," would suggest a more august, overtly theological locution.) The key to Gimpel's final profession of faith lies not so much in the invocation of God's name as in his own. In the world-to-come, he says with conviction, when the stigma of *opnarn* is erased, his true, projected, assembled and unfinalizable self will be revealed, and not just to a group of beggars in the flophouse.

The actively dialogical medium of Gimpel's monologue was its restorative message. Writing "as if" Yiddish were still the warp and woof of everyday life, Bashevis created an idealized transcript of Yiddish folkspeech, a reincarnated speech act. One voice successfully orchestrated multiple utterances: communal and individual, male and female, natural and supernatural. Knowing full well that the Yiddish heartland was no more, Bashevis produced a richly nuanced monologue designed to showcase Yiddish as the culture of *yidishkayt*: sublime in its earthiness, a civilization-in-miniature.

Even as "*Gimpl tam*" obeyed Bashevis's credo that "Yiddish literature must look backwards ... for theme, plot, setting, and character," it also heeded his call to betray the past in the name of a modernist sensibility. "Psychoanalysis," he went on to state in his 1943 manifesto, "can be applied to a story from the past just as well as to a slice of life still warm with reality."[31] To give a psychoanalytic reading more play, he even threw in a double dream sequence in which the id is disguised as a Devil and the superego appears as the penitent dead Elka. Were indeed the story to have ended with Gimpel's psychological triumph over the Devil, the resolution of his anger at society and the working through of his mourning for Elka, his therapy would be deemed a complete success. But what has been driving Gimpel's deathbed confession all along was not the healing of his psyche

---

31. Bashevis, "Problems of Yiddish Prose in America," 12.

but the journey of his soul—a journey whose ultimate destination would complete and possibly alter the meaning of his monologue outside of its very narration.[32]

5. Gimpel as a Neo-Hasidic Narrative

"*On letsónes*, without ridicule." These words spoken by Gimpel in 1945 had been uttered once before—130 years earlier to be exact—by a fictional character who was known simply as the *Tam*. By labeling Gimpel a *tam*, Bashevis linked him to a chain of exemplary figures: to Jacob (Gen 25:27), "a quiet man (*ish tam*) dwelling in tents; to Job (1:1), "blameless (*tam*) and upright; he feared God and shunned evil"; to the third of the Four Sons in the Passover Haggadah (the story's first publication appearing in honor of Passover); and last but not least, to the hero of Nahman of Braslav's "Mayse bekhokhem vetam."

Bashevis himself stood in an illustrious line of born-again storytellers who found in Reb Nahman ben Simhah of Braslav a kindred spirit. Peretz and Der Nister, Buber and Kafka, Pinchas Sadeh and Aharon Appelfeld, to name but a few, each mined Reb Nahman's metaphysical parables in fairytale garb. In 1943 alone, two American-Yiddish poets revived the figure of Reb Nahman by presuming to speak in his voice: Jacob Glatstein in his cycle of dramatic monologues "The Bratslaver to His Scribe," and Ephraim Auerbach, who wrote his own ending to the famously unfinished "Tale of the Seven Beggars."[33] Bashevis's attraction was twofold. In the Poland of his youth, the Braslaver Hasidim were a marginal bunch, despised by other Hasidim.[34] Unlike today, the words "N-NAH-NAHM-NAHMAN MIUMAN" were not pasted on storefronts, car fenders, lamp posts and billboards everywhere. For Bashevis, the smaller and more marginal they were, the better. In a world hell-bent on destruction, Braslav Hasidism represented a tiny but indomitable counter-offensive, an ongoing mini-revolution against the powers of darkness.

Braslav Hasidim make a cameo appearance at the end of his sweeping panoramic novel, The *Family Moskat* (1945–50), which tries to capture all of Polish Jewry—rich and poor, the Polonizers and the pietists, left and right, high society and the underworld—on the eve of its annihilation. On the first day of Rosh Hashanah, 1939, with German bombs falling on the Polish metropolis, one member of the Moskat clan makes his way to the Uman *shtibl* on Dzielna Street.

---

32. Cf. *Mikhail Bakhtin: Creation of a Prosaics*, 160, on the concept of a "loophole."

33. See Jacob Glatstein, "Der Bratslaver tsu zayn soyfer," in *Gedenklider* (New York: Farlag Yidisher kemfer 1943), 7–16, and Ephraim Auerbach, "Di mayse funem zibetn betler," *Yidisher kemfer* (November 12, 1943): 12–16.

34. See David Assaf, *Ne'ehaz basvakh: pirkei mashber umevukha betoldot hahasidut* (Jerusalem: The Zalman Shazar Center, 2006), chap. 3.

> The Dead Hasidim, as the followers of Reb Nahman of Braslav were called, celebrated as they did every year. They danced before prayers and studied together the *Likkutei Moharan*. An old man, Reb Menakhem, explicated a text for the gathering. The Hasidim applauded, artfully snapped their fingers, hopped along, and gesticulated. One Hasid reminded another of Reb Nahman's warning: There is no such thing as despair. As long as the fire glows, nothing is lost![35]

Menashe Dovidl is so swept away by their religious fervor that he joins the young Braslaver in the nearby ritual bath and is the first to immerse himself in its ice cold waters, proclaiming as he does so: "Who was this Hitler anyway? It was the same old Satan." In stark contrast, we last see the novel's intellectual hero, Oyzer-Heshl Bannet, still clutching his copy of Spinoza's *Ethics*. Like his father before him, he has destroyed the manuscript he labored over for years.

Against a backdrop of annihilation and universal despair, only two tiny groups uphold a vision of hope: the Halutzim preparing for the ardors of agricultural work in Palestine and the Dead Hasidim, whose blind, utterly irrational faith signals a metahistorical turn in the narrative. The novel ends, for those reading it from right-to-left, with a tableau of biblical scenes, which turn the Nazi apocalypse into a new and terrible genesis. Not so in the left-to-right version of the novel with a potential mass-market appeal. Better a truncated ending, without a modicum of hope, than an ending deemed too intertextual, too encoded, and too parochial.[36]

Written for an elite reader, the metahistorical tales over which Bashevis labored so diligently throughout the 1940s were deeply enmeshed within the Jewish textual tradition. ("More and more," Bashevis had written in his 1943 manifesto, "the Yiddish writer will have to draw material from sacred tomes.") Bridging the sacred and profane were the *Tales* of Reb Nahman, whose form preserved the cadences and idioms of Podolian Yiddish, and whose content was fiercely antimodern—none more so than "The Tale of the *Khokhem* and the *Tam*."[37] Bashevis essentially rewrote this very long story by splitting it into two: Standing in for the *khokhem*, the fastidious philosopher, medical doctor, and master craftsman was "*Zaydlus der ershter*" (1943), the brilliant Talmud scholar who wanted to be pope.[38] Stand-

---

35. Yitskhok Bashevis, *Di familye Mushkat* (New York: Sklarsky, 1950), vol. II, 756; Isaac Bashevis Singer, "*The Family Moskat*: Chapter 65," trans. Joseph C. Landis, *Yiddish* 6, no. 2–3 (1985): 112, with slight emendations.

36. See I. Saposnik, "Translating *The Family Moskat*: The Metamorphosis of a Novel," *Yiddish* 1, no. 2 (1973): 26–37.

37. For a detailed comparison of the Yiddish and Hebrew versions of the story, which comes down strongly in favor of the Yiddish, see Shmuel Werses, "Milashon el lashon ba'Sipurei maasiyot' shel R. Nahman miBraslav," *Khulyot* 9 (2005): 9–47.

38. Yitskhok Bashevis, "Zaydlus der ershter (fun a serye dertseylungen u.n. 'Dos gedenk-

ing in for the *tam* was Gimpel (1945). *"Nor on letsónes,"* says Reb Nah-man's Tam whenever smart-alecky townspeople ridicule his naïve behavior. At story's end that naiveté is spectacularly vindicated, even as the *khokhem* is made to suffer grievous torture at the hands of the Devil. As a stand-alone character, Reb Zaydl Cohen is a man of pure reason whom Bashevis con-signs to hell. As a stand-alone character, Gimpel the Orphan is a man of faith for whom a place is reserved in heaven. Gimpel, it emerges from an inter-textual reading of the story, stands on the shoulders of spiritual giants. With Jacob and Job, he is one of the moral pillars of the universe. With Reb Nah-man's *tam*, he is a lonely little-man of faith.

* * *

While three right-to-left readings by no means exhaust all interpretive possibilities, they do add up to a composite Yiddish-in-Yiddish portrait of Gimpel the Simple. Two orphans, completely mismatched, are thrown together by the vagaries and vanities of the society in which they live. They marry, they separate, and they get back together, the husband predicating his love on faith rather than fidelity. The wife dies, and only then do the bereaved husband and the deceased wife become one, on the way to becoming One.

This oneness, in turn, is embodied by the monologue form, which is "closed" only insofar as Gimpel's deathbed confession requires no outside validation. Hermeneutically, orally, it is wide open, orchestrating voices that are at once mundane and metaphysical. Gimpel is a dialogical being, who makes communal, learned, shrewish, and devilish speech into a vehi-cle of self-transcendence. No matter if his command performance falls on deaf ears. Its chief addressee (Elka, God, or God-as-Elka) is in heaven, not on earth.

The unconsummated, celibate love that is one, as narrated by manifold voices that are one, are further reinforced by the intertextual matrix of Braslav Hasidism. The Tam belongs in the pantheon of heroes because he is a solitary seeker of truth, because he is the subject of constant ridicule, and because alone among the faithful, he can face the Void with joy. "When the time comes," proclaims Gimpel at the (merely) visible end of the road, "I will go joyfully." At the nadir of Jewish historical time, Yitskhok Bashevis created a fully realized, many-voiced, open-ended, Yiddish-speaking charac-ter that could arrive at a hard-won, radically individualized profession of faith.

In English, Gimpel the Fool is less of a male, less of a folk artist, less of a Jew. The cup that Bellow handed the English reader in 1953 was at best half

bukh fun yeyster-hore')," *Svive* 1 (1943): 11–24; "Zeidlus the Pope," trans. Joel Blocker and Elizabeth Pollet, in *Selected Short Stories of Isaac Bashevis Singer*, ed. Irving Howe (New York: Modern Library, 1966), 341–353.

empty. Not so, Gimpel the Simple, who is endowed with the fullness of years, of voice, of human emotion, and of mystical knowledge. In celebration thereof, on the eve of the Passover festival in 1945, Yitskhok Bashevis presented the Yiddish reader with an Elijah cup, filled to overflowing.

Isaac Bashevis Singer's Short Story "Androgynous"

SUSANNE KLINGENSTEIN

On September, 29, 2003, when the attention of the United States was focused on its war in Iraq, *The New Yorker* magazine ran a short story entitled "Androgynous," by Isaac Bashevis Singer. This was an oddity on several counts, since *The New Yorker*'s editors usually preferred unpublished works by the young, hip, and socially critical. In September 2003, Bashevis would have been an unsexy ninety-nine years old. English readers would have been hard-pressed to know that he had been dead a dozen years, since from the grave Bashevis had been issuing a steady stream of publications, including a national bestseller, *Shadows on the Hudson* (1998). His story "Androgynous," though, had first appeared in Israel in 1975, in a Yiddish collection of his shorter works, edited by Khone Shmeruk.[1] Singer had not commissioned an English translation during his lifetime. Hence the publication of the story's superb translation by the Oxford-based scholar Joseph Sherman in *The New Yorker* could be considered something of a coup: a brand-new story had been pulled out of a very old hat.

The New Yorker's presentation of Bashevis's story was accompanied by Irving Penn's stunning 1966 photograph of the author. Penn, a Jew from Plainfield, N.J., published his first *Vogue* cover photo in 1943, the year Bashevis articulated his literary program in two important essays; Penn opened his own studio in 1953, the year Bashevis crashed into the awareness of America's literary intellectuals with Saul Bellow's translation of "Gimpel the Fool," published in the May issue of *Partisan Review*. In 1958, Penn was voted one of the world's ten greatest photographers; Bashevis was twenty years away from receiving the Nobel Prize. To have your picture taken by Penn meant that you were a celebrity. Penn, who had trained to be an artist, shot fashion advertisements for money, and nudes for the sake of art; in his business, sex, art, and commerce were the holy trinity, and it was

---

1. Isaac Bashevis-Singer, "Androygenus." *Der shpigl un andere dertseylungn*, edited and with an introduction by Khone Shmeruk (Jerusalem: The Hebrew University, distributed by Tcherikover Publishers, 1975), 180-193. In his '*bibliografishe protim*," Shmeruk notes that "Androygenus" was "*geshribn shpetsiel far dem bukh, London, May 1974*" (p. 284). Two months after the story's first English publication in *The New Yorker*, the story appeared also in the book by Sandra Bark, ed., *Beautiful as the Moon, Radiant as the Stars: Jewish Women in Yiddish Stories: An Anthology* (New York: Warner Books, 2003), 153-170.

one that Bashevis certainly knew much about, having been accused by his Yiddish colleagues of using sex in art for the sake of commerce.

Penn's portrait is a spare, stylish study of Bashevis's white face above a black wool coat topped by a plaid scarf. The face isn't soft. It resembles a hairless egg, smooth and white and inaccessible. Its strong features do not invite play: straight horizontal lips, strong, broad-ridged nose, left eye reduced to a dot of light in the shadowed left side of the face, right eye unrimmed by lashes looking straight at you, unblinking, uninquisitive, unsmiling. The overall impression created by the photo is one of complete silence. The face does not admit you and it does not speak to you. This is not the portrait of a "grandfatherly imp" or "Yiddish Yoda,"[2] but of a shrewd man who demands that you work hard to know him. Penn got it right.

The story itself starts conventionally, unpromisingly: "In the study house in the Polish village of Pilev, Hasidim sat around swapping Hasidic anecdotes."[3] The Yiddish original begins more laconically: "*Khsidim zenen gezesn un geshmuest khsides.*"[4] In the Yiddish version we don't learn until the second sentence in the second paragraph that the story takes place in the "*Pilever shtibl.*" (180) We understand, though, that in a modern American magazine, readers will want to know right away where they are. In Yiddish, the tautological beginning of *khsidim shmuesn khsides* ("Hasidim talking *hasidut*") signals that we are among generic Hasidim in Eastern Europe. It is precisely the run-of-the-mill pitted against the original, individual, and authentic that will turn out to be one of the story's central themes.

By the second sentence, however, things are looking up for *New Yorker* readers. They encounter contemporary relevance: "Someone mentioned a rebbe who taught that a Jew ought to be prepared to lay down his life for Kiddush Ha-Shem, the Sanctification of the Holy Name." Just two years earlier, in September 2001, Americans had witnessed several stunning acts of voluntary martyrdom as Muslims lay down their lives for the greater glory of their god. When the story ran, Muslim sanctifiers of Allah's name were blowing themselves up almost daily in the Middle East. Did *The New Yorker* editors pick Bashevis's story as a Jewish perspective on the sanctification of God's name? Such a perspective, if offered by the story, would amount to a tremendous moral and political critique of the Muslim martyrdom since the Jewish view of *kiddush ha-shem* is entirely defensive, rather than offensive, requiring, in its most extreme form, that a Jew lay down his life only if oth-

---

2. Tom Teicholz, "'Fabulous Invalid'," *The Jewish Journal of Greater Los Angeles* December 19, 2003; posted at www.jewishjournals.com/home/print.php?id=11529.

3. Isaac Bashevis Singer, "Androgynous." *The New Yorker* September 29, 2003: 94. All further references to this edition are cited in the text.

4. "*Androygenus,*" in Bashevis-Singer, *Der shpigl*, 180. All further references to this edition are cited in the text.

erwise forced to commit idolatry, adultery, or murder. In all other cases, a Jew is forbidden to kill himself.

Like a sentence in the Mishna, the anonymous rabbi's teaching "*az a yid darf yede rege zayn greyt zikh moyser-nefesh tsu zayn al-kidesh ha-shem*" serves as the starting point for a sophisticated multilayered commentary delivered by one Reb Leyzer Walden, "*an alter kotsker khasid*," against the prevailing *opinio communis*. The layering includes an initial one-word rebuttal, a historical reflection, a historical exemplum, and a moral parable, each loaded with short-hand allusions to events, people, and texts well known to (students of) prewar Polish Jewry.

As a page in the Talmud may contain all layers of commentary simultaneously—Mishna, Gemara, Rashi, Tosafot—so the multilayered commentary in "Androgynous" is held together by the voice and mindset of a single speaker, Leyzer Walden. The story is largely a monologue, like Joseph Conrad's *Heart of Darkness*, in a setting of mostly silent listeners representing the norms of ordinary society to whom both Marlowe and Walden pitch a tale of the extraordinary for their contemplation and edification.

What got the old Kotzker hasid's goat was the casual smugness with which a group of small-town smart-alecks discussed the greatest demand that can be made of a Jew, that of giving up his life.[5] Walden challenges the communal consensus in the study house with a single "So?" Surprised that there could be any dissent on *mesires nefesh*, a wealthy and impudent young man calls on Walden either to justify his "So?" or to submit to the general sentiment.

Before Walden launches into his three-part answer, Bashevis takes time out to describe the speaker, since his answer is an outcropping of his *weltanschauung* and our openness to it will depend on our evaluation of his character. Before we are told anything about him as an individual, we learn that he is an "*alter kotsker khasid*," meaning a follower of R. Menakhem Mendel Morgensztern (1787–1859), a "brooding iconoclast and radical theologian,"[6] who, according to Gershom Scholem, was one of the most significant Hasidic masters and one of the strangest.[7] He was born in Goray to a father who opposed Hasidism. After his marriage he settled in

5. Walden's older German contemporary, the writer Theodor Fontane, once found a classic formulation for this ubiquitous phenomenon: "Alle Stubenhocker dringen beständig auf Opfertod" (all homebodies urge heroic self-sacrifice). Theodor Fontane, *Vor dem Sturm: Roman aus dem Winter 1812 auf 13*. 1878 (Frankfurt: Insel, 1981), 163.

6. Gershon David Hundert, *Jews in Poland-Lithuania in the Eighteenth Century: A Genealogy of Modernity* (Berkeley: University of California Press, 2004), 231.

7. Gershom Scholem, *Die jüdische Mystik in ihren Hauptströmungen*, 1957 (Frankfurt: Suhrkamp, 1980), 378. Scholem, *Major Trends in Jewish Mysticism*, 1941 (New York: Schocken, 1971), 345.

Tomaszóv, where he was pulled into the movement. He became a distinguished disciple of R. Yaacov Yitzhak Halevy Horovitz (?–1815), known as
the *Khoze*, or the Seer of Lublin, and after the *Khoze's* death, of R. Simkha
Bunim of Pshiskhe (1765–1827). R. Bunim, who rebelled against the *Khoze*,
saved Hasidism from spiritual stagnation "by elevating it into a movement of
nonconformist young scholars who detested pose and pride, superficiality
and mechanical ritualism."[8] R. Bunim's court was known to contain the
sharpest minds in Jewish Poland, including R. Menakhem Mendel, who radicalized R. Bunim's principles.

Like his teacher, R. Menakhem Mendel saw Hasidism in steep decline.
He despised its emotionalism and sentimentality and he detested the movement's catering to the needs of the masses. He wanted Hasidism to remain
the purview of a small spiritual elite. After his move to Kotzk, he chose to
surround himself with few disciples of whom he demanded much. He hated
hypocrisy and dishonesty, which he considered variants of selfishness. He
favored a rationalist approach. His teacher R. Bunim had been learned in
worldly matters, especially medicine and pharmacology. Scholem points
out that the Rebbe of Kotzk pushed Hasidism to return to scholarship. In his
wake, *tsadikim* emerged who wrote responsa and works of pilpul. He himself wrote nothing, but cultivated an extremely laconic form of expression
as cutting as it was witty (his sayings were later collected by disciples).
When his extremism came under fire from other Hasidic masters, he said:
"Only horses go in the middle of the road."[9] Although (or because) he was a
rationalist, he demanded authenticity of faith. Not ritual observance, but
only a genuine movement of the soul, the soul on fire, enabled a Jew to
move toward God. When other Hasidic masters criticized that at the Kotzker's court prayers were not recited on time, he shot back: "In Kotzk, we
have a soul, not a clock."[10]

The Kotzker Rebbe was extreme in his effort to keep the movement
fresh and authentic. He offered no pabulum and little solace to ordinary
Jews in spiritual and earthly distress. Finally, in late 1839, his best friend and
most distinguished disciple R. Mordekhai Yosef Leiner revolted against him
and seceded with a group of the brightest Hasidim to set up his own court.
Angry and embittered, the Kotzker Rebbe shut himself up in his study for
the last twenty years of his life, granting access to two disciples only, one of
whom was his son-in-law Abraham Bernstein.

I am spending so much time on the Kotzker Rebbe, because both Leyzer
Walden and Reb Mottele, the protagonist in Walden's longest commentary,
are essentially sharpened portraits of the Kotzker Rebbe, whose failed

---

8. Milton Aron, *Ideas and Ideals of Hasidism* (Secaucus: Citadel Press, 1969), 240.

9. Quoted in Aron, *Ideas and Ideals of Hasidism*, 254.

10. Ibid., 254.

renewal of Hasidism and the systemic reasons for that failure are the submerged core issue of Bashevis's story. Once the story is recognized as a critique of Polish Hasidism executed with the help of its own rhetorical means—metaphor, allegory, satire, polemics—all contemporaneity vanishes and the cognoscenti of *khsides* are enabled to reenter the world of Polish Jewry before its destruction and continue the debate. Thus the story fulfills what Bashevis articulated as his cultural program and artistic desideratum in his two 1943 essays: preservation of an authentic core of Jewish thought and experience that is accessible through study.[11]

Leyzer Walden cultivates the Kotzker Rebbe's laconic style and his contempt for the *tsadikim* who cater to the *hoi polloi*, rich and poor, indulging them with advice and thus generating cheap forms of religiosity. Walden realizes that he lives in a time of decline and it irritates him. In turn, he wishes to irritate those who go easy on themselves. When the Jews sit down to eat and drink on Purim, he sits down to study the dry civil laws in the *Shulkhan Arukh*. On Tisha be-Av he smears cheese into his beard to goad the mitnagdim into thinking he was ignoring the fast. Although the wit and arrogance of Walden's extremism bear the hallmark of the Kotzker Rebbe's

---

11. Although the essays are well known among Yiddish literary scholars, it is worth recalling their main points since they are the key both to Bashevis's artistic program and to his later success (and misreading) as an American modernist. In the essay *"Problemen fun der yidisher proze in amerike,"* published with a disclaimer by the editors in the March-April 1943 issue of *Svive*, Bashevis argued that in America Yiddish as a sophisticated secular and literary language was as good as dead. Bashevis's assessment was guaranteed to offend the Yiddish-speaking community in New York. He, a newcomer from Warsaw, was rather arrogantly discounting decades of Yiddish literary effort in America not only by scores of journalists and writers, such as Abraham Cahan, but also, and more important, by the Yiddish literary giants of the day, such as Sholem Asch (see Yitskhok Bashevis, *"Problemen fun der yidisher proze in amerike,"* Svive 2 [March-April 1943]: 2–13; translated as "Problems of Yiddish Prose in America" by Robert H. Wolf, *Prooftexts* 9 [1989]: 5–12). In August 1943, five months after the *Svive* article, as the Warsaw ghetto stood empty and devastated like the *mishkan* after the Roman assault, the Yiddish literary monthly *Di Tsukunft* put out an issue to honor Polish Jewry. Among the expressions of sorrow and nostalgia, Bashevis's essay was a sobering blow to the head, in the manner of the Kotzker Rebbe, who had wanted to rid Polish Jews of sentimentality and emotionalism. Bashevis's essay *"Arum der yidisher literatur in poyln"* was a merciless critique of the shortcomings of modern Yiddish literature in Poland. Bashevis ridiculed the Polish Jewish modernists' aping of artistic fads, such as Italian Futurism, and argued that the Yiddish language was ill suited to such experiments. He declared that the modernist experiments in Yiddish letters were evidence not of cosmopolitanism but of provincialism. What propelled Bashevis's critique in both essays was his recognition that some sort of literary repair work would have to undo the damage sustained by the Yiddish language and its literature in both America and modernist Jewish Poland and that he was the man to undertake that work. Creative repentance became his calling. (See Yitskhok Bashevis, *"Arum der yidisher literatur in poyln,"* Di Tsukunft [August 1943], 468–475).

idiosyncrasies, Walden is himself an example of Hasidism's decline since he acts to spite rather than, as the Kotzker Rebbe did, to restore authenticity of feeling. Walden suspects, perhaps knows, that the new generation has no desire to achieve the Kotzker's goals.

Walden attempts to escape his belatedness by dressing "in the fashion of bygone times." The irony here is that R. Bunim already rejected the traditional dress of Eastern European Jews, but that in his belatedness Walden needs to hang onto it. In a final move to establish Walden's authenticity as a Kotzker hasid, Bashevis has him correspond with Reb Abraham Sokhatshever, in whom cognoscenti will recognize R. Abraham Bernstein of Sokhatshev (1839–1910), the son-in-law who had access to the secluded Kotzker Rebbe. But Bashevis goes wittily over the top. It isn't Walden who asks the Sokhatshever for advice on fine points of rabbinic law, but *"avrom sokhatshever hot geshribn tsu im shayles-tshuves."* (181)[12]

This, then, is the man who delivers a three-part commentary on the issue of self-sacrifice when faith is at stake. We can expect radicalism and idiosyncrasy for the sake of restoring Jewish authenticity, which, incidentally, also describes Bashevis's own Yiddish literary program in the wake of 1943. In the heady atmosphere of American literary high culture in the 1950s, the romantic, the radical, and the idiosyncratic, essential elements in early Hasidism, were in Bashevis's fiction often mistaken for "modernism."

Walden's first answer, "So?", exposes the conventional, routinized piety of the *"khsidim [vos] shmuesn khsides."* Challenged by an "insolent whippersnapper" (*"khutspenik"*), Walden understands that he has just been asked a *kashe*, a question concerning faith. In his role as elder he is obligated to answer, *"az a kashe muz men entfern a terets"* ([because] one is obligated to provide a justification for a question regarding faith; 181).[13] And so he begins.

He first interprets *kiddush ha-shem* to establish a principle that reflects his particular view of Judaism. "Certainly self-sacrifice is a matter of grave importance, but the manner in which it is performed is not important." (94/6) By this he means that it is not important that you actually kill yourself. Walden then bows piously to the martyrs of 1648 (and Bashevis nods to Asch's novel *Kiddush Ha-shem: An Epic of 1648*, which imagined the self-sacrifice): "Whole communities have sacrificed themselves." (96) He points

---

12. Sherman translates this as "Reb Abraham Sokhatshever had written asking for his opinion on questions of rabbinic law." My sense is that because *shayles-tshuves* literally means "question-answers" (responsa), it is ambiguous who wrote to whom first. Sherman also published the first and very fine close reading of Bashevis's story. Although I ultimately disagree with Sherman, his reading was an immensely valuable guide through the thicket of Bashevis's prose. Cf., Joseph Sherman, "What's Jews? Isaac Bashevis Singer's '*Androgynous*'," *Prooftexts* 14.2 (May 1994): 167–188.

13. Sherman's translation, 94.

out that this is not so special since the Gentiles do it too. "One general sends a whole camp of soldiers into battle, and they fight to the last drop of blood." (96) The thought can give rise to rebellion. Why go like sheep to slaughter? Why submit to rituals and constraints that go against your inner certainties, your faith?

Rebellion is one of the leitmotifs in this story about the authenticity of faith. In *hasidut*, rebellion and authenticity of faith are inseparable. Only rebelliousness proves that the believer hasn't become a complacent, unthinking conformist. Those who rebel against conformism and ritualized expressions of faith are moved to do so by the fire of genuine faith. Hasidism is full of rebels who see their masters slide into routine piety or get stuck and encrusted in idiosyncratic points of view. Then disciples secede to set up new courts of authentic *khsides* only to be rebelled against in turn.

Given the interdependence of rebellion and authenticity of faith, it makes perfect sense that after his comment about the Gentile soldiers going into battle like sheep to slaughter, Walden argues that the really difficult thing is to break away from mindlessly accepting death. Not dying, but living and deriving *simkhe-shel-mitsve* (181, joy from observing God's commandments) defines one's authenticity as a Jew. A dead Jew is a wasted Jew. Torah is of this world only; and because it is only of *oylem haze*, it is its own reward: "He who knows the true taste of being a Jew [through joyful observance, or *simkhe-shel-mitsve*] doesn't need to be encouraged with a pinch on the cheek." (96) We are now in the depth of *kotsker khsides*, where faith is expressed through an idiosyncratic worship of God that is often so non-normative that it seems rebellious, but for that reason is all the more credible and authentic. It is easy to see that such a construction of faith is inherently unstable and destructive to communal bonds, which is why the mitnagdim opposed it with utmost determination.[14]

Having established his interpretation of *kiddush ha-shem* as joyful worship of God, however non-normative, Walden supplies his first example. "In Shebreshin at one time there was a heretic, Yekel Rayfman, an atheist, who used to wear a rabbinical fur hat and spend his days and nights absorbed in Torah study. It was said that on the Sabbath he would read over the portion of the week while smoking a cigar." (96) Joseph Sherman pointed out that Walden refers here to the Polish *maskil* Jacob Reifmann (1818–95), an older contemporary of Abraham Bernstein.[15] As a *maskil*, however, Rayf-

---

14. Cf. Raphael Mahler, *Hasidism and the Jewish Enlightenment: Their Confrontation in Galicia and Poland in the First Half of the Nineteenth Century* (Philadelphia: The Jewish Publication Society of America, 1985).

15. Smoking on Shabbat is, of course, one of the best-known violations of Jewish observance, one favored by political, intellectual, and bohemian *apikorsim* alike. In his memoir, Gershom Scholem quotes the mid–nineteenth-century German Jewish Reform scholar Raphael Kirchheim as having said: ""Nothing surpasses the pleasure

man is barely a step above the Gentile general for Walden's Hasidic audience. But he appeals to Walden because of the principle he sees at work here: "rebellion ... as the true measure of faith."[16] That's interesting, but not Walden's central point. He adds that the *maskil* had a "devout wife" (*frum vayb*), who asked Reb Sholem Belzer[17] whether she should divorce her husband. The *sar sholem* (prince of peace), as the first Belzer Rebbe was known, told her to tough it out with Rayfman. She did, and had children with him, one of whom became a rabbi. Thus Rayfman is safe because of his wife's personal sacrifice (i.e., commitment to life with him). She is the hero of the story because her decision assured not only the birth of children, but also the quotidian workings of the household, which (as we will see) is the basis of spiritual fulfillment.

The Rayfman story was only preparatory to Walden's third and most complicated answer, which involves a couple like the Rayfmans, except that the husband is a morose recluse and the wife can neither bear children nor offer conventional sexual pleasure because she is an androgyne. Here then is the famed sexual perversity that repelled the proper Yiddish community[18] but might have rather attracted the urban and urbane *New Yorker,* in whose pages the outré is frequently brought into the mainstream.

Joseph Sherman suggests that Bashevis's story is largely about the accommodation of the sexual Other within Jewish law. He observes that

> this tale, set in the past, takes on a sharp contemporaneity. By presenting the uniquely idiosyncratic experience of two strikingly non-normative individuals through the narration of a third, it makes the point that monolithic unity, crumbling in consequence of apathy from within and socioeconomic pressures from without, must accommodate in proper balance—but within established halakhah—a range of expressions of faith if it is to survive.[19]

---

of pondering a *blat gemore* on Shabbes afternoon while enjoying a good cigar" [my translation]. Gershom Scholem, *Von Berlin nach Jerusalem* (Frankfurt: Suhrkamp, 1977), 197.

16. Sherman, "What's Jews?" 170.

17. Sholem Rokeakh of Belz (1779–1855), a disciple of the *Khoze* (Seer of Lublin).

18. Yankev Glatshteyn famously argued that Bashevis "dehumanized" his characters, "forcing them to commit the most ugly deeds. He brutalizes them and makes them so obnoxious that the Jewish reader is repelled." Glatshteyn, "Singer's Literary Reputation," *Congress Bi-Weekly* 32 (December 27, 1965): 17; quoted in connection with Bashevis's "grotesque eroticism" by Naomi Seidman, *Faithful Renderings: Jewish-Christian Difference and the Politics of Translation* (Chicago: University of Chicago Press, 2006), 254.

19. Sherman, "What's Jews?", 184. Sherman writes: "Including the 'Other' on condition that the core values of faith and Torah teaching are observed is the teaching of the prophet Isaiah in respect [to] the eunuchs (Isaiah 56:3–5). I read Bashevis's story as

To Sherman's mind, Bashevis produced "a critique not only of conventional Jewish observance, but of Hasidism itself."[20] Sherman argues that Bashevis is, retrospectively, making the case against Eastern Europe's normative Judaism (both mitnagdim and Hasidim accepted the norms of *halakhah*), urging it to open up (say, to homosexuals) and be more "humane." This reading fits into the liberal profile of *The New Yorker*.

To me this is a profound misreading. Bashevis was not interested in opening up unity to multiplicity, just as he wasn't interested in producing a hybrid version of his Yiddish stories for English readers to preserve "the artistic value" of the Yiddish original.[21] Yiddish was Yiddish and English was English. "*Der guf iz a guf un di neshome iz a nehome.*" (188) What he was interested in was the extraordinary potential of non-normative behavior to be both liberating and destructive, and although he was toying with it, he ultimately didn't like it. The hair-trigger proneness to rebellion and secession in Hasidism guaranteed the freshness and authenticity of the Hasidim's faith and was thus their conduit to God. Constant alertness protected from the soul-deadening ritual of observance and its accompanying hypocrisy. But the constant alertness and watchfulness for authentic, heart-felt expression was also exhausting and destructive, because it put the emphasis on individually felt expression at the expense of the communal bonding in quotidian ritual that provides comfort and security and reins in excess.

Bashevis's story is about finding the right balance between the rebellious, authentic inner life and the necessity to live in an orderly, ritualized way. It is thus deeply conservative. In the Rayfman anecdote, Walden's second *terets* (justification), the job is split along gender lines—the man behaves rebelliously while the wife creates the material conditions that allow him to be rebellious, to smoke his Shabbes cigar in the comfort of his study. Yekel Rayfman's non-normative *narishkayt* sinks into oblivion, while the wife's offspring continues in her materially observant way. It's a nice, though non-feminist, anecdote about the power of women and of matter over mind.

Walden's third *terets*, his story about Reb Mottele and the androgyne, moves from historical anecdote to moral example. Reb Mottele Partsever is a hardened version of the Kotzker Rebbe in his old age. He is a bitter recluse who extols his isolation. He has a running argument with the Master of the

---

a kind of midrash on that teaching." Email to the author, June 16, 2006. I want to thank Dr. Sherman for so generously sharing via email information and ideas about Bashevis and "Androgynous."

20. Sherman, "What's Jews?" 183.

21. Khone Shmeruk, "The Use of Monologue as Narrative Technique in the Stories of Isaac Bashevis Singer," appears as introduction to Isaac-Bashevis Singer, *Der shpigl un andere dertseylungn*, vi.

Universe ("*r'motele hot gefirt makhloykes mitn reboyne-sheloylem*," 182), and, like the Kotzker Rebbe, he "said such radical things that conventional Jews fled to the other ends of the earth." (96) But as in early Hasidism, "worship and rebellion went hand in hand." (96) Walden cottons to R. Mottele's rebelliousness and delineates its pedigree: "As long as he knows who his Master is, it does no harm for him to rebel. What was Job? What was Korach? Why did Moses break the tablets?" (96)[22]

In the manner of all romantics, R. Mottele's rebelliousness privileges self-ishly individual feelings over communal cohesion and causes strongly non-normative behavior. Using souls not clocks, the Partsevers *daven* at odd hours ("we pray so late it turns out to be early," 96) and "every man devised his own tune, both for prayer and for study." (96–97) The communal institutions, synagogue, study house, and *mikvah*, have fallen into disrepair; the community, never asked to assemble for a ritual meal, disintegrates. The *shammes* prefers the spirits he brews to the spirituality R. Mottele seeks to conjure. Rituals and routines hold communities together; but the Hasidic emphasis on authenticity of feeling denies their importance. Instead of giving rise to genuine spirituality, non-conformism leads to nastiness and decline.

Naturally, R. Mottele, like the Kotzker Rebbe, is deeply contemptuous of the masses. "Six hundred thousand ... journeyed out of Egypt, and as a result, they made the golden calf and longed for the fleshpots of Egypt." (96) Only in rare individuals, he assumes, is true spirituality found. His wife, dead after a year of marriage, seems to have been particularly devoid of metaphysical potential, since R. Mottele refuses to remarry, saying "piety and property don't go together," (96) a variant of "poor is pure" that proves his arrogance to be as profound as his selfishness. There is nothing attractive about Mottele Partsever, although Walden seems to admire his reckless willingness "*zikh tsu reytsn*," (180) which resembles Walden's own disposition.

Being intellectually foolish, like Rayfman, is one thing, but being disdainful of *simkhe-shel-mitsve*, joyful living as the path to God, is quite another thing, bordering on the sinful. Twice Walden calls attention to Mottele's insistence on celibacy after his wife's early death. The second time we hear the reason: "Mating, he used to say, is contempt of Torah." (97) Of course, the opposite is true. "Mating" is commanded by the Torah (be fruitful and multiply); kabbalistic lore even perceived its unique potential as a path to God. But because of Mottele's *makhloykes* with the Master of the Universe, he isn't going to oblige his general by providing him with more canon-fodder. The result of Reb Mottele's rebelliousness is not only that "in Partsev, everything was inside out and upside down," (97) but also that he remains

---

22. Cf. Sherman, "What's Jews?" 172–173 for some excellent comments.

stuck, like so many of Bashevis's characters, in an infantile narcissism. He never grows up, never moves from mating to conducting a marriage, never learns the ways of the quotidian world and is thus incapable of giving advice to those suffering quotidian hardships ("he gave such contrary responses that [the advice seekers] hurried away, bitterly disappointed," 97).

Mottele's *makhloykes* with God leads to ignorance of and contempt for the quotidian problems of his fellow Jews. It lands him in a decrepit, empty home with a drunk for company and a set of ideas that is not so much childish as anhedonic and destructive. The world is irrelevant to him and he is irrelevant to the world and soon utterly forgotten. In the characterization of Mottele, if anywhere, lies Bashevis's critique of Hasidism. The last sentence in Walden's introduction of Mottele sums up his subject's dead-end worldview: "female is flesh and flesh is slavery" (97; *nekeyve iz guf un guf iz avdes*," 185). Placed at the very end of Mottele's portrait, the sentence contains the seed of his redemption.

The stage is now set for delivery not only of the *coup de grace* to Reb Mottele, but also of Walden's teaching point. We remember that he wants to deliver a *terets* on the issue of *kiddush ha-shem*. As a good storyteller, he wants to mask the moral message and build suspense, so he delays delivery by starting to spin a new yarn. "Now hear a story" (97; "*itst hert a mayse*," 185). It takes place in the worldly world of material goods and productivity. A successful *arendar* (a lessee of a large estate) with five daughters and a son turns over the business to the son so he can study Talmud. The son, Leybele, becomes successful himself, travels on business to the cities, and one day comes home with a bride. She is an orphan named Shevach, not pretty but brainy.

She behaves oddly when the groom's mother tries to instruct her in the laws of ritual cleanliness and when the girls from the village come for the customary prenuptial visit. Like Reb Mottele, she answers her visitors at cross purposes and "they went away embarrassed." He disappoints; she embarrasses. Both fail as human beings. The wedding of Leybele and Shevach takes place and the bride embarrasses her husband at the feast when he forgets his speech and she "delivers the entire discourse from beginning to end and even adds an original bit of her own." (98) Immediately the wedding jesters poke fun at the couple because of the gender role reversal.

Shortly afterward the couple withdraws to a bedroom described as pitch dark ("*khoyshekh-finster*," 187), symbolic for the exclusion of all enlightening spirituality and the reduction of the human beings within to their bodily functions. That vulgar folk (*ameratsim*) are trying to peep in confirms that nothing spiritual takes place there.[23] The mismatch is soon discovered. Expecting a woman's body, the husband discovers an androgyne. Just as

---

23. Sherman in "What's Jews?" has some astute observations on that point (176).

Mottele's visitors run away bitterly disappointed and Shevach sent the girls away embarrassed, she now causes the groom to fly out of the room both disappointed and embarrassed as he shouts the news to the assembled wedding guests. Consternation ensues.

The physical oddity of Shevach is established. "Shevach was an androgyne—half man, half woman, neither one thing nor the other." (99) Her own assertion, "I don't want to be a woman. I'm a man" (98) is ignored. She is reduced to non-functional womanhood, which puts her low on the social totem pole, since she can't produce children ("no bread would rise from this dough" 99). She is divorced, given a bit of money, and sent away from Partsev.

It's easy to see why Shevach wants to be a man. She compensates for her physical defect through learning and by scoffing at the physical world of women (at the laws of *tahara* and at the girls who come to visit her). Yet she hasn't given up hope altogether. She agreed to the marriage, because she "imagined ... it might help." (99) Uncharacteristically for someone as learned as Shevach, she doesn't spell out just what sort of help she had expected. Her groom, an ordinary man from the material world, had only the most conventional expectations and was thus ill-suited to help her.

Having been rejected as a wife, Shevach naturally demands men's clothing. She puts on the ritual fringed undergarment and wants to don phylacteries. But the local rabbi prohibits it. "You can do as you please, but not here in Laptsev." (99) For spiritual sustenance "he reminded her of the passage in Isaiah regarding eunuchs," (99) which, conveniently for Laptsev, doesn't require the Laptsevers to do anything, since it states only that the Lord promises to give those eunuchs an "everlasting name" who keep the Sabbath and observe the covenant.

As a case in point, Walden mentions one Reb Hanoch Alexandrover "not only a saint but a great sage" of whom "everybody knew that he was a eunuch." (99)[24] Walden is probably thinking of R. Hanokh Henikh of Aleksander, a disciple first of R. Bunim, then of the Kotzker Rebbe, and finally of R. Yitskhak Meir of Ger, before overcoming his modesty and setting up his own court, where R. Abraham Bernstein of Sokhatshev was one of his disciples.[25] R. Hanokh Henikh's main teaching point was, unsurprisingly, the importance of humility and the service of the heart. Walden concludes his portrait of Shevach by summarizing the Laptsevers' resignation before the

---

24. The reference is probably to R. Hanokh Henikh Levin of Aleksander (1798–1870), the most important disciple of Yitskhak Meir of Ger. But I could not find any mention in the literature about Hasidism that he was a eunuch. For an excellent overview, see David Assaf, "Hasidism." *The YIVO Encyclopedia of Jews in Eastern Europe* forthcoming from Yale University Press; Assaf's article is available on the web at http://www.yivo.org/downloads/Hasidism_Overview.pdf.

25. Aron, *Ideas and Ideals of Hasidism*, 267, 316–317.

seemingly insurmountable physical obstacle Shevach presents: "The body is a body and the soul is a soul. The couple were divorced" (99); "*Der guf iz a guf un di neshome iz a nehome. M'hot dos porfolk opgeget.*" (188) I don't see Kabbalah at work in this sentence, as Sherman does; what we have here is a resigned recognition that boys will be boys, that you can't change a leopard's spots or make a silk purse from a sow's ear. The groom is all body (*guf*)–his name Leybele ("little lion") is a pun on *laybele* ("little body"). The bride is all soul (*neshome*); although her name is a near-homonym of the Yiddish adjective *shvakh* ("weak"); it derives from a Hebrew word meaning praise or compliment (shin-bet-khet). The groom, unimpaired in his material plenitude, is a *guf* who feels no need for a *neshome*.

The word *guf* had been used before in the story. When Reb Mottele defined women he offered the syllogism: "*nekeyve iz guf un guf iz avdes.*" (185) In light of what we know about the groom, we can see that Reb Mottele's definition is quite simply wrong: women *are* not *guf*, but the conventional male expectation of women is limited to *guf*. Liberation from such *avdes* is a matter of changing one's definition of *nekeyve* and thus one's horizon of expectation.

Leyzer Walden takes a break to light his pipe before he continues his narrative to let the inevitable happen. Shevach comes to Reb Mottele's court and he is smitten with her. His *shammes*, the drunk, conveniently dies, and the androgyne takes his place. The healing process starts. The seed of redemption comes up. Almost dutifully, Walden mentions that the "Kabbalah makes clear that both male and female attributes are present in every human being." (99) His Hasidic listeners, however, have already been sufficiently prepared–knowing the respective deficiencies of Mottele and Shevach–to anticipate the kabbalistic mechanics of the healing process, that is, the *tikkun* (the restitution of the scattered divine sparks to their legitimate place),[26] and they jump the gun: "I suppose the rebbe married Shevach," one of the youths calls out. "You guessed it, smart aleck," Walden replies.

Although the kabbalistic implications are clear to the listeners and they can now anticipate a description of restitution and fulfillment, what they really want to know is "What possible sense does it make in the quotidian world?" "*Vos iz der seykhel, ha?*" (190) *Seykhel* refers to the faculty of reasoning and is used here to inquire into the underlying rationale of such a union (from whence no children can issue). But Walden returns the story to the world of *khsides*. "*Nisht in alts iz do a seykhel, un oyb s'iz do a seykhel, must du im nisht visn*" ("Not everything makes sense. And even if it does, you don't need to know it"; 190).[27] This alludes both to the principle in Deut 28:29 that the mysterious things belong to the Lord and to the

---

26. Scholem, *Hauptströmungen*, 296.

27. Sherman's translation, 99.

Hasidic hermeneutic principle stated by Nathan Hertz, editor and printer of
R. Nahman of Bratslav's *Sippurey Maasioth*, that the stories of Hasidic masters are "far above the grasp of normal human intelligence."[28]

Walden's listeners who want *seykhel* instead of *tikkun* are very far away
from the *khsides* that is Walden's ideal. But Walden is determined to deliver
the pedagogical goods. He now shifts from telling a story (*mayse*) to
explaining "the nub of the matter" (*inyen*), beginning the final section of his
terets with the sentence "*der inyen is geven azoy* ("the nub of the matter
was as follows"; 190).[29] What follows is a description of Shevach's performance at Reb Mottele's court. It isn't a spiritual performance; it is a housewifely one that is not only *seykheldik*, but also takes on spiritual dimensions: she cooks and thus restores life to the decrepit courtyard. True, she
also lays *tfilin*, wears men's clothing, and dances with the Hasidim. But she
is compared to "Hodel, the Baal Shem's daughter," who is above reproach.

It is after Shevach has proven her femininity by restoring life to the court
and ensuring its quotidian functioning that Mottele, not fearing enslavement
by Shevach's *guf*, decides to marry her. Only then do things turn around fully. Shevach sheds her male clothing, and it is Mottele who writes to the
Sokhatshever for a responsum; he gives permission for the union, the wedding takes place, and Mottele is promptly accused by conventional minds of
succumbing to lust. But *guf* is not an issue in this union. Physical sustenance, of course, is assured (through Shevach's efforts) and acknowledged
as the basis of the soul's well-being, but beyond that *guf* is recognized for
what it is: a mere garment (*malbesh*, 191) for the soul. In fact, Walden
explains, "*der gantser inyen ziveg iz rukhnies, nisht gashmies*" (191; "the
core of that union was spirit, not flesh," 100), meaning Mottele's and Shevach's union was spiritual, not physical. "There are certain unions," he adds
later, "who have no need to couple." The spiritual congruence of two souls
is its own reward, like Torah study, which needs no physical remuneration
like a "*knip in bekl*" (182, 96).

After her marriage, Shevach reveals the full meaning of her name,
"praise." She becomes a Woman of Valor who is praised by all. She establishes even more firmly the physical basis of joyful living and intellectual pursuits. She restores the synagogue, study house, and ritual bath; she replaces
torn books; she studies to become a scholar and collects her husband's
teachings in seven books. They work on them together, but she undertakes
the manual labor of writing the words down and, after his death, goes to
Warsaw to have them published. The books are the couple's offspring and
Walden has them on his bookshelf.

---

28. Aryeh Kaplan, ed., *Rabbi Nachman's Stories* (Jerusalem: Breslov Research Institute,
     1983), 5.

29. Sherman's translation, 99.

Suddenly, Reb Mottele's pedigree consists no longer of Job, Korach, and the tablet-smashing Moses, but includes King Solomon and the Gaon of Vilna (100), because it turns out that Reb Mottele, like R. Bunim, is learned in worldly matters. In his union with Shevach he is perfectly responsive to her needs (as she is to his) and nurtures aspects of his own gender in her. Reb Mottele supports and sustains Shevach's intellectual and spiritual needs; Shevach, in turn, devotes herself entirely to his physical well-being (in providing housewifely services). Their union is androgynous and each behaves "androgynously" in it. Thus the story can be read as a paean to ideal marriage (Bashevis's own long marriage with Alma remained childless but produced many books).

More important, perhaps, is that Shevach's commitment to Mottele, her submission to domesticity to gain unimpeded access to spirituality, restores Mottele's authentic Hasidism, his joyous connection to the Master of the Universe, his *kiddush ha-shem* through *simkhe-shel-mitsves*. As Sherman points out, "Reb Mottele becomes the embodiment of that pristine *khsides*."[30] As he faces old age, sickness and death and his body weakens, his joy and readiness for ecstasy increase: "*vos shlafer der guf, alts freyle-kher iz gevorn di neshome*" (192; "the more feeble his body became, the more joyful grew his soul," 100). The rage, misanthropy and melancholy of his youth and manhood have been replaced by joy and tranquility. "Those who heard him singing on his deathbed said that no ear had ever heard such sounds before" (100; "*azoyne tener hot nokh keyn oyer nisht gehert. azoy zingn melokhim*," 193). In Partsev, then, Mottele, encounters in the infinitely complicated process of *tikkun*, a kabbalistic *partsuf*, a particular manifestation of the Divine.[31]

This was a strange story for *The New Yorker* to publish, a story about marital harmony and spiritual fulfillment. Written in May 1974, shortly after the Yom Kippur war and while fighting continued in Vietnam and American society was torn apart, the story was published in English as the specter of a new Vietnam in Iraq was just dawning on Americans. Was the story a response to war (and was that the reason *The New Yorker* ran it in 2003)? We must recall now that the entire story is a three-part refutation of the teaching that "a Jew ought to be prepared to lay down his life for Kiddush Ha-Shem, the Sanctification of the Holy Name." But what does the refutation finally amount to? The refutation was: "So?" – don't follow the herd. The second refutation in the anecdote about Rayfman's wife was: recognize where you are truly needed and accept your place, even if it goes against what you think is good for you. The third refutation in the Mottele and Shevach parable was: once you recognize your place, occupy it, even if it goes

---

30. Sherman, "What's Jews?" 180.

31. Scholem, *Hauptströmungen*, 295–299.

against *opinio communis*. Yet you must also accept the parameters of ordinary existence, because the requirements of the body are the basis for the well-being of the soul. It was a thoroughly unromantic answer. It claimed that the conditions of spiritual fulfillment were found in the ordered existence of the material world. This was a good thought, but more helpful perhaps to a people emerging from a war than to a people engaged in fighting one; and it didn't really solve the problem of obedience.

Bashevis, uncharacteristically, did not reprint this story and did not commission an English translation. I don't think he feared being accused of favoring homosexuality.[32] He would probably have found such a misreading rather amusing. The dense net of allusions to a particular niche of Hasidism might have been a deterrent to translating the story. What, after all, would an English-speaking audience get out of it? Ignorance of the Hasidic and kabbalistic concepts at work in the story would, indeed, show Shevach's sexual oddity in a different light.

Why did Bashevis not reprint the story in Yiddish? Was it too optimistic? Too harmonious? Conceived too much as a nostalgic wish fulfillment about the restitution of lost authenticity? Kafka, too, cut a short chapter from *The Trial* as unsatisfactory because it was too optimistic and harmonious a dream in which the hero got to live the author's fantasy of his body's perfect translation into pure writing.[33] Bashevis knew that Mottele's Hasidic fulfillment, never realized by the Kotzker Rebbe himself, was a sugary fantasy and he took care to append his skeptic's signature, choosing as the story's final word "*moyre-shkhoyre,*" "melancholy."

---

32. Sholem Asch had long beaten him to the punch on that score. Asch's successful 1907 play *Got fun nekome* (*God of Vengeance*), performed on Broadway in 1923, when it was already standard fare in European Yiddish theatres, featured a lesbian relationship.

33. Franz Kafka, "Ein Traum," *Erzählungen. Gesammelte Werke*, ed. Max Brod (Frankfurt: Fischer, 1983), 137–139.

Building Bridges Destined to Fall:
Biological and Literary Paternity in
Appelfeld's *The Ice Mine*

PHILIP HOLLANDER

Western intellectuals' adoption of Auschwitz as a symbol for a pan-European dystopia challenging the very idea of Enlightenment has led to the gradual defacement of the diverse Holocaust experiences of Jewish victims and survivors.[1] Viewed as passive objects loaded onto cattle cars and subsequently gassed and burned following their arrival at their final destination, these Jews cease to be bearers of a distinct cultural memory and serve as useful props in the portrayal of "the defeat of hope and the victory of meaningless death."[2] Consequently critics, such as Lawrence Langer, who concur with this view of the Holocaust have judged works of Holocaust literature "according to the strength of their refusal to derive meaning."[3]

Since the early 1980s, critics of Hebrew and Yiddish literature who object to the depersonalization and deracination of the Holocaust's Jewish victims and the delegitimization of efforts at meaning in Holocaust literature have attacked Auschwitz's synecdochal use and the effort to employ it as the primary criterion for assessing Holocaust literature. David Roskies's *Against the Apocalypse* and Alan Mintz's *Hurban* serve as important examples of this trend. With the publication of *The Modern Jewish Canon* in 2000, Ruth Wisse offered a cogent presentation of this position. Drawing on the framework she provides for the understanding of Holocaust literature and the setting of its canon, this essay will discuss the important place occupied by the novella *The Ice Mine* in Israeli writer Aharon Appelfeld's oeuvre. Rather than supporting Langer's linkage of aesthetic merit to a Holocaust work's refusal to derive meaning, this work combines aesthetic merit with an affirmation of life and Jewish community in its portrayal of Jewish existence in the ghettoes and camps. Its restrained use of language and its promotion of a "feminine" form of heroism return subjectivity to previously objectified survivors and victims and help the novella to promote a message

---

1. David Roskies, "What is Holocaust Literature?" *Studies in Contemporary Jewry* 21 (2005), 164.

2. Alan Mintz, *Popular Culture and the Shaping of Holocaust Memory in America* (Seattle: University of Washington Press, 2001), 50.

3. Mintz 2001, 50; Roskies defines "Holocaust literature," as "all forms of writing,...which have shaped the public and private memory of the Holocaust and been shaped by them" (Roskies 2005, 166), and usage of the term throughout this article will be in accordance with this definition.

of Jewish continuity to its Hebrew readers. As a result, it advocates the rejection of Langer's monolithic view of Holocaust literature in favor of a more contextual approach.

Wisse identifies context, social function, and literary period as three different facets of works of Holocaust literature that evaluating critics need to address. As she reminds us, "Holocaust writing obeys the internal laws of culture, not the imposed laws of Hitler."[4] Although it seems self-evident to stress the importance of linguistic and cultural context to literary judgment, Holocaust literary anthologies, such as Langer's *Art from the Ashes*, use translation to strip works drawn from various traditions of their particularistic features. Yet knowledge of Hebrew and the long tradition of Jewish responses to catastrophe help to inform readings of Hebrew works responding to the Holocaust. In addition, knowledge of external events shaping the Hebrew literary tradition, such as the formation of a modern secular Jewish identity in pre-state Palestine and the State of Israel's creation, help to inform one's understanding of Hebrew literature as a whole, including specific works responding to the events of the Second World War.

One's view of literature's proper social function also influences the evaluation of Holocaust literature and the establishment of a canon of Holocaust literature. While critics, such as Langer, stress aesthetics, many critics of Jewish literature, who recognize the contributions made by literary responses to catastrophe to Jewish continuity, as well as to Jewish efforts at collective and individual self-definition, view evaluation based solely on aesthetic grounds as overly limiting. As Ruth Wisse argues, "if we are to accept as a category the literature of the Holocaust, we should be equally prepared to recognize its function of reversing Hitler's plan of annihilation and overturning his definition of the Jews." (Wisse 2000, 197) Following the Holocaust, Jewish survivors and other concerned Jews were rightly worried about the Jewish people's continued survival. Writing in Hebrew or Yiddish, numerous Jewish writers engaged the Holocaust and attempted to move beyond the negative stereotyping imposed upon them by Nazi power. Instead, they asserted the possibility of continued Jewish life regardless of the incomprehensible suffering and death perpetrated against the Jews. While such writing contradicts Langer's opinion that the Holocaust should demonstrate hope's defeat and the victory of meaningless death, it should not prima facie deny the value, or the potential canonicity, of such writing.

Finally, one of the most innovative contributions made by Ruth Wisse in expanding upon earlier Jewish literary critics' work involves her introduction of periodization into the discussion of Holocaust literature. She discuss-

---

4. Ruth Wisse, *The Modern Jewish Canon: A Journey through Language and Culture* (New York: Free Press, 2000), 50. For similar remarks see Roskies 2005 and Mintz 2001.

es the commonalities of works written by ghetto diarists, as well as the commonalities of the works of a generation of young writers who emerged in the late 1950s and early 1960s whose literary efforts involved the transmission of their Holocaust experiences in an adopted language—efforts that brought forward the difficulties of Holocaust writing. This paper will transfer the discussion of periodization from literary groups to the individual author.

The inclusion of Aharon Appelfeld's 1987 short story "Tzili" in Langer's Holocaust anthology *Art from the Ashes* demonstrates that certain works by Appelfeld have satisfied the aesthetic criteria of proponents of the exceptionalist approach to Holocaust literature. Yet Appelfeld's novella *The Ice Mine* (1998) problematizes the use of this approach in evaluating his oeuvre and in developing a canon of Holocaust literature. Despite a portrayal of the ghetto and labor camp experiences that bring Appelfeld's writing into its closest proximity to "the heart of epistemological darkness" embodied by Auschwitz, *The Ice Mine* produces a hopeful and life-affirming work supportive of continued Jewish life. Rather than detracting from the novella's aesthetics, its positive message contributes to it. More than many of Appelfeld's translated works, *The Ice Mine* points to the need for readers to be more attentive to the developing context and changing social function of Appelfeld's work that divide it into separate stages.

Notwithstanding a sixty-year tenure in Israel and more than fifty years of Hebrew literary activity, efforts to place Appelfeld within a Hebrew and Israeli literary context have been limited. Even Alan Mintz, a critic who stresses the need to look at Holocaust literature in Jewish languages in a broader context, places Appelfeld outside of the Hebrew literary tradition of catastrophe.[5] Similarly Gershon Shaked, who made an important contribution by first noting the affinity of Appelfeld's early work to that of other young writers challenging Zionist orthodoxies, looks at Appelfeld's writing as largely disconnected from its Israeli context.[6] Shaked argues that Appelfeld has employed the archetypal image of Ahasuerus, the Jew cursed to wander until the second coming of Jesus, to create an image of the modern Jew that runs counter to models of prewar acculturated European Jewish identity and modern Israeli identity.[7]

These Jewish literary critics view Appelfeld as disconnected from a Hebrew and Israeli literary context due to the stress placed upon rupture in

---

5. Alan Mintz, *Hurban: Responses to Catastrophe in Hebrew Literature* (New York: Columbia University Press, 1984), 238.

6. Gershon Shaked, *Gal hadash basipporet haivrit* (Merhavyah: Sifriyat Poalim, 1971), 149–167.

7. Gershon Shaked, *Hasipporet haivrit 1880–1980*, Vol. 5 (Tel Aviv: Hakibbutz Hame'uhad, 1998), 269–271.

the early phases of his writing. As a result, their evaluations of his work bear a striking similarity to those of critics advocating the exceptionalist model of Holocaust literature. Yet as Mintz himself argued nearly twenty years after the publication of *Hurban*:

> The widespread phenomenon of continuity has been underrepresented and underreported. Continuity does not mean sameness, nor is it necessarily a product of repression, denial, and emotional constriction. Reconstructing a life after the war and striving to incorporate in that new life elements of prewar identity and belief deserve to be seen as a struggle as dramatic as the struggle to survive in the camps, in hiding, or in the forests during the war. To take the reconstructed life seriously does not mean to minimize the infinite suffering that preceded it nor the unending effects of that suffering. (Mintz 2001, 75–76)

Although the essence of Appelfeld's Holocaust experience has remained constant, it has found variant aesthetic representations. As Appelfeld has matured and the Israeli context in which he lives has undergone change, the message proffered by his writing has changed. As a result, one discerns three distinct phases in Appelfeld's writing that alternatively stress the Holocaust's disruptive nature or the possibility of Jewish continuity. *The Ice Mine*, the prime example of the emerging third phase in Appelfeld's writing, offers a message of Jewish continuity that connects it to earlier Jewish responses to catastrophe, despite a lack of faith characteristic of premodern examples.

The confrontation between emergent Israeli society's efforts to assimilate a vast immigrant influx and Appelfeld's personal need to make sense of his Holocaust experiences dominates the first phase in his writing.[8] Although Erwin Appelfeld changed his name to Aharon and worked on the land for years to help "make the desert bloom," neither the Zionist utopian vision nor the secular nationalist norms linked to this vision proved capable of offering him solace, understanding of his wartime experience, or an effective way of coping with his European past. While many Holocaust survivors in Israel, including Appelfeld, made a concerted effort to succeed in Israel through effective acculturation to the dominant secular norms, Appelfeld eventually rejected this path. He viewed it as unable to reconnect with the idealized Jewish past that he associated with the Hebrew language. Recognizing the sharp divergence between Zionist slogans and Israeli reality, Appelfeld attacked Labor Zionism's hegemonic discourse.

By challenging the way that Zionist ideals found expression in the new state and the way that contemporary Hebrew literature employed Zionism's

---

8. For a discussion of Appelfeld's poetic juvenilia not considered here, see Yigal Schwartz, *Aharon Appelfeld: From Individual Lament to Tribal Eternity* (Hanover, N.H.: Brandeis University Press, 2001), 8–14.

utopian aspirations in support of the status quo, Appelfeld joined the Israeli literary avant-garde in the early 1960s. Characters whose repressed Holocaust memories come back to disrupt and overturn their efforts to acclimate to Israeli society populate his debut collection *Smoke* (1962). These characters problematized the confident belief in the possibility of unlimited self-reinvention then predominant in Israel, and challenged the social organization of the Israeli state that had failed to effectively integrate Holocaust survivors. Meanwhile the static dystopian world of his follow-up collection *In the Fertile Valley* (1963) presented an implicit challenge to Labor Zionism's utopian strains and pushed contemporary Hebrew literature to look at life as it was, as opposed to how its writers wished it to be.

Key figures, such as S. Y. Agnon and Dov Sadan, pushed Appelfeld to explore the prewar European Jewish world from which he emerged and helped him to move into a second phase in his writing. The desire to make sense of this world came to dominate his writing. This new direction underlies the creation of important works of the 1970s, 1980s, and 1990s, including *Like the Pupil of the Eye* (1973), *The Age of Wonders* (1979), and *At One and the Same Time* (1985). By painting a huge multi-volume canvas portraying the evolution of modern Jewish life in German-speaking Central Europe, Appelfeld provided a larger context in which to understand his life and life in Israel.

Implicitly rejecting the idea of "Negation of the Exile" found in more extreme forms of Palestinian Zionism, Appelfeld reintroduced the European origins of Jewish modernity into Israeli discourse. Seen in historical perspective, Zionism proves to be only one form of Jewish modernity and Appelfeld's work helps to portray the wide variety of options open to secularizing Jews within the European context. By refusing to employ the Holocaust as a measuring rod against which to judge these variant forms of Jewish modernity, Appelfeld resurrects them and the plight of individual Jews who tested these various options in pre-Holocaust Europe as they attempted to find stability in their lives. Through revivification of Jewish modernity's variant forms and the portrayal of modern Jews' Kafkaesque struggles for meaning, Appelfeld returned dignity to those stigmatized by their victimization at Nazi hands. No longer disregarded for their inability to imbibe and act in accordance with Zionist "truth," survivors, such as Appelfeld, could refute the utopian claims of secular Jewish ideologies, including Zionism, which proved equally powerless in the face of the Nazi onslaught. The unchecked optimism characteristic of so many secular Jewish ideologies fell victim to the Holocaust, leaving a discursive cacophony seemingly at odds with Jewish continuity.

Paradoxically, when Appelfeld seemed most in accord with his surroundings, he distanced himself from them and entered into a third literary phase. By the 1990s, the Holocaust had made its way to the center of Israeli discourse. Its perceived impact on Israeli society rivaled that of the state's establishment. The ranks of those writing about it had swelled, and a second generation indirectly affected by the events of the Holocaust had emerged and helped turn it into a popular subject in Israeli fiction.[9] Simultaneously the Zionist orthodoxy that Appelfeld had earlier found so dangerous was in decline, while the catchphrase "Post-Zionist" entered into wide usage to describe Israeli society's fractured and diverse nature. With rupture and discontinuity no longer just a personal experience, Appelfeld shifted his attention to the maintenance of continuity in the face of rupture and produced the novella *The Ice Mine*.

In *The Ice Mine*, Erwin, the first-person narrator, recounts a nearly three-year period in his life. Chronologically, the narrative begins during his incarceration in the Czernowitz ghetto and concludes a short time after his liberation from a labor camp. Prior to the ghettoization of Czernowitz Jewry and the deportation of tens of thousands of Jews from the city, German-speaking Erwin studied at the local gymnasium. Following the city's conquest by Romanian and German troops, Erwin, his high school sweetheart Aida, and their parents serve the Third Reich as slave laborers. Despite the ghetto's difficult conditions, Erwin and Aida's love blossoms, and the couple marry after Aida becomes pregnant with Erwin's child. Then Erwin is unexpectedly deported. Together with additional inmates, Erwin and a large group of his townsmen who are deported with him find themselves in a labor camp on the far side of the Bug river building a bridge across the river. Despite numerous casualties, Erwin and other townsmen survive and find liberation following the camp guards' flight upon the advance of Soviet troops. After a period of paralysis, Erwin and others wander along the bank of the Bug until they arrive at a bridge. The novel ends with the beginning of the group's journey across the bridge.

Although the novella's protagonist shares a given name and has the same place of origin as the author, Erwin is a fictional figure nearly a decade older than Appelfeld, whose experience differs radically from that of his creator, and readers should be wary of biographical fallacy.[10] Nonetheless, central to an effective understanding of the novella is the way in which Appelfeld employs autobiography's retrospective premise to communicate the process of development that Erwin undergoes through the narration of his experience. The use of fictional autobiography allows Appelfeld to exploit the wide gap existing between Erwin as an experiencing character and Erwin as a retrospective analyst to help create a work of resistance that

---

9. Iris Milner, "A Testimony to 'The War After': Remembrance and Its Discontents in Second Generation Literature," *Israel Studies* 8.3 (2003), 194–213.

10. Budick argues that *The Ice Mine* attempts to fill in a lacuna in Appelfeld's memoir *The Story of a Life*. I question her designation of the novella as autobiography. Previous works by Appelfeld employ fictional biography to report events that are not part of the author's experience. See Emily Budick, *Aharon Appelfeld's Fiction: Acknowledging the Holocaust* (Bloomington: Indiana University Press, 2005), 158.

returns dignity and diversity to Hitler's Jewish victims while documenting a survivor's difficult return to life.[11]

The novella does not provide the reader with enough information to identify the length of time that separates the experiencing and narrating selves, but the traumatic issues introduced by the text lead the reader to conclude that a substantial time gap separates them. Two hundred seventy-four days in a labor camp, following an even longer ghetto confinement, leaves Erwin barely capable of independent action. Renewed individuality and identity, as well as the desire for continued life, will only gradually be achieved through painful retrospective analysis that culminates with production of the narrative of *The Ice Mine*.

Erwin's loss of individuality begins in the ghetto. There the Nazis stress his Jewish difference and his unworthiness. Even his right to exist must be earned through labor in the Third Reich's service. When the Nazi who oversees his factory demands that all Jewish workers cover their heads and pray daily, Erwin's identity comes under attack. Erwin's secular worldview must be abandoned, so he can conform to the overseer's view of Jews. Erwin resists such efforts to transform him and negate his individuality. Others, such as his intellectual cousin Felix, are not as successful: "Sometimes a wave of speech arises from within him and he repeats the cliches that wander around the workshops, as if he wasn't a thinking man but a word-spitting machine."[12]

With Erwin's deportation, his loss of individuality and identity intensifies. Forced work in a squad required to carry heavy seven-foot beams binds Erwin to his fellow Jewish prisoners. With his survival and others' survival tied to his ability to endure pain throughout the long workday, Erwin feels obligated to suppress his individuality. With identical blood and pus-browned uniforms sticking tightly to their bodies, the prisoners lose readily identifiable marks. Their animal-like movements and grunts mask their humanity. Only when lying awake at night do Erwin and the others allow themselves to imagine their liberation. Nonetheless, their suppression of their identities manifests itself in the predominant use of first person plural in novella sections relating life in the camp.

Although the prisoners help each other solve many of the difficult problems they face and maintain a sense of their humanity through communal living, the commune proves incapable of protecting the individual from his unconscious. Dreams bring out suppressed feelings, such as guilt, anger,

---

11. For a more detailed discussion of the interplay in fictional autobiography of "experiencing character" and "retrospective analyst" see Alan Mintz, *"Banished From Their Father's Table": Loss of Faith and Hebrew Autobiography* (Bloomington: Indiana University Press, 1989), 22.

12. Aharon Appelfeld, *Mikhreh hakerah* (Jerusalem: Keter, 1998), 40. This, and all following citations, translated by the author of this article.

and betrayal, tied to loved ones left behind. Left to fester, these feelings bring about self-loathing and a desire for death. To survive, the prisoners are forced to suppress their pasts even more strongly. Consequently the prisoners gradually become individuals tenuously connected to the past that formed them who cling like animals to the collective for survival.

With their liberation, Erwin and his fellow prisoners continue to function like an animal flock. Individuality's return remains far off. Some, who contemplate the death that they have witnessed and imagine the destruction wrought, commit suicide. Others exchange the flock shepherded by devout Pinchas for ones that enable them to better suppress their experiences. The option of individual and collective transformation advanced by Stahlnacht, a former military officer, proves tempting to many Jewish survivors. When Erwin and the other survivors locate a well-stocked bunker after liberation, Stahlnacht arms the men and has them swear fealty to a militaristic masculine ideal. His words are exact and his pronunciation chiseled. Anything less than a readiness to martyr oneself for group survival will show that the Jews are no better than insects.

Despite the direct nature of Stahlnacht's argumentation, many, including Erwin, do not accept it. In the camp, Stahlnacht embraced Nazi rhetoric that argued that camp life was meant to transform the Jews and prepare them for integration into general society. Thereafter he did his best to excel, but, when the Nazis punished him for his sincere efforts, the emptiness of their rhetoric became clear. Cowed by his treatment, Stahlnacht did not know how to respond and he renounced his efforts at leadership. Yet, when liberated, Stahlnacht attempts to impose a masculine discourse of transformation similar to the one preached in the camps and it leaves a bitter taste in Erwin's mouth.

The reemergence of Erwin's individuality begins with his decision to forgo the discourse of power preached by Stahlnacht in favor of the commitment to truth, "even if it is as cold as ice." (Appelfeld 1998, 136) Rather than covering over his labor camp and ghetto experiences with a facade of masculine power, Erwin looks for a way to positively reintegrate his death-drenched experiences into his life, cognizant of the potential pain involved. He will eventually succeed when he comes to recognize and portray a "feminine" form of heroism defined by David Roskies as "the heroism of small deeds, of parental sacrifice, bonding, loyalty, love." (Roskies 2005, 163) Yet communication of this form of heroism will not come as easily as Stahlnacht's pronouncements. Perceiving himself as indelibly marked by his experience, Erwin initially believes that his "legs will tell what has happened to [him] and [his] hands will add details." (Appelfeld 1998, 180) Unfortunately Erwin's flesh fails to communicate his inner experience. He must communicate in a different way. Falling back upon the language of interiority that he employed before the war, Erwin senses a "block of silence" (Appelfeld 1998, 180) inhibiting his speech. Rather than allowing himself to be brought to suicide by this inability to speak, like Dr. Buchbinder, who commits suicide when unable to effectively respond to accusations of collaboration that question his leadership in the camp, Erwin works toward a new approach to language that will enable him to integrate silence into his narrative. To arrive at this new approach to language, Erwin must separate himself from his fellow survivors to confront the trauma that acts as the linchpin of his silence.

Erwin's role in the death of his wife and their unborn child traumatizes him and inhibits his ability to both think and talk about the past. During Erwin's long incarceration in the ghetto, the love that he shares with Aida helps him to endure and even take pleasure in his life. Instead of allowing the filthy aspect of Aida's work in a munitions factory to detract from his appreciation of her, Erwin's love assists him in having it add instead. As he notes, "the suet accentuates the attractive lines on her face and I love her more." (Appelfeld 1998, 17) Myriad Nazi efforts to undermine the lives of the ghetto inhabitants function like a pesticide, but Erwin informs us that his "happiness [grew] like wild grass and [renewed] itself every day." (Appelfeld 1998, 23) It is this happiness, not a mere animalistic passion, which lies behind Erwin and Aida's decision to have sexual intercourse together. Yet when informed of Aida's pregnancy, Erwin proves incapable of celebrating the news of his first child, who will give physical expression to the love that he and Aida share. All that he can do is turn to her and apologize. While Erwin did not think about it at the moment of sexual union, Aida's pregnancy puts her life and the life of their unborn child in immediate danger: "Children and pregnant women are the first to be deported. The screams of children at home entrances will still be screaming within us when we are reincarnated and return as plants or birds." (Appelfeld 1998, 47)

Instead of viewing himself as an expectant father, Erwin views himself as a murderer. The imagined screams of his wife and his unborn child haunt him. Erwin feels that he has betrayed Aida, instead of protecting her as he promised. While conditions in the labor camp enable Erwin to successfully repress his past, liberation pushes his feeling of betrayal and his unconscious recognition that his wife and his child have been put to death toward consciousness. This sense of betrayal and Erwin's knowledge of his wife and child's deaths are what inhibit his ability to narrate his experience. Only by confronting them will his retrospective analysis of past events move forward.

Despite the pain involved in analyzing the events surrounding Aida's pregnancy and death, this analysis helps Erwin to give narrative form to his experience. Mistakenly viewing his efforts to procreate as an act of murder, in accordance with the logic of the genocidal Nazi imagination, Erwin hesitates to create a narrative of his experience, perceiving it too as a potentially lethal form of paternity. Only by reexamining the events leading up to and following the announcement of Aida's pregnancy from a new perspective does Erwin succeed in removing the false linkage between his act of paternity and the death of his wife and child. Rather than being a murderous act, his fathering of a child in the ghetto guiltlessly voiced the Jewish people's desire to live on and garnered the support of ghetto residents who viewed pregnant Aida with pleasure. The Nazis viewed this desire as a form of resistance, but this view and the Nazis' subsequent murder of Aida and her child point to the very illegitimacy of their rule. While neither Erwin's act of paternity nor Aida's determined effort to nurture her unborn fetus meet the standards of "masculine" heroism, proper attention to these and similar acts allow for the creation of a narrative concentrating on Jewish acts of "feminine" heroism and love rather than victimization and deadened emotion. By embracing this possibility through a form of selective narration, Erwin finds his voice. The completion of this narrative provides him with a substitute for the child that the Nazis denied him, which also serves as a memorial to Aida and others whose selfless efforts helped him to survive. This narrative cannot resurrect the dead, but it offers them a positive role in the promotion of the Jewish future.

Erwin's strategy of selective narration draws on the model Aida employs during her pregnancy. He comes to recall this strategy only when he reflects on their time together in the ghetto. Instead of allowing the difficulties of the present to bring her or Erwin down, Aida uses her memory to communicate experiences that buoy them and help them to continue on. As Erwin explains, "Aida remembers feelings in me that were put away or died out in their splendor. She preserved them, and now when she raises them from the depths they have a new type of vitality in them." (Appelfeld 1998, 36) Many of Aida's happiest memories are those of time spent together with her parents in the resort town of Kimpolong and, when recalling its verdant landscape, "she speaks words that give off the scent of pasture." (Appelfeld 1998, 45) Aida draws on her ability to present her experience in new and engaging ways to bring those experiences to life for her listeners' benefit, as hinted at above through the use of synesthesia. Considering her technique, Erwin recognizes the pleasures of poetic language and its usefulness for communicating the "unspeakable." Poetic language and a Spartan style, which provokes the reader into filling in missing details, provide Erwin with an effective way of voicing truths too painful or too sublime for direct communication. Although Erwin could reserve these techniques for portrayal of the devastating nature of his Holocaust experience, he prefers to follow Aida's lead and promote examples of beauty, human kindness, and love present amidst the darkness that prove capable of nourishing his audience.

Not surprisingly, Erwin employs a Spartan style, frequently using poetic language, in his portrayal of his mother to produce poignant expressions of care and affection experienced during his ghetto incarceration. Even though she works the same long hours as her husband and son, his mother stills finds a way to provide them with tasty meals: "Mom's food always has a conquering taste, and now, in this poverty, it is as if the taste has become more varied. Even her pancakes fried without oil melt in the mouth, and her soup fills the bones with warmth and spreads a concealed hope." (Appelfeld 1998, 39) The face of absence does not prevent Erwin's mother from embracing the present and provoking thoughts of the future seemingly cooked into her soup.

Erwin's Spartan style helps him to avoid sentimentalism and voice his mother's subtle expression of deep emotion at critical times, such as at the moment of his sudden removal from the ghetto. After his name is called and he is commanded to line up with those to be sent to "the central tailor shop in Munich," his mother takes leave of him: "My name was called and my mother held me with both arms. My name was called again and I released myself from her and I ran to the wall." (Appelfeld 1998, 68) Erwin leaves it to his reader to interpret his mother's grasp and his decision to pull free. One can view her grasp as a mother's refusal to part with her son, one last parental effort to shelter a child from potential danger, a final goodbye, or some combination thereof. Simultaneously Erwin's decision to break free can be seen as juvenile embarrassment at a mother's public expression of love, a son's desire to exert his independence, or his desire to protect his mother from punishment for obstructive behavior, or some combination of these emotions. Nobody speaks a word, but Erwin's restrained style evokes a full gamut of emotions communicating the complex relations between mother and son.

Erwin provides a similar restrained expression of love in the camp when Honig, one of his distant relatives, conveys his awareness that he will not make it home:

> "Erwin, my dear," Honig whispered.
> "What," I said and stretched out the small canteen in my pocket.
> "It's clear that I won't be returning home, tell them that you saw me."
> "No," a scream let forth from my mouth.
> Honig was shocked by my scream and he held my hand.
>
> (Appelfeld 1998, 125-126)

Erwin's continued strength, expressed through the canteen's extension, enables him to nurture others. Yet when confronted with the possible loss of Honig, who serves as a surrogate father, his fear of abandonment causes him to act like a child. With Honig's arrival, Erwin reestablishes and strengthens his ties to the past through information Honig provides about his family. His aid enables Erwin to maintain a hold on his unique nature, a fact emphasized by the first mention in the novella of Erwin's name in a letter to Aida prompted by Honig months after arriving in the camp. Despite his growing weakness, Honig decides to continue in the paternal role by holding Erwin's hand, as Erwin absorbs what he has just be told, aware that Erwin will communicate his death, like a son, once he is gone.

In order to best present examples of human kindness and love, such as these, Erwin structures his narrative to emphasize the continuing vitality of Jewish community both during and after the Holocaust. When looking to recount his wartime experiences, Erwin could have begun his narrative with the arrival of Romanian and German troops to his hometown, the ghettoization of the Jews, or his deportation, but he purposely avoids giving these events narrative primacy, because focusing on these events would unduly emphasize his lack of agency and the Jewish people's lack of agency. By choosing to open his narrative *in medias res* nearly three months after his arrival in the labor camp, Erwin instead emphasizes the mental and physical strength of the Jewish inmates, as well as their cooperative efforts, that enable them to endure the conditions that they face even as comrades and friends die around them. The heavy use of the iterative in the first chapter enables the reader to acclimate quickly to the highly regulated camp routine, just as Erwin and his townsmen have done. In the second chapter, Erwin shifts his narrative back to the ghetto prior to his deportation and once again employs the iterative to lend an air of normalcy to the regulated daily lives of ghetto Jews prior to his deportation.

After presenting the effectively organized and vital communal life existing among labor camp and ghetto Jews, regardless of the extreme conditions that their largely absent persecutors impose, Erwin provides a chronological narrative of his ghetto life, his deportation and labor camp arrival, and his life in the camp and immediately thereafter. This narrative purposely eschews an easy ending. Through selection of the liberation of the labor camp prisoners or the homecoming of the townsmen to Czernowitz as possible end points for his narrative, Erwin could have given his readers the impression that the world of the ghetto and the labor camp were what writers, such as Ka-Tzetnik 135633, have referred to as "a different planet," but, by having his narrative conclude with him making his way across a bridge over the river Bug with two companions, Erwin hints that the events of the war end with neither liberation nor homecoming. Instead the events of the war must be understood as part of a larger ongoing narrative.

By starting his narrative *in medias res*, quickly presenting the "normal" and "routine" worlds of the ghetto and the labor camp, and concluding his narrative with an open ending, Erwin retrospectively challenges the simplistic view of the pre-Holocaust world as an Eden forever torn asunder by the abnormality of war. While Erwin perceived his life in the German cultural milieu of Czernowitz as highly stable, his war-time encounter with hundreds of other Jews maintaining a panoply of different forms of Jewish identity helps him to recognize the rapid and revolutionary change undergone by Jews in his hometown and its environs over the course of the last few generations. The nurturing world of his childhood, like the community of the ghetto and labor camp, was merely a temporary haven created in a turbulent time from which he benefited.

With the encroachment of modern forces that undermined the social and economic foundations of Eastern European Jewish society, each succeeding generation faced new challenges that demanded new approaches to Jewish continuity. After reflecting on the war and what preceded it,

Erwin makes use of narrative ending to voice his approach. The innovations of Hasidism employed by his grandfather, the rebbe of Zjadover, helped him to provide spiritual sustenance to his followers. Yet Erwin's father viewed Hasidism as irresponsive to change and he painfully broke with it. Traveling to the city, he became an engineer, employing reason to earn his livelihood and support his family. Viewing his Jewishness as little more than ethnicity, he takes little from his father's home. Instead he provides Erwin with a secular upbringing that he sees as best able to help him find his way. Yet this rational worldview does not sustain Erwin during the war. Although he yearns for his ancestors' religious faith, which is revealed to him for the first time in the ghetto, he fails to embrace faith or any form of ideological certainty. In the absence of any clear plan, Erwin joins Pinchas and Salo in their crossing over the Bug river. Only later does he grasp the symbolism of this crossing and its value. The Bug represents death and despair in the novella. When Erwin chooses to make his way across it he embraces the nurturing environment of Jewish community, despite differences in belief that separate him from his companions, and highlights his recognition of the vitality and beauty of Jewish life even in the worst of times, as well as the confidence in the future shared by both his grandfather and father. Although incapable of negating death and the despair that derives from it, Erwin employs aesthetics to build a bridge across the abyss of the Holocaust for readers of his narrative aware of the inherent instability of his message. Nonetheless he proffers this message until a better bridge can be built.

Through creation of a mature survivor retrospectively mining his ghetto and camp experiences for exemplary moments of humanity from which to construct his future-oriented narrative, Appelfeld enters a new stage in his writing. *The Ice Mine* presents selective employment of memory as a viable Holocaust response alongside repression and total submission to the past. As a result, Erwin's aesthetic presentation of vital Jewish communities composed of colorful and disparate individuals challenges the limitation of the canon of Holocaust literature to works best able to express the rupture caused by the Holocaust. Simultaneously it meets the demands of late twentieth-century Israeli culture while working to reverse Hitler's plan to destroy the Jews by showing a path to a viable Jewish future through "feminine" acts of heroism—two basic criteria advanced by Wisse for Holocaust literature. Yet Appelfeld's presentation of viable seeds of hope in death's kingdom challenges the Holocaust's uniqueness and presents it as another catastrophic challenge to Jewish survival that can be overcome. Can continuity and the Holocaust canon coexist, or should Holocaust literature in Jewish languages be allowed to become a mere subset of modern Jewish writing driven by creative betrayal? Neither question has a simple answer, but *The Ice Mine* should surely be part of the debate.

Life/Writing:
Aharon Appelfeld's
Autobiographical Work
and the Modern Jewish Canon

NAOMI B. SOKOLOFF

No mapping of the modern Jewish canon can be complete anymore with-out mention of life-writing. Various related genres—autobiography, mem-oirs, diaries, autobiographical fiction and more[1]—have gained increasing vis-ibility in Jewish literature in recent years. Holocaust memoirs, no doubt, are the most recognized category; examples appeared shortly after World War II and have proliferated decades later. Moreover, autobiographical writing in Israel has attained new prominence since the 1990s.[2] Scholars have also discovered immense riches in autobiographical strains of American Jewish writing, from its beginnings till today.[3] At one time, recounting one's life may have been a negligible genre, considered less than central to Jewish tra-dition; now it seems to be everywhere, early and late, in writing by Jews.[4]

My thanks to Susan Shapiro for her discussion of these questions with me. Thanks also to Yael Kampf of the Appelfeld archive at Ben Gurion University, for helping me to locate useful secondary material.

1. Sidonie Smith and Julia Watson list 52 varieties of life-writing in their book *Reading Autobiography: A Guide for Interpreting Life Narratives* (Minneapolis: University of Minnesota Press, 2001).

2. Major Israeli writers who have turned to autobiographical modes include Amos Oz, Hayim Gouri, Shulamit Hareven, and Yoram Kaniuk, as well as Aharon Appelfeld. For discussion of this trend, see Gershon Shaked, "A Monument for the Fathers, a Beacon for the Sons," *Modern Hebrew Literature* 1 (2004/2005), 133–148.

3. For example, two special issues of *Prooftexts* (18, 2 and 18, 3 [1998]) were devoted to the topic of autobiography. Essays collected there by editors Hana Wirth-Nesher and Janet Hadda cover nineteenth-century immigrant writing, memoirs by more recent immigrants (such as Eva Hoffman), the fictional autobiography of Philip Roth, and more. Also of interest: the recent republication of autobiographical work written in the early twentieth century; see *My Future Is in America: Autobiographies of Eastern European Jewish Immigrants*, eds. Jocelyn Cohen and Daniel Soyer (New York: NYU Press, 2006).

4. Alan Mintz' path-breaking work *Banished from their Father's Table: Loss of Faith and Hebrew Autobiography* (Bloomington: Indiana University Press, 1989) argues that autobiography only belatedly entered modern Hebrew letters, because it was a mode of writing not integral to Judaism or classical Jewish texts. Taking issue with that stance, Michael Stanislawski concludes that forms of Jewish autobiography have, in fact, appeared frequently over the centuries but have been under-recognized. See his book *Autobiographical Jews: Essays in Jewish Self-Fashioning* (Seattle: University of

Aharon Appelfeld's life-writing merits particular consideration with regard to the Jewish canon. His work is centrally preoccupied with the writing of a life and with a life devoted to writing, and it is marked by a keen struggle for self-definition and reclamation of Jewish identity in relation to literature and Jewish texts. These qualities come to the fore above all in *Sippur hayim* (1999)[5] and in *'Od ha-yom gadol* (2001).[6] Both books complement and expand richly on the autobiographical dimensions of Appelfeld's published essays and on the numerous interviews he has given over the years.[7] They showcase how Appelfeld, as a survivor of the Holocaust, created a future for himself through his engagement with and disengagement from literary traditions while fashioning his own imaginative vision.

Ruth Wisse, in arguing the importance of defining a modern Jewish canon, remarks that the Jews will share a common future insofar as they can recognize and transmit works that embody their collective past. She writes, "A people that intends to participate meaningfully in the world would first have to know itself and be able to represent itself through a creative cultural continuum," and she privileges the literary canon in this mission for she considers it a unique repository of modern Jewish experience.[8] Appelfeld enacts this idea profoundly, on an individual level; he is, as it were, a test case of her thesis. Because he came from an assimilated home and had little formal or religious education, and because he survived the war by passing as a non-Jew (thus being removed even further from external Jewish identity), he starts from a position of Jewish cultural deficit. Then, once given the opportunity to make a new life after the Holocaust, he goes about forging a new identity through extraordinary determination to acquire Jewish literacy. To an important degree it is through immersing himself in great books

---

Washington Press, 2004). For an in-depth study of Jewish autobiography, especially as it developed in Hebrew and Yiddish in the nineteenth century, see Marcus Moseley, *Being for Myself Alone: Origins of Jewish Autobiography* (Palo Alto, Calif.: Stanford University Press, 2006).

5. (Jerusalem: Keter, 1999). Translated by Aloma Halter as *The Story of a Life* (New York: Schocken, 2004).

6. (Jerusalem: Keter, 2001). Translated by Aloma Halter as *A Table for One: Under the Light of Jerusalem* (London: The Toby Press, 2005).

7. Among his essays are *Masot beguf rishon* (Jerusalem: WZO, 1979); an English version is available as *Beyond Despair: Three Lectures and a Conversation with Philip Roth* (New York: Fromm International, 1994). For a biographical sketch and a list of interviews, see my entry on Appelfeld in *The Holocaust Novel: The Dictionary of Literary Biography*, ed. Efraim Sicher (Gale Pub., 2005), 17–30. In addition, several outstanding films feature interviews with Appelfeld: Adi Japhet Fuchs' "Appelfeld's Table" (2006), Nurit Aviv's "From Language to Language" (2004), and Zolton Terner's "Transnistria: the Hell" (1996).

8. *The Modern Jewish Canon: A Journey Through Language and Culture* (New York: The Free Press, 2000), 4.

that he acquires the tools for his own art and for crafting his own distinctive voice. In this way he lives out Wisse's conviction that literature is an indispensable way of "knowing the inner life of the Jews." He attempts to know himself and his people by coming to know the canon, and then weaving into it his own narrative art.

In many ways, Appelfeld's self-presentation in *Sippur hayim* and *'Od ha-yom gadol* also provides a compelling illustration of issues at the heart of contemporary debates about autobiography. He epitomizes at once three, sometimes competing, theories about the telling of the self: (1) a model that holds that narrative is constituent of the self; (2) an approach that emphasizes how the self emerges in cultural contexts; and (3) the insight that there is more to selfhood than can be expressed in self-narration. In this essay I examine these three strands in Appelfeld's work to suggest what a riveting contribution he makes to the corpus of Jewish life-writing and to explore aspects of his interactions with the canon: how it shapes his art and how he reinforces it, while also transforming and expanding its boundaries.

The dramatic events of Appelfeld's early life are widely known. Born in Bukovina in 1932 to a loving and financially comfortable family, he suffered enormous shocks and losses in the Holocaust. When he was eight, his mother was murdered by the Gestapo. He and his father were interned in a ghetto and sent on forced marches. At age ten he escaped from a camp, then he lived through the war wandering alone in the Ukrainian forests, at times seeking refuge with Gentiles, and later following the Red Army. Concealing his Jewishness was crucial for his survival. In 1946, at the age of fourteen, he arrived in Palestine as an illegal immigrant with the aid of Youth Aliya. This is the background that became the basis for much of his fiction, which has dealt with the world of European Jewry destroyed by the Holocaust and with the approach of catastrophe, as well as with the aftermath of liberation and the experiences of survivors and refugees.

My focus here, however, will not be on Appelfeld's early ordeal, but rather on the years of recovery and self-discovery in language and literature that figure so importantly in *Sippur Hayim* and especially in *'Od ha-yom gadol*. Those texts recount how, in refugee camps and later in agricultural schools, Appelfeld began to learn Hebrew. With this renewal of his formal education (which previously had extended only to first grade), he entered a new life in a new language. In fact, between 1946 and 1952 he gained enough knowledge to pass entrance exams and gain acceptance to the Hebrew University of Jerusalem. This was not an easy process. Losing a mother tongue and acquiring a new language, under any circumstances, is trying. For Appelfeld it was fraught with trauma. He lived a radical disruption and suppression of his native tongue, German, as he endured years of enforced or wary silences. His displaced childhood left him with but a smattering of various languages—including some Ukrainian, some Romanian, and some Russian—but no proper schooling in any of them. Not surprisingly, he describes his inner state after the war as a realm of chaos, crippling confusion, and fear. Lack of coherent language led him to a shaky sense of self, and so he writes, "Without a mother tongue, a person is defective" (*"belo safat em, adam hu ba'al mum,"* 88). In this way he recalls his own struggles and those of other child refugees who stuttered, withdrew into silences, or swallowed their words. The struggle to master Hebrew was titanic, and he compares the experience to climbing a sheer mountain wall. In time, he found his way in his adopted tongue and ultimately emerged as one of Israel's most prolific and celebrated authors. Yet, even after living in Israel for more than fifty years, he noted that writing in Hebrew still felt to him like sculpting hard stone.[9]

The way back to language and forward with his life, as Appelfeld presents it, unfolded through an encounter with literature. He appears in his memoirs, especially in *'Od ha-yom gadol*, as a bookworm. An introvert who read voraciously after his arrival in the Yishuv, he read first in German (despite discouragement from teachers) and then, with difficulty, in Hebrew. In his university studies Appelfeld focused on Jewish literature and Yiddish, which meant that he read widely from the Bible, Talmud, and Hasidic tales, as well as from the modern Jewish canon. Along with traditional religious texts he took in works by Mendele, Ch.N. Bialik, S.Y. Agnon, Jacob Glatstein, Haim Grade, and others. He speaks, with special fondness, also of writers who were his teachers, such as Eliezer Steinman, Leib Rochman, and Leah Goldberg; and he makes particular mention of Kafka. Altogether he presents himself as finding meaning through a rebirth into reading and writing. Literature helped him gain a greater sense of control over his inner life. As he explores Hebrew, the sacred tongue and the key to a vast tradition of Jewish texts, he discovers a religious and cultural world that was neither part of his upbringing nor a matter of his own personal practice, but that he welcomed as a reminder of his grandparents' lives. Similarly, immersing himself in Yiddish, he absorbs a language spoken by his grandparents as well as by many of the refugees he met in his youth. And, as he forges connections to the riches of the past, modern Hebrew helps him express in fiction and essays some of the turmoil, alienation, and wordlessness of the war years.

---

9. Aviv, "From Language to Language" (2004). It is striking that Joseph Conrad, another author famous for his creativity in an adopted language, also invokes imagery of unyielding rock to describe the process of writing. A native speaker of Russian, he observed, "I had to work like a coal-miner in his pit quarrying all my English sentences out of a black night" (quoted on p. 153 of Stephen Kellman's "Lost in the Promised Land: Eva Hoffman Revises Mary Antin," *Prooftexts* 18, 2 [1998]: 148–159). For discussion on the relation between creativity and loss of mother tongue in Appelfeld's art, particularly in connection to the novel *Laylah ve-'od laylah*, see Naomi Sokoloff, "Aharon Appelfeld and the Translingual Imagination," *The World of Aharon Appelfeld/ 'olamo shel Aharon Appelfeld*, eds. Risa Domb, Ilana Rosen, and Itzhak ben Mordechai, *Mikan* (2005).

It is important to keep in mind that, as Appelfeld articulates experiences of the Holocaust and of Jewish life in pre-war Europe, his storytelling is less a remembering than a reconstructing of a lost world. Yigal Schwartz points out that Appelfeld's art is never simply a recollection of the past, for his memories from a very young age are too fragmentary to be entirely accurate.[10] Consequently, even at its most autobiographical, his writing is an act of imagining what was or might have been, rather than a reporting or re-collecting of facts. In addition, we can conclude that, while looking backward, Appelfeld writes his way into the future. This is a process of vital importance. In effect, it is through writing that Appelfeld makes a life for himself—not just in the sense of rebuilding his experiences, nor even in the additional sense of making a living at reading and writing (his activities as an author only after a long struggle brought him a livelihood). Most fundamentally, he makes a life by gathering up the fragments of memory and casting them into stories, thus slowly knitting together a sense of self and gathering the strength to move on with living in the present. Narrative psychologists have argued that the self is "defined by and transacted in the narrative process"[11] and that crafting the story of one's life is not only "descriptive of self but fundamental to the emergence and reality of that subject."[12] If this is true of all life-narratives, Appelfeld's case is exemplary, since language for him was so hard won, the past so filled with upheaval, and his grasp of selfhood so shattered during the war.

Tellingly, Appelfeld remarks that he feels most at peace when he is writing: "When I write, I feel anchored to a time and a place; but when the writing no longer flows, it is as if a cloud descends and my world darkens and narrows" (*Table for One*, 100). This powerful statement seems straightforward enough in English; the original Hebrew, however, is both more forceful and also revealingly multifaceted. Take the words "*keshe 'ani kotev, 'ani mehubar*" (116). The word *mehubar* does not signify "anchored" so much as "connected." It comes from the root *h-b-r*, meaning "to compose"—that is, both "to put together" and also "to write." Here, since the root functions as an adjective describing the self, it suggests that writing is what keeps Appelfeld together—*is* indeed, what constitutes him. Composition, the composing of narrative, is what enables him to construct a life, and in the process of constructing texts, to feel calm and grounded. Much as in English "to be composed" means to be calm, in this case the Hebrew, too, implies composure. Moreover, the original text is especially emphatic, for *h-b-r* also underlies not only words related to texts, such as *hibbur* (a composition),

10. *Aharon Appelfeld: From Individual Lament to Tribal Eternity*, trans. J. M. Green (Hanover, N.J.: University Press of New England for Brandeis University Press, 2001).

11. Paul John Eakin, *How Our Lives Become Stories: Making Selves* (Ithaca and London: Cornell University Press, 1999), 101.

12. Anthony Paul Kerby, quoted by Eakin (1999), 21.

but also words that denote social bonds, among them *hevrah* (society or company) and *haverut* (friendship). Consequently, the sentence cited speaks to Appelfeld's hard-won sense of belonging. As a refugee who suffered multiple displacements and dislocations, he wrote his way into the hearts of his countrymen. This was no small accomplishment, he tells us, for Israel in the 1950s was a society that often looked on Holocaust survivors as outsiders, more to be rescued than respected. Through his writing Appelfeld earned a place of respect in that world, and he came to feel that Jerusalem was his true home.

The notion of writing and narration as constitutive of life is encapsulated also in the title *Sippur hayim*. Though translated as "The Story of a Life," this phrase implies much more in Hebrew. First, it suggests story as something lived (the words *sippur hayim*, with *hayim* a verb, could be understood literally as "a story is lived," "we live a story," or "a story is something we live"). As the language of psychotherapy would have it, people live storied lives; they find meaning and form their identities as they recount their experiences.[13] Emily Miller Budick has noted that this term applies aptly to Appelfeld's writing and that *Sippur hayim* "concerns the way in which life is a story and how, without its storied quality, it ceases to be a life at all."[14] She argues that Appelfeld's art thereby counteracts the Nazi assault on individual imagination; as he endows each of his fictional characters with the capacity for memory, hopes, and dreams, Appelfeld acknowledges the humanity of Holocaust victims and celebrates their lives.[15] We may add that the words "*sippur hayim*" can be understood in another way as well; this phrase suggests stories are something living. Writing possesses a magic that brings the past to life and endows it with vitality. Appelfeld explains his art this way: "Literature is an enduring present—not in a journalistic sense, but as an attempt to bring time into an ongoing present" (*Story of a Life*, 125; "*sifrut h'i hoveh bo'er l'o be-muvan jornalisti el'a ke-she'ifa lehavi et ha-zmanim le-nokhehut matmedet*," *Sippur hayim*, 114). Similarly, he notes, "*ha-zman sheli h'u hoveh nimshakh*"—"my time [or, verb tense] is present continuous" ('*Od ha-yom gadol*, 63). In other words, stories are not only that which we live on, that which sustains us, but that past that lives on in us. Keep in mind, furthermore, that *sippur hayim*, with *hayim* as a noun,

---

13. See, for instance, George C. Rosenwald and Richard L. Ochberg, *Storied Lives: The Cultural Politics of Self-Understanding* (New Haven: Yale University Press, 1994).

14. *Aharon Appelfeld's Fiction: Acknowledging the Holocaust* (Bloomington: Indiana University Press, 2005), 157–158.

15. Appelfeld's novel *Pit'om ahavah* (Jerusalem: Keter, 2003) would lend itself readily to analysis in these terms. It features a protagonist who, in his old age, devotes himself to writing and, in the process, reworks his understanding of his entire life, tells his way into the future in defiance of death, and recognizes how Communism took his story away during his youth.

can mean "a story of life," that is, a story that promises hope and renewal. Altogether, Appelfeld conceives of literature as something profoundly life-affirming. In a sense, all his artistic output is life-writing. His corpus of writing, in its entirety, emerges in creative ways from his lived experience and stands as an affirmation of his survival. Through it he constructs a path in the present and a bridge into the future.

These qualities present themselves notably in *Sippur hayim* and *'Od ha-yom gadol*, where Appelfeld highlights that he is a product of his own toil, that he forges his self as he writes. In the process Appelfeld reworks the conventional "autobiographical pact"—Philippe LeJeune's oft-cited term for the understanding that in autobiography the author, the narrator, and the subject are one and the same. Putting into relief his own multiple positions as author, narrator, and subject, Appelfeld also subtly effaces their differences and merges them.[16] All three are indeed unified, not because Appelfeld entertains a naïve notion that he is accurately chronicling the past, but rather because the act of composing contributes to the ongoing evolution of the self.

Altogether, Appelfeld presents a remarkable example of the general principle that self and story are "complementary, mutually constituting aspects of a single process of identity formation."[17] This is a principle that has multiple ramifications not only for literary studies and psychology, but even for neurobiology, which has examined ways in which people who suffer amnesia, autism, or other cognitive deficits suffer inabilities to narrate.[18] The idea that the self is "narratively structured"[19] has special resonance in regard to Appelfeld, who experienced devastating early deprivations, who reports that loss of native language meant loss of a coherent sense of self, and who nevertheless went on to rebuild a life through writing. How exactly did he reach this achievement? One factor, certainly, is that he overcame difficulties through his mighty efforts to write; another factor is that he did not undertake this challenge in isolation. He pointedly arrives at a sense of self-

---

16. Many Holocaust memoirs more emphatically uncouple the present from the past, insisting on ways in which the self is fragmented. Lydia Kokkola discusses this phenomenon in *Representing the Holocaust in Children's Literature* (New York and London: Routledge, 2003), 27–100. Citing Rose Zar's autobiography, *In the Mouth of the Wolf* (1983), this study shows how that author adopted different names and different roles at different points in her life. As a Jewish girl she was Ruszka; she was Wanda when passing as a Catholic; and when she began a new life in America after the war, she became Rose. For an illuminating essay on the invention of the self in Jewish autobiography of a different era, see Suzanne Shavelson, "Anxieties of Authorship in the Autobiographies of Mary Antin and Aliza Greenblatt," *Prooftexts* 18, 2 (1998): 161–186.

17. Eakin (1999), 100.

18. Ibid., 101.

19. Ibid., 100.

hood through an acquired language that carries an extraordinary heritage of cultural richness. Without the Jewish literary canon Appelfeld could not have made sense of his own experience. A second approach to autobiography is, therefore, also helpful in analyzing Appelfeld's life-writing. This is a social constructivist line of thinking that draws on Bakhtinian notions of dialogue, Vygotsky's psycholinguistics, and theories of intertextuality. Its proponents go so far as to suggest that not only written texts, but deep inner experiences as well are molded through the models of received texts: "To report on one's memories is not so much a matter of consulting mental images as it is engaging in a sanctioned form of telling."[20] Such insights reinforce the conclusion that it is through give-and-take with the canon, through his discovery of centuries of abundance in Jewish texts, that Appelfeld achieves his own voice.

Literature is, explicitly, one of the grand themes of Appelfeld's autobiographical work. In 'Od ha-yom gadol he situates his life-story almost entirely in relation to his acts of writing and presents his personal evolution expressly in terms of literary events: what he read, the curriculum he followed at Hebrew university, the Jerusalem cafes he frequented and in which he has written his books, the writers he met and the critics who encouraged or berated him (including S.Y.Agnon, Uri Zvi Greenberg, Hayim Hazaz, Shlomo Zemach, Shimon Halkin, Gershom Sholem, and an assortment of unnamed detractors). To this he adds the lessons he derived about writing, as well as his decisions about what to tell his students, his children, his audiences. He frequently cites dialogue with other authors and how he responded (or chose not to respond) to their comments. Such storytelling, which invests so much importance in a life of books, emphasizes Appelfeld's absorption and rejections of canonical models, and ways in which he aims to insert himself into the tradition.

Indicative of his pervasive ties to literature, he notes that when he travels abroad he always carries with him a book by Kafka and either Hasidic tales or a mystical text. "I can't be," he says, "without a Jewish book" (Table for One, 59). And he often acknowledges mentors. Strolling in Meah Shearim with Agnon, he admires the master's loyalty "to the heritage of his forefathers" (62) and identifies with his religious seriousness. Having expounded at length on the importance of close observation as the foundation of his art, Appelfeld uses these words to appreciate Agnon's attention to detail and intimate knowledge of Jerusalem: "In this, as in other ways, Agnon and I spoke the same language. Agnon's world had its roots in local surroundings, which provide him with a foothold and an anchor through all his wanderings." (36) Appelfeld also deeply respects Leah Goldberg, and he is grateful for her kindnesses to him. But he is especially glad that she defers to him when it comes to writing about the Shoah—for he is a survivor, not she—and

---

20. Kenneth Gergen, quoted by Eakin, 111.

that she concedes he is right to break away from previous models of writing. She tells him that those who criticize his stories do so from "lack of understanding—and vulgarity" (36), and he notes, "She herself had written a play about the Holocaust, but in her heart of hearts she knew that what she had written about the Holocaust was not exactly 'Holocaust' and did not penetrate the essence of the tragedy." (36) Appelfeld is quite clear about some of the ways he departed from predominating literary trends. He resented the themes, so prominent in fiction in the early decades of the Jewish State, which were (in his view) too narrowly committed to the tenets and values of Labor Zionism. He goes out of his way to note that he was educated on, and then became disaffected from, the writing of Moshe Shamir, S. Yizhar, Hayim Gouri, and others who, in their endorsement of the *sabra* ideal, also contributed to negation of the Diaspora and so proved dismissive of refugees and survivors.

Informed readers, familiar with Appelfeld's fictional oeuvre, can readily fill in more detail to identify what he has drawn from his precursors. Like Kafka, he crafts an aesthetic of the absurd that relies on eerie subtleties. There are echoes of Agnon in the musicality of his prose, and, like Agnon, Appelfeld creates a collective vision, populating his imaginary worlds with a panoply of Central European characters. From Bialik and others comes an appreciation for the longevity of the Hebrew language and its continuities with the religious past. Intertextual resonance and references to classical texts come boldly into play in the titles of his fictional texts.[21] And yet, well known, too, are ways that Appelfeld's art rebels against previous norms. Filled with reverence as he is for the canon, Appelfeld's famously understated prose distances him from a tradition of overflowing allusiveness. Appelfeld's prose is known also for its stylistic oddities and subtle idiosyncrasies of syntax, vocabulary, and grammar. As one of the first Israeli writers dedicated to conveying the perspective of Holocaust survivors, Appelfeld found early in his career that the reigning modes of narrative did not do justice to his material. Centrally concerned as he is with Holocaust themes and upheavals in European Jewish life, Appelfeld's fiction often cultivates a uniquely expressed poetics of trauma and alienation.

At the root of Appelfeld's departure from precedent and convention is his conviction that much of his childhood experience remains outside the bounds of what he can express. He insists time and again that part of what makes him a writer is his sense of that which he can't recount.[22] Always

---

21. Gila Ramras-Rauch elucidates many of these titles in her study, *Aharon Appelfeld: The Holocaust and Beyond* (Bloomington: Indiana University Press, 1994).

22. Masha Itzhaki, "Aharon Appelfeld/Histoire d'une vie, autobiographie d'une ecriture," *Yod* 9, Nouvelle serie (2003) comments on those elements of Appelfeld's writing as they produce instability and uncertainties in *Sippur hayim*, thus challenging the promise of accuracy implied in the autobiographical pact.

hovering nearby are physical sensations and phenomena he has observed that impel him to write and that

> [m]ore than my conscious mind does, my body seems to remember (*Story of a Life*, 51).

> I have forgotten much, even things that were very close to me—places in particular, dates, and the names of people—and yet I can still sense those days in every part of my body. Whenever it rains, it's cold, or a fierce wind is blowing, I am taken back to the ghetto, to the camp, or to the forests where I spent many days. Memory, it seems, has deep roots in the body (*Story of a Life*, 50).

Consequently, received conventions of storytelling go only so far in giving voice to his inner world. He openly acknowledges his indebtedness to literary tradition and to his studies, but he concludes on repeated occasions that what he learned in the university was *not* what taught him to write. He claims, for instance, "It was not [...] from books that I drew knowledge and understanding, but from life itself" (*Table for One*, 133). On another occasion he remarks that in his student days he loved to spend time in Meah Shearim—not so as to live an observant Orthodox life, but simply to observe, to watch traditional Jews and to study in them a kind of faith that he "hasn't been able to learn in the university and from books" (80). Similarly, he attributes his voice in prose to the simple words and the silences of people he overheard in Jerusalem cafes. "Café Peter was my school for writing," he notes, acknowledging gratefully that conversations there were models for his prose and that they enabled him to walk away from the high stylistic register that was in vogue in Israeli narrative of the 1950s. In sum, aware as he is of the redemptive role that Hebrew and Hebrew literature have played in his life, he nonetheless implores the reader to let him be himself, to accept his rebellion against the literary fashions of his era, and, above all, he asks them to acknowledge nonverbal dimensions of his existence that elude familiar conventions of storytelling. Given the profound memories that impel him to write but defy expression, his own writing must break out of previous literary molds and, even then, leave much unsaid.

That the self expressed in self-narration is not coextensive with all of selfhood is an idea that has gained considerable traction in the contemporary study of autobiography. Paul John Eakin explains that every individual has many selves or multiple registers of selfhood, some of which are pre-linguistic or inaccessible to reflexive consciousness. Developmental psychologists observe a well-developed kind of intersubjectivity in children even as young as two months old.[23] Yet storytelling (the kind of verbalization that involves memory and imagined futures) is usually characteristic only of people ages three and up. Accordingly, Eakin argues, narrative cannot encom-

---

23. Eakin (1999, 23) cites the work of Ulric Neisser on this topic.

pass many dimensions of personal interaction that begin early and continue throughout life. He goes on to claim that literature scholars for too many years overlooked such matters. Focused as it was on how the human subject is constituted through discourse and ideology, literary theory paid too little attention to ways in which people live as embodied beings.[24] Post-structuralist and post-modernist critics worked for decades to dismantle naïve notions of a unitary self, but an informed understanding of autobiography now can be greatly enhanced by exploring ways in which multiple selfhoods exceed the post-structural subject. In short, story and life may be inextricably intertwined, overlapping, interpenetrating, but there's much more to life than can be told. These are points to bear in mind as Appelfeld insists repeatedly that words are not enough and that literature is inadequate to express what he remembers—of the ghetto, the camp, wandering in the forests, and more. He remarks, "I still haven't found the words to give voice to those intense scars on my memory" (2004, 50). It is through indirection and through distortions of the literary norms of his day that he conveys his sense of this other dimension of life, hinting at unspoken sensations and bodily memories.

Altogether, Appelfeld's life-writing acutely highlights the riches of canon and its limitations, the importance of absorbing literary tradition and also undermining it so as to break out of its conventions. In a number of ways, Harold Bloom's model of canonicity aptly elucidates aspects of Appelfeld's self-presentation. Bloom sees canon in terms of a fierce struggle with precedent, of an indebtedness to and competition against precursors that entail strong misreadings of received literary traditions. Bloom's chief point is that important literary figures, those worthy of being included in the canon, fight against that which came before and succeed to the degree that their originality fosters new, unfamiliar ways of seeing the world. This new vision must be so compelling that, eventually, what was novel or innovative in it becomes accepted and is no longer deemed strange.[25] Such a dynamic is evident in Appelfeld's art, marked as it is by central tensions between, on the one hand, respect for forerunners and the generative powers of canon, and, on the other, claims for the embodied self that eludes language and strains against literary convention. Moreover, his artistic vision, which seemed so quirky and idiosyncratic at the outset of his career, over the decades moved from the margins of Israeli literature to its center. In fact, while retaining its own unique voice, Appelfeld's writing helped reshape the Israeli canon in significant ways. Bringing the Holocaust to the forefront in Hebrew literature, it contributed to a sea change of attitudes in Israeli

---

24. Eakin (1999, 64) cites the work of Ian Burkitt on this matter.

25. *The Western Canon: The Books and School of the Ages* (New York, San Diego and London: Harcourt Brace & Co., 1994).

society that became especially pronounced in the 1980s and 1990s. In those years survivors gained new visibility and new empathy. At the same time, because he was welcomed with great enthusiasm in Europe and in America, Appelfeld further transformed the modern Jewish canon by bridging Israel and the Diaspora. The indispensable Jewish bookshelf is defined quite differently in Israel than it is in North America; Israeli writers rarely attain a high profile in English translation, and so there is remarkably little literary consensus between the two most important contemporary centers of Jewish life.[26] Yet, Appelfeld is an exception, a point of convergence. Readers on both sides of the Atlantic hold him in high esteem as a spokesperson for the experience of survivors. Both societies in the 1980s came, in part through Appelfeld's writing, to a new admiration, even lionization, of survivors and to a new appreciation for their testimony of the war years. Highly celebrated at home and in translation, Appelfeld enters the canon from both directions.

To be sure, Appelfeld's conception of canon differs in significant ways from Bloom's, and not just because he is dealing with a different corpus of texts. In addition, whereas Bloom emphasizes adversarial struggle between the generations, Appelfeld gathers about him evidence of how individual writers, the Hebrew language, and the city of Jerusalem have created a home for him, not one free of struggle and without tension, but yet, unequivocally, a home. In some measure his work recalls Robert Alter's formulation of canon as an elective "transhistorical textual community."[27] The communal bonds Appelfeld describes have a decidedly personal quality, as he combines references to the Jewish classics and reports of his interactions with authors and critics in his immediate milieu. Appelfeld's account of immersing himself in Yiddish and Hebrew texts is perhaps most akin to an orphan's search for parents, for substitute family, for a world of literary and cultural abundance to compensate for overwhelming personal loss. As such, his work resists a number of other understandings of canon that have recently gained currency. For example, in his study *Cultural Capital* John Guillory defines canon as a zealous guarding of the gates of privilege, and he presents canon formation as a process that entails its own dynamics regardless of the contents of texts.[28] Such concerns are not the driving force behind either *Sippur hayim* or *'Od ha-yom gadol*. Nor does Appelfeld's life-

---

26. On the failures of conversation about literature between Israelis and North American Jews, see Alan Mintz's *Translating Israel: Contemporary Hebrew Literature and Its Reception in America* (Syracuse: Syracuse University Press, 2001) and Sidra Ezrahi, "Canon Fodder," *Tikkun* 19, 1 (February 2004): 67–73.

27. *Canon and Creativity: Modern Writing and the Authority of Scripture* (New Haven and London: Yale University Press, 2000).

28. *Cultural Capital: The Problem of Literary Canon Formation* (Chicago: University of Chicago Press, 1993).

writing present a view of canon as cultural agenda—meaning, ideological coercion, a set of rules and standards to follow. (Indeed, this kind of canon is specifically what Appelfeld chafed at as a young man.)[29] Ultimately, Appelfeld discusses canon less as a struggle over power and taste than as a search for belonging.[30]

Of course, Appelfeld's own choice of what to include and what to exclude in his memoirs leads to interesting re-mappings of canon and to telling redefinitions of centers and margins. In his life writing he mentions many writers of importance to him, but he leaves out major names, too. As Gershon Shaked has pointed out, *Sippur hayim* and *'Od ha-yom gadol* make no mention of Amos Oz, A.B. Ychoshua, or other contemporaries of Appelfeld's who helped form and define the cultural context in which his work found significance. Nor does Appelfeld acknowledge many of the honors he won or the praise he received from critics during his career. Instead, he creates a personal mythology that heightens divisions between survivors and *sabras*, insisting on his own outsider status within Israeli society. What comes to the fore are the difficulties he had in overcoming marginalization, as a writer dearly attached to his Diaspora past. Such a selective, at times myopic, view of his relation to literary currents yields more of an autobiographical myth than an accurate memoir or record.[31]

Emerging from this version of events is a portrait of an artist who, as a young man, shaped himself meticulously out of his encounters with a strik-

---

29. Several critics make a strong case that the modern Jewish canon has always been fluid, with constantly shifting boundaries and no set cultural agenda. See, for instance, Hillel Halkin, "Writing Jewish," *Commentary* 110, 3 (Oct. 2000): 37ff. and Dan Miron, *Harpayah letsorekh negi'ah: likrat hashivah hadashah 'al sifruyot ha-yehudim* [From Continuity to Contiguity: Toward a New Theorizing of Jewish Literatures] (Tel Aviv: Am Oved, 2005).

30. The formation of the modern Hebrew canon has become the focus of extended research and debate, though that debate has not yet dwelt much on Appelfeld's writing. For discussions in English, see, for instance, Chana Kronfeld, *On the Margins of Modernism: Decentering Literary Dynamics* (Berkeley: University of California Press, 1996); Hanan Hever, *Producing the Modern Hebrew Canon: Nation-Building and Minority Discourse* (New York: NYU Press, 2002); and Michael Gluzman, *The Politics of Canonicity* (Palo Alto, Calif.: Stanford University Press, 2003). After this article went to press, I discovered one very useful discussion of Appelfeld's relationship to Hebrew literary traditions, in particular his links to Ch. N. Bialik and to Natan Zach. See Lincoln Shlensky's "Lost and Found: Aharon Appelfeld's Hebrew Literary Affiliations and the Quest for a Home in Israeli Letters," *Prooftexts* 26 (2006): 405–448. See also Risa Domb, *Identity and Modern Hebrew Literature* (London and Portland: Vallentine Mitchell, 2006), 57–66, for some comments on Appelfeld's *Story of a Life* in relation to other recent Israeli autobiography.

31. "A Monument for the Fathers, a Beacon for the Sons." Another blatant omission from the memoirs is that Appelfeld makes almost no mention of his reception abroad, such as the stellar reviews he received in the *New York Times*.

ingly sophisticated array of texts. The salient features of his history as a reader are rupture and hiatus in his education, followed by an immersion in
texts that were classics or part and parcel of an established modern Jewish
corpus. This dramatic jump into adult books, with scant mention of juvenile
reading, sets him apart from a number of other authors whose memoirs
present them as insatiable bibliophiles and report at length on developmental stages in their reading.[32] Saul Friedlander, for instance, presents an
instructive contrast. Another young boy who survived the Holocaust passing as a non-Jew, Friedlander likewise came to discover Jewish texts and
identity after the war. However, his account of his youth, *When Memory
Comes* (1978), includes references to children's literature, Jack London
adventure tales, church teachings foisted on him in a Catholic school in
France, a plethora of non-Jewish writers from his father's library, and more,
as well as his belated introduction to the Bible and Jewish traditions. Friedlander's tale is fascinating as an account of personal, intellectual, and spiritual awakenings, but Appelfeld's project is of a different order of magnitude.[33] Although in *'Od ha-yom gadol* Appelfeld does make brief mention
of reading Jules Verne before the war–suggesting that in actuality he was
once a precocious reader–the memoirs deliberately position him primarily
as an adult reader who measures himself in relation to major Hebrew and
Yiddish literature. His life-writing presents his self-discovery and literary
endeavors as an accelerated, ongoing, and authoritative process of re-estab-
lishing continuities with Jewish tradition, imagining community, and acquiring expressivity in Jewish languages so as to reconnect with the past
and build a future.[34]

Appelfeld's autobiographical texts do not present themselves as comprehensive, definitive accounts of his life, but as highly crafted, selective memoirs that present certain experiences and not others. Strikingly, for example, *'Od ha-yom gadol* acknowledges that it avoids almost all mention of
Appelfeld's father. Michael Appelfeld, in fact, survived the war, and father

32. Consider, for example, Amos Oz' *A Tale of Love and Darkness*.

33. Hana Wirth-Nesher (1998, 2: 117) points to a number of contemporary American
    Jewish autobiographies in which the self that emerges is as much a product of what
    the author has read as it is of what that individual has "lived," among them: Eva Hoff-
    man, Alice Kaplan, and Nancy Miller.

34. Much post-Shoah Jewish writing seeks to re-establish links to a severed past. Appel-
    feld's life-writing would make for a telling comparison and important contrasts, with,
    for example, post-war French Jewish writing. Using a term coined by writer Robert
    Ouaknine, critic Thomas Nolden speaks of "autojudeography," to suggest how
    authors construct their identity through writing and present themselves more as prod-
    ucts of what they have read than of any Jewish traditions or historical experiences they
    have lived. See *In Lieu of Memory: Contemporary Jewish Writing in France* (Syra-
    cuse: Syracuse University Press, 2006).

and son were eventually reunited in Israel. But, Appelfeld notes, this book is not the place to tell about that (ch. 33) and so his life-writing quite openly calls attention to the fact that it is not the whole story. More than that, it is intentionally incomplete; rather than "tell all" narratives, these are works in progress that attempt to reconstitute the self as to be able to live into the future. The unfinished quality of Appelfeld's life-writing is clear from the fact that *Sippur hayim* ends abruptly, with a final chapter that skips over many decades of experience. This deliberately curtailed account of his life then serves as a point of departure for *'Od ha-yom gadol*, a memoir that picks up were the earlier one left off. It returns a number of times to familiar terrain, recounting how Appelfeld emerged as a writer. Each time the text elaborates, points out new subtleties, enhances and brings fresh nuances to the story begun in *Sippur hayim*.

The very title of the text confirms the idea of ongoing composition, insofar as it suggests that more work remains to be done. The phrase *'od ha-yom gadol* "it is still broad daylight" comes from Genesis 29:7, a passage that recounts how Jacob first met Rachel at the well. Jacob comments that it is not yet time to bring the flocks in from pasture, not yet time to call it a day. As an autobiographical title, *'Od ha-yom gadol* implies that Appelfeld's work isn't yet done; telling his story is an ongoing challenge. Since, in Hebrew, *ha-yom* indicates not just "the day" but "today," the title calls attention yet once more to the importance of the present, and to "present continuous," as a central element in Appelfeld's self-definition as a writer. All this reinforces the impression that for this author life-writing is part of a larger, constantly unfolding project of self-invention through a life of writing. (It is worth noting that Appelfeld continued to write prolifically, after the publication of this memoir, with many manuscripts completed and not yet in press.) Combining its reliance on allusion to the Bible with an emphasis on what is yet to come, the title *'Od ha-yom gadol* concisely indicates a fundamental dynamic described in Appelfeld's memoirs: the author conceives himself as moving forward toward the future, with an eye ever on texts of the past, creating an imagined life that is simultaneously shaped by and shaping the modern Jewish canon.

Henry Roth, Hebrew, and the Unspeakable

HANA WIRTH-NESHER

"Roth did not have the choice of Jewish writers before him of writing in a Jewish language," observes Ruth Wisse in her essay on Henry Roth's *Call It Sleep*. "By the time he was brought to America Yiddish was reserved only for use inside the home and Hebrew remained for him a dumb mystery."[1] By describing his connection to Hebrew as "a dumb mystery," Wisse has articulated the power of Hebrew for Henry Roth. Not a language of fading indifference, Hebrew retained the kind of magnetism associated with mystery. What was Hebrew for Roth that he should care for it, fear it, and finally submit to it?

Hebrew has played, and continues to play, a far more significant role in Jewish American writing, or any Jewish writing for that matter, than has generally been acknowledged. In the spirit of Ruth Wisse's *Modern Jewish Canon*, particularly in the close and nuanced attention that she gives to the role of languages in Jewish literature (exemplified in her reading of Kafka in light of the affinity between Yiddish and German), I would like to highlight those traces of Hebrew in English that testify to a rich dimension of the works that we treat as Jewish writing. According to David Damrosch in his essay "Scriptworlds": "Alphabets and other scripts continue to this day to serve as key indices of cultural identity, often as battlegrounds of independence or interdependence."[2] In terms of modern Jewish writing, Robert Alter, in his study of the German Jewish writers Kafka, Scholem, and Benjamin, has noted that "the historical attachment of Jews to the stubborn particularism of their own graphic system is mirrored in their practice of clinging to Hebrew script even when they converted one of the surrounding languages into a distinctive Jewish language, as they did with Yiddish in Central and Eastern Europe."[3]

Since Jewish civilization has always tended to be at least bilingual, if not multilingual, this has often meant that Jews have negotiated more than one

---

This research was supported by the Israel Science Foundation (grant No. 622/06).

1. Ruth Wisse, "The Classic of Disinheritance," *New Essays on Call It Sleep*, eds. Michael Kramer and Hana Wirth-Nesher (Cambridge: Cambridge University Press, 1996), 73.

2. "Scriptworlds: Writing Systems and the Formation of World Literature," *Modern Language Quarterly*, 68:2 (2007): 195.

3. Robert Alter, *Necessary Angels: Tradition and Modernity in Kafka, Benjamin, and Scholem* (Cambridge, Mass.: Harvard University Press, 1991), 27.

language, and often more than one alphabet. Since the Hebrew alphabet has been intertwined with Judaism as religion, even Jews who are not literate in Hebrew have often treated the letters as signs of their ancient culture, and American Jews have been no exception. They dwell in the English language and its Roman letters, yet the Hebrew alphabet has remained a unique sign of their Jewishness. Attitudes toward Hebrew have been as divergent as the world views of American Jewish writers, ranging from the transgressive and parodic to the romantic or sublime. Yet the rupture of Hebrew into English, in Hebrew typeface or in transliteration, is seismic. It telescopes out in time and space; it locates modern secular writing in an ancient universe of sacredness and mystery. Not every appearance of Hebrew refers to the reification of language as it developed in Jewish mysticism, but in its double role as foreign and ancestral, Hebrew calls into question the seeming universality of its surrounding culture. Henry Roth's writings, from his by-now classic novel *Call It Sleep* to his four-volume autobiographical fiction *Mercy of a Rude Stream,* are all haunted by Hebrew.

Roth's biographer Steven Kellman chose to begin the biography with a Hebrew epigraph, an inscription by Roth himself in a notebook used to teach himself Hebrew in 1978: "*kol hahatkhalot kashot*" ("All beginnings are difficult"). With this phrase Kellman goes right to the heart of Roth's life and work in a biography that he aptly entitled *Redemption.* Difficult, agonizing, self-scrutinizing beginnings marked Roth's early years, beginnings that preoccupied him throughout his life. Hebrew, the sacred beginnings and redemptive ending of the collective story of Roth's people, was a language and an alphabet that would also haunt Roth from his beginning to his end. How much Hebrew did Roth know, and what did it mean to him?

He began his Hebrew study in *cheder* on the Lower East Side, cut short by his family's move to East Harlem. His *melamed* regarded him as gifted, and praised him to Roth's mother Leah. As he approached the age of thirteen, he submitted to his parents' pressure to resume his studies in order to prepare for his bar mitzvah, and he was called to the Torah on February 8, 1919. The Torah portion that day was *Parshas Truma* (Exodus 25 to 27), which recounts God's instructions to the Hebrews about the raw materials they needed to obtain to construct their portable sanctuary in the desert. The *haftorah* accompanying *Trumah* is Kings I, describing the construction of a permanent sanctuary, King Solomon's building of the Temple. The resonant and highly charged section from Isaiah, therefore, that serves as a site of Jewish and Christian theology and teleology in *Call It Sleep* was not part of Henry's compulsory training toward his bar mitzvah. It was a biblical passage (*b' shnot melekh Uziyahu*) that he purposefully chose to serve his theme and his artistry. As Wisse points out, "Chapter 6 is one of the most remarkable dramatic passages of the Bible. Its images of the Lord on a throne high and exalted, the fiery angels calling each to the other 'Holy, holy, holy is the Lord of Hosts,' and the lone prophet in the Temple crying, 'Woe is me, for I am lost, for a man of unclean lips am I,' form part of Jewish daily liturgy."[4] Roth found this notion of language as holy or profane to be so compelling that he wove it into both this novel and his later works.

In 1972 in Albuquerque, after his newfound identification with Israel, he returned to the study of Hebrew, this time with his wife Muriel with whom he would read passages in the evening after supper. His notebooks from that period, the source of the epigraph to the biography, show painstaking care in the Hebrew script, carefully punctuated by a hand that knows these letters but not the definitions recorded to the left of each word. In one of his workbooks, he begins a series of Hebrew exercises by writing the word "Shibboleth" at the top of the page, a reference to the Ephraimites' inability to pronounce "sh" (Judges 15), a story that has come to stand for speech performance as betrayal of identity in situations where boundaries are strictly enforced. The difference between spoken and written language and the accent marks in dialect writing that produce bilingual word games are trademarks of Roth's inventive prose. In addition to phrases from the Bible, most of the Hebrew words that appear on the pages of *Call It Sleep* and all four volumes of *Mercy of a Rude Stream* are drawn from religion, among them the monotheistic credo (*Shma*), the morning prayers (*Modeh ani*), the *Shmona esrei* (the 18 blessings that form the core of the *Kedusha* taken from Isaiah 6:3: "*kadosh, kadosh, kadosh*"), the prayer marking the arrival of an event (*shekhiyoon*), and the commands for different shofar blasts, such as *tekiya*.

Although Hebrew occupies a central place in all his writings, his attitude toward it shifted dramatically in his later years, reflecting his changing attitude toward his Jewish identity. Before turning to *Mercy of a Rude Stream*, written during the last two decades of his life, I will need to review his dazzling use of Hebrew in *Call It Sleep*, the work of his youthful years. Roth was acutely aware of the restrictions and taboos around the uttering and writing of God's name, the sacred tetragrammaton, because in *Call It Sleep* one boy cautions another in the outhouse not to commit a sin by using the Yiddish "noospaper" for toilet paper. "It's a Jewish noospaper," he says, "wid Jewish on id"[5] (239). Obviously, the boy is referring to the Hebrew letters, because there is nothing in the Yiddish language itself that could be defiled except the alphabet of which it is comprised. In this exchange, Roth gestures toward the holiness of that alphabet, from talmudic commentary on the significance of each individual letter to the kabbalistic cosmologies in which the letters are the source of God's creation of the universe. Furthermore, David Schearl's first lessons in Hebrew demonstrate Roth's consciousness of the sacredness attached to the alphabet and his strategy for deconstructing that tradition by reducing the words to childlike babble. Here are David

---

4. Wisse, "The Classic of Disinheritance," 69.

5. *Call It Sleep* (Farrar Straus Giroux, 1991).

Schearl's thoughts in *cheder*: "First you read, Adonoi elahenoo abababa, and then you say, And Moses said you musn't, and then you read some more ababa" (226). David moves from the words that denote God but do not invoke his unutterable name, *"Adonoi elahenoo"* ("the Lord our God"), to the word for father (*aba*) to the gibberish of an infant (bababa)—the reverse of acquiring literacy in Hebrew, to an unraveling of the divine into nonsensical bilabials. Later David will associate God's presence with Hebrew typeface in his prayer book, locating the divine on its pages: "That bluebook. Gee! It's God"[6] (227).

For David, Hebrew is identified with the patriarchal Jewish deity, who sometimes takes the form of his own father, an immigrant compensating for his loss of manhood by terrorizing and abusing both his son and his co-workers. What David seeks throughout the book is to still "the whirling hammer," to be free of this patriarchal authority (427). As the child of immigrants for whom Yiddish was mother tongue and Hebrew (more precisely *loshn-koydesh*) was paternal prohibition, Henry Roth identified English as the ultimate power that would liberate him. More specifically, he recognized in the author James Joyce the literary father whose language experiments had taught the young Jewish writer that "it was possible to create great art out of urban squalor."[7] Having devoured *Ulysses* cover to cover, Roth sutured Joycean techniques onto Jewish themes (what he ironically called "Hybrew" in *Mercy*),[8] primarily through bilingual transgressive wordplay with the Hebrew name of the father.

This is in part achieved by transcribing Yiddish accented speech in such a way that the auditory sharply contrasts with the visual. When David and the other boys in *cheder* prepare for the Pesach seder, they chant "Chadgodya!" which appears in American English *haggadot* as "one kid." Since David, the kid, is the weakest figure in the chain of power in his urban world (the *Chad Godya* being a chain of power), he is associated with the Passover kid, underscored by the fact that he has been awarded two pennies that day (two *zuzim*), one for performing as a Jew (for accurate recitation of the *Chad Godya*) and the other for performing as a Gentile (for acting as a Shabbes goy and lighting an old woman's stove after sundown). Within the Hebraic/Aramaic world of his father, David is the "gadya," [*gdi*] the goat (or lamb) to be sacrificed. Yet within the world of English, Joyce, and modernist literature, he is "god" the artist, the creator of the phrase "chadgodya," which, if read bilingually, signals the monotheistic credo for

---

6. For an extensive discussion of Hebrew and Yiddish wordplay in *Call It Sleep*, see Wirth-Nesher, *Call It English: The Languages of Jewish American Literature* (Princeton: Princeton University Press, 2006).

7. Unpublished interview with Hana Wirth-Nesher, February, 1992.

8. *From Bondage: A Novel*, 70.

the name of the Father, which must not be uttered, the *Shma*—as in "one God, ya" (which his *melamed* shouts at the first clap of thunder, "*Shma Yisroel!*"). Moreover, the deity associated with the "one only kid" has been cut down to lower case, and converted into a bilingual pun—the Aramaic "godya" to the American "gotya" or "got you." Since "getting someone" is an idiom for cornering or defeating them, this phrase refers to his own father's intention "to get" him, the act that sends the panic-stricken boy to the streets to seek God between the car tracks. A Gentile passerby who sees the child prostrate on the cobblestone cries "Christ, it's a kid!" identifying David as an American child and, for the reader, also as the "kid" in the Passover liturgy (420).

This crossing of languages and religions at a critical juncture in the work, however, does not mean that Roth has rehearsed, and endorsed, the move from Judaism to Christianity, sliding into a belief in the one kid of the Christian God (Christ, it's a kid!"). Given Christianity's highly charged relation to its father religion, Judaism, Roth takes his linguistic and religious boundary crossings one bold step further, as he parodies the Crucifixion, rewriting it as a Jewish story. After his electrocution by the sparks between the tracks that he mistook for divine light, David hallucinates that a blond man appears in a tugboat, writhing and groaning, purple chicken guts slipping through his fingers, as he morphs into the image of Jesus of the Sacred Heart, which shocked David when he first saw it on the wall of his Polish neighbor's tenement flat. Earlier in the novel this same blond figure on a tugboat shouted "Wake up, Kid!" to the dazed boy on the riverbank. Now he utters one phrase, "Chadgodya" (427). Voiced by the "kid" of the Hebrew father, the God of Moses, the phrase "one only kid" restores the Jewish context of Passover as Jesus reverts back to practicing Jew at the Passover ritual. Placing this particular Aramaic phrase into the mouth of Christ, who thereby affirms the name of the Hebrew God in that this is a bilingual sign of the "Shma," rewrites the script of the Passion by translating Jesus back into a Jew. This brilliant undoing of the Passion is mediated by the bilingual English-Hebrew Haggadah with its "One Kid, One Only Kid."

Not content to re-Judaize Jesus by having him recite the monotheistic credo with its unutterable name of God, Roth invests David's dreamlike perceptions with the image of his father's wooden cigar box, focusing on its sliding cover "whereon a fiery figure sat astride a fish" (the pictogram of Christ in Greek) and "The voice spelled out 'G-e-e-o-o-o d-e-e-e!'" (428). The representation of God's name in English, on the father's cigar box, and in Roman letters, highlights the vast difference between David's old and new languages when it comes to signifying divine patriarchal authority. Insofar as this is God's name in English, this is not a transgressive moment, but its force comes from the taboo in Hebrew that it invokes. Although English and Joyce emerge as Henry Roth's literary fathers in this modernist wordplay, Roth's English text is always entangled in "Adonoi elahenoo abababa."

Written from the perspective of a Communist atheist in the 1930s, *Call It Sleep* parodies all religion: the Christian Passion, the Jewish seder, and the text in Isaiah that both religions identify as the source of the prophecy of the coming of the messiah. In a wholly secular universe, sacred and profane are only constructs of religious systems spun out of human minds, and, therefore, linguistic wordplay circling around religious taboos undermines them. The only "sin" that the child protagonist of *Call It Sleep* commits is mistaking car tracks for God, which in Roth's technological urban secular world may not be a mistake at all, and uttering unclean words that Roth swiftly reduces to non-referential sounds devoid of the power to offend. But when Henry Roth began to write *Mercy of a Rude Stream*, a guilt-ridden writer embarked on a confession of sin, and for that reason Hebrew returned to his pages with the power of sacrilege and transgression.

Roth insisted that all the volumes of *Mercy of a Rude Stream* were novels. Readers have not been able to resist calling this extraordinary series an autobiographical fiction. The books are reconstructions of a version of Henry's past beyond the age of David Schearl, into adolescence and early adulthood, including a relationship with an Edith Wells, modeled on Eda Lou Walton, his muse, mistress, and mentor/mother. The main character is named Ira Stigman (stigma), for good reason, as we will soon see. Interspersed throughout the narrative are sections set apart by bold typeface in the form of a diary of the writer addressed to his computer Ecclesias. In these intervals, the author comments on the thinly veiled autobiographical episodes while recording minutiae of his writing present, from conversations with his wife M (Muriel) and visits from his sons, to the painful maintenance of his aged body.

Although the most provocative and charged use of Hebrew takes place in the second volume, the first book, subtitled *A Star Shines Over Mt. Morris Park*, paves the way for what is to come. It is laced through and through with Yiddish, with more than one hundred fifty words appearing in the glossary, nearly all of them associated with his family, home, and, in particular, his mother. Like an adolescent version of *Call It Sleep*, this first volume of *Mercy* traces Ira's journey away from his stifling Jewish family toward America. He recalls his bar mitzvah as "his halting, stumbling recital of a brief portion of the Sabbath reading from the Torah scroll in the synagogue, with an embarrassed Zaida at his side prompting...deprecating over his woefully ignorant grandson, he who had once been so glib and praiseworthy at producing the sound of the language—*lushen koidish*, it was called"(159).[9] His Bar Mitzvah brought into sharp focus what he knew then as "*Jewishness*, detested it, was held to it, to the extent that he was held by a single bond: his attachment to Mom, his love for her, for the artless eloquence that imbued so much of her speech" (161). Ira and Leah Stigman appear to be

---

9. *Mercy of a Rude Stream* (New York: St. Martin's Press, 1994).

models of David and Genya Schearl, Leah representing beatific and maternal Yiddish, an image tarnished by the boy's witness of her as erotic object through the male gaze of her young brother-in-law Louie, the biographical source of Luter in *Call It Sleep*. Hebrew is reserved for the lips of his grandparents, often in the blessings and prayers that characterize Eastern European conversation and social practice. His grandmother, Baba, will greet her son, returned from the front in WW I, with "Oy, baruch ha shem [Blessed be the Name]" (Mercy, 154). So far there seems to be no marked difference in the role of Hebrew between this late book and the attenuated Jewishness of *Call It Sleep*.

But all of this changes with the second volume, *A Diving Rock on the Hudson,* because in this confession he reinstates the sister he had erased in *Call It Sleep* to atone for his sins. In this volume he reveals repeated acts of incest during their adolescence. He paves the way for this confession by divulging another sin, as if to set the stage by portraying Ira Stigman as a bad character. Just as Augustine's pears and Rousseau's ribbons are substitutes for the graver sins perpetrated in their confessions, Ira Stigman first steals a fountain pen in class and hides it in his parents' bedroom, for which he is expelled from high school, much to his and their shame: "his stealing of the fountain pen only part of the forbidden he felt within himself, only part of the corroding evil. Stealing was easily overcome ...The other was amalgamated, was fused with bodily rapture, with a name never to be named...Oh, the unspeakable, the abominable act" (55).[10] That the stolen object is a pen extends the shame, and guilt, of incest to the guilt of writing about it. His merciless exposure of his family for the sake of his art in *Mercy* shadows all of its volumes.

Ira's forbidden act is so detestable as to be unspeakable; even to utter the word would be shameful. Insofar as their act is an abomination, it is tantamount to the rites of idol worship that bring down the wrath of God in the Bible. Although Roth employs extreme language for his extreme act, one of the most disorienting aspects of this book is the dramatic shift in register between narrating the acts of incest and reflecting upon them. The acts themselves are depicted as mechanical, lacking in eroticism or mystery, two pranksters driven by physical desire and sensation devoid of all affect except the thrill of possible discovery by their mother or the dread instilled by a defective condom. She giggles, is casual and perfunctory, annoyed if he comes prematurely and indifferent to his apologetic "So once I got too excited... You wanna again?" She is quick to put him down with "*Briderl.* You stink, if you wanna know" (147). This is not the language of romantic rebellion. Minutes after such episodes on the parental bed, their mother arrives, "Noo, *kinderlekh.* You must be hungry by now" (147). Although Roth

---

10. *A Diving Rock on the Hudson* (New York: St. Martin's Press, 1995).

refers to both legendary and mythic acts of incest with his allusions to Byron and then to Amnon and Tamar, there is neither mystique nor tragic ending in his confession. On the contrary, in the next volume Ira and Minnie behave like ordinary siblings, giving each other advice about their dates, with the protective older brother comforting his sister when she fails the New York teaching license examination due to her accented English.

However, in the later reflections the narrator relentlessly insists on the rhetoric of confession: "I might as well confess to what has been all along a kind of spirit beneath the deep..." (148). He calls these scenes "the revelation, the frightful disclosure"... "and the story cannot continue without this admission" (148). "The unspoken and unspeakable must become spoken and speakable, and the taboo broken and ignored" (128). The issue is not whether this really occurred; it is what role it plays in this final magnum opus and what this has to do with Hebrew. To do that we will need to take a closer look at how Roth breaks not only the moral framework of his world but also the linguistic one.

Mercy of a Rude Stream encompasses many more non-English words than does *Call It Sleep,* so many that he affixed a glossary of Yiddish and Hebrew terms to the end of each volume. The first *loshn koydesh* to enter the text are the opening lines of the *Kaddish*, when his shame at having been caught for theft of the fountain pen makes him contemplate suicide (which he never considers in relation to incest). "If he could only think. *Yisgadal, v'yiskadash, sh'mey rabo*, the mourner's chant, was that how it went? What did it mean? That's how it sounded. Pop would sit on a wooden box, the way he did when his father died, ...and Mom, Mom, Mom, Wait—" (19). The thought of inflicting such pain on his mother leaves him speechless; separation from his mother is unthinkable and, therefore, suicide is untenable. Within a few pages he will return to the mourner's prayer, but in a perverse about-face that mourns the unborn: "Say *Kaddish* not only for your grandchildren, but for your great-grandchildren; rend your garment now, sit humbled by bereavement, sit *shiva*...in a word, mourn for the unborn, for the departed of the future" (45). In other words, *Kaddish* is invoked both for the death of a person and for the anticipated death of a people by abandonment of customs, beliefs, and language.

When Ira discusses his own possible future as a schoolteacher, he does so by belittling both the vocation and the Old World where it was practiced. "I'm a *melamed*, that's all," he tells his Americanized friend Larry. "That's the guy who teaches you to read Hebrew. My father calls me that" (215). A parochial calling. Although his Americanized friend Larry knows far less Hebrew than does Ira, and no Yiddish whatsoever, he explains to Ira that "Yale is a Hebrew word: *ya* standing for Jahveh, and *El*, the Lord." After Ira frequents the rooms of a black prostitute, he takes notice of the wall hangings as if through his mother's eyes. "Shmattas, Mom would have said...Who put the *shma* in *shmattas*?" (135). So great is Ira's guilt that he summons *both* parents here, his Mother as Yiddish in *shmattas* and his Father as

Hebrew in *shma,* the credo of Judaism. Whoring, he thinks, is "Horrible bad. Unspeaka-babble bad. Abomination bad" (130). The task of the *melamed*, in Ira's self-deprecating remark to Larry, is to introduce Jewish children to the Hebrew of a religious world whose authority has been super-seded by the educational elite of the New World, exemplified by Yale University's insignia, the mark of Christian Hebraism at the heart of Puritan America. When the author castigates his younger self for whoring, he does so by the standards of the Hebrew God, for whom Ira's sin is tantamount to the abomination reserved for the worship of foreign gods (Baal and Baby-lon). It is a sin against God.

Yet this sin pales besides incest, an "abomination" linked with the sacredness of Hebrew and with a punitive Hebrew God. At a Greenwich Vil-lage party where Ira meets Tamara Kahane, Sholem Aleichem's granddaugh-ter, she mentions the popular American poet Robinson Jeffers, who uses "my name, which happens to be Hebrew" (342). She is undoubtedly refer-ring to Jeffers' volume of poems *Tamar and Other Poems* (1925):

> "It means 'date,' the fruit," she explains, "but it means something else to Jeffers." "What?" asks Ira. "Tamar in the Bible is raped by her brother....She was King David's daughter, and the whole thing fits into Jeffers' incest symbol." *Incest symbol.* The way they used it, it didn't mean anything...a symbol? Putting a newspaper, *Der Tag,* under Minnie when she was bloggy, and then pitching it out the window down the airshaft....Now that was the real thing... "Where's *Der Tag*?" Mom kept hollering, accusing: 'Did you see Friday's Tag?' 'Me? No. Not me. What do I want with *Der Tag*?'" (342)

I want to take a look at Roth's dismissal of incest as a symbol, which he relegates to Jeffers' poetry, in contrast to what he calls "the real thing," the act of incest in a text that is, according to Roth, a novel, and according to what we know of his biography, a fictionalized autobiography. If we take him at his word about the genre, a novel, then he too is employing "*the incest symbol*," because at this moment two frames are being broken, the social and moral by committing incest with his sister, and the linguistic by placing a Yiddish newspaper under their bodies and over the sheets on the parental bed. The Yiddish newspaper, as Roth has already signaled in *Call It Sleep*, is a secular object with a remainder of the sacred by virtue of its alpha-bet. The double violation in this scene poses a question about symbolism in *Mercy of a Rude Stream*. If the autobiographical "fact" of incest with Rose (here renamed Minnie) is driving this multi-volume confession, a recurring motif in the bold diary-like sections where the aged Roth repeatedly reveals his sin to his readers, then the violation of the Hebrew letters is the vehicle or symbol for the sin that is being confessed. But if this is a *novel*, then the incest itself can serve as "*the incest symbol*," as the vehicle for the tenor of the suffocating incestuous Jewish family that Roth can toss down the air-shaft with the Yiddish paper that represents it, the paper, significantly, that his mother reads. The absent father, whose chronic absence makes these incestuous acts possible, can signify the Hebrew on those violated pages that are discarded along with Yiddish, the last remnant of Jewish sacred tradition for Roth in America.

The confusion, or interchangeability, of tenor and vehicle on this resonant page is symptomatic of the confusion or ambivalence of genre in *Mercy of a Rude Stream*. What Roth's character so blithely calls "the real thing" cannot be disentangled from that other story in the book, the one about the languages of Yiddish and Hebrew and what they signify in this narrative of family drama, assimilation, and Americanization. By calling his behavior with his sister "abominable" and "unspeakable," by calling it "with the name never to be named," he is placing it in a religious context. By committing the act on a Yiddish newspaper, he can violate two taboos at once, each a symbol for the other; he can abuse both his sister and Hebrew (as each can stand in for the other). The Yiddish newspaper serves as an instrument of concealment. Although the secular language Yiddish appears to have desacralized Hebrew, and is, therefore, a correlative for the desacralized sister in a world devoid of divine moral authority, it bears traces of the sacred, just as Ira (I–Ra, I am evil) is aware that sibling incest, no matter how mechanical its depiction, bears traces of sacrilege. This double move is exemplified elsewhere in the book. In another scene of profanation as incestuous Jewish family life, he describes sex with his cousin Stella: "Ram-ram-ram, *tikyoo, tikyoo*. Sound the shofar. *Tikeeyoo, matryoo*" (*Bondage*, 331). Casting himself as the butting ram, whose horn, the shofar, is sounded on the High Holy Days marked by confessions of sin, Ira parodies the Hebrew liturgy, "tikyoo" (tekiyo). By transliterating in two different ways he calls attention to bilingual punning: the "English" approximates "tickee you" (tickle?), and, more importantly, the rhyming "matryoo" (not part of the liturgy) gestures toward the Latin "maternal," *the* incest that underlies all of the other transgressions in *Mercy of a Rude Stream*.[11]

In *Call It Sleep*, Hebrew serves to parody religion, to empty sacred moments like the Passion of any vestige of religious sentiment. In *Call It Sleep*, Christianity reverts to its parent religion (as Jesus moans the *Chad Godya* from the cross), which is then also portrayed as false magic, the raw

---

11. That incest in this work conveys the incestuous and suffocating drama of the Jewish immigrant family has been pointed out by Morris Dickstein and Marshall Berman. According to Dickstein, "As Roth sees it, they represent his inability to break out of the cocoon of the family and the ghetto. This is where Roth's own history typically carries with it a large chunk of social history as well. There is some evidence that incest and sexual abuse were more prevalent in immigrant families precisely because they were so isolated—cut off by their poverty, ghettoization, and linguistic barriers." Morris Dickstein, "Memory Unbound: Henry Roth and the Philosopher's Stone," *Threepenny Review* 110 (Summer 2007), 10–11. Berman writes, "as a Jew living through a Jewish family, he also saw...the family imploding, crashing in on itself, with a love so intimate that it was incestuous, perishing from its very richness of being." Berman, "The Bonds of Love," *The Nation* September 23, 1996: 25.

material for secular modernist writing and the making of the artist. In *Mercy of a Rude Stream*, Hebrew serves to restore the sacred (as he restored his sister) without which there can be no sacrilege. Insofar as incest is an abomination, it is a sin against God, and the violation of his sister is analogous to the violation of Hebrew. This is the Hebrew of the punitive God of the Old World, and the adult Ira-Henry (I evil) feels compelled to write a confession in the Christian genre of Augustine about a sin that he associates with abandoning his Hebrew world. Without the Jewish prerequisite for atonement, namely asking forgiveness of the injured party, this act remains an abomination.

Whereas Hebrew in the narrative of Ira Stigman is entangled with the incestuous Jewish family, in the boldface commentary of the aged author Henry Roth Hebrew is a vehicle for articulating his newfound Jewish identity, the Zionism of his later years. By the time that Roth began composing *Mercy of a Rude Stream*, he had repudiated his former political beliefs and he had recovered his Jewish identity through the discovery of his bond to Israel at the time of the Six Day War. In contrast to Hebrew in the context of his adolescent transgression in the Ira Stigman narrative, the commentary passages are consumed with contemporary Middle East politics, with fear and concern for the fate of the Jewish homeland. "Let's imagine my father, a Zionist. In a few months, the Balfour Declaration will be published. Let's away to Israel, let's away to a kibbutz. I would know chiefly hard work, rigor, danger, but also kinship, precious kinship. But alas, I wouldn't have known M—[his Gentile wife]" (*Mercy,* 127). In fact, Roth had planned to immigrate, and in 1978 he preceded his wife Muriel on a trip to Israel that was to be the first step in that process. In a letter to Muriel from Tamara Kahana, who had by then settled in Tel Aviv and helped Roth arrange his stay, she writes that "he was determined to learn Hebrew."[12]

He and Muriel had been studying Hebrew arduously in their mobile home in New Mexico. With a cataract in one eye and a lens implant in the other, Muriel made the effort to read a paragraph or two of a Hebrew textbook in the evenings:

> She misread continually, not that Hebrew was easy to read at any time, the damned print with its *gimels* looking like *nuns*, and its *beths* like *kaphs*, and its *daleths* like *reshes* and its *khets* like *hehs* and its *vahv* like *zion*, but she even confused the more distinct letters, the *tets* and the *mems*, the *mems* and the *sameks*. He regarded her with astonishment—and with grief and apprehension....Dear M, dear patient, steadfast, objective M, weighing her options, deciding on her priorities, bravely abiding by them—abiding *him* these many, many years. (*Bondage*, 212)

---

12. Letter dated February 13, 1978. Henry Roth Papers; Box 4, folder 13; American Jewish Historical Society, Newton Centre, Mass. and New York, N.Y.

The most tender moments in all four volumes of *Mercy* are reserved for contemplating his Gentile wife's struggles with Hebrew to accommodate his dream of immigrating to Israel, a dream that his ill health and age made impossible to realize.

From his earliest years, Roth's refuge from what he perceived as incestuous, noisy, and unsightly Jewish family life would be the sheer beauty of English. On Friday night, his character Ira would bury his face in Milton's *Paradise Lost* to drown out his parents' squabbling and his father's rebukes, ""Spare us your *fahr Crite secks*. It's a Jewish home here. It's Friday night. The candles are still burning" (79).[13] He is passionate about Milton, his language, his sensibility, and his vision, "how he loved Milton...There was nobody like him; not even Shakespeare" (118). In *Requiem for Harlem*, the fourth volume of *Mercy,* Roth quotes passage after passage from *Paradise Lost*, as Milton's words about Adam's sin strike a chord in Ira's heart: "O Conscience, into what abyss of fears/And horrors has thou driven me; out of which/I find no way, from deep to deeper plunged!" (144). Beyond Adam's sin, Roth is drawn to Satan's denial of the authority God invested in Jesus: "Satan wasn't to blame if he objected to the dichotomy. So did Jews. *Shmai Yisroel, adonoi elohenu edonoi ekhud!* Every Jew knew that: it was the Credo: God is one...Object, and you're on the side of Satan" (149). And beyond Satan's stubborn monotheism, Henry Roth identifies with Milton because he "was a Puritan—unlike Shakespeare—and Ira himself was a Puritan...That was it. And Milton was bound. As Ira himself once was, still wanted to be, no longer could be. Mystique, devotion, sanctity—he was always running up against them, couldn't rid himself of them" (118). This identification with Milton, the Christian Hebraist bound to sanctity, amplifies Roth's recurring theme of sacrilege as violation of the Jewish family and of Hebrew.

Both exquisite English and exquisite Hebrew stand in sharp contrast to the mutilated accented speech of Ira's Jewish neighborhood in Harlem. On the one hand, he is aware of the beauties of Hebrew out of his reach as he contemplates the road not taken linguistically, just as he had nationally when he imagined himself on a kibbutz, "Supposing he himself had gone on studying *Khumish* in the *cheder* on 9th Street, could he have said to himself in Hebrew: 'Though they forget Thee, yet will not I forget Thee. Behold, I have graven Thee upon the palms of my hands?' Ah, how beautiful that was" (79). On the other hand, English paradise is restricted to reading and writing, and off limits to Jews as legitimate speech. In *From Bondage*, Ira's sister Minnie bursts into their home sobbing and throwing herself into Ira's arms: "My *s*...The speaking test, I failed...I have a lateral *s*...They don't want me...It was only the Jewish girls" (202). (Boards of Education did indeed add speech tests for licensing exams specifically designed to keep Jews out, in

---

13. *Requiem for Harlem* (New York: St. Martin's Press, 1998).

response to the large number of Jews who were passing their teaching exams.) In a rare instance of brotherly protectiveness, Ira consoles Minnie for being excluded from the Gentile English-speaking world.

On the closing pages of *From Bondage*, English and Hebrew, incest and marital love, prayer and intimacy converge. Admitting to Muriel that *The Rime of the Ancient Mariner* enchanted him when he first read it in the ninth grade, Ira recites, "He prayeth best, who loveth best, and all that sort of blarney...Thank God, I prayeth worst." "Oh no," she contradicts him. "When did you ever hear me pray?" She insists that "you're always appealing to the best in you, your conscience...I never saw a man struggle with himself so. Isn't that what you do?" Ira isn't persuaded. "What's praying about that?" As they reminisce about the first days of their love, she reminds him that her life was already settled when "you came along and ripped it all to pieces." True to his penchant for quotation, he replies, "This is all I have to say to thee," and notes for the reader that it is "Jocasta's last speech in Sophocles' *Oedipus*" (385). By shifting from sibling to maternal incest, Roth intensifies his sin. In *Requiem*, where the loving presence of his mother throughout all four volumes reaches its apex, he imagines her crying out, "How could you bring yourself to do such a thing!" And then he reassures himself: "She'd forgive him, she'd forgive him" (116).

"Ok, tell me," he turns to M, after dinner, Hebrew lessons, and conversation about life and their love for one another ("and when I love thee not, chaos is come again"), "what do you understand by the 'He prayeth best' stuff?" "Life's all unique and the same at the same time. I think that's what Coleridge meant...Every speck of consciousness is precious." "Say," he adds, as the book comes to a close: "while we're talking of specks of consciousness, maybe love is the highest thing in the speck. Or the best...How's that?" "I like the idea," she replies. "Glory be," Henry Roth exclaims. "You mean it? Hosanna!" (*Diving Rock*, 388). His last word in this book is in Hebrew, the return of prayer and the sacred. Transliterated from "Hoshia na," Hosanna is a plea to be saved that appears in Hebrew scripture and liturgy. Filtered through its Greek transliteration in the Gospels where it came to mean "Praise God," and twice removed from its Hebraic source in King James English (and in Milton), Hosanna is *almost* an English word. It does not appear in the appended glossary of Hebrew and Yiddish terms. As Hebrew-inspired English, it is Roth's prayer at the end of his confession. It means redemption.

The Modern Hero as Schlemiel:
The Swede in Philip Roth's
American Pastoral

MICHAEL KIMMAGE

In her 1971 book *The Schlemiel as Modern Hero*, Ruth Wisse describes two contradictory strains in Jewish-American literary culture. One originated in Europe and is devoted to the schlemiel, the fool who lives two realities, simultaneously inferior and superior to the Gentile world around him. In story, joke, folklore, and literature the schlemiel measures out "ironic balance for psychic survival," the title for chapter three of Wisse's study. The schlemiel enabled Old World Jewish writers to contend with the insecurities of their environment—with an anti-Semitism intended to make fools out of Jews—while affirming an embattled Jewishness. The schlemiel, and the schlemiel's appreciators, can "reinterpret his weakness as its opposite, for how else could a weakling survive?" The schlemiel was among the Jewish immigrants to America: "somehow, the policies of tolerance and the slow, steady climb into the middle, even upper-middle class, have not prevented Jews in America, including those of the third generation, from sharing many of the insecurities of their European forefathers." One can even refer to "the tenacious hold of the schlemiel on the American Jewish consciousness."[1] In the hands of a modern writer like Saul Bellow, the schlemiel is American-born. Bellow's novel *Herzog* (1964) tracks the foolishness of Moses Herzog, whose job and marriage and intellectual pretensions are all in disarray, though his can be a higher foolishness, the alchemy of humor and irony transforming his weakness into a sly strength.

For all the schlemiel's mobility, the final chapter of Wisse's study is a requiem for the schlemiel, a record of the effort by Jewish-American writers other than Bellow to retire the schlemiel, to banish him, along with his ironies and follies, from the American strand. One example is Norman Podhoretz, who, in his memoir *Making It*, celebrated success above failure, demonstrating that, for Jews, psychic survival in America need not depend on irony and mockery. Survival could now countenance vigorous self-assertion: Podhoretz's story of American success is a story of gain in almost every way, not the tale of a weakling. Similarly, Philip Roth deconstructed the schlemiel in his 1969 novel *Portnoy's Complaint*. Its protagonist, Alexander Portnoy, is, it seems, the last of the schlemiels. After all, he is not so

---

1. Ruth R. Wisse, *The Schlemiel as Modern Hero* (Chicago: University of Chicago Press, 1971), 70, x, 72.

much rooted in the Jewish past as standing in "the bright ahistoric present," as Wisse argues. The novel tells us that "we are back in a new enlightenment, and as the group is thought to have control over its destiny," Wisse writes, "it must be satirized for failing to execute its proper task."[2] The group is satirized for the vestigial schlemiels within it.

The last few paragraphs of *The Schlemiel as Modern Hero* outline the contradiction of a strangely modern figure, ill at ease in modern America. The schlemiel is fading away; the schlemiel has a tenacious hold. Jewish writers such as Podhoretz and Roth exploited American opportunity to intone the schlemiel's obsolescence, to reject the "balanced irony" that was the schlemiel's larger cultural function, the message behind his superficial ridiculousness. Why define Jewish character as it had been defined (if only in part) by an anti-Semitic past, a past that denied full civic and psychic agency to Jews? The neurotic Alexander Portnoy—disfigured by his parents' Old World fears and inhibitions, by a cultural inheritance suitable to the Pale of Settlement but comically inappropriate to northern New Jersey—was the schlemiel as cultural failure, victim of ironies unsuited to the American atmosphere. Portnoy is a schlemiel who struggles to liberate himself from unnecessary limitations. The American reader of *Portnoy's Complaint* may fare better, especially if the reader can see exactly how artificial the limitations facing Alexander Portnoy are. Norman Podhoretz was, in this sense, Roth's ideal reader. Long before *Portnoy's Complaint* was written, Podhoretz saw how few limitations there were between himself and a grand American success, a loud American voice, an American swagger: no inevitable poverty, no need to languish in provincial obscurity, no insuperable anti-Semitism; in their place, a path leading from working-class Brooklyn to Columbia University and from there to the upper reaches of Manhattan and Washington, DC. As much as Wisse appreciates the magic trick in *Making It*—Podhoretz makes the schlemiel disappear—she is herself reluctant to abandon the schlemiel to the world of our fathers. Success and failure, Europe and America, history and post-history, are not the only issues at stake: "the natural buoyancy of the schlemiel," Wisse argues, "certainly encourages belief in his long-range survival."[3] This sentence carries a hint of relief.

Philip Roth published *Portnoy's Complaint* in 1969. He was thirty-six, an established but still young writer. Roth has since been so prolific that few

---

2. Ibid., 119, 112. Wisse argues that the schlemiel rose to an unexpected American importance after the Second World War, and not simply because so many Jewish-American writers began to make their mark in the 1940s and 1950s: "when America as a whole began to experience itself as a 'loser' after World War II and ever more insistently in the 1950s, the schlemiel was lifted from his parochial setting into national prominence" (*The Schlemiel as Modern Hero*, 75).

3. Ibid., 123, 124.

meaningful generalizations can be sustained about his literary oeuvre. One generalization that can be sustained is Roth's growing interest in history.[4] The bright ahistoric present Wisse ascribes to *Portnoy's Complaint*, a pre-condition for dismissing the schlemiel, has given way to darker historical terrain. This is an evolution that has several dimensions in Roth's writing. One was his discovery of communist Eastern Europe as antipode to America, where, in the early 1970s, the author of *Portnoy's Complaint* experienced a tawdry and fleeting celebrity. A trip to Eastern Europe in 1972 altered the way Roth thought about literature. It was not a sentimental journey back to the *shtetl* but an education in the troubled present, filled with historical tension and, in Prague, suffused with the historical sensibility of its literary scene.[5] Another dimension to Roth's growing interest in history was autobiographical, beginning with *The Facts: A Novelist's Autobiography* (1988) and continuing with *Patrimony: A Memoir* (1991), which do not trade in history as high politics but in history's arc as lived by individuals and families. In *The Plot Against America* (2004), Roth merged family life with national history by writing historical fiction, having America sour with anti-Semitism along with Nazi Germany, as if there were no such thing as an ahistoric present or an ahistoric country as far as Jews (and others) are concerned, no enduring protection from the ravages of history. A fascination with Jewish history—with the diaspora, with the Holocaust, with Zionism—had already underscored Roth's 1993 novel, *Operation Shylock: A Confession*. If Philip Roth has a "late style" as a writer, separating his more recent books from *Portnoy's Complaint*, one of its elements would be a marriage of the literary and the historical, a layering of history within the practice of fiction.

Roth continued with this marriage in a trilogy of novels published in quick succession—*American Pastoral* (1997), *I Married a Communist* (1998) and *The Human Stain* (2000)—each immersed in a different area of postwar American history.[6] *The Human Stain* is the most gently historical

4. On the absence of history in Roth's early fiction, see Irving Howe, "Philip Roth Reconsidered" *Commentary* v. 54 no. 6 (December 1972), 69–77.

5. In Roth's own words: "They [Eastern European writers] made me very conscious of the difference between the private ludicracy of being a writer in America and the harsh ludicrousness of being a writer in Eastern Europe. These men and women were drowning in history. They were working under tremendous pressure and the pressure was new to me—and news to me, too. They were suffering for what I did freely and I felt great affection for them, and allegiance; we were all members of the same guild." See: http://books.guardian.co.uk/review/story/0,,1300982,00.html.

6. An excellent recent study of these three novels is Till Kinzel, *Die Tragödie und Komödie des amerikanischen Lebens: Eine Studie zu Zuckermans Amerika in Philip Roths Amerika-Trilogie* (Heidelberg: Universitätsverlag Winter: 2006). For an analysis of Jewish questions in Roth's fiction, see Alan Cooper, *Philip Roth and the Jews* (Albany, New York: SUNY Press, 1996) and Ruth Wisse, "Writing beyond Alien-

of the three. Its immediate context is the Monica Lewinsky scandal of 1998, a self-righteous persecution of libido that comes, in this novel, from the Right and from the Left. President Clinton is persecuted for his indiscretions, and the novel's protagonist, Coleman Silk, is persecuted for a non-existent thought crime and then for a sexual affair with a younger woman. *I Married a Communist* is a novel about American communism in its confrontation course with McCarthyism. In the pattern of this novel's tragedy, the blunt force of ideology crosses the lines of family history. Its hero, Ira Ringold, damages himself by adopting a delusional communist idealism. Others then destroy him for reasons of vengeance and ambition. The richest novel of the trilogy is *American Pastoral*, and it is also the most insistently historical. Its protagonist could almost be the city of Newark, awash in postwar optimism, at least in its Jewish neighborhoods, until all optimism is reversed in the 1967 riots, the precipitous rise of its Jewish inhabitants a precursor to their city's sudden fall. There is a surfeit of irony etched into the novel's laconic title. The American pastoral is real enough, close enough, to tantalize; America seems more than an ocean away from fascist Europe during the Second World War, a veritable garden for its Jewish residents. But the sinister mechanics of history cannot be eliminated and the pastoral myth only obscures the irrationality and rage beneath the surface, awaiting the right provocation to come into full view. Roth intends these rhythms to be Miltonic or simply biblical, titling the novel's three sections: Paradise Remembered, The Fall, and Paradise Lost. Jewish Newark of the 1940s is the Eden from which its postwar residents are banished.

At the heart of this drama is the novel's protagonist, the unlikeliest of schlemiels, Seymour Levov. From adolescence on, he is known as the Swede, because of his Scandinavian good looks, his athletic grace, and his physical strength, each attribute intensified by the coincidence of his adolescence with the Second World War and Holocaust. This Jewish boy from Newark, New Jersey is not consumed by moral and intellectual questions; his face and body do not betray the rigors of an academic youth; his bearing and his thoughts reveal not the slightest trace of historical persecution and suffering. Far from being a schlemiel in the classic sense of the term, he first appears to be its opposite, a hero from within the tradition of Western culture, not enraged enough to be an Achilles or wily enough to be an Odysseus but more in their mold than in the mold of Menakhem Mendl, Tevye the dairyman, Moses Herzog, or Alexander Portnoy. In *The Schlemiel as Modern Hero*, Ruth Wisse turns to Hemingway for a credible example of the hero, finding it in Romero the Bullfighter, who "is still the traditional Western hero in this work [*The Sun Also Rises*], a man of dignity, truth-to-

---

ation: Saul Bellow, Cynthia Ozick and Philip Roth," in *The Modern Jewish Canon: A Journey through Language and Culture* (New York: Free Press, 2000), 295–322.

self, physical courage, romantic polish, masculine beauty, the old-fashioned virtues."[7] This sentence could be applied to the Swede as well. The Swede may not be exceptional in his heroism or his success, but his achievements are formidable: star athlete in high school, a marine, marriage to Miss New Jersey, head of the family business, warmly assimilated into America, content in his patriotism. In *The Sun Also Rises*, the pathetic Robert Cohn, who tries and fails to imitate the traditional Western hero, may be only a few decades younger than the Swede in cultural time, but he is of another era, consigned to being a schlemiel when the Swede has the option to be a hero.

And yet, the simple story of the Swede's heroism is inconclusive. To his own horror, his life unveils "the raw potential for becoming a schlemiel, that is, the potential for suffering, submitting to loss, pain, humiliation, for recognizing himself as, alas, only himself," as Wisse writes, not about the Swede, but about the schlemiel.[8] The Swede's wife proves unfaithful. His city, home to the family glove business, undergoes an awesome decline, forcing him to move the factory out of country, depriving him of continuity between the world of his childhood and his adult world. He must exchange an unfettered patriotism for something more ambiguous during the Vietnam War. Over time, the American certitudes of his adolescence devolve into disappointment and cynicism. The most acute cause of the Swede's loss, pain and humiliation—which do indeed force him to recognize himself as only himself—involve his daughter, Merry. As a teenager, she joins the Weathermen and commits terrorist acts in its name. She abandons her family, lives as a vagabond, is raped and reduced to a life of utter destitution in, of all places, the slums of Newark. Like Moses Herzog, in Saul Bellow's *Herzog*, the Swede must learn to live "according to a twofold perception of himself in relation to the world," even if this is the last lesson he ever wished to learn from life.[9] The twofold perception is not of himself as Jew and as American; there is little content to the Swede's Jewishness. The twofold perception is of his own success and failure, strength and weakness, the dilemma of a man who has been admired and then ridiculed by fate. With the body of a Western hero, he is forced to look at the world, and at himself, through the eyes of the schlemiel.

Before the Swede can discover himself as schlemiel he must first be discovered as such by the author-within-the-novel, Nathan Zuckerman. Zuckerman is a recurrent character in Roth's novels, and he plays a pivotal role in *American Pastoral*, for he imagines the inner life of the Swede, whom he knew and revered as a child growing up in Newark. As the novel begins, Zuckerman is being drawn back further and further into the Proustian world

---

7. Ruth Wisse, *The Schlemiel as Modern Hero*, 76–77.

8. Philip Roth, *American Pastoral* (Boston: Houghton Mifflin, 1997), 111.

9. Ibid., 111.

of memory. Touched with a new awareness of mortality, Zuckerman is newly enlivened by the past, by his past, by the past of Jewish Newark. After his fiftieth high school reunion, Zuckerman receives a mug filled with *rugelach*, hoping to "find vanishing from Nathan what, according to Proust, vanished from Marcel the instant he recognized 'the savor of the little *madeleine*': the apprehensiveness of death... So, greedily I ate... but, in the end, having nothing like Marcel's luck." Instead, Zuckerman is left with a searing nostalgia. There is no escape from the past, or from mortality, but there is a solace in the sweetness of the past. "Am I completely mistaken," Zuckerman wonders, "to think that living as well-born children in Renaissance Florence could not have held a candle to growing up within aromatic range of Tabachnik's pickle barrels?" Zuckerman is a writer, and the reference to Proust is anything but accidental. *In Search of Lost Time* begins, literally and figuratively, with the older author tasting his childhood in the *madeleine*. Zuckerman is similarly inspired by the flavor of Jewish Newark.[10]

At first glance, the Swede is an unlikely vehicle for Zuckerman's nostalgic or historical purposes. The Swede is remarkable for his flight from Jewish Newark, a flight into the post-ethnic ether of American success. It was for his American power and grace—above all, in sports—that he had thrilled his Newark neighborhood and no one more than the young Nathan Zuckerman. To his Jewish admirers, with their World War II anxieties, the fact that the Swede was Jewish mattered, precisely because he transcended it so brilliantly, to the extent of taking on a Nordic name:

> in our idolizing the Swede and his unconscious oneness with America, I suppose there was a tinge of shame and self-rejection. Conflicting Jewish desires awakened by the sight of him were simultaneously becalmed by him; the contradiction in Jews who want to fit in and want to stand out, who insist they are different and insist they are no different, resolved itself in the triumphant spectacle of this Swede who was actually another of our neighborhood Seymours and Sauls who would themselves beget Stephens who would in turn beget Shawns. Where was the Jew in him?

The Swede's "unconscious oneness with America" synthesized and effaced Jewish contradictions. In Zuckerman's imagination this was the role the Swede was supposed to play, and it was the role he played from World War II on into the postwar American pastoral. The Swede raises his family in rural New Jersey, an affluent bucolic area far from the city streets of Newark. Hence, Nathan is surprised (in the year 1985) when the Swede sees him at a baseball game and follows up with a letter, asking to meet. The Swede wants to talk about his father, whom everyone thought was "indestructible." The Swede writes, "a thick-skinned man on a short fuse, not everyone knew how much he suffered because of the shocks that befell his loved

---

10. Philip Roth, *American Pastoral*, 47, 42.

ones."[11] They meet for dinner and talk about nothing. This brief glimpse of the Swede's outwardly impregnable father as schlemiel, out of harmony with public perception, suffering untold shocks, is not a subject the Swede can discuss with Nathan.

It is not the Swede's father who dominates Zuckerman's novel but the Swede himself, whose story Nathan discovers after the Swede has died. As a child, Nathan had been friends with the Swede's brother, Jerry, whose childhood burden was being the brother of the celebrated Swede. Where the Swede was heroic and adored, Jerry was brooding and troubled; the Swede's optimism borders on naiveté, while Jerry's cynicism is bottomless. Nathan meets up with Jerry at his high school reunion, and Jerry tells him the shocking story of the Swede's family, of his daughter Merry the terrorist. In Jerry's unsentimental words: "My brother thought he could take his family out of human confusion and into Old Rimrock, and she put them right back in." The unperturbed flight into America, projected onto the Swede by Nathan's ignorant imagination, looks altogether different from Jerry's point of view. Jerry speaks with scorn about the Swede's Irish-American wife, Dawn:

> Knockout couple. The two of them all smiles on their outward trip in to the USA. She's post-Catholic, he's post-Jewish, together they're going to go out there to Old Rimrock to raise post-toasties. Instead they get that fucking kid.

Jerry tacitly blames the Swede and his wife for the crimes of the daughter. It was folly to avoid human confusion, a folly that only created human confusion. It was dangerous to cast aside the markers of ethnic identity and to rear a child as if these signposts did not matter to the child, to the child's parents and to others. Where Jerry sees error, Nathan sees tragedy, the tragedy of the Swede's will to heroism:

> It all began—this heroically idealistic maneuver, this strategic, strange spiritual desire to be a bulwark of duty and ethical obligation—because of the war... It all began for the Swede—as what doesn't?—in a circumstantial absurdity.[12]

It began, in other words, in the schlemiel's natural habitat, in absurdity, and it will end there as well.

American Pastoral is not a *Bildungsroman*. The progression from hero to schlemiel is, without any question, a voyage of self-discovery for the

---

11. Ibid., 20, 18. The Swede's name, a cardinal fact of *American Pastoral*, describes an assimilation into American life that is more loss than gain, a mark of invisibility: "he carried it [his name] with him like an invisible passport, all the while wandering deeper and deeper into an American's life, forthrightly evolving into a large, smooth, optimistic American such as his conspicuously raw forebears—including the obstinate father whose American claim was not inconsiderable—couldn't have dreamed of as one of their own" (Philip Roth, *American Pastoral*, 208).

12. Ibid., 73, 80.

Swede, but it is not a voyage on which he learns any sustaining lesson or arrives at any lasting conclusion. It is not a voyage from sickness to health and may, in fact, be a voyage from health to sickness.

The Swede's voyage from hero to schlemiel is almost unbearably arduous. The Swede must suffer the consequences of his daughter's actions as well as the mystery of these actions. In their aftermath, he must suffer the dissolution of his marriage, the break-up of his house. He must accept that he has misunderstood more than he has understood. The accumulation of wisdom, assimilated in childhood from a disciplined family, making its way in America, was actually the accumulation of something other than wisdom. He has misunderstood his family and perhaps his country as well. Hard-won wisdom was closer to fantasy or fairy tale:

> you had only to carry out your duties strenuously and unflaggingly like a Levov and orderliness became a natural condition, daily living a simple story tangibly unfolding, a deeply unagitating story, the fluctuations predictable, the combat containable, the surprises satisfying, the continuous motion an undulation carrying you along with the utmost faith that tidal waves occur only off the coast of countries thousands and thousands of miles away—so it had all seemed to him *once upon a time*, back when the union of beautiful mother and strong father and bright, bubbly child rivaled the trinity of the three bears.

The result is a painful double-ness. Suffering has opened an abyss of disharmony, transforming him into "a riven charlatan of sincerity, an artless outer Swede and a tormented inner Swede, a visible stable Swede and a concealed beleaguered Swede, an easygoing, smiling sham Swede enshrouding the Swede buried alive." It is this Swede who inspires Zuckerman to write his novel, who makes the Swede worthy of a novel, but never is his suffering spiritually glamorous, the bridge to a better, wider, more profound self. Suffering educates the Swede, not in the intricate deeper meanings of life, but in its possible meaninglessness. Suffering circumscribes "an inner life, a gruesome inner life of tyrannical obsessions, stifled inclinations, superstitious expectations, horrible imaginings, fantasy conversations, unanswerable questions...Enormous loneliness."[13] Suffering here is sternly commensurate with loss; it does not make a sage out of a businessman.

Though the Swede's suffering does not yield spiritual majesty, it does yield a singular insight. For much of his life he has been a fool. Ensconced in the American pastoral, before Merry's explosions, the Swede is a myopic judge of character. His sweetness and generosity are his undoing. A boy who came of age during World War II might have been more attuned to malice; a Jewish boy in the early 1940s was spared senseless murder only by the accident of geography. Yet the Swede's most intense experiences, in the early 1940s, were on the ball field and the basketball court, honing a Stoic

---

13. Ibid., 412–413, 206, 173.

physical heroism that would leave him ill prepared for the non-physical challenges of an adult life. He is a poor judge of character. Contemplation of his daughter's life reveals "the evil ineradicable in human dealings," but this is after his pastoral fantasies, rooted in life's ineradicable bounty and goodness, have exacted their terrible price.[14] He has been foolish in his marriage, in his choice of homes, and in his friends. Here the Swede's Jewishness is no simple fact, to be bypassed in the rush forward into American opportunity. He is a fool for not realizing that non-Jews see him as Jewish, that his Catholic wife and affluent home confuse his not-quite-Jewish daughter, that his friend, Orcutt, looks down on him for being a Jew and seduces his wife in part because he, Orcutt, is a WASP, with access to an American authenticity that the Swede cannot claim. Not all the malice directed toward the Swede refers to his Jewishness; perhaps only a small portion of it does. But the Swede sees neither the malice nor its relation to Jewish facts. The Swede is thus a fool without the resources of the schlemiel.

With wife, daughter, and friends, the Swede's folly contributes to the eventual tragedy. His ambition gives his family a fraudulent aura, against which both wife and daughter will ultimately rebel. The Swede is intent on marrying a non-Jewish woman. Marrying within the fold would disrupt the logic of his ambition: "Dawn was the woman who had inspired the feat for which even his record-breaking athletic career had barely fortified him: vaulting his father. The feat of standing up to his father." With Dawn, he lives in a historic American home, among wealthy WASP families. On the grounds of their estate, Dawn raises cattle, Dawn who had grown up in working-class Elizabeth, New Jersey and who distinguished herself as a contestant in the Miss America pageant. Theirs is a gentility they can afford without occupying it naturally; it is tinged with absurdity. At one point, Dawn is featured in the local newspaper, photographed before the mantelpiece of her home, the genteel farmer at rest. The caption beneath the photograph reads: "'Mrs. Levov, the former Miss New Jersey of 1949 loves living in a 170-year-old home, an environment she says reflect the values of her family.'"[15] This is a kind of *arriviste* playacting, all the more absurd for being presented so earnestly by Mrs. Levov. The Swede has vaulted his Jewish father, launching himself into a sea of self-deception. The values of the family are a smokescreen, meant to obscure the family's background. The cultural comedy of Mr. and Mrs. Levov would be obvious, and delightful, to the born schlemiel. In the Swede's case, they expose a mid-life schlemiel, who is not in on the joke.

Cultural comedy shades into tragicomedy and then into outright tragedy with Merry, the daughter who must perpetuate "the values of her family." Merry occupies the terminal point of the heroic immigrant trajectory, "the

---

14. Ibid., 81.

15. Ibid., 411, 76.

flight of the immigrant rocket, the upward, unbroken immigrant trajectory from slave-driven great-grandfather to self-driven grandfather to self-confident, accomplished, independent father to the highest flier of them all, the fourth-generation child for whom America was to be heaven itself." She is herself unaware of this trajectory, ignorant of the immigrant rocket. Before Dawn and the Swede marry, Dawn must negotiate with the Swede's father, settling the question of family religion. They work out a compromise: almost no Jewish affiliation and limited Christian affiliation. After this, Merry is secretly baptized, taken to church by her Catholic grandparents, and raised in a semi-secular home; her name is almost Mary. When her troubled adolescence becomes apparent to others, the Swede's father believes "that what lay behind Merry's difficulties all along was the secret baptism: that, and the Christmas tree, and the Easter bonnet, enough for that poor kid *never* to know who she was."[16] With Merry, the Levovs' cultural pretensions take on a more serious hue. Self-deception is handed down and becomes, with the daughter, an enervating condition. Her beautiful accomplished parents stand atop the hierarchy of meritocratic success, wherever their grandparents were born. The awkward adolescent has neither family name nor family tradition and is, by birth, an exile in her own home.

If the Swede indulges folly within his family, he is made the fool by his friend Bill Orcutt, scion of their expensive region. They are friends but not equals. Orcutt admires the athletic prowess of the Swede when they play touch football, but he is the teacher and the Swede the student, when they walk their way through local history. Orcutt is far less professionally successful than the Swede. He is a failed artist, a cultured charlatan, a WASP schlemiel. But all this is irrelevant to Orcutt when "recounting the glory days of the nineteenth century," to which he feels the intimate tie of blood and culture. Without uttering a rude word, Orcutt conducts an endless tour of *his* New Jersey, necessary training for those who have moved up and out of Newark. The ironies of the situation are alive to the Swede, though they are not especially potent. When Orcutt discourses about the Morris canal, it reminds the Swede of his uncle Morris, compelling the Swede to associate "the name of the canal with the story of the struggles of their family rather than with the grander history of the state." The Swede's father, Lou, had regaled him with stories of Newark throughout his childhood; Lou Levov is an aficionado of local Newark history, an expert in the history of the glove business, no less a man of memory than Bill Orcutt. Yet it is Orcutt's historical patrimony that the Swede wants his daughter to inherit. Listening to another man's stories, the Swede "thought when Merry got to be a schoolgirl he'd inveigle Orcutt into taking her along this very same trip so she

---

16. Ibid., 122, 389.

could learn firsthand the history of the county where she was growing up," the family history of another family.[17]

The Swede's punishment for this folly is disproportionate to the crime. If the hero's tragic flaw—his fantasies, his blindness, his misplaced trust in others, including wife and friend—is itself without malice, it brings an eternity of suffering down upon the Swede's shoulders, robbing him of his heroism. His daughter opens a new world to him. He had thought he was perfectly assimilated; after Merry set off her bombs, "he receives anti-Semitic mail. It is so vile it sickens him for days on end." He had thought he was living out the American pastoral; his daughter introduces him to "everything that is its antithesis and its enemy, into the fury, the violence, and the desperation of the counterpastoral—into the indigenous American berserk." The Swede's degradation culminates in a meeting with his daughter, who has become a Jain, renounced all material possessions, material appetite, and is living in filth. She is also living in Newark, a city whose downward spiral mirrors the Swede's fall from grace. On his way to meet her, he sees a devastated Newark:

> It was Newark that was entombed there, a city that was not going to stir again. The pyramids of Newark: as huge and dark and hideously impermeable as a great dynasty's burial edifice has every right to be.

The pyramids of Newark are the burial edifice of a small dynasty, the Levov family, gone to seed after just three American generations:

> Three generations. All of them growing. The working. The saving. The success. Three generations in raptures over America. Three generations of becoming one with a people. And now with the fourth it had come to nothing. The total vandalization of their world.[18]

When father and daughter meet, it is as emissaries of foreign countries. Theirs is a family entirely out of balance, with no hope of ever regaining it, just as they are individuals entirely out of balance. Father and daughter relate to each other without hostility, and their meeting is the dramatic climax of *American Pastoral*:

---

17. Ibid., 302, 303. His father's story-telling comes back to the Swede with a vengeance when he meets his daughter, after years of separation, in her Newark slum. These are the stories of a paradise never to be regained: "Mulberry the Swede could recall as a Chinatown slum as long ago as the 1930s back when the Newark Levovs... used to file up the narrow stairwell to one of the family restaurants for a chow mein dinner on a Sunday afternoon, and, later, driving home to Keer Avenue, his father would tell the boys unbelievable stories about the Mulberry Street 'tong wars' of old. Of old. Stories of old. There were no longer stories of old. There was nothing. There was a mattress, discolored and waterlogged, like a cartoon-strip drunk slumped against a pole. The pole still held up a sign telling you what corner you were on. And that's all there was." Philip Roth, *American Pastoral*, 236.

18. Ibid., 168, 86, 219, 237.

> They are crying intensely, the dependable father whose center is the source of all order, who could not overlook or sanction the smallest sign of chaos— for whom keeping chaos far at bay had been intuition's chosen path to certainty, the rigorous daily given of life—and the daughter who was chaos itself.[19]

The daughter does not come home. *American Pastoral*, which does not progress in chronological order, ends with Bill Orcutt's drunken wife stabbing Lou Levov in the face with a dessert fork. It ends with irrational violence.

The Swede's life ends—not with this stabbing, not with his daughter's tragedy, not in the indigenous American berserk—but back in the American pastoral. In his inner life, he is the schlemiel *par excellence*, and so he must live out the pain of his family's break-up. His story has a certain universality, "the tragedy of the man not set up for tragedy—that is every man's tragedy."[20] We are all schlemiels. The Swede is not evasive in his suffering and his inner life bristles with intelligence and alertness, but neither can he find a public language for the experience of being a schlemiel, of having been rendered a schlemiel. He lives out his suffering in silence. After his father's death, he writes to his brother's childhood friend, Nathan Zuckerman, skirting the truth, hoping to talk over his suffering with a novelist, and retreating, when they do talk, into banal conversation. The Swede has gone on to have a second family, two normal sons who seem very much like the young Swede—athletic, enterprising, decent. Surely, their suburban life is an American pastoral of sorts, and they will act on the opportunity, advocated by Norman Podhoretz and many other postwar Jews, *not* to be a schlemiel. America, in its beneficence, will not demand that they be schlemiels. Philip Roth inverts irony (so dear to the schlemiel) by having the Swede change from hero to schlemiel, spinning a fine story from the change, and then restoring the Swede to a hero, or at the very least to an affluent, well-adjusted family man. In this instance, the modern hero is no less wily than his ancient Western ancestors, with an array of survival tricks, and a reconstituted Ithaca that Odysseus might have envied.

The Swede is in most ways an admirable character, his virtues more substantial than his failings. Roth does not begrudge him his limitations. These limitations cast an interesting light on the career of the schlemiel, however, for the Swede is not especially admirable in his return to normalcy or his inability to speak the schlemiel's truth, which is that life's irrationality is frightening, that it can bear down upon you, that it can elude your control and smash to pieces what you most cherish. The schlemiel's truth is also the

---

19. Ibid., 231.

20. Ibid., 86. This sentence anticipates the title of Roth's most recent novel, *Everyman* (New York: Houghton Mifflin, 2006). In *Everyman*, mortality makes every man into an existential schlemiel.

schlemiel's weapon. If his harsh vision of life can be articulated rather than evaded—it cannot always be subdued—perhaps it can also be survived. Moses Herzog may write unsolicited letters to Heidegger and Adlai Stevenson; his doing so is comic; yet the letters protect his sanity. The schlemiel, educated in the schlemiel's truth, may be physically weak and the very harshness of his vision may derive from physical weakness, but he is strong in his truth. History has testified to the enduring force of irrationality, and, in the midst of this grim record, the schlemiel has the humor by which "psychic balance" can be restored, the humor that softens and ennobles the darker wisdom behind it. This humor is entirely inaccessible to the Swede. He survives, ultimately, by virtue of his brute strength, leaving the ruin of one family behind in order to build up another better family.

By immersing us, the readers, in the Swede's limitations, which are the limitations of the traditional Western hero, Roth is writing as a modern and as a Jewish novelist. He is not making the case for religious Judaism in *American Pastoral*. What the Swede needs, the synagogue cannot give, not to the Swede. Jewish ritual cannot help the Swede when he is suffering, for these rituals mean as little to the Swede as they do, presumably, to the resolutely secular Philip Roth. When arguing about Judaism with his mother, about the status of his future wife, the Swede says that "a man to whom practicing Judaism means nothing, Mother, doesn't ask his wife to convert."[21] Nowhere in *American Pastoral* does Roth suggest disapproval for this candid admission. The Swede's limitation is not theological but cultural. He has rejected his father's stories for his neighbor's stories, his father's voice for his neighbor's voice. In his rush to be an American, he has adopted America's more brittle modes of heroism, which break to pieces under pressure, even if the pieces can later be reassembled. He has alienated himself from the long line of schlemiels that disappeared into his father's generation of strivers and successes. He has done what Alexander Portnoy should have done but could not do. He has shed Jewish neuroses, whether of the Old World or the New. He has made it: and none of this saves him from becoming a schlemiel himself, at least for a while. His refusal to remain a schlemiel, his rush to restore the mood of success, may be the gravest of the Swede's limitations, a limitation, not of physical, but of cultural strength.

Philip Roth does not invite comparison with Sholem Aleichem, and the Swede does not invite obvious comparison with Sholem Aleichem's Tevye the Dairyman, protagonist not of a novel but of a few exceptional short stories. Yet a comparison of the two, of Tevye and the Swede, sheds light on the literary schlemiel. Both Tevye and the Swede are Jewish fathers who undergo great suffering on behalf of their daughters. In both cases, childhood certainties, markers of an earlier historical era, dissolve around them. History befriends neither Tevye nor the Swede: indeed, it makes schlemiels

---

21. Ibid., 314.

of them. The crack-up of the Swede's family and the decline of Newark are no less profound than the crack-up of Tevye's Jewish world, the world of the fathers' fathers, disrupted by the dual pressures of assimilation and anti-Semitism. Unlike the Swede, though, Tevye can give full voice to his suffering. He is a prolix schlemiel with a voice rich in humor, intended and unintended, self-deprecating and at the same time self-confident and resilient, mingling the exalted biblical quotation with the lowly joke, sadness with joy—often in the same sentence. Tevye is no obvious hero; he does little that is classically heroic; but his voice is the hero of his literary domain, less a medium of private suffering than the robust vehicle of his culture. The Swede, by contrast, cannot speak his suffering aloud; he cannot utter the schlemiel's truth, much as he is compelled to live it; he can only suffer as a schlemiel. And, for this reason, he cannot achieve psychic balance.

III.
CONVERSATIONS:
ACROSS CANONS AND BETWEEN TEXTS

Innovation by Translation:
Yiddish and Hasidic Hebrew
in Literary History
KEN FRIEDEN

Yiddish, like a dybbuk, haunted the evolution of modern Hebrew. The enlightened, or *maskilim*, tried to exorcise the Yiddish spirit by eliminating Yiddish words, phrases, and grammar that entered Hebrew. In doing this, they often drained the blood out of their Hebrew texts. It was inevitable, however, that Yiddish would become an integral part of modern Hebrew as it emerged in the nineteenth century.[1] Some linguists have accepted this view,[2] but Hebrew literary history has seldom acknowledged the role of Yiddish. Zionist ideology and an anti-hasidic bias contributed to a neglect of the Yiddish contribution.

During the Enlightenment *(Haskalah)*, most Hebrew authors emulated biblical models and strove to write in a supposedly "pure language" *(lashon tsaha)*. The result was a stiff, ornate style that worked better for poetry than for prose. In contrast, hasidic Hebrew narratives often sounded as if they had been translated from Yiddish. Although this was considered "barbaric" by many secular Hebrew authors,[3] hasidic Hebrew successfully tapped the

---

This article originated as a lecture for a panel on Yiddish literature at the 2006 Modern Language Association convention in Philadelphia. I would like to thank Lewis Glinert and the editors of this volume for helpful comments on an earlier draft.

1. One remarkable early study, a dissertation written in Berlin in the 1920s, touches on Yiddishisms in modern Hebrew. See Irene Chanoch, *Fremdsprachliche Einflüsse im modernen Hebräisch* (Berlin: n.p., 1930), especially 30–32 and 80–82, citing examples from Abramovitsh, Brenner, Bialik. For many examples of Yiddish in colloquial Hebrew speech, see Dan Ben-Amotz and Netiva Ben-Yehuda's *Milon 'olami le-'ivrit meduberet* (Jerusalem: Lewin-Epstein, 1972).

2. Paul Wexler refers to many pertinent articles in his book, *The Schizoid Nature of Modern Hebrew: A Slavic Language in Search of a Semitic Past* (Wiesbaden: Otto Harrassowitz, 1990). Wexler basically argues that there was no revival of Hebrew in the late nineteenth century. Instead, Yiddish speakers retained Yiddish grammar and substituted Hebrew words for the Germanic component of Yiddish. I am skeptical about Wexler's further argument that Yiddish is essentially a Slavic language. But I do think that his approach shows how hasidic Hebrew writing anticipated later developments that led to Israeli Hebrew.

3. For examples of this negative evaluation of hasidic Hebrew, see Nathan Gordon, "Joseph Perl's Megalleh Temirin," *Hebrew Union College Annual* (1904): 235, and Israel Davidson, *Parody in Jewish Literature* (New York: Columbia University, 1907), 61–62.

linguistic and cultural resources of Yiddish. With the help of Yiddish, hasidic writers and anti-hasidic authors such as Joseph Perl and I. B. Levinsohn created colloquial-style Hebrew writing. It was impossible to write Hebrew in a conversational mode on the basis of Enlightenment principles alone and without imitating any living language. As a result, Yiddish contributed to some of the liveliest Hebrew writing in the nineteenth century.

In the twentieth century, a dominant view of Hebrew literary history was established by H. N. Bialik's theory of "Mendele's *nusaḥ*."[4] According to Bialik, S. Y. Abramovitsh (or Mendele Moykher Sforim) moved beyond the *Haskalah* model after 1886 and became the "creator of the *nusaḥ*."[5] Bialik argued in 1910–12 that Abramovitsh established the basis for a new kind of Hebrew style by bringing together biblical, mishnaic, midrashic, and later rabbinic layers. His synthetic style was an advance that superseded the neo-biblical style of the *maskilim*. Embracing a diachronic, amalgamated Hebrew, Abramovitsh helped to lay the foundation for the Hebrew of the "revival" *(teḥiya)*. But Bialik left out two essential elements that played a key role in modern Hebrew literature: Yiddish and hasidic writing.[6]

Abramovitsh's Hebrew fiction of the 1860s could not convey the vibrancy of his Yiddish work from the same period. He had not yet surpassed the maskilic style of authors such as Avraham Mapu. While Abramovitsh's later synthesis facilitated his advance beyond the one-dimensional Hebrew of biblical epigones, this does not adequately explain his accomplishment. One missing link was inspiration from his Yiddish novels written between 1864 and 1878. Abramovitsh innovated, in part, by embracing a model of translation from Yiddish, rather than just by combining prior Hebrew styles. In fact, the opening chapter of Abramovitsh's first Hebrew novel, *Limdu heitev* (1862), shows his effort to emulate Yiddish speech. He uses many calques—Hebrew phrases that are literal translations of Yiddish idioms—and he draws attention to them by adding footnotes to indicate the underlying Yiddish. If he could, Ephraim would bring his wife *ḥalav tzipor (feygl-*

---

4. In English, the best study of this tradition is Robert Alter's *The Invention of Hebrew Prose: Modern Fiction and the Language of Realism* (Seattle: University of Washington Press, 1988), especially chapter 1, "From Pastiche to *Nusakh*."

5. H. N. Bialik, "Yotzer ha-'nusaḥ'" in *Ha'olam* 5, no. 50 (23 Dec. 1910 / 5 Jan. 1911): 6–8. See also Bialik's essay "Mendele u-shloshet ha-kerakhim," in *Kol kitvei Mendele Mokher-Sfarim*, vol. 3 (Odessa: Moriah, 1912), iii–xi.

6. Differences between the styles of Abramovitsh and Bialik became evident when Bialik translated the early chapters of *Fishke the Lame (Fishke der krumer)* into the Hebrew version, *Sefer ha-kabtzanim*. Abramovitsh purportedly commented that "the bride is too beautiful" because Bialik's style "is too rich, abounding in too many idioms, expressions, and words." See Moshe Ungergeld's *Bialik ve-sofrei doro* (Tel Aviv: Am ha-sefer, 1974), 169.

milkh) and *ka'arat shamayim (dos telerl funem himl)*. His wife *noset ha-kov'a (geyt in spodek)* and *tolikheihu be-ḥotmo (firt im bay der noz)*.[7] Because she is so dominant, locals call him *Ephraim ish Ma'aka (Ephraim Make's)*, and a well-off boy is called *ben-av (dem tatens a kind*; ibid., 10). All this indicates that colloquial Yiddish lies beneath the Hebrew text.

The connection to Yiddish is not usually so evident in Abramovitsh's later Hebrew writings, but in many ways it is present. In 1968, Menahem Perry convincingly showed the implicit Yiddish in Abramovitsh's Hebrew texts.[8] He wrote that Abramovitsh's Hebrew writing "depends in an essential way on meanings and phrases from the Yiddish language" (92). Perry enumerates several ways in which this occurs. First, "Mendele's Hebrew text holds many Hebrew words that penetrated into Yiddish and that in that language underwent a shift in their central meanings or received additional connotations"; the author "gave the words a 'Yiddish' meaning within the *Hebrew* text" (ibid.). Some examples of this phenomenon are *gazlan, goles, kabtzan.* Second, in other instances, the Hebrew meaning remains but is supplemented by a secondary meaning from Yiddish. For example, *l'hazi'a* means "to sweat," but a secondary meaning is linked to the Yiddish connotations of *shvitsn* (93). Third, Perry refers also to Yiddish expressions that, appearing in literal Hebrew translation, can be understood only by processing their meaning in Yiddish. Perry gives the example of the implicit saying *aynredn emitsn a kind in boykh* (93), and another is the literal and metaphorical *firn in bod arayn*. Perry's overall point is that Abramovitsh wrote in Hebrew for "a reader for whom Yiddish is the spoken language that echoes in the background of his reading" (ibid.).

One of the easiest ways to see the dependence of nineteenth-century Hebrew fiction on Yiddish is to look closely at the dialogue. As one might expect, represented speech is often most convincing as dialogue when it sounds like Yiddish. At one point in *Fishke the Lame*, for example, Reb Mendele asks Alter incredulously, "Ma ata saḥ?" corresponding to the Yiddish "Vos redt ir?"[9] On the other hand, Abramovitsh sometimes moves in the opposite direction, trying to suggest a colloquial register by using Ara-

---

7. See the reprint edited by Dan Miron, *Limdu heitev fun Sholem-Yankev Abramovitsh* (New York: YIVO, 1969), facsimile 5–6.

8. "Ha-analogia u-mekoma be-mivne ha-roman shel Mendele Mokher-Sfarim: 'iyunim ba-poetika shel ha-proza," in *Ha-sifrut* 1 (1968): 65–100.

9. See *Kol kitvei Mendele Moykher-Sforim (S. Y. Abramovitsh)*, vol. 1 (Odessa: Bialik and Borishkin, 1911), 14, and *Ale verk fun Mendele Moykher Sforim (S. Y. Abramovitsh)*, vol. 11 (Cracow: Farlag Mendele, 1911), 29. Earlier in *Sefer ha-kabtzanim,* when Mendele meets Alter he asks him: "Le'an holekh yehudi?" (4). In the Yiddish original *Fishke der krumer*, Mendele asks "Fun vanen kumt es a yid?" (14). These phrases have different meanings; the Hebrew phrase seems to echo Pirkei Avot: "Da' mi-ayin ba'ta ve-le'an 'ata holekh" (3:1).

maic. I have argued elsewhere that the use of Aramaic in this way was an unsuccessful experiment.[10]

There are many examples that show how influential Hebrew works benefited from their connection to Yiddish. Aharon-Halle Wolfsohn's *Kalut da'at u-tzevi'ut* is the Hebrew version of his well-known Yiddish/German play *Laykhtzin un fremelay*. The Yiddish version dates to about 1796; it is not clear when the Hebrew translation was made.[11] The Hebrew translates, explicitly or implicitly, from Yiddish. For example, at the beginning of the play, the phrase " 'Ata nofel be-ra'yoni hamtza'a" translates from the Yiddish "mir falt do a hamtsokhe [sic] ayn."[12] Dan Miron notes this and other passages in which the Hebrew seems to calque the Yiddish. For example, Reb Henoch's impatient words, "gedenk hin, gedenk her" (Yiddish version, 41) becomes "zakhor heina ve-zakhor heina" (Hebrew version, 66).

Because he is trying to capture the liveliness of everyday speech, Wolfsohn cannot rely on the biblical style that was typical in his time. He anticipates some of the devices Perry noted in Abramovitsh's Hebrew, such as using Hebrew words with a meaning that had developed in Yiddish (e.g., *hamtsa'a*), in a Yiddishized form (e.g., *shtusim*), or in a direct translation of a Yiddish phrase (e.g., *tzei tomar lekha*, from the Yiddish *gey zog dir*). As Miron shows, Wolfsohn adapts his Hebrew dialogue to the social level of the speaker.

Almost no one reads the Haskalah Hebrew authors today. In contrast, the number of readers of hasidic works is increasing. There are religious and ideological reasons for the continuing spread of hasidic texts. But from a literary-historical perspective I would emphasize the power of the folk Hebrew in their texts. The hasidic authors anticipated Abramovitsh's use of Hebrew that in some ways echoed Yiddish. Bialik didn't want to validate this aspect of Abramovitsh's writing, but it continues to influence Israeli Hebrew.

The hasidic texts *Shivḥei ha-Besht* and Nahman's tales are in some ways the antithesis of Haskalah Hebrew writing. With the exception of the open-

---

10. "'Nusaḥ Mendele' be-mabat bikoreti" ["A Critical Look at 'Mendele's *nusaḥ*'"], *Dappim le-meḥkar be-sifrut* 14–15 (Haifa, 2006): 89–103.

11. The Hebrew text was first published by Bernard D. Weinryb in *Proceedings of the American Academy for Jewish Research* 24 (1955). Weinryb argues that the play "was originally written in Hebrew by Wolfsohn, apparently even before his Yiddish-German version" (ibid., 166). Dan Miron republished the work as *Kalut da'at u-tzevi'ut [R. Hanokh ve-R. Yosefkhe]* (Tel Aviv: Siman kri'ah, 1977). In *Antonio's Devils: Writers of the Jewish Enlightenment and the Birth of Modern Hebrew and Yiddish Literature* (Stanford: Stanford University Press, 2004), Jeremy Dauber accepts Weinryb's view (197). But even if this is correct, there is clearly an implicit Yiddish model behind the Hebrew.

12. *Laykhtzin un fremelay*, in Zalman Reyzen, *Fun Mendelssohn biz Mendele* (Warsaw: Kultur-lige, 1923), 38. Cp. Miron's discussion, ibid., 36.

ing section of *Shivḥei ha-Besht,* which uses biblical phrases, these narratives are the epitome of "low Hebrew." They are based on mishnaic grammar more than on biblical grammar and often use post-biblical vocabulary. Hasidic Hebrew writing is heavily influenced by Hebrew *as it appears within Yiddish.* A Yiddish-speaking Hebrew author could easily draw from thousands of Hebrew words that were used in Yiddish.

Rabbi Nahman of Bratslav told his tales in Yiddish, and his scribe Nathan Sternharz recorded Nahman's narrative writings by translating them into Hebrew. In translating from Yiddish, Nathan used a lively and straightforward Hebrew that was shaped by the Yiddish source. He was aware that his Hebrew style broke some conventions of the times. At the end of the posthumously published second preface to the *Tales* (*Sippurei mayses,* 1850), Nathan refers to the "coarse expressions" *(leshonot gasim)* that appear in some of the tales. A later editor elaborates on the reason Nathan gave for using them, explaining that he "lowered himself to simple language" (*horid et atzmo lelashon pashut*) to remain as close as possible to the original Yiddish. Nathan did this "so that the matter would not be changed for the person who reads them in the Holy Tongue."[13] In the interest of conveying Nahman's Yiddish words accurately, then, Nathan fashioned a Yiddishized Hebrew.[14] Nathan subsequently wrote biographical accounts and travel narratives using a simple and Yiddish-tinged Hebrew style. Maskilic contemporaries saw the result as corrupt Hebrew, but it was effective and reached a broad audience, although distribution was uneven because of mitnagdic opposition and Czarist censorship.

To understand how Yiddish pervades Nathan Sternharz's Hebrew writings, consider the beginning of his account of Nahman's journey to the Holy Land in 1798. First published following the *Sippurei mayses* in 1815, this account is Hebrew writing by a Yiddish speaker for other Yiddish speakers. The narrative uses simple sentences and the choice of words relies heavily on Hebrew that was present in everyday Yiddish. For example, it begins:

> Kodem she-nas'a le-Eretz-Yisrael, haya be-Kaminetz. Ve-ha-nesi'a shelo le-Kaminetz haita pli'a gedola. Ki pit'om nas'a mi-veito, ve-amar she-yesh lo derekh lifanav linso'a.... Be-'erev ḥag ha-Pesaḥ (1798) yatza Admor z"l mi-

---

13. *Sefer sippurei mayses* (Jerusalem: Hasidei Breslav, 1979), second preface, 14. Mendel Piekarz attributes this final segment of the second preface to Rabbi Nahman of Tulchin. See his book *Hasidut Breslav: prakim be-ḥayei meholelah, be-ktaveiha u-ve-safiḥeiha,* second ed. (Jerusalem: Mossad Bialik, 1995), 178. Thanks to Zeev Gries for providing this reference.

14. Compare Lewis Glinert, "The Hasidic Tale and the Sociolinguistic Modernization of the Jews of Eastern Europe," in *Studies in Jewish Narrative: Ma'aseh Sippur (Presented to Yoav Elstein),* ed. Avidov Lipsker and Rella Kushelevsky (Ramat Gan: Bar-Ilan University Press, 2006), especially 23–25.

ha-makom ve-amar le-zeh she-halakh 'imo she-be-zot ha-shana yehiyeh beva-
dai ba-Eretz ha-kadosha.[15]

If you listen closely, you can almost hear Nathan telling us in Yiddish:

> Far dem vos er iz geforn keyn Erets-Yisroel, iz er geven in Kaminetz. Zayn
> nesiye keyn Kaminetz iz geven a groyse pele. Vayl plutsling iz er avekgeforn
> fun der heym, un er hot gezogt, az er hot a veg tsu forn far zikh. Erev Peysekh
> (1798) iz Admor z"l aroys funem ort un hot gezogt tsu dem, vos iz gegangen
> mit im, az in dem yor vet er avade zayn in Eretz-Yisroel...

This is a rough guess at the implicit Yiddish original. In any event, Nathan's
Yiddishized Hebrew is very effective and, because of its simple grammar
and vocabulary, it was accessible to a wide readership.

Later writers such as Joseph Perl saw the Hebrew of the Hasidim as corrupt, but Perl's greatest accomplishment was in mimicking their written
style. Their non-standard innovations enabled Perl to create the illusion of a
colloquial-style Hebrew. Hence Perl's parodic fiction was a conduit that
made hasidic Hebrew more acceptable to secular Hebrew authors. One way
to see this is to look at the evolution of oral-style narrative and dialogue in
nineteenth-century Hebrew fiction. In a recent article I emphasized the
importance of dialogue in Perl's *Bohen tzadik* and in Levinsohn's *Divrei
tzadikim.*[16] Perl's and Levinsohn's parodies of the hasidic style they intended to mock were more effective than their writings in their own voices.

The hasidic writers were not constrained by the maskilic bias against
Yiddish. As a result, they had no qualms about incorporating Yiddish words
and syntax into their Hebrew texts. Moreover, they embraced the new
meanings of some Hebrew words that had developed in Yiddish. In this
way, they made significant contributions to the creation of a modern Hebrew style.

A phenomenon I would call "innovation by translation" helps to explain
the accomplishments of authors who diverged from the Haskalah style.
Instead of emulating the biblical prophets, they transferred the colloquial
quality from Yiddish to Hebrew. This involved creating Hebrew texts that
sounded like Yiddish—something that was at odds with Haskalah ideas. Yet
there are many instances of this in nineteenth- and early twentieth-century
fiction, extending far beyond scattered words and phrases. Most essential is
the development of a simpler, more European syntax that is distinct from
melitza as it was practiced by the *maskilim.*

---

15. "Seder ha-nesi'a shelo le-Eretz-Yisrael," in *Shivhei ha-Ran* (Jerusalem: Agudat
    meshekh ha-nahal, 1981), 19. This travel narrative was first published together
    with the first edition of Nahman's *Sippurei mayses* (Ostrog, 1815), part two (new
    numbering), 4b.

16. "Joseph Perl's Escape from Biblical Epigonism through Parody of Hasidic Writ-
    ing," *AJS Review: The Journal of the Association for Jewish Studies* 29 (2005):
    265–282.

The canon of "post-hasidic" Hebrew writers, following Perl and Levinsohn, includes authors such as I. L. Peretz, Ahad Ha-am, Berdichevsky, and even Y. H. Brenner. There are also elements of a post-hasidic style in some of Agnon's fiction. However, because of an inevitable mixing of styles, it is not always easy to distinguish clearly between the descendants of the *maskilim* and the Hasidim.

Bialik was part of the problem when it came to understanding what the modernist Hebrew authors were doing. His essays on "Mendele's *nusah*" created a false impression that Abramovitsh's style was the only solid foundation for modern Hebrew literature. As a result, the modernist authors were sometimes misunderstood as writing anti-*nusah*. But they were not only rejecting "Mendele's *nusah*"; they were also continuing a counter-tradition that began with hasidic writing. While Abramovitsh superseded Haskalah Hebrew, some of the modernists innovated by drawing from hasidic Hebrew. Authors such as Peretz, Berdichevsky, and Brenner did not merely take Abramovitsh's Hebrew as the starting-point from which they deviated; instead, they based their alternate style on a transformation of hasidic Hebrew and an incorporation of Yiddish elements. For example, when Brenner translated the first of Sholem Aleichem's Tevye stories, he was open to calquing Yiddish expressions—later avoided by Berkovitz in his Hebrew translations.[17]

We need to supplement Bialik's theory of "Mendele's *nusah*" with another model. It was not merely the diachronic layering that contributed to a new style, but also implicit or explicit translation from Yiddish. Ideological biases blocked recognition of the role of Yiddish and the Hasidim in contributing to modern Hebrew style.

Moving from literary history to historical linguistics, I offer some examples that show how Hebrew continues to be inhabited by Yiddish.[18] The evolution of spoken Hebrew in the twentieth century recapitulated some elements of hasidic Hebrew writing. Focusing on the lexicon, I want to sketch a few ways in which Yiddish is present in modern Hebrew. Linguists such as Paul Wexler have discussed some of the syntactical issues.

One of the most interesting categories is the case of ancient Hebrew words that were used in Yiddish, took on a new meaning, and then came to be used with the new meaning in modern Hebrew. For example, *hokhma* is a perfectly good classical Hebrew word, but when it returns as in the ironic

---

17. See Yitzhak Bakon, "Be-shulei tirgumo shel Brenner le-perek mitokh 'Tuvya ha-halvan," *Siman kri'a* 1 (1972): 211–222. Bakon writes that "Brenner's version is closer to a literal rendering of Sholem Aleichem's version. He allows himself to include things that Berkovitz would have seen as Yiddishisms" (218).

18. See Israel Rubin, "Vegn di virkung fun Yiddish afn geredtn Hebreyish in Erets-Yisroel," *YIVO Bleter* 25 (1945): 303–309, and Hillel Halkin, "Hebrew as She Is Spoke," *Commentary* 48:1 (July 1969): 55–60.

Yiddish reference to *khokhmes*, it has the opposite meaning. *Rogez* occurs in ancient texts, but *brogez* as an adjective is a modern usage taken from the Yiddish. Y-Ḥ-S (yod-ḥet-samekh) is a familiar Hebrew root, but the noun *yikhes*, meaning "pedigree," derives from Yiddish. *Klei-zemer* did not refer to a musician until the Yiddish *(klezmer)* initiated this usage. *Ba'al* was used in mishnaic Hebrew in expressions such as *ba'al ḥokhma*, but other expressions such as *ba'al guf* derived from Yiddish. *Simḥa* describes an emotional state in ancient Hebrew, but thanks to Yiddish it can now refer also to an event. The meaning of *'olam* extended from "world" to "people, audience, public." (Putting these two words together in his account of Nahman's travels, Nathan Sternharz writes: *"Ve-sham 'asu kol ha-olam simḥa gedola"*).[19] There are also many cases of mishnaic Hebrew and Aramaic that, via Yiddish, reached modern Hebrew: *hefker, davka, 'am-ha-'arets,* and many constructions with *beit-*. In addition, dozens of Yiddish words have entered Hebrew vocabulary, ranging from *alte zakhn* to *kunts, frayer, nebekh, litvak, vayter,* and many other essential words like *glitsh, makher,* and *shlimazl* that have also entered English.

One might argue that these are just isolated words that did not have a significant influence on the language. But it would be hard to say that about grammatical borrowings such as suffixes and nominalized verbs. Many suffixes were introduced from Yiddish (and other European languages), including -ke, -nik, -lekh, -le, -ist, -te, and -tzia.[20] The Yiddish verbal form *me-XXX zayn* influenced a distinctive use of nouns such as *mitnaged, matmid,* and *maḥmir*.

A significant influence on nineteenth-century Hebrew style was a simple Yiddish sentence structure that was at odds with Enlightenment *melitza*.[21] The hasidic authors epitomized this and were often mocked for it, but contemporary Hebrew owes a debt to Yiddishized Hebrew style. In 1937, Z. Kalmanovitsh pointed out the connection:

19. See "Seder ha-nesi'a shelo le-Eretz-Yisrael," section 18, in *Shivhei ha-Ran* (Jerusalem: Agudat meshekh ha-nahal, 1981), 35; in the first edition of Nahman's *Sippurei mayses* (Ostrog, 1815), part two (new numbering), 7b.

20. See Haim Blanc's discussion, "Some Yiddish Influences in Israeli Hebrew," in *The Field of Yiddish,* vol. 2, ed. Uriel Weinreich (The Hague: Mouton, 1965), 185–201; William Chomsky, *Hebrew: The Eternal Language* (Philadelphia: JPS, 1957), 193–198; Yudel Mark, "Yiddish-Hebreyishe un Hebreyish-Yiddishe nay-shafungen," *YIVO bleter* 41 (1958): 124–157. I am especially interested in the use of *et 'atzmo* to express the Yiddish reflexive *zikh*; see Shmuel Nobel, "Yiddish in a Hebreyishn levush," *YIVO bleter* 41 (1958), 158–175.

21. For an analysis of the Hebrew style in *Shivhei ha-Besht,* see Lewis Glinert, "The Hasidic Tale and the Sociolinguistic Modernization of the Jews of Eastern Europe," in *Studies in Jewish Narrative,* xx–xxiii. Glinert cites an unpublished Masters thesis by M. Grunzweig, *Behanim leshoniyim be-sefer Shivhei ha-Besht* (Jerusalem, 1974).

If one may say that Hebrew also lived among the Jewish people before the recent attempt to revive it as a spoken language, it lived in exactly this form of a 'folkloristic' Hebrew, as one could characterize it. And it still [that is, in 1937] sounds this way in the Land of Israel, in the mouths of adults who come from among the Yiddish-speaking communities.[22]

Linguistic history repeated itself, though not necessarily by direct influence of hasidic writing. As the Yiddish speakers arrived in Palestine and expressed themselves in Hebrew, they naturally contributed more elements of a Yiddishized Hebrew. Hasidic Hebrew was a forerunner of this development, and it provided written precedents.

Following eighteenth-century ideas about language, the German *maskilim* rejected Yiddish as an illegitimate "jargon" and strove to recreate a "pure" Hebrew in emulation of biblical Hebrew. Yiddish was, in fact, a fusion language combining Germanic, Hebraic, and Slavic elements. Two centuries later, Yiddish-style Hebrew has defeated Haskalah Hebrew, and Israeli Hebrew has attained a multicultural quality, with the infusion of elements from Yiddish, Arabic, English, Russian, German, and French, to name only the most obvious influences. One could almost say that Israeli Hebrew is the new Yiddish.

The presence of Yiddish in other literatures is a neglected topic and the influence of Yiddish on modern Hebrew writing has been especially neglected. In spite of efforts to suppress it, Yiddish haunts much of the best Hebrew writing of the past two centuries. The Haskalah writers tried to exorcise the Yiddish spirit, but without success—their patient died. Hebrew during the period of the Haskalah was lifeless until hasidic and anti-hasidic authors revived it with the help of Yiddish. Hasidic and neo-hasidic authors brought Hebrew back to life, in part, by injecting Yiddish back into its bloodstream. For centuries, Hebrew lived as it was spoken within Yiddish. Now, in spite of the time-honored suppression of Yiddish in Palestine,[23] Yiddish is being spoken within Israeli Hebrew.

---

22. *Yosef Perl's Yiddishe ksavim*, ed. Israel Vaynlez and Z. Kalmanovitsh (Vilna: YIVO, 1937), xcix.

23. See Yael Chaver, *What Must Be Forgotten: The Survival of Yiddish in Zionist Palestine* (Syracuse: Syracuse University Press, 2004).

Creating Yiddish Dialogue for
"The First Modern Yiddish Comedy"

MARION APTROOT

The literary historian Max Erik regarded Isaac Euchel's *Reb Henokh, oder vos tut me damit* as the first modern Yiddish comedy.[1] In order to create a new type of Yiddish comedy, or at least a comedy with Yiddish dialogue, in the last decade of the eighteenth century Euchel had to find an appropriate forum for the representation of spoken Yiddish. He did not do so in a literary vacuum; there was a series of linguistic options available to a maskilic writer of the period that he could consider. Several factors may have played a part in the stylistic decisions a maskil made writing Yiddish dialogue for the characters in a comedy: the spoken Yiddish with which he was familiar, representations of Yiddish on the stage, stylistic conventions of written Yiddish, ideologically motivated considerations, and the dramatic structure of the play.

I. Spoken Yiddish and the Berlin Haskalah

The Berlin Haskalah, which emerged around 1770, aimed for Jews to have a two-fold "national" identity: as Jews, and as citizens of the state in which they lived with rights equal to those of other citizens. Therefore they could have only two "national" languages: Hebrew for the religious realm and other aspects of Jewish culture, and the language of the state in order to be able to take part in the culture and politics of the country in which they lived. For German Jewry this language was High German. Yiddish was not part of the equation; it was regarded as a form of German that was on a par with other dialects or group languages. Unlike *Bildungsdeutsch* (the High German of the educated classes) Yiddish was not deemed suitable for high cultural purposes. A competence in High German was necessary for the emancipation of the Jews, and Yiddish or Yiddish remnants in German were regarded as impediments in the emancipation process. Yiddish was regarded as obsolescent, but it was by no means obsolete. The process of abandoning Yiddish for German had set in before the Haskalah and it would only be completed among German Jewry at the beginning of the twentieth century.[2] For most of the maskilim Yiddish was one of the languages they had

---

1. Max Erik, "Di ershte yidishe komedye," *Filologishe shriftn* 3 (Wilna, 1928), 554–84. I would like to thank Alyssa Quint and Jeremy Dauber for their helpful comments on an earlier draft of this paper.

2. See Steven Lowenstein, "The Yiddish Written Word in 19th Century Germany," *Leo Baeck Institute Yearbook* 24 (1979): 179–192.

grown up with–it usually was their mother tongue–and, although they rejected it ideologically, the reality of Jewish life was such that Yiddish did not disappear overnight. German maskilim used it occasionally for internal oral exchange, sometimes even in writing,[3] but not for contacts with non-Jews or for formal internal communication.

II. Yiddish on the German stage

From the sixteenth century on, it was widely known in Germany that Jews spoke differently from other Germans. "The Jewish dialect" or *Judendeutsch*–what we now call Western Yiddish–as well as German with Yiddish influences were used in literature, at least from the early eighteenth century on, for the sake of curiosity, exoticism, and comical effect. For example, in the comic opera *Die Hamburger Schlachtzeit* (1725), a satire on Hamburg's wealthy merchants, the local Low German dialect is used to give the impression of authenticity, and a Jewish character uses Yiddish words and can be identified by his speech.[4] In the late eighteenth century, German dramatists, reacting against French classicism, tried to create characters that were realistic, not least in their language, and thus Jewish characters were characterized by the way they spoke.[5]

Although the Jewish characters in German comedies, farces, and burlesques were usually characterized by their speech, which was a form of non-standard German, this does not mean that they spoke Yiddish. The mock Yiddish of the German stage contained some Yiddish words and expressions that cannot be found in German, but mainly relied on a pronunciation that was recognized by the audience to be that of native speakers of Yiddish trying to speak German.[6] The pseudo-Yiddish dialect served to iden-

---

3. In his memoirs (1792) Solomon Maimon notes that Mendelssohn used Yiddish words and expressions when talking with East European Talmud students. See Zwi Batscha, ed., *Salomon Maimon's Lebensgeschichte. Von ihm selbst geschrieben und herausgegeben von Karl Philipp Moritz* (Frankfurt am Main, 1995), 160. In his "Jewish-German" correspondence Mendelssohn also uses Yiddish expressions. Cf. Werner Weinberg, "Language Questions Relating to Moses Mendelssohn's Pentateuch Translation," *Hebrew Union College Annual* 105 (1984): 236–241; Dan Miron, *A Traveler Disguised: The Rise of Modern Yiddish Fiction in the Nineteenth Century*, 2nd ed., (Syracuse, 1996), 43.

4. See Hans Peter Althaus, *Mauscheln. Ein Wort als Waffe* (Berlin, 2002), 29–30.

5. Althaus, *Mauscheln*, 30–32. On the mock Yiddish performed on the German stage and in private performances, see also Jacob Katz, *Out of the Ghetto. The Social Background of Jewish Emancipation*, 2nd ed. (New York, 1978), 86; Sander Gilman, *Jewish Self-Hatred. Anti-Semitism and the Hidden Language of the Jews* (Baltimore and London, 1986), 156–160. The best-known play in which mock Yiddish plays an important role postdates *Reb Henokh*. Carl Borromäus Sessa's *Unser Verkehr* was first performed in Breslau in 1812 or 1813 and its first edition appeared in 1815.

6. Often it was enough to use little more than expressions such as "*Vay geshrien*" and the indefinite article *e(n)* or *a(n)* to create the impression that a Jew was speaking.

tify characters as Jews and the sub-standard mode of expression was intended to highlight their marginal position in society and ridicule perceived moral and spiritual deficiencies.

III. The Purimshpil

Creating Yiddish dialogue for stage characters, or at least for characters in a play that was to be read aloud, was not a new task for an Ashkenazic writer. Performances in Yiddish were part of Purim traditions. The *purimshpil*, although often considered a rather homogenous and decidedly premodern genre, had not been static during the time leading up to the period in which Euchel wrote his comedy, and innovations in the non-Jewish theater influenced developments in the Yiddish Purim plays, even if the Purim play did not develop as a genre following major trends in European drama.[7] Some of the more modern Purim plays made use of linguistic registers, multilingualism, or a single standardized language (German). For example, a *purimshpil* in the form of an opera, *Akhashveyresh shpil oyf eynen nayen oyfn glaykh eynen opera* was published in Amsterdam in 1718 and some decades later a modern *Akhashveyresh-shpil*, *Er retung der yudn durkh Ester und Mordkhe* (Amsterdam 1780) was written in the form of a "tragedy with a happy ending" interspersed with songs. This play is completely in Standard High German.[8] The German is stilted, not least because the author has, for the greater part, observed a strict *abab*-rhyme scheme. Even Mordkhe, who in many *purimshpiln* is a buffoon speaking a coarse but lively Yiddish, speaks formal German.[9] For a serious play, theatrical conventions adopted from other European theatrical traditions meant that the use of "dialect," including Yiddish, was undesirable, even unimaginable. The rejection of Yiddish here is not a result of maskilic views—this play is not maskilic in content—but part of a tendency to view Yiddish as a German dialect and High German as the more appropriate language for serious literature, which coincides with the maskilic perspective on the use of Yiddish and German with regard to High Culture. Serious plays and even lighter pieces by maskilim, for example by Jacob Dessauer (1764–1837), were in German only. Jacob Dessauer, a German Jew who was director of a professional Jew-

---

7. For a recent study on the development of the *purimshpil*, see Ahuva Belkin, *Ha-purimshpil:. Iyunim ba-teatron ha-Yehudi ha-amami* (Jerusalem, 2002).

8. For the development of the *Akhashveyresh-shpil*, see Yitskhok Shiper, *Geshikhte fun yidisher teater-kunst un drame fun di eltste tsaytn biz 1750* (Warsaw, 1923–1928), vol. 3, 262–293.

9. On a few occasions *mir* instead of *wir* ("we") is printed and there are other minor lapses in the High German that indicate that someone, probably the typesetter, was more familiar with Yiddish than German. In many respects, the typesetting of this booklet is haphazard.

ish theatre company in Amsterdam around 1800, wrote all his plays in German in Hebrew characters.[10]

In the late eighteenth century, comedies and farces, unlike tragedies and other serious works for the stage, often included characters who spoke dialect or other "imperfect" forms of the language of High Culture. This conformed to contemporary conventions. The comedy *Az der sof iz gut iz ales gut*, which uses different forms of speech (High German and Yiddish dialects), is more or less contemporary with *Reb Henokh*[11] and its unrhymed dialogue is not as stiff as that of *Er retung der yudn durkh Ester und Mordkhe.*

In this comedy of errors, set in the home of *parnes* Reb Lipman, hardly a visitor is what he seems or pretends to be. The director of a Talmud school, Reb Yokesh, runs into Lipe Yentes, the woman he has abandoned and left destitute; the *Yerushalmi*, a Hebrew-speaking emissary from Israel, turns out to be a fraud and a thief from Eastern Europe and the first husband (Reb Yokesh being the second) of Lipe Yentes, who had received forged proof of his demise years earlier; the manservant of the *Yerushalmi* is a young girl named Teymerl, who has left her father's home after having been promised marriage by the *Yerushalmi*. Eventually the confusion is resolved and "all's well that ends well": the cantor of Fingerloch, looking for his lost daughter Teymerl, happens to visit Reb Lipman and is reunited with her. The false *Yerushalmi* takes back his wife, who is given a divorce by her second hus-

---

10. Whether his actors pronounced the texts in such a way that they were still recognizably German or if they pronounced them like Yiddish, even changed them while on the stage, is not known. See Hetty Berg, "Thalia and Amsterdam's Ashkenazi Jews in the 18th and Early 19th Centuries," in Jonathan Israel and Reinier Salverda, eds., *Dutch Jewry: Its History and Secular Culture (1500–2000)* (Leiden 2000), 191–199. A number of works by Dessauer in manuscript and print can be found at the Bibliotheca Rosenthaliana, the Judaica division of the library of the University of Amsterdam.

11. It was performed at the house of Rabbi Jacob Moses Loewenstam (1747–1815), who became chief rabbi of the Ashkenazi community of Amsterdam in 1793. *Az der sof iz gut iz ales gut. All is well that ends well or the uncovered threefold deceit*, an anonymous Yiddish comedy from the end of the 18th century; introduction, notes, and modernized Yiddish version by L. Fuks (Paris, 1955). Since the title page of the manuscript is missing, Fuks gave the play the title by which it is now known. Fuks assumed the play was written in Amsterdam since a Yiddish dialect from southern Germany as well as Eastern Yiddish is parodied, but since there is no parody of the local Dutch Yiddish dialect, Hartog Beem thought this unlikely and assumed the play to stem from Germany. A few Dutch words in the manuscript would rather indicate that a play from Germany was copied and adapted in Amsterdam, where it was performed as is indicated in the manuscript. See Hartog Beem, "Als der sof is gut, is alles gut," *Nieuw Israelietisch Weekblad*, Dec. 2, 1955, p. 4. See also Renate Fuks-Mansfeld, "West- und Ostjiddisch auf Amsterdamer Bühnen gegen Ende des achtzehnten Jahrhunderts," in Astrid Starck, ed., *Westjiddisch. Le Yiddish occidental* (Aarau, 1994), 112–118. Fuks-Mansfeld repeats the views of her late husband and fails to mention Beem's criticism.

band, who in turn is prepared to take Teymerl for his wife, thus saving her honor. In a joyous final scene the cantor of Fingerloch and his future son-in-law sing a hymn in honor of Purim.

Different languages and linguistic registers are used: Reb Lipman and the young Teymerl speak (more or less) High German; the *Yerushalmi* speaks Hebrew (as does Teymerl in her role as servant) and after being unmasked, Eastern Yiddish; Lipe Yentes and Reb Yokesh speak Yiddish; the cantor of Fingerloch Franconian Yiddish dialect. The languages serve to illustrate the person's background and level of education; the Franconian Yiddish in addition adds a comic touch.

IV. Yiddish and German:
Component consciousness and stylistic considerations

Max Weinreich's theory of Yiddish as a fusion language in which components derived from different stock languages are fused together to form a whole also suggests that speakers of Yiddish have a heightened component consciousness.[12] Even if Ashkenazic Jews may have been more aware of the etymological origins of parts of their vocabulary—and the hybrid spelling system certainly helped to foster this consciousness—this knowledge was haphazard. The degree of component consciousness is dependent on the multilingual capabilities and the education of the individual speaker. Yet, however flawed the component consciousness of Yiddish authors was, it played an important part in the aesthetics of Yiddish style.

Yiddish and German are closely related and, although there is no doubt that by the sixteenth century Yiddish had become an independent language, spoken and written Yiddish would always maintain a relationship with German that is different from that with other languages. Especially in Germany, speakers of Yiddish were in close contact with German. Throughout the history of Yiddish, Yiddish was a language spoken by a minority and always compared to a German that not only had a much higher number of speakers, but also had higher prestige. Therefore, literary German has had an influence on written Yiddish from the very beginnings of Yiddish literature. The most easily recognized feature that clearly separates Yiddish from German is the vocabulary. In modeling their texts on German examples, some Yiddish authors concentrated on avoiding non-German vocabulary. A considerable number of Yiddish literary and sub-literary creations by Ashkenazic Jews from the Middle Ages through the nineteenth century boast an all-Germanic vocabulary—and elements that were mistakenly believed to be of Germanic origins.

Not only the German example, but also the aesthetic principle, according to which mixing elements from different components was undesirable in literary texts, played a part in this. The idea that words from different

---

12. Max Weinreich, *Geshikhte fun der yidisher shprakh* (New York, 1973), vol. 2, 318–320.

components should not be mixed was clearly expressed by Joseph ben Jacob Maarssen in *Sheyne artlekhe geshikhtn*, a selection of tales from Boccaccio's *Decameron* in Yiddish (1710).[13] In its preface, which is itself full of words of Hebrew or Aramaic origin, Maarssen stated that he had avoided the use of words from Hebrew in the main text because he thinks it is a "sin" to mix the Holy Tongue with other languages, as is the practice among Jews. However, even as Maarssen wrote, another view of the mixing of elements of different components had literary precedent. Hebrew grammarian Elye Bokher (Elia Levita, 1469–1549) was a pioneer in writing a literary Yiddish incorporating words and expressions of the Hebrew-Aramaic component as rhyme-words in his literary works,[14] which are stylistically among the most refined of older Yiddish literature.

The lack of formal education in Yiddish, which was taught as a subject in traditional education in the *kheyder* only, at best, briefly and just in order to be able to correspond in the mother tongue, meant that Yiddish authors had to seek out stylistic examples of literary style without having been offered any in their education that they could adopt or reject. Inspiration by German writing styles did not always result in the elimination of Semitic component words. Isaac Wetzlar's (1680–1751) *Libesbriv* (1749),[15] for example, boasts long, baroque sentences that were in fashion in German at the time, but the author also makes use of Semitic-based vocabulary and recognizably Yiddish turns of phrase. For Wetzlar, being understood by his audience was of greater importance than a notion of language purity. The use of vocabulary that was rooted in Jewish tradition was possibly also intended to give his call for reforms a less revolutionary character. The stylistic choices of a pre-Enlightenment thinker thus already contain elements that can be recognized in the works of East European maskilim, who resorted to Yiddish in order to reach the unenlightened audience they could not influence in Hebrew or in the official language of the state. It is known that the Galician maskil Joseph Perl (1773–1839) replaced German-sounding expressions and turns of phrase with expressions that were associated with and gave the impression of natural, spoken Yiddish. Chone Shmeruk, while researching Perl's language in the Yiddish stories and letters imitating the language of the Hasidim, noted that Perl had himself replaced certain (not

---

13. See Marion Aptroot, "'I Know This Book of Mine Will Cause Offence...': A Yiddish Adaptation of Boccaccio's Decameron (Amsterdam 1710)," *Zutot* (2003): 152–159.

14. Older works such as *Melokhim-bukh* (printed in Augsburg 1554 but written earlier) also incorporate Hebrew-Aramaic words.

15. *The libes briv of Isaac Wetzlar*, edited and translated by Morris M. Faierstein, Atlanta, Ga., 1996. On this text, see Faierstein's introduction and Stefan Rohrbacher, "Isaak Wetzlar in Celle—Ein jüdischer Reformer vor der Zeit der Aufklärung," in Brigitte Streich, ed., *Juden in Celle. Biographische Skizzen aus drei Jahrhunderten* (Celle, 1996), 33–66.

all) expressions taken from literary High German.[16] Mendel Lefin (1749–1826), a Podolian maskil, did not write a language emulating High German while working on his Bible translation, but he did not avoid words from German either if they were also current in contemporary Podolian Yiddish and part of the language of his intended readership; for Lefin, it was of the utmost importance to be understood by his readers.[17]

Prevalent examples of Yiddish stylistics were the chancery and epistolary styles. The chancery style could be so heavily Hebraized that some texts appear at first glance to be written in Hebrew, and only on closer inspection does one find that the Yiddish element, although accounting for a relatively small percentage of lexical items, provides most of the grammatical function words such as auxiliaries and conjunctions and thus dominates the structure of the sentences. The epistolary style, which according to Uriel Weinreich was influenced by the chancery style,[18] could employ grammatical units taken from Hebrew and longer sequences of Hebraisms. The style of letters could range from the informal writing down of Yiddish as it was spoken to a highly formal style using many fixed formulae in Hebrew and Yiddish, with most letters containing at least some fixed formulae at the opening and closing.[19]

Whether an author chose to avoid words from the Semitic component, to use them freely or even to write a heavily Hebraized Yiddish, component consciousness played a part in the stylistic decisions nearly every Yiddish writer made.

V. The structure of vernacular Yiddish as a model of good style

Where component consciousness on the level of the vocabulary had been one underlying criterion for deciding what constituted good Yiddish style, another was syntactical. Jekuthiel Blitz and Joseph Witzenhausen, the translators of two rival Tanakh editions in Yiddish (Amsterdam, 1678–1679), claimed to have written Yiddish in a pure and clear language.[20] In

16. Chone Shmeruk, "Halashon vehasignon shel hatekst beyidish" [The Language and the Style of the Yiddish Text] in Joseph Perl, *Maasiot veigrot mitsadikim heamitiim umianshei shelomenu* [Hasidic Tales and Letters], ed. by Chone Shmeruk and Shmuel Werses (Jerusalem: Academy of Sciences, 1969), 70–75. I would like to thank Roland Gruschka for drawing my attention to this.

17. Roland Gruschka, *Übersetzungswissenschaftliche Aspekte von Mendel Lefin Satanowers Bibelübersetzungen* (Hamburg, 2007), 80–81.

18. Uriel Weinreich, "Nusakh ha-soferim ha-ivri-yidi," *Leshonenu* 22 (1958): 54–66.

19. Cf. the letters published by Alfred Landau and Bernard Wachstein in their *Jüdische Privatbriefe aus dem Jahre 1619* (Vienna and Leipzig, 1911).

20. See Andrea Schatz, "Entfernte Wörter. Reinheit und Vermischung in den Sprachen der Berliner Maskilim" in Michael Brocke, Aubrey Pomerance, and Andrea Schatz, eds., *Neuer Anbruch. Zur deutsch-jüdischen Geschichte und Kultur* (Berlin, 2001), 243–261.

their case this refers to the syntax of their translations. Unlike the preceding Yiddish Bible translations, the language of Blitz and Witzenhausen is based on the implicit rules of their own vernacular Yiddish rather than the typical Bible translation syntax that was dictated by Hebrew word order through the practice of translating word-for-word. Both express in their respective prefaces that they have translated into "pure," "clear" and "beautiful" Yiddish, qualities that the language did not possess in the eyes of the maskilim. Other authors would look to German syntax and morphology as a model of written language, a practice that has created a continuum between written Yiddish and German.

VI. Creating Yiddish dialogue: the example of Isaac Euchel's Reb Henokh

Reb Henokh, oder vos tut me damit?, the play that Isaac Euchel (1756–1804) wrote in 1793 or shortly thereafter, is a multilingual comedy in which Yiddish is one of the main languages employed.[21] Euchel, a native of Copenhagen, was sent, following the death of his father, to an uncle in Germany at the age of twelve. Although his mother wanted him to become a rabbi, he used his Jewish religious and scholarly education to find positions as a tutor in rich Jewish homes in cities where he could obtain a modern, secular education. He spent time in Berlin, where he joined the circles around Moses Mendelssohn, and in Königsberg (1781–1786), where he studied Philosophy (with Emanuel Kant) and Oriental Languages at the university. Disappointed with the limits of emancipation since even a temporary appointment at that university was not within the reach of a Jew, he made the Jewish Enlightenment the main aim of his working life. As a founder of scholarly societies and the journal *Hameasef,* Euchel is now considered as a man who was pivotal in spreading the ideas of the Berlin Haskalah.[22] He wrote *Reb*

---

21. Isaak Euchel, *Reb Henoch, oder: Woß tut me damit. Eine jüdische Komödie der Aufklärungszeit*; text edition by Marion Aptroot and Roland Gruschka, with introductory contributions by Marion Aptroot, Delphine Bechtel, Shmuel Feiner, and Roland Gruschka, 2nd ed. (Hamburg, 2006). An earlier text edition was provided by Zalmen Reyzen [Reisen] in Yankev Shatski [Jacob Shatzky], *Arkhiv far der geshikhte fun yidishn teater un drame* (Wilna, 1930), 94–146. Reyzen's edition is based on the manuscript held in the Bibliotheca Rosenthalia in Amsterdam, which is of later date than the manuscript at the Royal Library in Copenhagen. For a comparison of manuscript versions of *Reb Henokh* see Aptroot and Gruschka, "Die Handschriften und Druckfassungen der Komödie" in Euchel, *Reb Henoch*, 67–85. Since this comparison of manuscripts and print versions was published, we have studied two more manuscripts and to date the Copenhagen manuscript remains the "most authentic."

22. See Shmuel Feiner, "Isaac Euchel: 'Entrepreneur' of the Haskalah Movement in Germany," *Zion* 58 (1987): 427–469 (Hebrew: "Yitskhak Aykhl—ha'yazam' shel tenuat hahaskala beGermania"); ibid., *The Jewish Enlightenment* (Philadelphia 2002), 221–242; ibid., "Isaac Euchel—Der Gründer der jüdischen Aufklärungsbewegung" in *Reb Henoch*, 1–17.

Henokh in 1793 in Berlin, where he had settled six years earlier. The Enlightenment had not had the results for which he had hoped; the maskilim had not been able to introduce modern Hebrew education on a wide scale, and especially in Berlin the offspring of the financial elite were not modernized in the sense of the Haskalah but rather mostly lost all attachment with Jewish religion and education. Torn between hope and disappointment, even despair, Euchel wrote *Reb Henokh, oder vos tut me damit,* "a portrait of a family,"[23] which deals with social and ideological problems caused by major changes in Jewish society in contemporary Berlin.

Reb Henokh is a wealthy Jewish merchant, married to Yitl. The traditional, conservative couple are the parents of four children: two sons, Hertskhe and Shmuel, and two daughters, Elke and Hodes. Shmuel is to all appearances a traditional religious Jew and he is his father's favorite. The other three are "falsely" enlightened: they have picked up some of the new ideas of acculturation and rejected old Jewish values, but they have not adopted modern Jewish and general enlightened ideas and values. They speak German, have adopted German names (Hertskhe–Hartwig, Elke–Elisabeth and Hodes–Hedwig), and are morally adrift. Jewish secondary characters include truly enlightened Jews (a doctor, a student named Marcus, and a relative, Nathan, who is a provincial deputy), a conservatively religious Jew (Reb Orn), a religious Jew who is willing to compromise his principles when in financial need (Modl, Elke's husband), a falsely enlightened Jew (Braytenboukh), and a hypocrite who pretends to be deeply religious (the "Zwicker," the traditional Jewish barber). Non-Jewish characters serve to illustrate the place Jews occupy in general society, further the plot, provide comic relief, or fulfill a combination of these functions.

During the action, which takes place in less than twenty-four hours, Reb Henokh's world falls apart: he finds out that his daughters spend Friday night at a public venue in the company of non-Jews, his eldest son Hertskhe is arrested and locked up in debtor's prison, his confidant the barber turns out to be a swindler and a thief, and he learns that the non-Jewish maid-servant is pregnant from his favorite son Shmuel.

The play uses language to characterize the background or outlook of the characters.[24] The main language of the play, which is written in Hebrew characters, is German. The descriptions of the scenery and the stage directions are all in German. The non-Jewish characters of the play speak Ger-

---

23. The subtitle of the play is "Ein Familiengemälde."

24. See, most recently, Delphine Bechtel, "Reb Henoch, oder: Woß tut me damit?– Hybride Sprache, Zwittergestalten: Kulturen im Kontakt in einer jüdischen Komödie der Aufklärungszeit," in Euchel, *Reb Henoch*, 19–44; Roland Gruschka, "Der Sprachenkosmos in Isaak Euchels Komödie *Reb Henoch* und die Sprachverhältnisse der Berliner Haskalah," in Euchel, *Reb Henoch*, 45–66.

man, German dialects, or, in the case of foreigners, a broken German mixed
with elements from their mother tongue. The languages spoken by the Jewish characters reflect their position within the spectrum, ranging from a
form of rabbinical orthodoxy that stubbornly hangs on to irrational ideas
and practices, to Enlightenment with different forms of incomplete or false
Enlightenment in between.[25] Those stuck in the traditional way of life and
impervious to the new ideas of Enlightenment speak Yiddish; the enlightened Jews (and the falsely enlightened ones) speak High German; and a
character like Hedwig, "a silly creature"[26] who believes herself to be more
enlightened than she really is, occasionally lapses into the local low city dialect.

   Reb Henokh is often mentioned with Aaron Halle-Wolfssohn's (1754–
1835) *Laykhtzin und fremelay* (or, since it is a German play with Yiddish in
it, *Leichtsinn und Frömmelei*) and the two contemporary plays are indeed
closely related. Both deal with the problems in a Jewish family with a conservative patriarch, falsely enlightened children, a hypocrite who pretends
to conform to traditional ethical standards and a character embodying the
ideals of Enlightenment named Marcus.[27] In both *Laykhtzin und fremelay*
and *Reb Henokh*, the Jewish characters are the embodiment of different
types of Jews on a scale defining them from enlightened to poorly or falsely
enlightened to traditionally Orthodox. Wolfssohn's play, with its small number of characters and its more condensed action, can be staged.[28] Euchel's

---

25. Delphine Bechtel analyzes the spectrum displayed in *Reb Henoch* according to the
    five categories described by Aaron Halle-Wolfssohn in *Jeschurun oder unparteyische
    Beleuchtung der dem Judenthume neuerdings gemachten Vorwürfe* (Breslau,
    1804), see Bechtel, "Reb Henoch, oder: Woß tut me damit?–Hybride Sprache, Zwit-
    tergestalten: Kulturen im Kontakt in einer jüdischen Komödie der Aufklärungszeit,"
    in Euchel, *Reb Henoch*, 19–44. Suse Bauschmid more recently demonstrated that the
    range of Euchel's Jewish characters fits the scheme that Lazarus Bendavid proposed
    in his *Etwas zur Charackteristick der Juden* (Leipzig, 1793) perfectly. Bau-schmid,
    "Etwas zur Charakteristik der Figuren in maskilischen Komödien," Paper presented at
    the Ninth Symposium for Yiddish Studies in Germany, Düsseldorf, 9–11 October
    2006.

26. Describing his failed education, Hartwig (Hertskhe) describes his sister Hedwig as an
    "albernes Geschöpf, das aber die Gutmütigkeit selbst ist," "a silly creature that is good-
    ness in person," Euchel, *Reb Henoch*, 192–193.

27. Cf. Jeremy Dauber, *Antonio's Devils: Writers of the Jewish Enlightenment and the
    Birth of Modern Hebrew and Yiddish Literature* (Stanford, 2004),185.

28. Indeed, Wolfsohn had practice directing student drama performances at the Breslau
    seminary and wrote a monolingual Hebrew version of *Laykhtzin und fremelay*. For
    their anthology of Yiddish plays that work in translation and can be staged, Joel
    Berkowitz and Jeremy Dauber, therefore, chose to include Wolffsohn's *Laykhtzin
    und fremelay* rather than Euchel's *Reb Henokh*; cf. Joel Berkowitz and Jeremy
    Dauber, *Landmark Yiddish Plays: A Critical Anthology*, New York 2006. *Reb
    Henokh* may only have been read, not staged. The markings in one of the manuscripts

comedy, with its large cast and the overlong monologue of the prodigal son, cannot hold the dramatic tension as well, even though every act ends with a climax.[29] *Reb Henokh* may not be as dramatically successful as *Laykhtsinn und fremelay*, but this play, in which linguistic subtleties are of greater importance, offers valuable material for an analysis of Yiddish dialogue.

For a maskil such as Euchel or his colleague and contemporary Aaron Halle-Wolfssohn the use of Yiddish was not self-evident. At first sight, the use of Yiddish by maskilim who favored using New High German and Hebrew may be surprising, but, given the function of Yiddish in these comedies, Yiddish was as obvious a choice as the German dialects or the broken German of foreigners in the plays that served as models for Wolfssohn and Euchel, and in Euchel's *Reb Henokh* itself. Euchel's satirical family portrait contains elements of the "rührende Lustspiel" (moving or touching comedy) as well as elements that follow the dramatic theories of Gotthold Efraim Lessing (1729–1781) and it may, in addition, have been influenced by popular adaptations of foreign works.[30] The use of High German and dialects in comedies serves to illustrate different levels of education and social standing. In addition, dialects or the broken German of foreigners also served as a comedic ploy. Language competence is a token of education and, in the case of Jews and foreigners, a sign of their decree of acculturation. Once the choice for creating Yiddish-speaking characters had been made, the authors saw themselves confronted with the problem of creating a literary Yiddish suited for the purpose.

With *Reb Henokh*, Euchel was one of the first authors to create a vernacular mode of Yiddish emulating the spoken language. This style had to illustrate the inferior nature of Yiddish when compared to High German—from the maskilic perspective—as well as to create the illusion that it was lifelike Yiddish.

Plays that are completely or in part in Yiddish and that predate *Reb Henokh*, i.e., the Purim plays, are not written in a language that testifies to similar literary ambitions. Authors who did want to write dramatic works of

---

indicate that the play was read with divided parts. See Marion Aptroot and Roland Gruschka, "Zur Rezeption und Gebrauch: Varianten, Zusätze und Eingriffe" in Euchel, *Reb Henoch*, 87–88.

29. In the original, three-act structure, every act goes out with a bang. The second and third act were later divided in two by a copyist who probably made these changes to conform to the influential theory of author and critic Johann Christoph Gottsched (1700–1766), according to whom five acts were the most appropriate structure for comedy. See Marion Aptroot and Roland Gruschka, "Die Handschriften und Druckfassungen der Komödie" in Euchel, *Reb Henoch*, 75.

30. Cf. Roland Gruschka, "Der Sprachenkosmos...," in Euchel, *Reb Henoch*, 55. Wolfssohn's more schematic play is in the tradition of the "sächsische Typenkomödie" (Saxon comedy of manners).

literary quality chose to write in other languages, preferably Hebrew,[31] but in the late eighteenth century German could also be the language of choice. Euchel indeed did write his play in German and used other languages and dialects as was common in German comedies, but he probably did not write *Reb Henokh* with the intention of composing a work of enduring quality. It was not printed during his lifetime and the author's name was not written on the manuscripts by copyists but added at a later date; so Euchel probably did not put his name on the autograph(s). Nevertheless, *Reb Henokh* has withstood the test of time extremely well. The charm of the play lies not least in the fluent and lively language, including those parts that are in Yiddish.

Reb Henokh is modeled on German comedies that did not contain Yiddish dialogue and thus could not serve as examples in this respect. In contrast to the stage Yiddish that can be found in German plays written by non-Jews, the Yiddish spoken in *Reb Henokh* is not mock but "real Yiddish." The Yiddish of *Reb Henokh*, which may at first appear to be a naturalistic rendering of the way traditional Jews spoke in Northern Central Europe in that period, is, in fact, honed in order to set off the Yiddish against German and to characterize the symbolic value of Yiddish through its structure.

Even if Euchel did not intend to connect or identify primarily with the tradition of the *purimshpil* but rather with that of the contemporary German theater, Euchel, like Wolfssohn, who suggested in the preface to his edition of *Laykhtzin und fremelay* (Breslau, 1796) that his play should replace the base traditional Yiddish Purim plays,[32] certainly was familiar with plays performed at Purim. Both also wrote plays that, like some Purim plays, take great liberties to criticize Jewish society in a satirical way and both have elements of the farcical and grotesque, including sexual innuendo, which would make the plays meet more of the expectations of a Purim audience than if they had nothing in common with traditional Purim entertainment.[33]

---

31. Ben-Ami Feingold, "Makhazei hahaskala vehamikra," *Teuda* 7 (1991): 429–449.

32. In his preface to *Laykhtzin und fremelay*, a comedy contemporary with *Reb Henokh* and written by a fellow maskil, Aaron Halle-Wolfssohn expresses his contempt for the unenlightened plays. His inclusion of a German play in the first edition of *Laykhtzin und fremelay*, Friedrich Wilhelm Gotter's (1746-1779) *Die stolze Vasthi* (1st. ed. 1789), of which he removed certain overtly anti-Jewish elements, is a further indication of German drama serving as a model for enlightened Jewish dramatic entertainment. For the adaptation of Gotter's play, see Chone Shmeruk, *Sifrut yidish: prakim letoldoteha* (Tel-Aviv, 1978), 149-151.

33. On the tradition of including "low" elements, see Evi Butzer, *Die Anfänge der jiddischen* purim shpiln *in ihrem literarischen und kulturgeschichtlichen Kontext* (Hamburg, 2002), 170-189 and Ahuva Belkin, "The 'low' culture of the Purimshpil," in Joel Berkowitz, *Yiddish Theatre: New Approaches* (Oxford, 2003), 29-43.

The use of German and Yiddish, even different forms of Yiddish, in the contemporary *purimshpil* was not unique, as can be gleaned from *Az der sof iz gut iz ales gut*, but this comedy is stylistically less refined than *Reb Henokh* and *Laykhtzin und fremelay*. Even if it or similar plays predate the two better-known plays, it is unlikely that they would have served as a direct model for Euchel, although influences cannot be ruled out.[34] No autograph of *Reb Henokh* exists and since all extant manuscript copies date from the nineteenth century, no analysis of the style of Euchel can be made without allowing room for speculation. Nonetheless, even if some of Euchel's formulations may have been scrambled during the process of transmission, the text was carefully crafted by its author and subtleties of expression play an important part.

Different styles of Yiddish had been parodied in earlier Yiddish texts, but the stress was mainly on dialect differences or different written styles, on the unusual and the exotic. Their aim was not the emulation of spoken Yiddish as it was familiar to the intended audience and, therefore, these texts do not offer models for a vernacular mode needed in a comedy of manners.

For his purpose—creating a Yiddish that would still be recognizable as natural speech but would also be clearly contrasting with Standard High German and German dialects—Euchel had to resort to the rules inherent in the Yiddish language itself. In this respect there is a similarity with stylistic principles of Blitz and Witzenhausen's translations, the language of which had been harshly criticized by Mendelssohn,[35] rather than the traditional form of language purism that excluded the "mixing of languages," i.e., the combination of elements from the different linguistic components of Yiddish. Euchel also relied on component consciousness, but he did not eliminate the elements that are not part of the Germanic Component. Indeed, to enhance the contrast between the language ideal of Standard High German (which according to his ideals was to be used by Jews alongside grammatically correct and stylistically refined Hebrew), the Yiddish spoken by his

---

34. The Purim plays of the late eighteenth century are a subject that is largely unexplored. Among the undated manuscripts in research libraries and private collections there may be a number of plays from this period that have not yet come to the attention of scholars.

35. In the prospectus for his own translation, *Alim literufa* (1778), Mendelssohn writes about Blitz's translation, which he thought worse than that of Witzenhausen, that the translator did a poor job because he was ignorant not only of Hebrew but of German (Yiddish) as well and so "with stammering lips did he speak to his people" (Isaiah 28:11). See Alexander Altman, *Moses Mendelssohn: A Biographical Study* (London, 1963), 369. He was to repeat his criticism in the introduction to his translation, *Or lanetiva* (1783); see Moses Mendelssohn, *Gesammelte Schriften*. Jubiläumsausgabe, vol. 14 (Berlin, 1972) [facsimile reprint of Breslau 1937], 242, quoted after Schatz, "Entfernte Wörter," 252. Mendelssohn did not distinguish between *loshn ashkenaz* as German and as the language traditionally spoken by the Jews (Yiddish).

non-enlightened Jewish characters had to be as much unlike German as possible without giving his audience, mainly native speakers, the impression that this was not Yiddish as they knew it.

The linguistic panorama of *Reb Henokh* is almost naturalistic and, therefore, all the characters had to speak a language that was crafted such as to be easily recognized but not exaggerated so much as to no longer ring true to an audience that was familiar with the different languages and dialects that are employed. The figures that speak Yiddish had to be characterized by a language that did not deviate from existent and recognizable syntactic patterns, vocabulary, and idioms.

To heighten the contrast between Yiddish and German, there is hardly a Yiddish sentence in *Reb Henokh* that does not include Semitic component elements. The first spoken dialogue of the play, uttered by the hypocritical barber, is a fine example:

> *Und reb Henokhs Hertskhe vird virklikh a khoysem-shtekher? Dos halt ikh for a khokhme. A melokhe iz a melukhe. Tsu a soykher hot er—zayt mirs moykhel—zoy kayn seykhel-hamoyled.*

> And Reb Henokhs [son] Hertskhe is really going to be a seal engraver? I think that is a wise decision. A craft is a sure way of earning a living. In order to be a merchant—please forgive me—he wasn't born with the practical intelligence.

Reb, *khoysem-shtekher*, *khokhme*, *melokhe*, *melukhe*, *soykher*, *moykhel*, and *seykhel-hamoyled* are all words and word combinations from the Semitic component of Yiddish and are not part of the High German vocabulary of the period. The use of these words serves to highlight the contrast between Yiddish and German, as do the names Henokh and Hertskhe.[36] The common idiomatic expressions "*a melokhe iz a melukhe*" and "*zayt mirs moykhel*" help to give the impression that this is natural speech.[37] One Germanic element, the adverb *zoy*, is clearly marked in its Yiddish dipthongal pronunciation by the spelling *zayen-vov-yud-alef* (and not *zayen-alef*, which would be pronounced *zo*, indistinguishable from the German *so*). In other instances, Euchel not only uses the different pronunciation but also the flexion of Germanic elements in Yiddish, e.g., *dray monat* (127), which contrasts with High German *drei Monate*, since the Yiddish form lacks the plural ending *-e*.

---

36. The names may sound Germanic-Yiddish. Henoch sounds like German Hennig and the name Hertskhe is all Germanic in origin. They are not known as personal names among non-Jews.

37. The text abounds with lively (Western) Yiddish expressions such as *bevounes* ("alas"), *gut shabes ... gut yor* (greeting and answer on the Sabbath), *kloumer kez* ("apparently cheese," an expression of skepticism), *a krie iber dem!* (a curse), and *shander-debander [der ayner vi der ander]* ("neither of them is any good").

The use of Semitic component words in the speech of the unenlightened characters appears to be higher than expected in a secular text of the late eighteenth century, although it is not possible to use statistics to prove anything in this matter. The use of Hebraisms is dependent on the education of the speaker/author, on the text genre and on the intended audience and the impression the speaker or author wants to make on his audience (whether he wants to communicate clearly or impress his audience with highly learned utterances). Since the number of Hebraisms that were part of spoken Western Yiddish was high—unfortunately we don't know much about their frequency—this left Euchel much leeway when writing the Yiddish dialogue.

Euchel was well aware of the use of Hebrew elements in the traditional Yiddish chancery style, as can be seen in the letter that Henokh receives from the community

> *Meakher zikh getsaygt, dos kame balebatim vebokhrim bebeys-hakneses hagdoyle kumen beshabes-koydesh in shtifl, veyesh mehem trogn gor shokher zaydn hals-tikher, voran tsu erkenen, dos zi onfangen, khokrim vefilosofim tsu verden, asher beafkoruse nikhe lehem, umetokh kakh dasyisroel nishtakakht min ho-orets, al-ken hot hagoen av-beys-din vealufey parnosey umanhigey-hakehile mazhir gevezen, dos zolkhes apikorses beknas-goydl nikht mer geshen zol. Vehaskhoynim yirun veloy yisiden od.*

> After it became evident, that many householders and young men enter the great synagogue on the holy Shabbat in boots and that some of them even wear black silk scarves from which can be recognized, that they are beginning to become thinkers and philosophers, that free-thinking is pleasant to them, and because it follows from this, that the faith of Israel disappears from the country, therefore the Learned President of the Religious Court as well as the community leadership and representatives have warned, that such apostasy will no longer take place or be sanctioned with high penalties. Those who hear this may be afraid and sin no longer.[38]

The letter is a parody of the Yiddish chancery style with its mixing of Hebrew and Yiddish. This style, which must have displeased an expert in Hebrew grammar such as Euchel, is clearly different from that of the vernacular style that represents the speech of the characters. The epistolary style was, however, connected to written Yiddish and could only be parodied as such. It could not be used as an example for dialogue without disturbing the dramatic illusion. In the speech of characters longer Hebrew units may be used in their function as quotations, but not as part of dialogue *per se*.

Euchel here distinguished clearly between the two ways Hebrew-Aramaic elements could be part of Yiddish, in what Weinreich called Whole Hebrew and Merged Hebrew.[39] In the vernacular mood they have clearly

---

38. Euchel, *Reb Henoch*, 111.

39. Max Weinreich, *Geshikhte*, vol. 2, 5–7.

marked functions: Whole Hebrew for Hebrew quotations such as the ones the apparently religious son Shmuel utters regularly[40] or the one verse Reb Henokh uses to impress his visitors with his new (unwittingly hilarious) interpretation,[41] and Merged Hebrew as part of the spoken style. Chancery style integrates larger and more units of Hebrew than other Yiddish styles, thus blurring the boundaries between Whole and Merged Hebrew and probably creating an extremely bad Hebrew style in the eyes of the maskilim.

Since the Semitic component in written Yiddish of the Early Modern Period can range from zero to about 85 percent, it is difficult if not impossible to say if the high number of Semitic component elements in the Yiddish spoken by characters in *Reb Henokh* really gave the contemporary audience for whom Euchel wrote—probably primarily his own friends—the impression of being either a faithful imitation of what they knew from their own experience or a recognizable parody of the speech of traditional Jewry.

In the attempt to create a "larger than life" Yiddish style, there is a similarity with the stage Yiddish that existed at the time Euchel wrote his play and that had anti-Semitic undertones. But unlike stage Yiddish in the Christian theatre, the Yiddish of the characters in *Reb Henokh* was to be judged by an audience conversant with the language from within. The mock Yiddish of the German stage mainly relied on a recognizably "Jewish" accent and less on a specifically Yiddish vocabulary. Euchel uses a Yiddish pronunciation of words that Yiddish and German have in common as well as a Yiddish abundant with words and expressions that cannot be found in German, a vocabulary his audience would have understood, unlike the non-Jewish audience that was the main addressee of German comedies.

VII. Parallel developments

The formation of a Yiddish literary style based on vernacular, spoken Yiddish would take flight in Eastern Europe in the second half of the nineteenth century, but there were attempts at creating a Yiddish style that emulated spoken Yiddish in Western Europe during the late eighteenth century. Closely related to the efforts of creating Yiddish for the stage, or at least for reading aloud, were the Dutch *Diskursn*,[42] which were written shortly after *Reb Henokh*. The *Diskursn* were polemical pamphlets published weekly by two rivaling factions in the Ashkenazic community of Amsterdam. One of them had split off from the main community and tried to persuade more

---

40. E.g., Act II, scene 18.

41. Act III, scene 9.

42. A selection from the two main series of *Diskursn* can be found in *Storm in the Community: Yiddish Polemical Pamphlets of Amsterdam Jewry, 1797–1798*. Selected, translated and introduced by Jozeph Michman and Marion Aptroot (Cincinnati, 2002).

members of the "old community" to join it. These pamphlets were apparently successful, because soon other series of similar brochures appeared that represented the point of view and the interests of the "old community." They served propaganda purposes, and in order to reach the intended audience—those Ashkenazic householders who had the money to pay membership fees in the community—the pamphlets had to be entertaining. They were written in the vein of a popular genre of Dutch pamphlets that purported to consist of faithfully reported conversations. The authors of the *Diskursn,* therefore, also created a Yiddish written style that was intended to convey the illusion of natural speech shortly after Euchel, but probably without knowing his play. The aim of these texts was to reach Jewish householders in a language they recognized and identified with. Although multilingualism also plays a part occasionally, the illusion of reality was of prime importance here, not the contrast with other languages. Here too, depending on the character speaking, the number of elements that do not stem from the Germanic component (words, turns of phrase, syntax and morphology) may be very high, but overall they are less concentrated than in the dialogue of the Yiddish-speaking characters of *Reb Henokh.* This is probably because the function of the imitated Yiddish speech is different from that in *Reb Henokh* and heightened contrast with German was not an important factor.

VIII. The Yiddish dialogue in Reb Henokh: mimesis or parody?

The high number of Semitic component elements in the spoken Yiddish style of *Reb Henokh* could create the impression that the Yiddish resembles the "mock Yiddish" of the German anti-Semitic literature. Max Weinreich was under the impression that the number of *loshn-koydesh*-derived periphrastic verbs in the anti-Semitic literature mimicking Yiddish was much higher in such texts than in "natural" Yiddish and that on occasion some periphrastic verbs may even have been invented.[43] However, Israela Klayman-Cohen has demonstrated, in her study of the Semitic component in Glikl Hamel's memoirs, that a relatively high percentage of Hebrew component words and expressions were not necessarily uncommon, and that most of the Hebraisms in Glikl's memoirs and the Christian books on Yiddish were indeed part of spoken Yiddish.[44]

In *Reb Henokh* the differentiation between the style of speech of the individual Yiddish-speaking characters is not very marked, even if its content is. It consists mainly of specific exclamations such as Henokh's *"Vos tut me damit!"* Euchel's aim was not primarily to draw individuals who all had

---

43. Max Weinreich, *Geschichte der jiddischen Sprachforschung,* ed. of his doctoral dissertation (Marburg, 1923) by Jerold Frakes (Atlanta, 1993), 150–151.

44. Israela Klayman-Cohen, *Die hebräische Komponente im Westjiddischen am Beispiel der Memoiren der Glückel von Hameln* (Hamburg, 1994), p. 27.

their personal oral style. His characters are types representing categories that are characterized by the language or dialect they speak (High German, Low German dialect, broken German of foreigners, Yiddish).[45]

Euchel edited the Yiddish speech of Reb Henokh and the other unenlightened characters in order to highlight the differences between German and Yiddish by using those characteristics of Yiddish that set it off from German without sacrificing the "authentic" quality of the Yiddish. He did this through the use of vocabulary and idioms as well as morphosyntactical structures that were part of the vernacular, and selecting the "exotic" elements with enough caution so as not to disturb the illusion of natural speech. The Yiddish of *Reb Henokh* necessarily had to reject German as a stylistic model and to model the Yiddish dialogue on the spoken language. Euchel could employ such a lively Yiddish because it was put into the mouths of characters that did not represent his own views and with whom he did not identify,[46] and therefore he was free to enjoy crafting the language according to its own rules. He may even have perceived Yiddish as inherently ugly, but since this would have fit the function of the Yiddish dialogue in his play, he did not have to change the language, only to show it at its best (dis)advantage. Although Euchel did not consider Yiddish a literary language, this did not keep him from being an accomplished Yiddish stylist who carefully crafted the language that the unenlightened characters in *Reb Henokh* speak.

---

45. Sometimes the unassimilated Jewish characters try to speak High German, and theirs too is a broken German, e.g., the duplicitous barber in I,9, Henokh in II,17. This, like the language of foreigners, indicates that merchants like Henokh could not pass as assimilated even if they tried and, therefore, cannot take a position in society commensurate to their wealth—the stage directions describing the furniture, clothing, and drinks (coffee!) indicate that Henokh is a wealthy merchant.

   When the barber, however, turns out to be capable of speaking whichever form of language may please his audience (in II,11 he speaks perfect German and then "lapses" into the local dialect to make a favorable impression on the watchman), this mainly serves to illustrate that he cannot be trusted.

46. There are some similarities to the considerations with which Sholem-Yankev Abramovitsh struggled, but, unlike Abramovitsh, Euchel used Yiddish only as part of one literary work and was mainly a German and Hebrew writer. On Abramovitsh using the "mask" of Mendele Moykher-Sforim and the search for aesthetic support, see Dan Miron, *A Traveler Disguised*, 16–17, 47, 75–76, 80, 92–94, 130–248, 264–268.

The Smoke of Civilization:
The Dialectic of Enlightenment in
Sh. Y. Abramovitsh's *Di Klyatshe*

MARC CAPLAN

There is an episode of *The Simpsons* in which, confronting the liquidation of the local library due to budget cuts and the public indifference to literacy, Marge narrates historical anecdotes to her children, accompanied by characters from the animated series parodically portraying the stories she tells. Among the incidents dramatized in this broadcast is an account of Henry VIII and the establishment of the Church of England. When Henry, depicted by Homer, decides to divorce his first wife (Marge), Sir Thomas Moore—Ned Flanders—implores the king not to disregard papal authority. Henry/Homer congratulates Sir Thomas/Ned for his wise words and assures him, "because you stuck to your principles, I'm going to canonize you." The next frame shows Flanders being fired out of a cannon.[1] This program, insightful for its commentary on the fate of history in a post-literate era and virtuosic in its use of multiple discourses and cultural codes, offers an enduring metaphor on the ambivalent nature of literary canons: canons, as the demise of Sir Thomas/Flanders demonstrates, can simultaneously sanctify and destroy.

A less compact sense of the canon's Janus-faced status emerges from a comparison of two works that, regardless of the disparities of their cultural affiliations and institutional classifications, reveal a common preoccupation with the political and social values encoded within literary traditions, and as such prefigure current questions about literary canons, particularly with respect to the position of Jews within Western culture: Sh. Y. Abramovitsh's

This article was conceived and researched under the auspices of a 2005–2006 Harry Starr Fellowship at the Center for Jewish Studies at Harvard University; the Center, its staff, and my colleagues there have my sincere gratitude for their generous support of my work. Among the individuals who offered their insights and encouragement for this article, I wish to thank Professor Mark M. Anderson of Columbia University, Professor Nico Israel of Hunter College, and, as ever, Dr. Beatrice Lang Caplan of Johns Hopkins. Particular and profound thanks are due to Professor Sara Nadal-Melsió of the University of Pennsylvania for her thoughtful and insightful reading of this article in draft form.

1. For further information on this episode, see "Margical History Tour" (episode #FABF06 / SI-1506, written by Brian Kelley and directed by Mike B. Anderson) at http://en.wikipedia.org/wiki/Margical_History_Tour, which originally aired in the United States on the Fox Television Network, February 8, 2004.

1873 novel *Di Klyatshe*[2] and the collection of philosophical fragments assembled in 1947 by Max Horkheimer and Theodor W. Adorno as *Dialektik der Aufklärung*.[3] A comparison of these works indicates the common pressures placed on Jews by modernity, as well as the role played by literature in mediating between Jews and the dominant culture. There are, nonetheless, obvious challenges to be addressed at the outset of this discussion, paramount among them the question of cultural *location*. Whereas Abramovitsh writes in a minor language on the periphery of Europe at the outset of East European Jewry's engagement with modernity, Horkheimer and Adorno are established intellectuals at work in Los Angeles, the center of the modern mass culture, writing in German, one of the essential languages of European modernity. Nonetheless, precisely because of his peripherality, Abramovitsh articulates a critique of modernity that Horkheimer and Adorno only formulate from a position of *exile*, more than a half-century later. The following analysis, which will consider the role of myth, phantasmagoria, and the uncanny in subverting enlightenment assumptions, will thus use *Di Klyatshe* and the *Dialektik* to expand the chronological and formal parameters, as well as to identify the preoccupations, of a specifically Jewish modernism.[4]

---

2. Mendele Moykher-Sforim, *Di Klyatshe*, in *Geklibene verk*, *Band* 2 ("The Mare," in "Selected Works, Volume 2," New York: YKUF, 1946). Translated as *The Mare* in *The Great Works of Jewish Fantasy and Occult*, compiled, translated, and introduced by Joachim Neugroschel (Woodstock, N.Y.: The Overlook Press, 1976; 1986), 545–663. References to this work incorporated in text as "Y" and "E," respectively, though translations will be my own.

3. Max Horkheimer and Theodor W. Adorno, *Dialektik der Aufklärung: Philosophische Fragmente* (Frankfurt am Main: Fischer Taschenbuch Verlag, 1988; 2003). Translated as *Dialectic of Enlightenment: Philosophical Fragments*. Translated by Edmund Jephcott; edited by Gunzelin Schmid Noerr (Stanford, Calif.: Stanford University Press, 2002). References to this work incorporated in text as "G" and "E," respectively.

4. Two hermeneutical questions emerge from the outset of this comparison: Would Horkheimer and Adorno wish to be considered as Jewish writers, and can they even be considered Jews? Certainly their research at the time of the *Dialektik* was funded and supported in part by Jewish organizations, particularly the American Jewish Committee. Although the support of Jewish institutions is not sufficient to demonstrate that the authors are embarking on their critique of modernity from a specifically Jewish perspective, the purpose of this comparison is to suggest in what ways their work can be *read* as a Jewish critique, even in those instances when they might most have wished to be seen as "universal" or objective. But first, to confront the question of their Jewish identity in precisely the tribal terms they would have found most objectionable, Horkheimer's Jewish origins are unambiguous. Adorno's father was apparently an apostate Jew and his mother was Catholic; Adorno came of age intellectually without a specific religious identity but in a predominately Jewish milieu. And it was not as a half-Catholic that he was forced to leave Nazi Germany, a fact that determined, by his own acknowledgment, the subsequent trajectory of his writing. For a sensitive

Before embarking on this comparison, it is perhaps helpful to summarize the contents of the two books under consideration. A novel in 24 chapters,[5] *Di Klyatshe* describes the misadventures of Yisrolik, a would-be university student who has been driven to madness by the stress of preparing for his entrance exams. While returning home after a particularly difficult study session, Yisrolik encounters a mare being abused by a band of juvenile delinquents. After Yisrolik rescues her, the mare reveals to him that she is not really a horse after all, but a Jewish prince that has been transmogrified by an evil spell. Promising to help protect the defenseless animal, Yisrolik contacts the local *tsar baley-khayim*, a Jewish equivalent of the S.P.C.A. The *tsar baley-khayim*, here intended to represent the St. Petersburg-based "Society for the Advancement of Enlightenment Among the Jews,"[6] responds that before they can intervene on the mare's behalf, she must learn to conform better to society's expectations for horses. When the mare balks at this prescription, Yisrolik responds that the devil must have gotten into her. In the instant, the demon Ashmedai takes over the narrative and leads Yisrolik on a balloon journey over all of Europe, explaining to him that all the technological, political, and cultural apparatuses of the modern world are, in fact, the devil's tools. As the devil's workshop expands to engulf the entire world, Yisrolik wakes from his nightmare to find his still-traditional mother, together with a hasidic *baal-shem* and a Ukrainian faith-healer, keeping watch over him, lamenting his pitiful condition.

---

discussion of Adorno's complicated relationship to Judaism, see Martin Jay's *Adorno*. (Cambridge, Mass.: Harvard University Press, 1984), 19–23. For an insistent argument against essentializing Adorno's identity as either Jewish or otherwise, see Evelyn Wilcock, "Negative Identity: Mixed German Jewish Descent as a Factor in the Reception of Theodor Adorno," *New German Critique*, 81 (Autumn 2000): 169–187. In response to Wilcock's assertions, one should not only consider her comment that "Max Horkheimer embraced orthodox Judaism towards the end of his life and he claimed in an interview in January 1970...that the virtues of the Frankfurt School were characteristically Jewish..." (Wilcock, 172–173), but also acknowledge that incorporating Adorno into a modern Jewish canon—a *fait accompli* that prompts Wilcock's essay—rather than essentializing Adorno, perhaps provides a conceptually productive and historically rigorous means of *de-essentializing* Jewishness.

5. The original, 1873 edition of *Di Klyatshe* was published in 16 chapters, but like most of Abramovitsh's major works, it was reworked and expanded over the remainder of his career. The version under consideration here is based on the "Jubilee edition" of the author's writings, published from 1911 to 1913; the expanded edition of the novel was first serialized in the Warsaw Yiddish newspaper *Der Yid* in 1902. See Dan Miron, *A Traveler Disguised: The Rise of Modern Yiddish Literature in the Nineteenth Century* (Syracuse, N.Y.: Syracuse University Press, 1973; 1996), 316–317.

6. For an analysis of the social milieu out of which this organization emerged, see Benjamin Nathans's definitive *Beyond the Pale: The Jewish Encounter with Late Imperial Russia* (Berkeley: University of California Press, 2004).

In formal terms, *Di Klyatshe* is noteworthy for its literary structure, which though based on the protagonist's first-person narration nonetheless divides into three equal parts dominated in succession by Yisrolik's perspective (chapters 1–8), the mare's (chapters 9–16), and Ashmedai's (chapters 17–24); in metaphorical, associative terms the juxtaposition of these perspectives suggests, through the trope of madness, that Yisrolik's pursuit of enlightenment, which blinds him to the sufferings of the mare and to his own oppression within the Czarist system, is, in fact, a mistaken attraction for a culture of destruction masquerading as progress and civilization. This sequence of associations unfolds in different terms but to similar effect in the *Dialektik*; Horkheimer and Adorno thus replace the philosophical principles of logical causality with a series of metonymies more familiar to works of prose fiction than the methodologies of German Idealism, which they at once lay claim to and critique. The continuous juxtaposition of civilization with brutality is the thematic point of correspondence between these two works. In both, the underlying organizational principle is analogical, rather than logical: where *Di Klyatshe* uses a succession of voices to develop its subversive critique of modernity, the *Dialektik* consists of an unhomogenized collection of five complete essays discussing in turn the concept of enlightenment, Homer's *Odyssey*, the Marquis de Sade's novel *Juliette*, contemporary popular culture, and anti-Semitism, followed by a concluding but deliberately inconclusive selection of "notes and sketches."

For both works, the associative structure of ideas and opinions is intended to resist the totalization of rational thinking; as critiques of rationalism, they each seek through separate discourses an alternative to sequential logic. For this reason Horkheimer and Adorno, having established the philosophical principles for their study in the introductory essay, devote nearly a third of their collaboration to works of belletristic literature; their choices call attention to the role of canon-formation in the enlightenment's self-definition by juxtaposing the most venerable poem of classical civilization with a notorious yet seldom-read narrative at the outermost fringe of modern literature, a novel that at the time of their analysis was still illegal in many jurisdictions.[7] Both the *Odyssey* and *Juliette* illustrate crucial, and ultimately common, correspondences between moral selfishness and the enlightenment's definition of self, yet Homer's epic is taken by the aesthetic standards of the enlightenment to be the foundation of Western literature, whereas Sade's novel, as a work of pornography—a word Horkheimer and Adorno never use when discussing it[8]—is routinely dismissed as the antithe-

---

7. For this reason they base their citations from *Juliette* on a 1797 edition of the novel published in Holland. Reliable Anglophone translations of Sade first appeared in the late 1950s, in Paris.

8. Adorno, however, does describe Sade's writing as pornography in a nearly contemporaneous reference: "How intimately sex and language are intertwined can be seen

sis of culture. The pairing of Homer and Sade provides the only instances in the book of textual readings on culture as such. From these crucial literary "excurses," they then turn their attention to mass culture and the Holocaust, a trajectory intended to suggest, via the discourse of German idealism, that the ability to objectify human subjectivity through commodification is the mechanism that links rationality to mass murder; significantly, they do not exempt the practices of idealist thought itself from this process, hence their efforts to construct an analogical argument as a means of standing outside, however tenuously, of the system they critique.

The seeming contradiction in the term "modern canon"—the modifier placing into a historical continuum a noun that purports to signify the timeless and unchanging—is itself a manifestation of enlightenment thought, articulating a liberal desire to replace the *law* of religion with the *consensus* of culture, to substitute art for belief, and to rationalize faith as a *species* of culture. Although the concept of a literary canon dates apparently only as far back as the last quarter century—Robert Alter notes that as late as 1955 the *Oxford English Dictionary* registers no references to secular literature in its definition of "canon"[9]—the task of identifying the central works of an essentially pan-European tradition, encompassing the Bible at its easternmost and oldest extreme and a select few American writers at its most westerly and modern, was a preoccupation of literary criticism throughout the twentieth century. But the process by which literature becomes established institutionally serves as an extension of the dominant political system, as Abramovitsh states explicitly in *Di Klyatshe*. There the protagonist, Yisrolik, experiences his exclusion from the intellectual life of the Czarist empire as both a linguistic and cultural consequence of his inability to master Russian literature and culture. As Yisrolik explains:

> It was most difficult for me to approach history, what they call in their language *slovesnost* [literature]. From memory I had to learn ridiculous stories about wars, how people have from since the world began down to

---

by reading pornography in a foreign language. When de Sade is read in the original no dictionary is needed." See Theodor Adorno, *Minima Moralia: Reflections on a Damaged Life*, translated by E.F.N. Jephcott (London: Verso, 1951; 2005), 48. In general, the inclusion of Sade's work in Horkheimer and Adorno's critique of enlightenment is intended as an *anti-canonical* gesture, using the petty, largely fantasized obscenities of Sade's writing to indict the greater, real-life obscenities of Western civilization in their era.

9. Robert Alter, *Canon and Creativity: Modern Writing and the Authority of Scripture* (New Haven: Yale University Press, 2000), 21. To the extent that one believes in the concept of Zeitgeist, it may be noted that this book was published in the same year as Ruth Wisse's *The Modern Jewish Canon*, however different the actual content of these two books in fact is.

the present day killed one another, brutalized, battered, and beat each others' brains out, all recited with precisely the right date, and precisely the right place!... On top of that I had to learn all kinds of wild fables, stories about horrible strongmen, notorious drunkards, world-renowned bandits, stories about transmigrations, with witches and warlocks, stories about living and dead waters, golden apples and golden horses. (Y 20–21; E 550)

This passage exposes the problem of culture implicit in Horkheimer and Adorno's critique: the history of a civilization is a chronicle of brutality; its literature is a rationalization of the irrational. Yisrolik formulates his rejection of culture in rationalistic terms, yet it is precisely the cultural productions he rejects that provide the key to enter the intellectual world.

At the same time, these remarks indicate Yisrolik's frustration at having to master a cultural canon that comprises a literature and history that systematically exclude him. Although the Russian national culture defines itself via literature and history, as well as religion, in explicitly non-Jewish terms, there is no countervailing modern Jewish "nationhood" from which Yisrolik may position himself; as a *maskil*—a proponent of *haskole*, the "Jewish enlightenment"—determined to abandon Jewish isolation and irrationality, he must nonetheless pursue a dominant culture that is no less irrational than the tradition he rejects, yet that offers him at best only the hope of a superficial and passive inclusion within its precincts. In historical terms, this passage underscores the fact that significant numbers of young Jews had already begun, as early as a generation prior to the publication of this novel, the difficult process of engaging with Russian culture and the demands of the Russian higher education system.[10] The root of the problem for Jewish intellectuals in the latter half of the nineteenth century, as Abramovitsh suggests, is the futility of their efforts to participate equally in a contemporary Russian society for which any concept of equality could be only a fantasy, or in the discourse of the novel itself, a phantasm. No sooner had they abandoned the medieval parochialism of the shtetl than they encountered the chauvinism of nineteenth-century modernity.

This paradox finds explicit articulation in Yisrolik's description of his unsuccessful efforts to prepare for the university matriculation exam; as he continues, "I had to be able to chatter away, just like a parrot, over whosoever's high-flown expressions and fancy phrases, making sure thereby to

---

10. As Michael Stanislawski writes, "The fact that the latter [*maskilim*] read more Russian books and adopted more Russian attitudes was a consequence of the substantial transformation of the Russian intelligentsia itself...on the one hand, the turning inward to Russian sources and the Russian nation; on the other, the dissemination of the intelligentsia's new views from the rarefied preserve of the capitals' salons to broad segments of society in the provinces." See Michael Stanislawski, *Tsar Nicolas I and the Jews: The Transformation of Jewish Society in Russia 1825–1855* (Philadelphia: Jewish Publication Society of America, 1983), 118.

include nuances, allusions, and such hidden meanings that neither I, nor the author himself, nor he who had taught me, could understand" (Y 21; E 550). Part of Yisrolik's complaint derives from, or at least is indicative of, his refusal to *parrot* the dominant culture. In order to avoid the risk of mere imitation, the condition of being reduced to a recipient or *consumer* of the dominant culture, the minority subject must be able to forge some sort of synthesis between his or her native culture and the discourse of hegemonic power. The inability to create such a synthesis is the central challenge confronted not only in Abramovitsh's dialectic of enlightenment—which anticipates Horkheimer and Adorno's modernist sense of the dialectic as a conflict between thesis and antithesis *incapable* of achieving synthesis—but in modern Jewish writing generally.

As *Di Klyatshe* continues to develop, Abramovitsh makes the connection between culture and power still more explicit. In this regard, one of the most significant incidents occurs when Yisrolik finally takes his matriculation exam. Abramovitsh writes:

> The teachers were...clothed in uniforms with brass buttons, looking at me with such severity, such malice, as if I were either a thief or a murderer.... What is the sense in having teachers, whose very profession obligates them to make from us, their students, rational and compassionate human beings...wear uniforms with brass buttons?... Can you imagine Socrates, Plato, or Aristotle wearing such buttons, or such sour expressions...? Such was the respect they showed me, such was the expression that the chief examiner wore when he turned to me with a quotation from here, another from there, until he finally arrived at the story of the Baba Yaha herself! I was left confused, mixed-up, up a creek without a paddle! (Y 56; E 581)

One can gauge the ideological distance Abramovitsh has traveled over the preceding decade by contrasting this scene to Itsik-Avreyml's interrogation in the *kheyder* in the first edition *Dos Kleyne mentshele* (1864).[11] Whereas in the earlier narrative Itsik-Avreyml was questioned on a verse from the Torah by a benign agent of the modern world—a *maskil*—in order to expose the deficiencies of traditional Jewish education, thereby advertising the ostensible compatibility between the objectives of the *maskilim* and "pure, authentic" Jewish piety, here Yisrolik must answer questions on Russian folklore by a uniformed officer of the imperial state, a militarized pedagogue who resembles an inquisitor. Just as *Dos Kleyne mentshele* had shown the *maskil* as the true champion of the Torah over the benighted teacher in the

---

11. *Dos Kleyne mentshele* was first published in installments by the Yiddish weekly newspaper *Kol mevaser* in 1864; an invaluable scholarly edition was prepared by the Literature Department of the University of Haifa (Israel) in 1994, edited by Shalom Luria. For an English translation of the 1864 edition, see Joachim Neugroschel's *No Star Too Beautiful: an Anthology of Yiddish Stories from 1382 to the Present.* (New York: W.W. Norton & Company, 2002), 190–218.

kheyder, so Yisrolik here identifies himself with the original authorities of non-Jewish wisdom, the philosophers of ancient Greece, in his complaint against the debasement of secular knowledge. The stakes for the adult Yisrolik in the fully modern world of the university are nonetheless much higher than for the child Itsik-Avreyml in *kheyder*. Abramovitsh in this scene turns an educational interview into a confrontation with ultimate, dehumanizing power.[12]

Into this unequal showdown between the putative *maskil* and the imperial state enters the mare herself. The horse motif first appears when Yisrolik considers the status of a herd at pasture after a particularly intense study session: Abramovitsh habitually juxtaposes his protagonist's intellectual pursuits with two antitheses, madness and the behavior of animals. Yisrolik thus states:

> One of them had a grandfather who was an English stallion that had in bygone days, while traveling through the land of Canaan, married an Arabian filly. Another's grandmother came from a famous family that had in its time smelled its share of gunpowder, while yet another's great-grandmother had received a good education somewhere on a renowned stud farm and was so learned that she gave dance recitals...together with other such worthy, well-trained horses. From all this you can plainly see that among horses lineage plays a significant role, and among themselves they look closely at aristocratic blood, and those with the right pedigree are known as nobility or thoroughbreds.[13] (Y 24; E 553)

In the context of the novel as a whole, the association between Yisrolik's impending humiliation at the hands of a rigidly codified, hereditary class system and the fixation on horses' lineage suggests that class and pedigree as such are as "crazy" as Yisrolik is, or at least, that they can only be properly understood through the eyes of a madman.[14] More generally, the anthropo-

---

12. However much Abramovitsh exploits the symbolic association of knowledge and power in this scene, the educational system, like all aspects of the Russian bureaucracy, *was* intimately connected with, and organized along the lines of, the military hierarchy—particularly during the thirty-year reign of Nicolas I.

13. In another setting, this passage could serve as the basis for a comparison with the fourth part of Jonathan Swift's satire *Gulliver's Travels*, "A Voyage to the Country of the Houyhnhnms." This narrative, which famously describes a society of civilized horses governing a tribe of savage human Yahoos, initiates the modern critique of rationality, the burgeoning class system, and colonialism, while at the same time serving as one of the foundational works of enlightenment literature. Without a doubt, the Enlightenment satires of eighteenth-century England and France exerted a significant influence on *haskole* narrative in general and on Abramovitsh's writing in particular; one can safely assume that Swift's work was familiar to him in either German or Russian translation.

14. It should be noted that the talking, or more precisely *writing*, dogs in Nikolai Gogol's great short story "Diary of a Madman" (1834) similarly function as a parallel and parody

morphization of animals, in both folklore and modern satire, inversely suggests the ultimate bestiality of people and thus the dialogue of the purebred
horses reveals the brutishness of class relations, as well as the need for a
social order founded on something other than physical force or lineage.

In the face of these polemical implications, Abramovitsh's mare stands as
a figure for the contradictions that the enlightenment had attempted to
smooth over with the veneer of reason: simultaneously male and female; an
animal, yet rational. This status places the mare in the domain of what Sigmund Freud identifies as "the uncanny," although Freud's essay on the subject curiously overlooks a consideration of the phantasmagoric in its definition of the concept. Freud nonetheless writes, "Everything which now
strikes us as 'uncanny' fulfils the condition of touching those residues of animistic mental activity within us and bringing them to expression."[15] The
"uncanny" occupies an explicitly liminal condition, one that is a function of
the linguistic associations between the *unheimlich* and the *heimlich*: a
mare is *heimlich*, a talking mare is *unheimlich*, but either can be uncanny
insofar as it serves as a *double* for the protagonist in a phantasmagoric tale
and identify his condition *between* life and death, animate and inanimate,
real and imagined, internal and external, good and evil.[16] To the extent that
the instability of the line separating human and animal in *Di Klyatshe* parallels or recapitulates the uncanny—and Freud's literary discussion of this
theme, focused primarily on the works of E. T. A. Hoffmann, underscores
how integral this motif is to the fantastic tradition of German romanticism,
which influenced both Abramovitsh and the Frankfurt Marxists—the novel
calls attention to what Freud diagnoses as the *residue* of animism lingering

---

of the rigid, dehumanizing class system that drives the narrator of that story insane.
Gogol's influence on the development of nineteenth-century Yiddish literature was
enormous and fully acknowledged by Abramovitsh's disciple Sholem Aleichem.

15. Sigmund Freud, "The 'Uncanny'," *Writings on Art and Literature*, trans. Alix Strachey
(Stanford, Calif.: Stanford University Press, 1997), 217.

16. Not so, according to Tzvetan Todorov's definition of fantastic literature, in which the
uncanny—which Todorov, by his own admission, defines differently from Freud—
stands *in opposition* to the phantasmagoric, or as he terms it, "the marvelous" (i.e.,
the purely imaginary and supernatural). For Todorov, the uncanny is "uniquely linked
to the sentiments of the characters and not to a material event defying reason. (The
marvelous, by way of contrast, may be characterized by the mere presence of supernatural events, without implicating the reaction they provoke in the characters.)" See
his *The Fantastic: A Structural Approach to a Literary Genre*, trans. Richard Howard
(Ithaca, N.Y.: Cornell University Press, 1970; 1975), 47. One can argue, by way of
response, that discrete taxonomies such as Todorov's, however illuminating they may
be to a precise *definition* of literary concepts, fail to account for the ultimate *continuity* between the uncanny and the phantasmagoric insofar as both literary modes
maintain a genetic relationship to the *pre-differential* mode of animistic, *mythical*
thinking.

beneath the surface of rational, categorical thought, and therefore the phan-tasmagoric narrative represents, in Freudian terms, the *return of the re-pressed* mythical component unarticulated but ever present in modern, rational consciousness.

Of course, the repression that the mare resists by embodying the liminal is as much political as it is psychological, as real as it is fantasized or project-ed out of Yisrolik's psyche: the mare is a victim of the class system, but because of her marginalization, she is also the most objective critic of it; this in turn is a richly suggestive metaphor for the role of Jews in modern Europe. Like the sphinx invoked at the start of the *Dialektik*, the mare typ-ifies the domain of the supernatural, "spirits and demons...taken to be reflections of human beings who allow themselves to be frightened by nat-ural phenomena" (G 12–13; E 4). As Horkheimer and Adorno contend, with implications for their interpretation of the *Odyssey*, such apparitions are the province of myth—the domain of collective, oral, pre-rational narratives that the epic, as an expression of a rational, calculating, and ultimately written culture, has struggled against in order to chronicle man's mastery over nature. This battle, which though seemingly primeval or pre-historical has nonetheless determined the course of enlightenment and modernity in terms as relevant to Abramovitsh as to Horkheimer and Adorno, is at last a conflict between two modes of narrativity, expressed in *textual* terms. If Abramovitsh's mare signifies the return of a repressed mythical mode of thought, then Yisrolik represents in complementary terms the *mock-epic* failure of an anti-Odysseus to control his destiny, or even maintain his rea-sonableness in the face of irrational historical circumstances.[17] Horkheimer and Adorno's reading of Homer, therefore, offers perhaps unexpected insights into *Di Klyatshe*'s satirical strategies, just as Abramovitsh's novel anticipates the *Dialektik*'s critique of modernity.

Horkheimer and Adorno thus consider Homer's *Odyssey* to be a repudi-ation of myth, constructed out of the remains of myth, insofar as the epic substitutes the singularity of the hero's destiny for the multiplicity and simultaneity of mythic thought and representation. The dialectical process by which epic articulates the conquest of mythical space is not one of syn-thesis or transcendence, but rather dislocation. As they write:

> The hero's peregrinations from Troy to Ithaca trace the path of the self through myths, a self infinitely weak in comparison to the force of nature....
> The primeval world is secularized as the space he measures out; the old demons populate only the distant margins and islands of the civilized Medi-terranean. (G 53; E 38)

---

17. As Bertolt Brecht memorably formulates this predicament in "The Jewish Wife," more than sixty years after Abramovitsh, "Yes, I know I'm being unreasonable, but what good is reason in a world like this?" See his *Fear and Misery of the Third Reich & Senora Carrar's Rifles: The Collected Plays; Volume Four, Part Three*, ed. John Willett and Ralph Mannheim (London: Methuen London Ltd., 1983), 51.

Anson Rabinbach suggests that their identification of the epic form with its hero's wandering exile reflects the authors' historical condition as refugees from Nazi Germany: "In a work of exile that makes Homer's ancient exile its 'hero,' the narrative of Odysseus provides a kind of allegory of the theory [through which subjectivity is constituted through 'homesickness'] elaborated in the first chapter [of the *Dialektik*]."[18] The specific problem of Jewish exile, which motivates a consideration of the Holocaust as an ultimate act of *displacement* in the history of enlightenment, is itself *displaced* onto Horkheimer and Adorno's ostensibly allegorical reading of the *Odyssey*. In Abramovitsh's novel, by contrast, though the crisis of Jewish exile had not yet reached the devastation of the Holocaust, another sort of displacement— internalized rather than projected—occurs simultaneously in the *body* of the mare and the *mind* of Yisrolik. This double, "uncanny" dislocation likewise illustrates in phantasmagoric terms a dialectal process of *subjectification*, the radical disjuncture of the self.

Through the process of *dis*location, epic anticipates a notion of *national* space dividing the world between civilized Greek rationality and the rest of humanity still enthralled by myth, a separation that itself forms another recurring tension within European modernity. Horkheimer and Adorno write:

> At the turning points of Western civilization, whenever new peoples and classes have more heavily repressed myth, from the beginnings of the Olympian religion to the Renaissance, the Reformation, and bourgeois atheism, the fear of unsubdued, threatening nature—a fear resulting from nature's very materialization and objectification—has been belittled as animist superstition and the control of internal and external nature has been made the absolute purpose of life. (G 38; E 24)

Implicit in the epic dialectic of man against nature—though explicit in a later work such as Euripedes' *Medea*—is the conflict between Greek and Barbarian: from the "mastery" of nature, Greek civilization moves inevitably to the domination of other groups of people, a process duplicated in every other imperial culture. The spatial metaphor for this process of mastery is the home itself. Home in this dialectic embodies civilization against nature, the human against both the animal and the supernatural, repose against labor. The epic dynamic initiated in the *Iliad* by a rupture in the domestic order of the Achaeans (Menelaus and his brother Agamemnon) returns to a reconfigured harmony in the *Odyssey* with the re-establishment of domestic order at Ithaca, with every incident intervening serving as a correlative to this domestic crisis.

---

18. Anson Rabinbach, *In the Shadow of Catastrophe: German Intellectuals Between Apocalypse and Enlightenment* (Berkeley: University of California Press, 2001), 171.

These dialectics also surface in *Di Klyatshe*, which begins, of course, with Yisrolik's *resistance* to the domestic order of the traditional Jewish family, and leads inexorably to his intermingling with the fantastic, the animal, the irrational, which supposedly had been subordinated by the epic, "enlightened" mentality. As the novel begins, Yisrolik states:

> Just as Noah long ago in the ark was at the time of the Flood the sole survivor among all the drowned creatures of the world, so I, Yisroyl the son of Tsipe, am the last remnant in my shtetl, the solitary bachelor among all my friends, who through the pestilence of the matchmakers have all become young householders before their time, and thus have sunk up to their necks in pitiable poverty and paupery. (Y 19; E 549)

This long, expertly structured—at least in the original—sentence reaches back to the Bible, the Jewish counterpart to Homer in the Western canon, in order to evoke the contemporary poverty of the traditional Jewish family. The reference to Noah thus calls attention to an ultimately *mythical* image of the shtetl, while at the same time suggesting the proximity of the protagonist with animals. Yisrolik's comparison of his condition with Noah suggests, in turn, that the traditional life of the shtetl to which he opposes his own modern ambitions is analogous to the corrupt condition of the world that preceded the Flood. More fundamentally, Abramovitsh presents Yisrolik's "madness" as a consequence of his isolation from humanity, his inability to enter the adult world by forming a genuine, conjugal relationship. Nonetheless, by underscoring the hardship and poverty incurred by marrying "before their time," the author presents his protagonist essentially trapped between historical conditions of competing misery.

The enlightenment and rationalism, therefore, offer Yisrolik no way out of his phantasmagoric madness and are revealed instead to be the most primitive form of mystification in the devil's arsenal. By contrast, the mare successfully extricates herself both from the tyranny of the "reactionary" masses and the restrictions that the "progressive" intellectuals such as Yisrolik would place on her; why, then, is Yisrolik left, at the novel's climax, still in the devil's clutches?[19] At this point, the maskilic dichotomy of tradition and the folk, opposed to modernity and the intellectual, collapses. And when this dialectic fails, everything falls with it, including the individual intellectual's sense of self and his or her place in the world. As Abramovitsh demonstrates, fantasy is the most durable and suggestive narrative strategy to address the failure of modern rationality. And since fantasy has already

---

19. Of course, the mare does return to the novel at the climax of Yisrolik's encounter with the devil (Y 147–148; E 659–660), but even here she stands primarily as a figure of *resistance*, challenging the devil who would again make of her a beast of burden, and encouraging Yisrolik similarly to resist the devil's efforts to make of him another parasitic agent of the organized community. The mare in her essence resists all authority, whether reactionary, progressive, or demonic.

been identified by *haskole* as a province of the tradition,[20] the reclaiming of fantasy for the modernizing writer entails trespassing the boundary between tradition and modernity in two directions simultaneously. In this newly created no-man's-land, where mares and demons rush in, and angels and human beings fear to tread, a newly elastic concept of the individual and his relationship to the world outside his own consciousness emerges.

However flexible the categories of internal and external, imaginary and real, may have become for Yisrolik, he nonetheless remains *bound* to the shtetl and the conventional relationships he maintained there. In the absence of a marital relationship like those of his peers, Yisrolik's most meaningful relationship, significantly enough, is with his mother. This fact in itself suggests both the fundamentally unproductive, stunted nature of his personality and of his aspirations, as well as the inability of the Russian *maskilim* to emerge fully into the modern world. As Yisrolik explains to his mother:

> I'm despised in the eyes of my own people, the Jews, and in the eyes of the others, the gentiles. When one hates me for not being the right kind of Jew, the other hates me for being a Jew like every other Jew. I'm alive and I want to live; I long to escape this confinement to live with people, equal in God's great world, to do whatever is possible, so that Jewishness shouldn't be a liability in my efforts at self-improvement. (Y 52; E 577)

The fact that Yisrolik's mother—a traditional Jewish woman incapable of understanding and unwilling to sympathize with his aspirations—is the only human to whom he can confide his frustrations indicates the reflexivity of his aspirations. His efforts to escape the confines of the shtetl thus demonstrate how much he remains trapped there; his efforts to join with a larger

---

20. In a magisterial, but uncollected, essay, Ruth Wisse captures the paradox of Abramovitsh's return to folklore when she writes, "Isrolik learns folklore, just as his Russian examiners had intended, but from the Jewish rather than the Russian folk imagination." Abramovitsh thus signifies his awareness of Russian populism by rejecting the assimilation of Russian values among Jews in favor of a reinvigoration of Jewish folk motifs—mythology in reconfigured, demotic form—in his own writing. See Ruth R. Wisse, "The Jewish Intellectual and the Jews: The Case of *Di Klyatshe* (The Mare) by Mendele Mocher Sforim," The Daniel E. Koshland Memorial Lecture of the Congregation Emanu-El, San Francisco, March 24, 1992: 12. This essay, which brilliantly traces Abramovitsh's intellectual trajectory away from *haskole* in light of the political relationship of Russian Jews to the czar during the 1860s and 1870s, is to date the best available discussion of *Di Klyatshe*; the present analysis differs from Wisse's essay, however, by considering the implications of Abramovitsh's narrative for a philosophical critique of European modernity, in contrast to Wisse's ideological reading of the novel as a proto-nationalist protest against the Russian empire. In terms either fully in keeping with the premise of a modern Jewish canon, or else diametrically opposed to its secularizing logic, *eyle v'eyle divrey eloykim khayim, v'halokhe kibeys hilel* (B. Eruvin 13b)!

humanity as part of "God's great world" likewise serve only to underscore his essential and immutable isolation.

Just as the scene in which the Russian educational bureaucrats interrogate Yisrolik evokes and inverts the *kheyder* scene in *Dos Kleyne mentshele* to underscore the inequality mandated by the Russian educational system, so too does the novel as a whole ridicule both the possibility of escaping the shtetl and the desirability of such an escape. Modernity in these terms no longer signifies a utopian promise of individual liberation, but is instead another institution that traps the protagonist and frustrates his efforts at self-determination. Although this theme receives its full development only after the devil makes his appearance in the novel, Yisrolik foreshadows this idea when he states, "Perhaps I'm in the hand of another power, which dwells in me, and I'm not the master of my own self, not someone who does everything according to his understanding or will, but this power rules over me and coerces me to do what he wants" (Y 39; E 565). To rebel against the unseen power dwelling within him, Yisrolik can only declare war against himself by abandoning his rationality; insanity, in this context, is a *revolt* against reason—in Yiddish, *seykhl*—and, therefore, also *haskole*.

The object of this rebellion comes into focus when the devil makes his appearance in the novel, taking over from the mare the task of externalizing Yisrolik's fractured consciousness. In the devil's monologue, both the diabolical nature of modernity and its seamless connection with the *kahal*, the institutional Jewish community, becomes explicit. Significantly, the mare introduces the demonic dimension of the narrative by offering a review of ethical philosophies to justify her rejection of the demands of the modern world, as represented by the *tsar baley-khayim*. As she says to Yisrolik:

> Of course, when the world begins to consider itself, that's when people start to speak about *humanism*...about mercy, about compassion; a little later, when the world begins slowly to become more practical, the fashion turns to *utilitarianism*, which means usefulness, the uses to which one can put other people. Only later, when the world receives both reason and fairness, and it better understands the ways of nature and all her creatures, can one begin to speak of *truth*, of *justice*. I don't want to hear any talk about mercy or about usefulness: mercy and usefulness can't sustain the world. I'm the equal of anyone...we're all just flesh and blood, our needs are identical, and everyone has the same right to live. (Y 100–101; E 619–620)

Yisrolik's reaction is to attribute these remarks to the devil (*der riekh*), and in the next chapter, the devil appears, taking over the remainder of the novel.

Horkheimer and Adorno ruefully offer a similar critique of liberal sympathy when they argue in their reading of *Juliette* that pity [*mitleid*] proposes the alleviation of suffering on an individual basis and thereby makes an exception to the general condition of exploitation while concretizing the subordination of the individual sufferer to his or her ostensible benefactor. They thus argue, "Just as the Stoic indifference on which bourgeois coldness, the counterpart of pity, has modeled itself was more loyal, however wretchedly, to the universal it had rejected than the compassionate baseness that adapted itself to the world, so it was those who unmasked pity who, however negatively, espoused the Revolution" (G 110; E 80–81). In this formulation, the repudiation of pity serves as the first step, even if a regressive one, toward a fundamental change in social conditions. The *Dialektik*'s explication of Sade's philosophy—as demonic a body of thought as anything articulated by Abramovitsh's Ashmedai or anyone else's—corresponds to the mare's discourse on utilitarianism as a simultaneous representation and refutation of enlightenment reason. Of course, Sade's rejection of pity as a superfluous emotion issues its critique from the perspective of the powerful, whereas the mare more urgently exposes the *inadequacy* of mere pity from the perspective of the oppressed. Indeed, the mare's attack on *rationalizations of pity* that shift the burden of change from society onto its victims calls into question the relationship between human reason and moral behavior, just as Horkheimer and Adorno disentangle the presumed affinity between a reason premised on *self*-interest and the obligations of the individual to those lower than he, or she, on the chain of being.

Ashmedai further develops the mare's critique by calling attention to the *baley-toyves*, the "professional philanthropists" who administer the shtetl's institutional organizations, the *kahal*:

> The kosher meat-tax is absolutely essential to my work. Because of it a whole troop of *baley-toyves* have emerged to lead all of you by the nose and leave you without a head on your shoulders....Through the meat-tax you have the clearest sign that with all the expenses that go toward communal necessities you are irrevocably separated from all the other nations of the world; and because of that you will never be able to unite with other people in loyalty to the state, and in turn truly you will always give evil men the excuse to attack you, and your situation will always be hopeless and degraded. (Y 138–39; E 652)

This, of course, is the central argument of previous, conventionally maskilic critiques of the shtetl, such as Abramovitsh's own desk-drawer drama *Di Takse* ("The Meat-Tax," 1869), to which *Di Klyatshe* was billed, deceptively, as a sequel. Here, though, the devil delivers the arguments that the *maskilim* had previously marshaled against the meat-tax. Does this, in fact, align the devil with the *kahal*, as he claims, or with *haskole*?

Abramovitsh foregrounds this ambiguity when he connects the devil both to the modern institution of the press as an industry and to the act of writing in general. Thus, Ashmedai describes for Yisrolik a "river of ink":

> I created this river that you see, and the woods it runs through, especially for your brothers. As long as the river provides ink and the trees pens, there will be writers to write without rest. Look! From the inkwells flow canals.... That canal, number 999,999, which you're considering now, flows directly to the inkwells of the journalists in Dneprovits. I have ink and pens to fill the ocean, and as many writers as grains of sand on the shore! (Y 137; E 651)

The explicit object of Abramovitsh's satire here is the anti-Semitic press, then inspiring discrimination and pogroms throughout Europe. As such, this passage bears comparison with Franz Kafka's "The Penal Colony," in the sense that writing itself is portrayed as a form of torture, with Yisrolik, the Jew who will bear the blows inspired by the press, as the victim.

The ambivalence of this passage stands in contrast to the most problematic chapter in the *Dialektik*, on the culture industry. Horkheimer and Adorno's essay offers a critique of "totalization" that nonetheless totalizes the mass culture as a monolith, remaining oblivious not only to the exceptions to this totality within contemporaneous cultural production,[21] but also to the idea of examining works of culture on their own terms and not just as functions of marketplace logic. In contrast to the nuanced readings of Homer and Sade preceding this essay, "The Culture Industry" presents an abstract and homogenous image specifically of American culture, which betrays both the authors' inattentiveness to the contradiction of a Marxian theory of mass culture that expresses elitist contempt for the masses that it would ostensibly serve to liberate, as well as a seeming nostalgia for the work of art *prior to* the era of mechanical reproduction.[22] Abramovitsh's "river of ink," by contrast, performs a mediating function between the author and the ideas he proposes to critique: unlike Horkheimer and Adorno, Abramovitsh implicates himself in his satire of the "culture industry" of his day. After all, Abramovitsh, like Horkheimer and Adorno, uses the same means of production as the journalists who create rivers of ink to justify the rivers of blood flowing already throughout late–nineteenth century Europe, and beyond; like the anti-Semitic journalists of his day, Abramovitsh also creates rivers of ink. Unlike Horkheimer and Adorno, Abramovitsh acknowledges his position within the culture industry by means of the metaphors he chooses to make *literal*. This is not just the luxury of satire over philosophy, but more crucially a function of the fantastic as a literary discourse.

Indeed, an aptly "Satanic" narrative strategy for *Di Klyatshe* positions the pastiche that Abramovitsh creates among competing *rationalizing* modes of discourse—allegory, parody, polemic, etc.—tempting the reader with each of them, but also allowing them to compete with one another disharmoniously, so that none of these discourses characterizes the novel in its entirety. All the rationalizing strategies of the novel are ultimately subsumed under the trope of madness, itself a negation, ostensibly, of the rational.

---

21. In what sense, for example, is be-bop part of the "jazz machine"?

22. Note, for example, "Even when the art business was in the bloom of youth, use value was not dragged along as a mere appendage by exchange value but was developed as a precondition of the latter, to the social benefit of works of art. As long as it was expensive, art kept the citizen within some bounds. That is now over. Art's unbounded proximity to those exposed to it...completes the alienation between work and consumer, which resemble each other in triumphant reification." (G 169–170; E 130)

Where Abramovitsh's narratives of the 1860s, such as *Dos Kleyne mentsh-ele*, dramatize the classic *haskole* trajectory from "Jew" to "man," *Di Klyat-she*, like Kafka's various animal parables, illustrates via the phantasmagoric a post-enlightenment anxiety over the status of the human: the man unmasked in *Di Klyatshe* is caught between beast and devil, with no angel to redeem his potentially monstrous character As such, the elaborate paro-dy of the class structure in the dialogue of the horses indicates not only the specific absurdity of the social relations in the Czarist Empire, but also the implicitly bestial nature barely repressed in every exercise of power. Abram-ovitsh presumably would have hated Friedrich Nietzsche's philosophy, but like Nietzsche he recognizes that at the origins of every governing order lie savagery, conquest, and greed. In schematic terms crucial to the argument of this comparison, Nietzsche is the primary influence on Horkheimer and Adorno's conception of the enlightenment,[23] yet Abramovitsh *anticipates* Horkheimer and Adorno while *surpassing* Nietzsche in his critique of ratio-nality; this positioning of Abramovitsh in advance of Horkheimer and Ador-no is precisely a function of his location, as a Yiddish writer, at the periph-ery of European modernity.

It is, therefore, necessary to emphasize that Ashmedai takes credit not only for the folly of the shtetl, but also for the excesses of modern, industrial life. Indeed, he defines himself as unmistakably modern when he states, "I'm that person who paves the way to a new world, so that the old should continually become new" (Y 103; E 622). One feature of the devil's moder-nity, surely, is his cosmopolitanism. As Yisrolik describes the panorama that Ashmedai unveils for him, "And immediately I recognize before me whole companies of evil spirits, devils, and all sorts of demons and tormentors, among them magicians, jugglers, tricksters, fortune-tellers of all nations together with water-nymphs, witches, gypsy queens, card-readers of all faiths" (Y 113; E 630). The "universality" of this *Walpurgisnacht* not only extends his parody beyond the confines of the Jewish tradition and its dis-contents, but suggests that the "beyond," the cultures outside the Pale, is as demonic, as much in need of ridicule, as the Jewish tradition itself.

In fact, Abramovitsh is just getting warmed up with this inventory of evil spirits and black magicians, an inventory that, in its catholicity, underscores the fact that superstition and fantasy exist in every culture. This insight itself

---

23. As Jürgen Habermas writes, "Point-for-point correspondences with Nietzsche are found in the construction by which Horkheimer and Adorno underpin their 'primal history of subjectivity.'" Habermas nevertheless insists that Horkheimer and Adorno's relationship to Nietzsche is ambivalent—appropriately so, given that they, like Nietzsche, are in like manner ambivalent toward the enlightenment itself; as Habermas states, "How can these two men of the Enlightenment...be so unappreciative of the rational content of cultural modernity...?" See Habermas's *The Philosophical Discourse of Modernity: Twelve Lectures*, trans. Frederick Lawrence (Cambridge, Mass.: The MIT Press, 1985; 1990), 121.

restores to the Jewish tradition an ironic equality with other cultures, including the Western tradition to which the Jewish intellectual was previously expected to elevate himself. As Ashmedai's monologue continues, the devil takes Yisrolik on a balloon tour of Europe, and en route he takes credit for the economic apparatus of the modern world:

> Look now and you will see smokestacks. From them my thousands of factories spew smoke and manufacture cannons, guns, and every conceivable implement of death; factories that cater to every need; and also factories that make every product you don't need; factories to make devices and machines, to save human labor, to render professions obsolete and deprive workers of their jobs; factories to make every sort of gadget to save time and shorten distances, and more often than not to shorten people's lives in the bargain; factories to print and spread over the whole world all sorts of foolishness—lies, slanders, libels, impossibilities, baseless hatreds, and every other conceivable manner of ugliness and vileness.... Simply stated, this is the smoke of "civilization," as it's known by the likes of you. (Y 122; E 638)

At least a half-century before Horkheimer and Adorno, Abramovitsh here articulates the central insight of the *Dialektik*—the same social, technological, and material circumstances that create modernity and the individual's awareness of the world at large potentially sow the seeds of civilization's destruction.

Aptly enough, Abramovitsh signals a crossing of the threshold between folklore and modernity in literary terms, as Wisse states:

> In a thorough study of the demonological sources of *The Mare*, Shmuel Werses has identified several Hebrew and European works including Goethe's *Faust*, Heinrich Zschokke's *Die Walpurgisnacht*, and Rene Alain's [Alain René Le Sage, 1668–1747] *Gil Blas*.... A more immediate literary source...was the Yiddish adaptation that Abramovitsh and his friend Bienstok had just published of Jules Verne's *Five Weeks in a Balloon*, in which representatives of British civilization observe the dark continent of Africa from their delightful, precarious balloon-perch.[24]

Abramovitsh had apparently translated Verne's adventure story for pedagogical reasons, to educate his readers about geography through a popular narrative about the European conquest of Africa.[25] This same narrative, however, now becomes an object of parody, as Abramovitsh reveals the real "dark continent" to be Europe itself. The true barbarians are the perpetrators of a modernity at once industrial and imperial, who have, as Abramov-

---

24. "The Jewish Intellectual and the Jews," 17.

25. For more on this translation and its place in Abramovitsh's ideological development, see Dan Miron and Anita Norich, "The Politics of Benjamin III: Intellectual Significance and Its Formal Correlatives in Sh. Y. Abramovitsh's *Masoes Benyomin Hashlishi*," *The Field of Yiddish: Studies in Language, Folklore, and Literature*, Fourth Collection eds. Marvin I. Herzog, Barbara Kirshenblatt-Gimblett, Dan Miron, and Ruth Wisse (Philadelphia, Pa.: Institute for the Study of Human Issues, 1980), 27–28.

itsh's complex allusion to Jules Verne suggests, disrupted and subjected the cultures of Africa and the Pale of Settlement equally.

The implicit connections between the colonization of Africa and the oppression of East European Jewry serve to ground a critique of global modernity viscerally in the lived experience of the author's own culture. This is precisely what is missing from Horkheimer and Adorno's first effort to come to terms with the Holocaust. Surprisingly, the least interesting section of the *Dialektik* is the chapter on anti-Semitism, which shares with its existentialist doppelganger *Anti-Semite and Jew*,[26] and implicitly with anti-Semitism as such, an inability to conceive of Jews or Judaism as anything other than a projection of the anti-Semite. In Sartre's case this distortion is both a sign of methodological weakness—his own ignorance, in 1946, of Jewish culture and Jewish people—and an enduring legacy of European anti-Semitism; in spite of Sartre's salutary efforts to critique this prejudice, Judaism in Sartre's essay ultimately exists only in negative terms, as the anti-Semite's last recourse to myth. For Horkheimer and Adorno, however, the consideration of Judaism as the mere inversion of anti-Semitism is indicative of the enlightenment they sought to analyze: nowhere are they more beholden to the limitations of the enlightenment than in the internal compulsion to be objective, "universal," about the self. Claiming to offer an objective analysis of the other, the anti-Semite, they demonstrate their own estrangement from the experience and condition that brought them into exile and motivated their collaboration on this work.

Because Abramovitsh, the Yiddish-speaking "recovering *maskil*," is most fully caught in the contradictions of enlightenment, he recognizes the dialectic on which enlightenment is premised so many years before his more formally trained German-Jewish counterparts. Abramovitsh's mare stands as a figure able to finesse the dilemmas of the enlightenment through its embodiment of myth, phantasmagoria, and the uncanny; the mare, and by extension its eponymous narrative, uses rationalistic devices such as polemic and parody to critique modernity, and in this act of assimilating the tools of rationality it straddles the line, uncannily, between traditional Jewish culture and European civilization. *Di Klyatshe,* therefore, offers a model for a critique of the other, most profoundly the other already assimilated by the self. More significantly, it illustrates the critical capacities of the *literary* as a mode of discourse that is neither philosophical nor allegorical (two competing modes of rationalization), but rather subjective, exceptional, and individual. By exposing the historical, social, and metaphysical limitations of enlightenment subjectivity, Abramovitsh restores the dignity of the individual as both an ethical ideal and a dramatic potentiality. This is perhaps the

---

26. Jean-Paul Sartre, *Anti-Semite and Jew: An Exploration of the Etiology of Hate*, trans. George J. Becker (New York: Schocken Books, Inc., 1948; 1995).

great achievement of the novel as a literary form and, therefore, the triumph of *Di Klyatshe* is nothing less than the triumph of literature as such, an achievement that, as Adorno himself might acknowledge, always calls attention to the limits of the absolute and, in so doing, achieves the paradoxical victory of rejecting all "fictions of salvation."[27]

In his classic story *Bontshe shvayg*, Y. L. Peretz offers through the character of the *kateyger*, the accusing angel, a variant on the theme developed in *Di Klyatshe* of a demonic voice speaking ultimate truths. It is nonetheless significant that the *kateyger*'s last words in Peretz's story are, "Gentlemen, he was always silent—and now I too will be silent."[28] By analogy—the governing analytical tool of the preceding discussion—just as Abramovitsh and the authors of the *Dialektik der Aufklärung* resist the temptation to facile conclusions, so too will this comparison end on a radically inconclusive note. Rather than attempt to neutralize the tensions generated by the juxtaposition of these dissimilar yet sympathetic works under the demands of a totalizing synthesis, it would perhaps be best simply to return to the original question of canon that has inspired this collection and motivated this contribution. It is worth considering in this light that for many of the people reading this volume, *Di Klyatshe* is a long familiar, perhaps even overly familiar classic of Yiddish literature, whereas the *Dialektik* might be an unknown and ostensibly irrelevant philosophical study; this relation of known and unknown would be diametrically reversed in any discipline of the humanities other than the study of Jewish literature. Yet as the preceding discussion has attempted to demonstrate, both works benefit from a consideration of one another.

To the extent that a modern Jewish canon exists, classic Yiddish fiction should serve as its foundation, and the *Dialektik* deserves a place within it, despite its problematic status as either a Jewish or a literary work; the *Dialektik der Aufklärung* is Jewish in a profound and agonistically modern way. If the *Dialektik*'s place in the modern Jewish canon is thus on the periphery, is it not the periphery that provides the best location for critique? The preceding comparison is, therefore, by no means intended to critique the concept of canon. Quite the contrary: the extraordinary relevance these two works share with one another points to their centrality in a "meta-canon" of the modern experience, particularly the experience of Jews in modernity. The canon as a concept thus functions best when it is conceived

27. Theodor W. Adorno, *Mahler: A Musical Physiognomy*, trans. Edmund Jephcott (Chicago: University of Chicago Press, 1992; 1996), 135.

28. Y. L. Peretz, *Bontshe shvayg, Ale verk*, vol. II (New York: CYCO Bicher-Farlag, 1947), 419. Translated by Hilde Abel as "Bontshe the Silent" in *A Treasury of Yiddish Stories*, ed. Irving Howe and Eliezer Greenberg (New York: Penguin Books, 1954; 1990), 229.

of as a vehicle of inclusion, one that opens within itself a continuous *path of escape* for figures, like Abramovitsh's mare, of resistance to authority and the burdens of repressive rationality. In this regard, the best precedent for a literary canon, to recapitulate the terms with which this comparison began, is neither the ecclesiastical canon nor the military cannon, but the musical canon.[29] As in music, the literary canon should function as a vehicle for imitation, echo, and counterpoint, in which the stated melody of the leader is less significant than the transformations of the theme from the margins.

29. Under these terms perhaps the most representative figure in a modern Jewish canon should be neither a belletristic writer nor a philosopher, but the composer Arnold Schoenberg. As Adorno demonstrates in his writing on modern music—the domain in which he was best able to transcend the contradictions of philosophy via an approach to the ineffable—Schoenberg's music deploys a mastery of contrapuntal devices, primary among them the *canon*, to give voice to the despair over modern rationality's failure to alleviate misery or provide a home in the world for the displaced person. For a treatment of the role of Judaism in his music, see Alexander L. Ringer, *Arnold Schoenberg: The Composer as Jew* (Oxford: Clarendon Press, 1990; 1993).

Yiddish Canon Consciousness and the Dionysiac Spirit of Music

JED WYRICK

From the self-proclaimed first work of Sholem Aleichem to the last and possibly most critically acclaimed work of Y. L. Peretz, classic Yiddish literature has been haunted by theories about the origins of European literature in music that have circulated since the time of Aristotle. Despite Peretz's desire to find models for his Jewish writing in the prophetic poetry of the Bible, and notwithstanding Sholem Aleichem's attempt to avoid genres and themes without significance to the Jewish world, elements of this literary history are treated in their works with a mixture of fascination and dismay. As I will argue, their works that meditate on the place of pagan and musical themes most centrally are among the works that exhibit the greatest degree of "canon consciousness" and that are most crucial in constructing a literature in Yiddish. The broad outlines of the Yiddish literary canon as conceived by Sholem Aleichem and Peretz were formulated by practically incorporating and symbolically rejecting what were assumed by both authors to be the universal building blocks of literature.

What I am referring to as "canon consciousness" is the self-awareness of writers who were attempting to create a literary canon, a set of agreed-upon works whose artistic merits and topical concerns conveyed enduring answers to the challenges faced by Jewish culture.[1] This "canon consciousness" was also a pressure felt from without. It represented an awareness of the need to create a first-rate literature in Yiddish that was in some way comparable to the Greek and Latin "classics" and the newly forming canons of

---

An early version of this essay, "Satyrs, Choruses, and Violinists: The Jewish Problem with Dionysiac Poetics," was delivered at the Association for Jewish Studies conference in 2002.

In special recognition of the individual to whom this essay and volume is dedicated, I would like to note that Professor Wisse has been the most devoted intellectual mentor and life coach that one could hope for and continues to be a tremendous source of strength and comfort to me. I am extremely grateful for Professor Wisse's championing of the anti-universal concerns of Jewish literature in the context of the study of comparative literature, the discipline in which I studied as a doctoral student at Harvard. In addition, many thanks go to Professor Wisse for helping me form the ideas I have attempted to express here.

1. The idea of "canon consciousness" is discussed in David G. Meade, *Pseudonymity and Canon: An Investigation into the Relationship of Authorship and Authority in Jewish and Earliest Christian Tradition* (Tübingen: J. C. B. Mohr, 1986).

the individual European vernaculars.[2] The approach to the notion of canon developed in this essay is primarily anthropological rather than aesthetic. Because I find it difficult as a student of comparative literature to assess works from different cultures using a single, universal aesthetic measuring rod, I prefer to examine how canons help cultures define themselves. As I will argue, the Yiddish literary canon at the outset had its own anxiety about universal aesthetic standards on the grounds that they were non-Jewish in essence. Put somewhat differently, the new Yiddish canon exhibited an awareness of and resisted the cultural particularity of allegedly universal aesthetics.

Because the contents of all modern literary canons are not really universally agreed upon, they differ from the canons of the Hebrew Bible or New Testament or even the canons of classical authors created in antiquity. The biblical canons were shaped by ritual and institutional forces, such as the archival practices of the priests of the Jerusalem Temple in the case of the Hebrew Bible and the liturgical collections of a small number of influential churches in the case of the New Testament, more than they were the products of an all-powerful synod at Yavne or ecclesiastical council, even if rabbinic and ecclesiastical traditions granted such a role to these assemblies after the fact.[3] For its part, the Alexandrian canon of classical Greek authors is comparable to the idea of canon as applied to the modern languages only to the extent that some modern national institution of like authority to the ancient Alexandrian Museion could stand as guarantor of such a list. In contrast, "canon" in its modern sense is a heuristic category rather than an actual list. Its individual components are continually subject to dispute, even if the existence of a general category and some of its component parts are universally granted. It is this more unstable and hypothetical notion of "canon," one aesthetically comparable to the emerging canons of other modern literary cultures and yet culturally authentic and true to Judaism, that Sholem Aleichem and Y. L. Peretz can be said to have had a consciousness of and to have helped create for Yiddish. Another feature typically associated with canons involves the creation of a set of works that might endure for all time. Was the Yiddish canon of Sholem Aleichem and Peretz intended as an ultimately self-effacing creation like the Yiddish literature of the Haskalah that preceded it, or was it was created "under the aegis of eternity"?[4] Peretz did

---

2. On the Latin term *classici* 'first-rate authors', see Jed Wyrick, *The Ascension of Authorship: Attribution and Canon Formation in Jewish, Hellenistic, and Christian Traditions*, Harvard Studies in Comparative Literature 49 (Cambridge: Harvard University Press, 2004), 346–347.

3. For a fuller discussion of this view of the history of ancient Western canons, see Wyrick, *The Ascension of Authorship*, 32–45, 185–200, and 345–353.

4. The phrase "under the aegis of eternity" was uttered by Joseph Wulf, author of a book composed as a tribute to Peretz's style that was begun five months after the occupation

evince a distinct "canon consciousness" in his writings with regard to literary quality, contrasting the opportunistic "artist" and the prophetic "poet" and lamenting the small number of true poets and books, a number that he felt must by all means increase.[5] But it is uncertain whether he felt his tragic drama, *Bay nakht oyfn altn mark* (*A Night in the Old Marketplace*), for instance, to be a work that would be eternally meaningful, considering the changes in the Jewish world that he envisioned at the date of its publication and even dramatized within its verses. Moreover, the actual legacy of Peretz inspires little confidence in the ability of history to make adequate judgments about literary value, considering his near eclipse as a writer in recent times (at least prior to Ruth Wisse's influential study) and, of course, the disappearance of Yiddish as a spoken language itself. It might even be said that Peretz's tremendously influential notion of secular Jewish culture, what Wisse calls the "determination of modern Jews to flourish as a minority in Poland, and perhaps elsewhere, with a language and culture of their own," outlasted his literary works to the extent that it continues to survive in any form other than nostalgia.[6] More could be said about the way Sholem Aleichem and Peretz's writings dramatize the tentative quality of the historical moment in which they found themselves, as well as the impact of this historical and cultural pessimism on their hopes for the future reception of their works.

Sholem Aleichem and Y. L. Peretz are both acknowledged to be crucial in creating a Yiddish literature, although they managed to do so using different means and without collusion.[7] As Dan Miron has shown, Sholem Aleichem was responsible for creating not only his own authorial persona but helped design a significant dimension to the persona known as Mendele Moykher-Sforim (Mendele "the Bookpeddler") by fashioning him as the *pater familias* of Yiddish writers and as Sholem Aleichem's own literary

---

of Cracow; cited in Ruth R. Wisse, *I. L. Peretz and the Making of Modern Jewish Culture* (Seattle and London: University of Washington Press, 1991), xvi. On the self-effacing quality of the Yiddish writings of the Haskalah, see Dan Miron, "Folklore and Antifolklore in the Yiddish Fiction of the *Haskalah*," in Frank Talmage, ed., *Studies in Jewish Folklore* (Cambridge, MA: Association for Jewish Studies, 1980), 219–249.

5. See, for example, "*Der dikhter, dos bukh un der lezer*" (1910) and "*Vos felt undzer literatur?*" (1910), both cited in Khone Shmeruk, *Peretses yiesh vizye* (*Peretz's Vision of Despair*): *Interpretation of Y. L. Peretz's Bay nakht oyfn altn mark and Critical Edition of the Play* (New York: Yivo Institute for Jewish Research, 1971), 104–105.

6. Wisse, *I. L. Peretz*, xiv–xv.

7. On their conflicting views of the ideal nature of Yiddish literature, as well as the strained relationship between Peretz and Sholem Aleichem, see Wisse, *I. L. Peretz*, 5–11 and 28–29; see also Dan Miron, *A Traveler Disguised: The Rise of Modern Yiddish Fiction in the Nineteenth Century* (Syracuse University Press: Syracuse, N.Y., 1996 [1973]), 71–74.

precursor. He did so in the prologue to *Stempenyu*, published as a supplement to the first volume of the *Di yiddishe folksbiblyotek* in 1888 and dedicated to Mendele Moykher-Sforim, the "grandfather" (*zeyde*) of Yiddish literature.[8] The narrator who graced the Yiddish works composed by S. Y. Abramovitsh was by this act transformed into a classic writer and mentor (and, I would add, the canonical forbearer of Sholem Aleichem). Miron notes that this creation had a spiraling effect on the self-awareness of the literature as a whole: "In 1880 Yiddish writers did not suspect that they had a history; by the early 1890s they already had produced one 'classic' writer; before the century ended *The History of Yiddish Literature in the Nineteenth Century* was written in English for American readers by a Harvard instructor."[9]

In its foreword, Sholem Aleichem declares *Stempenyu* to be his first novel, although this was not, in fact, the case; he had written five other novels before *Stempenyu*.[10] Sholem Aleichem envisioned the work to be the first in a trilogy of novels about Jewish artists. He went on to create *Yosele Solevey* (*Yosele the Nightingale*) about a cantor, and *Blondzhende shtern* (*Wandering Stars*) about the theater (the latter, however, appeared some twenty-two years later, and exhibits a much different writing style and set of concerns, despite Sholem Aleichem's early plan to create a coherent trilogy about Jewish artists). The intention to create a trilogy of novels, voiced in 1889 in his "A briv tsu a gutn fraynd" (A Letter to a Good Friend) and published in the same volume of *Di yiddishe folksbiblyotek* as *Yosele Solevey*, was itself a classicizing aspiration common in European literature that ultimately derived from the Greek tragic trilogies of Aeschylus, Sophocles, and Euripides.[11]

---

8. On the importance of the preface to *Stempenyu* in the history of modern Yiddish literature and the creation of the Sholem Aleichem persona, see Miron, *A Traveler Disguised*, 31. Miron points out that the preface recasts Mendele into the supreme artist rather than satirist or natural scientist and designates Sholem Aleichem as his disciple. "Grandfather Mendele" was as important a creation of Sholem Rabinovitch as was Sholem Aleichem himself.

9. Ibid., 31. The Harvard professor noted by Miron was, of course, Leo Wiener, whose collection of Yiddish works formed the centerpiece of the exhaustive Yiddish collection at Harvard's Widener Library. I would also note that the advent of the first Harvard professor specializing in Yiddish literature, Ruth Wisse, represents another milestone in the history of the field of Yiddish, as well as the field of Jewish literature in general.

10. See the extensive discussion in Dorothy Bilik, "Love in Sholem Aleykhem's Early Novels," *Working Papers in Yiddish and East European Jewish Studies* 10 (1975): 1–20.

11. Sholem Aleichem, "A briv tsu a gutn fraynd," *Yiddishe folksbiblyotek* (Kiev, 1889), 308; cited in Khone Shmeruk, *Eyarut ve-Karakhim: Perakim be-Yetzirut shel Sholem Aleichem* (*Studies in Sholem Aleichem's Writings*) (Jerusalem: Hebrew University Magnes Press, 2000), 92–93. On the different concerns of the third novel, see Sholem

Not all literary canons are lists of *works* judged to be the masterpieces of a tradition. The Alexandrian Greek canon, to take a prominent example from antiquity, was rather a list of first-rate *authors*.[12] This was precisely the kind of canon that Sholem Aleichem succeeded in creating in the prologue to his "first novel" and the legend it spawned.[13] Sholem Aleichem's accomplishment was thus not only to fashion what Dan Miron calls "the semblance of tradition" or the sense of Yiddish literature as "a grand literary institution," but also to inaugurate a new and instantly authoritative canon of authors, a succession of masters consisting of only two individuals at the time of its creation. By way of comparison, Sholem Aleichem's own literary legacy would eventually consist of his characters even more than his books; in the eyes of both critics and popular culture, Tevye, Menakhem Mendl, Motl the Cantor's son, and the narrative persona of Sholem Aleichem himself supersede the works in which they are found as enduring creations of the author.

Although neither *Stempenyu* nor *Yosele Solevey* are as powerful as *Tevye the Dairyman*, they both had an incomparable impact on the evolving shape of Yiddish literature, owing to the way that they presented Sholem Aleichem the author as a discrete voice and as an iterable and imitable entity: an incomparable author with a certain replicable style (only replicable by himself, to be sure).[14] Similarly, even if one could grant that *Bay nakht oyfn altn mark* is among the most significant literary creations of Y. L. Peretz (and the same might with good reason be said for his other important drama, *Di goldene keyt* [*The Golden Chain*]), nevertheless the reputation of Peretz hardly rests on either of these works.[15] Rather than being gov-

---

Aleichem's letter to Mordechai Spektor dated September 10, 1910; printed in Shmeruk, *Eyarut ve-Karakhim*, 91. Sholem Aleichem had also intended to create a trilogy of novels about the Blank family; see the letter to Dubnow dated Sept. 2, 1888; cited in Anita Norich, "Portraits of the Artist in Three Novels by Sholem Aleichem," *Prooftexts* 4 (1984) 237–251, on 249 n. 4.

12. The ancient Alexandrian Greek canon was also a canon of authors rather than a canon of texts; the idea of a canon of texts entered the Western tradition from Judaism via Christianity. See Wyrick, *The Ascension of Authorship*, 344–353.

13. Miron, *A Traveler Disguised*, 32.

14. On the idea of "iterability" and "imitability" as defining characteristics of authorship, see Wyrick, *The Ascension of Authorship*, 11, where authorship is discussed with reference to Jacques Derrida's definition of a signature: "In order to function, that is, in order to be legible, a signature must have a repeatable, iterable, imitable form; it must be able to detach itself from the present and singular intention of its production." Jacques Derrida, "Signature, Event, Context," in *Margins of Philosophy*, ed. Alan Bass (Chicago: University of Chicago Press, 1982), 328. The true accomplishment of both *Stempenyu* and *Yosele Solevey* was thus to render their author's voice equivalent to a signature that could be used again and again but only by himself.

15. *Bay nakht oyfn altn mark* has received scholarly treatment worthy of a canonical

erned by a single set of criteria (either their role in canon formation or some standard of artistic worth determined in hindsight), my selection of these three works as crucial in understanding the nature of Yiddish canon consciousness rests not merely in their tremendous influence on subsequent Yiddish literature, but on the way they articulate a consistent position on the relationship between this literature and the (alleged) *Ursprung* of poetry as formulated by Aristotle and his successors.[16] All three works, in a manner appropriate to a newly inaugurated canon, stake out a territory that does battle with the literary conventions and artistic vocabulary of competing traditions. In addition, they articulate a consistent and nuanced position on the compatibility of Jewish art and European culture. This meant, among other things, considering the affinity of Jewish characters to the genres of drama and novel, the suitability of romance and melodrama to the authentic Jewish world view, and even the degree to which Jewish literature might tolerate the racy subjects of popular European art.

Sholem Aleichem accomplished this aspect of his "canon consciousness" partly in the pamphlet *Shomers mishpet* (*Shomer's Trial*), published in the same year as *Stempenyu*, in which he puts Shomer (N. M. Shaykevitsh), the Yiddish author of pulp fiction based on European romance models, on trial for his sins against Jewish literature. Sholem Aleichem's ambivalence toward European literature may be seen elsewhere as well. In the prologue to *Stempenyu*, he cites a letter that Mendele Moykher-Sforim had once writ-

---

work; Professor Wisse calls Khone Shmeruk's *Peretses yiesh vizye* (*Peretz's Vision of Despair*) the "definitive edition and interpretation," stating that it is "one of the few reliable editions of Peretz and an invaluable source for the study of all Peretz's writings" (Wisse, *I. L. Peretz*, 124 n. 37). Shmeruk's documentation of the influence of the drama on subsequent Yiddish literature, particularly in the younger generation of Yiddish poets, is also worth citing here: see Shmeruk, *Peretz's Vision of Despair*, 214–216 for a general discussion, and 216 n. 37 for a list of allusions and citations of the drama in Yiddish poetry. Particularly interesting is the judgment of Israel Shtern, who considered *Bay nakht oyfn altn mark* to be Peretz's highest achievement. With regard to *Di goldene keyt*, Professor Wisse states that the play "became the most nationally significant, if not necessarily the best of Peretz's works" (Wisse, *I. L. Peretz*, 62).

16. It should be noted that Peretz, despite being a personal favorite, is not treated by Professor Wisse in *The Modern Jewish Canon*, since he did not compose an extended work of fiction (see R. Wisse, *The Modern Jewish Canon: A Journey Through Language and Culture* [New York: The Free Press, 2000], 347–348). Although *The Modern Jewish Canon* highlights "big books," the extended works of fiction that are at the center of many contemporary approaches to the Western canon, other articulations of the canons of Jewish and Yiddish literature should accommodate the short story, drama (both tragic and comic), and poetry of both lyric and epic scope, out of consideration of the place of these genres in ancient literary canons, the literary and cultural influence of the individual works in question, and an estimation of their aesthetic value.

ten, calling on him to avoid writing novels.[17] Accordingly, his novel *Sender Blank* (1888) was preceded by the epigraph *a roman on a roman* "a novel without a romance" or "a novel without a novel" (an earlier version had received the epigraph *a roman on a libe* "a novel without a love affair"). His ambivalence can also be seen in the narratorial interventions of his novels, for example in *Stempenyu*:

> Readers, who are used to "highly interesting" modern romances, have suffered enough from this novel, which has had no tearful scenes, no assignations. No one has shot himself, no one has poisoned himself, we have met no counts or marquis. We keep seeing only ordinary people, musicians and everyday Jewish women. These readers must be looking forward to Saturday night, they are waiting for a piquant and titillating scene on Monastery Street....But I have to say in advance that their expectations are useless. There won't be any piquant and titillating scenes because our Rachel hasn't come here for any sinful purpose, God forbid, she hasn't come here like a debauched woman, hurrying to kiss her lover in the darkness, heaven forefend! (*Stempenyu*, 355)[18]

While Sholem Aleichem struggled with the predicament of how much romance (and, I would add, how much of the European novel as a genre) could be tolerated in his Jewish *romanen*, Y. L. Peretz similarly undercuts the theme and genre of romance in a number of discrete episodes involving the impossibility of romantic love that pepper his drama, *Bay nakht oyfn altn mark*.[19] In one such episode in Act I, a young girl reads aloud a letter, ostensibly from her beloved, that praises her blue eyes, much to her delight. The pathos is, however, immediately undercut by her female companion, who counters that the girl's eyes are in fact gray, exposing the hypocrisy of the discourse. As Khone Shmeruk has shown, these scenes are relatively unchanged in each successive version of the play, revealing their centrality in the original conception of the work.

In bridging the gap between Jewish and European literature, both Sholem Aleichem and Y. L. Peretz avoided a discussion of the Christian role in European art and literature. Ingrained resistance to Christian persecution and the need to avoid religious assimilation might have unfairly prejudged the conflict and resulted in a premature and out-of-hand rejection of Europe-

---

17. According to the prologue, Mendele's argument had been, "your taste, your genre, is something different. If there are indeed *romanen* in the lives of our folk romances, they are something completely different (*gor andersh*) from those of other peoples. One must understand this well and write completely differently (*gor andersh*)." Mendele repeated this advice to Sholem Aleichem in a letter dated Jan. 17, 1889, cited in Norich, 249 n. 3.

18. Translation of *Stempenyu* by Joachim Neugroschel in Joachim Neugroschel, ed., *The Shtetl* (Woodstock, N.Y.: The Overlook Press, 1989), 287–375.

19. See the discussion in Shmeruk, *Peretz's Vision of Despair*, 66–75.

an traditions. Instead, I would assert that both authors broached the subject in more neutral territory, by asking how much of the ancient Greek classical substrate of the European tradition should be tolerated in the construction of modern Jewish artistic culture or, more primally still, by investigating whether Yiddish literature has any affinity to the forces that, since Aristotle, have been assumed to have created this substrate: song, dance, wine, and Dionysus.

There is no reason to believe that Sholem Aleichem and Peretz literally feared paganism or pagan influence on Jewish literature and culture. Rather, they employed paganism as a metaphor to speak about those elements of literature that were potentially non-Jewish in origin and thus by nature. It should also be specified that in no way do I mean to claim, as some of these European successors to Aristotle actually did, that the philosopher had correctly revealed the Greek and pagan or Dionysiac origins of all literature. Instead, I would suggest that the anxiety felt by these two authors derived from the Eurocentric and false assumption that the creation of a new literature required a return to the Greco-Roman classics. Both authors were capable of arguing in other contexts that song, dance, wine, and, indeed, all poetic tropes can be found in the Hebrew Bible and midrash and are thus native to Judaism. Yet, the idea of music as pagan and foreign is nevertheless taken up in these influential works as if it were both a necessary element in Jewish art as well as an element that Jewish art had to combat.

To be sure, neither Sholem Aleichem nor Peretz dealt with Greek culture in an extended fashion. Their approach to the correct degree to which Jewish literature ought to be open to the world of music and paganism is qualitatively different from the response to Hellenism evinced by many Haskalah writers (who had unreserved praise for the classical canon) or from the way that many writing in Hebrew subsequently dealt with Greek culture (one has only to think of the poetry of Saul Tshernichowsky).[20] Nevertheless, the response of modern Jewish culture to Hellenism parallels the approach of both authors to foreign literary influence. Yaakov Shavit locates four approaches in Jewish culture to the question of the value of outside and specifically Hellenic components of European culture.[21] The first position "views Judaism as a totally closed and sovereign metaphysical cultural entity, uncontaminated by any outside influences" or Greek traits. The second approach views Jewish culture as "living in symbiosis with the outside

---

20. On the Haskalah's approach to Greece, see Yaakov Shavit, *Athens in Jerusalem: Classical Antiquity in the Making of the Modern Secular Jew* (Portland, Oregon: Vallentine Mitchell, 1997[1992]), 119–145. Shavit, whose work has brought the importance of the connection between Hellenic and Judaic thought to the fore, also highlights the influence of the Homeric heroic ideal on M. Y. Berdichevsky, Ze'ev Jabotinsky, and the authors of the Zionist collection entitled *Kehiliyatenu* 'Our Congregation'; see 146–154.

21. Ibid., 218–219.

world" and Greek culture in particular; this approach has an entirely positive view of Hellenization, which it sees as capable of bringing Jewish art to an even higher level. The third approach asserts that something analogous to the Hellenic dimension already exists within Judaism and that there is no need to look to the outside world to furnish it. The fourth approach internalizes the criticism of Judaism, viewing Jewish culture as flawed, unidimensional, and worthy of being replaced.

Using this scheme, it might be said that both authors represent a unique combination of the first and third approaches. Sholem Aleichem's works depict a musical, primal force analogous to Hellenism that is at once inimical to Judaism and yet comparable to a force already present within the tradition; whatever its origin, this primal force is dangerous and irreconcilable with the Jewish forces that it threatens to overwhelm. Nevertheless, Sholem Aleichem is repeatedly drawn to this dangerous realm in order to fashion a literature. In the world of Peretz's drama, the pagan spirit of music that serves as an analogue to Hellenic influence, though recognizably alien and malevolent, is one of the preconditions of the tragedy that has befallen the Jewish world, and yet in the end may also aid society in coming to grips with this tragedy. The drama's mad and primal forces of song, dance, and wine are treated as the externalized internal, a voice originally found within Judaism that is now trapped within a recognizably non-Jewish domain located at the center of this diaspora community and governed by a pagan statue.

Although previous critics of Sholem Aleichem's trilogy of novels about Jewish artists have explored the self-referentiality of these works, only the way in which they represent externalized authorship models has been highlighted. According to these scholars, Sholem Aleichem was drawn to the idea of the romantic artist as the individual struggling with his world and employed the figure of the artist as an opportunity for self-presentation and definition. In the end, however, the artist fades out of each novel because, in their view, the artist is mainly an opportunity for romance, which Sholem Aleichem felt to be antithetical to Jewish life.[22] However, it seems more

---

22. Dorothy Bilik, who convincingly describes the author as uncomfortable with romance in a Jewish context, is less persuasive in arguing that the purpose of the novels about artists is therefore to reintroduce romance into the Jewish novel by the back door: "Sholem Aleichem seems to be most comfortable with the theme of love when it concerned artists, thieves, people removed from the more customary and traditional folkways of Jewish life" (Bilik, "Love in Sholem Aleykhem's Early Novels," 16). Similarly, according to Norich, the figure of the artist emerged as the natural embodiment for solving Sholem Aleichem's problems with the novel (as a genre meaningless without romance that is itself, at least as conventionally understood, foreign to the Jewish world). Norich supposes that the artist "was unrestricted enough to cover geographical and psychological distances even when rooted within traditional Jewish life by marriage or family" (Norich, "Portraits of the Artist in Three Novels by Sholem Aleichem," 238).

likely that Sholem Aleichem was attempting to discover an authentic ground on which a genuinely literary Jewish literature might be built, rather than simply thinking about his own authorial predicament, played out in the parallel worlds of klezmer, cantorial tradition, and the stage. To interpret the turn to artistic subjects as merely a convenient means by which romance could be realistically re-introduced into the Jewish novel would seem to emphasize Sholem Aleichem's problems with love at the expense of his anxiety about creating a Yiddish literature and canon. Instead, I would assert that these Jewish works about artists are meditations on the fortunes and perils of Jewish belles-lettres broadly understood (with the inception of a Yiddish literary canon being the particular concern lurking behind these works).[23]

The arts that Sholem Aleichem intended to explore in each artistic novel are parallel to those highlighted in Aristotle's *Poetics* as traditions from which tragedy developed: choral song and dance (related by Nietzsche to his notion of "the spirit of music"), dithyrambic poetry (a genre of ancient liturgical poetry sung by a single individual), and the primitive, ritualistic genre known as Satyr Drama (a bawdy drama featuring a chorus of Satyrs and stock mythical scenes involving Dionysus). The trilogy of *Stempenyu* (which features a Jewish musician), *Yosele Solevey* (depicting the life of a cantor) and *Blondzhende shtern* (describing actors in the Jewish theatre) thus replicates Aristotle's theory of the threefold origin of literature in music, liturgical performance, and popular drama. By creating such a trilogy, I would suggest that Sholem Aleichem hoped to demonstrate that Jewish literature could be no less vibrant or organic than the literature of Europe.[24]

The Aristotelian (and Nietzschean) figure of the satyr, the half-goat creature known for its voracious sexual appetite and musical abilities and connected by Aristotle to the origin of the genre of tragedy, is oddly suggestive

---

23. Of course, such an interpretation, like all interpretations, runs the risk of simply turning these works into a cipher in which the coded message lying underneath is the concern surrounding the formation of a Jewish literature. On this tendency of interpretation, see Frederic Jameson, *The Political Unconscious* (Ithaca, N.Y.: Cornell University Press, 1981), 17–102. Jameson discusses the dangers of "a system of allegorical interpretation in which the data of one narrative line are radically impoverished by their rewriting according to the paradigm of another narrative, which is taken as the former's master code or Ur-narrative and proposed as the ultimate hidden or unconscious *meaning* of the first one" (22).

24. It is difficult to ascertain exactly how Sholem Aleichem learned about Aristotle's theory; however, the enormous impact of the *Poetics* on European theories of the history of literature and views on the proper nature of drama is discernible beginning from the writings of Scaliger (who combined the views of Horace with those of Aristotle), Castelvetro (inventor of the "three unities"), Jean de la Taille (who insisted on them in France), and numerous others from the sixteenth century on.

as a model for the violinist Stempenyu, whose name provided the title of Sholem Aleichem's "first" novel. In *The Birth of Tragedy from the Spirit of Music* (published in 1872), Friedrich Nietzsche extended the Aristotelian argument about the importance of satyrs to literature, claiming that the function of the satyr was to bring man in contact with his roots in nature.[25] "The satyr was man's true prototype, an expression of his highest and strongest aspirations...a symbol of the sexual omnipotence of nature."[26] He is also "a replica of nature in its strongest tendencies and at the same time a herald of its wisdom and art. He combines in his person the roles of musician, poet, dancer, and visionary."[27]

Similarly, Stempenyu is the Jewish embodiment of paganism and sexual liberation:

> People tell so many different stories about Stempenyu. They say he hobnobbed with wizards and with all the demons, and if he wanted to take a bride away from a groom, he knew a special sort of incantation, all he had to do was give her a look, the right kind of look—and the girl was done for, Lord preserve us! (*Stempenyu*, 296)

Stempenyu's power is not just physical but also verbal:

> And talking was something Stempenyu could really do. He had the gift of the gab—that rascal! His words spun round and round a person, like the words of a demon (*vi a guter mazek*), and he stared into the eyes—the eyes? What am I saying? The heart. Deep, deep into the heart. (*Stempenyu*, 297)

As a sexual threat to the shtetl's women, Stempenyu, perhaps a little more prepossessing than the standard satyr, is described as being "busy with himself all the time: bedecking and bedizening himself, curling his hair—in a word, making himself a 'bachelor.'" But he is equal to a satyr in his lasciviousness and insatiability, wooing bride away from groom with his penetrat-

---

25. The reception of Nietzsche in Hebrew literature was highly charged, beginning with M. Y. Berdichevsky's espousal of Nietzschean ideas in the 1890s and the first Hebrew essay on Nietzsche, written by David Neumark and published in *From East to West* in 1894. Nietzsche's influence reached a high point in the poetry of Saul Tshernichowsky and Zalman Shneur. See David Ohana, "Zarathustra in Jerusalem: Nietzsche and the 'New Hebrews,'" *Israel Affairs* 1.3 (1995): 38–60. On the parallels between Nietzsche's ideas and the writing of Y. L. Peretz, see Shmeruk, *Peretz's Vision of Despair*, 194–195. Shmeruk points out the resemblance between the ancient Greek philosopher Diogenes, the Madman of Nietzsche's *The Gay Science* who pronounces the death of God, and the Jester of *Bay nakht oyfn altn mark*. On 194 n.2, however, Shmeruk cites the passages in which Peretz often exhibits explicit reservations about Nietzsche's ideas; he also claims that Peretz's allusions to the "death of God" may have originated from the modern theater rather than from Nietzsche.

26. Friederich Nietzsche, *The Birth of Tragedy and the Genealogy of Morals*, trans. Francis Golfing (Garden City, NY: Doubleday, 1956), 52.

27. Ibid., 57.

ing eyes and passionate words and immediately setting her aside to make room for his next sexual conquest.

The impact of his music on the sexuality of the entire community is profound:

> Yontel the slaughterer performed a kazatska, and opposite him the mother-in-law herself was letting go with lots of pluck and belly (pardon me!), and the entire crowd was clapping to accompany Yontel, who didn't even notice that he was dancing with a woman, and he squatted up and down like a daredevil, and opposite him, the mother-in-law was hippity-hopping with her arms akimbo, and grinning at Yontel, with a broad grin across her broad face like the moon at midmonth—Things got even wilder after that. Men were dancing in just their (excuse the expression) breeches. (*Stempenyu*, 299)

Despite its sexual excessiveness, Stempenyu's fiddling is occasionally assimilated into traditional and sacred modes of Jewish expression. His playing is described as "a religious service, a divine labor, with a lofty feeling, a noble spirit!" The passage goes on to state that "Stempenyu stood opposite the bride and played a sermon on his violin, a long, lovely sermon (*drosha*)." At times, he too is described with acceptable Jewish imagery: "And his eyes burnt like Sabbath candles, and his beautiful face shone in ecstasy" (289). Moreover, despite his obvious danger to the community, Stempenyu has been officially sanctioned by the community's rebbe as kosher, owing to an incident in which he demonstrated his resistance to Christian influences.

> But Stempenyu replied in French (he knew German and French) that even if the count offered him a torrent of ducats, he wouldn't take a single drop of baptismal water for love or money. (And that was why he was so greatly respected by all pious Jews, even the rebbe.) (*Stempenyu*, 301)

While walking along the boundaries of the Jewish world (a practice symbolized by his knowledge of French and German), there is one boundary at least that Stempenyu will not cross.

At one point in the novel, Stempenyu's music is translated into words, revealing that it is ultimately a force of human nature rather than an articulation of Judaism. Its message constitutes

> a poignant sermon about the bride's free and happy life until now, about the dark, bitter life in store for her, later, later. Gone was her maidenhood and girlhood! Her head was covered, her long, beautiful hair was out of sight, forever and ever....No more joy! Farewell, youth. Now you're a married woman!....How bleak and cheerless—may God forgive me! That was what came from Stempenyu's fiddle. All the wives understood the wordless sermon, all the wives felt it. They felt it and wept for it with bitter tears. (*Stempenyu*, 294)

In addition to voicing the novel's predominant social theme (the sad lot of marriage for the Jewish woman), the content of Stempenyu's song fits Nietzsche's point about the satyr as a means to bring mankind into contact with his roots in nature. Moreover, his playing is primal, universal, and belongs to the realm of nature, rather than that of Jewish tradition. Sholem Aleichem's novel as a whole has the same purpose as does the satyr-like violinist's plaintive song: to reveal the value of love between Jewish husband and wife, the necessity of marital communication, and the minimum rights to loving affection required by all human beings.

With an allusion to the fictitious prologue to *Stempenyu*, Sholem Aleichem claims in the prologue to *Yosele Solevey* (published in 1889) that the novel is his second. One would expect that in the context of cantorial singing, at least, music might be given a valued place in Sholem Aleichem's novel and, by extension, in Jewish literature. But this could not be further from the truth. The novel describes the dangers inherent to the position of cantor when its vocal and musical elements threaten to supersede its religious qualities. As the novel progresses, it becomes clear that Yosele is not a respectable Jew. He soon abandons the instruction of his father to maintain his Jewishness, put on his *tefillin* daily, and observe all the commandments.

Not only do the musical elements of the cantor's job overwhelm the occupation's religious significance, the novel depicts secular music as downright dangerous. Here, the threat does not lie in the Dionysiac qualities of music, its wild abandon and excessive masculine sexuality as in Stempenyu's playing. Instead, music often menaces by being overly refined and Victorian, qualities that (like the Jewish barons and princesses of Shomer's pulp fiction) Sholem Aleichem felt to be both foreign and absurd in a Jewish context. Anita Norich points out that Perele's reading of *shund* or trashy literature is her identifying characteristic; but it is surely in the author's descriptions of her playing of the piano that her allure is most starkly presented and critiqued.[28] The true nature of Perele, the calculating parallel to the character of Freydl in *Stempenyu*, is conveyed in the piano, that artificial and overly refined instrument:

> But later, when Perele was a little older, her piano playing became a liability. She wasn't just another girl; she had to dress elegantly, had to have a pretty hat, a parasol, gloves, and all the other accessories that a "mamselle" requires. And didn't she have to attend the theater? How would it look if a girl who plays piano failed to go to the theater? (*Yosele Solevey*, 129)[29]

Perele's very seduction of Yosele away from Esther is accomplished by means of her piano playing:

> For almost the first time in his life Yosele heard piano playing. He had heard it from a distance many times, but to be sitting so close to a beautiful woman as she played, her small, white fingers seeming to draw from the instrument such soft sounds, such tender melodies—that he could never have imagined.

---

28. Norich, 241.

29. All translations taken from Sholem Aleichem, *The Nightingale: Or, the Saga of Yosele Solevey the Cantor*, trans. Aliza Shevrin (New York: G. P Putnam's Sons, 1985).

> The room was soon filled with beautiful sounds, and Perele became even more charming in his eyes than before. As always happened with him, things quickly took on an entirely changed aspect: the house was transformed into a palace and Perele into a princess; in a state of ecstasy he arrived to the sound of miraculous, divine music that melted his heart, caressed his soul, renewed his vitality. He passionately desired to join her; he longed to blend his voice with the sounds of the piano. Yosele the Nightingale began to sing, following the same rhythm, the music pouring from his throat, his rare, accomplished voice forming such sweet, tender melodies that Perele the Lady stopped playing to listen to him sing. But Yosele insisted she keep on playing. As she accompanied him, his exquisite voice poured forth sublime supernatural sounds like a nightingale's. (*Yosele Solovey*, 134–35)

Eventually, the calculating and business-oriented Perele attempts to woo Yosele away from music altogether: "In place of singing, talk day and night of trade, percentages, profit, money, costs" (143). A novel about a cantorial singer features an individual drawn away from sacred Jewish music by means of the music of high culture, exposing Sholem Aleichem's anxieties about the shifting essence of music.

Sholem Aleichem may have wished to present a musical tradition native to Judaism that might serve as a model for Yiddish literature. Yet his novels depict music as a force that respects no religious or cultural boundaries and one that easily manifests the lure of the Gentile world. In this novel in particular, the artificiality of the piano in a Jewish context becomes equated to the absurdity of *shund* or pulp-fiction literature. Despite the artificial and highly improbable premises and inferior literary quality of *shund* (a feature that Sholem Aleichem believed to derive from its origin in Gentile popular culture and its distance from the reality of the Jewish world), the novel treats this literature as a threat to the integrity of Jewish literature no less seductive than Perele's piano playing. Both the fluidity and allure of music provide Sholem Aleichem with the opportunity to meditate on the difficulties faced by the new Yiddish literature in achieving literary respectability while still remaining a part of an authentic Jewish world.

The work ends as a full-blown tragedy. A discussion of Jephthah's sacrifice of his daughter begins the final section of the novel. Esther, the novel's sacrificial equivalent to the unnamed daughter of the book of Judges, is married off to a rich villain of the community. There is a sense that Sholem Aleichem wishes to claim that all Jewish celebration is animated by a kind of tragic energy: "A Jew, when he wants to be merry or celebrate a happy occasion, has to force himself to do so" (212). The narrator describes the downcast wedding party, whose members behave "in the manner of Jews who grow sad in the midst of joy even while fêting the bride and groom"; he then asks, "What is it in Jewish singing and Jewish music that evokes only sorrowful thoughts?" (220). Yosele arrives home to declare his true feelings for Esther too late and eventually goes mad. He is described as a person "crushed by tragedy, the kind of tragedy for which there are no words"

(226). The novel concludes with a complete loss of self-expression, as conveyed in Esther's funereal wedding and Yosele's exquisite vocalization punctuated with insane rooster calls that now replace his nightingale croonings. Its message is the impossibility of love and happiness (a version of the familiar theme of the infeasibility of romance in the Jewish world), as well as the inadequacy of art to withstand social pressures of the marketplace and entrenched traditionalism. Although the prospects of Jewish art (and hence, by extension, literature) are bleak, the novel articulates the challenges faced by this literature in an authentic and compelling way, opening a space in which a literary canon might be constructed.

An even more highly charged relationship to the Dionysiac roots of literature is apparent in I. L. Peretz's drama *Bay nakht oyfn altn mark* (*A Night in the Old Marketplace*) composed during the period 1907–1922.[30] This play depicts the dream of a wanderer visiting a Jewish town. The dream, a macabre vision in which the dead of the town are animated, is set into verse by a character called the Poet (*dikhter*) and presented on stage by other characters, including a stage manager, narrator, and director, in a self-referential and modernist manner. The town's corpses are brought to life by the drama's central character, a Jester who has been bewitched by a malevolent gargoyle, prominently featured in the middle of the marketplace and the center of the stage, according to Peretz's instructions. Peretz's drama offers a complicated critique of the troubles that plagued the Jewish community during his time by creating an upside-down dream world in which the many voices of the community prophetically condemn its ills while searching for meaning and redemption.

The play attempts to present the predicament of Judaism in the diaspora in microcosm, with characters and scenery that cover every aspect of Jewish life imaginable. That the play is also in some way *about* literature is clear from its meta-theatrical framing and from the fact that its characters are drawn from the world of popular art: the Folk Poet (*heymisher dikhter*), the Jester (*badkhn*), Musicians, and the Brody Singers.[31] Peretz appears to address a question that long troubled him: is literature a medium that is ade-

---

30. For a critical edition of the text, see Shmeruk, *Peretz's Vision of Despair*, 217ff. Hillel Halkin's translation is found in Ruth R. Wisse, ed., *The I. L. Peretz Reader* (New Haven and London: Yale University Press, 2002), 361–432.

31. As Shmeruk puts it, "The poet figures and their metamorphoses in *Bay nakht oyfn altn mark* are a direct expression of Peretz's thoughts about poets and poetry in general" (100). Shmeruk also emphasizes the idea of the Jester as a poet in Jewish culture, and points out that the Jester's speech incorporates elements of H. N. Bialik's poetic and prophetic world view. See Shmeruk, *Peretz's Vision of Despair*, 100–124. In addition, the character of the Wanderer has a certain poetic resonance, a relationship made plain in the second version of the play, where the Poet takes one of the Wanderer's speeches (Shmeruk, 108).

quate to addressing the overwhelming problems facing Judaism in the first decades of the twentieth century?

Abraham Novershtern's important interpretation of the drama focuses on one of its most productive oppositions. Throughout the play, the Jester searches for a particular word "for remaking, for overturning everything," namely, "the Word" (*vort*), a term that evokes the primal and foundational qualities associated with the *logos* in the Gospel of John and the angelic *memra* "Word" of the Targums, even as it highlights the inadequacy of a foundation or salvation that is not built on a *specific* word. At first, the Jester hits upon "dust" (*shtoyb*) as the word that would explain the predicament of Jewish life. Later, however, he wonders whether "dance" (*tants*) is that word. According to Novershtern, these two words are not used "as an either /or proposition, but as two antithetical poles inextricably yoked together."[32] This conclusion is bolstered by the Nietzschean energy that animates both concepts. Novershtern points out that *shtoyb* is "the one word which best embodies the extreme nihilistic impulse within the eschatological vision" and that the rising of the dead in Acts III and IV represents the "extreme realization of the nihilistic vision."[33] Likewise,

> The stirring dance, joined by living and dead, Jews and Gentiles, *pritsim* and ordinary people, is primarily meant to obscure any differences of ideology, class, and nation or religion. The overwhelming erotic energy released in the dance eradicates slogans and disempowers words. This dance of death is the anticlimax of the vision of redemption; the elimination of all accepted categories and the "harmonic anarchy" of the present replaces the hopes for a new harmonic order.[34]

This dance is thus a category-eliminating force that represents something of a letdown as a utopian recipe for earthly redemption. It might therefore be said that the central theme of the work is built around the search for an amelioration of the Jewish predicament, somewhere between decay and destruction (*shtoyb*) on the one hand, and the primal, category-eliminating force of the dance on the other. But "dance" is no more a realistic option than is "dust," as is revealed in the way that dance is contextualized in the drama as originating from a compromised "spirit of music."

---

32. Abraham Novershtern, "Between Dust and Dance: Peretz's Drama and the Rise of Yiddish Modernism," *Prooftexts* 12 (1992): 71–90, on 81. Novershtern cites the Bundist literary critic Leo Finkelshteyn as an example of the typical misunderstanding of this concept. Finkelshteyn wrote in 1928 that "In vacillating between 'dust' and 'dance' the Jester eventually prefers the dance, as dancing is the rebellion of *joie de vivre.*" (*Loshn yidish un yidisher kiem* [Yiddish Language and Jewish Survival] (Mexico, 1954), 166; cited in Novershtern, 90 n. 8).

33. Ibid., 79 and 80.

34. Ibid., 81.

Several important passages in the play invoke a putative prehistory for the dramatic events taking place in the marketplace, a prehistory involving the destruction of musical forces and their subservience to the demonic, non-Jewish idol from which the Jester calls forth the Wanderer's prophetic dream. These passages allude to a traumatic event that preceded the action of the play: the gargoyle sucked "the musicians" down the well to their death. The Folk Poet (*heymisher dikhter*), a character appropriate to recalling such a legendary event, turns the story into the following song (*lid*):

> Haven't you heard of the terrible event,
> What happened with the musical band (*kapele*), the one from here?
> At midnight, from the nobleman's ball,
> From the nobleman's ball, from Monastery Street!
> Without *tzitzes* came the troupe (*di klezmer*),
> Fiddle, trumpet, drum, and bass.
>
> The band of musicians (*klezmer*) come from the nobleman's ball
> (Having eaten across from the nobles),
> Having drunk a drought, eaten a pagan (*akum*) slice,
> Drunk from lust (*tayve*), drunk from wine.
> At midnight
> The idol (*getz*) awoke;
> It took them and pulled them into the well!
> They leapt one after another in order...

Bay nakht oyfn altn mark 311–24 (translation mine)

Instead of the birth of tragedy out of music, here we see the death of music, the sacrifice of the drunken band of musicians at the hands of the pagan deity, "a long forgotten god from before synagogue and church" (12–13) "who cast his spell and pulled them into the well" (6–7). Later, the musicians are pulled by the Jester from the well and resurrected. Noson the drunk runs over to the gargoyle, snatches the horn from its head, and uses it as a baton; the musicians strike up a polka, which turns into the prayer for the dead. It is this music that animates the general dance.

The very scenery of the drama depicts music (and, by extension, literature) as originating from a tradition antithetical to Judaism and capable of disrupting the categories upon which Jewish society is built. The idol or well-god (*brunemgetz*), a statue that dominates the central square of the town and serves as a conversation piece and mythological touchstone for the drama, is described as half man and half woman (*halb man un halb vayb*).[35] In Act I, a boy asks another about the nature of the statue, "A he or

---

35. This statue was only schematically represented in the few productions of the play, as a down-hanging hand in the Moscow production of 1925, or as a kind of abstract, Cycladic or Venus of Willendorf-like figurine by the Vilna troupe in 1928. In the Warsaw production, there was no trace of the statue.

a she?" and is answered "Both together!" (287). A girl replies, "I heard it from my mother" (288), confirming the superstitious quality of the tale. In earlier versions of the play, the statue is described as an *androginus* "hermaphrodite," a word of Greek origin that is fitting as an analogue to the effeminate Dionysus and to the widespread reputation of the ancient Greeks in general. Khone Shmeruk finds in the image an allusion to a powerful wave of romantic ideology promoted by Przybyszewski in Poland during the nineteenth and early twentieth centuries.[36] While the hermaphroditic gargoyle may thus in some refined way allude to the loss of Jewish intellectuals to the libertine culture of the time, I would argue that its androgynous qualities represent its ability to provoke madness, the same loss of boundaries and categories also promoted by the dance. The madness of the gargoyle is in some crucial sense the means by which the band of musicians, already drunk with wine and lust and missing their *tzitzes*, were enchanted and sucked into the well. Moreover, the well itself stands for the abyss of madness governed by the gargoyle; it is into this abyss that music is relegated. This image thus graphically depicts the ambivalence of Peretz's drama toward its own universalistic aspirations *qua* literature. The answer to the ills of the Jewish people lies in avoiding the Scylla of the category-eliminating features of music, dance, and the demonic forces that govern them, and the Charybdis of ultimate destruction and annihilation represented by *shtoyb*, "dust."

As Shmeruk has shown, Peretz engaged in a polemic against art for art's sake and against foreign influence on Jewish literature, advocating instead a return to the Bible and prophecy and upholding H. N. Bialik as a model.[37] In *Bay nakht oyfn altn mark*, this polemic against foreign influence and art for art's sake finds its symbolic analogue in the depiction of precisely the original elements of Greek tragedy, according to Aristotelian tradition: music, dance, and the specter of Dionysus. These elements are at once the ground and occasion for Peretz's drama, and yet are firmly rejected by it, as if the play is attempting both to make use of and distance itself from the universalistic claims of the Dionysian origins of tragedy, embodied in the hermaphroditic statue of the pagan deity. The problem is that the characters are drawn to the gargoyle; the Folk Poet is fascinated by its place in local legend; and Peretz's drama revels in the dancing corpses of the drowned musicians whose death was the precondition of the play's action. It would appear that vilifying the gargoyle is in its own way a return to Dionysus.

Sholem Aleichem and Y. L. Peretz, in response to Aristotelian and Eurocentric theories about the pagan roots of literature, were both attracted to

---

36. Shmeruk, *Peretz's Vision of Despair*, 176–180.

37. Ibid., 100–24, esp. 104–106 on foreign influence and the need for a return to the Bible, and 113–116 on the drama's invocation of the poetry and vision of Bialik.

and repulsed by the literary genres connected to European literature, the Greco-Roman classical tradition, and even Dionysus. In creating the Yiddish canon, Sholem Aleichem addressed this ambivalence by composing novels that speak to the centrality of Jewish music in Yiddish literature as well as to the dangers posed by music to Jewish culture. For Peretz, the bizarre mix of music, dance, alcohol, and paganism in *Bay nakht oyfn altn mark* represents a powerful marker of animosity toward the genre of tragedy. These "canon conscious" works of both authors meditate on the extent to which Yiddish literature might be analogous to music, an art pure and universal in theory, though certainly not in practice. They view music and the poetic force it animates as both native to Judaism and yet foreign and demonic, as a dangerous necessity for the creation of the Yiddish canon and a modern Jewish culture alike.

Joyce's Yiddish:
Modernism, Translation, and the Jews

RACHEL RUBINSTEIN

In *The Modern Jewish Canon* Ruth Wisse makes the conscious decision to include primarily those works of Jewish literature available in English translation.[1] While her decision is mainly utilitarian, a gesture to her generally North American, English-speaking readership, as well as a result of the book's genesis as a university course at Harvard, it still suggests a relationship between translation and canon formation that I intend to examine in this essay. I am not here concerned, however, with texts in Jewish languages that have been translated into English (and thus more easily assimilated into a Western literary canon), but rather with the relationship of specifically Yiddish writers with an English literary canon as articulated through the process of translation. I am also interested in what I discern to be occasional eruptions of Jewish language in a particular English canonical text, that is, James Joyce's *Ulysses*. What I shall discuss here is not translation, however, as much as non-translation: I am describing a series of absences, disjunctions, non-encounters, mistranslations, pseudo-translations, translations that never happened. Nevertheless, I am proceeding from the conviction that absences, silences, and gaps are important shapers of meaning, and that what a text seems to suppress can in turn become a reigning textual logic.

Yiddish modernists were energetic translators, particularly of other modernists and modernist intertexts. Translation of Greek, Latin, Old English, Chinese, Japanese, Egyptian, Italian, and other European and Eastern verse, largely through the influence of Ezra Pound, became a central characteristic of Anglo-American literary modernism and, indeed, in some accounts con-

---

I would like to heartily thank Alyssa Quint and Marilyn Reizbaum for their careful and generous readings of this piece in draft, Justin Cammy for many conversations about these materials, the conference participants and audience at the Third Annual Conference on Yiddish Culture at the University of California at Berkeley, where I presented an earlier version of this essay, and finally Ruth Wisse, an ever-inspiring teacher, for, among so many other things, introducing me first to the poets of *Di yunge* and thus to Yiddish-American modernism, and second to the great tradition of American Jewish literary criticism, both of which are in many ways the subject of this piece.

1. Among her other criteria: "As a start, I have limited myself to works of Ashkenazi Jews and their descendants that appeared in whole or in part in the twentieth century, and, except for the years of World War II, to books of prose fiction, which more than poetry pronounces its social context and cultural affinity" (Ruth Wisse, *The Modern Jewish Canon: A Journey Through Language and Culture*. The Free Press, 2000), 5.

stitutive of it.[2] "Translation," wrote Pound, "is good training, if you find that your original matter 'wobbles' when you try to rewrite it. The meaning of the poem to be translated can not 'wobble.'"[3] Translation for Pound was both a means of cultivating "modernist" poetic values such as linguistic precision, as well as fashioning an individual and collective sense of cosmopolitan, modernist authorial identity. To translate from other languages was to further dramatize the modern experiences of travel, exile, and expatriate sojourning that defined modernist expression.

For Yiddish poets in the United States, engagement with the modernist scene via translation could serve as an assertion of modern and American, as well as cosmopolitan and transnational, identity. Dovid Ignatov and Reuben Eisland, members of the aestheticist American Yiddish group *Di yunge*, left in their papers Yiddish translations of Pound alongside translations from the Chinese poetry in which he was so interested, plans to translate John Gould Fletcher for *Shriftn* (1912–26), and, in *Shriftn* itself, published translations of Rabindranath Tagore, Japanese haiku, Chinese and Egyptian poetry, Walt Whitman, and Native American chant. All their source materials were culled from American modernist journals.[4] Mikhl Likht, a member of the modernist group *In zikh*, translated T.S. Eliot's essay "Tradition and the Individual Talent" in 1927,[5] and the same year published in *Unzer Bukh* a group of translations of modernist American poets that included William Carlos Williams, Mina Loy, Marianne Moore, Carl Sandburg, Wallace Stevens, Eliot, Ezra Pound, John Gould Fletcher, Malcolm Cowley, e.e. cummings, Hart Crane, and, as proto-modernist model, Emily Dickinson. In his introduction to these republished translations in 1954, N.B. Minkov, another member of *In zikh*, explains that Likht had read these poems as they were emerging in magazines such as *Broom*, *Poetry*, *The Dial*, and *The New Republic* in the early 1920s. Minkov goes on to say that Likht chose to translate both famous and little-known poets that he felt were creating exemplary "modernist" poetry, which in his definition meant speaking in a natural, common, and democratic idiom: *"poetishe iberlebungen in der geredter shprakh"* ("poetic experiences in plain speech").[6] Thus, Eliot, Pound, Moore, and Sandburg

---

2. See, for instance, Steven G. Yao, *Translation and the Languages of Modernism: Gender, Politics, Language* (Palgrave Macmillan, 2002).

3. Ezra Pound, "A Few Dont's By An Imagist," *Poetry*, 1913.

4. See my essay, "Going Native, Becoming Modern: American Indians, Walt Whitman, and the Yiddish Poet," *American Quarterly* 58: 2 (2006).

5. David G. Roskies, "The Achievement of American Yiddish Modernism," *Go and Study: Essays and Studies in Honor of Alfred Jospe*, eds. Raphael Jospe and Samuel Z. Fishman (Washington D.C.: B'nai B'rith Hillel Foundation, 1980), 363.

6. N.B. Minkov, "Introduction," *Moderne Amerikaner Poezye Lider, Ibergezetst fun Mikhl Likht* (Buenos Aires, 1954), 11. I must here thank David Roskies, who introduced me to Mikhl Likht and gave me the volumes from which I quote.

are side by side in Likht's collection with the now less familiar Walter Conrad Arensberg and Clara Shanafeld. Yiddish poets, clearly, were engaged with Anglo-American modernism, and had their own arguments to make, via translation, about its models and practitioners. But was Anglo-American modernism at all engaged with Yiddish?

Perhaps one of Wisse's most endearing and enduring contributions to the field of Yiddish literature is her transcription and discussion, in a 1996 essay, of the first twenty-two lines of a Yiddish poem that had up until then been oral tradition, a piece of literary lore. I speak of course of Saul Bellow and Isaac Rosenfeld's "translation" of T.S. Eliot's "The Love Song of J. Alfred Prufrock." In *The Modern Jewish Canon*, Wisse mentions this Yiddish spoof briefly, using it to illustrate the point at which "American Jewish letters gave notice of its independence from Anglo-American modernism."[7] In her earlier essay, "Language as Fate: Reflections on Jewish Literature in America," she offers a more elaborate discussion of the translation/parody, "Der shir hashirim fun Mendl Pumshtok," composed sometime during the 1930s, when the two writers were students in Chicago. "How sweet it must have felt," Wisse begins, "to mock the Anglo-American snob in the Jewish immigrant vernacular!"[8] Eliot's poem, "a signature poem of twentieth-century modernism," is thus a particularly fruitful target. The parody is "packed with enough Jewish national-religious imagery to remind the upstart Christian of what constitutes true cultural resonance," and at the same time, "pungent Yiddish also pulls the poem downward, into the colloquial vitality of the Jewish everyday."[9] "Mendl Pumshtok" utterly deflates the original as it argues the richness of Yiddish's historical and religious resources and its linguistic flexibility; the poem asserts Yiddish as the ideal, and even more authentic, site of modernist expression.

The exemplary literary modernist who haunts Wisse's *Modern Jewish Canon*, however, is not Eliot—a rather easy target for the American Yiddish satirist because of his Anglophilia, elitism, and anti-Semitism—but rather James Joyce, whose position vis-à-vis the Jews was rather more complex and ambiguous. Joyce, after all, chose to make the Jew, Leopold Bloom, the central and emblematic figure of modernity and alienation in *Ulysses*, and readers have been struggling with the "Jewishness" of Joyce's hero, and his text, ever since. In Wisse's discussion of Jewish modernists in Hebrew, Yiddish and English, Joyce appears continually as both gold standard and

7. *Modern Jewish Canon*, 289.

8. Ruth Wisse, "Language as Fate: Reflections on Jewish Literature in America," *Literary Strategies: Jewish Texts and Contexts; Studies in Contemporary Jewry, An Annual*, ed. Ezra Mendelsohn (Oxford University Press, 1996), 130. The beginning of the Yiddish parody is also reproduced and briefly discussed by Gene Bluestein, "Prufrock-Shmufrock," *Yiddish* 7:1 (1987).

9. Ibid., 130.

bogeyman. In her discussion of Jacob Glatstein (Yankev Glatshteyn) and the poets of the American Yiddish modernist group *In Zikh*, she observes: "They exploited the suppleness of their vernacular by incorporating vocabulary and sounds from other languages, paralleling the modernists, like Ezra Pound and James Joyce, who had re-imagined English as the universal tongue."[10] In her discussion of S.Y. Agnon, Wisse writes that "the effect of totality that James Joyce achieves through stream of consciousness and a syncretic English...Agnon accomplishes through the interpenetration of symbolic, midrashic, homiletic, and realistic layers of narrative in the simultaneity of Hebrew."[11] In her discussion of A.M. Klein's *The Second Scroll*, Wisse comments that Klein's "adoration of language led him to its English master, James Joyce. As well as paying Joyce the compliment of imitation, Klein spent many years working on an interpretive commentary on *Ulysses* that applied the technique of talmudic exegesis to the modernist text."[12]

Joyce's "Jewish" novel even merits a discussion of its own in Wisse's modern Jewish canon. This "classic of modernism" pays "the cosmopolitan Jew the ultimate compliment by making so much of Bloom...what a welcome departure this magnification was from the unsympathetic Jewish portraits by T.S. Eliot, Wyndham Lewis, Ezra Pound, Ernest Hemingway!" On the other hand, Joyce worship would eventually give way to increasing skepticism: "Not until the end of the century did some Jewish disciples of Joyce perceive that he may have cuckolded the Jew politically as well as maritally at the cost of starring him in the modernist epic."[13]

This dramatic change in attitude toward Joyce is perhaps best exemplified by Henry Roth. If students of Anglo-American literary modernism come across Yiddish at all, it is generally through the scrim of his novel, *Call It Sleep*, published in 1934. The novel is written, for the most part, in English, though in its traces of actual Yiddish and in the stylized English it uses consistently to represent Yiddish, it impresses itself upon the reader as a "Yiddish" novel. It is experienced by the reader as if it were a translation. Yiddish, as Hannah Wirth-Nesher has suggested, "is the absent source language" of the text.[14] The "trace" of actual Yiddish that is at moments present in the text can be read then in a kind of Derridean sense, as the "essence of Being" that, in turn, haunts the language of the novel.

---

10. *The Modern Jewish Canon*, 167–168.

11. Ibid., 188.

12. Ibid., 259–260.

13. Ibid., 246.

14. Hana Wirth-Nesher, "Between Mother Tongue and Native Language: Multilingualism and Multiculturalism in Henry Roth's *Call It Sleep*," *Prooftexts: A Journal of Jewish Literary History* (1990). Reprinted as the Afterword to *Call It Sleep* (New York: Farrar, Straus, Giroux, 1991).

Call It Sleep, about the spiritual and sexual crises of a Jewish immigrant child, is most frequently described as "Joycean," and not long ago I tested the limits of this description by teaching the novel up against Joyce's *Ulysses*. I expected to find what Roth claimed he learned from Joyce: "this awed realization that you didn't have to go anywhere at all except around the corner to flesh out a literary work of art—given some kind of vision, of course."[15] That is, Roth applied Joyce's narrative strategies to the materials of Jewish immigrant New York, creating a messianic child hero who is both Bloom and Dedalus, both wandering Jew and artist in the making. What I rediscovered was something that, since my initial encounter with *Ulysses*, I had forgotten: there is, in fact, a trace of Yiddish (or rather a *representation* or evocation of Yiddish) in *Ulysses*, and that this, as much as anything else in the novel, might have provided Roth with his inspiration for *Call It Sleep*. Roth's novel, I began to think, was, in addition to all the other ways in which it rewrote *Ulysses*, also an elaboration and dramatization, if not a correction, of the trace of Yiddish in *Ulysses*: the novel whose strategies of linguistic play, intertextual quoting and adaptation, and use of stream of consciousness to represent the chaotic way in which the individual experiences modern urban life, we now think of as modeling what would become normative literary modernism.[16]

Yet if Henry Roth began his literary career as a disciple of Joycean modernism, several decades later, writing his autobiographical novel from a position of renewed Jewish affiliation and passionate Zionism, Roth criticizes his former "literary father" for depriving Bloom of any historical, linguistic, national Jewish content, thus creating as his representative Jew an "Irish quasi-Marrano of the year 1904." "What unspeakable gall that took, gall and insufferable egotism! Gall and ignorance!"[17] Wisse describes Roth as convinced that "it was Joyce's prose—more than Marxism, more than anti-Semitism—that lured him into the 'stupendous gravitational field' of modernism and erased whatever had made him and could have maintained him as a Jew."[18] Wisse suggests that Roth's imploded love affair with canonical modernism and with Joyce accompanies, or is the result of, his "repossession" of Jewishness and a "Jewish" literary style.

15. Bonnie Lyons, "An Interview with Henry Roth," *Shenandoah* 25:1 (1973), 60.

16. For this definition of modernism and a discussion of the relationship between "Joycean modernism" and *Call It Sleep*, see Brian McHale, "Henry Roth in Nighttown, or, containing *Ulysses*," *New Essays on Call It Sleep*," Hana Wirth-Nesher, ed. (Cambridge University Press, 1996).

17. Henry Roth, *Mercy of a Rude Stream*, vol. 2: *A Diving Rock on the Hudson* (New York: St. Martin's Press, 1995), 116; quoted in *Modern Jewish Canon*, 247.

18. *Modern Jewish Canon*, 248.

Maurice Samuel, on the other hand, represents an opposite trajectory, moving from condemnation of Joyce's representation of the Jew in 1929 to a kind of grudging admiration in 1966. Samuel, who is briefly discussed by Wisse in *The Modern Jewish Canon*, was a critic, translator of Yiddish and Hebrew literature (the translator, in fact, who introduced Peretz, Bashevis, Y.Y. Singer, Sholem Aleichem, and Asch to English-speaking audiences), novelist, and memoirist, and noted Zionist of his day. In his long essay "Bloom in Bloomusalem," published in two installments in the journal *Reflex*, Samuel reflects upon the theme of Jewishness in *Ulysses*. "Bloom is all (or nearly all) vulgarity, carnality, smallness, in his reflections, in his suffering, in his kindnesses."[19] Acknowledging the greatness of the novel, describing it as "too bitter, too wild and too difficult a book,"[20] Samuel nevertheless is "compelled to wonder what complex in the mind of Joyce explains this cosmic loathing for the little Jew, Bloom."[21] And in what serves as a deflating counterpoint in Samuel's catalogue of attacks upon Bloom over the course of *Ulysses*, the critic interjects a Yiddish punchline after one of his lengthy quotations from the novel: "*Es iz oich a standpunkt*" ("this is also a point of view").[22] Samuel's wry Yiddish has the same ironic and cutting effect as does Bellow and Rosenfeld's more elaborate Eliot parody. Samuel's Yiddish also serves to point out that despite the "magnification" of Bloom's Jewishness in *Ulysses*, there is a notable absence of Yiddish in Bloom.

History was to prove Samuel wrong, at least concerning Joyce's Jewish loathing: in France Joyce helped Jews escape Austria and Germany from the Nazi onslaught, and when he himself applied to enter Switzerland in 1940 he was initially refused an entry visa because the Swiss authorities believed he himself was a Jew.[23] In 1966, reviewing Saul Bellow's novel *Herzog*, Maurice Samuel compared the novel to *Ulysses*, and Herzog to Bloom. Samuel was not the first critic to discern this relationship between the two novels: Moses Herzog, after all, is the name of a minor character in *Ulysses*, a Jewish grocer who is mocked in conversation for suing a customer who won't pay a bill: "Jesus, I had to laugh at the little jewy getting his shirt out: *he drink me my teas. He eat me my sugars. Because he no pay me my monies?*"[24] Samuel calls Bellow's mode of narration "Joycean," and charac-

---

19. Maurice Samuel, "Bloom in Bloomusalem," *Reflex* (January 1929), 15.

20. Ibid., 11.

21. Maurice Samuel, "Bloom in Bloomusalem," *Reflex* (February 1929), 14.

22. Maurice Samuel, "Bloom in Bloomusalem," *Reflex* (January 1929), 19.

23. See Ira B. Nadel, *Joyce and the Jews: Culture and Texts* (University of Iowa Press, 1989), 230–232, 235. Also see Marilyn Reizbaum, *James Joyce's Judaic Other* (Stanford University Press, 1999), 25–26, 75.

24. *Ulysses* (Vintage International Edition, 1990), 292.

terizes both *Ulysses* and *Herzog* as "major modern studies in Jewish assimilation."[25] He suggests similarities between Bloom and Herzog, for one, a
"strain of masochism." But they are both "inveterate thinking men, interested in people, processes, and general laws." Herzog is "Leopold Bloom with
a Ph.D."[26] "The outstanding resemblance—and difference—between Leopold Bloom and Moses Herzog lies in their respective efforts to come to
terms with their self-identification as Jews while trying to leave their mark
on the world."[27]

At this point, however, Samuel departs from the genre of the conventional literary review and begins a narrative of his own, a kind of *midrash*
on *Herzog* in which Samuel recounts his own relationship with the "real"
Herzog. If there is "little of the Jew left in Bloom," who "has only bits and
snippets of Jewish information, fragments of Hebrew phrases and quotations, and no Yiddish at all," Herzog, on the other hand, comes from a "thoroughly Jewish home,"[28] and Samuel, during the course of their many conversations, is "astonished by the quality of his Yiddish."[29] In fact, in this
"reminiscence," Yiddish poetry becomes the site upon which Samuel and
Herzog develop their bond, particularly over Glatshteyn's modernist poetry:
"he did things with Yiddish," Samuel tells Herzog, "that had never been
done before, revealed in it an unbelievable range of styles."[30] The last time
Samuel sees Herzog, Herzog recites for him a Glatshteyn poem from memory.[31] Samuel's narrative thus attempts to rehabilitate the suppressed Yiddish
of Bellow's Herzog and, by extension, perhaps of Joyce's Bloom.

Whether or not to define Leopold Bloom as a "real Jew" was the very
subject of the earliest commentary on the Jew in Joyce, and subsequent
inquiries into Joyce and the Jews have hinged on Bloom's vexed, unfixable,
and ambivalent Jewishness. To sum up: Bloom is the son of a Gentile mother
and a Jewish father who converted to Protestantism. Bloom himself has con-

---

25. Maurice Samuel, "My Friend, the Late Moses Herzog," *Midstream* April 1966,
reprinted in *The Worlds of Maurice Samuel: Selected Writings*, Milton Hindus, ed.
(Philadelphia: The Jewish Publication Society of America, 1977), 410.

26. Ibid., 410.

27. Ibid., 411.

28. Ibid., 412, 415.

29. Ibid., 422.

30. Ibid., 431.

31. The Glatshteyn poem quoted in Samuel's piece is "Tsvey berglekh" ("Two Mounds").
Samuel "interprets" Herzog's interest in the poem as illustrative of his grief over his
dead mother and his lost heritage. It is not difficult, however, to make a leap from a
lost mother to a lost mother-tongue. Glatshteyn, as it turns out, was a Yiddish poet who
was particularly involved with Joyce and is the only one, to my knowledge, to have
produced a kind of "translation" or parody of Joyce in Yiddish. This will be discussed
later in the essay.

verted to Catholicism (twice, in fact), of whose rituals and philosophies, however, he still remains ignorant. He isn't circumcised. He remembers only fragments of incorrect Hebrew; he thinks about Palestine when he sees an advertisement in a Jewish paper, but ultimately rejects Jewish nationalism. There are, in fact, some suggestions in the novel that Bloom is rather active in Irish nationalist circles. Despite this, Bloom is constantly reminded of his Jewish difference by other characters in the novel, but only once gives way to a rebellious and transgressive rage, when he tells the ultranationalist and anti-Semitic Citizen that: "Mendelssohn was a jew and Karl Marx and Mercadante and Spinoza. And the Saviour was a jew and his father was a jew. Your God...Your God was a jew. Christ was a jew like me."[32]

As Reizbaum notes, "The men to whom Bloom compares himself are converts, revaluers of faith, apostates in one sense or another."[33] The open question of Bloom's Jewishness has thus been taken up in a number of ways by Joyce scholarship: racially, nationally, emotionally, halakhically, linguistically. It is this last category, language, with which I am primarily engaged. It seems that Joyce scholars have, by and large, taken for granted that Bloom's Jewish language is, and ought to be, Hebrew and not Yiddish. Bloom, as he moves through Dublin, remembers bits of the Passover Haggada, the Hebrew alphabet, snatches from Song of Songs, among other, usually incorrectly transcribed fragments. Bloom's incorrect and incomplete Hebrew is due either to his character's attenuated Jewishness or to Joyce's insufficient mastery of the language. If Bloom were "real," we might speculate, as the child of a Hungarian immigrant father, growing up in a Dublin that at the turn of the century was populated mainly by Russian-Jewish refugees fleeing violence in Eastern Europe, lacking a religious education, he would have arguably been as, if not more, familiar with Yiddish as with Hebrew. Joyce was perfectly aware of the immigrant Jewish neighborhoods in Dublin, where Yiddish was the vernacular, as is evident from his early prose.[34]

It seems then that Joyce deliberately chose to represent Jewishness linguistically through Hebrew for a variety of reasons that have been rather thoroughly catalogued by Joyce scholarship: he wanted to highlight and then interrogate the connections he saw between ancient Greek and ancient Semitic cultures, and between Hellenism and Hebraism; he was

---

32. James Joyce, *Ulysses*, 342.

33. Reizbaum, 72.

34. In an unpublished 1904 essay/fiction Joyce describes his hero writing "amid a chorus of peddling Jews' gibberish and Gentile clamour." Ira Nadel comments: "This conventional scene of Jews speaking to one another in Yiddish, often thought to be a 'secret language' by Gentiles, evokes stereotypes of Dublin Jewish merchants and markets of 'Little Jerusalem,' the Jewish neighbourhood near the South Circular Road, where the hero of *Stephen Hero* walks with Emma" (*Joyce and the Jews*, 57).

interested in the revival of Hebrew and of Jewish political nationalism as a cognate for the revival of Gaelic and Irish nationalism; he wrote *Ulysses* mainly in Trieste, Zurich, and Paris, where he encountered and befriended Sephardic and German Jews who were Hebraists and not Yiddishists. "Jewish" books Joyce had in his Trieste library included Herzl's *Der Judenstaat*, H. Sacher's *Zionism and the Jewish Future*, and George Foot Moore's *The Literature of the Old Testament*.[35] A naturalized link between Jewishness and Hebrew has now become rather commonplace in discussions of Joyce.[36] I mean here to disentangle this link and to unearth the buried traces of Yiddish in *Ulysses*, as well as to ask how various kinds of readers have chosen to manage the question of Jewish language in *Ulysses*. That is to say, it is not only the absence, or near-absence, of Yiddish in Joyce, but the subsequent near-absence of Joyce in Yiddish that constitutes my subject.

The first effort to translate *Ulysses* was as early as 1927, into German, and it has since been translated into French, Italian, Spanish, Chinese, Japanese, Latvian, Croatian, Czech, and Hungarian. Joyce was very interested in the translation of his own work, and worked with his German, Italian, and French translators. He himself translated from German, and into Norwegian and French, among other languages.[37] Joyce knew, as Yiddish modernist

---

35. See Reizbaum, 133, for a list of books in Joyce's Trieste library, and for books that he was known to have read.

36. One exception is in Neil R. Davison's *James Joyce, Ulysses, and the Construction of Jewish Identity: Culture, Biography, and "The Jew" in Modernist Europe* (Cambridge University Press, 1996) in which he notes that "on occasion Bloom underscores his thoughts with Yiddish. As Hebrew was primarily a liturgical language in 1904, these Yiddish terms again represent Bloom's cultural 'Jewishness'. He uses such expressions throughout the day, as in his estimation of Denis Breen as "Messhugga" (U8.314). These snippets of another language now become mostly an intimate inner voice, a manner of personal emphasis, perhaps parallel to the use of Gaelic of many turn-of-the-century Dubliners...Bloom thus appears to have a different mother tongue from other Irishmen—as will be confirmed in 'Ithaca' (U17.724–760)" (206–207). I think Davison imagines, to some degree, more Yiddish in *Ulysses* than actually exists in the novel, but this is a rare discussion in which Yiddish is mentioned as the probable "mother-tongue" of Leopold Bloom. Ira Nadel also mentions the scarcity of Yiddish, explaining it thus: "Yiddish is 'the language of Jewish exile and sorrow,' Hebrew the language of revived hope. In *Ulysses*, Bloom uses almost no Yiddish, only incomplete and incorrect Hebrew. In recalling this language of hope in the text, Bloom provides an optimistic glimmer of a Jewish present and future" (*Joyce and the Jews*, 193). A possible "hidden" source for Bloom's Yiddish is a 1904 Dublin trial, *Wought v. Zaretsky*, mentioned twice in *Ulysses*. In this case, a Jew was accused of masquerading as an emigration official and of obtaining money from another Jew for passage to Canada. The trial would have "caught Joyce's eye" not just because of its content, but because "the translator for a witness who spoke only Yiddish was named Bloom" (Reizbaum, 15).

37. See Yao, *Translation and the Languages of Modernism*. Also see *James Joyce Quarterly*, IV, 3 (1967), an issue devoted entirely to Joyce and translation.

translators did, that the translational encounter is also, at the same time, a mutually transforming encounter. When he "translated" the Odyssey in *Ulysses*, like Bellow and Rosenfeld, he both elevated his narrative and domesticated an epic.

Ulysses was never translated into Yiddish. However, in 1985, there was a translation of *Ulysses* into Hebrew. Despite the presence of Hebrew throughout *Ulysses*, Hebrew proved to be a difficult language in which to translate the novel, according to the translator, Yael Renan. The central problem, Renan explained in a letter to Joyce scholar Ira Nadel, was

> the relative poverty of Hebrew in both vocabulary and stylistic differentia-
> tion of "registers": slang is hardly existent (most of it is Arabic, Yiddish, etc.),
> nor is there a colloquial style that does not deviate too much from the correct
> rules of the Academia of Hebrew Language (rules that are commonly ignored
> in conversational styles of even educated Israelis). The most insoluble prob-
> lem, however, is the lack of a continuous history of Hebrew literature, a lack
> that leaves me without equivalents for the historical styles in "Oxen of the
> Sun."[38]

"Oxen of the Sun" is the episode of *Ulysses* that rehearses, through a par-
ody of literary styles, the history of English language and literature. By the climactic end of the episode, "proper" English has been taken over by a "frightful jumble" of, in Joyce's words, "Pidgin English, nigger English, Cockney, Irish, Bowery slang and broken doggerel,"[39] all this in addition to Latin, French, Spanish, Gaelic, and German. This linguistic and dialectical melee, Joyce seems to suggest, will be the Language of Modernism. This new language of modernism, however, has within it no Hebrew, but does indeed have a trace of Yiddish, or rather Yinglish. From amidst the babble of drunken voices at the pub a Yiddish-English hybrid emerges: "Vyfor you no me tell? Vel, I ses, if that ain't a sheeny naches, vel, I vil get misha mishin-nah."[40] Joyce, in a letter to his German translator, translates "Sheeny Na-ches" as "Jew Thing;" something a "Jew would do."[41] Joyce also translated the Yiddish idiomatic "misha mishinnah" ("misa-meshune"), correctly, as

---

38. Quoted in Nadel, *Joyce and the Jews*, 258 n. 61. This critique prompts some questions
    for me, one of which being why Renan evidently does not share Wisse's appraisal of
    the Joycean possibilities of Hebrew in, for example, S.Y. Agnon. Renan also doesn't
    seem to consider that an ideal translation of Joyce into a Jewish language might be
    multilingual, would involve Hebrew and Yiddish, as well as, perhaps, Arabic and
    Judeo-Spanish, and thus a mix of registers, idioms, dialects, and linguistic and literary
    histories. Henry Roth tried to do something like this in *Call It Sleep*, introducing Polish
    and Hebrew presences into his Yiddish-English narrative.

39. Quoted in Don Gifford and Robert Seidman, *Notes for Joyce: An Annotation of James
    Joyce's Ulysses* (New York: E.P. Dutton and Co., Inc. 1974), 362.

40. *Ulysses*, 426.

41. Gifford, 366.

"bad, violent, and unprepared for death or end." Joyce identified both these phrases as "jüdische."[42]

More flecks of Yiddish, or pseudo-Yiddish, appear in the "Circe" episode, which is usually read as the most wild, untamed, and disruptive episode in the novel. Bloom has protectively followed Stephen Dedalus, the young would-be writer, to the red-light district, called Nighttown, where they visit Bella Cohen's brothel. The episode, in the form of a play, chronicles both the "real" goings-on in the brothel and the hallucinations, bizarre imaginings, and physical projections of both Bloom's and Stephen's unconscious. Bloom either remembers or imagines his long-dead father rebuking him:

> Rudolph: "Second halfcrown waste money today. I told you not go with drunken goy ever. You catch no money. Bloom: Ja, ich weiss, papachi...Rudolph (severely). One night they bring you home drunk as a dog after spend your good money. What you call them running chaps? Bloom: ...Harriers, father. Only that once. Rudolph: Once! Mud head to foot. Cut your hand open. Lockjaw. They make you kaput, Leopoldleben. You watch them chaps. Bloom (weakly): They challenged me to a sprint. It was muddy. I slipped. Rudolph (With contempt) Goim nachez. Nice spectacles for your poor mother.[43]

A little later in the episode, Bloom hallucinates an exchange with his grandfather, who curses the Gentiles in a more *daytshmerish* (Germanic) Yiddish: *Verfluchte Goim!*[44]

Don Gifford, the annotator of *Ulysses*, identifies Bloom's line, *Ja, ich weiss papachi*, as Yiddish, as well as Bloom's father's line, the scornful "Goim nachez." Gifford translates this, not quite correctly, as "the luck of the Gentiles."[45] *Goyim nakhes* is more correctly to be understood as pride in an accomplishment that only a Gentile would feel, thus appropriate for describing the young Leopold's desire to run in races, or get drunk in pubs. This is a deliberate echoing of the earlier phrase "Sheeny naches," which is not a "Jew Thing," then, as much as pride in an accomplishment that only a Jew would feel.[46]

---

42. The letter to his German translator, Georg Goyert, is dated March 6 1927. See *James Joyce Quarterly* IV, 3, 194; quoted in Gifford, 366. My thanks to Anita Norich for confirming the accuracy of Joyce's translation, as well as for pointing out that "Goyim nakhes" was in fact a German-Jewish expression.

43. *Ulysses*, 437–338.

44. Ibid., 520. This is also identified by Gifford as Yiddish.

45. Gifford, 375.

46. Marilyn Reizbaum notes, "In part *goyim naches* in context is, in a variation on the original meaning, the pleasure non-Jews get off of Jewish apostasy as in Jews' betrayal of the faith through eating pork or running races (or, to put it another way, it is a goy thing to get such pleasure in un-jewing). This is my understanding of the term *nakhes* here—

These traces, or evocations, of Yiddish that erupt in the most wild and disorderly moments in *Ulysses* ultimately point to the palpable absence of Yiddish in the rest of the novel.[47] Toni Morrison has argued famously that white-authored American literature has been consistently shaped by an invisible, suppressed, and unacknowledged non-white Africanist presence.[48] Emily Budick, after Morrison, asks if African-American literature, and American literature generally, has, therefore, been shaped by a suppressed Jewish presence:

> Just as a repressed relation to black materials may be imagined to vibrate within much American narrative from the seventeenth century on, so within African-American fiction, as within white Christian writing generally, an unacknowledged relation (appropriative, displacing, and even hostile) can be understood to structure the text—at least when read by a Jewish reader through the perspective of Jewish history.[49]

For a Jewish reader interested in Yiddish modernism, it is difficult, when reading *Ulysses, not* to imagine Yiddish as the unacknowledged and suppressed linguistic presence that nevertheless shapes even as it threatens to disrupt both the novel and the normative modernism it came to model.

Yiddish may be an invisible and yet guiding presence in *Ulysses* scholarship as well. Marilyn Reizbaum, for instance, describes her first Joyce symposium in 1979, her initiation into the world of Joyce studies. She remembers meeting the eminent and prolific Joyce scholar Bernard Benstock, who was, she remembers, "the only Joycean ever to have addressed me in Yid-

---

it's one for the *verfluchte goyim*, as it were. *Sheeny naches* as Jew thing or, synonymously, a thing a Jew would do, is interesting too; it turns it about a bit, like a parody of the original, especially in that the term sheeny is the goyim's pejorative term for the Jew incorporated into the expression of what a Jew takes pride in—again, it seems to be one for the goyim, an internalization of their view. Appropriately, the subject there in the passage seems to be cuckoldry and apostasy and how they intertwine, as elsewhere in the text. The term *misa meshuna* is also interesting in that *meshuna* means "other," "weird" or "strange," from the Hebrew. I wonder how *meshunah* in Yiddish became interchangeable with *sof* from the Hebrew, also Yiddish, in a variation on that expression (*misa sof*). That whole phrase at the end of "Oxen" is a Yiddish translation of an English vernacular phrase, something like: "if that ain't a Jew, I'll be damned. Amen." In context, it seems to refer not only to the intertwining of the subjects of apostasy and cuckoldry, but the linguistic product of such intertwining" (email to author, June 20, 2007).

47. It is worth noting, as Alyssa Quint did upon reading this piece, that the retrievable Yiddish of *Ulysses* is both brothel-inspired and about Jewish superiority and the denigration of Gentiles, thus, markedly, and even radically, transgressive.

48. Toni Morrison, *Playing in the Dark: Whiteness and the Literary Imagination* (Cambridge: Harvard University Press, 1992), 4–5.

49. Emily Miller Budick, *Blacks and Jews in Literary Conversation* (Cambridge University Press, 1998), 216–217.

dish, my first language."[50] Reizbaum, elsewhere in her study, relies quite heavily on Sander Gilman's discussions of *mauscheln*, a term of German coinage used to describe what was often imagined to be a "hidden language" of Jews, and could be affiliated variously with Hebrew, Yiddish, or an undefined "ethnic linguistic trait of Jews by which they can always be identified."[51] Is Yiddish then a suppressed, invisible, and secret language among Joyce scholars? The language in which they greet one another at conferences but not the language into which *Ulysses* could be translated? The language that may inadvertently shape their readings of *Ulysses*? Even Reizbaum, who calls for a reassessment of Joyce's modernism as a poetics of hybridity and otherness that she describes in shorthand as a "poetics of Jewishness," stops just short of explicitly connecting this to her mother tongue, Yiddish.

Reizbaum also remembers, during that same symposium, being asked in an interview with a German journalist to account for the seemingly large Jewish constituency among the critics of Joyce. She tentatively proposed then what many years later seems to her self-evident: that it was the "Jewishness of Bloom and of Joyce's work" that drew Jewish critics to Joyce. As Wisse might observe, perhaps *Ulysses* offers an opportunity for the thoroughly Hellenized Jewish scholar, the scholar conversant in the languages and literatures of the British and European canonical traditions, if not those of the Jews, to be able to, dare I say, *shep* some *sheeny naches*: to declare: "Bloom is a Jew like me," or even more rebelliously, transgressively: "Joyce is a Jew like me."

Joyce's deliberate elision of Yiddish, even in his privileging of the experience of the Jew in modernity, resulted in a culture of normative modernism—and, it must be said, a culture of scholarship on Anglo-American modernism—that took no ostensible notice of Yiddish even as it translated widely from Eastern and European languages. Yiddish modernists, at the same time, seem to have refused to attempt to translate Joyce, even as Joycean modernism inflected their writing.[52] Perhaps it is possible to read the palpa-

---

50. Reizbaum, ix.

51. Reizbaum, 52. Also see Sander Gilman, *Jewish Self-Hatred* (Baltimore: Johns Hopkins University Press, 1986).

52. On the one hand, *Ulysses* was a very long piece of prose fiction and a daunting task for any translator, and Yiddish modernists experimented mainly with poetry (with a few exceptions, such as Glatshteyn and Likht) and mostly seemed to translate other poets (with, of course, notable exceptions, such as Kafka); *Ulysses* was banned in both the United States and Great Britain until 1934 and may have been difficult for those Yiddish writers living in America to access. On the other hand, *Ulysses* was serialized in the American journal *The Little Review*, which Yiddish modernists were reading, well before 1922, until the editors were forced to discontinue because of charges of obscenity. Joyce was a literary superstar by the time his novel, to great fanfare, was published in book form.

ble absence of Joyce in Yiddish as a response to the palpable absence of Yiddish in Joyce.

Mikhl Likht published poems to "T.S.E" (T.S. Eliot) and "E.P." (Ezra Pound), but not to the modernist ("J.J.") who would have completed this triumvirate. Instead, Likht dedicated a poem to "Y.G."[53] Yankev Glatshteyn is the poet and prose artist who has been compared the most to James Joyce, and who, indeed, is the only Yiddish writer to have "translated" Joyce, or more precisely, paid parodic homage to Joyce in a 1928 prose poem titled "Ven Joyce volt geshribn idish: A Par Ode" ("If Joyce wrote Yiddish: A Par-Ode (y)"), which appeared in *Inzikh*, the New York journal Glatshteyn co-edited with Aaron Leyeles.[54] Ruth Wisse discusses this poem in her essay "Language as Fate," describing it as a "cutting parody" whose object, however, was not Joyce but rather the "local Yiddish literary scene," which Glatshteyn refers to in the poem as "literatuches," a linking of literature and backside, quite the profane inversion of Itzik Manger's more sublime coinage, "literatoyre." Wisse writes: "The fun-filled literary style that James Joyce pioneered in English perfectly suited Yiddish, a European language that had integrated at least as many linguistic strands as English, and could take at least equal delight in showing off its wit."[55]

Glatshteyn's "Par/Ode/y" is identified by Benjamin Harshav as a rendering of *Finnegans Wake*, Joyce's later work that in 1928 had appeared only in sections in some little magazines under the title "Work in Progress."[56] The first and last parts of the prose poem are in the form of a dialogue between "Yolanzio" and "Patriziano," which Glatshteyn pretends are quotations (perhaps translations) from an imaginary medieval drama called "Der Shrobdalema" (which can perhaps be translated as "The Writer's Dilemma"). Yolanzio calls Patriziano a "shraybmeshugener" (a punning of *shraybmashin*—typewriter—and lunatic) as Patriziano performs acrobatic faux-Old Yiddish linguistic riffs in which "puns and word plays" go off "like firecrackers."[57]

The middle sections of Glatshteyn's Joyce-parody, like *Finnegans Wake* (which itself, it must be said, reads rather like a Joyce parody), intersperse songs, rhymes, twisted quotations, even a mathematical equation. One relatively explicable example: "gedank oder gezang dos iz di froyge," that is, "to think or to sing that is the question," except that "froyge" plays with both "woman" or "wife" (*froy*) and "question" (*frage*).[58] Shakespeare himself is

53. See Mikhl Likht, *Gezamlte lider* (Buenos Aires: Farlag Gelye, 1957).

54. *Inzikh* 5, July 1928, 68–70.

55. Wisse, "Language as Fate," 137.

56. See *American-Yiddish Poetry: A Bilingual Anthology*, eds. Benjamin and Barbara Harshav (University of California Press, 1986).

57. Wisse, 138.

58. *Inzikh*, 70.

not immune from Glatshteyn's wordplay. All these form a nonsensical, gleeful riff around a character named "Beshi Bezek," a cognate of Joyce's "Shem the Penman," the title of and central character in book I, chapter 7 of *Finnegans Wake*.[59]

"Shem is short for Shemus as Jem is joky for Jacob," begins the section that served as Glatshteyn's inspiration.[60] Shem (Noah's son/ Semite) is short for Shemus (Seamus), which is, of course, the Irish version of James (Jem), which is "joky for Jacob," that is, the Anglicization of the biblical Jacob, just as Yankev is the Yiddish diminutive for the Hebrew Ya'akov. The kinship between Glatshteyn's and Joyce's names certainly served as the inspirational spark for Glatshteyn's Joycean riff. This section of *Work in Progress* features also a dialogue in the form of a play between "Justius" and "Mercius," in which "Mercius" (Shem) is called upon to defend himself from charges of fakery, of being "Pain the Shamman." At the end of the section Mercius demonstrates his writerly powers; he "lifts the lifewand and the dumb speak."[61] In Glatshteyn's "translation:"

Voila—Es kumt der groyse kishefmakher
Far a tsveyer un far a drayer
Makht er hokus pokus

---

59. "Beshi," built upon the Biblical Hebrew root *bosh*, "shame," clearly uses Joyce's own Shem/Shame pun. "Bezek" is the Hebrew root for "lightning," and was, in addition, a Canaanite city named in the book of Judges. *Beshi Bezek* as a phrase also perhaps recalls the phrase *bezi-bizyones*: "a great shame." Glatshteyn writes "Beshi Bezek" in Hebrew, as opposed to Yiddish orthography; it seems meant to evoke faux-Aramaic or Mishnaic Hebrew (my thanks to David Braun for pointing out this, as well as Glatshteyn's inventive "Old Yiddish" throughout the piece. He observes also that Beshi— perhaps Boshi—sounds a bit, possibly, like "Bosyak," Yiddish for barefooted person, or vagabond).

60. James Joyce, *Finnegans Wake* (New York: Viking Press, 1939), 169. This section had appeared in several little magazines before 1928, including: *This Quarter*, Milan, I.2 (Autumn-Winter 1925-1926) 108-123; *Two Worlds: A Literary Quarterly Devoted to the Increase of the Gaiety of Nations* (New York, June 1926), 545-560; *transition*, Paris, October 1927, 34-56. See James Fuller Spoerri, *Finnegans Wake by James Joyce: A Checklist* (Evanston: Northwestern University Library, 1953).

61. *Finnegans Wake*, 195. Ira Nadel argues the fundamental "Jewishness" of this chapter of the *Wake*, as well as the Jewishness of Shem (James Joyce) himself, suggesting that Shem is here linked to Moses through word plays on Semite, on circumcision, on the sacrificial lamb of Passover, on Moses' staff, and finally, a pun on Shem/Sham/asham (Hebrew for sin-offering), which suggests for Nadel that Shem, the writer-artist, is also sacrificial artist-victim (*Joyce and the Jews*, 101-102). Many Joyce critics agree with Nadel that "Shem the Penman" is both James himself and the Semite: Neil Davison writes, for instance, that "Joyce suggested through 'Shem the Penman'...that the position of the Jew was analogous to that of the twentieth-century writer, the fragmented voice (re)defining itself through the word" (*James Joyce, Ulysses, and the Construction of Jewish Identity*, 7).

Ober tsu lebn eyvik kumt dos nit.
Kumt dos nit amen sela....

(Yolanzio un Patriziano kleytern oyf di himlen)
Yolanzio: Ikh shtrav nokh ru.
Patriziano: Kleyter hekher, bruder.
Yolanzio: Di propelern fun lebn royshn un ikh her nokh
Patriziano: kleyter nokh hekher, bruder.

Voila—the great magician comes
For two or three cents
He makes some hocus-pocus
But it doesn't measure up to eternal life
Doesn't measure up amen sela...

(Yolanzio and Patriziano climb into the heavens)
Yolanzio: I am streving for peace.
Patriziano: Clemb higher, my man.
Yolanzio: The propellers of life roar and I am still listening.
Patriziano: Clemb even higher, my man.[62]

The sorcerer's "hocus pocus" fails to win him eternal life; Yolanzio and Patriziano find themselves clambering with great effort into heaven. Like "Shem the Penman," Glatshteyn's piece is about the literary anxieties of the rarefied writer.

Joyce the sorcerer appears again in Glatshteyn's poem "Nayvort," ("Newword") published in his 1929 collection *Kredos*.[63] In this poem, the poet declares his intention: "*Farshraybn alts vos iz umbagrayflakh volt ikh/ mit dem gli fun a vort*" ("I would describe all that is inconceivable / with the glow of a word"). But whose words shall the Yiddish poet use? Tolstoy's, whose words the poet describes as a "*shos fun kleyngever*" ("a shot from a pistol") or Joyce's words: "*Farplantertsoyber fun dem urgeheym*" ("tangledmagic of ancientmystery")? The poet's effort to disentangle himself from the enchantment of such forbears as Joyce prompts a crisis: "*Gornit ikh veys gornit ikh ze gornit ikh farshtey*" ("I know nothing I see nothing I understand nothing"). But the poet regroups and declares again his determination: "*Katalogirn volt ikh dos umfarshteyn/ mit dem flater mit dem gli fun a vort*" ("I would catalogue the unfathomable/ with the flutter with the glow of a word"). Here Glatshteyn, after Joyce, experiments with neologisms and with mysticism. But Joyce is treated here as a vexed forbear; the Yiddish poet must create his own language, his own "newword" to describe his own unique experience.

---

62. Again, my thanks to David Braun for inventing this way of approximating Glatshteyn's faux-Old Yiddish.

63. Yankev Glatshteyn, *Kredos* (New York: Verlag Yiddish Leben, 1929), 39.

It wasn't until the 1930s that any critical assessment of Joyce would appear in Yiddish. In 1935, Nakhmen Mayzel published a two-part consideration of Joyce in *Literarishe bleter*, Europe's leading Yiddish literary weekly published out of Warsaw. He begins: *"James Joyce—a nomen, vos hert nisht oyf tsu interesirn un intrigirn di kultur velt zint yorn, un bay unz— ingantsn umbakant."*[64] An entire literature, Mayzel observes, has sprung up around Joyce's work, but *"bay unz,"* in Yiddish, nothing had yet been written. The first installment of the article discusses Joyce's earlier works through *Ulysses*; the second installment is entirely concerned with his *Work in Progress*, not yet titled *Finnegans Wake*. Mayzel spends quite a bit of time on *Ulysses*, describing the novel's epic symbolism as a sharp delineation of the indignities of bourgeois urban life. Mayzel is one of the first critics in any language to argue that it is Bloom, *"an irlandisher yid,"* and not Stephen, who is the central figure in *Ulysses*: *"a guter, a bal-toyve, a vulgarer un mit a neygung tsu filozofirn"* ("a good man, a benefactor of others, a vulgar man with an inclination to philosophize"). He "willingly swims in a swamp, thinks it magnificent, and uses it for his own ends." The conflict of the novel, Mayzel observes, evolves in the elaboration of Joyce's own feeling of being "from no place and in no place." The protest of *Dubliners* and the searching of *Portrait* have become in *Ulysses*, he argues, an immense hollowness and hopelessness. In *Ulysses,* the chronicle of an "very ordinary day in the lives of very ordinary people," for Joyce becomes a portrait of a "world poised in intense anticipation of a catastrophe."[65]

Bloom's Jewishness merits hardly a mention in Mayzel's discussion (though he does call Molly Bloom "Miriam"). Rather, he argues that Joyce's novel is a parody of English and Western high culture as filtered through English school examinations, through his referencing of the *Odyssey*, of older forms and writers both famous and forgotten, of an entire "canon" of English literature. For Mayzel, Joyce is a radical innovator of form, offering a radical critique of petite-bourgeois morality, and existing in a kind of radically ambivalent and often oppositional relationship to canonical European literature. Mayzel here intuits what Deleuze and Guattari would later characterize as the political, social, and aesthetic experiments constitutive of "minor literature."[66] Joyce's sense of dissent and dislocation, that is to say, his *Irishness*, is articulated in his very use of language; he becomes, ironically, the "Irish English master."[67]

---

64. Nakhmen Mayzel (writing as A.B.), "James Joyce," *Literarishe bleter* 12: 25 (June 21 1935), 395.

65. Ibid., 395.

66. See Deleuze and Guattari. *Kafka: Toward a Minor Literature*, trans. Dana Polan (Minneapolis: University of Minnesota Press, 1986).

67. This phrase is borrowed from Reizbaum. My thanks to Marilyn Reizbaum for pointing

As Ruth Wisse observes in *The Modern Jewish Canon*, "the most com-plicating feature of modern Jewish literature as I conceive it is its relation to language."[68] Unlike other national literatures, Jewish literature cannot be limited to only those texts written in Jewish languages. After Wisse, we might also say that one of the defining features of Yiddish literary modern-ism is a heightened sensitivity to the precariousness of language as a trans-mitter of culture. The most complicated and complicating feature of Joyce, as Mayzel observes, is his relation to language. All this is to say that Yiddish writers entertained as ambivalent a relationship with the modernists who influenced them and ignored them, as did Anglo-American literary modern-ism with so-called "minor" traditions whose alterity threatened even as it inspired. Joyce represented the normative and canonical modernism that Roth, Samuel, and Glatshteyn strained against even as it defined their own literary efforts. For Mayzel, Joyce himself strained against those literary norms and canons. I thus read these moments of Joyce-Yiddish contact as encounters between faintly antagonistic modernisms that, however unac-knowledged, shaped both.

---

out the convergences of minor writing, Joyce's Irishness, and Yiddish. See Reizbaum, "The Minor Works of James Joyce," *James Joyce Quarterly* 30 (Winter 1993): 177–189.

68. Wisse, *The Modern Jewish Canon*, 5.

The Transmission of Poetic Anger:
An Unexploded Shell
in the Jewish Canon

JANET HADDA

I admit it: I'm fascinated by anger. For Jews, anger is not a sin for which we must atone on Yom Kippur. So why is such a natural, understandable, and universally present emotion frowned upon, even forbidden? Why is it "out of control" to feel and express anger? And why is women's anger, in particular, so frightening? Conceivably, precisely because women's writing—and women's poetry, in particular—tends to be more personal and confessional than that of their male counterparts; women's literary anger seems especially immediate. It may be more acceptable to be angry about general injustice or persecution than to be enraged at a lover or at a child. Moreover, in Yiddish literature, if not in Jewish life in Ashkenaz, depression is preferable to fury.

Perhaps because of her focus on collective experience, Ruth Wisse has excluded poetry from her concern. Her choice is understandable, since the idiosyncratic voice of the poet generally eschews plot and character and also usually stresses private knowledge. Nonetheless, many poets do draw heavily upon their own sustaining culture. In Yiddish literature, Yankev Glatshteyn as poet springs immediately to mind, as do Itsik Manger and Peretz Markish.

"Modern Jewish literature is the repository of modern Jewish experience. It is the most complete way of knowing the inner life of the Jews."[1] I find myself captivated by the implications of Wisse's statement. Can Jews as a collective have an inner life? Or does any generalization miss the uniqueness of each Jew's inner life? And what form of inner life do we mean: conscious, unconscious, cognitive, affective, physical, psychological, political, philosophical, religious, cultural, sexual? And can this inner life be reflected and transmitted in poetry, individualistic though it tends to be?

As the jumble of Jewish literary voices reaches the ear, the reader may discern a number of distinctive feelings or "affect states" (in the language of psychoanalysis). These states emerge either explicitly or elusively in the form of the reader's subtle shifts of mood and they certainly play an important, if often understated, role in cultural transmission. I want to argue, however, that this connection remains individual, not communal. Whereas

---

1. Ruth R. Wisse, *The Modern Jewish Canon: A Journey Through Language and Culture* (New York: The Free Press, 2000), 4. Hereafter cited as Wisse.

an individual reader may have a powerful sense of recognition and under-standing of such feelings, the experience is not, and cannot be, collective. In this essay, I examine affect states revealed and transmitted in two poetic voices, those of Tsilye Drapkin and Allen Ginsberg. In addition, I will sug-gest that the link between these voices is anger, and even rage, an affect state that is definitely not highlighted in most discussions of Jewish litera-ture.

Discussing poetry in one of her asides, Wisse comments, correctly I believe, about Yiddish writing in interbellum Warsaw:

> Though female poets and writers were still a rarity in Yiddish and Hebrew, women were among the leading liberal voices in Polish literature—hence greatly beloved by Jewish readers—and their work confirmed the woman's particular ability to sympathize with children and the disadvantaged. (147)....The women of this generation...were as socially and politically engaged as the men, but in taking women's experience as the special prov-ince of their writing, they often favored the solitary, isolating emotions, choosing poetry over prose, and the domestic and erotic veins of language...The Jewish emphasis on study and learning that had done so much to develop male intellect had curtailed competing forms of emotional experience, so confessional writing of Jewish men consisted of complaints of stifled hunger for physical release. The women, conversely, exulted in their sex.[2] (148)

Wisse is accurate in her omission of anger as one of the overriding female preoccupations in Yiddish literary expression, not because it didn't exist, but because it was considered unseemly. Indeed, in one of the few prose creations that explicitly deal with a woman's anger, I.L. Peretz's *A kaas fun a yidene* ("A Jewish Woman's Anger"), the woman in question is told by her husband that she has lost the world-to-come because, in desperation, she has indulged in an outburst against him. The story ends with the protago-nist's conclusion that, since she has nothing in this world and she has for-feited the next world, the only solution to her plight of poverty and an unre-sponsive husband is suicide. But as she is about to commit this act, she real-izes that she cannot take that step because she cannot imagine abandoning her child. So much for her anger.[3]

During my Yiddish education at Columbia University and the YIVO Insti-tute, all my professors of Yiddish were male, although I did have a wonder-

---

2. Wisse, 147, 148.

3. Peretz, I.L. "*A kaas fun a yidene.*" *Ale verk*, vol. 3 (New York: Farlag yidish, 1929), 70–76. See also my book, *Passionate Women, Passive Men: Suicide in Yiddish Liter-ature* (Albany: SUNY Press, 1988). There, I explore the suicides of several female liter-ary characters who commit the forbidden act of suicide because they cannot bring themselves—or they are forbidden—to express their authentic emotions, including rage over the limitations thrust upon them by social rules.

ful tutor, Shoshke Erlich, who introduced me to many literary works. So I don't know what would have happened if I had studied with one or more female professors (or for that matter, if I were to be studying now, rather than in the early 1970s). In any event, I do not recall reading a single female author as a graduate student. I was first introduced to the poet Tsilye Drapkin during my first or second year of teaching at UCLA, when a student inquired why we weren't reading any of the female poets in Howe and Greenberg's *Treasury of Yiddish Poetry*, and particularly the poems of Drapkin (Dropkin). The answer to the student's question, I am embarrassed to admit, was that I had simply not noticed those poems because of my own biases, however innocently acquired. The discovery of Drapkin in the Howe and Greenberg anthology led to an abiding love for her work. She remains my female poet of choice, in large part because she is so adamant about allowing her emotions to emerge poetically.

In thinking about Wisse's canon and about the non-inclusion of Drapkin, another angry woman came to mind, Naomi Ginsberg. Tsilye Drapkin and Naomi Ginsberg have some aspects in common. Both were born in Russia, Drapkin in 1888 and Ginsberg in 1895. Both were secular, left-leaning Jews. Both were teachers at an early point in their lives. Both died in New York in 1956. Both Tsilye Drapkin and Naomi Ginsberg could be very angry. Drapkin left a poetic, prose, and painting legacy that has attracted to her a limited but enthusiastic following. Naomi Ginsberg would not be remembered today had she not been memorialized by her famous son, Beat poet Allen Ginsberg. Because Allen immortalized Naomi poetically, she, like Tsilye Drapkin, remains alive for today's reader. Indeed, I argue that Naomi Ginsberg's Eastern European Yiddish voice, anger and all, is an integral part of Allen Ginsberg's American voice.

Tsilye Drapkin's anger did not come easily to her. Often, as I have discussed elsewhere,[4] before she let the anger out, she prohibited it, and the result is poetry of intense depression and even suicidality. Sometimes, however, she could hold back, and the rage—usually at a man—flowed out of her. Listen to *In koyt fun dayn fardakht* ("In the Dirt of Your Suspicion"):

Vos ikh zog un tu,
Alts toyvlstu in koyt fun dayn fardakht
Un lakhst oys mit kalte shvere blikn.
Zhabes heybn mit a mol on shpringen fun mayn moyl.
Verim glitshn zikh arop fun mayne finger;
Vi bay a farzeenish a makhesheyfe, vern mayne oygn,
Mayne hent, vi shlangen,

---

4. Janet Hadda, "The Eyes Have It: Celia Dropkin's Love Poetry," in *Gender and Text in Hebrew and Yiddish Literature,* eds. Ann Lapidus-Lerner, Anita Norich, and Naomi Sokoloff (New York: The Jewish Theological Seminary of America, 1992), 93–112.

Vos viln dikh dershtikn,
Nor mayne fis, farshemte
Shteyen tsugeklept tsum dil,
Umzist pruvn zey antloyfn
Fun dayne kalte oyslakhndike blikn.[5]

All that I say and do
You immerse for ritual purification in the dirt of your suspicion
And ridicule with cold, heavy looks.
Suddenly frogs begin to spring from my mouth,
Worms slide down from my fingers;
My eyes become like those of a monster, a witch,
My hands, like snakes
Which want to strangle you,
But my legs [feet], embarrassed [ashamed],
Remain glued to the floor,
In vain they attempt to flee
From your cold, ridiculing looks.

The poem begins with a strong accusation: the use of the verb *toyvlen*, which means to immerse ritually and is familiarly used for the ablutions in the *mikve* at the end of a woman's menstrual cycle, when juxtaposed with *koyt fun dayn fardakht* indicates the harshest irony. If I were to ritually immerse myself, the poet implies, I would be pure for you. But you, who dare suspect me, turn purity to dirt. The focus of her anger is a person, a man, I assume, who is not only suspicious, but also cold and contemptuous.

The woman's reaction is rage, but notice (it's hard not to) how she describes that rage. Out of her mouth jump, not words, but frogs. Worms slither from her fingers and her eyes become monstrous, witchy. This is anger—frightening, cold-blooded, even disgusting. Her hands, which Drapkin elsewhere describes playfully as nests of white snakes,[6] are now murderously snake-like. Is it her female sexuality run amok? Anger transforms this woman into a grotesque and horrifying creature in her own eyes.

The final price that the poet must pay is her own shame. Paralyzed, she must continue to endure her partner's frigid disdain. Perhaps her punishment is the outcome of her alleged, possibly sexual, wrong-doing. Or perhaps she is guilty for no more than her very expression of anger. In the end, though, her outburst neither moves nor influences the man. Is he unmovable or has she undercut herself with the conviction that her anger is reprehensible? Drapkin does not provide an answer to that question, but her his-

---

5. Tsilye Drapkin, *In heysn vint* (New York: Shulsinger Bros.,1959), 57. Hereafter cited as Drapkin.

6. Drapkin, 13.

tory yields a clue. Having been brought up without a father, Tsilye was forced to rely on a distant and difficult mother. Demanding mother and spirited daughter would engage in ferocious battles, but, inevitably, Tsilye would find herself overcome with guilt, begging her mother for forgiveness. This troubled attachment became the model for Drapkin's understanding of intimate relationships, wherein she raged at and hated the other, only to retreat, disgraced, in the end.

Accounts by Drapkin's children make clear that she, like so many artists, needed her poetry and her writing as an outlet for her inner turmoil and misery. As she explains in *Ikh shrayb lider* ("I Write Poems"), her creations clear her mind and soul. She is compelled to create, but the compulsion is psychological, rather than aesthetic, political, theoretical, ideological, or communal:

Ikh shrayb lider—
Ver darf zey?
Ober af mir faln zey
Vi veykh-vayser shney.

Falt af mayn shtern un lipn,
Falt, shneyelekh tsarte,
Ot hot ir fartribn
Verter harbe un harte
Falt af mayne lipn,
Vi mayn shvesters kushn,
Ot hot ir fartribn
Di sharfkeyt fun mayne khushim.

I write poems—
Who needs them?
But they fall on me
Like soft white snow.
Fall on my brow and lips
Fall, tender snow flakes,
Now you've banished
Harsh, hard words....

Fall on my lips,
Like my sister's kisses,
Now you've banished
The sharpness of my senses.

The snow softens and purifies, revealing the extent to which the narrator, true to Drapkin, experiences her inner self as unclean and dangerous. Drapkin was able to pour her uncensored emotional states—her depression, anguish, rage, and, for that matter, her joy—into her poetry, and her life became more livable as a result, even though she was never a peaceful person.

While Tsilye Drapkin was enduring her inner struggles and describing them in poems of immense vibrancy and emotionality, a woman I believe she was never to encounter was growing up not far away. Naomi Levy, born Naomi Livergant in the vicinity of Vitebsk, came to the United States in 1905, seven years before Tsilye Drapkin arrived. The ten-year-old Naomi lived with her family, first on the Lower East Side and then in Newark. She and Louis Ginsberg met when they were both seventeen and still in high school. Their lives seemed off to a good start: she would be a teacher; she would be engaged in Communist party activities; she would marry Louis. Louis would be a teacher and a poet. But in 1918, when Naomi was twenty-three, she experienced a strange malaise: she became massively sensitive to light and spent weeks lying in a darkened room.

When Naomi recovered, the couple married. They moved to Paterson and had two sons. Allen was born in 1926. But that malaise in 1918 was probably Naomi's first schizophrenic break. Over the next 38 years, she gradually declined, often institutionalized for years at a time. When she was at home, she terrified her family with her screams. She mortified and confused them with her nakedness. She plunged them into hopeless conflict with one another, insisting that Louis and his mother were trying to murder her. Allen Ginsberg grew up with Naomi's Yiddish-accented madness in his ears and in his heart. His father tried, unsuccessfully, to tame Naomi, and his brother, Eugene, tried, unsuccessfully, to run away from any awareness of the problem. But Allen, who had immense resources of empathy, simply accepted Naomi.

Ginsberg is, of course, an American icon, known for his political radicalism, his embrace of unpopular causes, his Buddhist-inspired patience, and his poetic fearlessness. He had many influences, from Walt Whitman to William Carlos Williams, from the junkie William Burroughs to his meditation teacher, Chögyam Trungpa, all of which are painstakingly well-documented.[7] Just a glance at Ginsberg's own words, however, in his poetry and journal entries, proves without a doubt that the influence of his mother's rage and insanity, which she articulated in Yiddish and Yiddish-accented English, marked him indelibly.

From the time he was a boy, Ginsberg kept a diary,[8] in which he recorded the events of daily life with spooky composure. When he was just eleven, he wrote:

7. See, for example, Barry Miles, *Ginsberg: A Biography*, revised edition (London: Virgin Publishing Ltd., 2000; reprinted 2002). Hereafter cited as Miles.

8. Allen Ginsberg, Unpublished manuscript (1937). Series 2, Box 1, Folder 1. Allen Ginsberg Papers, M0733, Dept. of Special Collections, Stanford University Libraries, Stanford, Calif. Dates will be included in text.

Went to the movies and saw "Parnell" and "Hotel Haywire." My mother thinks she is going to die and is not so good. (June 19, 1937) Diary, went to the movies again and saw "This is my Affair" and "Oh Doctor" the latter would set a good example for my mother as she is pretty bad today. Her sickness is only mentally. However and she has no chance of dying. My brother still has the idea that he is big. (June 30, 1937)

Thurs. June 24, 1937. I stayed home from school again today only today I went to high school and saw my father teach, my mother locked herself in the bathroom early in the morning and my father had to break the glass to get in. She also went back to the sanitarium [Greystone, a state hospital near Morristown, N.J.]. I saw a news reel of the Louis Braddock fight, also "Dangerous Number," and another picture in the movies. I also developed a sty below my eye.

This acceptance came at some cost to Ginsberg. In 1949, when he was just twenty-three years old, he was hospitalized at New York's Psychiatric Institute and remained in the hospital for seven months. The need to be hospitalized was a result, I believe, of the cumulative strain of coping with the effects of his mother's illness. Shortly before he was admitted, he revealed that he, like Tsilye Drapkin, may have believed that his anger was bad:

I dreamed of a madhouse, and now tomorrow I am going to New York to a medical hospital....I have been wrathful all my life, angry against my father and all others. My wrath must end....[9]

However, like Drapkin, Ginsberg was able to use that anger to invigorate his poetry. Later in life he came to embrace the plight of those who didn't fit in, whether politically, sexually, or mentally. While he trained himself to behave pacifically through intense Buddhist discipline, he allowed his alternating rage and despair to emerge in his poetry. Indeed, I would argue that part of what made Ginsberg's voice unique was his ability to convey rage in his poetry with control and just the right amount of restraint.

Ginsberg's *Howl* heralded a completely new voice in American poetry. And that voice contains Naomi. A few years later, in *Kaddish*, Ginsberg documents, with heart-breaking clarity, the anguish of watching helplessly as his mother succumbs to terrifying paranoia. On the way, she rages, accuses, and lashes out physically:

"I am a great woman—am truly a beautiful soul—and because of what they (Hitler, Grandma, Hearst, the Capitalists, Franco, Daily News, the 20s, Mussolini, the living dead) want to shut me up—Buba's the head of the spider network —

Kicking the girls, Edie & Elanor—Woke Edie at midnight to tell her she was a spy and Elanor a rat....

9. Allen Ginsberg, Unpublished manuscript (1949) Series 2, Box 3, Folder 8. Allen Ginsberg Papers, M0733, Dept. of Special Collections, Stanford University Libraries, Stanford, Calif., 7.

The relatives call me up, she's getting worse—I was the only one left—Went
on the subway with Eugene to see her, ate stale fish —

"My sister whispers in the radio—Louis must be in the apartment—his mother
tells him what to say—LIARS!...Elanor is the worst spy! She's taking orders!"[10]

The anger and indignation that Allen heard in Naomi's desperate ravings
spill out clearly in the opening lines of *America*:

America I've given you all and now I'm nothing.
America, two dollars and twenty-seven cents January 17, 1956.
I can't stand my own mind.
America when will we end the human war?
Go fuck yourself with your atom bomb.
I don't feel good don't bother me.[11]

In *Howl*, Ginsberg's ability to shout out literally leaves the reader breathless:

What sphinx of cement and aluminum bashed open their skulls and ate up
their brains and imagination?....

Moloch the incomprehensible prison! Moloch the crossbone soulless jail-
house and Congress of sorrows! Moloch whose buildings are judgment!
Moloch the vast stone of war! Moloch the stunned governments![12]

Seeking to describe post-World War II capitalism and the heartless lust for
power that crushes delicate souls, Ginsberg uses Moloch, the Canaanite fire
god, in praise of whom parents burned their children. In their raw ugliness,
Ginsberg's descriptions defy any attempt to evade his meaning. While Ginsberg's point here is clearly political, the poem is dedicated to Carl Solomon,
a man Ginsberg met when he himself was hospitalized at New York's Psychiatric Institute. And later on in *Howl*, Ginsberg switches his focus of
indignation to the hospitalizations of Solomon and Naomi, whom he con-
flates:

Carl Solomon! I'm with you in Rockland
          where you're madder than I am
I'm with you in Rockland
          where you must feel very strange
I'm with you in Rockland
          where you imitate the shade of my mother
                    ...

10. Allen Ginsberg, *Kaddish and Other Poems* (San Francisco: City Lights Books, 1961),
    26. Hereafter cited as *Kaddish*.

11. Allen Ginsberg, *Howl and Other Poems* (San Francisco: City Lights Books, 1956,
    1959), 39. Hereafter cited as *Howl*.

12. *Howl*, 21.

I'm with you in Rockland
>   where there are twenty-five-thousand mad comrades all singing the
>   final stanzas of the Internationale[13]

Whatever intellectual, literary, and political influences Ginsberg absorbed
through his rich education and important friendships, I suggest that the specific articulations that make his work unique are a conscious, and perhaps
also unconscious, evocation of his mother. And her voice, shaped though it
was by insanity, nonetheless stemmed originally from her life as a Yiddish-
speaking immigrant and as a free woman—free to choose her politics, her
profession, and her husband.

The spirit and tone of Ashkenaz granted Ginsberg's work an unparalleled
quality. Late in life he turned to reading Yiddish poetry, especially that of
Avrom Sutzkever, and I like to think that he was recognizing an early source
of his own creativity. The appeal of Ashkenaz, and of Yiddish, as a wellspring for imaginative expression in English, is alive today, one generation
after Ginsberg, in such writers as Pearl Abraham, Allen Hoffman, Dara Horn,
and Steve Stern. As we face the inevitable demise of Ashkenaz, we can rest
assured that its soul will continue to thrive in the voices of artists such as
Ginsberg and more recent talents.

Allen Ginsberg, like Tsilye Drapkin, used his poetry to balance himself—
indeed, if we believe him, to conquer insanity. As he says toward the end of
Kaddish, his monumental memorial to Naomi:

> O glorious muse that bore me from the womb, gave suck first mystic life &
> taught me talk and music, from whose painted head I first took Vision—
>
> Tortured and beaten in the skull—What mad hallucinations of the damned
> that drive me out of my own skull to seek Eternity till I find Peace for Thee—
> O Poetry—....[14]

Ginsberg had had an auditory hallucination of sorts while still a student:
he heard the voice of William Blake, and he understood the possibility that
poetry could be eternal. Years later, he was still reflecting on that moment
and still using it to emphasize the essential role of poetry for him: it was
more, but certainly nothing less, than the result of his reaching a state of
calm, of preparedness, whereby his emotional turbulence could find a safe
means of expression.

Ginsberg wrote directly about the place of Naomi within him. A few
days after her death, in 1956, when he was thirty years old, he wrote:

> Everything changes toward death. My mother. Myself...My childhood is gone
> with my mother. My memory becomes less clear. My body will go. There is

---

13. *Howl*, 24, 25.

14. *Kaddish*, 29.

no me left. Naomi is a memory. Naomi is a memory. My thirty years is a
memory to me.[15]

Ginsberg's capacity to regain and retain the spirit and the expression that
came to him through the energy of Naomi, furious and paranoid though she
might have been, was both a creative gift and a source of depth for him. He,
like Tsilye Drapkin, turned a troubled and painful mother-child relationship
into a blessing instead of a curse. Drapkin described that link with exquisite
sensitivity in her famous poem *Mayn mame*, "My Mother," and the process
she articulates fits for Naomi and Allen Ginsberg as well.

Mayn mame,
A tsvey-un-tsvantsik-yorike,
An almone mit tsvey kleyninke kinder geblibn,
Tsniesdik hot zi bashlosn tsu keynem a vayb mer nit vern.
Shtil hobn zikh ire teg un yorn getsoygn,
Vi fun a kargn vaksenem likht baloykhtn.
Mayn mame iz tsu keynem a vayb nit gevorn,
Nor ale filtegike,
Filyorike, filnakhtike ziftsn
Fun ir yungn un libendn vesn,
Fun ir benkendik blut,
Hob ikh mit mayn kindershn hartsn farnumen,
Tif in zikh ayngezapt.
Un mayn mames farborgene heyse benkshaft
Hot zikh, vi fun an untererdishn kval,
Fray in mir arayngegosn.
Itst shpritst fun mir ofn
mayn mames heyser, heyliker,
Tif-farbahaltener bager.[16]

My mother,
A twenty-two-year-old,
A widow left with two tiny children,
Modestly she decided never to be anyone's wife again.
Quietly her days and years stretched,
As if lit by a short [stingy] wax light.
My mother became the wife of no-one,
But all the many-dayed,
Many-yeared, many-nighted sighs
Of her young and loving being,
Of her longing blood,

---

15. Mile, 203–204.

16. Drapkin, 11.

I perceived with my childish heart
Absorbed it deeply.
And my mother's hidden hot longing
Flowed into me freely
As from an underground source.
Now my mother's hot, holy
Deeply hidden desire
Spouts from me openly.

Mayn mame discusses transmission at its most basic and visceral level: it is the passing of affect from mother to child through their physical and emotional proximity. Similarly, readers may perceive the affect states of the writers with whom they are engaged. They also have unique reactions to what they read because of emotional evocations that are distinctive to their experience.

Tsilye Drapkin is not angry in this poem about her relationship with her mother. Instead, she concentrates on the effect of her mother's emotional and sexual constriction upon her own creative freedom. She is the recipient, thanks to her child's unmitigated heart, of the passion that her mother repudiated. The image of the stingy candle is central to the poem: light and heat are allowed to exist, but only in muted and inhibited form. Despite Drapkin's acceptance of her mother here, I speculate that she had to struggle against this very narrow and withdrawn presence throughout her life. The deprivation led to depression, on the one hand, and to anger, on the other.

Allen Ginsberg, too, had to contend with an impossible and depressing mother. He, too, had to learn to master overwhelming affect states. Both Drapkin and Ginsberg managed to transform their depression and rage into art that vividly conveys their suffering without annihilating them in the process. Their emotional courage is their gift to their readers.

One of the lessons I have learned from Ruth Wisse is that being an honest scholar requires that one express whatever is on one's mind, regardless of how it will be received. To her immense credit, Wisse has written and spoken her mind with increasing vigor and clarity, despite the reaction of her critics. She has been angry, and she has accepted the anger of her opponents. Even in her articulation of a modern Jewish canon, she has not avoided controversy. While I do not agree with all her positions, I know that she can handle the disagreement. To me, personally and professionally, this is her greatest gift. May she continue to get angry and inspire anger *biz hundert un tsvantsik*.

Guilt, Mourning, Idol Worship, and Golem Writing: The Symptoms of a Jewish Literary Canon

EMILY MILLER BUDICK

In taking leave of her subject in *The Modern Jewish Canon*, Ruth Wisse suggests that her readers take the book as an "invitation to set out on their own journeys through Jewish language and culture." I want to accept Wisse's invitation in relation to one of the writers she specifically laments having left out of her study, Bruno Schulz, of whom she astutely asks: "has any writer exerted greater influence on emerging Jewish literature than the enigma from Drohobycz?" She goes on to say, "In what must be the highest form of literary appreciation, the American Cynthia Ozick made a lost manuscript by Schulz the centerpiece of her novel *The Messiah of Stockholm* (1987) at almost the same time that the Israeli writer David Grossman animated his deathless spirit in the novel *See Under: Love*" (1987).[1] To this list of Schulz's influences on major contemporary authors Wisse might well have added Philip Roth, who creates a Schulz-inspired character in "The Prague Orgy," the fourth in the Nathan Zuckerman novels and the culminating piece in the publication entitled *Zuckerman Bound* (1991).[2] Not for naught does Ozick dedicate her *Messiah* to Roth. It is Roth whose "Writers from the Other Europe" series first brought Schulz's novels to worldwide public notice: *The Street of Crocodiles,* originally published in Polish under the title *Cinnamon Shops* in 1934 first appeared in English in 1963, but was republished as part of the Penguin series in 1977, while *Sanatorium Under the Sign of the Hourglass,* which was originally published in Polish in 1937, was brought out for the first time in English in 1977. Roth returns the favor of Ozick's gratitude by constructing part of his plot in "The Prague Orgy" along the lines first set out by Ozick in *The Messiah.*

I want to put at the center of my discussion a Jewish canon comprised by Ozick's, Grossman's, and Roth's novels and by the two writers, Schulz and Kafka, who inform their texts, not to mention the writings of a second Israeli author who seems to me to belong to this canon, Aharon Appelfeld. Although Appelfeld is not directly influenced by Schulz, Schulz's voice can

---

1. N.Y.: The Free Press, 2000, 347–348. Naomi Sokoloff has considered the Ozick and Grossman texts in relation to each other in "Reinventing Bruno Schulz: Cynthia Ozick's 'The Messiah of Stockholm' and David Grossman's 'See Under: Love'," *AJS Review* 13 (1988): 171–199.

2. Another text to be added to this list, which I will not be discussing, is Danilo Kiš, *Hourglass.*

be distinctly heard speaking through Appelfeld's, most especially in the text
I want briefly to refer to here, his *Age of Wonders.* Appelfeld explains in an
interview with Roth:

> Kafka spoke to me not only in my mother tongue, but also in another
> language which I knew intimately, the language of the absurd....To my
> regret, I came to Bruno Schulz's work years too late, after my literary
> approach was rather well formed. I felt and still feel a great affinity with his
> writing.[3]

That Appelfeld should experience this affinity and already (as Roth's question to him suggests) speak in a recognizably Schulzian voice in advance of
his having heard that voice directly testifies to what Roth in *The Ghost Writer* refers to as the "family resemblance" among Jewish writers.[4] It also suggests that the features they share are not a matter of influence only. For this
reason Appelfeld's comment also points to the connection between Schulz
and Kafka, despite Schulz's biographer's vehement disclaimers to the contrary and despite the fact that Schulz did not, as is often assumed, translate
The Trial into Polish (Ozick's *Messiah* repeats this error).[5] As Jerzy Ficowski
notes, Schulz lent his name and authority to his fiancée's translation; he may
not even have read Kafka until after he had begun writing his own fiction.
Yet Ficowski doth protest too much in disclaiming Schulz's Kafkaesque
qualities, as evidenced by his locating in Schulz, immediately after his vituperative disclaimer, just those subjects and images that most define Kafka:
fantasy, the grotesque, cockroaches, and fathers.[6] That Ficowski, who is
also a writer, is so defensive of his idol Schulz might suggest, especially
given Ozick's and Roth's concerns with literary idols, Ficowski's own affinities with this canon, which include as well, I suggest, Roth's "I Always
Wanted You to Admire My Fasting; or, Looking at Kafka" and his *Ghost
Writer* (the first of the Zuckerman novels, which might be understood as a
wacky take on Kafka's *Trial* and has everything to do with idols).

I want to suggest that a defining feature of this canon and a quintessential mark of its Jewishness is a quality of tormented and incomplete mourning and what, for want of a better term, I want to call in relation to this
mourning "survivor guilt." To invoke and negate a key term from *The Messiah of Stockholm,* these works are not lamentations or elegies. Rather, as in
the image at the beginning of the "Bruno" section of *See Under: Love,*

---

3. *Beyond Despair: Three Lectures and a Conversation with Philip Roth*, trans. Jeffrey
M. Green (Chicago: Chicago University Press, 1988), 63–65.

4. *The Ghost Writer* (New York: Vintage Books, 1995), 47.

5. *The Messiah of Stockholm* (New York: Random House, 1988), 33; references hereafter in text.

6. *Regions of the Great Heresy: Bruno Schulz, a Biographical Portrait*, trans. Thedosia
Robertson (New York: W. W. Norton & Co., 2003), 115–126.

which Grossman takes from the paintings of Eduard Munch, these texts are nothing more and nothing less than a "scream," of the type Rosa in "The Shawl" squelches by shoving her daughter's baby blanket into her mouth.[7] Ozick writes of her protagonist in *The Messiah* when he reads through the manuscript he believes to be the lost text of Schulz's *Messiah:*

> Lars fell into the text with the force of a man who throws himself against a glass wall. He crashed through it to the other side, and what was there? Baroque arches and niches, intricately hedged byways of a language so incised, so *bleeding*—a touch could set off a hundred slicing blades...Lars did not resist or hide; he let his flesh rip. (105)

Insofar as Munch is himself much reviled by the Nazis as a degenerate artist (to pick up a key term from Appelfeld's *Age of Wonders*)[8] and, therefore, were he Jewish, an author much like Schulz, Kafka, and, as we shall see, Father in Applefeld's novel, we might want to grant him honorary status in this canon. Be that as it may, Grossman's and Ozick's texts are as barbed, brilliant, and sharp as the texts by Schulz, Kafka, and Munch that they invoke.

In thus identifying this canon through the emotional, psychological work that the texts do as opposed to the subjects or themes they seem to concern, I want to suggest that the texts themselves all perform the work of mourning, and that they do so inadequately and incompletely, which, I hasten to add, is not a sign of their inferiority as texts, but rather of their brilliance as works of art. Mourning in all these texts is blocked because of their own expression of just that symptom they identify as problematical in their protagonists, a survivor guilt that prevents them (characters and authors alike) from putting the dead to rest and that produces instead a tendency toward an idolization of the dead past—a phenomenon not unknown within the psychoanalytic literature concerning mourning, especially in cases of trauma.

Since the ancestral voices of grieving that emerge anew through the writings of Ozick, Roth, and Grossman are those of writers who write before the Holocaust, such survivor guilt as I want to discover in these texts cannot have to do exclusively with the guilt of those who survived the devastation of European Jewry, to which the term generally refers. This is so even though the later writers in the series are all in different ways "survivors" in the usual sense of the word. Nonetheless, survivor guilt (at least as the later writers interpret it, and I for one would agree with their analyses) emerges in the writings of Kafka, who dies before the Holocaust; Schulz, who is murdered in a wild action during the Holocaust; and, to add one more name to this list of authors, I. B. Singer, who escapes the catastrophe to America. By

---

7. Trans. Betsy Rosenberg (New York: Washington Square Press, 1989), 89–92.

8. *The Age of Wonders*, trans. Dalya Bilu (Boston: David R. Godine, 1981), 72, 75, 133.

survivor guilt, then, I wish to refer to a more general response to the condition of Jewish life in Europe long preceding the Holocaust, a guilt concerning survival itself in a world that has for countless generations communicated to the Jews that not only was their existence (personally and communally) precarious, but that they had no right to survive, either on the communal or personal level—a communication by Christians to Jews that had everything to do with the figure that emerges as central in Ozick's as in Schulz's work before her: the messiah. This is the guilt expressed, for example, by the typical Austrian Jewish writer in Appelfeld's *Age of Wonders*, who is himself a Kafkaesque, Schulzian writer, and who damns himself for just those Kafkaesque qualities he idolizes in Kafka. Since Appelfeld is himself a child-survivor and the major protagonist in that novel, the writer's son, is a child-survivor as well, this representation of the writer as suffering from Jewish anxiety and guilt before the war and before it is evidenced in the sons of such fathers is a significant gesture toward acknowledging the preexisting condition within European Jewry of this *symptom* I am calling survivor guilt.[9]

As with the term "survivor guilt," I use the word "symptom" in a very deliberate way. I mean by a symptom the ways in which a text might be an expression *of* something and not simply *about* something. Let me be clear from the outset. By thinking of these or other fictions as symptoms I do not mean to diagnose some pathology either of the authors or of their characters or even of the works themselves (as if literary texts were themselves human minds). This is so even though in the case of, for example, the protagonist of Ozick's *Messiah,* we are speaking of a highly neurotic character, only slightly more bizarre than the other characters in that novel and only slightly less crazy than the more certifiable madmen of Schulz's short stories. Despite this, I do not intend by looking at the symptomology of these text to psychoanalyze the characters, let alone the author or the work itself, as if the canon of Jewish writers writing about Jewish suffering and death was itself hopelessly deformed or that the language of psychoanalysis provided the authentic text of which literary texts were only defensive, allegorical, and somewhat weak transcriptions into other (less compelling) words. This kind of reductive Freudianism characterized much early psychoanalytic criticism, and it recurs still, even in more Lacanian modes of psychological interpretation of literary works.

Rather, my interest in texts as expressing symptoms and Jewish texts as expressing specifically Jewish symptoms derives from my sense of literature as fundamentally an expression of the human mind in all its multifaceted and diverse manifestations, and of Jewish texts as being distinctive from literature generally insofar as the mind it expresses is informed by Jewish his-

---

9. For a discussion of this see my book *Aharon Appelfeld's Fiction: Acknowledging the Holocaust* (Bloomington, Ind.: Indiana University Press, 2005), 78–105.

tory. This history includes not only the private, personal, familial history of any particular Jew, but the collective history in which individual biography takes place, including the textual traditions (both religious and secular) that also constitute a part of an individual's everyday lived experience. In the psychoanalytic view of literature, as of life, every human expression is personal and unique. It originates furthermore not only in our conscious intellects, though such rational, intentional thought is clearly a major facet of our human expressions, but also in the unconscious contents and processes of mind, which inform reason and are indeed inseparable from it. Yet, as Stanley Cavell has so aptly put it, there are conditions that condition the utterly specific individual life.[10] We are, as humans, like-minded, which is why we are capable of "reading" and responding to another person's similarly conditioned thoughts.

For these reasons the word *symptom* serves better than the word *expression* to convey the depth and complexity of literary texts. It carries with it a sense of the ways in which expression does not originate only in our conscious intellects. Just as importantly, the word symptom signals the need of a response on the part of the witness of the symptom. Writes Slavoj Žižek in an essay entitled "The Truth Arises from Misrecognition":

> The symptom not only can be interpreted but is, so to speak, already formed in view of its interpretation....In other words, there is no symptom without its addressee. ...the symptom is not only a ciphered message, it is at the same time a way for the subject to organize his enjoyment....In other words, the symptom is the way we—the subject—"avoid madness," the way we "choose something...instead of nothing"...through the binding of our enjoyment to a certain signifying, symbolic formation which assures a minimum of consistency to our being in the world....[I]n the real of [the] symptom [is] the only support of [an individual's] being.[11]

By reading a series of texts in terms of Jewish symptoms, I am applying to this double function of the symptom: how the symptom organizes the writer's Jewish experience, especially under conditions of extreme suffering as has so often (far too often) characterized Jewish life; and how the expression of that symptom addresses itself to a reader (in the case of Kafka and Schulz: Ozick, Roth, Appelfeld, and Grossman; in the case of Ozick, Roth, Appelfeld, and Grossman: us).

The symptom is always unique and personal. Yet, insofar as we humans live among other people, the symptom can also be constructed by, contain and express, the equally unique and personal symptoms of others. In the

---

10. Stanley Cavell, *Contesting Tears: The Hollywood Melodrama of the Unknown Woman* (Chicago: University of Chicago Press, 1996), 94–96.

11. *Lacan and the Subject of Language*, ed. Ellie Ragland-Sullivan and Mark Bracher (New York: Routledge, 1991), 206–208.

case of the Jewish symptom, the communal formation is deeply historical as well. It often bespeaks an inherited and not only or even primarily a personal trauma, although inherited trauma must be understood in its expression and experience as being as personal and unique as any other traumatic experience a human being may endure. There is a condition that Maria Torok and Nicholas Abraham refer to as a transgenerational phantom, in which the secrets of others enjoy encrypted existence within the individual:

> What haunts are not the dead, but the gaps left within us by the secrets of others....the tombs of others....The phantom's periodic and compulsive return lies beyond the scope of symptom-formation in the sense of a return of the repressed; it works like a ventriloquist, like a stranger within the subject's own mental topography.[12]

The idea of a transgenerational phantom accords very nicely with Ozick's aesthetics, as articulated in an essay such as "I. B. Singer's Book of Creation," in which she defines the particular tradition of Jewish writing in which I would like to place her own writing, including *The Messiah of Stockholm*. This is a tradition, Ozick suggests in still another essay, aptly entitled "The Phantasmagoria of Bruno Schulz," that places Singer and Schulz alongside each other—Schulz's *Sanatorium* has everything to do with what he calls "the Book," as in the title of the essay on Singer; it is an image that Grossman picks up as well in *See Under: Love*—and she places both Singer and Schulz alongside Kafka, Isaac Babel (who figures in Roth's *Ghost Writer*), and Jerzy Kosinski (Zuckerman's PEN Club card is signed by Kosinski in "The Prague Orgy"). In Ozick's words, this is a tradition that is pitted by "the black crevices of nihilism [and] animalism" and spurred on by the condition of "homelessness" and "pariahship," conditions that defined the lot of European Jewry long before the war. As Ozick writes in "I. B. Singer's Book of Creation," Singer's fictions:

> contain the whole human world of affliction, error, quagmire, pain, calamity, catastrophe, woe....[H]e cracks open decorum to find lust [and] peers past convention into the pit of fear....This phantasmagorical universe of ordeal and mutation and shock is, finally, as intimately persuasive as logic itself.[13]

"Phantasmagorical" is the key word here. It finds its way also into the opening pages of Ozick's *The Messiah* and describes as well the texture of the

---

12. Nicholas Abraham and Maria Torok, *The Shell and the Kernel*, ed. and trans., Nicholas T. Rand (Chicago: University of Chicago Press, 1994), 171-174.

13. "Phantasmagoria of Bruno Schulz," *Art and Ardor* (New York: Dutton, 1984), 227; the essay originally appeared in *The New York Times Book Review* Feb. 13, 1977, upon the occasion of the publication of the English translation of *The Street of Crocodiles*. "I. B. Singer's Book of Creation," *Art and Ardor*, pp. 219-222; the essay was originally published in 1981 as the introduction to *The Collected Stories of Isaac Bashevis Singer*.

novel as a whole, not to mention David Grossman's *See Under: Love*. Ozick's observations concerning Singer, in other words, define a quintessential quality of Singer, Schulz, Appelfeld, Grossman, and her own writing. The phantasm or phantom that haunts these texts, pictured in the final words of Ozick's *Messiah* as "the man in the long black coat, hurrying with a metal garter box squeezed under his arm, hurrying and hurrying toward the chimneys" (144), is not, however, only Bruno Schulz (or, for that matter Franz Kafka), nor even all the many victims of the Holocaust whom Schulz might be thought to represent (or Kafka to have escaped joining). Rather, it is the long line of Jewish dead, about whom Schulz also writes and whose death he would somehow undo, like Lars in *The Messiah* vis-à-vis Schulz, or Rosa in *The Shawl* vis-à-vis her daughter or Nathan Zuckerman in both *The Ghost Writer* (vis-à-vis Anne Frank) and in the epilogue to that story *The Prague Orgy* (in relation to a fictive Schulz-inspired Yiddish writer); and, I want to add, like their authors. The characters would undo death through acts of conjuring, rescue, translation, and resurrection; their authors would undo death through writing itself, which these writers also—as much through their incorporation into their texts of phrases and images from Schulz and Kafka as through their subjects—imagine as acts of recuperation. For this reason, all the writers of Jewish phantasmagoria are, to use Roth's title, ghost writers of one sort or another. They write about the ghosts of the past; they speak as if haunted by those ghosts; and they are themselves ghostly presences, preferring residence among the dead rather than among the living.

By several ordinary criteria Ozick's *Messiah* is an identifiably Jewish text. The author is one of the leading American Jewish writers and its subject is that unmistakably Jewish subject, the Holocaust. The protagonist is a survivor refugee, living in Sweden, who, bereft of family and family history, fabricates as a father no lesser a figure than the murdered Bruno Schulz. As numerous critics have pointed out, there are clear affinities between *The Messiah* and other of Ozick's writings, including the temptation to and wariness concerning paganism so brilliantly expressed in her very early "Pagan Rabbi"; the mourning of Jewish Yiddishist culture, which occupies her in "Envy; or, Yiddish in America" and *The Cannibal Galaxy*; and the sheer horror of Holocaust devastation and loss described in *The Shawl*. Like these other writings, *The Messiah of Stockholm* is a work of Holocaust fiction in which Ozick conjures the ghosts of the past. Indeed, as if in a frenzy of endeavor to recover or resurrect the dead author, or at least the tradition he represents, Ozick imagines not one but two heirs to the murdered Polish writer; or, more precisely, she creates three heirs, because it is her book, finally, which is *The Messiah* (albeit *of Stockholm*) and not the manuscript that Schulz's other (illegitimate) daughter in the text professes to have found and for which the illegitimate son has been searching. As if to draw our attention to the fact that this *Messiah* is the one and only *Messiah*, Ozick also produces a plot summary of what she imagines Schulz's lost manuscript to have been about. As in "Envy; or Yiddish in America," in which the Sing-er-inspired Yiddish story-writer's story is given whole in the text, thus merg-ing the text within the text with the text itself, Ozick's rendition of Schulz's *Messiah* has a lot in common with her own novel entitled *The Messiah*, especially as pertains to idols, which come, through her own novel, to include the idolized Schulz himself.[14]

It is in the text's move to inherit Schulz as one more illegitimate heir (a move that repeats a major feature of the short story "Envy; or, Yiddish in America," in which Ozick situates herself in several ways in the tradition of Yiddish and American Jewish writing that she is discussing) that Ozick's text becomes less a study in survivor guilt and, one would have to add, sib-ling rivalry among Jewish authors than itself a participant in this odd family romance of thwarted mourning. The novel incorporates the rumors Ficow-ski records in his biography of Schulz having to do with the lost manuscript having surfaced in Sweden in the year of the novel's composition, 1987. It also, almost bizarrely, incorporates obliquely certain details of Ficowski's story as recorded in his biography of Schulz, including the fact that the per-son who first contacted Ficowski about the lost manuscript seems to have been the illegitimate son of Schulz's brother, who produced as well letters from the brother's legitimate daughter, Schulz's niece (Ficowski 158). Like its predecessor "Envy," this is a novel that proceeds under the weight of its belatedness and loss, and there is here as in the other story a good measure of envy being expressed, not only by the fiction's characters, but by the text itself, concerning who has the right to inherit and speak for this tradition. Ozick's text puts itself in the line of the family quarrel concerning the con-tinuity of Jewish literature.

In the *Messiah*, therefore, we cannot ignore the fact that Ozick empha-sizes the illegitimacy of inheritance by producing, within the novel, not one but two illegitimate heirs. Nor can we ignore the even more startling fact that she also doubles the illegitimate daughter with herself, doubling that doubling with her being herself also a double both of the sister's brother and double Lars, but also Heidi's husband Dr. Ecklund. To further com-pound the mathematics, Dr. Ecklund is, as Mrs. Ecklund puts it, also Lars's psychological twin (95), not to mention the father of Schulz's illegitimate daughter (perhaps his illegitimate daughter as well). For a story in which, as Lars puts it, "there's no room...for another child" (54), Ozick has made room for even one child more, not to mention grandchildren and multiple possible parents. Ozick's *Messiah,* like Ecklund's, is a forgery, for which she nonetheless, like him, desires legitimization of some sort; otherwise why publish it? But, insofar as the manuscript of Ecklund, born Eckstein (and if

---

14. I have developed this and other points concerning Ozick's short story in "Literary Symptomology and Jewish Fiction: Envy; or, The New Yiddish in America," *Anglo-phone Jewish Literature*, ed. Axel Stähler (London: Routledge, 2007), 79–92.

born Eckstein, why not born Schulz?), may be authentic, so too may Ozick's, for who is to say who or what is the false *messiah*? Given the history of Christian anti-Semitism, certainly Christianity cannot be allowed the last word on messiahs, hence Ozick's quotation of the Polish accusation concerning the lost manuscript, which could be taken as echoing the essential prod to anti-Semitism throughout the ages: "*The Messiah,* it's the Jews cursing Our Lord" (76).

If there is a messiah or an author thereof, why not a female messiah or author? There is a gender issue here as well. "It was being *saved,*" Adela says to Lars of the found manuscript, "for the daughter" (79). The intrusion of the gender issue is no more incidental to this text than it is to the short story "Envy," in which, as I have argued elsewhere, Ozick also insinuates herself as the female inheritor into the line carrying on the murdered tradition of Yiddish and Jewish writing. Critics have noted the affinities between Ozick's story and James' *Aspern Papers.* Herein lies another connection between the two works: the male protagonist, who is obsessed with recovering the texts of his master, whom he idolizes, dismisses all too quickly the intelligence of the women, who might lend him access to those texts (Heidi and Adela/Elsa forming in Ozick's rendition the parent [aunt? mother?]-child pair represented by Miss Juliana and Tina/Tita in James's story). These are women who might, in some way at least, even be the authors of those texts, not only their inspiration (as in the case of Adela for Schulz or in *Sanitarium* Elsa [Ozick's Adela's other name]).

The Jamesian influence is even more prominent in Roth's "Prague Orgy," which, insofar as it concludes the narrative begun in *The Ghost Writer,* has everything to do with the problematical idolization of past writers, for whom it seems impossible otherwise to mourn. For the American Jewish public in *The Ghost Writer* that idol was Anne Frank, whom Roth/Zuckerman resurrects from the dead in order to authorize or legitimate (to pick up the language of *The Messiah*) his own Jewish loyalty. This idolization is repeated in the young Zuckerman's reverence for the Jewish writer Lonoff (so like Isaac Babel and Bernard Malamud), which itself emulates Lonoff's own reverence (which is Roth's, not to mention Ozick's, as well) for James himself. This possibility of self-serving idolization of previous authors recurs toward the end of "The Prague Orgy," when the possessor of the manuscripts that Zuckerman is trying to smuggle out of Czechoslovakia hurls at him the following not-so-easily-to-be-dismissed accusation (either by us or by Roth himself):

> So *that's* what you get out of it! *That's* your idealism! The marvelous Zuckerman brings from behind the Iron Curtain two hundred unpublished Yiddish stories written by the victim of a Nazi bullet. You will be a hero to the Jews and to literature and to all of the Free World." (700)

By the Epilogue to *The Ghost Writer* the stakes for Zuckerman (and Roth) have become very high indeed.

The Aspern plot to which Ozick's *Messiah* applies to make a certain point about the tendency to turn writers into idols appears in Roth's text in a more fully Jamesian way. Zuckerman courts Olga, the abandoned wife of the refugee Czechoslovakian writer who sets Zuckerman on his quest to acquire his father's manuscripts, which are now in her keeping. Zuckerman even imagines, like the narrator in the James story, that they might become his by way of a "dowry" (767) should he marry her. From the initial conversation with the ex-patriot writer Sisovsky, who Zuckerman doesn't initially realize is (half-) Jewish, Zuckerman feels guilty. His troubles with his American critics cannot hold a candle to the censorship, censure, and finally exile Sisovsky has had to suffer. Jews are privileged in America, even Jewish writers like Zuckerman/Roth, who are the target of public attack. But by implied extension, Eastern European writers are also not suffering what Jews and Jewish writers suffered in the Holocaust. Hence the invention by Roth (not Zuckerman) of the Eastern European Sisovsky's Jewish Yiddishist father.

It is in order to acknowledge this other past and more primarily Jewish event that Roth's text has the story of Sisovsky's father recall that of Schulz (who did not write in Yiddish but was identifiably Jewish). In one popular retelling of that story Schulz was murdered by one Nazi in retaliation for another Nazi's murder of the first Nazi's Jew. Hence the line: "he shot my Jew, so I shot his" (718), a line that is repeated several times in the Roth text, as it is throughout Grossman's *See Under: Love,* as testimony to the odd economy of Holocaust logic.[15] Yet, Sisovsky's story is ultimately refuted by his abandoned wife Olga as "another lie. It happened to another writer, who didn't even write in Yiddish. Who didn't have a wife or have a child;" "Sisovsky's father," we are told, "was killed in a bus accident" (757). This serves to bring the fictional story back to the factual reality of Schulz. But it does more; it reduces the frame narrative to a cover story for the ever-Jewish Roth's inner plot, which is the almost obsessive and guilt-ridden post-Holocaust rescue (as in and by Ozick's *Messiah*) by Jews of Jewish texts. Hence Roth's own involvement, in his own interpretation, in the Other Europe project.

In Roth's text Sisovsky plays the role of Lars (and Ozick) in Ozick's novel: "My father's stories," the Czech ex-patriot writer tells Zuckerman, "were in Yiddish. To read the stories, I taught myself Yiddish." "He himself," Sisovsky tells us, "read Lessing, Herder, Goethe, and Schiller, but his own father had been, not even a town Jew like him, he had been a Jew in the farmlands, a village shopkeeper. To the Czechs such Jews spoke Czech, but in the family they spoke only Yiddish. All of this is in my father's stories: homelessness beyond homelessness. One story is called 'Mother Tongue.'"

---

15. *Zuckerman Bound* (Ferrar, Straus & Giroux, 1985), 716; references hereafter in text.

And he continues, bringing not only Schulz but Kafka into this story: "Kafka's homelessness, if I may say so, was nothing beside my father's" (719).

Just as the author of *The Messiah of Stockholm* comes to double both the murdered author of *The Messiah* and those heirs who would resurrect their idol and thus become its author, so Roth comes to replicate both the Yiddish writer and his ex-patriot writer son. In a scene that anticipates a Zuckerman novel yet to be written, *The Counterlife,* Zuckerman discovers his lost homeland, not in Israel, but in the destroyed alleyways of Kafka's and Schulz's devastated Europe:

> This is the city I imagined the Jews would buy when they had accumulated enough money for a homeland. I knew about Palestine and the hearty Jewish teenagers there reclaiming the desert and draining the swamps, but I also recalled, from our vague family chronicle, shadowy, cramped streets where the innkeepers and distillery workers who were our Old World forebears had dwelled apart, as strangers, from the notorious Poles—and so, what I privately pictured the Jews able to afford with the nickels and dimes I collected was a used city, a broken city, a city so worn and dim that no one else would even put in a bid....What was to betoken a Jewish homeland to an impressionable, emotional nine-year-old child...was, first, the overpowering oldness of the homes, the centuries of deterioration...the leaky pipes and moldy walls and rotting timbers and smoking stoves and simmering cabbages ....Second were the stories, all the telling and listening to be done, their infinite interest in their own existence, the fascination with their alarming plight, the mining and refining of *tons* of these stories—the national industry of the Jewish homeland, if not its sole means of production .... The construction of narrative out of the exertions of survival. (760–761)

The Jewish national agenda as Roth imagines it is very much Roth's own. Thus, hurrying with a "candy box full of Yiddish manuscripts" (770), recalling both the JNF collection box of his youth and the "garter box" in *The Messiah,* Zuckerman is like that "man in the long black coat," "hurrying hurrying" toward an escape that will be only another form of entrapment, albeit one that Zuckerman/Roth (like Lars/ Ozick) invites. This is Zuckerman's (and Roth's) Kafkaesque inheritance. Writes Roth in the aptly entitled story "'I Always Wanted You to Admire My Fasting'; or, Looking at Kafka" (1973), in which he resurrects the dead Kafka (the move that anticipates his resurrection of Anne Frank in *The Ghost Writer,* which is recalled in "The Prague Orgy" by the fact that Sisovsky's mistress plays the role of Anne Frank in the theatrical production of the play): "[Kafka] died too soon for the holocaust. Had he lived, perhaps he would have escaped....But *Kafka* escaping. It seems unlikely for one so fascinated by entrapment and careers that culminate in anguished death."[16] To be sure, Roth is far less anguished a writer than Kafka, but the identification is strong, and the bid to be admired for

---

16. *Reading Myself and Others* (London: J. Cape, 1961), 248.

taking on Jewish suffering characterizes not only Zuckerman's fantasy in *The Ghost Writer* and "The Prague Orgy," but Roth's fantasy as well in these and other writings.

For this reason Roth not only specifically recalls Schulz in the primary narrative of the recovery of the lost manuscript, but permits the text to be, as it were, infected by the other texts in the tradition to which he would attach it. Novak's (the minister of culture) "soft, fine hair white hair," for example, is described as being "like the fluff of a dry dandelion" (773), echoing the word *dandelion*, which no less than punctuates Ozick's *Messiah*. There is also the reference to an airport official as wearing an "hourglass" suit, echoing this prominent term in the titles not only of Schulz's but Danilo Kiš's novels (Kiš being one more writer from the other Europe). Says Novak, invoking both the Germany of the dandelion lamp and the writers such as Schulz, Kafka, and Kiš: "The ordinary Czech citizen does not think like the sort of people you have chosen to meet .... Who are they? Sexual perverts? Alienated neurotics. Bitter egomaniacs .... At least their blessed Kafka knew he was a freak" (777), at which point Zuckerman fantasizes Kafkaesquely: "As Nathan Zuckerman awoke one morning from uneasy dreams he found himself transformed in his bed into a sweeper of floors in a railway café" (778). If Sisovsky is Zuckerman's "counterpart from the world that my own fortunate family had eluded" (774), Novak is this text's counter-writer in the sense of its anti-writer. He represents the literary tradition that disdains Kafka and all that Kafka represents, which is expressed ironically in his straightforward respect, admiration, and love for his father, whom, damning with faint praise, he labels a "little man" (779). The relationship between fathers and sons in Kafka, Schulz, Appelfeld, and Roth may be highly vexed and fraught, but there is no way in which the fathers of these sons (either literal or literary) are, in their views of them, little men. Indeed, they are more like idols whom they both worship and despise, a complexity of feeling—indeed, a complex in the Freudian sense—not only about fathers but about idolatry (even the idolatry of literature) with which Ozick is keenly familiar.

In keeping with the dominant subjects and tropes of Schulz's published writings and certain of his comments concerning his lost manuscript, the encapsulated version of Schultz's *Messiah* in Ozick's text is all about idols. Like the Harold Bloom she produces in her essay entitled "Literature as Idol" Ozick is both Terach and Abraham; she is both a maker of idols and one who sees through them and smashes them. "A Jew," writes Ozick, "is someone who shuns idols" (188). And messiahs: "*The Book of Creation* has been returned to the Creator," Ozick quotes Singer as writing, "Messiah did not come for the Jews, so the Jews went to Messiah" ("I. B. Singer's Book of Creation," 221). For Jews there is no Messiah, and idol worship went out with Abraham. And yet, Ozick's writing everywhere makes clear, the temptation to idolatry perseveres and the wish for a Messiah remains strong. Otherwise, why in the Jewish tradition the recurrence to golems, to which Ozick's own fiction recurs again and again, who also, in Ozick's view, like the messiah, might just be a woman, especially since a golem (like an idol in Ozick's definition in relation to Bloom) has so much in common with a text. In Ozick's tale-within-a-tale version of Schulz's *Messiah,* the messiah in the world of idols is none other than a Book: "No human beings remained...only hundreds and hundreds of idols....Then...the Messiah arrived....More than anything else...he resembled a book–The Book" (108–110).

As female author in this male tradition, Ozick's take on this idolizing relation to the past is somewhat different, and this difference is reflected very powerfully in another one of the male members of this canon: David Grossman. In her essay on Singer, Ozick offers the following provocative comment that suggests something about the male / female aspects of this canon:

> [W]hat are we to think of the goblin cunning of a man who has taken his mother's given name–Bashevis (i.e., Bathsheba)–to mark out the middle of his own?...Does the taking-on of "Bashevis" imply a man wishing to be a woman? Or does it mean that a woman is hiding inside a man? (218)

The identification of Yiddish with the *mamaloshn* or *mother tongue,* which features prominently in Ozick's story "Envy" (a story that is actually about Singer and that also has to do with the relationship between the feminine Yiddish and the more masculinist Hebrew) takes a new turn in Grossman's novel, in which Hebrew recovers its relationship to the feminine aspects of the *mamaloshn.*[17] This feminization is already evidenced in the name of the protagonist. *Momik* recalls the Yiddish and Hebrew term of endearment whereby a child (male or female) is called *mommy,* in this way wishing the child long life and a procreative future by calling the child by the name through which his or her children will know him/her.

See Under: Love is typical of one genre of Holocaust novels. It deals with the child of survivors, for whom "Over There" and the "Nazi Beast," as Grossman's novel refers to Europe and the Nazis, remain terrifying in their mysteriousness, for the ways in which the realities can be neither spoken nor named (17, 13). Grossman's novel, thus, is, like Art Spiegelman's *Maus,* a classic study in inherited trauma, such as Abraham and Torok describe. It dramatizes the devastating consequences of inherited trauma, as it is passed on from generation to generation. Nor does inherited trauma either begin or end with the parent-child generation. Momik's dysfunctional fathering, born of his parents' dysfunctional parenting, threatens to perpetuate the inheritance of trauma, while the origins of Momik himself extend further back, or at least more broadly, than his parents. His grandfather Wasserman (i.e., Schulz) is thus a central character in his story.

---

17. Once again see my essay on this story.

Like the protagonist of Ozick's novel and like Ozick's novel itself, Grossman's Momik sees the world through the "murdered eye" of the dead "father"—in Momik's case a grandfather—the phrases referring to the dead "father's eye" recurring almost like a mantra throughout Ozick's novel (8, 31, 40, 41, 64, 68, 74, 83, 86, 90, 91 115). To be sure, Lars and Momik, who is only slightly less orphaned than the literally orphaned Lars, have endured the unendurable bereavement and dislocation produced by the mass slaughter of the Jews during the Holocaust. Thus Lars' fantasy, for example, that his father is the dead author, like Momik's weird games and obsessions in *See Under: Love*, may seem to us less symptoms of psychosis or even of neurosis than understandable and forgivable fantasies. Yet these fantasies do not serve these protagonists' best interests. Like hysterical symptoms (which, of course, they are, however much we might understand and sympathize with them), they keep these characters pinned in a place of devastation and loss, unable to grieve properly and hence unable to move on. Like Rosa in *The Shawl*, the images through which Lars and Momik perceive themselves and the world make of the world itself an unending extermination camp and themselves its eternally suffering victims: "that roasting in the air," writes Ozick, somewhere between her voice and Lars's; "His own sweat. The exertion. His legs like gyros. O the chimneys of armpits, moist and burning under wool" (18). The imagery repeats throughout the text.

In a similar way Momik lives his parents' trauma over and over again. Thus Momik, like Lars, discovers himself unable to father (or mother) the future, except in the most minimalist and compromised way. "On account of this father," *The Messiah* records, "Lars shrank himself. He felt he resembled his father: all the tales were about men shrinking more and more into the phantasmagoria of the mind" (5). In this way he acquires "the face of a foetus; it was as if he was waiting for his dead father to find him, and was determined to remain recognizable" (6). The (male) child Lars would father himself; he would virtually *become* his own father in a very literal way. So would Momik, whose major fantasy in the Bruno section of the novel has to do with a virtual return to the womb-like sea, who is both the speaker of the maternal tongue that, we are to understand from the text, Schulz spoke too, and who is also the maternal presence who might give birth to a new procreative son—namely, the author Momik, not to mention the writer whose text this is: Grossman. Might we not understand Grossman, by recasting himself as Momik, to be attempting to rid his name of both its gross and masculinist components, making him, like his protagonist, more a *mommy* than a father?

To remain recognizable is the inner burden of this family of texts, for if they do not back up out of time and if they do not recapitulate in their own being the murdered fathers, how then will their fathers know them to give birth to them again? Roth's "family resemblance" turns out to be paramount to the survival of family itself. "No more sins, no more temptations! ...There is no further need for demons," Ozick quotes Singer in his short story "The Last Demon" (220–221). Singer's own fiction belies this statement, as does Ozick's, Grossman's, and Roth's. Ozick's messiah of Stockholm is no messiah, but, in a recurrent image for Ozick, in *The Messiah* and elsewhere, a *golem*—perhaps, as in *The Puttermesser Papers,* a female golem. A golem is the Jew's version of a messiah. It is a mud-and-clay zombie, stirred up from the depths (of an ocean or an earth: they are sisters in Grossman's novel), who, like Grossman's Schulz-inspired grandfather Wasserman, is doomed to keep himself alive by his storytelling despite his equally powerful wish to die; in *See Under: Love* the man Bruno wishes to die, while the storyteller in him struggles to live. That survival through literature, Roth tells us in "The Prague Orgy," is the Jewish homeland, telling the story that is survival itself. And yet, as Kafka made so clear, storytelling is not escape, but entrapment instead (whether in sea or myth or fantasy or writing). This is Grossman's, Ozick's, Appelfeld's, and Roth's fate and homeland as well. For the story the Jewish storyteller finds himself or herself telling is just that story of doomed and detested survival, which doesn't so much exhaust itself in the telling as drain the teller of all energy and life.

To reformulate the imagery of Roth's *Ghost Writer* and make it more applicable to the texts we have been discussing, might it not be possible to claim that these writers and their characters do not so much ghostwrite the past as they *golem*write it, producing an embodied ghost that is something between idol and messiah and that is identical to the text itself. Literature, Ozick insists in the Bloom essay—and her own writing and Roth's confirms this—may well be a form of idolatry. And neither idols nor messiahs nor even golems constitute viable options for the Jewish writer. Indeed, as more than one story of the golem has indicated, the very creature designed to save the Jewish people might just swing out of control and threaten their destruction instead. Book, idol, messiah, golem—all run the same risk. Yet, how, then, keep the past alive? How produce that text that is the homeland of the Jewish people and the instrument of their survival and that will enable a future that is not merely a dead and deadening repetition of the past?

"Yet it happened on occasion, not very frequently, that Lars grieved for his life." And in the text's final sentence, simply, "he grieved" (143–144). Grieving for these writers may constitute only an occasional respite from the phantoms that haunt Jewish history. Those phantoms, captured in the image of "the man in the long black coat," are for them, and through them for us, always "hurrying...hurrying...hurrying toward the chimneys" (144). Yet, occasionally, like Lars, we may simply grieve, "not" (to use the word the text repeats four times in the penultimate paragraph) for any specific loss, but as a response to the history that he (like the Jewish people itself) cannot help but inherit. Ozick's, Roth's, and Grossman's texts, like Kafka's and Schulz's before them, bring the reader to the place of inconsolable grief. Then they leave us, to determine for ourselves, how and when and what we will mourn.

IV.
INTERVENTIONS:
EXPANDING WISSE'S CANON

What's So Funny about Yiddish Theater?
Comedy and the Origins
of Yiddish Drama

JEREMY DAUBER

In a volume of this sort, personal reminiscences regarding the honoree are, if not obligatory, at least permissible; so permitted, I will begin this essay by setting the scene of my first encounter with the study of Yiddish drama: a small seminar room in 6 Divinity Avenue, under Ruth Wisse's instruction. My admittedly hazy memories of that particular seminar are shot through with a recollection of the awe I had—and have—of her incisive intelligence and her remarkable insight into the materials we discussed. I was an undergraduate and just beginning to learn the language; and as a result, the textbooks for the course, ordered from the National Yiddish Book Center, were among the very first Yiddish volumes I ever purchased: the two-volume *Di yidishe drame fun der tsvantsiktn yorhundert*.[1]

Looking through the plays chosen by the editors for inclusion provides a remarkable overview of the great plays and playwrights of the first half of the twentieth century, the zenith of secular Yiddish culture. In its pages, the reader finds Isaac Leib Peretz's Hasidic family drama and meditation on the birth pangs of Jewish modernity, *Di goldene keyt* ("The Golden Chain"); Peretz Hirshbein's pastoral excursion *Grine felder* ("Green Fields"); Jacob Gordin's *Mirele Efros*, sometimes known as the "Jewish Queen Lear," which takes old English wine and fits it, perhaps uncomfortably, into modern Jewish bottles; Dovid Pinski's *Yankl der shmid* ("Yankl the Blacksmith"), which substitutes the urges and temptations of the Jewish *baal-guf*, the powerful man, for typical tales of yeshiva students (as does, in its own way, the also included *Yankel Boyle*, by the noted American Yiddish writer Leon Kobrin); H. Leivick's *Shmates* ("Rags") focusing on the dehumanization of American Jewish immigrants under the heel of capitalism; and perhaps the apotheosis of twentieth-century Yiddish drama, S. Ansky's *Der dibek* ("The Dybbuk"), that star-crossed combination of Jewish ethnog-

---

A version of this essay was first delivered as the Jacob Pat Memorial Lecture at Harvard University in February 2005. I would like to thank Dr. Charles Berlin of the Harvard College Library for his generous invitation and hospitality in that instance. My thanks also to the editors for their considered and incisive comments, as well as to Ruth Wisse, for more than I can say.

1. Hyman Bass, ed., *Di yidishe drame fun der tsvantsiktn yorhundert* (Alvelt-lekhen yidishn kultur-kongres, 1977), 2 vols.

raphy and Shakespearean doomed romance.[2] After a decade of greater exposure to Yiddish literary and theatrical history, however, perusal of the anthology yielded an additional observation: of the eight plays the editor chose to purportedly represent the range of twentieth-century Yiddish theater, only one could truly be considered a comedy, Sholem Aleichem's *Dos groyse gevins* ("The Jackpot").[3]

This is hardly to suggest that the Yiddish theater's sense of humor vanished in the twentieth century; such a claim would be demonstrably untrue. Even a glimpse at the plays produced at New York's Second Avenue Yiddish theaters reveals that many popular light comedies were on offer; comic writers such as Sholem Aleichem and Moyshe Nadir were writing important plays; and satirical *kleynkunst* (cabarets), with notable contributors and performers such as Moyshe Broderzon and the team of Dzigan and Shumacher, were highly influential and popular in interwar Europe.[4]

Popularity and influence notwithstanding, though, certain imbalances seemed to exist on what, following Professor Wisse, we might call the canonical level, the works of Yiddish theater that tell the story of Jewish experience the best.[5] It seems eminently possible to list the great works of the Yiddish theater after, say, 1900, and, as Hyman Bass did, feature almost no comedies in doing so. The converse, though, is precisely not the case. If one were to take a look at the Yiddish theater before, say, 1890, and propose a list of the canonical works—even, arguably, almost all of the works, since they are fairly limited in number—not only would it be impossible to exclude comedies, it would be very difficult to find works that were *not*, by some definition or other, comic.

---

2. One indisputably great twentieth-century Yiddish play, notable for its absence in the volume but, as I recall, not in the class reading, is Sholem Asch's controversial *Got fun nekome* ("God of Vengeance"), with its prostitution and discreet lesbianism. My memories of discussing *Got fun nekome* may, however, stem entirely from the fact that Caraid O'Brien, who went on to retranslate the play into English, was also present in these Yiddish seminars.

3. The complexities inherent in the translation of the word *drame* in Yiddish as it appears in the anthology's title as, variously, any kind of theatrical genre or dramas more specifically, are, it seems to me, reduced here by the inclusion of the Sholem Aleichem play in the first place, clearly suggesting the word's more universal sense.

4 See, for example, Nahma Sandrow, *Vagabond Stars: A World History of Yiddish Theater* (Harper & Row, 1977), 91-131, 323-333; Moyshe Broderzon, *Oysgeklibene shriftn* (Literartur-gezelshaft baym yivo in argentine, 1972), passim; Jacob Weitzner, *Sholem Aleichem in the Theater* (Symposium Press, 1994).

5. See Ruth R. Wisse, *The Modern Jewish Canon: A Journey Through Language and Culture* (The Free Press, 2000), esp. 14-15, for her significantly more elegant and nuanced formulation of these canonical conditions.

From the late eighteenth-century Berlin Haskalah and what Max Erik has referred to as "the comedies of the Berlin Enlightenment"[6] to the anonymous *Di genarte velt* ("The Fooled World"), probably written in the first quarter of the nineteenth century in Galicia, to the Eastern European tradition—Isaac Ber Levinson's *Di hefker-velt* ("The Topsy-turvy World"), Ettinger's *Serkele*, Gottlober's *Der dektukh* ("The Bridal Canopy"), S.Y. Abramovitsh's *Di takse* ("The Tax"), and the early work of Avrom Goldfadn, most notably *Di tsvey kuni-leml* ("The Two Kuni-Lemls")—the overwhelming majority of the works under discussion are pointedly satiric. They traffic in comic stereotype, often delight in farcical situations or physical comedy, and frequently parody other literary texts or dramatic material.[7] And yet this particular type and genre of Yiddish comedy largely disappears at the end of the nineteenth century.

Describing and explaining its rise and fall, in part, necessitates an overview of the main trends shaping Yiddish theatrical culture's first century and, following Professor Wisse's example of constantly grounding general questions in specific works, viewing those trends through three authors' notable variations of standard conventions. In reading their plays in slightly less conventional ways, I hope to suggest how taken together they contribute to the relationship of Yiddish, the theater, and Jewish comedy, the last a topic of particular and lasting interest to this festschrift's honoree from her first book to the present day.

First and foremost, all modern Yiddish theater of this period is fundamentally conditioned by the contours of the general trends of contemporary Jewish literature, that is, by the Haskalah. I have discussed maskilic literary approaches more generally elsewhere.[8] Aspects of the movement relevant to our purposes, though, include first the creation and designation of literary material as polemic material to change the actions and the mindset of traditional, unenlightened Jewry; second, the common usage of subversive humor, most frequently parody and satire, to effect that change, particularly given the resistance of traditional communities to material viewed as frivolous at best and heretical at worst; and third, the establishment of aesthetic and generic criteria resulting in the elevation of material modeled on Western European (or, to a lesser extent, Russian) work over internal Jewish literary structures.

---

6. Max Erik, *Di komediyes fun der berliner ufklerung* (Melukhe-Farlag, 1933).

7. For more bibliographic information about these works, see Joel Berkowitz and Jeremy Dauber, "Introduction," in Joel Berkowitz and Jeremy Dauber, eds., *Landmark Yiddish Plays: A Critical Anthology* (SUNY, 2006), 1–71, passim.

8. See Jeremy Dauber, *Antonio's Devils: Writers of the Jewish Enlightenment and the Birth of Modern Hebrew and Yiddish Literature* (Stanford University Press, 2004), passim.

Theater provided a particularly challenging medium for the maskilim. Its stark circumscription by traditional Jewish authorities and, paradoxically, its extreme popularity in the form of the subversive outlet of the *purim-shpiln* or Purim plays offered remarkable opportunity to pursue their ideological agendas.[9] After all, the eighteenth-century German culture they wished to emulate certainly valued the theatrical form. Drama is as suited as any medium, if not more so, to the polemic, and the *purim-shpil* provided an extant and wildly popular genre for them to subvert. Their task was to find, in these new successors to old Purim theatricals, a means of balancing their cultural conservatism (since, though regarding the *purim-shpil*'s excesses as deeply offensive and counterproductive to the Enlightenment project, they required traditional continuity to attract their traditional targets) and their progressiveness (using the theater to advocate social and religious reforms).

At least part of the solution must have been to maintain some analogous version of the original plays' spirit of comic reversals, to suggest that the Purim theme, that of topsy-turviness,[10] of reversal of established hierarchies (including social and religious hierarchies), is not limited to creating safety valves within traditional culture—the role played by the *purim-shpil* in generations past—but can extend to transvaluing that same culture. Comedy, then—a mode of subversion and disruption, but that, through the vicissitudes of the particular theatrical culture facing the maskilim, also stands for cultural continuity—was precisely the dramatic medium needed by the maskilim in their balancing act between cultural conservatism and progressiveness.

One of the foundational plays of modern Yiddish theater, Aaron Halle Wolfssohn's *Laykhtzin un fremelay* ("Silliness and Sanctimony"), is a case in point. Wolfssohn was a member of the Berlin Haskalah and contributed to many of its flagship projects, but, most importantly for our purposes, headed the Königliche Wilhelmsschule in Breslau along with his fellow maskil Joel Bril.[11] The school taught Jewish and secular subjects according to new, Enlightenment-oriented, pedagogical principles and thus sparked

---

9. For some accounts of the well-known rabbinic bias against theater and the history of the Purimshpiln, see B. Gorin, *Di geshikhte fun idishn teater* (Literarishe farlag, 1918), 7–63; Evi Bützer, *Die Anfänge der jiddischen purim shpiln in ihrem literarischen und kulturgeschichtlichen Kontext* (Helmut Buske Verlag, 2003); Jean Baumgarten, *Introduction à la littérature yiddish ancienne* (Paris, 1993), 443–473, and Khone Shmeruk, ed. *Makhazot mikraiim be-yidish, 1697–1750* (Israel Academy of Sciences and Humanities, 1979).

10. See Esther 9:1.

11. For a fuller treatment of Wolfssohn and his work, see *Antonio's Devils*, 164–206, and Jutta Strauss, "Aaron Halle-Wolfssohn: A Trilingual Life" (Ph.D. dissertation, University of Oxford, 1994). The play is available in translation in *Landmark Yiddish Plays*, 81–111.

controversy within the local Jewish community. As part of his work there, Wolfssohn composed plays for the students of the school to perform in the period around the holiday of Purim, plays designed to replace the old *purim-shpiln* with a new theatrical paradigm. Whether *Silliness and Sanctimony* was one of those plays is a matter of speculation, but seems reasonable.

In the play, Reb Henokh, deeply influenced by the Polish rabbi and Hasid Reb Yoysefkhe and his constant perversions and misinterpretations of Jewish tradition, has decided to marry off his daughter Yetkhen—and thus give his new-made fortune—to Reb Yoysefkhe, despite the warnings given him by his solid and sensible wife, Teltse, and her enlightened brother Markus. When Reb Yosefkhe reveals her father's intent to Yetkhen, she becomes so enraged and terrified that she runs away from home with an ardent admirer, a non-Jew named Von Schnapps (who is never seen). Von Schnapps betrays her trust, however, and places her in a brothel. She is saved from a fate worse than death by the timely intervention of Markus, whose actions cause Reb Henokh to reevaluate his position and arrange a marriage between his daughter and Markus. His reevaluation is aided by the fact that Reb Yoysefkhe, the supposedly pure and holy Reb Yoysefkhe, is revealed as a regular visitor to the brothel, having even offered to pawn his phylacteries to help pay the large bill he has run up.[12]

Real continuities exist between the story of the Book of Esther and *Silliness and Sanctimony*. Both feature hypocrites who, as the play opens, are firmly ensconced in the good graces of the ruling authority, but are unmasked due to efforts of the hero and heroine. In both cases the revelations occur at locations ostensibly designed for entertainment and pleasure (a feast or wine party in the Bible, and a bordello in *Silliness and Sanctimony*) and both attempt to represent Jewish existence in societies that seem to vacillate between tolerance and hostility. Here, of course, the solution is to remove the traditionalist hypocrite-turned-Haman and replace him with a reformed, Enlightened approach.[13] Wolfssohn's return to the biblical story as a template accords well with the maskilim's love of classicism and their bibliophilia (a sentiment that itself had ideological roots and effects), but probably also has much to do with his desire for the play to serve as a replacement for the contemporary *purim-shpiln*, which demanded the thematic continuity.

But continuities of theme do not necessitate continuities of tone and the choice of tone—particularly in the choice of language, and choices within that language—are vital in further understanding Wolfssohn's work and its importance to our discussion. *Laykhtzin un fremelay*, one of the first Yid-

---

12. I have taken this plot summary from my *Antonio's Devils*, 186–187.

13. The play is remarkably subtle about the nature of that chosen approach; see Dauber 189–206 for details.

dish plays, was Wolfssohn's second version of the work; he had written a Hebrew version some years before. I've written about this switch in more detail elsewhere.[14] Suffice it to say that Wolfssohn's Hebrew dramatic work—both here and in his philosophical dramatic dialogue *Sicha be'eretz hachayim* ("A dialogue in the land of the living [dead]"), published in the journal *Hameasef* between 1794 and 1797—shows his struggle with the limitations of the theatrical genre as it had heretofore been presented in the literature of the Berlin Haskalah, which is to say, as a Hebrew-language genre.

In the dialogue, Wolfssohn attempts to provide his characters with stage directions and offers a certain intensification of the dialogue through punctuation and the occasional interjection. But ultimately these characters fail to serve as anything more than mouthpieces for a set of ideological positions. Such failure, perhaps stemming at least in part from the employment of elevated, classically resonant Hebrew, may be excused (or at least excusable) in a dialogue set in the abstracted land of the dead, whose characters' preoccupation with things ultimate may lead to a kind of absence or effacement of tics and character, as well as an undue gravity on the protagonists' part. In the real land of the living, however—the living, breathing social situation of Northern Prussia, in which Wolfssohn sets his bourgeois family drama—conflict and comedy come not only from the clash of ideas, but from the lived characters who speak and represent those ideals; and as such Wolfssohn must have become highly sensitized to the intimate relation between language and character.[15]

Yiddish, then, or more precisely the multivocal production that is *Silliness and Sanctimony*, with its mixture of Hochdeutsch, Western Yiddish, and Eastern European Yiddish, might have been looked upon by Wolfssohn as a comic alternative to reflect the most serious questions of Jewish Enlightenment, its prospects and its stumbling blocks. And, in this reading, he would have done so precisely *not* for the reasons that "Yiddish" today is often tarred as a comic language, fit only for jokes, but rather because its ability to express character and societal realia rendered it a far more appropriate alternative, aesthetically speaking, besides the other historical factors we've mentioned, than the Hebrew favored by other writers of the time, and, indeed, Wolfssohn himself originally.

With the eastward move of the Haskalah into Galicia and the Russian Pale of Settlement, the themes of maskilic literature shift to reflect the changed historical situation of the Jews. The most notable change is the literature's

---

14. See Jeremy Dauber, "The City, Sacred and Profane: Between Hebrew and Yiddish in the Fiction of the Early Jewish Enlightenment," *Jewish Studies Quarterly* 12 (March 2005).

15. Such sensitivity is highlighted further if we consider Wolfssohn's relation to his other source material, Moliere's *Tartuffe*; see *Landmark Yiddish Plays*, 13, and the notes there. One may, perhaps, view the transition from Moliere's rhymes to Wolfssohn's prose as an analogue to the switch from Hebrew to Yiddish.

(and the movement's) marked anti-Hasidism, only natural given the new and enormous popularity of a movement whose features, particularly the worship of a charismatic figure who claimed to be capable (or whose followers claimed him capable) of miracles, were particularly offensive to the rationalist forces of the Enlightenment. Joseph Perl, the Galician Haskalah's best-known figure, left behind no dramatic writings; however, his early essay *Über das Wesen der Sekte Hasidim* ("On the Nature of the Hasidic Sect") has much to say about the role of theater in its broadest sense in this period, and inaugurates a sensibility of vital importance to the next stage in Yiddish theater.[16] In the work, submitted to the Austrian authorities in the hope that they would take an active role in combating the newly powerful movement, Perl portrays the general Jewish community as credulous simpletons misled by malicious and brilliant impersonators (or perhaps I should say impresarios) who misrepresent their holy abilities for (primarily) financial profit.

My point here is not to judge the accuracy of Perl's claims or even to judge the influence of his work (which in this case was minimal, since the Austrian authorities refused to allow him to publish it). Rather, it is to suggest that in the eyes of maskilic figures of the time there was again a theatrical enemy at once to be combated and to serve as creative inspiration. But now the enemy was not only (or even primarily) traditional Purim plays but rather the theatrical performance inherent in everyday Hasidic life. Hardly surprising, then, that plays of the period bear titles such as *Teatr fun khsidim* ("Theater of Hasidim") and *Di genarte velt* ("The Fooled World"). The latter's title suggests that the world's problematic constitution stems from a surfeit of deception, of artifice, and, therefore, there must be deceivers and artificers, in this case, the Hasidim. Its (anonymous) author's introduction accentuates the maskilic characterization of Hasidic behavior as theatrical and performed:

> Our holy Talmud says, *mefarsemin et hachaneifim mipnei khilul hashem*, that is, it is proper to reveal the shame of false people, who disguise themselves (*farshteln zikh*) and who say that they are pious, but in truth they are great evildoers; they bow down to the ground and contain matters of blasphemy to heaven's peak. Such men disgrace God's name in the world, and through them it emerges that even someone who is in truth a honest Jew can become shamed. One must not be ashamed, but rather one must openly let the world know that they are swindlers and that their piety is pure deception (*batrigerai*). So says our Talmud, and this is in truth the main purpose of this small volume....Concerning them [these deceivers] it is a great *mitzve* to tear the false masks off these people's faces..."[17]

---

16. See Joseph Perl, *Über das Wesen der Sekte Chasidim.* ed. Avraham Rubinstein (Publications of the Israel Academy of Sciences and Humanities, 1977). On the work, see Avraham Rubinstein, "Al mahut kat khasidim," *Kiryat Sefer* 38 (1964): 263–272, 415–424; 39 (1965): 117–236.

17. M.Viner, ed. *Di genarte velt* (Melukhe-farlag, 1940).

Such perspectives reveal an expansionist impulse in the comic sensibility of the Haskalah. Though Wolfssohn's play was intended as a vehicle of social and theatrical change, the scene in which that change played itself out was a small one: one household in a city in Northern Prussia. True, the current situation of Reb Henokh's household may have stood *metonymically* for strains and stresses in Jewish society, but in Wolfssohn's play society at large is stable (if slightly problematic) until the entrance of the masked, theatrical Reb Yoysefkhe, who threatens to disrupt the situation entirely. When he is removed, order is restored and the world runs as it should. Given trends of acculturation and Jewish cosmopolitan presence in Prussia at the time, as well as the maskilic desire to present Prussian Jews as inherently assimilable over and against their Eastern European counterparts, this perspective seems reasonable. As befits the maskilic view of the situation in East and East Central Europe, however, matters are here entirely reversed: it is the world itself that is masked and theatrical, and the figures of virtue—the unmasked and the unmaskers—who are few and far between.

The resulting transformation of Yiddish theater into a darkly comic reflection of a skewed, theatricalized Jewish universe becomes the basis for even further development in the next great Yiddish play, Shloyme Ettinger's *Serkele*. Ettinger, dubbed "the merry Solomon" by friends, may have been a man for whom comedy came naturally; but it was still serious business to him. His good friend Anthony Eisenbaum, submitting a request for permission to publish Ettinger's *Serkele* and *Fables* in 1843, said that "these works are accessible to all classes of Jews, they present in living colors their failings and their lacunae, they picture pointedly and comically the entire Jewish way of life and therefore they can have a redeeming effect on the brain."[18] Eisenbaum's peculiarly anatomical turn of phrase finds its reflection in Ettinger's own distinctive biography; the latter apparently attended medical school in Lemberg in the late 1820s and cut his teeth as a practitioner in the cholera epidemics that swept Poland in the summer of 1831 and once again in 1855.

Ettinger's epidemiological experiences enabled him, it seems to me, to take a peculiarly medical view both of the problems he and other maskilim saw afflicting the traditional Jewish community and the possibility and dimensions of its cure. Moreover, the widely circulated story that Ettinger read *Serkele* aloud to his patients, insisting that it and the laughter it evoked had medicinal value, seems to be so perfect in this vein that it is tempting to assume that it is apocryphal. But it is certainly significant that the medical Ettinger created a comedy of hypochondria—the eponymous Serkele, one of the great characters of the Yiddish theater, though constantly bewailing her

---

18. For a more detailed biography of Ettinger and a more detailed introduction to *Serkele*, see Berkowitz and Dauber, 23–35, and the bibliographical material cited there; the analysis here, however, complements the discussion there.

weakened state, has enough strength to swat her servants around the stage like flies, and enough presence to chew scenery with the best of them.

The play's Yiddish subtitle is *a yortsayt nokh a bruder*, literally, the anniversary of a brother's death. The entire action takes place on the anniversary of the day Serkele's brother Dovid Goodheart reputedly died at sea on a business trip. Prudently, Dovid had provided a substantial fortune to see that his daughter Hinde would be raised as befits a girl of her station, and he had named Serkele and her husband, Reb Moyshe Dansker, as her guardians. However, Serkele had a fake will drawn up that redirected those funds into the guardians' own pockets. Hinde, knowing nothing of her inheritance, lives a Cinderella-like existence, more overworked servant than adored niece. By contrast, Serkele dotes elaborately on her own daughter, the foolish (but now well-dowered) Friederika. Friederika is being courted by a sly young fortune hunter named Gavriel Hendler, who steals a box of Serkele's jewels and then helps to throw the blame on Hinde and her beloved, the enlightened Markus Redlekh. Things look grim for our heroes until a stranger comes to town, who, of course, turns out to be none other than the long-lost brother. By the play's end, the falsely accused have been cleared of wrongdoing and given Dovid's blessing and the true villains have been punished.[19]

Normally, given the typical understanding of the play, the Haskalah, and Yiddish comedy entirely, we might formulate our approach to the play as follows. What indeed is the sickness that attacks the Jews and what is its cure? A standard reading of the play—a reading that has much to recommend it—locates the themes of the play quite conventionally along Enlightenment-oriented lines. The sickness is the hypocrisy and falsehood that obtains among the powerful and empowered in traditional society; that, following in the example of *Di genarte velt* (which, parenthetically, Ettinger mentions reading while in Lemberg), the world as a whole consists of those wearing masks, engaging in theatrical activity within the play.

Serkele, of course, would figure then as our hypocritical and theatrical Typhoid Mary, pretending to be the rightful heir, and pretending, perhaps, to mourn her brother's death, when in reality exulting in the chance it gives her to increase her economic status. Indeed, even the haughtiness Serkele displays is a kind of theatrical act. A number of characters comment that she has "forgotten her place" as someone who once worked with corn and meal, but a more accurate assessment would be that she only acts as though she has forgotten that place. In reality—as is commonly the case in negative portrayals of the noveau riche—she remembers it all too well and would do anything to avoid returning to it. One might even argue that it is from this schizoid stress of acting that illness arises. Certainly this is the case with Ser-

---

19. I have largely taken this plot summary from *Landmark Yiddish Plays*, 30–31.

kele's husband, who, as a result of his participation in the fraud, has become ill and has extremely vivid nightmares.[20]

If the illness has indeed been diagnosed correctly, then the cure is apparently evident: one big dose of truth, exemplified by the enlightened figure's arrival (in the form of the absent virtuous man), and the infection of theatricality will clear right up. Certainly this is a standard reading of the play, according to notions of maskilic comedy articulated earlier: the world is fooled by those in masks, illness goes hand in hand with theatricality, and truth and enlightenment are the cure. But the play is more complex than that and, in examining its complexities, we may see how it represents yet another transition in this constantly evolving tradition. Serkele, of course, is not ill; she only says she is. Yet the play remains remarkably unclear as to whether she believes herself to be ill or merely uses it as an excuse to achieve her own goals, whether those goals be the seduction of Markus—a doctor whom she insists provide her with hands-on treatment—or simply the opportunity to excoriate and hit her servants. What's more, the equivalence of theatricality to evil or illness is also complicated by Dovid, who masquerades as a stranger upon his return rather than announcing himself to his family immediately.

The latter concern is more easily dismissed. We may take Goodheart's decision to disguise himself—a decision expressed in the play as a purely instrumental choice born of necessity—as a reference to the means maskilim must employ, even and especially if they find those means problematic, in order to achieve their ultimate goals. This dynamic of using problematic means to achieve desirable goals by Eastern European maskilim is generally applied to the decision to use Yiddish, as Dan Miron has famously shown.[21] Our knowledge of Ettinger, though, indicates that the hypothesis that the anxiety reflected is a linguistic one seems unlikely. In fact, Ettinger is generally accepted as one of the few Yiddish writers of the nineteenth century to be genuinely comfortable with his use of the language.[22] Instead, the anxiety may come from the same source Baruch Kurzweil famously anatomized in nineteenth-century Hebrew satire: once a satirist takes up his arrows against any position, it becomes very difficult to keep one's searching gaze away from one's own positions and cherished ideals as well.[23]

Unlike his predecessors, Ettinger may, in *Serkele* and with Serkele, be starting to ask more profound questions about the nature of comic literature

20. See, for example, his long monologue at the beginning of the second act.

21. See Dan Miron, *A Traveler Disguised* (University of Syracuse Press, 1996 [2nd ed.]).

22. On Ettinger's positive attitude toward Yiddish, see the discussion in *Landmark Yiddish Plays*, 28–30.

23. See Baruch Kurzweil, "Al hasatira shel Yosef Perl," in his *Bemaavak al erkhei hayahadut* (Jerusalem: Schocken, 1969), 55–85.

and the dangers of its use for causes other than for its own sake, and, perhaps, may suggest that comedy digs at the very foundations of identity itself. The knowing position of the eiron, so essential to early maskilic comedy, is beginning to crumble. Wolfssohn's play, after all, has a character who renders the ultimate judgment of the playwright, and the author of *Di genarte velt* tells us, in a highly explicit introduction to the play, exactly who is fooling whom and how. As we become less certain whether Serkele believes herself to be ill or not—a condition befitting a hypochondriac—even we become less certain of her status, as a figure of evil or of pity (she is graciously forgiven at play's end, after all), and less certain, then, of where precisely we stand as observers. The dangers posed by the adoption of the comic technique for sincere and idealistic purposes become clearer as the plays become less so.

Serkele's comedy follows the Shakespearean comic mode, itself, of course, heavily influenced by Roman New Comedy, with its clever servants, frustrated lovers, and even its multiple marriages. Alyssa Quint has aptly demonstrated the ways in which *Serkele* resonates with that most deeply troubled, from a Jewish context, of Shakespeare's comedies, *The Merchant of Venice*.[24] As is well known, the message of the caskets of Belmont is not "Who chooseth me shall gain what many men desire" or even "Who chooseth me shall get as much as he deserves," but "Who chooseth me must give and hazard all he hath." When the censor, in response to Eisenbaum's 1843 request for publication, suggested massive changes to his manuscript, Ettinger refused to accede and as a result died without seeing any of his Yiddish work in print. It is easy to take this as the sign of a proud artist insisting on the quality of his work, and perhaps rightly so. But it may also be the case of a doctor particularly attuned to the lethal power of medicine inaccurately calibrated by hands other than his own.

The most expert hands at comedy are well aware of its dangers. As all readers of *The Merchant of Venice* know, Act V, when Jessica enters Belmont, can be seen as putting a powerful lie to Puck's promise in another of Shakespeare's comedies that "Jack shall have Jill/Nought shall go ill" (III.ii.461–62). Endings are rarely neat; theater impressed into the service of history rarely does what one expects it to; any sense of an uncomplicated comic vision begins to crumble. With the last work to be discussed in detail, the process of internal disintegration reaches its apex, marking the end of a type of Yiddish theater and the real beginning of a new type of Jewish comedy.

Avrom Goldfadn is generally referred to as the father of modern Yiddish theater. The works discussed here, of course, tend to suggest that such assignment of paternity is, at the very least, somewhat complex. But Gold-

---

24. See Alyssa Pia Quint, "The Currency of Yiddish: Ettinger's *Serkele* and the Reinvention of Shylock," *Prooftexts* 24:1 (Winter 2004).

fadn's responsibility for manifold and multiple developments in the Yiddish theatrical tradition, such as his innovation and institutionalization of a performing tradition within Yiddish theater, especially a tradition that features his preferred modes of operetta and melodrama, make him worthy of an honored, perhaps the most honored, place in that tradition.[25] However, the discussion here will focus on just one, significantly less marked aspect of his contributions: the increasingly horrific nature of his comedy, particularly around the issue of identity, and the transformation of his farce (and he is one of Yiddish's great farceurs) into nightmare. Considered this way, Goldfadn may be seen (along with his prose counterpart in exploring the terrors of Jewish identity through black humor, Sholem Aleichem) as a central figure in the creation of a kind of modern and uncompromising dark comic vision that will characterize Yiddish—and Jewish—comedy of the twentieth century.

This may be, to put it mildly, a surprising way to characterize Goldfadn, a man best known for his light operettas and happy songs, but it may serve as a way into another side of this enormously multifaceted talent. Such exploration is best accomplished by looking at the process of creation of one of his great characters, Kuni-Leml, one (or both) of the title characters in his most famous play, *The Two Kuni-Lemls*. From early in his dramatic career, Goldfadn seems to have been interested in presenting a monstrous image of an unfit, unreconstructed pre-enlightened Jew, in a fashion not too dissimilar to Wolfssohn's Reb Yoysefkhe or Hasidim in the fiction of the Galician Haskalah. An early play features this figure, whose name, Shmendrik, has become a by-word.

The 1877 play of the same name features a beautiful, intelligent young girl from a distinguished but impoverished family willing to accept any candidate with money. Certainly one would find it hard to imagine anyone less suitable than Shmendrik, who, according to Golfadn's description, is "fifteen years old, not tall, a *yarmulke* on his head and two long, straight earlocks, in red underwear that buttons in back. Over the underwear a *taliskotn*, and a long string of lead amulets, parchments, and wolf's teeth hangs around his neck, and a silver hoop in one ear. His foolish face is framed by large black eyebrows, with redness around his nose and various scratches scattered about his face and neck." He says "s" instead of "sh" and "t" instead of "k." Shmendrik's intelligence is as disfigured as his Yiddish, and his stunted sense of sexuality matches. In a scene with his bride to be, Rivke, he responds to her question of "What good would a bride do you?" by saying "What do you mean, what good would a bride do me? Get a load

---

25. For a brief discussion of Goldfadn's biography, his achievements, his links to Ettinger, and his dramatic work, see *Landmark Yiddish Plays* 35–46 and the bibliographical notes there; see especially Alyssa Quint, "The Botched Kiss: Abraham Goldfaden and the Literary Origins of the Yiddish Theatre" (Ph.D. dissertation, Harvard University, 2003).

of her, the crazy girl! My rebbe bought me a dreydl, so I'll play dreydl with her! Heh heh heh— ...", and then, when she bursts into tears, cries for his mommy.[26]

But Goldfadn's attempts to paint this representative of the old world in lurid colors succeeds too well. Shmendrik comes off as little more than a monster, and though we share the characters' vision of horror at the potential mesalliance that might result, Shmendrik is so caricatured that he never transcends the black and white world in which he resides. The result is that the play never truly emerges above simple polemic. It essentially serves to reiterate the fairly common warning in maskilic literature to avoid issues of wealth and social standing when it comes to marriage, and urge instead to follow the dictates of the heart and like-mindedness.

It is perhaps because of this perceived aesthetic failure on his part—Goldfadn later wrote in his memoirs about the play: "Shmendrik! What sort of diseased notion got into my head? I frightened myself, was ashamed of myself"—that he felt it necessary to return to the theme, which he did in one of the most famous and important plays in the Yiddish theatrical repertory.[27] Despite Kuni-Leml's similarities to Shmendrik—similarities of both the plays as a whole and the title characters—the new play, written after over thirty others by Goldfadn, reaches aesthetic heights the former never could.

Those heights, which mark the fundamental transformation of Yiddish comedy in the theater, are apparent in what is arguably the most famous scene in the play. Through a series of plot devices too confusing to relate in full, Max, the lover of Carolina, who is about to be married off to the foolish, disfigured Kuni-Leml, has plotted to dress up as Kuni-Leml in order to foil Carolina's father's plans. While in full costume, he comes face to face with the original Kuni-Leml. In the scene, Max, taking the bull by the horns, asks Kuni-Leml to prove that the latter is indeed Kuni-Leml. When Kuni-Leml is unable to do so, in the face of the disguised Max's claims to the contrary and his threats to drag Kuni-Leml to the police, he collapses:

KUNI-LEML (*runs after him and stops him*): Reb K-kuni Leml, come here. (*pleading*) What do you need the p-police for? I'll run home right n-now to get the proof in b-black and white. But is it f-fair for me to leave here without a name?

MAX (*grabs him by the lapels and speaks to him as if angry*): No, no, y-you're a swindler. C-come with me to the police.

KUNI-LEML (*afraid*): Oy, oy, Reb K-kuni-Lemele, may you enjoy g-good health, don't t-take me to the p-police. I'll run home right now without a name and bring proof in b-black and white that I am Ku—no,

---

26. See *Landmark Yiddish Plays*, 38–39.

27. See *Landmark Yiddish Plays*, 39–40 for the fuller quote.

no, you are K-kuni-Leml! I am Mocks—no, no, that I am...that I am
me! But I beg of you, Reb Kuni-Leml: until I c-come back, please
don't squeeze my fiancée. (*starts to go, looks Max over, says to
himself*) Apparently he really is K-kuni-Leml. (*starts to go again,
turns back*) Reb Kuni-Leml?

MAX: W-what is it now?

KUNI-LEML: I m-meant to ask .... For example, if I walk down the street and
someone c-calls out to m-me, "Reb K-kuni- Leml! Reb K-kuni-Leml!"
should I answer or not?

MAX (*with an angry tone*): No, you m-mustn't answer, since you're not
K-kuni-Leml! Now r-run along home!

KUNI-LEML: So he r-really is Kuni-Leml, and I am...me. (*he exits right*)[28]

When considered on its own, the scene can be viewed simply as an
excuse to wring laughs from a highly contrived situation, a common (if shining) example of farce. Given our discussion about theatricality, identity, and
its relation to comedy in the nineteenth-century Yiddish theater, we can see
how the trick played on Kuni-Leml is deeper and far more profound. Max is
able to strip Kuni-Leml of nothing less than his own self, in a twist that transforms the moment from simple farce to nervous comic genius. Though
establishment of the contours of one's identity—passing what psychologists
refer to as the "mirror stage"—is one of the most obvious and essential stages
in human development, Kuni Leml's regression to a time before that developmental milestone is the work of a moment.

Full appreciation of the scene's comic dimensions, then, depends on the
recognition of twin horrors. The first, as just suggested, is that our own
notions of identity are less stable than we might like to think. In Goldfadn's
expansion of Shmendrik's idiocy and Serkele's hypochondria to Kuni-Leml's
complete personal disintegration, he has done nothing less than present to
us a sobering example of the precariousness of Jewish identity in this changing, hectoring modern world, how quickly it can happen that others telling
you who you are and what you can be threatens to turn you into someone
else, or, more subversively and frighteningly, into nobody at all. (After all, at
scene's end, what name can Kuni-Leml come up with when he searches to
identify himself?) Though this same joke would be used more famously and
more masterfully in Sholem Aleichem's story "On Account of a Hat," Goldfadn got there first, with a canny example of physical comedy turned epistemological horror story.[29]

---

28. Translation taken from *Landmark Yiddish Plays*, 234.

29. On that classic story, see now David Roskies, "Inside Sholem Shachnah's Hat," *Prooftexts* 21:1 (Winter 2001); Roskies notes (44) that the story is based on an old joke, which
Goldfadn may have also heard.

Bringing up Sholem Aleichem's masterpiece, though, a story that is often read as a parable about the consequences of the rapid pace of Jewish modernization, enables us to move to the second unsettling consequence of this scene: the realization that our ideas about the successfully transformative nature of comedy and of theater are inherently shot through with doubt. This doubt stems from the fact that this Jewish comedy, far from simply unmooring the firm holds the problematic forces have over Jewish society, ends up demonstrating that, at bottom, there's nothing for anyone at all to hold onto, in part because the people who are doing the uncovering are themselves problematic. In this play, it is Max who is the comedian, the director, the arranger of masks that he can take off and put on. He directs Carolina; he pretends to be Kuni-Leml as well as a hidden saint; he pretends to fly; he corrals fellow students to become ghosts in a theatrical tableau. But he does so at some cost. To slightly misquote a character in another, earlier play, Max is not who he is. And as these lines are spoken by Iago, we may well believe that his efforts to confuse Kuni-Leml, efforts that result not only in bewilderment but in some sense a catastrophic annihilation of his identity, are tainted with some of Coleridge's motiveless malignity as well.

Indeed, Max takes just a bit too much relish in the theatrical tricks he plays. Compare this to *Serkele's* Goodheart, for whom disguise is a constant burden to be borne until things get back to normal. Here, our ostensibly sympathetic hero-character disguises himself as Kuni-Leml. But we may feel that when the Kuni-leml mask comes off, the Max face is a mask as well, and there's something a bit Kuni-lemlish behind it there, in the monstrous, Shmedrik-like sense. Max is, as the play takes pains to point out, Kuni Leml's cousin, and there's more of a familial resemblance than he'd like to admit. If Serkele's hypochondria means she is unclear about her theatrics, Max's actions leave no such doubt. Goldfaden leaves us with the feeling that theater as means has been replaced by an unrestrained pleasure in the theater in itself.

These observations—that everyone loves the greasepaint, and the resulting sneaking, somewhat horrifying suspicion that such an unrestrained love of greasepaint means a commitment to characterological arbitrariness and a lack of fixed identity, that it's all greasepaint, all masks, all the way down—have significant implications for maskilic dramatists. After all, how can they mesh with classical maskilic ideology, where, first, the greatest good lies in the unvarnished truth, and second, that such truth is ultimately recoverable by men of good will whose cause is just? It would seem that the authors of maskilic drama found no good answer to these questions once they truly realized their dimensions. Given their proclaimed cause and their chosen vehicle, the questions were unanswerable and so this period marks an end to the Haskalah play, or, more precisely, the Haskalah comedy as well. By the early 1880s, when Goldfadn wrote *Di tsvey kuni-leml*, Yiddish authors such as S.Y. Abramovitsh were already beginning to reflect on the failures of the Haskalah, on both its inability to attain its stated goals of Jewish emancipation and, more subtly, the deformations it worked on the characters of its practitioners with little or no positive return. The brightness of the Enlightenment's knowledge, the ability to mock and satirize, may have done a number of things, but it didn't provide useful, powerful, and satisfying answers; hence the development of the literature featuring the uprooted, dissatisfied, and certainly unfunny character known as the "uprooted man," or *talush*.

In this sense, Goldfadn serves not only as the harbinger of a kind of new Yiddish theater, but the end of the beginning of a new kind of Jewish comedy, one for which change is not only to be welcomed and assisted with the winged gifts of satire and the joys of graceful ends, but to be viewed with some trepidation, with irony, with the knowing second glance. This kind of corrupting gaze from within, when staged and taken seriously, ends up creating plays of problems, not solutions, of questions, not answers. This may explain why Goldfadn's work was taken up so strongly by the avant garde of the interwar period including (though by no means limited to) the figures of the Moscow State Yiddish Theater.[30] Writers such as Itzik Manger and Mikhl Weichert use nineteenth-century material in works such as Weichert's *Di Tanentsap-trupe* ("The Tanenstap Trupe," in which the actors play a troupe performing Goldfadn's *Kuni-Leml*), and Manger's *Hotzmakh-shpil* (a postmodern take on Goldfadn's *Koldunye*), and are able to adopt a kind of meta-theatrical approach—theater reflecting on theater—that revels in the fissures the comedy creates rather than trying to paper them over.[31] Only when the Yiddish theater was able to find its Pirandellos and, to a lesser extent, its Stoppards would it be able to take up the questions that the late comic geniuses of maskilic theater posed.

The nineteenth-century history of Yiddish theatrical comedy is, then, in many ways, a history of the Haskalah and its attempts to use that comic material for its own fairly straightforward agendas. But comedy doesn't fit easily into straightforward frameworks, and that realization becomes more and more evident as the decades continued and the notion of the Haskalah becomes more and more fraught. Once fully acknowledged, it was up to the masters of Yiddish writing to craft comic works, both on the page and on the stage, that dealt with new concerns, new audiences, new desires in very different ways. But these are different jokes altogether, and for a different time.

---

30. See Jeffrey Veidlinger, *The Moscow State Yiddish Theater* (Indiana University Press, 2000), esp. 163.

31. See *Vagabond Stars*, 320–321, 328.

Naked Truths:
Avrom Goldfaden's
The Fanatic or the Two Kuni-Lemls

ALYSSA QUINT

Scholars of the modern Yiddish theatre fall silent during talk of canons, or hum a familiar tune and drum their fingers distractedly. Though we sit on a large trove of fascinating cultural artifacts in the form of unpublished and published dramas and operettas, few of us are prepared to argue their artistic value. But canon talk raises the question: What are we to do with works that should not be dismissed as mere historical artifact–that require formal analysis to be fully appreciated–but are excluded by the canon because of their lack of literary excellence? How to approach works that were once popular but whose literary power has since faded?[1] An expansive reading that accounts for what cultural phenomenon a text refers to beyond itself allows us to probe text and context in tandem and, in this particular way, shore up the relevance of an otherwise outmoded work. One of Avraham Golfaden's (1840–1908) most popular Yiddish-language operettas, entitled *Der fanatik oder di tsvey kuni-lemlekh* (The Fanatic or The Two Kuni-Lemls), lends itself to such a methodology. Moreover, in the way in which it implicates history, the way it plays to a variegated audience, and the way it puts forward the modern Jew as a socially constructed being that resists stable definition, the operetta poses a challenge to the idea of a modern Jewish canon.

I delivered an early version of this paper at a conference on Yiddish theatre hosted by the University of Washington in 2006. My gratitude to Rachel Rubinstein, Dara Horn, Justin Cammy, Rebecca Kobrin, and Avrom Noveshtern for their valuable comments on an earlier draft and to Olga Litvak for her insight and knowledge.

1. Arguably the operetta under discussion became canonical by measure of its popularity. Early critics considered it a cheap knock-off of substandard European operetta fare but its continued resonance with audiences made it into a kind of classic. For a discussion of Goldfaden's canonic stature on the Yiddish stage as well as a list of adaptations of *The Two Kuni-Lemls* in translation, see Joel Berkowitz and Jeremy Dauber's "Introduction" in their *Landmark Yiddish Plays: A Critical Anthology* (Albany: SUNY Press, 2006) 46, n. 120. Quoted in this essay are, most importantly, Jacob Mestel's "Goldfadn als traditsye af der bine" and Nokhem Bukhvald's "Goldfadens a shpil modernizirt," which speak to the question of the play's monumentality. For the best discussion of the canon question as it pertains to nineteenth-century Yiddish theatre more generally, including the issue of class and cultural gate-keeping see Michael Steinlauf's important article, "Fear of Purim: Y. L. Peretz and the Canonization of Yiddish Theater," *Jewish Social Studies* 1(1995), 44–65.

This essay explores nineteenth-century Russian Jews as creatures of cal-
culated self-fashioning and demonstrates these calculations to be an abiding
preoccupation of *The Two Kuni-Lemls*, which was written by Goldfaden
not long before it premiered in Rumania in 1878. Max, the dashing young
medical student, tutors Carolina in the German classics, and they are in love.
By the end of Act I, Carolina has discovered that her father Pinkhes, a
devout Hasid who belongs to a fictional Cracow-based Hasidic sect Goldfaden ironically calls Shakhreyvke ("City of Swindlers"), has arranged a
match for her. To accrue the prestige of marrying into the family of the
Hasidic sect's *gabbay*, Sholem, Pinkhes has agreed to a match with
Sholem's hapless stepson Kuni-Leml, who stammers, is half-blind, and
limps. Max and Carolina plot to undermine the marriage by having Max disguise himself as Kuni-Leml to take the intended bridegroom's place. Mud-
dles ensue and denouement restores order—or at least to some extent. The
comedy demonstrates, however, that all its characters are pretenders or dis-
semblers for whom a return to lives of authenticity is impossible. (In fact,
who each of the operetta's characters is, is hardly a simple matter.) *The Two
Kuni-Lemls* goes out of its way to suggest that identity is unstable, and that
the apparently deep and obvious divisions among Jews—Hasidic and modern, pious and lapsed—are, in fact, better understood as myriad and ever-
shifting fault lines. In *The Two Kuni-Lemls*, Jews are what they wear and
what they appear to be—and there are no "naked" Jews. This is not a play
about identities temporarily mistaken and restored, but about the absence
of essential identity, an undermining of the fixity of the sign.

In both the way it contests the notion of a modern Jewish essence and its
demands on today's interested reader, *The Two Kuni-Lemls* poses a challenge to Ruth Wisse's *The Modern Jewish Canon*, especially its "Jewish"
claim. Underlying *The Modern Jewish Canon* is Wisse's conviction that a
work of canonical modern literature contains a Jewish ethos and, in her
words, "illuminates Jewish experience from within."[2] Beautifully and persuasively crafted, Wisse's book is a series of canonical Jewish readings that
discipline the texts they discuss according to a set of values (literary taste-
making, nationalist ideology) that are the foundation of what is reflexively
referred to as "modern Jewish identity." In this fashion, Wisse constructs a
community of readers bound by ideological kinship. *The Two Kuni-Lemls*
proposes that "Jewish" identity is instead messy, mired in the particulars of
ever-evolving social history, a mixture of individual manipulation and
impossible social structures. Only a fresh reading of the play makes such
meaning legible.

---

2. For a cogent critique of the framework of Wisse's book, see Mikhail Krutikov's review
"Jewish Literature between Future and Past," *Prooftexts* 21 3 (1991): 409–423.

Previous Critics on The Two Kuni-Lemls

Defenders of *The Two Kuni-Lemls* have read the operetta as a work informed by a mixture of Enlightenment ideology and Jewish nationalist sentiment akin to the ideological underpinnings of Wisse's canon. The Enlightenment motif they point to in the play is the didactic mirror. The climax of the operetta's largely standard comedic plot line arrives when Kuni-Leml, the hapless Hasid, encounters his double in Max, the young medical student disguised as Kuni-Leml. Hence "The Two Kuni-Lemls": the one "real," the other an imposter. Both dressed in full Hasidic regalia, they size each other up; each gazes at the other, the mirror-image of himself. Critics invoke Goldfaden's own purported view of this and his other comedies as attempts to put his drama to the service of lessons in modern bourgeois life and the evils of Hasidism:

> I sought to serve the moral imperative: my nationalistic instinct drove me to create a public school, a stage of mirrors in which everyone could see their reflections, how beautiful or how ugly they appear in the context of their private family or their social life.[3]

For most critics, the image of the theater as a mirror, a central trope in the *bourgeois drame* and the theoretical writings of its expounders, is reinforced by the prominence that the motif of the mirror assumes in *The Two Kuni-Lemls*. When Max insists he is the real Kuni-Leml, Kuni-Leml quickly assumes he is someone else but cannot figure out who that might be. "One can argue that Goldfaden had brought the satirization of Hasidism to its logical conclusion; in his hands, Hasidism had seen itself in the mirror, and was left with no identity of its own."[4] So write Joel Berkowitz and Jeremy Dauber in their distillation of the body of criticism that the play has attracted since its debut. Michael Taub offers a gentler ideological diagnosis, asserting that the operetta's concluding moment of reconciliation expresses a national Jewish ethos.[5] With his bride securely at his side, Max sheds his disguise and Kuni-Leml recovers his identity and accepts another bride in the place

3. Avrom Goldfadn, "Fun shmendrik biz ben-ami (autobiography)" in *Avrom Goldfadn: oysgeklibene shriftn*, ed. Shmuel Rozhinski (Buenos Aires: YIVO, 1907), 6. See Yiddish theatre critic Sholem Perlmutter, who writes: "Goldfaden did more to disabuse the fanatic his blindness than the teacher...in [*The Two Kuni-Lemls* and *Shmendrik*] he had but one goal: the struggle against fanaticism....He turned all his strength against Hasidism, against obsequiousness and masked faces." In his *Yidishe dramaturgn un kompozitors* (New York: IKUF, 1952).

4. "Introduction" in Berkowitz and Dauber's *Landmark Yiddish Plays,* 44.The weight of Berkowitz and Dauber's original analysis of the play consists of a comparative study of *The Two Kuni-Lemls* and an earlier Yiddish play by his teacher Avrom Gottlober called *Dos dektukh: tsvey khasenes in eyn nakht*, which they reveal to be an important source of the operetta.

5. "Yiddish Theatre in Romania: Profile of a Repetoire" *Yiddish* 8 (1991): 59–68.

Book cover for *Di Tsvey Kuni-Lemls*

of the first; both marry and thus both Hasid and maskil claim the future of
the play's society. *The Two Kuni-Lemls* is, then, an anti-Hasidic play, in
which hero rescues heroine from a Hasidic groom, which then dissolves
into one that highlights the peaceful co-existence of Hasid and modern,
albeit in a universe where Hasid plays only a marginal role. These analyses
lock neatly into a normative reading of this play that has characteristics of
both the Enlightenment and Jewish nationalism, in which "modern Jewish"
is defined by the operetta as Max.

Max's Mirror Experience

Scholars take Kuni-Leml's encounter with "himself" as emblematic of the
normative ethos of the operetta. Yet Max's mirror experience—given equal
weight in the play—is ignored. Why forget that when Kuni-Leml looks at
Max and sees his double, Max does the same? Max's desire drives the plot

that, as comedic convention has it, concludes in the hero's success as he weds his betrothed in the final scene. Early in the play Max says to Carolina: "[W]hen you can't succeed either by being nice or getting rough you have to rely on desire."[6] His procreative impulse, however, plays out preemptively in the mirror scene as Max successfully reproduces himself in a way that cuts Carolina out of the process. As Max's mirror image, Kuni-Leml is identical to him as well as a radically alien self-image, undermining of Max's previous self-image. On display is Max's split subject that expresses a desire for wholeness, specifically with himself as Kuni-Leml. Seeing himself as a Kuni-Leml, however, triggers in him "the desire to overcome what is different and unassimilable in the Other."[7] In other words, Max's desire to reproduce goes askew and the result of his desire, Kuni-Leml, becomes the object of his loathing. The scene, then, simultaneously projects the love and loathing with which the modernized "Western" Jew looked upon his unassimilated "Eastern" co-religionist.[8]

Just how far afield *The Two Kuni-Lemls* roamed from the Enlightenment values previous critics believe it represents may be measured in Max's relationship to Y.L. Gordon's canonical dictum of the Russian Jewish Haskala, "Be a man on the street and a Jew at home." With it, Gordon called for a self-integrated, authentic Russian-Jewish self:

> The modernization of the Jews, therefore, requires their assimilation to Russian culture, their becoming loyal and equal citizens of the tsar, *and* their remaining proud, loyal, and creative Jews. Only by combining all these elements, moreover, will the Jews be true to themselves.[9]

But reflected in the funhouse mirror that is Goldfaden's operetta, the dictum sponsors a brand of social opportunism and suggests that one manipulate one's behavior and appearance depending on the social context.[10] If

---

6. I rely on Berkowitz and Dauber's fine translation, "The Two Kuni-Lemls," in *Landmark Yiddish Plays*, 213. Further quotes from the play are parenthetical.

7. Judith Butler, "'Desire" in *Critical Terms for Literary Study*, ed. Frank Lentricchia and Thomas McLaughlin (Chicago: University of Chicago Press, 1995), 369–386, supplies an overview of philosophical theories on "Desire," some of which feature the mirror as an important motif. Perhaps most relevant to Max's experience is Hegel's interpretation of desire: "self-consciousness is Desire in general." When consciousness turns into self-consciousness, it is accompanied by the lure on the part of the subject to generate more selves. It also "precipitates desire into a life and death struggle" with this reflection, as Butler explains since, ironically, it threatens the singularity of the subject. (379)

8. I am grateful to Rachel Rubinstein for this insight.

9. Michael Stanislawski, *For Whom Do I Toil? Judah Leib Gordon and the Crisis of Russian Jewry* (New York: Oxford University Press, 1988), 52.

10. As Stanislawski explains, critics of the motto believed that Gordon "called on the Jews to limit their Jewishness to the home or synagogue and to suppress it in public" and

only accidentally, the motto incisively captured identity dilemmas that would play out in the lives of the *maskilim* explored in this essay, just as much as it stood for their integrationist aspirations. The play, in any case, does not prescribe Enlightenment self-consciousness as a cure for what ails the modern Jew, but poses the problem of self-consciousness against the background of the modern religious Jewish condition. Self consciousness is Max's undoing.

Setting off the ingredients of Max's identity dilemmas are the other characters of the play, particularly Sholem the *gabbay*, whose behavior is characterized by an easy-going social chameleonism, and Carolina's provocative embrace of modern life and its social and material accoutrements. Self-consciousness—and, for that matter, Haskala—neither hampers nor enables either of them. All three (Max, Sholem, and Carolina) are theatrical; but only Max is psychologically invested and ultimately divided by the demands of the Haskala. Why is Max, the apotheosis of the Russian Jewish Enlightenment movement, so portrayed? Goldfaden explores this very question in the peculiar construction of his characters, each of whom represents a brand of theatricality that thrived as part of nineteenth-century East European Jewish life. Max—not Kuni-Leml—stands at the center of them all. The context of a largely unexplored theatricality is critical to understanding the operetta in this way.

My approach synthesizes a close-reading of the operetta with the cultural history of Jewish attitudes toward their appearance and clothing in the late-nineteenth-century Russian Empire. By "culture" I mean the shared beliefs and habits that Eastern European Jews associated with their clothing and that policed the limits of their social behavior. Particularly useful to a contextualizing of *The Fanatic or the Two Kuni-Lemls* is a sensitivity to what critic Stephen Greenblatt calls the "the symbolic economy [of a culture] made up of the myriad signs that excite human desire, fear and aggression."[11] Clothing and appearance, for instance, played an important role in

that "in the pathological course leading from the Haskalah to assimilationism to self-hatred, Gordon's dictum early on epitomized the psychic damage inflicted on modern Jews by the specious distinction between man and Jew." (51) Also, see Olga Litvak, *Conscription and the Search for Modern Russian Jewry* (Bloomington: Indiana University Press, 2006), 94, who writes, "Celebrated and vilified as the motto of maskilic integrationism, Gordon's dictum epitomized the "bifurcation of Jewish identity"... that potentially divided the modern Jew against himself." (94) For a parsing of the motto and an analysis of its frequent deployment, see Dov Sadan's *"Betsetekha u-be-ohalekha: toldot sisma ve-shevura"* (Tel Aviv: Masada, 1966).

11. Stephen Greenblatt "Culture" *Critical Terms for Literary Study*, ed. Frank Lentricchia and Thomas McLaughlin (Chicago: University of Chicago Press, 1995), 230. See also Greenblatt's *Renaissance Self-Fashioning: from More to Shakespeare* (Chicago: University of Chicago, 2005) and his *Learning to Curse: Essays in Early Modern Culture* (New York: Routledge, 1990).

the lives of the first modern Yiddish actors and was key to their celebrity. Actors Jacob Adler (1855–1926) and David Kessler (1860–1920) were first dazzled by the off-stage demeanor and attire of the early Yiddish theater's actors as much as by their performances.[12] The actors' theatricality in everyday life bewitched them. Always impeccably attired in public, Goldfaden was trained at a government-sponsored Russian-Jewish seminary, where he learned that costume was an essential component of polite society.[13] Moreover, in his plays, Goldfaden describes many of his characters' costumes with great care and refers to clothing in their dialogue immersing us in the greater culture of clothing of his day. What if *The Two Kuni-Lemls*, beneath a template of stylized convention, and through its language—through Goldfaden's word choices—steers us toward a rich cultural and discursive context that, in turn, provides a key to layers of the play that have been lost to generations of its readers and viewers?

> Works of art...contain directly or by implication much of [their cultural contexts or situations] within themselves, and it is this sustained absorption that enables many literary works to survive the collapse of the conditions that led to their production.[14]

Falling short of canonical, *The Fanatic or the Two Kuni-Lemls* is, nonetheless, such a text. Under analysis, it demonstrates how Goldfaden contemplates the condition of his fellow Jews living under the force of unprecedented dilemmas of selfhood.

---

12. Adler recalled that "[e]verywhere they went they were pointed out with a whispered, 'Evraiski Aktiory' –Jewish actors!" In Lulla Adler Rosenfeld's *The Yiddish Theatre and Jacob P. Adler* (New York: Shapolsky Publishers Inc., 1977), 70. Kahan writes, "Kessler was attracted to Abba Sheyngold, then an important star on the Yiddish stage before the ban [of 1883], he loved his acting and his fur-trimmed cape." In *Arkhiv far der geshikhte fun yidishn teater un drame* (New York: YIVO, 1930), 305.

13. According to his colleague in the Zhitomir teachers' seminary, Menashe Margolies, for instance, dance instruction (a staple of the enlightened education of the Jew) enabled students to attend masquerade balls that took place at the Zhitomir theatre. "...it became a real challenge: with little means at all, to create gracious (*gratsieza*) costumes, especially ones that captured the most attention." Quoted in *Avrom Goldfadn*, 11. See R. V. Liber's description of a dandified Goldfaden in his "Zikhroynes vegn Avrom Goldfadn" in *YIVO Bleter* 35 (1951): 245–251. See also Goldfaden's then-future brother-in-law David Silberbusch's description of him in which he likens him to a rebbe. "Visiting Goldfaden, Father of the Yiddish Stage," *The Golden Tradition*, ed. Lucy S. Dawidowicz (Syracuse: Syracuse University Press, 1996), 321–326.

14. Another model of analysis for me that blends literary analysis and cultural investigation is the work of Russian semiotician Yu. M. Lotman, who argues the importance of everyday behavior as a historical-psychological category. He demonstrates the usefulness of understanding codes of individual actions that animate larger historical movements. See "The Decembrist in Daily Life (Everyday Behavior as a Historical-Psychological Category" in *The Semiotics of Russian Cultural History* (1985), 95–149.

Goldfaden might have conceived of his theatre in the vein of Lessing's didactic Enlightenment stage, but *The Two Kuni-Lemls* advances these values only to destabilize them. Instead of creating a uniform community of "readers" (as Wisse suggests of canonical Jewish texts), his theater drew an audience of diverse opinions, classes, and ideologies whose members each interpreted the play according to his own beliefs. Membership in a "community" requires identification with it, membership in an "audience" requires five rubles or the like. One can, therefore, read *The Two Kuni-Lemls* as a secular and comedic comment on the construction of Jewishness as a feature of Eastern European Jewish life. Rather than an unshakable sense of Jewish uniqueness, the play demonstrates varying degrees of likeness and difference among its characters, and within its audience.

The Russian Sartorial Laws of 1844 to 1851

The language of *The Two Kuni-Lemls* reflects the discourse about Jews and clothing generated in the wake of sartorial laws passed by the Russian government between 1844 and 1851 to regulate the appearance of its Jewish subjects.[15] This was not the first law of its kind. As early as 1804, Jews recruited to the army or traveling beyond the Pale were obliged to adopt a non-Jewish appearance and did so without resistance. Most Russian Jews, however, residing within the borders of the Pale, were untouched by such reforms. In 1839, the czar passed a law extending a privilege to all local Jewish communities to tax the production of Jewish clothes, instituting a *korobka* (tax) on any new Jewish clothing item produced. The tax, structured to pass to the consumer through the tailor, would be kept by the community and was meant to serve as an incentive for traditional-minded community leaders who were otherwise unlikely to discourage the Jewish traditional appearance. Historians know of no community that adopted the tax.[16] Jewish reformers, eager to cultivate secularizing social mores, pushed for the regulation of Jewish clothing, but quickly came to the conclusion

---

15. There is no comprehensive history of the 1844 sartorial law and its effects throughout the Russian Empire. Historian Shaul Ginzburg tries for thoroughness in his chapter on the subject, *"Redifes af yidishe begodim"* in Shaul M. Ginzburg, *Historishe verk: yidishe layden in tsarishn Rusland,* vol. 3 (New York: S. M Ginsburg Testimonial Committee, 1937), 273–314. On Vilna see Israel Klausner "Ha-gezeira al talboshet ha-yehudim, 1844–1850," in *Vilna 'Jerusalem of Lithuania' Generations from 1495–1881,* ed. Shmuel Barantchok (Tel Aviv: Ghetto Fighters' House, 1981), 278–288. Jacob Lippman Ha-levi Lipschitz, *Zikhron Ya'akov* (Kovno-Slobodka: N. Lipschitz, 1924), 135–143. On the decree as it played out in Warsaw, see Jacob Shatsky, *Geshikhte fun yidn in Varshe,* vol. 2 (New York: YIVO, 1948). For a recent treatment of this topic, see Eugene M. Avrutin, "The Politics of Jewish Legibility: Documentation and Reform during the Reign of Nicholas I," *Jewish Social Studies* 11, no.2 (Winter 2005): 136–169, and especially 150–155.

16. Ginzburg, *Historishe verk: yidishe layden in tsarishn Rusland,* 292–293.

that the law could not be left to the discretion of communal leaders; enforcement of the law, they felt, had to be placed into the hands of the local Russian government. In the 1840s, the issue gathered momentum. In 1841, the Nicholas Committee agreed to pass a law reforming Jewish appearance as part of its larger project to reform Jewish life in the empire, but it was shelved. Finally in 1844 the government did pass a dress code that would effectively transform the appearance of at least some Russian Jews in some of the larger cities throughout the Pale, although the law was applied differently and with varying intensity in each province.

In 1844, the government informed its Jewish population that by 1850 they would be expected to appear *"daytsh geklaydet,"* dressed German or according to a modern style, and that so-called Jewish clothing would be outlawed completely. During the intervening years, the government forced local communities to levy a tax of three to five rubles on any Jew who insisted on donning his traditional clothing in public. Jews were expected to adopt their new appearances gradually and buy the necessary new articles of clothing as they could afford them. The tax on traditional garb was nonetheless intended to act as an incentive for such a change. Exactly which garments were considered "Jewish," and thus offensive, and which other garments could be used to replace them, was generally not so much stated as assumed. Jewish clothing for men included "silk hoods, belts, fur hats, yarmulkes, short trousers and boots." Side-locks, beards, or long hair would not be officially tolerated.[17] Jewish women were forbidden from wearing turbans (*turbanen*), *shterntikhlekh* or other such "Jewish fashions" to which they had been habituated. Instead, they were ordered to wear simple garments "similar to what Russian women wear," including bonnets. They were likewise forbidden to wear wigs of any sort that matched their own hair color.[18] The shaving of brides' heads, customarily done on the day after the bride's wedding day, was forbidden in 1851.

How the government was to deal with those who did not conform to the law became a matter of improvisation and gave way, at least in some instances, to episodes of violence. While some reports of police persecution may be based on actual episodes, others might have been generated by rumor. Due to the difficulties associated with enforcing them, the decrees eventually languished—but not before they became "a symbol of an assault on Jewish life and traditions" on a par with Czar Nicholas's attempt to convert underage recruits.[19] Thus, "the dress reforms contributed more to the

---

17. As quoted in Avrutin, "The Politics of Jewish Legibility," 152. For the law as it appeared on the books, see M. U. Mysh, *Ruskovodstvo k russkim zakonam o evreiakh* (St. Petersburg: Frolov, 1898), 435.

18. Avrutin, "The Politics of Jewish Legibility," 152.

19. Ibid., 155.

history of ideas, to the debates between enlightened and conservative camps during the reign of Nicholas I, than to a social history of cultural change."[20] On the one hand, the events associated with these decrees exaggerated the Jews' concerns over modernity and observance and polarized relations between reformers and traditionalists. They also contributed to the reframing of the debate as one between Hasid and maskil. But these events also confused internal Jewish relations as different regions and communities adopted discrepant standards of appropriate dress, while the emotional and ideological investment in appearances mounted.

The symbolic economy of Jewish clothing in nineteenth-century Eastern Europe, in and beyond Russia, was deeply informed by these decrees, the various attempts at enforcing them throughout the ensuing years, and the reactions they provoked on the part of Jewish communities.

Max's Mirror Experience

Toward the middle of the play, as Max's plan reaches full tilt, he is disguised as Kuni-Leml and positioned in Pinkhes's home, in private and intimate company with his bride. We have, by this time, gotten to know both Kuni-Lemls: the short-sighted, stuttering, limping fool whose own stepfather (Sholem) is surprised at his having earned a match, and Max, the dashing trickster. Stealing a moment alone, Max (dressed up as Kuni-Leml) and Carolina are interrupted by the return of the real Kuni-Leml. Carolina frets that their discovery by Kuni-Leml will be brought to her father's attention and will undermine their plan. But Max reassures her and asks Carolina to leave him alone with the hapless Hasid. The mirror-like encounter of Kuni-Leml and Max-as-Kuni-Leml is thus created: "If I wasn't sure I am me, I would think he is me," Kuni-Leml says aloud about Max. (43) Max is immediately hostile and says something rather jarring to the crippled and stuttering groom:

> Max: You can walk and see and speak like everyone else, you're just
>   in disguise.
> Kuni-Leml: I can swear on my f-father and m-mother that I was born b-blind
>   and l-lame and with a s-stutter.
> Max: Q-quiet you liar. You better tell me right now why you d-
>   disguised yourself... What are you doing here? (43)

Max's logic is simple: if Max is Kuni-Leml (and Kuni-Leml *isn't* Kuni-Leml) then presumably Kuni-Leml must be *other* than stuttering and crippled; he must "walk and see and speak like everyone else."

Max's words also invoke the maskilic propaganda campaign against Jewish appearance as it called on sartorial reform in the name of sameness. *Maskilim* argued that beneath a kind of artificial surface, Jews look like their

---

20. Ibid.

Yosele Cutler's poster for
the Art Theater's performance of the play in 1925.
(Courtesy of YIVO)

non-Jewish countrymen and they should act similarly to Jews of other lands by shedding their distinctive costume. Mordechai Ginzburg wrote the following: "Throughout the world, the Jews of other lands have adopted the costume of their non-Jewish neighbors so why should it be the case that the Jews of Lithuania, Poland and Raysn [Belarus] be different from those of their Christian neighbors?"[21] If only the Jew appreciated that he was like the Christian, Samuel Fuenn and his colleagues in Vilna wrote in a letter to the Russian Ministry of Interior, "the Christians in their different garb would not seem so alien to him."[22] Also putting it in terms of sameness—if more cynically—the radical maskil Isaac Kovner, brother of maskil and Hebrew literary critic Uri Kovner, wrote: "Many of the self-styled believers know well that secretly (*beseter*) they are surely not passionate Jews but are like regular people enjoying and engaging in all kinds of amusement."[23] Reformers

21. Quoted in Klausner, "Ha-gezeira al talboshet ha-yehudim," 21.

22. Ibid., 21.

23. Aisik Kovner, *Sefer ha-matsref*, ed. Shmuel Feiner (Jerusalem: Mosad Bialik, 1998),

argued that Jews must return to a "natural" state of looking and seeming the same, in order to be accepted as the same by their Gentile neighbors.

Max's posture toward Kuni-Leml is characterized by a brand of trickery with which we are familiar from previous anti-Hasidic Enlightenment dramas. But the stridency in his posture, coupled with his insistence on written proof, recalls, once again, the specific elements that marked the harassment of Jews after the tax on Jewish clothing went into effect:

> Max: Q-quiet you liar. You better tell me right now why you d-disguised yourself as me. What are you doing here?
>
> Kuni-Leml: What am I doing here? Reb P-pinkhesl wrote me a l-letter that I should c-come and take the one thousand rubles' dowry and take his girl for my w—oh here's the letter (*Takes a letter out of the breast pocket of his coat and shows Max.*)
>
> Max: (*Skims through the letter.*) Now I see what a s-schemer you are. This letter is c-counterfeit....I'm taking this letter to the p-police, and I'm g-going to show them what a s-swindler you are unless you bring a s-signature from home that this is you.
>
> Kuni-Leml: (*Runs after him and stops him.*) Reb K-kuni-Leml, come here. (*Pleading.*) What do you need the p-police for? I'll run home right n-now to get the proof in b-black and white. But is it f-fair for me to leave here without a name?
>
> Max: (*Grabs him by the lapels and speaks to him as if angry.*) No, no, you're a swindler. C-come with me to the police. (233–34)

During the period of forced taxation, policemen were instructed to stop Jewish-looking men on the street and demand to see a receipt as evidence they had paid for the privilege of wearing Jewish clothing. According to some stories, if the Jew could not produce a receipt, the police would arrest him or take out scissors right then and there and bluntly cut off the end of his caftan or his *payes*. One report cited by a number of historians recounts policemen cutting the *payes* off a man by laying him on the ground and grinding them off with two stones.[24] According to Klausner, for instance, "rumors quickly circulated that police officials shaved beards, cut side-locks, and removed women's head-coverings."[25] In Vilna, the government gave directives to its police to pursue and to incarcerate those pious Jews who hid themselves indoors rather than appear outside in modern costume.[26] "I still remember the tumult and uproar," remarks Kovner, who

---

173. This was not published before 1998; it was probably penned in the 1870s. I am grateful to James Diamond for helping me with the translation of this difficult text.

24. Lipschitz, *Zikhron Ya'akov,* 142.

25. Klausner, quoted in Avrutin, 154.

26. Kovner, 171. Kovner's reports seem most reliable since he is unsympathetic toward traditionalists who were persecuted by authorities. On the physical harassment of the

describes the policemen beating, cursing their subjects, and "dragging them into jail." Jacob Shatsky recounts that in Warsaw, where the traditionally-garbed paid the tax—and richer Jews subsidized the payment of the tax for poorer Jews who could not afford it—the wearer received a *kvitl* or receipt that proved he had paid the tax in case he was approached by a law enforcement officer. For contemporary viewers, Kuni-Leml's reliance on a note from home to prove his identity to a hostile force might have invoked this chapter of recent history. As in the scene, *kvitlekh* were by no means enough to protect the wearer from police harassment. In an incident that a Christian observer likened to an Italian carnival, policemen with the help of Cossacks stormed a synagogue during prayer services demanding receipts: "Those who didn't have receipts immediately jumped out of the window to save themselves."[27]

If Max's rhetorical and physical aggression is a stand-in for the harassment of Jews by the Russian authorities, it also captures the Jewish reformers' anger that fueled this harassment. Reformers could only imagine that traditionalists resisted the laws out of spite. Kovner, for instance, was frustrated over this issue some twenty years after the 1844 sartorial laws were passed. He notes in his memoirs, thick with sarcasm, that "even now the pious protest short clothing and every moment they can (on *shabes* and *yontef*) they deck themselves out, and restore themselves to their former glory and celebrate as if they have just been released from Egypt."[28] Kovner's aggravation over the failure of Jews to willingly modernize their appearance was shared by non-Jews, including the Volhynia (non-Jewish) Governor Kaminskii, who in a public speech encouraged the Jews to reform their clothing, even as he expressed doubt that his listeners would heed his advice. His description of them resembles the portrait of Kuni-Leml: "While the Jews of other lands dress like their countrymen, Russian Jews' eyes are blinded by superstition....[they] are without language, egoists and fanatics."[29] For Jewish reformers like Max, however, the psychological pressure was greatest. The reformers' anxiety about the traditionally-clad stemmed from their own need for acceptance by the larger community and their concern about how they were perceived by Gentiles. No matter how much Kovner or his confrères modeled their manner and appearance after Gentiles, fellow Jews with *payes* reminded them of something they wanted to

---

Jews of Vilna, Kovner adds that if it were publicized in Jewish newspapers, it would have only given the impression that the Russians were persecuting Jews, without properly communicating the obstinacy of the pious, and so reform-minded Jewish journalists refrained from reporting compromising episodes in their newspapers.

27. Shatsky, *Geshikhte fun yidn in varshe*, 91.

28. Kovner, *Sefer ha-matsref*, 172–173.

29. Quoted in Ginzburg, *Historishe verk*, 297.

suppress, and reminded them that others saw them as Jews, undifferentiated from the traditionalists.[30] In his six-volume collection of vignettes entitled *Yidishe neshomes*, A. Litvin recounts a story about the clothing decrees and the involvement of the rabbi of Volozhin and Max Lilienthal, the German-Jewish reformer, who presented themselves before the Russian Minister of Interior Uvarov:

> In 1843 a group of Jewish community leaders was assembled in St. Petersburg. Reb Itsele Volozhiner came in a long silken *talis-kotn* (much like the rise of the Russian monk)... In it, he approached Minister Uvarov with pride. The Russian government wasn't content with Jewish clothing. They wanted the Jew to wear German clothing, more European, and be "like all others." The minister asked the rabbi: "Why do you wear this crazy-looking '*tales*' to the ground while Lilienthal wears nothing of the sort? Is Lilienthal not the same Jew (*der zelber yid*)?[31]

Uvarov sees two Jews standing before him and cannot grasp what set of differences the *talis-kotn* signifies. Likewise, Max looks up at the Hasid Kuni-Leml in caftan, knee socks, and side-locks and sees—to his horror—himself.

Theatricality in Shakhrayvke: Sholem

Max's alter ego is Sholem the *gabbay*, a kind of permanent dissembler. Max is in disguise only temporarily—he is a committed Russian who is loyal to the czar and a Jew who is committed to showing his co-religionists the error of their ways. As a character in a maskilic play, Sholem is *sui generis*.[32] Typical maskilic literature portrays *gabbayim* as villains who hoodwink their hasidic followers in order to extract money from them. In sharp contrast, his kinship with both Max and Kuni-Leml (he is Max's uncle and Kuni-Leml's stepfather), and the prestige he accrues in the community as the powerful *gabbay* (chief advisor to the rebbe) and *parnes-khoydesh* (the highest level of elected Jewish community officialdom) makes him the ulti-

---

30. Arguably, the laws *forced* traditionalists into investing their differentiating garb with more value than it previously had to them in order to salvage it—but in doing so, the meaning of clothing transformed altogether. As Barbara Kirshenblatt-Gimblett explains, "Defensiveness doesn't simply protect the status quo. It actually produces something new—theologically, socially, culturally, politically—even as it imagines itself in conservative terms." See her "Introduction" in *Life Is with People: The Culture of the Shtetl*, by Mark Zborowski and Elizabeth Herzog (New York: Schocken, 1995), 7.

31. (New York: Arbeter Ring), 2–3. Litvin must have enjoyed likening a *talis-kotn* to a monk's rise.

32. For a far more conventional depiction by Goldfaden of a Hasidic *gabbay* who controls the rebbe's court life, see his *Ni me ni be ni kukuriku* (Odessa, 1881) published in Russian translation; a Yiddish manuscript of this play did not survive. For a discussion of the power exerted by the *gabbay* in the Hasidic court, see David Assaf's "Money for Household Expenses," *Scripta Hierosolymitana* 38 (1998): 14–50.

mate authority in the play's universe. Sholem the *gabbay*, however, is not always who he pretends to be. As Max explains privately to Carolina:

> Don't think my uncle is a Hasid like your father assumes him to be. He is a free thinker like my father. But, because he was the eldest brother, he never had the opportunity to study and was left to play the pious role (*er iz geblibn shpiln di frume role*) and leads the rebbe and his followers by the nose. (212)

The second most important man in the Hasidic community is not a Hasid at all, according to Max, but a free thinker. Goldfaden does not suggest that Sholem is corrupt as an apparent Hasid or as a supposed maskil. In fact, his moral uprightness and accrual of authority is contingent upon modulating his behavior according to the perceptions and expectations of the communities within which he moves. Sholem is a social chameleon.

Nineteenth-century memoiristic literature provides evidence of a trend of social chameleonism, specifically of Jewish men manipulating their clothing so they could be perceived to be more pious in some circles and less so in others. The maskil Mordechai Guenzburg provides an early example. According to his personal letters, we know he habitually carried with him two sets of garments. In 1825, after being robbed one night while asleep at an inn, he wrote to a friend with great distress, "I lost my Polish and German costumes that I would change into from day to day to be worn as emprimateur cut to the desires of the people among whom I move."[33] The city of Odessa (where much of the operetta's action takes place) became famous for studied social chameleons. According to the Russian-Jewish writer Osip Rabinovitch, "Dandies who paraded around Odessa in the latest fashion, would for a time before leaving to visit home let their beard grow, leave behind their frocks and their [modern] waist-coats and set out in their traditional caftans."[34] In *Di geshikhte fun yidn in varshe*, Shatsky explains that business trips to the west more frequently embarked upon by Belorussian and Lithuanian Jews (in contrast to Warsaw Jews, for instance) "allowed pious Jews of these areas to taste the art of masquerade (*kleyder maskarad*) and, with time, to feel more familiar with it."[35] Newspaperman Alexander Zederbaum (1816–1893), who serialized his *Rayze geshikhtn* in the early 1870s in *Kol mevaser*, was struck by a comparable studied nonchalance among bourgeois Hasids from even small and medium-sized towns of the Russian Empire who depended on regular interaction with the non-Jewish world and dressed accordingly:

---

33. Joseph Klausner, *Historia shel ha-sifrut ha-ivrit ha-khadasha* vol. 3, 125.

34. This is quoted in Steven Zipperstein's *The Jews of Odessa: A Cultural History 1794–1881* (Stanford: Stanford University Press 1985), 44.

35. Shatsky, *Geshikhte fun yidn in varshe*, 82.

It is undeniable that in most every shtetl—not to mention the larger towns—
there are wholly practical and worldly people even under the mask of Hasidism, most of whom must deal with the world, with Christians....and if his
extreme Hasidic allegiance does not allow for him to announce his worldliness openly, he still may dress in the European fashion.[36]

The "Sholems" of the East European cultural reality came up against limits that Sholem of *The Two Kuni-Lemls* never experiences. In other words,
their negotiations, when grasped by certain authorities, were deemed transgressive. Consider Hasid-cum-maskil Yekhezkel Kotik's (1847–1921) account of one of his first trips to the big city of Grodno. His growing ambivalence about his traditional clothing and his observance prodded him to temporarily modernize his appearance while he was doing business among
Grodno's Jewish reformers. Reformers harassed him about his long caftan.
"[S]omewhat willingly, and somewhat unwillingly (truthfully, more willingly than unwillingly) I began to wear short clothing, in the German style, and
I wore my pants over my boots."[37] Even retrospectively (Kotik penned his
memoirs many years later), he could not be sure how much he was shamed
into modernizing his appearance and how much he did so according to personal motivation. Instead, he demonstrates, like Zederbaum, the negotiation of personal conviction and perceived convention in self-fashioning. In
any case, Kotik's wardrobe adjustments are minor. But Kotik could not control for chance, and he comes to feel the negative consequences of his transgressive behavior. According to his memoirs, as he walks down the city
street, Kotik comes upon a friend of his grandfather's from his hometown
Kamenets with whom he sends greetings to his family. Soon after this brief
encounter he receives a letter from his father:

> My son,
>
>   I met Sholem the Baker and he sent me your greetings. I asked him "How
> is my son? How does he look?" He answered, "Nuuu...what can be done? He
> is already wearing his pants over his boots." My soul almost collapsed. I felt
> as if a plague seized my heart, as if I was hit by a bullet....Never in my life
> had such a tragedy befallen me. For three days I could scarcely eat due to
> overwhelming despair. When I returned home, the rebbe's bride Hadas was
> over for a visit and saw the grief on my face. When I told her about the greet-
> ings from you I received from Sholem the Baker, there was an outburst of
> crying. (120–21)

No doubt the "audience" of Kotik's theatricality was also capable of great
drama, which was further embellished by the author in the episode's retell-

---

36. *"Rayze geshikhte" Kol mevaser* 1870 (2): 12.

37. Yekhezkel Kotik, *Ma she-raiti: zikhronotav shel yehezkel kotik*, ed. and trans. David
    Assaf (Tel Aviv: Tel Aviv University, 1998), 120. Originally published in Yiddish in
    1922.

ing. Kotik's wearing of his pants over his boots brought him acceptance by the modern Jews with whom he wanted to socialize just as it was taken by his father as an emboldened sign of rejection. To judge by Kotik's parents, one might say that to reject *looking* like a Jew in late-nineteenth-century Russia was tantamount to rejecting *being* a Jew, at least in some circles. Notably absent from the narrative is any curiosity on the part of Kotik's father as to his son's religious practice and beliefs. The possibility, taken for granted by historian Klausner for example, that the maskil's desire was to change traditional Jewish behavior "without affecting the religious foundation" would have been foreign to Kotik's father.

In *The Two Kuni-Lemls* there is no comparable disciplining of Sholem the *gabbay*'s two-sidedness, but Goldfaden does touch upon it. After the denouement of the plot, after Sholem has identified himself as sympathetic to the maskilic cause even before the eyes of the play's Hasids, Pinkhes runs his hasidic entourage out of his home. As they leave they threaten, "We are going to tell the rebbe everything..." (245) In such throwaway lines, the operetta registers the mechanisms of social discipline that were at work just beyond the happy world of the final scene. There, as we shall see below, Sholem validates Max as Max validates Sholem, each of them running parallel courses through the drama by slyly negotiating the Hasidic and maskilic worlds in which they want—and do not want—membership. But Sholem is a kind of utopian character, absorbing the benefits of both worlds, while Max embodies the strife that divides them.

Theatricality in Odessa

A second foil to Max is his girlfriend Carolina, whose stance is one of quiet rebellion and provocative theatricality. In contrast to Max, the son of a progressive-minded medical doctor who raised him according to his maskilic worldview, Carolina's freshly acquired habits are a product of her family's upward mobility. Her character reflects the gendered encounter with modernity of Eastern European Jewry: her behavior is shaped more profoundly by trends of urbanization and embourgeoisement rather than ideology.[38] Goldfaden inscribes in her character various dimensions of this phenomenon: the considered adoption of nontraditional manners and appearance and nontraditional sexual mores.

Soon before the "mirror scene," Carolina's arranged groom Kuni-Leml arrives at the house to claim his dowry and meet his bride. Before this point, we have come to know Carolina for her embrace of Max and for her resentment of her father Pinkhes. Reluctantly, he allows her a modern tutor but forbids her from marrying Max when he discovers that they have fallen in

---

38. See Paula Hyman's *Gender and Assimilation in Modern Jewish History: The Roles and Representation of Women* (Seattle: University of Washington Press, 1995).

love. She sings her first aria in the solitude of her bedroom, in which she complains that her father imprisons her in the shadows of his Hasidic superstitions. Her parents are justly surprised, then, when Carolina consents to meeting Kuni-Leml. She does so expecting he will be Max disguised as Kuni-Leml. When he arrives, Carolina plays the provocateur, scandalizing her father and—as the audience quickly deduces—the *real* Kuni-Leml who arrived at the house faster than Max. She insists on introducing herself by her non-Jewish name, Carolina, and not by her Hebrew name Khayele:

Carolina: ...Allow me the honor of presenting myself to you—your bride Carolina!

Kuni-Leml: Why is she using such funny language?

Carolina: (*with a smile*) I am your bride.

Kuni-Leml: My b-bride? ...What's this C-crinolina? (*To Pinkhesl who has been gesturing to Rivke this entire time as if they are arguing*) Reb P-pinkhesl, oy, she is a he-r-etic! Can a Jewish girl have such an aristocratic name?

Pinkhesl: (*Goes to Carolina and whispers in her ear*) You should have said "Khayele" to him. .... (226)

Coded with cultural nuance, this brief exchange speaks to social conduct and attitudes peculiar to Goldfaden's day. As Kuni-Leml's comment hints— "Can a Jewish girl have such an aristocratic name?"—Carolina was a name popular among contemporary Polish nobility that implied to Goldfaden's original audience a criticism of Khayele as a striver. Jews more conservative or traditional expressed their disapproval of their fellow Jews by calling them "aristocrats" when they changed their appearances too quickly. Later in the century, writer Nahum Shaikevitsh (1849–1905), for example, uses this ironic usage in the first line of one of his novels:

Do you recognize that aristocrat running there along Canal Street? You don't recognize him? Take a closer look and you will surely recognize our friend Mr. Abraham Katerman.... It's no wonder that you didn't recognize him since overnight he became another person entirely...[39]

Kuni-Leml's speech also picks up on Carolina's evolved sexuality when he confuses her name with "crinoline," the hoop-like petticoat that women wore beneath their dresses and a word that became a shibboleth of Jewish Eastern European sartorial tensions. The Jewish battle with the crinoline is dated by Ginsburg to be almost a century old by the 1870s when Goldfaden wrote his operetta, but it still continued to raise the ire of the rabbinic establishment. Pauline Wengeroff records her parents' rage against the makeshift crinoline that her sister crafted on her own and modeled for her parents. Furious, Wengeroff's parents quickly made kindling of it. Her last words on

---

39. *Der zhentlemen oder sof ganef letliye* (New York: 1889), 1.

the subject hint at the item's sexual connotations: "...the flames grabbed eagerly at the new fashion."[40] Multiple articles in the conservative maskilic organ *Ha-magid* alone evidence the suspicion traditionalists assigned to this piece of clothing. One community leader claimed its wearing to be responsible for the spread of cholera while another rabbi put the garment in *herem*. A brief article that did not condone the reported eruption of violence also reminded readers that the donning of crinolines had been recently outlawed by a judicious rabbi:

> Recently, the rabbi and leader of the community of K— issued judgments (*sayagim*) that were both good and just among the people...and he raised his voice in the camp of the Hebrews to declare that no female Israelite will enter the synagogue in a crinoline (*be-malbush krinolina*) [kri-no-lin] (sic) These days, even girls of Israel, in order to appear plump and healthy of flesh, wear crinolines. This is a wild custom that is unprecedented among Jews.[41]

Another rabbi simply dismissed it as "dissolute clothing" (*malbushim prizut*). And as evidence of its corrupting nature, he points out that it is clothing "in which our forefathers (*avot avoteynu*) never walked."[42]

Through Kuni-Leml, Goldfaden refers to the discourse on the crinoline among Eastern European Jews only obliquely in the operetta; we do not even know if Carolina's character actually wears a crinoline since Goldfaden did not indicate as much in his costume notes. And yet, in one word—and as one reference to a garment among many—Goldfaden refers to the competing opinions on and formulations of self-fashioning he observed around him. Invariably, the crinoline among Jewish women of this time had much in common with its initial resistance by, say, the English, and its role in women's asserting their control over their appearance. As the historian Kimberly Chrisman explains:

> The origins, innovations, fluctuations, and failings of the hoop demonstrate the tenacity of eighteenth-century Englishwomen in their struggle for sexual autonomy. Although it is tempting to condemn the hoop as yet another example of female subjugation through dress, such as the medieval chastity belt or the crippling corsets of the nineteenth century, the hoop actually had quite the opposite function. In the face of widespread and violent protest from men, women willingly adopted the hoop as a means of protecting, controlling, and, ultimately, liberating female sexuality.[43]

---

40. Pauline Wengeroff, *Rememberings: The World of a Russian-Jewish Woman in the Nineteenth Century*, trans. Henny Wenkart; ed. Bernard D. Cooperman, (Bethesda, Md.: University Press of Maryland, 2000), 110.

41. *Hamagid* (1861): 180. See Ginzburg for other references to the crinoline in Hamagid in the same year.

42. Ginzburg, *Historishe verk*, 281.

43. Kimberly Chrisman, "Unhoop the Fair Sex: The Campaign against the Hoop Petticoat

Kuni-Leml's stuttered slippage from "Carolina" to "crinoline" signifies his attentiveness to his betrothed's sexual awakening as it comically expresses his fear of and instinctive outrage for it.

In contrast to Max, Carolina's desire to scandalize her father are fundamental to her modern experience. In Act I, Scene 2, when Carolina puts her coat on and with her mother's encouragement leaves the house to get some "fresh air," Pinkhesl gets upset and resists Carolina's leave-taking, but to no avail. But the full freight of Carolina's rebellion is silently but effectively communicated to her father as it was decipherable to the play's contemporary audience. "Fresh air" is here not simply a vague metaphor for Enlightenment, but refers specifically to the type of leisure strolling that was ritualized in many nineteenth-century European cities: it took place in indicated picturesque areas, was intended for enthusiasts to "see and be seen," and played out according to prescribed rules of behavior. In Warsaw, for instance, taking fresh air was an affair so disciplined that Jews in caftans were considered dressed inappropriately and were denied entry to parks restricted to the bourgeoisie or nobility who were always dressed *comme il faut*:

> The Jewish women in Warsaw preferred to use the money [they may have spent on the Jewish clothing tax] to doll themselves up (*putsn zikh*). In the Warsaw gardens, Jewish dandies surfaced, especially in places where Jews with *kapotes* were forbidden to enter. [Traditional Jewish] husbands did not want their wives strolling alone in the gardens, and so, for the purpose of protecting their wives, they began dressing in the German fashion. In the provinces, however, where there were no gardens, this excuse of accompanying your wife to take some fresh air did not exist.[44]

At least initially, the money Jewish men spent on the clothing tax to maintain their traditional appearance and lifestyle, women spent on appearing *au courant*, thereby inviting the threat of intermarriage. No wonder Carolina's parents' surprise at her willingness to meet Kuni-Leml only hours later. Carolina signals to Pinkhes that she publicly and willingly identifies herself with society's modern, non-Jewish element and would not consort with traditional Jews who do not take part in such rituals as "walking along the boulevard." Moreover, while Carolina is concerned with gesture and appear-

in Eighteenth-Century England" *Eighteenth-Century Studies* 30.1 (1996): 7. My essay does not include discussion of Rivke's wig (mentioned in the description of the *Dramatis Personae*), which was also a controversial accessory in nineteenth-century Eastern Europe and about which rabbis issued many contradictory and passionate responsa. These are collected in an anthology called *Dat yehudit ke-hilkhata* (Jerusalem: Vad mishemeret ha-tsniut, 1973). For a good introduction to the eventual acceptance of the *shaytl*, see Leila Leah Bronner's "From Veil to Wig: Jewish Women's Hair Covering," *Judaism: A Quarterly Journal* 42.4 (1993).

44. See Shatsky, 97. Shatsky draws this from an unpublished Polish-language memoir that he refers to as "Papiery Hofmana" or the Hoffman Papers.

ance her character is a far cry from the female representatives of pseudo-Enlightenment we are used to from previous Enlightenment dramas. In fact, her preoccupation with appearances recalls those of the reformers.[45]

The tense drama that unfolds between Carolina and Pinkhes corresponds to similar theatrical gestures of the young and upwardly mobile that played out within Jewish families off the stage. They were not limited to women. Consider the experience of Yitskhak Librescu (1850–1926), who grew up in Bucharest and who would become the financier of Goldfaden's early theatrical efforts in the 1870s. By the time he was a young man in the 1860s, larger cities throughout Rumania, and Eastern Europe more generally, boasted communities of Jews who subscribed to modern values and who dressed in some modern key. Although he had wanted to change his traditional garb for a while before he was twenty-three, Librescu writes in his memoirs that he wanted to wait for "the best moment."[46] Once he was hired by a modern Jewish gentleman to be the sexton in the local reform synagogue, he felt he could rationalize to his pious family the switch of clothing for the practical reason of blending in and keeping his job; at that point, there was an expectation that he dress according to the dictates of the modern world.

Still, there is something decidedly gratuitous about the way Librescu goes about remaking his appearance. At this point, Librescu's memoirs record his "change of costume" as if he is preparing himself for entrance onto a theatrical stage. In the stretch of one day, he changed his name from the Jewish-sounding "Liber" to the Rumanian "Librescu," bought a gentleman's top hat or *silinder,* went to the family barber who reluctantly shaved off his beard and side-locks, and finally bought himself a modern-looking suit. As all this took place on a Friday, when the household was busy preparing for the Sabbath, Librescu secretly sneaked into the house with his packages. After getting dressed "utterly daytsh," he asked his wife to assemble everyone for his grand entrance:

> I opened the door and turned to the women: "Mother, mother-in-law, what do you think?"
>
> It is hard to depict the impression I made on my mother and my mother-in-law. Instantly, they both became hysterical....A similar scene, although more masculine, played out when my father and father-in-law returned home.[47]

---

45. On the pseudo-Enlightenment see Shmuel Feiner's chapter "On Frivolity and Hypocrisy" in his book *The Jewish Enlightenment* (Philadelphia: University of Pennsylvania Press, 2003), 342–356.

46. Yitskhak Librescu, *"Di zikhroynes fun Yitskhak Librescu der initsyator fun Goldfadns teater"* in *Hintern forhang*, ed. Zalmen Zilbertsvayg (New York: 1926).

47. Ibid., 18–19.

Many altered their dress, often over long periods and gradually, if for financial reason alone. But Librescu's memoirs of his involvement in the beginnings of the modern Yiddish theatre, starting with this chapter, "*Ikh ver a
daytsh*," mark his birth into a world of Jewish performance and represent
the manipulations of which Jews were capable on and off the stage. As
such, his narrative starkly illustrates a slippage between theater and theatricality explored in this paper. Librescu and Carolina perform "selves" that
they cultivated independent of the traditional society that bred them;
"selves" finely tuned in order to impress on their families their resistance to
their authority. The nature and role of Carolina's theatricality is important
because it shares specific patterns of behavior at play within the larger culture of East European Jewish society. It also allows us to define with greater
subtlety Max's performance as Kuni-Leml: in contrast to Carolina's performance as a heightened version of the bourgeois values to which she aspires
—the self she adores just more of it—Max's relationship to his performed self
may be described as an appropriation of a self that, on a more conscious level, he sees as patently other than himself.

False Signs in The Two Kuni-Lemls

Discussion of Sholem and Carolina's performances within the world of the
play and the cultural codes they reflect focuses and re-focuses Max-as-Hasid
so that he has no unified stable meaning throughout the play. Being Kuni-
Leml is not a means to the end of marrying Carolina, but an end in itself that
collapses multiple identities into one self. In this respect, Max as Kuni-Leml
is the Ashkenazic equivalent of a cross-dresser. Just like the transgender
cross-dresser, Max as Kuni-Leml challenges the binarism he seemingly represents, here Hasidic/maskilic. He is neither Max nor Kuni-Leml, maskil or
hasid, but a third term that "puts into question one, identity, self-sufficiency
and self-knowledge."[48] It thus puts into question "*Ikh bin ikh*," as Carolina
sings it in her flirty song to her beloved. In *The Two Kuni-Lemls*, the
dressed-up Max puts into crisis a comfortable binary of Hasid and maskil
that has been the conventional template with which we have sought to
understand a vital aspect of the modern Eastern European Jewish experience. It is a template that is both illuminating and obscuring, because the
behaviors that defined both these groups, as this play suggests, were both

---

48. Marjorie Garber, *Vested Interests: Cross-Dressing and Cultural Anxiety* (New York:
Routledge, 1992), 10. Also relevant is her discussion of the movie "Yentl," 77–84. This
sense of crisis is picked up on by later Yiddish playwrights who riff on this theme of
multiplication in homages to Goldfaden. See, for instance, Itsik Manger's (1901–1969)
Hotsmakh shpil, in which there are three of the eponymously-named traditional
haberdashers and four Kuni-Lemls appear in Mikhl Vaykhert's *Trupe tanentsap: a
Goldfadn-shpil in a galitsish shtetl*, which was first staged in 1933. See Berkowitz and
Dauber for bibliographic information, "Introduction," 66 n.120.

rigid and flexible, reassuring to both sides when it communicated meaning and anxiety-producing when it failed to explain and define the realities of social relationships.

Finally forced to sort out the two Kuni-Lemls, Sholem takes control of the situation at the end, lending his imprimatur as a Hasid (although not a Hasid) to legitimate Max's machinations. So who is who? Sholem confirms what Max says about him, but hedges. He begins with the following admonition: "Don't think I am a Hasid of the kind you think I am." And he continues:

> More than once I have envied my brother who attained such a high level, and made of his children *layt*. We must play old roles since we are of the old world, but in our heads, we need not be deceived.

In an attempt to convince Pinkhes of Max's quality as a groom, Sholem does what Max did earlier in the play—that is, Sholem likens him (Max) to himself. When Max and Carolina first conceived of their machinations, Max likened his uncle to himself, a "free-thinker," as discussed earlier. Now, Sholem depicts Max as the same as himself: "he is as pious, possibly as much as I am, besides which he is also educated. That is, to God and to People." Who Max and Sholem are can only be expressed as a series of likenesses. Kuni-Leml, in contrast, affirms his identity in a way no other character can or does: "*Ikh bin Kuni-Leml*" ("I am Kuni-Leml"). Of course, Kuni-Leml asserting his authentic selfhood functions as a kind of punch-line given all that has come before.

Signs proliferate in *The Fanatic or the Two Kuni-Lemls* but are mostly false, unstable, or so novel so as to render them less than universally legible. The kiss, a symbol of love between Max and Carolina, becomes a botched kiss between Carolina and Kuni-Leml. Through Max, Goldfaden introduces other secular signs to the play as well, such as the shaking of hands between Max and his fellow-students when they agree to help him in his attempt to win Carolina's hand in marriage. But the handshake itself is a sign that is new to its context and Goldfaden takes pains to clarify its meaning. In stage directions, Goldfaden explains, "They all shake his hand as a sign that they are ready to serve him."(213) Later, Pinkhes and Max as Kuni-Leml shake hands on his betrothal to Carolina, but this sign, too, is arguably empty, since Pinkhes believes Max to be Kuni-Leml at the time. There is a scene in which Max as Kuni-Leml, presented as a lamed-vovnik, "resurrects" the ancestors of Pinkhes in order to prove the couple's fatedness, but the "resurrected" are Max's colleagues disguised—another false sign.

The trickiness of signification infiltrates the operetta's full title. We know who the two Kuni-Lemls are, but who is the fanatic of *The Fanatic or the Two Kuni-Lemls*? The most obvious response would be the real Kuni-Leml, who is portrayed as a devoted Hasid. But what if Max is the fanatic? *Maskilim* and *hasidim* came to mirror each other in their discursive tactics, each accusing the other of displays of distasteful ostentation through their clothing, of trickery (City of Swindlers), and both invoked the authority of their ancestors to prove why the Jews should or should not dress in traditional garb: "Jews did not wear these clothes at Sinai," explained the *maskilim* in their petition to the Russian government; while the traditionalists wrote, in response to sartorial reforms, "Why should we wear these German clothes if 'our forefathers did not wear them'?" In *The Two Kuni-Lemls*, Max accuses Kuni-Leml of submitting a false document to him, but manipulation of documents occurred on all sides of these cultural battles. In Vilna, for instance, *maskilim* became notorious for manipulating a petition to the government that called for reform of the Jews' dress by collecting signatures of the pious under false pretenses, since they often could not read the Russian-language documents they were being asked to sign.[49] *Maskilim* called Hasids "fanatical" more often than the reverse, but Hasids knew the word to be deployed as that much self-serving propaganda. As Lipschitz writes "the maskilim wrote a letter to the government that poured fire and brimstone on the People of Israel, saying that they were lazy, and dull-minded, and that "all this was caused by their clothes, and their [so-called] 'fanaticism.'" Curiously the English usage of the word "fanatic" (imported to Yiddish as *fanatik*) denotes a "religious zealot," a description that fits only loosely on Kuni-Leml, as well as "dissembler," a label better suited to Max.[50] The disequilibrium of the title's construction, in any case, underscores the ambiguity of language that infuses the entire operetta.

Conclusion

Instead of a tidy didactic play born of well-worn Enlightenment conventions, *The Two Kuni-Lemls* is a product of the specific milieu of active Yiddish theater life. It thus breaks radically from the earlier, mostly salon-based tradition of the anti-Hasidic maskilic play. Unlike in the salon, the theater's viewers were not ideologically bound but, rather, assembled for the purpose of seeking entertainment. Michael Steinlauf has shown that Jews in pious garb were avid attendees of the Polish stage during the last decades of the nineteenth century.[51] Other traditionalists considered theatre *"treyf."* The Hasidic parents of Isaac Loewy, a future actor on the Yiddish stage and, through his theater career, a friend of Franz Kafka, believed the theatre to be for *goyim* and sinners. Loewy nonetheless took in non-Jewish theater in

---

49. Lipschitz, *Zikhron Ya'akov*, 138.

50. *Oxford English Dictionary on-line* "fanatic," http://dictionary.oed.com/cgi/entry/ 50082098?single=1&query_type=word&que-word=fanatic&first=1&max_to_show=10, accessed March 1, 2008.

51. See his article "Black Coats and Beards in the Polish Shrine: Jews and Turn-of-the-Century Warsaw Theater," *Cross Currents* 8 (1989): 40–52. On the attendance of Jews "even with side curls" at the opera in Odessa during the first half of the nineteenth century, see Zipperstein, *The Jews of Odessa*, 66.

Warsaw secretly, for which he bought "a collar and a pair of cuffs for every performance" to blend in with the audience only to "throw them into the Vistula" on his way home. Then Loewy discovered theater in the Yiddish language:

> That completely transformed me. Even before the play began, I felt quite different from the way I felt among "them." Above all, there were no gentle-men in evening dress, no ladies in low-cut gowns, no Polish, no Russian, only Jews of every kind, in caftans, in suits, women and girls dressed in the Western way. And everyone talked loudly and carelessly in our mother tongue, nobody particularly noticed me in my long caftan, and I did not need to be ashamed at all.[52]

Goldfadn's theater validated its Jewish viewers, no matter their appearance or their self-image. Joseph Latayner (1853–1935), a successful Yiddish playwright who claimed to have written an earlier version of *The Two Kuni-Lemls* (entitled *Di tsvey Shmuel Shmulkes*) that he asserted Goldfaden later plagiarized, felt similarly to Loewy.[53] He had not dared to visit the non-Jewish theater despite a deep desire to do so because he felt too alien wearing his caftan and *payes* among non-Jews. Goldfaden's theater was the first theater he saw. No doubt his early audiences took in those around them just as much as they took in what played out on stage. The Russian non-Jewish journalist N. D. Shigarin, who was in Romania to cover the Russo-Turkish War (1876–77), which coincided with Goldfaden's first productions, decided to find out what all the fuss was about. He noticed its amateurish aspects, but was generally impressed with how well Goldfaden's troupe reproduced the elements of seasoned theater. One of his observations is particularly noteworthy:

> Only one thing struck me as strange. During intermissions, the actors and actresses emerge from backstage and appear publicly, mingling with the audience; they talk, drink and smoke and then return to the stage to appear in the next scene. Such behavior weakens the impression of their performance, at least insofar as it struck me.[54]

In fact, as we have seen, it was not at all counterintuitive for the actors to blur the worlds of stage and audience. Participants on both sides of the curtain did not conform to theater etiquette because theater was both novel and all too familiar.

---

52. Quoted in Franz Kafka's unfinished record of actor Isaac Loewy's life story, "Concerning the Jewish Theater," in *The Blue Octavo Notebooks*, ed. Max Brod, trans. Ernst Kaiser and Eithne Wilkins (Cambridge: Exact Change, 1991), 82–83.

53. Latayner is one of a number of playwrights and Yiddish theatre producers who has been arguably overshadowed by Goldfaden's legend. See Perlmutter on his importance and contribution, *Dramturgn*, 65.

54. Quoted in Uri Finkel and Nokhem Oyslender's *A. Goldfadn* (Minsk: Institute of White Russian Culture, 1926), 96.

Given the motley makeup of the Yiddish theater's first audiences, it should not be surprising that the operetta lends itself to multiple and contradictory interpretations. If one were inclined toward modern thinking, manner, or appearance, one might see Max as a hero, Sholem as a maskil, Pinkhes as a Hasidic buffoon, and Kuni-Leml as a metaphor for Hasidism (crippled and laughable). And most critics and historians, leaning as they do toward the secular and modern, see the play in just such a light. If one were Hasidic, however, one would notice the trickery of Max, his sycophantic love for the czar, his mean-spirited mimicking of Hasidic manner, and, in contrast, interpret Kuni-Leml as a kind of hapless but lovable hero who despite his naiveté is authentic, truth-telling, and unapologetically Hasidic. When Max's colleagues reveal themselves to be behind the resurrection of the dead, all orchestrated by Max, almost everyone on the stage laughs as if to cue the audience that this has been a maskilic hoax at Pinkhes's expense and that this is funny. But the trickery of which the *maskilim* accused the Hasidic establishment is, in the play, all the handiwork of *maskilim* themselves. That is to say, Max's young friends successfully mock the institution of the resurrection of the dead and the *lamed-vovnik* but themselves come off as slippery tricksters. For the traditionalist, the true laugh might come when Kuni-Leml sees that Max's friends are still decked out in their ghost costumes and, with his signature literalism, calls them "*meysimdike daytshn*" or "deathly Germans." He does not see spirits raised from the dead, because they are not, in fact, spirits raised from the dead, but rather modern-clad Jews in death shrouds. Kuni-Leml (incapable of understanding metaphor) might not have meant it as a witty criticism of his victimizers but *meysimdike daytshn* would certainly be grasped by the audience as a knock against reformers. Finally, consider the equation Goldfaden makes between Hasidism and the theater, a flourish that introduces the operetta and may even be a coded defense of the Yiddish theater itself:

We *yehudim*.
Pious Hasidim.
Follow the Lord's good name.
The rebbe is our joy,
But those other men and boys
Their pleasures just aren't the same.
Sabbath and holidays, they ruin absolutely.
"Who needs it?" they ask. "Where's the beauty?"
Oy do we enjoy it!
Every minute,
There's a meal,
A flask and a cask,
A song, what a deal!
Oy, come eat, come drink, have a sip and a bite,
Everyone taste—what a delight! Sing and dance, jump and prance,
For the love of God tonight!

Who better to appreciate the joy, celebration, food, and drink, singing and dancing but those assembled in a tavern to watch a Jewish operetta?

No text is ideologically neutral or without its structures of authority. With Wisse's canon book in mind we might ask, "What does *The Two Kuni-Lemls* deem 'modern Jewish'?" I have argued that the play answers such a question with a multiplicity of answers: Max, the ambivalent maskil; Sholem, the negotiator of multiple worlds; Carolina, liberated from the patterns of her traditional family; and Kuni-Leml, navigating modernity by clinging single-mindedly to his piety. But the "answers" are coded with inside jokes and subtle cultural references such as Kuni-Leml's slip of the tongue ("c-c-crinoline") and Carolina's need for "fresh air," as well as the layers of historical experience Goldfaden knowingly or otherwise folded into the character of Max. Even the mirror-like encounter between Max and Kuni-Leml had a pedigree with which "in-the-know" audience members were familiar: a classic Yiddish folk performance staged in the taverns that pre-dated Yiddish theater played out between a modern Jew or *"daytsh"* and his plant in the audience who would play a Hasid. They would argue with each other until the Hasid furiously stormed on stage. Instead of throwing punches at the insulting performer, however, he danced a mazurka while the *daytsh* did a Hasidic jig. In the choreographed exchange and its punch-line is the psychological complexity of the Hasid/maskil relationship telegraphed in Max's performance as Kuni-Leml. Yiddish theatre, like operettas in any language, might have held itself out to non-Yiddish speakers, but only to an extent. Only viewers who knew Yiddish and came from the Yiddish speaker's cultural world had access to the operetta's most sophisticated jokes. In the end, then, the play deems "modern Jewish" those who are clued into its secrets. To the religious as well as the bourgeois establishments Goldfaden was considered a loose cannon, if you will. They understood that for Goldfaden an audience that laughed at the right places was more important than one that left with a lesson. The enduring question the operetta asks is: Do you get the joke?

Memory as Metaphor:
Meir Wiener's Novel *Kolev Ashkenazi*
as Critique of
the Jewish Historical Imagination

MIKHAIL KRUTIKOV

Meir Wiener's historical novel *Kolev Ashkenazi* presents one of the most provocative and problematic examples of that genre in Yiddish literature. Conceived in Vienna in the early 1920s and published in Moscow in two editions in 1934 and 1938, the novel is a sarcastic parody of the so-called "bourgeois-nationalist" concept of Jewish history that was developed by such historians as Simon Dubnov, Meir Balaban, and Max Weinreich, and utilized by the Yiddish historical novelists in America and Poland. By focusing his attention on internal social conflicts and showcasing the corruption in the Krakow Jewish community of the late seventeenth century, Wiener produced a fictional deconstruction from a Marxist point of view of the myth of the national and religious unity of the Jewish people.

One of the finest and most erudite scholars of Jewish culture, a talented writer, and an original Marxist thinker, Wiener set out to expose the social and economic roots of anti-Semitism and demonstrate in a historical novel the confluence of the economic and political interests of Jewish and Christian ruling classes that jointly oppressed the Jewish and Christian poor. But underneath that scheme one can discern yet another layer of critique. By demystifying the aura of power and authority of the old Jewish oligarchy, Wiener inadvertently invited his reader to question the validity of any ideologically motivated interpretation of history. He portrayed the ruling class as criminals who used ideological rhetoric to cover up their crimes by turning their victims into martyrs. Published at the height of the Stalinist terror, *Kolev Ashkenazi* can be read, rather paradoxically, both as a model socialist realist historical novel and as a subversive critique of the ways in which history can be utilized for political and ideological means. Perhaps even more paradoxically, both readings appear equally valid. This ambivalence reflects the contradictory nature of Wiener's world view in the 1930s, when he was at the height of his Soviet career.

Born in 1893 into a well-off traditional Jewish family in Krakow, then part of the Austro-Hungarian Empire, Meir Wiener underwent several dramatic ideological and linguistic transformations. His family moved to Vienna on the eve of World War I, and after receiving an exemption from military service on health grounds, he went to neutral Switzerland to study. Around 1917 he began publishing articles on medieval Hebrew poetry, Kabbalah, and Zionism in German Jewish publications, including Martin Buber's prestigious journal *Der Jude*. Upon his return to Vienna in 1919 he became involved in a variety of cultural and political projects, such as an anthology of Hebrew mystical poetry in German translation *Die Lyrik der Kabbalah* (The Poetry of the Kabbalah, 1920) and a cultural-philosophical treatise *Von den Symbolen* (On Symbols, 1924), as well as a short book of his own poetry *Messias* (1920). Together with the prominent Prague scholar Rabbi Heinrich Brody, Wiener edited *Anthologia Hebraica* (1922), which for many years remained the standard collection of post-biblical poetry in the original Hebrew. Politically Wiener was sympathetic to radical left-wing Zionism, but eventually turned to Communism. His radical views did not prevent him from socializing in various cultural and political circles in Vienna and Berlin. He had a wide range of interests in Judaism, Hebrew literature, German modernism, and Oriental cultures. In Berlin he became friends with the Soviet Yiddish writers Leib Kvitko and Der Nister, and, probably under their influence, began writing poetry and novellas in Yiddish. Frustrated by his inability to find an intellectual job and to publish his Yiddish fiction in Europe, Wiener accepted an offer from the Soviet Union and moved to Kharkov in October 1926.

In the Soviet Union Wiener built a remarkable academic career in Yiddish studies, first at the Kiev Institute of Jewish Culture and later at the Moscow State Pedagogical Institute, where he headed the Department of Yiddish Language and Literature until its closing in 1938. He was also a member of the Union of Soviet Writers and coeditor of *Sovyetish*, the most prestigious Soviet Yiddish periodical. The main area of his academic interest was Yiddish literature of the nineteenth century, as well as contemporary literary criticism. In 1929 he published his first novel, *Ele Faleks untergang* (The Downfall of Ele Falek), written in Berlin in 1923, but soon had to renounce it as "decadent." *Kolev Ashkenazi*, his second novel, proved to be more successful and appeared in two different editions. His second historical novel, titled *Baym mitlendishn yam* (At the Mediterranean Sea), about the seventeenth-century Venetian rabbi and scholar Leon da Modena, was published only in fragments and remained unfinished. His major work of fiction, a 450-page novel that portrayed Jewish bohemian life in Berlin of the early 1920s, also remained unfinished and has never been published. Shortly after the outbreak of the Soviet-German war in June 1941, Wiener enlisted in the writers' battalion and was killed in action in the autumn. Today Meir Wiener is remembered mostly for his works about classical Yiddish literature, while his fiction remains largely unknown and his major work is awaiting publication.[1]

---

1. A more detailed account of Wiener's life can be found in my article "A Yiddish Author as a Cultural Mediator: Meir Wiener's Unpublished Novel," in Ritchie Robertson and Joseph Sherman (eds.), *The Yiddish Presence in European Literature: Inspiration and Interaction* (Oxford: Legenda, 2005), 73–86.

Meir Wiener vs. Georg Lukács on the Theory of Historical Fiction

Wiener's interest in the historical genre was both practical and theoretical. He developed his concept of historical fiction within the theoretical framework of Soviet Marxist discourse, which during the 1930s was dominated by Georg Lukács and his circle. Another important factor was the Yiddishist theory and practice in Poland and America, to which Wiener responded with scathing criticism. Both contexts are equally important to our understanding of Wiener's critical and artistic mindsets. The most coherent exposition of his views on the historical novel can be found in his essay on the popular Russian historical novelist Aleksey Pavlovich Chapygin (1870–1937), the author of two novels of Russian history set in the seventeenth and eighteenth centuries.[2] This essay, which appeared in 1940 in the leading Soviet literary monthly *Novyi mir*, was to remain Wiener's only critical foray into the field of Russian literature. The essay opens with a theoretical statement that echoes Wiener's pre-Marxist views: "The historical theme in general is a kind of gigantic metaphor, through which the author expresses his attitude to the events and the very essence of his time."[3] To adjust this view to Marxism, Wiener defines the metaphor in socio-historical rather than aesthetic terms. He argues that historical events are important not for their own sake but only in their relation to the present: "a poetic narrative about the past is at the same time, to a larger or lesser extent, a story of the present" (218). The genuinely positive hero of historical fiction can be only an epic character who embodies the "most exalted aspirations of the people" (219). This means that the plot of a "positive" historical novel has to be based not on a romantic story of individual passions, but on the "social aspirations of the depicted period" (219). The true aspirations of the time, Wiener continues, are to be found in the consciousness of the suppressed underclass rather than in that of the ruling elite. To bolster his argument, Wiener invokes Marx's idea that the social energy of change in the late medieval period was located in the urban plebeians.

These arguments bring Wiener to the conclusion that a genuine folk character is both national and universal. A plebeian protagonist serves as a pivot for the entire novel, with other characters revolving around him and personifying the variety of social types of the age. The authority of that epic folk hero is rooted in "his ability, by means of free, just, resolute, and steadfast action, to overcome the contradictions of life, danger, and death" (222). The "naïve" folkloric idea of heroism produces an "epic" literary quality,

---

2. *Razin Stepan* (1926–1927; Stepan Razin, an English translation by Cedar Paul, New York: Hutchinson, 1946), and *Guliashchie lyudi* (Vagabonds, 1935–1937).

3. Meir Viner, "Master epicheskogo povestvovaniia: ob istoricheskikh romanakh A. P. Chapygina," *Novyi mir*, 9 (1940), 218. Further references in brackets are to this publication.

harmonizing emotions with intellect, and engaging the reader with the characters and their struggle for redemption. One of the features of this naïve style is its unmediated way of depicting cruelty and passions, which does not, however, degenerate into a decadent naturalism. The portrayal of the extreme forms of passion elucidates the most dramatic qualities of the folk character. Propping up his point with an appropriate quote from *Das Kapital*, Wiener points out the progressive role that was played by paupers and beggars in the historical transition from the Middle Ages to early Modernity. It was that underclass, rather than the more privileged social group of artisans and craftsmen, who gave birth to the modern proletariat. Similarly, it was the picaresque novel rather than more "cultured" genres that gave birth to the modern European novel. Chapygin's achievement, Wiener concludes, lies in his ability to incorporate picaresque elements into the Soviet historical novel and to provide them with a new ideological meaning. In Chapygin's works, "the old picaresque novel receives a new development in the form of the revolutionary Odyssey of the rebellious medieval peasantry and urban plebs" (228).

Wiener's concept of the plebeian underclass as the primary moving force of historical progress and of the vagabond intellectual and artist as the voice of this force can be interpreted as a response to Georg Lukács' theory of the historical novel, developed during the second half of the 1930s.[4] In contrast to Wiener, Lukács had little interest in the masses as a historical force. In his view, the masses had possessed no historical consciousness until the French Revolution and the Napoleonic Wars shocked, for the first time in history, the whole of Europe and awakened the sense of historic change among its nations, offering them "a concrete opportunity to understand that their entire existence is historically conditioned, to see history as something that intrudes in their everyday life."[5] This awakening of the historical consciousness, Lukács argues, gave rise to two opposite but complementary ideological paradigms, nationalism and universalistic humanism: "on the one hand, the national element gets connected with the problems of social transformation; on the other hand, an awareness spreads in wide circles that the history of each nation is merely a part of world history."[6] Contrary to Lukács, Wiener regards both types of historical awareness, the national and the universal, not as an ideological product of a new historical experience, but as the inherent feature of mass consciousness, something that every national community possesses naturally. These "hidden qualities

---

4. Lukács formulated his ideas in a series of essays that appeared first in Russian in the Moscow journal *Literaturnyi kritik* in 1937 and 1938, which served as the basis for a later German monograph.

5. Georg Lukács. "Istoricheskii roman," *Literaturnyi kritik*, 7 (1937), 52.

6. *Literaturnyi kritik*, 7 (1937), 53.

and abilities of the folk character" contribute to the "national realization of
the advanced aspirations of the whole humanity."[7]

Another difference between Wiener and Lukács is the role and place of
the central character in the historical novel. Lukács's favorite historical novelist is Sir Walter Scott, who introduced the "mediocre" protagonist character as a mediator between different forces in the novel, enabling the author
to maintain equilibrium in the portrayal of the different sides of the historical struggle.[8] Wiener admires Scott's use of folk poetics but criticizes his idealized portrayal of the Scottish nobility, the "gang of perjurers, thieves and
bandits," as noble folk heroes.[9] Wiener's notion of the "epic hero" as the
embodiment of the eternal energy of the masses is the opposite of Lukács's
concept of a "mediating" character. For Lukács, the task of the historical
novel is to show how the dominant conflicts of a particular age shaped people's characters and affected their actions, rather than to portray extraordinary historic personalities.[10] By depicting ordinary people in ordinary circumstances, a skillful writer can recreate the authentic atmosphere of an
age. Wiener, on the contrary, privileges the extraordinary character capable
of overcoming the limitations imposed on his freedom by the historical forces and conditions of his age. According to Wiener, such a character is to be
found not at the top nor in the middle, but at the very bottom of the social
pyramid.

As a Hegelian thinker with a penchant for authoritarian leadership,
Lukács divides humanity into two categories. The overwhelming majority of
people are ordinary "maintainers" (*Erhaltende*), capable merely of repro-
ducing the existing order but unable to change its course, whereas a few
heroic "world-historic" (*welthistorische*) personalities have the ability to
affect the course of history by forming and leading mass movements. Lukács
believes that the protagonist of a historical novel can be only a "maintainer."
Due to its genre limitations, the historical novel has no artistic means for an
adequate representation of the grandiose intellectual and practical activity
of a "world-historic" leader. Literature can show history only through its
reflections on the surface of ordinary everyday reality, the way life is perceived by ordinary people.[11]

Unlike Lukács, Wiener has little interest in the heroic characters of the
"world-historic" scale. He believes that the energy of historical change is
concentrated in the masses rather than in individuals. In his unpublished

---

7. Viner, "Master epicheskogo povestvovaniia," 221.

8. *Literaturnyi kritik*, 7 (1937), 64.

9. Viner, "Master epicheskogo povestvovaniia," 220.

10. *Literaturnyi kritik*, 7 (1937), 70.

11. Ibid., 72.

"Notitsn vegn historishn roman" ("Notes on the Historical Novel," 1930s)
Wiener criticizes non-Soviet Yiddish writers for creating a national Jewish
version of the "world-historic" character: "a central figure of the contemporary historical themes in the capitalist abroad is the historical 'national Jewish' 'hero'—the 'saint' in different shapes (*a tsentrale figur fun di haynt-
tsaytsike historishe temes in kapitalistishn oysland iz der historisher 'nats-
ional-yidisher' 'held'—der 'heyliger' in di farshidene geshtaltn*)."[12] For
Wiener, an example of the ideal Jewish folk character is Sholem Aleichem's
Tevye the Dairyman, and this is also a type that he tried to recreate in his
own fiction.

Wiener and Lukács differ in their views on the issue of the relevance of
the image of the past for the present. Lukács believes that the historical
novel has to produce an "animation of the past as the prehistory of the
present, an artistic animation of those historical forces that have, in the
course of a long development, formed our life the way it is now. A genuine
artist makes this process as tangible and visible as if we experience it ourselves."[13] According to Lukács, most historical fiction, from the nineteenth-
century Romantics to the early twentieth-century German modernists, suffered from what he called "psychological modernization," an inability to
represent historical reality adequately to its time. Wiener is less interested in
the dynamics of the historical process than in certain stable metaphorical
structures that link the past to the present and show the way into the future.
Like Lukács, Wiener is critical of "psychological modernization"; he proposes instead a different kind of artistic modernization, which one can call
"metaphorical modernization." In historical fiction, Wiener values the ability to discern timeless symbolic images behind historical reality, not to create an "animated prehistory." For Wiener, who in his early works rejected
Hegel's dialectical view of history in favor of Goethe's "morphological" concept, metaphors constitute the symbolic foundation of reality. In contrast,
Lukács regarded symbols and metaphors as technical devices that help to
produce an artistic illusion of reality. He sees the function of the artistic
form as a "recreation of the immediate image of external life by means of
art, a new individualization of regular and common elements in human relationships."[14] For Wiener, metaphors and symbols are metaphysical entities
that transcend historical reality; for Lukács, they are merely projections of
infinite reality onto the finite medium of literature.

---

12. Quoted in Leyzer Podryadtshik, "Vegn Meir Viners literarisher yerushe," *Sovetish
    heymland*, 10 (1968), 60.

13. *Literaturnyi kritik*, 7 (1937), 80–81.

14. Lukács, "Istoricheskii roman i istoricheskaia drama," *Literaturnyi kritik*, 9 (1937).

From Theory to Practice: Wiener's Historical Fiction

Like some other Russian literary historians of the twentieth century, most notably Yuri Tynianov, Wiener tried his hand at historical fiction.[15] Among his unpublished Yiddish works of the pre-Soviet period is a historical novella titled "Valenty Gulveyts" (1924). In the Soviet Union Wiener considerably expanded this early text, turning it into a short novel, which appeared in the first issue of the Moscow Yiddish almanac *Sovetish* and was published by the Moscow Emes press in two different editions in 1934 (168 pages) and in 1938 (254 pages). A Russian translation by B. Cherniak was prepared for publication in 1938 and reached the galley stage, but never appeared in print, for reasons that remain unclear. The original novella is a story of a mentally unstable Polish aristocrat, Valenty Gulveyts, who tries first to rape a Jewish woman at his own wedding and then stabs her musician husband. Unable to free himself from the ghost of the dead Jew, Gulveyts decides to convert to Judaism and rid himself of his pursuer using Jewish remedies. Disguised as a vagabond, he disappears among the shtetl Jews. In the meantime it transpires that the Jewish musician did not die, but was secretly sent to a Jesuit seminary, where he became an ardent Christian, while the Jewish community received a nailed casket filled with stones instead of his body. As a result of the complicated plot, which involves a lot of intrigues and machinations by the Krakow Jewish community leaders and Polish aristocrats, Gulveyts, now a Jew, ends up being murdered by his supposed victim and proclaimed a martyr who gave his life for the sanctification of God's name (*kidesh-hashem*). He is buried near the previous "martyr," the musician.

The ger-tsedek *and* kidesh-hashem:
Motifs in Jewish History and Yiddish Fiction

The primary target of Wiener's satire is the popular Polish-Jewish legend about the *ger-tsedek*, the eighteenth-century story of a Polish aristocrat Walentyn Potocki, who supposedly converted to Judaism and was burned at the stake in Vilno. Analyzing the origins, the structure, and the significance of the legend, the historian Magda Teter arrives at the following conclusion: "The legend of ger zedek [*sic*] of Wilno, though said to be a true story, appears to be a carefully crafted tale of conversion, a polemical and apologetic response to a number of challenges that the Polish Jewish community

---

15. Analyzing the phenomenon of literary scholars writing historical fiction and Russian novelists engaging in historical studies, Andrew Wachtel argues for "the existence of a specifically Russian literary tradition of intergeneric dialogue on historical themes." See his *Obsession with History: Russian Writers Confront the Past* (Stanford: Stanford University Press, 1994), p. 219.

faced from the mid-eighteenth century."[16] As Teter demonstrates, the *ger-tsedek* legend is constructed as a reversal of the classical Christian tale of martyrdom. In contrast to the situation in which a Jewish convert to Christianity gains a higher social status (in medieval Poland those converts were as a rule elevated to the nobility), "the righteous convert, son of a duke, Potocki openly acknowledged his decline in status when he stated that he was a Jewish man dwelling in the exile."[17] Teter interpreted the *ger-tsedek* legend as a response to a variety of external and internal challenges faced by Polish Jewry in the second half of the eighteenth century: Catholic propaganda, the Frankist and Hasidic movements, the Haskalah. The Jewish community "needed religious stability, and the legend of *ger zedek*, which affirmed the truth of Judaism in no uncertain terms, served the purpose." But at a different level, Teter argued, the legend could be read also as evidence of "permeability of social and cultural boundaries, between Jews and Christians, not only because it tells of Christians who become Jews, but also because it illustrates Jewish appropriation of Christian literary topoi."[18]

By the time Wiener turned to the *ger-tsedek* legend, it had already become a popular motif in Jewish literature in various languages.[19] Thanks to his broad erudition in both Christian and Jewish cultures, Wiener must have been familiar with a range of interpretations of the legend, so that his irreverent rendition of it was a deliberate subversion. In fact, Wiener was not alone in treating the *ger-tsedek* legend this way. A strikingly similar interpretation was offered by the Polish Yiddish author Alter Kacyzne in his play *Der dukus* (The Duke), which received a controversial welcome when it was performed in Warsaw in 1925. The play was criticized by some Yiddish critics for its "*goyish*" approach to the theme, and lack of stylistic uniformity.[20] In his preface to the play, Kacyzne explained that he used the story of the *ger-tsedek* of Vilno not as a "theme" but as an "outline" for his psychological drama, because the story itself was good only for a sentimental national melodrama: "The tale of the Righteous Convert inspired me not as a legend born in the Jewish imagination but rather as a plausible event that is psychologically extraordinary."[21] Kacyzne explained that his primary

16. Magda Teter, "The Legend of Ger Zedek of Wilno as Polemic and Reassurance," *AJS Review*, 29:2 (2005), 238.

17. Ibid., 252.

18. Ibid., 263.

19. For a brief bibliography, see Teter, 237, n. 2.

20. Zalman Reyzen, *Leksikon fun der yiddisher literature, prese un filologye*, vol. 3 (Vilno: Kletskin, 1929), col. 534.

21. *Landmark Yiddish Plays: A Critical Anthology.* Edited, translated, and with an Introduction by Joel Berkowitz and Jeremy Dauber (Albany: State University of New York Press, 2006), 293.

goal was to create a "social Jewish drama" rather than a "personal drama of the convert": "The Righteous Convert with his aristocratic fantasy of becoming a Jew interested me only to the degree that it allowed me to illuminate the background of the Jewish community."[22]

Like Wiener's Valenty Gulveyts, Kacyzne's Young Duke is portrayed as a mentally and psychologically unstable personality. His identity undergoes a complete change after his conversion to Judaism, which has turned him into a religious scholar with strong messianic aspirations. In his final confession before the court of noblemen, the Young Duke proclaims that the true goal of his conversion to Judaism is martyrdom:

> It is not my life, but my death, that is necessary, for myself and for my Jewish faith. [...] I want to die now, for my whole life's work lies in these last few steps to the pyre. [...] Though I have immersed my soul in the waters of Judaism, my back has not borne the Jewish yoke, and my aristocratic spine remains unbent. [...] I am strong enough to die as a Jew, but too weak to live as one.[23]

In the introduction to their English translation of *The Duke*, Joel Berkowitz and Jeremy Dauber describe the historical determinism of the play as "essentially congruent with Communism," adding that "it may also be that Kacyzne's own attraction to Communism may be related to his interest in characters as archetypes."[24] Although some Marxist theorists would question the congruence between Communism and historical determinism, one can clearly see the parallel between Kacyzne's story, Wiener's conversion to Communist ideology and the legend of a Catholic aristocrat's conversion to Judaism. Kacyzne and Wiener, to different degrees, chose to reject their precarious status as bourgeois intellectuals and instead to identify with the struggle of the downtrodden proletarian masses. But they realized also that they would never fit into the new community, and their conversion must have seemed like an act of madness from a "normal" point of view. And yet, with all remarkable parallels between *The Duke* and "Valenty Gulveyts," it is difficult to see how one work could influence the other, because both texts were written practically simultaneously.

Wiener's sarcastic treatment of the martyrdom motif challenged the mood that prevailed in Yiddish culture in the aftermath of the Russian Revolution and the Civil War. As his primary target Wiener chose the highly popular historical romance by Sholem Asch entitled *Af kidesh hashem* (*In Sanctification of God's Name*, 1919). For Asch, the historical setting of seventeenth-century Ukraine was merely a backdrop for a contemporary tale of collective Jewish suffering. According to Ellen Kellman, Asch's novel had a

---

22. Ibid.

23. Ibid., 351.

24. Ibid., 70.

modern political agenda: "Asch apparently intended to draw a parallel between issues of Jewish power and powerlessness in mid seventeenth-century Eastern Europe and in post-World War I Europe and America, thus seeking to warn contemporary Jewish leaders not to repeat the costly mistakes of their predecessors."[25] Contrary to Asch, Wiener in "Valenty Gulveyts" seems to be highly skeptical about both the efficiency of Jewish politics and meaningfulness of Jewish martyrdom. A brief personal encounter in Paris in 1926 only reinforced Wiener's negative impression of Asch. In a letter to the Hebrew writer David Vogel, Wiener reported: "Yesterday I was at Asch's. He invited me. He owns a villa, nice household—disgusting. A kind of newly decorated salon belonging to a nouveau-riche innkeeper."[26] As we shall see, Wiener's dark artistic worldview deepened even more after his emigration to the Soviet Union, in spite of his embrace of Communist ideology.

From "Valenty Gulveyts" to Kolev Ashkenazi: Composition and Characters

The conclusion of "Valenty Gulveyts" touches upon the problem of the reliability of a historical memory that is produced by the authorities and transmitted through official channels. The invented stories of two "martyrs" are utilized for propaganda purposes by the communal leadership, yet the folk memory preserves a trace of doubt, which is hinted at by the sly smile of the female caretaker at the old Krakow Jewish cemetery. The conflict between the collective memory of the people and the official history of the community becomes more prominent in the subsequent expanded versions of the novella. In *Kolev Ashkenazi* Wiener presents a broader picture of the social transformation of the Polish Jewish community at the turning point in history when the Polish-Lithuanian Commonwealth began its decline. The novel's main hero is not Valenty Gulveyts but the powerful *parnas* of the Krakow Jewish community and the financial agent of King Jan III Sobieski (1629–1696), the last great ruler of Poland. The story of Gulveyts turned into a subplot within a broader historical narrative, being connected to the main plot through the figure of Bendit Sirkis, the nominal head of the community.

Sirkis and Ashkenazi personify two different types of Jewish leaders who are struggling over dominance of the Jewish community. Ashkenazi is a medieval Jewish financier who provides the ruler with money, whereas Sirkis represents a new socio-economic force, the emerging industrial capital. Ashkenazi derives his influence and prestige from his closeness to the

---

25. Ellen Kellman, "Power, Powerlessness, and the Jewish Nation in Scholem Asch's *Af kidesh haShem*." Nanette Stahl (ed.), *Sholem Asch Reconsidered* (New Haven, Ct.: The Beinecke Rare Book and Manuscript Library, 2004), 106.

26. Mikhail Krutikov, "From Vienna to Kharkov via Paris: Five Letters of Meir Wiener to David Vogel, 1925–26," *Jews and Slavs*, 17 (2006), 101.

king, whereas Sirkis builds his economic and social power base by investing in the development of salt mines that he leases from the Polish magnates. To circumvent the medieval prohibition on direct commercial dealings between Jews and the nobility, which safeguarded the power of the old communal oligarchy, Sirkis secretly employs the impoverished aristocrat Gulveyts as a front for his business. This example demonstrates, in accordance with the Marxist theory, how common economic interests unite, across religious and ethnic boundaries, the members of the emerging capitalist class, a Jew and a Pole, in their desire to exploit Polish serfs who are forced by economic necessity to become miners. Wiener's novel explores the very beginning of the process of the proletarization of peasants, which will eventually bring about the end of capitalism.

Kolev Ashkenazi opens with two Polish peasants coming to Krakow to seek protection from ruthless treatment in the mines. In the Marxist scheme of the novel, the peasants signify the victimization of the masses under the joint economic exploitation by Polish nobility and Jewish entrepreneurs. In the course of the novel these peasants are cheated, abused, accused of false crimes, and finally executed by the authorities. Their tragedy conveys the ideological message of the novel: it is the peasants and not the fake Jewish "martyrs" who are the true victims of history. By exposing the collaboration between the Jewish oligarchy, the Polish aristocracy, and the Christian city authorities in their cruel intrigue against the innocent peasants, Wiener highlights the supremacy of the economic interests of the ruling classes over religious and ethnic divisions. But the emerging capitalist system affects not only the lower classes. It also undermines the authority of the king as the leader of the nobility and his factor Ashkenazi as the leader of the Jewish community. While the noblemen wrestle ever more new concessions and privileges from the king, the Jewish entrepreneurs struggle for more independence from the community. For his analytical exposition of the economic links between the Jews and the nobility, Wiener skillfully adapts the grand historical narrative of the Marxist theory to the specific conditions of late–seventeenth-century Poland. Such "accidental" events as the Chmelnicki uprising or the messianic movement of Sabbatai Tsvi, which are central for Jewish historians, have no relevance for this narrative, which sees history as a process driven by class struggle.

The clear-cut ideological scheme of the novel does not prevent Wiener from creating a complex psychological portrait of the controversial main character, Kolev Ashkenazi. Scrupulously honest in his religious observance, he can be cunningly ruthless in his political and economic dealings. One of the greatest intellects of his generation, famous all over Jewish Europe for his expert knowledge in religious and secular affairs, Ashkenazi holds no formal position of power in the Jewish community. He exercises his authority in a quiet way, relying mainly on his wealth and a direct access to the king. In contrast to Ashkenazi, who inherited his wealth and power, Sirkis has had to work his way up from a modest horse dealer to a wealthy lessee of salt mines. His reward is the title of the head of the Krakow community, which carries no real power. Now Sirkis's situation is dangerous, because the peasants threaten to expose his real position as the lessee of the salt mines, which, in turn, will endanger the entire Jewish community. Quickly realizing Sirkis's predicament, Ashkenazi starts an elaborate intrigue whose aim is both to weaken his opponent and to rescue the community. To achieve his goal, Kolev uses the communal *rekim*, criminal convicts who are protected from their punishment for as long as they perform useful services for the communal oligarchy.

Kolev maintains close personal relationships with the members of the underclass on the margins of the Jewish community. As a pious Jew, he invites all those who have nowhere to go every Friday evening to his house for a Sabbath meal. Even the *rekim* are there, although they are served in a separate room. The depiction of the beggars' meal at Kolev Ashkenazi's home is one of the most memorable episodes in the novel. It is based on Wiener's own childhood memory of a banquet that his grandfather Binyomin Lande used to give for the Krakow beggars once or twice every year. Kolev emerges in this episode as a patriarchal authority, genuinely committed to the welfare of his people regardless of their social standing. This aspect of his personality comes through particularly vividly during the plague epidemic, when all other leaders abandon their community, and only a few individuals, among them Kolev and some of the *rekim*, remain true to their religious and human duty and continue to care for the ill:

> *Dos zaynen geven yene mentshn, vos vayzn zikh plutsem fun zikh aleyn in a tsayt fun groyser noyt, greyt yedn noytbaderftikn guts tsu ton mit layb un zel. Genit un bahavnt in mentshlekher payn, in di shoydern fun krenk un toyt—farlangt fun zey yederer, az zey zoln alts un dos shverste ton, vi opgebn an antlienem khoyv, vos me hot a rekht tsurik tsu fodern. Un zey tuen alts mit yenem gelasenem mut, vos dremlt in di tifenishn funem folk.*[27]

> Those were the kind of people who appear unexpectedly by themselves in a time of great need, ready to offer help with their body and soul to anyone who needs it. They were experienced and skilled in dealing with human pain, with the horrors of disease and death—and everybody demanded from them the most difficult things, as if they had to repay a debt. And they performed everything with that relaxed courage that is dormant in the depths of the people.

As Wiener makes clear in this fragment, the time of need is also the time of individual heroism, when even people like Kolev and *rekim* realize their human potential. As an act of repentance, Kolev forgives the debts that are owed to him by dying people.

---

27. Meir Viner, *Kolev Ashkenazi* (Moscow: Emes, 1938), 127.

Kolev's spiritual antagonist in the novel is Shepsl Gets, a vagabond who wanders from one community to another. A committed enemy of the establishment and the rich, Gets is also a folk poet whose songs give voice to the sufferings and aspirations of the people. In the course of the novel Kolev and Shepsel have two encounters, first at the beggars' table in Kolev's home, where Gets shows his independent character by arguing with Kolev, and then during the plague, when they work together to help its victims. From the point of view of the Marxist scheme of the novel, the relationship between Kolev and Shepsel has an ambiguous significance. Socially they represent two antagonistic classes within the Jewish community, yet spiritually they share the sense of common responsibility for the collective fate of the Jewish people. Shepsl personifies the worldliness, the open-mindedness, and the social energy of the Jewish masses, whereas Kolev embodies the patriarchal notion of communal responsibility as a religious duty, something that is no longer shared by the upcoming bourgeoisie.

During the plague the figure of Shepsl reaches almost mythological proportions: "Shepsl Gets behaved as if the plague could have no power over him (*Shepsl Gets hot zikh azoy gefirt, vi di mageyfe volt iber im nit gekont hobn keyn makht*)." As part of the eternal world of nature rather than mortal humanity, he seems to be immortal: "nothing bad happens, wild weeds do not wither (*Epes beyz geshet nisht, vildgroz fardart nisht*)" (131). During his last encounter with Kolev, Shepsl explains to him his notion of Judaism, which he regards as a mere translation of the social order of exploitation and inequality into the language of religious discourse. He sarcastically notes that he will be expelled from paradise in the same way he has been expelled from all Jewish communities, for the lack of a "residence permit." While his message confirms the Marxist idea of religion as part of the ideological superstructure determined by a socio-economic basis, the character of Shepsl as a symbolic image of the eternal Jewish people certainly contradicts this materialist interpretation of history. The first edition of *Kolev Ashkenazi* makes the ideological message of the novel explicit by quoting from Karl Marx's essay "On the Jewish Question" in the epigraph: "Let us consider the real secular Jew, not the *Sabbath-Jew* [...] but the *Jew of everyday*."[28] This epigraph is notably missing both in the expanded second edition of the novel and in the proofs of its Russian translation. The removal of the epigraph may suggest that between 1934 and 1938 Wiener's concept of history underwent some transformations and became less class-deterministic, a trend that can be observed in his scholarship as well.

The first edition of the novel was positively reviewed by two prominent Soviet Yiddish scholars. The historian Osher Morgulis (1891–1976), who collaborated with Wiener on a number of projects, praised the novel for its

---

28. Karl Marx, "Zur Judenfrage," in Karl Marx, Friedrich Engels. *Werke*, vol. 1 (Berlin: GDR: Karl Dietz, 1976), 372.

objective portrayal of the tragic life of peasants and the artistic representation of the contradictions between the city and the country and between
different religious and ethnic groups.[29] But Wiener's greatest achievement
as a historical novelist was, in Morgulis's view, the detailed analytical picture of the Jewish community. Kolev Ashkenazi was portrayed in accordance with Marx's prescription, in his everyday garb rather than in his Sabbath attire, which was a big step forward in comparison to the idealized
images of Jewish leaders in the works of the bourgeois nationalist historians
such as Graetz, Dubnov, and Balaban. Wiener was also the first Jewish writer to throw light on a social group that had until now been ignored by the
Jewish historians, the déclassé Jewish plebs who had no place in the communal structure. But, Morgulis noted, Wiener's narrative did not include the
class of working Jews—the artisans, their apprentices, and the coachmen—
who were part of the communal structure. In conclusion he expressed hope
that Wiener would produce another, larger historical novel that would
cover all aspects of Jewish life in the old Poland.

Morgulis was critical of Wiener's image of the Polish nobility, which he
found artistically weaker than that of the peasants. He pointed out that the
mentally deranged character of Valenty Gulveyts was by no means typical of
his class. He also complained that the story of Gulveyts had no clear meaning in the conceptual framework of the novel: Was it meant to be a rationalist critique of the romantic ger-tsedek legend, or was it a depiction of the
psychological disorder caused by the bad conscience of the landowner? As a
result, Morgulis argued, Wiener's critique of the bourgeois-nationalist concept that viewed Jewish history as a chain of religious persecutions and sufferings was not as convincing as it could be. Nor did the distorted image of
the Polish nobility match the masterful portrayal of the peasant characters,
who had a symbolic significance.

The literary scholar Aron Gurshteyn (1895–1941) in his review concentrated on the literary aspects of the novel.[30] He commended Wiener for
introducing the historical genre into Soviet Yiddish literature, "dealing a
blow" to the bourgeois-nationalist concept of Jewish history that found its
expression in the works by the foreign authors Sholem Asch, H. Leyvick, I. J.
Singer, and, to a lesser extent, Y. Opatoshu. Gurshteyn noted the element of
parody in Wiener's treatment of the kidesh-hashem theme, but found it flat
and formal. Gurshteyn regarded the character of Valenty Gulveyts merely as
a literary construction in accordance with the genre conventions of parody,
rather than as a realistic portrait of a Polish nobleman. But as a whole, the
novel had overgrown the limitations of parody and developed into a full-
scale realistic portrayal of the social reality of the age. Gurshteyn saw this

---

29. Osher Morgulis, "A raykhe arbet," *Sovetish*, 4 (1937), 341–356.

30. A. Gurshteyn, "Tsu der problem fun der geshikhtlekher teme," *Shtern*, 12 (1934), 85–
    92.

internal stylistic shift in *Kolev Ashkenazi* from parody to realism as an indication of Wiener's artistic development as a creative writer. By turning to
the historical theme, Wiener had successfully overcome the limitations of
the "subjectivist-psychological" style of his first novel, *Ele Faleks untergang*, and achieved a synthetic fusion between psychology and realism. The
next stage in Wiener's artistic development was to be, and here Gurshteyn's
view coincided with Morgulis's, a large historical epic novel in the style of
socialist realism.

As both Morgulis and Gurshteyn point out, Wiener shifts the mode of the
Jewish historical narrative from celebration to criticism. Instead of eulogiz-
ing the virtues of the old communal solidarity as a mechanism of defense
and preservation, as was common among Jewish historians and writers of
nineteenth and early twentieth century, Wiener focuses his artistic lens on
an analysis of the internal conflicts and economic interests that underlie
them. He exposes the communal administration as an instrument of socio-
economic oppression and ideological dominance in the service of the oligarchy. Eager to preserve their control over the masses, the communal leadership uses the cult of martyrdom to produce the illusion of unity in a situation
in which economic conflicts drive the community apart. The true martyrs in
his novel are not Jewish victims of religious persecution but Polish peasants
who suffer from economic oppression. Religion is merely a pretext for false
accusation. Indeed, the Christian peasants who were falsely accused of robbing and desecrating a Christian church were set up with the help of the
Jewish leaders.

The archetypal Jewish story of *kidesh hashem* had already been turned
into a travesty in "Valenty Gulveyts." In *Kolev Ashkenazi* the accent shifts
from the sphere of pathological psychology to the area of socio-economic
relations. The mentally unstable *"ger-tsedek"* Gulveyts becomes an instrument in Sirkis's economic exploitation of the peasants. To stress the theme
of social antagonism within the Jewish community, Wiener adds in *Kolev
Ashkenazi* a third "martyr" to the two who were already present in "Valenty
Gulveyts." This is the communal *rek* Vrome Druker, who has been used by
Sirkis to set up the peasants as suspects in the church robbery, who are then
handed over to the Christian authorities, tortured, and executed on direct
orders from Sirkis. But the sociological scheme of the novel leaves Shepsl in
an ambivalent position. On the one hand, as a wandering Jewish artisan, he
is a victim of the medieval socio-economic order, an embodiment of the
large Jewish underclass of paupers, who have no place in the communal
structure. The naturalistic portrayal of the Jewish underclass as a "state within a state" in *Kolev Ashkenazi* has parallels in Yiddish literature, from Mendele's *Fishke the Lame* to Der Nister's *Family Mashber*. On the other hand,
Shepsl, like some of his literary counterparts, symbolizes the eternal values
of justice, morality, and vitality, which Yiddish writers ascribed to the collective psyche of the Jewish people and which had no place in Marxist soci-
ology.

Kolev Ashkenazi *and the Ideological Battles of the 1930s*

To understand the polemic significance of Wiener's interpretation of Jewish history in *Kolev Ashkenazi*, we should turn to his 1929 essay on Shloyme Etinger. Wiener began his analysis of that early nineteenth-century Yiddish author with a sharp attack on Max Weinreich's introduction to the first academic edition of Etinger's works, which was published in Vilno in 1925. Wiener accused Weinreich of disregarding the broader socio-historical context of Etinger's life and concentrating instead on small details and personal circumstances. Wiener regarded Weinreich as an heir to the petite-bourgeois tradition in Yiddish literary scholarship, which extolled national virtues but played down class conflicts in the Jewish society: "It is clear that Weinreich wants Etinger to be regarded as a great-grandfather not just of Yiddish literature, but also of the entire bourgeois Yiddishist style of life and thought (*Es iz klor, az Vaynraykh vil, me zol banemen Etingern vi an elter-zeydn nit bloyz fun der yidisher literatur, nor funem gantsn balebesldik-yidishistn nusekh in lebn un inem trakhtn*)."[31] Wiener and Weinreich shared the conviction that the study of Yiddish literary history had direct relevance for contemporary affairs, but they differed in their understanding of this relevance. In the charged ideological atmosphere of pre-war Eastern Europe, Yiddish literary history was turned into another ideological battlefield between Soviet Marxists and Polish Yiddishists.

One particular episode in *Kolev Ashkenazi* leads to the suggestion that Wiener used his fiction to carry out his polemics against Weinreich. When Vrome Druker is arrested by the city's Christian authorities for his role in the church robbery, the communal leadership begins to prepare for his future sanctification as a martyr. This task is entrusted to Yoyzl Brandayz, the intelligent and shameless communal secretary.[32] In the name of the community, Brandayz declares a public fast and composes special *kines* (liturgical elegies) for the occasion. The narrator sarcastically remarks that "owing to their beauty they were included in some of the rare prayer books (*zey zaynen dernokh tsulib zeyer sheynkayt arayn in gevise zeltene gebet-bikher*)."[33] Brandayz bribes the prison guards so that Vrome can get kosher food, and arranges for prayers to be read at the place of the execution. At the same time, Vrome is being cruelly tortured to prevent him from telling the truth about the real culprits, Sirkis and Brandayz. To commemorate the tragic event, Brandayz had composed a "beautiful *kine*, an elegy, to be recited in all synagogues and at the gallows at the moment of Vrome's execution (*a sheyne kine, a klog-lid, oyf tsu zogn in ale shuln un oykh in der noent*

---

31. Meir Viner, "Shloyme Etinger, zayn ort in der yidisher literatur," in *Tsu der geshikhte fun der yiddisher literature in 19tsn yorhundert*, vol. 1 (New York: IKUF, 1945), 211.

32. Viner, *Kolev Ashkenazi*, 191.

33. Ibid., 191.

fun der tlie, beshas me vet Vromen hangen)." In short, Yoyzl Brandayz "has taken care of everything to ensure that Vrome is not angry in the other world and the communal administration is satisfied (*hot altsding bahavnt un batrakht tsugegreyt, az Vrome Druker zol oyf yener velt nisht zayn broygez un az kohol zol zayn tsufridn*)."[34]

The detail about composing the special elegy on the occasion of the martyrdom seems to be aimed directly at Max Weinreich. In his book *Shturemvint*, Weinreich argues that Yiddish historical songs and legends must be recognized by scholars as an important historical source, because sometimes they are "the only witness of a historical event (*der eyntsiker eydes fun a historisher iberlebung*)."[35] Among examples of historical legends that Weinreich discusses in his book as evidence of true historical events is a story about a certain pious Jew named Reb Avrom from Moshchisk, who was falsely accused of church robbery:

> *Men hot gekhapt a ganev, vos hot genumen di heylike keylim fun a kloyster. Dos iz geven a gute gelegnhayt tsu makhn a bilbl oyf yidn, un men hot ongeredt dem ganev, er zol zogn, az dos hobn im yidn geheysn baganeven dem kloyster, vayl zey darfn hobn dos heylike broyt, vos iz loytn kristlekhn gloybn dem derleyzer Yezuses kerper.*[36]

> Once they caught a thief who stole the sacred utensils from a church. This was a good opportunity to blame the Jews, and they told the thief to say that the Jews asked him to rob the church because they needed the consecrated bread that, according to the Christian faith, is the body of Jesus.

Wiener's use of this tragic motif in *Kolev Ashkenazi* appears to be a direct critique of Weinreich's "bourgeois-nationalist" approach to Jewish history. In his fiction, Wiener claims to recreate the "true" reality by showing how the supposedly "historical" songs had been produced from ready-made clichés by a hired writer in the service of the communal oligarchy. Wiener turns the relationship between history and fiction on its head. His fiction claims to be true because it conforms to the Marxist scheme of history, whereas any historical evidence that contradicts this scheme can be dismissed as concocted.

It would certainly be an oversimplification to reduce the complex and ambiguous ideological content of *Kolev Ashkenazi* to a Marxist critique of

---

34. Ibid., 192.

35. Vaynraykh, *Shturemvint*, 169.

36. Vaynraykh, *Shturemvint*, 171. Krakow city records of 1682 mention the case of a certain Jew, Mark Michalowicz, who was accused of *swentokradstwo*, buying sacred vessels that were stolen from a church in Bochnia, and subjected to investigation with torture. Adam Kazimierczuk, *Materiały sródowe do dziejów Żydów w ksiegach grodzkich dawnego województwa krakowskiego z lat 1674–1696*. Vol. 1 (Kraków: Universitas, 1995), 73.

the "bourgeois-nationalist" concepts of Jewish history of Dubnov, Balaban, and Weinreich and their literary adaptation by the Yiddish historical novelists in America and Poland. Underneath the class-oriented Marxist scheme is another layer of critique, aimed at the notion of master narrative as an instrument of ideological domination. By deconstructing national myths, Wiener invites his reader to question the validity of any, not necessarily "bourgeois-nationalist," ideological interpretation of history that is produced by a dominant group. He describes in great detail how the authorities manipulate other people's lives, cover up their own crimes by turning victims into martyrs, and then control the use of that "usable past."

Writing a novel that implicitly challenged the idea of authority *per se* was a risky enterprise in the Soviet Union of the 1930s. Wiener made necessary precautions by locating the action of his novel in seventeenth-century Krakow and providing it with an explicit orthodox Marxist interpretation. But it does not require much imagination to see parallels between the situation of Krakow in the 1670s and that of Kiev, Minsk, and Moscow in the 1930s: old and new leaders struggle for power, innocent people suffer, and history is constantly re-written, with new myths being created every year. Yesterday's criminals are celebrated as today's martyrs, only to be struck out from history tomorrow. The only successful people are unscrupulous *apparatchiks* like Yoyzl Brandayz, equally ready to serve their master and to betray him. All these ideas are discussed in the new ending that was added to the 1938 edition of the novel. Sensing his approaching death, Kolev retreats from worldly affairs after the death of the "martyrs" but retains Brandayz as his companion. Kolev despises Brandayz for his opportunism but is attracted to his intelligence. Taking stock of his life, Kolev realizes that he has left no legacy. A great scholar, the spiritual leader of Polish Jewry, and the powerful banker of the king of Poland, he will be replaced by a non-entity like Yoyzl Brandayz. Kolev comes to accept this fate as punishment for the evil deeds he committed, believing, nonetheless, that they had been necessary for the good of the community. In a desperate attempt to break out of the depression of his last days, Kolev tries to solicit a response from his loyal servant Vaybl Bas, but the servant remains silent, echoing the silence of the people as the ultimate sign of disapproval of the ruler in the final episode of Pushkin's *Boris Godunov*.

Conclusion: Truth between Fact and Metaphor

As the historian Osher Morgulis demonstrated in his review, Wiener succeeded in producing a Marxist historical novel on a Jewish theme, focusing on the complex relations between the socio-economic and the cultural, ideological, and religious superstructure. Morgulis also noted Wiener's special interest in the Jewish underclass: vagabonds, represented by Shepsl Gets, who existed outside the limits of the organized Jewish community. This interest reflects Wiener's views on the historical novel, which he outlined in his essay on Chapygin. Aron Gurshteyn, as a literary critic, has described Wiener's literary style as an amalgamation of two different manners, subtle psychological "graphics" and epic realist "painting."[37] While the latter manner largely serves for presenting the Marxist master-narrative, the former one is often used to subvert and question this narrative. Kolev Ashkenazi is portrayed both as a typical representative of his class and as a complex and contradictory personality. Unable and unwilling to escape the pressure of the historical circumstances that have pushed him into his social role, Kolev engages himself in a psychological exercise of constructing a personal mythology that would enable him to justify his behavior in terms of religious ethics. A highly sophisticated political player during his entire lifetime, at the end of his days he wants to translate the results of his successful political practice into the metaphorical language of Jewish values, yet he fails the ultimate test of convincing the *folksmentsh*, his most loyal servant Vaybl Bas.

The issue of historical "truth" and its moral validity is a central problem in *Kolev Ashkenazi*. Using the Marxist methodology of socio-economic analysis, Wiener deconstructs the national myths that were so important for other Yiddish writers and scholars of his time. But his critique of the historical notion of truth does not stop there. In his artistic reconstruction of historical reality, he creates a conflict between fictional and historical truth. As an artist, Wiener is highly skeptical of the validity of historical documents. He shares this attitude with his fellow novelist Yuri Tynianov, who, like Wiener, was a prominent literary historian and theoretician. Tynianov once said: "there are ceremonial [*paradnye*] documents, and they lie like people."[38] Like Tynianov, Wiener distrusts the official, "ceremonial" side of life and seeks in his fiction to uncover the "real" truth beneath it by revitalizing the metaphorical discourse of the age. For Wiener, the metaphor is closer to truth than are the recorded facts, because the facts are often constructed by the authorities according to their needs of the moment. This real "truth" could be recovered by looking into the depth of the collective creativity of the people, by studying and analyzing the symbolic language of folklore and and literature. The true custodians of the national historical heritage are the beggars and the outcasts who live outside the official discourse.

---

37. Gurshteyn, "Tsu der probem fun der geshikhtlekher teme," 91.

38. Tynianov, "Kak my pishem," in *Ivrii Tynianov: Pisatel i uchenyi. Vospominania, razmyshlenia, vstrechi* (Moscow: Molodaia guardia, 1966), 196.

Shmuel Nadler's *Besht-Simfonye*:
At the Limits of Orthodox Literature

BEATRICE LANG CAPLAN

In the spring of 1933, the Yiddish writer L. Olitski saw a new volume in the window of a store selling Jewish religious books and articles entitled *Besht-Simfonye* (*Bal-Shem-Tov Symphony*). He was so intrigued that he purchased it, read it immediately, and reviewed it for the Bundist *Vokhnshrift*. It is not surprising that he was curious about the book. The title pairs the Besht, the founder of Hasidism and a figure representative first and foremost of a traditional Jewish way of life, with "symphony," a modern, Western musical form unknown in traditional Jewish culture. The author, Shmuel Nadler, was a rising star of the new Orthodox literature being created within the framework of the Orthodox political party Agudes Yisroel, a literature that itself paired Orthodox content with modern literary form.

The promising title apparently did not live up to Olitski's expectations. He offered a scathing critique of it:

> *Besht-Simfonye*—a name that's a crown on the head of a dwarf. It's not the Besht and it's not a symphony. It's: [Shmuel] Nadler and cacophony. [...] It's the gabbing of the "awakening" young Orthodoxy. A grating song of "Agudes Yisroel."[1]

The critique is justified; the portrait of the Besht in the book is inconsistent and often bears no resemblance to the way the founder of Hasidism is traditionally portrayed. The idea of a "symphony" is not explicitly developed. Parts of the book are very similar to the weaker efforts of young Orthodox authors to write modern literature. And yet, Olitski's dismissive tone is unfair. He criticizes the inconsistencies of the book without any interest in probing why they crept into the work, or seeking the book's strengths; he dismisses Nadler's portrait of the Besht because it throws no new light on this famous figure, complaining that the book seems to be more about Nadler himself. He does not pause to wonder what light Nadler's portrayal might throw on its author, or on his Orthodox literary project.

Had Olitski written the review a few months later, he might have been more interested in Nadler himself, whose life, as it turned out, also encom-

---

I would like to thank Marc Caplan, Paul Glasser, Avrom Novershtern, Eddy Portnoy, and Alyssa Quint for their help in ways large and small in the preparation of this essay.

1. L. Olitski, "Di muze in a sheytl mit a shterntikhl," *Vokhnshrift far literatur, kunst un kultur* 18 (May 12, 1933): 5. Olitski erroneously gives Nadler's first name as "Eliezer."

passed an odd pairing. In early January 1934, Nadler announced dramatically in the course of a lecture at the Warsaw Jewish Writers' Union on "Religion and its meaning in society" that he was rejecting Orthodox Judaism in
favor of Communism.[2] The embrace of Communism by a Jew from a religious background was a common enough occurrence at the time, but the
"defection" of someone as deeply involved in the Aguda as Nadler to the
opposite end of the political spectrum was highly unusual and, as reports of
Nadler's controversial lecture make clear, surprised both sides.[3]

This peculiar fact of Nadler's biography ensured that his work would be
all but forgotten. The Orthodox camp disowned him and his writing was
thus excluded from an anthology of Orthodox literature published after the
Holocaust.[4] The Communists were not interested in the bulk of his literary
work, written in his Orthodox phase.[5] Nadler participates, then, in this
Festschrift devoted to the notion of a modern Jewish canon as a writer who,
because of his choices in life, did not have a chance of being included in any
canon at all. This paper will argue that Nadler deserves a place at least in the
canon of modern Yiddish literature because his identification until 1934
with those who upheld religious tradition differentiates him from most
modern Yiddish writers who abandoned tradition as they embraced modern secular culture and began to write. Before he himself abandoned tradition, Nadler made a serious attempt in his writing to combine both a religious and a modern sensibility: "Besht" and *simfonye*." How successful
was his attempt? Did it fit into the parameters of the new Orthodox literature being written in the orbit of the Aguda? How do Nadler's biography
and his writing help to explicate each other? Why did he choose the Besht
as the central figure of his "symphony"? Was it, in the end, possible to write
modern literature within the parameters of Orthodoxy or did the would-be
Orthodox writer always find himself pushing against the boundaries of an
Orthodox world view?

---

2. "Shturmishe stsenes," *Undzer ekspres* 3 Jan. 1934: 6.

3. Moyshe Shulshteyn, in a memoir devoted to Nadler, recalls that the Communists did
   not try to recruit among the Orthodox since they were unlikely to be successful.
   Rather, they directed their propaganda at members of other Jewish leftist but non-
   Communist movements. See Moyshe Shulshteyn, *Geshtaltn far mayne oygn* (Paris:
   M. Szulsztein, 1971), 180–181.

4. Moshe Prager, ed., *Antologye fun religyeze lider un dertseylungen* (New York:
   Research Institute of Religious Jewry, 1955).

5. Memoirs recalling Nadler as a devoted Communist mention from his Orthodox phase
   only fragments of the *Besht-Simfonye* that can be read from a socialist perspective. See
   Shulshteyn 184–189 and Spero's article on Nadler in *Yisker-bukh tsum ondenk fun
   14 umgekumene parizer yidishe shrayber*, ed. Y. Spero, G. Kenig, M. Shulshteyn, B.
   Shlevin (Paris, Farlag "Oyfsnay," 1946). An example of such a text is given later in this
   essay.

Shmuel Nadler, known to his friends as Munye, was born in the Galician shtetl Glina in 1908 and had a traditional Jewish education at which he excelled.[6] He was among the first students of the renowned educator Rabbi Meir Shapiro,[7] with whom he developed a close personal relationship. He began writing poetry at a young age—by sixteen he apparently was already composing poems in the Aramaic of the Zohar. He published poetry, prose, and articles on literary subjects in the Hebrew and Yiddish journals of the Aguda, and edited the literary section of the *Ortodoksishe yugnt-bleter*, the journal of the Aguda men's youth movement. He published three books in Yiddish, and he edited and contributed to a Hebrew volume published in honor of the twenty-fifth anniversary of Rabbi Shapiro's rabbinical activity.[8] Around the time of his "conversion" he studied engineering at Cannes University, but made his career in the Communist phase of his life as a writer and literary editor for the Yiddish Communist paper in Paris, *Di naye prese*, writing copious amounts of journalistic material but little in belletristic genres. During the war he was active in the resistance and the underground press. He was shot by the Nazis in August 1942.

The Orthodox literature in which Nadler participated, indeed, that he helped to shape, came into being in the interwar period as a response to the fact that even traditional Jews, and young people in particular, were reading modern books. This reading was seen as an important factor in the vast defection of young people from tradition, and thus the Aguda sanctioned modern belles lettres in a limited way, as a means to help keep young people within the Orthodox fold. This strategy was parallel to the adoption by the Aguda of other modern forms, such as the political party, the press, and modern educational methods, adapting them in the name of strengthening the traditional way of life.[9] As a counter-balance to modern secular litera-

---

6. Biographical sources on Nadler are as follows: Moshe Prager, "Dos yidishe togblat," *Fun noentn over*, vol. 2 (New York: Kultur-kongres, 1956), 500–505; K. Tsetnik, "Vide fun a shrayber," *Di goldene keyt* 110–111 (1983): 34–40; Leyzer Ran, "Munye Nadler," *Leksikon fun der nayer yidisher literatur*, vol. 6: 133–135; Shulshteyn and Spero as above.

7. Founder of the famous yeshiva *Yeshivas khakhmey Lublin* and of the *Daf yomi* Talmud study program.

8. In Yiddish: a translation of the Book of Ruth (Lodz: Beys-Yankev, 1930), a book of poetry, *Der veg tsu zun* (Kolomyya: Yaades, 1930), and the *Besht-Simfonye* (Warsaw: Golder, 1933). In Hebrew: *Seyfer Hayoyvl* (Lodz: Moriya, 1930). In addition, he apparently left in manuscript a large work in Aramaic that has been lost (K. Tsetnik 36–37) and an unfinished autobiographical novel in Yiddish, one chapter of which was published with Spero's article.

9. For an account of the Aguda's adaptation of modern forms, see Gershon C. Bacon, *The Politics of Tradition: Agudat Yisrael in Poland, 1916–1939* (Jerusalem: Magnes, 1996). On Orthodox literature see my dissertation, "Orthodox Yiddish Literature in Interwar Poland," Columbia University, 2005.

ture, Orthodox literature took its models, its forms, and much of its content from secular literature rather than from traditional Jewish texts. Since, however, the existence of modern literature in the Orthodox context was justified only as a means for strengthening traditional life, aesthetic considerations were of secondary importance, as Hillel Zeitlin notes in a review of the volume Nadler edited in honor of Rabbi Shapiro:

> A large portion of the book is devoted to belles lettres. One cannot say more about this literature than about Aguda literature in general: its ideological direction is too strong and too marked and does not allow the writer's talent to come through, even if real talent is present.

In addition, certain subjects that one would expect to be of importance to the young readers and writers of this literature were effectively taboo, including relationships between the sexes, opposition to parents and teachers, and any critique of the traditional way of life. The few texts that succeed both aesthetically and ideologically use modern forms to convey traditional Jewish concerns.[10]

Nadler certainly conformed to the demands of Orthodox ideology in much of his work; he composed the text, for example, of the hymn of Bnos Agudes Yisroel, the Aguda organization for young women.[11] There are, however, many indications, both within his work and without, that he had been drifting away from Orthodoxy for some time before his dramatic announcement. In the late 1920s and early 1930s, Rabbi Shapiro wrote several letters to Nadler in which it is clear that he fears that Nadler is abandoning traditional religious life.[12] Nadler's first book of poetry was almost banned by the Orthodox establishment. It seems that only Rabbi Shapiro's intervention smoothed over the situation and allowed Nadler to continue writing for the Orthodox press.[13] It is surely significant that Nadler did not announce his conversion until after Rabbi Shapiro's death (October 27, 1933).

When Nadler published his *Besht-Simfonye* in 1933, then, he was still regarded as an Orthodox writer, but he had clearly been pushing at the boundaries of Orthodox literature for some time. An anecdote recalled by Moshe Prager, an Orthodox journalist and historian, suggests that Nadler

---

10. For example, the longing for redemption, as in a poem by Nadler entitled "Dos gezang, vos Shloyme-hameylekh hot gezungen..." ("The Song that King Solomon Sang"), *Der Flaker* 2 (1926): 44–45.

11. *Beys-Yankev* 46 (1929): 6.

12. These letters were published, with an analysis, by Rabbi Eliezer Katzman in *Yeshurun* 16 (2005): 270–275.

13. On the un-Orthodox content of the book, see B. Karlinius [Ber Karlinski], "Fun bikhertish," *Der moment* 241 (7 Nov. 1930): 5. The book is the subject of one of Rabbi Shapiro's letters quoted above. A copy of the book is held by the Lubavitch library in New York.

himself saw the work as belonging to the Orthodox phase of his life. Apparently Nadler took back a copy of the book he had given to a friend and wrote on the title page:

Opium-sam in klasndinst	Opium poison in service of class
Sentimentn-sakharin,	Sentiment-saccharine
Khaver,[14] *az du mishst dos uf —*	Comrade, when you open it —
Shpay deruf!	Spit on it![15]

Contemporary reviewers certainly saw it as the work of an Orthodox writer, although Y. Vild from the secular perspective and Yisroel Emiot from the Orthodox side sensed that something was lacking in his piety.[16] How, then, does this work combine "Besht" and "symphony"?

The *Besht-Simfonye* is divided into three main sections, each of which consists of a number of short, loosely related texts—some prose, some poetry—each with its own title. These three sections are framed by an introduction and, at the end, two additional sections, each of which contains a text on one theme. The first of the additional sections at the end of the book provides a clue as to why Nadler entitled his work "symphony." It is an assessment of Ernest Bloch's *Baal Shem Suite* for violin and piano (1923).[17] Nadler understands Bloch's music as being of a spiritual nature, expressing the faith of the Jews through the trauma of Jewish history and reaching, through *nign*, Hasidic song, toward the divine. (127) Bloch's understanding of the essence of the Besht comes, according to Nadler, from within the composer himself:

> Ernest Bloch understood where to seek the source of the Bal-Shem's affirmation of life. With his clearly perceiving eye, with his sixth musical sense, he pierced through all transformations that led to the wonderful revelation. And that which the geographer sought in vain in maps, the historian in musty pages, the man of letters in folk legends and wonder tales—he found in the strings of his violin and the trembling of his heart. (125)

This understanding of Bloch's music corresponds closely to the composer's own pronouncements on the nature of his so-called Jewish compositions:

> In all those compositions of mine which have been termed "Jewish," I have not approached the problem from without, i.e., by employing more or less authentic melodies...or more or less sacred "oriental" formulas, rhythms o[r]

---

14. Spelled phonetically, according to the Soviet system of Yiddish spelling.

15. *Fun noentn over* 501.

16. Y. Vild, rev. of *Besht-Simfonye, Globus* 10 (April 1933): 82; Yisroel Emiot, "Vegn un umvegn fun der nayer ortodoksisher literatur: Shmuel Nadler, *Di Besht-Simfonye,*" *Ortodoksishe yugnt-bleter* 44 (Aug. 1933): 9–10.

17. First published as an essay in *Beys-Yankev* 50 (1930): 30–31. The text is incorporated into the *Besht-Simfonye* unchanged.

intervals! No! I have hearkened to an inner voice, deep, secret, insistent, burning, an instinct rather than any cold, dry reasoning process, a voice which seemed to come from far beyond, beyond myself and my parents, a voice which surged up in me on reading certain passages in the Bible...[18]

Bloch thus helps Nadler to explain his own use of the figure of the Bal-Shem: not to engage in ethnographic reconstruction or a mission rescuing morsels of Jewish heritage for an alienated generation, or even conveying a new, nonreligious message, but rather as a key to the expression, within a Jewish context, of profound spiritual experience. The designation of the book as "symphony" seems to suggest that Nadler wanted in his literary work, modern and European in form, to express first and foremost the intangible, as music does, rather than, for example, to narrate a plot or to present a set of ideas.

This yearning toward the spiritual is both confirmed and undermined in the remaining framing texts of the *Besht-Simfonye*: the introduction and the concluding section. The concluding section, "Belz," is a lengthy narrative poem in which Nadler describes in the first person a visit to the Belzer Rebbe for the Sabbath. The mention of the narrator's name, "Shmuel ben Zisl," indicates that the reader is to identify the first-person narrator with the author himself. In the middle of the poem, in a section that takes place in the early hours of the Sabbath morning when Nadler is apparently alone, having just visited the mikvah, he makes a remarkable confession:

> Kh'bin mikh moyde umisvade: ikh bin aher ot gekumen
> Un in mayn harts hot gelakht un geshpet der lets fun der tume:
> – Shoyte! Vos vestu dort zen bay di brudike vilde azyatn
> Akhuts kapotes un blotes? – Fargib es mir, himlisher tate!
> Ikh dayn umverdiker zun un diner, Shmuel ben Zisl,
> Hob gezindikt akegn dayn makht, vos iz iber mayn tfise.
>
> I admit it and I concede: I came here
> And in my heart laughed and scoffed the jester of the impure:
> – Fool! What will you see there amongst the dirty, wild Asians
> Except long coats and mud? – Forgive me, Heavenly Father!
> I your unworthy son and servant, Shmuel son of Zisl,
> Have sinned against your power that is beyond my grasp. (136)

Nadler declares that he had made the trip to Belz with the intention of laughing at the Hasidim, recalling the stance of the maskilim who, among other things, railed against what they saw as lack of hygiene and outmoded forms of dress amongst traditional Jews. Such an admission by an author writing in the Orthodox context is shocking, although it is somewhat neu-

---

18. Quoted in Suzanne Bloch and Irene Heskes, *Ernest Bloch: Creative Spirit: A Program Source Book* (New York: Jewish Music Council of the National Jewish Welfare Board, 1976), 38.

tralized by being framed as a mistake and including the profession of God's unknowable power. Throughout "Belz," criticism of Hasidic life is tempered by appreciation of it. On the critical side, Nadler makes fun of the physical discomforts of the visit to the rebbe in the crowded study hall. Other moments in the poem, however, suggest that he participates in the spiritual journey on which the rebbe takes the Hasidim and appreciates the heights the rebbe enables them to reach. He thus presents both an insider's and an outsider's view of Hasidic life. It is as if he is at the same time both the Bialer Rebbe and the Brisker Rov in Peretz's "Tsvishn tsvey berg" ("Between Two Mountains"), seeing the spiritual glory of Hasidic devotion on the one hand and the torn clothes of the Hasidim on the other.

The introduction, however, presents the book as anything but spiritual. Dated Paris 1932, it presents literature in material terms, as a form of energy analogous to that of electricity, in which even the poet's "feeling" is the key to the "laws" of the "inner structure of life." (4) There is also an implicit distancing from the Aguda and traditional Jewish life. For one thing, no reference is made to the Aguda's goal of using literature to strengthen allegiance to tradition; this is apparently not a concern of the *Besht-Simfonye*. For another, the introduction proposes an objective, psychological approach to the Besht, not a traditional, pious view: "historical fiction should reconstruct the subconscious personality according to its conscious manifestations." (4)

The opening and closing texts of the *Besht-Simfonye*, then, present two very different approaches to the Hasidic subject matter of the book: material and secular on the one hand, spiritual and religious on the other. The main text is caught between the two. Because of the ideological parameters of Orthodox literature, the *Besht-Simfonye* does not address the tension between these two extremes directly, but rather by implication and juxtaposition. The presence both of an earnest secular approach to literature and a sincere appreciation of the spiritual potential in religious devotion (Nadler's critical distance in Belz makes this appreciation ring all the more true) suggests that the creative consciousness behind the *Besht-Simfonye* is unwilling to abandon one in favor of the other. Indeed, the very structure of the work implies a constant struggle: it is fragmented, divided into many small sections that are only loosely connected, leaving both continuities and contradictions dangling. The reader, with some difficulty, can plot a path through the work, as we shall see, but even as we try to discover lines of development, it should not be forgotten that the constant change of topic, style, and genre makes the *Besht-Simfonye* essentially a work of discontinuities, a work that is unable to settle around any one idea, stance, or mode of being.

This instability is clearly apparent in the figure of the Besht himself. In each of the three main sections of the *Besht-Simfonye* he is presented in different, and even contradictory, ways. The first section, "Karpatn" ("The Carpathians"), recalls the traditional image of the Besht by drawing loosely on early sections in *Shivkhey HaBesht* ("In Praise of the Baal Shem Tov"), the major hagiographical account of the Besht's life, that describe a period of seclusion in the Carpathian mountains before the Besht revealed himself. However, the stories in *Shivkhey HaBesht* view the Besht from the outside: what he said and did, or what happened on account of him (for example, the mountains are said to level out while the Besht walks deep in meditation so that he does not fall into the ravine[19]). Nadler, in his attempt to uncover the "subconscious personality" of the Besht, seeks to portray his internal spiritual experience. Indeed, by emphasizing this spirituality with little reference to the Jewish cultural framework, Nadler presents the Besht in this part of the book as a figure of universal appeal.

Nature, in particular, is shown to be the source of the Besht's spiritual feeling and the site of his encounters with the divine. Nonetheless, although God has a very strong presence in this part of the book, there is also room for a secular reading of the Besht's spirituality as an innate, human quality resulting from the encounter with nature. An example of this ambiguity arises from the juxtaposition of a pair of poems near the beginning of the section, "Di suke" ("The Sukkah," 13–16) and "Tfiles" ("Prayers," 17–18). In "Di suke" the first-person speaker calls together the trees of the woods as walls, the sky as roof, and flowers as decoration in a sukkah that is literally made from living things. The speaker then summons animals from all over the world to celebrate life in this living sukkah. Although it uses an image from traditional Jewish life, the sukkah, the poem does not have any specific religious content. There is no acknowledgment, for example, of God as the creator of nature or the sustainer of life. Such acknowledgment is, however, clearly stated in the poem "Tfiles": "A glowing sun / You have hung upon the skies, / Red roses, / Grass green, / And the trees and I / Draw strength from her [the sun's] burning. / Praised be God / Creator of light" (17). Is the clear presence of God in "Tfiles" supposed to inform our reading of "Di suke"? Or does the life-force that flows from nature in "Di suke" undercut the acknowledgment of God as Creator in "Tfiles"? The tension is not resolved.

In *Shivkhey HaBesht*, we are told simply that the Besht revealed himself when "the time came." Nadler, in keeping with his emphasis on the Besht's internal life, traces a process of development in which the Besht gradually discovers the spiritual resources within himself until he feels strong enough to enter the community and use this strength to help others. Thus, "Karpatn" begins with "Di zalbung" ("The anointing," 7–9), in which a youthful Besht is anointed by the sun as a free spirit within nature; reaches a turning point with "Hisgales" ("Revelation," 31–35), in which the Besht, still alone

---

19. *In Praise of the Baal Shem Tov*, trans. and ed. Dan Ben-Amos and Jerome R. Mintz (Northvale, N. J.: Jason Aronson, 1993), 22.

in nature, discovers within himself the strength to help others; and closes with "Un ven der heyliker Bal-Shem-Tov iz gegangen a rekide" ("When the Holy Bal-Shem-Tov Danced," 45–51), in which the Besht reaches spiritual heights, both for himself and for others, from within the community. The universal appeal of the Besht's spiritual qualities is emphasized by several encounters with non-Jews, and by the generic forms chosen for this section that, for the most part, do not derive from specifically Jewish writing traditions: folk song and folk tale on the one hand, and the forms of modern poetry and symbolic or psychological narrative on the other.

A generic change in the second section points to the very different image of the Besht present here. Far from the spiritually strong Besht of "Karpatn," a series of lyric poems in the first-person here expresses a sense of ambivalence, indeed, inadequacy. The section opens with a poem in which the speaker expresses an overbearing confidence in his spiritual strength (untitled, 53), but soon thereafter confesses to having sinned ("Vide," 56), questions the meaning of life ("A din-toyre mitn kivyokhl," 60–61) and even hints at doubt in the existence of God ("Muz zayn...," 62), although God is addressed directly in many of the poems. This section certainly emphasizes the discontinuities in the *Besht-Simfonye*, calling into question the spiritual confidence of the Besht in the first section and breaking the line of development from self to community that runs through the first section and is continued in the third. The first-person speaker is identified as the Besht only once, at the end of the section, and the image of the Besht presented here bears no resemblance to any traditional portrayal. Why, then, did Nadler include these poems in his *Besht-Simfonye*, in a section entitled "Azoy hot gezogt der Bal-Shem-Tov" ("Thus spoke the Bal-Shem-Tov")?

It seems that the best way to read these poems is to follow Olitski's lead in seeing the speaker as Nadler himself. Indeed, the poems do read as the expression of a young man's spiritual crisis, and they bear a strong resemblance to the lyric poems published in the pages of Orthodox journals. Like other Orthodox lyric poems, they convey only a vague sense of anguish, giving no clue as to the cause of the crisis and little indication of the identity of the speaker. This vagueness, most likely, results from the limitations of Orthodox literature; any thought or emotion that might be critical of Orthodox life or did not exactly match its mores could not be expressed. Nadler pushes at the boundary with his hints at a crisis in faith, but keeps the poems vague enough not to cross it. These poems thus seem to confirm that Nadler was struggling with his identity as an Orthodox Jew, but they provide almost no clues as to the origins or the nature of the struggle.

We return, then, to the question: Why did Nadler include these poems in a book about the Besht? I would like to suggest two answers. First, perhaps Nadler wanted to put doubts into the mouth of the Besht in order to suggest that even the spiritually great are prone to such questioning. Second, and conversely, perhaps this part of the book, which reads so strongly as the feelings of the author and not of the figure he sets out to portray, should alert the reader that the whole book is as much about the emotional, spiritual, and literary journey of the author as it is about the Besht. Of course, trying to extrapolate the author's intentions or various details of his biography from his work is a critical move that is not likely to meet with success, but, given the strong first-person voice in the second and final sections of the book, such an approach must at least be entertained. Indeed, the discontinuities and the ambiguous view of the source of spirituality in the first section also point toward a spiritual questioning on the part of the author. And the third part, to which we now turn, in which Nadler parodies diverse literary forms, may be read as conveying a process of literary discovery.

This third part, "Tsvishn talmidim" ("Among Students"), picks up where the first part ends, when the Besht, having discovered the spiritual resources within himself, turns toward the community. Unlike the universal image of the Besht in the first part and the very personal Besht in the second, here the Besht is presented as a Jewish national figure. The first few texts in "Tsvishn talmidim" combine Nadler's image of the Besht in "Karpatn" with elements of a more traditional view of him. The opening text, for example, "Der rov un der shames" ("The Rabbi and the Shames," 71-79), is a revelation tale in which the town rabbi, Reb Moyshele (known from *Shivkhey HaBesht*), becomes aware of the special spiritual powers of the Besht, here the young Israel serving as *shames*. In the traditional story, the Besht decides to reveal himself to the rabbi in the course of a discussion over ritual practice.[20] In Nadler's version, however, it is again the encounter with nature that brings the Besht into a heightened spiritual state that the rabbi can perceive. This text is also pivotal in a formal sense, combining the well-known European literary forms that characterize the first section of the book (a symbolic narrative that conveys the thoughts and feelings of the Besht) with elements of traditional Yiddish storytelling (beginning a paragraph with a word in *loshn-koydesh*, and continuing with the Yiddish translation of this word). The shift to forms taken from the tradition of Yiddish literature signals the major import of this third section: the significance of the religious and cultural role the Besht has come to play in Jewish life, even decades after his death.

Two texts, "A mayse noyre" ("A Terrible Story," 83-91) and "Di khasene in kretshme" ("The Wedding at the Inn," 94-102) present the Besht as he is seen in traditional tales, using folk forms—the chapbook tale and the ballad, respectively—with a literary polish. Both are tales of poor Jews whose plight is remedied by the Besht using his superior powers of perception, and both are told in a lively and engaging narrative. Like traditional Besht tales, they present the Besht through his words and his deeds rather than conveying his thoughts and feelings. It could be argued that these stories present a

---

20. See *In Praise of the Baal Shem Tov*, tale 14 (27-28).

socialist's view of the Besht, helping the poor, and indeed, Moyshe Shul-shteyn, who knew Nadler in his Communist period, cites "A khasene in kret-shme" with admiration. Such a reading would certainly not be out of place given Nadler's biography, and may stand alongside the function of these texts as representative of the Besht's image amongst traditional Jews.

The final two texts in "Tsvishn talmidim," by contrast, present ways in which the Besht has been incorporated into the cultural sphere of secular Jews. The first, "Neile" ("The Concluding Service of the Day of Atonement," 103–110), recalls in theme and tone the tales of I. L. Peretz, who popularized the Hasidic motif in modern literary tales that do not necessarily convey a Hasidic world view. The second, which we will consider in more detail, is entitled "Er un der fremder" ("He and the Stranger," 111–120), and recalls another classic writer of secular Yiddish literature, S. Y. Abramovitsh. The "Stranger" is none other than the Devil and, in a scene reminiscent of the tour of the modern world on which Ashmedai takes Yisrolik in *Di klyatshe* *(The Mare),* he shows the Besht what will become of his teachings. First, in the world of Hasidim themselves, a rebbe twists the meaning of the Besht's words in order to justify his indulgence in food and drink. Then, through the pen of secular men of letters, headed by Peretz, the Devil shows the Besht how his own teachings have been turned upside down, quoting directly (though without attribution) from Peretz's early, and bitingly satir-ic, Hasidic story "Mekubolim" ("Kabbalists"). Finally, the Devil shows the Besht what will become of him in the eyes of historians and literary critics. At a "literary evening" on the topic "Hasidism and the Jewish People" the speakers attempt on the one hand to understand Hasidism in its political and economic context, and on the other to dissect its legends in order to under-stand its essence. The Besht is extremely distraught by these scenes.

The Devil is portrayed in a way that connects the text both to Hasidic tra-dition and to the general European culture that had such a profound influ-ence on modern Jewish culture. It is headed by an epigraph from the Besht's famous letter to his brother-in-law, in which he describes an ascent of the soul. The epigraph recalls that on this mystical journey he encoun-tered the Devil: "And I beheld in a vision that Samael rose to give evil coun-sel with great delight as never before."[21] The Devil is "issuing decrees of forced conversion" and the Besht risks his life to investigate the matter, determining eventually that the Devil's intentions are for a "heavenly cause." The Devil's form is not described. The Devil in Nadler's work, how-ever, appears as a faun who specifically introduces himself as such and recalls that he had "worked for the Greeks." He shows the Besht how he has wreaked havoc with the Besht's teachings, and offers no purposeful expla-

---

21. Quoted from the translation of the letter in Immanuel Etkes, *The Besht: Magician, Mystic, and Leader*, trans. Saadia Sternberg (Waltham, Mass.: Brandeis University Press, 2005), 275.

nation for his actions. This European devil thus undercuts the image of the Devil implied by the epigraph: rather than evil that, in the grand scheme of things, is a force for good, the Devil/faun presents the perversion of the Besht's ideas as a negative force without any redeeming factors. Rather than stilling the Besht's distress, as in the letter, Nadler's devil abandons the distraught Besht to chase a doe. The implications of this European devil are not spelled out, but they seem to represent an indictment of the European culture through which secular Jews appropriated elements of Hasidic lore for their own ends.

We will return in a moment to the resolution of this piece. First, however, we must consider the questions of why the *Besht-Simfonye*, with its contradictory impulses, was considered to be an Orthodox work, and why Nadler chose the figure of the Besht. In many ways, the *Besht-Simfonye* does fit into the paradigm of the new Orthodox literature that was being created in Aguda circles in interwar Poland. Its subject matter is a great Hasidic master, a common and accepted theme in Orthodox literature. It uses modern forms to treat a traditional topic and the strong presence of God in the book seems to mark it as a religious text. Even the lyric poems that hint at doubt in God are comparable to other Orthodox poems in which the expression of individual struggle is apparently limited by what is considered acceptable within the parameters of Orthodoxy. In addition, references to secular treatments of Hasidic material fit in with the Orthodox imperative to "set the record straight."

We have seen, however, how Nadler in many ways pushes at the bounds of Orthodox ideology, and it may well be that Nadler chose to write about the Besht precisely because he could voice his own concerns and pursue his literary interests without straying too far from what was acceptable. The period of seclusion at the beginning of the Besht's spiritual development, about which little is known, enabled Nadler to explore a Jewish spiritual life outside the bounds of the organized community without openly criticizing the community. The popularity of the Besht in secular Jewish culture enabled Nadler to engage with this culture without declaring allegiance to it. Even if the book should be read as indicating a desire to move outside organized Orthodoxy and to engage with the secular world, even if the book's fragmentation and discontinuities indicate a consciousness struggling with basic questions of faith and identity, the Besht provides Nadler with a framework that can contain the struggle within a true appreciation of the traditional Jewish life of the spirit.

Indeed, it is the traditions originated by the Besht that provide the resolution to the encounter with the faun. After the Besht has been abandoned by the faun, he has another vision of the future from which he derives comfort. A poor Jew, a traditional Jew, who has been chased out of the *shtetl* through no fault of his own and is almost at the point of collapse, finds the strength to continue when he recalls a *nign* of the Besht that he had learned from his grandfather. It is highly significant that what should be emphasized at this climactic moment at the end of the final story of the final main section of the *Besht-Simfonye* is music, and not the modern symphony, but the Hasidic *nign*.

The Hasidic *nign* is also a central motif at the climactic moment of the first main section of the *Besht-Simfonye*, in the lengthy poem "Un ven der hcyliker Bal-Shem-Tov iz gegangen a rekide" ("When the Holy Bal-Shem-Tov Danced"). This poem conveys the power of the *nign* sung in a community of Hasidim to connect the singers to the spiritual achievements of the Besht and, through him, to the Jewish national past (Temple service) and biblical ancestors, and with the Carpathian nature that inspired the Besht. At the climax of the poem, the singing Hasidim and the Besht are linked in a mystical unity with God:

> Zeyer keyn mol oysgeloshn fayer glit in zayne oygn,
> Zeyer tsutsutrayb trogt itst arum dem shulkhn zayne fis,
> Nisht er iz er un nisht zey—zey, zey zenen nor der eyntsiker urtate: Got

> Their never-extinguished fire glows in his eyes,
> Their impetus now carries his feet around the table,
> He is not he, nor they—they, they are but the One Ultimate Father: God (51)

Moreover, this evocation of the Besht's dance is delivered in the poem by an anonymous first-person speaker who himself is engaged in Hasidic dance and song and has a *vision* of the Besht. In a symbiosis of past and present, then, the Hasidim draw inspiration from their collective memory of the Besht and in particular from his music, while the Besht is given new life, so to speak, through the Hasidic tune that owes so much to his memory. And the result of this symbiosis is the encounter with the divine.

The emphasis on a musical form that emerged within the traditional Jewish world, the Hasidic *nign,* as a means of reaching the divine at these climactic moments underlines the incongruity of the very notion of a Besht *symphony*, and points toward the limits of Orthodox literature, not in the ideological sense that literature associated with the Aguda was limited artistically because of the need to toe the party line, but in a fundamental sense, having to do with the striving toward the divine that is at the heart of religious life. The *Besht-Simfonye*, written in European forms in the spirit of Bloch's *Baal Shem Suite*, evokes the spiritual accomplishments of the Besht. The question remains, however, as to whether Bloch's music, or Nadler's writing, inspires a spiritual feeling, a closeness to God, in the listener or reader, as the Hasidic *nign* does in those who sing it within the Hasidic milieu. The fact that Nadler includes in his Besht "symphony" depictions of the spiritual heights that can be achieved through *nign* seems to suggest that, in the end, the modern work of literature or musical composition can only evoke religious spirituality, but cannot provide the means through which such spirituality can truly be experienced. This is the limit of Orthodox literature; it must always be at one remove from the heart of religious life. Nadler had, perhaps, turned to literature in an attempt to escape what he experienced as confining in the Orthodox world without abandoning it entirely and without giving up the path it provided to profound spiritual experience. In the attempt he managed to evoke this spirituality, adding a new nuance to modern Yiddish literature by portraying the encounter with the divine from within the religious world. But he also discovered that it was no substitute for the experience itself, the crowded *beys-medresh* in Belz. Nadler, it seems, tried and failed to make a space for himself within Orthodoxy through modern literature and, most dramatically, abandoned the attempt.

Chava Rosenfarb and *The Tree of Life*

GOLDIE MORGENTALER

In Chapter Six of *The Modern Jewish Canon*, Ruth Wisse discusses a number of works on the Holocaust that she considers canonical. Given that her list includes the work of writers most closely associated with Holocaust literature in the public mind—Elie Wiesel, Primo Levi, Anne Frank, Jerzy Kosinski, and Emmanuel Ringelblum—it is difficult to argue with her choices. But I would suggest that one important work has been left out of the discussion, although not from the list of suggested readings from the modern Jewish canon that can be found on page 382 of the paperback edition of Wisse's book.[1] That work is *The Tree of Life* by Chava Rosenfarb, originally published in Yiddish in 1972 as *Der boym fun lebn*, in Hebrew as *Ets Hahayim* (in 1978), and in English in 1985 and 2004-2006.[2] This epic novel—one of the few works of fiction about the Holocaust by an actual survivor—is little known and has been omitted from most major studies of Holocaust literature. (David Roskies, although aware of the novel's existence, does not mention it in either *Against the Apocalypse* or *The Literature of Destruction*.)

What I would like to do here is to make the case for this three-volume novel as a seminal work of both Holocaust literature and modern Jewish literature precisely because it undermines Ruth Wisse's observation that "the most impressive feature of Holocaust literature is its reliance on the first-person singular." (193) By this Wisse means that the vast majority of literature about the Holocaust, especially that written by the survivors themselves, takes the form of memoirs, autobiographies, diaries, and fictionalized accounts of personal experience. Very few of the survivors were moved to transmute their experiences into full-fledged novels and those few who did so have sometimes been accused of fabricating a reality that never existed. (I am thinking here of the controversy that surrounded Jerzy Kosinski's *The*

---

1. Ruth R. Wisse, *The Modern Jewish Canon: A Journey Through Language and Culture* (Chicago: University of Chicago Press, 2003).

2. *Der boym fun lebn*, 3 vols. (Tel-Aviv: Hamenora, 1972); *Ets Hakhayim*, 3 vols. trans. Shloyme Shenhod (Tel Aviv: Syfriat Poalim, 1978). The English version was first published in Australia as *The Tree of Life: A Novel about Life in the Lodz Ghetto* (Melbourne: Scribe, 1985). The more recent American edition is called *The Tree of Life: A Trilogy of Life in the Lodz Ghetto* and is published as three separate volumes (Madison: University of Wisconsin Press, 2004-2006).

Painted Bird, when it became known that, despite his claims to the contrary, Kosinski's own war experiences were markedly different from those of his first-person narrator.[3]) Presumably the reason for this shying away from fictional recreation is that the kind of distance and objectivity required to create novels was lacking among the survivors, for whom the experience of the Holocaust was too immediate, too personal, and too raw.

And yet, for Chava Rosenfarb, the opposite was true. She was never able to write about her experiences as either a memoir or an autobiography. All her accounts of the Holocaust and its aftermath are presented as fictions, even though many of the events described are historical and biographical. "Memoirs," she said, "are in the service of history. Fiction is in the service of the imagination and it can go to places where no memoir has the right of entry."[4] In the case of *The Tree of Life,* Rosenfarb's motivation was also to recreate the experience of an entire community rather than just her own experience, and only a novel on the scale of *The Tree of Life* could do that.

Thus, although written by a Holocaust survivor and based to some extent on personal experience, *The Tree of Life* is most emphatically a third-person novel in that it draws more on the imaginative resources and narrative strategies of the professional fiction writer than it does on the personal memories of its author. While some of its fictional characters write letters or use the diary form and so recount their experiences in the first person, the effect of this is to mimic the documentary style; the narrator's primary stance remains objective.

Chava Rosenfarb was born in Lodz, Poland in 1923. She was educated at the Bundist Medem School in Lodz, where all instruction was in Yiddish; thus her formative training, though secular, was intensely Jewish. In 1940, when she was seventeen, she, her parents, and younger sister were incarcerated in the Lodz Ghetto. When the ghetto was liquidated in August 1944, Rosenfarb and her family were deported to Auschwitz. From Auschwitz she, her mother, and sister were transported to the forced labor camp at Sasel, on the outskirts of Hamburg, where they built houses for the bombed-out Germans of that city. As the Allies approached, Rosenfarb, her mother, and sister were transported to Bergen Belsen, where they were liberated by the British Army in April 1945. In 1950 she emigrated to Canada and settled in Montreal.

Although she had begun writing *The Tree of Life* in the Lodz Ghetto, those first attempts had been confiscated at Auschwitz and it was not until she was settled in Brussels immediately after the war that the real work on the novel began. At the same time, Rosenfarb was writing poetry and her first published books were collections of poems. Between 1947 and 1965

---

3. See James Park Sloan, *Jerzy Kosinski* (New York: Penguin, 1997), 190–195.

4. Interview with Chava Rosenfarb, July 2006.

she published four volumes of poetry in Yiddish, some of it dealing with the Holocaust, although for the most part her poems are more personal, expressing the joys and sorrows of daily life.[5] Feeling, however, that poetry could not adequately express all that she felt about her experiences during the Holocaust, that it could not serve the function of re-creation in the same way that prose fiction could, she concentrated most of her literary energies on writing her novel *The Tree of Life,* which was finally published in Yiddish in 1972.

The three volumes of *The Tree of Life* chronicle the destruction of the Jews of Lodz, the second largest Jewish community in Poland (after Warsaw). Because the subject is so vast, the structure of the novel, its breadth and scope are vast as well. *The Tree of Life* is, in fact, an epic, a form of prose fiction that does not appear often in Yiddish literature, although it has been attempted by such male writers as I. J. Singer in *The Brothers Ashkenazi* and Sholem Asch in *Three Cities* and his Christian trilogy. Epics are traditionally national and heroic in scope, interweaving the fates of individual characters with important historical events. This description certainly applies to *The Tree of Life.* But one must add to it the obligation felt by the memorialist to chronicle the destruction of a way of life and a community that has vanished forever. That this community was also intimately known to the author, who had been one of its members, lends both an urgency and an authenticity to the novel.

The Tree of Life presents the inner workings of the ghetto, the daily frustrations and humiliations of ghetto life, in unflinching, precise, and often horrific detail. It chronicles the barbarous cruelty of the Nazis, the constant hunger barely relieved by concoctions made from turnips and potato peels. It chronicles torture, betrayal, and degradation. But it also documents the tenderness of human love despite these conditions. It illuminates the complexities of relationships between husbands and wives, parents and children, lovers and friends. It describes the cultural life of the ghetto, the establishment of a library in a two-room flat, attendance at concerts and plays, meetings of the writers' group, political agitation and resistance. Most importantly, it peoples the ghetto with complex human beings whose individual stories make for compelling reading. In short, *The Tree of Life* provides

---

5. For instance, *Dos lid fun dem yidishn kelner Abram* [*The Song of the Jewish Waiter Abram*] (London: Moshe Oved, 1948) is a book-length narrative poem about Rosenfarb's father. The other books of poetry are: *Di balade fun nekhtikn vald* [*The Ballad of Yesterday's Forest*] (London: Moishe Oved, 1947), republished a year later as *Di balade fun nekhtiken vald un andere lider* [*The Ballad of Yesterday's Forest and Other Songs*], in conjunction with *Fragmentn fun a tog-bukh* [Fragments of a Diary] (Montreal: H. Hershman, 1948); *Geto un andere lider* [*Ghetto and Other Poems*] (Montreal: H. Hershman, 1950); and *Aroys fun gan-eydn* [*Out of Paradise*] (Tel-Aviv: Peretz farlag, 1965).

as complete and authentic a portrait of what it was like to have lived and died in the Lodz Ghetto as literature can. And in this way it also demonstrates the extent to which fiction can both transcend and animate history.

The narrative of *The Tree of Life* chronicles the fate of ten individuals from various walks of life who live through the terrible events of the years 1939–1944. The main characters include the impoverished Itche Mayer, a carpenter with four sons, each of whom is a member of a different political party; the wealthy Samuel Zuckerman, a rich factory owner before the war; and Adam Rosenberg, a pre-war industrialist who becomes a Kripo (German criminal police) spy in the ghetto. There is the assimilationist Miss Diamand, a high school teacher and Polish patriot; Esther, a great beauty and ardent Communist, who is active in the ghetto underground and whose wish to have a baby in the ghetto seals her doom; and the doctor, Michal Levine, who compulsively writes letters that he never sends to a woman he loved in Paris before the war. The most autobiographical characters are Rosenfarb's alter ego Rachel Eibushitz, a politically committed high school student, and her boyfriend David, a diarist, who is modeled on Henry Morgentaler, the man who became Rosenfarb's husband after the war. In addition to these central characters, the novel is replete with memorable secondary portraits, so that the overall effect is of a community of individuals all responding in individual ways to the torments inflicted on them by powers that they cannot control nor propitiate. It is the incomprehensible cruelty and capriciousness of Nazi rule that produce much of the horror the Jews endure: the ever decreasing rations of food permitted the ghetto inhabitants, the issuing of one evil decree after another.

For all the complexity with which Rosenfarb depicts her Jewish characters, for all her probing of their faults and their motives, there is never any doubt—as there is sometimes in the writing of Aharon Appelfeld, for instance—that for Rosenfarb the Nazis are the enemy. She is always aware of the beast at the door. Although the focus of *The Tree of Life* is on the Jewish community of Lodz, the Nazis are not a shadowy presence in the novel. On the contrary, they appear as themselves, terrifying and all-too-human, enforcing barbaric decrees, shooting randomly into the ghetto as if it were a fish pond. In one particularly chilling instance they shoot a young boy sitting near a water pump quietly reading on a very hot day, because he has removed his shirt with its identifying Star of David.

Several of the characters in *The Tree of Life* are based on actual people, which makes the novel both an imaginative and a factual recreation. Among the most significant of these are Rosenfarb's mentor, the poet Simkha-Bunim Shayevitsh (1907–1944), whose long poem "Lekh Lekho" was found on a garbage heap in the ruins of the Lodz Ghetto after the war.[6] *The Tree of*

---

6. Most of the information on Shayevitsh is in Yiddish and dates from soon after the war, including Nakhman Blumenthal's Introduction to *Lekh-Lekho* (Lodz: Central Jewish

Life supplies some of the only available information of what is known of Shayevitsh's life in the ghetto. Shayevitsh himself appears in fictionalized form under the name of Simkha-Bunim Berkovitch.

And then there is the one historical character who keeps his real name, Mordecai Chaim Rumkowski, "the eldest of the Jews," the de facto king of the Lodz Ghetto. Rumkowski is one of the novel's most powerful and ambiguous creations, a self-styled savior of the Jews, who nevertheless aided the Nazis in sending tens of thousands of them to their deaths. *The Tree of Life* describes the road that Rumkowski traveled from being the founder and director of the Helenowek orphanage in Lodz before the war to being the puppet leader of the ghetto, put in place by the Nazis and compelled to do their bidding even as he tried to "save" the ghetto.

The Tree of Life is organized chronologically, which allows for a logical progression through time even as each chapter concentrates on another major character. Book One (subtitled "On the Brink of the Precipice, 1939") begins with a New Year's Eve party at the home of the rich factory owner Samuel Zuckerman, shepherding in the year 1939. Among Zuckerman's guests are most of the characters whom we will meet again on more intimate terms in subsequent chapters and whose fates we will follow throughout the novel's three volumes. Book One ends on New Year's Eve 1940, thus encompassing a year of extraordinary change in the fortunes of Lodz Jewry, a year that sees the Nazis march into Poland and that signals the beginning of the end of the Jewish community of Lodz. By beginning her novel in the months before the Nazi invasion of September 1939, Rosenfarb enables her readers to see what that community was like in "normal" times, when people still had the luxury of going about their daily activities, when they could still experience the joys and sorrows of peaceful times, when they could still act out their social roles and assume their public faces. This first book of the trilogy thus gives a sense of what will be lost, of the vitality and creativity of this community, which, within the space of a few short months, will be reduced to fighting for the bare essentials of survival.

The subsequent two books of *The Tree of Life*, each of which encompasses two years in the life of the ghetto, describe in vivid and meticulous detail the deterioration and dismantling of this once vibrant Jewish commu-

Historical Commission, 1946) and Ber Mark's *Di umgekumene shrayber fun di getos un lagern un zayere verk* [*The murdered writers of the ghettos and concentrations camps and their works*] (Warsaw: Yidish Bukh Farlag, 1954). See also Khaim Leyb Fuchs, *Lodzsh shel mayle: dos yidishe gaystige un derhoybene Lodzsh* [*Lodz of the Heavens: The Spiritual and Sublime Jewish Lodz*] (Tel Aviv: Y. L. Peretz, 1972). Chava Rosenfarb also published a long essay about Shayevitsh under the title "A vide fun a mekhaber" ["An author's confession"] in *Di goldene keyt* 81 (1973), 127–141 (in English). David Roskies writes about Shayevitsh in *Against the Apocalypse* (Cambridge: Harvard University Press, 1984).

nity. The social masks are dropped in response to ever increasing hardship as the ghetto is established and random killings, starvation, disease, deportation, and death become the norm. Each book of the trilogy depicts the noose tightening a little more. Book Two begins with the establishment of the ghetto and ends with another New Year's Eve retrospective. Book Three begins with the deportations from the ghetto, deportations that increase in intensity and number until the ghetto is finally liquidated. Because the narrative filters historical events through the experiences of its ten characters, by the time we reach the last pages the destruction of human life has become so personalized that it is difficult to avoid the sense of loss as one after another of Rosenfarb's characters is sent out of the ghetto to a fate we can imagine only too well. The chronological structure of the novel keeps readers tied to historical reality even as the events in the lives of the characters spiral out of control.

What Rosenfarb captures—perhaps too well, because it is so painful to read—is the constant anxiety that permeated every aspect of ghetto life, an anxiety about never knowing if one would survive to the end of the day, if one's loved ones would survive, if one would make it through the *Sperre* [house arrest] or the deportations, an anxiety brought on by ever harsher decrees and ever decreasing food rations. It is this basic anxiety about being able to live another day and having no control over one's fate, of being the sport in someone else's game, that gives this description of the Lodz Ghetto its nightmarish quality. And it is this psychological probing of what it is like to live with such an unrelieved sense of impending doom that is one of the novel's contributions to our understanding of the Holocaust. What the novel conveys most vividly is that intangible quality of atmosphere, an atmosphere of dread that permeates the life of the ghetto and contributes to what critic Irena Kohn has called the "haunting" quality of the novel.[7]

Another great accomplishment of this novel lies in its vivid presentation of character and in the range of characters it chooses to depict, from the lowest classes to the highest, from the young to the old. Because the ten major characters of *The Tree of Life* come from all walks of life, the novel recreates, in all its complexity, an entire Jewish ghetto community. In addition, it captures in detail the everyday life in the ghetto workshops and food distribution centers. It describes the gatherings of the ghetto intelligentsia and the Jewish underworld, as well as the ideological responses of the various political parties—the Zionists, Communists, and Bundists. Most importantly, Rosenfarb gives a portrait of that section of ghetto society that she knew well from personal experience, the Lodz Ghetto's artistic community. Her portrayal of the tenacity and bravery of this community includes fiction-

---

7. Irena Kohn, "Late Mail from Lodz: Chava Rosenfarb's Literary Witness Account of Jewish Life in the Lodz Ghetto, Book Two" *Outlook* (Mar/April 2006): 28.

alized portraits of the real-life painter Israel Leizerowicz, who appears here under the name Guttman, and the real-life Miriam Ulinover, who appears as the elderly woman poet Sarah Samet.[8]

Questions about the role and value of art and culture in the face of barbarity permeate the narrative and fuel debate throughout the novel. Arguments about the "Jewishness" of Jewish art, about the insularity of Yiddish literature versus the "international" quality of European literature, about the relative qualities of Yiddish versus Hebrew as appropriate languages for the Jews, about the value of theatre and concerts in the ghetto, are all raised and discussed by various characters throughout the novel. One theme in particular arises at crucial moments: the significance of Western non-Jewish culture for the Jews. For instance, when news reaches Lodz that the Nazis will be entering the city the following day, the father of the high school student David—a man whose political activities as a Bundist council member mean that he has the most to fear from the Nazis—suddenly takes to reading the Roman poet Horace. He annoys his terrified children with constant requests for help with the translation from Latin. "Garbage!" exclaims his exasperated daughter and throws the Latin book onto a heap of books to be burned. But the father responds, "What are you so mad at the book for? Don't you think the words are quite appropriate for the occasion?"[9]

The elderly literature teacher Miss Diamand uses Shakespeare's *The Tempest* to try to comfort the students in the newly reopened Jewish high school after the Nazi invasion. The students initially respond to the play's love story between Ferdinand and Miranda; but then some of the boys are pulled out of their classrooms by the Nazis and sent out to forced labor. After this, none of the remaining students can concentrate on *The Tempest,* which is suddenly as remote and meaningless to them as a fairy tale. As with David's father's attempt to use Horace as a way of shutting out present reality, Miss Diamand too offers her students the fruits of Western civilization as a way of making them forget their present situation.

> She wanted them to hold on, as she did, to eternal indestructible values. [...]
> She was aware of what was going on around them, in their homes and in town. But [in school] at least, all that must be made to fade out of their minds, for only in this manner, she felt, could they acquire the strength and dignity

---

8. Israel Leizerowicz (b. 1902) is pictured on the cover of the University of Wisconsin Press edition of *The Tree of Life*. In August 1944 he was deported to Auschwitz, where he perished. Many of his paintings and drawings survived the war and are housed today at the Jewish Historical Institute in Warsaw. Miriam Ulinover (b. 1888), a poet, was the author of a collection of poems called *Der bobes oytser* [Grandmother's Treasure]. She too perished at Auschwitz, where she was deported in August 1944.

9. Chava Rosenfarb, *The Tree of Life: A Trilogy of Life in the Lodz Ghetto. Book One: On the Brink of the Precipice,* trans. the author in collaboration with Goldie Morgentaler (Madison: University of Wisconsin Press, 2004), 180.

to deal with the storm raging outside. She had therefore begun the first literature lesson by choosing the giant Shakespeare to assist her task. She spoke
of Caliban and Prospero; she discussed Prospero's dialogue with Ariel. The
students listened to her, but their faces told her that she had not achieved
what she desired. (Bk. 1, 211)

Both of these examples force us to question the value of Western culture
in addressing the problems of being Jewish in a world that despises Jews.
Both David's father and Miss Diamand turn to non-Jewish texts in an
attempt to find comfort and healing in the cultural heritage of Europe and in
doing so are accepting and perpetuating assumptions about the value of
that heritage. But the younger generation rejects these assumptions, so that
the argument about the value of Western culture takes on a generational
tinge. In every confrontation of this type in the novel, it is the younger generation that is the more "Jewish" and the more inclined to question the
humanistic assumptions of its elders about the value and inclusiveness of
Western culture.

The Tree of Life is not particularly sentimental in its depiction of the
ghetto inhabitants. Rosenfarb's characters may be victims of the Nazis, but
that is incidental to their essence; they are victims, but they are not inno-
cents. Their natures partake of all the usual complexities of the human
psyche, both good and bad. Thus the novel does not shy away from describing the activities of the Jewish ghetto spies and informers. Rosenfarb's great
strength is as a psychological realist and she is at her best in delineating the
personalities of those characters of whom she approves least. Thus, the
stool pigeon, Kripo spy, and sadist Adam Rosenberg is the most pathetic,
the most despicable, and one of the most compelling of the characters in
The Tree of Life. He is an uncaring husband and father, who loves his dog
more than his family and does nothing to save his wife and son from deportation. He is a manipulator and an exploiter of the weak. When we first meet
him he is the self-indulgent owner of a Lodz factory, who spends his days
playing with the fish in his aquarium, thinking up ways to humiliate his
female secretary, and burying his head in the sand. The result of this last
propensity is that, despite his vast wealth, he defers leaving Lodz until it is
too late and the Nazis have occupied the city.

But once incarcerated in the ghetto, the weak Adam proves to be an
adept survivor, because he has no moral compunctions. He betrays whom-
ever he needs to betray in order to survive. Adam also has a sadistic streak.
In one extraordinary scene, he gives a bath to his young lover Sabinka,
because he has convinced himself that she is always dirty. The water in the
bath is scalding hot and Adam rubs Sabinka's naked body with a scrub brush
until she faints. His thoughts throughout this scene vacillate between the
pleasure of inflicting pain and the tenderness and pity evoked by the pain
that he inflicts. In this short, horrific episode Rosenfarb chillingly anatomiz-
es the mixed emotions that animate the torturer. Suffering does not make

Rosenfarb's characters kinder or nobler than they were before; it merely highlights the qualities that were there before the war and in some cases turns those qualities into their opposites. At the same time, *The Tree of Life* never allows us to lose sight of the fact that this is suffering brought on by an outside force, that the ultimate evil belongs to the Nazis.

Adam Rosenberg is a fictional character. But Rosenfarb attempts a similar psychological dissection of the Lodz Ghetto's puppet dictator Mordecai Chaim Rumkowski, with the result that if Rumkowski does not appear as particularly likable, he at least emerges in these pages as knowable. When we first meet him at Samuel Zuckerman's New Year's Eve party, Rumkowski is soliciting funds for the orphanage he runs. In some ways he is similar to Rosenberg in that he too loves the adulation of those who are weaker than he, a fact brought home in our next view of Rumkowski during the festival in honor of the establishment of the orphanage. Rumkowski has a weakness for young girls and in the culminating episode of this chapter he attempts to seduce a young girl from the orphanage, the aforementioned Sabinka, whom he has treated to an afternoon at the fairgrounds of Luna Park. Rumkowski's near-rape of the innocent fifteen-year-old Sabinka in the outlying bushes of the park is interrupted by some Polish boys, chanting "Hep, hep, give it to her old Jew boy! Give it!" (Bk 1,102). The reminder here is that the Jewish world of pre-war Poland is hedged around with anti-Semitic hatred, even before the Germans march into the country. And the irony here is that this same anti-Semitism of the Polish thugs saves the innocent Jewish girl from assault by a Jewish predator.

Rosenfarb's Rumkowski is a man with a mission: "He had come into this world to fulfill a mission, to become a Moses [...]. He had been created not in order to direct an orphanage, but to direct an entire people" (Bk 1, 247). He is a man who is dangerous because he is so completely convinced of his own importance that he can blind himself to any reality. He is, ironically, an admirer of Hitler: When the *Sperre* starts, he realizes with regret that: "He now knew clearly what the Germans wanted and what they needed him for. He knew that he would never sit with Hitler at the same table, discussing the establishment of a Jewish state."[10]

Yet Rumkowski is not an out-and-out villain. Convinced as he is that only he can rescue the Jews, he nevertheless does act, at least some of the time, for altruistic reasons. And he has a modicum of bravery, as when, early on, he saves a number of Jews from the hands of the Nazis despite the fact that he is beaten for his efforts; and he puts up with the contempt and physical abuse of his Nazi overlords. But, as life in the ghetto becomes progressively

---

10. Chava Rosenfarb, *The Tree of Life: A Trilogy of Life in the Lodz Ghetto. Book Three: The Cattle Cars Are Waiting, 1942–1944,* trans. the author in collaboration with Goldie Morgentaler (Madison, Wisc.: University of Wisconsin Press, 2006), 116.

more desperate, Rumkowski's position becomes ever more untenable as the Nazis demand that he hand over larger and larger numbers of Jews for deportation to the death camps. Rosenfarb describes in chilling detail the kinds of accommodations with his own conscience that Rumkowski must make in order to justify handing over, first the children from his beloved orphanage, then all children under the age of ten, then the sick from the hospitals, the elderly, the Western Jews, the Jews whose partners had been deported before, and so on. In one of the novel's most horrifying accounts of a historical event, the *Sperre*, Rumkowski demands that the mothers of the ghetto willingly give up their children to the Nazis for the good of the collective.

Clearly it is the moral ambiguity of Rumkowski's position that fascinates Rosenfarb, the human kernel of good overlaid with layers of self-delusion, megalomania, and petty cruelty. This propensity for trying to imaginatively get under the skin of characters whom she despises in order to see how they tick occurs in other of Rosenfarb's fictions. For instance, the long short story "Edgia's Revenge" is told from the point of view of a former kapo who after the war must come to terms with the guilt she feels for persecuting her fellow Jews during the Holocaust.[11] The attempt to understand and convey evil from the inside suggests a wish on the part of the author to come to terms with it, to fictionalize cruelty as a way of defanging the monster.

Rosenfarb's presentation of this type of negative Jewish character also has another dimension. It insists on the humanity of the Jews both for good and ill and, in so doing, makes an implicit argument that what happened to the Jews during the Holocaust was an abomination, not because Jews are inherently saintly or inherently evil, but precisely because they are *not* exempt from all the failings of humanity. All the more reason, then, that they should be treated as equal to other human beings. For this reason, Rosenfarb does not shy away from portraying negative Jewish characters, nor is she reluctant to portray the disintegration and self-delusion of even the most admirable among them, such as the well-meaning Samuel Zuckerman.

As a novelist, Rosenfarb was clearly influenced by the epics of the great Russians Tolstoy and Dostoevsky, by the French Victor Hugo and Romain Rolland (especially his *Jean Christophe*), and by the Scandinavians Knut Hamsen and Sigrid Undset—works that she originally read in Yiddish. Her style was thus strongly influenced by nineteenth-century European realism. But, while her fiction falls broadly within the parameters of realism, it does not adhere completely to realist tenets. Rosenfarb often adds a symbolic dimension that seems to translate her fiction into the realm of supra realism

---

11. "Edgia's Revenge" in *Survivors: Seven Short Stories*, trans. Goldie Morgentaler (Toronto: Cormorant, 2004), 81–165.

or magic realism. In one section of *The Tree of Life*, for instance, we learn of the tortures in the Red House from the perspective of newly born ants who happily set out on a journey of discovery by crawling along a prisoner's body only to drown in the castrated void between his legs.

> Through a yellowish roundness covered with a prickling needle-like forest— a human four-day-old beard—the ants descended into a valley that was a human neck, reaching a rocking surface covered with soft curling hair-weeds: a man's chest. A long and fascinating march over skin and cloth finally brought the ants to a point where they could have gone in one of two directions: along two spread out human legs. They chose instead to descend straight from the belly into the depths between the two legs—and suddenly they lost the ground under their ant-feet, finding themselves in water that was sticky and red—in a deep sea of human blood oozing through the cloth between the thighs. Ants were not created with the ability to swim in human blood. For a moment they quivered. Finally they drowned. All that they had seen on their long and daring road drowned along with them. (Bk. 3, 64)

The ants are ants, but they also represent the ghetto inhabitants in microcosm, crawling their way through a precarious life toward a bloody death. The tendency to animate symbols, which doubtless owes much to Rosenfarb's literary beginnings as a poet, is more pronounced in her short fiction, but even in *The Tree of Life* there are characters whose existence is clearly symbolic as well as three-dimensional. One such character is the Toffee Jew, who makes a living from selling ersatz candy made from his sugar rations. While this character has a recognizable existence in the real world, he does not quite belong to reality and his function in the novel is symbolic. All his pronouncements have a meaning beyond the literal, including the way in which he hawks his wares: He is selling hope, he declares, a remedy for the heart, a little bit of sweetness on the brink of hell. These same words make up the novel's last spoken dialogue, this time addressed by a ghetto inhabitant to Rumkowski as he too is loaded into a cattle car: "Here, Mr. Rumkowski, taste a cherry from our cherry tree... It's a remedy for the heart." (Bk. 3, 361)

The Tree of Life limits its narrative perspective to the ghetto; it ends with the liquidation of the ghetto and the deportation of all the characters, including Rumkowski. The death camps that await outside the barbed wire fence of the ghetto are indicated simply by a short inscription: "AUSCHWITZ. WORDS STOP. UNDRESSED. NAKED. THEIR MEANING, THEIR SENSES SHAVEN OFF. LETTERS EXPIRE IN THE SMOKE OF THE CREMATORIUM'S CHIMNEY..." (Bk. 3, 362) This is followed by a series of blank pages and an epilogue. In the epilogue, which is set in Brussels ten years later, we are told that three of the characters have survived. One of the survivors is the author of the novel we have just read and we see her sit down to begin her book with its actual first paragraph. But, of the fates of the other characters we learn nothing. Can we assume that some of them survived? The narrative is silent on this, and so allows readers to hope that some of those deported to Auschwitz may have survived. Silence allows for irresolution, which in turn allows for hope. But when asked about this, the author herself gives no hope. As far as she is concerned all the characters except for the three mentioned in the epilogue perished at Auschwitz, because "that's the way it was."[12]

When it was published as *Der boym fun lebn* in 1972, the Yiddish press immediately acclaimed *The Tree of Life* as a masterpiece, repeatedly emphasizing its unique place in the literature of the Holocaust. Isaac Jonasovitch, writing in the quarterly *Folk un medine* (Tel-Aviv, Summer 1975), announced that, *"The Tree of Life* is a work that surpasses everything that has been expressed up to now on the tragedy of Eastern European Jewry, or more precisely, surpasses everything that has been written in prose on this topic." And the jury that unanimously awarded Rosenfarb the 1979 Manger Prize, Israel's highest literary honor for Yiddish literature, concurred, noting that: "[*The Tree of Life*] is a work that rises to the heights of the great creations in world literature and towers powerfully over the Jewish literature of the Holocaust, the literature which deals with the annihilation of European Jewry, in particular Polish Jewry." Numerous other international prizes were conferred on Rosenfarb for this novel, including the Canadian Segal Prize and the Argentinian Niger Prize.

Yet despite the excitement in the Yiddish press, in the world at large the novel went unheralded and largely unknown. In effect, it suffered the fate of the language in which it was written. Ironically, its very strengths—the all-encompassing epic structure, the complexity, the detail, and the length—made it a difficult book to publish in a non-Jewish language. While *Der boym fun lebn* was soon translated into Hebrew as *Ets hahayim,* for many years the English version could not find a publisher. An English translation was finally published by Scribe Publications of Melbourne, Australia in 1985, but without distribution rights in North America. The Australian edition also eliminated the introduction and compacted the novel's three volumes into one large tome. In 2004 the University of Wisconsin Press began publishing a paperback reissue of this Australian edition, this time returning to the original format of three separate volumes. That version is now available in North America.

I collaborated with Chava Rosenfarb on the English translation of *The Tree of Life,* a process that took about two years of intense labor. Rosenfarb herself realized early on in the writing of *The Tree of Life* that if she wanted to be read by a wider audience her work would have to be translated and so she herself produced a first draft of the translation from Yiddish to English. This first draft formed the basis for the subsequent translation. In the meantime, publisher after publisher turned down the manuscript as being too expensive to publish, too unwieldy, too much of a risk. Jack McClelland of

---

12. Interview with Chava Rosenfarb, April 1984.

the respected Canadian publishing firm McClelland and Stewart was wildly enthusiastic about the manuscript itself, but eventually decided against publishing because of the costs involved.

The need for translation and the arduous and lengthy process by which the translation eventually found a publisher underlines still further Ruth Wisse's suggestion that, where writers are concerned, language is destiny. Rosenfarb's decision to write in Yiddish illustrates perfectly Wisse's contention that the nature of literature during and after the war depends in large part on the language and context in which it was written, as well as on the author's relationship to his or her language. Rosenfarb's decision to write *The Tree of Life* in Yiddish was a fateful one, given that it contributed to the obscurity of the work. But it was also unavoidable, not only because Yiddish was the author's mother tongue and the language in which she felt most at ease, but also because of her desire to memorialize the lost Jewish community of Lodz, a community that lived its life in Yiddish. As Rosenfarb has said:

> I write in Yiddish out of fidelity to a lost language. If writing is a lonely profession, the Yiddish writer's loneliness has an additional dimension. Her readership has perished. Her language has gone up with the smoke of the crematoria. She creates in a vacuum, almost without a readership, out of fidelity to a vanished language and a lost community; as if to prove that Nazism did not succeed in extinguishing that community's last breath and that it is still alive.[13]

Thus, a number of factors have contributed to the obscurity that has surrounded *The Tree of Life*, including the fact that it was for so long unavailable to a non-Yiddish-speaking readership. It is my contention that this obscurity is undeserved and that the Yiddish critics were right: there is nothing quite like *The Tree of Life* in the vast corpus of Holocaust literature. I can only hope that this essay has gone some way toward illustrating just why I believe this. But, as with all fiction, the proof is in the reading and *The Tree of Life* is very good reading indeed. It is so vast, its narrative so engrossing, its depiction of the horrors of the Holocaust and the bravery of the human spirit despite these horrors so compelling that it is impossible to do it justice in a short essay such as this. I can only hope that I have given enough of a sense of the magnificence of this work to justify its inclusion in the Jewish canon.

---

13. Excerpted from unpublished speech delivered at the Genocide Conference of the University of Lethbridge, Oct. 2005.

Fiddles on Willow Trees:
The Missing Polish Link
in the Jewish Canon

MONIKA ADAMCZYK-GARBOWSKA

When I first received a review copy of Ruth Wisse's book about the modern Jewish canon, my natural impulse was to check what Polish authors she had included—that is, Polish Jews writing in the Polish language. I was not particularly surprised to find only two names: Bruno Schulz and Henryk Grynberg. I did not expect to find many other authors from among those who are considered the most important Polish Jewish writers in Poland today, for they are little known in the United States, even though some of their works have been translated into English.

It is interesting to note that these two "canonized" authors represent two very different directions in Polish literature of the twentieth century. Although brought up in a Jewish milieu, Bruno Schulz consciously aspired to become a Polish writer; Henryk Grynberg became a mainstream Polish writer by (or in spite of) consciously emphasizing his Jewish identity. Obviously this basic difference in their aspirations was caused by the completely different times and environments in which they were born and raised.

Remarkably enough, Schulz seems to be better known in the United States than Henryk Grynberg in spite of the fact that the latter has lived in the United States for almost forty years. Has Schulz's fame, first facilitated by Philip Roth and his series "Writers from the Other Europe," and enhanced through fascination with him on the part of foreign critics and fiction writers, been caused by the quality of his prose or rather his tragic life story? One may ask a hypothetical question: If Bruno Schulz had survived the war and continued to write, would he still attract so much attention? Wouldn't he share the fate of other Polish or Polish Jewish writers? What if his legendary novel *The Messiah* had been written and published (and eventually translated) rather than supposedly lost?

In the context of Polish literature, Bruno Schulz together with his contemporary Witold Gombrowicz are considered major innovators. It does not seem that they are perceived in the same way in the West, as the limited reception of Gombrowicz's prose testifies. (This might be attributed also to the alleged untranslatability of his prose, but not only that; what was considered innovative in Polish literature might have seemed artificial or derivative in American literature, where modernism was much more advanced.)

Artur Sandauer, whose important concise study under a provocatively clumsy title *O sytuacji pisarza polskiego pochodzenia żydowskiego w XX wieku (Rzecz, która nie ja powinienem był napisać ...)* ("On the Situation of the Polish Writer of Jewish Descent in the Twentieth Century [It Is Not I Who Should Have Written This Study]") has appeared recently in English translation, defines Bruno Schulz as "a Polish writer with an Old Testament Subconscious."[1] Sandauer considers him the "only innovative Polish writer of Jewish origin to emerge in the thirties" and offers a psychoanalytical explanation to his complex and contradictory personality:

> As a person he drew on the conscious, as a writer on the subconscious. As a person he was a European, as a writer he was stuck in myths and rites. A gap separated the person from the writer; it was as if his subconscious was acted upon by dark magnetic forces [...] The European in Schulz condemned the *ur-Semite*, and the progressive condemned the deviant. Hence his dream of self-destruction. His masochism—for he was a masochist—was a form of self-denial.[2]

Paradoxically then, Bruno Schulz is the only writer of Jewish origin writing in Polish who "made it" in America. Perceived as a Jewish writer, he is often included in Jewish literature surveys, although he himself, like numerous other assimilated Jews of his generation, wanted to be treated as a mainstream Polish writer. He is sometimes discussed in a Holocaust literature context although he never wrote about the war experience. To a great extent this popularity was facilitated by his tragic life story,[3] which has stimulated the imagination of a number of American authors, including Cynthia Ozick and Philip Roth (as well as the Israeli author David Grossman) and the poetic, ahistorical, and apolitical character of his prose, which allows for various interpretations. Other authors, those constituting the so-called Jewish school[4] in Polish literature, such as Julian Stryjkowski, Adolf Rudnicki, and Bohdan Wojdowski, are known only to a narrow group of specialists, and the same is the case with the younger generation, perhaps with the

---

1. See Artur Sandauer, *On the Situation of the Polish Writer of Jewish Descent in the Twentieth Century (It Is Not I Who Should Have Written This Study...)*, trans. Abe Shenitzer (Jerusalem: The Hebrew University Magnes Press, 2005), 37–39. The edition seems to contain a number of typographical errors (including the title on the cover) and the translation is somewhat stilted, but it is good that this important work has become available to English-language readers.

2. Ibid., 38.

3. Bruno Schulz (b. 1892), an accomplished writer and graphic artist, was shot in the streets of his native Drohobycz in November of 1942 by a Gestapo officer who had a grudge against another Nazi, the artist's temporary "protector" who liked his paintings and who ordered him to paint frescoes in his children's bedroom. Before WWII two collections of Schulz's stories were published in Poland in 1934 and 1937. Supposedly he was working on a novel, entitled *The Messiah*, but there is no proof or any remains of the manuscript.

4. See Jan Błoński, "Is There a Jewish School of Polish Literature?" *Polin* 1 (1986): 196–211.

exception of Henryk Grynberg, but even he has been recognized in the English-speaking world only recently.

In 1974 Julian Stryjkowski (1905–1996), the best-known Polish Jewish writer, well established in the Polish Jewish literary canon, published a collection of three stories/novellas under the title *"Na wierzbach...nasze skrzypce"* ("On Willow Trees... Our Fiddles").[5] What might have helped avert the eyes of the censor, which were particularly sensitive to Jewish topics at that time, was a very critical vision of America contained in this volume. Stryjkowski looks at the United States through California, with Los Angeles as a present-day Sodom marked with a desert-like highway without sidewalks or passers-by, where no one is allowed to look back. Dead branches of palm trees hang down like black fans, and high above, dead motionless stars look out from behind the smog. Having arrived in this milieu, Stryjkowski's narrator visits old friends, Holocaust survivors, whom he has not seen for many years. Most of them lead secure lives, enjoying material comforts, and they assume that the visitor from the Old World will remain with them. However, he is too old to start anew. To the question of why, in spite of the pogroms, poverty, and humiliations that Polish and European Jews had experienced, he does not want to settle down in sunny California, he responds that it is too late to start a new life and, what is more, he is a writer who happens to exist in the Polish language. Emigration to America would deprive him of his frames of reference, and it would not bring him closer to his Jewish roots, because Jewish tradition in its Californian version seems to him like a parody of the old way of life.

Stryjkowski is not the only Polish Jewish writer voicing such sentiments. One can find similar tones in Grynberg's or Hanna Krall's works. Although Polish literature as a whole is very little known in the United States, one might think that Polish Jewish writers would be received with more interest because of the large Jewish reading audience. This is not the case by any means, so the authors' disappointment should not surprise us.

What are the reasons for this state of affairs? First of all, one must admit that this is also the case with other literatures of minor languages. If we apply Itamar Even-Zohar's polysystem theory,[6] we may state that Polish literature occupies a marginal position in the American literary polysystem. But to some degree the situation after World War II contributed to this absence: to a smaller or greater extent some of these writers were involved in Communism and generally they were treated with suspicion for the very fact that they had remained in Poland rather than emigrated to Israel or the West. The resentment on the part of Jewish critics from the United States is

---

5. Published by Czytelnik Publishers in Warsaw; it contains the following works: "Martwa fala," [A Dead Wave] "Syriusz" [Sirius] and the titular novella.

6. See his "Polysystem Theory," *Poetics Today* 1 (1990): 9–26 as well his earlier works.

most strikingly evident in Lucy Dawidowicz's reaction to Hanna Krall's book-length interview with Marek Edelman, one of the leaders of the Jewish Fighting Organization in the Warsaw Ghetto who decided to stay in Poland after the war, working as a cardiologist in Lodz. In the late '70s he became involved in the opposition movement in Communist Poland and since that time has been politically involved and considered a highly respected public figure of moral authority. Here we have an example of drastically different responses. A work that has become part of the canon of Polish literature on the Holocaust together with stories by Tadeusz Borowski and Zofia Nalkowska met with a devastating critique from the well-known Jewish historian, who criticizes both Edelman and Krall, the former for staying in Poland after the war, the latter for what Dawidowicz considers the writer's confusing style, bordering on "chatter" and mixing "matters of importance" with "trivialities."[7]

But even favorably inclined critics such as Timothy Garton Ash reveal indirectly the problems with reading Polish literature. In the preface to the first English language edition of Krall's book *Shielding the Flame: An Intimate Conversation with Dr. Marek Edelman, the Last Surviving Leader of the Warsaw Ghetto Uprising*,[8] he foresees that

> the English speaking reader may at first be a little baffled by Hanna Krall's style of writing, a kind of Polish "New Journalism," leaping, sometimes breathlessly, and without explanation, from past to present and back again [...] All I can say is: please persevere, do read on. The author has good reasons. The point of this mixing will soon become clear. In the end, through all the doubt and questioning, Marek Edelman's story does itself, triumphantly, "show as an affirming flame."[9]

How many readers, however, will listen to this plea, persevere, and read on?

And yet sometimes the lack of translations of certain Polish authors makes it hard for American readers to comprehend some Jewish authors writing in English. For instance, a very important reference in Cynthia Ozick's novella *Rosa* is that to Julian Tuwim (1894–1953),[10] a celebrated

---

7. Lucy S. Dawidowicz, "The Curious Case of Marek Edelman," *Commentary* 3 (1987): 66.

8. The second edition was published under the title *To Outwit God* together with *The Subtenant* in 1992.

9. Timothy Garton Ash, "Preface" in Hanna Krall, *Shielding the Flame: An Intimate Conversation with Dr. Marek Edelman, the Last Surviving Leader of the Warsaw Ghetto Uprising*, trans. Joanna Stasińska and Lawrence Wechsler (New York: Henry Holt and Co., 1986), xiii.

10. "In school she had read Tuwim: such delicacy, such loftiness, such Polishness." In Cynthia Ozick, *The Shawl* (Vintage International, 1990), 20.

poet, one of those assimilated Jewish authors who entered the mainstream of Polish literature in the '20s. Before World War II Tuwim devoted very little attention to Jewish topics and even distanced himself from Jewishness. For this reason he was often castigated by Yiddish writers or Polish Jewish writers (those who used the Polish language as their primary medium of expression but identified themselves as Jews).[11] Simultaneously, he was sometimes attacked by Polish nationalists, who would accuse him of "Semitic sensuality" and argue that Tuwim wrote in the Polish language but not in the Polish spirit. This was an absurd claim, sometimes raised in reference to other authors as well, and based on a belief in supposed "alien elements" present in the literature created by assimilated Jews. Such accusations would lead them to special concern about their use of Polish. No wonder then that Ozick's Rosa, an assimilated Jewess, completely acculturated from the traditional Jewish community, brags that she spoke better Polish than the majority of Christian Poles.

For many years Tuwim's Jewishness was downplayed in Communist Poland. He was cherished as the most important poet of the twentieth century, but his texts concerning the Holocaust and the question of his mixed identity were practically unavailable. In Israel he had a very mixed reception because of his attachment to Polish culture, which some critics considered a form of betrayal.[12] In the United States he is largely unknown due to the untranslatability of his poetry, characterized by complex rhymes, musicality, and lexical experiments. He deserves more attention both in terms of his work and his biography, which in a striking way reveals a confused identity. It is arguable if he could be included in the Jewish canon (but why not, if Schulz has been included?) but he undoubtedly can serve as a key figure in understanding the intricate situation of an assimilated Jew in Poland before and after World War II.

In my book on Jewish literature as a multilingual phenomenon,[13] in which I discuss, among other things, Ruth Wisse's Jewish canon, I propose my own Jewish canon, in which from among Polish works I include Adolf Rudnicki's *Summer, Voices in the Dark* by Julian Stryjkowski, *Bread for the Departed* by Bohdan Wojdowski, *The Jewish War* and *Victory* by Henryk Grynberg, and *Subtenant* by Hanna Krall. I did not include Bruno Schulz in

---

11. For more on this topic see Eugenia Prokop-Janiec, *Polish-Jewish Literature in the Interwar Years (Judaic Traditions in Literature, Music, and Art)*, trans. Abe Shenitzer (New York: Syracuse University Press, 2003).

12. On Tuwim's reception in Israel see a very interesting discussion in Ryszard Löw, *Hebrajska obecność Juliana Tuwima: Szkice literackie* ["Julian Tuwim's Presence in Hebrew: Literary Sketches"] (Oficyna Bibliofilów: Lodz, 1996).

13. See Monika Adamczyk-Garbowska, *Odcienie tożsamości. Literatura żydowska jako zjawisko wielojęzyczne* [Shades of Identity: Jewish Literature as a Multilingual Phenomenon] (Lublin: Wydawnictwo UMCS, 2004).

that canon as I would rather consider him, like Tuwim, part of the mainstream Polish canon (which does not mean that the other writers could not be included in the latter as well). Could these works, very well established among Polish readers and critics, be incorporated into the Jewish canon for the American reader? And what other Polish works could be of interest for the American reader who would like to look at Jewish literature from the multilingual perspective?

Among the selected names are two authors who started writing before the war, when Jewish culture in Poland was trilingual in Yiddish, Hebrew, and Polish, and who consciously chose the Polish language, and three who survived the war as children and, therefore, did not have a chance to make a linguistic choice because history had decided for them.

Adolf Rudnicki (1909–1990) knew Hebrew and Yiddish from home, but like a number of Jewish writers in the interwar period, chose Polish as his language of artistic expression. As he stated about himself much later: "I belonged to those creatures that started worshipping two gods rather early. Polish legends interposed themselves on Jewish ones, got entangled, mixed together."[14] After the war he did not change his technique of elaborate psychological realism, in which he combined elements of fiction with reportage, memoirs, and autobiography, but adapted it to the new subject matter. For approximately a decade he focused mainly on recording the Holocaust experience in the cycle *Epoka pieców* ("The Epoch of Crematoria"). This cycle constitutes one of the most compelling voices on the topic of the Holocaust in Polish literature and is comprised of collections of stories and novellas of different length and character. Some critics, such as the merciless Artur Sandauer, accused Rudnicki of narcissistic tendencies (going as far as calling him a kind of "martyrological *prima donna*") and excessive pathos and moralizing.[15]

However, what might seem interesting to the American reader is *Lato* ("Summer"), a literary reportage from the late '30s, perhaps the only Polish Jewish work from the interwar period (apart from Schulz, if we classify him as a Polish Jewish author) that has passed the test of time. After the war Rudnicki looked critically at his own works written before its outbreak, claiming that the events of the war and Nazi occupation made them look as if they were from a completely different era. He writes that he looks at them with disgust, as if they were some worthless and lifeless manuscripts left somewhere in an attic:

> The war has aged what I have written by a thousand years. I read myself full of astonishment. I read with anger and disapproval. I read and do not recog-

---

14. Adolf Rudnicki, "Stara ściana" [The Old Wall], in *Sto jeden*, vol. 3 (Kraków: Wydawnictwo Literackie, 1988), 27.

15. See Sandauer, 90–93.

nize... [...] The war has already destroyed them, though it has not touched their physical form. The impact of the great conflagration has deprived their pages of readability, deformed them like a bridge into whose trusses a missile has been fired. Life has left them, as it has left the steppes under the crushing weight of tanks. My art seems to be wretched. Wretched![16]

Lato, published in 1938, is almost the only pre-war work in which Rudnicki treats Jewish topics, specifically in scenes of Jewish life in Kazimierz on the Vistula (known in Yiddish as Kuzmir), a picturesque *shtetl* frequented by artists and literati, and in a description of a pilgrimage to the *shtetl* of Ger (Polish Góra Kalwaria), the seat of the famous Hasidic rebbe. In the preface to the re-edition of *Lato* in 1959, Rudnicki states that he finds comfort in the fact that he recorded at least this much and he treats his prose devoted to those topics as a small memorial candle. One must add, however, that the writer looks at the Jewish world from the point of view of the outsider, an assimilated artist who by no means identifies himself with the presented milieu. Nevertheless, when read today, some of its fragments receive a new meaning and resonate with ominous tones.

What is more, his work can be juxtaposed with Jacob Glatstein's travel novel *Ven Yash iz gekumen,* as the question of the portents of the future becomes very prominent in both works. Glatstein paid a visit to Kuzmir in 1934, which found its reflection in his novel published in 1940. Rudnicki was a frequent visitor there both before and after the war, but they probably never met nor even knew of each other, just as Bashevis Singer did not know about Bruno Schulz until he reviewed his book in the 60s.[17] Contrary to Rudnicki's, Glatstein's narrator spends only one day in the *shtetl*, but, perhaps thanks to this, he is able to offer a very clear and sharp vision, presenting the town as beautiful, but simultaneously artificial, theatrical, and rotting from the inside, as well as threatened from the outside. Rudnicki's vision is strikingly similar, although he approaches the town from a different angle. Whereas Glatstein assumes the pose of an accidental traveler who distances himself from what he happens to see, Rudnicki looks at Kazimierz from the point of view of someone well settled. He attempts to read the minds of the local inhabitants: Jews, Poles, pauperized gentry, and vacationers. He creates a sharp contrast between the outsiders and the local inhabitants, presenting them as two antagonistic groups, stating, "Painters walk

16. Adolf Rudnicki, "Kartka znaleziona pod murem straceń" ["A Sheet of Paper Found at the Execution Wall"], in *Sto jeden*, vol. 1 (Kraków: Wydawnictwo Literackie, 1984), 207.

17. Singer claimed he learned of Bruno Schulz only in the United States in 1963 when he reviewed the English translation of his prose for *Forverts*. See Yitskhok Varshavsky [Bashevis], "A bukh fun poylish-yidishn shrayber in English," *Forverts*, December 1, 1963. See also Philip Roth, "Roth and Singer on Bruno Schulz," *New York Times Book Review*, February 13, 1977, 50.

over this nest of poverty as if in the garden of Eden."[18] Both authors dwell on the failures of assimilation. In Rudnicki's account the "ghetto" triumphs along with the growing anti-Semitism. And in both works the theme of death is present, as apart from individual deaths; there is foreboding of the demise of the whole community.

The final scenes in Rudnicki and Glatstein are strikingly similar. In the latter the narrator, Yash, is seen on a summer morning, just before his departure for America. A pale light settles on his suitcases leaving the rest of the room blurred and insubstantial. The suitcases are "the only solid objects in this world of shadowy forms."[19] Rudnicki concludes his *Summer* with the image of winter approaching together with the smell of moth balls: "We are going back to the matters that are closest to us. Everybody knows that. We are going back to the city to die."[20]

Contrary to Rudnicki, from the very beginning of his writing career Julian Stryjkowski dealt with Jewish topics. His masterpiece (as it is perceived in Poland), *Voices in the Dark*, describes the breakdown of the closed world of the *shtetl* under the impact of modern political ideas and the growing impoverishment of the small-town Jewish community, whose members' role as intermediaries between the village and outside world was being superseded by the development of a modern capitalist economy. Stryjkowski's description of this process takes place in Habsburg Galicia in 1912 and is accompanied by a complex account of the relations between Jews and Gentiles in the context of the growing conflict in the eastern part of this province between the dominant Poles and the increasingly politically conscious Ukrainian majority. The action is seen through the eyes of the six-year-old Aronek (clearly an autobiographical portrait), and it documents his growing self-awareness.

The core of the novel is an account of the downfall of Aronek's father, Reb Toyvye, a *melamed* and teacher of Gemara in the town, a self-styled "policeman of God" who sees himself as duty-bound to rigorously uphold His Law. In his youth he was himself attracted to "forbidden books" and his fascination with the secular world is strongly felt by members of his family.

Stryjkowski was a man marked by a sense of difference. He felt estranged in Poland because of his Jewish origin, and because his language was Polish he was a stranger also in Israel and in the Jewish communities of America. Finally, he felt different because of his homosexuality, to which he referred

18. Adolf Rudnicki, "Lato" ["Summer"], in *Sto jeden*, vol. 1, 145.

19. Jacob Glatstein, *Homecoming at Twilight*, trans. Norbert Guterman (New York-London-Toronto, Thomas Yoseloff, 1962), 271. The Yiddish original was published by Farlag Moshe Shmuel Shklarski in New York in 1940.

20. Rudnicki, *Lato*, 198.

in his writing only late in his life.[21] These differences, however painful and traumatic for him as a human being, gave rise to his unique writing. An outsider by so many standards, he left a strong impression on postwar Polish literature and enriched its canon with his distinct and needed voice. Juxtaposing Stryjkowski's works with those by the Singer brothers or Shmuel Agnon could be a fascinating research topic. Unfortunately, only one novel by Stryjkowski, *Austeria*, is available in English translation.[22] And I doubt if *Voices in the Dark*, even if published in English in book form, would fare well. Perhaps some scholar could juxtapose it with Henry Roth's *Call It Sleep* because of the shared figure of the child narrator and observer and Stryjkowski's use of Yiddish-inflected Polish, which creates a similar effect to Roth's use of Yiddish-inflected English. But, on the other hand, it might meet criticism similar to that voiced by some Yiddish critics against Isaac Bashevis Singer, who suspected him of selling himself out to a Gentile audience. Similarly, in the Polish context Sandauer criticized Stryjkowski as a "eulogist of the language manglers," accused him of ignorance, and offered the following summary of his work:

> [...] Stryjkowski's novels are imitations of an authentic item. Included in the calculation are the "goy's perspective," his ignorance, his greed for exoticism, his notion—possibly well-intentioned but rooted in the era of contempt—of Jews as simpletons, and of their language as a jargon that is flawed by nature and lacks grammar and an established vocabulary and, in addition, is rather nauseating. In a word, it all adds up to an attempt to create a philosemitic whole out of allosemitic notions.[23]

This description resembles some of the tirades against Bashevis Singer and, as in the case of Singer, since most of Stryjkowski's readers are "goyim" or highly assimilated Jews, they dismissed this type of criticism, additionally suspecting Sandauer of professional jealousy characteristic of a frustrated fiction writer.[24]

It is worth emphasizing that Stryjkowski, especially in his later years, underlined his Jewish identity. In the '80s he would start every meeting with readers with the words, "I am a Jewish writer." And immediately after this introduction he would tell the story of his first day at school and the first

---

21. See *Milczenie* ["Silence"], published by Wydawnictwo Literackie in Kraków in 1993 three years before Stryjkowski's death.

22. See *The Inn*, trans. Celina Wieniewska (New York: Harcourt Brace Jovanovich, 1971). Fragments of *Voices in the Dark* were included in *Contemporary Jewish Writing in Poland: An Anthology*, eds. M. Adamczyk-Grabowska and A. Polonsky (Lincoln, Neb.: University of Nebraska Press, 2001). Some of the issues discussed in this article were first addressed in the introduction to this anthology.

23. Sandauer, 96.

24. Sandauer aspired to be a novelist and short-story writer himself, but his fiction is generally regarded as much less interesting than his literary criticism.

Polish word he learned, *Jestem* (literally meaning "I am," used also in the school context as an acknowledgment of being present), which ever since symbolically accompanied him in his writer's career.

For a number of years I kept mentioning to my Jewish American fellow literary historians the novel by Bogdan Wojdowski (1930–1994), a writer belonging to the generation of Polish Jewish writers who were children during the war. Born in Warsaw, he spent three years of his childhood in the Warsaw Ghetto and later in hiding on the "Aryan" side. In my opinion, *Chleb rzucony umarłym* (Bread for the Departed)[25] is perhaps the best fictionalized account of the Warsaw Ghetto ever written and I thought it would meet with much interest as soon as the English translation became available.[26] However, although the novel was published in Madeline G. Levine's superb rendering in 1998, it seems to have met with very little interest and almost no attempts have been made to include it in Holocaust courses at universities. This might be caused by purely practical reasons, as it as a rather long work and its style may be considered difficult. And yet it could be treated as an excellent introduction to teaching literature on Nazi ghettoes, as it covers the period from the establishment of the Warsaw ghetto in 1940 until January 1943, the time of the "little action." It relates a number of crucial events, such as the "great action" of summer 1942, when thousands of the inhabitants, including the Polish-Jewish doctor and educator Janusz Korczak, were transported to the death camps. The young narrator, David, perceives the world of the ghetto as it is; the most abnormal situations are a part of his reality. He never comments but gives us all the details, which together form a nightmarish image. However, there is plenty of commentary, often quite ironic, in numerous dialogues included between the inhabitants, or between the latter and the Nazis, as well as scraps of German orders quoted in the original. Wojdowski does not glorify the ghetto; on the contrary, he shows it in all its misery, ugliness, and corruption. The "bread" referred to in the title is a leading motif, becoming a symbol of survival.

The action of the novel rarely crosses the wall, focusing on the situation inside the ghetto and emphasizing the isolation of its inhabitants. Wojdowski attempts to penetrate the core of human cruelty and degradation by creating sharp and clear visions of the apocalypse and by restrained, non-judgmental analyses of people's behavior in extreme conditions. His technique resembles that of Tadeusz Borowski in his camp stories, as the most grue-

---

25. The English title is somewhat euphemistic and less powerful than the original one, which literally means "bread thrown to the dead."

26. Another Polish novel concerning the Warsaw ghetto that deserves wider recognition both in Poland and abroad is *Bomby i myszy: Powieść mieszczańska* [*Bombs and Mice: A Bourgeois Novel*] by Mina Tomkiewicz, published in Polish in London in 1966.

some events are described in a matter-of-fact way, with a conscious detachment.

All in all, I could imagine using this novel or portions of it in Holocaust literature courses juxtaposed with, for instance, Elie Wiesel's *Night* to compare ghetto and camp experience as seen through the eyes of juvenile survivors, the more so since Wojdowski and Wiesel (b. 1928) were almost the same age when the war broke out. And, because the structure of the novel is loose and fragmentary and the language often consciously incorrect in order to render the Polish Jewish idiom and stress the fact that most of the characters speak Yiddish as their native tongue, Wojdowski's novel, like Stryjkowski's, could be paralleled in different respects to Henry Roth's *Call It Sleep*. His tragic end, on the other hand, resembles that of Primo Levi's, as Wojdowski committed suicide on the fifty-first anniversary of the Warsaw Ghetto Uprising.

Henryk Grynberg (b. 1936), the only Polish-Jewish writer apart from Bruno Schulz included in Ruth Wisse's Jewish canon, fully embodies the complicated position and predicament of a post-Holocaust Jewish writer. As Ruth Wisse states in the introduction to her book, "The most complicating feature of modern Jewish literature [...] is its relation to language."[27] Polish Jewish writers up until the Holocaust had faced the dilemma of choosing a language: Yiddish, Hebrew, or Polish. Sometimes they wrote in two or even three languages, as did Peretz. Henryk Grynberg belongs to the generation of those who had been deprived of such a choice, although theoretically he could have tried to switch to English, as did some émigré authors, including Vladimir Nabokov and Jerzy Kosinski before him. But for him the mother tongue is Polish:

> Of course, it would be better to write in English, French or Spanish. I would be much happier writing in Hebrew, and much better off if I wrote in German. But my medium, my main ingredient, is the words I had received from the lips of that beautiful young woman from Dobre and they are deeply embedded in me. A scientist can be born from a test-tube, but a poet has to come from a mother. In a doctoral dissertation I was called a "Jewish writer writing in Polish" and "a Jewish poet writing in Polish." Antisemites used to gall Tuwim—who was one of the masters of Polish poetry—like that, wounding him deeply. But I don't feel wounded. It's an honor to belong to Polish literature, but it's not so bad to be part of Jewish literature, either. [...] In Tuwim's time in order to become a Polish poet, one had to abandon one's Jewish heritage. In my time this is no longer true, and even Tuwim changed his mind after the Holocaust calling himself a "Jew doloris causa."[28]

27. Ruth R. Wisse, *The Modern Jewish Canon: A Journey through Language and Culture* (New York: The Free Press, 2000), 5.

28. Henryk Grynberg, *Holocaust as a Literary Experience*, Occasional Paper (Washington, D.C.: Center for Advanced Holocaust Studies, United States Holocaust Memorial Museum), 10–11.

In the same text, a published lecture delivered in 2004 at the United States
Holocaust Memorial Museum in Washington D.C., Grynberg underlines his
complicated identity:

> I am a Jew who lives in America and writes in Polish about Jewish fate. For
> the Poles I am a Jewish writer, for the Americans a Polish writer, for the Jews
> a Polish-Jewish writer, for the Chinese—an American writer. [...] My soul is
> Jewish, and Polish, and Polish-Jewish, but my mentality has become Amer-
> ican. Americans are my brothers, with the Jews I share my fate, with the
> Poles—my language and wounds (without my wounds I could perhaps forget
> to be Jewish). I am a child of the Jewish fate who has been adopted by Amer-
> ica but the most important part of myself has remained in my Polish
> language.[29]

Who can ask for a better description of a Jewish writer's complicated situation both in terms of the language and identity? At the same time Grynberg's
reflections excellently pinpoint the radically different situation of the Polish
Jewish writer of modern times as compared to that from the interwar period.

Grynberg's exceptionally strong involvement with the Holocaust—apart
from his linguistic, cultural, and territorial displacement—makes him an
embodiment of a contemporary Jewish writer. In a number of his works he
presents variants of the same life story, one marked by the protagonist's survival as a child under the most difficult conditions, gradual discovery of
one's identity, struggles with the imposed ideology of Communism,
encounters with anti-Semitism, and, finally, exile. Although he draws upon
his own autobiography a great deal, the stories have a universal dimension.
A number of critics have called him a writer of one theme, a statement that
has been corroborated by Grynberg's own declarations. For instance, in an
interview published in the major Polish national newspaper *Gazeta
Wyborcza* in 1998, he stated:

> Until something more horrible than the Holocaust takes place, there is no
> more important topic for mankind, but let's hope that nothing like this
> happens. The Holocaust is a great lesson and warning for our civilization, a
> turning point. Although the history of the Jews is quite unique, everybody
> can draw conclusions from it because it did not take place in a vacuum and
> concerns everybody who participated in it.[30]

On other occasions he has called himself a guardian of the graves, the great
Jewish cemetery Poland was turned into by the Nazis, and adds that this mission prevented him from committing suicide, as his will to commemorate
the dead is stronger than the repulsion to the world he knows. Ironically he

---

29. Ibid., 10.

30. Henryk Grynberg, "Najważniejszy temat" [A Most Important Topic: An Interview with
    Henryk Grynberg by Michal Cichy], *Gazeta Wyborcza* 225 (1998): 18–19.

claims that he became the writer of the dead because the living had enough of their own writers.

Thus Grynberg's search for national identity consists of a struggle between Polishness and Jewishness, which is a recurring motif in other writers as well. He expresses himself in the Polish language and feels quite attached to the Polish landscape and culture, but he also has a great deal of resentment and many "accounts" to settle with Poland. Some roots of his mixed identity lie in the fact that he had to play the role of an "Aryan" in order to survive. His mother created a whole new family for him, telling him numerous stories about fictitious grandparents of Polish stock. This was also accompanied by religious confusion, as Polishness implied Catholicism and necessitated taking the first Communion as a preventative measure. No wonder that in his prose Christian symbols are often combined with Jewish religious imagery.

Ruth Wisse includes in her canon and discusses in her book *Victory* Grynberg's sequel to his first novel, *Żydowska wojna* ("The Jewish War"), which was first published in English under a rather kitschy and simplified title *Child of the Shadows*. The original title alludes to Joseph Flavius and Lion Feuchtwanger and bears ironic implications: the Jews who are "at war" have to constantly hide. It presents a child narrator in hiding with his family and friends. He observes the gradual disappearance of people close to him. *Victory* covers the postwar experience of his mother and himself. As in the earlier novel the title is ironic: the war has ended, but soon after the initial exhilaration doubts arise as to who actually won.

Grynberg's style is generally marked with irony and black humor and he has a rare talent for drawing vivid and semi-comic characters, such as the memorable Śliwa from *Fatherland*, a Polish peasant who helped a Jewish family to survive. In an ironic manner the writer explains in various contexts why the Jews could not conform to the traditional Polish stereotype of the heroic resistance fighter. For instance, his mother, who is a real heroine, making every effort to secure the survival of her son, has him conform to the stereotypes of Polish society and assume a Polish identity, inventing "a grandma who played the piano, and a grandpa who died of cancer, the illness of gentlefolk."[31] Grynberg's presentation of his mother deserves attention and could be compared to portraits of mothers drawn by other Jewish writers of different languages and traditions.

In *Życie ideologiczne* 1975 ("Ideological Life") Grynberg describes the pressures of Stalinism during his young years, while in *Życie osobiste* ("Personal Life") we encounter the same narrator as a young adult deeply affect-

---

31. Henryk Grynberg, *The Jewish War* and *The Victory*, trans. by Celina Wieniewska with the author and Richard Lourie (Evanston, Ill.: Northwestern University Press, 2001), 44. Literal translation from the Polish: "of cancer of the stomach, the noble disease of noble people."

ed by the experience of the Holocaust. These two works can be read inde-
pendently, but they are linked by the narrator and his environment. He lives
in fear of death and with a strong sense of guilt that he has survived while
others perished. As he resides in the country where his community has
ceased to exist, all kinds of daily events evoke in him the vision of the Holocaust, such as the damaged gas stove or bugs that infest his apartment. The
Holocaust experience taught him that Jews did not die a "natural death." As
he relates in *Kadisz*, a novella that takes place in America and surprisingly
enough has not been published in English so far (perhaps for "diplomatic"
reasons of tact, for like Bashevis Singer's posthumously published *Shadows
on the Hudson,* it offers a rather critical image of America): "In our family
everybody died a violent death. We didn't know another one. Both grandfa-
thers and both grandmothers, all uncles and aunts, my half-year-old brother."[32] Paradoxically, the narrator's stepfather is shot in America by a gun-
man. Therefore, the fact that his mother, who survived the Holocaust
thanks to her enormous courage, strength, and inventiveness, is now dying
of cancer in sunny California seems to him to be a return to normalcy, but,
of course, this does not alleviate the pain.

Hanna Krall is the only woman among the presented writers and the
most popular author from among them with contemporary readers in
Poland and other European countries, including Germany and Sweden. She
herself dislikes most national or gender categorizations. For this reason, she
did not grant her permission to have samples of her work included in an
anthology of "Jewish Women Writers from Europe."[33] (However, she did
not object to being included in an anthology of Polish-Jewish writers.)[34] I
know that she is surprised that her work has met with so little attention in
the United States in spite of the fact that she often writes about survivors
who live in America or Israel. Just recently a collection of her stories *The
Woman from Hamburg and Other True Tales* (2006) was published in
Madeline G. Levine's translation, but I would not be surprised if it shared
the fate of other Polish Jewish authors. Subsidized by Instytut Książki (Book
Institute) in Poland and published by the Other Press in New York in a very
modest edition, without any preface or postscript, it is not very likely to
draw the attention of many readers nor, most importantly, of university
teachers, who help to create canons by incorporating texts into their courses. Moreover, perhaps what is considered in Poland an innovative style does
not necessarily impress American readers used to Ernest Hemingway or Ray-
mond Carver, both of whom have been widely imitated.

32. Henryk Grynberg, *Kadisz* ["Kaddish"] (Kraków: Znak, 1987), 23.

33. The anthology in question is *Voices of the Diaspora: Jewish Women Writing in
Contemporary Europe*, edited by Thomas Nolden and Frances Malino (Evanston, Ill.:
Northwestern University Press, 2005).

34. See her stories and note about her in Polonsky, Adamczyk-Garbowska, 301–320.

Krall was born in 1937 in Warsaw into an acculturated Jewish family. Her parents and other relatives perished in the Majdanek concentration camp while she survived outside the camp, helped by a number of Polish people. She graduated from the School of Journalism at Warsaw University and for a number of years worked as a reporter for major Polish newspapers. Her career was launched by the above-mentioned book interview with Marek Edelman. The interview was also the beginning of a phase for Krall to which she has remained faithful ever since. In her books that followed, for instance in *Taniec na cudzym weselu* ("A Dance at Somebody Else's Wedding") and in *Dowody na istnienie* ("Proofs of Existence"),[35] she combines stories about the Holocaust with describing Jewish life in Poland before the destruction, recreating minute details of that existence. In this manner the stories of destruction become even more real and devastating. A large group of her protagonists are "children of the Holocaust," now in their late fifties and sixties, who often do not know how they survived, who their parents and grandparents were, and what had happened to them. Some of them have labored for many years to learn this, others have just discovered their origin, and there are some who prefer not to dwell in the past at all.

Krall calls these people the co-authors of her stories and, as she has repeated on numerous occasions, she wishes to save them from oblivion. She is afraid, as she has mentioned in a number of interviews and on public occasions, that a purely historical and statistical approach to the Holocaust focusing on mass murders, deportations, descriptions of death camps, gas chambers, and other atrocities, might create fear and a sense of horror in modern readers, rather than evoke real compassion, and might possibly even have the reverse effect of causing them to avoid the topic in the future. Real empathy, according to Krall, can rather be evoked by recalling individual fates and concentrating on feelings and emotions. In her stories she writes not only about survivors, but also about their rescuers, informers, more and less indifferent witnesses, as well as perpetrators. Indirectly, she raises the question of how readers would behave in similar situations, but does so in an unobtrusive albeit sometimes provocative way.

Krall focuses on the paradoxical vicissitudes of her characters (most of them based on real people), a number of them having been children during the Holocaust. In *Sublokatorka* ("Subtenant"), her only novel so far (first published in Paris in 1985 because of strict censorship in Poland at that time), she ironically contrasts the tragic disparity between the Polish and Jewish experience under the Nazi occupation through the symbolic "brightness" (stereotypically perceived "heroic" deaths of Polish resistance fighters) and "darkness" (the equally stereotypical "passive" fate of the Jews in the ghetto). Again, as with the Edelman story, the novel may constitute rath-

---

35. Selected stories from these two particular collections were included in the new American edition.

er difficult reading for the Western reader because of numerous historical references to political events in Poland after World War II, presented by means of a multiple-layered plot.

Krall's style is characterized by brief, restrained narrative, with a focus on characters' dialogues and monologues, and very little authorial comment (hence my reference to Hemingway and Carver). She might be blamed for repeating certain patterns and narrative strategies, as well as overusing a restrained manner of presentation. But in a sense this is her consciously and carefully crafted voice selected to describe the tragedy of the Holocaust via multiple voices of survivors and witnesses. Critics have noticed her growing use of the fairy tale convention, which makes some of her stories read like documentary fables. For instance, in "Dybbuk" a handsome middle-aged Jewish American professor develops a passionate interest in Poland and wooden synagogues. Behind a seemingly innocent story lurks one from the Warsaw ghetto, where the professor's baby step-brother, born a long time before his own birth, perished and the thought of whom has now entered the post-Holocaust sibling's mind. By exploiting the dybbuk motif she establishes a connection to Yiddish literature (in other stories she also makes references to the Singer brothers) and her story was adapted for the theatre, juxtaposed with An-sky's famous play.

Like other Jewish literatures created in non-Jewish languages that draw both from the Jewish tradition and the majority's cultural milieu, Polish Jewish literature is marked by its relationship to the Polish mainstream literary tradition. When Polish Jewish writers use the Polish language, they draw from its variegated literary resources. They make frequent references to Polish Romantic poets or those from the interwar period.[36] Contrary to non-Jewish writers creating in Polish who also reveal interest in Jewish topics, Jewish authors present the latter as intimate and familiar, rarely showing distance to and fascination with it as unknown and exotic. At the same time, Polish Jewish literature sustains a link to Jewish writings in other languages, by drawing on symbols and images of Judaism, Yiddish folklore, and humor, and by exploring such universal Jewish topics as the search for identity, the conflict between tradition and secularization or urbanity and the *shtetl* existence, exile and alienation, and more recently the impact of the Holocaust on survivors and their descendants. There is no room in this essay to conduct a thorough comparative analysis with Jewish works written in other languages, but I have at least attempted to indicate some possible connecting themes that deserve more attention and that could enrich our knowledge and understanding of this complex international phenomenon that we tend to call "Jewish literature."

---

36. Polish Yiddish poets also drew from these sources (e.g., Avrom Sutzkever) and it would be interesting to compare the ways both groups of authors use such references.

In his drama *Esterke* Aaron Zeitlin makes the most esteemed Yiddish writer Yitzkhok Leyb Peretz address the greatest Polish Romantic poet Adam Mickiewicz with the words: *"Ver du bist—dos veys ikh, nor ver ikh bin—dos veystu nisht"* ("I know who you are, but who I am—you do not know.")[37] Not only did Polish writers not know Yiddish writers, Jews writing in Poland in different languages did not know each other, as the example of Bruno Schulz and Isaac Bashevis Singer testifies. Perhaps now, after a long delay caused by manifold historical and political factors, scholars of Jewish literature in various languages will attempt to find the missing links by examining one another's canons.

---

37. Used as a motto in Chone Shmeruk's comparative study *The Esterke Story in Yiddish and Polish Literature* (Jerusalem: The Zalman Shazar Center for the Furtherance of the Study of Jewish History, 1985), 5.

The Kvetcher in the Rye:
J. D. Salinger and Challenges to
the Modern Jewish Canon

LEAH GARRETT

When I was a doctoral candidate at the Jewish Theological Seminary, David Roskies invited me to be a teaching assistant in his graduate course "Modern Jewish Literature." The class had developed out of a similar one that his sister Ruth Wisse was then teaching at Harvard (which she had first taught at McGill University), which would serve as a basis for her book *The Modern Jewish Canon: A Journey Through Language and Culture.*[1] Seeking a cohesive framework for the modern Jewish novel, the class crackled with questions about what constitutes modern Jewish literature and how one defines a Jewish canon. The readings in the course, for the most part, presented Jewish life from an insider's perspective that challenged the prevalent notion that modern Jewish culture meant the years leading up to, during, and immediately after the Holocaust. These texts instead showed that Jewish writers around the world were at the forefront of modern literary culture and were creating ground-breaking works in a host of languages.

Upon graduating from JTS, I became an assistant professor of Jewish literature at the University of Denver, where I developed my version of the Wisse/Roskies class. While I continued to teach the majority of texts used by Wisse and Roskies (Sholem Aleichem's *Tevye*, Kafka's *The Trial*, I. B. Singer's *Satan in Goray*, Babel's *Red Cavalry*, Agnon's *A Guest for the Night*, Primo Levi's *Survival in Auschwitz*), I also made some amendments. For instance, I dropped A. M. Klein's *The Second Scroll*, finding it too difficult for undergraduates with little to no background in Jewish studies, while adding Orly Castel-Bloom's controversial *Dolly City* to show the students the extraordinary level of self-questioning and literary inventiveness in recent Israeli writing. The year that the Hungarian author Imre Kertesz unexpectedly won the Nobel prize for literature, I added his book *Kaddish for a Child Not Born* in place of Primo Levi's *Survival in Auschwitz*, although I found it an inferior substitution.

As in Roskies's course, the students were always fired up with questions about the meaning of "Jewish," "modern," and "canon." As the class progressed, both the questions and their answers would inevitably change, although, fortunately, the heated exchanges never died down. We all know the basic questions. If an author is Jewish, is his/her text Jewish literature,

---

1. Ruth R. Wisse, *The Modern Jewish Canon: A Journey Through Language and Culture* (New York: The Free Press, 2000).

or must the characters or cultural milieu be explicitly Jewish? What exactly do we mean by "modern" when relating it to the Jewish experience? For my own definitions, I relied heavily on my training at JTS, where "Jewish" was consigned a positive locale in the center of the cultural universe, rather than marginalized as the site of otherness, and where a Jewish text grew out of a dynamic, multilingual, and multicultural tradition stretching back to the Bible. Nearly all the works I included were self-evidently Jewish because they explicitly examined questions about modern Jewish identity from a variety of angles based on the author's location in time and place. The exceptions were Franz Kafka's *The Trial* and J. D. Salinger's *Catcher in the Rye*. Although *The Trial* was not explicitly Jewish, the selection could nevertheless be "rationalized" by Kafka's persistent personal examination of his Jewish identity. *Catcher*, in contrast, was problematic not only because Holden Caulfield (like Joseph K) was not overtly Jewish, but because Salinger (unlike Kafka) distanced himself from his Jewish upbringing. Yet, *Catcher* so forcefully presented the postwar American Jewish experience and fell so obviously in my mind into the tradition of Roth, Bellow, and others, that it had to be included. Moreover, it challenged the entire framework of the course and led to extremely productive discussions on the nature of Jewish literature.

To my surprise, however, in teaching the class I discovered that there existed virtually no critical examinations of American Jewish literature that included J. D. Salinger or *Catcher in the Rye*.[2] It was understandable why *Catcher* was excluded as a Jewish text, but why omit Salinger the author? After all, he was raised as a Jew in a Jewish home, and his grandfather was even a rabbi. Moreover, throughout his childhood and adolescence, Salinger confronted anti-Semitism, particularly at a military boarding school in Pennsylvania. Was the problem that after his bar mitzvah he discovered that his mother, the Jewish Miriam, was in reality the Irish Catholic Marie? Was he thus excluded because his mother was not a Jew (although she lived as a Jew throughout her married life)? Or because as an adult Salinger distanced himself from his Jewish upbringing, instead, like so many other American Jews, embracing eastern religions?[3] Was the only explanation for Salinger's

---

2. The only criticism I could find that asserted outright that Holden's family was really "middle-class urban Jewish" even though Salinger had "Anglicized them" was a 1958 piece by Maxwell Geismer in which he condemns Salinger outright for hiding the Jewishness in the text. See Geismer's chapter "J. D. Salinger: The Wise Child and The New Yorker School of Fiction" in his book *American Moderns: From Rebellion to Conformity, A Mid-Century View of Contemporary Fiction* (New York: Hill and Wang, 1958), 195–209.

3   There is little biographical information on Salinger and most (if not all of it) is not considered entirely reliable because of Salinger's extreme reclusiveness. For recent biographical information that I referred to when compiling information on Salinger's

exclusion his identity? Why were his other writings overlooked? For instance, his later work *Franny and Zooey* is about the experiences of a family with a Jewish husband and a gentile wife, and some of his stories, particularly "Down at the Dinghy," deal explicitly with what it means to be Jewish in America. It seemed to me that even if one was understandably uncomfortable calling Salinger an American Jewish author, nevertheless, some of his writings were overtly Jewish American literature.

In preparing this essay, I decided to contact three of the most central authorities on Jewish American writing and canon formation, to ask why they had not included Salinger and *Catcher* in their configuration of Jewish American literature. John Felstiner, who compiled the section on postwar American Jewish writing for *Jewish American Literature: A Norton Anthology*, wrote me that he had not included Salinger because of copyright issues (Salinger refuses to allow his works to be reprinted). Yet even if Salinger had agreed to have his work republished, he probably would not have included his writing since it really did not speak to the nature of the Jewish American experience. Felstiner's selection criteria thus did not have to do with the author's identity, but the content of his works. This position matches that of the *Norton* anthology. As Jules Chametzky writes in the introduction:

> Finally, Jewish American literature may simply or strictly derive from the author's identity as a Jew. But this most reductive definition again begs the essential question—that of identity. This anthology means to expand the question of identity to encompass all its turns and folds.[4]

It is an "inclusive vision," which focuses on literature that covers all facets of Jewish life in America. Hana Wirth-Nesher, editor of the *Cambridge Companion of American Jewish Literature* and *What is Jewish Literature?*,[5] shared with me that she was reluctant to label a writer Jewish who did not label him or herself as such and whose works "do not provide much

---

life, see the (extremely controversial) biography by Salinger's daughter Margaret entitled *Dream Catcher: A Memoir* (New York: Washington Square Press, 2000). Another recent biography is Paul Alexander's *Salinger: A Biography* (Los Angeles: Renaissance Books, 1999). There is also Norma Jean Lutz's essay "Biography of J. D. Salinger" in *J. D. Salinger*, ed. Harold Bloom (Philadelphia: Chelsea House Publishers, 2002), 3–44; Warren French's *J. D. Salinger Revisited* (Boston: Twayne, 1988); Michael A. Sommer's *J. D. Salinger* (New York: Rosen Publishing Group, 2006).

4. Jules Chametzky, "General Introduction," in *Jewish American Literature: A Norton Anthology*, eds. Jules Chametzky, John Felstiner, Hilene Flanzbaum, Kathryn Hellerstein (New York: Norton, 2001), 1–16.

5. *The Cambridge Companion to Jewish American Literature*, eds. Michael P. Kramer and Hana Wirth-Nesher (Cambridge: Cambridge University Press, 2003) and *What is Jewish Literature?*, ed. Hana Wirth-Nesher (Philadelphia: Jewish Publication Society, 1994).

evidence for Jewishness." Yet she suggested that one could find a tie between Salinger and African American literature, as well as see Salinger's work as mirroring many of the "values, world views, and rhetoric" of the "ambitious Anglophones" of his generation, such as Delmore Schwartz, Bellow, Kazin, and Rosenfeld. In other words, Salinger potentially could be grouped with other Jewish American writers of his generation because of their shared rhetorical strategies. Harold Bloom, who recently edited books on Holden Caulfield and J. D. Salinger,[6] emailed me that Salinger "seems devoid of Jewish traces." In a recent essay, Bloom instead locates Holden in the tradition of American protagonists as found in Hemingway and Fitzgerald.[7]

For Wisse, both *Catcher* and Salinger would clearly have no place in the Modern Jewish Canon since they do not fall into her definition of Jewish literature: "I mean simply that in Jewish literature the authors or characters know and let the reader know that they are Jews."[8] There is nothing overtly Jewish about the text and, as with Proust, J. D. Salinger seemingly has no interest in labeling himself either as a Jew or a Jewish writer. (Salinger's extreme reclusiveness means we must assume this from the little information we have.) The case of *Catcher*, in fact, mirrors in numerous ways the situation of Lionel Trilling's 1947 novel *The Middle of the Journey*, which seems to address a "Jewish set of themes" but in which, to quote Wisse, he "removes his character from the Jewish milieu where this movement actually ripened, thereby depriving the book of its social substantiveness." Wisse's decision not to include the Trilling novel in her modern canon is based on a desire to not "reinject into any work the lifeblood of a people that its author emptied out."[9]

First, I want to state that I am in complete intellectual agreement with Wisse's goal not to reinject Jewishness into a work, as well as her aversion to locating Jewish culture on the margins of the mainstream, instead seeking to show how the Jewish people construct their worldview from a standpoint of the center.[10] The two-thousand-year-long cultural continuum of Jewish life is well documented and solid, and bespeaks a tale of internal transmission that challenges the idea that Jewish writing was created from a

---

6. See *Holden Caulfield*, ed. Harold Bloom (Philadelphia: Chelsea House Publishers, 2005) and *J.D. Salinger*, ed. Harold Bloom (Philadelphia: Chelsea House Publishers, 2002).

7. In Bloom's "Introduction" in *Holden Caulfield*, 1–4.

8. Wisse, *The Modern Jewish Canon*, 15.

9. Ibid., 17.

10. My book *Journey beyond the Pale: Yiddish Travel Writing in the Modern World* (Madison: University of Wisconsin Press, 2003) took this perspective as its central thesis.

peripheral standpoint. Certainly the Jews were politically, socially, economically, and culturally marginalized and were disenfranchised in every possible way. But generally the response, rather than retreat, was to construct cultural means of keeping the distinctiveness of Jewish life intact, although there are, of course, numerous instances in which assimilation became more widespread, with early modern Germany and France the most obvious cases. Yet even there Jewish intellectuals sought to find specifically Jewish tropes of assimilation.

Nevertheless, *Catcher* and the case of Salinger offer important insights into theories of canon formation and their relationship to the modern Jewish experience. The canon, a Christian notion, becomes in the Jewish realm extremely complicated because of the unique history of Jewish cultural transmission. The debates of the last twenty years about what the canon is and what purposes it serves have tended to position it as a weapon of white, male, Western society, to suppress the voices of people of color and women. Yet as Jan Gorak has documented, there has never been one canon, but multiple ones.[11] Moreover, rather than viewing the canon as a negative force of domination, Gorak asks us to consider it as a means by which a culture transmits to itself from one generation to the next what is important.[12] Gorak thus suggests that "instead of presenting the canon as a servant of larger ideological forces or as an assembly of texts invested with the authority of tradition," the canon can be seen "as a coherent work of art, a body of texts larger than the sum of its members, a grand cultural narrative not so different from the Hebraic canon that emerged in Ancient Israel."[13] It is in this positive position that Wisse locates her canon and by so doing enables the Jewish people, often considered to be the marginalized "other" who are disenfranchised by the perpetuation of a canon, to take on the power to pick and choose what is essential to their own cultural transmission. She thus writes that "readers have every right to classify works according to diverse criteria, and finding a usable tradition for their own group or polity is one of the highest critical functions they can undertake."[14]

---

11. For a discussion of how critics have viewed the canon as a weapon of suppression, which contradicts the historical evidence of the multiplicity of canon formation, see Jan Gorak's *The Making of the Modern Canon: Genesis and Crisis of a Literary Idea* (New Jersey: Athlone, 1991). For a series of recent discussions about canon formation, see Gorak's edited volume *Canon Versus Culture: Reflections on the Current Debate* (New York: Garland, 2001). I would like to personally thank Jan Gorak for the illuminating discussions he had with me about canon formation as I prepared this essay.

12. See in particular his discussion in the chapter in *The Making of the Modern Canon*, "Conclusion Cultural Studies: Towards a New Canon?" 221–259.

13. Gorak, *The Making of the Modern Canon*, 259.

14. Wisse, *The Modern Jewish Canon*, 3.

Wisse's selections will be the works that best transmit the experience of modern Jewish life. Once the reasons for the canon have been formulated, the questions and answers about what to include become much trickier, because this is a canon that is narrowed by the term "Jewish." And it is around this question that Salinger and *Catcher* throw up so many interesting ideas.

The term Jewish has been contested, particularly in the last two hundred or so years, on religious, cultural, artistic, political, and social grounds. As intermarriage has become common, even in Israel the Law of Return has had to be amended to include those with a Jewish grandparent (rather than the traditional concept of a Jewish mother) in order to enable some families from Russia to emigrate intact. The American experience throws a spanner in the works when considering the term Jewish. At the end of the nineteenth century, responding to the endemic poverty, pogroms, and persistent anti-Semitism in Eastern Europe, the Jews responded by embracing socialist universalism (often at the expense of Jewish particularism), or its seeming opposite nationalism in the form of Zionism, or searching out the promise of America as the land of rebirth. America, while outwardly responsive to the Jews' plight, was nevertheless a location that also encouraged the dissipation of Jewish distinctiveness.

In America, particularly during the rise of nativism in the 1920s (when J. D. Salinger was a child), to be "American" was not a blank slate on which anyone could claim any unique ethnic or religious identity. To be American was to follow the model of a white, Anglo-Saxon Protestant. This bias was actualized in the 1921 and 1924 Johnson Acts, which created a quota system that virtually closed the door to Jews and Southern European Catholics, while continuing to keep the door wide open to Northern Europeans.

In America, the land of limitless self-reinvention, being Jewish has thus often meant a religious, cultural, and ethnic identity, at times relegated to a minority stance, and more recently representative of a mainstream white ethnicity, much like Italian Americans. Nowadays in America, anti-Semitism is a relatively rare scourge in comparison to the treatment of African Americans, and Jews have been able to navigate into nearly every position of power. Yet when *Catcher* was written, Jews were still considered to be members of a minority rather than mainstream white, and anti-Semitism in WASP strongholds, such as universities and country clubs, was endemic.

As I have noted, the main problem with including Salinger in the canon is his identity. Salinger, although raised in a New York City Jewish home, discovered after his bar mitzvah that his mother was not Jewish. Moreover, as an adult, he embraced eastern religions rather than Judaism. Yet, in his childhood and adolescence at the military school he faced anti-Semitism, and as a soldier in the Second World War he not only had to deal with the general anti-Semitism in the military, but the horrors of the Holocaust were propelled right into his personal realm when a young woman whom he had loved in Vienna before the war was killed, along with her family, in Auschwitz. Moreover, his battles throughout the war certainly brought him into close, if not direct, proximity to the destruction of European Jewry. For his daughter Margaret, Salinger's Jewishness is absolutely central to his identity, as one sees in the large space given to it in her biography *Dream Catcher*, and in her insistence in seeking out the Jewish aspects of his texts.[15] The biography, however, is extremely controversial because of its negative portrayal of Salinger as a father (so much so that his son felt compelled to write a letter to *The New York Observer* stating that the portrait does not reflect the father whom he knows and loves). One could suppose that his daughter's decision to make Salinger's Jewishness so central may have been inspired by the negative motivation to stress the importance of something that Salinger has distanced himself from (although most of the statements about Salinger's Jewishness supposedly came from his own sister Doris, which gives them an element of truthfulness). Other biographers, while always noting his Jewishness, don't give it the centrality his daughter does.

In perusing the amount of "Jewishness" ascribed to Salinger by biographers, one enters the minefield of trying to pinpoint Jewish identity in contemporary America. However, excluding Salinger merely on the basis of his identity is highly problematic, as Hana Wirth-Nesher writes in her compelling essay "Defining the Indefinable: What is Jewish Literature":

> The simplest formula for identifying Jewish literature is also the least satisfactory—literature written by Jews. Such a reductive approach, by its indiscriminate inclusiveness and its biological determinism, begs the question of what constitutes Jewish culture as a matrix for Jewish literary texts.[16]

In other words, to decide that a work is Jewish if its author is reduces Jewish literature to the locale of individual identity rather than the much richer, broader matrix of culture.

There are means of defining a canon that don't rely on the author's identity. Rather than locating a Jewish text in the identity of the author, I would suggest that we locate it in the "family of resemblances" between it and other works of art. In *Catcher* we have a forceful expression of the alienation so common at the time in modern American Jewish writing. One need only to peruse the pages of *Commentary Magazine* in the late 1940s, when *Catcher* was being composed, to see how often Jewish writers described the American Jewish experience as typified by the alienated young man.

---

15. Margaret A. Salinger, *Dream Catcher: A Memoir* (New York: Washington Square Press, 2000). The chapter that focuses most extensively on Salinger's Jewishness is "Landsman," 16–42.

16. Hana Wirth-Nesher's examination of the difficulties of pinpointing the term Jewish literature is found in her essay "Defining the Indefinable: What is Jewish Literature?" in her edited volume *What is Jewish Literatur?* 3–12. This quote is from page 3.

Thus Irving Howe wrote in his seminal 1946 essay "The Lost Young Intellectual: A Marginal Man, Twice Alienated":

> Usually born into an immigrant Jewish family, he teeters between an origin he can no longer accept and a desired status he cannot attain....He has largely lost his sense of Jewishness, of belonging to a people with a meaningful tradition, and he has not succeeded in finding a place for himself in the American scene or the American tradition.[17]

It is this "unattached intellectual," as Howe labels him, who predominates in Jewish writing. He suffers from a general sense of "alienation" to quote Nathan Glazar's 1947 *Commentary* essay, which is "a unique facet of the crisis of our times: the widespread belief that there has been a revolutionary change in the psychological condition of man, reflected in the individual's feeling of isolation, homelessness, insecurity, restlessness, anxiety."[18] This assortment of feelings matches exactly *Catcher's* "lonely as hell" (149) Holden Caulfield, composed when this trope was so prevalent in the pages of *Commentary*.[19] Moreover, both Howe and Glazer conflate the "alienation" of the young American Jewish male with the general feeling of malaise prevalent in the postwar years, as we see in the titles given to their essays wherein they make the Jewish experience universal: "The Lost Young Intellectual: A Marginal Man, Twice Alienated" or "The Alienation of Modern Man: Some Diagnosis of the Malady."[20] As in these essays, so too in *Catcher* the experience of alienation is universalized into the general experience of the modern young man.[21] Yet, it is also particularized, one could say Judaized, in

---

17. *Commentary* 2.4 (Oct 1946): 361-367. This quote is from page 361.

18. "The 'Alienation' of Modern Man: Some Diagnoses of the Malady," in *Commentary* 3.4 (April 1947): 378-385. This quote is from page 378.

19. Another way of looking at the angst expressed in *Catcher* is to read it in light of Salinger's very recent military service, when he fought in some of the most intense and horrific battles of World War II. Salinger was part of the bloody D-Day campaign, and also spent months fighting nightmarish battles in the Huergten Forest, where "Salinger saw many of his friends and comrades killed and wounded in action" ("Biography of J. D. Salinger" by Norma Jean Lutz, 6). His experiences in the war led Salinger to be hospitalized briefly in Nuremberg for a "nervous breakdown" (Lutz, 7). For a brief discussion about viewing the book in light of the war, see Carl Freedman, "Memories of Holden Caulfield—and of Miss Greenwood" in *Holden Caulfield*, ed. Harold Bloom. The essay is found on pages 165-181, while the discussion of its relationship to the war is on pages 175-177.

20. One could counter that since they were writing in *Commentary*, a Jewish journal, there was no need to specify that their essays referred to the Jewish experience. However, the majority of essays in *Commentary* that discuss Jewish themes mention it in their titles.

21. For an insightful discussion of how Jewish American writers in the 1940s associated alienation with Jewishness, see Ruth Wisse's essay "Jewish American Renaissance," in *The Cambridge Companion to Jewish American Literature*, 190-211, esp. 200-203.

that Holden's alienation is specifically against the surrounding WASP culture that he encounters at boarding school and in Manhattan. The phonies are those who embrace that culture without even being aware of it, the jocks, the upper class, the snobs, the "Ivy League bastards" (85). It is a culture in which adults don't protect the children, in which cruel jocks discriminate against the weak, the intellectuals, and those who look different to such an extent that it even leads an unpopular student at Holden's prep school to commit suicide as his only means of action against the bullies (170). It is specifically against this phony culture that he is rebelling.

Yet if Salinger is constructing a novel around a Jewish *talush* or dangling intellectual, a man who is intellectually rich and physically weak, who excels at literature (in other words, at the culture of words) and fails at sports, who is a great talker always in a position of being "alienated" by the mainstream society, then why not make him explicitly Jewish? Surprisingly, Holden may in fact be. He states in a rarely noticed clause that his "parents are different religions, and all the children in our family are atheists" (100). Later he tells us that "my father *was* a Catholic once. He quit, though, when he married my mother" (the italics are Salinger's, 112). His mother, then, may well be Jewish, making Holden Jewish and his father a convert who gave him an anglicized first name. But it is never made clear if this is in fact the case, since it is possible his mother's "different religion" is Protestantism (although it is more likely she is Jewish, since Salinger supposedly told his daughter that all his characters are at least half Jewish like him). Although we are not explicitly told that Holden's mother is Jewish, nevertheless we are shown Holden directing frequent, intense sarcasm against Christians. Thus he "kvetches" about the lecture of a bigwig donor at his prep school:

> He told us we ought to think of Jesus as our buddy and all. He said he talked to Jesus all the time. Even when he was driving his car. That killed me. I can just see the big phony bastard shifting into first gear and asking Jesus to send him a few more stiffs. The only good part of his speech was right in the middle of it (when) Edgar Marsalla, laid this terrific fart. It was a very crude thing to do, in chapel and all, but it was also quite amusing. (17)

For Holden, authentic Christians, like some impoverished nuns he meets, are fine. Jesus is fine as well. What he dislikes is the hypocritical use made of Christianity by the phonies. He thus describes going to a Christmas pageant at Radio City Music Hall with his love interest Sally Hayes:

> It's supposed to be religious as hell, I know, and very pretty and all, but I can't see anything religious or pretty, for God's sake, about a bunch of actors carrying crucifixes all over the stage. When they were all finished and started going out of the boxes again, you could tell they could hardly wait to get a cigarette or something....I said old Jesus probably would've puked if He could see it—all those fancy costumes and all. Sally said I was a sacrilegious atheist. I probably am. (137)

Why this tactic of obfuscation, of suggesting but not stating outright that Holden may be Jewish? Foremost, Salinger is mirroring what Howe and other American Jewish intellectuals were doing at the time, conflating the alienation of the male Jewish intellectual in America with the general alienation prevalent in society.[22]

One can also see the obfuscation as a rhetorical strategy, best illuminated by considering *Catcher* in light of the other great Jewish novel of alienation (which Wisse does include in her canon), *The Trial*.[23] In fact, the texts have so much in common that the only way to include *The Trial* and not include *Catcher* in the modern Jewish canon is to consider the Jewishness of the authors: Kafka was then delving into, and embracing, his Jewish identity, whereas Salinger was not. But back to their similarities. In both works the main character's Jewishness must be read into the work. The protagonist is a character drawn in opposition to the center. In *The Trial*, the center is the legal system, in *Catcher* it is WASP culture. The male protagonist's job is to discover what the insiders want, what the larger game is, and whether or not he is able or willing to play it. Yet both are "guilty" of playing the game poorly, and their alienation is profound.

The endings are reflections on the same theme of searching out an authentic truth in a world where meaning is slipping away. Yet the protagonists reach opposite conclusions. In *Catcher*, Holden refuses to disappear from the scene by running away. Instead, he chooses to stay and reconnect with his sister in order to build a stronger family (and community) out of the one shattered by the death of his brother. Holden's seemingly positive act suggests a search to belong somewhere, to find an authentic sense of home in a world of WASP phonies, matching Howe's rendering of the alienated man as one who the more he withdraws, "the more he feels unhappy about his withdrawal and desires a sense of community."[24] However, the final chapter makes it clear that Holden is telling his tale from a mental hospital after having suffered a nervous breakdown. Much like Philip Roth's Eli in his tale "Eli, the Fanatic," the world at large has decided the only "solution" for a young (Jewish) man totally at odds with broader society is to institutionalize him. In the end it becomes clear that the narrative voice is generated in therapy to a psychoanalyst about the events leading to his breakdown. It is a

---

22. Salinger's daughter Margaret believes that he disguised the Jewishness of his characters as a reaction to the anti-Semitism prevalent at the time that made him ashamed to admit their true identity. See her discussion on pages 24–42 in *Dream Catcher*.

23. For Wisse's discussion of Kafka, see *The Modern Jewish Canon*, 68–87. For an extremely compelling essay asserting the brilliance of Salinger's much maligned *Franny and Zooey* that considers in part how his writings share aspects with Kafka, see Janet Malcolm, "Justice to J. D. Salinger" in *The New York Review of Books* 48.10 (June 21, 2001).

24. Howe, "The Lost Young Intellectual," 367.

ruptured voice that is now trying to salvage itself and its sanity. At the end of *The Trial* (although there is no set ending since it was unfinished), in contrast, Joseph K. is slaughtered (or one could say sacrificed). In both cases, there is the possibility that the original protagonist has not succeeded in joining the society and instead is utterly destroyed, though in *Catcher* with the possibility of redemption through therapy.[25]

The Trial and *Catcher* also resemble one another in the rhetorical strategy of hiding, which imparts the alienation of the central character. In both cases there is a disjunction between the action and the voice describing it. In Kafka the voice is the narrator, who both mirrors and seems to refute the judges who are condemning Joseph K. It is a narrative strategy that creates an uncomfortable awareness in the reader that there are signs that must be decoded in order to uncover the real text, the real story, which lies just below the surface. Yet the narrator gives the reader no key with which to unlock the meaning. In *Catcher* we also have a narrative distance from the occurrences, with a narrator who is most likely unreliable, since, as he tells us, he is "the most terrific liar you ever saw in your life" (16). Where in *The Trial* the reader tries to use the narrative distance to discover levels of guilt, in *Catcher* the distance becomes a bridge with which to try and gauge who the real Holden is and what he really wants. In both tales, the writers employ a system of codes to push the reader to decode the root causes of the alienation. In neither case is it shown that being Jewish may be a cause.

We return to the issue of employing a rhetorical system of obfuscation to impart the Jewish American experience. I refer to a 1949 tale by Salinger, "Down at the Dinghy," which deals overtly with anti-Semitism in America.[26] The story begins with a maid, Sandra, conversing with another household employee, Mrs. Snell, in the kitchen of a lakefront home. Sandra announces to Mrs. Snell that "I'm not gonna worry about it" (57), although it is clear that she is deeply distressed about something, since she constantly repeats how she is not worried about it. There is a four-year-old in the house who

---

25. Seeing therapy as the means to self-improvement is, of course, an extremely Jewish American take on things.

26. The story was originally published in *Harper's* magazine in 1949 and later collected in J. D. Salinger's *Nine Stories* (New York: Signet Press, 1953), 57–66. For a brief discussion of the publication history that mentions the interesting fact that the story was originally called "The Killer in the Dinghy," see Paul Alexander, *J. D. Salinger: A Biography*, 132–134.

The reluctance to label anything Jewish about Salinger's work is manifested in a brief discussion of "Down at the Dinghy" by the critic Clifford Mills in Harold Bloom's edited volume *J. D. Salinger*. Mills refuses to mention the anti-Semitic occurrence around which the story revolves, instead stating obscurely that Lionel is "running away from a slur he overheard and does not understand about his father." See his essay "A Critical Perspective on the Writings of J. D. Salinger" in *J. D. Salinger*, 45–66. This quote is from page 54.

has overheard something she said. However, it is his fault (not hers), because he sneaked up on her (something a maid would normally cherish: having a quiet rather than rowdy child in the house). After Mrs. Snell responds that he is a handsome child, the reader gets the second clue when Sandra snaps back that "He's gonna have a nose just like his father" (58). The third clue is that, unlike other lakefront dwellers, this family rarely if ever goes into the water (another source of consternation to Sandra). Finally Sandra wonders if she should come clean about what she has done, while Mrs. Snell suggests that she look for another job.

In the act of reading the opening scene, we are only slightly aware that we are picking up clues as to what has occurred. Instead, we jump in mid-conversation to an event that has already transpired. The feeling is that we are "bad" readers, that we have somehow missed clues that should reveal to us what has happened. This leaves us in a mood of anticipation to find out the meaning just below the surface, and puts us in the position of a detective trying to solve the text's mystery, as occurs in *The Trial*.

In the second scene, the boy's mother, Boo Boo Tanenbaum, enters the kitchen, trying to find a pickle with which to lure her son out of a boat down by the water. As Boo Boo lightheartedly discusses other times when the boy has run away, it becomes evident to the maid Sandra that Boo Boo does not know about the incident that is worrying her.

In the final scene, Boo Boo is down at the lake trying to get her son Lionel out of his father's dinghy. She jokes with him, pretending to be a boat's admiral to get him to leave, but he won't play along, since his father (her husband) has told him she is not an admiral but a "lady." She asserts that his daddy is the biggest "landlubber" she knows (62). She keeps teasing him, and the portrait the reader sees is of an extremely kind and gracious mother who loves her child and will use any means to make him feel better. She keeps pretending to be an admiral in the army and offers to blow "every secret bugle" (63) for him if he will tell her why he ran away.[27] He still refuses to come clean, not even allowing her into the boat. She has a brainstorm. She offers him a keychain with ten keys on it that he can throw into the lake. Once he defiantly tosses them into the lake, he bursts into tears and tells her what happened (the "keys" he tosses are a symbol for the reader gaining the tools to unlock the text's real meaning):

> "Sandra—told Mrs. Smell—that Daddy's a big—sloppy—kike." (65)
>
> Boo Boo flinches at this, and draws the boy close. She says:

---

27. This mimics, certainly without Salinger's knowledge, Mendele's famous novella *The Brief Travels of Benjamin the Third*, in which Benjamin pretends to be a Russian officer.

"Well, that isn't *too* terrible... That isn't the *worst* that could happen." She bit the rim of the boy's ear. "Do you know what a kike is, baby?"

Lionel was either unwilling or unable to speak up at once. At any rate, he waited till the hiccupping aftermath of his tears had subsided a little. Then his answer was delivered, muffled but intelligible, into the warmth of Boo Boo's neck. "It's one of those things that go up in the air," he said. "With *string* you hold." (65)

Lionel does not know what the word "kike" means, but understood from the tenor of Sandra's voice that it was used negatively. Even though he misread the word as "kite," he understood the hidden meaning. In this instance Jewishness is coded and then decoded, while the relationship between the sign and signified is not direct or primary but distanced. Jewishness becomes in the Salinger text something below the surface, unlocked, even when the words used to show it don't express it directly. We saw this in *Catcher*, when rather than saying outright that Holden may be Jewish, Salinger dropped clues: his father (like Salinger's mother) quit being Catholic; Holden disparages Christians; his parents are of different religions. In the same way in "Down at the Dinghy," the reader is able to discern the hidden meaning behind the earlier statements of the anti-Semitic Sandra, that the boy will have a "big nose" and that the family is not water-loving or athletic. The little boy knows the full force of the hidden text in an indirect way. "Kite" as "kike," "kike" as "kite," they are the same things but with different signifiers. And the mother, Boo Boo, does not even try to disavow him from his reading. Instead, she diverts Lionel by telling him that if he leaves the boat, they'll go meet his father at the train station and then will have the father bring them out for a boat ride. She thus replaces the father blighted by Sandra's anti-Semitism with the one he loves and is excited to see. Although the tale began from the perspective of Sandra, Salinger effectively undermines her anti-Semitism by replacing it at the conclusion with the image of a Jewish family that can resist her poison from a loving position.

In his tale Salinger creates a commentary on anti-Semitism in America as a hidden negative force that the reader at first can see only by noticing the clues that present it indirectly. As in *Catcher*, Salinger employs a similar rhetorical strategy (also used in *The Trial*) of a coded text to present individuals at odds with the dominant society. This, however, is not to locate *Catcher* in the rhetoric of otherness, of the Jew on the margins of the center. In fact, it is quite the opposite. The voice of Holden is insistent, powerful, unique, frequently funny. It is not the voice of a weak, marginalized "other." Instead, in every word, in every sentence, it takes on a centered position of power. Here, the alienation is the voice of the world. It is the whole world. Salinger has not transformed a Jewish voice into an American one, but instead made the American voice Jewish, much as Howe and Glazer did during the same time period. In this case, THE great American novel that

would help to bring in the disaffected voice of youth of the 1950s and Ker-
ouac, Ginsberg, James Dean, and Elvis Presley, is Jewish.

Holden need not be overtly Jewish, because to make him so would be to
put him in the position of the "other," on the margins of the mainstream.
Better to keep his true identity hidden, since Salinger clearly does not want
to place every aspect in the oppositional tone of the repressed minority.
Instead, he draws Holden as seemingly a member of the center, one of the
WASP culture's very own, down to the boarding school education and the
Upper East Side apartment. A member of the power center, he is able to
look at and verbalize all the foibles of that society from a seemingly insider's
position. Yet a true member of that society would never be able to see it
with the distanced perspective of Holden. *Catcher* works by making Holden
appear to be an insider who is able to navigate the center and show its problems from within, although, as I have said, Salinger drops numerous clues to
suggest that Holden is not a WASP. I would suggest that, in fact, he is the
"kike" transformed into a "kite" rising above the phony society to invent a
more true self.

Why give Salinger a spot in the modern Jewish canon? It enables us to
reorient the notion of the Jewish canon from the minefield of identity to a
theory of family resemblances in which works that fall under the rubric of
"Jewish American" share certain traits, in clear evidence in *Catcher*: the
constant recourse to humor and the obsession with the perspective of
youth that Wisse notes as so prevalent in Jewish American writing;[28] the
monological tone; the image of total alienation documented in the pages of
Commentary. In fact, it is a parallel text in numerous ways to Philip Roth's
Portnoy's Complaint, but with the Jewish narrator passing himself off as a
Gentile, while trying to unpack the broader WASP culture that he is both
attracted to and despises (as shown in the love interest Sally). It teaches the
reader that the American Jewish experience in the postwar years was often
one in which Jews were given access to the localities of mainstream society,
but remained sufficiently aloof that they could navigate with an extraordinarily critical, often profoundly funny eye (as we also see in the ascendance
of Jewish American comics in the postwar period).

Yet it is also a coded text, as in *The Trial*, that reflects the talmudic literary tradition of multiple readings, of a disavowal of a univocal interpretation, of layered meanings, which points out its relationship toward not only
Jewish American writing but Jewish European discourse. And, moreover, to
agree with Wisse's suggestion that we choose the finest pieces to represent
the canon, *Catcher* is ground-breakingly brilliant in so many ways that it

---

28. For her comments on the theme of the perpetual adolescent in Jewish American writing, see Wisse, *The Modern Jewish Canon*, 25 and 269. For her comments on humor,
see "Jewish American Renaissance," 202.

continues to speak to generations of readers, as shown in its perennial placement in the top one hundred best-selling books. Moreover, it is considered one of the great American novels, such as *Moby Dick*, that critics still dissect and analyze as seen in the large number of critical editions that continue to be published about it.

To include it also challenges the idea of a pure Jewish text. *Catcher* shows us that in the American scene in particular, to be Jewish could mean something other than being all Jewish or all Gentile, to be located somewhere beyond the author's identity in the text's strategies of meaning. Thus in the American milieu, which called for the submergence of the ethnic into the WASP-fashioned melting pot, one could detect in *Catcher* the insistent survival of the Jewish dangling intellectual at odds with the society seeking to subsume him. Moreover, we see Holden as a clear member of "a community that has traduced its values and followed strange gods,"[29] to quote Wisse's description of Jewish American discourse. In the end, however, Holden learns that to authentically be Holden is not to be beholden to the values of the "strange gods" of WASP society, but only to his and his sister's needs. Viewing *Catcher* as part of the modern Jewish canon makes Holden Caulfield–and the Jewish experience–the universal experience of alienation in America. The American tradition of rebellion against the dominant society, stretching back to the founding fathers, is so essentially both American and Jewish that Holden is Salinger's perfect amalgamation of the two.

---

29. Wisse, *The Modern Jewish Canon*, 322.

Israeli Identity in a Post-Zionist Age

YARON PELEG

Much of the literature that was written in Israel in the late 1980s and 1990s has been labeled postmodern or post-Zionist. Both of these terms are elusive and cannot be easily defined. Postzionism, which is more relevant for the discussion here, has generally been understood either as a rejection of Zionism as a valid ideology or more benignly as the understanding that Zionism has succeeded in its mission and needs to be replaced with a more relevant, cultural paradigm.[1] Either way, as a local, Israeli version of postmodernism or postcolonialism even, one of the primary drives of postzionism has been the debunking, dismantling, or deconstruction of the grand Zionist narrative/s of the past. One of the earliest and most obvious examples of this drive, though perhaps unjustifiably so, would be Benny Morris' 1987 *The Birth of the Palestinian Refugee Problem*, in which Israel's image as a chaste David fighting an overwhelming Arab Goliath was challenged both militarily and morally.[2] A more recent and more appropriate example would be the work of Hanan Hever, who has published a number of articles in the past few years charging some of Israel's most venerated authors of complying indirectly with the dispossession of Palestinian Arabs during Zionism's formative years.[3]

In some ways, the criticism of post-Zionists is neither new nor unique, of course. In fact, much of the canonical literature that was written after 1948 can be labeled "post-Zionist" in some fashion. The early works of both Amos Oz and A. B. Yehoshua contain a harsh critique of Israel post-independence. Oz's short story "Where the Jackals Howl" and Yehoshua's story "Early in the Summer of 1970," for instance, published in the early 1960s, draw pointed attention to the gap between the lofty ideals of Zionism and their realization after 1948.[4] The difference between the earlier and the later critics of Zionism lies in the motivation behind the criticism. Whereas Oz, Yehoshua, and other writers of the so-called State Generation were in many

---

1. See Laurence J. Silberstein, *The Postzionism Debates: Knowledge and Power in Israeli Culture* (New York: Routledge, 1999).

2. Cambridge and New York: Cambridge University Press, 1987.

3. For a representative article, see Hanan Hever, "Mesifrut Ivrit lesifrut Yisre'elit," *Te'oria uvikoret* 20 (2002).

4. Amos Oz, *Where the Jackals Howl* (New York: Harcourt Brace Jovanovich, 1981); A.B. Yehushua, *Early in the summer of 1970* (Garden City, N.Y.: Doubleday, 1977, 1976).

ways frustrated romantics who were angry at a disappointing reality that did not hold up to Zionist ideals, some contemporary post-Zionists question the validity of the ideology itself. This is an important difference that changes the very role and function of criticism. Because one of the most problematic aspects of both postmodernism and postzionism is a tendency toward moral relativism, a misguided attempt to do away with *any* kind of value judgments; a *de*-constructive drive that often results merely in *destruction* and does not go beyond. Literary and other critics do not necessarily have to provide a solution for problems they engage with. But in order to make their criticism meaningful, they do have to ground it and provide a perspective that would give their critique sense. One of my aims in this essay is to suggest such a perspective and to contextualize Israeli literature once again within the old Zionist narrative that has fallen into disrepute in the last two decades.

Since the conclusion of Gershon Shaked's synoptic literary study, which ended in 1980, most of the studies dedicated to the literature of the ensuing decades emphasized the dissolution and fragmentation of Israeli identity along ethnic, gender, and other lines.[5] While this very process of fragmentation seems to defy broad mapping endeavors like those of Shaked, I think that the attempt to create a more comprehensive Israeli identity within the context of Zionist history still animates several of Israel's major writers today and I would like to examine the works of three of them: Orly Castel-Bloom, Etgar Keret, and Ronit Matalon. While all three writers acknowledge the breakup and disintegration of a coherent and unified Israeli culture and identity—their works are often cited as examples of this very process—they also offer new definitions of Israeliness and even of canonicity that counter these trends. Orly Castel-Bloom, in her 2002 novel, *Human Parts*, presents an amalgamation of various parts of Jewish, Israeli society that are woven into a tapestry of separate identities that nevertheless make a cohesive, if tenuous whole. Etgar Keret, in his numerous collections of short stories throughout the 1990s, attempts to redraw the contours of an urban, secular, and ethnically inclusive Israeli middle-class. Ronit Matalon, in her 1995 *The One Facing Us*, ultimately transcends the rich Mizrahi identity at the heart of the novel and offers more varied and complex ways of creating [Israeli] identity. Common to all three writers is the attempt not only to draw a picture of the specific group or groups they focus on but to consider those groups as part of an Israeli collectivity as well.

I begin with Orly Castel-Bloom, whose work has often been used to announce the arrival of postmodernism and even postzionism in Israel. Castel-Bloom began publishing in 1987, a few months before the first Intifada

---

5. I am referring to Shaked's five-volume literary history, *Hebrew Fiction, 1880–1980*, which appeared between 1977 and 1988 (Jerusalem: Hakibutz Hame'uhad, Keter, 1977, 1988).

broke out, and received immediate and wide public attention as the voice of a new generation.[6] Focusing primarily on her style, the critical establishment declared Orly Castel-Bloom a prominent existential writer already by 1990. Her language was described as "tin-like," that is, language that does not try to be mimetic or expressive but focuses instead on its automation, its clichéd quality, the fact that it no longer expresses depth or emotion.[7] Castel-Bloom's stories, it was said, are a cruel parody on the kitschy desire for meaning, a rejection of any illusion of depth in language, in culture, in the human experience, in the privacy of the human soul, in society, in tradition and in the past. All she sees before her is a reality "made up of a thin and dull layer of automatic and quotidian existence that hides an abyss of chaos below it."[8]

The fact that Castel-Bloom's works were found to express an "existential anxiety" is at first glance strange because the young author was not only part of a relatively affluent generation, but a generation that grew up during a comparatively peaceful period in Israeli history. Castel-Bloom was twenty-seven when she published her first collection of short stories, *Not Far from the City Center* (*Lo rachok mimerkaz ha'ir*). Yet almost every year or so for the next decade, she continued to publish frenzied texts, short stories and then novels that presented a hellish Israel: chaotic, incomprehensible and especially mean. Consider, for instance, the following opening to her short story, "The Woman who Wanted to Kill Someone" (*Ha'isha sheratzta laharog mishehu*): "There was a woman who wanted to kill someone, preferably someone fat. Don't get her wrong," the story continues, "she didn't want to kill someone fat so that the broken children of New Delhi would have more food. She had other motives, secret, obscure."[9] The story disabuses readers of any causality that may exist between the woman's wish and her motives. She has no personal vendetta nor is she a deranged activist

---

6. Castel-Bloom's first publication, a collection of short stories titled *Not Far from the City Center* (*Lo rachok mimerkaz ha'ir*, Tel-Aviv: Am Oved, 1987) received wide attention and was critiqued frequently and in numerous publications, including *Yediot Aharonot*, May 22 and again on August 5, 1987; *Ha'ir*, May 22, 1987; *Al Hamishmar*, June 17, 1987; *Ha'aretz*, July 3, July 24, July 27, 1987; *Koteret Rashit*, August 12, 1987.

7. Dan Miron, "Something about Orly Castel-Bloom" (*Mashehu al orly castel-blum*), *Al Hamishmar*, August 16, 1989.

8. Miron, ibid. Ariel Hirshfeld concurred in his review of Castel-Bloom's first novel, *Where Am I?* (*Hechan ani nimtzet?*, 1990), which he saw as a "large and horrifying image of the world as it is imprinted on the soul." The book imparts to the reader "a sense of insult of such vast proportions that it suffuses the world with its shrieking darkness," Ariel Hirshfeld, "Castel-Bloom in Wonderland" (*castel-bloom be'eretz hapla'ot*), Ha'aretz, May 18, 1990.

9. See Orly Castel-Bloom, *Selected Stories 1987–2004* (*Im orez lo mitvakchim*) (Kineret, Zmora-Bitan Publishers, 2004).

for human rights. Her secret motives continue to be obscure and inexplicable until the very end.

These are clearly postmodernist techniques; language is no longer mimetic but becomes a fetishized medium, senseless, circular, a collection of signifiers without signifieds. Yet, surprisingly, the intention or meaning behind this and many of her other hyper-real texts seems much more conservative, even idealistic since the pastiche and the exaggeration in Castel-Bloom's works are used first and foremost as allegorical distortion.[10] Castel-Bloom's stories are obviously trapped in a harsh and grating reality, made up from the worst of Israeliana: brutality, violence, detachment, and evince the desperation of a dead-end or no-win situation.[11] At a certain point, however, the accumulated pastiche becomes an internal critique against the oppression of absolute kitsch and the system of values it represents.[12]

One of the most important clues to Castel-Bloom's hysterical narratives can be found in the surrealistic gap that opened up during those years between the increasingly comfortable lives of most Israelis, especially in the Jewish urban center, and the growing misery of Palestinians; a gap that became ever more apparent as the first Intifada dragged on.[13] Indeed, Castel-Bloom showed an uncanny ability to articulate precisely the inchoate angst of the Israeli bourgeoisie, "to express the emptiness it feels and its inability to define exactly what bothers it behind the comforts of its privileged existence."[14] In various interviews, Orly Castel-Bloom herself acknowledged her agenda, the motives behind her writing. "I ask moral ques-

---

10. Ortzion Bartana, "Where Are We" (*Heichan anachnu nimtsaim*), *Moznayim*, June-July, 1992. As a literary stratagem, writes Ortzion Bartana, [Israeli] postmodernism "is a satirical-allegorical protest against a harsh reality. The evil and the ugly are embellished in order to be derided and condemned." Bartana identifies precisely the postmodernist aspects in Castel-Bloom's works but is skeptical of their efficacy as literary devices. In his opinion, the hyper-realism of postmodernism undermines the text's ability to redeem.

11. Amnon Jacont, "Bad Aura" (*Hila ra'ah*), *Yedi'ot Aharonot*, Feb. 8, 1989.

12. Gurevitz, ibid.

13. See, for example, some of the items in the local Tel-Aviv newspaper *Ha'ir*, which emerged during the 1980s as the venue of Israel's new and young urban culture, an irreverent and aggressively apolitical culture. The cover of the Yom Kippur edition from September 16, 1988 is a paraphrase of the holy day's prayer of *Ashamnu* ("We are guilty"). Instead of the usual litany of trespasses Jews recite on Yom Kippur, the cover alludes directly to the Intifada and begins: *atamnu, ba'atnu, gerashnu, dikinu...trinsfarnu* etc., meaning respectively, we sealed [houses], we beat up, we expelled [Palestinians], we oppressed, we transferred. The edition also includes an insert for the holiday, a mock Monopoly board (78–79) whose new categories like roadblocks and other obstacles players must pass through.

14. Unsigned, *Ha'aretz*, July 3, 1987. One of her most important contributions, wrote Ariana Melamed, was the skillful way she mapped the modern soul, delicately,

tions; questions about our ability to live in a world like ours. I want to protest, to unite people through some action; I want justice, a sense of brotherhood. I have naïve hopes that I don't think we should give up on. I am an idealist."[15]

This is precisely why I do not think that Castel-Bloom's works can really be labeled "post-Zionist," that is, that they portray a morally deteriorating Israel in order to negate it or, on the other hand, that they demand a new cultural paradigm. The value of Castel-Bloom's works resides instead in the loud cry they raise, a terrible lament of prophetic proportions about the dismal state of the country, its politics and its culture. Thus, the very terror that her stories raise actually becomes one of their most redemptive aspects because it is a terror that expresses an inherent inability to make sense of an Israeli world that lost its anchoring in a grand national narrative. This is not to say that Castel-Bloom is a reactionary who wishes to reinstate a parochial Zionism, but rather that she expresses a profound sense of loss on the brink of a new era.

For all these reasons, Castel-Bloom's first novel in the twenty-first century, the 2002 *Human Parts* (*Chalakim enoshiyim*), stands apart from her previous works with its [relative] realism, in which a contemporary Israel under the relentless attacks of suicide bombers is decidedly recognizable.[16] I put "relatively" in parenthesis because *Human Parts* like Castel-Bloom's other works still depicts a world that fundamentally does not make sense. This time, however, the source of surrealism is more a product of the impossible political and social "situation" as Israelis call it (*hamatzav*) than Castel-Bloom's own literary construction. This is an important difference. Although the novel is fantastically set in an Israel beset by incessant rain and snow storms and sub-zero temperatures, the literal Ice Age is a metaphor for the political limbo of the country, the perpetual cycle of violence. The bitter effects of the harsh winter draw attention to the impossibility of the political quagmire by aggravating its impact. "It was an exceptional winter," begins the novel,

> In the mountains the temperature was almost always below zero....Raindrops the size of olives fell in multitudes... hailstones were gigantic.....Owing to the heavy snow drifts, trees planted by the pioneers early in the previous century fell to the ground... Yet as if the outlandish winter wasn't enough...

---

precisely, and subversively "through the deliberate deconstruction of linguistic and conscious clichés and the paradoxical construction of a nightmarish world made up of the most common and immediate Israeli materials," Ariana Melamed, "Hallucinations from the Depth of Oppression" (*Hazayot mima'amekey hadikui*), *Ha'ir*, June 9, 1996.

15. Orly Toren, "Love Is a Depth Charge inside the Soul" (*Ahava ze ptzatzat omek bema'amekey haneshama*), *Yerushalayim*, January 6, 1989.

16. Orly Castel-Bloom, *Chalakim enoshiyim* (Tel-Aviv: Kinneret, 2002).

> the peace process with the Palestinians ... collapsed like one of the houses
> whose roof gave way under the weight of the snow. (3–5)

The Israel of *Human Parts* is a merciless place that is plagued externally and internally. The characters that populate it have little understanding and compassion for one another, not even in the face of the deadly fate that threatens them all. What separates them are not so much ethnic or political differences as much as wealth, widening gaps between the rich, who isolate themselves from the harsh winter in their plush apartments and luxurious cars, and the poor, who have no money for heating or warm clothes. Many of the commonalities that held them together before, despite their differences, seem to have disappeared. In this new and cruel Israeli universe of dog-eat-dog, the only thing that holds everything together is the narrator or language. The obvious connection that binds the alienated characters is their common fate, the suicide-bombing death that threatens them at random whether they are rich or poor. But in addition to that, the characters are linked by intricate geographic, biographic and textual relationships that hold them tightly together making Israeli society itself the central character of the novel.

This was a novelty for Castel-Bloom. A central feature of her previous works from the 1980s and 1990s, which earned her postmodern credentials, was her penchant for eliminating the logical connections between syntax and lexicon. Look again at the opening sentence of her story "The Woman who Wanted to Kill Someone": "There was a woman who wanted to kill someone, preferably someone fat." Although both syntax and lexicon are proper, they are inconsistent and make no sense. Grammatically speaking, the qualifier "preferably" further explains the "someone" in the sentence, and adds meaning to it. Only, it does not. It destabilizes the alarming sentence by further stripping it of coherence—fatness is not a capital offense. To make sure no one missed the illogic, the next sentence spells it out clearly: "Don't get her wrong, she didn't want to kill someone fat so that the broken children of New Delhi have more food. She had other motives, secret, obscure."

Contrary to that, *Human Parts* reestablishes the connections between syntax and lexicon. But now, the described reality itself does not make sense: "The country was drenched with every form of precipitation....Navy ships were anchored in places no one could have imagined possible before the onslaught....Sailboats were seen in Petah-Tikva, in Or Yehuda, in Mazkeret Batya, in Kfar Saba..." (4) This is a logical description of an extremely bizarre situation. The surrealism is external, not linguistic and internal. If the country is flooded, it makes sense that ships would be seen in what were formerly dry, low-lying lands. The same surface or superficial tightness holds the novel's disparate characters together.[17] The wealthy siblings Adir

---

17. A similar device is used by Ya'acov Shabtai, for instance, in *Past Continuous* (*Zichron*

and Liat Dubnov, Adir's former girlfriend, the divorcée and increasingly poorer Iris Ventura, his new girl friend, the Ethiopian supermodel Tasaro, and the destitute Kati Bet-Halahmi and her husband Boaz, have little in common save for the proximate lives they lead in an ever shrinking Israel. But as the tight text makes very clear, these are strong ties that bind these people together nevertheless.

Thus, after more than a decade of writing strident prose about the dissolution and fragmentation of Israeli society, *Human Parts* presents for the first time in the works of Castel-Bloom a picture of a more cohesive Israel. This is not the picture of a strong and integrated society by any means. Rather it is a patched-up union that is comprised of different groups of different people who are held together by fear and by a shared, dismal, fate. At the same time, the inclusion of the various groups that make up *Jewish* Israel— the founding, Ashkenazi elite of the country, working class Mizrahim as well as recent Ethiopian and Russian immigrants—renders the novel more than a little symbolic, so that the close proximity of the characters and their collective destiny also have a comforting and perhaps even a redemptive message, which, as vague and intangible as it might be, holds the promise of a more united and constructive future.

The second writer, Etgar Keret, has long been regarded as one of the most expressive voices of what has alternatively been called the Oslo generation, the postmodern generation, and sometimes the post-Zionist generation in a confusing mixture of terms.[18] The four collections of short stories he published, beginning with *Pipelines* (*Tzinorot*) in 1992 and ending with *Cheap Moon* (*Anihu*) in 2002 were widely embraced in Israel, especially by younger readers who were born after the Six-Day War and grew up in a relatively secure and increasingly affluent Israel.[19]

---

dvarim), in which the disintegrating Ashkenazi elite is held together only by the long and thin run-on sentences that go on for pages on end.

18. *Tzinorot* (Tel-Aviv: Am Oved, 1992), *Anihu* (Lod: Zemora-Bitan, 2002). The representative qualities of Keret's stories have been acknowledged almost immediately. See for example one of the earliest critiques of his first collection of stories, *Tzinorot*, by Rachel Dana Fruchter, *Iton 77*, October 1992: "Keret severs the dichotomy that existed since 1948 between the individual and the group. His stories repeatedly deal with outcasts so that these misfits eventually become the most well-defined group of the 1990s; the We of the present." Two years later, after Keret published his second anthology of short stories, *Ga'agu'ay le-Kissinger* (*Missing Kissinger*) (Tel-Aviv: Zemora-Bitan, 1994), Gideon Sammet complained about the inanities of the young Israeli generation and named Keret as one of its representatives; see *Ha'aretz*, August 19, 1994.

19. Keret's appeal to young readers is mentioned already in one of the first reviews of his work. In an interview with Gil Hovav in *Kol Ha'ir* (Feb. 28, 1992) Hovav relates a story about students in a problematic Bat-Yam high school, who, despite their usual disdain for literature, reacted enthusiastically after their teacher introduced them to some of

Very early on, Keret's writing, together with the writing of Orly Castel-Bloom, was labeled postmodern and it is easy to see why. It is not just that many of the stories seem to be short TV commercials—something they were often compared to. Neither was it just the plethora of borrowings from and allusions to the mass media: popular television series, comic books and detective films that abound in his stories. What earned Keret and Castel-Bloom the postmodern label was also the creation of what appears to be a morally relative Israeli universe in which good and evil have lost their meaning, a truly pluralistic fictional world in which all values are leveled. The story "My Brother Has the Blues" (*Ach sheli bedika'on*) is a good example, because of the casual way it deals with random violence:[20] After the narrator's rotweiler mangles a toddler in a peaceful Tel-Aviv city park,[21] the narrator's little brother clubs the dog to death with a crowbar and continues to smash the face of the toddler's complaining mother. "It's okay," the narrator explains, "my brother has the blues."

Another story, "Shlomo, You Mother-Fucking Fag" (*shlomo homo kus el omo*) reads almost like a prolonged joke that deals much more crudely and harshly with a similar theme.[22] Shlomo is a miserable schoolboy who is picked on by his classmates during a class trip to the park. The teacher, who ostensibly is the only one who feels compassion for him, tries to comfort him some during the trip. But when at the end of the day Shlomo asks her pathetically: "Miss, why do all the kids hate me?" the teacher shrugs her tired shoulders, puffs on her cigarette, and replies casually: "How should I know, I'm only the substitute teacher." While the story deals flippantly with a harsh injustice, it offers no explanation or consolation for it. In many ways it even exacerbates the injustice and the atmosphere of violence and aggression by adding the epithets from the title to Shlomo's name every time it is mentioned. The teacher, who significantly is a substitute teacher, not a "real" one, like the park with its artificial lake and the giant statue of an orange—all mock-ups of Zionist achievements—goes through the motions and helps Shlomo only because it is part of her job description. That she has

---

Keret's stories. Hovav reports that they exclaimed to their teacher: "See, that's the way to write! Short, with a little violence, a little sex, and some humor beside. Now, that's literature!"

20. *Ga'agu'ay le-Kissinger*, 36–37.

21. The park is called Ginat Shenkin, a small urban garden in the middle of the fabled Shenkin Street, which in the early 1990s became the symbol of Israel's new urban youth culture. Shenkin Street still stands for these values, although the concept has been commercialized. See, for example, the Shenkin shopping-as-lifestyle website that was launched last year at http://www.sheinkinstreet.co.il. The website's homepage states clearly that "Shenkin street is more than a Tel-Aviv street or neighborhood. It is a place that represents the spirit of urbanism in Israel."

22. *Tzinorot*, 130.

no real compassion for the child becomes clear in the end, when she cannot or will not offer the boy any words of consolation. The boy is thus left alone in the desert of a new Israeli society that does not make a real effort to provide a meaningful message that would unite its disparate elements under a redeeming narrative.

Still, the moral relativism in Keret's works is merely a surface affect. That is, it only functions as a stylistic element that is part of a surprisingly conservative and even old-fashioned morality that permeates his works. "Down with integration – let the wicked back into Hell" (*Tvutal ha'integratzia – yuchzeru harsha'im lagehenom*) concludes one of his other stories, a slogan that succinctly expresses Keret's romantic vision, his nostalgic desire for the moral clarity and simplicity of a pre-Intifada Israel where it was possible to tell the bad guys from the good.[23] Indeed, the story's protagonist, Avigdor, finds himself displaced in a bizarre and hellish universe, where vile and slimy science fiction creatures probe his body and tear pieces of his soul away to the heavenly sounds of a concerto: "Avigdor screamed with pain. For the first time in his life he had experienced a real sense of loss, and understood the meaning of emptiness." Hinting at the bygone world of clarity, order, and fixed values, the classical music exacerbates Avigdor's alienation, pain, and loss in the new world into which he is suddenly thrust.

The nostalgia for simpler, morally clearer times cloaked in postmodern parlance is one of the most powerful draws of Keret's literature, and accounts, probably more than anything else, for the wide appeal of his stories. By staying away from the problematics of Israel's uncomfortable position vis-à-vis the Palestinians, Keret both protests it and offers a way to escape it in his urban love stories, which make up the vast majority of his prose. This is a generalization, of course. Some of Keret's stories do struggle with the cultural and political complexities of Israeli life, like the story "The Son of the Head of the Mossad" (*Haben shel rosh hamosad*), which protests Israel's excesses of power not by escaping it but through a direct engagement with the most recognizable symbol of that power, the head of the Mossad, who manages to turn even his sensitive son into a killing monster like himself.[24] In any event, it is this nonconforming that lent Keret the ear of a young generation that has often been called *hador hamezuyan, hador hashavuz,* or *hador hashafuf* and that can roughly be translated as "the burnt-out generation," a generation that found little meaning in the old Zionist narrative after the first Intifada in 1987 and more so after the 1993 Oslo Peace Accord, and sought to substitute it with less parochial narratives.[25]

---

23. From the story "Rahamim and the Worm Man – an Evil Story" (*Rachamim ve'ish hatola'im – sipur merusha*) in *Tzinorot*, 60–61.

24. *Tzinorot*, 45–48.

25. The name comes from one of Aviv Gefen's songs, "It's Cloudy Now" (*Achshav me'unan*), which was released in 1993. Gefen was a teen idol in Israel in the 1990s,

Not everyone applauded this contribution to the Israeli literary discourse. The critic Yitzhak La'or, for instance, saw Keret as a modern Palmachnik, a reactionary writer who strikes a similarly contrived pose of cutesy, adolescent bravado in order to ingratiate himself with grown-ups.[26] Although I do not think Keret's writing is contrived, La'or's analogy is telling. The Palmachniks were the first generation of native-born Israelis and their literature, as simplistic and juvenile as it may seem today, was one of the first expressions of a new generation that was less troubled by the difficult experiences and complex differences that burdened their immigrant parents. Keret's insistence on writing differently, on abandoning the old paradigms and introducing a new literary and linguistic discourse, can be seen in a similar light. And while his current popularity may pass in time, one cannot ignore the chord it had struck or its authenticity as a popular, cultural expression.

The escapist qualities of Keret's new narrative may be problematic in some ways, but in other ways they also unite readers in different configurations that do away with more traditional and troubling divisions into Jews and Arabs, Ashkenazim and Sephardim (or Mizrahim), and so on. This can be seen most clearly by the new social paradigm that Keret promotes in his stories, which increasingly focus on relationships or coupling, not just with women actually, but with male friends and sometimes even with pets, but always and repeatedly relationships involving two.[27]

Keret uses love, romance, or abiding friendships as answers to some of the existential confusion his stories raise, to a world that lost its moral compass and makes little sense. This happens in the last story in his first anthology, *Pipelines*, a magic-realist story called "Crazy Glue" (*Devek meshuga*) in which a married? couple is isolated from everyone and everything around them in a brief moment of connubial bliss. In the story, the couple's relationship is threatened by an affair the husband has with a colleague at work. Fearful that his wife suspects the affair, the husband decides to come home early one day instead of staying out late with his mistress. On his return he

---

and his hit song was very influential. It came to define the mournful mood after the 1996 assassination of Premier Yitzhak Rabin, and inspired the title of Gadi Taub's important cultural study of that era, *A Dispirited Rebellion – Essays on Contemporary Israeli Culture* (*Hamered hashafuf*, Tel-Aviv: Kibbutz Me'uhad, 1997).

26. *Ha'aretz, Yoman Tel-Aviv*, Nov. 13, 1998.

27. The number of love stories alone increases from a fifth of the stories in the first anthology, *Pipelines*, to two-thirds of the stories in the last anthology, *Cheap Moon*. Historically, within the context of Hebrew literature, Keret's focus on romance stands out. Because of the unusual history of the Jews, especially in the modern era, most Hebrew writers were preoccupied with other matters and had little time for the kind of romance that was often at the center of other European literatures in the nineteenth century.

discovers that his wife glued down everything in the house and attached herself to the ceiling. Confused and annoyed at first, he tries to peel her off but then gives up and sees the humor in the situation. "I laughed too. She was so pretty and illogical, hanging upside down like that from the ceiling. Her long hair falling down, her breasts poised like two drops of water under her white T. So beautiful." He then climbs on a pile of books in order to kiss her. "I felt her tongue touching mine, the pile of books pushed away from under me; I felt that I was floating in the air, touching nothing, hanging only by her lips."

Keret's construction of an alternative social unit, the shift in focus he makes from the traditional tensions between the individual and the group to the more limited but more even relations that exist between two is a constructive protest. This, among other things, is one of Keret's important contributions: the wish to modify the old narrative to suit a changing Israel, not an Israel that subjects the individual to the service of the national-ethnic community, nor an Israel in which individual and separate group identities undermine the national community, but a more pluralistic society that makes room for individuals as part of a greater whole.

The third and last writer, Ronit Matalon, belongs in this discussion precisely because her preoccupation with identity comes from her refusal to deal with it on a political level.[28] This is perhaps surprising as many of Matalon's stories and certainly the first of her two novels, *The One Facing Us* (*Ze im hapanim elenu*) deal very obviously with Mizrahi history, identity, and culture.[29] *The One Facing Us* literally follows the dispersing of her Egyptian-Alexandrian family after the Second World War across the globe to Israel, Europe, Africa, and North America, and deals minutely with the consequent legacy of their Levantine origins and the different meanings it takes wherever they go.

On the biographical level Matalon can be easily associated with some of the major writers who brought the Mizrahim to the center of Israeli culture and to the pages of Hebrew literature. Men like Eli Amir and Sami Michael are the most obvious examples of writers who used their personal stories to break into the consciousness of an Ashkenazi-dominated culture.[30] But even more recent writers, such as Sami Shalom Chetrit in his collection of *Poems in Ashdodian* (*Shirim be'ashdodit*) and Yitzhak Gormezano-Goren in his

---

28. Matalon derisively labeled efforts to promote a Mizrahi cultural autonomy separate from Israeli culture as a whole as "Mizrahi Disneyland." See her interview with Rona Ra'anan-Shafrir, "No One Has to Read This" (*Af echad lo chayav likro et ze*), *Kolbo*, 20.3.92.

29. Ronit Matalon, *Ze im hapanim elenu* (Tel-Aviv: Am Oved, 1995). By "Mizrahi" I mean non-Ashkenazi Israeli.

30. See for instance Sami Michael's *Hasut* (Protection, Tel-Aviv: Am Oved, 1977) and Eli Amir's *Tarnegol Kaparot* (Scapegoat, Tel-Aviv: Am Oved, 1993).

Alexandrian Trilogy (*hatrilogia ha'alexandronit*) still use autobiography
for personal and political reasons as much as for "pure" literary reasons, if
such a division can even be made.[31] That is, they use literature to announce
their very existence as non-Ashkenazim and to legitimize their difference.[32]

Matalon, on the other hand, does something else, I think. Rather than
protest her discrimination as Mizrahi through various modes of expression
(indignation, blame, self-righteousness), she arouses readers' empathy by
the patent lack of pathos, commiseration, or a sense of grievance. Not that
her characters lack reasons to protest the economic and political disadvantage they experience in Israel. Yet discrimination is never understood as
being directed at a specific group of people because of the kind of people
they are or the places they came from. Rather, the characters' reactions to it
are used to explore alienation as a human condition.

This becomes very clear as Esther, the teenage narrator, tells the stories
of her various family members who are scattered throughout the globe.
Esther's visit to her wealthy uncle in Cameroon in the 1970s paints a picture
of an existentially displaced man who lives in time rather than in a specific
place. A refugee of the great Levantine tradition of early twentieth-century
Alexandria, Jacqou Sicourelle is an Egyptian Jew who lives as a white
Frenchman in post-colonial Africa. Married to a non-Jewish Frenchwoman,
Jacqou consorts neither with the white ex-colonialists nor with the black
natives, preferring instead the company of Lebanese merchants who are
similarly displaced. Esther's search for her missing aunt Nadine in New
York, at the end of the book, is just as tragic. Severed from the family early
on to marry a wealthy American Jew, Nadine seems to lead a virtual life,
existing, like the books she works with in the New York public library, on
paper only, in the letters she sends over the years to her brother in Israel.
Indeed, her demise is a fitting closure to the imaginary life she led: Nadine is
reported to have literally vanished into thin air, rising into the sky one day
outside of her apartment building.

Against the insubstantial and tortured existence of these and other characters in the novel, the members of Esther's family who emigrated to Israel
and reside in it seem to fare much better. This is not to say that their lives
there are easy—her uncle Moise leaves his kibbutz because he is discriminated against as Mizrahi—but they do seem to have the weight and the meaning
that is missing from the lives of the others. The Zionist Moise expends great
efforts to bring his family to Israel and remains one of the only common
points of contact between its scattered members. More importantly,

---

31. *Shirim be'ashdodit* (Tel-Aviv: Andalus, 2003), *Mosheh-Moris-u-Musa : o Pesach
    Aleksandroni* (Tel-Aviv: Bimat Kedem Lesifrut, 1986).

32. A good analogy would be the preoccupation with the shtetl in maskilic and even in
    revivalist literature in which the writers announce their secular existence in the midst
    of a traditional Jewish world.

Esther's mother, Ines, has one of the book's most poignant and revealing exchanges with her American niece Zouza, who is visiting Israel in search of her roots. "Are you sorry you left Egypt, Tante?" the niece asks. "Sorry?" the mother is surprised at the question. "No, I'm not sorry. Sure, I miss it—I miss it like crazy. But I'm not sorry. Our life there was over, Zouza," the mother reflects. "But what about your roots there," the niece insists, "what is there for you here?" to which the mother replies emphatically and somewhat curtly, "roots shmoots. A person doesn't need roots, Zouza, a person needs a home" (277–278).

Although biography is certainly the point of origin in Matalon's works, it is primarily used as the colored pieces of glass in a kaleidoscope, in order to refract alienation and estrangement in its various permutations. Any connection between Matalon's biography and the lives of her characters remains forced, resisted by her very text that stands in the way of such facile associations. If there is one definite statement in Matalon's writing, then, it is that identity is not only fragmented, but also constantly evolving, despite the incessant quest for a peaceful, familiar, and safe place, in other words—a home. *The One Facing Us* questions the ability of ever finding one.

This does not mean that Matalon gives up on it. But the paradox that animates her writing, especially in this novel, is that while the creation of identity is inevitably linked to specific national, ethnic, local, political, or gender values, these must never be allowed to dictate it in any rigid way. While Matalon's characters are informed by all these predetermined connections, they nevertheless remain free to reconfigure them privately. This is also the point at which Matalon and Keret converge. Both reject the former narratives not so much because of their Zionist or national-Jewish content as much as for their tendency to rigidly define and fix Israeli Jewish identity. Neither Keret nor Matalon want to throw the baby out with the bath water. They do not give up their duty and their privilege to define such identity. But they insist on doing so in their own way and demand that what they have to say be accepted as legitimate, though not binding definition of "who's an Israeli."

While none of these writers offers a decisive or coherent picture of a new Israel, their refusal to engage in simplistic identity politics of either schools—the parochial Jewish identity politics of the old Zionist school as well as the minority identity politics of the more universalist, postmodern school—is promising, especially given Israel's own obsession with identity and the region's preoccupation with it in general. Taken together, then, the three writers I mentioned offer a picture of an emerging pluralistic society in Israel; a society that hints not only at the chance of a more harmonious coexistence between its disparate parts, but perhaps also between itself and its neighbors at some point in the future.

V.
WRITERS, CRITICS, AND CANONS

Bellow's Canon

JONATHAN ROSEN

> And now as new anthologies came out I went down to Brentano's
> basement and checked them. Humboldt's poems were omitted. The
> bastards, the literary funeral directors and politicians who put
> together these collections had no use for old-hat Humboldt.
>
> Saul Bellow, *Humboldt's Gift*

Saul Bellow has Charlie Citrine chide the "literary funeral directors" for leaving out poor Humboldt, but when he came to edit *Great Jewish Short Stories*, Bellow himself left out Delmore Schwartz, who provided the literary model for Humboldt and whose story "In Dreams Begin Responsibilities" certainly deserves a spot alongside Isaac Rosenfeld's "King Solomon" and Philip Roth's "Epstein."[1] Bellow wasn't neglecting Schwartz, of course; he was leaving a space for *Humboldt's Gift*, published ten years later and one of the great literary shrines in modern fiction. And it is important to note that Bellow left himself out of *Great Jewish Short Stories*, too. Was this an act of modesty? Is it a reflection of his own sense of himself as a great American writer, not a great Jewish one? Or is the whole book a statement of his literary project—an arrow pointing toward his future work?

It is perhaps unfair to look at an anthology as an act of canon formation, but how often does a great Jewish writer put together a book called *Great Jewish Short Stories*? Bellow's anthology offers a useful way of looking not only at this greatest of twentieth-century writers, but at particular problems facing modern Jewish writers and their relationship to a modern Jewish canon.

Great Jewish Short Stories was published in 1963, the year of my birth, and so I feel a special connection to it. The book was on my parents' shelf, and though it is out of print at present, it passed through more than 11 printings and is constantly invoked, if only for the famous anecdote it contains about Bellow's meeting with Agnon, in which Agnon tells Bellow that to be "safe" he must be translated into Hebrew. *Great Jewish Short Stories* is a remarkable artifact of American Jewish writing in the middle of the last century. In certain ways it anticipates Ruth Wisse's seminal *Modern Jewish Canon* but in others it resists the idea of a Jewish canon altogether, even as it bundles Agnon, Peretz, Sholem Aleichem, Isaac Babel, I.B. Singer, Grace

---

1. I am grateful to my mother, Norma Rosen, for pointing out the irony of Schwartz's exclusion.

Paley, and Philip Roth all under the same roof. It is, almost in the manner of a complex novel, a work at odds with itself.

For a long time I saw *Great Jewish Short Stories* as a way for Bellow to create for himself a sort of Jewish literary family tree, perhaps in the way Sholem Aleichem did when he called Mendele the grandfather of Yiddish writing. But the closer I looked, the stranger that family tree seemed—and not simply because Bellow isn't part of it. Bellow's descriptions of the writers he includes offer keys to his ambivalence about the existence of a modern Jewish canon. Consider his assertion that Sholem Aleichem "was a great humorist, but a raconteur rather than a literary artist." It is hard to imagine Bellow making this comment about Mark Twain. Though he clearly loves Sholem Aleichem—he used to read his work aloud in Yiddish to his father—he accepts the persona adopted by the author over the artistry involved in creating that persona. He relegates Sholem Aleichem to a folk realm, though surely he knew otherwise.

Bellow's way of distancing himself from the very authors he includes is felt even more keenly in his introductory remarks about Agnon. "Mr. Agnon feels secure in his ancient tradition," he observes. Is "his" ancient tradition not also Bellow's? Does it not belong to all the writers Bellow includes? Bellow is speaking specifically about the Hebrew language, but "tradition" is a strange word to use, as if Hebrew were a metonym for an entire religious tradition as well and one that in this context is not Bellow's but Agnon's.

The story Bellow tells about Agnon and translation is introduced as "an amusing and enlightening conversation" that Bellow had with Agnon in Jerusalem. What makes it amusing and the word "enlightening" ironic is the obvious fact that Bellow is clearly the more famous, more widely read author. It is assumed, correctly, that the reader will share Bellow's gentle bemusement before the idea that until he is gathered back into the bosom of Hebrew he will not quite exist as a writer. Bellow is like the lion in Aesop's fable, laughing with kingly generosity at the mouse that says that perhaps some day he will save the lion's life.

The humor in that story enacts the humor that Bellow describes as a common heritage of all Jewish writers. He retells a joke his father used to tell about the Angel of Death and an old woodcutter, and so makes humor his literal as well as his cultural patrimony. But when he turns Agnon's Hebrew into "his ancient tradition," he is not merely speaking up for multilingual Jewish culture but resisting the idea of a core particularist culture that shapes a sense of shared destiny. As Wisse observes in *The Modern Jewish Canon,* language is the most complex element of the canon. There is a healthy iconoclasm in resisting the authority of any language, even one's own, but it is shadowed as well by a resistance to any core, identifying element of Jewishness.

Perhaps all Jewish writers have a little of the wicked son of the Haggadah in them, since to write you must step outside your own tradition, whatever it is. Bellow simultaneously emphasizes the multilingual nature of Jewish writing, referring to, if not including, the French André Schwartz-Bart and the Italian Italo Svevo, as well as making a place for Yiddish writers and Russian writers and German writers and English-language writers in his anthology. But the suggestion of a primary Jewish language, and one anchored in the specificity of a religious tradition, makes Bellow uncomfortable and this is obvious in the story he tells about Agnon.

Bellow is respectful, certainly, and even admiring of Agnon, who would precede him by a decade to the Nobel prize, but in addition to his comment about "his" ancient tradition, he gets further revenge in his thumbnail introduction to the lone Agnon story—which is also the lone modern Hebrew story—included in the anthology: "A great Hebraist, he is also a student of Ghetto traditions." Bellow does not specify what he means by "Ghetto" traditions—Jewish folklore, perhaps? Diaspora culture? Bellow himself seems to be putting Agnon in the ghetto when he adds: "Entirely immersed in Hebrew and Yiddish literature, he apparently has little interest in Western literary traditions."

Even the slightest acquaintance with Agnon's work, which Bellow surely had, contradicts that statement. Bellow mentions Agnon's eleven-year period in Germany, spent between Jerusalem sojourns, without mentioning how deeply immersed Agnon became in western literary culture. It was in Germany, attending philosophy lectures, that Agnon (who had been tutored in German as a child) met his eventual publisher, Zalman Schocken. And even if Bellow had not read Agnon's letters to Schocken—in which Agnon describes reading an essay by Zola on Flaubert in one breath "because anything on Flaubert goes straight to my heart"—and requests from Schocken a copy of the "Chanson de Roland"—Bellow surely would have been aware of the powerful influence on Agnon of another of Schocken's authors, Kafka. Even a cursory encounter with Agnon tells the reader that Kafka is as powerful a presence in Agnon's work as Nachman of Bratslav, and that an aspect of his literary project is to add Jewish signposts to Kafka's anonymous labyrinth. But Kafka is himself absent from *Great Jewish Short Stories*, despite the fact that Kafka was quite interested in "Ghetto traditions."

Writers are notoriously unreliable when it comes to canon formation because, among other reasons, they wish to be their own parents. This is as true for Agnon as for Bellow, who can't necessarily be blamed for mistaking Agnon's literary origins because Agnon, who took his own name from one of his own short stories, was busy inventing himself too. He also pretended to the world that he had sprung from "ghetto traditions" and not, therefore, literary ones, much as Robert Frost seemed to many to have risen out of the New Hampshire soil, despite the fact that he grew up in San Francisco and knew Latin and Greek better than T.S. Eliot did.

Writers are usually divided against themselves. Bellow has Augie March declare, "I am an American, Chicago-born," at the beginning of *The Adventures of Augie March*. Though the sentence reads from left to right, its linguistic undertow pulls in the other direction, so that by the time it ends—"sometimes an innocent knock, sometimes a not-so-innocent"—the sentence, like the entire novel, has been tugged toward the Yiddish that Bellow spoke as a child. The challenge for any canon-former is corralling so many divided selves into a unified tradition without the whole thing falling apart.

Agnon is tweaking Bellow when he urges Hebrew translation on him, but Agnon was in turn tweaked by I.B. Singer. Singer's son, Israel Zamir, in his memoir *Journey to My Father,* recalls going with Singer to the 92nd Street Y to hear Agnon in 1967. Afterward, Zamir reports:

> Dozens of admirers crowded around Agnon, and my father, who had wished to shake his fellow writer's hand, had to forgo that pleasure. "Too bad there aren't any translators so his books could be distributed widely," said my father.

This comment is even more appropriate to Bellow's anthology because Bellow includes "Gimpel the Fool," in his own translation. In that sense, Bellow is present in the volume, not as an author but as the person launching Singer's career by gathering him into American literature and guaranteeing that his work will be, in Agnon's words about literature smuggled into Hebrew, "safe."

The three great Jewish writers of the twentieth century, each a recipient of the Nobel prize in a different language, each uncomfortable with an aspect of the other's existence, are all bound together not merely by rivalry but by an anxiety over their relationship to tradition, to language, and even to geographical choices; it is this anxiety and ambivalence that perhaps renders them quintessentially Jewish writers as much as anything else they might share.

Writers are the real canon creators, even though they are self-serving and unreliable, because the books they champion and absorb trail them into eternity. Sholem Aleichem decided that Mendele—missing from Bellow's anthology altogether—was the grandfather of Yiddish literature because he needed a family tree. I.B. Singer, for his part, unmade a Jewish canon altogether by focusing on Dostoyevsky, Knut Hamsun, and Baudelaire when speaking in his Nobel Prize address of the influences on him. He owned that the Yiddish language and its speakers were an influence, but not other Yiddish writers, with the exception of his long-dead brother. Singer ignores other Jewish writers completely in his address. Since writers want the comfort of tradition and precedent, and simultaneously long to be self-created, they are constantly defying the very thing that created them. Singer, while speaking up for Yiddish, in Yiddish, nevertheless plants the suggestion that Yiddish might just be the language fate translated him into but that, in fact, he is a modernist master whose true language is literature and whose true home is with Baudelaire and Dostoyevsky. English is, therefore, no more a traduction of his deepest purposes than is any other language.

Every Jewish writer wrestles with the secret fear that the letter killeth and the spirit sets you free. Since Jewish tradition is not a literary tradition, the closer you get to it the closer you get to a world in which it is commentary and not new creation, repetition not invention, adherence not deviation, that is most prized. This is feared most keenly of all in America, where tradition itself is suspect, and the prevailing cry is "make it new."

Bellow begins his anthology with *Tobit*—apocryphal for Jews but canonical for Catholics—and notes in *Tobit* a mixture of "laughter and trembling" that for Bellow has been the hallmark of Jewish writing for 2000 years. He notes that one finds this mixture in the stories of I.B. Singer, too, and in all the stories he's included. But when he offers his thumbnail introduction to *Tobit*, he ends by observing, "Tobit, in exile, cannot forget that he is a Jew. It is possible to compare him with Joyce's Leopold Bloom." It is fascinating that Bellow, at the moment he identifies an ineluctable core Jewish consciousness, closes the circuit from *Tobit* to the present not with Malamud or Singer or Roth but with Leopold Bloom, the half-Jewish character of a lapsed Catholic author. But Leopold Bloom is in many ways the literary father of Bellow's *Herzog*. Whether Bellow is Judaizing the entire Western canon or baptizing Herzog in it—or doing a little of both—is one of those unresolvable ambiguities that lives inside the complexity of all Jewish fictional creation and perhaps all fictional creation in general.

No canon is ever complete for a writer or the writer could not write. All novelists look at their shelves the way Artur Sammler looks at his in the first sentence of *Mr. Sammler's Planet*. Sammler "took in the books and papers of his West Side bedroom and suspected strongly that they were the wrong books, the wrong papers." The answers in books are insufficient to the world Sammler finds himself in—a post-Holocaust nightmare where contemporary American urban decay is dusted with memories of fallen European culture, and where modern diversions seem like a profanation of human suffering and the dire state of civilization. What's missing from Mr. Sammler's shelf is *Mr. Sammler's Planet*.

It is tempting to say that what is missing from *Great Jewish Short Stories* is Bellow himself. But is Bellow creating a club he himself does not wish to join? Or is he creating a space for himself to which he can someday retire? Perhaps the best answer is that he is doing both. He is like Walt Whitman, whom Bellow invokes in his introduction: "both in and out of the game and watching and wondering at it."

But there is one element of *Great Jewish Short Stories* that challenges the notion of a living Jewish canon so thoroughly that the book almost fails to recover from it. In his introduction, Bellow focuses on the place of laughter in Jewish stories. (He never really says there is a literary tradition, only individual "stories," but his book implies one anyway.) The laughter Bellow means may be intermingled with, and at times indistinguishable from, trembling, but it is there, a sly, ironic response to the universe that is life-affirming. As Bellow puts it, "The real secret, the ultimate mystery, may never reveal itself to the earnest thought of a Spinoza, but when we laugh (the idea is remotely Hassidic) our minds refer us to God's existence. Chaos is *exposed*."

The last story in Bellow's anthology, Isaiah Spiegel's "A Ghetto Dog," shares certain ironic elements with the other stories. But it is a story that extinguishes laughter, and its position in the anthology is important.

After conventionally ironic American stories, after Isaac Rosenfeld's "King Solomon," Grace Paley's "Goodbye and Goodluck," Philip Roth's "Epstein," there is Isaiah Spiegel's "A Ghetto Dog." Roth, whom Bellow defends for his irreverent humor in his general introduction, might well have ended the anthology with a promise of the future, though "Epstein" is a silly burlesque that does not in fact hold up very well. But Bellow breaks the rough chronology of his anthology, and he breaks the sense that America is the new direction of Jewish fiction, with "A Ghetto Dog," which was published in English in 1954 and written in Yiddish by a writer living in Israel whose work can scarcely be classified as Israeli. There is something so final in "A Ghetto Dog" that it serves more as a gravestone than a capstone and threatens to undermine the very tradition Bellow is, however ambivalently, defining.

"A Ghetto Dog," a story of astonishing power, is a seemingly straightforward account of an assimilated Jewish Pole driven out of the Christian neighborhood where she has lived for many years and forced into the Lodz ghetto. She is old and widowed and she brings her old, devoted dog, Nicky, with her. She is housed with a Jewish whore named Big Rose, who resents her presence and hates the dog but who softens when the old dog comes back one night, bloodied and torn by barbed wire. The two women together care for Nicky.

The dog, already a half-human reminder of the old woman's deceased husband, takes on larger and larger symbolic meaning. Nicky is the emblem of the two women and the whole beaten Jewish people. The once-pampered companion of deracinated Jews, Nicky is nevertheless a "ghetto dog" in the end, and so is the woman who shares her dog's fate: the old woman refuses to let go of the leash when forced with all the other Jewish inhabitants to hand her dog over to the Nazis. She winds up inside a pen, encircled by a pack of Jewish animals destined for slaughter.

One might say that this story fits perfectly well in the tradition Bellow has established, where trembling and laughter mingle. In the very first paragraph of his introduction, Bellow notes, as an especially Jewish, comic element, the fact that a dog trots after the angel in *Tobit*, and there are so many symbolic dogs in Jewish literature one could almost create a canine canon to accommodate them. But the ghetto dog is in the end indistinguishable from the Jewish woman, and this final dehumanization contains no glint of comic redemption because there is no distinction between man and beast, even if one decides that the dog-like Jews are more human than their bestial Nazi degraders. The dog may represent the old woman, but the old woman just as fully represents the dog.

"A Ghetto Dog" is about nothing less than the death of humanity:

> The widow and Big Rose halted before the German. He was waiting for the old woman to let go of the leash. But, instead of letting go, she wound the leash still tighter about her wrist and even her forearm. She did this with her eyes closed, the way a Jew winds the straps of a phylactery on his forearm. The German snatched the leash. The widow staggered on her old legs, since Nicky was by now pulling her into the pound. She let herself be dragged along.

This is more than an old woman facing her fate. Wound around her arm, the leash is like the strap of *tefilin*. The "ghetto traditions" of Agnon have become traditions of another ghetto; the thing that elevated Jews now is invoked as a thing that sinks them. The allusion is more than a bitter way of gathering the old assimilated Jew into a religious fold she resisted her whole life. It is Judaism itself that is dying. And there is the suggestion too that perhaps even the yoke of the commandments, the shut-eyed devotion, the mark of Jewish difference, has bound the Jews for slaughter.

Though we know that the story was written by a man living in Israel, which is important, and though we know that the story was written by a survivor—and so whatever finality that happens in the story is perhaps over-ridden by our knowledge of a recording consciousness—the story itself issues a challenge to the very tradition Bellow has been exploring in his own complex way. It issues a challenge to the recording voice as a sign of survival.

Bellow notes in his introduction that, "In defeat, a story contains the hope of vindication, of justice." But there is no recovery from this final story, and no justice. All thoughts of Philip Roth's randy old man and Grace Paley's wise-ass, Yiddishe Wife of Bath vanish in the face of it. The end of Spiegel's story, which is the end of Bellow's book, is a challenge to the reader—and to Bellow, which is to say to the Jewish writer, himself:

> Big Rose saw another wicket fly open on the other side and someone begin driving the dogs out into an open field. The widow stood up, leaned on her small silver-knobbed cane, and, with Nicky leading, started toward the field....
>
> Big Rose wrapped the small black shawl more tightly about her head. She did not want to hear the dull, tinny sounds that came from the sharp-edged shovels scooping up the frozen ground of the Balut. It was only the wind, playing upon the shovels that delved the narrow black pits—only the wind, chanting its chill night song.

The graves that Big Rose hears being dug, but that she ignores, are being prepared for her, and for all the Jews, as much as for their dogs, but she does not wish to hear it and turns away.

In 1991 I interviewed Bellow for the *Forward* and, in the course of a wide-ranging conversation, I asked him if he had any regrets about his career. To my surprise Bellow told me that he had one that was particularly keen. In the late 1940s he had been living in Paris working on *The Adventures of Augie March*. Paris, Bellow noted, was full of Holocaust survivors and, as a Yiddish-speaker, Bellow was aware of their stories. But, he told me, he shut them out. He wanted to write his freewheeling America picaresque. In his words, "I wanted my American seven-layer cake." If he had incorporated the stories of those survivors, he could not have written *Augie March*, his breakthrough book; he could not have become the writer he wanted to be. One might say he was Big Rose in "A Ghetto Dog," turning away from the gravediggers.

It is fascinating to wonder what sort of novel he might have written had he incorporated the stories of those survivors but one doesn't have to wonder too hard. *Mr. Sammler's Planet*" published seven years after *Great Jewish Stories*, places a Holocaust survivor at the center. Sammler is, as Wisse has observed in *The Modern Jewish Canon*, a highly Westernized survivor, steeped not in Agnon's "ghetto traditions" but in the London of H.G. Wells. His voice is not Yiddish but Oxonian English. But he is also someone who has literally sprung from one of those graves we hear being dug in "A Ghetto Dog."

In some sense, what is missing from *Great Jewish Short Stories* is a story like *Mr. Sammler's Planet*, which combines American insouciance and dark European tragic awareness. What is unanswerable in "A Ghetto Dog," the bleak acknowledgment of tradition-ending finality—both Jewish and literary—finds not an answer but a dialogic expression in *Mr. Sammler's Planet*.

In a wonderful essay called "Where Do We Go from Here: The Future of Fiction," Bellow finds hope for the novel in a statement by Dostoyevsky:

> When he was writing "The Brothers Karamazov" and had just ended the famous conversation between Ivan and Alyosha, in which Ivan, despairing of justice, offers to return his ticket to God, Dostoyevsky wrote to one of his correspondents that he must now attempt, through Father Zossima, to answer Ivan's arguments. But he has in advance all but devastated his own position. This, I think, is the greatest achievement possible in a novel of ideas. It becomes art when the views most opposite to the author's own are allowed to exist in full strength.

Bellow, in this remarkable passage, does a little of what Singer did: he is enlisting an anti-Semitic Russian to articulate what is in many ways a talmudic enterprise. But it renders the talmudic ability to hold contradictory elements in hand simultaneously a literary project. Bellow locates in a western novelist an idea that is as central to Judaism as the combination of wit and trembling that Bellow identifies. Indeed, Judaism's ability to balance wit and trembling is itself a testament to this rabbinic, dialogic concept that for Bellow is the height of novelistic achievement.

Mr. Sammler's Planet holds together not only the horror of the Holocaust and the diversions of modern American life, it manages to merge western literary traditions with ancient Jewish impulses. The last line of *Mr. Sammler's Planet* is an evocation of the last line of Joyce's *Ulysses*, in which Molly Bloom, remembering what it felt like to say yes to sex with Leopold Bloom, declares, ecstatically, "yes I said yes I will Yes." This becomes transformed into Sammler's post-Holocaust, theological affirmation in the last sentence of *Mr. Sammler's Planet*: "...we all know, God, that we know, we know, we know."

Bellow has reversed the conventional pattern of modern Jewish literature; he hasn't secularized religious forms, he has transformed a secular modernist formulation back into a religious one. One might almost say that, the "ghetto traditions" of Agnon have come calling on Western literary traditions. The mouse has indeed rescued the lion. Bellow found a way to double back to an older religious tradition that underpins and transcends a modern Jewish canon and in doing so found a way to keep it going. And this religious impulse offers a way past the finality of "A Ghetto Dog." Bellow invokes and affirms the impossibility of a tradition that nevertheless endures.

Bellow is in some sense like the old woodcutter in the joke he tells in the introduction to *Great Jewish Short Stories*, who, unable to shoulder his burden of sticks, calls for the Angel of Death. But when the Angel of Death appears and asks what he wants, the woodcutter, thinking fast, asks only for Death to give him a hand with his wood. Bellow starts out like one of the "literary funeral directors" who make up the anthologies in *Humboldt's Gift*. Anthologies, like the canon itself, spell a sort of death for the living writer. But somehow, in the very process of spelling out the end, the anthologist-writer, which is to say the tradition-conscious Jewish writer, discovers a desire to keep going. And perhaps Bellow's father, who told him the joke about the woodcutter, deserves the last word not merely about his joke but about modern Jewish writing: "'So, you see, when it comes to dying...,' my father said, 'nobody is really ready.'"

The Eicha Problem

DARA HORN

One learns a lot from one's children, but not always in the ways one expects. When my daughter was born in 2005, a friend who, like me, is an American Jewish novelist gave her a picture book called *Doctor De Soto*, by the children's author and New Yorker cartoonist William Steig. Despite knowing no English (or any other language, for that matter), my daughter became absolutely riveted to this book at the age of five months, which means that I have been compelled to read it to her twelve times a day almost every day since then. Through the potent combination of receiving a doctorate in literature from Ruth Wisse and being forced to commit this picture book to memory, I have thought about this particular literary work far more deeply than anyone should. And with Ruth Wisse's and William Steig's help, I have diagnosed the deepest and most disturbing problem of Jewish history and culture, one to which Wisse has devoted her entire career, but which she has never actually named. No, I'm not joking. Allow Doctor De Soto to explain.

Doctor De Soto, a mouse, is a dentist working in a town with a diverse population of anthropomorphic animals. Although his patients range from chipmunks to horses, he quite logically refuses to admit predators into his practice. But one day he makes an exception when a fox, weeping in pain from a toothache, appears at his office door. While under anesthesia for an extraction, the dreaming fox rather unsubtly announces his intent to eat the dentist upon completion of his two-day treatment, with the help of the new gold tooth the dentist will provide for him. That night, the dentist's wife suggests to Doctor De Soto that this patient might perhaps be too dangerous to readmit. Yet the dentist is insistent: "'Once I start a job,' said the dentist firmly, 'I finish it. My father was the same way'."[1]

This being a children's book, of course, a clever plan is hatched, and no one is eaten in the end. But there is something deeply disturbing about the entire plot of this apparently conventional story. In trying to decipher my unease with the book, my husband commented that it seemed odd that a society advanced enough to have dental care would be so primitive that its members would be regularly eaten by their fellow citizens. At first I agreed. But then I thought of my husband's own grandparents, whose families were murdered in Europe by a society with excellent dentistry, and I realized that

---

1. William Steig, *Doctor De Soto* (New York: Farar Straus & Giroux, 1982), n.p.

Doctor De Soto's world isn't odd at all. No, what is odd in this book is the dentist's insistence that it is his moral obligation to offer treatment to a known predator with a stated intention to eat him—and not merely to relieve the predator's pain, but, in fact, to *arm his own murderer* by providing the fox with the tooth that he knows full well will be used to eat him. Suddenly I was reminded of an uncomfortable moment in Ruth Wisse's popular lecture course on modern Jewish literature at Harvard that served as the basis for *The Modern Jewish Canon*. In an aside concerning the Oslo Accords and Israel's subsequent assistance in the creation of a Palestinian security force, Wisse, her passion tempered only by cold logic, announced to the class that "the Jews are the only nation in the world that has ever armed its enemies in the hope of achieving peace." She then repeated this statement, and even instructed the students to write it down.[2] Most students simply stared at her, puzzled as to what on earth this might have to do with Saul Bellow. But this was in 2002, at the height of the second intifada in Israel and just months after the 9/11 terrorist attacks in the U.S., and the sense of siege on campus among Jewish students was higher than I had ever felt it in my short lifetime. I suddenly looked at the course's reading list and understood what Wisse meant. Despite its omission from Wisse's canon, *Doctor De Soto* (whose author, it is worth mentioning, was Jewish) is a deeply Jewish book. The absurdity it presents is a simple illustration of a profound Jewish psychological illness, which I will call the Eicha Problem. And the most disturbing part of this problem is that, just like Doctor De Soto's, our fathers were the same way.

Eicha, or the Book of Lamentations, is one of the Hebrew Bible's shortest books, but the punch in the gut that it gives the Jewish people has caused the longest-lasting stomachache in the history of the world. The book is purportedly a song of mourning, a five-chapter alphabetical acrostic poem lamenting the destruction of the first Temple by the Babylonians, their sacking of Jerusalem, and the subsequent exile of the Jews to Babylonia for what became half a century. But it isn't an elegy of mourning as much as it is a rant of regret and vengeance—and its regretful vengeance, oddly, isn't primarily directed against the Babylonians, but against the Jews themselves. Despite the poem's graphic depictions of what today might be called war crimes perpetrated by the Babylonian forces against Jewish civilians, Baby-

---

2. Wisse had already publicly expressed this sentiment in the Zalman C. Bernstein Memorial Lecture in Jewish Political Thought, delivered in Jerusalem on January 20, 2000. She later adapted the lecture for print, where the sentiment appears in writing: "The Oslo Accords of 1993 made Israel the first sovereign nation in memory to arm its declared enemy with the expectation of gaining security." Ruth Wisse, "The Brilliant Failure of Jewish Foreign Policy," *Azure* 10 (Winter 2001): 141. Her most recent monograph, *Jews and Power* (New York: Schocken, 2007), a further exploration of these ideas, had not yet been published when the present essay was written.

lonia is never mentioned by name in the book's five chapters. While "the enemy" occasionally merits a reference, such references are often delivered with no more anger than one might direct at a hurricane or any other "act of God," which is, of course, precisely the point. Even Nebuchadnezzar, the Babylonian tyrant who surely would qualify as the Slobodan Milosevic or Saddam Hussein of his day, merits no mention in Eicha. So who are the villains in this catastrophe of biblical proportions? The Jews! According to the logic of Eicha, the destruction of Zion was not a catastrophe at all, but (if the reader will permit the anachronism) a tragedy in the classical sense: it was not the Babylonians but the Jews themselves who brought about this destruction, by provoking God into a dramatic demonstration of divine justice to punish them for maddeningly unspecified sins.

One can appreciate, to a point, the theological imperative of Eicha's interpretation of events. If one is to believe in a just God, it might be argued, one must accept on faith that one's suffering is somehow deserved, because otherwise one might be stranded with the possibility that life on earth, with its alarming frequency of apparently arbitrary pain and loss, has no significance at all, that our actions carry no consequence whatsoever in the shaping of our own destinies. But this is hardly the only theologically meaningful interpretation of suffering. In fact, it isn't even the only interpretation of suffering within the theologically manifest world of the Hebrew Bible itself. Flipping just a few pages away in the Tanakh, we find a very different understanding of disaster in the Book of Job. Job is explicitly tortured by God without deserving it, and he ultimately dismisses his peers' suggestions that he has somehow earned his pain. God's subsequent response to Job, containing some of the Bible's most beautiful poetry, suggests the limits of human reason and imagination in understanding undeserved destruction. Yet Job has never represented the Jewish national outlook. In fact, he is so distanced from Jewish culture that he is not even an Israelite; talmudic rabbis argue about where he fits into Jewish history precisely because he fits nowhere at all.[3] There is no melody designated for reading the Book of Job aloud, because unlike most books of the Hebrew Bible, it is never even publicly chanted. Eicha, on the other hand, merits not only its own melody, but an entire annual fast day in which the whole nation repeatedly invokes its interpretation of history. We are regularly reminded that it was all our fault. And, as any parent of young children knows, repetition works, because thousands of years and many cultural and religious revolutions later even the most secular among us, whether we realize it or not, still believe it is our fault.

The Eicha Problem is the tendency of Jews to believe that anti-Semitism—causeless hatred inevitably leading to sadistic violence against them—is actu-

---

3. Bavli Bava Batra 14b.

ally their fault. It is a problem that spreads itself far and wide across Jewish literature, appearing everywhere from the Mishnah to modern Hebrew poetry to articles on yesterday's blogs. In Eicha itself, of course, the concept could not be more obvious: the priests slain in the sanctuary (2:20), the raped girls (5:11), the captive princes (5:12), the orphans and widows (5:3), the starving children (4:4), and the women who boil their own children for food (2:20), along with all the other demeaned ones of Israel, are simply enduring divine punishment, for "Jerusalem has severely sinned" (1:8). But the self-flagellation of Eicha, which also appears in like-minded biblical books such as Jeremiah and Judges (where God is similarly portrayed as using neighboring nations as weapons to punish the people for their sins), is only the opening salvo against the Jewish psyche. The Talmud makes it even worse. What really caused the destruction of Jerusalem? asks Tractate Shabbat 119b, offering ample answers from renowned rabbinic minds. According to Abayye, "Jerusalem would not have been destroyed except that they [the Jews] violated the Sabbath." According to Rabbi Abahu, "Jerusalem would not have been destroyed except that they [the Jews] neglected to recite the Shema morning and evening." According to Rabbi Hamnuna, "Jerusalem would not have been destroyed except that they [the Jews] neglected the children of the house of study [i.e. religious education]." According to Ulla, "Jerusalem would not have been destroyed except that they [the Jews] were not ashamed in front of one another." According to Rabbi Shimon bar Aba, "Jerusalem would not have been destroyed except that they [the Jews] did not rebuke one another." And, most famously, Rabbi Yochanan in Tractate Gittin 55b–56a, referring to the destruction of the Second Temple by the Romans, insisted that Jerusalem would not have been destroyed except for "causeless hatred," by which he meant causeless hatred *among the Jews themselves*. It is worth noting that none of these brilliant rabbis ever claimed that Jerusalem would not have been destroyed except for the Babylonians' superior weaponry. Or except for Nebuchadnezzar's megalomania. Or except for a very different sort of causeless hatred—the causeless hatred of the Babylonians (or Romans) against the Jews. But in the world of Eicha—a world where Jews have now lived for millennia and that is reflected in Jewish religious literature from biblical times through the present day, covering aggressions ranging from the Romans to the Nazis and beyond—it is inconceivable that the destruction of the Jews is anything other than a divinely ordained punishment for Jewish sins. The perpetrator is irrelevant, since the real perpetrator is God. And justice is also irrelevant, since the sadistic aggression is itself believed to be an act of justice. The way to stop anti-Semitism is to stop sinning against God.

This way of thinking is so ancient, so religious, so unironically divorced from the tangible world, that it really ought to have nothing whatsoever to do with Ruth Wisse's decidedly modern *Modern Jewish Canon*, particularly since Jewish modernity was supposed to be defined by a radical revision of precisely this sort of traditional thinking. Modernity for the Jews was supposed to involve their drastic repossession of their own destiny through the Zionist revolution, expressed through a physical repossession of their own land, a cultural repossession of their own language, an intellectual repossession of their own religion, and a psychological repossession of responsibility for their own fate. Brave men and women achieved all this in what can only be described as one of the most successful revolutions in modern history. But the canon of modern Jewish literature tells us a great deal about what did not change, and how the Eicha Problem survived.

Consider, for instance, the literary work that is often considered one of the loudest clarion calls to the Zionist movement: Hayyim Nachman Bialik's "Ba'ir haharegah," or "In the City of Slaughter," a harrowing poem about the 1903 Kishinev pogrom. A modern-day Eicha, the poem, written in a biblically toned Hebrew, echoes the pattern of descriptions in Lamentations as it provides graphic detail of a town in ruins, property destroyed, and bodies ravaged. But it saves its greatest vituperation for the victims of the pogrom themselves. After its descriptions of arson and gang rape, it reaches its lyrical apex with its description of the Jews' responses to the pogrom: the *kohanim*, whose major concern for their raped wives is whether they are still halakhically permitted to have sex with them; and the congregations who return to the synagogue specifically to recite the traditional confession of sins in the hope that God will forgive them for their own iniquities, which surely caused the pogrom. God's response to these pathetic supplicants, as addressed through the poet-prophet, is to chastise them for lacking the self-asserting anger that would prove their humanity: "And here they are beating their breasts and confessing their sins / "Saying: 'We have trespassed, we have betrayed'—and their hearts do not believe their mouths. / Can a shattered idol sin, and can shards of pottery have trespassed? / And why do they pray to me?—Speak to them and make them roar!"[4]

This brutal condemnation of traditional religion was not new. But the mercilessness of applying it to the victims of a real pogrom certainly was. Bialik's poem was not motivated by the idea that the Jews brought the pogrom upon themselves by failing to fulfill their obligations to God, as in Eicha, but by the idea that the Jews brought the pogrom upon themselves by failing to fulfill their obligations to themselves, specifically by failing to fight back, despite historical evidence to the contrary. In fact, it was this powerful message that informed Bialik's reputation from that point forward: after Bialik published "In the City of Slaughter," critic David Aberbach has noted, "what [Bialik] wrote was not as important as what he stood for: a

---

4. H.N. Bialik, "Ba'ir haharegah" (1904), *Kol shirey h.n. bialik* (Tel Aviv: Dvir, 1952/1953), 371.

new, aggressive, self-critical, forward-looking Jewish creativity."[5] The poem's grand chastising of the Jews for their passive acceptance of victimhood, lambasting them for their self-destructive faith in divine justice and punishment, was meant to be a radical departure from the words that the poem's Jews recite to God, the repetitive Eicha-logic of the Jewish liturgy of repentance (the Jews in the poem even recite Eicha after the pogrom), with its assumption that divine reward and punishment are consistent and real.

But despite its apparent demonization of traditional Jewish life and of the Eicha attitude itself, "In the City of Slaughter," radical though it may have been, is, in fact, just another reenactment of the Eicha problem, this time with a new twist on why anti-Semitism is actually the Jews' own fault. Like Eicha, "In the City of Slaughter" never mentions the pogrom's perpetrators by name, and like Eicha, it aims its primary anger and regret directly at the Jews themselves. If the Jews were fools for believing that their suffering was caused by their sins against God, as Bialik suggests, they were apparently not fools for believing that their suffering was caused by their sins. It was, of course, still their fault.

Bialik's tone of self-criticism—apparently dramatically new, but actually quite tediously old—set the stage for much of the Hebrew literature that followed in what became the foundations of the Israeli literary canon. The major founding writers of Israeli literature—from Yosef Hayyim Brenner, whose greatest novel is about a decidedly impotent pioneer in Ottoman Palestine, to Nobel laureate S.Y. Agnon, whose signature tale is about the loss of a private paradise in the Land of Israel due to inherently Jewish failings—are perhaps unique among the founding writers of modern literatures worldwide in the astonishing prevalence of their criticism of the very national experiment of which they are a fundamental part, and the canonized writers who followed Israel's statehood have typically continued this tradition. It could be argued, of course, that non-critical "patriotic" literature simply does not make for very good art, but readers of major world talents like Walt Whitman and William Blake must recognize the shallowness of this claim.

And here we discover the roots of the discomfort that Ruth Wisse, perhaps today's greatest anti-Eicha activist, so obviously feels when reading and teaching canonical Israeli literature. Wisse's sidestepping of Israeli literature in *The Modern Jewish Canon*—her book, ostensibly about the grand sweep of the Jewish novel in the twentieth century, ultimately discusses only one Israeli novel written after 1948—is something that puzzled and occasionally angered even those critics who otherwise admired the book. Yet Wisse's avoidance of so large and obvious a topic in the realm of Jewish literature was not faulty scholarship, but rather an act of deference to her readers as well as to the canonical Israeli writers whose works she has criticized else-

---

5. David Aberbach, *Bialik* (London: Peter Halban, 1988), 98.

where. *The Modern Jewish Canon* was conceived as a celebration, and on the subject of Israeli literature, Wisse is reluctant to celebrate when she so vividly perceives the Eicha problem afoot. While the Eicha approach to Jewish history has been analyzed and interpreted as a means of both providing comfort and creating continuity in a persecuted and often-ruptured Jewish community, most notably by David Roskies in his 1984 literary history *Against the Apocalypse*,[6] Wisse's work differs by not merely identifying this trend, but actually condemning it—and one cannot canonize the condemned.

If Wisse sidesteps the Israeli canon in *The Modern Jewish Canon*, there can be no mistaking her attitude toward it—or, better, her diagnosis of it—in other parts of her oeuvre. In her polemic-cum-novel *If I Am Not for Myself...: The Liberal Betrayal of the Jews*, Wisse includes a chapter called "The Ugly Israeli" in which she lambasts some of the most central works of the Israeli canon for the Eicha problem that these works so clearly display. One sample target of her vituperation is S. Yizhar's very canonical 1949 story "Hashivui," or "The Prisoner," about a group of Israeli soldiers in the 1948 War for Independence who capture an innocent Arab man as a gratuitous prisoner-of-war. Wisse's critique of the story identifies the Eicha problem at work within it: In a war of independence that Israel did not start, in a moment when the new state has been simultaneously attacked by the armies of five Arab countries, in an Israeli army where a significant number of soldiers are themselves survivors of previous sadistic attacks on Jews, in a context in which foreign Arab states as well as domestic Arab residents have declared a total war on civilian and soldier alike and where enemy attacks included the murdering of doctors and hospital patients and the slaughter of civilians in the millennia-old Jewish neighborhoods of Jerusalem, the most canonized literary product of the historical moment, *on the Israeli side*, is a story about a few Israeli soldiers who have committed the grave sin of humiliating a Bedouin man.[7] Wisse's discussion in this vein extends to other Israeli works as well, from the works of the acclaimed David Grossman to the most minor of mystery novels, in which, she says, she can detect the "unmistakable whiff of rot"—that is, evidence of the Eicha problem at work.[8]

Murder mysteries aside, the literature that engenders such resentment from Wisse has been canonized and lionized by her Israeli colleagues almost without exception. The tradition of self-criticism within Israeli literature is usually seen by literary critics simply as one of Israeli literature's unique and intriguing qualities, or even as a sign of Israel's moral vision. But few critics

---

6. David Roskies, *Against the Apocalypse: Responses to Catastrophe in Modern Jewish Culture* (Cambridge, Mass.: Harvard University Press, 1984).

7. Wisse, "The Ugly Israeli," in *If I am Not For Myself...: The Liberal Betrayal of the Jews* (New York: Free Press, 1992), 152.

8. Ibid., 146.

have expressed as clearly as Wisse does how this peculiar literary quality is more than literary, or how it is part of a larger political illness within Jewish history itself. Criticizing a colleague's assessment of Jewish politics, Wisse openly states the Eicha problem: "[T]he Jews never did 'conceal their moral failures by blaming others.' Their problem was rather that they blamed themselves."[9]

It must be said that Wisse does occasionally overstate the Eicha problem within her critique of the Israeli canon. If one looks carefully enough, one can find in some of contemporary Israeli literature's most significant canonical works an implied rejection of the Eicha problem—even in those works that at first seem to epitomize it. In Wisse's Harvard seminar on the intersection of literature and politics in Zionist thought, for instance, Wisse concluded the course with a reading of A.B. Yehoshua's *Mar Mani* (*Mr. Mani*, 1989), which is perhaps the best novel by one of today's most canonical living Israeli writers. It is also the only novel published in the past quarter-century to make Wisse's list of suggested reading in *The Modern Jewish Canon*, where it is placed as the capstone of a list of masterpieces. But at the seminar table, Wisse roundly criticized the novel for taking what she considered (with support from the language of the novel itself) the "back way" when it came to describing Zionism, and this criticism is certainly a fair one. Structured by rather experimental (some would say elliptical) one-sided conversations between minor characters over the course of a century, the novel moves backward through time to track five generations' worth of suicidal members of a single Jewish family. The "back way" Wisse alluded to does not merely refer to the novel's chronologically backward trajectory or the presentation of events from minor characters' points of view, but also to the deliberately bizarre historical situating of the Mani family itself. The novel's obligatory Holocaust victim, for instance, unlike the overwhelming majority of Holocaust victims, is not an Ashkenazi Jew from Eastern Europe but a Sephardi living on the island of Crete; the Mr. Mani who lives in 1918 Palestine is no transplanted pioneer draining swamps, but rather a native Palestinian Jew and a turncoat spy among Jews, Britons, and Turks alike; the Mani family's delegate to the historic World Zionist Congress is a resident of Jerusalem who must travel to diasporic Switzerland in order to rally to the Zionist cause. But there is something very potent about the novel's centering of its personal unrolling of Jewish history as a tale of a recurring suicidal gene, ultimately leading all the way back to the biblical binding of Isaac. Despite its apparent alienation from the conventional truths of Jewish national history, the novel deserves canonical credit for diagnosing the Eicha problem through its Jewish characters' pathological will to self-destruction. But the prevalence of non-self-consciously Eicha-tinged works in the rest of Yehoshua's oeuvre (such as his 1970 novella *Mul haye'arot,* or

---

9. Wisse, "The Brilliant Failure of Jewish Foreign Policy," 123.

Facing the Forests, which casts its Israeli-Jewish protagonist as an almost-unconscious blundering conqueror who redeems himself only by becoming complicit in an act of Arab terror), Wisse's reluctance to address this litera-ture becomes clearer. And those looking for Jewish literature that diagnoses the Eicha problem, as Wisse always is, can find far more vivid examples else-where in the canon.

There does exist in modern Jewish literature a small yet persistent strain of what I will call anti-Eicha literature—works that explicitly expose the Eicha problem within Jewish culture. One, Hayyim Hazaz's short story "Hadrashah," or "The Sermon" (1945), is the story of a man who goes to the board of his kibbutz to make a speech about how he is opposed to the entire idea of Jewish history and believes it should not be taught to children. The story itself is an essay proclaiming the Eicha problem and the disaster it has wrought on Jewish history—and Hazaz does merit mention in Wisse's canon. Another canonical story, I.L. Peretz's "The Shabbes-Goy," a rewriting of a Chelm tale, spells out the problem with equal clarity, though with irony rather than rage. Its title character is a Christian sadist who repeatedly attacks the same Jewish man. The victim repeatedly asks the local rabbi why he has been targeted and how he can avoid further abuse. Each time, the rabbi advises the victim that something the victim did was the cause of the attack—that his smiling provoked the sadist into knocking out his teeth, for instance. The story concludes with the rabbi's horrifyingly true-to-life con-clusion that what would really prevent future attacks would be to give the *shabbes*-goy a raise. Yet I would like to call the reader's attention to two par-ticularly shocking stories from Yiddish literature that proclaim the Eicha problem in an even more devastating fashion: Dovid Bergelson's "Tsvishn emigrantn" or "Among Refugees," and Lamed Shapiro's "Der tselem" or "The Cross."

"Among Refugees" (1924) is the story of a self-proclaimed "Jewish terror-ist"—and if the term sounds like an oxymoron, it is even more of one by the story's end. A twenty-five-year-old man enters a Jewish writer's house in Ber-lin, announces that he is a Jewish terrorist, and says he needs the writer's help. And then, as the reader listens in, the terrorist tells the writer his story. He is a refugee from a city in Ukraine that was wracked by a pogrom. Prior to the pogrom, the man lived with his grandfather, across the street from the Pinskys, a wealthy, happy family with many beautiful daughters. During the pogrom, his grandfather was murdered and the Pinsky daughters raped. Afterward, he and many others, including the Pinskys, fled to Berlin. But in the story, the pogrom isn't even described. Instead, we hear about what the self-proclaimed terrorist has just noticed in the boarding house where he lives, which is that the leader of the pogrom has moved into the room across the hall. And now the aspiring terrorist plots to kill him in revenge. But how will he do it? A knife is no good, he decides, since the pogrom lead-er is much stronger than he is. What he needs is a gun. But how can he, a penniless refugee in Berlin, buy a gun without arousing suspicion? He turns to Berl, a wealthy Jewish man from his old hometown, to describe his plan and ask for support. Berl seems enthusiastic and offers to meet him the following day. The next day, Berl leads him to the boardroom of an abandoned office building, where a group of important Jewish Berliners are waiting for him. But when the eager Jewish terrorist tells them about his plan, all of them leave the room but one. The one who remains tells him that he is a psychiatrist and would like to help him, and, in fact, the Pinskys themselves have offered to pay for his stay in a mental hospital. After this devastating setback, the terrorist decides to come to the Jewish writer's home for help with his rather literal plot. We aren't told what the writer answers, but it's clear enough at the story's end. A few days later, the writer receives the disappointed terrorist's suicide note in the mail. He has hanged himself, explaining that he no longer wishes to live "among refugees."

It is the location of the horror in this story that makes it one of the most powerful anti-Eicha stories of all time. That the murderer is happily ensconced in Berlin, and right across the hall from one of his potential victims, isn't even the scary part. What's horrifying is that the Jews are completely incapable of indignation, that Jewish self-respect is so alien a concept that the desire to kill an anti-Semitic murderer is considered a sign of insanity. The story shows how anti-Semitism is internalized, how the man who wanted to be a Jewish terrorist instead becomes the pogrom leader's last victim. The political implications of this story alone make it worthy of being the only story in the modern Jewish canon that anyone ever reads again.

But this story is outdone by Lamed Shapiro's "Der tselem" or "The Cross" (1909). The story's protagonist is a Jewish hobo in America, with a scar on his forehead in the shape of a cross, who recounts how he acquired this mark of Cain. A would-be Russian revolutionary, he had fallen in love with a non-Jewish woman in his revolutionary cell. In part to impress her, he announces to his cell that he will take on a dangerous, life-threatening secret mission on behalf of the revolution, and he is assigned to his task. But our hero's prospects for both revolution and love hit a snag when pogromists invade his home, brutally beat him, scratch a cross into his forehead, and tie him to the foot of the bed in which they proceed to rape his mother and shred her face and body into a pulp of blood and flesh while he watches. Regaining consciousness hours later, our hero writhes out of his bonds, mercy-kills his own mother, and flees his home. On the streets, he sees none of his non-Jewish revolutionary colleagues who had vowed to defend the Jews, but he does see one Jewish "self-defender" who aims a stolen gun at a pogromist before changing his mind and firing the gun at his own head. Our hero then proceeds to his would-be girlfriend's house, to whom he describes what has happened. In a moment that reveals her complete lack of regard for anything he has just experienced (as well as the revolutionary cell's complete failure to respond to the pogrom), she replies not by expressing any anger or even any pity, but merely by asking him if he will still complete his mission for the revolution. And in a moment unique in all Jewish literature, he responds by raping and murdering her.

In teaching this text to college students, I have discovered that the power of this story is in the innate response it evokes in the reader. Most of my students respond to this story with horror, and understandably so. But what is remarkable about this response—and what is the entire trick of the story itself—is that their horror is directed at the actions of the Jewish character, and not at all at the pogromists, despite the fact that the actions of the Jewish character and the pogromists are absolutely identical. (In fact, the Jewish character's actions might even be considered technically less violent, since they are the actions of a lone criminal rather than those of a nationwide sadistic movement with the capacity to attack large numbers of people. And from a literary point of view, they are also far less vividly described.) It might be said that this response to the hero's actions is simply a natural reaction to the story's first-person orientation; the Jewish protagonist is, after all, the character we know best and care about most. But this explanation is a fallacy; if it were true, we ought to care even more about the violence perpetrated against him. Moreover, readers tend to explain their horror at the narrator's choices not in terms of point-of-view, but in terms of morality. The outrage of these readers against the Jewish protagonist, as I have heard it expressed by my own students, is often couched in terms like "two wrongs don't make a right"—a phrase that exposes a failure to acknowledge that one wrong doesn't make a right either. Some of my students (most often, I must say, the Jewish students) have even insisted that their revulsion at the Jewish character's actions, as opposed to those of the pogromists, is due to the "higher moral standard" to which they would hold this Jewish character above a Russian pogromist. But such a claim, common among those who have unwittingly inherited the ethos of Eicha, is not only chauvinistic but also downright false. People who care about ethics do not turn a blind eye to murder and rape. There is no "higher moral standard" in allowing the most heinous crimes known to man to go unnoted, uncriticized, and essentially treated as though they were normal or even expected. This so-called "higher moral standard" amounts to nothing more than a buried version of the belief that the Jews can take it, and therefore should. It is precisely this false logic—the juncture at which the intelligent Jewish reader's opinion of what Jews "deserve" coincides precisely with the opinions of the anti-Semites themselves—that the reader's response to the story throws into high relief. In "Among Refugees," it was the would-be Jewish terrorist who came to this realization and hanged himself in despair. Here, it is the Jewish reader who has metaphorically hanged himself, by revealing his failure to believe in his own right to live.

These anti-Eicha stories do exist in the modern Jewish canon. Yet these stories, despite their astounding power, are still, small voices compared to the vast corpus of both religious and secular Jewish literature suggesting that anti-Semitism is something that Jews have brought upon themselves. So what accounts for the longevity of the Eicha problem, in both literature and life? Why do Jews, with their culture of brilliant rational analysis, continue to believe, against all logic, that anti-Semitism is in fact their own fault?

Well, partly because of their culture of brilliant rational analysis, of course. Today we speak of rationalists as those who believe that events in our world are directed by understandable, transparent forces of logic; we tend to exclude religious thinking from the realm of the rational. But it is important to recognize that Jews who believe explicitly (whether in ancient times or today) in the Eicha understanding of the world—that events beyond our control are actually acts of divine agency—are also engaging in a type of rational thinking, for both they and modern rationalists agree to an understanding of the world in which events are motivated by both logic and justice, whether divine or human.

This appears to be a noble way of regarding the world, whether in a secular or religious context, because it demands that one maintain a tremendously high standard of behavior for oneself, regardless of how one is treated by others. In fact, it even demands that one's behavior follow an *inverted* trajectory of that of one's aggressors—that the greater the pain inflicted by the aggressor, the greater the victim's responsibility for the aggression becomes, and the more generous and noble he must be in his superhuman toleration of torture without "stooping to the level" of actually fighting back. But in the Eicha-assumption that suffering is a logical consequence of one's own actions, it is a world view that is dramatically and horrifyingly flawed. Anti-Semitism's radical irrational sadism—whether practiced by the Babylonians, the Romans, the Crusaders, the Nazis, the Soviets, the Arab League, Hamas, Hezbollah, al Qaeda, or any sadist in between, before, or since—flies in the face of any rational understanding of how the world works. A rational understanding of the world cannot accept that sadistic aggression is simply sadistic aggression, whose causes, while perhaps discernible by reason, are *completely irrelevant* to the actions of the victim. The Eicha problem makes Jews believe in a solipsistic view of the world, contending that the perpetrator of violence against them is irrelevant, that it is their own behavior that counts. In fact, precisely the opposite is true. It is the victim whose behavior is irrelevant. The victim can try to appease the sadistic aggressor or to fight him off, but the truly sadistic aggressor—unlike, say, one's pugilistic-yet-loving eight-year-old brother, or a government that is truly invested in the advancement of its citizens, or even the traditional conception of God—does not act in response to the victim's choices. A fight might damage or even destroy the sadistic aggressor's physical capacity for inducing destruction, but such a victory can be achieved only physically, not through a winning-over of ideas. The sadistic aggressor does not modify his sadism because the victim chooses to be gentle, or become even more riled because the victim chooses to fight back. He simply wants to kill him. And it has nothing to do with the victim's choices at all.

That is the truth, but no one wants to think it, because it leaves us with nothing left to think. Jewish civilization is at its heart an inward-looking one, set up to self-evaluate, self-examine, self-criticize, but not necessarily to self-respect. In the great refinement of its ethical traditions, it is not set up to deflect blame, even when such deflection is warranted. As a result, it sees itself as profoundly "moral." But as Wisse has repeatedly reminded us, it too often forgets the morality of one's obligations to oneself. Doctor De Soto may think himself the noblest dentist in town in his generosity to provide a predator with new teeth. But he is actually the stupidest dentist in town, because it is difficult to practice dentistry at all, noble or otherwise, after one has been eaten alive.

This is what Ruth Wisse has been arguing for decades. It is often thought that Wisse's career is bifurcated into two accomplished but unrelated tracks—her academic career, in which she analyzes Jewish literature, and her polemical career, in which she argues ardently and provocatively for conservative politics in both the Jewish and the national context. But for Wisse, these two careers are actually one and the same, motivated by her profound reading and experiencing of the Eicha problem of destructive self-criticism in both Jewish literature and Jewish life. As Wisse once announced in a lecture at Harvard, "Yiddish literature is the history of Jewish mistakes." It is her passion for correcting these mistakes—or really, the single mistake of the Eicha problem—that has motivated her every move as scholar, writer, teacher, and advocate.

Yet in some small way, like all of us, Wisse too falls victim to the Eicha problem. In devoting her career to the cause of ridding Jews of this illness, she has painted herself into a bit of a corner, having no choice but to blame the Jews for their sufferings as well. Her compelling essay on the subject of Jewish power, entitled "The Brilliant Failure of Jewish Foreign Policy," ends with—you guessed it—an indictment of the Jews. Concluding her analysis of Jewish political behavior in the Diaspora and beyond, Wisse finishes her essay with these lines: "The Jews had tried to make a virtue of adapting to foreign power in order to perpetuate their own way of life with the least interference. Instead, their deferment of power engendered unique conditions for genocide."[10] Even in Wisse's hands, it seems, it is still the Jews' fault. Here, though, this fault is not guilt, but rather responsibility—not merely Bialik's "modern" idea of the Jews' responsibility for defending themselves, but a deeper responsibility to continue the conversation about how to change Jewish history. Speaking to a Jewish audience, Wisse is still part of the ongoing conversation within the Jewish community about what Jews can do to alter a hostile world, even though she recognizes the vast his-

---

10. Wisse, "The Brilliant Failure of Jewish Foreign Policy," 136.

torical failures of this conversation in the past, and the fact that, in essence, it is not our problem to solve. The problem with the Eicha problem is that no Jewish argument, once begun, can ever really end. And it is the passion of that argument that engages her and will forever engage us.

There is one part of Eicha that actually takes on an anti-Eicha tone. In the third chapter of Lamentations, the poem cries out to God not only with guilt, but also with anger, asking God to take revenge on the enemies of Israel. One of these verses is ritually recited near the end of the Passover seder, where, along with two preceding lines from Jeremiah and Psalms, it urges an angry release that rarely appears elsewhere in the Jewish liturgy:

> Pour out your wrath on the nations that do not know you, and upon the nations that do not call upon your name. For they have devoured Jacob, and laid waste his habitation. Pour out your indignation upon them, and let the wrath of your anger overtake them. Pursue them with anger, and destroy them from beneath the heavens of the Lord.[11]

These verses are recited formulaically every year, just as the rest of Eicha is recited. But how can one engage with this call to anger when faced with a God, or with enemies, who do not respond—a God whose motivations we surely cannot fathom, or enemies whose motivations we surely cannot change? How can we even ask God to pour out this wrath that we have failed to pour out ourselves? What is the truest response to the agonies of the Jewish past, or to those of the Jewish present?

One year at my family's seder table, just as my daughter's picture book inspired adult questions, a child provided the best response to this ancient dilemma. It had been a very long seder, and as the service continued after the meal had ended, my five-year-old cousin began to get restless. As the solipsisms of Jewish history were narrated before him, he repeatedly asked if he could be excused. But, as we have seen, no one is ever excused. We reached the page of the Haggadah with the famous lines from Eicha, and recited them together. "Pour out Your wrath," my family called out, as our ancestors had for millennia before us, without any response. And at that moment, my five-year-old cousin stood up on his chair and vomited over the entire seder table. As every good teacher knows, the wisdom of children has something to teach us all.

---

11. Jeremiah 10:25; Psalms 69:24; Lamentations 3:66.

The Grand Explainer

CYNTHIA OZICK

Fortunate is the generation that has burning in its midst a robust and independent temperament of the kind Saul Bellow memorably named "reality-instructor"; unfortunate is the generation that requires one. Significantly, the term is a novelist's invention, since the concept, and especially its rare living incarnations, are so uncommon as to be discovered missing when most needed. But Bellow is elusive: his mercurial recognitions never cleanly identify the often idiosyncratic earmarks of the reality-instructor, so it is up to us to pursue him in formation, or to catch him in the act. Stepping outside the freer bounds of fiction into precarious life, I take the reality-instructor to be a Grand Explainer: one who opens us not only to intelligent understanding, but also to that resistance to pusillanimity that comes of saying out loud what is true. Ah, truth: not your truth, or my truth, or their truth (those equivocal unequals), but unambiguous, indisputable, adamantine here-is-what-happened. Or call it history—not capitalized, not metaphorical, not metaphysical, insusceptible to revision, distortion, or erasure; simply recorded, known, and remembered.

Ruth Wisse is the Grand Explainer of our time. What she explains is the place of Jewish literature in the history of Jewish civilization; and also the imperatives of the response to the war against the Jews.

The war against the Jews, as the historian Lucy Dawidowicz indelibly framed it, did not end with the Allied victory over Nazi Germany or with the implosion of the Soviet Union; and for millions of European Jews, whether victims of Hitler's atrocities or of Stalin's, these events came too late in any case. Besides, this same period (and the decades before it) was roiled by a parallel war across the Mediterranean, in another part of the world infected by annihilationist Jew-hatred. It is this latter war, or series of wars, that endures, unabated, into the twenty-first century. Though both had their enthusiasts, Hitler's genocide and Stalin's Doctors' Plot (including the terrors, imprisonments, and murders it continued and unleashed) could hardly lend themselves to easy apologetics. By contrast, the war against the Jews in its present form, even when it is most violent, is a war of apologetics. Which is to say that those who kill, and those who calumniate, maintain that they have nothing to apologize for: the Jews are to blame for the violence perpetrated against them.

This succinct and powerfully illuminating formulation—that the Jews are being held responsible for the deeds of their attackers—is the governing manifesto of contemporary reality-instruction. Ruth Wisse is the chief author of this necessary insight; without it, one becomes vulnerable to the omnipresence of obfuscation, slander, and lie: the insidious apologetics of Jew-hatred. Astonishingly, this apologetics has currently taken on an extraordinary vocabulary. Certainly the German death factories and the Soviet gulag could not have been defended in the sacrosanct idiom of "human rights"; yet the rise of anti-Zionism, a malignant movement prevalent in the West and ubiquitous among Muslim societies, has succeeded in defaming the Jewish state as a human rights violator, as a colonialist interloper, as a usurper, as an agent of apartheid. Forgotten—suppressed—is the long record of attempts at partition, negotiation, compromise, concession, all on the Jewish side, and wholesale rejection on the Arab side. Forgotten—suppressed—are the repeated Arab attacks that began most vehemently as long ago as 1920, with the consistent purpose of destroying in its cradle the Jewish national liberation process—a process that, against all odds, and under the fire of five invading Arab armies in 1948, culminated in the United Nations' recognition of a sovereign Israel. Continuing intransigence on the part of Arabs and the entire Muslim world led ultimately to the present shameless questioning, or outright denial, of a living nation's "right to exist" —an utterance one would hesitate to apply to a dog or a horse.

Accordingly, Jewish self-defense against programmatic Arab assaults, whether by Fatah, Islamic Jihad, Hamas, or Hezbollah (and both Iran and al-Qaeda are increasingly influential in Gaza), is termed aggression. Jewish victims of incursions, abductions, rockets, missiles, and suicide bombers are excoriated as victimizers. The self-declared International Parliament of Writers, founded by Salman Rushdie and including a Nobel prizewinner, defines its aims by its adherents, who traversed oceans to honor and shield an infamous terror chieftain during a war he instigated. Members of the International Solidarity Movement, which happily hosted the British Muslim bombers of Mike's Place, an eatery close to the American Embassy in Tel Aviv, shelters hidden weapons depots and their users; lauded as "peaceniks," they publicly announce their encouragement of "armed struggle." Campuses all over the civilized world become propaganda mills for anti-Semitism, urging divestment and boycott. A tear-jerker theatrical performance defames and defames, earning standing ovations in London and New York.

Meanwhile, the verbal storm accelerates, and instances of cant—i.e., dishonesty—multiply even in respected journals. To cite merely a single passage: in a recent issue of *The New York Review of Books*, Robert Paxton, writing with admirable precision and authority on the Vichy regime of the 1940s, comments in an aside on the current "widespread criticism in France of policies pursued by the government of Israel, which some people call anti-Semitism, apparently blind to the fundamental difference between criticism of a government's policy and a belief in the inherent harmfulness of an entire people." This willful distinction is by now a stale charade that no one who reads, listens, and observes can any longer pretend to be valid.

When Lawrence Summers, the ousted former president of Harvard University, rightly noted that proposed divestment pressures against Israel were "anti-Semitic in their effect, if not in their intent," he was far too lenient: anti-Semitic in their effect surely, but also, and primarily, in their intent. Though there were other intemperate charges against him, these remarks, received with angry resentment by the proponents of divestment, cannot be irrelevant to Summers's forced resignation.

Yet a segment of American Jews, academics in particular, are either cowed or co-opted. Many are simply cowardly or callous. More have relinquished sympathy with or interest in Jewish history and culture. Of these, few—very few—are open to reality-instruction; some indulge in reality-obstruction. And beyond the dubious intramural, the purveyors of the familiar old canards hawk their noisome wares—currently, the professorial team of John Mearsheimer and Stephen Walt, who, under the risible rubric of Realpolitik, have become notorious for conspiracy-mongering. Reviewing the Mearsheimer-Walt indictment of what they term "the Lobby," Wisse instructs these realists in the reality of their telltale omissions. Among their prosecutorial incitements, she writes,

> The twenty-one countries of the Arab League with ties to 1.2 billion Muslims world-wide are nowhere present as active political agents. There is no mention of the Arab rejection of the United Nations's partition of Palestine in 1948; and no 58-year Arab League boycott of Israel and companies trading with Israel; no Arab attacks of 1948, 1967 and 1973; no Arab-Soviet resolution at the U.N. defining Zionism as racism; no monetary and strategic support for Arab terrorism against Jews and Israel; and no Hamas dedication to destroying the Jewish state. The authors do not ask why Arab aggression and Muslim "rage against Israel" should have morphed into a war against the U.S. and the West.

Thus the Grand Explainer. In essay after essay, indefatigably, heroically, coolly, eloquently, with factual exactitude, she dissects and disposes of public liars. She is not a journalist; she is not associated with any advocacy group; she has no professional role in politics. She is a literary scholar with a free, honest, and honorable mind; and it is this freedom, this honesty, this scrupulously truthful honorableness, that is the source and fabric of her power. She is undaunted in addressing—in exposing—the recrudescence, even as late into modernity as the twenty-first century, of an obscurantist medieval anti-Semitism cloaked in the ferociously betrayed language of humanism.

What propels this unparalleled heroism? Perhaps the course of literature itself, the remarkable literature of (the phrase is commanding) Jewish peoplehood. The development of Yiddish fiction—and here Wisse's mastery is uniquely authoritative—is ineluctably embroiled in the society and politics of its era. In reflections introducing the work of I. L. Peretz, a classical Yiddish writer wrestling with modernity, Wisse describes how, in Poland toward the close of the nineteenth century, anti-Semitism became an effective tool of nationalist politics, while the revolutionary movements insisted that Jews be the avant-garde of the International. From a socialist-internationalist perspective, those nations that already occupied a place on the map would have to make a gradual transition from national to class consciousness. But because the Jews had no land, they were to dissolve themselves at once. Any attempt on the part of the Jews to regroup as a nation would be a setback to the cause of world revolution.

As for the Jews, who were the simultaneous targets of both these powerful competing forces, they tried frantically to find a solution to their dilemma. Many emigrated, and many assimilated. Jewish political parties proliferated, and the tensions between them increased in direct proportion to the pressure against the Jews from the outside. Peretz, who stood at the center of Jewish life in Warsaw, had to confront not only the mounting hostility to the Jews on the part of his native Poland, but spreading demoralization in the Jewish community itself.

"Had it been possible to ensure the continuity of the Jewish people through literature in a Jewish language," she goes on, "or to fashion out of literature a weapon of cultural resistance sufficiently forceful to stave off those who hated the Jews, the collected works of Peretz might have secured the Jews to the end of time." She concludes: "Peretz's idea of culture as a guarantor of Jewish national survival did not prove viable."

Whatever the reigning social context, as Wisse penetratingly shows us, the moment a consciously Jewish literature entered the modern world, it was caught in the vise of a brutishly hostile politics. Hence the necessity of Jewish sovereignty in its historic land. And that this sovereignty, once achieved, was instantly warred against, and continues to be warred against, bespeaks unreason. Nationalists once attacked Jews for being landless interlopers; nationalists today attack Jews, again as interlopers, for having a land. Internationalists once demanded that Jews as a people vanish. Internationalists today (often designated as universalists) characterize Jewish sovereignty as anachronistic and recommend that it vanish.

It may be that all literature, with the exception of the frivolous, the purely lyrical, and the immaculately aesthetic, is hostage to politics. The difference for Jews—as Kafka knew, as Babel and Mandelshtam knew, as Bellow's Mr. Sammler and Ravelstein knew—is that the tangled darkness of a pernicious history, and the proliferations of contemporary defamation, inescapably intrude. Inescapably? Perhaps not. *The Modern Jewish Canon*, Wisse's dazzling landmark study of the ascent of Jewish literature in Yiddish and in other tongues (Russian, Polish, German, Spanish, English, Hebrew), closes with a ripeness that contradicts and overturns every untoward intrusion. "Not all Jewish writers," she avers in a voice both admonitory and prophetically transcendent, "were inspired by their Jewishness—but many were. Not all Jewish writers sought beauty in truth, but a surprising number created it....As in the Bible, the world will also value what the Jews find of value to themselves."

Still, the world goes on doing its worst, and the reality-instructor, whether as peerless professor of Yiddish or as fearless Grand Explainer, will never want for work. In Ruth Wisse they are intertwined, and the times, the bloody times, bleed and plead for both.

Ruth R. Wisse Bibliography*

BOOKS

The Schlemiel as Modern Hero. University of Chicago Press, 1971.

A Little Love in Big Manhattan: Two Yiddish Poets. Harvard University Press, 1988.

I.L. Peretz and the Making of Modern Jewish Culture. University of Washington Press, 1991.

If I am Not for Myself: The Liberal Betrayal of the Jews. Free Press, 1992.

The Modern Jewish Canon: A Journey Through Literature Language and Culture. Free Press, 2000. National Jewish Book Award for Scholarship. Paperback edition, University of Chicago Press, 2003; Dutch edition, 2005; Russian edition, forthcoming.

Jews and Power. Nextbook/Schocken, 2007.

BOOKS EDITED OR TRANSLATED

The Well, by Chaim Grade. Translator from the Yiddish. Jewish Publication Society of America, 1967.

The Best of Sholem Aleichem. Edited, with an introduction by Wisse and Irving Howe. New Republic Books, 1979.

A Shtetl and Other Yiddish Novellas. Edited, with an introduction.Wayne State University Press, 1986.

The Penguin Book of Modern Yiddish Verse. Edited, with an introduction by Wisse, Irving Howe and Khone Shmeruk. Penguin, 1987.

The I.L. Peretz Reader. Edited, with an introduction. Schocken, 1990. Republished by Yale University Press, 2002. The volume appeared while Wisse served as Senior Editor of the Library of Yiddish Classics, Schocken (4 vols. 1987–1996).

Jacob Glatstein*, The Yash Novels.* Edited, with an introduction. Yale University Press, forthcoming.

---

* The bibliography includes works published through December 2007. Though we strove for comprehensiveness, Wisse's activities as a public intellectual precluded inclusion of every article or editorial appearing in the press, especially in publications in which she served as contributing editor or regular columnist.

On Literature and Literary Culture

"Kminhag yid: an umbakanter ksav-yad fun Mendele Moykher Sforim" (Study of
a variant ms. of a play by Mendele Moykher Sforim). *For Max Weinreich on His Seventieth Birthday: Studies in Jewish Language, Literature and Society.* Mouton, 1964: 337–344.

"Stil un politik bay Dovid Bergelson" (Style and Politics in the Work of David Bergelson). *Yugntruf* (December 1968): 16–20.

"Itsik Manger: Poet of the Jewish Folk." *Jewish Heritage* (Spring 1970): 27–37.

"Vegn Dovid Bergelsons dertseylung 'Yoysef Shor'" (A Study of David Bergelson's story "Joseph Shor"). *Di goldene keyt* 77 (1972): 133–144.

"The Prose of Abraham Sutzkever." In Avrom Sutzkever, *Griner akvaryum:
dertseylungen.* Hebrew University of Jerusalem, 1975: v–xxxiii.

"American Jewish Writing, Act II." *Commentary* (June 1976): 40–45.

"The *Yunge* and the Problem of Jewish Aestheticism." *Jewish Social Studies*
(Summer/Fall 1976): 265–276.

"In Praise of Chaim Grade." *Commentary* (April 1977): 70–73.

"The Ghetto Poems of Abraham Sutzkever." *Jewish Book Annual* 36 (1978/
1979): 26–36. Republished as the introduction to *Burnt Pearls:
Ghetto Poems of Abraham Sutzkever.* Mosaic Press/Valley Editions, 1981.

"Singer's Paradoxical Progress." *Commentary* (February 1979): 33–38.
Reprinted in *Studies in American Jewish Literature* I (SUNY
Press, 1981): 148–159.

"Introduction." *Voices Within the Ark: The Modern Jewish Poets.* Howard
Schwartz and Anthony Rudolf, ed. Avon Books, 1980: 236–242.

Sholem Aleichem and the Art of Communication (B.G. Rudolph Lecture in
Judaic Studies). Syracuse University Press, 1980: 31 pages.
Reprinted in *Judaism in the Modern World.* Alan L. Berger, ed.
New York University Press, 2004.

"Reading About Jews." *Commentary* (March 1980): 41–48.

"A Yiddish Poet in America." (On Moyshe-Leyb Halpern) *Commentary* (July
1980): 35–41.

"Isaac Bashevis Singer: A Reconsideration." *Studies in American Jewish Literature* 1 (1981): 148–159.

"Di Yunge: Immigrants or Exiles?" *Prooftexts* (January 1981): 43–61.

"Philip Roth, Then and Now." *Commentary* (September 1981): 56–60.

"Jewish Culture and Canadian Culture." *The Canadian Jewish Mosaic.* M. Wein-
feld, W. Shafir, and I. Cotler, eds. J. Wiley, 1981: 315–342.

"Saul Bellow's Winter of Discontent." *Commentary* (April 1982): 71–73.

"Aharon Appelfeld, Survivor." *Commentary* (August 1983): 73–76.

"The Last Great Yiddish Poet?" (On Abraham Sutzkever) *Commentary* (November 1983): 41–48. Reprinted (in Polish) in *ARCA*, 1984.

"Two Jews Talking: A View of Modern Yiddish Literature." *Prooftexts* (January
1984): 35–48. Reprinted in *What Is Jewish Literature?* Hana Wirth-
Nesher, ed. Jewish Publication Society, 1994.

"Introduction."*The Selected Stories of Meir Blinkin*. SUNY Press, 1984: vii–xviii.

"What Shall Live and What Shall Die: The Makings of a Yiddish Anthology." Twelfth Annual Feinberg Memorial Lectures in Jewish Studies, University of Cincinnati, 1989: 31 pages.

"Jewish Guilt and Israeli Writers." *Commentary* (January 1989): 25–31.

"Introduction." *Di nevue fun shvartsuplen: dertseylungen* (Prophecy of the Inner Eye: Stories) by Abraham Sutzkever. Magnes Press of the Hebrew University, 1989: v–xix.

"Introduction." *The Fiddle Rose: Poems 1970–1972,* by Abraham Sutzkever (Translated by Ruth Whitman). Wayne State University Press, 1990.

"A Monument to Messianism" (on I.L. Peretz). *Commentary* (March 1991): 37–42.

"The Jewish Intellectual and the Jews: The Case of *Di Kliatshe* (The Mare) by Mendele Moycher Sforim." Daniel E. Koshland Memorial Lecture, Congregation Emanu-el, San Francisco. March 1992: 28 pages.

"1936: A Year in the Life of Yiddish Literature." *Studies in Jewish Culture in Honour of Chone Shmeruk*. Israel Bartal et al., ed. Zalman Shazar Center, 1993: 83–103.

"The Jewish Writer and the Problem of Evil." *Terms of Survival: The Jewish World since 1945*. Robert S. Wistrich, ed. Routledge, 1995: 412–427.

"Jewish Writers on the New Diaspora." *The Americanization of the Jews*. Robert M. Seltzer and Norman J. Cohen, ed. New York University, 1995: 60–78.

"Not the 'Pintele Yid' but the Full-Fledged Jew." *Prooftexts* (January 1995): 33–61.

"Introduction." *Satan in Goray* by Isaac Bashevis Singer. Noonday Press/Farrar, Straus & Giroux, 1996: viii–xlviii.

"The Classic of Disinheritance." *New Essays on Call it Sleep,* Hana Wirth-Nesher, ed. Cambridge University Press, 1996: 61–74.

"Language as Fate: Reflections on Jewish Literature in America." *Literary Strategies: Jewish Texts and Contexts*. Ezra Mendelsohn, ed. Oxford University Press, 1996: 129–147.

"'English Literature' Was More Fragile Than We Knew" (in memory of Peter Shaw). *Academic Questions* 9:5 (1996): 85–88.

"The Maturing of *Commentary* and of the Jewish Intellectual." *Jewish Social Studies* 3.2 (Winter 1997): 29–41.

"Preface." *A Garment Worker's Legacy: The Joe Fishstein Collection of Yiddish Poetry.* McGill University Libraries, 1998: x–xiii.

"Introduction." *Holocaust Chronicles: Individualizing the Holocaust through Diaries and Other Contemporaneous Personal Accounts*, Robert Moses, ed. Ktav, 1999: xiii–xviii.

Preface to *The Range of Yiddish: Catalog of an exhibition of the Harvard College Library*, Charles Berlin et al. Harvard College Library, 1999.

Some Serious Thoughts about Jewish Humor. Leo Baeck Institute, 2001: 18
        pages.

"The Yiddish and the Hebrew Writers Head Home." *Ideology and Jewish Iden-
        tity in Israeli and American Literature.* Emily Budick Miller, ed.
        State University of New York Press, 2001: 147–175.

"The Yiddish and American-Jewish Beat." (On *Prooftexts* at Twenty). *Prooftexts*
        (Winter 2001): 135–143.

"Speaking of the Devil in Yiddish Literature." *Studies in Contemporary Jewry*
        18 (2002): 59–73.

"A Prayer of Homecoming by Abraham Sutzkever." *History and Literature: New
        Readings of Jewish Texts in Honor of Arnold J. Band.* William Cut-
        ter and David C. Jacobson, eds. Program in Judaic Studies, Brown
        University, 2002: 339–349.

"Abraham Sutzkever." *Holocaust Literature.* S. Lillian Kremer, ed. Routledge,
        2002: 1234–1240.

"The Pain and the Gain of Proposing a Canon." *Jewish Studies* 42 (2003–2004):
        5–16.

"The Political Vision of I.L. Peretz." *The Emergence of Modern Jewish Politics.*
        Zvi Gitelman, ed. University of Pittsburgh Press, 2003: 120–131.

"Jewish-American Renaissance." *The Cambridge Companion to Jewish Ameri-
        can Literature.* Michael P. Kramer and Hana Wirth-Nesher, eds.
        Cambridge University Press, 2003: 190–211.

"The Function of Memory: Keeping Body and Soul Together." *Figures de la
        Memoire dans la Litterature es les Arts Juifs Americains des XXe
        et XXIe Siecles.* Martine Chard-Hutchinson, ed. Institut d'Etudes
        Anglophones, Universite Paris VII-Denis Diderot, 2004: 9–28.

"The Jewishness of *Commentary*." In *Commentary in American Life,* ed. Mur-
        ray Friedman. Temple University Press, 2005: 52–73.

PERSONAL ESSAYS

"Hurra! Hurra!" (A Study of Family Folklore). *Moment* (December 1975): 21–23.

"A Golus Education." *Moment* (January 1977): 26–28; 62.

"The Most Beautiful Woman in Vilna." *Commentary* (June 1981): 34–38.

"Between Passovers." *Commentary* (December 1989): 42–47.

"Love and Loyalty: A Story." *Commentary* (October 1992): 40- 47.

"What My Father Knew." *Commentary* (April 1995): 44–49.

"My Life Without Leonard Cohen." *Commentary* (October 1995): 27–33.

"Bellow's Gift." *Commentary* (December 2001):43–53.

"An Unheralded Zionist" (on Gershon Shaked). *Commentary* (June 2007): 49–54.

"How Not to Remember and How Not to Forget." *Commentary* (January 2008):
        37–44.

REVIEW ESSAYS AND BOOK REVIEWS

"Yiddish Fiction Re-Examined" (Review of *A Traveler Disguised: The Rise of Modern Yiddish Fiction in the Nineteenth Century* by Dan Miron). *Midstream* (May 1975): 70–72.

"Jewish Herstory" (Review of *The Jewish Woman in America* by Charlotte Baum, Paula Hyman and Sonya Michel). *Commentary* (July 1976): 68–70

"The Pen and the Sword" (Review of *Truth is for Strangers* by Efraim Sevela, and *A Hero in His Time* by Arthur A. Cohen). *Commentary* (October 1976): 92–94; 96.

Review of *Letters to an American Jewish Friend* by Hillel Halkin. *Moment* (September 1977): 46–48.

Review of *Image Before My Eyes* by Lucjan Dobroszycki and Barbara Kirshenblatt-Gimblett, and *An Illustrated Sourcebook on the Holocaust* by Zosa Szajkowski. *Commentary* (March 1978): 80–82.

"Suburban Kitsch" (Review of *Rachel, the Rabbi's Wife* by Silvia Tennenbaum). *Commentary* (June 1978): 76–78.

"Fairytale" (Review of *King of the Jews* by Leslie Epstein). *Commentary* (May 1979): 76–78.

"Jewish Dreams" (Review of *The Refusers* by Stanley Burnshaw and *The Book of Lights* by Chaim Potok). *Commentary* (March 1982): 45–48.

"Rediscovering Judaism" (Review essay of current Jewish American fiction). *Commentary* (May 1982): 84–87.

"Religious Imperatives and Mortal Desires" (Review of *Rabbis and Wives* by Chaim Grade). *New York Times Book Review* (14 November 1982): 3, 18.

"Return to the Fold?" (Review of *An Orphan in History* by Paul Cohen). *Commentary* (February 1983): 70–75.

"Bearing False Witness" (Review of *The Longest War* by Jacob Timmerman). *Commentary* (March 1983): 74–77.

Review of *Short Stories* by A.M. Klein. *The Montreal Gazette* (10 September 1983): 14.

"Matters of Life and Death" (Review of *In the Land of Israel* by Amos Oz). *Commentary* (April 1984): 68–70.

"The Jew of Prague" (Review of *The Nightmare of Reason: A Life of Franz Kafka* by Ernst Pawel). *Commentary* (November 1984): 62–64.

"Sholem Aleichem's Treasure is Life" (Review of *From the Fair*). *The Montreal Gazette* (3 August 1985).

Review of *A Certain People: American Jews and Their Lives Today* by Charles E. Silberman. *Commentary* (November 1985): 108–112.

Review of *The Family Mashber* by Der Nister. *New York Times Book Review* (12 July 1987): 15–16.

"Life Became the Greatest Feat" (Review of *The Magic We Do Here* by Lawrence Rudner). *The New York Times* (7 August 1988): 7:8.

Review of *See: Under Love* by David Grossman. *Boston Globe* (26 March 1989): 45–46.

"A Romance of the Secret Annex" (Review of *The Diary of Anne Frank: The Critical Edition* and *Eva's Story,* Eva Schloss). *New York Times Book Review* (2 July 1989): 2.

"The Survivor's Voice" (Review of *From the Old Marketplace* by Joseph Buloff). *The New Republic* (24 June 1991): 40–42.

"Advertisements for Himself" (Review of *Chutzpah* by Alan M. Dershowitz). *Commentary* (September 1991): 54–56.

"The Art of the Possible?" (Review of *On Modern Jewish Politics* by Ezra Mendelsohn). *Commentary* (March 1994): 55–57.

"Found in America" (Review essay of Jacob Glatstein's *The Holocaust Poems of Jacob Glatstein*, trans. Barnett Zumoff, and *Selected Poems of Yankev Glatshteyn*, Richard Fein, ed.) *The New Republic* (18 and 25 September 1995): 52–57.

"The Lost Word" (Review of *Portrait of a Lady* by Henry James). *Washington Times* (8 October 1995).

"Sex, Love & Death" (Review of *Sabbath's Theater* by Philip Roth). *Commentary* (December 1995): 61–64.

"By Their Own Hands: How the Jews of Russia Outwitted Themselves to Death" (Review essay on Soviet Jewish Literature). *The New Republic* (3 February 1997): 34–43.

"The Individual from the Ashes: Hitler and the Genre of the Holocaust Memoir." *The Weekly Standard* (21 April 1997): 29–31.

"Recovery" (Review of *Drawing Life: Surviving the Unabomber* by David Gelernter). *Commentary* (December 1997): 60–63.

"The Joy of Limits" (Review of *Kaaterskill Falls* by Allegra Goodman). *Commentary* (December 1998): 67–70.

"Testament" (Review of *A Passion for Truth* by Eric Breindel). *Commentary* (May 1999): 70–72.

"The Smell of the Greasepaint, the Roar of the Torah" (Review of books on Yiddish theater and klezmer music). *The New Republic* (1 May 2000): 33–38.

"Delayed Impact" (Review of *The Holocaust and the Canadian Jewish Community* by Frank Bialystok). *National Post* (Toronto, 30 September 2000): E8.

"Back to Uganda" (Review of *His Brother's Keeper: Israel and Diaspora Jewry in the Twenty-first Century* by Yossi Beilin). *Commentary* (November 2000): 60–63.

"A Loss of Confidence" (Review essay on *The Jewish State: The Struggle for Israel's Soul,* by Yoram Hazony, *From Herzl to Rabin,* by Amnon Rubinstein, and *The Blood-Dimmed Tide,* by Amos Elon*). Times Literary Supplement* (2 March 2001): 1–2.

"Torn in the USA" (Review of *Jewish American Literature: A Norton Anthology*). *The New Republic* (2 April 2001): 36–42.

"Lost Illusions" (Review of *Commies: A Journey Through the Old Left, the New Left, and the Leftover Left* by Ronald Radosh). *Commentary* (July 2001): 62–66.

"In Nazi Newark" (Review of *The Plot Against America*, by Philip Roth). *Commentary* (December 2004): 65–70.

"Slap Shtick" (Review of *The Yiddish Policemen's Union* by Michael Chabon). *Commentary* (July/August 2007): 73–77.

COMMENT AND OPINION

"The Anxious American Jew." *Commentary* (September 1976): 47–50.

"Quebec's Jews: Caught in the Middle," with Irwin Cotler. *Commentary* (September 1977): 55–59.

"Poland Without Jews." *Commentary* (August 1978): 64–67.

"Women as Conservative Rabbis?" *Commentary* (October 1979): 59–64.

"Liberalism and the Jews: A Symposium." *Commentary* (January 1980).

"'Peace Now' and American Jews." *Commentary* (August 1980): 17–22.

"Judaism for the Mass Market." *Commentary* (January 1981): 41–45.

"Portrait of a Hero." *Commentary* (March 1981): 53–56.

"The Delegitimization of Israel." *Commentary* (July 1982): 29–36.

A Critical Look at the Jewish Condition in North America, with Chaim Potok and Vivian Rakoff. Council of Jewish Federations and Welfare Funds, 1984: 17–26.

"Blaming Israel." *Commentary* (February 1984): 29–36.

"The Politics of Yiddish." *Commentary* (July 1985): 29–35. Republished in Yiddish in *Di goldene keyt* (Autumn 1985).

"My Father, My Self." *The Montreal Gazette* (1 February 1986).

"Poland's Jewish Ghosts." *Commentary* (January 1987): 25–33.

"Letter to a New Israeli." *Commentary* (June 1987): 44–49.

"Israel: A House Divided?" *Commentary* (September 1987): 33–38.

"The New York (Jewish) Intellectuals." *Commentary* (November 1987): 28–38.

"A Light Unto the Nations?" *Commentary* (December 1987): 30–35.

"Ha'ivrim yod'im." *Ma'ariv* (25 December 1987): 9.

"American Jews and Israel: A Symposium." *Commentary* (February 1988): 75.

"Israel & the Intellectuals: A Failure of Nerve?" *Commentary* (May 1988): 19–25.

"Why Should a Secular Jew Marry a Jew?" *Proceedings of the Institute for Distinguished Leaders.* Brandeis University, July 1988: 18–23.

"Living with Women's Lib." *Commentary* (August 1988): 40–45.

"No Left Turn: The Case Against Jewish Liberalism." *The New Republic* (22 May 1989): 23–27.

"The Hebrew Imperative." *Commentary* (June 1990): 34–39. Republished in *Hebrew in America.* ed. Alan Mintz. Wayne State University Press, 1992: 265–276.

"The 20th Century's Most Successful Ideology." *Commentary* (February 1991): 31–35.

"A Truer Internationalism." *Jerusalem Report* (12 and 19 September, 1991): 62.

"The Feminist Mystery." *Jerusalem Report* (9 January 1992): 40.

"Incurably Correct." *Jerusalem Report* (21 May 1992): 63.

"A Purim Homily." *Commentary* (May 1992): 53.

"The Unchosen: Political Anti-Semitism Anew." *The New Republic* (15 June 1992):15–17.

"Crimes of the Past: For a Truer Reckoning." *Jerusalem Report* (13 August 1992): 54.

"Israel Watch: The Might and the Right." *Commentary* (September 1992): 48–50.

"The Liberal Betrayal of the Jews: an exchange (with Robert Alter)." *The New Republic* (19 April 1993): 44–45.

"Peace Not." *The New Republic* (4 October 1993): 15–16.

"Holocaust, or War Against the Jews?" *Approaches to Antisemitism: Context and Curriculum.* Michael Brown, ed. American Jewish Committee, 1994: 24–31.

"'Schindler' and the Victim Image." *Jerusalem Report* (10 March 1994): 55.

"A Degree of Freedom." *Jerusalem Report* (30 June 1994): 54.

"Return of the Defeatist." *Jerusalem Report* (12 January 1995): 48.

"The Moral Minority." *Jerusalem Report* (5 October 1995): 71.

Symposium on "The National Prospect." *Commentary* (November 1995): 113–115.

"Making War with the Word 'Peace'." *The Weekly Standard* (20 November 1995): 28–30.

"Shul Daze: Is Yiddish Back from the Dead?" *The New Republic* (27 May 1996): 16–19.

"Journalistic Fundamentalism." *The Wall Street Journal* (5 June 1996).

"The Times Got It Wrong." *Jerusalem Report* (8 August 1996): 60.

"Zionism at 100: A Symposium." *The New Republic* (8 and 15 September 1997): 23–24.

"Yiddish: Past, Present, Imperfect." *Commentary* (November 1997): 32–39.

"The Politics of Denial: Israel, the United Nations, and the Anniversary That Should Have Been." *Harvard International Review* (Spring 1998): 88–94.

"War against Jews." *The Montreal Gazette* (25 April 1998): B5.

"A Debate about Teaching the Holocaust (with Steven T. Katz)." *New York Times* (8 August 1998): B7.

"Teaching the Living Language of Israel." In *Zionism: The Sequel.* Carol Diament, ed. Hadassah: the Women's Zionist Organization of America, 1998: 385–392.

"The Virtue of Virtue." *Wall Street Journal* (7 January 1999): A8.

Symposium on "The Jewish State: The Next Fifty Years." *Azure* (Winter 1999): 223–226.

"The Cultural Contribution of Jews to the Twentieth Century (in Hebrew)." *Ha'am Hayehudi Beme'ah Ha'esrim.* Mordecai Naor, ed. Am Oved, 2000: 524-527.

"The Brilliant Failure of Jewish Foreign Policy." *Azure* (Winter 2001): 118-145.

"Standing Up for Israel." *The Harvard Crimson* (25 February 2002).

"The U.N.'s Jewish Problem: Anti-Semitism Has Found a Comfortable Home on the East River." *Weekly Standard* (8 April 2002): 27-29.

"On Ignoring Anti-Semitism." *Commentary* (October 2002): 26-33.

"Flip-Flop Not About Free Speech." *The Harvard Crimson* (26 November 2002).

"Israel on Campus." *Wall Street Journal* (13 December 2002): A16.

"At Home in Jerusalem." *Commentary* (April 2003): 44-50.

"Jews and Anti-Jews." *Wall Street Journal* (16 June 2003): A14.

"On Declarations of Independence." in *Renewing the Jewish Social Contract* (American Jewish Committee, 2004): 48-50.

"John Kerry U." *Wall Street Journal* (25 October 2004): A18.

"Gender Fender-Bender." *Wall Street Journal* (21 January 2005): A8.

"'Dear Ellen'; or Sexual Correctness at Harvard." *Commentary* (April 2005): 31-37.

"Women's Choices." *Commentary* (July/August 2005): 14-16.

"A Dangerous Combination." *The Harvard Crimson* (17 February 2006).

"Coup d'Ecole." *Wall Street Journal* (23 February 2006): A17.

"Israel Lobby." *Wall Street Journal* (22 March 2006): A16.

NON-PRINT

The Poetry of Abraham Sutzkever: The Vilno Poet: reading in Yiddish. (Sound recording), editor. Folkways Records, 1991.

The Next Generation: Responding to the Challenges Ahead. (Videorecording) Charles Bronfman. United Jewish Appeal, Department of Communications, 1992.

Abraham Sutzkever: The Uncrowned Poet Laureate, Three Recorded Lectures. (Sound recording) National Yiddish Book Center, 1994.

A bas-Vilne: dos liderbukh fun Mashe Roskes / Daughter of Vilna: the life in song of Masha Roskies. (Videorecording) David G. Roskies, Ruth R. Wisse, and Joshua Waletsky. National Yiddish Book Center, 2000.

Compiled by Justin Cammy and Debra Caplan

Contributors

David Aberbach is professor of Hebrew and Comparative Literature at McGill University, Montreal, and (since 1992) a visiting academic at the London School of Economics and University College, London. His books include *Surviving Trauma: Loss, Literature and Psychoanalysis* (1989), *Imperialism and Biblical Prophecy 750-500 BCE* (1993), *Charisma in Politics, Religion and the Media* (1996), and *Jewish Cultural Nationalism* (2008). He and Ruth Wisse introduced a course on Holocaust literature at McGill, from which this article derives.

Monika Adamczyk-Garbowska is professor of Comparative Literature, and head of the Center for Jewish Studies at Maria Curie-Skodowska University in Lublin, Poland. Her books include *Isaac Bashevis Singer's Poland: Exile and Return* (1994, in Polish), *Contemporary Jewish Writing in Poland: An Anthology* (with Antony Polonsky; 2001), *Shades of Identity: Jewish Literature as a Multilingual Phenomenon* (2004, in Polish), and *Kazimierz vel Kuzmir: A Shtetl of Various Dreams* (2006, in Polish).

Edward Alexander is professor emeritus of English at the University of Washington. Among his more recent books are *Irving Howe: Socialist, Critic, Jew, The Jewish Wars: Reflections By One of the Belligerents*, and (with Paul Bogdanor) *The Jewish Divide over Israel* (2008).

Marion Aptroot is professor of Yiddish Culture, Language and Literature at the Heinrich Heine University in Düsseldorf, Germany. Her publications include *Storm in the Community: Yiddish Polemical Pamphlets of Amsterdam Jewry, 1797–1798* (with Jozeph Michman; 2002) and a critical edition of *Isaac Euchel's Reb Henoch, oder: Woß tut me damit* (with Roland Gruschka, 2004).

Emily Miller Budick holds the Ann and Joseph Edelman Chair in American Studies and is chair of the American Studies department at The Hebrew University of Jerusalem. She has published five books and over fifty essays on American literature, Holocaust writing, and Jewish fiction.

Justin Cammy is assistant professor of Jewish Studies at Smith College, where he also teaches in the Program in Comparative Literature. He is the translator and editor of Hinde Bergner's *On Long Winter Nights: Memoirs of a Jewish Family in a Galician Township*, and is complet-

717

ing a book on interwar Yiddish literature in Vilna, *When Yiddish Was Young*. Cammy is an associate editor of *Prooftexts: A Journal of Jewish Literary History*.

Beatrice Lang Caplan currently teaches at Johns Hopkins University. Her dissertation examines Orthodox Yiddish literature in interwar Poland. She has taught Yiddish language and culture at the Uriel Weinreich Program (YIVO/NYU), the Jewish Theological Seminary, and Harvard University.

Marc Caplan is the Tandetnik Professor of Yiddish Literature, Language, and Culture at the Johns Hopkins University. He is working on a book comparing Yiddish writers in Weimar-era Berlin with contemporaneous figures from German-language literature, philosophy, and film.

Jeremy Dauber is the Atran Associate Professor of Yiddish Language, Literature, and Culture at Columbia University. He is the co-editor of *Prooftexts: A Journal of Jewish Literary History*.

Ken Frieden is the B. G. Rudolph Professor of Judaic Studies at Syracuse University. His publications include the scholarly book *Classic Yiddish Fiction* (1995) and a popular anthology, *Classic Yiddish Stories* (2004). He has been a visiting professor in Tel Aviv, Haifa, Jerusalem, Heidelberg, Berlin, and Davis, California.

Leah Garrett is the Loti Smorgon Research Chair in Contemporary Jewish Life and Culture at Monash University, Australia. She wrote *Journeys beyond the Pale: Yiddish Travel Writing in the Modern World* (University of Wisconsin, 2006) and edited the volume *The Cross and Other Jewish Stories* by Lamed Shapiro (2007).

Janet Hadda is professor of Yiddish emerita at the University of California, Los Angeles. She is also a practicing psychoanalyst and a training and supervising analyst. She is the author of *Isaac Bashevis Singer: A Life* (1997, 2003).

Hillel Halkin is a literary critic, political commentator, and translator of many works of Hebrew and Yiddish literature. He is a columnist for *The New York Sun* and a frequent contributor to *Commentary* magazine and many other publications. His most recent book is *A Strange Death*.

Philip Hollander is assistant professor of Hebrew Literature and Language at Tulane University.

Dara Horn is the author of two award-winning novels: *In the Image* (Norton, 2002) and *The World to Come* (Norton, 2006).

Michael Kimmage is an assistant professor of history at The Catholic University of America in Washington, D.C. His dissertation was *The Conservative Turn: Lionel Trilling, Whittaker Chambers and the Lessons of Anti-Stalinism*, which he will be publishing as a book.

Susanne Klingenstein is a lecturer in the humanities in the Harvard-MIT Division of Health Sciences and Technology. She studied with Ruth Wisse in the early 1990s and wrote about her life and work in her book *Enlarging America: The Cultural Work of Jewish Literary Scholars, 1940-1990.* She is currently working on a book about Jewish writers in the Weimar Republic.

Mikhail Krutikov is the author of *Yiddish Fiction and the Crisis of Modernity* (2001) and is a columnist for the Yiddish *Forverts.* Currently assistant professor in Slavic and Judaic Studies at the University of Michigan, he is completing an intellectual biography of Yiddish scholar and writer Meir Wiener.

Ezra Mendelsohn is professor emeritus at the Hebrew University, having taught in the departments of Contemporary Jewry and Russian and East European studies. He specializes in modern Jewish history in Eastern Europe, Jewish cultural history, and Jewish politics. He is the author of five books and editor or co-editor of another fourteen on these and other subjects, and is co-editor of the journals *Studies in Contemporary Jewry* and *Zion* (Hebrew).

Alan Mintz is the Chana Kekst Professor of Hebrew Literature at the Jewish Theological Seminary. He is the author of *Translating Israel: Contemporary Hebrew Literature and Its Acceptance in America* and *Popular Culture and the Shaping of Holocaust Memory in America.* He is completing a critical introduction to American Hebrew poetry.

Dan Miron is a literary critic and a scholar and literary historian in the field of modern Jewish literature. He has published more than thirty scholarly books and monographs and hundreds of articles and papers. He has taught Jewish literature at the Hebrew University of Jerusalem, Tel Aviv University, Columbia University, and the YIVO Institute of Jewish Research in New York.

Goldie Morgentaler teaches nineteenth-century literature at the University of Lethbridge. She has published prize-winning translations from Yiddish to English, primarily of the work of Chava Rosenfarb.

Avraham Novershtern is Professor of Yiddish Literature at the Hebrew University in Jerusalem and the director of Beit Sholem Aleichem in Tel Aviv. His books include *The Lure of Twilight: Apocalypse and Messianism in Yiddish Literature* (2003; Hebrew); *The Rise of Modern Yiddish Literature* (2000; Hebrew), and a critical edition of Anna Margolin's *Poems* (1991).

Cynthia Ozick is the author of novels, stories, essays and a play. *Dictation: A Quartet* is her newest fiction, and her most recent collection of essays is *The Din in the Head.* Her novel *The Shawl* has been selected by the National Endowment for the Arts for its nationwide Big Read project, which has produced it as a critical and dramatic CD.

Yaron Peleg is assistant professor of Hebrew at George Washington University. He is the author of *Derech Gever: Homoeroticism in Hebrew Literature 1887–2000* (2003) and *Orientalism and the Hebrew Imagination* (2005).

Alyssa Quint is a lecturer at Princeton University and a columnist for the English-language Forward newspaper.

Jonathan Rosen is the author of two novels, *Eve's Apple* and *Joy Comes in the Morning*, and two works of non-fiction, *The Talmud and the Internet* and *The Life of the Skies: Birding at the End of Nature*. He is the editorial director of *Nextbook* and general editor of the *Nextbook/Schocken Jewish Encounter* series.

David G. Roskies is the Sol and Evelyn Henkind Chair in Yiddish Literature and Culture at The Jewish Theological Seminary. With Alan Mintz, he edited *Prooftexts: A Journal of Jewish Literary History*. His major books are *Against the Apocalypse* (1984), *The Literature of Destruction* (1989), and *A Bridge of Longing* (1995). In *Yiddishlands* (2008), the Roskies family saga is retold from his mother's perspective.

Rachel Rubinstein is assistant professor of American Literature and Jewish Studies at Hampshire College, and an associate editor of *Prooftexts*. Her work has appeared in *Shofar: An Interdisciplinary Journal of Jewish Studies* and *American Quarterly*.

Sasha Senderovich is a doctoral candidate in Slavic Languages and Literatures at Harvard. He is working on his dissertation on Russian-Jewish literature in the Soviet Union.

Naomi Sokoloff teaches modern Jewish literature and Hebrew at the University of Washington in Seattle. She is the author of *Imagining the Child in Modern Jewish Fiction* and co-editor of *Gender and Text in Modern Hebrew and Yiddish Literature*, *Infant Tongues: The Voice of the Child in Literature*, *Traditions and Transitions in Israel Studies*, and *The Jewish Presence in Children's Literature*.

Ilan Stavans is Lewis-Sebring Professor in Latin American and Latino Culture and Five College-Fortieth Anniversary Professor at Amherst College. His books include *On Borrowed Words* (2001), *Spanglish* (2003), *Dictionary Days* (2005), *Love and Language* (2007), and *Resurrecting Hebrew* (2008). He has edited *The Oxford Book of Jewish Stories* (1998), *Isaac Bashevis Singer: Collected Stories* (2004), and *The Schocken Book of Sephardic Literature* (2005).

Miriam Udel-Lambert is assistant professor of Yiddish language, literature, and culture at Emory University.

Hana Wirth-Nesher is the Samuel L. and Perry Haber Chair on the Study of the Jewish Experience in the United States and professor of English and American Studies at Tel Aviv University. She is also the head of the Goldreich Family Institute for Yiddish Language, Literature, and Culture. Her most recent book is *Call It English: The Languages of Jewish American Literature* (2006).

Jed Wyrick is associate professor and chair of the Department of Religious Studies at California State University, Chico, as well as coordinator of its Humanities and Modern Jewish and Israel Studies Programs.